# FOREIGN TRADE POLICY

COMPENDIUM OF PAPERS ON
UNITED STATES FOREIGN TRADE POLICY

COLLECTED BY THE

STAFF FOR THE

SUBCOMMITTEE ON FOREIGN TRADE POLICY

OF THE

COMMITTEE ON WAYS AND MEANS

GREENWOOD PRESS, PUBLISHERS
NEW YORK

Originally printed in 1956 by U.S. Government Printing Office.

First Greenwood Reprinting, 1968

Library of Congress Catalogue Card Number: 68-55108

PRINTED IN THE UNITED STATES OF AMERICA

# CONTENTS

# FOREIGN TRADE POLICY

---

## INTRODUCTION

This compendium has been assembled in connection with the program of study of the Subcommittee on Foreign Trade Policy of the Committee on Ways and Means. Study of the compendium will make it manifest that it represents a great deal of thought and effort on the part of individual contributors. Personally, and on behalf of the subcommittee, I wish to thank those who have thus contributed to the subcommittee's work.

The subcommittee was first established (under the name of the Subcommittee on Customs, Tariffs, and Reciprocal Trade Agreements) by the Committee on Ways and Means on July 6, 1956—shortly before the adjournment of the 84th Congress. It was authorized:

> To conduct an investigation and study of all aspects of our customs, tariff and reciprocal trade agreement laws and trade agreements entered into thereunder and the administration thereof, with particular reference to the relationship and effect of such matters on the foreign economic policies of the United States and their effect upon domestic producers and employment.

During the adjournment period of the 2d session of the 84th Congress the subcommittee held public hearings in Washington and some of its members engaged in conferences in Europe with foreign government officials and the representatives of foreign and American commercial interests while other members engaged in similar conferences in Japan. The record of these hearings and conferences was issued in four volumes which are available at the Government Printing Office.

The subcommittee submitted a report to the full Committee on Ways and Means on March 15, 1957. That report undertook to describe the main features of our existing foreign trade and tariff legislation and to discuss the questions that have arisen regarding the interpretation and administration of that legislation. The report did not attempt to evaluate the legislation or its administration or to make recommendations with respect thereto.

The subcommittee was reestablished by the Committee on Ways and Means for the duration of the 85th Congress under its present name but with the same jurisdiction and membership as its predecessor. The subcommittee agreed that its current studies should involve analysis of the economic and political considerations pertinent to the country's foreign trade policy and also agreed on a compendium, panel-discussion procedure in the conduct of its studies.

The following five topics or groups of topics were especially identified for attention in the subcommittee's current studies.

(1) Analysis and evaluation of the trade agreements program including appraisal of the adequacy and usefulness of the annual reports of the President and the Tariff Commission on the program.

(2) The trade and payments restrictions in use by foreign countries and their relation to the trade agreements program with special attention to the European common market project and other developments.

(3) Analysis of the regulation of imports by quotas.

(4) Trade agreements procedures and administration:

(*a*) Preparatory and negotiating procedures,

(*b*) The escape-clause concepts and procedures,

(*c*) The peril-point concepts and procedures,

(*d*) The National Security Amendment,

(*e*) Protection of programs of the Department of Agriculture from import interference.

(5) Import competition with domestic industries with special attention to different levels of wage rates here and abroad and related elements of cost as they affect the competition of imports with domestic industries.

The papers included in this compendium have been prepared in response to the subcommittee's invitations which were intended to secure up-to-date information and analysis of recent developments relevant to the many issues and problems involved in the formulation and implementation of foreign trade policy. These are matters of particular importance in this time because, in the absence of further legislation, the President's authority to enter into trade agreements with foreign countries will expire June 30, 1958, and because there is much controversy as to whether the authority should be extended and, if so, in what ways if any the controlling legislation should be amended. The present studies of the subcommittee are in large part directed to the formulation of conclusions and recommendations with respect to the country's future foreign trade policy and more particularly with respect to the trade agreements program and legislation. With this end in view, the subcommittee, in selecting people and organizations to invite to contribute to this compendium, was motivated by the hope of securing papers which would set forth the reasoned bases of the diverse opinions held by those who have given much attention to the problems of United States foreign trade policy.

The subcommittee was anxious to have the cooperation and assistance of the executive branch in its studies. In this connection the President was requested to have his office prepare an analysis of the requirements and objectives of foreign trade policy as viewed by the administration and of the manner in which the various instruments of policy are designed to effectuate these objectives. The correspondence of the subcommittee with the White House on this matter and the report prepared in response to the subcommittee's request is included in the first section of this compendium.

The subcommittee also requested agencies of the executive branch particularly concerned with the administration of our foreign trade policy and tariff legislation or particular features thereof to provide information on their experience in these matters. The material submitted in response to these requests has been included in the appropriate sections of the compendium.

In the invitations to contribute to this compendium the subcommittee requested the persons addressed to deal with specific items in the foregoing list of topics. The subcommittee was aware, however, that the topics are interrelated in many ways and that their analysis would involve consideration of collateral matters. The subcommittee also understood that to be analyzed adequately the various topics would have to be considered in the context of our general economic policy and in relation to the domestic economy. Nevertheless, the content of many of the papers submitted has been, no doubt, controlled by the subcommittee's invitation rather than by what the particular author might have chosen to discuss if he had been asked simply for a paper in the whole field of the subcommittee's studies.

In connection with topic 5 identified above, the subcommittee invited papers from various industry groups in an effort to develop "case studies" which would provide a comprehensive analysis of the problems of foreign trade policy in the light of the experience of such groups. These papers will be found at the end of the volume.

A further statement should be made about the organization of the papers in the compendium. The attempt has been made to assemble together papers relating to particular subjects. As already suggested, however, the analysis of the various subjects overlap so that the papers could be arranged only imperfectly on the basis of their special subject matter.

It is planned that this compendium will be widely distributed as soon as the printed edition becomes available—early in October. Comments in writing on the compendium or particular sections thereof are invited from interested persons. The subcommittee plans to hold public panel discussions during the first 2 weeks in December and this compendium is expected to provide much of the basic information and analysis on which these panel discussions will be based. The subcommittee plans to organize the panels to particpate in the discussions of the various subjects from contributors to the compendium and from persons who submit comments thereon. It is further contemplated that the comments pertaining to particular panel discussions will be distributed to the participants in the discussions in advance of such discussions. By this means it is hoped that the panel may approach the discussion of particular subjects with a common background of pertinent reading material and that, as a result, time may be saved in arriving at areas of agreement and establishing the irreconcilable elements in the opinions of the participants.

HALE BOGGS, *Chairman.*

OCTOBER 7, 1957.

# I

# UNITED STATES FOREIGN-TRADE POLICY—GENERAL—EVALUATION OF THE TRADE-AGREEMENTS PROGRAM AND ITS RELEVANCE TO THE COUNTRY'S GENERAL FOREIGN POLICY AND TO THE DOMESTIC ECONOMY UNDER PRESENT-DAY CONDITIONS

# FOREIGN ECONOMIC POLICY AND THE TRADE AGREEMENTS PROGRAM[1]

Office of the President

## I. OBJECTIVES OF FOREIGN ECONOMIC POLICY

The broad objective of United States foreign economic policy is identical with that of our general foreign policy and, in fact, of the overall policy of the United States Government: to protect and advance the national interest, to improve the security and well-being of the United States and its people.

This broad objective of our foreign economic policy has three major components:

### (a) *To promote the economic strength of the United States*

This is the traditional objective of foreign economic policy: expanding foreign markets for the products of our factories, mines, and farms; insuring ready access to overseas sources of supplies needed by our economy; permitting the Nation to take reasonable advantage of the economies which flow from specialization in production throughout the world; improving conditions for United States citizens to invest and do business abroad.

Foreign trade is one of the most important business activities of the United States. Statistics tell an impressive story of the vital role of our international commerce. It is estimated, for example, that the families of at least 4½ million American workers, or about 7 percent of our labor force, gain their livelihood from foreign trade. A commensurate share of the profits of American business firms is traceable to foreign-trade activities. As for exports alone, the value of United States goods marketed abroad last year exceeded that of all nonfarm home building, or of consumer purchases of automobiles, or of farmers' gross receipts from either crops or livestock.

---

[1] The correspondence between the chairman of the subcommittee and the White House relating to this report follows:

APRIL 8, 1957.

The PRESIDENT,
*The White House.*

MY DEAR MR. PRESIDENT: I am writing you to invite the assistance and participation of the executive branch in the work of the Subcommittee on Foreign Trade Policy of the Committee on Ways and Means.

As you probably know, the subcommittee was first established on July 6, 1956, to function during the remainder of the 84th Congress as the Subcommittee on Customs, Tariffs, and Reciprocal Trade Agreements. The subcommittee was authorized "to conduct an investigation and study of all aspects of our customs, tariff, and reciprocal trade agreement laws and trade agreements entered into thereunder and the administration thereof, with particular reference to the relationship and effect of such matters on the foreign economic policies of the United States and their effect upon domestic producers and employment." During the adjournment period of the 2d session of the 84th Congress the subcommittee conducted public hearings and made such a study as was possible in the limited time available of the major features of our customs, tariff, and trade agreements legislation. I am sending you under separate cover a copy of the subcommittee's report to the full committee which was published on March 15, 1957. Along with that report I am also sending a copy of the three volumes of the subcommittee's hearings and we will send you the fourth volume reporting on the conferences abroad as soon as it is available.

The subcommittee has been reestablished in this Congress as the Subcommittee on Foreign Trade Policy with the same jurisdiction and membership as its predecessor in the

Exports comprise about 9 percent of the value of our production of movable goods—8 percent for manufactured goods and 11 percent for agricultural products. For many specific commodities, the proportions of United States output sold abroad run substantially higher than the average—for example, according to the latest available annual figures in each case, about 19 percent for trucks, 40 percent for tracklaying tractors, 11 percent for machine tools, 26 percent for construction and mining equipment, 14 percent for coal, and between 25 and 40 percent for cotton, wheat, rice, fats and oils, and tobacco. The vital importance of exports in such cases is beyond dispute; and even among those manufacturing industries with below-average ratios, the great majority depend upon foreign markets for at least some significant share of their sales, profits, and jobs.

It should be noted that the available ratios for many specific commodities seriously understate the true importance of export markets for their producers, since they cover only exports of an industry's products in the form in which they leave that country. Much of an industry's output may be exported only in some other form after further processing by other industries, or, even though not physically exported, may be utilized by other industries in production for export. This is particularly true of such primary manufacturing industries as iron and steel or nonferrous metals.

Through foreign trade the United States obtains from abroad a wide range of goods which are not otherwise available here at all or not in adequate quantities for industrial needs or consumer demand. Many of these imports are vital to keep factory wheels turning and assembly lines moving. We obtain from foreign sources about one-sixth of our crude petroleum, almost one-fourth of our iron ore, one-third of our copper and rubber, over one-half of our raw wool, and the great bulk of our supplies of tin, nickel, and newsprint. Most of our supplies of various ferroalloying ores and metals come from abroad as do industrial diamonds, mica, and asbestos.

Altogether, about one-fifth of the crude and semimanufactured goods imported by the United States in 1956 were officially classified as strategic materials for stockpiling purposes, and another one-fifth consisted of materials (other than those in the stockpile group) obtain-

---

84th Congress. The subcommittee has drawn up a program of work for the 1st session of the 85th Congress. I enclose a copy of a press release dated February 27, 1957, which describes this program. As indicated in the press release, the subcommittee has identified five principal topics or groups of topics in the field of foreign trade and tariff policy for study. You will note that the proposed studies cover a wide range of subject matter. Moreover, the subcommittee proposes to study the various topics in the context of the overall foreign economic policy of the United States. The subcommittee has further agreed that its studies should be conducted by assembling a compendium of papers from selected scholars and interested observers on the various topics included in the agenda. This compendium of papers will be published and will provide the basis for public panel discussions subsequently to be held for the purpose of further exploring matters relating to foreign trade policy and the implementing legislation and to serve as an aid to the subcommittee in arriving at conclusions and recommendations thereon.

The subcommittee has also agreed to request the cooperation and assistance of the executive branch, and it is in this connection that I am writing to you. As one feature of such cooperation it would be very desirable to have a report from the executive branch for inclusion in the compendium of papers above referred to. The subcommittee believes that this study should be directed at an analysis of the requirements and objectives of foreign economic policy as viewed by the executive branch, the manner in which the various instruments of policy are designed to effect these objectives, including the relationship of our trade and tariff policy to other components of foreign economic policy, whether the various components of foreign economic policy constitute an integrated and adequate program, and what our foreign economic policy in general and trade and tariff policy in particular can properly be expected to accomplish.

As you know, your trade-agreement authority will, in the absence of new legislation, expire on June 30, 1958. One of the objectives of the subcommittee's work in this Congress must therefore be directed to consideration of questions relating to the extension

able wholly or almost exclusively from foreign sources. Many other raw material imports also represent high proportions of United States requirements, and still others supplement predominantly domestic supplies to an important degree.

Imports of foods and manufactured goods bulk smaller in the total than those of industrial materials. Nevertheless, every American household enjoys the variety contributed to our established consumption pattern by imports both of foreign foodstuffs and manufactured consumer goods.

(b) *To promote the economic strength of the rest of the free world*

This objective has become of major importance within the past decade. We recognize, first of all, that a prosperous world brings economic advantages to our own country. Furthermore, foreign economic growth is necessary for the establishment and maintenance of stable, peaceful, and friendly societies abroad. Economic stagnation is a source of unrest which can threaten political stability and, eventually, the peace of the world we are so earnestly seeking to make durable and just. The moderate leadership groups which are in power in most of the less developed countries are under tremendous pressure to speed millions of their countrymen into the 20th century. Failure of these leaders to achieve reasonable economic progress would result in these governments being replaced by others more extreme, more likely to be totalitarian, either of Communist or indigenous origin, and more likely to resort to violence as a means of achieving their objectives. Economic strength abroad also is a prerequisite to the building of solid military forces with which to deter potential Communist subversion or aggression.

(c) *To build and maintain cohesion in the free world*

Our present foreign policy is built upon a web of relations among virtually all of the free nations. Through the North Atlantic Treaty Organization and the Baghdad Pact, through the Organization of American States, through a variety of other organizations and treaties, we have undertaken to work with friendly countries in building our common strength and in defending ourselves against Communist aggression.

---

and possible amendment of the trade-agreements legislation. You will recall that there were some very close votes in the House on the trade-agreements legislation in 1955 when the Trade Agreements Extension Act of that year was enacted. You are also, no doubt, aware that the trade-agreements program and its administration have been subjects of increasing citicism in recent years and that, in the present climate of public and congressional opinion, the continuance of the program is by no means assured.

Inasmuch as the trade-agreements legislation provides substantial discretion to the President in the fields of trade and tariff policy, it is important that the subcommittee should have an authoritative report from the executive branch setting forth the basis of the administration's views with respect to the objectives of the trade-agreements program, its relation to other components of our foreign economic policy, and the appropriateness of the existing trade-agreements legislation and its administration in the light of general policy objectives.

Some of the criticisms of the trade-agreements program and its administration involve a challenge to the basic concepts and objectives of our foreign economic policy as viewed by this and previous administrations. I refer here to the fact that a fundamental and long-run objective of the trade-agreements program, as implemented through the General Agreement on Tariffs and Trade, as well as of other components of our foreign economic policy, has been to encourage a nondiscriminatory or multilateral system of trade among countries of the free world. The question has arisen as to whether this orientation is realistic in view of present conditions in this and other countries—whether, for example, such an outlook is consistent with our policies with respect to domestic agriculture and other institutional factors influencing the price system. It is on account of such considerations that the subcommittee believes that its studies of tariffs and trade policy must be broadly conceived, and that the report we are requesting should be similarly broad in scope.

Among the specific features of the trade-agreements legislation and its administration which the subcommittee believes should be covered by the report of the executive branch

These ties have not been and could not be purely political or military. Without adequate economic support they would be weak and unreliable. Modern power depends upon the basic economic strength of the nations involved. This in turn depends upon the efficient use of domestic and foreign resources, and is reduced when each nation tries to build on its own resources alone.

Moreover, economic disputes can weaken or destroy political and military alliances. For most countries, it is vital to have easy access to foreign markets and foreign sources of basic materials and capital. The jobs and well-being of their people depend on it. Most of our allies are particularly sensitive to this because they depend much more on foreign trade than does the United States.

Countries of the free world are under external and internal pressure to aline themselves with the Communist bloc or at least to become neutral in the great power struggle between communism and the way of life represented by the democracies. To oppose this pressure the United States has used its economic resources and political leadership.

The most difficult problems are posed in the developing countries, particularly those in Asia and Africa. Between our country and those countries today are vast differences in culture, language, and social tradition as well as economic attainment. Mutual confidence must be established. This cannot be achieved by words alone.

By working together with the free-world countries for their and our economic advancement and for the building of a durable and just international economic order, we can do much to achieve our broad as-

---

are the escape clause, peril point, national security amendment, sec. 22 of the Agricultural Adjustment Act, and the questions connected with the regulation of imports by quotas. The question was frequently raised in the subcommittee's previous hearings as to whether the present legislation relating to the application of the escape clause and of the peril-point concept was an adequate expression of the policy that should be represented by these provisions and as to whether the administration of these provisions by the executive branch had been in accord with their clear implications. On the other hand, these provisions of the legislation were the subject of numerous criticisms on the ground that they could provide a complete reversal of the basic policy represented by the Trade Agreements Act.

It therefore seems to me that a basic reappraisal of our present trade agreements and tariff laws must be made and where appropriate either legislative or administrative changes must be adopted. Accordingly we are asking that the ideas of the executive branch on these matters be authoritatively stated and that proposals for revision and amendment of the existing legislative provisions where appropriate be offered. I believe that the work of our subcommittee can have an important bearing on the future of the country's trade and tariff policy and indeed on even broader aspects of our foreign economic policy. We seek the cooperation and support of the executive branch because such cooperation is essential if the work of our subcommittee is to be fully effective.

As in the case with respect to the other papers and materials that we are requesting for inclusion in the proposed compendium, it is our present expectation that such material should be submitted to the subcommittee by the 1st of August of this year.[a] Likewise the subcommittee and its staff intend to discuss in some detail the subjects and questions to which these various papers should address themselves in order to yield the most meaningful and helpful presentation. Accordingly we would be very pleased to discuss this matter further with anyone you may designate to handle the matter.

Yours respectfully,

HALE BOGGS,
*Chairman, Subcommittee on Foreign Trade Policy.*

[a] This date was subsequently changed to the 1st of September.

THE WHITE HOUSE,
*Washington, April 15, 1957.*

Hon. HALE BOGGS,
*Chairman, Subcommittee on Foreign Trade Policy,*
*Committee on Ways and Means, House of Representatives,*
*Washington, D. C.*

DEAR MR. BOGGS: The President has asked me to acknowledge your letter of April 9th and to express his appreciation for the work your subcommittee is doing in the vital area of foreign trade.

The President has instructed me to say that the executive branch will be glad to cooperate by preparing the report you request to aid the subcommittee in its work. While the detailed views of the administration with respect to the form of the trade-agreements

pirations as a nation. We can demonstrate the community of interest of the peoples of the free world. We can encourage the growth of the idea of democratic and limited government and the basic values on which this rests.

II. THE ROLE OF ECONOMIC POLICIES

To achieve these objectives the United States Government has followed three basic economic policies: the expansion of trade, in both goods and services, through the gradual and reciprocal reduction of unjustifiable governmental and private barriers; the promotion of private investment; and the provision of mutual assistance. These policies and their roles are discussed below.

These three policy subjects, however, do not begin to exhaust the immense range of economic matters that are dealt with in our international relations. There is the complex and difficult field of aviation policy. There are problems of shipping, telecommunications, agricultural surplus disposal, currency exchange, east-west trade, and special problems surrounding key commodities such as petroleum, cotton, wheat, and rubber. Our participation in United Nations economic programs is a subject in itself. Foreign policy today is pervaded by economics, and in all these activities the Government seeks closer cooperation with other peoples to the mutual advantage of them and us.

These various components of foreign economic policy are inextricably interrelated. Actions taken with respect to one have a bearing on one or several other components. None can be treated in isolation. They form an integrated whole.

---

extension legislation next year will not be determined until late this year, the President believes that useful comments can be made on the points you raise. His representative will be in touch with you or your staff to work out the arrangements for the report.

Sincerely,

I. JACK MARTIN,
*Administrative Assistant to the President.*

THE WHITE HOUSE,
*Washington, September 6, 1957.*

Hon. HALE BOGGS,
*Chairman, Subcommittee on Foreign Trade Policy,*
*House of Representatives, D. C.*

DEAR MR. BOGGS: In your letter to the President, dated April 8, 1957, you requested from the executive branch "an analysis of the requirements and objectives of foreign economic policy * * *, the manner in which the various instruments of policy are designed to effect these objectives, including the relationship of our trade and tariff policy to other components of foreign economic policy, whether the various components of foreign economic policy constitute an integrated and adequate program and what our foreign economic policy in general and trade and tariff policy in particular can properly be expected to accomplish." You also asked for the administration's views on "the appropriateness of the existing trade-agreements legislation and administration in the light of general policy objectives," and proposals for revisioon of existing legislative provisions where appropriate.

Attached is a report, submitted on behalf of the executive branch in response to your request, for the use of the subcommittee on Foreign Trade Policy. This matetrial is supplemented by the more detailed reports from the various departments concerned and the Office of Defense Mobilization, prepared in response to your separate requests to them.

As noted in the letter to you of April 15, 1957, from Mr. I. Jack Martin, Administrative Assistant to the President, the detailed views of the administration with respect to the form of the trade-agreements legislation next year will not be determined until later this year. For this reason, it has not been possible to include in the report comments on specific features of the trade-agreements legislation. It may be said, however, that the executive branch strongly favors the continuation of the reciprocal trade-agreements legislation.

It is hoped that the attached paper together with the reports from the various departments annd agencies will be usefuul to the subcommittee.

Sincerely yours,

WILTON B. PERSONS,
*The Deputy Assistant to the President.*

*(a) Expansion of trade*

The trade and financial policies of the United States Government are designed to help to achieve all three basic objectives of foreign economic policy; to increase the economic strength of the United States, to increase the strength of other countries and to promote the unity of the free world. To the fullest practicable degree they call for the gradual and reciprocal reduction of unjustifiable public and private barriers to trade and payments.

Government restriction have in the past throttled mutually profitable world commerce to the detriment of the United States and of every other nation. To remove unjustifiable barriers and to promote the productive interchange of goods and services is a major task of United States policy.

This task is undertaken primarily through the trade agreements program including the General Agreement on Tariffs and Trade (GATT) and through the International Monetary Fund (IMF). Through the trade agreements program we seek the gradual, selective, and reciprocal reduction of tariffs and the elimination of quantitative restrictions on imports and of other governmental barriers to trade. Through the fund, we seek the promotion of a sound financial basis for the development of international economic relations, including the maintenance of equitable, stable exchange rates, the provision of short-term financial resources to countries short of foreign exchange, and the elimination of governmental restrictions on international payments. Experience through the years has demonstrated clearly the superiority of multilateral discussions and negotiations over bilaterals in achieving the objectives of United States policy in these fields.

By removing or reducing barriers to foreign trade, the United States contributes materially to its own economic advancement and, simultaneously, to that of other countries. When foreign nations reciprocate in tariff reduction, as they must do, and remove restrictions on international payments, the stimulus to our and their economies is increased.

The United States over the years has taken the lead in this program. We have undertaken this task not only because our foreign commerce is greater than that of any other country, but also because of our basic philosophical attitude toward the role of government in economic life. The general philosophy underlying the GATT and the IMF is a practical application of the emphasis in our political thought on the importance of limiting the role of government in economic life and expanding the opportunities for individual choice, initiative, and experimentation.

GATT and the IMF are important forums for considering differences which now frequently arise between friendly nations in the area of trade and payments. These differences are largely created as governments, attempting to protect the industrial, agricultural, or financial resources of their countries, adopt measures which come in conflict with the objectives of other nations.

Finally, there are United States Government policies designed to reduce or eliminate abroad nongovernmental barriers to trade, that is, private restrictive business arrangements, and to encourage free competitive enterprise. Policies in these fields are designed to aid American businessmen to operate more freely in foreign commerce and to strengthen the economies of the free world countries.

(*b*) *Private foreign investment*

In the interest of United States economic growth—the development of foreign markets and sources of supply—and in the interest of assisting foreign economic growth, the United States has encouraged the outflow of private capital. Private investment not only provides financing but it also takes with it the managerial, entrepreneurial and technical talents which are essential for successful enterprise but are seriously lacking in the less developed countries.

Some of the measures employed, such as treaties of friendship, commerce, and navigation, are designed to improve the investment climate abroad. Others, such as loans to business from the International Finance Corporation and the Export-Import Bank, and the removal of tax impediments, offer a direct stimulus to United States private capital to go abroad.

As the less developed countries achieve a substantial degree of economic growth and as they achieve a greater degree of trust in us and confidence in themselves, the opportunities for private capital will grow. The opportunities are already large in much of Latin America. In the long run, private capital can reduce the demands on the United States Government for financial assistance to foreign countries.

(*c*) *Foreign economic and technical assistance*

The Marshall plan, the United States economic assistance programs for the underdeveloped countries of the free world, the technical cooperation programs, the Export-Import Bank, and the International Bank for Reconstruction and Development have been major factors in the growth of both economic strength and a sense of community in the free world.

The success of the Marshall plan in Western Europe was striking. Economic output quickly reached and exceeded prewar levels. Economic nationalism, which in the prewar and immediate postwar periods dominated European governmental policy, has had serious setbacks. Quantitative restrictions upon European trade have been substantially reduced. Limitations on the use of the major European currencies, particularly in the nondollar world, have been virtually eliminated. United States economic aid there, of course, has ceased.

The problems of the less developed countries are much more difficult than those of Western Europe. Many of the former are already overpopulated in relation to their low levels of production. Moreover, the populations are growing rapidly as death rates fall sharply with the introduction of low-cost health measures. Capital is lacking and domestic savings are low. The labor force needs to acquire the basic skills required for a modern economy; these requirements vary from learning to read simple instructions to the strengthening of high-level manpower resources, especially managerial, supervisory, technical, and scientific talents. A business or entrepreneurial class must be created or enlarged. In general, basic changes in attitudes and institutions are necessary. Many of these problems can only be resolved slowly and require long-term and persistent measures for their solution.

## III. THE TRADE AGREEMENTS PROGRAM

Modern United States trade policy has its roots in the Trade Agreements Act of 1934. Our trade policy rests on the doctrine of reducing unjustifiable Government interference to allow international trade to expand in response to market forces. Foreign trade allows nations to take advantage of the specialization of production which is the distinguishing feature of modern economic life. It is the international counterpart of the domestic specialization of function which has been one of the foundations of United States national strength.

As discussed above, foreign trade is of great importance to the American people both as consumers and producers. The world's largest economic power, the United States, is also the world's largest foreign trader. We have a large stake in a healthy, expanding international trade.

As important as foreign trade is to United States employment, production, and consumption, it is of even greater importance to most of the nations of the free world which cannot match the size and diversity of United States natural and human resources. For the major industrial countries such as the United Kingdom, West Germany, and France, the ratio of exports to gross national production is 3 to 4 times as great as for the United States. For smaller advanced nations, such as Belgium, the Netherlands, Sweden, and Switzerland, it is 5 to 9 times as great. For many of the underdeveloped countries, exports are the single largest component of the market part of their economy.

In fact, trade with the United States alone is of significant proportions for many countries. Over two-thirds of total exports of Colombia, Mexico, and Cuba go to the United States. For Canada the ratio amounts to 60 percent, while for Brazil and the Philippines it is at least 50 percent.

For many particular commodities the United States is the dominant market. For example, Chile sends two-thirds of her total copper production to the United States; Cuba sells us half of her sugar; Indonesia sells one-quarter of her rubber; Bolivia, one-third of her tin; Brazil, over one-half of her coffee production.

Even western European countries with relatively large markets on the Continent depend to an important extent on exports to the United States. Specific industries depend heavily upon the American market. For example, Switzerland exports to the United States over half of her total production of Emmenthaler and Gruyere cheese and over one-third of her production of watches and watch movements; United Kingdom sends about one-third of her total production of Scotch whisky to America; Portugal exports about 40 percent of her cork production to this country.

These facts suggest the extent to which the United States has come to occupy a dominant role in critical segments of the economies of many foreign countries. A decline in sales to the United States fundamentally affects income and savings abroad. The availability and growth of the American market is of vital importance to them.

The trade agreements program is designed to contribute to the development of mutually beneficial international trade. In so doing it plays an important role in the achievement of our foreign economic policy objectives. Experience with the program since 1934 demonstrates this conclusively. The executive branch strongly favors continuation of the trade agreements program including the extension of the Trade Agreements Act. The life of the program should be extended by the Congress for a sufficient period to provide the essential stability to the program and adequate authority to vouchsafe and expand the gains that have been made in world trade.

The trade agreements program is designed to be realistic and practical. It is recognized that abrupt lowering of barriers to trade can create serious problems in our own as well as foreign economies. Some United States industries are particularly sensitive to import competition. A sudden increase in imports may have relatively important effects on their output, profits, and employment. The fact that these industries tend to be localized in particular areas of the country increases the magnitude and seriousness of the problem. Thus, the policy of the United States Government has been one of gradual and selective tariff reduction, one which gives public consideration to each item before any reduction in tariffs is made, and which provides opportunity for reconsideration when serious injury occurs or is threatened.

The case-by-case approach to tariff reductions permits the executive branch to administer the program in a way to provide reasonable assurance that serious injury will not be threatened any industry as a result of a tariff negotiation. The peril point findings of the United States Tariff Commission, as required by the trade agreements legislation, play an important role to this end. Likewise, provision for reconsideration of a tariff reduction when serious injury does occur or is threatened makes possible the use of appropriate measures for the removal of such threat or serious injury. The executive branch subscribes fully to the principles underlying both the peril point and the escape-clause provisions of the Trade Agreements Act.

The special consideration given in the act to protecting essential defense industries has the full support of the executive branch. So also do the limitations on imports of agricultural products as provided for within the trade agreements program, and in the controlling legislation, in those instances in which this country has a policy of supporting domestic prices and as a result limits the production or sale of the domestic products.

The GATT has been the instrument by which 35 nations, accounting for 80 percent of world trade, have agreed to reduce tariffs and to eliminate quantitative restrictions and other harmful discriminatory practices. It has provided a forum where governments can discuss their trade problems and submit complaints. In this forum differences of policies can be discussed and discord among friendly countries can be reduced. The effectiveness of the GATT can be greatly increased by establishment of an administrative unit, the Organization for Trade Cooperation. The executive branch will again urge the Congress to authorize membership in the OTC.

The results of the trade agreements program have been gratifying in terms of reductions in unjustifiable trade barriers, the expansion of world trade, the economic growth of the entire free world, and the development of closer, friendlier international relations. Continuation of this record of achievement depends on the ability of the United States to carry on a constructive program. This is in our own interest as well as that of the entire free world.

Much has been accomplished but much remains to be done. Moreover, there is always the danger that if momentum is lost there will be a lapse into economic nationalism around the free world. This lapse may be confined to individual countries or may be expanded to groups of nations which would have as a major objective discrimination against American goods.

Regional trading plans of all sorts are being proposed throughout the world. Whether such plans, particularly the European common market and free-trade area, will contribute their full potential to the development of world trade or become restrictive depends very largely on the attitudes and outlook toward trade adopted by the member countries. In part, this depends on the example the United States sets in its own trade policy.

# THE ROLE OF FOREIGN TRADE IN THE UNITED STATES ECONOMY

United States Department of Commerce

The Subcommittee on Foreign Trade Policy, in Chairman Boggs' letter of June 1, 1957, to Secretary Weeks, asked for comment from the Department of Commerce on the role of foreign trade in the domestic economy including the relation of imports and exports to the national income and on the importance of various categories of our import and export trade to domestic industry, agriculture and commerce.

Foreign trade is one of the most important United States business activities. Although this fact may readily be taken for granted, it deserves wider and more emphatic recognition.

The vital role of our international commerce can be demonstrated only in part by reference to the key statistics available on relationships of foreign trade to the domestic economy. There are inherent in these relationships some important qualitative characteristics which cannot be adequately reflected in quantitative measurements. The available statistics, nevertheless, tell an impressive story.

Altogether, it is estimated that the families of at least 4½ million American workers, or about 7 percent of our labor force, gain their livelihood from foreign trade. This figure covers those who are engaged directly or indirectly in production or service for export markets, or in the handling and distribution of imported goods, or in the first factory processing of imported materials. A commensurate share of the profits of American business firms is undoubtedly traceable to the same activities.

A more commonly cited, if somewhat more limited, indicator of the importance of United States foreign trade is the ratio of exports to the gross national product.[1] In 1956, total United States exports of both goods and services (exclusive of military aid) represented some 5½ percent of the Nation's output; merchandise exports alone (also exclusive of military aid) were more than 4 percent. While the size of this ratio is well known, its significance is not always fully appreciated.

Proper perspective calls for realization that no single homogeneous component of such a huge and comprehensive aggregate as the gross national product constitutes a very high percentage of the total. The ratio for exports looms large in comparison with similar ratios for a number of other economic variables which are of universally recognized importance, but which also fall in the range of 3 to 5 percent of the gross national product. The value of United

[1] Comparisons of this type are usually based on the gross national product, rather than on the alternative measure of total United States output—the national income—mentioned in Chairman Boggs' inquiry. The technical reason for this preference is that reported foreign trade values are more appropriately comparable with the market price valuation of the GNP than with the "factor cost" valuation of the national income.

States goods marketed abroad last year, for example, exceeded that of all nonfarm homebuilding, or of consumer purchases of automobiles, or of farmers' gross receipts from either crops or livestock. It equalled the Nation's entire output of crude or prepared minerals, valued at the mine, well, or plant; and it was not far below the retail value of all clothing and shoes purchased by American consumers.

Much of the gross national product, of course, consists of services, construction, and retail distribution values which are not by nature exportable. It is therefore pertinent to emphasize the much higher proportion which exports comprise of the value (at early stages of distribution) of our production of movable goods alone. This ratio was around 9 percent last year. It is somewhat higher for agricultural than for nonfarm products, but a separate estimate for manufactured goods would probably be not less than 8 percent in 1956.

Because of the difficulty of tracing the productive contributions of various industries to the values of exported merchandise in which they are finally embodied, accurate estimates for broad segments of the economy are not available. The foregoing comment is based upon a rough comparison of agricultural exports[2] with the value of agricultural output.[3] The ratio indicated by this comparison was about 11 percent last year, and that suggested above for manufactured goods is simply inferred from a comparison of nonagricultural exports with the remaining value of movable goods output apart from agricultural production (but without accurate allowance for the value of agricultural materials incorporated in manufactured goods).

For many specific commodities, of course, the proportions of United States output sold abroad run substantially higher than the average—for example, according to the latest available annual figures in each case, about 19 percent for trucks, 40 percent for tracklaying tractors, 11 percent for machine tools, 26 percent for construction and mining equipment, 14 percent for coal, and between 25 and 40 percent for cotton, wheat, rice, fats and oils, and tobacco. The vital importance of exports in such cases is beyond dispute; and even among those manufacturing industries with below-average ratios the great majority depend upon foreign markets for at least some significant share of their sales, profits, and jobs. Ratios corresponding with those cited above for a large number of additional exported commodities have been published by the Bureau of Foreign Commerce in an annual bulletin (Exports in Relation to United States Production, World Trade Information Service, pt. 3, No. 56–31).

It should be noted, however, that the available ratios for many specific commodities seriously understate the true importance of export markets for their producers, since they cover only exports of an industry's products in the form in which they leave that industry. Much of an industry's output may be exported only in some other form after further processing by other industries, or, even though not physically exported, may be utilized by other industries in production for export. This is particularly true of such primary manufacturing industries as iron and steel or nonferrous metals. While there is a very sizable volume of direct exports of the products of these two

[2] Not, however, including agricultural materials incorporated in exports of manufactured goods, such as textiles and apparel.
[3] Adjusted to a valuation basis corresponding approximately to that of exports at the point of exportation.

industries, as a percentage of their output it is perhaps somewhat below the average for all manufacturing industries. According to the Labor Department's interindustry studies[4] based on the 1947 Census of Manufactures, however, it is clear that both the iron and steel and the non-ferrous-metals industries have a total stake in export markets which is several times as large as their direct stake. If that part of their output embodied indirectly in export shipments of more advanced manufactures, such as machinery and vehicles, were included in the calculation (as it was in the Labor Department's estimates of employment attributable to exports in 1947), these two industries would show a much higher than average reliance upon export markets.

Another similar example, also drawn from the 1947 analysis of interindustry relationships, is the paper and allied products industry. As far as direct exports are concerned, this industry sells abroad only about 2 percent of its production—a very low proportion in comparison with the average for the manufacturing sector. However, owing chiefly to the ubiquitous use of the industry's products in the packaging of goods for export, it has an unusually large indirect stake in the foreign sales of others. Inclusive of this indirect share, the reliance of the paper and allied products industry upon foreign markets appears to be pretty close to the average for all manufacturing industries.

In terms of fairly broad generalization, a list of the principal nonagricultural industries which are markedly above the Nation's average in their reliance—indirect as well as direct—upon export trade would include the following: Ocean transportation; agricultural, mining, construction, metalworking, and other nonelectrical machinery manufacturing; motors and generators; motor vehicles (primarily trucks rather than passenger cars) and other transportation equipment; iron and steel; nonferrous metals manufacturing; chemicals; products of petroleum and coal; and rubber products. On the other hand, nonagricultural sectors with relatively low degrees of dependence upon export markets include, apart from trade and construction, the following: Communications; printing and publishing; food processing; apparel manufacturing; leather and leather products; furniture and fixtures; and plumbing and heating supplies.

While the foregoing discussion has been focused on exports essentially from the traditional standpoint of the American businessman viewing them as sales outlets for his products, sight should not be lost of another point of view which brings out certain even more fundamental—if somewhat theoretical—aspects of the role of exports in the United States economy. This is the broad, national frame of reference in which the function of exports is to pay, in real terms, for our imports and our foreign investments (and also, during and since World War II, for the aid granted to other countries by the United States Government. The fact that individual export, import, and foreign investment transactions take place independently in a money and credit economy tends to obscure the basic function of exports in this respect, as does the persistent tendency, apparent since the latter part of the 19th century, for the United States to export more goods

[4] See staff papers of the President's Commission on Foreign Economic Policy (February 1954), pp. 374–376.

than it imports. Moreover, much public discussion in recent years has centered on the superficially opposite (but correlative and equally valid) concept of United States imports as a means of payment by foreigners for our exports. Nevetheless, for the Nation as a whole, the most fundamental role of its exports is as a means of payment either for goods and services currently obtained from abroad or for United States investments abroad which are also expected eventually to yield returns in relative as well as monetary, terms.

In other words, the overall national economic gains from foreign trade are centered essentially in the imports for which our exports are exchanged, rather than in the sale proceeds from the latter. The immediate monetary earnings are vitally important to the workers, managers, and owners of the individual firms receiving them, and constitute a key element in the dynamic mechanism of an economy, but what exports contribute to the economic welfare of the whole Nation is an efficient means of obtaining goods which are either not otherwise available here or are producible domestically only at higher total costs, in terms of human, capital, and natural resources, than those of the exports exchanged for them.

The importance of imports to the United States economy is quite inadequately reflected by simple measures of their magnitude in relation to domestic output or consumption. In the aggregate, their value (as recorded in the official foreign trade statistics, generally f. o. b. foreign port of exportation) has been equivalent to about 3 percent of the gross national product, or to a little over 6 percent of the estimated value (at early stages of distribution) of movable goods produced in the United States. There are several major reasons, however, for looking beyond these broad ratios in assessing the pervasive role of imports in our economy. Directly or indirectly, imported goods are in daily use in virtually every American household, factory, and office.

The composition of imports is radically different from that of domestic production, and the predominant types of imports are much larger in relation to corresponding domestic output than is suggested by the above percentages. Well over half of all merchandise imports in 1956 consisted of crude or semiprocessed materials,[5] while foodstuffs accounted for about one-fourth and finished manufactures for only one-fifth. Imports of raw materials represent a far higher percentage of those processed by United States industry than total imports as a percentage of all United States consumption.

According to estimates prepared originally for the President's Materials Policy Commission for each year from 1900 through 1950 and later extended through 1952 by the Bureau of the Census, imports of nonfood raw materials during the years 1950–52 were equivalent to more than one-sixth of total United States production of raw materials other than foods. This proportion was more than double that prevailing 50 years earlier. The estimates were based on measures of the volume of raw materials imports and production of individual commodities, aggregated in terms of values expressed in constant 1935–39 dollars. Corresponding statistics for later years have

[5] Including newsprint and burlap, which are treated as finished manufactures in the standard classification of imports by economic classes, but are better regarded in the present context as industrial materials.

not been prepared, but estimates of the ratios prevailing since 1952 would clearly be of the same order of magnitude as those for the early 1950's.

For many specific commodities, of course, reliance upon imported supplies is much greater than the average for all industrial raw materials. We now obtain from foreign sources around one-sixth of our crude petroleum, almost one-fourth of our iron ore, one-third of our copper and rubber, over half of our raw wool, and the great bulk of our supplies of tin, nickel, aluminum,[6] and newsprint. Numerous other examples are listed in a bulletin published by the Bureau of Foreign Commerce (Contribution of Imports to United States Raw Material Supplies, World Trade Information Service, pt. 3, No. 57-1).

Another major consideration is that the dependence of United States industry upon imports of many technologically strategic materials is highly disproportionate to their dollar value. They are literally essential to keep factory wheels turning and assembly lines moving under existing technological conditions.

This is perhaps most emphatically illustrated by reference to the metallurgical industries upon which our high production of capital equipment, consumer durables, and military "hardware" is founded. We obtain from abroad, in addition to the substantial shares of our basic iron ore and major nonferrous metal requirements, most of our supplies of various ferroalloying ores and metals which impart to steel the heat-resistant, rust-resistant, and other special characteristics imperative for the operation of so much modern equipment, from machine tools to jet aircraft. Examples of metals supplied chiefly from abroad, other than those mentioned in a previous paragraph, include manganese, chrome, antimony, and cobalt (all in the neighborhood of 80 to 90 percent imported), as well as tungsten, lead, zinc, and cadmium.

The list of vital industrial materals obtained wholly or primarily from abroad is not, of course, confined to metals. Industrial diamonds, mica, asbestos, quebracho extract, and extra-long staple cotton are among numerous other examples noted in the bulletin cited above.

Altogether, about one-fifth of the crude and semimanufactured goods imported by the United States in 1956 were officially classified as strategic materials for stockpiling purposes, and another fifth consisted of materials (other than those in the stockpile group) obtained wholly or almost exclusively from foreign sources. Many other raw materials imports also represent high proportions of United States requirements, and still others supplement predominantly domestic supplies to an important degree.

United States imports of foods and manufactured goods are of somewhat less fundamental importance, either qualitatively or in terms of relative magnitudes, than those of industrial materials. Nevertheless, every American household enjoys the variety contributed to our established consumption pattern by imports both of foreign foodstuffs and of manufactured consumer goods.

Among the foodstuffs, some three-fifths consists of tropical products—coffee, tea, cocoa, bananas, spices, and nuts—for which imports represent the whole supply. While they can scarcely be regarded as

[6] Including the aluminum produced from imported bauxite, the principal form of importation.

absolutely indispensable, they certainly enrich not only our diets, but also our social customs. In addition, roughly half of our sugar and one-third of the fish marketed here come from abroad. The remaining food imports consist mainly of out-of-season produce and of such specialty items as European cheeses, meat products, wines, and spirits. Generally speaking, items in the latter group represent relatively small proportions of total United States supplies of similar foods and beverages, though many of them are of distinctive types not strictly identical with any domestic products.[7]

Many imports of foreign manufactured goods share the salient economic characteristics of the tropical and specialty foods. They are neither essential nor directly competitive, in a strict sense, with domestically produced goods; yet they contribute appreciably to the embellishment of our consumption patterns.

Imports of manufactured goods also include a number of types which are more or less directly competitive with similar domestic products. Watches, bicycles, musical instruments, tableware, photographic goods, cotton and woolen fabrics and apparel, automobiles, sewing machines, and some categories of industrial machinery are among the examples of this sort. There is no doubt that imports of such goods often create problems for the particular groups of Americans engaged in producing competitive articles. These imports, however, also play a role which is distinctly beneficial to other groups of Americans. In addition to increasing the dollar exchange available abroad to potential customers for United States exporters, they increase the range of free choice available to American consumers, reduce the prices at which the merchandise is available, or both, either through direct fulfillment of demand or through responses of domestic producers to the competitive challenge of imports.

This last point is one of general applicability, to competitive imports of raw materials as well as finished goods. The United States economy as a whole has benefited in wide areas from reductions in cost or improvements in design which actual or potential imports have stimulated United States producers to achieve. Such increases in efficiency, of course, reflect the power of competition to create better products at lower costs—a broad tendency upon which great reliance is normally and properly placed in our free-enterprise economy. The role of imports thus goes beyond the impact of those which actually enter American markets. Other potential imports exert a qualitative influence upon United States productive efficiency and living standards which is never reflected in the foreign trade statistics.

Apart from basic structural relationships between foreign trade transactions and the domestic economy, it is obvious that exports and imports also play dynamic roles both in cyclical fluctuations of business activity and in long-term economic growth. Brief comment on these points is in order.

With respect to long-term trends, a number of implications are clearly indicated by what has already been said. It may be emphasized here, however, that a salient feature of our economic history during the past century has been the way in which the changing

[7] For further details on foodstuffs, see the bulletin, published by the Bureau of Foreign Commerce, Contribution of Imports to United States Food Supplies (World Trade Information Service, pt. 3, No. 56–49).

pattern of United States foreign trade has both reflected and facilitated the transition of the United States from a primarily agrarian economy to the world's leading industrial economy.

During this interval, our needs for industrial raw materials have expanded enormously, and we have shifted from large net exports of raw materials to sizable net imports. Without the availability of foreign supplies to make up the deficit of domestic supplies in relation to recent rates of industrial consumption of raw materials, the expansion of the United States economy would certainly have been inhibited. At best, it would have been much slower and more costly than has been the case. Moreover, the thorough study of our raw materials position which was conducted a few years ago by the President's Materials Policy Commission strongly suggests continuing increases in our reliance upon foreign sources in order to obtain larger raw materials supplies at economically practicable costs.

While shifting from a surplus to a deficit position in raw materials, the United States has altered its international position with respect to manufactured goods in the opposite direction. The historical change in the pattern of United States exports has been toward progressively higher proportions of advanced manufactures. The capacity of foreign markets to absorb expanding amounts of such goods, and especially of those produced by our newer and more rapidly growing industrial sectors, has helped to accelerate the development of some of our more efficient industries, and thus to raise the productivity of the economy as a whole. Without this element of selective stimulus for high-productivity industries, the reallocation of national economic resources to them would have been somewhat less rapid and more limited in scope.

With regard to the role of foreign trade in short-term fluctuations of United States business activity, it is difficult to generalize. Current trends in exports and imports depend in considerable measure upon diverse conditions and developments abroad, as well as here, and these influences upon our trade are not necessarily nor consistently coordinated in a complementary way with purely domestic trends.

During the 1953-54 dip in United States economic activity, for example, the impact of changes in foreign trade was clearly advantageous. Rising exports and a shrinkage of imports helped to cushion the effects of declining tendencies in certain segments of the domestic economy. This factor, while perhaps not a decisive element in the early reversal of that downtrend, certainly provided appreciable support to the economy during the critical period of readjustment.

On the other hand, during the inflationary spurts of both 1946-47 and 1950-51, waves of heavy foreign demands for United States exports coincided with upsurges of domestic demand in the face of stringent supply conditions. The result in each case was to add fuel to inflationary fires and to complicate further an already tight supply situation. It may also be noted, however, that the influence of foreign trade upon the problem of inflation after the outbreak of the Korean conflict was by no means completely one-sided. For instance, an unprecedented influx of European steel-mill products in 1951 mitigated the supply stringency and was of notable assistance in avoiding serious production bottlenecks during that mobilization period. Similarly, the subsidence of effective exports demand after mid-1947 tended to ease the upward pressure on United States prices before the crest of the postwar inflationary spurt was reached. On the other hand, rising exports were an expansive, inflationary factor in the 1956 boom.

It is probably fair to say, in general, that the cyclical influence of foreign trade is usually wholesome for the United States. Unless cyclical swings (induced or occurring independently) in other countries are synchronized with our swings, changes in United States imports and exports tend to produce definitely countercyclical cushioning effects, at least during a mild United States business downturn of the type experienced since World War II—i. e., one initiated by internal factors, such as slackening of business investment in plant and equipment, retrenchment in business inventories, or curtailment of Government defense expenditures. Under such circumstances, part of the drop in spending by certain segments of the United States economy tends to be absorbed by declines in imports, rather than in domestic procurement and production. At the same time, the volume of exports is likely to be steady or even somewhat stimulated by more aggressive selling efforts by United States exporters, easier supply conditions in this country, and perhaps also by reductions in United States prices. Conversely, during a boom phase of the business cycle, increasing imports tend to relieve supply shortages and mitigate inflationary price movements.

# RECENT DEVELOPMENTS IN UNITED STATES FOREIGN TRADE

United States Department of Commerce

The Subcommittee on Foreign Trade Policy, in Chairman Boggs' letter of June 1, 1957, to Secretary Weeks, asked the Department of Commerce to supply a "* * * description and analysis * * *" of "* * * changes in the volume and composition of our merchandise trade."

United States export trade has expanded vigorously since 1953—following the letdown after the Korean war boom—and there has also been a substantial concurrent rise in imports. In export trade rates of expansion both in total foreign marketings of individual products and in total sales of United States goods in particular markets have varied widely. There has also been considerable diversity in the trends of United States demands for various categories of foreign products and in the geographic distribution of United States foreign purchases, which are the primary source of dollar availabilities for most countries.

The principal developments after 1953 along the above lines in United States exports and imports are the main concern in this paper. They can be better viewed, however, in the perspective of the broad historical changes of the preceding quarter century of economic growth and fluctuation. The broad changes in United States exports from 1929 to 1953 are summarized below, as a preface to a fairly detailed survey of export tendencies since 1953, and a similar introduction precedes the outline of recent import tendencies which follows in the latter part of the paper.

## BACKGROUND: BROAD CHANGES IN EXPORT TRADE, 1929–53

United States export trade expanded greatly in value in the quarter century ending with 1953; in that year, the earliest postwar year reasonably comparable with prewar periods with respect to United States foreign trade, United States commercial exports were 2½ times those of 1929. Foreign shipments of all United States products in 1953, including those of military equipment and supplies under the mutual-security program, which began in 1950, were 3 times the total value of 1929 exports. The expansion was even greater relative to levels in the depressed 1930's, when exports persisted at levels well below those of the preceding years of prosperity.

Much of the value rise from levels in prewar periods, of course, stemmed from price inflation, but in volume terms the gains were, nevertheless, large. Nonmilitary exports in 1953 averaged 50 percent greater in volume than in 1929 and 80 percent higher than in 1939.

The expansion of exports from 1929 to 1953, although large, was considerably smaller than that in total United States domestic output. From 1939 to 1953, however, exports and gross national product increased in about the same degree. Nonmilitary exports were 3.4 percent of the gross national product in 1953, or barely as large in these relative terms as in 1939, as compared with a 5-percent ratio of total exports to gross national product in 1929. The smaller relative size of exports in 1939, as in other prewar years after 1929, despite weaker trends in the United States economy than in most other industrial countries, reflected the extreme slump in United States exports, as in international trade generally, in the course of the great depression of the early 1930's. Persistence of exports in the prewar decade at a much lower level even relative to United States output than before the depression is explained by a comparable drop in the relative size of United States imports, particularly reflecting protracted underutilization of United States production capacity and technological advances which substituted domestic output for certain raw-material imports, and by the collapse of United States private investment abroad after 1929.

The shift to a much higher level of exports in the postwar period was marked by considerable fluctuation. Mainly owing to the United States lend-lease program, wartime exports soared by 1944 to $14.4 billion, or 6.8 percent of gross national product, but with the winding up of the war were reduced to $10.5 billion in 1945. Relief and reconstruction needs in Europe and the Far East, coupled with extensive United States Government financing, supplemented by the spending of accumulated dollar balances by countries outside the war areas to meet deferred needs, boosted exports by 1947 to a peak of $15.3 billion, or 6.6 percent of gross national product.

Subsequent to 1947, exports fell to lower levels, particularly relative to gross national product (the export gross national product ratio in 1950 was little above that of 1939) until 1951, when they were boosted sharply again, owing to the Korean war boom and rising military-aid shipments. Nonmilitary exports reached $14 billion in that year, and total exports mounted to $15 billion. In the succeeding 2 years, although total exports continued at or above their 1951 level, nonmilitary exports fell off, with most of the decline registered in agricultural exports.

Both before and after World War II there were noteworthy shifts in the relative importance of the major foreign areas as markets for United States goods. In 1939 continental western Europe was the destination of 22 percent of United States exports as compared with 26 percent in 1929, and the proportion going to Canada also dropped, while the Far East became much more important despite a large relative contraction in United States sales to Australia and New Zealand. In 1947, on the other hand, continental western Europe was more important as an export destination even than in 1929, reflecting the area's emergency needs and large-scale United States financing, while much sharper upward shifts in relative importance were evident for the Latin American market and the total market in the Near East and Africa. On the other hand, the United Kingdom in 1947 bought less than half as large a proportion of United States exports as in 1939 or 1929, and there were relative declines as destinations for United States exports also in the cases of Canada and the Far East.

There were sharp differences in the geographic distribution of the total United States foreign market in 1953 as compared with 1947.

Most striking were the near doubling of the percentage of United States exports shipped to Canada and the elimination of the Soviet bloc countries as United States markets.

The principal net effects of these shifts on the relative position of the various United States foreign markets in 1953 as compared with 1929 were substantial gains on the part of the Canadian and the Latin American markets and the total market in the Near East and Africa, and a decline by two-thirds in the percentage of United States foreign sales made to the United Kingdom.

Reflecting the altered geographical distribution of foreign demand for United States goods, there were substantial changes in the composition of United States exports by economic class. The proportion of finished manufactures in total exports (excluding military goods) rose progressively, apart from short-term fluctuations, from 49 percent in 1929 to 61 percent in 1953. Offsetting this change there was a sharp relative contraction in crude materials as a class, owing to the declining position of United States cotton in world markets, and also some lessening of semimanufactures in relative importance.

### EXPORT TENDENCIES SINCE 1953

In the last several years a major new advance has developed in United States commercial exports, both in absolute terms and in relation to United States domestic output. Following a moderate rise in 1954, an accelerating upward trend set in, and from 1955 to 1956 the increase was over 20 percent. By the latter year total nonmilitary exports had mounted by 41 percent to $17.3 billion. The uptrend continued in 1957; exports in January–June exceeded those of the first 6 months of 1956 by 22 percent. The 1957 rise, it should be noted, stemmed to a considerable extent from extraordinary and temporary increases in shipments of cotton and petroleum.

The export rise since 1953, particularly from 1955 to 1956, has been somewhat steeper than that in gross national product. In relation to gross national product, nonmilitary exports increased from 3.4 percent in 1953 to 4.2 percent in 1956.

The advance in the total value of all United States good supplied to foreign countries, including shipments of military equipment and supplies under the mutual-security program, was somewhat less than that in commercial shipments alone, amounting since 1953 to 20 percent. Military-aid shipments, which commenced in 1950, reached their peak in 1953, and subsequently have been at much lower levels.

The volume advance in commercial exports since 1953—36 percent—has been nearly as great as that in their value. For finished manufactures the average volume gain was 20 percent, while those for crude materials, semimanufactures, and foodstuffs all were considerably in excess of 50 percent.

Reflecting the particularly rapid increases in the latter three economic classes, the proportion of each in the commercial export total was higher in 1956 than in 1953, with semimanufactures, owing to substantially higher prices, showing the largest relative gain—from 12 to 16 percent of total nonmilitary exports. The offsetting contraction was in the proportion of finished manufactures, from 61 to 54 percent of all nonmilitary exports.

The 1953–56 export rise was characterized by a growing excess of exports over imports as United States purchases from abroad tended less strongly upward. The export surplus in commercial merchandise trade was particularly low in 1953, reflecting the sizable decrease in exports from their Korean war peak. It amounted to $1.4 billion—except for that of 1950, by far the smallest trade gap of the entire period since World War II. With the dip in imports in 1954 as exports picked up again, the trade balance mounted to $2.6 billion. Subsequently, it soared to $4.7 billion in 1956 as exports accelerated upward in the face of a slower—even though substantial—rise in imports.

The great rise in the nonmilitary export surplus from 1953 to 1956 was counterbalanced by noteworthy increases in several types of foreign dollar receipts through transactions with the United States, although there was no gain in net foreign earnings from those of a service nature. The net upward shift in new United States private investment abroad alone amounted to $2.6 billion. About two-fifths of this increase appeared in new direct net investment, which jumped to $1.8 billion in 1956—by far the highest annual amount on record and more than double the previous high of $850 million in 1952. The spurt in United States direct investment abroad in 1956 in part reflected unusual transactions centering particularly in petroleum. That year was also marked by substantial upward shifts in net United States purchases of foreign securities and in net short-term foreign lending.

As regards foreign dollar receipts from United States Government sources over the interval, there was little change in nonmilitary grants, which were fairly steady at $1.7 billion to $1.9 billion. However, there was a sharp rise of about $0.8 billion in net short-term United States Government credits outstanding, reflecting sales of agricultural surpluses for foreign currencies.

Throughout the period 1953–56, total United States funds made available through imports of goods and services, net capital outflow, and United States Government grants and other unilateral transfers substantially exceeded foreign payments to the United States for goods and services. Accordingly, through all transactions with the United States, the rest of the world increased its holdings of gold and dollar assets by $7 billion. Even in 1955 and in 1956 the annual surplus of foreign dollar receipts amounted to about $1.5 billion despite the large rise in foreign purchases of United States goods.

*European market expansion strongest*

Nearly half the entire recent $5 billion expansion in United States foreign markets occurred in Western Europe. Shipments to destinations there rose $2.4 billion, or 81 percent, from 1953 to 1956, an increase reflecting progressive liberalization of dollar imports as the area's reserves in United States currency accumulated, as well as rapidly rising underlying demands especially for United States raw materials and foodstuffs. Among the greatest percentage gains by individual countries were those for West Germany and the Netherlands, to which shipments rose by 1956 to well over double their levels of 1953. The relative increases to the other important destinations were also very large—53 percent for the United Kingdom, 65 percent (nearly all in 1956) for France, and 83 percent both for Italy and for Belgium.

Another large segment of the export rise—nearly $950 million—stemmed from a 29-percent expansion in the Canadian market, centering particularly in producers' durable goods. Shipments to Canada of industrial machinery rose 62 percent over the interval, and those of iron and steel rose 87 percent. There were broad gains also in other categories of both producer and consumer goods, notably in motor vehicles and parts and in foodstuffs.

Nearly as substantial an expansion was evident in the Latin American market. Increases ranging from 20 to 30 percent in shipments to Mexico, Venezuela, and Cuba were responsible for over half the total rise of about $720 million in exports to Latin America, and the average gain to other destinations apart from Brazil was similar in percentage terms. Although that country purchased heavily in 1954 when coffee prices soared, it held imports of United States goods subsequently to not more than the very low level of 1953. The increase for the entire Latin American market, which expanded by a fourth, was distributed over a broad range of capital goods, raw materials, and consumer products, with advances in machinery, automobiles, and chemicals predominating.

By 1956 the rise in exports to Latin America was exceeded in degree by that in shipments to the Far East. Although exports to destinations in the Far East rose little above their 1953 level until 1956, in that year they jumped to 33 percent more than 3 years earlier. A third of the expansion of around two-thirds of a billion dollars stemmed from the sharp advance of 1956 in exports to Japan, but outstanding gains also appeared in total exports to India, which reflected large shipments of surplus wheat and cotton, and to the Republic of Korea, destination of increased shipments of cotton, fertilizers, and machinery. There were other substantial gains in the area, notably for Viet-nam, Laos, and Cambodia and for Hong Kong, Indonesia (which permitted greatly increased importation following price inflated receipts for rubber in 1955), and Pakistan. Iron and steel-mill products, raw cotton, chemical products, and industrial machinery accounted for most of the rise in exports to the Far East, while shipments of textile manufactures fell by a third, partly reflecting a cutback in purchases by the Philippines.

The 1953–56 advance in exports to Western Asia was particularly strong, amounting to 40 percent. A high percentage rise in shipments to Iran led the gains in that area. Total exports to destinations in Africa increased 30 percent; about half the rise was recorded in those to the Union of South Africa, which comprises almost 50 percent of the entire United States market in that area.

The geographic distribution of the total United States foreign market was materially shifted after 1953 by the great increase of sales to Western Europe. In 1956 that area was the destination of 31 percent of all commercial exports as compared with 24 percent in 1953, while the percentages of exports to Canada, Latin America, the Far East, and Africa, were in each instance a reduced part of total exports.

Among the leading individual countries, substantial upward shifts in the percentages of United States exports despatched to Western

Germany, the Netherlands, Belgium-Luxembourg, Italy, France, the United Kingdom, and India, were offset by noteworthy declines in the proportions destined for the Philippines, Brazil, Colombia, Cuba, Mexico, Venezuela, and Japan.

*Agricultural exports increase strongly*

The United States nonmilitary export gain from 1953 to 1956 reflected particularly strong increases in agricultural products. From their postwar low in 1953, agricultural exports rose somewhat in the succeeding 2 years, then jumped $1 billion from 1955 to 1956 to a total of nearly $4.2 billion, or 46 percent more than 3 years earlier. Nevertheless, relative to the commercial export total, agricultural exports showed little change, amounting to 24 percent of all nonmilitary exports in 1956 as compared with 23 percent in 1953.

The expansion in agricultural exports is attributable to new supply shortages abroad, rising income levels in important markets, liberalization of dollar imports, ample United States supplies, sales for foreign currencies and other surplus disposal measures under Public Law 480, and more competitive United States export pricing.

Over a fourth of the increase of $1.3 billion was contributed by fats, oils, and oilseeds, exports of which soared by 1956 to almost 2¼ times their value in 1953. Factors in this expansion include high and rapidly increasing United States soybean production, surplus stocks, favorable export pricing, and sales for foreign currency coupled with increasing basic demands in Europe, in part owing to income gains there, and reduced supplies of olives in the Mediterranean Basin and of sunflower seed in the Argentine. Exports of soybeans and other oilseeds, the most important type of export in the category, rose by nearly three-fourths, while those of refined vegetable oils, which were at a very low postwar level in 1953, rocketed to a value six times as high and shipments of inedible vegetable oils tripled. In addition, there were substantial percentage gains in shipments of tallow and lard. A sizable portion of all fats and oils shipped—in volume several times the typical level of 1946–52—was exported under Government programs, as compared with a minor amount in 1953.

Another fifth of the agricultural export expansion from 1953 to 1956 resulted from a steep rise in exports of grains in 1955–56, following the decline of 1953–54 with the expansion of agricultural output in Europe and termination of emergency-aid shipments of 1952 and 1953 to south Asia. The upturn of grain exports in 1955 reflected principally a near doubling of coarse grain shipments from their very low level in 1954, owing to a sharp drop in supplies available to Europe from Argentina. In 1956, however, most of the margin of grain exports over those of 1953 was contributed by wheat, shipments of which were valued at 35 percent more than 3 years earlier. Wheat shipments mounted in 1956 from their relatively low volumes of 1953–55 to a level typical of the early postwar years. This rise is traceable to weather damage to the European wheat crop early in 1956 and at harvesttime, and larger sales for local currencies to countries in Asia and South America. About half the wheat shipped in 1956 went under Public Law 480 programs. Rice exports, after a rapid decline from their very high level of 1952–53, turned sharply upward in 1956 with large Public Law 480 shipments to Pakistan and Indonesia. Despite the huge shipments in 1956 to destinations outside Western Europe, nearly all of the margin of total grain exports over those of 1953 was afforded by those to that area.

Cotton also contributed much of the 1953–56 gain in total agricultural exports. Exports of that commodity in 1956 were greater in volume than in any year subsequent to 1951, although in value they were under those of 1952 and 1954. Foreign sales of United States cotton had been very low in both 1953 and 1955, owing mainly to availability of relatively large supplies of foreign cotton at prices below United States support levels. Following open market sales from Government stocks for export, shipments soared in 1956 as purchases abroad were increased, partly to rebuild depleted mill stocks.

In contrast to wheat and cotton, exports of unmanufactured tobacco did not gain over their value in 1953, apart from a peak in 1955 which partly reflected sizable foreign currency sales. The high export figure for 1953 had been affected, however, by the delay of certain shipments to the United Kingdom which normally would have been made in the preceding year. On the whole, in recent years tobacco exports have manifested little tendency to grow in volume. Despite growing cigarette consumption, foreign purchases of United States cigarette tobaccos—the bulk of exports—have been held in check by expanding production in other exporting countries and by increasing United States demand for some export grades owing to consumption shifts in favor of the filter cigarette.

The high total value of agricultural exports in 1956 as compared with 1953 also reflected great increases in foreign sales of United States fruits and dairy products. Shipments of fruits and preparations rose 71 percent, as European markets, especially in the United Kingdom, expanded, partly as a result of liberalization measures. Moreover, poor harvests in 1956 in Canada and in other producing areas limited some competing supplies. Exports of dairy products, classified as such, rose even more percentagewise, also reflecting improved European demand. In addition, there was a great increase in private shipments of surplus foodstuffs, largely dairy products, donated from United States Government surplus stocks to private welfare agencies for foreign distribution. Increased foreign demand became evident after 1953 also for certain other types of agricultural products, particularly feeds and vegetables.

*Nonagricultural exports expand*

Nearly as substantial a rise as that in exports of farm products has developed since 1953 in sales abroad of nonagricultural products, which constituted over three-fourths of the nonmilitary export total in 1956. After a horizontal course from 1951 to 1954, apart from a minor dip in 1953, a strong advance set in which lifted commercial exports of nonfarm products to a total of $13 billion in 1956, or 40 percent more than in 1953.

The underlying economic factors in this rise, in addition to growth of dollar recipts abroad, included the rapid expansion of manufacturing production in Europe and Japan coupled with inadequacies of certain internal raw material supplies, high rates of capital formation (in some instances reflecting substantial inflows of United States private capital) in numerous primary supplying countries in response to rising exports to the manufacturing countries, and resultant increases in internal incomes, profits, and consumer spending.

The gains were particularly great for iron and steel, coal, and copper, to supply rapidly growing metal products industries in Europe and Japan, where deficiencies of local supplies, particularly of coal, pig iron, and scrap steel, became acute. Shipments of iron and steel scrap soared from a minor figure in 1953 to nearly $300 million in 1956, while coal shipments more than doubled in value, owing almost entirely to a fivefold gain in those to Europe, which were at a low postwar level in 1953. Shipments of nonferrous metals, primarily consisting of copper and copper-base alloys including scrap, jumped to over 2⅓ times those of 1953, reflecting large gains recorded for destinations in Europe and the Far East. There were also very strong rises in exports of chemical products, which as a group, apart from medicinals and pharmaceuticals, mounted by 70 percent, owing to particularly sharp advances in shipments to Europe, Latin America, and the Far East. Exports of synthetic rubber and of paper base stocks advanced even more strongly than those of chemicals. There was a decline in exports of petroleum and products until 1956, but their annual total in that year exceeded that of 1953 by $69 million. Mainly owing to the Suez crisis, the annual value of crude petroleum and of gas oil and fuel oil exports alone in 1956 was $92 million above that of the preceding year.

Increases in exports of the foregoing commodities accounted for nearly all of the $1.5 billion total expansion in the value of nonagricultural raw materials exported (apart from iron and steel other than scrap), which in turn contributed two-fifths of the $3.7 billion overall increase in nonagricultural exports. Around another two-fifths of this rise stemmed from larger exports of capital goods.

Capital formation in Canada, Latin America, and the Far East was responsible for much of the 60-percent rise in exports of iron and steel-mill products (exclusive of scrap), which contributed about a fifth of the total increase in exports of capital goods.

The largest gain in capital goods, however, was that in industrial machinery—around 40 percent of all United States exports of capital goods. Industrial machinery exports rose nearly $600 million, with most of the gain appearing in 1956. While close to half of the increase was recorded in shipments to Canada, which mounted by 63 percent, those to most other areas also increased very substantially. The expansion in industrial machinery reflected high percentage gains for construction, mining, and many other varieties of industrial machinery. On the other hand, shipments of metalworking machines and machine tools, which in 1953 were at a peak total for recent years, were subsequently at substantially lower levels.

There were substantial advances also in other categories of capital equipment. Although shipments of railway equipment did not rise, particularly high increases were evident for other transportation equipment; exports of trucks and buses rose by two-thirds and those of civilian aircraft nearly doubled. Relatively strong gains were registered also in certain other equipment categories—notably office machines and equipment and scientific and professional instruments—and in metal manufactures, much of which consist of producers' items including building supplies. A rise of 20 percent appeared in shipments of electrical apparatus other than household appliances and radio and television apparatus, with particularly strong percentage gains in those dispatched to Canada and the Far East.

Export sales increases were narrower in the principal categories of manufactured goods for consumer use, owing in part to import and economic development policies in many countries giving higher priority to needed raw materials and capital goods. Shipments of passenger automobiles were increased in 1954 and particularly in 1955, but were reduced in 1956 to a level 20 percent over that of 1953. Smaller gains were evident for radio and television apparatus and for household appliances. Shipments of textile manufactures in 1954–56 were a little lower than in 1953; those to the Far East fell by nearly a third, but some increase appeared in textile exports to Europe and to Africa. Exports of medicinals and pharmaceuticals were relatively high both in 1954 and in 1956, in the latter year exceeding those of 1953, the lowest year since 1950, by 13 percent.

*Industrial materials bulk larger as export components*

The strong recent uptrends in exports of a number of products have resulted in some noteworthy changes in the commodity composition of the United States nonmilitary export total. In terms of broad classes, exports of nonagricultural raw materials became considerably more important by 1956 than they were in 1953, while finished manufactures—the greater part of the total—fell off somewhat.

Total exports of crude and semimanufactured materials of nonfarm origin were boosted from 15½ to nearly 21½ percent of the value of all nonmilitary exports, chiefly by the steep uptrends in coal and metals. Coal shipments expanded from 2¾ to 4¼ percent, those of iron and steel scrap jumped from a negligible fraction to 1.7 percent, and nonferrous metals also expanded substantially as an export component. In addition, relative expansion in exports of chemical semimanufactures (chiefly of synthetic rubber, plastics and resin materials, nitrogenous fertilizer materials, and industrial chemicals) and of iron and steel (excluding scrap), also contributed to the expansion of raw materials in total United States foreign sales.

The comparatively moderate rise in commercial exports of finished manufactures reduced their proportion in total nonmilitary exports in 1953–56 from 61 percent to 54 percent. Most categories of finished manufactures were smaller components of the nonmilitary export total in 1956 than in 1953. Reflecting horizontal tendencies or declines in actual shipments, machine tools and metalworking machinery, tractors and parts, agricultural machinery and implements, railway transportation equipment, textile manufactures, and lubricating oils were all considerably reduced as export components in the later year. Electrical apparatus and passenger automobiles also declined relative to the export total. The only noteworthy gains were those for construction and mining machinery, which rose from 4.1 to 4.6 percent of total nonmilitary exports, for motortrucks and buses, and for civilian aircraft.

There were other noticeable differences between 1953 and 1956 in the composition of exports. Among agricultural raw materials, about 9½ percent of total nonmilitary shipments in both years, a relative increase in oilseeds and inedible vegetable oils was offset by a decline in the tobacco component. Foodstuffs increased a little—from 14 to

15 percent—reflecting principally relative expansion in edible vegetable oils, fruits and preparations, and dairy products (including those donated for foreign relief), partly offset by shrinkages in the percentages of wheat, rice, and coarse grains.

BACKGROUND: BROAD CHANGES IN UNITED STATES IMPORTS, 1929–53

The upward shift in the annual value of imports from 1929 to the threshold, in 1953, of the latest upsurge of United States foreign trade was about equal in degree to that in exports, apart from military aid shipments. Imports in 1953 were valued at $10.9 billion—2½ times their value in 1929. Compared with just before World War II, the rise of imports to a level nearly 5 times as high by 1953 considerably exceeded the percentage increase in commercial exports, but the import shift was from an abnormally low level which in part reflected a marked reduction from 1936–37 levels in imports originating in Europe owing to the increasingly disturbed situation there.

Nevertheless, in volume terms the change in imports from prewar levels to 1953 was not as great as that in exports, while import prices, on the average, rose considerably further than those of exports. The volumes of foreign goods arriving in the United States in 1953 averaged about 36 percent above those of 1929 and nearly 70 percent higher than in 1939, as compared with gains of 50 and 80 percent in commercial exports.

In comparison with United States gross national product or expenditure, the expansion in imports, like that in exports, was much smaller between 1929 and 1953. As compared with the late 1930's, however, the value expansion in imports, as for exports, was about equal, in percentage terms, to that in gross national product.

From 4.2 percent of GNP in 1929 imports fell sharply in the early 1930's, and throughout the depression decade, except for 1937, tended to remain at about 2.8 percent, or only around two-thirds their size relative to GNP as in the prosperous, expanding 1920's. Explanations for this large drop in relative magnitude are to be found in relatively decreased prices for imports, excess production capacity at home, the substitution of domestically produced synthetic fibers for silk, and the decline of the luxury market.

Subsequent fluctuations in the magnitude of imports in relation to total United States output were roughly the reverse of those in exports. Shipping shortages and the cutting off of supplies from extensive areas of the world while United States output expanded cut import/GNP ratios in 1941–45 to 1.9 percent. By 1948, however, imports had recovered to their prewar value relationship to GNP of about 2.8 percent, reflecting greatly increased prices and a relatively small rise in average volume. Even in that year volume was not much above the 1937 level, partly as a result of inadequacies of supply both from areas subjected to war damage and from others which had to forego expansion and even replacement of capital equipment. United States imports in the early postwar period were also held in check by high restocking demands abroad, the prolonged suspension of prewar marketing relationships, and the substitution of domestic United States sources of supply.

During the Korean war imports rose considerably relative to GNP, as a result of sharply higher prices as well as substantial volume gains. With the reversion from hot to cold war by 1953, the import/GNP ratio settled down to about 3.0 percent, or a little under the average of 1936–37, prior to the distortions of the 1938 recession and the intensifying international crisis.

The factors explaining the low level of imports relative to GNP in 1953 as compared with 1929 center primarily in raw materials. Imports in that economic class in the later year were only 1.6 percent of GNP, as compared with 2.7 percent in 1929. This downward shift stemmed from the virtual elimination of raw silk as an import item, large relative declines in imports of crude rubber, hides and skins, undressed furs, and fats and oils, and substantial relative shrinkages also in imports of a number other less important raw materials. In some instances there were actual decreases in import volume, while in others there was an absence of growth commensurate with the doubling in real terms of total United States domestic output and expenditure. Over the whole quarter century, these relative declines, which resulted principally from substitution of new domestic products for imported materials and from changed international supply-demand relationships, far exceeded in weight the noteworthy relative gains in imports of petroleum and fuel oil, nonferrous and ferroalloy ores and metals, newsprint, and several other commodities.

Imports of finished manufactures also shifted after 1929 to a much lower level relative to GNP. From a ratio of 0.7 percent, these imports fell in the 1930's by a third to a half in relative size. The relative contraction may be attributed to excess productive capacity at home, intensified domestic competition with imports, and the depressed condition of the domestic market for luxury goods. After World War II, relatively low levels of imports of finished manufactures persisted as late as 1953, when they remained no greater than 0.4 percent of GNP. Formidable obstacles, often unrelated to tariffs, faced by foreign manufacturers in endeavoring to enter or to reenter the United States market, and the incompleteness of economic reconstruction in several countries, were among the factors responsible for the comparatively small United States purchases of manufactured goods from abroad.

Corresponding shifts took place between 1929 and 1953 in the commodity composition of the United States import total. Crude materials fell off from 35 percent of all imports in 1929 and nearly as high a fraction in 1939 to 24 percent in 1953, while the proportion of semimanufactures, which include nonferrous metals as refined from their ores, expanded from 25 percent to 31 percent. Raw material imports as a whole, therefore, were a somewhat reduced proportion of all imports in the later years. Finished manufactures (excluding newsprint and burlap, classified for present purposes as raw materials) also were a smaller fraction of all imports in the later year, although up considerably from that of early postwar years; they were 14 percent of total imports in 1953 as compared with 18 percent in 1929. Foodstuffs, on the other hand, were a substantially increased segment of the import total in 1953—nearly 31 percent; most of the increase in this component from 22 percent in 1929 is traceable to coffee, which approximately doubled from prewar as a percentage of total imports.

Substantial shifts from prewar to postwar in the geographic distribution of United States imports by area of origin resulted from the varying commodity developments summarized above. The impact of war, United States technological advances, and Chinese communism on United States purchases of raw materials produced in the Far East was responsible for much of the decline from 30 percent in 1939 to 15 percent in 1953 in the proportion of all United States imports originating in that area. Destruction of manufacturing plants in Japan and the effects of the war on market relationships were also factors. Similar developments in Europe and the substitution of domestic United States sources of supply reduced western Europe's share in the United States market for imported goods from 25 to 21 percent. Above-average increases in United States import demands for newsprint, metals, and sawmill products were important in the expansion of Canada's share from 15 to 23 percent. The rise in expenditures for foreign metals and, more important, similar gains for petroleum and fuel oil and for coffee contributed to the rise of imports originating in Latin America from 22 to 32 percent of all imports. There was also a relative expansion in purchases from western Asia and Africa; imports from those areas rose from 4 to 7 percent of the total.

### IMPORT TENDENCIES SINCE 1953

Since 1953 imports have grown at about the same rate as that for United States domestic output and expenditures. The import/GNP ratio in 1956 was 3.0 percent—just equal to the ratio 3 years earlier.

In absolute terms the import rise has been considerable. After a dip in 1954 with the domestic business readjustment of that year, imports mounted by 1956 to $12.6 billion—$1.7 billion or 16 percent more than in 1953. In volume the rise amounted to about 11 percent.

The average rise in the import volumes of nonfood materials to supply domestic production—over half of all imports—was considerably smaller, amounting to about 6 percent. The fluctuations in the volume of raw material imports from 1953 to 1956 were approximately parallel to those in domestic manufacturing production.

Although imports of manufactured foodstuffs expanded steadily, those of crude foodstuffs did not gain over the period in average volume, and in 1956 remained below their peak in 1953. Imports of consumer and other finished manufactures, on the other hand, after a hesitation in 1954, increased rapidly to a 1956 total more than 60 percent, both in volume and in value, above their 1953 level.

The expansion in imports of manufactured goods maintained the 1953 relationships of total imports to GNP as the ratio for foodstuffs fell off and that for raw materials showed little change. There were corresponding shifts in the composition of imports by economic class; the proportion of finished manufactures rose from 14 to nearly 20 percent, with the offsetting decline in foodstuffs, which were a fourth of all imports in 1956. Reflecting substantially increased prices, raw material imports increased sufficiently in value to hold steady as a percentage of the total.

The rise in imports of raw materials after 1953 amounted to nearly $900 million, or 15 percent, to a total of $6.8 billion in 1956. Over half of the increment was contributed by the accelerated uptrend in imports of petroleum and residual fuel oil, which together accelerated upward to nearly $1.2 billion, or 62 percent more than 3 years earlier. Iron ore was prominent among the other raw material import gains; imports of that material soared to 2¾ times their volume in 1953. Imports of diamonds also rose steeply, and there were sizable value gains in sawmill products, newsprint, paper base stocks, rubber, and nonferrous metals, but deliveries of wool were considerably lower.

The percentage advance in nonferrous metals and ferroalloys was minor, despite the strong long run uptrend of United States foreign purchases in this important group of commodities. Nonferrous metal imports were particularly high in 1953, in part owing to the program for stockpiling strategic and critical materials, which attained its peak rate of total annual expenditure in the fiscal year ending in mid-1953. Nevertheless, imports of nickel, lead, and zinc were substantially greater in value by 1956, although higher prices were responsible for much of these increases. The value of copper imports also rose considerably, but annual volume was lower not only in 1954 but also in 1955 and 1956 when competing European demands for that metal were particularly strong. On the other hand, imports of tin after 1953 were reduced in volume but still more in value, and deliveries of ferroalloy ores and metals, which also were very high in 1953, likewise were subsequently much lower, owing mainly to cutbacks in purchases of manganese and tungsten. There was a somewhat similar pattern of variation in the case of aluminum and bauxite, but by 1956 imports of these items rebounded to their 1953 level in value, although volume remained considerably lower.

There were some indications in 1953–56 that imports of all raw materials used in nondurable goods production (mainly fibers and leather) may have continued their apparent tendency after 1929 to lag in volume relative to domestic nondurable goods production. A similar though less clear tendency in imports used in durable goods production seems also to have persisted.

Total imports of foodstuffs—nearly half of which consist of coffee—were nearly 3 percent lower in value in 1956 than in 1953. Those of coffee, which exhibited a declining trend of per capita volume in the present decade as the price advanced, showed little net change in either total value or in volume in the period under review; appreciably lower prices in 1956 were reflected in a value 2 percent under that of 1953. Considerably lower prices for cocoa with no gain in volume reduced the value of imports of that commodity. The principal reduction, however, was recorded for grains and feeds, which were cut sharply following the imposition of quotas late in 1953 and 3 years later were only half those of that peak year. Meat imports also fell off, but those of fish and some alcoholic beverages registered substantial gains. There was little evidence in the period of a modification in the very broadly horizontal long-term trend in the volume of per capita imports of foodstuffs other than coffee.

The $0.9 billion rise in total imports of finished manufactures stemmed to a considerable extent from very large increases in United States purchases of foreign industrial and electrical machinery, vehicles, and textiles. Total deliveries of machinery and vehicles increased $278 million, or 79 percent, with about a third of this rise recorded for automobiles, imports of which nearly tripled. Machinery imports rose by over $100 million, and deliveries of aircraft were $55 million in 1956 as compared with $10 million in 1953. Virtually all of these gains appeared in imports from Western Europe. Imports of textiles rose about $165 million, or nearly 60 percent, with the bulk of the rise appearing in those from the Far East, chiefly Japan. Those of cotton finished manufactures—over a third of all finished textile imports—more than doubled, with almost two-fifths of the increment in cloth alone. An increase of nearly 50 percent appeared in wool finished manufactures. Imports of finished iron and steel mill products amounted to over $170 million in 1956, or about 15 percent above their relatively large value in 1953; domestic demands for steel were at peak levels in both years.

The commodity composition of imports in 1956 was noticeably different from that of the initial year of the period under review, reflecting the varied tendencies outlined above. The outstanding expansion as a component of total United States imports was that of petroleum and products—from 7 to 10 percent. Machinery and vehicles, iron ore, textile manufactures, and fish also shifted upward considerably in relative importance. Compared with 1953, imports of coffee, which bulks larger than any other single commodity in United States foreign purchases, were rather less important in 1956 in the total value of goods delivered from abroad. Tin, grains and feeds, wool, fertilizers and explosives, iron and steel-mill products, cocoa, and meat products also fell off noticeably in relative importance.

*Purchases from most areas rise*

The diversity in commodity import tendencies after 1953 is reflected in the varying increases in total United States purchases from the major foreign regions. By 1956 imports from Europe mounted to one-fourth more than 3 years earlier, while somewhat lesser gains were apparent in total deliveries from Canada and the Far East and those from all Latin America increased only moderately. Imports from western Asia soared, in contrast to no gain in deliveries from Africa.

Over a third of the $1.7 billion expansion in United States imports in 1953–56 was contributed by the expansion in purchases from Western Europe. In addition to a $256 million increase in deliveries of machinery and vehicles, increments appeared in those of textile manufactures, paper and paper materials, steel manufactures, glass, and whiskey and other distilled spirits. Moreover, there were extensive increases amounting to over $200 million in a variety of other classifications, mainly of manufactured products, apart from declines in nonferrous metals, ferroalloys, and fertilizers.

Imports from Canada mounted by $431 million over the period despite 1956 imports from there of grains and feeds valued at over $100 million below those of 1953. The rise stemmed chiefly from increased United States purchasing of newsprint and paper-base stocks, crude petroleum, iron ore (imports of which were minor as late as 1953), nonferrous metals, and sawmill products.

A virtual doubling of textile sales to the United States market was responsible for half the total addition of almost $270 million to imports from the Far East. The increased value of rubber imports in 1956 despite a reduced volume, and greatly enlarged deliveries of Japanese plywood, also contributed noticeably to this expansion.

The $187 million augmentation in the total value of goods arriving from Latin America was considerably exceeded by the increase in crude petroleum and residual-fuel oil alone. Imports of iron ore also soared, rising by $61 million. Other important shifts over the period included a $71 million lower value in 1956 of coffee imports from the area, and a $52 milion decrease in those of wool.

The greater part of the $238 million expansion in imports from all other areas (Western Asia, Africa, European territories in the Western Hemisphere, and the Soviet bloc) centered in petroleum and products, which are imported from the Netherlands Antilles in the Caribbean area as well as from Arab oil countries. There was a noticeable rise also in imports of coffee from African sources.

Expressed in terms of shares of the United States market, or percentages of total imports, the relative importance of the major world regions as sources of foreign supplies to the United States did not change much after 1953. Canada remained the source of close to one-fourth of all United States imports, while Latin America, a somewhat more important supplying area in value terms, slipped from 32 to 29 percent. In the Eastern Hemisphere, Western Europe received an increasing proportion of United States expenditures for imports, by 1956 matching Canada as a source, and imports from Western Asia mounted to over 2 percent of total imports, while those from Africa fell off in 1956 to under 5 percent.

There was great variation in the trends of United States imports from at least the leading individual countries of origin in the period 1953–56. Purchases from Japan more than doubled and those from West Germany mounted by three-fourths. Imports from Venezuela, Italy, the United Kingdom, Belgium-Luxembourg, and France all registered substantial gains, while more moderate increases characterized those from Canada, Mexico, and Cuba. On the other hand, purchases from the Netherlands, Colombia, India, and the Philippines declined after 1953 and persisted at lower levels. The total value of Brazilian products delivered to the United States also was reduced in the 2 middle years, but in 1956 recovered most of the lost ground.

The most important individual country sources of foreign supplies to the United States in 1956, apart from Canada, were Brazil, the United Kingdom, and Venezuela, each with between 5½ and 6 percent of the United States market. Other comparatively important suppliers included Japan, Western Germany, Mexico, Cuba, and Colombia. The percentages of all imports in 1956 which originated in Japan and West Germany, of course, greatly exceeded those of 1953, and relative gains were evident also for Venezuela and the United Kingdom. On the other hand there were reductions in the proportion of imports supplied from Brazil, Colombia, and Cuba.

## A TARIFF TRUCE—PLUS

Samuel Lubell

In preparing for next year's battle over the extension of the reciprocal trade agreements program we might do well to turn back our memories to 1955 when the extension of the act was debated last.

At the time both side tried to frighten the public with dire prophecies of what would happen if they lost the legislative battle. Those who favored lower tariffs warned that if tariffs were not cut foreign nations would be unable to earn enough dollars to pay for their imports; some of these countries would have to impose restrictions on United States goods other countries would have to show their economic development. The unity and prosperity of the Western World would be undermined.

From the high tariff camp came equally exaggerated forecasts of a threatened flood of imports which would drive American producers to ruin unless tariffs were raised.

*So what happened?*

Actually the continuation of the reciprocal trade program in 1955 did little more than leave things as they were. The trade agreements program was extended for 3 years with only relatively small changes. Since then a few duties have been lowered and a few raised, but, in the main, the general tariff level has remained unchanged through the last 3 years.

And on the whole the world has not done badly economically.

Neither the high nor low tariff advocates had their way. Yet the calamitous prophecies of neither side materialized.

This is not surprising. Any detached study of the effects of tariff changes on trade would show that the importance of the tariff has long been exaggerated by both its friends and its foes. The decisive factor determining how much this country imports has always been the level of our economic prosperity. If our economy continues to expand, our imports can be expected to rise even as they have in the last few years. If our economy were to take a nosedive, no adjustment of tariff rates could avoid a precipitous decline in our imports.

*The tail and the dog*

To put it colloquially the tariff is the tail not the dog.

The experience of the last 3 years has confirmed the fact that the tariff is only a part—and by no means the decisive part—of the whole of our foreign economic policy.

This may be recognized as the view put forward 3 years ago in my The Revolution in World Trade. The facts assembled at that time indicated that our military expenditures and economic aid abroad would provide enough dollars for most countries to balance their accounts with us and even to build up their dollar reserves.

As far as tariff policy was concerned, the course urged was to maintain a virtual tariff truce, with no abrupt changes in tariff rates. The period of this tariff truce was to be used to reexamine the whole of our foreign economic policy so it could be made to serve our strategic needs in a world threatened constantly by war or subversion.

*Extend tariff truce*

That was the sensible course to have followed 3 years ago. It remains the most sensible course to follow today. The tariff truce that has prevailed since the end of World War II should be continued by a further extension of the reciprocal trade agreements. But we should not stop there.

We should use this economic breathing spell to develop a completely thought-through foreign econmic policy which will support a global peace strategy and then proceed to put that policy into operation.

*Stability beyond trade*

The central problem of foreign economic policy which the United States and its allies face is not the dollar gap. It is the strategic gap—the fact that in many parts of the world our strategic interests are far heavier than any possible economic interest than can be developed through trade and investment.

The underdeveloped countries of Asia, for example, can supply us with only limited quantities of raw materials that we do not already obtain from other parts of the world like Latin America and Canada. Yet we have a crucial strategic interest in promoting political and economic stability in these countries so they do not succumb to subversion. To met this challenge could require a more rapid rate of growth in these underdeveloped countries than could possibly come from normal trade and investment.

Again, in our lifetime we have seen this country forced into an ever more intimate strategic alliance with Western Europe because of the changing nature of war, and the development of new weapons of even greater destructiveness and wider geographical range. Yet for almost a century the United States and Western Europe have been moving apart economically. Where Western Europe once supplied this country with machinery in exchange for food and raw materials, we now produce most of our own machinery and look to Europe for relatively little of our basic economic needs.

*Can the twain meet?*

The main reason why it is so difficult to devise the right kind of foreign economic policy in relation to Europe is not our tariffs. It is the fact that strategic and economic trends have been moving in conflicting directions.

Militarily we have been made more dependent upon one another because of the threat of Soviet aggression. But at the same time it has become more difficult to settle our trade balances with Europe because Europe no longer produces what we are most eager to buy.

*The dollar bloc*

The strategic gap takes a third form when we think of trade with the Soviet Union and her satellites. Here we face the harsh realization that trade opportunities which might yield a money profit could hurt us dearly in terms of our efforts to prevent war.

In fact, as we glance around the world there is only one area where our strategic and economic needs dovetail rather well—that is the Western Hemisphere.

The defense of Canada and Latin America are considered part of our own national defense, and Canada and Latin America remain our prime source of imported raw materials as well as our best single customer and the main center of American investment abroad.

What all this means is that we cannot take for granted that our strategic interests can be safeguarded simply by expanding trade and investment. In some parts of the world our strategic and economic interests can be balanced with ease. But in other parts of the world our strategic concerns are certain to remain heavier than any possible opportunities for profitable trade and investment that can be developed.

*Managing a revolution*

The main reason why our strategic interests do not parallel our economic interests is the revolutionary transformation that has taken place during our lifetimes of both world trade and the nature of war. The chief elements of this revolution might be summarized as follows:

1. The surge for economic independence among former colonial countries which has short circuited old trade wirings.
2. The ever-quickening technological and scientific revolution which is undercutting the advantages of international specialization making our world ever more fiercely competitive, but without forging adequate mechanisms of adjustment.
3. The narrowing of Western Europe's trading space by the rise of overseas industrial powers.
4. The further narrowing of that trade space by the emergence of a new Soviet economic imperialism which seeks to sever what it can from the free trading world.
5. A desperate race of population and production in many parts of the world with the winner still undetermined.
6. The terrible physical destruction of World War II which left Western Europe in a Malthusian squeeze—in desperate need for more intensive investment at a time when its people hungered for more abundant spending.
7. The shift in the center of economic gravity within Britain's old empire and her struggle to find a new balance within her Commonwealth.
8. Modern warfare's increasingly totalitarian nature.
9. The development of a whole new arsenal of economic weapons which makes the tariff seem like a tank or artillery piece in a world of atomic armaments.
10. The memory of the great depression, which pressures for more intensified Government intervention in a period when the Nation itself has become an ineffective governmental unit.

*The tariff riddle*

None of these forces [1] can be brought under control by tariff changes. If our foreign economic policy is ever to become more than a package of hastily improvised stopgap measures we need a bolder and larger frame of thinking.

[1] For a full analysis of these forces see Lubell, The Revolution in World Trade; Harpers, 1955.

We could do without most of the slogans that are brought forth ostensibly to enlighten us. For example, trade cannot be a substitute for economic aid, if aid is really needed. If the problem is one of finding means of exchanging what nations produce then expanded trade can be a solution. But if nations really need aid it means that they need additional resources above and beyond what they can produce and trade.

This is one question to ask—is it markets that our allies need or additional economic resources? We do ourselves and the rest of the world a grave disservice if we fail to recognize the distinction between aid and trade.

*The dollar illusion*

The "dollar gap" is another misleading label. It implies that the solution of the economic difficulties of foreign nations rests with the United States, when the heart of the difficulty may be inflation in the home economies of these nations or how they channel their exports to different parts of the world.

Another concept that needs reexamination is the widely held assumption that the lifting of all trade controls is the ideal goal toward which we should move. This belief is a hangover of the old laissez-faire, free-trade philosophy which regarded every act of Government intervention as bad and even immoral.

*Nostalgia no policy*

Today, however, we live in a world of managed economics, with Government intervention a constant force. This paper is not the place to argue whether Government intervention is good or bad. But our economic philosophers might be asked how do they reconcile the philosophy of a managed economy at home and free trade abroad?

If Government is to be charged with the responsibility of maintaining a high level of prosperity, must not control over foreign trade and the value of a nation's currency be numbered among the most powerful tools that a Government may use?

Must we not also expect different nations to use these and other tools in different ways to protect their own interests? Should we not then reexamine trade policies in the realistic light of what is needed to serve our interests and those of our allies and not on the basis of an obsolete assumption that any restriction is bad and free trade is the state of perfection?

*Morality versus realism*

The issue, in short, is not a moral one of how to return to a Garden of Eden which may be free of the original sin of having tariffs. The issue is the highly practical one of managing trade controls, along with other economic controls, so our best interests are served.

II

With what should we concern ourselves in framing the larger foreign economic policy we need?

The full answer to that question can be developed only through years of trial and learning. But this paper might try to set forth a frame of reference that may be of some help in organizing our thoughts.

*Survival comes first*

Our prime consideration must not be trade for the sake of trade but how to strengthen our capacity to defend ourselves from war, subversion or enslavement.

Within such frame of reference, every part of the world cannot be treated identically. The policies we follow in regard to the Soviet Union and her satellites cannot be our policies for allies and other nations. How we deal with our allies is not how we should deal with the Soviets.

As far as the Soviet Union is concerned we should begin by facing up to the bitter fact that the Soviets are at perpetual economic war with the rest of the world. One basic principle should guide any trade we may have with the Soviets—nothing for nothing.

No resources should go into the Soviet area without resources of equivalent value coming back.

*Keep strategic ban*

This means that no credits should be extended to Russia or her satellites. We should also continue to bar the shipment of items of strategic importance to the Soviets since anything we get back in exchange will be a poor deal for the West. It is hardly evidence of Yankee trading shrewdness to buy furs from Russia, for example, and to give the Soviets in exchange high-precision machinery that will strengthen the Soviet military might.

The furs may warm some of our women. What the Russians get in exchange may cause the whole world to shiver.

High on the verboten list should be machinery and equipment which incorporate the latest technological advances. When the Soviets buy such equipment they immediately copy it. This spares them the costs of developing these machines themselves. The further behind the West that the Soviets lag in the technological race, the greater will be the assurance that they will not start a war.

*Fool's gold from Russia*

It is also a mistake to continue to take gold from the Soviet Union in payment for goods. Inside Russia this gold is of no more productive use to the Kremlin than the gold which lies buried at Fort Knox is to us. Through this gold, however, the Soviets are able to acquire resources which they otherwise would not be able to obtain. Those resources in turn, increase Russia's capacity to make trouble all over the world.

Right now may not be the opportune time to cut off these gold purchases. Most of the Soviet gold goes to other countries and not directly to us. These Soviet gold shipments have helped Britain and other nations build up their gold reserves. Still let us not forget that these gold sales strengthen Russia as well. Perhaps the good the West draws balances out the harm that is done. But this is something that should not be taken for granted and should be reexamined from time to time.

In urging such a nothing-for-nothing trade policy, perhaps it should be emphasized that I do not do so in any belief that economic sanctions can bring the Soviet Government to its knees. Foreign trade is simply not that important to the Soviet Union, which has always striven for the maximum degree of economic self-sufficiency. What I am urging is that we recognize that the Soviets operate a perpetual war economy. They permit no trade that is not calculated to strengthen their war machine or their policies of imperialistic expansion. We should be sensible enough to limit our trade to what is to our advantage, or at least to what is of equal value to both sides.

*Trade is a weapon*

Some people, of course, believe that expanded trade, in itself, makes for peace. They argue that removing trade barriers anywhere would help reduce the tensions which, we are told, make war likely. But can this belief be justified by the experience of the last half century? The scrap iron we sold to Japan did not make her any less belligerent. What is traded to the Soviet Union will not make her war machine any less formidable.

Governments which want peace will use trade to further their interests of peace. Governments which are bent upon war, aggression, or subversion will use trade to strengthen their ability to commit war, aggression, or subversion.

Nor should it be forgotten that the main reason for the low volume of trade between Russia and the West is the decision the Soviets made to cut themselves off from the rest of the world and build Russia into a self-contained war economy.

*Butter over guns*

It would be wonderful if expanded trade could lead to a liberalization of the Soviet regime domestically. I doubt that any trade policy the West adopts can accomplish this aim. Still, it might be worth making the effort. We could propose to select trade restrictions if the Soviets agreed to devote a larger proportion of their resources to improving the living standards of their own people, using less for war preparations.

If the Kremlin really moved to put butter over guns—to demobilize the Russian economy and turn it into a welfare rather than a warfare state—we could aid the process through various other measures. But as long as the Soviet rulers systematically depress the living standards of their own people to built a more menacing war machine any trading with Russia is trading with the enemy.

To the extent that we contribute to the Soviet ability to maintain heavy war preparations we add to the defense burden which we ourselves must bear.

*Strategy for the satellites*

What of the Soviet satellites?

In general we should treat the satellites as we do the Soviet Union except for one question which arises—can trade or other economic means be employed to increase the independence of these countries vis-a-vis the Russians?

Certainly this is a worthy goal. But one precaution is worth sounding—let us be certain the methods employed will in fact accomplish the objective sought. Trade, for example, would be a far more effective weapon in attaining this aim than economic aid.

As long as the bulk of any satellite's trade is channeled to the Soviet Union the economic dependence of that satellite on Russia will remain high. If a larger proportion of satellite resources can be drawn into trade with the West, the economic bonds between the satellites and the Soviets will be weakened.

One drawback in extending economic aid to a satellite is that it may not redirect the flow of resources away from the Iron Curtain countries. Economic aid means sending additional resources into a country. If nothing is shipped out in exchange, it leaves the trade pattern unaffected.

*Trade for independence*

Important political advantages may flow from the extension of economic aid. In the case of Poland for example, the assistance we render the Gomulka regime may help keep in power those Polish leaders who want to be independent of Russia.

This gamble in favor of political independence may be worth taking. But the move will be all the stronger if economic aid is supplemented by an increase in actual trade.

Even if the West cannot gain much of the satellite trade we would do well to bid for it, if only to stiffen the economic bargaining power of the satellites in relation to the Soviets.

Take Polish coal for example. To the extent that the western nations show themselves willing to pay a decent price for this coal, they strengthen the hand of the Poles in demanding a decent price for coal sold to Russia.

A systematic examination might be made of all things that the satellites sell to the Soviet Union and what they buy in return. Wherever possible we and our allies ought to bid fair prices for goods going to Russia—to force the Soviets to pay fair prices. We also ought to offer to supply the things the satellites get from Russia at fair prices, to prevent the Soviets from making exorbitant charges for these goods.

*Russian "giveaway" programs*

This same line of reasoning can be applied to the problem of economic aid being extended by the Soviet Union. From time to time newspapers run scare headlines of a so-called Soviet offensive through economic aid. The implication in such headlines usually is that we must outbid the Soviets by promising more than the Soviets are promising.

But is it entirely to our national disadvantage for the Soviets to embark on a large-scale program of economic aid to other countries? Whatever resources the Soviets ship out of Russian, without getting anything in exchange, are resources which the Soviets cannot use for building up their own war machine.

Given the internal strains in the Soviet economy, one wonders how much such aid could be sent out of Russia before the Politburo would be split between those who favored imperialistic adventures abroad and those who wanted to keep Russia's resources at home for Russia's own domestic development. I am sure that within the Kremlin there are powerful Russia-first interests which will prove as cold to giveaway programs as are the America firsters in this country.

*Is it really a gift?*

In reading reports of Soviet economic aid a vigilant eye should be exercised to determine how much of such aid is really a gift and how much of it represents loans that must be repaid or are merely trade arrangements.

A distinction should also be drawn between what the Soviets promise and what they deliver. Remember the Soviet assurances of aid to Egypt to build the Aswan Dam if we refused to finance it. We did refuse to finance it and what happened? The Soviet "promises" proved a mere bluff.

It may help us keep a proper sense of perspective if one concept is stressed. We should think of trade with the Iron Curtain countries in terms of physical resources and not money. This, of course, is one of the main lessons of wartime economies, that under conditions of war it is not money that matters but things, like raw materials, machinery, food, and other needed resources.

If we can learn to think in terms of resources we will realize that the same resources cannot be in two places at the same time. What is used for military production leaves less for the civilian economy; what is used at home leaves less to go abroad; what is shipped to one country leaves less to be shipped to other countries.

*The new arms merchants*

In short, there are limits to the resources the Soviets can make available from their domestic economy, even as there are limits to what this country can do.

Let me emphasize that these points are not made to argue against a foreign-aid program of our own. Continued economic aid abroad is needed. But what we do will be most effective if it is applied against the backdrop of a realistic appraisal of what the Soviets can do—and cannot do.

Currently, at least, our real concern with Soviet economic aid is not so much with the fact that the Soviets are ready to give away things that are economically useful, as with the fact that it is military weapons the Soviets want to ship out.

To combat this Soviet arms traffic will require quite different measures than if the competition were one of extending productive economic aid.

III

What of our allies and the "uncommitted" neutral nations? What kind of foreign economic policy should we follow in regard to them?

*Unite the free world*

Our broad aim should be to see that the preponderant part of the free world's resources can be exchanged for mutual benefit within the free world.

Along with the widest possible interchange of trade should go a thought-through program to speed the economic progress of the underdeveloped countries.

New sources of supply should be sought within the free world for anything of importance that now comes from behind the Iron Curtain. New markets should be opened inside the free world to offset any dependence on the Iron Curtain countries. This is particularly important, of course, with Japan. In view of the changes that have already taken place in China's economy there is no possible way for Japan to regain her prewar markets in China. Other markets in the free world must be opened to Japan.

*Wanted: More homework*

As far as the underdeveloped countries are concerned, the main difficulties we face might be summed up as too much suspicion and not enough homework.

We still have not found a way of overcoming the legacy of distrust that persists in many underdeveloped lands because of the old imperialism. Nor have we learned how to do our homework before spending money in these countries to make certain that the available funds are used to the maximum advantage.

Nearly 6 years ago I was associated in a staff capacity with the International Development Advisory Board's study of the problem of the underdeveloped areas. The Board urged that joint commissions be established to work out country by country, a detailed program of what needed most to be done, what local resources were already available and where these local resources could be combined with outside aid to yield the best results.

Six years have passed and this detailed homework has still to be done. Our foreign aid officials still draw up requests for funds without having determined in advance and in specific detail just how the money is to be spent. For no country is there a master plan into which each individual project can be fitted.

*A competitive alliance*

In the more industrialized countries the main economic problem the free world faces is that of bringing so many competitive economies into balance. Strategically we and most of the Western World are allies; economically we remain highly competitive with one another.

This competition cannot be eliminated. Nor would we want to if we could since competition is essential to our economic system. What we must do is find the means of making sure that this economic competition with our allies works to our mutual advantage; that it strengthens our strategic alliance rather than weakening it.

*Not doctrine alone*

This goal will not be accomplished simply by proclaiming some economic doctrine. What is needed is the ability to balance our interests with those of other nations in countless situations most of which have to be dealt with case by case.

The reciprocal trade agreements are a considerable aid in this respect. More important than the actual tariff rates that we set is the fact that the trade agreements programs force us to determine in detail just where the interest of the whole country lies. It makes us think of the trade problems of other nations as well as of our own, of how the interests of individual producers in this country can be reconciled with the larger interests we all share.

*A board of economic defense*

Proposals have been made to terminate the trade agreements authority and, in this way, return the tariffmaking power to Congress. This would be an unfortunate move. The national interest will be served far more effectively if its definition is left to the executive, operating within guidelines and safeguards laid down by Congress.

*Global strategy needed*

The needed reform is to strengthen our ability to recognize our strategic and economic interests. This requires a permanent agency to develop foreign economic policy in the whole.

The nucleus for such an agency could be found in the present Foreign Economic Administration or it could be set up as an arm of the Office of Defense Mobilization or of the National Security Council. I have seen too much of governmental reorganization schemes to believe that it makes much difference into which box of the Government charts an agency is put. The essential ingredients are a vigorous directing head and a clear concept of the job to be done.

Our main need is to deal with all of our foreign economic problems as part of one whole effort, with interrelated actions on many fronts. Also we should not wait until our hand is forced by events, but should think through a global strategy which will stand up for years to come.

Only by thinking ahead will we be able to take the initiative in the cause of peace, using our economic strength wisely and in time. The alternative is to deal with problems in piecemeal fashion, as they come up, which means following the drift of least resistance and least effectiveness.

# EVALUATION OF THE TRADE AGREEMENTS PROGRAM[1]

The American Tariff League, Inc.

## HISTORY OF THE TRADE AGREEMENTS PROGRAM

The trade agreements program was a product of the great depression. Its sponsors may have been motivated by other reasons in proposing it, but the program was presented to Congress as one of the tools with which to build recovery.

The chief author of the program was the Honorable Cordell Hull. Formerly a Congressman and Senator, he was, in 1934, Secretary of State. He testified at the Senate Committee on Finance hearings on April 26, 1934, on H. R. 8687 (73d Cong.). This legislation, which had passed the House on March 29, proposed to amend the Tariff Act of 1930 by adding a new section 350, setting up the authority whereby the President might negotiate tariff concessions with foreign countries in a series of executive agreements.

Secretary Hull told the committee:[2]

> The proposed bill, H. R. 8687, would authorize the President to enter into reciprocal commercial agreements with other governments for the purpose of promoting international trade. The bill frankly proposes an emergency remedy for emergency conditions. Most persons, at least, will agree that this and other parts of the world, notwithstanding substantial improvement, are still passing through a grave economic crisis. If there be those who question the seriousness of existing conditions, or who, unwilling to do so, profess to believe that only normal policies applicable to normal conditions are necessary to cure the panic, they would naturally hesitate to support this bill.
>
> With respect to this opposing view, it is my judgment that extraordinary conditions call for extraordinary methods of treatment, and that the proposed measure of relief is urgently needed at this time.

The emergency nature of the measure was expressed in the very bill which created the trade agreements program. As enacted, the law (Public No. 316, 73d Cong.) began:

> Section 350 (a) for the purpose of expanding foreign markets for the products of the United States (as a means of assisting *in the present emergency in restoring the American standard of living, in overcoming domestic unemployment and the present economic depression, in increasing the purchasing power of the American public* * * *

This language persisted as the original act of 1934 was extended again and again, through the recovery of the late 1930's, the World War II period, and the postwar recovery period until, in the Extension Act of 1949, the above italicized words were deleted.

Section 350 was restated in the Trade Agreements Extension Act of 1955. The opening language, which establishes its objectives, is vir-

[1] The American Tariff League has underway a comprehensive study of the domestic and international aspects of our foreign-trade situation and expects to publish its findings and policy recommendations at a later date. Some of the material is presented herein, together with the tentative conclusions prompted thereby.

[2] Hearings on H. R. 8687 (73 Cong.), Committee on Finance, U. S. Senate, p. 4.

tually the same as that of the original act of 1934, omitting only the reference to the present emergency and the depression:

> For the purpose of expanding foreign markets for the products of the United States (as a means of assisting in establishing and maintaining a better relationship among various branches of American agriculture, industry, mining, and commerce) by regulating the admission of foreign goods into the United States in accordance with characteristics and needs of various branches of American production so that foreign markets will be made available to those branches of American production which require and are capable of developing such outlets by affording corresponding market opportunities for foreign products in the United States, the President, whenever he finds as a fact that any existing duties or other import restrictions of the United States or any foreign country are unduly burdening and restricting the foreign trade of the United States and that the purpose above declared will be promoted by the means hereinafter specified, is authorized * * *

Thus the purpose of the trade agreements program, in 1955 as in 1934, is primarily to foster United States exports. Increase in United States imports is auxiliary to that purpose. The Trade Agreements Act and its many extensions fail to declare that its purpose is to lower United States tariffs, or to provide the American consumer with cheaper goods, arguments which are frequently advanced by those advocating freer trade as reasons for their support of the trade agreements program. Rather, the emphasis is all on selling more American goods abroad.

*Two major provisions*

The original Trade Agreements Act of 1934 had 2 major provisions for carrying out these purposes, 1 temporary, 1 permanent. The President was granted authority:

> (1) To enter into foreign trade agreements with foreign governments or instrumentalities thereof.

A later section of the act declared that—

> the authority of the President to enter into foreign trade agreements * * * shall terminate on the expiration of 3 years from the date of the enactment of this act (June 12, 1934).

Subsequent extensions of this authority were for definite periods of 3 years or less. Present authority expires June 30, 1958.

> (2) To proclaim such modifications of existing duties and other import restrictions * * * as are required or appropriate to carry out any foreign trade agreement that the President has entered into hereunder. * * * The President may at any time terminate any such proclamation in whole or in part.

No time limit was placed on this authority.

The agreements entered into under the President's authority could thus run indefinitely. Translated in terms of United States tariff rates and quotas, a rate or quota once proclaimed by the President could continue forever unless or until the President proclaimed otherwise, or, possibly, a pertinent foreign trade agreement was terminated, or, of course, Congress enacted a law changing such a rate or quota.

This permanence of effect, subject only to positive action of termination, applied to the bilateral agreements negotiated by the United

States from 1934 to 1943; and to the reductions on United States tariffs negotiated under the General Agreement on Tariffs and Trade from 1947 to date.

RESULTS OF THE PROGRAM IN TERMS OF ITS OBJECTIVES

How has the operation of the trade-agreements program compared with its major objectives: (1) To aid recovery from the depression, and (2) to increase markets for United States exports?

The program began life on June 12, 1934, when the depression was nearly 5 years old. Recovery had already begun and is generally considered to have been complete by 1937. In the 2½-year interval between the start of the program and 1937, the following trade agreements became effective:

| Foreign country, party to agreement: | *Effective date of agreement* |
|---|---|
| Cuba | Sept. 3, 1934 |
| Belgium | May 1, 1935 |
| Haiti | June 3, 1935 |
| Sweden | Aug. 5, 1935 |
| Brazil | Jan. 1, 1936 |
| Canada | Jan. 1, 1936 |
| Netherlands | Feb. 1, 1936 |
| Switzerland | Feb. 15, 1936 |
| Honduras | Mar. 2, 1936 |
| Colombia | May 20, 1936 |
| France | June 15, 1936 |
| Guatemala | June 15, 1936 |
| Nicaragua | Oct. 1, 1936 |
| Finland | Nov. 2, 1936 |

The four 1934–35 agreements would be the only ones that could have appreciably aided recovery in 1936, and they were of minor importance. While more important, the 1936 and later agreements cannot have had any real antidepression effect, particularly since 1938 was a year of recession, and World War II disrupted world trade thereafter.

In attempting an appraisal of the effect of these early agreements on United States foreign trade, the United States Tariff Commission declared in 1949:[3]

> These earlier agreements were, thus, of such scope that experience under them should afford a substantial basis for a study of the effects of the trade agreements. Such a study, however, would be difficult even if conditions were relatively stable and there were no important economic disturbances. As a matter of fact, conditions during the latter half of the 1930's were far from normal; many and profound economic changes were taking place both in this country and abroad, and these changes, taken together, had greater effects on United States foreign trade than the duty reductions and other trade agreement concessions. Moreover, these changes affected trade with individual countries, whether or not the United States had agreements with them, in widely different ways and to widely different degrees.

[3] Operation of the Trade Agreements Program, pt. I, summary, p. 51.

CHART A

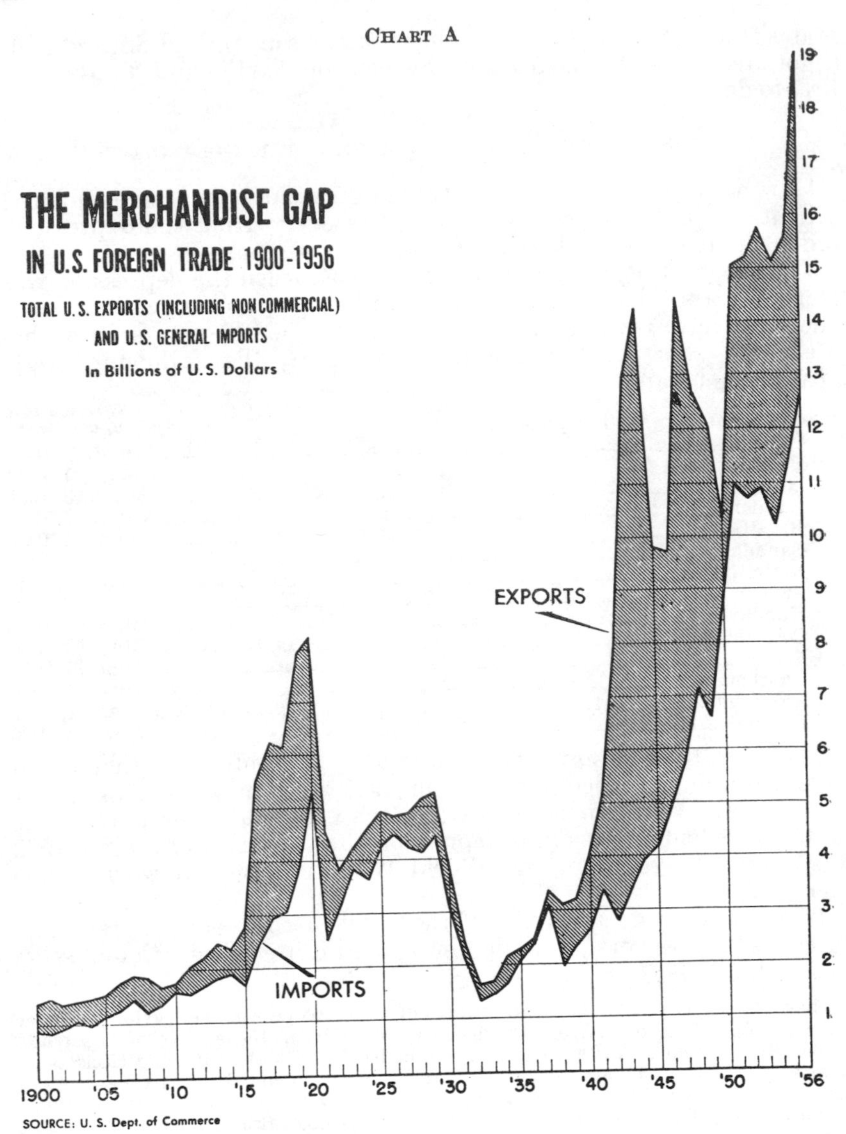


*Not responsible for recovery*

The only valid conclusion to be drawn is that the trade-agreements program was not responsible, in whole or in part, for our recovery from depression.

As to the long-term growth of markets for American products, the program presumably was expected to contribute in two ways:

1. By inducing foreign countries to lower their tariffs and, hence, let in increased American exports.

2. By lowering United States tariffs and inducing increased imports into this country, thereby permitting foreign countries to earn additional dollars with which to buy increased amounts of American goods.

There is no doubt that between 1934 and 1957, United States exports and imports have both increased tremendously in dollar volume. (See chart A.) The question is how much those increases are attributable to the working of the trade-agreements program.

Because the early trade agreements had no pronounced effect on our foreign trade in the brief interval before World War II began in 1939, and because the war itself completely disrupted patterns of world trade, only the postwar period, 1946 to date, provides any true measure of the results of the program in terms of United States imports and exports.

The period has been one of sharply increasing unit prices of both imports and exports, with United States imports showing an apparent increase of 67 percent in units value as compared with the lesser increase of 34 percent in the prices of our exports. (See table No. 1.) The effect of these divergent increases has been to give foreign countries a proportionately larger share of dollars with which they could buy our exports. That is to say, the proportionately higher prices of United States imports, quite aside from any increase in the total of goods received, might have the indirect effect of increasing our exports. This price effect, of course, is not due to the working of the trade-agreements program.

TABLE 1.—*Unit values of United States imports and exports, 1946–56*

[1936–38 average=100]

| | Imports | Exports | | Imports | Exports |
|---|---|---|---|---|---|
| 1946 | 173 | 158 | 1952 | 289 | 205 |
| 1947 | 213 | 188 | 1953 | 276 | 204 |
| 1948 | 235 | 200 | 1954 | 283 | 201 |
| 1949 | 224 | 186 | 1955 | 282 | 203 |
| 1950 | 243 | 180 | 1956 | 289 | 211 |
| 1951 | 305 | 206 | | | |

Source: U. S. Department of Commerce.

To measure the effect of the program on our imports and exports, it is necessary to eliminate the increases due to unit price rise. This can be done by showing imports and exports by quantity rather than value. Here, however, we run into a difficulty with Government statistics on United States exports.

*Foreign aid pays for exports*

Since World War II, a large portion of our exports have been paid for through grants or loans under our military and economic aid programs. Such aid, for the postwar period, has totaled approximately $60 billion to date, of which approximately $40 billion has been in economic aid. In recent years the Government has segregated military exports statistically, but has not segregated those paid for by our economic aid transfers. Hence, the nonmilitary exports in table No. 2 contain an unknown, but an undoubtedly substantial, amount of goods which would not have been purchased abroad if it were not for economic aid receipts from the United States. (The $60 billion in aid mentioned above equals nearly 40 percent of the $155 billion of United States exports for 1946–56.)

TABLE 2.—*United States imports and exports (including and excluding military), by quantity, 1946–56*

[1936–38 average=100]

| | Imports | Exports | | | Imports | Exports | |
|---|---|---|---|---|---|---|---|
| | | Excluding military | Including military | | | Excluding military | Including military |
| 1946 | 113 | ---------- | 206 | 1952 | 151 | 218 | 251 |
| 1947 | 108 | ---------- | 275 | 1953 | 158 | 204 | 263 |
| 1948 | 123 | ---------- | 214 | 1954 | 147 | 217 | 255 |
| 1949 | 120 | ---------- | 219 | 1955 | 163 | 239 | 259 |
| 1950 | 146 | 188 | 193 | 1956 | 176 | 279 | 307 |
| 1951 | 144 | 229 | 247 | | | | |

Source: U. S. Department of Commerce.

It appears from table No. 2 that, while imports by quantity increased 56 percent between 1946 and 1956, exports (including military and economic-aid items) increased by a lesser amount, 49 percent.

The makeup of 1956 (preliminary) quantitative figures for United States imports and nonmilitary exports appears in table No. 3.

TABLE 3.—*Components of United States imports and nonmilitary exports, 1956, by quantity*

[1936–38=100]

| | Imports | Nonmilitary exports |
|---|---|---|
| Crude materials | 166 | [1] 162 |
| Crude foodstuffs | 116 | [1] 503 |
| Manufactured foodstuffs | 142 | [1] 459 |
| Semimanufactures | 228 | [1] 226 |
| Finished manufactures | 233 | 308 |
| Total | 176 | 278 |

[1] Export indexes are influenced by foreign sales of Government-owned surplus. Such sales may be made at prices well below market quotations and, sometimes, cover large quantities exported within a short interval of time. (From statistical reports of U. S. Department of Commerce.)

It is obvious from table No. 3 that what is swelling our nonmilitary exports are the foodstuffs, much of it our Government surplus sold abroad below the market.

According to the February 1957 Survey of Current Business, published by the United States Department of Commerce:

A large portion of the rise in agricultural exports during 1956 comprised accelerated shipments under Government programs, including sales for foreign currencies, exports under barter agreements, outright donations, and shipments financed by Government loans.

This portion of our export trade could not be much influenced by any concessions gained abroad through the trade-agreements program.

The increase in exports of nonmilitary finished manufactures may be substantially accounted for by the shipment of capital goods to foreign subsidiaries of American companies. American individuals and companies had $33 billion invested abroad at the end of 1956, an increase of $3.9 billion over the previous year, according to the United States Department of Commerce.

According to February Survey of Current Business:

Exports of capital equipment * * * scored an advance of about $900 million during 1956. Notable gains were recorded in sales of heavy equipment, such as construction, excavating, and mining machinery, and in electrical machinery, engines and turbines, tractors, trucks, and civilian aircraft.

The upswing in United States exports * * * may be attributed to the following major factors: The expansion of foreign demand as a result of the continued rise in foreign production and incomes, and larger foreign-dollar receipts to support this demand, the higher foreign investments by United States private business, and the accelerated Government programs to stimulate the exports of agricultural commodities. Toward the end of the year (1956) exports were also raised by the closing of the Suez Canal.

*Composition of imports changing*

Turning to imports as a generator of foreign dollar credits, we find that imports by quantity have been rising in a steady trend since 1921, broken only by the sharp swings of the depression and war periods. (See chart B.) This steady upward movement answers the growing needs of an expanded population which increased from 105 million to nearly 170 million in the 35-year period covered. This uptrend in quantitative imports, evident in the 1921–29 period before the trade agreements program began, and resumed in 1942, is obviously not due to the program but to population growth and basic economic forces. However, within the general upward trend, there have been shifts of pattern that may well be due to the trade agreements program.

CHART B

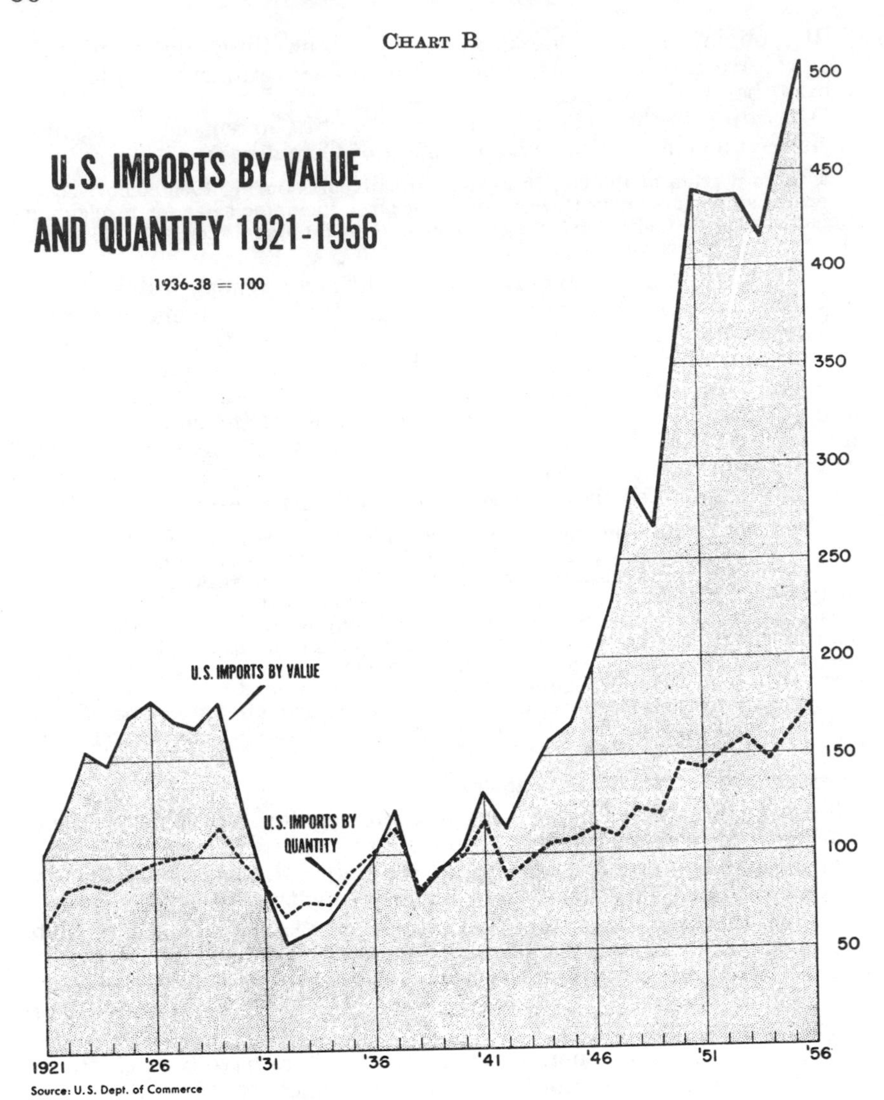


TABLE 4.—*Proportion of dutiable to total United States imports—1934–56*

| | *Percent* | | *Percent* | | *Percent* |
|---|---|---|---|---|---|
| 1934 | 39.4 | 1942 | 36.2 | 1950 | 45.5 |
| 1935 | 40.9 | 1943 | 35.3 | 1951 | 44.6 |
| 1936 | 42.9 | 1944 | 30.2 | 1952 | 41.8 |
| 1937 | 41,4 | 1945 | 33.0 | 1953 | 45.1 |
| 1938 | 39.3 | 1946 | 39.5 | 1954 | 44.7 |
| 1939 | 38.6 | 1947 | 39.2 | 1955 | 46.8 |
| 1940 | 35.1 | 1948 | 41.1 | 1956 | 50.2 |
| 1941 | 37.0 | 1949 | 41.1 | | |

Source: U. S. Department of Commerce.

Tariff reductions made under the trade-agreements program can only affect the dutiable portion of our imports. The dutiable portion has been rising (see table No. 4) since World War II, and may well reflect the drastic tariff cuts made under the program. This change in the complexion of imports is also reflected in the components noted in table No. 3. There the imported crude materials and foodstuffs, for 1956, show a smaller index figure than those for semimanufactures and finished manufactures.

This situation represents a shift in the composition of our imports from emphasis on raw materials not produced here at all, or in inadequate quantities, and much of which enter duty free, to greater proportions of finished and more competitive products, the tariffs on which have been sharply reduced under the trade agreements program.

This shift was commented upon in the February Survey of Current Business, as follows:

Among the commodities which best illustrate this change are rubber, certain metals, and lumber. The more than 5 percent drop in rubber consumption during 1956 was almost entirely in the use of imported natural rubber. The proportion of synthetic to total rubber consumption continued to advance again in 1956. * * * While purchases of practically all types of imported nonfood consumer goods expanded still further during 1956, greater deliveries of textiles and automobiles continued as in 1955 to lead the overall rise in this category of imports. * * * With the exception of agricultural machinery, every major import item in the producers' durable-equipment group scored advances in 1956.

This shift in the composition of imports is partly due to technological changes, greater proportionate use of synthetic materials, and changing tastes of consumers. The shift has been going on for a considerable period of time, and, insofar as it results from these causes, of course, has no relationship to the trade agreements program.

Table No. 5 shows the relative position of major groups [4] of imports for selected years during a 30-year period. Not only does it show the changes in composition of major import categories, it reveals that these groups together account for an increasingly greater proportion of total imports. In 1928 they accounted for 53 percent of total imports; in 1956, 76 percent.

---

[4] The groups selected were those that accounted for $100 million or more of imports in 1956.

TABLE 5.—*Major United States imports by commodities or commodity groups for selected years*

[Millions of dollars]

| | 1956 | | 1951 | | 1947 | | 1938 | | 1934 | | 1928 | |
|---|---|---|---|---|---|---|---|---|---|---|---|---|
| | Rank | Value | Rank | Value | Rank | Value | Rank | Value | Rank | Value | Rank | Value |
| Coffee | 1 | $1,438 | 1 | $1,367 | 1 | $601 | 2 | $138 | 1 | $133 | 1 | $310 |
| Petroleum and products | 2 | 1,269 | 4 | 601 | 6 | 250 | 9 | 39 | 9 | 37 | 5 | 134 |
| Standard newsprint | 3 | 688 | 5 | 513 | 3 | 343 | 4 | 101 | 4 | 76 | 4 | 139 |
| Copper and manufactures | 4 | 501 | 9 | 278 | 8 | 176 | 10 | 38 | 11 | 28 | 8 | 98 |
| Sugar and related products | 5 | 494 | 6 | 444 | 2 | 442 | 1 | 141 | 2 | 118 | 3 | 207 |
| Crude rubber | 6 | 398 | 2 | 809 | 4 | 317 | 3 | 130 | 3 | 102 | 2 | 245 |
| Paper base stocks | 7 | 342 | 7 | 414 | 5 | 294 | 5 | 86 | 5 | 71 | 6 | 112 |
| Sawmill products | 8 | 306 | 10 | 229 | 13 | 102 | 20 | 14 | 18 | 12 | 17 | 41 |
| Vehicles and parts | 9 | 276 | 28 | 57 | 28 | 13 | 26 | 2 | 25 | 1 | 26 | 3 |
| Ferroalloys, ores, and metals | 10 | 271 | 18 | 133 | 17 | 67 | 18 | 18 | 19 | 9 | 22 | 14 |
| Precious, semiprecious stones, industrial diamonds | 11 | 264 | 13 | 176 | 12 | 124 | 13 | 33 | 15 | 18 | 13 | 75 |
| Iron and concentrates | 12 | 250 | 27 | 60 | 25 | 22 | 25 | 5 | 24 | 3 | 25 | 5 |
| Unmanufactured wool | 13 | 243 | 3 | 714 | 7 | 209 | 16 | 23 | 16 | 17 | 11 | 80 |
| Steel mill products | 14 | 240 | 8 | 342 | 29 | 5 | 22 | 11 | 21 | 6 | 20 | 19 |
| Fish and fish products | 15 | 238 | 17 | 157 | 15 | 83 | 15 | 28 | 13 | 23 | 18 | 39 |
| Beverages | 16 | 201 | 19 | 128 | 16 | 68 | 6 | 58 | 6 | 50 | 27 | 2 |
| Fruits, nuts, and preparations | 17 | 192 | 14 | 169 | 10 | 136 | 7 | 55 | 7 | 46 | 9 | 90 |
| Nickel and manufactures | 18 | 188 | 21 | 96 | 19 | 45 | 21 | 13 | 17 | 13 | 22 | 14 |
| Aluminum and manufactures | 19 | 184 | 23 | 82 | 26 | 18 | 24 | 7 | 22 | 5 | 24 | 10 |
| Tin | 20 | 178 | 16 | 158 | 14 | 86 | 8 | 45 | 8 | 45 | 10 | 87 |
| Industrial, textile, office machinery | 21 | 176 | 25 | 69 | 27 | 16 | 23 | 10 | 20 | 7 | 20 | 19 |
| Cotton manufactures | 22 | 154 | 25 | 69 | 23 | 24 | 13 | 33 | 11 | 28 | 14 | 63 |
| Wool manufactures | 23 | 145 | 22 | 93 | 22 | 33 | 19 | 15 | 17 | 13 | 15 | 62 |
| Meat products | 23 | 145 | 12 | 187 | 24 | 23 | 14 | 30 | 17 | 13 | 19 | 36 |
| Cocoa and cocoa beans | 24 | 144 | 11 | 197 | 9 | 152 | 17 | 20 | 14 | 19 | 16 | 47 |
| Wood manufactures | 24 | 144 | 26 | 67 | 21 | 34 | 23 | 10 | 23 | 4 | 23 | 11 |
| Lead and manufactures | 25 | 143 | 24 | 80 | 18 | 51 | 26 | 2 | 25 | 1 | 21 | 16 |
| Zinc and manufactures | 26 | 119 | 26 | 67 | 21 | 34 | 27 | 1 | ---- | (1) | ---- | (1) |
| Jute and manufactures | 27 | 114 | 15 | 160 | 11 | 133 | 11 | 37 | 10 | 36 | 7 | 101 |
| Fertilizers and materials | 28 | 102 | 20 | 102 | 20 | 43 | 12 | 36 | 12 | 26 | 12 | 78 |
| Total for commodities | ---- | 9,547 | ---- | 8,018 | ---- | 3,944 | ---- | 1,179 | ---- | 960 | ---- | 2,159 |
| Total United States imports | ---- | 12,607 | ---- | 10,967 | ---- | 5,756 | ---- | 1,960 | ---- | 1,655 | ---- | 4,091 |
| Percent of total United States imports | ---- | 76 | ---- | 73 | ---- | 69 | ---- | 60 | ---- | 58 | ---- | 53 |

[1] Under $500,000.

Source: U. S. Department of Commerce.

Those groups which have advanced in relative position through the years are, for the lowest and highest ranks in the period covered:

Steel mill products, from 29th to 14th.
Vehicles and parts, from 28th to 9th.
Iron and concentrates, from 27th to 12th.
Aluminum and manufactures, from 26th to 19th.
Ferro-alloys, ores and metals, from 22d to 10th.
Sawmill products, from 20th to 8th.
Copper and manufactures, from 11th to 4th.
Petroleum and products, from 9th to 2d.

It will be noted that most of the products in these advancing categories are of the "hard goods" classification.

Those groups which have declined in relative position are:

Sugar and related products, from 1st to 5th.
Crude rubber, from 2d to 6th.
Beverages, from 6th to 16th.
Fruits, nuts and preparations, from 7th to 17th.
Jute and manufactures, from 7th to 27th.
Tin, from 8th to 20th.
Cocoa and cocoa beans, from 9th to 24th.
Cotton manufactures, from 11th to 22d.
Meat products, from 12th to 23d.
Fertilizers and materials, from 12th to 28th.
Wool manufactures, from 15th to 23d.

These are mainly foodstuffs and "soft goods."

## TARIFF REDUCTIONS UNDER THE TRADE AGREEMENTS PROGRAM

Have United States tariffs been widely reduced under the trade agreements program? The answer seems to be an obvious "Yes." Have the reductions been substantial? Again, a seemingly obvious "Yes." However, the fact that reductions have been substantial is difficult to prove statistically.

The problem is how to measure a tariff reduction. If an ad valorem rate of 50 percent is reduced to 25 percent, the reduction seems substantial. Yet the effect of such a reduction may be less on the imports involved than a reduction of a 10-percent rate to 5 percent. So much depends on the variables of relative price, and the country of origin. A Japanese product may easily surmount a 50-percent rate while a competing product from Great Britain might find the rate restrictive because of the higher labor and production costs in Britain as compared with Japan.

All that can be done is to apply the best measurements available and draw rough conclusions.

### *Scope of potential reductions*

Under the trade agreements program the President's authority to reduce tariffs by negotiation was delegated by Congress in three main stages:

*Stage 1.*—The Trade Agreements Act of 1934 permitted the President to reduce (or increase) by 50 percent "any existing rate of duty." Presumably that meant existing on the date of enactment, June 12, 1934, and that is the way it was administered. The Extension Acts of 1937. 1940, and 1943 did not alter this limitation.

*Stage 2.*—The Congress was advised by the executive branch that the United States had exhausted much of its bargaining power by the reductions made in the bilateral agreements negotiated up to 1945. Congress, accordingly, in the Extension Act of 1945, authorized the President to reduce (or increase) rates up to 50 percent of the "duty, however established, existing on January 1, 1945." The effect was to permit a compounding of rate reductions. As a maximum, a rate reduced the full 50 percent authorized in stage 1 could be reduced up to 50 percent of the resulting rate in stage 2, so as to effect a total 75-percent reduction of the rate existing on June 12, 1934. A multitude of compounded combinations less than the maximum was, of course, possible. The Extension Acts of 1948, 1949, 1951, 1953, and 1954 did not alter this second limitation.

*Stage 3.*—Congress in 1955 was again advised that our tariff bargaining power was exhausted. The Extension Act of 1955 thereupon authorized two kinds of further reduction:

(*a*) Reductions up to 15 percent below the rates existing on January 1, 1955.

(*b*) Reductions to 50 percent of any rates higher than 50 percent.

The 15-percent reductions had to be made in 3 annual steps of no more than 5 percent each, so that to achieve the maximum, a reduction would have to be made in each of the 3 years ending June 30, 1958. Any 1934 rate that had been already fully reduced under each of the 2 previous stages, for a compound reduction of 75 percent, could thus be further reduced to a maximum compound total of 78.75 percent.

A reduction of more than 78 percent seems substantial. Of course, only a minority of 1934 rates will have received that full compounded reduction by June 30, 1958. Most will be in the range of compound reductions up to 78 percent.

*Depth of reductions*

To determine how deep were the cuts made, two rough measurements are possible, both of them employed by the United States Tariff Commission.

One of these consists of analyzing the rates actually cut and applying statistically the reduced rates to imports received during a representative year. For example, the Tariff Commission noted that on January 1, 1953,[5] using import statistics of calendar 1952, 89.4 percent of the dutiable imports would have been appraised at reduced duty figures. These showed total reductions from an average ad valorem equivalent of 25.3 percent in 1934, to 11.6 percent on January 1, 1953, a compound average reduction of 54 percent.

Since the effect of the stage 3 authority cannot be fully measured until after June 30, 1958, the above figures are still the latest available under this method of tabulation.

The second method of measurement consists of noting actual duties collected as a proportion of dutiable imports for certain years.

Thus, for 1934, before any duty reductions under the trade agreements program, the average incidence of duties collected to total dutiable imports was 46.7 percent. For 1956 it was 11.7 percent, the

[5] All major reductions of United States rates had been effected by that date under stage 2.

lowest in our history. This represented an apparent reduction of 75 percent.

These figures do not exactly express the extent of tariff reductions between 1934 and 1956 for this reason: The relatively low unit prices of dutiable imports in 1934 would result in abnormally high ad valorem equivalents of specific duties. Similarly, the relatively high unit prices of imports in 1956, would result in lowering the incidence of applicable specific duties even if they had not been actually reduced. (For example—an import item valued at $1 and subject to a duty of $0.20, would show an incidence of 20 percent ad valorem equivalent. If the same item is reduced in value to $0.50, the same duty of $0.20 works out to a 40 percent equivalent.)

Allowing for the approximate nature of these measurements, the resultant figures (54-percent reduction under the first calculation; 75 percent under the second) indicate that substantial total reductions did take place even though their magnitude cannot be determined with mathematical certainty.

Perhaps as significant in demonstrating that tariff reductions have been substantial is the fact that 28 bilateral trade agreements were negotiated under stage 1 of the program (1934–45); 4 major multilateral agreements negotiated under stage 2 (1945–55); and one moderately important multilateral agreement under stage 3 (1956 to date). It is inescapable that this considerable activity, with duty cuts superimposed one upon another, would result in total overall reductions of sizable proportions.

RECIPROCAL ACTIONS BY FOREIGN COUNTRIES

The trade agreements program was expected to accomplish its objective of expanding American exports by offering to reduce United States tariffs as an inducement to other countries to reduce their tariffs and restrictions on their imports of American goods.

As to tariffs, the negotiations under both bilateral and multilateral trade agreements consisted of one country offering to reduce a tariff, or to bind a tariff against increase, or to bind an item on the free list, against similar commitments by the other negotiating countries.

As to import restrictions such as embargoes, quotas, currency licensing, state purchasing, and other devices, many of them discriminatory against United States products, there was no provision for bargaining. These restrictions were largely ignored in the bilateral agreements. In the multilateral agreements they were also not subject to bargaining; the covering General Agreement on Tariffs and Trade was supposed to eliminate them.

There is no doubt that other countries did reduce a considerable number of their tariffs in return for reductions in ours. However, our reductions were not always the prime inducement; rather, our grants and loans of foreign aid after World War II were made, in some instances, on condition that the foreign country involved would negotiate with us on tariffs.

Attempting to measure how much other nations have reduced their rates offers the same difficulties present in measuring the extent of our own reductions. The only method readily available, approximate though it is, is to compare the incidence of customs collected to total imports for foreign countries at the beginning and end of a period covered by the trade-agreements program.

The league has made such a study, comparing the ratios of customs duties collected to total imports for 1937, a prewar year of relatively large imports and one early in the program, and before any trade agreements could have had much effect, and for 1955, the latest year for which there are figures for most foreign countries. The results are shown in table No. 6. They are to be taken as relative rather than as absolutes.

From this tabulation it appears that the United States has exceeded most other countries in reducing tariffs during the period studied.

TABLE 6.—*Ratios of customs duties collected to total value of imports, 1937 and 1955, for comparable countries*

[Expressed in percentages]

| Country | 1937 | Country | 1955 | Percent change from 1937 |
|---|---|---|---|---|
| 36. Haiti | 63.3 | 36. Haiti | 47.7 | −25 |
| 35. Venezuela | 62.2 | 35. Guatemala | 37.3 | +4 |
| 34. El Salvador | 48.0 | 34. United Kingdom | 30.4 | +43 |
| 33. Turkey | 46.6 | 33. Costa Rica | 28.3 | +13 |
| 32. Iran | 41.5 | 32. Ireland | 27.4 | +26 |
| 31. Guatemala | 35.9 | 31. India [1] | 26.3 | −19 |
| 30. India | 32.5 | 30. France | 25.3 | +37 |
| 29. Brazil | 30.4 | 29. Honduras | 21.3 | −3 |
| 28. Thailand | 29.4 | 28. El Salvador | 19.6 | −59 |
| 27. Argentina | 28.5 | 27. Turkey | 19.4 | −58 |
| 26. Iraq | 27.7 | 26. Colombia | 19.0 | −6 |
| 25. Australia | 25.9 | 25. Thailand | 17.9 | −39 |
| 24. Greece | 25.4 | 24. Iran | 17.6 | −58 |
| 23. Portugal | 25.1 | 23. Iraq | 16.4 | −41 |
| 22. Costa Rica | 25.0 | 22. Mexico | 16.2 | −24 |
| 21. Panama | 25.0 | 21. Peru | 14.4 | −11 |
| 20. Germany | 24.4 | 20. Panama | 14.3 | −43 |
| 19. Honduras | 22.0 | 19. Greece | 13.8 | −46 |
| 18. Ireland | 21.7 | 18. New Zealand | 12.7 | −34 |
| 17. Mexico | 21.4 | 17. Portugal | 12.6 | −50 |
| 16. United Kingdom | 21.3 | 16. Venezuela | 11.0 | −82 |
| 15. Sweden | 21.0 | 15. Switzerland | 10.1 | −34 |
| 14. Colombia | 20.3 | 14. Australia | 9.2 | −65 |
| 13. New Zealand | 19.1 | 13. Canada | 9.1 | −13 |
| 12. France | 18.5 | 12. Italy | 9.0 | −24 |
| 11. Peru | 16.1 | 11. West Germany | 7.4 | −70 |
| 10. United States | 15.8 | 10. Union of South Africa | 7.3 | −32 |
| 9. Switzerland | 15.3 | 9. Argentina | 6.8 | −76 |
| 8. Italy | 11.8 | 8. United States | 5.4 | −66 |
| 7. Norway | 10.9 | 7. Netherlands | 5.0 | −15 |
| 6. Union of South Africa | 10.8 | 6. Norway | 4.9 | −55 |
| 5. Canada | 10.4 | 5. Sweden | 4.8 | −77 |
| 4. Denmark | 6.5 | 4. Brazil | 4.2 | −86 |
| 3. Netherlands | 5.9 | 3. Belgium-Luxembourg | 3.3 | −43 |
| 2. Belgium-Luxembourg | 5.8 | 2. Japan | 2.8 | −39 |
| 1. Japan | 4.6 | 1. Denmark | 2.6 | −60 |

[1] Average 1955 ratio for 4 countries, Burma, Ceylon, India, and Pakistan, for comparison with India in 1937.

Sources: U. S. Department of Commerce, Tax Research Foundation, United Nations Statistical Yearbook, International Monetary Fund, Foreign Consulates in the United States.

TABLE 7.—*GATT countries, their shares of external trade, ratio of tariff collected to total imports, and ratio of reduction of tariff, 1937–55*

[Each expressed in percentage]

| Country | Share of trade | 1955 tariff rate | Tariff reductions |
|---|---|---|---|
| Australia | 3.0 | 9.2 | −65 |
| Austria | .8 | ---------- | ---------- |
| Belgium-Luxembourg | 4.2 | 3.3 | −43 |
| Brazil | 2.4 | 4.2 | −86 |
| Burma | .3 | 29.8 | ---------- |
| Canada | 6.5 | 9.1 | −13 |
| Ceylon | .5 | 43.0 | ---------- |
| Chile | .6 | ---------- | ---------- |
| Cuba | 1.1 | ---------- | ---------- |
| Czechoslovakia | 1.4 | ---------- | ---------- |
| Denmark | 1.4 | 2.6 | −60 |
| Dominican Republic | .1 | ---------- | ---------- |
| Finland | 1.0 | ---------- | ---------- |
| France | 8.5 | 25.3 | [1] +37 |
| Germany, Federal Republic of | 5.2 | 7.4 | −70 |
| Greece | .4 | 13.8 | −46 |
| Haiti | .1 | 47.7 | −25 |
| India | 2.4 | 19.7 | ---------- |
| Indonesia | 1.3 | ---------- | ---------- |
| Italy | 2.8 | 9.0 | −24 |
| Japan | 2.3 | 2.8 | −39 |
| Netherlands | 4.6 | 5.0 | −15 |
| New Zealand | 1.0 | 12.7 | −34 |
| Nicaragua | .1 | ---------- | ---------- |
| Norway | 1.1 | 4.9 | −55 |
| Pakistan | .8 | 37.6 | ---------- |
| Peru | .4 | 14.4 | −11 |
| Rhodesia and Nyasaland | .6 | ---------- | ---------- |
| Sweden | 2.4 | 4.8 | −77 |
| Turkey | .6 | 19.4 | −58 |
| Union of South Africa | 1.8 | 7.3 | −32 |
| United Kingdom | 19.8 | 30.4 | [1] +43 |
| United States | 20.1 | 5.4 | −66 |
| Uruguay | .4 | ---------- | ---------- |

[1] Increase.

Sources: Same as for table 6, plus General Agreement on Tariffs and Trade.

Table 7 reveals that the major trading countries, except for the United States, and 1 or 2 others, have not cut their tariff levels sharply.

The United Kingdom, next to the United States in magnitude of world trade, appears actually to have increased her tariff levels by 43 percent. It is true that much of her tariff consists of revenue imports on items like tobacco and oil.

France, the third greatest trader, also increased her duty levels by 37 percent.

The fourth in magnitude, Canada, reduced her levels by a relatively modest 13 percent.

The fifth, West Germany, made a substantial reduction of 70 percent.

The Netherlands, sixth in trade, reduced her levels a modest 15 percent.

Belgium and Luxembourg, seventh, show a fairly substantial cut of 43 percent.

Of course, tariff cutting by most of these countries, even where substantial, has been largely nullified by the various import restrictions imposed on American goods. A majority of these major trading countries have only allowed entry to those American goods which were paid for under our military or economic aid programs, or which were not made or grown in the country of import, or which were considered by the foreign governments to be vitally needed at one time or another.

GATT is its own best witness of the extent of these practices. Its publication, International Trade 1956, declares on page 250:

> Twenty-five of the governments which are contracting parties to GATT still maintain import restrictions to protect their balances of payments and monetary reserves and 23 of these apply their restrictions in a discriminatory manner.

The United States Tariff Commission in its ninth report, Operation of the Trade Agreements Program, July 1955 to June 1956, states on page 231, et seq:

> Of the 43 countries with which the United States had trade agreements in force during all or part of the period from July 1, 1955, to June 30, 1956, 27 restrict imports for balance-of-payments reasons and discriminate between sources of supply. There are 23 general agreement countries in this group, as well as 4 countries with which the United States has trade agreements on a bilateral basis. The general agreement countries are Australia, Austria, Brazil, Burma, Ceylon, Chile, Denmark, Finland, France, the Federal Republic of Germany, Greece, India, Italy, Japan, the Netherlands, New Zealand, Norway, Pakistan, the Federation of Rhodesia and Nyasaland, Sweden, Turkey, the United Kingdom and Uruguay. The bilateral trade-agreement countries are Argentina, Iceland, Iran, and Paraguay. The remaining countries—those that do not restrict imports for balance-of-payment reasons and that do not discriminate between sources of supply—comprise 10 general agreement countries and 6 bilateral-agreement countries. The general agreement countries are Belgium, Canada, Cuba, the Dominican Republic, Haiti, Indonesia, Luxembourg, Nicaragua, Peru, and the Union of South Africa. The bilateral-agreement countries are Ecuador, El Salvador, Guatemala, Honduras, Switzerland, and Venezuela.
>
> Although the general agreement lays down the rules for the relaxation and final elimination of quantitative trade restrictions, it is not intended to be an instrument for the solution of the basic problems that make such restrictions necessary. It therefore remains for other agencies to bring about such improvements in the internal economic and financial conditions of countries as will assist them to overcome their external economic and financial difficulties. The reduction of tariffs under the general agreement, although a type of cooperative effort among countries for a particular purpose, does not in itself lead to cooperation in the use of financial aid from the United States or in the solution of such problems as the increasing of production and productive efficiency, improving the balance-of-payments position by increasing exports, combating inflation, and attaining a balanced external financial position that will permit currency convertibility. Solution of these problems has been the special responsibility of agencies that have no direct or necessary connection with the General Agreement on Tariffs and Trade, yet have worked toward the same general objectives as those sought by the general agreement. * * *
>
> Most of the countries with which the United States has trade agreements made additional progress during 1955–56 in overcoming their external financial difficulties. They continued to match this improvement by further relaxing quantitative trade controls and exchange restrictions originally imposed for balance-of-payments reasons. * * *
>
> General tariff revisions by a few countries during 1955–56 and numerous upward adjustments in individual rates of duty by almost all countries reflected the general tendency—noted in the Tariff's Commission's last two reports—for countries to increase the protective incidence of their tariffs as they progressively eliminate the more direct forms of trade control, such as quotas and import licensing.

All of which is to say that substantial progress toward eliminating foreign restrictions on American goods usually has to be generated outside the trade agreements program and, when such progress is made, foreign countries raise their tariffs despite the program.

The executive branch of our Government has recognized this state of affairs. On February 12, 1957, the State Department announced that it was sending delegations to Geneva in June and October to discuss with 20 GATT nations the status of their import restrictions. Indeed an earlier United States delegation had sponsored this proposal at the 11th session of GATT in late 1956.

Whatever the net effect of the trade agreements program on removing foreign restrictions to United States exports, the situation, may become chaotic for a time with the formation of the proposed European common market and with free trade zones envisioned for Great Britain, Scandinavian countries, Latin America, and perhaps other areas. These proposals contemplate gradual average reduction of tariffs and elimination of quotas as among the participating countries, thereby creating preferential trading areas that discriminate against the United States, at least during the preliminary stage over the next decade or more. In the tariff averaging process, duties of some countries will be raised against United States exports.

The trade agreements program was incapable in 23 years of achieving much progress in wiping out discriminatory restrictions abroad against American products. With much weaker potential bargaining power available to it, the program is even less capable of coping with the formidable discriminatory restrictions that will face United States trade abroad over the next few years.

CONCLUSIONS AS TO THE RESULTS OF THE TRADE AGREEMENTS PROGRAM

1. The trade agreements program did not make any appreciable contribution toward recovery of the United States economy from the depression of the early and mid-1930's.

2. The program did effect substantial reductions in United States tariffs.

3. These reductions were not followed by any increase in total imports, measured on a quantitative basis, above those induced by our expanding population and economy. However, they apparently assisted in changing the composition of imports, by increasing the dutiable proportion which, in general, is directly competitive with Amercan goods, and increasing the proportion of durable consumer goods which heretofore have not entered in sufficient quantities to threaten injury to many American producers of competitive goods.

4. The program is only an ancillary cause of increased United States exports, which have been largely generated by—

(*a*) Military and economic aid;
(*b*) United States private investment in foreign plants;
(*c*) Recovery of areas from war damage.

5. The program has not produced much net reduction in the restrictions which other countries have raised against United States exports. The major trading nations have, in general, reduced their tariffs to a lesser degree than has the United States, and have nullified these reductions by the imposition of discriminatory import restrictions. As they have eliminated these direct controls they have increased their tariffs. Whatever the past net result of our program in reducing foreign restrictions to our exports, there is the certainty that the situation will be completely scrambled by the European com-

mon market and the proposed free trade areas in various sections of the world.

SAFEGUARDS IN THE TRADE AGREEMENTS PROGRAM

The presence of safeguards for the American producer and worker in the trade agreements program stems from the very nature of United States tariff policy. The purpose of our tariffs has been mainly protective. The revenue-producing aspects, except in the early years of our history, have been secondary and, lately, comparatively negligible, considering total Federal revenue demands.

The fact that tariffs raise revenue, however, is important in a procedural sense. The United States Constitution, article 1, section 7, states: "All Bills for raising Revenue shall originate in the House of Representatives * * *" Today's basic Tariff Act of 1930 has as its title "An act to provide revenue, to regulate commerce with foreign countries, to encourage the industries of the United States, to protect American labor, and for other purposes." The 1930 act and its many amendments accordingly have originated in the House.

The real purposes of the 1930 act are, of course, those recited after the reference to the revenue. This fact becomes of great importance because the Trade Agreements Act, with its authority and machinery for negotiating duty reductions (and increases also, but this is an almost totally unused power), is a part of the basic 1930 act. The latter's title and intent thus apply to the subsequent tariff-cutting provisions of the Trade Agreements Act as well as to the original setting of the statutory rates.

Consequently the trade agreements provisions of the 1930 act should be administered so as to "encourage" American industry and "protect American labor."

This inherent responsibility was publicly recognized at the outset when President Roosevelt, in a March 2, 1934, message to Congress, requested that the trade agreements authority be added to the 1930 act. He said:

> The exercise of the authority which I propose must be carefully weighed in the light of the latest information so as to give assurance that no sound and important American interest will be injuriously disturbed. The adjustment of our foreign-trade relations must rest on the premise of undertaking to benefit and not to injure such interests.

Thus the Congress, the people, and foreign nations were early put on notice that the trade agreements program was to be administered in a way noninjurious to American interests. As a corollary, they were all to infer that any action that proved to be injurious—being contrary to intent—would be rescinded or modified. There were to be no vested interests, either here or abroad, in the rates reduced under the program.

Noninjurious administration of the trade agreements program requires attention to safeguards of two kinds:

1. Preventive safeguards.
2. Remedial safeguards.

The first should provide machinery to assure that tariff concessions are not likely to be injurious to domestic industry. The second should provide a method whereby concessions that nevertheless do prove injurious may be withdrawn or modified, or other remedial action taken.

Although the same safeguards can be made applicable to both bilateral and multilateral trade agreements, their effectiveness differs with the type of agreement.

In a bilateral agreement the United States negotiates with country A, and need consider only the effect of a concession in terms of imports from A. After an agreement is concluded, and injuries to American producers result, the United States need only deal with A, in withdrawing or modifying the offending concession. A is, of course, free to take compensatory action, but the negotiations are relatively simple, confined, as they are, to two parties.

In a multilateral agreement the United States negotiates with countries A, B, C, D, and E simultaneously. Frequently the countries involved number 30 or 40. In granting a concession that may benefit A, the United States must also consider whether it may benefit B or C. Also, there is pressure upon the United States to grant concessions to all, instead of only to this and that country, because all parties to an agreement are urged to give and take equally, all around the table. Thus the United States may be induced to grant more and deeper tariff reductions in one such multilateral agreement than we would make in separate bilateral negotiations.

Consequently, a United States attempt to withdraw or modify a concession made in a multilateral agreement becomes a complex process. Countries A, B, and C may have benefited from the concession and so take compensatory action by withdrawing concessions made for our benefit. However, their withdrawn concessions may also have benefited D and E, and the latter also take compensatory action. This action, in turn, adversely affects others in the agreement, and so it can go indefinitely until a large part of the fabric becomes unraveled. Reluctance to start this chain reaction is a real obstacle to invocation of the remedial safeguards in a multilateral agreement.

*Preventive safeguards—Peril points*

According to the Tariff Commission's publication, Operation of the Trade Agreements Program, June 1934 to April 1948, part I (p. 5)—

> Before 1937 the formal announcement of intention to negotiate was accompanied by a list of the principal items imported from the foreign country concerned. Since 1937 that list has been replaced by a so-called public list,[6] which names all import items on which the grant of a concession will be considered. Items which do not appear on that list are not considered for a concession. The list, prepared initially by the country committee, is reviewed and revised by the Committee on Trade Agreements.

That committee is headed up by the State Department.

These preliminary findings, based, in part, on testimony of interested parties, appear to be safeguards against injurious concessions, and have often been cited as such by those administering the trade agreements program. However, these investigations and reviews have always been secret, and it is not known what weight is given to this or that economic element, or to considerations of an international political nature.

Early in 1947 peril point findings were among the recommendations made by Senators Millikin and Vandenberg, which will be referred to

[6] Commonly called the bargaining list.

hereafter. They suggested that the Tariff Commission determine, for each rate suggested as a possible subject of a concession in a forthcoming trade agreement, the maximum reduction possible that would not result in probable injury to American producers of the pertinent products. However, this particular suggestion was ignored by the President in his Executive Order 9832 of February 25, 1947, setting up procedures for negotiating the 1947 Geneva Agreement.

Congress indicated it wished to be sure that no injury would follow tariff concessions, and it included in the 1948 Extension Act a peril point provision. This required the Tariff Commission to set the points below which our negotiators should not cut United States duties. It did not prevent reductions below the points, but if the President subsequently proclaimed rates reduced below the points, he was required to so advise Congress, giving reasons for his action.

Peril points were actually set for the tariff negotiations held under GATT, at Annecy in 1949. However, before the results were proclaimed a newly elected Congress had repealed the peril-point provisions. Whether the points set by the Commission were honored at Annecy was not made known to the public. The negotiations at Torquay in 1950–51 were not made subject to peril-point determinations.

Congress, in the 1951 Extension Act, reestablished the peril-point procedures. Since then all negotiations have been preceded by peril-point findings and the President has publicly stated that no United States rate has been cut below the points set, although, in two instances, rates were not increased in negotiations when the Tariff Commission found that the peril points were higher than their current levels.

*Remedial safeguards—Escape clause*

In the beginning no provision in a trade agreement permitted either party to withdraw or modify a concession by unilateral action because the concession had resulted in injury to one of its domestic industries. Such a provision was first included in the agreement with Mexico, which became effective in 1943. A later bilateral agreement with Paraguay also contained this clause, which became known as the standard escape clause and was the prototype of the clause inserted in the later multilateral agreements.

As described in the Randall Commission staff papers (pp. 266–267):

> Under this clause either party to the agreement could suspend or modify any concession if, because of unforeseen circumstances, increased imports threatened serious injury to the domestic industry. The administration agreed, in committee hearings before Congress in 1943, to include such an escape clause in all subsequent trade agreements.

The Randall staff papers describe how, in early 1947, escape-clause policy was decided:

> Following extensive discussion between Senator Millikin, the late Senator Vandenberg, and Under Secretary of State Clayton, the President, by Executive order,[7] stipulated that an escape clause would henceforth be included in every new trade agreement.

Accordingly a provision, modeled on the standard clause, was incorporated as article XIX of the General Agreement on Tariffs and Trade, which was negotiated at Geneva later in 1947. GATT has

[7] No. 9832 of February 25, 1947.

conducted all subsequent multilateral trade agreements to which the United States is a party.

Article XIX is further recognition by, and notice to, GATT countries that the United States, as well as the other member nations, negotiates a tariff concession subject to the express proviso that it will be withdrawn or modified if "any product is being imported into the territory of" a member country—

in such increased quantities and under such conditions as to cause or threaten serious injury to domestic producers in that territory of like or directly competitive products * * *.

United States domestic procedures for invoking this escape clause were set forth in general terms in Executive Order No. 9832. The Tariff Commission was to investigate escape clause applications by domestic producers "when in (its) judgment * * * there is good and sufficient reason therefor." If, after investigation, the Commission finds injury or a threat of injury it—

shall recommend to the President, for his consideration in the light of the public interest, the withdrawal of the concession, in whole or in part, or the modification of the concession * * *.

Thus both the Commission's and the President's roles were originally discretionary. This situation, which persisted essentially unchanged until 1951, proved unsatisfactory. Of 21 applications filed between 1947 and 1951, 14 were dismissed by the Commission on preliminary examination; i. e., without investigation. Four were investigated during that period, resulting in findings of injury and recommendations for relief for 3, to the President, who rejected 1 and acted favorably on 2.

The Trade Agreements Extension Act of 1951, for the first time, made the escape clause a matter of legislative directive. The act required an escape clause in every new trade agreement, and directed the President to negotiate for the inclusion of such a clause in earlier agreements, "as soon as practicable." It eliminated the former prima facie determination and provided that the Commission "shall promptly make an investigation" of applications and "report thereon not later than 1 year after the application is made."

The President's discretionary role was continued. However, the act provided that if the President does not put into effect any Commission recommendation for relief to an applicant within 60 days he must advise the House Ways and Means and Senate Finance Committees why he has not done so.

In determining injury to an applicant the Commission "without excluding other factors" was to "take into consideration" a number of criteria of injury. It was also required to publish its findings and conclusions when they were unfavorable to the applicant.

In the period 1951–53, when the law was further amended, 21 applications were investigated and reported by the Commission, with 4 findings of injury and recommendations for relief. Of these, the President put one into effect.

The Commission occupied the full year allowed for investigations in most cases. There had been several split decisions by the Commission from 1947 to 1953, including 3 evenly divided (3 to 3), which were, in effect, unfavorable to the applicant.

The 1953 Extension Act reduced the time allowed for the Commission investigation to 9 months and provided that in the event of an evenly divided Commission vote, the recommendations of both groups of Commissioners would go to the President, who then could put into effect or reject either.

There were 14 applications on which investigation reports were made by the Commission between 1953 and 1955, when the law was next amended. These resulted in 8 Commission recommendations for relief (including 2 by 3 to 3 vote). The President put into effect relief for 3 of these (but not for the 2 tied cases).

In the 1955 Extension Act the Commission was required to make public its findings and recommenadtions when they are favorable to the applicant. Theretofore it had been left to the President to make public these reports. The injury definition was amended and the term "domestic industry" defined. From 1955 to date, 14 applications have been reported by the Commission, after investigation, 9 of them finding injury to applicant and recommending relief (2 by 3 to 3 decision). Of these the President put into effect the recommendations for 1 (which was not one of the 3 to 3 decisions).

From 1947 to date 83 escape-clause applications have been filed, of which 6 are pending. There were 25 Tariff Commission findings of injury with recommendations for relief. (Of these 5 were 3 to 3 split decisions.) The President put into effect relief recommendations in whole or in part in seven cases.

The above results show that:

1. The bulk of Commission recommendations for relief were reported after Congress had enacted the escape clause in 1951, and that these reports favorable to applicants have grown each time Congress has amended and perfected the escape clause criteria and procedures, thereby reexpressing its intent that injury from tariff cuts shall be relieved.

2. Presidential actions favorable to the applicant have been relatively few, and have decreased as favorable Commission reports have increased.

*Postponement of cases*

One of the trends in the handling of escape-clause cases has been the growing recourse on the part of the President to postpone decisions on Tariff Commission recommendations favorable to applicants. The 1951 act provided that, after the Commission reports to the President, if he "does not take * * * action within 60 days" he must report to the congressional committees "stating why he has not made such adjustments," etc., as the Commission recommended.

It may have been intended by Congress, and it was so interpreted by domestic producers, that this language required the President either to reject the Commission's recommendations, or to implement them in whole or in part, within 60 days of their receipt.

However, the President has read this language as meaning that he need not make a decision in 60 days, but only report to the congressional committees if he has not acted by the end of that period. Beginning in 1953, the President has postponed action on 8 Commission recommendations for periods from 1 to 10 months, reporting to Congress that he had done so. Five of the postponed cases he referred back to the Tariff Commission for further information; the remaining three were deferred pending study by other executive agencies.

In only one of the postponed cases did the President grant the relief recommended by the Commission, and then only in modified form.

*Remedial safeguards—section 22, Agricultural Adjustment Act*

A special channel of potential relief leading to the escape clause of the trade agreements is open to American producers of agricultural commodities under section 22 of the Agricultural Adjustment Act.

A concise description of these provisions appears in the United States Tariff Commission's Operation of the Trade Agreements Program, as follows:

> Section 22 authorizes the President to restrict imports of any commodity, by imposing either import fees or quotas, whenever such imports render or tend to render ineffective, or materially interfere with programs of the United States Department of Agriculture relating to agricultural commodities. Before the President takes any action under section 22 he is required in ordinary circumstances to await an investigation (including a public hearing) and recommendations by the Tariff Commission. The Trade Agreements Extension Act of 1951 (sec. 8) provides that, upon report by the Secretary of Agriculture that emergency treatment is required because of the perishability of an agricultural commodity, the Commission's report to the President and the President's decision must be made not more than 25 calendar days after the case is submitted to the Tariff Commission. In such circumstances, however, the President is authorized to take immediate action if he deems it necessary, without awaiting the Commission's recommendations. The Trade Agreements Extension Act of 1953 provides further that the President may take immediate action under section 22, without awaiting the Commission's recommendations, in any case where the Secretary of Agriculture reports to the President that a condition exists requiring emergency treatment.

Beginning with 1939, there are publicly recorded 46 individual investigations by the Tariff Commission of cases under section 22, Agricultural Adjustment Act. Many of these are supplementary or continuing investigations after recommendations have been made. The Commission itself lists 19 separate commodity investigations.

Of the 46 cases, the Commission recommended relief in 34, and against in 3. Four cases are pending; the remainder withdrawn or terminated by some other way.

The President took action favorable to the applicants in 30 cases; unfavorable in 3; no action, 1.

If the separate cases are considered to number 19, then it should be said that only 3 were turned down by the Commission, and of those favorably reported, only 3 were turned down by the President.

As compared with the record of regular escape-clause cases, this is an extremely high proportion of results favorable to the applicant.

An explanation for the difference probably lies in the nature of the commodities involved (an agricultural commodity producer, having a choice between remedies, would naturally choose sec. 22, Agricultural Adjustment Act, as faster than the regular escape channel); the fact that injury to an industry does not need to be proved, but only that imports are interfering with a support program; and that the Secretary of Agriculture's prior intervention is a Cabinet level decision carrying great weight with the President.

*Safeguards, ODM*

A special safeguard that is partly preventive, partly remedial, is provided by amendments to the trade agreements laws in 1954 and 1955.

The first declares:

No action shall be taken * * * to decrease the duty on any article if the President finds that such reduction would threaten domestic production needed for projected national defense requirements.

The second provides, in effect, that whenever the Office of Defense Mobilization "has reason to believe" that imports of an article are threatening "to impair the national security," he shall so advise the President. "If the President agrees" he "shall cause an immediate investigation." If, then, the President finds such a threat "he shall take such action as he deems necessary to adjust the imports of such article to a level that will not threaten to impair the national security."

No procedures, or time limits, are provided in the law, so that ODM has made its own rules for handling cases.

There appear to have been 14 cases filed with ODM from 1955 to date, the earliest in June 1955. None has been finally disposed of. One, filed in July 1955, involving cordage, had an initial negative decision in March 1957; that is, a finding that ODM has no reason to believe that imports of the commodity involved were threatening to impair the national security. The applicant filed an appeal in July 1957, and the case is to be reopened.

A second case, involving oil, which was filed in August 1956, was determined to have met the prima facie test, and so a "reason to believe" report was sent to the President in April 1957. Thereafter the oil-importing companies were urged to make voluntary reductions in imports.

ODM is a Cabinet level agency. Its Defense Mobilization Board includes the Secretaries of State, Defense, Treasury, Interior, Agriculture, Commerce, and Labor. Hence, almost any decision of ODM is in essence a decision representing executive branch policy.

*Summary of remedial safeguards*

Of the avenues open to American producers to obtain relief from the impact of imports, the section 22, Agricultural Adjustment Act channel appears to be the most productive of results favorable to the applicant; the ODM channel least productive; and the general escape clause channel not much more productive.

These laws appear to express adequately and in detail the intent of Congress, except possibly in the case of the ODM directive, that domestic industry should not be injured by the workings of the trade agreements program. However, the law vests wide discretionary authority in the Executive. Hence, practical application of these safeguards is a matter for administrative decision and a decision may be gravely affected by considerations not written by Congress into the statutes.

# IMPORTS, THE TARIFF, AND THE NEED FOR ADJUSTMENT

Charles P. Kindleberger, professor of economics, Massachusetts Institute of Technology

It is the burden of this paper that the tariff has been used in the United States, by and large, to prevent desirable economic adjustments and as a means of redistributing income among various industries, various parts of the country, and between consumer and producer. Other effects of tariffs, and other arguments in their behalf, it is argued, are unintended and illusory, respectively.

The economic theorist recognizes as many as seven effects of a tariff. These may be listed briefly:

1. Revenue.
2. The reduction of consumption of a given article.
3. Forcing foreigners to sell their goods more cheaply; that is, taxing the foreigner.
4. Improvement in the balance of payments on current account; that is, reducing imports of goods and services relative to exports.
5. Increasing domestic expenditure and employment in general.
6. Increasing production of a commodity, or preventing a reduction in its output which would otherwise take place.
7. Redistributing income within a country.

### THE REVENUE EFFECT

Underdeveloped countries typically raise revenue through import duties, and occasionally through export taxes (which are unconstitutional in the United States). In the United States in the 19th century, customs duties have provided as much as 75 percent of the income of the Federal Government. Today, however, this source of revenue is unimportant. In the usual case, the higher the revenue the less effective the tariff, since imports have been maintained rather than reduced. Neither the Tariff Commission nor the Congress are interested in using customs duties to offset Federal expenditures. This effect is, accordingly ignored.

### THE CONSUMPTION EFFECT

While it is generally true that the tariff reduces domestic consumption of the taxed article, this is not the intention when it is levied. Typically, a tariff raises the internal price, and the higher the price the less is consumed. Any expansion in domestic output is more than offset by the reduction in imports. But the effect is incidental, rather than sought. It is a clear loss to the consumer. It is a cost of tariffs, rather than an object.

### TAXING THE FOREIGNER

It will sometimes happen that a customs duty is paid by the foreign supplier, rather than by the domestic consumer. After the tax, the country gets the same, or almost the same, amount of goods from abroad, but the foreign supplier offers them more cheaply. This will occur because the supply cannot readily be contracted or sold in another market, or sometimes because the foreign supplier was a monopolist who was making a substantial profit, and would have been willing to accept a lower price for his goods rather than reduce his sales. When this result occurs, economists call it the terms-of-trade effect; the tariff has enabled the taxing country to obtain its imports more cheaply, and has, therefore, improved its terms of trade, or the relationship between its export prices and its import prices.

Taxing imports to improve the terms of trade and enrich a country at foreign expense could occur as a result of a conscious policy decision. Typically, however, it happens as an unsought-for result, and one which defeats the primary purpose of levying the tariff. The United States, for example, is not concerned to tax foreign suppliers or to improve its terms of trade; it typically wants to raise domestic prices and expand domestic output. When the foreigner absorbs the entire duty, however, and sends the same amount of produce as before, the price in the home market will not rise, and no increased production will take place. The higher the terms-of-trade effect, that is, the lower the protective and redistribution effects, which, as set forth below, are the main motivation for tariff increases.

Examples of tariffs being paid by the foreigner and thus preventing any increase in price or expansion of output are not lacking. The denunciation of the Mexican trade agreement raised the tariff on petroleum products from 10½ cents per barrel to 21 cents, until a new agreement with Venezuela could be negotiated. But the price of petroleum did not rise in the United States as a consequence of this increase in the tariff; it fell in Venezuela.

Similarly, the increase in the tariff on watch movements under the escape clause produced very little in the way of price increase, since much of the tariff was absorbed by Swiss producers.

The possibility that the terms-of-trade effect will defeat the intended protective purposes of a tariff, even though it achieves a gain for the country as a whole at the expense of foreigners, is one of the major factors why quotas are sought in many agricultural products and currently in petroleum products. If there were not a rigid limitation on quantities, the foreigner would pay the tax and still ship the goods.

### THE BALANCE-OF-PAYMENTS EFFECT

Tariffs are sometimes recommended in some countries as a means of improving the balance of payments. It is occasionally believed that, if a tariff succeeds in keeping out certain foreign goods, it will improve the balance of payments by this much. This is the reasoning in reverse underlying the British slogan, "Trade, not Aid," coined by the former Chancellor of the Exchequer, R. A. Butler, Trade, not Aid, as a slogan, assumes that if United States tariffs are lowered, the United States balance of payments, which shows a surplus of exports of goods and services over imports of goods and services, would be restored to a closer balance and eliminate the necessity for the United States to make aid available to foreigners.

There is likely to be a balance-of-payments effect resulting from the new imposition of a tariff, but it is smaller, in the typical case, than the amount of goods which are directly excluded. Consumers who might otherwise have bought the imported goods, spend their income on other domestic products, and on other imports. That part additionally spent on domestic products creates new incomes, as will be elaborated presently, and this in turn leads to an increase in imports. If all the income diverted from imports by the tariff were spent at home or abroad, and none of it saved, there would be no balance-of-payments effect at all. Income would be increased by the repeated spending at home (though not by the portion spent on imports) until the income which spilled over into new imports equaled the amount diverted from the taxed import commodities. Only to the extent that the income diverted from imports is saved, either in the first instance, or out of the income created by the new domestic spending, will the balance of payments be improved. This balance-of-payments effect, moreover, depends upon the readiness of the market to finance the export surplus through gold flows or movements of reserves and upon the existence of unemployed resources which can expand output. If there is full employment in the taxing country, the additional spending at home may be purely inflationary and prevent the improvement in the balance.

This balance-of-payments effect of a tariff is both conditional as already indicated, and not normally an objective of policy, certainly not in the United States. The gain for one country is a loss for another, and the attempt is therefore properly regarded as a "beggar-thy-neighbor" type of policy. In the depression some countries undertook to prevent a deterioration in their trade balance resulting from depression abroad by taxing imports. This policy was defensive. In the United States, however, we have had a surplus in the current account of the balance of payments for an extended period. Even were the balance of payments to turn adverse, it seems likely that the adverse balance could be financed by further foreign acquisitions of dollar liabilities of the New York market, or of gold. In either case, there would be no reason to regard the movement as disturbing. And if monetary authorities after a long cumulative deficit in the balance of payments were to become disturbed, the tariff is probably the most inefficient method to use to improve the balance.

Other countries then may use tariffs as a means of controlling their balance of payments, and may be conscious of the balance-of-payments effects of tariff action in the United States. Moreover, the surplus in the United States balance of payments may constitute an argument in favor of tariff reduction by the United States on a unilateral rather than a reciprocal basis. But the United States balance of payments is not and should not be used as a justification for imposing tariffs in this country.

### THE INCOME EFFECT

It is sometimes argued that tariffs can be applied to increase or restore national income or employment. This argument can be dismissed in large part on the same grounds as the argument just discussed. It is likely that under ordinary conditions expenditure diverted from imports would raise domestic income and employment but it is not certain that tariffs could systematically be used to achieve that result. At any rate such a tariff policy would be one of beggar-thy-neighbor designed to export unemployment. It would be virtually certain to elicit retaliation and reduce employment in United States export industries. There would certainly appear to be better means of restoring or maintaining domestic income and employment than tariffs or restrictions on imports.

### THE PROTECTIVE OR REALLOCATION EFFECT

We are left then with the two principal reasons for imposing a tariff: to achieve a certain allocation of resources, and to achieve a certain desired internal redistribution of income. This section will deal with the various reasons why a country might want to impose a tariff to achieve a reallocation of resources. In particular it will discuss:

(1) noneconomic arguments, such as defense
(2) the infant-industry argument
(3) to defend against dumping
(4) to slow down the rate of change to manageable proportions

### A. NONECONOMIC ARGUMENTS, INCLUDING DEFENSE

It is entirely appropriate for a country to undertake steps to achieve noneconomic ends, such as the preservation of certain industries or certain methods of production, even though the goods involved can be acquired more cheaply in other ways. The only stipulation which the economists should add is that the cost of achieving the noneconomic objective be recognized, and that some attempt be made to insure that this cost be minimized, and borne in equitable fashion. As a rule, this means that the economists prefer a subsidy to a tariff. A subsidy can be restricted to the particular increased production being sought, rather than given to the industry as a whole, as is the case with a tariff; more, a subsidy is raised in taxes which are levied in some fashion regarded as appropriate for expenses by the community and its budgetary institutions, whereas a tariff imposes the taxes in arbitrary fashion on the consumer and distorts the pattern of consumption as well as that of production.

The defense argument raises peculiarly difficult questions for analysis. No one quarrels with the need for national defense. But the same industries will not be needed to meet every possible kind of war. Ships, for example, are appropriate to a long-drawn-out war in which production can rely on supplies imported from overseas, but have virtually no relevance to nuclear-bombing-type hostilities. Another important question is raised by timing: Today's ships will be of almost no help in any war which occurs 20 years from now. Equally, a subsidy to oil exploration maintained by quota restrictions may help if war occurs in a relatively short space of time, but exhaust United States reserves if the defense need is potential, but not actual for a longer period, such as 20 years.

The defense argument is generally advanced by particular economic interests in their own behalf. Were the major concern really the national defense as a whole, these interests would be prepared to allow the additional profits created for private firms by the artificial scarcity to be collected for the society as a whole. In the discussion of import quotas for oil, for example, a difficult problem is created by the allocation of the quotas. Since quotas raise the price of oil inside the United States, and may lower it abroad, licenses representing permission to import under the quota have a scarcity value. The firms with foreign producing interests are naturally interested in keeping this scarcity value for themselves, buying cheap and selling dear. Some refining interests have suggested informally that if imports of crude petroleum are to be limited to 10 percent of oil refined, the licenses might be issued to the refineries, and sold by those which did not want to import crude petroleum, such, as for example, as those in Texas or the Central United States. But it is clearly more equitable, if the import restriction is undertaken in the national interest, rather than the interests of particular groups of producers, to have the benefits of the scarcity value accrue to the country as a whole, and have the United States Government auction off the limited licenses, and apply the revenues therefrom to the general welfare.

The fact is that the national defense, and other noneconomic purposes such as the preservation of the countryside or the family farm, the prevention of the depopulation of a particular region, etc., are typically introduced into tariff discussion to support arguments which rest, at basis, primarily on the case for a particular interest. National defense is cited in tariff discussions primarily as rationalization, rather than basic justification. In watches, oil, and a number of other products the Defense Department, under great pressure from legislative and other representatives of particular interests has reversed its position. Manufacturers of many peacetime products ranging from paper to candles and thumbtacks have insisted that the country will be unable to defend itself against aggression from overseas unless they get tariff protection. There may be solid arguments for support of certain industries in the national defense. If so, it should be done by subsidy, stockpiling, or manufacture in national arsenals, and not by raising the price to the consumer in general by limiting imports.

### THE INFANT-INDUSTRY ARGUMENT

The infant-industry argument is another which is intellectually respectable in a limited number of circumstances but which has been used in a large number of instances where it does not really apply. Industries which today insist that the country's defense will turn on their preservation through tariff protection were earlier claiming special consideration in the form of tariff protection on the basis of conditions which appear only in the case of industries with long-run decreasing costs. Like the national-defense argument the infant-industry argument is sometimes justified but more frequently claimed. Many branches of the chemical industry, such as pharmaceuticals and dyestuffs, needed protection after World War I but are now able to export in competition with German industry which indicates that they have grown up. But promotion of infant industries, whether or not such industries are important to national defense, would be more equitably supported by subsidies than by tariffs; subsidization would permit assisting the high-cost plants only, rather than those which have already achieved efficient size, and putting the burden of the cost on the taxpayer rather than the consumer.

### ANTIDUMPING TARIFFS

Antidumping tariffs will commend themselves to people who believe in retail-price maintenance and other fair-trade legislation. This excludes the majority of economists who view price competition as desirable in improving the real income of consumers and the most efficient allocation of resources.

Sporadic dumping, of the sort which is involved in distress selling, clearly poses problems for competitive producers. But it is difficult to see that one should legislate against it, any more than against January white sales, or the selling of retailers' stocks from other parts of the country in Filene's basement in Boston.

Persistent dumping, involving long-run differential pricing, is a familiar practice in national trade and should pose no particular international problems. The United States itself claims the right to sell surplus agricultural stocks at the world price, while holding the domestic price at whatever level it chooses. This benefits foreign consumers, since the sales actually depress the world price, though they hurt foreign producers. But if the price discrimination is persistent, of the sort that first-, second-, and third-run movie houses practice, or that doctors indulge in when they vary their fees with the patient's income, there is no reason why the country should not adjust to it and benefit from cheaper imports.

The problem arises with so-called predatory dumping, where a foreign competitor reduces selling prices to drive a domestic producer out of the market and is expected thereafter to raise prices and capture exorbitant profits. This is possible, but not likely. It requires an irreversibility, that is, that it is easy for a domestic producer to be driven out of the market by low prices, but impossible for him or other potential competitors to go back into production when prices go back up. Such situations are not unknown. If mines are closed down, it may be that flooding will make it impossible to reopen them except at exorbitant cost. Or, as in the early claims against the Standard Oil Co., predatory dumping may be combined with economies of scale found in the infant industry, and the foreign producer gains an efficient scale which the domestic producer cannot hope to achieve. In this case, however, the foreign producer may produce the goods at a permanently reduced cost so that the problem is akin to the less troublesome one of persistent dumping.

In general, however, the case against predatory dumping is not strong enough to make it worthwhile to support the enormously complex machinery needed to establish the facts in an area—price data—where facts are notoriously difficult to establish. Few antidumping cases present themselves in the United States for administration through the Treasury's procedure, and fewer antidumping duties are imposed. The possibility of dumping is one which every domestic industry faces internally, where fair trade laws do not apply; and there is no particularly different reason it should not face this from foreign competitors. The only basis for such an exception could be that it was claimed that a producer entering a business should be expected to take into account the possible action and reactions of domestic, but not of foreign producers. As the world shrinks, this basis of differentiation makes less and less sense.

### SLOWING DOWN THE RATE OF CHANGE

Today's world is one of change. New goods, new processes for making known goods, new means of transport, new skills threaten old at the same time that they offer the new producers and the consumers new gains. Much of the argument for tariff protection is to fend off, or sometimes to slow down the rate of adjustment to these changes.

Samuel Lubell has argued in his book, The Revolution in World Trade, that these changes have become so widespread and frequent as to undermine the classical argument for free trade and to establish a presumption that trade should be administered rather than allowed to adjust through the price system. Don D. Humphrey, on the other hand, in his study of American Imports, contends that adjustment must be undertaken to new circumstances, but that sometimes the market mechanism strains the capacity of the system to bring about such adjustments, and that a tariff or some similar device must be used to slow down the rate of change. Such a tariff, for example, might be one which was imposed when the impact of a change was fully felt, and recognized to be too great for the system to adjust too smoothly, but disappeared over 2 or 3 years. The escape provision to the general rule that tariffs should be held down, and in fact lowered, through reciprocal trade agreements or unilaterally, would then call for the application of a disappearing tariff to slow down the rate of change, in circumstances where the private-enterprise system was overwhelmed by the speed and extent of the required adjustment.

It must be underlined that this concept would differ profoundly from the present escape-clause provision which is based on a finding of serious injury to the import-competing industry. The serious-injury doctrine calls for resistance to adjustment. Any foreign innovation, reconstruction, or recovery from depression, which threatens an industry in the United States is to be resisted in toto. To slow down the rate of change, on the other hand, recognizes that adjustment is desirable, that change and growth are the well-springs of economic vitality, and that the attempt to protect import-competing industry in the condition of prosperity to which it had become accustomed is subversive of the underlying doctrines of the free enterprise system.

A Boston jeweler has argued that the troubles of the Waltham Watch Co. sprang in some considerable measure from the Dingley tariff on watches imposed in 1909, and that the funds which the industry then spent on lobbying for the tariff should rather have been devoted to endowing a chair or a department of horological research in a technical university. It has often been asserted that the backwardness of much of European agriculture in the present century before World War II was due to the protection accorded to peasant farmers in the 1880's and 1890's against cheap wheat from North America, Australia, Argentina, and the Ukraine. To defend an industry against serious injury runs the grave risk of lulling it into obsolescent comfort. This is a world of change, calling for adjustment. Governmental intervention should promote adjustment, rather than frustrate it.

An analogous situation has been presented by domestic technological change and the specter it has posed of technological unemployment. Economist and legislator are joined today in the recognition that it is futile and even absurd to attempt to prevent technological change, and that the only problem is how to overcome the transitional difficulties for particular localities and governments. Labor unions, craft and industrial, in a few cases resist technological innovation, although most labor spokesmen are reluctant to justify such action. But a wide number of the same people will support the doctrine of a tariff to prevent serious injury in an import-competing industry, without recognizing its kinship to now discarded arguments in behalf of resisting technical change.

Transitional problems are not to be ignored in the interest of the long-run benefit. It is argued below that general measures for promoting adjustment of resources to internal as well as to external change are preferable to tariffs, even disappearing ones. But the disappearing tariff, based on the doctrine of slowing down the rate of adjustment in the few cases where the transitional difficulties are particularly obdurate, is preferable to withdrawal of tariff concessions in order to forestall serious injury.

A good many tariff problems arise from a peculiar set of dynamic circumstances. There is a war. In the particular trade vacuum left by the disruption of trade through war, new enterprises are created in new lines. After war, with the restoration of trade, there is a question whether these enterprises should be maintained by tariffs or allowed to decline. The national-defense argument is brought into play, and has some merit if there is a valid expectation that a subsequent war will follow the pattern of the previous one, and if there is no possibility of employing a subsidy. The infant-industry argument is also adduced, although the question is not one of giving birth to new industries so much as preventing industrial infanticide. But United States tariffs have risen after the Napoleonic, and civil wars and after World War I. It is inevitable that the demand for protection should increase after World War II. It is remarkable, in the light of this history, that it has been possible to renew the Reciprocal Trade Agreements Act even with the substantial emasculation through the escape clause and peril points.

The tariff as a means of slowing down economic adjustment runs the risk of becoming a tariff which will prevent economic change. It is argued later that this is a mistake; that the short-run gains in avoiding the costs of readjustment are almost invariably overwhelmed by the long-run losses of misallocation which keeps land, labor, capital, and business enterprise engaged in industries where they earn smaller returns than are available to them elsewhere. Costs of readjustment are an inevitable accompaniment of a world of change. It is imperative to adjust to basic changes in the structure of production at home and abroad. The costs of this adjustment should be borne widely by the economy, to the extent that it is possible to transfer them from the individuals directly affected. But a net loss for the community is involved in taxing consumers and exporters to subsidize producers in inefficient import-competing industries, since total output in value terms is reduced by the misallocation.

### TARIFF AS A MEANS OF REDISTRIBUTING INCOME

In my opinion, the major social and political forces making for the imposition, and the removal, of tariffs are concerned with the redistribution of income inside the community. All other arguments in the United States today have secondary force as compared with this one. Individual producers, industries, groups of industry, factors of production, and regions are interested in levying or removing tariffs from the point of view of increasing their income at the expense of others in the community. The effect on the foreign producer is frequently regretted, but is regarded as secondary. The tariff is a domestic, not an international issue.

Tariffs redistribute income in various ways. The increase in price on the existing domestic production is a tax on the consumer for the benefit of the producer. The reduction in exports which comes about through the loss of imports and the consequent inability of foreigners to buy to the same extent, lowers export prices and transfers income from the export industry to import-competing. If exports consist of agricultural produce and the output of mass-production industries, while imports represent largely the output of labor-intensive industries, a balanced reduction in imports and exports will lower the return to agricultural land, and capital and labor in mass-production industries, and improve the incomes of labor and capital in small-scale industries. In the 19th century, the tariff assisted the northeastern manufacturing States at the expense of the agricultural South and the West. Today, some tariffs and quotas benefit the oil-producing States at the expense of the consuming centers; others help the States engaged in the production of older products like textiles, hats, gloves, pottery, hand-blown glass, and so forth, and hurt the exporting interests in machinery, consumers' durable goods, wheat, cotton, and so forth.

If it is desirable in any case to assist hard-pressed producers in an import-competing industry, there are better means of doing so than the tariff. The tariff raises prices for the efficient producer as well as for the one who is having difficulty covering costs. It has been asserted that, while the purpose of much farm legislation is to help the family-size farm, the major benefits of price supports and soil conservation accrue typically to the large-scale commercial farm which could survive without them. Whether this is true in farm legislation is not known to me, but it is typically the case in tariffs. In many industries, the plight of the struggling marginal producer who may be put out of business by imports is headlined, while the fact that a number of other producers are successfully competing with foreign suppliers with existing protection is ignored. An additional tariff helps those who do not need it at the expense of the consumer and of the exporter.

Further export interests gain from freer trade at the expense of importing-competing industries. Mr. O. Strackbein has complained that the import-competing proponents of tariffs are characterized as vested interests when they advocate protection, while export industry is not regarded as self-seeking when it seeks to lower trade barriers. There is merit in this position. Export interests which advocate lower trade barriers do not usually reveal the special benefits which would accrue to them as they proclaim the general interest. But in these cases there is a presumption that to divert income from import competing to export industry by lowering tariffs enlarges total income and is thus beneficial, in an overall sense, whereas a transfer of income from export industries to import-competing ones lowers national real income on balance. Accordingly, it cannot be justified in welfare terms unless there are special circumstances which call for a transfer in this particular direction.

To say that the major purpose of tariffs is to transfer income from one group to another within the country is not necessarily to condemn them. Income transfers are appropriate under various circumstances, and government is the appropriate agency to undertake them. The progressive income tax, which falls more heavily on large than small incomes, social insurance, and a considerable amount of collective consumption in education, housing, et cetera, represent just this sort of transfer. In these circumstances, however, it is important to identify what groups in the economy are to be taxed, what groups are to benefit, and to have clear criteria for assigning costs and gains. The difficulty with the tariff as a means of redistributing income is that it is highly arbitrary in its incidence on consumers, having no systematic relation to ability to pay or to the nature of consumption, on the one hand, and is fairly erratic in the distribution of its benefits, on the other. Where in an industry there are some prosperous firms and some encountering real difficulties, it fails to distinguish among them. To encourage efficient import-competing firms to spend their energy in raising tariffs may lead them into neglecting the attention to research and to production and marketing efficiency, which are the basis of desirable business success.

These redistributive considerations can be illustrated in a number of industries. In watches, for example, one struggling and admittedly inefficient and backward company provided the excuse for the tariff even though there were in the industry a number of other efficient firms which were able to hold their own against Swiss imports. The emphasis on the demand for quotas on oil imports is so strongly on national defense as to conceal the fact that a politically powerful group of independent oil producers in a key political State, most of them already rich, demand still higher prices for oil at the expense of the refining industry, the producers with foreign supplies, most of which have also been very profitable in recent years, and consumers in all parts of the country.

As the oil industry indicates, these struggles can take place within a single industry; one group able to export, or with access to foreign imports, interested in freer trade, while another group, less efficient or with different resources, is entirely import competing and interesting in keeping out foreign competition. Such struggles may even take place between labor and enterprise in the same industry, as the example of the movies now illustrates—Hollywood organized labor being opposed to the making of pictures abroad, while the larger companies with access to foreign facilities are interested in freer trade. A similar split may occur in the automobile industry if all domestic producers team up with foreign suppliers to import cars made with United States capital, United States and foreign technology, but with foreign labor.

There is nothing, perhaps, which can be done in a democracy to stop the use of tariffs for redistributing income among industries, regions, factors of production, producer, and consumer. Our form of government constitutes a standing invitation to any group which regards itself as hurt by these methods to organize politically and to present its case for or against any tariff in as clear and effective manner as it can. But it should be recognized in this that the consumer typically organizes very little, and rather ineffectually on the whole, as compared with the producer, and that battles among producers, while they have the chance of coming out beneficially for the consumer, if the exporting interests defeat the import-competing, can on occasion end up in producers' agreements concluded at the expense of the general interest. Such was the Smoot-Hawley Tariff Act of 1930, which attempted to provide something for everyone. In addition, the link between the gain of the import-competing producer and an increase in a tariff is closer and more easily demonstrable than the gains of the exporting producer from maintaining freer trade, so that the latter tends to exert himself less against any particular duty than the former does in its favor.

There are strong reasons for using other means than the tariff to effect redistribution. One is political morality. Exclusion of imports designed to raise or maintain incomes of a particular group is frequently masked as national defense, infant industry, repelling of dumping, maintaining the United States standard of living, et cetera, without the check of any political Federal Trade Commission which can halt misrepresentation. The nature of a subsidy in enlarging incomes is evident. Typically, such subsidies will be given only to the marginal producer whose output is deemed needed or whose incomes would fall below some normal level, and not to the efficient producer who could make a profit at the lower price but would prefer to have more. Another is the impact on consumption. To subsidize the marginal producer enlarges total consumption by expanding output, while the tariff contracts consumption overall.

The appropriate means for redistribution, therefore, are governmental taxes and expenditures, including subsidies, not governmental price fixing which distorts the pattern of production and consumption while it arbitrarily taxes one group for the benefit of another. To invite all groups to interfere with the distribution of income by persuading the Government to alter prices is to subvert our economic system. This should distribute rewards on the basis of people's contribution to the national economic well-being, not on the basis of political effectiveness.

## TRANSITIONAL MEASURES IN THE PROCESS OF ADJUSTMENT

This analysis can be summarized by saying that it holds that the operational motives for raising tariffs are to expand production in a given item, or, more generally, to resist contraction, and to improve the income of one group of producers at the expense of other producers and of consumers. The redistribution motive is the more effective one, and operates in an area which would normally be handled through the budgetary mechanism of government.

It is contended that this is not satisfactory in a world of change, and that the role of government ought to be one of assisting economic forces to adapt to new circumstances rather than resisting them. In particular, so long as the balance of payments as a whole is not seriously adverse, the availability of imports at a price cheaper than they can be produced in this country is a sign that we have resources working in a wrong industry and an opportunity to improve our real income by shifting them into other lines. The serious injury suffered by this economy is not that done by the expansion of imports, but arises through misallocation and unwillingness to adust. It is time that the United States changed its basic philosophy of imports from one of serious injury to reallocation and readjustment of those resources which are badly located.

The problem is by no means limited to the import-competing industries, and there is no reason why remedies which are needed to improve the mobility of capital and labor among industries should be limited to situations where attention is called to the malallocation by an increase in imports. Technological change based on domestic innovations, both new products and new ways of producing old goods and services; shifts of capital to new and more efficient locations, leaving labor and ancillary services stranded; cancellation of defense contracts, such as those recently carried through by the Air Force, and particularly in the Navajo guided missile and the F–100; a change in taste against an established industry in favor of another, such as the loss of the motion-picture distributor to the television industry, or the smaller automobile producers to the Big Three and the foreign car; all of these present similar problems. They call for adaptation and change rather than resistance. To continue to manufacture the Navajo merely because the cancellation of the contract displaces 11,000 workers would be unthinkable. Similarly, it should be unthinkable to limit imports to maintain company profits or employment in import-competing industry.

The problem presented by technological unemployment is universally recognized as a transitional one. Equally transitional is the problem presented by cheap imports. The problem of technological unemployment is likely to be accentuated in coming years by the spread of automatic methods of production which reduce the demand for relatively unskilled labor as they increase the need for highly educated and skilled technicians. It may be appropriate, therefore, for the United States to give more attention to easing transitional and reallocation problems for the economy as a whole. The tariff is only part of a broad domestic problem of increased mobility.

In the field of labor, mobility requires a variety of steps: retraining; wider use of the United States Employment Service; possibly increased unemployment benefits; in large-scale firms producing a variety of products, perhaps a guaranteed annual wage or supplementary unemployment benefits; and in extreme cases, where a highly specialized locality is very hard hit, some means of preventing or slowing down a potential collapse of real-estate prices and of service industries by inducing new plants to locate in such an area.

The allocation of responsibility and costs for these various measures to separate institutions: the Federal Government, State and local governments, private enterprise, public-spirited citizens, and labor itself, is a most complex question in which an economist interested in international issues has no expertise. It is recognized that the present administration is disposed to place a minimum of responsibility on the Federal Government and as much as possible on other agencies. Nonetheless, I believe that alternative opportunities for employment of labor outside of the affected community, or means of bringing to the community new enterprises frequently lie beyond the capacity of local governments or groups of citizens to affect. It may therefore be that some national means are required to expand the effectiveness of the Employment Service, and for calling attention to opportunities for new locations where labor of various calibers is available.

A particular difficulty is posed by the difference in the capacity of large and small firms to develop new ways of reducing costs; develop new profitable lines of output; retrain workers and to pay or contract for supplementary unemployment benefits. Where there are large firms, workers may expect greater resourcefulness in meeting the competition of imports or shifting into new lines and attempt by collective bargaining to load much of the risk on employers. Where, on the other hand, firms are typically small, there is little research, output tends to be limited to traditional lines, and guaranteed annual wages, or supplementary unemployment benefits are usually out of the question. For the worker this means that the possibility of loading the cost of adjustment on the firm is excluded.

Where the basic economic position is changed by technological change, loss of a major contract, change in taste, or new competition from imports, management and ownership need: new technology and/or new products, as already mentioned; or assistance in salvaging the maximum amount of capital from the existing enterprise and starting afresh elsewhere. For small firms, which typically undertake no research, the first two paths are closed in the absence of research departments. Some substitute can occasionally be found through buying research from profitmaking firms or supported at universities. But there is missing in the assistance to small firms the kinds of aid the farmer has received through the research undertaken by the Department of Agriculture and the land-grant colleges. It might be desirable for the budget of the Small Business Administration to be enlarged for the purpose of supporting research on a small scale needed by firms in difficulties which seek aid in particular directions.

For the rest, firms may need loans, which are available under certain circumstances through the Small Business Administration. In addition, financial assistance might be given them under limited conditions at the expense of the taxpayer (who should bear it rather than the consumer) by designating certain industries hard hit by innovations or by new imports as qualified for limited periods of time for doubling their losses for carryover purposes on the corporate income tax. This would make them more attractive for mergers, which would salvage more of the capital; enable them to earn higher returns on new projects, if these were successful; and would encourage a more venturesome attitude toward research, new products, etc. It would be limited, moreover, to those firms which incurred losses, and would not benefit the inframarginal efficient firm which did not need the help so much. The writer is not sufficiently expert in the area of taxation to know what the full effects of such a device might be, what safeguards it requires, and whether it might be considered practical. But if it could be made to operate effectively, it would tend in the right direction of expediting adjustment, rather than thwarting reallocation.

Even if the Congress and the administration are not now ready to enlarge the program of aid for displaced workers and small business affected by technological change, contract cancellation, change in tastes, etc., it would still be useful as an alternative to the imposition of tariffs under the escape clause or quotas under the national defense procedure to develop procedures for adjustment required by increases in imports of a substantial sort, where capital and labor are stranded and are not in a position to help themselves. Such industries might be designated by the President as entitled to special assistance from the Small Business Administration, in unemployment compensation, supported by the Federal Government through the States, in retraining programs, in the doubling of tax losses for carryover, etc. Such a designation and the benefits accruing under it should be limited in time, and should be made available only after special study and published findings by an adjustment board, as contemplated in some bills before the Congress, and especially the Williams-Kennedy bill. If the so-called Douglas bill giving special consideration to depressed areas were enacted, its provisions could readily be broadened to cover the adjustment problem created by sudden large changes in imports.

### THE DISAPPEARING TARIFF FOR ESCAPES

If the main purpose of legislation in this area is to free trade, the renewal of the Reciprocal Trade Agreements Act should provide that if the escape clause is invoked, and returns a tariff to the level of the Smoot-Hawley Act, the exception should be limited in time, and used only to assist the industry during the period of transition—say 18 months or 2 years. It would be desirable to use the adjustment mechanism instead of a tariff, since the invoking of tariff changes is very disturbing to international trade as it creates uncertainty for foreign producers who might otherwise spend time in developing a market in the United States. The presumption should rest in favor of leaving the tariff unchanged. But when the President, on recommendation of the Tariff Commission, decided that the long-run salvation of the industry lay in increased efficiency in existing lines, based on the employment of new techniques or new machinery, rather than relocation into other employments, then, and only then, there is something to be said for invoking the escape clause on a disappearing basis. A possible formula would be 100 percent for 6 months, 75 percent for 6 months, and 50 percent for 6 months, following which the tariff would fall to zero, where 100 percent represents the Smoot-Hawley tariff level, and zero represents the level embodied in the latest trade agreement.

### VOLUNTARY EXPORT QUOTAS ABROAD OR IMPORT QUOTAS IN THE UNITED STATES

Equally, of course, voluntary export quotas negotiated with foreign producers or import quotas among importers in the United States should be limited in their effect to a relatively short period of adjustment. I cannot forbear indicating my thorough disapproval of the device of asking foreign exporters to limit their exports to this market as a means of enabling this country to slide out of the necessity to violate its international obligations to the General Agreement on Tariffs and Trade, violate its own laws regarding the application of the antitrust laws to exports to the United States, and in general behave in an illegal and inconsistent way. We have a tradition of objecting to foreign cartels; it is inconsistent, then, to promote their establishment. In one case of Switzerland, we both asked the Swiss to limit exports to this market and prosecuted them for violation of the antitrust laws on the allegation that they had done so. If we insist on limiting imports, it is less hypocritical to do so openly rather than ask exporters "voluntarily," but under threat of compulsion, to limit their exports. But if we still persist in this behavior, which started in the 1930's, let us limit our requests in each case to a finite time period, with 2 years as a maximum. Change is inevitable, even though we may need time for adjustment.

### TARIFF REDUCTIONS

The new legislation renewing the Reciprocal Trade Agreements Act should also provide new scope for tariff reductions. In industries which are recognized to be using obsolete and inefficient methods, these reductions should be accompanied by the designation of the industries as qualified for assistance from the Adjustment Board. The writer desires that such reductions should be substantial. At a minimum, they should be 5 percent a year for 3 years, of the 1955 level, not the level in existence in 1958. But if the emphasis is turned to adjustment, as it ought to be, it should be possible to resume the progress toward freer trade which was interrupted in 1953.

### THE MAINTENANCE OF PROSPERITY

It goes without saying that the major means for assisting adjustment out of inefficient import-competing industries into lines where the resources can be more effectively used, is to maintain high levels of prosperity and employment. No economists recommend tariff reductions in periods of slack. It should be clearly understood by the executive branch of the Government that the Congress does not intend the powers for tariff reduction to be used when business is in recession. When business is prosperous, however, as it has been for the most part for the period since the war, with exceptions in 1949, 1951, and 1954, and prospectively parts of 1957 and 1958, adjustment is readily undertaken in all but a few cases where labor and capital are stranded in a depressed area remote from alternative opportunities. These cases cannot be helped in any effective way by tariffs. They need the resources of Government to be brought to bear to shift them to centers of adequate business activity. Adjustment, not injury, should be the touchstone.

# DO DISPARITIES BETWEEN REAL AND MONEY PRICES MODIFY TRADITIONAL ARGUMENTS FOR FREER TRADE?

Stephen Enke, chief, logistics department, The Rand Corp.

It is a commonplace that, in the mid-20th century, real costs are often not reflected by money costs, or real benefits by money gains. The main cause of these discrepancies is the intervention in price making of governments, large corporations, labor unions, etc. As a consequence, it is sometimes alleged that the economic efficiency that is supposed to flow from policies of freer trade cannot be relied upon in the world of today. However, it can be shown that, from the selfish viewpoint of a single country, the existence of discrepancies abroad between money and real costs and gains in no way modifies traditional arguments for free trade. Moreover, for a country like the United States, which has full employment, a strong current account in its balance of payments, and a highly mobile labor force, it can be shown that import restrictions are usually not the answer when real values and money prices are disproportionate at home.

## IRRELEVANCE OF DISPARATE REAL AND MONEY VALUES IN FOREIGN COUNTRIES

From the selfish viewpoint of the United States, it makes no difference whether real values and money prices abroad are equivalent or in correspondence. The prime concern of those responsible for the United States economy, and the gains it can attain from foreign trade, is whether certain products can be obtained for United States use more economically as imports than as domestic production. Imports must be acquired indirectly from the sale of exports, and so the cost of these imports is the cost of producing the exports for which in effect they were exchanged. The cost of domestic production is the money value of the productive factors employed in such production.

Let us suppose that, in the absence of foreign trade, the real costs of producing a barrel of A or a ton of B in the United States are $5 and $10 respectively. Let us suppose that international trade among various producing and using countries has established a world price for A and B, respectively, of $9 a barrel and $12 a ton. Moreover, let us suppose that these world prices do not reflect real costs of production and real use values in the other trading countries.

Despite this fact, it will be in the interests of the United States to export A and import B. After all, it costs $10 of resources to produce a ton of B in the United States. But a ton of B can be bought on the world market for 12/9—i. e., 1.33—barrels of A. And 1.33 barrels of A can be produced in the United States with 1.33 times $5—i. e., $6.65 worth—of resources. The saving that results for the United States from acquiring goods for use indirectly, through purchasing imports with exports, is clear in the case of B.

It is worth repeating that these conclusions follow independently of the real costs of producing A and B in foreign countries. Suppose we are now told that, in the other countries principally concerned, the real costs of producing a unit of A and B are, respectively, $10 and $15. But from the selfish viewpoint of the United States, we do not need this information. As long as we know the relative prices of A and B on the world market, and the relative real costs of producing A and B domestically, a lot can be said about policy. If, at the present scale of producing and exporting, the cost of making a unit of A is disproportionately low (as defined above), more production and exports can normally be assumed beneficial. Similarly, if the unit production cost of B is disproportionately high, at the present scale of production and importation, less producing and more importing is in order.

The moral is that if trade is profitable to United States exporters and importers, the United States Government should generally not intervene, and certainly not because of supposed discrepancies between money prices and real costs or gains abroad. Profitable trade should be presumed beneficial until proven otherwise.

However, there are three broad classes of exceptions—other than those based on moral and health considerations—that merit the examination given below. The first is when United States threats to impose trade restrictions can be used to induce foreign governments to take action favorable to our interests. The second is when the production costs of certain domestically made goods are artificially overpriced or underpriced. The third is when the United States has some marked monopoly power, whether as importer or exporter, that it tries to exploit.

### IMPORT RESTRICTIONS AS A BARGAINING WEAPON

Following the example analyzed above, suppose another country alters the world market prices of A by instituting an import duty on A. As a result, the amount of B that the United States can acquire indirectly, through exporting A for B imports, is lessened. Or the other government by subsidizing exports of B may "hurt" producers of B in the United States. These actions of the foreign government are of concern to the United States Government, even though it cannot intervene in a way that would benefit the United States directly. In an indirect way, however, and if the bluff is not called, the United States Government may be able to induce foreign government to take certain actions that are favorable to different United States interests. However, it must be stressed that this is a dangerous game, one that may be beyond the capabilities of our system of government, and one that other foreign governments can play more effectively than ours.

The case of the subsidy on B exports, granted by the other government, can be passed over briefly. As a result of this subsidy the United States can acquire more B imports for the same quantity of A exports. The users of B in the United States, because they can now obtain it at a lower price, obtain a user's surplus. The domestic suppliers of B in the United States—and it can be assumed that some of the United

States use is home produced—now obtain a lower net price for their output and so suffer a reduction in their aggregate suppliers' surplus. However, as more units of B are used than made in the United States, the increment in users' surplus exceeds the decrement in domestic suppliers' surplus. On balance, so far as dollars can measure the incidence on these various domestic interests, the United States gains from the foreign subsidy. There is nothing that the United States Government need do except be grateful.

The converse case of a foreign import duty on A is more complex. The domestic play of interests is the opposite of that just examined. The net price received by United States producers and exporters, allowing for the duty, is reduced, lessening their suppliers' surplus. Against this, as a partial offset, is the fact that domestic users benefit from the reduced world and domestic prices, and so gain a modest users' surplus. The United States economy must now export more units of A to obtain a given quantity of B imports. Moreover, part of the customs duties on A imports received by the foreign government comes in effect from the producers of A in the United States. The United States producers of A are probably better organized politically than the domestic users of A, and for this reason alone, despite the conflicting interests in this matter of United States producers and users, the United States Government would probably like to do something about the duty on A imposed by the foreign government.

What can it do? Of the many possible things that it might sensibly consider, three obvious possibilities are to threaten to (1) pay an export subsidy on A, (2) levy an import duty on B, and (3) impose duties on other imports of which the foreign country in question is a major supplier of the United States.

*Export subsidy on A.*—The United States Government might seek to placate domestic exporters of A, on units sold to the foreign country, with a per unit subsidy equal to the per unit duty imposed by the foreign government. This, if it were done without further reactions abroad, would restore the original situation as regards the United States domestic price, production, consumption, and exportation of A. However, the United States Government would find itself in the galling position of paying out as many dollars as subsidy on A exports as the foreign government was collecting from the duty on A imports. In effect, the United States Treasury would be providing the other government's duty revenues on the commodity in question. This can also be a dangerous policy for the United States, especially if this were ever to become the normal United States reaction to a new foreign duty; such a policy would then be an invitation to foreign governments to finance their operations through duties against United States exports.

*Import duty on B.*—Conversely, if the United States Government imposes a duty on imports receiving export subsidies from the foreign government, the United States Government would, in effect, receive duty revenues paid by the foreign government. Hence either the threat or the actuality of the United States duty may well result in eliminating the subsidy on A. The problem for the United States, however, is that it probably does not want the subsidy eliminated. If the United States threatens a tariff duty, and the foreign subsidy is eliminated, United States buyers no longer benefit, and on balance the United States economy has suffered too. If the United States does impose the tax, the foreign subsidy will almost certainly be withdrawn; the United States Treasury then gains some ordinary duty revenues, but primarily from domestic users and producers, and not from the foreign government.

*Impose duties on other imports from the foreign country.*—Inasmuch as the United States maintains an unconditional most-favored-nation policy toward imports, the United States Government, unless it violates this policy, is limited to imposing import duties on those goods (other than B and irrespective of country of origin) for which the United States constitutes an important market for the "hostile" country's exporters. The danger is that the bluff may be called. As we shall see, there are only a few special instances in which it is to the benefit of the United States to impose restrictions on imports. These we shall call justified import restrictions. Supposedly they are all imposed already. To impose unjustified import restrictions will injure the United States interests on balance. Hence, if the United States exercises its threat, it is in the position of a man who "cuts off his nose to spite your face," for the injury done to the foreign economy also injures the United States economy.

### DISPARATE REAL AND MONEY VALUES WITHIN THE UNITED STATES

#### *Money costs that are disproportionately higher than real costs in the United States*

Many a United States trade association has claimed that its industry must bear unnaturally high costs because of Government actions. Excise taxes, high minimum wages, and price-supported inputs are some of the examples advanced. These assertions are usually coupled with requests, in the name of "equality," for protection against imports.

*Excise taxes on output.*—There is general agreement that, if the United States Government levies an excise tax on a good, this tax should be remitted on exported units and applied comparably to competing imports. However, there are sometimes conceptual difficulties when subordinate jurisdictions levy taxes on output, and applications of this principle can create problems. For example, a timber State may have a stumpage tax, justified perhaps on the grounds that the State's forestry activities are beneficial and must be supported. Should logs imported into any one of the United States pay an equivalent tax, either as an excise or import duty, and what shall the rate be if different States have different stumpage taxes?

*Minimum wage laws.*—The Federal Government, and many of the State governments, have minimum wage and overtime work laws that increase hourly wage rates, and so it is argued by some industries that this should be offset by import restrictions or export subsidies. But what if the main producing States have different wage-and-hours laws? And what of differences among rules and laws of the major competing nations? Supposing the major domestic producers offset much of this supposed special and artificial burden by substituting capital for labor and introducing new processes of production? To what extent are United States workers, partly because of their higher pay scales and shorter hours, more productive per hour worked?

*Safety regulations and workmen's compensation.*—Some of the more dangerous occupations, such as mining, incur special costs for safety devices and workmen's compensation in the United States, as they do in varying degree in most of the more "advanced" countries. (Of course, to some extent, safety measures and workmen's compensation are alternative ways of bearing the special costs of hazardous occupations.) The question is whether, if in fact these costs are substantially higher in the United States than in some unenlightened lands, they constitute a valid reason for special help from the Federal Government? In this instance, in addition to all the usual problems of measurement, there is a nice conceptual point. Is not this really an example of a foreign country not fully reflecting its true costs in its money costs? If some foreign country permits its minerals to be extracted in dangerous ways, and has no system of compensating for injuries and fatalities, is it not in the selfish interests of the United States to accept imports from that country if they are cheaper?

*Material inputs that are overpriced.*—The United States Government has artificially raised the prices of many materials in the United States, sometimes through price-support buying and sometimes through tariffs and other restrictions on imports. These high-priced inputs are used by industries that must often sell their outputs in competition with foreign goods. Should there be some Federal relief, perhaps through "drawbacks" or "compensatory" duties, as is now done to some extent?

For example, if a woolen textile manufacturer uses imported wool that has paid duty, should he not receive a rebate if and when he exports, and should he not have enough protection against woolen textile imports to offset this handicap? In principle, these two kinds of relief are probably sound, but in practice they are likely to be most unpopular with different domestic interests. The export rebate could eliminate some of the protection now enjoyed by domestic woolgrowers. And protection for woolen textile imports just adequate to offset duties on processed wool would probably result in a lower woolen textile tariff than at present. In this case, as so often, a sincere attempt to apply a valid principle will not provide the special benefits sought by some of its advocates.

A related example might be a cotton textile manufacturer that is disadvantaged by having to pay prices for cotton that are artificially high because of cotton price-support programs. If there is not to be an underemployment of resources in cotton textile manufacturing in the United States there should be some rebate for the cotton content of exported textiles. Also, there should be some protection against cotton textile imports.

These two cases may be more alike than they superficially seem. If the domestic output of cotton has its price supported at an artificial level, there will usually be a tariff enacted so that domestic output does not create even larger surpluses. Similarly, if a tariff is placed on wool, the price of domestically produced wool will tend to rise to a comparable level.

In both cases growers will tend to produce their last bale of cotton and pound of wool with resources roughly equal in value to the price of this output. However, in the absence of further intervention, such as the Government selling wool and cotton to domestic textile manufacturers at world prices, the employment of resources in textile making may be too low. It is the old story of one Government intervention creating a distortion that invites another intervention.

*Tax burdens occasioned by health and welfare services.*—Tax burdens are higher in the United States than in all save a few countries. Also, the social services provided by the Federal and State Governments are considerable. These two facts are sometimes combined into an argument for import restrictions, on the grounds that these taxes are added to real costs of production, and so in turn make many United States products too highly priced to face competition from less advanced countries.

This argument, to be sustained, requires some demonstration that these services do not raise productivity and that these domestic taxes have a marked effect on prices of home-produced goods.

Most State and local expenditures, and a modest fraction of Federal expenditures also, increase productivity to some undetermined extent. The United States working force is literate—unlike that of some Asiatic countries having very low-tax burdens—and our economy could not operate effectively or for long if a majority of employed people could neither read nor write. The professional people educated by the State universities are needed by industry, business, and government; their education probably represents a very profitable investment for the American economy; however, no other country makes comparable per capita investments. In the more primitive countries, the high death rates permit only a small fraction of the population to reach a productive age, and hence a large fraction of the national output of these countries is devoted to rearing children who never live long enough to be economically useful. In contrast, in the United States, a relatively high percentage of people born enter the labor force and survive to retirement age. Government expenditures for transportation—e. g., harbors and highways—are usually productive investments for the economy.

Even if the tax receipts of all Government units in the country always fell on production, it is not clear that rising tax burdens over the past decades would have caused an increase in output costs per unit. However, such a calculation cannot be made because of the need to subtract the influence of the depreciating dollar and the changing state of technology. There can be no doubt, though, that labor and capital funds are now far more productive than 50 years ago, and this is partly the result of many Government activities, financed from taxes.

Actually, a large part of the cost of Government does not fall on production in any way that obviously deters it and raises costs. A considerable fraction of Government revenues are raised from estate and inheritance taxes and from personal and corporate income taxes. Another large fraction comes from personal consumption, through taxes on services, personal property taxes, and taxes on real estate used for housing. These taxes that Americans pay are not included in the prices of the goods and services that they help to produce, some of which compete with foreign goods and services.

*Money costs that are disproportionately lower than real costs in the United States*

It is also possible for money costs of production to be less in some sense than the real costs of production. Some industries, especially in the past, have occasioned various kinds of costly damage for which they have not had to pay: these instances may arise, for example, from pollution of air and water, damage to the health of workers and people in the community, et cetera. In these cases it may be that production is greater than it would be if all real costs had to be met by the producers.

Goods of this kind, if in competition with foreign goods, are likely to be sold at too low a price, whether sold for domestic use or for export. Hence, if the competitive imports are restricted by duties or quotas, these inhibitions should be eliminated. And if the goods are exported, some consideration should theoretically be given to reducing these exports, perhaps through an export quota, an export duty being unconstitutional.

Little attention is generally given to the need for reductions in the domestic output and export of goods having disproportionately low money costs, relative to their real costs, of production. In part this is probably because the obvious remedies tend to run counter to the immediate interests of the producers concerned. Nevertheless, in any sincere and impartial investigation of disparate real and money costs within the economy, these goods constitute a category that should not be ignored by Government.

### UNDERVALUATION OF THE DOLLAR RELATIVE TO OTHER CURRENCIES

Many foreign governments attempt to keep their national currencies overvalued, relative to the United States dollar; and, to the degree that they are successful, the dollar becomes undervalued, on official exchanges, compared with other moneys. The motives of these foreign governments are mixed, one element sometimes being national prestige, another being a desire to reduce the quantity of goods that their countries must export to the United States to obtain a given quantity of United States goods. Whatever the motive, the effect is to elevate equivalent dollar prices of United States imports and exports as seen from the United States economy.

As regards potential exports, the effect of this official foreign undervaluation of the dollar, assuming foreign buyers can acquire the necessary dollars, is to encourage United States exports unduly. The United States objection to these excessive exports is that they do not earn enough foreign exchange for the United States economy. One possible remedy, were it constitutional, would be to impose some export tax. (Of course, because the dollar is undervalued abroad, it is in short supply relative to the demand for it, and so United States exports are not as great, given prices and official exchange rates, as foreign buyers would like.)

Because imports tend to be overpriced, when expressed in dollars, they tend to be imported in too small a quantity; and the United States-produced goods, with which they compete, also tend to be overpriced and overproduced. If these imports are currently being inhibited by tariffs or quotas, one obvious solution is to lessen or eliminate these restrictions, depending on the percentage undervaluation of the dollar abroad. One difficulty, though, is that the foreign misvaluation of the dollar varies from currency to currency, and so some average adjustment would have to be made.

Increased imports will tend to give foreigners more dollars exchange. Some of this will be used to bolster central bank reserves abroad. Most of it will be spent for United States goods and services, or debt repayment, although not necessarily by the persons or countries initially earning the dollars.

Revaluation of the dollar by the American Government is, of course, one alternative that should be explored when it seems to be generally undervalued or overvalued by foreign governments. However, this course of action also involves many practical difficulties that will not be explored here. The simplest and healthiest remedy in the case of foreign undervaluation of the dollar may be to encourage imports into the United States in the hope that this will in time strengthen foreign currencies, increase their convertibility into dollars, and remove at least some of this disparity between real and dollar costs of goods within the American economy.

### EXPLOITATION OF UNITED STATES MONOPOLY AND MONOPSONY POWER

In viewing United States trade policy from this country's selfish interests alone, mention at least should be made of the conceptual possibility of exploiting United States monopoly and monopsony power where it exists. However there are practical difficulties that may prevent this being done. And there are broader considerations of statesmanship that should perhaps preclude the adoption of such measures.

*Monopoly cases*

There are a few commodities that enter world trade of which the United States economy is a sufficiently important supplier that a reduction in the quantities of its exports would raise the world price for the goods in question. Conceptually, the last or marginal unit of such an export earns fewer extra receipts for the United States economy than the price at which it is sold: in more technical language, the marginal revenues of the United States economy are less than average revenues.[1] If there are many suppliers of the export in the United States, and they do not act in concert, this discrepancy between marginal and average receipts will be ignored, and it is very probable that the quantity exported will be such that the last or marginal unit to be exported will have cost more resources to produce than the foreign exchange that it earns. In short, there has been an overexport, and attention should be paid to the possibility of reducing this export quantity by some means. One outcome would be a higher price to the foreign buyer, and so a policy of this kind should

[1] Marginal revenue of an export is defined as the addition to total gross receipts earned by the home economy as a result of selling exports at a rate of one more unit, all units perhaps being sold as a result at a slightly lower price; average revenue refers to total receipts from exports divided by the number of units exported.

only be implemented cautiously; quite unexpected and alternative foreign sources of supply may become established as a consequence. History is replete with instances of supposed monopoly positions that were exploited only to disappear.

*Monopsony cases*

The United States economy, as distinct from the many firms that may act in competition with one another, has monopoly power as a buyer in the case of some commodities. This situation is often called one of "monopsony."

This monopsony power only exists to the extent that the prices received by foreign supplies tend to rise or fall as the United States buys respectively more or less. Such a situation may exist in the case of some of the commodities that we import from Central America and Canada.[2]

The logic of the problem is illustrated in figure 1, which shows the possible exploitation of United States monopsony power, through imposition of a tariff, in the case of a single commodity import. The essential requirement is that the supply schedule of the import to the United States is such that a smaller quantity of imports reduces the price that must be paid the sellers. If this is so, the marginal cost of imports will always be greater than the price paid.[3]

The art is so to reduce the quantity imported that the marginal cost of imports comes to correspond with the demand price that will be paid by United States buyers. There are reasons for supposing that the demand price will roughly reflect real use value, and that the marginal cost does indicate the extra money cost of importing an extra unit into the United States economy; and so, apart from exceptional circumstances, there is a presumption that a correspondence of these two values is desirable for the economy. One obvious way to reduce imports from $Q_1$—which would be the expected rate in the absence of intervention—to $Q_2$ is to impose a tariff per unit of import represented by $P_bP_s$. This has the merit that the United States economy derives customs duties, partially paid by foreign supplies, for the price to sellers is depressed from P to $P_s$. This is the conceptual argument for an import tariff on a goods when the quantity of United States imports definitely influences the foreign price.

[2] It should be remembered too that these "foreign" suppliers are often the subsidiaries of United States corporations, and the profits of the former are of some concern to United States policymakers.

[3] For example, if the United States imports $Q_2$ quantity, the price may be $10, but the marginal cost may be $20; this is because the very slightly lower price that would prevail if the United States imported at a slightly lower physical rate will apply to the entire quantity of imports, all of which will now cost a slightly lower price too, so that the total payment for the import may be $20 less.

P-1154
8-15-57
-20-

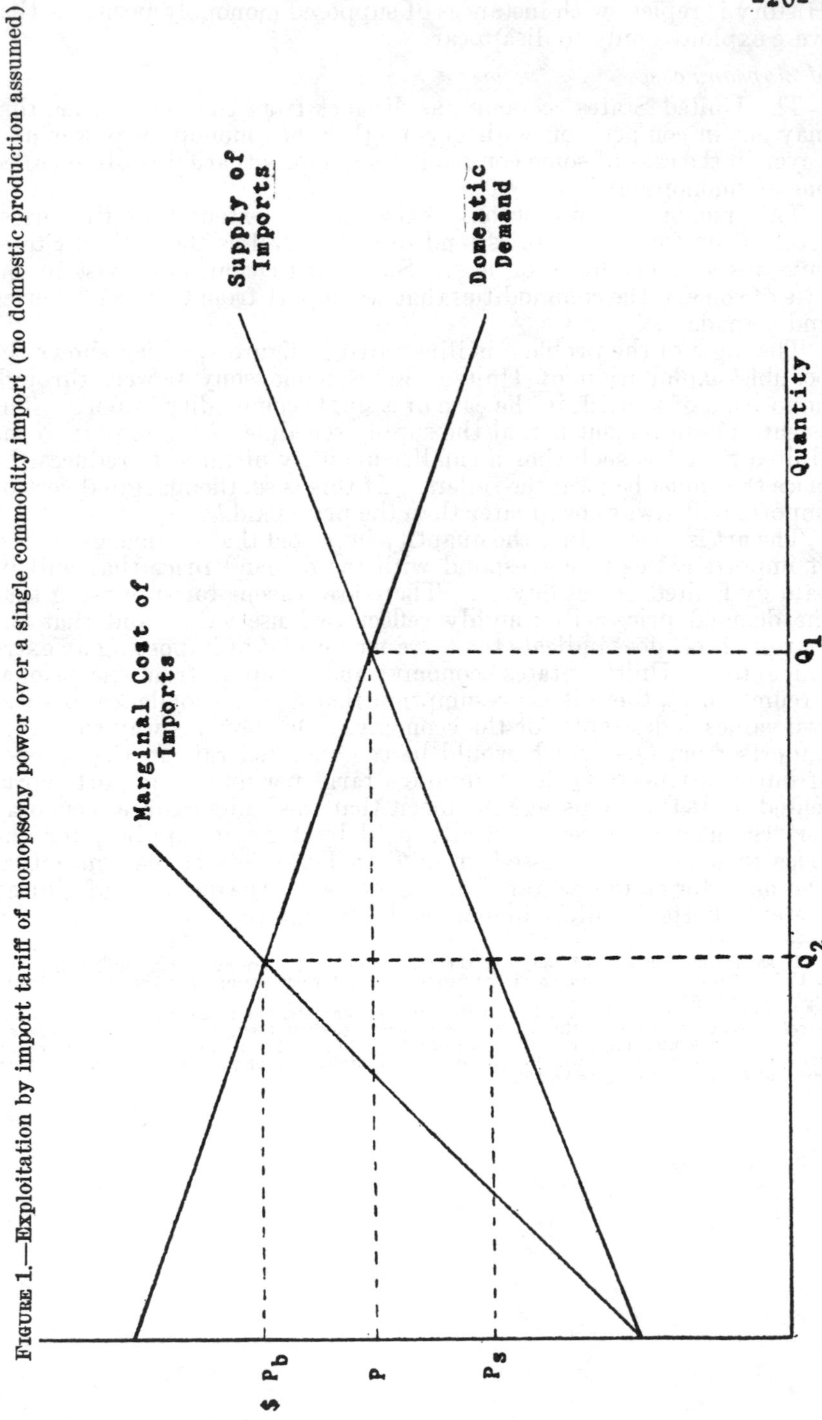


FIGURE 1.—Exploitation by import tariff of monopsony power over a single commodity import (no domestic production assumed)

*Practical difficulties and objections*

There are many reasons for supposing that the United States cannot apply these principles as a national trade policy and should not exploit those few instances in which it has marked monopoly and monopsony power.

(1) The character of foreign supply schedules and domestic demand schedules of a particular import commodity are not precisely known. The slope and locations of the schedules shown in figure 1 will always be guesswork. It would be a matter of luck if the duty applied in these instances was the appropriate one. Moreover, supplies and demands can alter more rapidly than Congress can alter tariffs.

(2) A systematic exploitation of monopoly and monopsony power, even if possible, might instigate retaliation by foreign governments. The final position of the United States might then be worse rather than better. (But, in a few cases, the exploitation duty might be less than the currently imposed one.)

(3) It ill behooves the United States, as one of the leading importers and exporters in the world, to set a bad example by adopting beggar-thy-neighbor policies; this is especially true in that the United States has a stronger balance of payments position and larger exchange reserves than any other nation.

MONOPOLY, DISCRIMINATION, AND DUMPING

Disparities between real and money costs sometimes occur, and are frequently alleged in connection with supposed instances of monopoly, price discrimination, and dumping.

*Domestic monopoly protected from imports*

There is an old adage to the effect that tariffs are the mother of monopoly. For certain products, the United States market may be sufficiently insulated by transportation costs and import restrictions to enable a domestic producer to exploit the relation between the reduced quantities of his output sold at home and the higher prices that he can charge. This situation, if and when it occurs, is likely to be marked by patent control and the absence of any close substitute, and the company is likely to stress price manipulation rather than sales promotion.[4] Given these circumstances, there is a presumption that the producer of this good is restricting output, with the result that the worth of the resources used to make the last unit of output are worth far less than the use value of the same unit. Foreign-trade policy as such can only deal with this situation to the extent that the producer's monopoly position depends upon import restrictions, the indicated remedy being to remove such restrictions. It would be a wise precaution, from time to time, to revise the protection enjoyed, if any, by the makers of products for which there are either (1) no close substitutes, or (2) are produced by a very few firms which do not compete actively regarding price or sales promotion.

[4] Excluded from this case are branded products with negatively inclined demand schedules which are in active sales competition with close substitutes and which have high cross elasticities of demand.

*Discrimination by United States exporters*

Many large United States firms produce for the home market and for export. In both markets it tends to be true that more can be sold at a lower price and vice versa. Theoretically, if such a firm knows how to maximize its profits, it will try to adjust its selling prices in the domestic and foreign markets such that the last (or marginal) unit sold in each market yields the same addition to receipts (and, of course, is equal to the extra costs incurred to produce it). Usually the effect on sales of a price cut will not be the same in the home and foreign markets. Hence some United States producers will wish to sell at different net prices in these markets.

This allocation between the home and foreign market is not in the best interests of the United States under the usually assumed conditions. The main objection is that domestic sales are too low, and that from the national viewpoint the producer is selling too much abroad. The social goal is to have the producer adjust sales in the foreign and domestic market so that (1) the price in the home market equals the extra receipts earned by the last unit sold abroad, and (2) all these in turn are equal to the costs of producing the marginal unit destined for both markets. The first rule assumes that the price paid by domestic buyers for a unit roughly reflects its worth and that the addition to export proceeds of selling one more unit of export will be used to buy imports worth about their cost.

Even with adequate knowledge of demand and cost schedules, it would be difficult to effect this special outcome, and to make timely revisions to meet altered circumstances. Export sales can be curtailed by means of a quota, but this serves no useful purpose unless domestic sales are increased, and this would probably require the imposition of a lower domestic price ceiling. All in all, while discrimination by United States producing firms that also export probably occasions some malallocations, it may be impractical for the Federal Government to attempt a remedy. This class of problem is likely to remain little more than a theoretical curiosity.

*Dumping by foreigners in United States*

Protectionist interests in the United States would like to define dumping in either of two ways that are not acceptable if dumping is to be prevented by law. One of these definitions of dumping is selling foreign produce in the United States market at prices below home costs of production; the difficulty here is not that United States costs vary among plants and firms but an important objection of principle, namely, that the United States economy should accept imports if they can be obtained more cheaply from abroad. The second unacceptable definition of dumping is selling foreign produce in the United States market at a price below the foreign cost of production; not only are these foreign production costs peculiarly unascertainable to United States officials, but the application of this rule penalizes overestimates of sales and prevents the moving into use of unplanned and unwanted surpluses. Analytically, it is more useful to view dumping as a special form of discrimination. Accordingly, dumping in the United States is defined here as sales of foreign produce in the United States market at net prices, after deducting transportation costs and import duties, etc., lower than the net prices received for equivalent goods sold under similar conditions during the same time period in the producer's home market. We shall distinguish between predatory, preclusive, and persistent dumping.

*Predatory (including sporadic) dumping.*—Occasionally a strong foreign firm or cartel might seek to destroy an existing United States industry by temporarily selling in the United States market at very low prices in an effort to secure an unchallenged monopoly position. This is the traditional atrocity case that is often mentioned but so seldom documented. Obviously it is desirable to prevent predatory dumping of this sort.

Sporadic dumping is somewhat akin to predatory dumping except that the sinister motive is largely lacking. The producers in one nation—especially in the case of agricultural crops and other perishables—may be unable to predict supplies and demands except very roughly: when there is an excess of supply, rather than spoil the home market, they may try to sell the entire surplus in another national market. All the uncertainties of the home market are hence focused on the neighboring market, which experiences unnaturally violent price fluctuations. These price uncertainties contribute to risk and real costs; further, if factors of production in the neighboring (dumped) market are specialized and rather immobile, dumping will lead to unemployed resources and waste in the country of import from time to time.

Hence, the Executive should probably be granted powers in such cases to assess special dumping duties, set temporary import quotas, or establish interim minimum prices. However, there will always be domestic pressures upon the customs to overuse these powers, and their administration is rendered difficult by the necessity of inferring the foreign sellers' motives and capabilities.

*Preclusive dumping.*—It may be that a foreign firm is steadily dumping—in the sense defined here—with the object of precluding the establishment of a domestic industry in the United States. In this case, no existing United States industry is threatened. Dumping of this kind may not be contrary to the general economic interests of the United States. The low price benefits domestic consumers, or using industries, as the case may be. If it seems that the low price will endure there is no apparent economic gain in restricting such imports and raising prices in the American market to a level that will bring forth domestic production. The practical difficulty again is one of assessing the intent of the foreign dumper, who is compelled to maintain his low price for so long as he wishes to prevent the establishment of a competitive United States industry.

*Persistent dumping.*—This is a special and reverse example of the case of discrimination by a United States exporter already examined, except that in the present instance foreign goods are being exported to the United States at a net price lower than that received from sales in the country of origin. Discrimination (or dumping) under these circumstances is likely to be persistent and there is no intent to destroy or prevent production in the United States. (Actually, as we have seen, this kind of discrimination is likely to run counter to the interests of the exporting country.) There are no clear economic reasons for the United States to deter this sort of dumping—however much it may discomfort United States producers—because in effect this country is benefiting from an apparently dependable source of supply that at the best is more economical and at the worst will eliminate inefficient United States producers. The pruning function of competition is just as useful when exercised internationally.

If there is any valid reason for restricting dumped imports, it arises from probable price uncertainties, and not because of any special relation between real and money prices and costs in the foreign exporting country. If another economy will supply goods more cheaply than the United States can produce them, not just temporarily but for a long time into the future, it is wisest to accept them as a general rule. Dumping is injurious when it leads to aggravated price fluctuations combined with price discrimination between the exporting and importing markets. The existence of both these circumstances should be suspected before antidumping measures are applied. Moreover, it should be noted, this definition of injurious dumping makes no references to production costs, whether at home or abroad, for they are irrelevant.

PROTECTION IN THE NAME OF SECURITY

During the past decade many familiar special interests have based their pleas for import protection in a novel way, stressing the supposed needs of national security, and asserting that the military power of the United States in future wars depends upon greater self-sufficiency in such things as ships, wool, watchmaking, crude-oil production, lumber, and cotton, but not as yet tobacco. Expressed in more scientific terms, it is argued that the domestic peacetime prices of these goods do not fully reflect their real value to the country in wartime, when overseas supplies may for some reason be unavailable, so that there is an economic justification for making more of them in the United States, even though their peacetime production costs exceed their selling prices in the absence of protection. This sort of argument cannot be evaluated without an excursion into the possible nature of future wars, and although such essays are inevitably controversial, the time is overdue when these military possibilities should be translated into foreign-trade policy.

United States policy, whether concerned with national defense or foreign trade, cannot prepare simultaneously for every possible war. Responsible authorities must seek to identify the most probable wars in which the United States might be engaged during the coming decade.

Only three possible kinds of war will be considered here, although there are certainly others: These are (1) an all-out United States-Soviet Union war; (2) a Korea-type war; and (3) a European satellite war. The question is whether any of them are likely to involve a long period of economic mobilization and military deployment, as characterized United States participation in World Wars I and II, and whether the United States will have to practice a greater degree of economic self-sufficiency during their prosecution than in peacetime.

*All-out United States-Soviet Union war*

This kind of war would truly constitute world war III. It would include the Soviet Union and the United States as belligerents from the first hour of hostilities and would be marked by atomic bombing of each other's interior zones, these attacks shifting from strikes against enemy bomber bases to enemy populations. Both the United States and the Soviet Union might lose their hundred largest cities, and radioactive fallout would incapacitate many additional millions residing downwind from their targets. The air, sea, and land war would be fought with forces in being, and mostly from initial positions. Within a few weeks or months the will of the survivors to remain alive may well exceed their desires for victory. Cessation of hostilities will then be followed by a prolonged period of recuperation, during which the United States is partly succored by Canada, Australia, South America, and even perhaps Western Europe.

There is a strong possibility that the active phases of such a war will be concluded long before interdiction of the sealanes by Soviet submarines could prove effective. Soviet air strikes against United States metropolitan areas and cities will prevent any effective economic mobilization. Substantial losses of United States petroleum refinery capacity will render the country largely dependent on imports of petroleum products despite the availability of crude petroleum from domestic wells. The existence or nonexistence of an American merchant marine during active hostilities will be of almost no consequence, partly because allied and neutral shipping will be available, partly because major port facilities will have been destroyed. The presence of domestic stockpiles of many raw materials will be of little significance if the United States lacks adequate processing facilities and internal transportation means after air attacks. (Even the peacetime preservation from foreign competition of a few hundred domestic watchmakers may not serve to stem the tide of war.)

Any contemplation of the economic requirements of an all-out war, such as has been briefly outlined, reveals that most protectionist pretensions in the name of national defense are ridiculous. And yet, of all the wars that can be conceived, it is a war involving a nuclear exchange between the United States and the Soviet Union. That appears to be the primary preoccupation of the Department of Defense. Perhaps, if the foreign-trade policy of the United States is truly to be shaped according to national defense requirements, an attempt should be made to ascertain what these needs really are, not from industry spokesmen, but from military planners.

*Korea-type wars*

There are several peripheral areas of the world into which China or a Soviet satellite, aided by the Soviet Union itself, might push. In addition to Korea, other examples are Thailand, Iran, and Finland. It is possible that the United States would then become a belligerent in a limited war that excluded strategic bombing, with or without atomic weapons. For the same motives the Soviet Union would not initiate an unlimited submarine campaign. The military emphasis would be on ground actions and tactical air war.

The support of a limited war of this kind would not place a serious drain on the economy of the United States or its allies. There would be no need for full-scale economic mobilization in these countries. The sea lanes would be open and, except insofar as support of the theater of hostilities absorbed allied and neutral ship and airlift capacity, the resources of the free world would be available and accessible. Raw material stockpiles in the United States at most would have a very limited usefulness. Not having to be self-sufficient, the United States would be no better off and might well be rather worse off, from having protected various kinds of uneconomic domestic production in peacetime.

The best economic preparation for these kinds of wars may be to increase the economic power and political cooperation of the United States and its allies through permitting freer geographic specialization of production. Economic efficiency has a military value, and especially in wartime when capacities are strained and resource limitations are more obvious. The main counter consideration would be the availability of shipping—not just American shipping—and in this connection the Korean war revealed no serious shortage despite the effect on charter rates for marginal shipping.

*A European satellite war*

It is barely conceivable that an attack on a NATO power in Europe, by a Soviet satellite, might remain a limited conflict that excluded atomic strategic bombing of each other by the United States and the Soviet Union. For example, East Germany and Poland might invade Norway. A prime factor in determining the spread of the war would be the geographic extent of Soviet submarine operations. So long as the area of hostilities continued to be confined to the territory of the attacking satellite and the attacked NATO member, the military and economic requirements would not be too unlike those of a Korea-type war, already described briefly.

Most protectionist arguments in the name of national security assume that the United States will fight a major war in which it will have economically to be rather more self-sufficient for a considerable period of time. It is difficult, though, to conceive of a major all-out war that will be prolonged. It is difficult to conceive of a minor war in which the United States will not have access to the economies of all nations outside the Soviet bloc, whether these countries are cobelligerents, allies, or neutrals. These countries will be ready to sell to the United States and the likelihood of inadequate shipping facilities appears rather remote. The main threat to transoceanic communications comes from Soviet submarines, and an all-out submarine war off our coasts and directed against the United States would presumably be, or become, part of an all-out strategic air war of short duration. It seems unlikely that essential military and economic demands on allied and neutral shipping will exceed availabilities in the absence of submarine sinkings. However, if this is considered a serious danger, there are more effective ways for the United States to increase its wartime control of shipping than those provided by the Merchant Marine Act of 1936, as amended. Properly evaluated, the needs of national security are not more self-sufficiency and higher prices and income for certain domestic producers; the need is rather for freer trade, especially with allies and Latin America.

### THE OPPORTUNITY OF THE UNITED STATES

Today the United States, of all nations, has an especially favorable opportunity to lower or eliminate many of its customs duties, quotas, and other import restrictions that prevent a full development of its own economy and wartime potential.

*Strong balance-of-payments position combined with large foreign reserves*

The United States has a strong balance-of-payments position and the dollar is probably the most sought-after currency in the world today.

To the extent that United States imports goods and services of greater value, foreign earnings of dollar exchange are increased. Additional foreign receipts of dollars must either be held or spent, and in many countries private dollar earnings must be sold to the central authorities: for so long as these dollars are held, rather than spent, the United States is temporarily enjoying free imports for which no exports need be exchanged. To a limited extent, the dollars may be used by foreign interests to repay dollar debts to the United States, and this is generally to our advantage, especially if these debts have been in jeopardy because our debtors lacked foreign exchange. Primarily, though, these dollars will be spent, directly or indirectly, for United States goods and services, thereby stimulating our export industries.

The undervaluation of the dollar and the very large holdings of gold in the United States remove the two fears associated with extra imports in most countries, namely depreciation of a weak currency and loss of scarce foreign-exchange reserves. Extra dollar earnings of foreigners must go into central bank reserves, be used for repayment of United States debts, be employed to buy United States exports, or be sold on foreign-exchange markets. Insofar as this last leads to a real appreciation of foreign currencies—as distinct from their formal overvaluation—this may promote fuller convertibility of more foreign currencies and hence contribute to multilateral trade. In the unlikely event that the foreign-exchange value of the dollar has to be supported by United States authorities, gold can be sold to foreign central banks, thereby strengthening their currencies and eventually liberalizing exchange controls. Both routes lead to healthier and expanded trade among our allies and the other nations of the free world.

*Full employment of a mobile labor force*

The labor force of the United States is now about as fully employed as one could expect or want. This is not to say, of course, that everybody who could work is employed in the job that he favors. Many old people, wives, and youngsters could work who should not work if the economy is to provide reasonable opportunities for retirement, homemaking, and education; this view is apparently widely shared, for statistics indicate that few acknowledged members of the labor force are unemployed. Much of the unemployment that is recorded is transitional or seasonal: this unemployment is usually temporary for the workers concerned, and most of it is inevitable in any dynamic economy. There is almost no chronic unemployment now—in 1957—that can be attributed to foreign trade policy.

However this is not to say that a sudden elimination of nearly all import duties and quotas would not eliminate many current jobs and reduce the capital values of many plants and natural resources. The sudden cessation of what is, in effect, a complicated set of subsidies, paid not by American taxpayers but by United States users of protected goods, is bound to cause losses. On the other hand, employment and capital values in the export industries will increase. So one important question is to what extent there will be only a small net loss, or even a net gain, in any given State, community or family, because of a boom in the exporting trades.

The answer to this question requires a detailed examination of many locality-industry combinations, and so only some general observations can be made here.

*Transfers among industries without changing occupations.*—Many different industries provide jobs requiring the same human skills and functions. Workers are increasingly becoming machine tenders. Plant construction has many common elements that are independent of the industry that is to use the facility. A great deal of office work is common to almost all business. A substantial fraction of workers can change industries without having to learn new skills.

*Direct transfers from import-threatened to export-expanding industries not necessary.*—Necessary adjustments can take place in the United States economy without a direct transfer of labor from import-threatened to export-expanding industries. Thus a lumber-mill worker in Washington State does not have to find work in an exporting industry like airplane construction. Instead, he may become a construction worker, taking the job of a man who instead goes to work in an airplane plant. These "triangular" industry adjustments are more the rule than the exception.

*Changing industry of employment without changing residence.*—The American worker, thanks to "car pools" and commuter facilities, has an increasing number of potential jobs requiring his skills within practical daily transportation of his home. This is markedly true within metropolitan areas. A change of job today is less likely to require a change of residence than 50 years ago when most industrial workers had to live within walking distance or streetcar ride of their job.

*Geographic mobility of United States labor.*—The rapid growth of certain areas of Texas and the Pacific coast during the past two decades testifies to the readiness of many single workers and families to move to new regions of employment. In almost all instances private housing construction has kept pace with this shifting pattern of population. There are no reasons to suppose that the expanding export industries, even when located in sparsely populated areas, would have to wait long for labor to arrive.

*Decentralization of United States industry.*—Several United States industries, and some of the larger United States corporations, have evidenced a marked willingness, since the depression, to decentralize and construct new plants in areas of lower labor cost. One very familiar example is the shift of the textile industry to the South from New England. While some industries are inextricably tied to natural resources, there are reasons for supposing that pockets of unemployment that continued for any length of time would, in part, be eliminated by the plant decentralization of expanding industries.

*Only partial transfers needed from import-threatened industries.*—An elimination of import restrictions might eliminate some domestic industries. But in a vast majority of cases the result will be reduced output, and a percentage redistribution of industry receipts away from profits or returns to natural resources and toward salaries and wages. Thus the free importation of Australian wool would primarily affect the owners of sheep grazing land, which would lose much of its capital value, but sheep ranch labor and wool brokers would find other work. Of all the factors of production, labor probably has the least to fear from increased imports, being less specialized and more mobile.

*Gradual elimination of import restrictions.*—No responsible person has ever proposed a sudden elimination of all import restrictions. The United States might, as various European countries are scheduled to do, reduce some fraction of its duties each year for a stated number of years. Duties that are already less than 10 percent might be eliminated by a few annual decreases. In the case of quotas, some percentage increase might be scheduled for each successive year. There are many reasons for supposing that these steps toward trade freedom could be taken in stride by the American economy. After all, some protected industries employ only a few hundred people, whereas the Department of Defense has been known to cancel projects employing over 10,000 people in a single locality with little public protest. Perhaps the best course is to experiment with a gradual relaxation of import restrictions, with Congress establishing a schedule of annual reductions that can be collectively continued or deferred by a single vote each year.

### CONCLUDING COMMENT

It is axiomatic that the foreign trade policy of the United States cannot be considered apart from its military alliances and the general objectives of its foreign policy. Most of the important trading nations of the free world are actual allies of the United States, which consequently has a concern in their economic progress, partly because this increases their ability to contribute to the common-defense establishment. Moreover, these countries, to a greater or lesser extent, are characterized by private investment, and the United States has a vested interest in demonstrating, to the Soviet bloc and various Asiatic countries, the economic benefits to these countries of free enterprise. Finally, in order to be strong and prosperous itself, the United States has a stake in realizing the economic efficiencies that can be gained through a national division of labor.

On the other hand, it is well known that in economic affairs, producer interests—except perhaps when in conflict with organized labor—tend to determine national policy. Producer interests have always outshouted consumer interests on questions of foreign-trade policy; the former are organized and have a large and obvious interest in specific Government decisions, whereas the latter have only a general interest which is too diffuse to be brought to bear effectively on any one issue. Under the circumstances, it is not surprising if Congressmen often forget the general interest and give way to protectionist pleas.

This is particularly true when many arguments for protection come wrapped in the flag. It takes moral courage to resist a case that is presented in the name of national security. And yet a careful consideration of most of the cases in which national security is invoked reveal that the kind of war that is assumed by the pleader is not the sort of war for which the Military Establishment is preparing. Many industry spokesmen seem to assume a long period of economic mobilization, followed by deployment across the oceans, during which time we will need many raw materials that must be brought across submarine-infested areas. Against this the national strategy, if deterrence fails, appears to assume a short all-out war, fought with forces in being and placing heavy stress on atomic bombing. Either the Joint Chiefs of Staff or the lobbyists for protection are correct, but they cannot both be right, and the Congress has a responsibility to reconcile foreign trade policy and military preparedness.

Our military security to some extent depends on allies to stage our bombers, give early warning of air attacks, and provide ground troops under certain contingencies. It is hard to maintain effective allies at the same time as one is conducting a cold trade war with some of them. And yet postwar history contains instances in which penetration of the American market by foreign producers has led to effective agitation for protection by affected United States producers. In the case of branded goods, requiring national sales promotion, foreign firms will not attempt to expand their sales to the United States if there are good reasons for supposing success will bring extra duties or quotas against their products. Foreign exporters are especially anxious for some guaranty that free international competition will be permitted in the United States when it is effective.

As for the clash of special domestic interests, the issues of foreign-trade policy range producers who must compete with foreign goods against three other citizen groups. These last are (1) producers of export goods whose sales are limited by the inability of foreign countries to export to the United States and so earn dollars; (2) industrial users of imports, many of whom have obtained free entry for the goods they need; and (3) consumers, unorganized, as usual, to whom freer imports offer some hope of better quality goods, more choice of styles, and lower retail prices. Unfortunately, the play of political forces on Washington does not fully reflect the importance and nature of all these domestic interests, so that the Nation's need for congressional discernment and economic statesmanship is great, indeed.

Finally, and in summary, most free-trade arguments are incontrovertible in the abstract, and, so, opponents of freer trade have often relied on at least three arguments. One of these is that institutional distortions have rendered money prices a poor reflection of money costs. But the preceding review suggests that there are not enough circumstances of this kind to justify the numerous import restrictions that special pleaders have induced the Congress to enact, especially when it is realized that the existence of such disparities in foreign countries does not subtract from the selfish interest of the United States in freer imports and trade. A second argument is that national defense, in contemplation of a war without allies and without access to other national markets, requires a higher degree of United States self-sufficiency in many lines of production; a sketchy examination of possible wars indicates that the opposite may be closer to the truth. A third special argument is that, given the desirability of freer trade in the long run, such a reform would so dislocate the economy as to be impracticable at this time, but the current and prospective state of the United States balance of payments and employment of labor are such that few nations during recent history have been better situated to make the adjustments required of freer trade.

# TARIFF AND THE UNITED STATES FOREIGN TRADE POLICY

Lewis E. Lloyd, economist, the Dow Chemical Co.

This paper is prepared in response to an invitation to submit a memorandum for the subcommittee's study on foreign trade. The subcommittee is doing an important service in preparing the study, which will be available for Congress when it considers foreign-trade legislation at the next session. In order to have sound legislation, Congress must have all the pertinent facts and make a careful and objective analysis. The subcommittee study can be of maximum value in both supplying the facts and thoughtfully analyzing the problem.

In all probability, interested trade associations and Government bureaus will furnish adequate statistics for the factual background of United States foreign commerce. Moreover, they will relate this to the importance and influence on the particular industries. I plan to direct my attention primarily to the basic economics involved and to an analysis of some of the arguments concerning the effect of tariffs which seldom are mentioned in committee hearings.

## BASIC TERMINOLOGY

A large part of the misunderstanding which has developed in this country on the tariff problem arises from a loose use of terminology. Semantic traps must be avoided in analyzing the information if Congress is to arrive at a sound national trade policy. To avoid semantic traps, it is essential to define terms carefully and use words precisely. Many of the arguments for free trade (or freer trade) can be made to seem plausible by the simple expedient of using the words "embargo," "protection," and "tariff" more or less interchangeably. These words, however, are not synonymous. An embargo, or a quota, is a quantitative restriction on imports. Protection, as used in foreign-trade discussions, means to shield from competition.

A tariff, on the other hand, is merely a tax on imports. It may or may not restrict trade; it may or may not shield domestic producers from foreign competition, depending on the level of the tariff and on many other factors. Even the expression "freer trade" or "liberalized trade" leads to many interpretations. To those who look forward to ultimate free trade, these terms are synonymous with tariff reduction. To those who believe in a reasonable equalizing tariff under present world conditions, the expression "freeing of trade" means reducing quantitative and monetary restrictions so there is more freedom to trade. Careful analysis will show that many of the arguments put forth on foreign-trade questions evaporate when attention is given to accurate use of words and careful terminology.

### WORLD TRADING CONDITIONS TODAY

The proper frame of reference is another essential factor in sound analysis of any problem. It is important to examine the foreign-trade problem in the light of the real world as it exists today. Too often the exponents of free trade examine the problem in the light of an idealized world situation rather than in the light of real conditions.

As we examine the real world in which we live, we find it divided into sovereign nations, each intent on developing its own self-interests. Examination of the record shows that, whereas most nations in the free world have been willing to join with us in GATT and negotiate tariff reductions, they have not been willing to hand over to an international agency the control of imports into their economy. If they found the reduced tariff levels inadequate to control imports which they felt were not in their best interests, they have raised quantitative barriers or exchange restrictions which accomplish their objectives even more effectively than tariffs could. Consequently, today, particularly with respect to our freedom to export, quantitative barriers and currency restrictions are the prime deterrent to freedom to trade and tariffs are only a minor or secondary factor. Even in our own case, export subsidies and quotas on agricultural products are a major digression from acceptance of a world market place on these products.

Walter Lippmann[1] brought the foreign trade problem clearly into focus when he reminded his readers that:

> The main trouble today is not the level of the tariff rates. In the United States they are by and large not exorbitantly high any longer * * *. The real problem is economic warfare. All the governments have armed themselves with legal powers which they use to interfere with the international markets for goods. They use them offensively and they use them defensively to cut down, to cut off, to divert, to penalize, to subsidize buying and selling so that the pattern of transactions is different from what it would be under the free operation of supply and demand * * *. There is no inherent reason why the level of tariff rates should be determined by reciprocal bargains.

It is equally essential to recognize the fact that the world situation is in constant flux and that our policies need to be designed to permit freedom to meet changing situations—for example, the establishment of the European common market. Not only has a six-member European common market been established, but discussions are underway for a whole series of common markets. One would result in a free-trade area in Europe, adding to the European common market, the United Kingdom and the other countries in the OEEC. Discussions have been initiated on formation of a South American common market, on formation of a Central American common market, and on a Near East common market. The unspoken objective in each of these cases is to advance the interests of producers in the area involved in their efforts to compete with exporters from other areas. In the last analysis,

[1] New York Herald Tribune, January 13, 1954; H. R. 1 hearings, pt. II, p. 1712.

this means that each of these common areas which have been or may be established are a direct threat to the competitive position of United States exporters. The establishment of the European common market and the addition of any other such regional groupings as may develop in the future will greatly alter historic trade relations between nations involved and other nations. All of this may require an extensive reevaluation of some of our trade legislation.

NO REAL DOLLAR SHORTAGE EXIST

Another factor in the world situation which needs to be given increased attention is the matter of dollar availability. The "freer traders" have, for some years, been proposing tariff reductions to make the United States market more easily accessible to foreign exporters, to assist them in obtaining dollars. However much there may have been a dollar shortage in the free world at the end of the war, the condition has now greatly changed. In fact, foreign dollar holdings have increased steadily for more than 10 years and are at the point where foreign nationals now have claims against almost two-thirds of our total gold reserve. The problem is not that there is a shortage of dollars abroad, but rather that many countries choose to use the dollars they have for uses other than purchases of United States merchandise. Foreign nations hoard dollars to stabilize their own currency or for use as exchange with other countries. Figure No. 1 shows the steady growth of foreign claims against the gold of our money credit base. If at any time, for whatever reason, foreign nationals began to prefer gold to our dollars, we could end up with a financial crisis the likes of which this country has not seen in half a century. In discussing this subject, E. C. Harwood, head of the American Institute for Economic Research, concludes that—

* * * the fact that so much was transferred in the form of short-term claims on United States gold presumably reflects relatively higher prices in the United States and a resulting preference of foreigners for gold or claims on gold rather than for United States goods.

Thus, we see that no longer is the shortage of dollars outside the United States a deterrent to more United States exports.

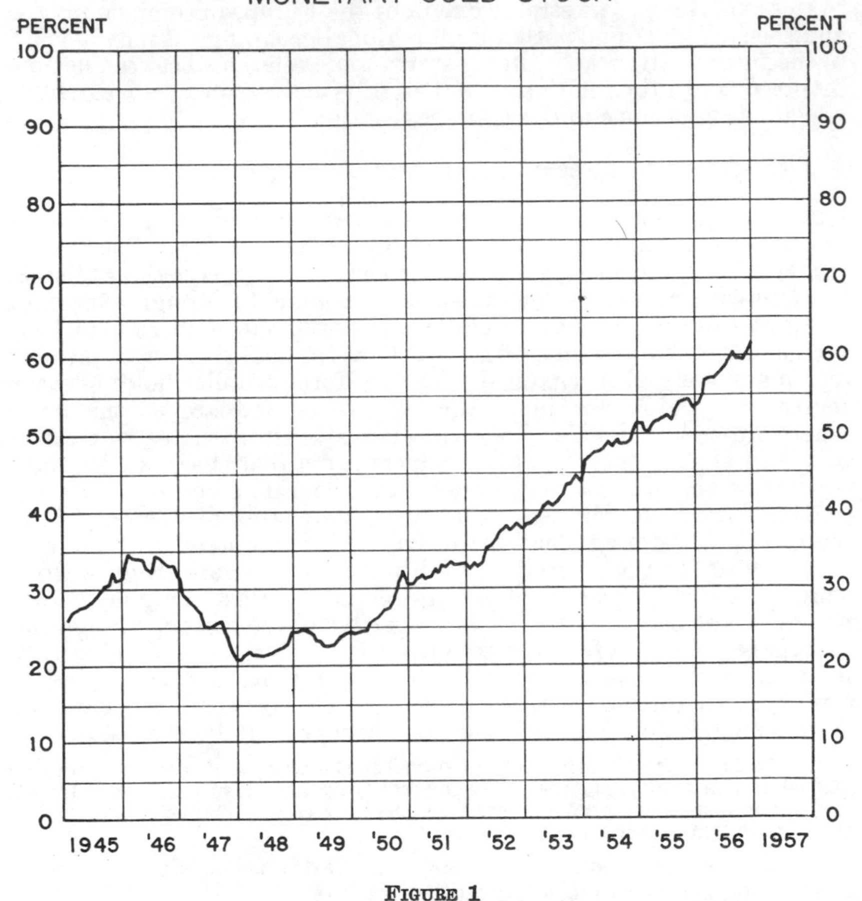


FIGURE 1

JAPAN'S LOGICAL TRADING SPHERE

Another aspect of the international situation which we must face if we are to develop a sound foreign trade policy has to do with natural trading areas. There is, for example, much talk by the free-traders about arranging in Europe and in the United States adequate markets for Japanese exports. It is scarcely economically sound to expect that Japan will long continue to conduct most of its trade with other highly industrialized nations halfway around the world, when nearby is underdeveloped China and southeast Asia which can supply an abundance of raw material and has hundreds of millions of consumers who need cloth, utensils, and other manufactured goods. In the long run, the economic principles of self-interest require that trade primarily develop between complementary nations and regions of the world rather than between competitive areas. Japan has recently completed a trade agreement with Australia and is actively pursuing closer trade relations with other Asiatic nations. Any sound United States foreign policy must accept the fact that, ultimately, Japanese trade will be oriented toward the East even though some of these nations are Communist and we would not like to see the Japanese trading with Communist countries.

### BASIC ECONOMIC FACTORS

With due regard for the kind of world in which our foreign trade must be conducted, let us turn our attention to some economic factors relating to tariffs and their influence on trade. Writers and speakers on tariff questions often seek to arouse opposition to tariffs with statements about their detriment to the consumer. For example, many writers claim tariffs are a tax on the consumer. Let us examine this. We should note, first of all, that the tariff is a revenue to the Federal Government. If the tariff is reduced or eliminated, an equal amount of revenue must be obtained from some other source. It will obviously come in some other form of tax, and, for the most part, be paid by the consumer. So, even if the tariff were a tax on a consumer, elimination of the tariff would not eliminate the collection of an equivalent amount of tax. However, in most instances the tariff is actually paid by the foreign manufacturer or his agent and not by the United States consumer. To understand why this is so, we need to remind ourselves that whenever there is production of a given item in this country, the foreign exporter can seldom sell a competing item here for more than the American market price. Consequently, if his cost (including transportation and tariff) will make a sale at the going American price unprofitable, he will not export. If, however, his cost (plus ocean freight and tariff) is well below the American market price, he finds it profitable and will export. Being a good businessman, however, he will place his sales price in the American market just sufficiently below the going price to capture as much of the market as he desires. If the tariff is lowered, he need not lower his price to the United States consumer. He merely receives a larger spread between his total cost and selling price; namely, he makes a larger profit. In cases where the foreign producer's cost is much below United States production costs—and this is the general rule today—the tariff is actually paid out of the foreign exporter's profits. If the tariff rate is reduced, it means that less is collected by our Federal Treasury from foreign producers and more must be collected from the American taxpayers to replace this reduction in revenue.

A few examples will illustrate how this works in actual cases. Magnesium sulfate is being imported into the United States, principally from Germany. Most of this material shows a declared valuation of $8 or $8.30 per ton. This product, however, is offered to American consumers on the east coast at from $49 to $64 per ton. Some forms of magnesium sulfate are duty free, but in any case the maximum tariff rate is three-eights cent per pound, equivalent to $7.50 per ton. It is obvious that with a spread from $8 to $50 or $60 per ton, the foreign producer is asking what the United States market will stand and it seems unlikely that a tariff of $7.50 per ton, whether paid or not, would have no effect on the price which the United States consumer would pay but would have a small effect on the net profit of the foreign producer.

Another example of more interest to the ultimate consumer would be that of Japanese sewing machines. Many of the Japanese machines which reached the American consumer have sales markups of as much as 300 percent above the import price in this country. The Norelco electric shaver, made by the Phillips Co. in Holland, sells there for 39 guilders (equivalent to $9.75). These shavers are also exported to the United States and recently have retailed at $29.95. At the same time, the comparable Remington shaver was selling for $29.95 and the Shick at $29.50. Thus, the imported product is priced in the American market competitively with standard United States electric shavers. Many other similar examples could be cited. These all demonstrate what any practical businessman knows; namely, that sales prices are set by what management judges the market will bear. In the case of imports from low-cost countries, this generally bears little relation to actual production cost but does show a close relation to the market price established by United States producers. In these cases, which are rather typical, the markup has been determined not by the foreign producer's cost (plus ocean freight, plus tariffs, plus a small profit) but rather by an established American market price for similar products which represents a 100 to 200 percent markup over the selling price in the foreign producing country. Under these conditions, is it reasonable to expect that reduction or even elemination of a tariff of 10 or 20 percent would be passed on to the American consumer? Under such conditions, reduction of tariff generally results in larger profits by either the foreign exporter or his American agent.

### THE CONSUMER IS THE PRODUCER

Except for children, most consumers are also producers. In this case, the term "producer" is used in the economic sense and includes production of both goods and services. There is no such thing as a consumer's interest separated from and at variance with his interest as a producer also. The consumer's well-being, on the average, is determined by the amount of production in this country which can be distributed. If some of the goods to be distributed are imported, this means that they are not produced in this country and so the average consumer has produced less; in other words, he has less income to spend. So what he has gained by lower prices of imported goods as a consumer he has lost in the form of lower income as a producer. Even if he produces goods for export, the foreign exporter having sold the goods at, let us say, lower prices has relatively fewer dollars to spend for the export goods.

### TARIFFS ARE NOT A SUBSIDY

Another argument which is commonly put forth by the freer traders but is seldom openly discussed in committee hearings is the allegation that tariffs are a subsidy to United States producers. Here again loose use of terminology is what makes the idea seem plausible. If the word "subsidy" is to have any real meaning, we must be consistent in its use. *A subsidy is a payment by the Government to an individual or group of individuals. A tariff, on the other hand, is a payment to the Government—not from the Government.* It obviously could not be a subsidy.

In order for a tariff to shield a domestic producer from competition, it must be at or above some threshold value. This threshold value would be a tariff which just offsets the difference between the domestic producer's costs and a foreign producer's cost plus ocean transportation. If the tariff is any less than this, then obviously the foreign producer's profit margin is greater than the American producer's profit margin, at any given selling price in this country, and such a tariff would offer no assistance to a domestic producer faced with foreign competition. At best, a tariff below the threshold value will only retard the rate with which foreign producers will capture the United States market. Even if tariffs exceeded the threshold value and it were unprofitable for a foreign exporter to sell in the United States market, there would be little or no assist to domestic firms which were not monopolies. Competition from United States producers, paying the same level of wages and operating under the same business laws and taxes, would keep prices to the minimum commensurate with good business practice. Thus, careful use of terminology and recognition of the actual business effects of tariffs reveals that tariffs not only are not subsidies but cannot even assist in raising domestic producers' profits if there is United States competition.

### TARIFFS AND COMPETITION

This brings to mind another antitariff argument which does not stand up under careful examination. It is often claimed that tariff must be reduced so that the goad of foreign competition would stimulate progress and efficiency. As we pointed out above, unless a tariff is at least equal to the threshold value at which the foreign producer has neither a competitive advantage nor disadvantage in the domestic market, it offers no protection whatsoever to the American producer; so that if the tariff were a little below the threshold value, the efficient foreign producer can, in time, take the whole market. However, in the case of most American production there is ample, adequate, intense competition from other American producers. The drive for higher profits is a constant goad to management to keep up with or beat out domestic competition. This assures efficiency, technological advance, and progress. If import competition becomes much more rigorous than the competition which domestic competitors offer, it proves to be destructive and results in cutbacks and retrenchment in domestic production rather than industrial growth.

### EXPORTS DO NOT INCREASE TOTAL UNITED STATES MARKET

One other economic principle which seems to be little understood in foreign-trade discussions has to do with the influence of exports on the total domestic market. Many of those who urge a tariff reduction policy claim that tariff reduction will result in increased imports, which will give other countries more dollars with which they will buy from us and thus increase our exports. It is contended that export markets must be added to the domestic demand in order for our economy to expand. This concept is a type of economic perpetual motion idea. Over the long run, exports cannot increase the total demand in any country.

What a trading of exports for imports can and in fact does accomplish is shift the demand from some sectors or industries in the economy to others. Some who favor freer trade are those who think or hope that their industries will benefit at the expense of other industries if more of our total trade is at the international rather than the national level.

In a purely economic sense, however, the dollars spent to buy imported goods have no more influence in creating markets for domestic manufacturers than the same dollars spent in the domestic market place. As a matter of fact, instead of having some pyramiding effect to increase demand for United States goods, experience of the past decade has shown a fractioning factor. Only part of the dollars which we have supplied foreign nationals through trade, aid, travel, investment, and the like have returned through purchases of goods. The rest have been hoarded—used to increase foreign dollar claims against our gold.

In recognition of the principle that foreign trade does not automatically expand the economy, Woytinsky[2] in his book, World Commerce and Government, concludes as follows:

> The foreign trade of the United States was overexpanded after the war; exports were maintained on a high level by grants and credits to foreign countries and, in 1951 and 1952, by the vast defense and rearmament program. Stabilization of military expenses may be followed by a reduction of United States exports, but such a reduction would not necessarily endanger full employment and a high level of economic activity in the country. Indeed, if it were possible to divorce commercial policy completely from broad considerations of world peace and welfare, a strong argument could be made in favor of balancing the United States foreign trade at a comparatively low level—perhaps no higher, or even lower, than $10 billion—without endangering the continuous growth of its industrial production and rise of its standard of living. The United States depends, of course, on imports of certain metals and minerals and tropical products but could pay for them with 2 to 3 percent of its production.

UNITED STATES FOREIGN COMMERCE POLICY CONSIDERATIONS

In the light of these and other factors which have an influence on our trade relations, what would be a sound long-range policy for our foreign commerce? There is much evidence to indicate that the market place is the most efficient device for leading to progress in the regulation of a division-of-labor society. Not only does the outstanding economic growth in this country justify such a conclusion, but the experiences in postwar Europe support the same conclusion. The record shows that in the postwar years, economic progress has been positively correlated with freedom for the market place to operate. In the light of all this, it is clear that our foreign trade policy should foster a truly competitive market place in the United States.

In the regulation of our foreign commerce to assure a competitive market place here, we must take into account two factors: One has to do with natural advantage and the other with unnatural advantage or government-made advantage. We should continue our traditional recognition of the value of imports of commodities for which foreign sources represents a true natural advantage. Thus, for example, we should continue on the free list products which are not indigenous to our climate and soil and can be produced much more

[2] W. S. Woytinsky and E. S. Woytinsky, World Commerce and Government, pp. 105–112.

efficiently elsewhere. In general, these natural or fundamental economic advantages are associated with natural resources, including soil and climate. In some cases, however, even where there is a slight natural advantage in foreign production, national defense factors may require that we maintain domestic production adequate to meet critical defense needs.

It is the second factor which the free traders often overlook but which requires careful consideration, namely, the artificial or unnatural advantages which result from the legal actions of sovereign nations. It is well known in natural science that when man artificially disturb's nature's balance, the consequence is often unexpected and sometimes very undesirable. In a similar way, when a sovereign nation takes actions which impinge upon the natural action of a completely free market, some counteraction may be called for. Many United States laws place domestic producers at a disadvantage in competition with manufacturers from other countries who are not faced with the same legal or tax requirements. Our minimum wage laws, our antimonopoly laws, our national standards of health and safety in industrial employment, our high corporate income taxes, the effective enforcement of our laws regulating commerce, and our aggressive unions which bid up wages—all combine to place the United States producer at a disadvantage with respect to his competition in many other countries. These are manmade differences and not the result of natural advantage or differences in economic efficiency.

A bill now pending before Congress illustrates the dual standard of many of our trade laws. S. 11 has been proposed as an amendment to the Robinson-Patman Act. The proposed amendment would greatly restrict domestic manufacturers who sell in interstate commerce in freedom to meet localized price competition. This restriction would not apply against foreigners who export to this country and sell in interstate commerce throughout the 48 States. This is characteristic—the foreign manufacturer need not comply with our minimum wage or working condition standards either.

Added to the differences in the legal restrictions which producers face in different countries, there are also many differences in business ethics and practices. For example, differences, in income distribution can have an important bearing on the results of foreign versus domestic trade. In many foreign countries, the workers get a considerably smaller portion of the sales dollar for their company than is characteristic in the United States. This means that purchasing power is not as broadly distributed and does not build a satisfactory mass market. Extensive export sales are thus less effective in building demand for major American-manufactured items than similar dollars spent for American-produced merchandise.

## A CONSTRUCTIVE UNITED STATES FOREIGN TRADE POLICY

However satisfactory our foreign trade policy of the past has been, it does not meet the present situation. Some important changes are needed. We need to develop a new long-range trade policy which is based on sound economics and can be followed consistently into the future.

There is no question but that we need foreign trade. The questions to be answered are: How much foreign trade is needed and under what conditions will it operate? In developing the rules for control of our foreign commerce, we need to devise a policy which will be in the best interests of all our citizens, which will take due account of national defense requirements, and which faces the realities of world conditions.

We should regulate our foreign commerce so that foreign producers do not gain a competitive advantage in our markets by skirting some or all of the rules and conditions which we have established to make our mass market the foundation of our high standard of living. Our policy should insure that jobs of American workers are not forfeited merely because foreign workers receive a lower wage. To accomplish this objective, the foreign trade policy of the United States should develop along the following lines:

1. We should reaffirm the principle of equalizing tariffs so that tariff rates can sufficiently equalize competition between American producers and foreign producers having lower labor costs (wage rates adjusted for productivity). Our tariff rates should be set on the basis of Tariff Commission studies so that foreign producers have no competitive advantage in our markets unless it results from their having a greater economic efficiency in their production.

2. Administration of tariffs should be returned to Congress, working through the Tariff Commission. The Tariff Commission should be strengthened and given the job of establishing tariff rates, much as the Interstate Commerce Commission is responsible for establishing rail freight rates. By having the Commission thus determine tariff rates subject to suitable congressional review, the tariff question could largely be removed from politics but yet remain sufficiently responsive to reflect consideration for local problems.

3. The most-favored-nations policy should be abandoned and for it should be substituted a formula for calculating tariff rates, which would be based on the labor cost differentials between the country of origin and the United States. Of the several factors of unnatural advantage which foreign producers enjoy, their lower wage rate is often the most important. By arranging tariff rates in relation to foreign wage rates—properly adjusted to their national economy—our foreign trade policy would encourage rather than discourage increases in foreign wage rates. This would assist in broader distribution of incomes and expanding of mass markets in our industrial neighbors. In this way our tariff policy could serve a dual purpose. In the first place it would result in fair competition within our own market place, and secondly, it would encourage the distribution of mass buying power throughout the world.

4. The General Agreement on Tariffs and Trade, to which we have given provisional approval, and the Organization for Trade Cooperation, for which United States membership has been pending before Congress for the last 2 years, should both be replaced by an international tribunal of the sort proposed by the Randall Commission. Such a tribunal would be restricted to the collection of international trade

data, arranging for consultation between members, and proposing broad principles for improving international trade relations. It should have none of the quasi-legislative and judiciary characteristics of GATT and OTC.

5. We should completely overhaul our antidumping laws. They need to be improved so that they can be enforced to really prevent dumping on the United States market. We could do well to imitate the Canadians in their antidumping legislation.

# WORLD COMMERCE AND UNITED STATES FOREIGN TRADE POLICY

W. S. Woytinsky, Washington, D. C.

SUMMARY

The introduction (sec. 1–4) to this paper points out that the decision of Congress to review all aspects of national foreign-trade policy calls for clarification of the objective of this policy.

Part I of the paper, Purposes of Foreign Trade (sec. 5–14), attempts to give basis for the ideology of our foreign-trade policy by restating the general principles, purposes, and advantages of international exchange of goods. The emphasis is on the advantages of international competition and division of labor and on the limits beyond which such division of labor and specialization may become harmful for a nation.

Part II, Recent Trends in World Trade (sec. 15–32), describes the structure of world commerce and the main trends in its development as the background for an analysis of the unique position of the United States. It deals with the growth of world trade, the relationship between imports and exports, the relative rates of growth of world exports and industrial production, the foreign trade of leading nations, the geographic pattern of world trade, the per capita import and export and ratio of foreign trade to national income in various countries, broad regional markets, the main commodities in world commerce and patterns in the composition of foreign trade.

Part III, United States Position in World Trade (sec. 33–42), starts with the general picture of world commerce given in part II and highlights the peculiarities of this country's position in comparison with other nations: largest in world import and export value, low in the per capita value of foreign trade, lowest in the world ratio of the value of foreign trade to national income, characterized by a tremendous surplus of exports over imports. The geographic pattern of the United States foreign trade is examined in detail and its regional character—concentration in the Western Hemisphere—is stressed. Its share in imports and exports of individual countries is analyzed. The characteristic features of our strong and weak industries are examined, and an hypothesis of the original of weakness of certain lines of production is ventured. Next, the structure of our tariffs is analyzed and it is shown that, despite radical cuts in import duties, they remain too high to permit our imports to keep pace with our increasing exports (excluding unilateral transfers).

Part IV, Principles of the United States Foreign Trade Policy (sec. 43–57), makes an attempt to formulate the general principles that emerge from the analysis of United States position in world trade:

First, United States foreign-trade policy must be integrated with the general domestic and foreign policy of the Nation; no decision on tariffs should be made wholly on considerations of the effects of foreign competition on domestic producers.

Second, the most urgent immedient objective of our foreign trade policy must be to reduce the gap between our exports and imports by encouraging imports.

If these two principles are accepted by Congress and announced in the new act, they would facilitate decision on pending controversial issues.

They would suggest—

That the United States must support both GATT and OTC;

That the practice of setting peril points as limits to tariff negotiations is sound, but these points should be set much lower than for the preceding negotiations;

That the principle of the escape clause is sound, but this principle should be applied only to whole industries which are unable to meet foreign competition by diversification of production, and only when interests of large groups of people or whole communities are involved;

That redress in the case of serious injury may require other measures than an increase in import duties;

That the maxim "Buy American" is contrary to the interests of the United States;

That the national-defense principle must be preserved;

That agricultural quotas are unavoidable as long as the Nation is pledged to support certain lines of agricultural production;

That import of metals and minerals which cannot be provided, in case of emergency, by local deposits must be encouraged;

That the principle "trade rather than aid" should become the basis of our foreign-aid and foreign-trade policy;

That more attention must be given to commodity agreements insuring stability of prices of essential raw materials;

That systematic efforts must be made not only to find new markets for our domestic products but also to encourage import of foreign products in payment for those which the United States exports.

## INTRODUCTION

1. The problem of tariffs was one of the main issues that precipitated the break between British colonies along the Atlantic shore of North America and their mother country. This issue played an outstanding role in domestic policy of the United States during the first century of its existence. Later it was dwarfed by other issues—wars, taxes, monopolies, labor, scope of the responsibilities of Government, foreign policy.

Public interest in foreign-trade policy has changed with fluctuations in business conditions. More often than not in the past 170 years, the people, Congress, and the administration have approached the issue empirically, from single cases rather than general principles. Policy shaped in this way has not always been internally consistent.

2. From time to time, however, attempts have been made to streamline United States foreign-trade policy by basing it on certain clearly announced principles. The earliest attempt of this kind is associated

with the name of Alexander Hamilton. In his famous report on manufacturers, presented to Congress in 1791 he outlined the principles of customs policy as part of a long-range economic program designed to transform the United States from a land of small farmers into an industrial power. The tariff of 1930 (Hawley-Smoot tariff) likewise had a clear leading idea. There was also a definite leading idea in the Reciprocal Trade Agreements Act of 1934 which proposed to open new outlets to United States products by liberalizing foreign tariffs and removing other trade restrictions. The United States, emerging from the great depression, proclaimed its return to world market. It promised cuts in its tariff rates and called on other nations to follow its example. The new foreign-trade policy seemed to be inspired by the faith that removal or reduction of trade barriers would be followed, automatically, by a revival of international exchange of goods, which in turn would create new demands, new jobs, and prosperity. As far as domestic economic policy is concerned, the philosophy of the reciprocal trade agreements was that increase in exports would be to the advantage of this country even if it had to cut down its prohibitive import duties. The contention that the act of 1934 aimed to increase exports and imports is not correct: its aim was to increase exports even at the cost of increasing imports.

This philosophy was characteristic of a definite phase in the development of our economic thinking and represented a reaction to the philosophy of high protectionism in the tariff of 1930. It came at the proper time, and the positive role of reciprocal trade agreements in restoring the position of this country in world markets is undeniable.

3. World War II has radically changed the situation in the world market and our domestic economy. The United States entered an era of economic expansion with full, or almost full, employment of human and natural resources, punctured by occasional minor setbacks, readjustments effected on a very high level of prosperity. The system of reciprocal trade agreements began to crack. Some amendments introduced in the original act by successive extension acts ran in the direction of concessions to protectionist interests. Even if the concessions were not very important and did not affect the structure of our new liberalized tariff appreciably, trend was against the philosophy of the original act. The foreign-trade policy lost its clear ideology, so that many observers at home and abroad began to have doubts about its aims and immediate purpose.

4. The decision of Congress to reexamine the whole field of problems of foreign-trade policy in their relation to our domestic policy and our stake in world affairs reveals its desire to put an end to this ambiguity. Its intention is obviously to develop guidelines for trade policy based on a definite conception of the position of this country in world trade and its long-run interests. This task cannot be accomplished without reference to certain theoretical notions, historical trends and facts and figures which are often disregarded in discussion of practical problems.

### I. THE PURPOSE OF FOREIGN TRADE

5. The effect of foreign trade on a nation is to offer it new opportunities for expansion and to expose its domestic industry to foreign competition. This double impact affects both production and

consumption and depends largely on the nature of exchanged commodities. Intertribal or international trade usually begins with the exchange of products which are found or produced in certain areas and are coveted by people in other areas. This type of trade prevailed in the ancient world and may have predominated in Europe and America until the 18th century. It occurs even now in commerce between industrial countries of the Temperate Zone and underdeveloped countries rich in certain tropical products or minerals, but most of the goods carried by modern international trade either could be produced in the importing countries or compete with comparable domestic products. They appear in international trade because consumers in the importing country prefer them to local products or local producers are unable to deliver goods of comparable quality at comparable prices. In other words, a large part of modern international trade is based on the international division of labor rather than the geographical incidence or the uneven distribution of certain rare commodities. Its role in fostering competition and international division of labor is at least as important as the exchange of goods which are found or produced in the exporting country but not in the importing nation.

6. The mutual advantages of trade in competing goods are less obvious than in the case of transfer of goods found in only one of the trading countries. Economic competition often ends with the triumph of one party and the defeat of the other. It can bring the elation of victory and the bitterness of failure, gains, and losses. Its ultimate advantage or disadvantage to a nation can be measured only by its impact on the whole national economy.

7. Adam Smith pointed out that the foundation of international trade is the difference in cost of production. He referred to an extreme case.

By means of glasses, hotbeds and hot walls—

he wrote—

very good grapes can be raised in Scotland, and very good wine too can be made of them at about 30 times the expense for which at least equally good can be brought from foreign countries * * * Whether the advantages which one country has over another be natural or acquired, is in this respect of no consequence. As long as the one country has those advantages, and the other wants them, it will always be more advantageous to the latter, rather to buy of the former than to make * * * .

In this question, Adam Smith saw no difference between international division of labor and specialization of individual producers.

8. Most modern students go beyond him. The situation is not identical in the two cases. Moreover, the cost-of-production factor in international trade is not as simple as in the case of raising grapes in Scotland and Spain. The key to international trade is not the difference in production costs of the same commodity in different countries, but rather the comparative costs of production of different commodities in each of the competing nations. David Ricardo illustrated this point by the following example:

Two men can both make shoes and hats, and one is superior to the other in both employments; but in making hats, he can only exceed his competitor by one-fifth, or 20 percent, and in making shoes he can excel him by one-third, or 33 percent; will it not be for the interest of both that the superior man should employ himself exclusively in making shoes, and the inferior man in making hats?

The law of comparative cost formulated by Ricardo is the guiding principle of international division of labor and foreign trade. The question is not in the cost differential of competitive commodities—for example, fabrics, chinaware, precision instruments, bicycles, or watch movements—in two countries but in comparative production costs of these and other commodities in each country.

9. The weakness of this reasoning is in its abstract character. Even if far-reaching division of labor were ultimately beneficial for mankind, there is no evidence that it would be good for all nations at all times. Furthermore, it is possible that the transition from the present structure of world economy—with limited division of labor—to the ideal state of specialization would be too expensive and too painful for individual countries.

Indeed, excessive specialization of production in a small country may be incompatible with its aspiration for economic independence. The existing pattern of relative costs that seems to demand such specialization may change.

Apart of this general consideration, a country may be interested in preserving a definite line of production for sociopolitical reasons or for reason of national defense. A nation may also decide to introduce a new line of production in order to substitute a domestic product for imports. If it has the necessary raw materials and possesses or hopes to acquire necessary skills, this policy may be perfectly sound. Then the country would reconcile itelf to paying too dearly for certain domestic products or to having them of inferior quality in the period of apprenticeship of its infant industry. The test of such a policy is its temporary character. Protection may be required for 3, 5, or 10 years, but misses its purpose if custom duties become permanent and the protected industry proves unable to stay on its feet.

10. Diversification of production is often preferable to specialization. A region or a nation that specializes in a single product—sugar, rubber, coffee, tin, or what else—is vulnerable to excessive fluctuations of prices in world market. It must try to develop other lines of production even if they seem uneconomical. It may make mistakes in selecting its targets but this does not invalidate the soundness of its drive toward some degree of self-sufficiency.

11. A special situation develops in the case of import of articles competing with domestic products subjected to excise tax. Free admission of such articles would endanger the tax structure in the country. If excise tax paid by local producers does not apply also to imports, it must be offset by a special duty on the imported articles.

12. In all these cases, limitation of the free flow of certain groups of goods seems not only defensible but necessary. There are other situations in which less selective restrictions may be required. Such are the restriction of luxury imports as a means of protecting the national currency, or preferential tariffs that serve political purposes, strengthening the ties between a country and certain politically related areas abroad. Such situations deserve serious considerations as exceptions from the general rule that competition is wholesome for both parties.

13. It must be recognized also that the exchange of goods across international boundaries is never completely free. Independent of custom duties and other restrictions to free exchange of goods, domestic producers in each country are protected against foreign compe-

tition, to some extent, by costs of transport, insurance, loading and unloading, promotion and distribution, and other overhead expenditures. There must be a substantial span between the f. o. b. price of an imported article and wholesale price of the comparable domestic product to give the imported merchandise an even chance. The minimum span varies with the product. Falling back to Ricardo's example, two countries would hardly establish a regular bilateral exchange of hats against shoes if the relative cost difference between them is as small as he assumed. Indeed, international trade in competitive products is not possible without considerable differences in relative cost of production in different countries. The classical concept of the world market as a continuous entity is misleading. What is designated as the "world market" is actually an agglomeration of national markets, each surrounded by a protective wall of transportation cost of, say, 5 to 10 percent ad valorem of imported commodities, with a superstructure in the form of customs barriers of different heights for different products, not infrequently reinforced by a chain of strongholds in the form of quota and embargoes.

14. Once admitted within this enclosure, imported goods behave precisely as local products do in trying to gain the attention of consumers and knock out competing articles. Local goods maintain certain advantages because local producers are closer to distributors and consumers, know better their habits and can more easily adjust their designs to changing demand. But superior quality or lower price in comparison with local products may give victory in the contest to the imported merchandise, to the advantage of consumers and distributors and the dismay of local producers. The latter can gain ultimately if they respond to the challenge by diversifying production, improving its methods and reducing its cost. If they are unwilling or unable to respond to the challenge, they must share a part of the market with foreign competitors. In this respect, the competition between imported and domestic products does not differ essentially from the competition between different regions within the national economy.

A healthy foreign trade in competitive goods hits inefficient producers on both sides of the international boundary line. Eventual losses suffered by such producers are not an annoying repercussion of foreign trade but one of its fundamental features. Without such losses, foreign trade would miss one of its essential purposes—to foster international division of labor and the economic development of participating nations.

## II. RECENT TRENDS IN WORLD TRADE

15. Despite continuous efforts of the League of Nations and the United Nations, statistics of international trade are neither complete nor internally consistent. Most countries report special exports and imports but few keep records of general trade (including certain reexports which are not counted as part of special trade). There is no universally accepted method of valuation of exported and imported merchandise except for the general agreement to record f. o. b. value of exported goods and c. i. f. value of imported. Serious difficulties arise in converting national import and export statistics into world currency, practically United States dollars, in countries that have mul-

tiple exchange rates. Furthermore, world-trade statistics computed by the U. N. either exclude Iron Curtain countries or include only their trade with free countries.

These reservations should be kept in mind with regard to the overall survey of changes in the value and volume of world trade in the past two decades. (See table 1.)

TABLE 1.—*Trends in world trade*

| Year | Value, in millions of United States dollars | | Volume of exports, 1953=100 | Year | Value, in millions of United States dollars | | Volume of exports, 1953=100 |
|---|---|---|---|---|---|---|---|
| | Imports | Exports | | | Imports | Exports | |
| 1937 | 26,450 | 23,400 | 72 | 1952 | 79,200 | 72,300 | 94 |
| 1938 | 23,300 | 20,650 | 69 | 1953 | 75,800 | 73,300 | 100 |
| 1948 | 58,500 | 52,700 | 70 | 1954 | 79,000 | 76,100 | 105 |
| 1950 | 58,200 | 55,300 | 85 | 1955 | 88,100 | 82,700 | 114 |
| 1951 | 80,200 | 75,000 | 95 | 1956 | 96,900 | 91,600 | 123 |

Source: U. N. Monthly Bulletin of Statistics, May 1957.

16. The value of imports and exports of the world (excluding the U. S. S. R., mainland China and other Iron Curtain countries) increased almost fourfold from 1937 to 1956. The volume of exports (i. e., their value at constant prices) rose more than 70 percent. Since world population increased about 25 percent in the same period, the volume of exports per capita of world population increased a little less than 40 percent. With allowance for possible errors in these figures, the average annual increment in volume of world trade per capita was between 1.5 and 2 percent.

Two features deserve attention—the disparity between the export and import values and the relation between the rising volume of foreign trade and the growth of production in the world.

17. Before World War II, world import exceeded export by more than 10 percent. The difference was reduced to about 6 percent in 1951–56. Apart from difference in valuation, especially in the 1930's the disparity between the value of imports and exports is due to the fact that the same goods are valued f. o. b. when they leave the exporting country and c. i. f. when they reach the destination country. The difference—assuming a correct valuation—represents the cost of transportation and insurance. It suggests that, independent of invisible export and import, i. e. exchange of services and similar operations, the normal flow of merchandise in world trade would give all countries an import balance. The absence of such a balance indicates that the f. o. b. value of goods exported from the country exceeds the f. o. b. value of its imports, i. e. the country exports more than the equivalent of its imports when both are evaluated similarly.

18. The simplest way of comparing the growth of foreign trade with overall economic progress would be to analyze the trend in volume of world exports in relation to world income. This method is impracticable, however, because there is no universal agreement on the measurement of world income.

It is possible, however, to compare the changes in the volume of world trade and industrial production over nearly a century. From 1867–68 to the outbreak of World War I, the volume of world exports grew at an average rate of 36 to 37 percent per decade and world industrial output, 47 percent per decade. Between 1913 and 1938, world industrial output increased by 37 percent while the volume of world trade gained only 20 percent. Thus the volume of trade was lagging behind the growing industrial output.[1]

The trends in more recent years are shown in table 2.

World War II did not stop the growth of industrial production but disorganized world trade. In 1948–49, when the Marshall plan was put in operation, the volume of world exports lagged far behind industrial growth in the world. In more recent years, international trade has been catching up with the world's industrial growth. From 1948 to 1956, world trade increased nearly 78 percent as compared with 60 percent for production, but in comparison with the prewar level, the rise in the volume of trade remained behind that in production (the indexes are 174 and 215, where the average for 1937 and 1938 equals 100). These increases represent an average rate of 34 and 48 percent per decade, respectively; both rates are amazingly close to the average rates for the period from 1867–68 to 1913.

19. The ranking of individual countries by their share in world trade changes slowly as time goes. From the end of the Napoleonic wars to the outbreak of World War II, the United Kingdom led, followed by France, the United States, and Germany. In the recent years the United States has advanced to the first place, with the United Kingdom second.

TABLE 2.—*Indexes of world industrial production and volume of export*

[Average 1937–38=100]

| | Industrial production | Volume of exports | | Industrial production | Volume of exports |
|---|---|---|---|---|---|
| 1948 | 136 | 99 | 1953 | 187 | 142 |
| 1949 | 138 | 106 | 1954 | 187 | 149 |
| 1950 | 157 | 121 | 1955 | 206 | 162 |
| 1951 | 170 | 135 | 1956 | 215 | 174 |
| 1952 | 174 | 133 | | | |

Source: United States Monthly Bulletin of Statistics, April–May 1957.

A large part of all world trade is attributable to a dozen countries arrayed in table 3 by their imports in 1956; the ranking would not change much if they were arrayed by exports. The main changes in ranking in 1956 as compared with 1938 have been as follows: The United States, Canada, and West Germany advanced to a higher ranking; the United Kingdom, France, and Japan dropped to a lower ranking. Changes for the other six countries did not exceed the magnitude of annual fluctuations due to changing business conditions, harvest, divergent trends in prices and similar factors. Apart from such fluctuations, the 12 nations listed in table 3, together with 7 other countries—India and Malaya, Union of South Africa, Brazil and Argentina, Denmark and Norway—account for more than two-thirds of world imports and three-fourths of world exports. The fact that they have a larger part in world exports than imports is due wholly to the export balance of the United States.

20. The net balances of the merchandise trade of individual countries—excluding invisible exports and imports, movement of capital,

[1] W. S. and E. S. Woytinsky, World Commerce and Governments, 1955, pp. 39–43.

unilateral transfer and similar operations—have fluctuated narrowly from year to year. The most recent annual data for the 40 countries with the largest imports are summarized in table 4.

It appears that 31 countries listed in this table had an import balance and 9 an export balance.

The last group included the United States, Australia, and Western Germany, on the one hand, and Brazil, Venezuela, Cuba, Malaya, Indonesia, and the Belgian Congo, on the other.

TABLE 3.—*Imports and exports of 12 leading countries, 1938, 1948, and 1956*

[Millions of United States dollars]

| Country [1] | 1938 | | 1948 | | 1956 | |
|---|---|---|---|---|---|---|
| | Imports | Exports | Imports | Exports | Imports | Exports |
| United States | 2, 180 | 3, 064 | 7, 163 | 12, 544 | 12, 635 | 18, 862 |
| United Kingdom | 4, 285 | 2, 446 | 8, 125 | 6, 362 | 10, 480 | 8, 882 |
| Western Germany | [2] 1, 004 | [2] 1, 135 | 1, 386 | 599 | 6, 617 | 7, 358 |
| Canada | 675 | 844 | 2, 637 | 3, 110 | 5, 804 | 4, 946 |
| France | 1, 330 | 880 | 3, 442 | 3, 307 | 5, 552 | 4, 538 |
| Netherlands | 803 | 593 | 1, 871 | 1, 024 | 3, 712 | 2, 862 |
| Belgium [3] | 767 | 730 | 1, 985 | 1, 690 | 3, 263 | 3, 162 |
| Japan | 1, 070 | 1, 109 | 684 | 258 | 3, 230 | 2, 495 |
| Italy | 593 | 553 | 1, 539 | 1, 077 | 3, 169 | 2, 157 |
| Sweden | 525 | 464 | 1, 377 | 1, 107 | 2, 207 | 1, 941 |
| Switzerland | 366 | 302 | 1, 163 | 799 | 1, 766 | 1, 442 |
| Australia | 507 | 562 | 1, 227 | 1, 653 | 1, 713 | 1, 896 |
| Total for 12 countries | 13, 835 | 12, 682 | 32, 599 | 33, 530 | 60, 148 | 60, 541 |
| Percent of world total [4] | 60 | 61 | 56 | 63 | 62 | 60 |

[1] Arrayed by imports in 1956.
[2] All Germany.
[3] Including Luxembourg.
[4] World total excludes Iron Curtain countries.

Source: U. N. Monthly Bulletin of Statistics, May 1957.

TABLE 4.—*Exports, imports, and balance of trade of 40 countries with the largest foreign trade, 1956*

[Millions of United States dollars]

| Country | Imports | Exports | Surplus of exports (+) or imports (−) | Country | Imports | Exports | Surplus of exports (+) or imports (−) |
|---|---|---|---|---|---|---|---|
| United States | 12, 635 | 18, 862 | +6, 227 | Finland | 885 | 774 | −111 |
| United Kingdom | 10, 480 | 8, 882 | −1, 598 | Venezuela [2] | 884 | 1, 912 | +1, 028 |
| Western Germany | 6, 617 | 7, 358 | +741 | Netherlands Antilles [2] | 830 | 803 | −27 |
| Canada | 5, 804 | 4, 946 | −858 | New Zealand | 804 | 724 | −80 |
| France | 5, 552 | 4, 538 | −1, 014 | Hong Kong | 799 | 563 | −236 |
| Netherlands | 3, 712 | 2, 862 | −850 | Mexico [2] | 792 | 668 | −124 |
| Belgium [1] | 3, 263 | 3, 162 | −101 | Algeria | 777 | 429 | −348 |
| Japan | 3, 230 | 2, 495 | −735 | Colombia | 657 | 538 | −119 |
| Italy | 3, 169 | 2, 157 | −1, 012 | Spain [2] | 619 | 446 | −173 |
| Sweden | 2, 207 | 1, 941 | −266 | Indonesia [2] | 604 | 931 | +327 |
| Switzerland | 1, 766 | 1, 442 | −324 | Egypt | 534 | 409 | −125 |
| Australia | 1, 713 | 1, 896 | +183 | Ireland | 507 | 301 | −206 |
| India | 1, 712 | 1, 267 | −445 | Philippines | 506 | 453 | −53 |
| Union of South Africa | 1, 385 | 1, 201 | −184 | Morocco [2] | 497 | 326 | −171 |
| Malaya | 1, 357 | 1, 361 | +4 | Cuba [2] | 496 | 495 | +98 |
| Denmark | 1, 311 | 1, 111 | −200 | Yugoslavia | 473 | 321 | −152 |
| Brazil | 1, 235 | 1, 482 | +247 | Greece | 464 | 190 | −274 |
| Norway | 1, 210 | 772 | −438 | Portugal | 441 | 299 | −142 |
| Argentina | 1, 123 | 944 | −179 | Turkey | 407 | 305 | −102 |
| Austria | 974 | 849 | −125 | Belgian Congo [2] | 379 | 454 | +75 |

[1] Includes Luxembourg.
[2] 1955.

Source: U. N. Monthly Bulletin of Statistics, May 1957.

Moreover, the surplus of exports over imports is less typical for Western Germany and Australia than for Cuba, Venezuela, Belgian Congo, Indonesia whose import-export position in 1952–55 was as follows:

[In millions of United States dollars]

| | 1952 | 1953 | 1954 | 1955 |
|---|---|---|---|---|
| Cuba: | | | | |
| Import | 618 | 490 | 488 | 496 |
| Export | 675 | 640 | 539 | 594 |
| Venezuela: | | | | |
| Import | 756 | 816 | 919 | 884 |
| Export | 1, 450 | 1, 445 | 1, 690 | 1, 212 |
| Belgian Congo: | | | | |
| Import | 401 | 363 | 371 | 379 |
| Export | 391 | 398 | 397 | 454 |
| Indonesia: | | | | |
| Import | 1, 000 | 765 | 629 | 604 |
| Export | 1, 012 | 840 | 867 | 931 |

The implications of the export balance in these countries and in the United States will be discussed later. (See pp. 63ff.)

21. The general geographic pattern of foreign trade can be illustrated by a world map on which the exports of each country are indicated by dots, say 1 dot for each $500 million. (See fig. 1.)

This map reveals two focal points of international trade, on the opposite shores of the Northern Atlantic—Great Britain and northwestern continental Europe on the one side of the ocean, the United Stats and Canada, on the other. It also reveals that northwestern Europe dwarfs North America in the value of its exports. The shortcoming of this map is, however, that it invites comparison of the density of the dots in the different parts of the world, which amounts to a comparison of the value of exports with the area of the various geographical regions, which does not make much sense.

FIGURE I.—*Geographic distribution of world trade.*

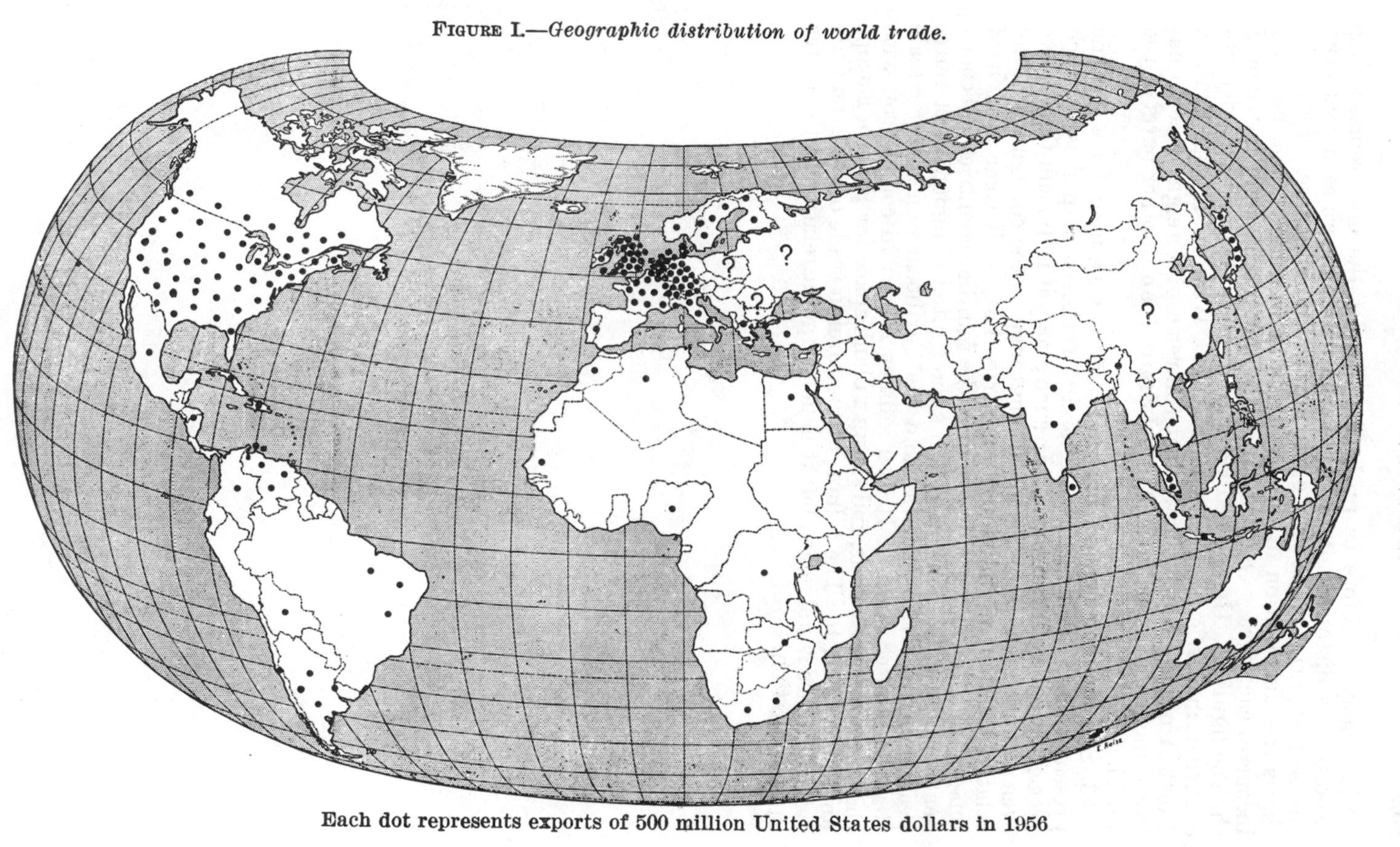

Each dot represents exports of 500 million United States dollars in 1956

22. It may therefore be preferable to plot the dots representing exports on a distorted map of the world which shows each continent and each country on the scale of its population or income. Figure II shows the distribution of foreign trade in relation to the national income of each area. On this map the dots are more evenly distributed than on figure I. Unexpectedly it appears that they are more densely clustered in Africa, Latin America, and Western Europe than in North America—which shows that the ratio of foreign trade to national income is lower in the United States than in other parts of the world.

23. Still another type of distorted map can be used for a graphic presentation of the structure of foreign trade—a map showing each area on the scale of its exports. In such a map it is difficult to preserve even a rough likeness to a conventional map in the configuration and relative location of individual countries but, with some stretch of imagination, the reader will recognize the familiar countries and continents on figure II. This map shows the United Kingdom, west European countries, Latin America and the Caribbeans on a larger scale than the United States. It also inflates Africa in comparison with the income of these areas, and shows a blank space for Eastern Europe and the U. S. S. R.: The volume of the foreign trade of the Iron Curtain countries is unknown, but it is not large in relation to their area and population.

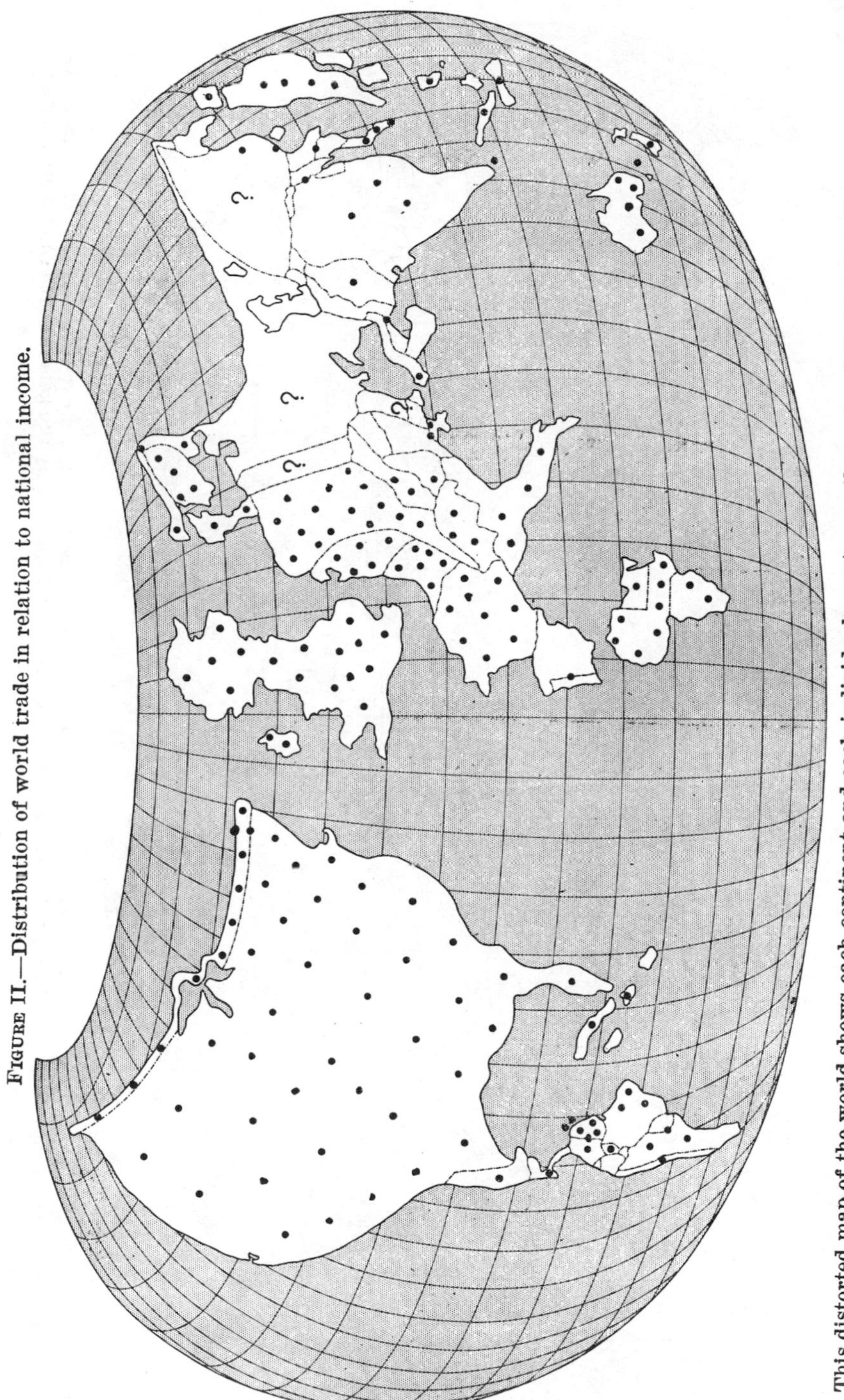

FIGURE II.—Distribution of world trade in relation to national income.

This distorted map of the world shows each continent and each individual country on the scale of its national income around 1950. Each dot represents exports of 500 million United States dollars in 1956

FIGURE III.—Distribution of world trade.

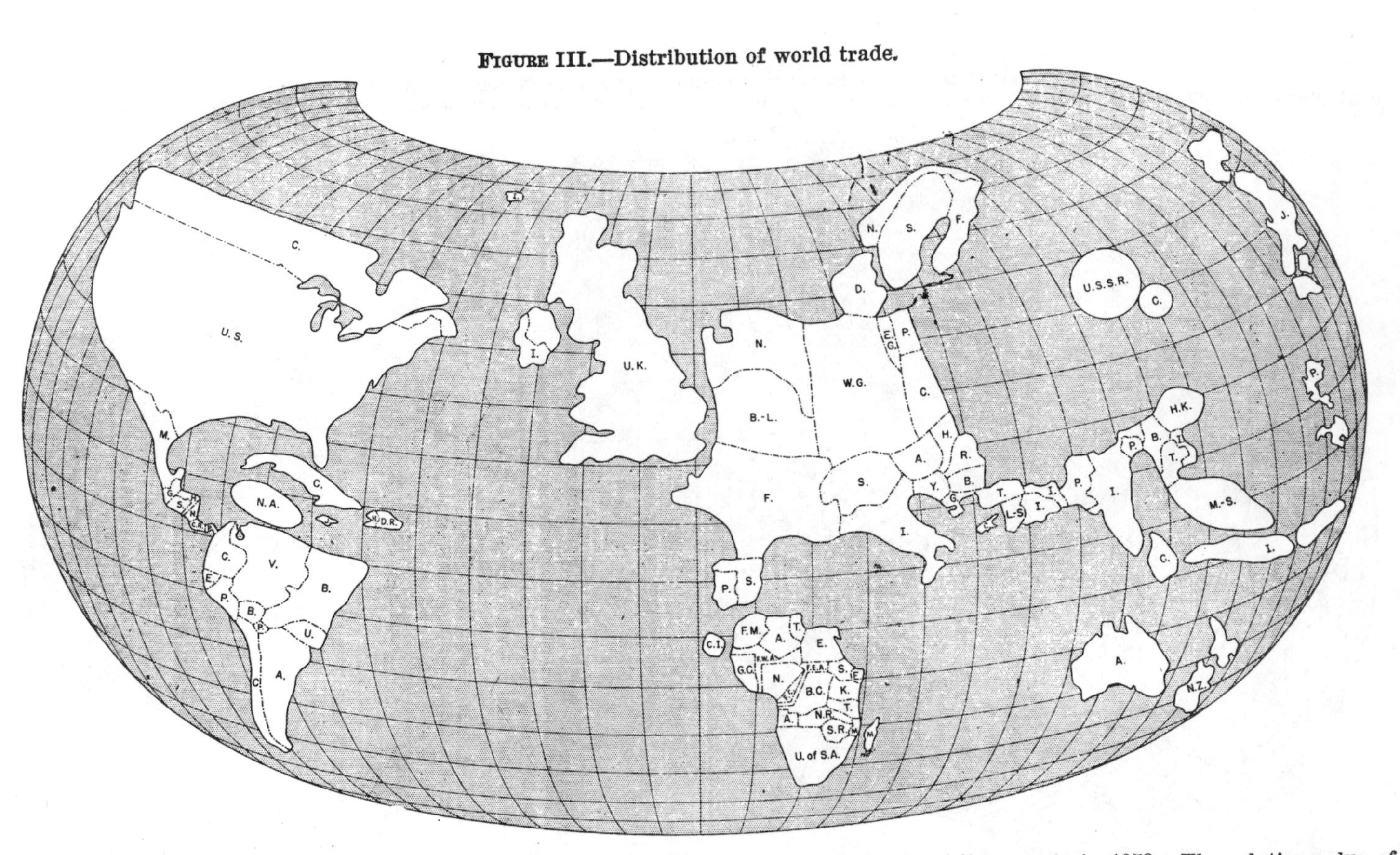


This distorted map shows each continent and each individual country on the scale of its exports in 1952. The relative value of exports of each area changes from year to year, but these changes do not affect appreciably the general pattern of distribution of world trade among different parts of the globe.

24. The value of exports or imports per capita of population depends on many factors. Generally, all other conditions being equal, the rate is higher in small countries than in big ones: the possibility of far-reaching division of labor and diversification of national economy reduces the dependence of a country on foreign markets. On the other hand, per capita imports and exports increase with economic progress in an area. There are, however, many exceptions to this rule. A country emerging from colonial bondage may possess a highly specialized economy geared to that of the economy of the colonial power. Its economic revival would bring diversification of its economy and may be followed by a decline in its per capita trade and the import-export ratio to national income.

25. In table 5, the 40 countries included in table 4 are arrayed by their per capita import in 1956 (or 1955).

Apart from the Netherlands Antilles, a place with less than 200,000 inhabitants and brisk international transactions in oil, the list is topped by comparatively small prosperous nations—New Zealand, Canada, Belgium, Switzerland, Norway, the Netherlands, Sweden, Denmark, Finland. Hong Kong and Malaya are also in this group, ahead of the United Kingdom, which ranks 13th in the table. France ranks 19th, Germany 18th. The United States comes 23d, after Cuba and Algeria. This fact must be remembered in analyzing the particular position of this country in the world market.

26. The ratio of the value of exports to national income (or gross national product) is not identical with the share of exports in national output. The nation may reexport imported goods after some processing or repacking. It also may export the products of mines and plantations in its territory that are owned by foreign capital and the value of which is only partly recorded in its national income. Yet the ratio of the value of foreign trade to national income is an important measure of the role of foreign trade in a country's economy.

In table 6 countries are arrayed by the ratio of the value of their imports and exports to national income in the last year for which the data are available, in most cases 1955.

TABLE 5.—*Per capita import and export in countries with largest foreign trade in 1956*

[United States dollars]

| Country | Import | Export | Country | Import | Export |
|---|---|---|---|---|---|
| Netherlands Antilles | 4,560 | 4,412 | Cuba | 83 | 99 |
| New Zealand | 376 | 339 | Algeria | 80 | 44 |
| Canada | 363 | 309 | United States | 75 | 112 |
| Belgium | 354 | 344 | Italy | 65 | 45 |
| Switzerland | 351 | 287 | Morocco | 57 | 38 |
| Norway | 351 | 223 | Greece | 58 | 24 |
| Netherlands | 341 | 263 | Argentina | 57 | 48 |
| Hong Kong | 335 | 236 | Portugal | 50 | 34 |
| Sweden | 302 | 265 | Colombia | 50 | 42 |
| Denmark | 293 | 249 | Japan | 36 | 27 |
| Malaya | 219 | 219 | Belgian Congo | 30 | 36 |
| Finland | 206 | 180 | Mexico | 27 | 23 |
| United Kingdom | 204 | 173 | Egypt | 23 | 13 |
| Australia | 182 | 202 | Philippines | 23 | 20 |
| Ireland | 173 | 102 | Yugoslavia | 21 | 18 |
| Venezuela | 157 | 331 | Spain | 21 | 15 |
| Austria | 139 | 122 | Brazil | 21 | 25 |
| Western Germany | 131 | 144 | Turkey | 16 | 12 |
| France | 127 | 104 | Indonesia | 7 | 11 |
| Union of South Africa | 100 | 86 | India | 5 | 3 |

Source: Table 4.

TABLE 6.—*Percentage ratio of the value of imports and exports to national income in selected countries, 1954–55*

| Country | Ratio | Country | Ratio |
|---|---|---|---|
| Hong Kong (1952) | 258.0 | Portugal | 41.3 |
| Malaya (1953) | 118.0 | Panama | 40.5 |
| Kenya | 117.7 | West Germany | 39.5 |
| Netherlands | 94.2 | Dominican Republic | 39.4 |
| Belgian Congo | 88.0 | Thailand | 38.3 |
| Mauritius | 83.6 | Colombia | 38.1 |
| Iceland | 80.4 | Australia | 37.8 |
| Gold Coast [1] | 78.9 | Egypt | 34.6 |
| Ireland | 68.6 | Honduras | 34.4 |
| Ceylon | 65.7 | Guatemala | 33.3 |
| Denmark | 65.5 | Greece | 30.8 |
| New Zealand | 64.5 | Ecuador | 29.5 |
| Union of South Africa | 63.5 | Italy | 26.9 |
| Norway | 63.0 | France | 26.7 |
| Jamaica (1952) | 60.0 | Indonesia (1952) | 26.4 |
| Cuba | 58.5 | Philippines | 24.3 |
| Belgium-Luxembourg | 56.6 | Mexico | 24.0 |
| Peru | 52.0 | Japan | 23.7 |
| Switzerland | 51.6 | Brazil | 20.9 |
| Austria | 51.2 | Turkey | 15.9 |
| Burma | 47.5 | Yugoslavia | 15.0 |
| Finland | 46.7 | Argentina | 13.2 |
| Sweden | 46.4 | Paraguay (1953) | 12.6 |
| United Kingdom | 44.6 | India | 12.5 |
| Canada | 44.1 | United States | 8.2 |
| Israel | 42.5 | | |

[1] Includes export of gold.

Source: United States Statistics of Foreign Trade and National Income.

The survey covers all countries for which more or less comparable statistics have been compiled by the U. N. The problem of converting the respective data into dollars has been eliminated by direct comparison of the original statistics in local currency. As the table shows, colonial areas with a highly specialized economy and areas acting as trading posts for a mother country head the list (Hong Kong, Malaya, Kenya, Belgian Congo, Mauritius, Gold Coast). The group includes also the Netherlands, which has a large reexport traffic; Iceland, which has practically nothing but fisheries to support its population; and Ireland, whose economy is strictly supplementary to that of the United Kingdom.

Next come comparatively small countries, rich and poor, industrial and agricultural. The United Kingdom ranks 24th, West Germany 29th, Italy and France 39th and 40th. And at the bottom of the list are two giants—India and the United States, one of the poorest nations and the richest nation on our planet. The position of the United States in this list—after Brazil, Argentina, and landlocked Paraguay—is one of the greatest paradoxes in the modern world economy.

27. The direction of world trade reveals a clear regional pattern. Four regional markets are of paramount importance.

(1) Western Europe, including the United Kingdom and overseas possessionsof continental European countries.

(2) The Americas.

(3) The Middle East and Southeast Asia, including Japan.

(4) The Soviet bloc.

Almost all countries trade mainly with one of these regions. A few have about equal commercial relations with two regions. The United Kingdom is the only country that distributes trade more or less evenly among three regions. The bulk of the foreign trade of the U. S. S. R. countries under its domination, and mainland China is carried out within the Soviet bloc. (See fig. IV–A.)

On a map of world trade, almost all Africa and the Middle East appear as gravitating to the West European market. This area, indeed, obtains a large part of its import from Western Europe which likewise absorbs a large part of its exports.

The map shows mainland China as attached to the Asian market, to which it seems to belong in accordance with geographic conditions, although currently, as a result of embargoes and other political factors, its trade is oriented toward the U. S. S. R. and its satellites.[2]

28. The geographic pattern of world trade comes into clearer relief when countries are classified by the prevailing direction of their exports on a distorted map of world trade which shows each country on the scale of its exports (fig. IV–B).

---

[2] This classification of China is, of course, open to criticism.

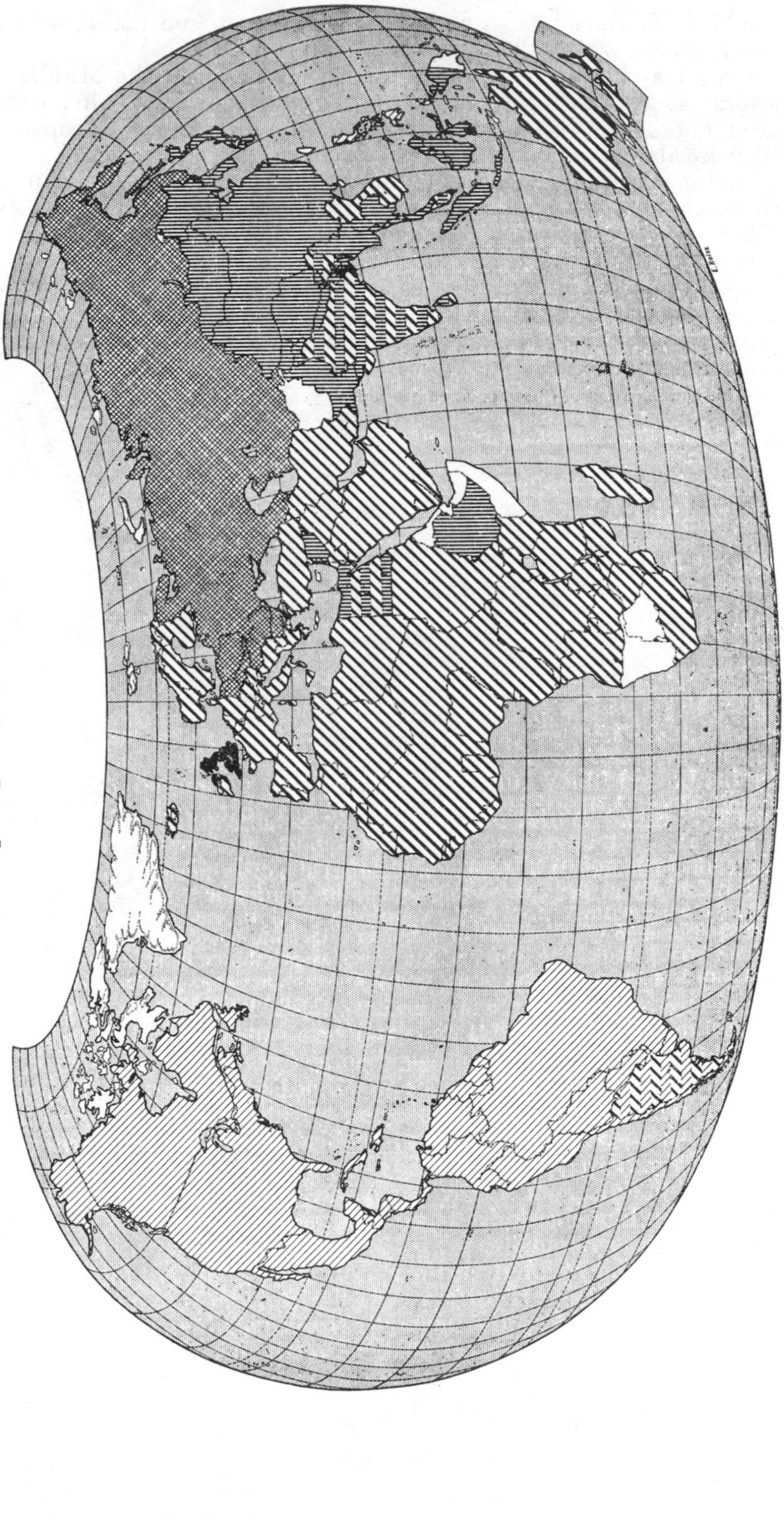

FIGURE IV.—Regional pattern of international trade: Distribution of the world by the orientation of exports from each area to the principal regional markets.

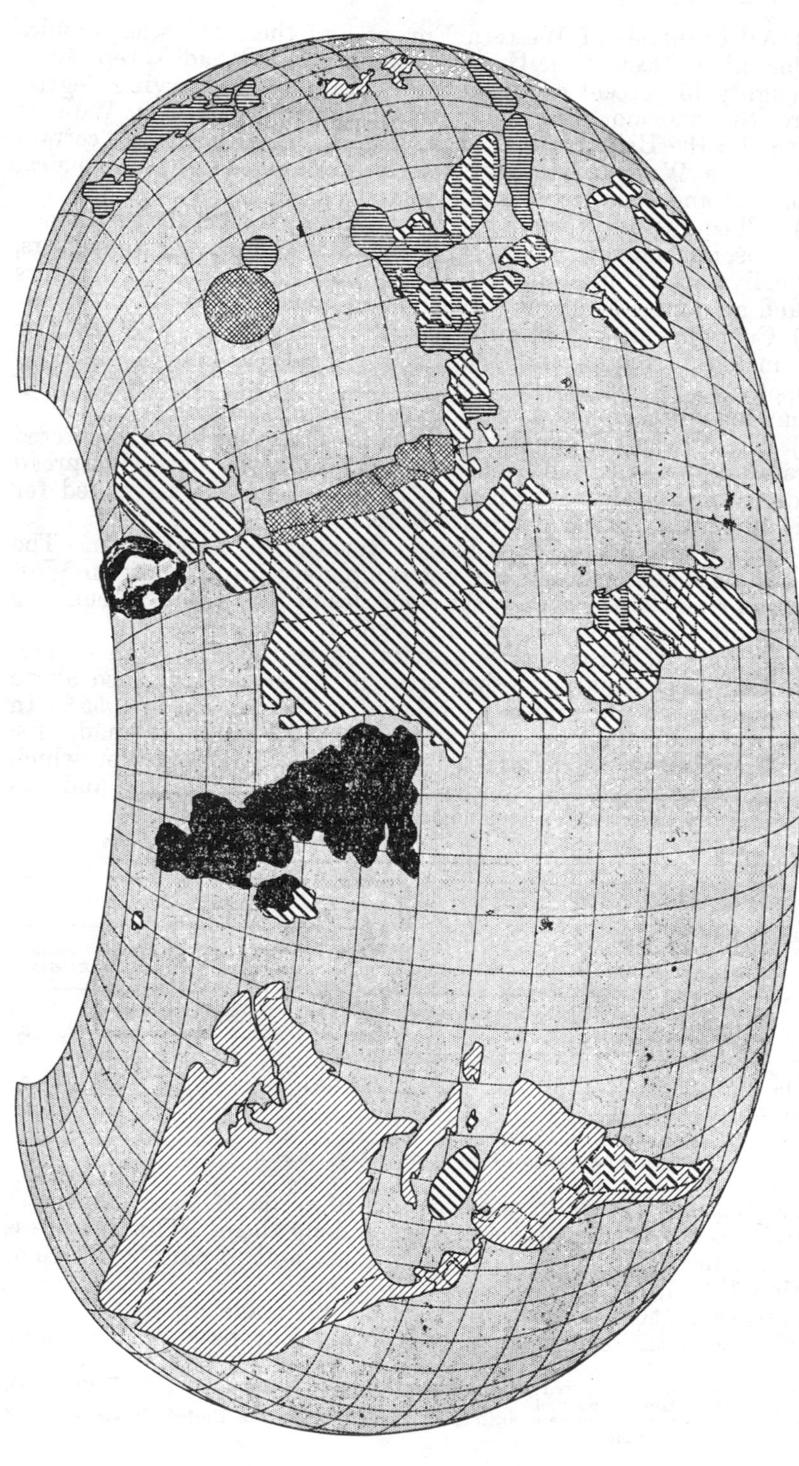

The United Kingdom is distinguished from other countries to show that its foreign trade is widely distributed among all three large regional markets outside the Soviet bloc.

(1) All countries of Western Europe and their overseas colonies and dominions (except the United Kingdom and Canada), representing roughly 45 percent of world trade, gravitate, in varying degree, toward the enormous market that embraces continental Western Europe and the British Isles. This market likewise attracts certain areas in the Western Hemisphere (Netherland Antilles, Jamaica, Argentina) and Asia (among others, India).

(2) All countries of North and South America with the mentioned exceptions, but including Canada, gravitate to the American markets, practically to the United States. This group includes the Philippines also and accounts for about 30 percent of world trade.

(3) Countries of the Middle East, Southeast Asia, and the Far East, including Japan and Indonesia, are either torn between the European and Asian markets or gravitate toward the latter. They account for a little more than 10 percent of world trade.

(4) The United Kingdom, despite the severe setback it has suffered as a result of two wars and the loss of colonies, has the most widespread and diversified trade with all parts of the world. It accounted for nearly 10 percent of world exports in 1956.

(5) The share of the Soviet bloc in world trade is unknown. The respective national markets are not completely insulated from West European trade. Altogether, the countries of this group account for hardly more than 5 percent of world exports.

29. Exports of all countries gravitating to the American market (excluding Argentina and other areas in America mentioned above but including the Philippines) totaled about $28 billion in 1955.[3] In this total, the United States accounted for $15.3 billion; Canada, for $4.3 billion; all other countries, for $8 billion. Exports for which data on destinations were reported[4] totaled about $24 billion and was distributed by source and destinations as follows:

[In billions of dollars]

| To— | From— | | | |
|---|---|---|---|---|
| | Total | United States | Canada | Latin America[1] |
| World | 23.7 | 12.5 | 4.3 | 6.9 |
| United States | 5.9 | ---------- | 2.6 | 3.3 |
| Canada | 2.4 | 2.2 | ---------- | .2 |
| Latin America[1] | 3.9 | 3.2 | .2 | .4 |
| Rest of the world | 11.6 | 7.1 | 1.5 | 3.0 |

[1] Excludes Argentina.

Source: U. N. Yearbook of International Trade Statistics, 1955, pp. 20–21.

The striking feature in the direction of trade of Latin American countries is the small volume of trade among them. This feature is explained in part by geographic conditions, and in part by the composition of their exports.

Contrary to this pattern, intracontinental trade predominates on the European regional market. All in all, Europe and its colonies,

[3] Based on estimates prepared jointly by statistical services of the U. N. World Bank, and International Monetary Fund.

[4] For security reasons, foreign military aid exports from the United States were not distributed by destination.

excluding the sterling area outside the United Kingdom, absorbed exports from continental Western Europe worth $17 billion. Europe's exports to the Western Hemisphere totaled $3.4 billion and those to the overseas sterling area, $1.7 billion; more than $800 million went to the U. S. S. R., its European satellites, and China, and $1.3 billion were distributed in the Middle East and other areas.

The geographic pattern of the foreign trade of the Middle and Far East is somewhat similar to that of European countries in its orientation toward European markets but differs from it in the extent of ties with local Asian markets.

Foreign trade of the United Kingdom is spread all over the world, with a strong emphasis on the members of British Commonwealth and other members of sterling area.

Its exports in 1955 were distributed as follows:

[In millions of United States dollars]

| | | | |
|---|---|---|---|
| Total | 8,468 | Europe and its colonies | 2,515 |
| America | 1,286 | Continental Western Europe | 2,142 |
| | | Other Europe | 233 |
| United States | 559 | Colonies [1] | 140 |
| Canada | 405 | | |
| Latin America | 322 | Middle East | 278 |
| | | Sterling area | 4,063 |
| | | Far East | 135 |
| | | Iron Curtain countries | 164 |
| | | Unknown | 27 |

[1] Excluding U. S. S. R. satellites.

Source: U. N. Yearbook of International Trade Statistics, 1955, pp. 2–25.

The universal character of the British foreign trade is illustrated by figure V, which shows the geographic distribution of imports and exports of the United Kingdom in 1955. (Similar maps for the United States are reproduced in figure VII.)

30. The direction of world trade is closely associated with its composition. As has been mentioned, world trade stems in part from the uneven distribution of natural resources, including soil and sunshine, and in part from the international division of labor. With the progress of science, the latter part has become increasingly important.

The 50 leading commodities, accounting for about two-thirds of world trade, are listed in table 7, with their estimated value in 1954 exports.

Many countries import and export goods which are registered under the same title in foreign-trade statistics but differ in quality and design. The United States, for example, reports petroleum products, machinery, fabrics, metals, tobacco, road motor vehicles, and many other articles in both imports and exports.

FIGURE V.—Foreign trade of the United Kingdom, 1955.

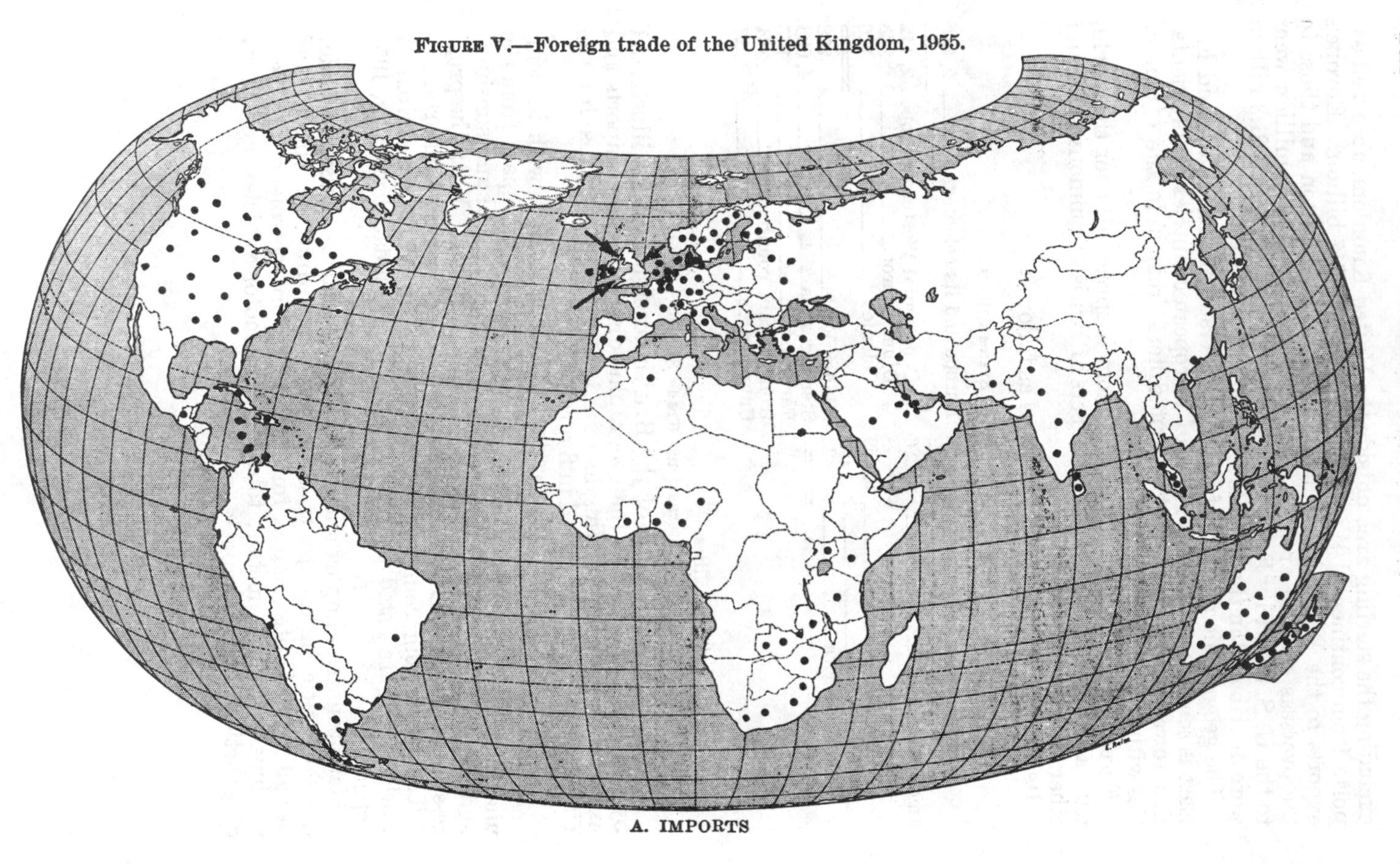

B. EXPORTS

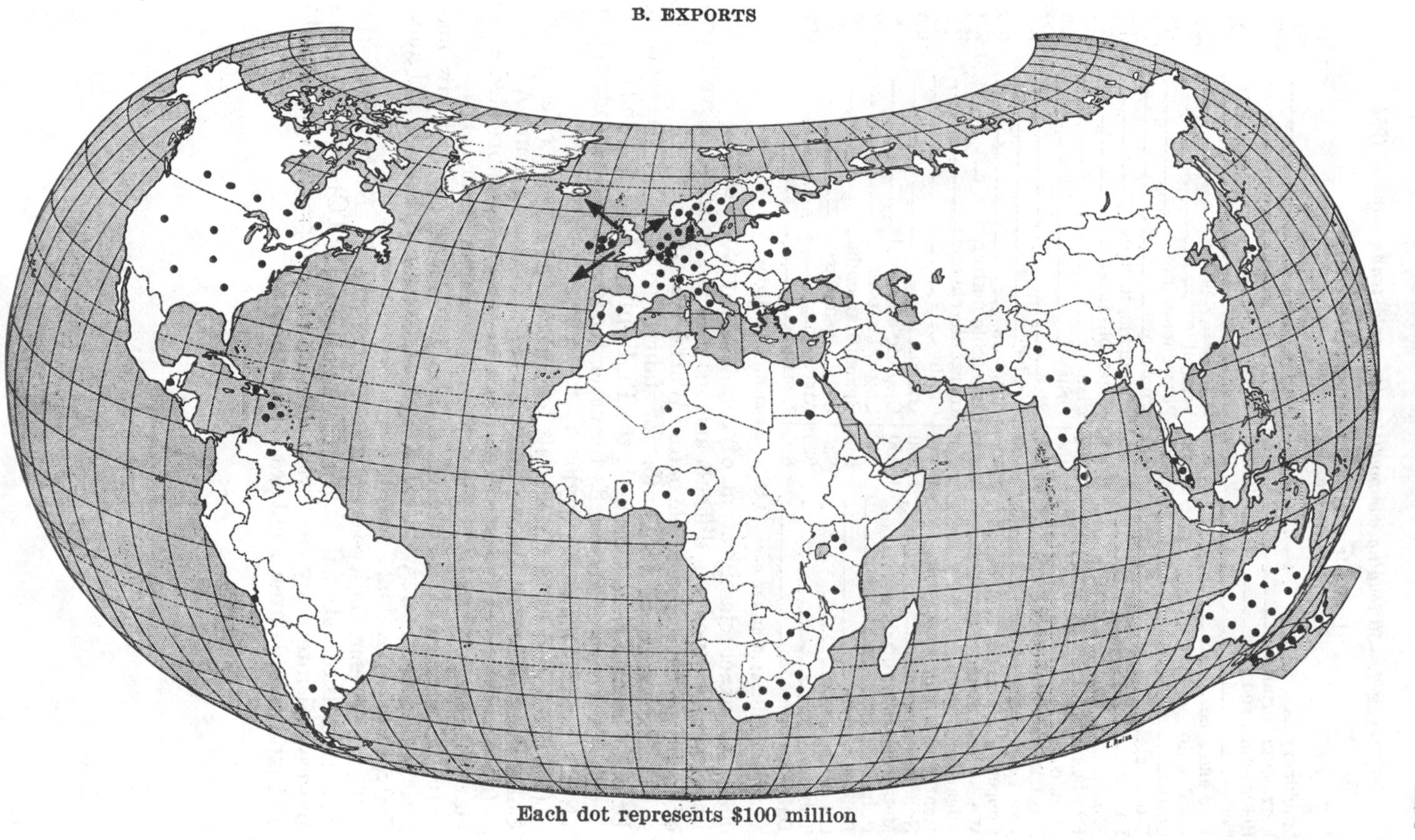

Each dot represents $100 million

TABLE 7.—*50 leading commodities in world trade import, 1954*

[Value in millions of United States dollars]

| | *Value* | | *Value* |
|---|---|---|---|
| Machinery | 3, 275 | Cocoa | 700 |
| Petroleum, crude | 2, 800 | Yarn | 625 |
| Petroleum products | 2, 775 | Beverages | 625 |
| Coffee | 2, 750 | Tea | 600 |
| Iron and steel | 2, 300 | Minerals, crude | 600 |
| Road motor vehicles | 2, 150 | Vegetables | 575 |
| Cotton | 2, 120 | Power machines | 575 |
| Wool | 2, 000 | Iron ore | 550 |
| Fabrics | 1, 950 | Chemicals, n. e. c | 550 |
| Wood | 1, 575 | Vegetable fats | 525 |
| Fruits, nuts | 1, 500 | Fish | 525 |
| Coal, coke | 1, 460 | Drugs | 525 |
| Electric machinery | 1, 460 | Rice | 500 |
| Paper and paperboard | 1, 450 | Fodder | 450 |
| Copper | 1, 400 | Tractors | 450 |
| Wheat and flour | 1, 350 | Vegetable matter, n. e. c | 425 |
| Sugar and prep. | 1, 225 | Inorganic chemical | 420 |
| Meat, fresh and preserved | 1, 100 | Clothes | 420 |
| Nonferrous ores | 1, 000 | Hides | 400 |
| Metal, manufactured | 1, 000 | Organic chemicals | 400 |
| Pulp | 950 | Ships, boats | 400 |
| Rubber, crude | 940 | Gems, diamonds | 400 |
| Oil seeds, crude | 925 | Soap, cosmetics | 375 |
| Tobacco | 820 | Aircraft | 360 |
| Dairy products | 800 | Instruments | 360 |

Source: Estimated on the basis of U. N. commodity statistics.

31. An exact classification of countries by composition of their imports and exports is difficult and may be misleading. Five types of exchange were discernible before World War II.

(1) Exchange of foodstuffs for fabricated articles (Argentina, Brazil, Cuba; Spain, Portugal; the Philippines, New Zealand).

(2) Exchange of foodstuffs for other foodstuffs and raw materials (Netherlands, Denmark; Ceylon).

(3) Exchange of raw materials for fabricated articles (Venezuela, Chile, Peru; Norway, India; Belgian Congo, Union of South Africa).

(4) Exchange of foodstuffs and raw materials for fabricated articles (Canada, Australia; China, Korea; Morocco, Tunisia).

(5) Exchange of fabricated articles for foodstuffs and raw materials (United States, United Kingdom, Germany, France, Belgium, Italy, Czechoslovakia, Japan).

The new commodity-trade statistics of the U. N. based on the Standard International Trade Classification (SITC) provide more precise and internally consistent data on the composition of imports and exports in 2 dozen countries. (See table 8.)

**TABLE 8.—*Foreign trade of selected countries classified by major groups of commodities (SITC), 1955***

[Millions of United States dollars]

A. IMPORTS

| Importing country | Total trade | Food, beverages, tobacco | Crude materials | Mineral fuels, lubricants, etc. | Oils, fats | Chemicals | Machinery, transport equipment | Other manufactured goods |
|---|---|---|---|---|---|---|---|---|
| United States of America | 11,334 | 3,176 | 2,841 | 1,041 | 89 | 347 | 447 | 3,129 |
| Canada | 4,774 | 466 | 423 | 496 | 29 | 276 | 1,584 | 1,290 |
| El Salvador | 92 | 15 | 2 | 6 | 1 | 12 | 21 | 36 |
| Netherlands Antilles | 830 | 24 | 2 | 732 | 1 | 19 | 16 | 37 |
| United Kingdom | 10,881 | 4,042 | 2,987 | 1,147 | 159 | 314 | 405 | 1,785 |
| Austria | 887 | 178 | 137 | 115 | 18 | 57 | 195 | 187 |
| Belgium-Luxembourg | 2,844 | 424 | 654 | 290 | 39 | 155 | 460 | 799 |
| Denmark | 1,173 | 210 | 126 | 222 | 10 | 82 | 171 | 345 |
| Finland | 769 | 153 | 72 | 95 | 10 | 58 | 178 | 205 |
| France | 4,688 | 1,081 | 1,341 | 837 | 92 | 183 | 490 | 661 |
| Germany, Western | 5,793 | 1,544 | 1,845 | 507 | 160 | 177 | 269 | 1,292 |
| Ireland | 572 | 118 | 56 | 78 | 5 | 36 | 109 | 139 |
| Netherlands | 3,208 | 484 | 545 | 455 | 60 | 154 | 570 | 907 |
| Norway | 1,089 | 139 | 98 | 109 | 12 | 48 | 369 | 315 |
| Sweden | 1,992 | 294 | 181 | 346 | 16 | 127 | 408 | 620 |
| Greece | 382 | 79 | 46 | 52 | 2 | 32 | 80 | 91 |
| Italy | 2,705 | 451 | 780 | 532 | 61 | 141 | 299 | 441 |
| Portugal | 398 | 45 | 74 | 49 | 3 | 33 | 101 | 94 |
| Turkey | 498 | 42 | 32 | 42 | 5 | 35 | 175 | 167 |
| Yugoslavia | 441 | 122 | 77 | 36 | 5 | 29 | 112 | 58 |
| Japan | 2,470 | 625 | 1,226 | 289 | 36 | 80 | 132 | 80 |
| Malaya X | 1,249 | 315 | 275 | 226 | 3 | 49 | 99 | 260 |
| Gold Coast | 246 | 50 | 1 | 15 | -------- | 15 | 42 | 118 |
| Nigeria | 380 | 50 | 5 | 18 | -------- | 20 | 78 | 203 |

B. EXPORTS

| Exporting country | Food, beverages, tobacco | Crude materials | Mineral fuels, lubricants, etc. | Oils, fats | Chemicals | Machinery, transport equipment | Other manufactured goods |
|---|---|---|---|---|---|---|---|
| United States of America | 2,103 | 1,562 | 1,132 | 246 | 1,121 | 5,394 | 3,488 |
| Canada | 901 | 1,342 | 59 | 11 | 246 | 284 | 1,538 |
| El Salvador | 94 | 10 | -------- | 1 | -------- | -------- | 1 |
| Netherland Antilles | -------- | 3 | 791 | -------- | 6 | 1 | 2 |
| United Kingdom | 482 | 282 | 396 | 30 | 652 | 3,033 | 3,000 |
| Austria | 12 | 193 | 15 | -------- | 30 | 90 | 359 |
| Belgium-Luxembourg | 104 | 203 | 187 | 22 | 187 | 310 | 1,725 |
| Denmark | 694 | 51 | 2 | 9 | 26 | 159 | 94 |
| Finland | 12 | 425 | -------- | 1 | 2 | 96 | 252 |
| France | 747 | 420 | 387 | 14 | 360 | 786 | 1,930 |
| Germany, Western | 147 | 176 | 532 | 27 | 680 | 2,457 | 2,113 |
| Ireland | 203 | 23 | -------- | 1 | 1 | 8 | 22 |
| Netherlands | 838 | 188 | 304 | 34 | 193 | 416 | 691 |
| Norway | 136 | 140 | 2 | 34 | 57 | 45 | 221 |
| Sweden | 49 | 755 | 1 | 9 | 45 | 380 | 485 |
| Greece | 121 | 42 | -------- | 6 | 6 | 1 | 7 |
| Italy | 412 | 123 | 166 | 7 | 127 | 371 | 650 |
| Portugal | 81 | 67 | 8 | 9 | 14 | 6 | 99 |
| Turkey | 196 | 103 | -------- | 1 | 3 | -------- | 11 |
| Yugoslavia | 80 | 75 | 3 | -------- | 14 | 5 | 78 |
| Japan | 136 | 98 | 7 | 18 | 94 | 247 | 1,403 |
| Malaya X | 95 | 811 | 126 | 35 | 13 | 21 | 209 |
| Gold Coast | 185 | 41 | -------- | -------- | -------- | -------- | 16 |
| Nigeria | 86 | 224 | 1 | 46 | -------- | -------- | 3 |

Table 8 suggests that the pattern of exchange of raw materials and foodstuffs for machinery and other fabricated goods or vice versa prevails in Greece, Turkey, El Salvador, Malaya, Gold Coast, and

Nigeria on the one hand, and the United Kingdom, Germany, and Japan, on the other.

The United States, Belgium, and France trade machinery and fabricated goods for other fabricated goods, foodstuffs, and raw materials. Canada, Austria, the Netherlands, Sweden, and Norway trade fabricated goods and foodstuffs or raw materials for other fabricated goods, foodstuffs, and raw materials. Denmark and Ireland export foodstuffs in exchange for other foodstuffs, raw materials (fuels), and fabricated goods. Finland exports raw materials (timber) and imports practically all other commodities. Italy exports manufactured goods and foodstuffs and imports raw materials and fuels. Portugal and Yugoslavia pay for manufactured goods with foodstuffs, raw materials, and manufactured goods.

32. Perhaps most significant is the classification of countries by the net balance of imports and exports of fabricated goods.

Before World War II, there were 10 countries with a net export balance in fabricated goods: the United States, United Kingdom, France, Belgium, Germany, Switzerland, Austria, Czechoslovakia, Italy, and Japan.

A similar computation for the postwar world is very difficult in view of the lack of information on the Iron Curtain countries.

Using prewar data, the countries with export balance in manufactured goods appear, on the conventional world map, as three islands in the ocean. (See fig. VI, A.) They look more impressive on the distorted map of world population (fig. VI, B).

When the same classification is applied to a distorted map of world trade, that shows each country on the scale of its exports in 1952, it appears that the 10 countries with net exports of fabricated goods account for the bulk of world trade (fig. VI, C). A large part of their foreign trade is carried out among themselves on the basis of a more or less voluntary division of labor.

The space and purpose of this paper do not permit a detailed analysis of balances of payment of different regions and individual countries and their foreign-trade policy. The facts and figures presented here may serve as a foundation for the following observations about the particular position of the United States in world trade.

FIGURE VI.—Countries with net export of manufactured goods.

A. CONVENTIONAL WORLD MAP

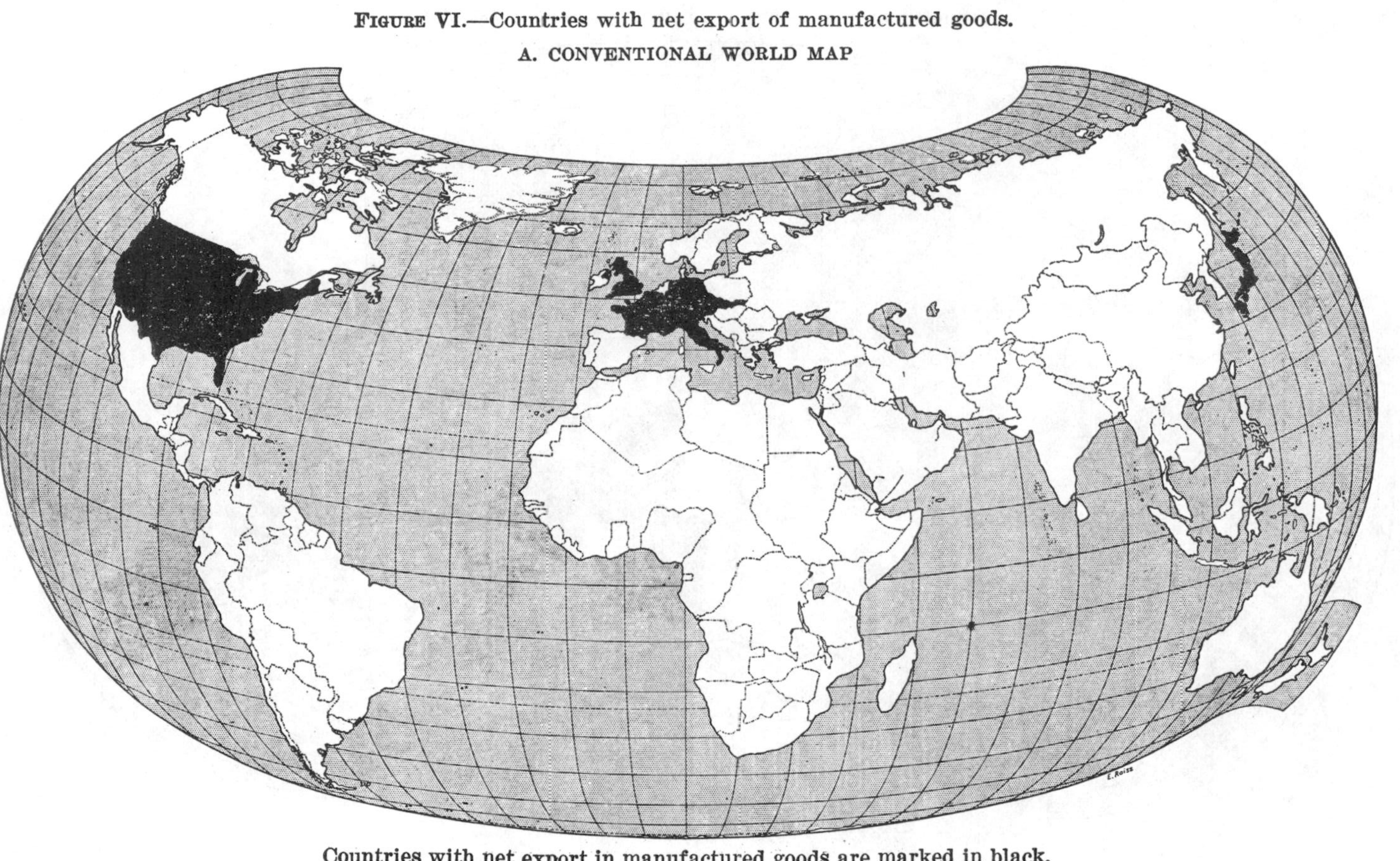

Countries with net export in manufactured goods are marked in black.

B. DISTORTED MAP OF WORLD INCOME

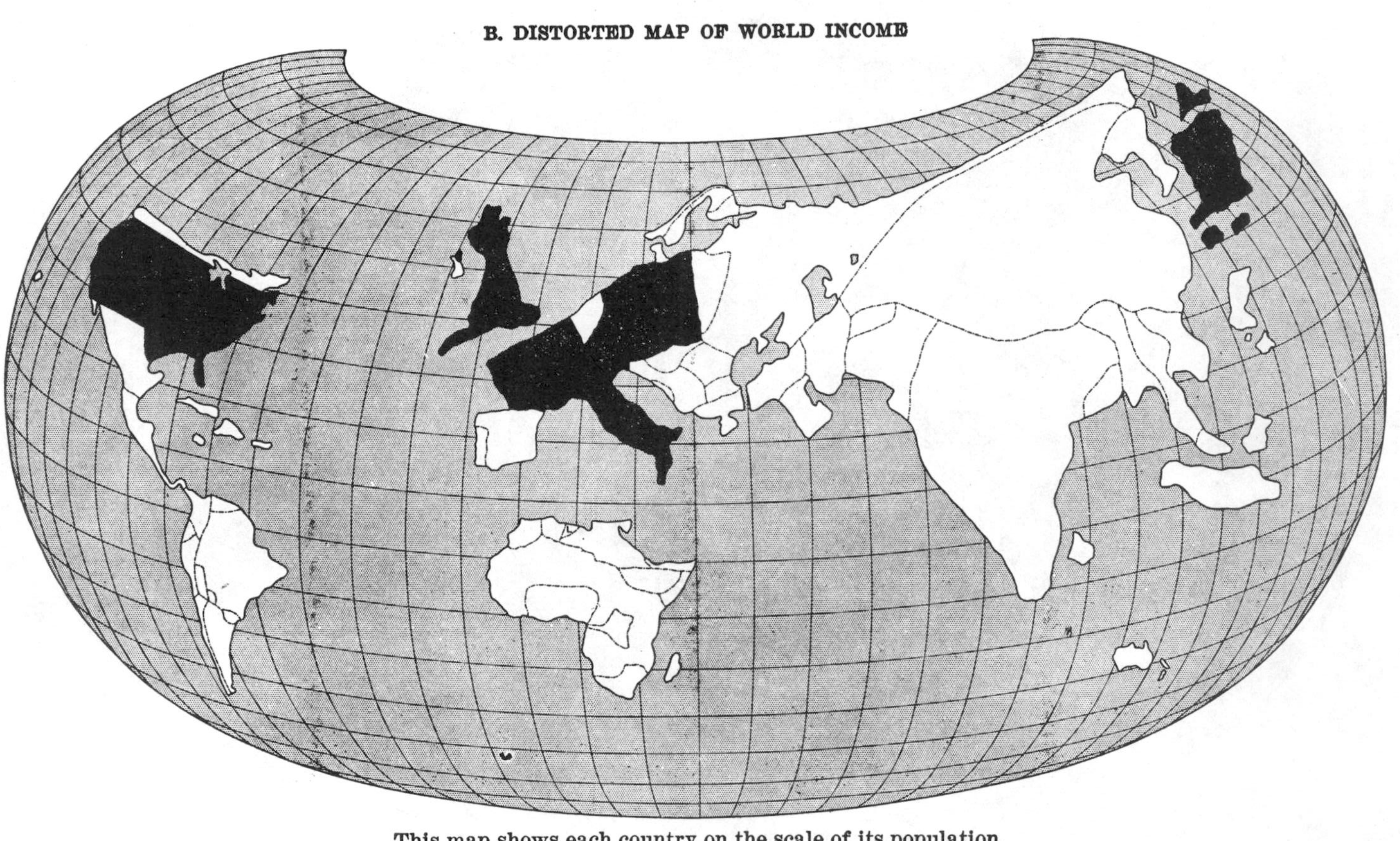

This map shows each country on the scale of its population.

C. DISTORTED MAP OF WORLD TRADE

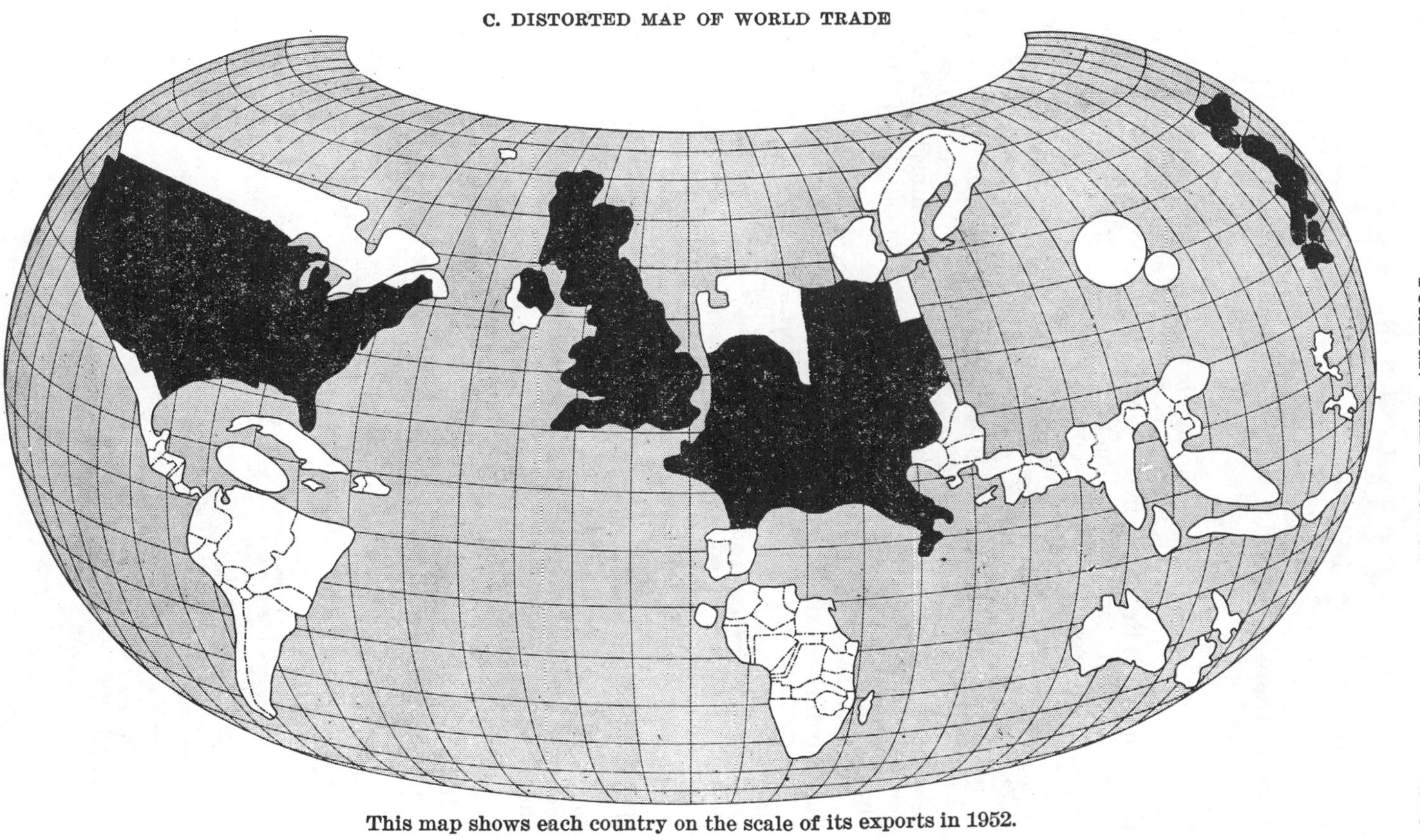

This map shows each country on the scale of its exports in 1952.

## III. UNITED STATES POSITION IN WORLD TRADE

33. The preceding survey of world trade shows the exceptional position of the United States.

(*a*) This country is the largest exporter and importer in the world. From its traditional position as the second greatest commercial power, after the United Kingdom, it moved to the top place after World War II.

(*b*) Its per capita value of foreign trade is comparatively low, however (see table 5), and its ratio of value of imports and exports to national income is the lowest in the world. (See table 6.)

(*c*) It dominates American markets as both a seller and buyer but is a second-rate customer in European markets.

(*d*) Like other industrial countries, the United States has a net export of machinery and other fabricated goods and a net import of foodstuffs and raw materials. But its net balance in imports of foodstuffs is negligible and unstable and the value of its imports of mineral fuels (mainly crude petroleum) about equals that of its exports of petroleum products. It has a huge net export in machinery and transportation equipment, and a small net export in chemicals and other manufactured goods.

(*e*) It is the only industrial country of the world with a continuous huge surplus of exports over imports. (See table 4.)

The combination of these features determines not only the exceptional position of the United States in world trade, but also the unique setting for its foreign-trade policy.

34. The United States ranks fourth in the world in size of population—after China, India, and the U. S. S. R.—and represents the world's largest aggregation of consumer purchasing power. It accounts, indeed, for about 40 percent of world income.[5]

While the share of the United States in world output and consumption varies from item to item, its overall share in the monetized world economy, both as producer and consumer, is at least as large as its share in world income and probably larger. In comparison with this ratio, its share in world exports (about 13 percent) and world imports (about 10 percent) is strikingly small.

This situation is explained, of course, by the high degree of self-sufficiency of the United States economy. Since its regional division of labor replaces the intracontinental foreign trade of European countries, its foreign trade is comparable with the trade of Western Europe with the rest of the world (excluding its trade with the United

---

[5] The rate is somewhat lower—probably 35 percent—if services are excluded and the comparison is limited to incomes spent for goods. It is considerably above 40 percent if outlays on food are likewise excluded and only outlays for manufactured goods are taken into consideration. The United States consumes 34 percent of all energy used in the world, including the U. S. S. R. (in terms of coal equivalent), and more than 40 percent of all electric energy. It absorbs one-sixth of the world output of wool, nearly one-third of that of cotton, more than half of the rubber output (natural and synthetic combined). It accounts for 43 percent of world consumption of steel (including the U. S. S. R.), 48 percent of the copper, 50 percent of the zinc and iron ore, 65 percent of the petroleum. It absorbs about 30 percent of the world output of phosphatic, nitrogeneous, and potash fertilizers, and accounts for about 70 percent of world production of passenger and commercial cars and for 55 percent of the radio sets.

It also consumes 17 percent of the world output of sugar, 40 percent of the coffee, 27 percent of the cacao, 13 percent of the bananas, and absorbs the lion's share of exports of the last 3 commodities.

Kingdom). For such a comparison, exports and imports of Western Europe should be classified as follows:

| Trade with— | Value, in millions of dollars, 1956 | |
|---|---|---|
| | Exports to Western Europe | Exports from Western Europe |
| World | 28,871 | 26,977 |
| Western Europe | 13,392 | 13,392 |
| United Kingdom | 2,390 | 2,273 |
| Other areas | 13,089 | 11,312 |

Source: U. N. Monthly Bulletin of Statistics, June 1957.

In the U. N. classification, continental Western Europe includes 13 countries with total population of about 250 million. Their per capita exports to other areas (excluding exports to the United Kingdom) appears close to $45; the respective rate of their import from these areas is about $52. Both rates are appreciably lower tahn those for the United States: $75 and $112 in 1956 (see table 5). United States foreign trade appears disproportionally small in relation to its income; but not in relation to its population, if its interregional division of labor is kept in mind.

35. The low ratio of the value of foreign trade to national income in the United States is obviously due to the diversity of climatic conditions and natural resources and the exceptional diversification of production, largely based on regional specialization.

This ratio has been declining since the middle of the 19th century. Apart from wide fluctuations during both World Wars and the Great Depression, it has changed as follows:

[Percent]

| | 1800 | 1850 | 1900 | 1950 | 1954 | 1955 | 1956 |
|---|---|---|---|---|---|---|---|
| Imports | 10.2 | 5.9 | 9.0 | 4.3 | 3.4 | 3.6 | 3.7 |
| Exports | 13.1 | 7.1 | 5.5 | 3.7 | 5.0 | 4.8 | 5.1 |

Source: W. S. and E. S. Woytinsky, World Commerce and Governments, 1955, p. 62; U. N. Monthly Bulletin of Statistics, May 1957.

The share of imported manufactured goods in the domestic consumption in this country is even lower than the ratio of the value of imports to national income.

In 1955, the United States imported manufactured articles worth $3,576 million—about 2 percent of total domestic consumption of finished goods.

36. The geographic pattern of United States trade is illustrated by Figure VII which shows the distribution of its imports by source and its exports by destination in 1955. Both distributions fluctuate from year to year, but the general pattern—except for convulsions caused by two world wars and the great depression—is fairly stable.

FIGURE VII.—Foreign trade of the United States, 1955

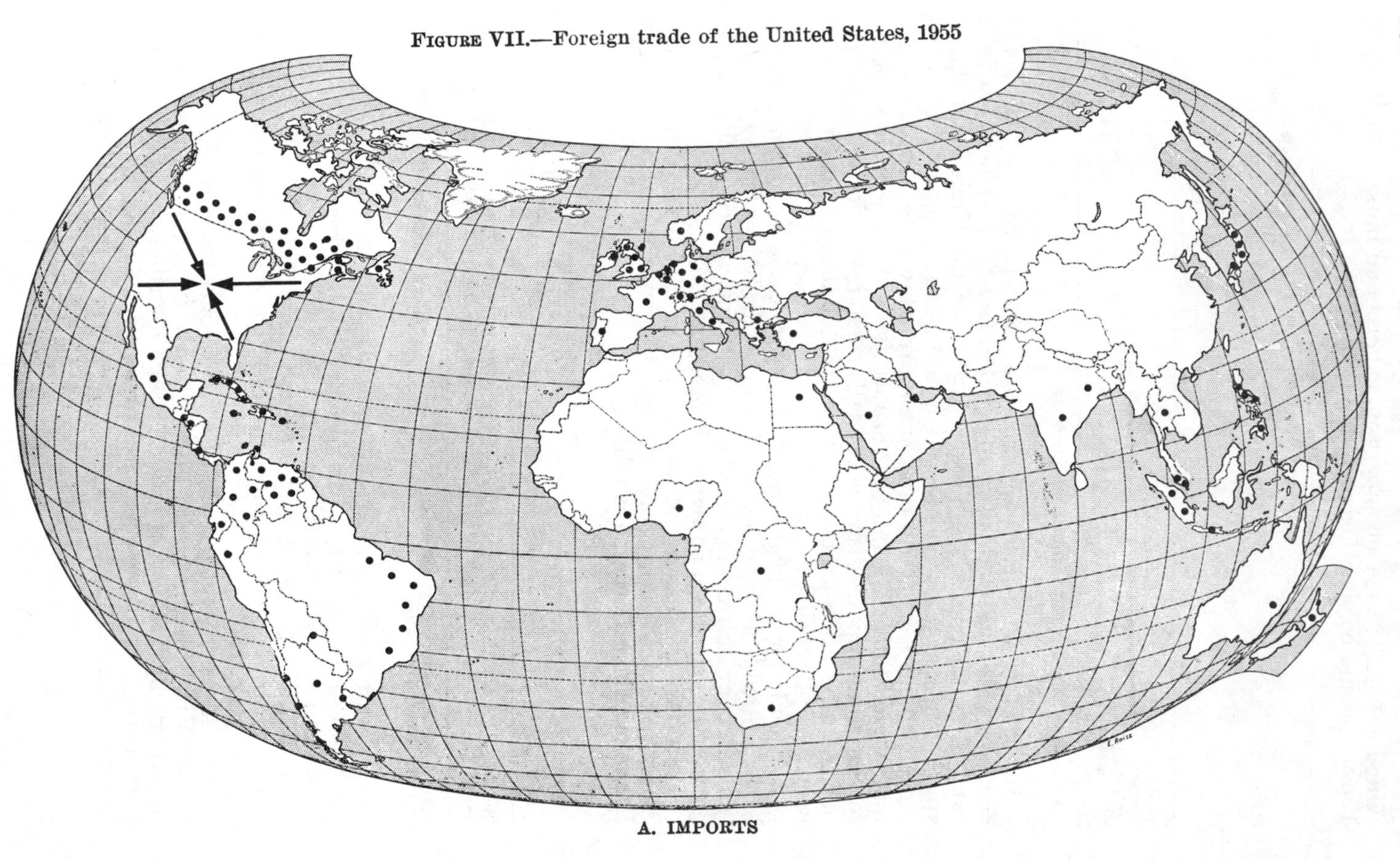

B. EXPORTS

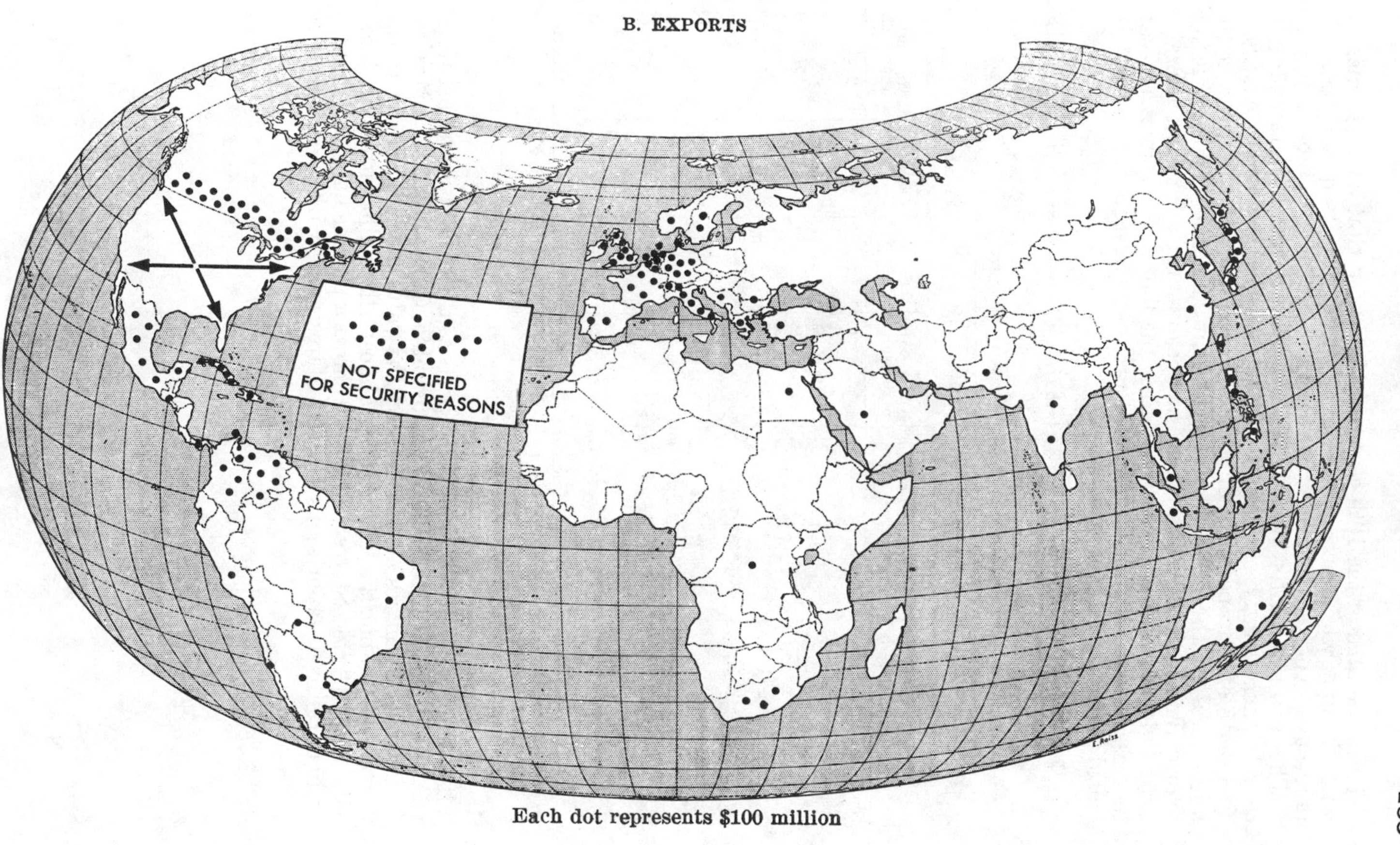


Each dot represents $100 million

Until the turn of the 19th century the United States traded mainly with Europe, which accounted for 52 percent of its imports and 78 percent of exports in the average for 1891–1900. (See table 9.)

The turn came after World War I, when the United States began to rely increasingly on imports from Canada and Latin America. The share of Europe in its imports shrank although European countries remained the main markets for United States exports. After World War II the significance of European markets for United States export declined further and that of Canadian and Latin American increased, conforming with the general trend toward regionalism in world trade.

TABLE 9.—*Trend in the geographic distribution of United States foreign trade, 1871–80 to 1955*

[Percentage distribution of imports and exports [1]]

| Period or year | Imports from— | | | Exports to— | | |
|---|---|---|---|---|---|---|
| | Other America | Europe | Other parts of the world | Other America | Europe | Other parts of the world |
| Average: | | | | | | |
| 1871–80 | 35 | 53 | 12 | 15 | 82 | 3 |
| 1881–90 | 32 | 56 | 12 | 15 | 80 | 5 |
| 1891–1900 | 32 | 52 | 16 | 16 | 78 | 6 |
| 1901–10 | 31 | 51 | 18 | 21 | 70 | 9 |
| 1911–15 | 35 | 47 | 18 | 27 | 64 | 9 |
| 1915–20 [2] | 48 | 20 | 32 | 25 | 63 | 12 |
| 1921–25 | 39 | 30 | 31 | 31 | 53 | 16 |
| 1926–30 | 37 | 30 | 33 | 35 | 47 | 18 |
| 1931–35 | 40 | 30 | 30 | 30 | 47 | 23 |
| 1936–40 | 39 | 25 | 36 | 35 | 41 | 24 |
| 1941–45 | 67 | 8 | 25 | 24 | 56 | 20 |
| 1946–50 | 58 | 15 | 17 | 42 | 35 | 23 |
| 1951 | 53 | 19 | 29 | 47 | 30 | 23 |
| 1952 | 56 | 19 | 25 | 50 | 27 | 23 |
| 1953 | 56 | 21 | 23 | 52 | 25 | 23 |
| 1954 | 58 | 20 | 22 | 50 | 28 | 22 |
| 1955 | 55 | 22 | 23 | 48 | 30 | 22 |

[1] For 1950–55 excludes exports not distributed by destination for security reason (cf. fig. IX–B).
[2] Period from July 1, 1915, to Dec. 31, 1920.

Source: Computed from Statistical Abstract for the United States, 1956, p. 911.

The countries with the largest imports to the United States are Canada, Brazil, the United Kingdom, Colombia, Cuba, Japan, and Mexico. In table 10, countries are arrayed by the value of their import to the United States, but the list includes almost all significant export markets of the United States. Table 10 shows a passive balance (surplus of imports over exports) in United States trade with such countries as Brazil, Colombia, Malaya, India, Netherlands, Antilles, Indonesia, Chile, Belgian Congo, Thailand, Kuwait, Guatemala, Dominican Republic, El Salvador, Gold Coast, Ecuador—all comparatively underdeveloped countries exporting raw materials and foodstuffs. France, with which the United States had an import balance in 1955, usually imports from the United States more than it exports to this country. A considerable surplus of exports over imports is typical of the trade of the United States with economically developed nations.

TABLE 10.—*Source of imports and destination of exports of the United States, 1955*

[In millions of dollars]

| Country of provenance or destination. | Imports from— | Exports to— | Surplus of imports (−) or exports (+) | Country of provenance or destination | Imports from— | Exports to— | Surplus of imports (−) or exports (+) |
|---|---|---|---|---|---|---|---|
| Canada | 2,646 | 3,134 | +488 | Australia | 126 | 201 | +75 |
| Brazil | 630 | 240 | −390 | Belgian Congo | 108 | 53 | −55 |
| United Kingdom | 615 | 915 | +300 | Thailand | 104 | 50 | −54 |
| Colombia | 442 | 328 | −114 | Peru | 103 | 120 | +17 |
| Cuba | 417 | 450 | +33 | Kawait | 95 | 16 | −79 |
| Japan | 416 | 642 | +226 | Union of South Africa | 87 | 260 | +173 |
| Mexico | 392 | 697 | +305 | Sweden | 85 | 161 | +76 |
| Western Germany | 362 | 587 | +225 | Guatemala | 71 | 56 | −15 |
| Philippines | 252 | 338 | +86 | Turkey | 62 | | |
| Belgium-Luxembourg | 244 | 312 | +68 | Dominican Republic | 62 | 60 | −2 |
| Malaya | 234 | 35 | −199 | El Salvador | 62 | 47 | −15 |
| India | 224 | 187 | −37 | Norway | 62 | 75 | +13 |
| Netherlands Antilles | 220 | 56 | −164 | Spain | 59 | 153 | +94 |
| Indonesia | 212 | 75 | −137 | Denmark | 58 | 68 | +10 |
| Chile | 202 | 90 | −112 | Saudi Arabia | 56 | 69 | +13 |
| France | 200 | 357 | +157 | Gold Coast | 55 | 7 | −48 |
| Italy | 177 | 354 | +177 | Ecuador | 53 | 46 | −7 |
| Netherlands | 148 | 472 | +324 | Finland | 44 | 40 | −4 |
| Switzerland | 147 | 161 | +14 | New Zealand | 43 | 52 | +9 |
| Argentina | 127 | 148 | +21 | Liberia | 40 | 21 | −19 |

Source: U. N. Yearbook of International Trade, 1955, p. 701.

37. As mentioned, the United States plays a secondary role as seller and buyer on the markets of Europe and Asia (except Taiwan, Korea, the Philippines, and Japan) but dominates the markets of the Western Hemisphere. Its role in some minor markets of this hemisphere amounts to almost monopolistic control. (See table 11.) It accounts for half or more than half of the imports of 13 American countries (with Canada close to the head of the list) and absorbs likewise half or more than half the exports of 13 such countries.

TABLE 11.—*United States share in imports and exports of selected countries, 1955*

| Country | Imports | Exports | Country | Imports | Exports |
|---|---|---|---|---|---|
| Mexico | 76 | 74 | Angola | 16 | 18 |
| Cuba | 75 | 68 | Indonesia | 16 | 16 |
| Canada | 73 | 60 | Italy | 15 | 9 |
| Honduras | 69 | 79 | Ethiopia | 14 | 24 |
| Haiti | 66 | 50 | Argentina | 14 | 14 |
| Dominican Republic | 66 | 60 | Netherlands | 14 | 6 |
| Philippines | 65 | 55 | Iraq | 14 | 4 |
| Nicaragua | 65 | 46 | Lebanon | 13 | 10 |
| Guatemala | 64 | 74 | Germany | 13 | 6 |
| Colombia | 63 | 74 | Switzerland | 13 | 12 |
| Panama | 62 | 93 | India | 13 | 14 |
| Liberia | 62 | 87 | Egypt | 12 | 7 |
| Costa Rica | 60 | 54 | Australia | 12 | 7 |
| Venezuela | 59 | 38 | Belgium-Luxembourg | 11 | 9 |
| El Salvador | 57 | 64 | United Kingdom | 11 | 7 |
| Ecuador | 52 | 61 | Austria | 11 | 5 |
| Paraguay | 50 | 34 | Syria | 11 | 5 |
| Taiwan | 47 | 4 | Portugal | 10 | 11 |
| Chile | 41 | 46 | Sweden | 10 | 5 |
| Bolivia | 38 | 59 | France | 10 | 4 |
| Korea | 35 | 42 | Jordan | 10 | -------- |
| Japan | 31 | 23 | Pakistan | 9 | 8 |
| Israel | 29 | 19 | Hong Kong | 9 | 4 |
| Brazil | 24 | 42 | Morocco | 9 | 4 |
| Iran | 24 | 9 | Ireland | 9 | 3 |
| Turkey | 22 | 16 | Trinidad | 9 | 3 |
| Union of South Africa | 21 | 8 | Norway | 9 | 9 |
| Jamaica | 20 | 16 | New Zealand | 9 | 6 |
| Thailand | 20 | 7 | Denmark | 8 | 7 |
| Belgian Congo | 19 | 17 | Netherlands Antilles | 8 | 26 |
| Uruguay | 19 | 9 | Finland | 6 | 6 |
| Greece | 18 | 13 | Gold Coast | 4 | 20 |
| Spain | 18 | 18 | Tunisia | 2 | 2 |

Source: Computed from U. N. Yearbook of International Trade Statistics, 1955, passim.

The striking feature of the United States position in foreign markets is that it absorbs only 7 percent of the exports from the United Kingdom, Denmark, and Australia, 6 percent from Germany, the Netherlands, Finland, and New Zealand, 5 percent from Austria and Sweden, 4 percent from France, and 3 percent from Ireland (fig. VIII).

38. The difference in the geographic distribution of United States imports and exports is determined largely by the composition of its foreign trade. (See table 12.) This country gets sawmill products, paper pulp and paper from Canada, coffee from Brazil, crude petroleum from Venezuela, cane sugar and southern fruits from the Caribbeans, tin from Peru, all in exchange for its fabricated goods. The bulk of its foreign trade is based on the complementary character of resources in different areas of the Western Hemisphere rather than the voluntary division of labor, which is the foundation of its regional economy and intracontinental trade in Europe.

TABLE 12.—*Leading import and export commodities, by provenance and destination, 1955*

[In millions of dollars]

| Commodity | Imports | | | |
|---|---|---|---|---|
| | Total | From America | From Western Europe | From other areas |
| Total | 11,334 | 5,963 | 2,385 | 2,957 |
| Agricultural: | | | | |
| Coffee | 1,356 | 1,228 | ---------- | 127 |
| Cacao | 185 | 94 | 1 | 90 |
| Cane sugar | 414 | 305 | ---------- | 109 |
| Other foodstuffs | 945 | 422 | 307 | 217 |
| Crude rubber | 440 | 1 | ---------- | 440 |
| Wool | 261 | 73 | 16 | 171 |
| Nonagricultural: | | | | |
| Machinery and vehicles [1] | 438 | 127 | 286 | 18 |
| Chemicals | 255 | 120 | 112 | 22 |
| Textile manufactures [1] | 586 | 38 | 300 | 237 |
| Iron and steel mill products | 151 | 37 | 99 | 15 |
| Petroleum and products | 1,032 | 599 | ---------- | 433 |
| Nonferrous metals | 1,527 | 820 | 253 | 450 |
| Paper and manufactures | 984 | 899 | 82 | 8 |
| Sawmill products | 323 | 303 | ---------- | 19 |
| Other [1] | 2,436 | 867 | 876 | 628 |

| Commodity | Exports | | | |
|---|---|---|---|---|
| | Total | To America | To Western Europe | To other areas |
| Total | 13,607 | 6,358 | 4,147 | 3,102 |
| Agricultural: | | | | |
| Grains | 940 | 136 | 537 | 268 |
| Fats and oils | 533 | 117 | 293 | 124 |
| Other foodstuffs | 808 | 342 | 272 | 194 |
| Cotton | 477 | 44 | 239 | 194 |
| Tobacco and manufacture | 418 | 25 | 269 | 125 |
| Nonagricultural: | | | | |
| Machinery and vehicles | 4,048 | 2,456 | 64 | 922 |
| Chemicals | 1,075 | 574 | 268 | 234 |
| Textile manufactures | 626 | 300 | 99 | 228 |
| Iron and steel mill products | 815 | 338 | 341 | 136 |
| Petroleum and products | 440 | 237 | 100 | 102 |
| Coal | 495 | 200 | 259 | 36 |
| Copper | 220 | 26 | 179 | 15 |
| Other | 2,713 | 1,565 | 623 | 525 |

[1] Includes small entries not distributed by area.

Source: Statistical Abstract of the United States, 1956, p. 913.

39. Many attempts have been made to explain why some industries in the United States are able to meet any competition on the world market and others are scared of competition of foreign products in the domestic market and can operate only behind the wall of protective tariffs.

The testimony of Prof. Irving B. Kravis before the subcommittee has shown that there is no meaningful difference in wage rates in exporting industries and those demanding prohibitive tariffs as a condition for meeting competition of imported goods.[6] Indeed, the difference in median wages in leading exporting industries and those pressed by import of competing articles are smaller than the differences in wages in individual industries within either group.

Prof. Wassily Leontiev has demolished another widespread contention that the United States exports products which absorb more capital and less labor than is required for production of an equivalent amount of goods now provided by imports. On the contrary, he found the inverse relationship and concluded that this country resorts to foreign trade rather in order to economize its capital and dispose of its surplus labor.[7] Even if the last contention is open to criticism, his analysis shows that the strength of industries is not correlated positively with the ratio of capital to labor input.

Perhaps, the comparative strength of various industries has little to do with their structure and depends on the comparative strength of various industries in different countries.

An industry may be beaten in international competition even if it is stronger than all its competitors except one. Thus certain lines of our textile industry may be strong enough to meet the competition of British and German factories but cannot compete with the respective lines of production in Japan. Our bicycles may be second best in comparison with the British, our watches, second best in comparison with the Swiss, and so on.

Such a situation is germane to international trade. Indeed, it is the basis of international division of labor.

40. Tariffs were originally established by the United States for fiscal purposes but their role changed as time went on. Our present tariff is considered purely protective. A little more than half of our imports are free of duty. The share of dutiable commodities was as low as 34 percent during World War II, in 1941–45, and inched up after the war, from 39 percent in 1946 to 47 percent in 1955. (See table 13.) At the same time the ratios of duties to the value of total and dutiable imports declined, the first ratio from 9.9 percent in 1946 to 5.6 percent in 1955, the second from 25.3 percent to 11.9 percent. The duties-to-import ratio has declined in the past two decades in all schedules. (See table 14.) In part this has been due to the marked rise in the price level since World War II, in part to the substantial duty reductions by the reciprocal trade agreements concluded since 1934.

[6] Hearings, pp. 307–311.

[7] Domestic Production and Foreign Trade: The American Capital Position Reexamined. Proceedings of the American Philosophical Society, vol. 97, No. 4, September 28, 1953, p. 343.

TABLE 13.—*Free and dutiable imports into the United States*

| Period or year | Value of imports, in millions, of dollars | Percentage distribution of imports | | Percentage ratio of duties | |
|---|---|---|---|---|---|
| | | Free | Dutiable | To all imports | To dutiable imports |
| 1851-60 | 268 | 15.2 | 84.8 | 20.4 | 24.0 |
| 1901-10 | 1,143 | 45.7 | 54.3 | 24.6 | 45.3 |
| 1931-35 | 1,704 | 63.1 | 36.9 | 18.5 | 50.0 |
| 1936-40 | 2,440 | 60.5 | 39.5 | 15.0 | 37.9 |
| 1941-45 | 3,476 | 66.0 | 34.0 | 10.9 | 32.1 |
| 1946 | 4,825 | 60.8 | 39.2 | 9.9 | 25.3 |
| 1947 | 5,666 | 61.0 | 39.0 | 7.6 | 19.3 |
| 1948 | 7,092 | 58.9 | 41.1 | 5.7 | 13.9 |
| 1949 | 6,592 | 58.9 | 41.1 | 5.5 | 13.5 |
| 1950 | 8,743 | 54.5 | 45.5 | 6.0 | 13.1 |
| 1951 | 10,817 | 55.4 | 44.6 | 5.5 | 12.3 |
| 1952 | 10,747 | 58.2 | 41.8 | 5.3 | 12.7 |
| 1953 | 10,779 | 54.9 | 45.1 | 5.4 | 12.0 |
| 1954 | 10,240 | 55.3 | 44.7 | 5.2 | 11.6 |
| 1955 | 10,334 | 53.2 | 46.8 | 5.6 | 11.9 |

Source: Statistical Abstract for the United States, 1956, p. 921.

TABLE 14.—*Average rate of duties by tariff schedule, 1935–55*

| Tariff schedule | 1935 | 1940 | 1945 | 1950 | 1955 |
|---|---|---|---|---|---|
| 1. Chemicals, oils, paints | 42.7 | 30.0 | 14.0 | 15.5 | 14.4 |
| 2. Earths, earthenware, glassware | 50.9 | 39.4 | 26.3 | 26.5 | 23.4 |
| 3. Metals | 34.3 | 30.5 | 25.7 | 13.0 | 12.1 |
| 4. Wood | 23.1 | 9.9 | 6.4 | 3.6 | 6.1 |
| 5. Sugar, molasses | 42.1 | 48.8 | 29.5 | 10.5 | 10.2 |
| 6. Tobacco | 84.5 | 60.4 | 34.3 | 24.8 | 20.5 |
| 7. Agricultural products | 40.0 | 31.3 | 13.6 | 10.7 | 10.9 |
| 8. Spirits, wines, other beverages | 92.8 | 60.9 | 66.8 | 25.1 | 23.1 |
| 9. Cotton manufactures | 40.0 | 35.1 | 17.2 | 23.8 | 21.7 |
| 10. Flax, hemp, jute | 24.2 | 15.1 | 22.3 | 6.4 | 7.0 |
| 11. Wool | 81.5 | 66.3 | 62.8 | 23.9 | 22.5 |
| 12. Silk | 58.9 | 52.7 | 48.1 | 30.6 | 28.2 |
| 13. Rayon, other synthetic textiles | 48.0 | 32.3 | 49.5 | 22.4 | 19.4 |
| 14. Pulp, paper, books | 24.3 | 16.9 | 14.4 | 9.9 | 9.8 |
| 15. Sundries | 32.6 | 25.7 | 19.4 | 18.2 | 19.5 |

Source: Statistical Abstract of the United States, 1956, pp. 922-923.

41. Our present tariff appears too low to the domestic producers affected by competition of imported articles, but it seems prohibitively high to some foreign producers. Appraisals of it depends ultimately on the yardstick used for measuring the overall level of duty rates.

When average duty rates for selected merchandise groups in the United States tariff are compared with corresponding rates in other countries, it appears that the general level of our tariff does not differ much from that of the French, German, or British.[8]

[8] W. S. and E. S. Woytinsky, World Commerce and Governments, 1955, pp. 286–292.

However, the range of duties for different commodities in all tariffs is so broad that the average rates depend largely on the method of computation, namely weighting single items.

42. Perhaps the best way of determining whether a tariff is high or low is through its impact on the trade balance of the Nation. Whatever the rates, the tariff is low if it permits access of foreign goods to the domestic market in an amount exceeding the value of the Nation's export. Inversely, it is high if it bars competition of foreign products with the similar domestic products so that imports are artificially depressed below the value of exports.

## IV. PRINCIPLES OF UNITED STATES FOREIGN TRADE POLICY

43. The foreign trade policy of the United States is embodied in the Tariff Act of 1930 (the Hawley-Smoot Tariff), the Trade Agreements Act of 1934 and the amendments of this act in Extension Acts of 1943, 1945, 1948, 1951, 1954, and 1955. In addition, the foreign trade policy of the Nation has found expression in the Buy American Act (passed in 1933 and amended in 1949), section 22 of the Agricultural Adjustment Act of 1935, repeatedly amended thereafter, and numerous administrative decisions and regulations. This system is extremely complex but has the advantage of great flexibility. This flexibility is evidenced by the amazing fact that the Hawley-Smoot Act of 1930 has never been repealed. Its duty rates remain, in principle, the law of the land. The duties actually levied—some of them only a fraction of those in the 1930 act—rest on trade agreements.

The administration is invested with far reaching authority in implementing and interpreting the existing laws. Since 1934 the general tendency of the administration has been to interpret such laws in a moderately liberal spirit. The hearings conducted by the subcommittee have revealed that the complaints of extreme protectionists are directed less against the existing laws that their interpretation by the administration.

The experience in applying the national defense amendments to the Trade Agreement Act of 1955 and the escape clause is characteristic in this respect.

44. Up to October 1956 the Office of Defense Mobilization received 11 formal requests to investigate the adverse effect of the reduction in duty rates on industries essential for the military potential of the United States. The industries claiming special protection included producers of balances, clocks, watches and thermometers, cordage and wooden boats, wool felt, textiles, and petroleum. No administrative action was taken in these cases. Only in the case of petroleum has the ODM informed the President that a high level of production by the domestic industry was essential for defense.[9]

45. The escape clause was invoked 60 times in the decade from 1947 to 1956. In 20 cases the Tariff Commission, found, after investigation, that the respective industry had suffered serious injury, but only in 7 cases did the President accept the recommendation of the Commission and order an increase in the duty rates. Some of

[9] The President is now having an interagency group working on a program of import restrictions which he might order.

the items involved were trivial, such as women's fur felt hats and hatters' fur, dried figs and alsike clover, but the list also includes three more significant items: bicycles, watch movements and towels. All in all, it must be recognized that the escape clause has been administered in the spirit of moderation and restraint.

46. The hearings held by the subcommittee headed by Representative Boggs have not resolved the controversial issues in our foreign-trade policy but have thrown them into sharp relief and have provided an enlightening poll of public opinion. They have proved that only a small part of the United States business community is afraid of competition. Organizations representing industry as a whole or large segments of it, such as the Committee on Economic Development, Committee for National Trade Policy, United States Council of International Chamber of Commerce, and United States Chamber of Commerce, have asserted unanimously that the United States is able to meet the challenge of foreign competition and have demanded a firm, liberal foreign-trade policy. This point of view has been strongly supported by the American Federation of Labor and CIO, leading farmers' organizations, the League of Women Voters, and the Cooperative League of the United States as spokesmen of consumers.

Particular industries have clearly divided into two camps. The campaign for increase in tariff protection, reduction of import quotas, wider application of the escape clause, curtailment of the President's authority to reject recommendations of the Tariff Commission, and so on, has been headed by spokesmen of the textile industry and representatives of localities in which this industry is concentrated. They have been seconded by the petroleum industry (which pleaded mainly against admission of residual oil to the United States), producers of china, bicycles, some chemicals, plywood, and precision instruments (including watches and photographic equipment), and representatives of a few minor industries such as producers of luggage locks, roasters, and grinders of chicory, producers of tung oil, fishermen. Their point of view has been supported by the protectionist lobby and by a couple of labor unions that have pleaded for protection of the respective branches of production.

On the other hand, spokesmen of the most advanced industries have argued for further liberalization of foreign trade. Such also has been the attitude of import trade, port authorities, confectioners, oilseed producers. Perhaps Mr. Percy of Bell & Howell Co., who most effectively pleaded for liberalization of our foreign-trade policy, was the spokesman not only of the fine mechanical and optical industry but of all captains of industry who have made the United States what it is—the greatest economic power of all time.

Careful reading of the records of the hearings gives the impression that the public and the business community in general back a liberal foreign-trade policy while a small but resolute and embittered minority of industrialists opposes it. There was no dissension, however, among the economists who testified before the subcommittee. All the 11 professors who appeared before it essentially supported the need to strengthen our foreign-trade policy by clarifying its purpose, in the direction of liberalization.

Such a result of the poll of public opinion conducted in the spirit of impartiality and with equal respect to all views professed by the witnesses seems to have laid foundations for proper decisions by Congress.

47. Before venturing any suggestion on the specific, highly technical problems the subcommittee will have to solve, I would like to call to mind the assignment of the subcommittee—

to conduct an investigation and study of *all aspects* of our customs, tariff, and reciprocal trade-agreement laws and trade agreements entered into thereunder and administration thereof, with particular reference to the relationship and effect of such matters *on the foreign economic policies of the United States and their effect upon domestic producers and employment*." [10]

The last task is particularly important in view of the role of administrative decisions in shaping the foreign-trade policy of this country. The Trade Agreements Act of 1934 has substantially transferred the right of changing import duties from the legislative to executive branch of the Government, retaining for the legislative branch responsibility for establishing the limits of the authority of the administration in this field. The act of 1945 and subsequent extension acts have in general left the authority to change duty rates in the hands of the President. Actually they have broadened his authority far beyond the limits indicated in the original Trade Agreements Act of 1934.

Recent amendments that changed the wording of certain provisions have not limited the discretional authority of the administration (since the new language of the law does not exclude different interpretations in its application) but serve as a general instruction to the executive branch in clarifying the intent of the legislative branch. Yet they have not made it clear enough.

48. The immediate objectives of foreign-trade policy may change as time passes. There is no evidence that in the conditions under which a new extension act is considered by Congress, its objectives are precisely the same as those 10 years ago, but a law establishing guidelines of foreign-trade policy for the next 3 years must have a definite aim in view and must be interpreted and administered in accordance with this aim.

The general objective of the Trade Agreements Acts of 1934 and 1945 was perfectly clear. The objective for the term of the new act is doubtful. Most certainly our objective is no longer to increase exports so as to bring orders to idle plants and provide jobs to the unemployed, but if trade policy is no longer geared toward this old aim, what is its new objective?

Many controversies will be avoided if the new act answers this question clearly stating its purpose.

Since all that foreign-trade policy can do is to influence the outflow and inflow of goods across national boundaries, it cannot be consistent and efficient unless the law gives it a definite assignment in this field. It is therefore of paramount significance, in my opinion, that the subcommittee submit to Congress an unambiguous definition of our immediate aims in the field of foreign trade. Should it be wise to promote further increase in our exports with as little increase as possible in imports?

Or should we attempt to reduce our imports as a measure to protect domestic producers?

---

[10] Report to the Committee on Ways and Means. Italic supplied.

Is our aim to increase the export balance or to close the gap between exports and imports?

The new Trade Agreement Act can pick any goal but it should not expect the administration to move in opposite directions simultaneously. Above all, it should give the administration a guideline for integrating foreign-trade policy with other national targets.

49. There is no doubt that foreign trade policy must be integrated with the needs of national defense, conservation of resources, fiscal policy (excise taxes), agricultural policy (import restrictions for price supported products and program for disposal abroad of surplus farm products), and so on. More controversial is its integration with the foreign policy. The controversy is about the question whether tariff decisions should be made wholly on the basis of an appraisal of their effect on the respective domestic industries or on the basis of broader considerations, as part of our foreign economic policy. All countries have faced this alternative in determining their foreign trade policy. I think that the choice between the two methods ultimately depends on two criteria: first, the significance of foreign economic policy for the Nation, i. e., its stake in world affairs; second, the significance of competition of imported goods with domestic products, i. e., the ratio of the value of imports to domestic production.

In the case of the United States, the first criterion indicates the tremendous stake of this country in global economic policy. Indeed, it is called upon to defend economic bastions on a line encircling the globe—in Europe, Asia, Oceania, and both Americas. It is particularly interested in sources of various raw materials, their long-range development and the lanes of communication with the respective areas. It is vitally interested in maintaining economic stability and promoting economic progress in the free world, and is the only power able to defend its integrity by economic measures.

The second criterion suggests that foreign competition is less of a threat to domestic production in the United States than in any other country. Apart from import of raw materials that do not compete with local products, our total import of fabricated goods is almost negligible in relation to the total capacity of domestic industries, and its possible increase—assuming a very liberal foreign trade policy—would hardly liquidate our present surplus of exports over imports.

The conclusion is inescapable that it would be against the vital interests of the United States to base its decisions on foreign trade policy and tariffs wholly on considerations relating to the competitive position of single industries or lines of production. Final decisions must depend also on broader considerations. A possible adverse effect on directly affected domestic industries must be taken into account, and serious attention must be given to the measures designed to minimize any hardships imposed upon them, but preoccupation with this aspect of change in tariffs should not overshadow other considerations which determine the orientation of our foreign trade policy.

I think that the new Trade Agreements Act should establish this scale of values in a clear, unambiguous form, restating at the same time that such was the general philosophy of the acts of 1934 and 1945 although neither stated it clearly enough to avoid misunderstanding and misinterpretation.

50. The next question that calls for clarification is the immediate objective of our foreign trade policy in the forthcoming years. The hearings have provided a sound foundation for solving this problem.

The hard fact of life is that our foreign trade is badly out of balance, with our imports lagging far behind our exports. The term "dollar gap" repeatedly used in the hearings means simply that the United States exports more than other countries are able—or permitted—to import into our country. Such being the structure of our foreign trade, the question arises, Which party suffers most from such disequilibrium?

This is what the report declares on the problem of dollar shortage in the world:

> Although the United States has had a surplus in its exports of goods and services since before World War I, it has been only since World War II that * * * attention has been focused on the dollar gap in discussions of United States foreign economic policy. The causes of the postwar dollar gap were many, but fundamentally they related to the disruption of industries of many foreign countries and the impact of these dislocations on world trade. The industries of Europe and Japan could not produce adequately to meet even domestic needs, so that their capacity to produce for export was seriously limited. Moreover, the needs for reconstructing foreign industries and maintaining reasonable standards of living after the war expressed themselves in increased demands for imports of capital equipment, raw materials, and consumer goods. For many of the needed imports the United States was the major, if not the only, source.
>
> Large-scale economic aid, particularly under the Marshall plan, provided the means by which much of the United States excess of exports over imports was financed. Had the United States not provided this assistance, foreign countries would have been obliged to undertake difficult and harmful adjustments in their domestic economies * * * [which] would have resulted in a depression of economic activity in those countries, unemployment and curtailment of social services * * * [11]

The report recognizes that the situation has changed in recent years and refers to the new ways of financing the dollar gap.

> The new element has been the increase in military expenditures abroad under the offshore procurement program and for the maintenance of United States troops and installations abroad. In addition, there have been sizable direct grants of economic equipment * * *

And it concludes:

> A liberal import policy on the part of the United States can be at most only a part of the prescription offered for solving the dollar gap problem. In the long run, countries experiencing a dollar shortage will be obliged to increase the efficiency of their own industries and undertake other policies * * * that will improve their competitive position in world markets. The adjustments toward closing the dollar gap must be made through an increase in United States imports relative to our exports. This may involve a decline in United States exports of certain types of goods as alternative sources of supply are developed outside the United States. * * * The basic solution of dollar gap problem must come from within [foreign] countries.

From this point of view the report considers the plans for economic integration of Western Europe as a step toward enhancing competition and productivity within Europe, increasing its competitive position in world markets, reducing Western Europe's dependence on imports from the United States.[12]

Ultimately this would narrow and close the dollar gap, according to the report.

[11] Report, pp. 44–46.
[12] Report, pp. 48–49.

51. Like many other economic processes, international trade has two aspects: movement of material goods and financial transactions. What appears as difficulty of payment for the receiver of goods, from the financical point of view, is a transfer of goods without equivalent compensation from the point of view of real phenomena constituting foreign trade. Indeed, export subtracts goods from the supply of a nation while import adds goods to its consumption funds.

From this viewpoint, the export balance may be a bitter necessity for a nation or may serve definite purpose under certain conditions and is a pure unrecoverable loss for the nation under other conditions. It is a necessity for a country dominated by foreign capital. It serves a definite purpose for a country engaged in liquidation of its debts or building up foreign assets in order to insure an import balance in the future. It is a net loss for a country that disposes over considerable assets abroad and, as in the case of the United States, has no intention of taking earnings of these assets in the form of a surplus of imports over exports.

Regardless of the way in which our surplus of exports over imports has been financed—foreign aid, Government loans and grants, or private loans and portfolio or direct investments—from a narrow economic point of view all the surpluses in our exports in the last decade have been a net loss for our national economy. Moreover, each billion dollars of such surplus in coming years will be a billion of net loss, unless unilateral transfer of exported goods is justified by broader political considerations, such as national security or promotion of peace and economic stability and progress in the world.

These are not theoretical generalizations but a blunt statement of hard facts.

52. The foreign-trade policy of a nation is determined largely, although not exclusively, by its trade balance and what it intends to do about it. In the early period of its existence, the United States had a net import balance in merchandise trade and paid for it partly in gold and partly by increasing its debts to foreign countries, mainly Great Britain. Since the United States mined gold, export of this metal did not differ from export of any other domestic produce. United States cumulative import balance for merchandise and gold was about $1 billion, for the period from 1790 to 1875. Since the middle of the 1870's the United States has generally had an export balance. The cumulative surplus of export over import from 1876 to 1950 was about $100 billion. This total, however, includes about $40 billion for military goods delivered by the United States to the Allies under lend-lease provision. This was an item in the military expenses of this country, its contribution to the war effort of the Allies. Of the rest, amounting to about $60 billion, one-third was covered by import of gold from abroad, an operation which brought no gain to the United States economy and resulted only in concentrating tremendous gold reserves in this country. It can be argued whether this export in return for gold was more advantageous for the United States than it would have been to dump the respective commodities, worth $20 billion, into the ocean or burn them.

An additional $24 billion went in part for payment of interest on old loans and their liquidation, in part for remittance of immigrants to their old countries, and in part for building up assets abroad. About

$16 billion was covered by unilateral transfer of funds through foreign-aid grants under the Marshall plan and other programs.

From 1951 to 1956 the United States has accumulated export surpluses in merchandise trade totaling $16.4 billion, not including military transfers. It had an additional $10 billion net income from the excess of earnings of private and public investments abroad over payments on the foreign investments in this country. On the other hand, it had a surplus of imports over exports totaling $2.4 billion in exchange of services (including transportation and travel). All in all, the exchange of merchandise, services, and incomes from investment in the past 6 years has left the United States with a net export balance of $24 billion.[13]

This time the United States did not take gold in payment for its exports. It accumulated a $4.6 billion increment in its private investment abroad, but at the same time foreign gold and dollar holding in the United States has increased by $5.7 billion.

Practically the whole surplus in exports has been covered by Government loans, grants, and other unilateral operations. Substantially, the bulk of this amount was met by the taxpayers' money, and the respective merchandise, labor, and capital were extracted from national economy without any real compensation. This total, however, includes $11.4 billion in military expenditures abroad (including offshore procurement) and export of agricultural surplus commodities for which producers were recompensed under special programs. These transactions, of course, have nothing to do with foreign-trade policy. That is concerned only with the remaining part of our net balance of payments, a surplus of exports over imports of about $10 billion in 6 years.

53. It may be argued that the surplus of exports stimulated our postwar economic growth. This is a fallacious argument. Our economy was working at full capacity and needed no props. The surplus of exports was harmful to it as a source of inflationary pressure. It tended to reduce the supply of goods in the Nation in relation to the disposable purchasing power. The resulting inflationary pressure has been particularly harmful in view of the fact that, independent of the balance of trade, inflationary forces have prevailed in our economy in recent years.

This situation illustrates again our statement that the objective of foreign-trade policy is bound to change with changing economic conditions. Its logical aim in 1934 may have been to increase exports and the surplus of exports over imports, as an inflationary—or more precisely, antideflationary—measure. The present situation, however, demands a radically different orientation of foreign-trade legislation.

54. The preceding analysis seems to justify the conclusion that the United States can gain nothing by maintaining the present gap between exports and imports and pays in full for each million dollars of this gap. The most urgent objectives of our foreign-trade policy is to reduce this gap in the exchange of goods and services to the amount of unilateral transfers demanded by other programs approved by Congress. In view of our active balance in the exchange of services (including earnings of investments abroad), the net balance in

[13] For 1951–55, see the report of the subcommittee, p. 45. For 1956, Survey of Current Business, March 1957, p. 16.

merchandise trade must be appreciably less than the amount appropriated for foreign economic and military aid abroad. If, for example, Congress decides to appropriate $4 billion for this purpose (including surplus farm products disposed abroad on the basis of grants), the economically sound surplus of exports over imports would be about $2–$2.5 billion (including farm products sold abroad), and the main objective of the foreign-trade policy would be to reduce the gap in this width.

55. In the passage quoted above, the report recognized the necessity of a drastic reduction of the present surplus of exports over imports, but it anticipates that the basic solution of the problem will come from abroad. I would put greater emphasis on increasing imports for the following reasons:

(*a*) It is preferable to seek equilibrium in foreign trade on a high level of imports and exports rather than a low level.

(*b*) Since the disequilibrium in United States foreign trade inflicts direct losses on our country, we should assume primary responsibility for restoring equilibrium between its exports and imports.

(*c*) The unwillingness or inability of certain industries in the United States to meet foreign competition is in striking contrast to the tradition of the great majority of businessmen in this country. The policy of closing the gap in our trade balance should be oriented by the sense of strength and responsibility.

56. To sum up, the new trade act should, first of all, firmly establish two principles:

(*a*) Foreign trade policy is a part of national domestic and foreign policy and its implementation must be coordinated with the activity of other agencies. With all regard for the justifiable interests of single industries and individual producers, it must be guided by recognition of the tremendous stake of this country in world affairs and its vital interest in promoting peace, economic stability, and economic and social progress in the free world.

(*b*) The immediate aim of our foreign trade policy in terms of the new Trade Agreements Act should be to narrow the gap between our exports and imports by encouraging and facilitating imports.[14]

The announcement of this objective of our foreign-trade policy should not be construed as abandonment of the principle of moderate protectionism, the procedure of reciprocal agreement negotiations, existing safeguards for certain industries and so on. It should rather serve as a general guideline to the administration in implementing and interpreting the law. To the extent that the new orientation of policy will demand changes in the structure of duty rates, it should be made clear that such changes must be effected gradually so as to minimize adverse effects on single industries.

57. The following remarks illustrate the application of the suggested general principles to some of the practical questions raised before the subcommittee.

### (*1*) *GATT and OTC*

The contention that foreign-trade policy is a part of our general foreign economic program excludes any possibility that the United States withdraw from the General Agreement on Tariffs and Trade

[14] Cf. hearings, pp. 45–46.

and suggests that this country should join the Organization of Trade Cooperation. The United States will, of course, defend its point of view in controversial issues before the latter organization. Perhaps it will gain less from it than the European nations, but a negative attitude on its part toward this organization would undermine its leadership in world affairs. United States participation in OTC would have an important psychiological effect on European nations and its absence from this organization would change the character of the latter, to the disadvantage of United States announced policy.

(2) *Peril points*

The idea of drawing in advance a limit beyond which the tariff concessions should not go, seems sound, provided the peril points are not established on a prohibitively high level so as to exclude the possibility of foreign competition with domestic producers. Peril points must be low enough to permit steadily increasing imports of goods coveted by American consumers and sound competition of such imports with local products.

(3) *Escape clause*

The principle of the escape clause seems sound. What it means is that the United States negotiators might make mistakes which will require corrective action by the Chief Executive. It is fairly probable that the number of cases requiring such action will increase if peril points are lowered and the whole foreign trade policy is conducted in a more liberal spirit.

It should be recognized, however, that the escape clause should not be applied to the normal and predictable effect of a reduction of tariff rates. If the objective of our foreign-trade policy is to restore equilibrium between exports and imports, the growing import of an article shows simply that liberalization of the tariff has served its purpose. Consumers must be permitted to choose between imported and domestic articles even if their preference for better or less expensive merchandise is injurious to local producers who would like to make them pay a higher price for an inferior product. A situation might develop, however, in which the reduction in the tariff rate proved to have a serious effect on the vital interests of an industry or a whole community. Such situation may demand intervention of the Government. The procedure used now for establishing serious injury under the escape clause may be successfully applied in such situations.

I do not think that "serious injury" can be recognized in the event of successful foreign competition with a particular product if the affected industry can recoup its losses by diversifying production or improving its methods. Similarly, no "serious injury" should be recognized if single concerns in an industry lose their market while other concerns in the same industry maintain their position despite foreign competition. No "serious injury" exists if an industry loses an increase in demand to foreign competition but maintains its old customers. The definition of "serious injury" must be fair to all three parties: the complaining industry, its foreign competitors, and the consumers who have acted as a jury in deciding in favor of the imported merchandise against the domestic product.

More thought should be given to help the injured industry or community by means other than withdrawal of concesesion in tariff duties or suppression of competition by import quotas. Such measures may include loans for diversifying and modernizing production, accelerated amortization allowances for the industry, loans for community development, promotion of retraining and resettlement of affected workers.[15] All such measures may meet with serious objections, but they seem preferable to the idea that consumers who prefer imported articles to the domestic product must be brought back to the domestic producers by high tariffs and low import quotas. Without insisting on any particular plan of rederess for serious injury inflicted to an industry by foreign competition, I believe that protection of single lines of production and individual products by raising import duties would be incompatible with the sound objective of our foreign-trade policy.

(4) *Buy American*

The principle behind the slogan "Buy American" seems unsound and conducive to abuses. Foreign bidders are sufficiently handicapped by transportation costs and unfamiliarity with local conditions. With this protection, local industries must be able to meet foreign competition. This is particularly true of the industries that seek protection under the Buy-American provision—some of the strongest industries in the Nation. The provision not only tends to reduce imports but also calls for deliberate waste of taxpayers' money.

(5) *The national defense amendment*

The idea is sound in principle. Although the provision so far has not been used for any administrative action, it may gain in importance if Congress and the administration accept a bold liberalization policy.

(6) *Agricultural quotas*

The policy of agricultural price support necessarily implies control over import of the supported articles. The question relates to agricultural policy rather than foreign-trade policy.

(7) *Metals and other strategic materials*

The long-run materials policy calls for encouragement of imports of raw materials and cautious use of scarce domestic resources. Research and development of local resources must be supported, but better methods of support may be devised than bolstering prices by prohibiting import.

(8) *Trade rather than aid*

The first fundamental principle of foreign-trade policy—its integration with our foreign policy—demands that greater attention be given to this slogan, often repeated in friendly countries. Indeed, for a country with unused reserve of labor power and raw materials, an opportunity to export its products to a value of, say, $100 million, means more than a loan or grant of the same magnitude. By stimulating production, the opportunity to export permits such a country to earn foreign currency without reducing the domestic supply of consumer goods, while at the same time it creates additional jobs and

[15] Cf. hearings, pp. 920–921.

strengthens the local economy and social fabric. A liberal trade policy does not exclude the necessity of foreign military and economic aid, but it reduces the need for such aid and makes it more effective.

*(9) Commodity agreements*

The same fundamental principle of foreign-trade policy suggests that more attention be given to international commodity agreements, especially agreements with our suppliers of foodstuffs and minerals. The core of the problem is that our purchases in these countries are of vital significance for them while for us the trade with each of them is a comparatively minor item (cf. table 11). Although excessive fluctuations in price are much more destructive for them than for the United States, stabilization of prices would be advantageous for both sides. Even if it required certain financial sacrifices on the part of the United States, such sacrifices would be justified by the effect of the agreements on the economic stability and development of friendly nations, especially in the Western Hemisphere.

*(10) Diversification of our foreign trade*

The promotion of imports from Europe and Japan requires particular attention. The urgent objective of our foreign-trade policy should be to eliminate or reduce our export balance in merchandise trade with the United Kingdom ($300 million in 1955), Japan ($226 million), Western Germany ($225 million), Italy ($177 million), Netherlands ($324 million), Belgium ($68 million), Switzerland ($33 million), and other countries in which we have no prospect for large direct investments. The United States Foreign Service should look for opportunities to increase imports from these areas with the same diligence it looks now for new export opportunities and especially for outlets for our agricultural surpluses.

# ECONOMIC AID AND TRADE POLICY AS AN INSTRUMENT OF NATIONAL STRATEGY [1]

Lincoln Gordon, William Ziegler professor of international economic relations, Graduate School of Business Administration, Harvard University

It is a commonplace today to say that America's foreign economic policy should be an integral part of general foreign policy and should be consciously designed to support our national strategy. This is, however, a concept of very recent origin. It is by no means universally accepted in public attitudes or reflected in all the phases of national action, especially legislative action, which go to make up foreign economic policy.

Our historic national tradition, back to the American Revolution, is rather the reverse of this concept, much of foreign policy being designed primarily to serve national economic interests. Obvious examples are the right to manufacture for ourselves, insistence on freedom of the seas in peace and war, and maintenance of an open door for American trade and investment.

Among the present array of foreign economic policies, foreign aid is one which reflects a deliberate attempt at serving the broader objectives of foreign policy. On the other hand, policies affecting trade, agriculture, and shipping are often heavily influenced by special domestic interests, seeking protection from imports or subsidy of exports.

The present discussion assumes that American interests will best be served in a world where free institutions predominate and where popular aspirations for material improvement and other social change are met by such institutions without recourse to force. Communist expansionism is the most obvious threat to such a world—a global and potentially mortal threat. There are also conceivable challenges from other forms of totalitarianism, perhaps based on the frustrated nationalism of newly independent peoples in Asia or Africa. It follows that our national strategy should pursue three broad lines: (*a*) to maintain and strengthen the positions and the alliance structure of those free nations recognizing the common danger; (*b*) to harmonize the interests of neutralist underdeveloped countries with the free world in the short run and to secure their identification with the cause of freedom in the long run; and (*c*) to contain Soviet expansionism in whatever form and to weaken the cohesion of the Soviet bloc.

Economic policy can play an important part in each of these three lines of national strategy. It might seem sufficiently obvious that any foreign economic policy at cross-purposes with this broad national strategy would be absurd. But some potential conflict is almost inherent in the structure of the American economy and our political institutions, and in the nature of America's role in the world economy.

The basic fact is that with 6 percent of the world's population we account for something like 40 percent of total production and about one-sixth of non-Soviet world trade. While we are thus the largest factor in the world economy by a substantial margin, foreign transactions account for only about 5 percent of our gross national product. Our prosperity is less dependent upon external economic developments than that of any other nation outside the Sino-Soviet bloc. It follows that the direct effects of American foreign economic policies on our own national well-being are far smaller than the effects on other nations; they are therefore less likely to be judged by Americans in terms of general national interest.

These policies do, however, greatly affect particular industrial, agricultural, or local interests. Given a constitutional structure which magnifies the influence of well-organized special interests, such interests are bound to play an important role in policymaking. Their weight is further magnified by certain mercantilist myths deeply ingrained in popular attitudes: that exports are good, imports potentially dangerous, and American living standards constantly exposed to undermining from the imported products of "sweated foreign labor." Such attitudes are apparently even more deep-seated and harder to dispel than political isolationism.

These facts pose serious problems for political leadership in seeking to integrate foreign economic policy into broad national strategy. General foreign and military policy have, of course, major domestic political repercussions in the form of national service arrangements, high defense budgets, and the risk of ar. They do not, however, impose an immediate burden on the pocketbook interests of particular regions or industries in the manner of a tariff reduction on Japanese textiles, quotas on Danish butter or cheese, or a refusal to strengthen domestic cotton and rice markets by dumping surpluses abroad—examples all having an important bearing on foreign policy repercussions.

The political problem has an administrative counterpart in the structure of our National Government. The President has the clear responsibility for general foreign and security policy making, with advice primarily from the Departments of State and Defense. In the foreign economic field, however, he must also be advised by agencies whose primary orientation is domestic: the Treasury, the Departments of Agriculture, Commerce, and the Interior, and others. For the reasons suggested above, moreover, the Congress is far more likely to take initiatives of its own in the foreign economic field than in broader foreign policy areas.

There is one further element inherent in foreign economic policy which makes it difficult to integrate fully with general foreign policy. Within broad lines, the latter is subject to a good deal of tactical flexibility. Much of diplomacy is concerned with making the best use of tactical opportunities and dealing promptly and skillfully with crises. For good or ill, however, foreign economic policies generally cannot be made responsive to very short-run political changes. Most such policies set the conditions for private commercial and financial transactions; their ability to achieve results depends on reasonable confidence in the durability of the policy framework. Aid policies, except for famine relief or other stopgap emergency measures, are likewise concerned with the necessarily slow process of investment and structural economic change, or the almost equally slow process of building up military strength. In these fields, consistent adherence to policy over substantial periods of time is simply indispensable to effectiveness. While backing and filling is hardly to be prescribed in any field of policymaking, in the economic field it becomes wholly self-defeating.

The present paper seeks to analyze the main strands in our foreign economic policy as it exists today and then to set forth the principal alternatives in three areas: (*a*) The general framework of international economic relations, which affects mainly our relations with other economically advanced countries in the free world; (*b*) economic policy toward the underdeveloped countries; and (*c*) economic policy in relation to the Soviet bloc. It concludes with some brief observations on the problem of policy coordination in the interest of an effective national strategy.

Certain important elements of foreign economic policy are mentioned only briefly or are omitted. They include the international espects of agricultural policy, shipping, civil aviation, telecommunications, and stockpiling. Military assistance, and economic aid in support of other nations' defense efforts, are also omitted, since they can be discussed only in a framework of poliitcal and strategic considerations which lie outside the compass of this paper.

## MAIN ELEMENTS OF CURRENT FOREIGN ECONOMIC POLICY

American foreign economic policy today is a compound of two major elements, not always fully reconciled. The first is the broad design for an international economic world order developed at the close of World War II; it might be termed the "Bretton Woods element." The second is a series of measures, some emergency improvisations and some longer run in character, to make good the postwar underestimation of the reconstruction problem, to cope with the economic aspects of the cold war, and to meet other unforeseen problems, especially in underdeveloped areas. In addition, there have been some halting efforts to consolidate the more durable of these measures and to reconcile the two lines of policy.

The Bretton Woods element (so named because of the international economic conference of 1944 at Bretton Woods, N. H.) can be viewed as an economic counterpart of the hoped-for United Nations kind of political world, in which the wartime allies would have cooperated everywhere to prevent the use of force and to promote equitable settlements of international political disputes. Its architects were also deeply influenced by the bitter experience of the 1930's. They were resolved to deal explicitly with the disorderly international economic practices engendered by the great depression, practices which had prolonged and intensified that depression. They recognized that the 19th century, gold standard, British-dominated, economic order was gone. In addition to immediate postwar rehabilitation, they sought to create a new international economic framework conducive to the steady growth of trade and investment on generally liberal, but not doctrinairely liberal, lines. They made provision to accommodate the special concern in various countries with such problems as the expansion of agricultural output or the maintenance of farm incomes, the need to protect industries vital to national defense, the curtailment of market fluctuations for primary commodities, and the conscious promotion of economic development.

In the field of trade, the Bretton Woods goal was orderly expansion on a multilateral and nondiscriminatory basis. Quotas and other quantitative restrictions were to be minimized if not eliminated. Tariffs were to be made nondiscriminatory and gradually lowered on the basis of simultaneous bilateral negotiations in a multilateral framework. Export subsidies, dumping, and other trade-distorting measures were to be suppressed.

In the financial field, a fully multilateral system was to be restored through the recreation of convertibility for all current account transactions, at least among the major world currencies. Competitive exchange depreciation would be ruled out, but there would be provision for orderly adjustment of exchange rates to help bring about fundamental equilibrium. There was to be an international pool of foreign exchange resources to supplement national reserves in order to tide over short-term swings in balances of payments without resorting to trade quotas or exchange controls. Controls on capital account were to be limited to the prevention of speculative excesses. In both the trade and financial areas, there was a sharp emphasis on nondiscrimination and worldwide multilateralism. There was also, however, provision for discrimination against imports from a country where severe internal deflation made its currency generally scarce in the world; this reflected fears of another major American depression.

In the field of investment and development, the main emphasis was on a free flow of private capital, with a code of rules to safeguard borrowing countries against undue exploitation and to safeguard investors against unreasonable harassment. Since it was clear that some types of investment in social and overhead capital would not be attractive to private investors, provision was made for international public investment to fill these needs and thus pave the way for an even larger flow of private investment.

In each major area there were to be cooperative international institutions. Their charters scrupulously avoided any interference with national sovereignty. They were not instruments of a proposed world government, but rather institutions to develop and supervise voluntary codes of conduct and to provide forums for consultation, advice, and the adjustment of disputes. The most elaborate was to have been the International Trade Organization (ITO), whose charter was negotiated at Habana in 1947–48. This project, however, died when the United States administration decided at the end of 1950 that it could not win approval from Congress. Its basic trade provisions are contained in the General Agreement on Tariffs and Trade (GATT), for which an administrative structure is currently proposed in the Organization for Trade Cooperation (OTC). The ITO provisions concerning private investment were especially controversial, and nothing has since been done to replace them on an international basis. The International Monetary Fund (IMF) and the International Bank for Reconstruction and Development (IBRD), both negotiated at the Bretton Woods Conference of 1944, have now been functioning institutions for 10 years.

It is easy to sneer at the "dream world of Bretton Woods," to carp at the loopholes and compromises which pervade its structure, to quarrel with particular provisions, and to condemn its preoccupation with the fear of an American depression and with deflation and unemployment generally rather than with inflationary pressures. Yet its construction and negotiation reflected great application and ingenuity. With all its loopholes and compromises, its realization would pretty clearly have been in the interests of the United States and of the world at large. Even in the much more gloomy and dangerous world of the past 10 years, this element of policy has made a not insignificant constructive contribution.

Nevertheless, the Bretton Woods element in our foreign economic policy certainly failed to meet the most urgent problems of the postwar decade. Hence the second major policy element—the series of economic measures designed to meet specific postwar foreign policy problems as they arose.

The main items are generally familiar. For immediate postwar rehabilitation, when UNRRA proved inadequate and politically objectionable in certain respects, it was supplemented by post-UNRRA American relief and special bilateral loans. When the ink was barely dry on the Articles of Agreement of the International Monetary Fund, it was already clear that its provisions alone could not restore sterling convertibility. The key currency line of approach was then employed, in the form of the Anglo-American Financial Agreement of 1945 with its $3.75 billion loan. In 1947, this effort too had to be written off as a failure. That same year, with the whole economy of Western Europe facing collapse and with evidence mounting that the Soviets were ready and eager to take political advantage of that weakness, the European recovery program was launched as a systematic cndeavor to bring about European economic recovery on a durable basis through a large-scale 4-year program. This program—the Marshall plan—worked almost incredibly well; the hoped-for results were more than met in less time and at lower cost than foreseen in 1947.

More directly related to the cold war, when it became evident in 1950 that physical security in Western Europe required large-scale NATO rearmament, massive direct military assistance and substantial indirect economic support were brought to bear through the mutual defense assistance program and later the mutual security program, including its provisions for defense support assistance, offshore procurement of certain munitions in Europe, and contributions to the joint financing of NATO military intrastructure. An attempt was made to hamper the growth of Soviet military strength by a cooperative embargo against the export of arms and strategic materials and equipment to the Soviet bloc. This was organized cooperatively through the consultative group-coordinating committee merchanism in Paris, backed up by American legislation in the form of the Mutual Defense Assistance Control Act of 1951 (the Battle Act).

With respect to the underdeveloped areas, finally, it became increasingly clear in the late 1940's that private capital and technical assistance were moving very slowly indeed into many of these areas, and that the United Nations specialized agencies and the International Bank were not alone sufficient to meet the needs. At the same time, these areas were apparently becoming important battlegrounds of the cold war. New American initiatives were then taken in the form of President Truman's point 4 address in 1949, the act for international development in 1950, support for an expanded United Nations program of technical assistance, wider authority for the Export-Import Bank to make development loans, and some bilateral development assistance as part of the mutual security program and in connection with the disposal of agricultural surpluses.

It will be seen that the first major element in our foreign economic policy consisted primarily of an orderly framework for private trade and investment on the basis of worldwide international cooperation, while the second or emergency element has consisted largely of foreign economic and military spending programs directed toward more specific and localized economic, political, or social objectives. In the interweaving of these two elements, certain crosscurrents have developed. Perhaps the most important is the conflict between regionalism, with its tolerance (or even encouragement) of discrimination in trade and exchange policies, and strict global nondiscrimination.

Trade discrimination against the Soviet bloc has not involved serious differences of opinion within the United States, although it has created certain problems in relations with some of our European allies and with Japan. In the other cases, however, there have been significant divisions of opinion within the United States itself. The postwar period began with vigorous American opposition to British imperial preference and considerable suspicion and hostility toward the whole sterling area system, with its freedom from internal exchange controls and more or less common exchange restrictions against the outside world, especially the dollar world. As the decade progressed, less and less was heard about the evils of imperial preference, and the sterling area arrangements became an object of affirmative American support. This shift in attitudes was gradual and at no stage a self-conscious change in policy. It rather reflected the growing political conviction that these economic arrangements were important to the cohesion of the Commonwealth, which in turn in a world of cold war and uncertain allegiance of Asia and Africa, might be as important to basic American political objectives as to British ones.

With regard to Western Europe, the conflict of approaches has been more clear-cut. The Bretton Woods world had no place for regional integration short of complete customs unions. On the European scene even the most ambitious customs union proposals were originally limited to small groups of neighboring countries such as Benelux, and possibly Scandinavia or France-Italy. Largely as a byproduct of the Marshall plan, however, the idea of European integration became a cardinal element in American foreign policy, and its proponents were quite prepared to make Europe a major exception to the Bretton Woods notion of global nondiscrimination. The desirable area for integration in American eyes has fluctuated with attitudes and possibilities in Europe, the emphasis sometimes being on the six continental members of the Schuman plan Coal and Steel Community, and sometimes on the 17 members of the Organization for European Economic Cooperation.

Other crosscurrents have resulted from conflicts between domestic and foreign economic policies, notably in the agricultural field. In spite of our general opposition to the use of import quotas for restricting trade, we have had to impose quotas on agricultural imports where domestic prices are kept higher than world market levels, in order to avoid supporting the entire world market and accumulating even greater surpluses in Government storage. Those same surpluses have led to heavy pressure, successful in some instances, for agricultural export subsidies and other disposal methods which in foreign eyes look like "dumping," and which sometimes undermine the markets of friendly countries we are simultaneously seeking to aid under other programs.

Shipping policy involves another such crosscurrent. The system of subsidies to shipbuilders and operators is based on national defense grounds and therefore falls within a recognized category of exceptions to the general Bretton Woods concepts, but the flag discrimination requirement of the foreign aid legislation (requiring 50 percent of all Government-financed cargoes to be carried in American-flag vessels) can scarcely be reconciled with those concepts.

There have also developed significant forces toward reaction against the broadly liberal foreign economic policy trend of the 1934–48 period. These are reflected in the peril-point amendments to the reciprocal trade legislation; the broadening of tariff reduction escape-clause criteria in 1955; the provision in the same legislation for import quotas to protect domestic industries essential to national security; uncertainties on application of the "buy American" legislation; increasing pressure for additional countervailing duties against allegedly subsidized imports; and the failure to press for a vote on adherence to the Organization of Trade Cooperation during the 1956 or 1957 sessions of Congress. At the same time that the Republican Party has become divided into protectionist and liberal wings, with the official leadership supporting the latter, the Democratic Party has also become divided and has developed significant protectionist elements, especially in southern industry. This dissolution of traditional alinements on the foreign trade front could have a net effect in either direction, but for the moment the drift appears to be protectionist.

The resultant of these two rather disparate major policy trends and the various crosscurrents is a somewhat uneasy coexistence of a series of foreign economic policies. The seemingly clear image of a world economic order which Americans pictured for themselves at the close of the war was not realizable, at least during the first postwar decade. There is no longer a coherent view of the kind of economic order which would best fit our broad foreign policy objectives. To the extent that we still pursue the Bretton Woods line, is it a valid and viable line in the world as it now appears? If valid for us, can it still enlist enough support elsewhere in the world to become a reality? Does our combination of policies effectively strengthen the free world alliances? Are we adequately dealing, insofar as economic policies can be of influence, with the problem of the underdeveloped areas and their long-run political allegiance? Is there sufficient clarity in both our ends and our means to create confidence and understanding at home and abroad?

Such questions might be dismissed on the ground that the world economy, for all its remaining restrictions and confusions, is by no means in desperate shape. Compared with the period of the 1930's, its condition in the early and middle 1950's has been remarkably good. There are, however, reasons to suppose that the current situation is not necessarily self-sustaining, that it might readily turn in directions sharply at variance with American interests, and that new American foreign economic policy leadership is very much in order if we are to influence events and not merely be carried along by them.

ECONOMIC RELATIONS IN A FREE WORLD

A decade ago, the makers of American foreign economic policy hoped that by now the world would long since have emerged from a period of wartime controls and postwar reconstruction into a global multilateral system of trade and payments free from arbitrary restraints on the movement of goods and capital. Instead, the year 1957 is ending with no major currency except the Canadian dollar and the Swiss franc freely convertible with the United States dollar; import quotas and some degree of exchange control are still the rule rather than the exception; there is substantial continuing discrimination against dollar imports, especially the less essential agricultural products and almost the whole range of consumer goods; complex multiple exchange rate systems are more common than not in Latin America; and private investment is still short of hoped-for levels. There is a major slowdown, if not a complete halt, in the movement toward a freer world system of trade and payments, and there are painful signs of a possible reemergence of worldwide dollar shortage.

Despite all this, a remarkable amount of real progress has been made. The volume of free world trade in 1956 and early 1957 has been at record levels, the increase in real terms amounting to almost 90 percent since prewar and about 45 percent since 1948, the first year of the Marshall plan. World production is likewise at record levels. In the nondollar areas of the free world, two great regional trade and payments systems, the sterling area and the OEEC–European Payments Union arrangements, have served to multilateralize payments and eliminate quantitative restrictions on the vast bulk of nondollar free world trade, or well over half of total world trade. Contrary to the fears expressed by many observers, the operation of these systems in practice has not intensified discrimination against the dollar, but has been accompanied by a reduction in such discrimination. Gold and dollar reserves of other countries have increased significantly during the last decade, and there has been a fairly steady relaxation of quotas on dollar imports, especially in Europe.

Moreover, since 1953, the leading trading countries have ceased to resort to new import restrictions as their first reaction to temporary deterioration in their balances of payments. They have instead sought to rectify the difficulties by anti-inflationary domestic fiscal and monetary measures which do not directly disrupt international trade and payments. While de jure convertibility of sterling is still not in sight, and may be pushed back much further by the consequences of the Middle East crisis of 1956 and the continuing inflationary pressures in Britain, India, and other sterling area countries, there has been something close to de facto sterling convertibility for all nonresidents of the sterling area since 1954. At that time, the British Government unified the transferable account areas and began to support transferable sterling in foreign exchange markets at only a slight discount from official parity rates; they also reopened the channels of trade on a wholly nondiscriminatory basis for the main basic agricultural and nonagricultural commodities.

In addition, as 12 postwar years have passed with only 2 minor and short-lived recessions in the United States, another world economic nightmare is slowly dissolving: the fear of a worldwide dollar shortage created by a major American depression. The recession of 1953–54 did not have a seriously multiplied effect abroad, and it is coming to be widely believed that future American recessions can and will be held within similar limits through domestic policy measures.

This is by no means a dismal picture. Does it follow that, in our economic relations and foreign economic policies toward the more advanced countries of the free world, we can and should simply rest on our oars, seeking to avoid any serious worsening of the situation but also refraining from any concerted effort to improve it? Or is it really more fragile and less stable than it looks, a condition possibly calling for new leadership exerted in this period of relative calm rather than awaiting new emergencies and once again improvising policies to deal with them?

There are unfortunately several elements making for basic doubts as to the long-term stability of the recent favorable developments.

The first is the problem of the United States balance of payments. Between 1951 and 1956, the problem of worldwide dollar shortage, which had been the central concern of foreign economic policy for almost all governments during the first 5 postwar years, receded into the background. The reasons can be seen in the accompanying table (p. 22), which summarizes the United States balance of payments for 1948 (the first year of the Marshall plan) and for 1953, 1955, 1956, and the first quarter of 1957. It will be noted, comparing 1955 with 1948, that our trade surplus had been cut in half, not through a reduction in exports but through a much larger increase in imports. Our current account surplus as a whole, excluding aid, was less than a third of the 1948 level. From 1953 until the latter part of 1956, the current surplus was much more than covered by the combination of Government grants, net Government loans, and private investment, so that during this 4-year period we sold \$1.3 billion worth of gold and also increased our short-term liabilities to foreign banks and official institutions by some \$4 billion. It is no wonder that so little was heard of the dollar shortage during those years, that foreign reserves generally were less straitened than in most of the postwar era, that conditions favored an approach to at least de facto convertibility of many foreign currencies, and that discrimination against American imports was reduced. There were even a few voices expressing concern about the "dollar surplus" which was reflected in the growth of our short-term foreign liabilities.

*United States balance of payments, 1948–56*

[Billions of dollars]

| | 1948 | 1953 | 1955 | 1956 | 1st quarter 1957 [1] (at annual rates) |
|---|---|---|---|---|---|
| Exports of goods and services (excluding direct military assistance [2]) | +16.8 | +17.1 | +19.9 | +23.5 | +26.5 |
| Merchandise (f. o. b.) | +13.3 | +12.3 | +14.3 | +17.3 | +20.3 |
| Services | +2.2 | +2.9 | +3.1 | +3.5 | +3.6 |
| Income on investments | +1.4 | +1.9 | +2.5 | +2.7 | +2.6 |
| Imports of goods and services | −10.3 | −16.6 | −17.9 | −19.8 | −20.2 |
| Merchandise (f. o. b.) | −7.6 | −11.0 | −11.5 | −12.8 | −13.2 |
| Services | −1.6 | −2.7 | −3.1 | −3.5 | −3.0 |
| Income on investments | −.3 | −.4 | −.5 | −.6 | −.6 |
| Military expenditures abroad | −.8 | −2.5 | −2.8 | −2.9 | −3.4 |
| Balance on goods and services | +6.5 | +.5 | +2.0 | +3.7 | +6.3 |
| Balance of trade | +5.6 | +1.3 | +2.8 | +4.5 | +7.1 |
| Balance of services and investment income | +1.7 | +1.7 | +2.0 | +2.1 | +2.6 |
| Military expenditures abroad | −.8 | −2.5 | −2.8 | −2.9 | −3.4 |
| Unilateral transfers (excluding direct military assistance [2]) | −4.5 | −2.5 | −2.5 | −2.3 | −2.3 |
| Governmental | −3.8 | −2.0 | −2.0 | −1.8 | −1.7 |
| Private remittances | −.7 | −.5 | −.5 | −.5 | −.6 |
| Net movement of United States capital (minus means outflow from United States) | −1.9 | −.6 | −1.5 | −3.6 | −4.2 |
| Private | −.9 | −.4 | −1.2 | −3.0 | −3.2 |
| Government | −1.0 | −.2 | −.3 | −.6 | −1.0 |
| Net movement of foreign capital (minus means outflow from United States) | +.3 | +1.1 | +1.4 | +1.8 | (3) |
| Long-term, United States securities, and miscellaneous short-term | −.1 | +.1 | +.7 | +.7 | +1.5 |
| Short-term liabilities to foreign banks and official institutions | +.4 | +1.0 | +.7 | +1.1 | −1.5 |
| Gold sales (+) and purchases (−) | −1.5 | +1.2 | +.1 | −.3 | −1.4 |
| Errors and omissions | +1.1 | +.3 | +.5 | +.7 | +1.6 |

[1] Preliminary.
[2] Direct military assistance financed by Government grants amounted to $0.3 billion in 1948; $4.3 billion in 1953; $2.1 billion in 1955; $2.6 billion in 1956; and a rate of $2.4 billion in the first quarter of 1957.
[3] Less than $50 million.

Source: Department of Commerce, Survey of Current Business, July 1954; June 1956; and June 1957

This last point ought not to have caused any serious concern, since the moderate increase in foreign reserves was badly needed to increase international liquidity and to safeguard expanding world trade levels against the shocks of minor fluctuations. From this viewpoint, in-
reversed in 1956.

During that year our trade surplus mounted quarter by quarter, reaching a level in early 1957 well above that of 1948. While it was substantially intensified during the Suez crisis, this disturbing new trend had begun before the canal nationalization and has persisted since the canal's reopening. Its predominant feature is a continuous and large-scale expansion of exports while imports increase much more slowly. The welcome increase in United States private investment abroad, which has doubled since 1954, has fallen far short of financing this expanded trade surplus.

In consequence, we have once more been accumulating monetary gold since the beginning of 1956, and foreign dollar reserves are also once more declining. In the first quarter of 1957, foreign gold and dollar holdings fell by almost $500 million, contrasted with an increase of similar magnitude a year before. This meant a net deterioration at a rate of $4 billion a year. For most other trading nations, moreover, the position was gravely aggravated by the large and steady increase of West Germany's dollar holdings, which was matched by even larger reductions elsewhere. A serious international financial crisis was averted during 1956 only through large loans and standby credits from the International Monetary Fund to Britain, France, and other countries.

It is too soon to disentangle from these events the role of short-term speculation. There has certainly been a flight from the French franc because of the Algerian troubles and domestic inflation, a process stemmed rather than stopped by the de facto partial devaluation of August 1957. There has likewise been a loss of confidence in sterling as a result of inflationary pressures in the United Kingdom and other sterling area countries. There has been a move into deutschemarks in hopes of an upward exchange rate revaluation. But underlying all this is the American export boom and import sluggishness. Once again the question has been raised in many minds whether there is a structural dollar shortage in the world—whether other leading countries can ever "live with the dollar" on ordinary terms or whether they must reverse the liberalizing trends of recent years and organize for permanent discrimination against the United States. These doubts and fears, it need hardly be added, would be greatly intensified by an American industrial recession.

This type of concern is also enhanced by the extent to which the 1953–56 period of relative dollar ease was a result of "abnormal financing" by the United States Government. Entirely apart from direct military assistance, such financing in 1956 comprised $2.9 billion in military expenditures abroad (this includes base construction, contributions to NATO infrastructure, the portion of troop pay spent overseas, and offshore procurement of military equipment in other countries) $1.7 billion in Government nonmilitary grants, and $100 million in net Government loans, or a total of $4.7 billion—more than one-quarter of our merchandise exports.

Thus the absence of an acute dollar shortage in recent years has been largely a result of our military expenditures overseas and the mutual security program in both its military and nonmilitary phases. On the military side, base construction expenditures are likely to taper off; offshore procurement is already drawing to a close; and any significant withdrawal of troops stationed abroad would immediately reduce the troop pay component of this large overseas dollar expenditure item. At the same time, the future of the foreign aid program is in doubt. To the extent that dollar availabilities in the rest of the world depend on these programs, therefore, the recent past must be considered more a breathing spell than a durable solution to the worldwide dollar shortage problem. If there is a resurgence of effective protectionism regarding American imports; if there is a domestic economic recession of any magnitude; or if inflationary pressures abroad are not brought under control satisfactorily, the present difficulties, already serious enough, will become acutely critical.

Another source of uncertainty is the unsatisfactory economic position of the United Kingdom. Here any weakness has a magnified effect abroad because of the key world position of sterling. After an excellent recovery from the balance-of-payments crisis of 1951—the third biennial crisis since the war—Britain has now suffered for almost 3 years from chronic weakness in her balance of payments resulting from domestic inflationary pressures. Strenuous monetary restraints and some reinforcing fiscal policy measures have operated only very slowly to improve this situation, and have by no means provided as assured remedy. Britain's troubles in the Middle East came on top of this already unsteady position. France and a number of other Western European countries—notably excepting Germany, Switzerland, and Austria—are in similar positions. There is a real danger that any further weakening may be followed by restrictionist foreign trade measures which could rapidly reverse the improvements of the past half decade.

Further weakness comes from uncertainty abroad on the future lines of American foreign economic policy. Our failure to ratify the OTC agreement in 1956 or 1957 is one element in this uncertainty. Another is the whole question of what sort of import policy will follow the expiration in 1958 of the Trade Agreements Extension Act. A third arises from the unsolved problem of agricultural surpluses.

There are also widespread doubts as to the adequacy of growth rates in the free world, not only in the underdeveloped but also in the advanced countries. Europe has enjoyed a 4-year boom in production and trade, with a growth rate higher than our own, but there are many doubts as to whether it can be sustained. There is also the shadow of the much more rapid growth rates in the Soviet world, backed by a prodigious rate of annual investment in heavy industry and by the large-scale and rigorous training of scientific and technological manpower. And in the Far East, there is the chronic question of whether the free world trading system can accommodate the needs of Japan as foreign military exepnditures there continue to decline, or whether Japan will be tempted increasingly to seek her economic future by new ties with the Chinese mainland.

These many uncertainties raise the prospect that, without renewed United States leadership, individual countries will relapse into autarkic methods of protecting their economies againsts outside influence or will seek anew to organize the soft currency countries as a whole against the dollar world. This latter idea, which has had many sponsors and taken many forms, including the Council of Europe's Strasbourg Plan, has always been one theme of believers in the inexitability of a permanent dollar shortage. It has won some support even in the United States, as well as a great deal abroad. Underlying it is the question, as much political as economic, whether the free world is to be divided sharply and indefinitely into hard and soft currency blocs, engaged in a kind of mutual economic warfare, or whether the basic pattern is to be a united free-world economy.

The most immediate policy problem in this area arises from the Rome Treaty of 1957 to create a customs union among the six European members of the Schuman plan Coal and Steel Community and the current initiatives to associate with this customs union the United Kingdom and other Western European countries in a free-trade zone. Despite its length the complexity of its trade provisions, the Rome Treaty leaves many questions unresolved. Its intentions regarding agriculture are especially obscure; they apparently contemplate not so much a free market in farm products as some form of internationally administered price supports. On the financial side the treaty is exceedingly vague, although much closer coordination of exchange rates and monetary policies would seem indispensable to a successful customs union. The free trade area arrangements have not yet been worked out in detail, and there is a major conflict between the British desire to exclude agriculture and the insistence of Denmark and the Netherlands that it be somehow included.

Will such a customs union and free-trade zone prove to be to the interest of the United States? There can certainly be adverse effects on some American interests. Exporters of such items as machine tools, electrical equipment, other machinery, chemicals, pharmaceuticals, and vehicles may find it substantially harder to compete for European markets against producers within the tariff-free area. Moreover, if successful in achieving its European purposes, a customs union may have some adverse effect on the terms of trade between the United States and Europe, and should strengthen European competition against American exports in third markets. It could also strengthen European bargaining power in negotiations with the United States on tariffs and other economic policies.

In short, many of the reasons impelling the British, Scandinavian, and Swiss Governments to get inside a European customs union system through the free-trade zone device, for fear of the effects of the creation of such a customs union excluding them, are also relevant to the United States. On the other hand, if the principal limitation on American exports to Europe is the availability of dollars to Europe, American exports as a whole ought not to suffer, even in the short run, while if the longer run effect were a substantially stronger European economy, this would be to our economic as well as our political interest. Much depends on the common tariff level of the customs union with the outside world, including the United States, and on the broad policies it might adopt with respect to dollar trade. In Professor Viner's terminology, a predominantly trade-creating European customs union would be desirable, while a predominantly trade-diverting one would not.

There is an analogy here between the economic and political movements for European unity. A united Europe acting as a neutralist third force would certainly not be in our political interests, and a European economy organized to minimize trade relations with the dollar world would likewise not be to our interests. By the same token, a stronger Europe firmly allied to the United States would be desirable from every viewpoint.

The policy line suggested by this reasoning is that the United States should support the new European movement if, and only if, it is firmly fit into a wider framework of multilateral trade and payments. This means that its common outside tariff should be moderate, and that discrimination through quantitative restrictions on dollar imports should be reduced rather than increased as a result of its formation. Nor should its creation be the occasion for any additional exchange controls or other steps away from the still valid goal of general currency convertibility. For many reasons, these results are more likely to flow from the wider free trade zone than from the narrower customs union alone; American influence should therefore favor the wider plan. On such a basis, the possible gains from added political and economic strength in Europe would seem to justify the risk of such comparatively small adjustments in the pattern of American trade as might be required. But such a basis is possible only if there exists a strong global framework to contain the regional arrangement.

The prospect of major new policy developments along these lines by the other leading industrialized countries is in fact one major reason for a fresh review of our own general trade policy. Unless a healthy wider framework is strengthened and assured, there is a real danger that the world economy will once again move toward cleavage and away from integration, with anti-Americanism a major theme of the organized soft currency world. This would not, to be sure, be an economic disaster for the United States, but its economic effect would be unfortunate alike both for us and for our free world friends, and the political effect might be very seriously adverse. In any event, certain questions are pressing for early decision. In 1958 we must take a final stand on the Organization for Trade Cooperation, and even more important, we must determine the future of the reciprocal trade agreements program.

During the past 15 years, an enormous amount of effort has gone into working out a long-run American commercial policy suited to our unprecedented position in the world economy, in keeping with our creditor status, and harmonized with our broad foreign policy objectives. This broad policy line has been supported by the leadership of both our political parties, but it has been increasingly an uphill battle. It has certainly not won general popular support of the kind which can be claimed for collective security policy through NATO and otherwise, provision of technical assistance to underdeveloped countries, or other important aspects of postwar foreign policy. Except in 1949, each extension of the reciprocal trade agreements legislation has been surrounded with additional limitations and broader escape clauses. While we officially favor freer trade, the structure of peril-point and escape-clause requirements in this legislation, especially since 1955, comes close to preventing any replacement of domestic production by imports, no matter how inefficient or unessential the domestic production concerned. And there is heavy pressure against permitting imports to absorb a larger share of any particular market, even if the total is expanding enough to avoid absolute decreases in sales of domestic output. Meanwhile, commercial policies of the rest of the world are still far short of the ideals we have proclaimed.

This situation has led some observers to argue that the whole liberal policy line is a theorist's dream, and its results clearly not commensurate with the effort. They say that tariffs are far too much emphasized; that adherence to unconditional most-favored-nation treatment reduces our ability to make effective bilateral bargains; that convertibility is an ever-receding mirage; and that we too should join the "realists" of the rest of the world and fight for our economic interests with quotas, export subsidies, and special bilateral deals.

The broad policy alternatives in the foreign trade field come down to either (*a*) abandoning the postwar liberalization effort, (*b*) seeking to keep things much as they now are resisting retreats but taking no new initiatives, or (*c*) trying to push ahead on the same lines with renewed vigor and ingenuity.

Of these three, the second would seem the easiest course, but developments elsewhere in the world, especially in Europe, will probably make it impossible. As between the first and the third, this writer is satisfied that the third is clearly preferable on both political and economic grounds. It can readily be admitted that American imports are more affected by the level of domestic business activity than they are by minor changes in tariffs. Domestic economic stability and growth are still the prime prescriptions for a sound foreign economic policy. But our role in the world economy is so powerful that the set of our policy line greatly affects economic policy throughout the free world. And it is a fact, not a theorist's dream, that the free world is economically healthier and its enterprise more vigorous under a system of multilateral than of bilateral trade, under conditions of nondiscrimination rather than discrimination, and with the market instrument of tariffs rather than administrative instruments of quotas or exchange controls as the normal means for such economic protection as is inevitable.

Compared with the late 1940's, the main structural economic adjustments among the advanced countries required for freer multilateral trade have been made. The German case is a striking example of the way in which, in a reasonably favorable, economically open environment, adjustments can be made rapidly to overcome seemingly hopeless conditions of balance-of-payments deficits and structural unemployment.

In specific terms, this policy line would mean ratification of the OTC, and a further extension of the trade agreements legislation in 1958. The extension should preferably be for a period of at least 5 years. If the peril-point and escape-clause provisions cannot be eliminated, they should certainly be amended to redress the balance of interest in their criteria, so that the Tariff Commission and the President could take into account benefits or injuries to exporters as well as import-competing domestic producers, and could give their proper weight to broader considerations of national interest. The agenda also includes tariff reclassification and further simplification of customs procedures. In the agricultural field, if the basic domestic policy cannot be made to bring home and world prices into accord, this policy line would not exclude a broader use of surpluses in conjunction with economic development programs. But it would have to mean abandonment of the "sell regardless" philosophy of certain recent proposals for agriculaural legislation. It would also mean a review of protective measures imposed for national security reasons to ensure that they meet a real and not pretended test of defense essentiality, not in

World War I or II terms but in a world of nuclear weapons and collective security alliances.

Finally, there is the question of a renewed attack on the problem of currency inconvertibility. Although most other major currencies, including sterling, the deutschemark, the Belgian franc, and the Dutch guilder are close to de facto convertibility, there is no doubt that, if it could be achieved without an intensification of trade restrictions, formal convertibility, even of limited to nonresidents of the countries concerned, would be a substantial forward step to a more stable world trading system. It cannot be forced prematurely, as the 1947 sterling experiment showed. But there is some evidence that a rather more encouraging attitude on the part of the United States might have brought about convertibility of sterling and the other leading European currencies in 1953 or 1954, and the question of policy is what our attitude should be if similar conditions again present themselves.

One prerequisite might well be further strengthening of the resources of the International Monetary Fund and arrangements and its even greater use for stabilization loans or standby stabilization credits. In the institutional field, moreover, it would be highly desirable to arrange for coordination of the work of the IMF and the OTC (assuming that the latter comes into existence), so that the financial and commercial aspects of balance-of-payments problems could be analyzed concurrently and complementary action taken on both sides.

Clearly no combination of American and international measures will serve as a universal prescription for continuous good health in the world economy. The economic repercusisons of the cold war, the complex and changing relations among more or less developed countries, and the dynamics of necessarily uneven growth will always call for new adjustments and new adaptations of policy. Neither the United States nor other nations have yet wholly solved the dilemma of reconciling growth with price stability. Varying degrees of inflation are bound tc create serious international disturbances, as the experience of 1957 makes all too plain. But there is a basic choice for the United States between a broad line of foreign economic policy which favors rapid adaptations and the maintenance of forces for growth, as against one which, by seeking to preserve obsolescent positions, encourages a downwar spiral of international retaliatory restrictions whenever any chill breeze ruffles the world economy. The program advocated here means clear-cut support for the first of these two lines.

Is a program of this type politically feasible for the United States? The difficulties should not be underestimated. This is a field of little public glamour. It is especially susceptible to effective political action by particular local or industrial interests exposed to adverse effects from further policy liberalization. Moreover, little effort has gone to public education and persuasion in this area, and the administration has not brought to bear on it all the resources of political leadership. Unless the public can be made aware of the basic interdependence of exports and imports, of the substantial affirmatice American interest in the healthy growth of international trade, and of the relation between free world trade and our political objectives, success can hardly be expected.

Economic aid to the advanced countries has not been discussed here because such aid is no longer an instrument of national strategy. And it ought not be, except in cases of compelling emergency. Military aid is quite a different matter. There is every reason to believe that a sound system of military specialization under a collective security policy will involve unreimbursed American provision of certain types of expensive military equipment as long as the cold war lasts. Apart from military aid, however, the lessons of the postwar decade strongly suggest that, given national policies which avoid serious unemployment or serious domestic inflation, and given a strong framework of cooperative international institutions to help maintain ground rules, resolve disputes, and tide over particular crises without destroying the fabric of cooperation, the forces of the market can be made to work toward multilateral equilibrium. Even more important than equilibrium as such, is the fact that it can be accompanied by substantial growth rates in the advanced countries. In the underdeveloped countries, to which we now turn, the situation is quite different. But there is a close connection between the two sets of issues. One of the strongest reasons for continuing to promote a liberal policy for the free world economy as a whole is to build a framework in which the underdeveloped countries can progressively take their place as factors in a mutually beneficial international economic order.

### RELATIONS WITH UNDERDEVELOPED AREAS

While the postwar trend of economic relations among the advanced countries has been broadly in accord with our basic foreign policy objectives, the same cannot be said with respect to the underdeveloped areas, especially those recently freed from direct or indirect colonial rule. The political problems of nationalist reaction against the West, and of aggressive neutralism often biased toward the Communist bloc, have deep-seated causes, by no means limited to economic factors. But the preoccupation of these areas with their desperate poverty and with the growing divergence between their living standards and those of the advanced countries gives to economic policy in this field unique potentialities as an instrument of national strategy.

Economic development has become one of the great talismanic phrases of our time. It is a leading, self-conscious political goal of most of the world's peoples and a central battleground of the cold war. The urge for accelerated development has become a major factor in world politics. Totalitarian and free institutions are in direct and visible competition to demonstrate their superiority as methods of fulfilling this urge. Economic policy in this field is at once the most readily available instrument for pursuing basic free world aims, the one in which the West has the greatest natural advantages, and the one whose importance is being increasingly recognized by the Soviets. Success for the methods of freedom would not only be of critical importance to the political future of the presently non-Communist underdeveloped areas, but could also be a major factor in weakening the cohesion of the Communist bloc itself.

No subject is more susceptible to oversimplification or misleading generalization than the problems of economic development. They are as much social, cultural, and political as they are strictly economic.

They range all the way from the almost undevelopable conditions of Libya to the potentially rich, still largely unexplored frontiers of Brazil, the Rhodesias, and even Canada and Australia. Even if consideration is confined to the very poor regions of Asia, the Middle East, Africa, and Latin America—those with an apparent per capita production of less than $200 per year—there is a vast variety in conditions, needs, and current rates of growth and change.

Most of these areas have shared to some extent in the postwar international trade boom and worldwide rise in economic activity. Most have gained by the general shift in the terms of trade since prewar times in favor of primary products as against manufactured goods. Some have benefited from the exploitation of oil, uranium, or other natural resources in very high world demand. In much of Latin America, although there are certain critical exceptions, the postwar decade has seen very substantial growth even though it has been marred by lack of balance, varying degrees of inflation, and political instability.

On the other hand, in most of Asia, the Middle East, and northern and tropical Africa, except for the oil countries, growth has been very slow indeed and is threatened by the formidable race of population increase. This expansion of population against a limited natural resource base, especially in agriculture, has led to consumption levels in some areas lower than those of the late 19th century. The contrast with advancing living standards in the Western World and with the prodigious rate of industrialization in the Soviet Union is becoming steadily more pronounced. Hence the critical urgency of accelerated economic development and the significance of outside assistance for political as well as economic relationships.

The concept of international governmental assistance to economic development is a postwar phenomenon. Developing countries in the 19th century did, of course, benefit greatly from foreign investment, but these were private funds moving abroad for profit. Only in rare cases, usually connected with political alliances, were government-to-government loans involved. International assistance on a public grant basis was unheard of. Moreover, much of the world accepted economic stagnation as the natural order of things. Today it is widely agreed that the economically advanced countries have, as a matter of public policy, an affirmative interest in promoting accelerated development, but there is much disagreement on the desirable magnitudes and means for such assistance.

Is this a valid consensus, and what in particular is the nature of the American interest in this process?

Our possible economic interests fall in the three standard categories: To provide new sources of required American imports, new markets for American exports, and new outlets for American investment. Both the first two are significant and of growing importance. The prospect for increased American dependence on imported raw materials has been thoroughly documented by the Paley Commission; it applies especially to Western Hemisphere minerals and Middle Eastern oil. The developmental process itself accounts for an important share of the export market for American, as well as for European and Japanese, machinery and other capital goods. This may be extended in due course to certain types of consumer goods, although most developing countries are seeking to meet a broader range of their domestic needs through industrialization and diversification.

On the other hand, the notion that increased investment in underdeveloped countries is required to maintain American economic stability carries little weight. Technological development and increasing population at home should continue to offer fruitful outlets for most of our domestic capital, and there are profitable investment opportunities in advanced as well as underdeveloped nations abroad. We do, of course, have an economic interest in having the rest of the world continue open to us economically, but this consideration merges into the political and security interest.

It is to this political and security interest that one must look for the main justification of an active American governmental policy in support of economic development abroad. Directly, the interest is in having these areas free and friendly. Indirectly, this is reinforced by the positive economic interests of our industrially advanced allies, whose future economic vitality is much more dependent than our own on accelerated growth in the underdeveloped countries and in their potential both as raw material sources and as markets. The political dangers are in the first instance Communist expansionism, but they may also arise from other forms of totalitarianism.

The evolution of postwar policy in this field can be very briefly summarized. While the extent and depth of the preoccupation of underdeveloped countries, especially the former colonial areas, with conscious promotion of development was hardly foreseen, the postwar plans for a world economic order gave this problem some attention in the creation of the International Bank for Reconstruction and Development and the investment provisions of the draft ITO charter. Some hope was also expressed for a restoration of international portfolio investment, although it was recognized that recovery from the collapse of the great depression would be slow. In addition, the United Nations specialized agencies were to provide technical assistance in their respective fields.

When President Truman announced his point 4 program in 1949, the world was heavily conditioned in its thinking by the example of the Marshall plan. It was widely expected that the new project would also involve billions of dollars of Government expenditures on a grant basis. This was a misreading of the point 4 proposal. By its own terms, point 4 was focused on expanded technical assistance as a basis for a greatly enhanced flow of private developmental capital, but not on a new program for public financing of capital assistance, either in loans or in grants. The Act for International Development of 1950, designed to implement the point 4 program, faithfully reflected this limited concept. It contributed to the expanded United Nations technical assistance program and also laid the basis for a very substantial bilateral technical assistance program. It was paralleled by the Colombo plan for development of south and southeast Asia, originally a British Commonwealth affair but later expanded to include non-Commonwealth countries on both the supplying and receiving ends.

From the start of the point 4 program, there was always some conflict between the advocates of "pure technical assistance" (i. e., provision of experts who would provide instruction, preferably to a cadre of local instructors, and occasional demonstration in techniques), and proponents of a more liberal concept of technical assistance who would associate with it a significant degree of capital assistance. To some extent the categories were inherently fuzzy, since effective technical assistance often required supplies for demonstration, and some types of demonstration had to be on a substantial scale to be meaningful. The use of Government funds to assist directly in economic development began in the Far East as a byproduct of the cold war, in the effort to keep friendly countries from following the fate of China. As a recognized explicit category in the mutual security program, development assistance dates only from 1953. And only in 1956 did the administration come to advocate such assistance as a part of American foreign economic policy for the indefinite future.

During this period of gradual evolution of American policy, the International Bank, with the encouragement of our Government, gradually expanded its lending criteria and its volume of loans. The Export-Import Bank began to make development loans to friendly governments and quasi-governmental enterprises, especially in Latin America, a major part of its activity. In 1955, under pressure from the other American Republics, we abandoned our longstanding opposition to the creation of the International Finance Corporation as an affiliate of the International Bank, able to lend to private enterprises without Government guaranty. In general expressions of American policy, steadily increasing recognition was given to the importance of economic development as a long-run objective, the most noteworthy pronouncements being the statements by both Presidents Truman and Eisenhower that, in the event of a general disarmament agreement, an important share of the savings would be devoted to promoting economic development. Apart from governmental policy, economic development has become a major concern of the large American foundations, of academic research, and of informed public discussion.

At the same time there has developed, both at home and abroad, increasing uncertainty as to the precise character of our purposes in this field and the methods we are using to accomplish them. The Congress has been voting annual mutual security authorizations and appropriations with growing reluctance. It was against this background that major official reappraisals were undertaken in 1956–57—on the executive side by the Fairless Committee and on the congressional side by the Senate Special Committee To Study the Foreign Aid Program. The conclusions of these bodies were paralleled by a number of important unofficial reviews. While differing in detail, they were in accord on three major points: That development assistance should be made an explicit instrument of United States foreign policy for a long period to come; that it should include substantial governmental provision of capital over and above more effective inducements to privately financed development; and that it should be established on a systematic basis as a long-term undertakeing. A program based on these points was submitted to the Congress in May 1957, but the resulting action fell far short of the recommendations.

In this whole field, too, there appear to be three possible lines of action: to abandon the effort; to continue from year to year within the present framework; or to define a new program. The first course is clearly incompatible with our basic political purposes. As between the other two, a fresh approach seems required alike by the doubt and confusion which still exist in the public and congressional minds and by the objective needs of national strategy. It would be worse than useless, however, to talk loudly about a new approach without following through with effective action.

The requirements for accelerated development are diverse and complex. They include in varying proportions education and training; the modification of cultural attitudes and institutions hostile to change; often land reforms; development of administrative talent and stimulus to enterprise, whether private or public. They also include mobilization of maximum domestic savings voluntarily or through taxation or forced saving; and capital accumulation of three kinds—(*a*) social capital for education and public health, (*b*) overhead capital in transportation facilities, communications, power and water supplies, and (*c*) directly productive capital in industrial, agricultural, and commercial enterprise, all applied in the most productive manner for balanced growth. Most of this must be done by means of policies and actions internal to the developing country, but the contribution of outsiders may be of critical importance in making development possible without resort to totalitarian controls.

Until a few years ago, it was generally hoped and widely expected that the foreign governmental role could be limited to technical assistance and a moderate amount of overhead capital provided through the International Bank, and that the rest could be done through domestic efforts and foreign private investment. Considering the general disruption of the war and postwar years, international private investment has been far from negligible. In the 3 years 1954 to 1956 alone, long-term net foreign private investment by the United States has amounted to some $4.7 billion, and in early 1957 it was running at an annual rate of over $3 billion. Most of this has been direct investment, but there has recently also been a growing and welcome component of portfolio investment, signifying the gradual restoration of an international market for securities. Of the total, however, almost half has gone to Canada, about two-thirds to Canada and Latin America taken together, and recently about one-fifth to Europe—leaving relatively little for the poorest areas with the greatest needs and the greatest current political importance. Moreover, the direct investment in these latter areas has been heavily concentrated in petroleum and other minerals, with little in general industry.

The obstacles to a larger and broader flow of private investment have often been rehearsed. They include the comparatively favorable opportunities at home, unfamiliarity of many American investors with conditions abroad, political risks resulting from unstable governments and unsettled international conditions, foreign governmental policies unfriendly to private enterprise in general and outside capital in particular, the danger of exchange controls preventing the repatriation of profits, and the possibilities of discriminatory taxation or other harassments. The Suez Canal nationalization has doubtless further dampened the enthusiasm of potential investors, at least in the Middle East.

Not all of these obstacles are incurable, and some progress has been made in reducing them. No effort should be spared in continuing this process. Tax incentives on this end could certainly be of some assistance; it is unfortunate that 3 years have passed without action since the Randall Commission's modest recommendations in this regard. Government guaranties against certain types of risk deserve further exploration, although it seems doubtful if the most serious real risks are susceptible of Government guaranty. There is also much to be done by private enterprise in learning how to conduct itself abroad so as to win recognition of the mutuality of interests between the investor and the developing country. In this connection it would be helpful to obtain and disseminate more information on successful experiments in joint ventures, the licensing of patents and industrial techniques, and other similar cooperative private investment activities.

The record strongly suggests, however, that the best that can be done on these lines will not suffice, and that governmental action is also required, especially in providing social and overhead capital. There is already a good deal of such action. At present the International Bank is lending some $300 to $400 million a year, of which 80 percent is in American dollars, but this magnitude seems to be about the ceiling under present project standards and loan terms. The Export-Import Bank is now putting a similar amount annually into development loans. The true development assistance component of the mutual security program is very difficult to disentangle, but its current yearly rate may be estimated at about $400 million. There is also the United Nations technical assistance program of $30 million, the United States bilateral technical assistance program of over $100 million, and some bilateral assistance from other countries under the Colombo plan and other arrangements. Under the Agricultural Trade Development and Assistance Act of 1954, local currency proceeds from sales of agricultural surpluses can be used for development assistance, and this is being done increasingly, especially in the very large programs for India and Brazil negotiated in 1956 and 1957. What seems called for is partly an increase in the volume of governmental assistance for development; but equally essential and now lacking is an explicit and long-term commitment to helping a necessarily slow process. The essence of a fresh approach would be clarity as to purpose, orders of magnitude, duration, forms and conditions of assistance, and organization to administer it.

What lines might such a fresh approach take? It is suggested that it be a commitment to assist the process of deliberate development in any non-Communist country below some reasonable poverty standard, on the basis of country programs demonstrating maximum self-help, presenting a reasonable pattern of investment priorities, and identifying the critical bottlenecks in skills or capital which can be supplied from outside. There can be no uniformity in detail. Each program must be tailored to individual country conditions. There cannot be an unlimited capital supply commitment, but there can be assurance for some continuing assistance over a sufficient time period to set a realistic programing process in motion where it does not exist or to give it some reasonable prospect of success.

In essence, the function of outside capital assistance should be to permit development under free institutions without the further squeezing of already fearfully low consumption levels which is achievable only by totalitarian methods. In the poorest countries with large population growth, the best that can be hoped for in the short run is to increase living standards 1 percent or 2 percent a year. Reducing the gap betwen underdeveloped and advanced countries is necessarily a much longer run goal, unless the advanced countries are to halt their own processes of growth, which would be disastrous. The important thing is to have a visible process in motion. To this end, popular demonstration projects should not be wholly ruled out even though they may not always represent the soundest use of capital.

The administration's proposals for a development loan fund, submitted to the Congress in May 1957, were generally in line with this approach. They called for lending authority of $2 billion over a 3 year period, segregating developments assistance from the military and defense support programs and also distinguishing it from economic aid to deal with short-run emergencies. The Mutual Security Act of 1957 accepted the device of the fund, but reduced to a 2-year authorization of $1,125 million and an appropriation of only $300 million for the first year, 1957–58. Both in magnitude and in duration, therefore, the new concept was gravely limited.

Nevertheless, a possible foundation for a new and more effective approach has been laid. An energetic program built on this foundation, given more adequate magnitudes and greater authority for forward commitments in the future, might transform the climate of development programing in the underdeveloped areas of key political importance.

The main content of such a program would be technical assistance and contributions to the financing of social and overhead capital, fields in which private investment is unlikely to be attracted for the foreseeable future. It is a sound principle to put the bulk of assistance for economic development on a loan rather than a grant basis. At the same time, although technical assistance and social capital may increase productivity as much as or more than directly productive investments, there might be considerable political and administrative advantage in providing these components as grants, requiring repayment for all other assistance. Where, as is likely generally to be the case, there are serious prospective difficulties in transferring repayments in dollars, there is much to be said for local currency loans on a revolving fund basis, with a commitment for reinvestment of the proceeds in further development projects extending over a very long period. This device would combine the advantage of requiring economic calculations of the productivity of each set of projects, while making the assistance in general a very long-term investment in the recipient country's development. Even in the early stages, certain types of industrial and commercial development could and should be reserved for private investment, either domestic or foreign.

As the recent Indian and Brazilian programs make clear, agricultural surpluses can play an important and constructive part in development programs if their supply is assured over time and if they are coupled with other balancing components. To avoid disruption of normal markets, their supply should be for emergency stockpiles or for increases in consumption demonstrably related to the development program. These are not impossible conditions to secure.

Is it right to make the main emphasis in such a program bilateral rather than multilateral? Among the underdeveloped countries themselves, there is widespread support for the Special United Nations Fund for Economic Development (SUNFED). But this organization as presently proposed does not seem capable of assuring proper conditions of self-help or other standards which can reasonably be claimed by assisting countries. Nonetheless, participation by other advanced countries would be highly desirable. The solution may lie in a general invitation to others to participate, with arrangements for coordination informally on a country-by country basis. In face of the dislocations to the European economy imposed by the Middle Eastern crisis and renewed balance-of-payments difficulties, large-scale participation in capital assistance by that important group of advanced countries can hardly be expected in the near future. In the technical assistance field, on the other hand, where the bottleneck is much more in personnel than in funds, serious consideration could well be given to shifting a larger share of the entire program to United Nations auspices.

The problem of Soviet rivalry in this field raises more difficult questions. No doubt the best answer to Soviet penetration is an adequate western program in whose significance and stability and underdeveloped countries have confidence. We clearly do not want to be subject to Soviet blackmail or to being played off against the Soviets by underdeveloped countries, but it is doubtful whether Soviet initiatives can be completely disregarded. Perhaps the wisest policy is to set a basic western program without regard to Soviet action, but to make some adjustments on an ad hoc basis when Soviet initiatives appear to offer real strategic dangers.

A word is in order, finally, on the problem of price and market instability for primary product exports of underdeveloped countries. In cases where they constitute the main source of foreign exchange earnings and of budgetary revenues, the notorious fluctuation in proceeds make sensible planning of a development program practically impossible. Except for wheat, sugar, and to a lesser extent tin, we have taken a resolutely hostile attitude toward international efforts to moderate these fluctuations, except for some adjustment of stockpiling policy. Since the entire stockpiling principle requires reexamination in the light of new weapons and changes in military strategy, it is questionable whether this device will continue to be available. While the record of international commodity agreements is dismal, and it is not easy to devise practical arrangements for stabilization, it is suggested that this policy also warrants reexamination to see whether in some instances a buffer stock arrangement could not be created which would lessen the market fluctuations without requiring production control or building up unworkable surpluses in the hands of international organizations.

## RELATIONS WITH THE SOVIET BLOC

The major element in our economic policy toward the Soviet bloc has been the effort to slow down the rate of Soviet military expansion through cooperation with other free industrialized countries in limiting or embargoing the export to the Soviets of arms, atomic energy materials, and strategic industrial goods. This problem, with its associations of steel scrap exports to Japan before World War II, easily arouses political emotion. Its proper appraisal would require intelligence information not publicly available. On the public record, however, it is hard to believe that the control arrangements have had a substantial effect in retarding Soviet military potential. It is also clear that they have created a good deal of interallied friction.

In the field of weapons themselves and of military technology closely related to weapons, it would obviously be undesirable to go out of our way to export to the Soviets. But in the general industrial field, even where there are strategic applications, the impossibility of keeping technology secret in open societies necessarily limits the results, even if the Soviet Union can still be regarded as technologically primitive. At the same time, developments in the past few years have largely dispelled the myth, once widely held in European countries and Japan and sedulously cultivated by the Soviets, that there was a gold mine of profitable trade being dammed back by the strategic embargo system.

In 1954, a major effort was made to reduce the control list to levels appropriate to a long-haul cold war situation and to make them more effective in administration. Another review of the same sort might well be in order. It would be an error, however, to regard this policy as a major instrument of national strategy.

The more serious problems of economic policy in relation to the Soviets arise from the comparative rates of growth in the Soviet and free worlds and from the new policies of Soviet penetration in the underdeveloped areas. The latter topic has been touched on briefly in the previous section. For the former, there is no specific prescription in the field of foreign-economic policy, since the essential need is the maintenance of conditions for steady growth in the free world as a whole. The era of most rapid Soviet advance in relation to the Western World was the 1930's, when for a decade they progressed rapidly while we stood still. The main lines of action indicated in this field, however, are measures to overcome the inadequacy of scientific and technical recruitment and training and other matters of essentially national concern outside the scope of this paper.

## CONCLUSION

If foreign economic policy is to be an effective instrument of national stategy, not only must its basic lines be set right but its day-today administration must also be integrated into national strategy as a whole. This has often not been the case, partly because of the technical character of many economic issues but even more because of the pressure of domestic interests and the preoccupations with domestic affairs of many of the Government agencies concerned.

Much has been done in recent years to rectify this condition through interdepartmental committees and coordinating experiments under the State Department, the Treasury, or the White House. Especially noteworthy was the institution in 1954 of the Foreign Economic Policy Council, chaired by a special Presidential assistant. The basic principle of this coordinating machinery is sound, provided that the committees are made effective conduits for the communication of policy and not merely devices for postponement or meaningless compromise of issues. That any specialized foreign economic policy committee must work within the framework of basic foreign policy as laid down in the National Security Council should go without saying.

At least of equal importance is the need for an altered climate of public opinion. There is little hope for an effective foreign economic policy, or for any effective foreign policy, without a dispelling of the complacency which mistakes the absence of hostilities for peace, or the absence of overt Communist revolutions for the vitality of free institutions. The lines of policy suggested here, although contributing to American prosperity in the long run, also involve their costs in human energies and material resources and in willing adjustments to help create a world environment conducive to the survival and growth of freedom. There must be better public and congressional understanding of the reciprocal relation between foreign economic policy and the broader interests of national strategy. There must above all be a renewed and widely shared sense of urgency. We are very far indeed from this necessary climate of public attitudes. Its creation is a major challenge to leadership in the Government and in the public at large.

# UNITED STATES FOREIGN TRADE POLICY IN RELATION TO ECONOMIC POLICY IN GENERAL

Arthur R. Upgren, Frederic R. Bigelow, professor of economics, Macalester College, St. Paul, Minn.; Formerly Dean of the Amos Tuck School of Business Administration, Dartmouth College, Hanover, N. H.

## Summary

The approach of this memorandum is—

(*a*) To consider the important methods whereby the United States may rationally meet its economic responsibilities in and to a world of which it is an indivisible part.

(*b*) To relate thereto the importance or relative unimportance of "our customs, tariff, and reciprocal-trade-agreement laws and trade agreements entered into thereunder and the administration thereof, with particular reference to * * * foreign economic policies of the United States and their effects upon domestic producers and employment." (The quoted section is a partial statement of the frame of reference, or program, of the subcommittee.)

The general nature of the conclusions reached are as follows:

(*a*) The trade-agreements policies and tariffs represent a desirable form of international economic cooperation for the United States. However, they are of relatively low importance in the short run and long run to other nations. Maintaining a highly productive domestic economy is of far greater importance to the world external to us. The consequences of this are given in the memorandum.

(*b*) Far more important to the rest of the world, particularly to the countries of Western Europe, is their tariff policy. This will affect their welfare in a ratio of 10 to 1 to the gains which might flow from any tariff action we can take.

## I. Context

The context within which the trade policies being investigated by the subcommittee operate can, first, be briefly given:

1. In the past 10 or 12 years, the imports of the United States have increased from about $6 billion to almost $16 billion. Only a small part of this immense increase in our imports can be imputed to the declining rates of our effective import duties. These duties have declined, in part, as the result of tariff-rate reductions and, in part, because the weight of our declining specific duties falls even more rapidly as the price levels of such goods have risen.

2. Scholarly studies made by Dr. Howard Piquet reveal that the increase in imports which would follow the complete removal of American tariffs would neither be large nor would the increase come more than very slowly.

3. The causes of our very large increase in imports since the end of World War II are to be found not in tariff reductions but in the maintenance of "high productive levels of output, employment, and incomes in the United States."

4. Desirable as it is to reduce tariffs in order to advance the general welfare of the people of the United States and to obtain the great fruits of specialization, of far greater importance is the entire set of policies whereby we maintain a high level of national income and production within the United States.

5. The great improvement in the imports of Western Europe is the result of internal economic recovery in Europe. The increase in the levels of production, real incomes, and welfare in Western Europe will depend, in the future, far more upon developing rational methods of production there than upon any reduction in American tariffs. Such rational action is primarily enlarging "the size of the market." Only in this way can the "cultural lag" in Europe be reduced. That "cultural lag" is the wide gap between modern, known methods of production which call for mass-producing industries, and the present social, political, and economic, or trading arrangements now prevailing in Western Europe.

## II. United States Effective Tariffs

The high point in the weight of our tariffs against imports was reached with the Smoot-Hawley Tariff Act of 1930. The average weight of ad valorem duties (effective) and the weight of specific duties (calculated as an ad valorem equivalent) was about 48 percent.

More recently this combined effective rate of our tariff duties on imports has been about 15 percent, at times being calculated as low as 12.5 percent.

A very rough calculation would probably show that as a result of cutting tariffs in trade agreements this average weight of duty fell from 48 percent to less than 30 percent and a figure of 27 percent can be suggested. The rest of the decline has been the result of the rise in prices of goods upon which specific, not ad valorem duties are levied. A "specific duty" is an absolute amount levied and stated in dollars and cents per physical unit of the article imported. Thus if a duty rate had been 20 cents per pound (or other unit) when the value of the article being imported was worth only 40 cents a pound, and that duty rate has been cut to 12 cents a pound in a time period when the price of the article has risen to a price of $1 a pound, the now effective ad valorem equivalent is 12 percent.

Here we observe that the original rate, specific, was 20 cents. The ad valorem equivalent was 50 percent with the imported article then being worth 40 cents a pound.

Now the tariff rate, specific, is cut to 12 cents. This is a reduction of 40 percent and well within trade agreement authorization. But the article imported has now risen in price to $1 a pound. The 12-cent specific duty has a weight of 12 percent on the present value of the article. The reduction in the effective rate has been from 50 percent to 12 percent. The actual cut in the tariff would have sent the rate down from 50 percent to 30 percent. The push downward the rest of the way to a 12-percent effective rate has been the consequence of the two facts: The rate of duty is stated in specific terms not value terms; the price of the article has risen.

The figures used in the foregoing assumed situation are not far from reality.

Clearly we have lowered our effective tariffs as the result of trade agreement action and as a further result of the worldwide inflation which has intervened between the time we last passed a General Tariff Act and today.

In these years when we have lowered our tariffs, other countries have increased theirs. We are probably midway on the list of countries and their effective tariffs. India, France, newly developing countries and older countries which believe they must depend upon tariff protection (France) today have higher tariff rates than the United States. In addition, where the United States has few direct limitations upon imports, many of these countries have many restrictions (import quotas, etc.).

### III. The Differential Impact of United States Effective Tariff Rates and the "Differential" Political Objectives We Have in World Areas

Our effective tariffs weigh most heavily against the countries of Western Europe, the countries of other like temperate climate areas, and Japan.

We positively discriminate against Czechoslovakia, the satellite countries, and the Soviet Union. The trade with the Soviet Union is small; the trade with the satellite countries, except Poland, has always been small; the trade with Czechoslovakia has been important and tariff rates against that country have been very high. Here considerations of high national policy go far beyond the matter of tariffs.

Our tariffs have always been high against Italy, Germany, France, and Britain in about that order of descent from their high levels. Our tariffs have been always the highest against Japan.

Next, our tariffs are high against competitive agricultural products of other countries with a like temperate climate. The rates are high against Australian wool, New Zealand butter, and Argentine flax, wheat, and corn. Lastly we have had extremely high effective rates against the world's sugar with a slight preference being afforded Cuba.

It must always be sobering to every American that when we increased our tariffs to an alltime high effective average rate against all dutiable imports in 1930, that the blow was far the most severe to Japan, Italy, and Germany—and in about that order. Those are the countries we faced in the last World War. They are precisely the "shoulder bastions" we want on our side henceforth.

Thus further substantial tariff reduction is most desirable "to win friends and influence people." I was serving in the Trade Agreements Section of the State Department in early 1935 when one of the last peace-loving delegations came to seek trade opportunities over here. Those opportunities were denied. Answering the denial on our part the members of the Japanese delegation askeed:

> In what directions do you suggest we turn to find trade opportunities for the output of the 700,000 workers we have entering our labor force each year?

The final country to be mentioned in this case is Canada. Her Prime Minister has spoken vigorously in his country's defense at the recent Convocation at Dartmouth College, September 5–7, when the subject in hand was Anglo-Canadian-American unity.

The force of his criticism was in part against our unthinking in foreign trade policy and in our taking actions adverse to Canada. The sale and dumping of our agricultural surpluses came in and always comes in for strongest Canadian criticism. Here the issue is agricultural policy, not trade policy. We might be frank though with respect to our premier place as world "dumpers." The term of course, we have never liked.

## IV. The Principal Ways in Which the United States Has Assisted, and Is Assisting the Rest of the World

### A. FOREIGN AID

The United States has assisted the rest of the world greatly by grants and aid. The total amount of aid granted since 1913, and aid for which we have got no return (unrequited gifts) is regularly reported by the Department of Commerce. The amount now is roundly $120 billion.

In the years since the end of the last war this aid has probably added up to about $60 billion or an average amount of $5 billion a year. This form of aid has been the most important aid we have given the world. It is described by both friend and former foe abroad as "unsordid," "most generous," and in such phrases as "never in the world's history has the victor treated the vanquished with such generosity." The foregoing are words from the lips of Sir Winston Churchill and Konrad Adenauer.

Perhaps in delicate situations such as textiles, wollens, and fine metal manufacturers, not to mention agricultural products we should have been more frank. We should have said we prefer billions for aid but not many millions for enlarged imports.

The aid we are now giving is lessening and most of it is for military defense purposes. We should, however, always make clear that military aid abroad is for the defense of the United States and not to be construed as gifts, aid, or import.

It must be abundantly clear to all that we could in no other way have assisted the rest of the world after 1945 than by direct aid. Talk of tariff reduction as a method of immediate alleviation of the difficulties of foreign countries; at that time would have been absurd. There were no goods to be imported from Western Europe and Japan which they did not need far more than we.

### B. UNITED STATES PROSPERITY

High productive levels of employment leading to a high national income and production is the most effective way, by far, to enlarge our imports.

When American industry is highly active it chews up record-breaking amounts of raw materials. Many of these we produce at home but many are imported. A high rate of industrial production means a high level of imports. This leads to a further gain to the rest of the world which is next considered.

### C. TERMS OF TRADE

The following comparisons of the terms on which we trade with the rest of the world will reveal how the United States has an automatic means for sharing the fruits of its increasing productivity and production with the rest of the world.

In all these comparisons the years 1936–38 are the base and consequently reckoned as 100 (1936–38 equals 100). The figures are from the President's Economic Report for January 1955, page 201.

From the base years just prior to the war when our exports in quantity are taken as 100, the increase was to 252 in 1954. The average price we received in 1954 was up to 202, or just double the price levels in the base years 1936–38.

Thus we exported 2½ times as much in quantity in 1954 (index 252) and the prices we received were just doubled (index 202). In contrast, our imports in quantity were increased in the same period only to an index of 148 and the price charged us for these imports was increased to an index of 283. Here we see we received only about 1½ times as much in quantity. The price was paid for these imports was almost tripled (index 283), whereas the price for our exports only doubled. Here we see how greatly the world gained from our rising productivity. The gain, in effect, consisted in receiving 100 percent more goods in quantity and being able to pay for them by charging us a very much higher price.

This is the way we share the fruits of our increased productivity with all the world automatically, without design, and generously.

Western European countries have resources, a skilled and trained population which compare favorably with ours. Their ability to produce is far less.

Britain's miners produce about 1¼ tons of coal per working day. For this they receive about $8.60 in wages. Our miners produced 10 tons of coal per day in 1955 and were paid about $21.45 a day. Our labor cost is about one-third of England's when expressed in tons of coal produced and it is the coal, not the laboring, that we want. As a result we exported 52 million tons of coal last year.

It is the common market we should promote in Western Europe to have them produce more, produce more more cheaply, export more to us, and so greatly increase their prosperity and production that they will be a far greater market for us. This need is "instantaneous, overwhelming, and not admitting of delay." Thus will the common defense be strengthened.

### D. PRIVATE FOREIGN INVESTMENT

Private foreign investment by United States nationals and American industry is encouraged on every hand. Its greatest discouragement at the present time comes from the unsettled political state—the polarization—of the world. Thus do we have national agencies

(American Export-Import Bank) and international agencies (IMF and the bank) assisting.

### E. POINT 4 OR TECHNICAL AID

Technical assistance is encouraged in every way but the amount of aid which can usefully be rendered is not large, important, and helpful as it is.

## V. Policies Recommended for the Subcommittee's Further Study and Formulation

The trade-agreements program is important, but it is not a solution for the imbalance in the world's international accounts with the United States. It is helpful in making a contribution to a larger world trade with more country specialization, but it will not cure the world's international economic difficulties. It should not be allowed to become a fetish which blinds us to other policies available to us.

The policy should be steadily adhered to, but with realization that politics being the art of the possible, there is not very much that can be done. We can however take better care of our friends in trade. They, however, can be well advised to seek our aid in other ways where a great deal more can far more easily be done. We are determined to protect jobs, we are not poor so thus we can afford this cost. This should be recognized.

The Swiss were not following the most desirable business policies when they put so many eggs in one basket by allowing so high a proportion of their exports of watches to come to us and in allowing watch production to become so high in Switzerland to their total production.

The British way of a little bit more here and a little more there has greatly expanded their trade.

When Sir Anthony Eden and Chancellor of the Exchequer R. A. Butler made their dramatic trip to the United States appealing for trade not aid they were neither well advised politically nor at all well advised economically.

Lowering of our tariffs is no assurance that a foreign country will make a gain. We may gain but in the present economic circumstances it is doubtful that the western European countries will gain much (it is against them that our highest tariffs prevail).

Today practically all industry in the United States is profitable with textiles to be sure a notable exception. Given our policies of maintaining and enlarging upon a growing economy we intend to keep industry profitable.

For industries operating profitably a lowered tariff in such cases as there is tariff protection does not make the industry like Rover roll over dead. The industry hangs on, probably lowers its market prices as long as it covers out-of-pocket costs and a little more. It retains the market. The foreign import is not greatly enlarged. It is not our imports which are consequently enlarged but our price level for such goods which is probably reduced. This may be desirable for us but it does not give aid to those for whose sake we lowered our tariffs.

This is the general line of reasoning which explains why the complete removal of all our tariffs would increase our imports so little and so very slowly.

These are the economic facts of life. They are other than are commonly held because our industries are profitable, we are efficient, and we do not give up easily. They are the consequence of changed conditions from those which prevailed when tariffs were adopted.

The greatest single fact that is different is that industry now has a huge investment in fixed plant, specialized more and more all the while. That plant is the dedication of capital to the continuation in retaining the American market by such industries, and of these the chemical industry is an outstanding example.

It is in education of the American people and peoples abroad that the subcommittee can be of great help. If, as a recent inquiry revealed, it is 10 times as important for their sake that European countries lower their tariffs than we lower ours, then a restored sense of proportion is needed.

This is not to say that persistent lowering of tariffs is not desirable. It is to say that the western world can move ahead far more rapidly by putting first things first and less important things, our tariffs reducing policy, farther down on the list of objectives we can politically achieve. The list must not be made too long lest progress be too slow.

### CONCLUSIONS: INVESTMENT AND BROADER MARKETS

In the forefront of our national international economic objectives should be the enlargement of international investment. We can be sobered by the fact that if the United States were to lend out of its present income as the countries of Western Europe did from 1883 to 1913 we should be lending not less than $15 billion a year. First should come broader markets, for Western Europe and the entire North Atlantic community and then the investment to fulfill this greater promise.

An import and but minor role will be played by the entire trade agreements policies, helpful and desirable as they are.

## PART II

### THE INTEREST OF AMERICAN FARMERS IN AMERICAN TARIFF POLICY

American farmers have hugely increased their efficiency, productivity, per man output, and per man-hour output in recent years. Since the end of the Second World War there are 25 million more of us in the United States. Despite that large increase in our numbers, we are all fed 13 percent better than only 10 years ago. This represents a remarkable increase in total production and in efficiency of American farmers.

The Department of Agriculture estimates that total output of American farms has increased 75 percent in the past 4 decades with 5 million fewer workers in agriculture. In the same 40-year period agricultural output per man has increased 175 percent. In the last 15 years per man-hour output has increased 91 percent. No important industry of such size has had an increase in productivity and output of so great a magnitude.

American farmers should ask that industry secure like efficiency in order that this large increased volume of farm output may continue to be profitably marketed.

What are the interests of American farmers in American industry and, through that, in American tariff policy, which can affect American industry?

Substantially more than half of our total agricultural or farm output consists of livestock and all its products. The share of these products in total farm production is probably about 60 percent today. In the Corn Belt States the share of total farm output represented by livestock and its products is in excess of 70 percent. In Minnesota it is 74 percent, possibly higher in Iowa.

The interests of farmers, therefore, in industry can be simply defined: American agriculture is interested that industry shall produce most efficiently, paying the highest possible wages in order that farmers may have profitable outlets for the products of the farm.

As American agriculture has shifted from a preponderance of cereal production to a preponderance of production of livestock and its products, American farmers can be said, briefly, to be interested that American industry shall pay sufficiently high wages to make meat eaters of the workers who produce our industrial output. Meat eating, or, in more general terms, the consumption of all forms of livestock products, requires that industry must be productive and pay high wages and that there be an efficient agriculture. These requirements are generally met in the United States, but American farmers should in their own proper interest be more insistent that American industry as a whole improve materially upon its present performance. Cereal consumption in a substantial degree is a feature of low-wage countries with inefficient agricultures.

Consequently, American agriculture has the primary interest that industry shall be efficient and produce high wages. What has American tariff policy to do with all this?

In the United States, without making invidious comparisons, we have high-wage industries and low-wage industries. Out of the high-wage industries come the wage payments which sustain families in a high-quantity, high-quality, food consumption, mainly of meat or livestock products. Out of low-wage workers' families comes a low purchasing power ability for these more desirable and of course, more expensive farm products.

Consequently American agriculture has the interest that it should support all economic policies which would increase the total efficiency of industry. One way in which this could be done is by reduced tariffs.

But can a guide be furnished for the way in which tariffs should be reduced? The guide would be to make an array schedule of the wages paid by the different industries in the United States. The rank order would be from those paying the highest wages; namely, all the building trades and the coal-mining industry, for example, when the latter enjoys full employment. Next perhaps would be the automobile industry, for example, in which the weekly wages last year were in excess of $92. The average weekly wage for workers in all durable industries in December 1954, was $80.15. In the nondurable goods industries, the average weekly gross earnings were $66.47. The average weekly wage for all workers engaged in manufacturing was midway between these 2 figures, $74.12. With wages for coal miners averaging more than $80 a week; with building construction workers averaging more than $95 a week; with wages of railroad workers averaging $78 a week, there naturally must be as many groups whose workers earn substantially less than average earnings ($74 for all factory workers in 1954).

Many studies in the past show the high and very increased consumption of meat, milk, dairy products, cheese, butter, and other poultry, dairy and livestock products which prevails in families where the breadwinner (a misnomer today) receives a high weekly wage. In contrast, the consumption of these products is necessarily low for those families whose breadwinner is earning low wages as the result of employment in those industries which, unavoidably and despite their best efforts, have a lower productivity and therefore can only pay lower wages.

Clearly the interest of agriculture is to maximize the number of workers in industries of average or better-than-average wages. A persistent lowering of tariffs upon the imported goods so that they may slowly displace the goods of our lower wage industries will gradually mean that our future industrial expansion will come from the higher wage industries. New workers will be attracted to the employment opportunities available in such industries and will be dissuaded from entering the fields which will be slowly declining as a result of the exercise of this type of tariff-reducing policy.

To the extent that our total imports can be enlarged our total exports wil be enlarged. Our exports are preponderantly the products of industries which are the high-wage industries. Thus there is the double gain by this method of tariff reduction that we expand employment in the more profitable industries and the higher wage industries and we discourage new employment in the less profitable, declining, and lower wage industries.

The key to the level of wages is not easily found. One extremely important factor, however, is the total investment per worker.

Such investment ranges from roundly $50,000 per worker in the utility industry, down through from $35,000 to $25,000 per worker in the petroleum industry, on through $20,000 to $15,000 in the chemical industry, to the national average of perhaps $10,000 investment per worker in all manufacturing industries. Other industries are to be found where the investment is perhaps unavoidably smaller than in the industries we have named. In consequence wages are lower too.

A third great advantage in the creation of high wage, high meat consuming families is to be gained by a policy which encourages industries which have a high capital investment. That high capital investment naturally if the industry is expanded, will be further enlarged. Thus the construction trades and machine making trades will increase their numbers of higher wage earning workers.

It is extremely interesting to observe that American agriculture itself is an industry of very high investment per worker. For all American agriculture the total gross investment today is more than $22,500 per worker. Taking the farms which produce the major share of the total supply of farm products marketed commercially, there is a per farm investment which will range very substantially upward from $25,000 per worker through $50,000 per worker and on up. This standard of investment per worker in farming compares favorably with the extremely higher investment level industries. Thus agriculture is already practising the policy it would preach for others.

In turn, other countries which are somewhat "long" on labor supplies and, somewhat "short" on capital supplies could, as a result, specialize in the industries in which they have for these reasons a greater advantage. We in turn in the United States could continue our specialization in the industries in which we have the greater advantage.

Such a policy would in no way discourage growth industries, or the growth in all more efficient industries. These growth industries and growing industries are needed for the very substantially increased volume of employment which wil be wanted soon as the very greatly increased numbers of young since 1940 move forward to the thresholds of their future employment. Industries which are growth industries or which are growing rapidly are almost certain to be large capital-using industries. It is their capital investment which makes not only an important contribution to total production in the United States but which makes a most important contribution to the number of workers in the high wage earning categories which further supply the high demand for farm production of today.

American farmers could secure a great gain from this guide to trade policy which calls for reducing tariffs upon the products of those industries unable, because of an inherent inability to use large amounts of capital per worker, to pay the high wages which create the demand to absorb the livestock products which make up the major share of farm output in the United States today.

## MISCELLANEOUS TABLES

***Selected United States tariff rates, 1930, present (1954), and decrease in them***

| Commodity | Unit of quantity | 1930 | Now | Percent change, down |
|---|---|---|---|---|
| Animals and animal products: | | | | |
| Sheep | Each | $3.00 | $0.75 | 75 |
| Poultry | Pound | $0.08 | $0.02 | 75 |
| Hogs | do | $0.02 | $0.01 | 50 |
| Cattle 200 and less 700 | do | $0.03 | $0.01½ | 50 |
| Lard | do | $0.03 | | 100 |
| Butter | do | $0.14 | $0.07 | 50 |
| Shoes—McKay sewed | Percent | 30 | 20 | 33⅓ |
| Luggage and related articles | do | 50 | 25 | 50 |
| Vegetable food products and beverages: | | | | |
| Barley | Bushel | $0.20 | $0.075 | 63 |
| Buckwheat | Pound | $0.25 | $0.10 | 60 |
| Corn | Bushel | $0.25 | $0.12½ | 50 |
| Oats | do | $0.16 | $0.04 | 75 |
| Rice | do | $0.01¼ | | 100 |
| Whisky | Gallon | $5.00 | $1.50 | 70 |
| Vegetable products, inedible: | | | | |
| Tires | Percent | 10 | 10 | |
| Turpentine | do | 5 | | 100 |
| Grass seed | Pound | $0.02 | $0.01 | 50 |
| Smoke-cured cigarette tobacco | do | $0.35 | $0.15 | 57 |
| Textile fibers, manufactured: Flax | Ton | $67.20 | $33.60 | 50 |
| Wood and paper: Plywood birch | Percent per square foot | 50 | 15 | 70 |
| Metals and manufacturing: | | | | |
| Aluminum bauxite | Ton | $1.00 | $0.50 | 50 |
| Copper | | | | |
| Brass rods, strips | | $0.04 | $0.02 | 50 |
| Heating and cooking stoves | Percent | 45 | 12½ | 72 |
| Machinery and vehicles: | | | | |
| Electric lamps | do | 30 | | 100 |
| Generators | do | 35 | 15 | 57 |
| Radio apparatus | do | 35 | ½ | 99 |
| Sewing machines | do | 15 | 10 | 33⅓ |
| Adding machines | do | 35 | ¾ | 98 |
| Trucks | do | 25 | ½ | 98 |
| Pleasure boats to $15,000 | do | 30 | ½ | 98 |
| Chemicals: | | | | |
| Crude coal tar products | | | | |
| Alcohol—ethyl | Gallon | $0.15 | $0.07½ | 50 |
| Cellulose acetate | Pound | $0.50 | $0.12½ | 75 |
| Enamel paint | Percent | 25 | 12½ | 50 |
| Miscellaneous: | | | | |
| Field glasses | do | 45 | ½ | 99 |
| Microscopes | do | 45 | | 100 |
| Phonographs | do | 30 | 15 | 50 |
| Golf clubs | do | 30 | 15 | 50 |
| Watch—15 to 17 jewels | Each | $1.25 | $0.90 | 28 |

[A set of figures to illustrate the foreign trade interests of the United States]

### *1. The direction of trade*

[In millions of dollars]

| Areas | 1952 exports [1] | 1952 imports | 1952 total trade | 1901–05 average total trade | Percent increase, 1937 to 1952 | Percent increase, 1901–05 to 1952 |
|---|---|---|---|---|---|---|
| Europe | 3,342 | 2,028 | 5,370 | 1,549 | 144 | 247 |
| Western Hemisphere | 6,318 | 6,022 | 12,340 | 573 | 443 | 2,054 |
| Asia and Oceania | 2,337 | 2,057 | 4.394 | 265 | 156 | 1,558 |

[1] Includes reexports, and excludes some special category exports which, for security reasons, are not reported by country of destination.

Source: 1953 Statistical Supplement, Business Statistics.

*2. Trade by classes of goods*

[In millions of dollars]

| | 1952 exports of United States merchandise | 1952 imports for consumption |
|---|---|---|
| Finished | 9,326 | 2,093 |
| Foodstuffs, manufactured and crude | 2,095 | 3,150 |
| Crude, semifinished | 3,604 | 5,502 |

Source: 1953 Statistical Abstract, p. 904.

*Commodity trade of the United States*

[In millions of dollars]

| *Commodity* | *Exports, 1952 (preliminary)* |
|---|---|
| Machinery | 2,824 |
| Petroleum | 800 |
| Automobiles [1] | 988 |
| Iron and Steel | 621 |
| Cotton | 874 |
| Meat products, and animal fats and oils | 199 |
| Wheat and wheat flour | 942 |

| | *Imports, 1952 (preliminary)* |
|---|---|
| Rubber | 619 |
| Sugar | 415 |
| Coffee | 1,376 |
| Paper and manufactures | 600 |
| Vegetable oils | 95 |
| Silk | 34 |
| Tin | 298 |
| Woodpulp | 271 |
| Wool and mohair | 382 |
| Cotton manufactures | 67 |
| Wool manufactures | 165 |

[1] Exclusive of machinery and vehicles manufactured to military specifications.

Source: Statistical abstract, 1953, pp. 910–911.

INTERNATIONAL ECONOMICS

[A set of figures to illustrate the foreign trade interests of the United States]

*1. The direction of trade*

| Areas | 1937 exports (in millions of dollars) | 1937 imports (in millions of dollars) | 1937 total trade (in millions of dollars) | Growth in trade from 1901–05 to 1937 |
|---|---|---|---|---|
| | | | | *Percent* |
| Europe | 1,360 | 843 | 2,203 | 42 |
| Western Hemisphere | 1,158 | 1,113 | 2,271 | 300 |
| Asia and Oceania | 679 | 1,036 | 1,715 | 550 |

*2. Trade by classes of goods*

[In millions of dollars]

| Classes of goods | Exports | Imports |
|---|---|---|
| Finished | 1,617 | 551 |
| Foodstuffs | 283 | 853 |
| Crude and semifinished | 1,400 | 1,047 |

*Commodity trade of the United States*

[In millions of dollars]

| Commodities | Exports, 1937 | Exports, average, 1901–05 |
|---|---|---|
| Machinery | 479 | 78 |
| Petroleum | 376 | 82 |
| Automobiles | 347 | ---------- |
| Iron and steel | 300 | 33 |
| Cotton | 369 | 335 |
| Edible animal products | 43 | 182 |
| Wheat | 64 | 131 |
| | **Imports, 1937** | **Imports, average, 1901–05** |
| Rubber | 248 | 35 |
| Sugar | 166 | 77 |
| Coffee | 151 | 69 |
| Paper | 137 | 4 |
| Vegetable oils | 112 | 7 |
| Silk | 107 | 45 |
| Tin | 104 | 22 |
| Woodpulp | 98 | 3 |
| Wool | 96 | 25 |
| Cotton manufactures | 57 | 48 |
| Wool manufactures | 32 | 17 |

*Surpluses of the Western Hemisphere (1937)*

[In millions of dollars]

| Commodity | United States surpluses | Total Western Hemisphere surpluses |
|---|---|---|
| Wheat | 64 | 376 |
| Meat | 43 | 216 |
| Cotton | 369 | 433 |
| Tobacco | 135 | 144 |
| Corn | ---------- | 196 |
| Coffee | ---------- | 213 |
| Linseed | ---------- | 93 |
| Copper | 94 | 253 |
| Petroleum | 376 | 571 |

*Absorption in imports by Europe of export surplus commodities of the Western Hemisphere*

| Commodity | Percent absorbed by United Kingdom | Percent absorbed by continental Europe |
|---|---|---|
| Wheat | 62 | 38 |
| Lard | 58 | 42 |
| Meats | 90 | 10 |
| Cotton | 37 | 63 |
| Tobacco | 32 | 68 |
| Corn | 40 | 60 |
| Coffee | ---------- | 100 |
| Linseed | 25 | 75 |
| Copper | 49 | 51 |
| Petroleum | 38 | 62 |

BALANCE OF PAYMENTS

(in billions dollars)

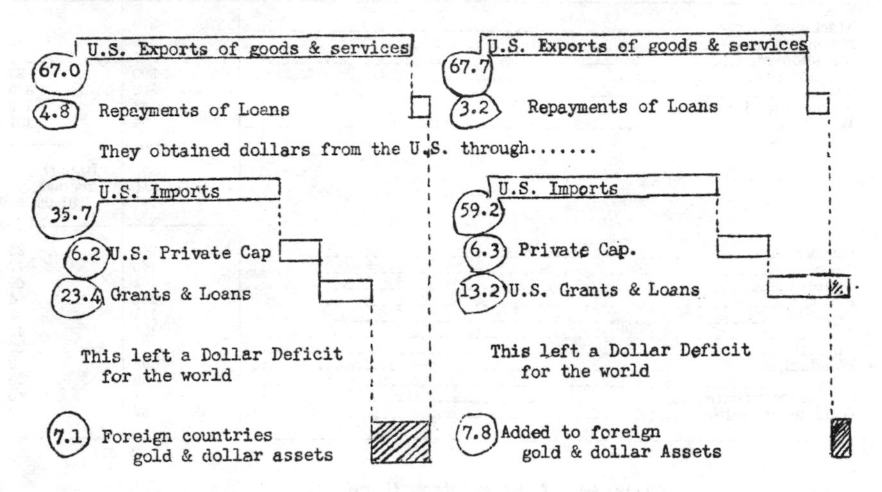


Source: Survey of Current Business July, 1954, p. 10,13

# II

# QUANTITATIVE APPRAISAL OF TARIFFS, TARIFF CHANGES AND THEIR EFFECTS—POSSIBILITIES AND LIMITATIONS

# THE ROLE OF THE UNITED STATES TARIFF AND THE EFFECTS OF CHANGES IN DUTY RATES

United States Department of Commerce

The Subcommittee on Foreign Trade Policy, in Chairman Boggs' letter of June 1, 1957, to Secretary Weeks, requested that the Commerce Department provide—

* * * analysis of the relation of tariff reductions under the trade agreements program to the changes in the merchandise trade of the United States—

together with—

* * * observations and information * * * on * * * the role of the tariff in relation to merchandise imports and domestic production; the degree of protection which the tariff affords domestic industries; [and] the extent to which the tariff restricts imports and the likely effects of further tariff reductions. * * *

These questions are certainly pertinent to intelligent appraisal or formulation of tariff policies. They are, however, extremely difficult questions.

Objective judgment of the effects—either past or prospective—of tariffs or of changes in them upon the volume and pattern of United States foreign trade presents some of the most intractable problems in the field of economic analysis. There are few questions on which informed individual judgments diverge so widely.

The extreme variation of judgments stems in part from the necessarily inconclusive character of available statistical information on the impact of tariffs or tariff changes. It also reflects the wide range of economic philosophies underlying particular opinions formed in the absence of definitive factual evidence.

Changes in United States tariff policies have not occurred in isolation; but have been associated more or less fortuitously with wars, political and social turmoil here and abroad, business cycles, technological developments, shifts in consumer tastes, and other phenomena of sweeping economic significance. Some of these factors have doubtless exerted more profound influences upon our foreign trade than have modifications in tariff rates; and it is virtually impossible to distinguish separately the effects of the latter in statistics which generally reflect only the composite results of all the relevant causal factors.

The dearth of factual evidence as to the weight properly assignable to each of a number of joint causal factors—many of them interrelated also with each other—gives rather free rein to inferences based chiefly on abstract theoretical considerations or personal prejudices. Moreover, the formulation of conclusions is further confused by an abundance of arguments founded upon rationalizations of self-interest by particular industrial groups or localities and their spokesmen, or upon doctrinaire positions with respect to broader national or international political issues.

The staff of the Department of Commerce is little or no better equipped than other serious students of these questions to cut through the morass of fragmentary and often ambiguous evidence at hand to clear-cut and demonstrable conclusions. It can only trace the outlines of the available data as far as they lead and suggest as objectively as possible the principal lines of interpretation which are compatible with them.

By way of background for this approach, there follows a brief description of the broad characteristics of the United States tariff. The subsequent section gives summary information indicative of the degree to which United States tariff rates have been reduced since passage of the Trade Agreements Act, together with comments regarding the impact of these changes upon United States foreign trade. These comments, of course, are necessarily somewhat speculative. They are illustrative of the range of plausible inferences which may be drawn from the recognized facts, rather than flat conclusions clearly derivable from them. A final section deals with the even more problematical question of the degree of restrictiveness still inherent in our tariff structure after the sharp rate reductions of the past two decades.

## GENERAL CHARACTERISTICS OF THE UNITED STATES TARIFF STRUCTURE

The provisions of the United States tariff schedule are extremely complex. There are some 3,300 different tariff rates, according to the most acceptable basis for counting them, with minutely specified distinctions, at many points in the schedule, among the commodity classifications to which separate rates apply. In addition, of course, there is a long list of items admitted free of duty. In the face of this detail, accurate generalization is not easy, since any concise summary risks oversimplification. The following comments, therefore, should be read as a rough outline of salient features in which numerous minor exceptions and qualifications are ignored.

In terms of actual imports during the last full calendar year, the total value of United States imports for consumption was divided almost evenly between dutiable and duty-free merchandise. The former amounted to $6,270 million, while the latter totaled $6,220 million.

Customs collections are no longer a principal source of Federal revenues, as they were for many decades earlier in our history. They now account for only about 1 percent of Federal tax receipts. Nevertheless, they still yield a significant amount of revenue in absolute, if not relative, terms. The total for calendar 1956 was well over $700 million, indicating an average tariff rate of somewhat under 12 percent on dutiable merchandise actually imported last year.

The average, however, is a composite of widely varying levels of duty on individual commodities. Many imports are subject to essentially nominal rates, equivalent to only a few percent of their value, while a good many others pay rates several times as high as the average. In brief, slightly more than half of our dutiable imports, on the basis of value, are subject to rates no higher than 10 percent and approximately another third to rates in the 10.1 to 20-percent range. Duties in the 20.1 to 30-percent bracket apply to about one-tenth of the total, leaving only a small proportion dutiable at more than 30 percent.

It should be remembered, of course, that these proportions, being based on actual importations, give no reflection of goods bearing duties which may be prohibitive, or nearly so. Small amounts of imports are recorded for a great many articles assessed at 50 to 100 percent or more, but there is no reliable means of gaging the degree to which the duty rate on these or other items is itself responsible for a low volume of imports.

By and large, levels of duties in the United States tariff schedule are at least loosely correlated with certain economic characteristics of the various types of merchandise imported. With many minor exceptions and a few major ones, it may be said that the rates tend to vary more or less directly with the degree of processing or fabrication to which the merchandise has been subjected. Moreover, the free list is composed predominantly of the same types of goods as those on the low-rate end of the dutiable scale. In general, items not obtainable domestically or urgently needed by United States industry are lightly assessed, if at all, while those competitive with United States production are subject to steeper levies.

For the most part, crude foodstuffs and raw or partly processed materials are admissible either duty free or at low tariff rates, while manufactured goods, including manufactured foods and beverages, fall mainly within the middle and higher duty brackets. Among the industrial materials, there is a general—though not entirely consistent—tendency for the cruder forms of a given material to carry lower rates than the partly or considerably processed forms. The tariff on aluminum metal, for instance, is intermediate between that on crude bauxite and the somewhat higher rate on aluminum plates and sheets. Similarly, the duties on crude petroleum and pig iron are much lower than those on gasoline and on steel bars or tubes.

Among finished manufactures, however, the same tendency toward correlation of tariff rates with the degree of physical processing between farm or mine and final product is not observable. Instead, the height of duty tends as a general rule to vary roughly with the ratio of direct labor costs to total costs in the industry performing the final stages of fabrication. Rates applicable to the complex products of our principal mass-production manufacturing industries are distinctly more moderate, on the whole, than those on goods produced by labor-intensive industries, particularly where the production process is characterized by skilled artisanship, rather than advanced engineering techniques.

Since tariff data on the several thousand dutiable items in the rate schedules are regularly summarized only in terms of categories based primarily on physical composition, it is not feasible to present exact statistics in terms of economic classes of merchandise. However, rough estimates based on a review of principal items accounting for around 75 percent of all dutiable imports permit a reliable outline of comparative duty levels among broad economic classes of imports.

With joint regard to both free and dutiable components, the class carrying the lowest average tariff rate is crude foodstuffs. Dominated by such duty-free tropical products as coffee, cacao beans, tea, and bananas, this group of imports as a whole is subject to an average tariff of only about 1 percent. The minute size of the average is chiefly a reflection of the fact that goods accounting for nine-tenths of the value of the class are nondutiable. Even on the relatively small dutiable components, however, rates are moderate, averaging about 8 percent.

Nonagricultural crude materials and semimanufactured goods[1] are also subject, for the most part, to rather low rates of duty. The average on dutiable segments of each of these classes is around 6 percent ad valorem, and roughly half or more of each total is duty free. The overall averages for both groups, therefore, are in the vicinity of 3 percent.

Dutiable imports of agricultural crude materials (other than foods) show an average tariff rate of approximately 18 percent. This contrast with other raw materials, however, is attributable chiefly to the inclusion of one major high-duty commodity—apparel wool. Moreover, dutiable items represent little more than one-fourth of the value of all imports of agricultural crude materials, so that the ratio of duties to imports for the class as a whole is only about 6 percent.

Manufactured foodstuffs, consisting chiefly of sugar, alcoholic beverages, and processed meat and dairy products, are nearly all dutiable. The average rate of duty—not far from 12 percent—is close to that for all dutiable United States imports, but about double the overall average in relation to combined dutiable and free merchandise.

As already indicated, it is on finished manufactures[2] (other than processed foods) that the highest average rate of duty is found. In relation to dutiable manufactures alone—four-fifths of the class total[3]—it is in the neighborhood of 20 percent. In relation to all manufactured imports, including the minority on the free list, the ratio is somewhat lower, of course, but farther out of line with corresponding ratios for most of the other categories mentioned above. Within the manufactures group, it is noteworthy that the principal types of machinery and vehicles are subject to rates below the group average, while the opposite is true of such items as watches, cotton and woolen fabrics and apparel, pottery and glassware, and some chemicals.

The above differences in typical tariff rates on the various economic classes of merchandise, in combination with contrasts in the commodity composition of United States imports from various regions of the world, result in marked differences among the principal supplying areas as to the average tariff burdens falling on their shipments to the United States. Our imports from Canada, Latin America, and Africa, consisting predominantly of industrial materials or crude foodstuffs, not only carry by far the lowest average rates in relation to dutiable imports alone (6, 7, and 10 percent, respectively, in 1956), but also include the highest proportions of duty-free goods—three-fifths of the totals from Canada and Latin America and four-fifths of that from Africa. The ratio of duties to total United States imports from each of these areas is under 3 percent.

Corresponding ratios for goods originating in Asia and Oceania are several times as high. Owing chiefly to the preponderance of manufactured goods in United States purchases from Japan and of apparel wool in those from Australia and New Zealand, dutiable mer-

[1] Newsprint and burlap are here regarded as semimanufactures, rather than finished manufactures.
[2] Exclusive of newsprint and burlap, here regarded as semimanufactures.
[3] See note 2.

chandise comprises over half of the total from Asian and other Far Eastern sources, and the average rates on such merchandise (13 and 17 percent, respectiveley, in 1956) are appreciably higher than on Canadian, Latin American, or African goods. Apart from Japan, however, the Asian picture resembles much more closely that for the three regions mentioned.

The highest average appears on imports from Europe, reflecting, of course, the concentration of manufactures in shipments from that area. Roughly three-fourths of these shipments were dutiable in 1956—a substantially higher proportion than for any other region—and these bore a higher average tariff (16 percent) than dutiable imports from any geographic area except Oceania. In relation to combined dutiable and free entries, the ratio for European goods (12 percent) was just about double that for United States imports from all sources last year.

The uneven geographic incidence of the United States tariff explains some of the apparent contradictions heard in discussions of its level. Especially from the standpoint of European businessmen and governments, it appears considerably higher than a global view would suggest.

TARIFF REDUCTIONS UNDER THE TRADE AGREEMENTS PROGRAM

It is well known that the United States tariff levels described above are far lower than those prevailing prior to the commencement of the trade agreement program some two decades ago. Much interest and considerable dispute has centered on the question of the effects which reciprocal reductions in duties here and abroad have had upon United States foreign trade.

Two sets of facts relevant to this question can be readily demonstrated: On the one hand, the dimensions of the reductions in United States tariff levels are reasonably well established, at least in relation to the actual import pattern; and somewhat rougher indications are available as to the extent to which tariff levels have also been lowered in other countries of the North Atlantic community. On the other hand, it is clear that United States foreign trade has prospered along with the domestic economy in the tremendous growth of business activity, both here and abroad, during the past two decades and especially since World War II. What is not conclusively demonstrable is the degree of causal connection between these two sets of facts.

Regarding the extent to which the United States has lowered its tariff through both bilateral trade agreements in the early stages of the program and multilateral agreements since inception of the General Agreement on Tariffs and Trade, a good summary was presented by Under Secretary of Commerce Walter Williams in an address to the opening session of the 42d National Foreign Trade Convention in the fall of 1955. While there have been small further reductions through GATT negotiations since the date of the Under Secretary's address, they do not significantly alter the substance of his remarks on this topic, which are quoted below as a convenient outline of major points with respect to the degree of reduction in the United States tariff level:

Because I believe that the facts regarding United States tariff reductions have not received adequate recognition, either here or abroad, I would like to review some of them for you. They constitute an impressive record of positive contributions to the lowering of trade barriers.

If United States imports in the past few years had still been subject to the tariff duties prevailing just before the passage of the Trade Agreements Act in 1934, the average rate on all dutiable imports would have been near 25 percent. In fact, however, under the reduced tariffs established through the whole series of reciprocal trade-agreement negotiations to date, the average rate on dutiable imports amounts to only about 12 percent. This represents a reduction of fully 50 percent in the average level of our tariff rates. Nearly two-thirds of this reduction has occurred during the decade since World War II, while the remainder reflects concessions negotiated in prewar trade agreements.

The comparisons I have just made reflect only such changes in the weighted average as have been brought about by changes in particular rates of duty, rather than by shifts in the import pattern or in the level of import prices for goods subject to fixed amounts of duty per unit of quantity. I shall comment further on the effects of price increases in a moment.

Before doing so, however, I want to point out how widespread the reduction of duty rates has been. The proportion of imports unaffected by trade-agreement concessions is very small indeed. Roughly nine-tenths of our dutiable imports now enter the country at lower tariff rates as a result of those concessions. Moreover, many of the remaining imports, both free and dutiable, have been bound against tariff increases by our trade agreements.

Furthermore, the reductions have been widely scattered among the various categories of imported commodities. Of the 16 tariff or import excise tax schedules into which dutiable imports are grouped for customs purposes, there is none for which the average rate reduction through trade agreements has been appreciably less than 40 precent. Average cuts in most of the schedules range between that figure and 60 percent.

A full story of reductions in the United States tariff level since inception of the trade-agreements program must take into account not only rate changes as such, but also the fact that unlike many other countries we have refrained from adjusting our specific duties upward in line with the worldwide inflation of prices during and after World War II. As I am sure you all appreciate, the relative level of a given specific duty, unlike that of a given ad valorem duty, will rise or fall with decreases or increases in import prices.

Average prices of United States imports today are, of course, several times as high as they were before inception of the trade-agreements program. Just since 1945, they have risen about 80 percent. By foregoing adjustment of specific duties to these sharp increases in prices, the United States has accepted very substantial cuts in the effective levels of those duties, quite apart from reductions in the rates as such. Since more than two-thirds of dutiable United States imports are subject only to specific duties, our restraint on this point has been of no small consequence. In fact, its effects on the average tariff level over the entire life of the trade-agreements program have been approximately as great as those of rate reductions.

Through the combination of factors which I have mentioned, the actual average ratio of United States tariff collections to dutiable imports, which exceeded 50 percent during the years when rates of the 1930 Tariff Act were fully applicable, has been reduced to less than 30 percent at the end of World War II, and to only about 12 percent today. Over the whole span, in other words, our tariffs have been lowered by an average of more than 75 percent.

Moreover, we must remember that well over half of our total imports enter free of any duty whatever. If these goods are weighted into the calculation of a comprehensive duty ratio for all imports, we find that it now scarcely exceeds 5 percent, as compared with 18 or 19 percent before the initiation of the trade-agreements program.

The United States, of course, is by no means the only country whose tariffs have been reduced through trade agreements concessions, especially following the adoption of the GATT by several dozen major trading nations. In Western Germany, for example, the average ad valorem rate of duty on that country's imports in 1956 was less than 8 percent, as compared with 28 percent for prewar Germany in

1937. In the United Kingdom, exclusive of the high British revenue duties on such items as tobacco and liquor, the overall average rate has been reduced from 4 percent in fiscal 1938 to about 2 percent in fiscal 1956.

Roughly similar data for France and Italy, covering approximately the same span of years, show declines from 17 to 6 percent and from about 12 to 8 percent, respectively. Even Belgium-Luxembourg and Sweden, whose tariff levels were already comparatively low before the war, show sizable reductions in their ad valorem averages—the former from about 6 percent in 1937 to less than 4 percent in 1956 and the latter from 9 to 5½ percent.

For reasons indicated at some length in another memorandum [4] to the subcommittee, extreme caution in the interpretation of the foregoing statistics is essential. In particular, because of the peculiarities of weighted tariff averages in which the weights depend upon the composition of imports, the data do not represent an adequate basis for comparisons between countries. Many of the reservations appropriate in that connection, however, apply with much less force to changes over time in a given country's tariff level. The data cited may therefore be accepted as meaningful rough indicators of the considerable extent to which tariffs have been lowered by western European industrial nations during the past two decades.

Generally speaking, similar reductions in average duty levels have not characterized the tariff schedules of underdeveloped countries. Many of these have maintained or increased their rates to protect local industries whose establishment and growth became objectives of governmental economic policies. At least among GATT members, however, reciprocal concessions have kept duties, even in underdeveloped countries, lower than they would otherwise probably have been.

In a number of both industrial and underdeveloped countries, direct quantitative restrictions on dollar imports and in some cases the institution of taxes other than customs duties have tended since World War II to negate in part the benefits to the United States of lower tariffs. Much progress has been made in the past 4 or 5 years, however, toward freeing dollar goods from restrictive governmental controls abroad. With this widespread relaxation of such restrictions, the lower tariff levels previously negotiated have facilitated gains in sales opportunities for United States exporters in important segments of their foreign markets and thus contributed to the sharp expansion of our commercial exports since 1953.

The reductions in both United States and foreign tariff rates since the 1930's, together with the recent progress in removal of direct restrictions on trade, have certainly been a part of the setting—if not necessarily major determining factors—for the enormous expansion of United States foreign trade which has taken place since passage of the Trade Agreements Act in 1934. The dimensions of this expansion can be sketched in a few paragraphs.

In 1956, the volume of our merchandise exports, measured in constant dollars and exclusive of military aid, was well over three times that of the early 1930's and more than double the level of the prosperous late 1920's. The volume of United States merchandise imports, also

[4] On the Nature and Significance of International Comparisons of Tariff Level.

measured in constant dollars, was in 1956 more than twice the 1930–34 average and some 70 percent above the level of 1926–29. In actual dollar values, of course, all of these increases were much more pronounced, owing to the very marked inflation of both export and import prices during the past two decades.

The expansion of our trade since 1947, the last year before the GATT came into effect, is more difficult to characterize because of postwar abnormalities in our trade during that year. The volume of exports in 1947 was temporarily almost as large as in 1956, but this was possible only by virtue of the availability of nearly $6 billion of United States Government grants and loans to foreign countries, plus the liquidation of some $4½ billion of foreign gold and dollar asset holdings. The slightly higher volume of exports (not counting military aid) which prevailed in 1956 was achieved, by contrast, with United States nonmilitary grants and credits amounting to less than $2½ billion, and with foreign countries, instead of liquidating their gold and dollar assets, inceasing them by $1½ billion. This vast shrinkage in abnormal financing, rather than the change in exports themselves, is perhaps the best index of improvement in our export position since 1947.

The principal factor permitting exports to rise over this interval despite a net drop of close to $9½ billion in extraordinary financing was, of course, the recovery and expansion of United States imports from levels of the immediate postwar years, when the capacity of normally important foreign sources of supply to deliver goods to us was severely impaired. In actual value, the rise in imports from 1947 to 1956 was nearly $7 billion, or some 120 percent. In terms of constant dollars, the increase was roughly 60 percent.

It cannot be reasonably claimed, of course, that the healthy growth of United States foreign trade since the early 1930's has been primarily attributable to the trade-agreements program, either in its early bilateral form or in the multilateral form of the postwar period. The past quarter century has been one of tremendous economic upheaval, embracing recovery from the depression, World War II and its aftermath, and the Korean war, as well as accelerated technological progress and the strong underlying growth trends in the United States and the world economy. These are the forces which have unquestionably predominated in determining the course of our foreign trade. In view of their magnitude, it is impossible to isolate and measure statistically the separate impact of the tariff policies which we have pursued.

Nevertheless, it is clear that the trade agreements programs—both bilateral and multilateral—have made valuable contributions to the great expansion of United States foreign trade broadly outlined above. The reciprocal reductions in tariff barriers, both here and abroad, have facilitated the international movement of goods to markets, and have widened the scope for application of free-enterprise principles in foreign commerce. The partial attainment of the goals established by the general rules of the GATT has further contributed to creation of opportunities which would not otherwise have existed for exercise of private initiative, not only by American traders, but by their counterparts abroad. Moreover, the original trade agreements program was a major factor in arresting and reversing a global spiral of increases in tariffs and other trade barriers during the early 1930's; and the GATT has been instrumental since World War II in preventing the reemergence of such a trend, from which the United States would perhaps suffer greater damage than any other nation.

Unfortunately, the effects of tariff reductions upon imports are much harder to distinguish than either the extent of changes in duty levels as measured by weighted average ad valorem rates or the magnitude of changes in exports and imports. The period since inception of the trade agreements program embraces too staggering an array of other developments strongly affecting United States and world trade trends to permit any possibility of tracing separately the specific quantitative influence of tariff changes. Nevertheless, it is almost inconceivable that changes on the scale involved here have failed to exert a material influence in facilitating expansion of our import trade.

In this connection, attention is sometimes called to the fact that dutiable imports as a class have increased considerably more sharply than total duty-free entries since the early 1930's or the late 1920's, and also—to a lesser extent—over the shorter interval since the first GATT negotiations. The proportion of total United States imports which falls in dutiable categories has risen from about one-third in the early 1930's (or in the late 1920's, under the pre-1930 Tariff Act) to approximately two-fifths in the late forties and just over half in 1956. This rising share of dutiable goods reflects a rather substantial difference between their composite growth rate and that of duty-free merchandise as a class. The value of dutiable imports in 1956 was 12 times that reported in 1933 (and over 4 times the 1929 total), whereas duty-free imports last year were less than 7 times the 1933 figure (and not much more than double that for 1929).

If there were any acceptable grounds for assuming that the two groups of imports would have shown, in the absence of tariff changes, approximately parallel growth (or any other given relationship), then these comparisons of growth rates would offer some promising clues. As it happens, however, the distribution of imports as between the free and the dutiable lists is by no means random. On the contrary, as indicated in an earlier section, there are rather pronounced and, to some extent, systematic differences in the typical economic characteristics and end uses of the goods on the two lists. These preclude use of the comparative growth rates as a basis for serious quantitative estimates, but do not invalidate the highly plausible inference that at least a part of the larger increase in dutiable imports is attributable to the stimulating effects of duty reductions upon their volume.

While the magnitude of the portion so attributable remains uncertain, there can be no doubt as to the direction of the influence. This has been recognized—and indeed sometimes exaggerated—by opponents as well as proponents of the reductions which have taken place.

Even if there had been no reciprocal concessions from foreign countries with whom the United States has negotiated agreements, the additional dollar exchange thus made available to our trading partners would have been an important stimulant to our export sales. But, in fact, as noted earlier, there have been broadly commensurate reductions in the duties applied to our goods abroad, and we have also benefited, under the multilateral approach of the GATT, from reductions achieved in agreements (to which the United States was not directly a party) among other members of that organization. These reductions have undoubtedly facilitated the increases in United States exports which have occurred.

Opponents of trade agreements reductions in United States tariff rates have frequently argued that whatever beneficial effects resulted in some respects were outweighed by a negative impact in other respects. They have alleged serious displacement of domestic production and employment by imported goods.

There is no reason to doubt the occurrence of a few cases in which particular American industries may have suffered injury primarily from imports increasing as a result of duty reductions. In general, however, the difficulty of identifying and measuring increases in imports attributable to duty reductions militates against the supposition that the latter may have induced enough additional imports to result in unfavorable effects on any very sizable or widespread scale. Further circumstantial evidence to the same effect may be found in the limited number of applications by domestic producers for restoration of high duties through escape-clause procedures. Over more than a decade, the cumulative total of such applications is only about 7 dozen, and the great majority of these have failed to establish their merit under a thorough process of Government review. This is true despite the fact that the escape clause is available for invocation, if needed, with respect to well over 3,000 commodity classifications involving more than $6 billion worth of imports.

Difficulties encountered in gaging the impact of the trade agreements program in an environment of major economic forces which outweigh and obscure its influence do not call for discounting that influence. On balance, it seems fair to conclude that United States and foreign duty reductions under the program have contributed valuably to the healthy status of United States foreign commerce. The high level of our foreign trade, in turn, is demonstrably one important element in the unparalleled period of sustained prosperity which the United States economy has enjoyed in recent years.

## PROBLEMS IN JUDGING THE RESTRICTIVENESS OF THE UNITED STATES TARIFF

Questions regarding the extent to which the tariff restricts imports and the degree of protection which it affords to domestic industries are different facets of essentially the same coin. Both involve inquiry into the additional volume—and the composition—of imports that might enter the United States in the absence of the tariff.

The obstacles to such an inquiry are even more formidable than those confronted in appraising the effects of duty reductions under the trade agreements programs. In the latter case, there is at least a "before and after" history extending over a relatively short recent period, and this furnishes—despite difficulties of identifying rate-change effects as such—considerable evidence from which individual observers may form subjective judgments, if not definitive conclusions. Speculation about possible imports in the absence of a duty which has been in effect at one level or another for many decades, however, is on a very infirm footing. In most cases, there has been no test, under anything resembling current supply and demand conditions, of the market as it might exist in the absence of the duty.

The aggregate volume of potential additional imports would presumably include both larger amounts of a great many dutiable goods already entering in substantial quantities despite the tariff and highly uncertain amounts of others now excluded, for all practical purposes, by prohibitive duty rates. For any individual item of either type, the additional import volume would depend upon various long- and short-term elasticities of demand and of supply, both domestic and foreign. These, in turn, would depend on complex combinations of factors, including the size, nature, and trend of the United States market and of world demand for the commodity in question; techniques of production in use or utilizable both here and abroad; the institutional organization of the producing industry both in the United States and elsewhere; profit margins, especially domestically; raw material sources and costs, as well as capital and labor requirements and costs, in each of the main producing areas; the existence and availability of closely similar substitutes; and so forth. Merely to enumerate a few of the relevant variables is to suggest the dubious nature of quantitative estimates in this field.

An estimate would have to begin—in the light of known background considerations—with assumptions as to how the United States price of the imported merchandise would change (if at all) with elimination of the duty, and perhaps also as to how much additional expenditure (if any) might be made for advertising and promotion of the foreign goods. Further assumptions would follow regarding the reactions of the domestic producers, as expressed in their own pricing and promotional policies, and of consumers, as expressed in the volume of their purchases. These developments, in turn, would have to be related to the size and flexibility of production abroad. Eventually, guesses regarding a new position of equilibrium would have to be developed.

In such a process, the pyramiding of hypothetical considerations tends to become unmanageable, even in dealing with a single commodity in isolation. With respect to the whole range of dutiable imports, there is not only the cumbersome problem of dealing with a multiplicity of commodities, each with its unique features, but also the further complication of making allowances for the way in which simultaneous developments in many fields might impinge on each other. The potential aggregate change would be considerably more limited than the sum of individual changes estimated independently.

Moreover, while an estimate of the potential increase in imports would be a necessary step in estimating the resultant displacement of domestic production, the latter volume would not usually be equal to the former. An increase in imports, whether through reduction in their prices or through more aggressive marketing methods, is likely to be associated with expansion of the whole market for the goods in question. The volume of any domestic production displaced, therefore, would rarely be fully as large as that of the increment in imports.

In the face of all these obstacles to more than conjectural judgment, it is not surprising that wide differences of opinion have developed. At one extreme, there is a school of thought holding that the experience of the past 10 or 20 years proves that sizable tariff cuts can be taken in stride without significant danger, generally speaking, of sharp and painful increases in imports. At the other extreme, it is held that United States tariff reductions have already been carried close to the breaking point, and that further cuts would produce much stronger effects on imports than have been observed heretofore. In effect, the latter viewpoint attributes a high degree of restrictiveness to the present tariff level, while the former tends to minimize its protective implications.

The truth, though varying widely from commodity to commodity, probably lies in an intermediate area somewhat closer to the first point of view, at least as far as the broad national picture is concerned. Some of the reasons why pervasive United States tariff reductions averaging about 75 percent have not induced a more readily visible and dramatic impact would be likely to continue operative with further reductions.

On the whole, it appears that United States demand for many types of imported articles has not proven particularly elastic, at least over the range of price changes attributable to tariff cuts put into effect to date. Especially in the field of finished consumer goods, a considerable proportion of the imports are destined for fairly narrowly limited markets which are insensitive to relatively small variations in price. A contributing factor to these limitations of market appeal and apparent inelasticities of United States consumer demand is the unwillingness or inability of many foreign producers to undertake extensive sales-promotional activities and expenditures, in line with American selling techniques, which might widen markets here for their goods.

The same type of conservatism and inadaptability to United States methods tends in a number of instances to limit effective elasticity on the supply side abroad. It is believed that many foreign producers neglect opportunities to enter United States markets primarily because of contentment with traditional levels of operations and reluctance to invest the necessary capital in expansion of facilities. Foreign observers, of course, have frequently pointed to the threat of United States escape-clause procedures as justification for conservative approaches to both sales-promotional expenditures and plant expansion for entry into the American market.

It is also probable that United States producers could in a significant number of cases match whatever price cuts on competitive imports might be associated with further tariff reductions, and thus preserve their own share of the market at the expense of their profit margins. If past experience is a reliable guide, such cuts in profit margins would frequently be short-lived, owing to cost-saving innovations or improvements in product design stimulated by the challenge of competition.

It should be remembered, too, that some two-thirds of our dutiable imports consist of crude foodstuffs and industrial materials on which the tariff rates are generally nominal or quite moderate. With such large quantities of these goods coming in under existing tariffs, it is difficult to regard the latter as very seriously restrictive.

The supposition that the volume of imports kept out of the United States by tariffs alone is, on the whole, fairly moderate, is supported by an intensive study made several years ago by Dr. Howard S. Piquet, former Chief Economist of the Tariff Commission staff and more recently a specialist with the Legislative Reference Service of the Library of Congress. In a privately published book entitled "Aid, Trade, and the Tariff," Dr. Piquet presented estimates of the range of potential increases in imports, over 1951 levels, that would probably occur in the course of 3 to 5 years, under conditions prevailing in 1951, if all duties (and import excise taxes) were temporarily suspended. These estimates were based on a detailed commodity-by-commodity analysis of well over 200 commodities, covering four-fifths of all dutiable imports and including all those amounting to $5 million or more in 1951.

While Dr. Piquet's figures were necessarily somewhat conjectural, his long experience in the tariff field, his thorough acquaintance with the information available, and his intensive consultations with commodity experts in the course of this project entitle his judgment to more than ordinary respect. Despite changes both in the size and composition of imports and in the general economic situation since 1951, his estimates remain the most comprehensive and plausible indicators available regarding the orders of magnitude of potential imports kept out by the tariff. He concluded that suspension of United States duties, under the assumptions made in his study, would probably induce an increase of between 17 and 38 percent in dutiable imports, or 8–17 percent in relation to total imports.

Even at the "maximum increase" end of this range, the implied volume of additional imports would be equivalent to only about half of 1 percent of the gross national product of the United States. If these imports were admitted, however, their impact would be centered to a considerable extent upon a relatively few domestic industries. Not many of them are very significant in relation to the economy as a whole, but some are quite important to particular localities.

Despite the many difficulties inherent in ascertaining the magnitude of potential imports which might enter in the absence of present tariffs, there is widespread agreement among tariff students as to the types of commodities for which the likelihood of displacement of domestic production by imports would be comparatively great and the types for which it would be relatively slight.

Apart from such agricultural products as raw wool, oats, barley, and cigar filler tobacco, the major part of the impact would probably fall on textiles and an assortment of other light manufacturing industries, especially those dealing in specialty lines. Reasonably clear examples would include: woolens and worsteds, rayon staple fiber, knit and crocheted woolen apparel, certain rugs and carpets, lace and lace-trimmed and embroidered articles, fur-felt hats, leather handbags and gloves, earthenware, chinaware, and handblown glassware, musical instruments, bicycles and motorcycles, cutlery, watches, and perhaps silk fabrics and optical instruments.

On the other hand, the principal mass-producing manufacturing industries of the United States would be very little affected. Among them are motor vehicles and other transportation equipment, iron and steel, electric motors, domestic appliances, rubber manufactures, most chemicals and related products, office equipment and supplies, paper products, metal furniture, and machine-made glass and glassware. Many of these industries compete successfully abroad, and should not experience greater difficulties at home.

# THE NATURE AND SIGNIFICANCE OF INTERNATIONAL COMPARISONS OF TARIFF LEVELS

United States Department of Commerce

The Subcommittee on Foreign Trade Policy, in Chairman Boggs' letter of June 1, 1957, to Secretary Weeks, asked for the Commerce Department's "observations and information * * * on * * * the relevance and meaning of comparisons of tariff levels here and abroad."

There is considerable interest in comparisons of relative tariff levels in various countries. In connection with negotiation of reciprocal tariff concessions under the General Agreement on Tariffs and Trade, for example, certain countries have insisted that given reductions in their duties would represent greater effective concessions than corresponding percentage reductions in duties of certain other countries, because their existing average rates of duty were already much lower than those of the others. The former countries have argued that they could not equitably be expected to exchange further cuts in their duties for merely proportionate cuts by the higher-tariff countries. In principle, there is doubtless a great deal of merit in this argument.

Comparisons between average tariff levels in the United States and elsewhere are also frequently injected into debates here in the United States regarding our own tariff policies. It is sometimes argued that the United States tariff is already lower than that of most other countries, and that this militates against further cuts in our duties by reciprocal negotiations or otherwise. Conversely, foreign representatives, placing different interpretations on the available statistics, have sometimes argued that the United States rates are relatively high, and that this is justification for more liberal concessions on our part.

Unfortunately, however, there is no practical method of objectively measuring with even reasonable accuracy the relative levels and degrees of restrictiveness of the tariffs levied by the world's trading nations. There are three classes of reasons for this: First, the difficulty of establishing a meaningful statistical measurement of individual countries' tariffs; second, the difficulty of obtaining comparable basic statistics for several countries; and third, the difficulty of appraising given tariff levels in the appropriate context of variations among countries in their revenue systems and general economic structures.

## INHERENT DIFFICULTIES OF STATISTICAL MEASUREMENT

The method most commonly employed for measuring comparative national tariff levels consists of relating the value of a country's total customs receipts to the value of its total merchandise imports so as to obtain an average ad valorem rate. In effect, this is a weighted average of detailed tariff rates in which the weight assigned to each individual duty is proportionate to the value of the importations upon which it is levied. A variation of this method involves relating duty collections to the total value of dutiable imports.

With respect to the United States, for example, 1956 data show customs collections of $739 million and total imports for consumption of $12½ billion, of which $6.2 billion, or just about 50 percent, were duty free. The duties collected thus represented almost 12 percent of the value of dutiable imports and around 6 percent of all United States imports. A choice between these measures depends upon the purpose at hand. The former ratio is obviously the relevant figure when interest is centered upon dutiable imports as a class; but in other contexts, when duty-free items may be regarded as merely special cases differentiated only in small degree from low-duty items, the more broadly based ratio is the appropriate selection.

There is, however, a serious fallacy inherent in these straight arithmetical calculations as a means of determining the overall level of a country's tariff, whether in relation to total imports or to dutiable imports only. This fallacy lies in the fact that merchandise values used in the calculations are based on imports, the flow of which is regulated to a significant degree by the tariff level, operating through individual rates levied on individual commodities. For any country the most restrictive duties fail to be fully reflected in the average, because they eliminate or depress the statistical weight, in the computation of the average, of the imports against which they are assessed.

To illustrate: If a country's tariff were composed of a free list, a schedule subject to a 10-percent rate, and another subject to prohibitive duties, all imports would enter at 10 percent or free, and the general average would be between 10 percent and zero—say, 5 percent if equal amounts of dutiable and free merchandise were being imported. Somewhat paradoxically, under a tariff comprising only prohibitive duties and a free list, all imports would enter duty free and the average tariff level would be zero.

It is this type of consideration which leaves open to some question the frequently stated notion that the United States tariff is low because half of our imports enter free of duty. The percentage of free imports could be raised to 100—and the statistical average of duties lowered to zero—merely by raising the rate on dutiable imports until it became prohibitive. Conversely, the proportion of duty-free imports might be lowered—and the average ad valorem rate raised—by reduction of the most restrictive duties to levels that permitted significantly larger importation of the goods in question.

Effects similar to those of prohibitive duties upon the arithmetical average of a country's tariff rates may also result from concentration of quantitative import restrictions upon a wide range of goods subject (if imported) to relatively high rates. The restrictions, by reducing or eliminating the goods in question from the actual imports upon which the statistical weights are based, prevent due reflection in the average of the high rates upon such goods. This is one of the reasons why the average ad valorem for France, for example, compares so favorably—on the surface—with corresponding averages for other countries generally recognized by tariff specialists as having much more moderate tariff levels.

This is not to say that average ad valorem rates may not, within their limitations, throw some light on the direction and rough order of magnitude of changes from one period to another in the tariff of a single country. Generally speaking, the influence of differences in the composition of imports tends to be much less marked in comparisons between different years for one country than in comparisons between different countries. The sharp drop in the average ad valorem rate on United States imports over the past quarter century, for instance, is a valid broad indicator of reductions in United States tariff rates, especially when reinforced by relevant information regarding various factors underlying the change. In 1933, the year before enactment of the first trade-agreement legislation, the ratio of United States duties to imports was about 20 percent for the total and 54 percent for dutiable imports only. The steep decline from these figures to 6 and 12 percent, respectively, in 1956 reflects both major reductions in most individual duty rates under the trade-agreement program and the sharp decline in average ad valorem equivalents of specific duties which has been brought about by price increases for goods subject to such duties.

### PROBLEMS OF STATISTICAL COMPARABILITY

Many difficulties are encountered in obtaining comparable import and customs statistics on which to base a comparison of tariff levels as between countries. These difficulties arise from differences in the definitions, sources, and methods used by countries in compiling both their import statistics and their customs-receipts data.

Several countries, including the United States, publish import values on a country of export (or f. o. b. foreign port) basis, while the majority record import values at their own frontiers (c. i. f. basis), including the cost of freight and insurance as well as the foreign value of the merchandise. In some cases, Government purchases and imports under special concessions are not tabulated as commercial imports, while in others they are included. Some countries import considerable quantities of merchandise under state trading arrangements, at artificial prices, on which import duties may or may not be paid. Also, in any given year, some countries may have in effect temporary suspensions of duties which throw the ratio for that year out of line with longer term levels.

Even greater difficulty arises in connection with obtaining comparable figures on customs receipts. Some countries include the proceeds of export duties, and others include excise taxes levied on imports at the point of importation and internally on domestic production, while other countries exclude not only these items, but also various types of taxes not regarded by them as tariff duties, even though they may have the same effect for all practical purposes.

On the whole, nevertheless, problems of international comparability in basic statistics are much less bothersome in the present context than either the types of problems discussed above or those mentioned in the following paragraphs.

### PROBLEMS ARISING FROM DIFFERENCES IN NATIONAL REVENUE SYSTEMS AND ECONOMIC STRUCTURES

In any attempt to compare not merely the average statistical ratios of tariff collections to imports, but degrees of restrictiveness in the tariffs of various countries, analysts are confronted with the fact that even an identical rate of duty on an identical item may have very different significance in different countries, depending on whether it is primarily a revenue duty or a protective duty. In a country where the item is not produced and the tariff is imposed only for revenue purposes, its restrictive effects may be negligible. In another country which produces the item on a substantial scale, exactly the same tariff on it may be highly restrictive. This consideration is especially relevant in comparisons between tariff levels of underdeveloped countries in Latin America, Africa, or Asia and of industrial countries in Western Europe or North America. While many high duties in the former area are decidedly protectionist, it remains true that many others are restrictive of imports only in the sense that any tax upon the purchase of a commodity tends to raise its price beyond the reach of some potential consumers. For countries in which high customs duties are an integral and important part of the revenue system, a fairly high average ad valorem may have much less restrictive implications than a lower average ad valorem in a major industrial country where customs duties play only a minor role in the nation's tax system.

The above point is not by any means confined to comparisons between industrial and underdeveloped countries. In fact, an outstanding example of major distortion (with respect to restrictive implications) of a country's average tariff rate by inclusion of large revenue duties is to be found in the case of the United Kingdom. In the fiscal year 1956, British customs collections amounted to £1,148 million, or 30 percent of total United Kingdom imports of £3,865 million. On the surface, this percentage is completely out of line with ratios of customs collections to imports in other major industrial countries. For the United States, Germany, France, Belgium, Sweden, and Italy, e. g., the percentages range from about 4 to 8. This does not signify, however, that the United Kingdom's tariff level is correspondingly out of line with all the others. Some £684 million, or 60 percent of the British customs collections, came from the revenue duty on tobacco, which is not produced in the United Kingdom; and another £377 million, or 33 percent, consisted of revenue duties on other items, such as liquors, which are also subject *alternatively* to excise taxes if produced domestically in the United Kingdom. If these items are excluded from both duty collections and imports, or if only a hypothetical share of the revenue duties based on the difference between the customs rate and the alternative countervailing excise-tax rate is included in British customs receipts, then the overall average ad valorem on United Kingdom imports drops to 7 percent—well within the range indicated for the countries mentioned above. In other words, the difference between the very high prima facie average for the United Kingdom and the 4–8 percent ratios for the other countries is not really an indication of differences in tariff levels as such, but primarily a reflection of (1) very high British taxation of tobacco, liquor, etc., and (2) contrasts between the United Kingdom and others as to administrative procedures or institutional arrangements for collection of revenues on these items. (The British collect them in one levy at the time of importation, whereas some of the other countries collect separate customs duties and excise taxes on such items, and France gets its tobacco revenue from operation of a Government monopoly, rather than from either a tariff or an excise tax.)

Interpretation of the statistics available for international comparison is further complicated by the fact that average rates of duty on all imports (or all dutiable imports) of a country depend in part upon the composition of the trade. It would be quite possible for two countries to have identical tariffs on each and every item imported by either, and yet for one of them to have a much higher overall average duty level than the other simply because proportionately more of its imports consisted of the items subject to high duties in both countries.

Distortions of this type are by no means purely theoretical possibilities. A good example may be found in the comparative average ad valorems for Belgium and France in 1954, which illustrates all too aptly the peculiarities of weighted averages in which the weights depend upon the composition of imports. Tariff specialists are pretty well agreed that France is one of the higher tariff countries; yet the average ratio of duties to imports for France was about the same in 1954 as that for Belgium, which is generally acknowledged to be a relatively low-tariff country. This specious result was due primarily to the fact that the French average was weighted downward by much higher proportions of imports entering duty free or at low rates in both countries. Actually, it is well known that French rates are characteristically higher on individual items, and rough calculations show that if both French and Belgian duties were applied to the same import pattern (either the French or the Belgian) then the French average would have been substantially higher than the Belgian in 1954. (As a matter of fact, the French average rose some 65 percent above the Belgian in 1955, when France's easing of restrictions on its intra-European trade admitted more high-duty merchandise into the country, and when special compensatory import taxes—actually in the nature of tariffs—were increased by the French Government.)

QUALITATIVE JUDGMENTS OF SPECIALISTS VERSUS STATISTICAL AVERAGES

Specialists who are constantly working with tariffs seem to be in rather general agreement on broad characteristizations of the relative tariff levels of most countries. They usually consider the below-average group to include Norway, Sweden, Denmark, Belgium, the Netherlands, the United Kingdom, South Africa, and Japan; and the above-average group to include France, Germany, Italy, Austria, New Zealand, Australia, and most Latin American and Near Eastern countries. The United States and Canada are usually considered to rank somewhere between these two groups. With some exceptions, these characterizations correspond loosely to those which emerge from comparisons of average ad valorem tariff ratios. Such ratios, however, embody too many qualifications and ambiguities to permit their use for any very exacting analytical purposes. As has been shown, serious errors with respect to individual countries are likely to occur, and there also remains the basic objection that the ratio of duty collections to imports is not in itself a true or adequate indication of a nation's tariff level.

# TARIFF REDUCTIONS AND UNITED STATES IMPORTS

Howard S. Piquet, senior specialist in international economics, Legislative Reference Service of the Library of Congress

SUMMARY

1. Since 1947 the administration has been moving more and more determinedly along the route of multilateral negotiating of trade agreements, while Congress has been restricting the President's power to reduce tariffs by enacting the escape clause and the peril-point and defense essentiality amendments. The caution of Congress is explained largely by the fact that, by 1947, most of the "excess" protection in the tariff had been squeezed out. Thereafter, tariff cuts began to be felt, in the sense that they stimulated imports.

2. This observation is supported by the fact that the Trade Agreements Act of 1955 restricted the power of the President more severely than any trade legislation since 1934. Most of the tariff reductions that have been made since 1955 have been by only 15 percent. In only 34 instances has the power conferred upon the President by the act of 1955 to reduce duties in excess of 50 percent to that level been utilized.

3. Tariffs have been reduced by trade agreements on almost 90 percent of all dutiable imports during the past 23 years.

4. The 418 items upon which duties have not been reduced are mostly products with which imports are competitive and on which tariff reductions would be vigorously contested.

5. There is no accurate way of determining how much of the decline in the ratio of duties collected to the value of dutiable imports since 1934 (from 47 percent in 1934 to 12 percent in 1953 and 1956) has been caused by trade-agreement reductions and how much by rising prices of products subject to specific duties. The Tariff Commission, by applying preagreement and postagreement rates to imports in a single year (1952) found that the ratio of duties collected to the value of dutiable imports declined from an average of 24.4 percent in 1934 to an average of 12.2 percent in 1953. This appears to be an approximate index of the decline in tariff duties that may be attributed to the trade-agreements program.

6. The amendments that have been added to the Trade Agreements Act since 1947, and repeated assurances by administration officials, make it clear that neither the administration nor Congress will allow any domestic producer to be injured by imports resulting from trade-agreement concessions. As long as this policy prevails there appears to be little more that can be accomplished in the way of effectively reducing tariff barriers. A choice must be made. Are we going to continue to avoid all injury and confine ourselves to token tariff reductions, or are we going to enact legislation that will make increased imports possible? Only Congress can decide.

7. While we have been lowering tariffs we have been imposing import quotas on a number of agricultural products in order to protect domestic support programs.

8. Compared with many other countries, the foreign trade of the United States is small relative to the size of the economy. In 1956, exports equaled 4.5 percent, and imports 3 percent of the gross national product.

9. Contrary to popular belief, the foreign trade of the United States since the close of World War II has been increasing more rapidly than the country's gross national product.

10. One of the outstanding facts of the post-World War II period has been the rapid growth of imports. Although imports are still considerably smaller than exports they have been expanding at a more rapid rate than either exports or gross national product. Moreover, dutiable imports have been growing more rapidly than duty-free imports, which is presumptive evidence that reductions of tariffs under the trade-agreements program have been moderately effective.

11. If all tariff duties were suspended, imports into the United States probably would increase by not more than $2 billion. If tariffs were permanently abolished imports might increase by as much as $4 billion.

12. Even if all tariffs were abolished, the proportion of the total domestic market that would be supplied by imports would be small and the area of likely displacement of domestic production would be even smaller. The great bulk of American industry, agriculture, and mining would not be seriosuly affected by such action.

13. Producers of probably not more than 30 or 40 products would be in a position to be injured by competition from increased imports, if tariffs were abolished.

14. This does not mean, however, that those who might be injured should be ignored. Injury is an individual matter and is not any the less painful because the overall statistical picture is favorable.

15. If the United States inaugurates a program designed to increase foreign trade, particularly imports, it will be necessary to evolve a formula whereby increased imports can be absorbed without hardship. Proposals for easing the adjustment from lines of production that are vulnerable to import competition to more profitable lines were made in 1954 by David McDonald, a member of the Randall Commission. The substance of his proposals for "adjustment assistance" have been incorporated in several bills that have been introduced in Congress.

16. Senator Payne, of Maine, has proposed that there be a "limited sharing" of the United States market with imports from low-wage countries, such as Japan. Under his proposal a stated proportion (say 10 percent) of the domestic market for specified goods would be open to imports with exemption from escape-clause action guaranteed.

17. The United States has not been clear as to what it means by a "liberal" trade policy. To some it means merely the lowering of tariff duties. To others it means virtually free trade, while to still others it means nondiscriminatory trade, even with tariffs. Confusion as to objective has made it difficult to pursue a policy that does not appear to be hypocritical to foreign nations faced with trade and currency difficulties.

TARIFF REDUCTIONS AND UNITED STATES IMPORTS

This memorandum has been prepared in response to an invitation by the Ways and Means Subcommittee on Foreign Trade Policy (*a*) to examine what has happened to United States tariffs since 1934, (*b*) to evaluate the changes with respect to the volume and composition of United States imports, and (*c*) to appraise their effects upon domestic-producing interests.

Economic cause and effect relationships are so complex that it is not possible to trace clearly the effects of tariff changes. About the best that can be done is to identify the forces at work and to draw some inferences as to which are most significant.

*Historical background*

Until 1934 Congress wrote its own tariffs, regardless of the tariffs of other countries and with little regard for foreign policy considerations.

As the country developed economically, it became more and more difficult, and finally impossible, for any Member of Congress to be conversant with all the problems of the thousands of commodities involved.

Some legislators, including many who have been emphatic in their criticism of the trade agreements program, have been outspoken in insisting that Congress not return to the old method of itself determining tariff rates. The late Senator Vandenberg felt so keenly about it that he said he would rather resign his seat in the Senate than to have to endure another general tariff revision similar to that of 1929–30.

It is inevitable, when Congress determines tariff rates, that increases in rates are more likely to result than decreases. The reason for this is that groups of people who seek special favors from Government, or who fear import competition, are more insistent in exerting pressure upon their representatives in Congress than are those who place the general welfare ahead of self-interest or those who take their prosperity for granted.

From the close of World War I to the great depression of the 1930's tariff levels were raised several times. The Emergency Tariff Act of 1921 and the Fordney-McCumber Tariff Act of 1922 both raised import duties to new high levels and, in 1930, the Smoot-Hawley Act raised them to the highest point in the country's history.

The new administration and the new Congress, which came into power in 1933, as the country was emerging from the great depression, brought about an abrupt change in tariff policy. The Trade Agreements Act of 1934, implementing a low-tariff philosophy, authorized the President, whenever he finds that existing import restrictions of the United States, or any foreign country, are unduly burdening the foreign trade of the United States, to negotiate with such country or countries for the reciprocal adjustment of tariffs and other trade barriers.

The law also provided that, in proclaiming such duties, it is not necessary for the President to secure the specific approval of Congress.

The act limited reductions in duty to 50 percent, and also prohibited the President from transferring commodities between the dutiable and the free lists.

From the start, the delegation of tariff-cutting authority to the President has been temporary. Each time the Trade Agreements Act has been renewed it has been for a specified period—1, 2, or 3 years. Congress thus has had opportunity to review the administration of the act at frequent intervals.

In 1945 Congress enlarged the President's power by authorizing him to grant tariff concessions, up to 50 percent of the rates in effect on January 1, 1945. Thus, duties which had been reduced by 50 percent prior to 1945, could be reduced by another 50 percent, or by as much as 75 percent below the rates in effect in 1934.

The year 1945 marks the legislative high point of the trade liberalization program of the United States. Since that time amendments to the Trade Agreements Act have been restrictive, rather than expansive, of the President's power.

Under the authority conferred upon him by the Trade Agreements Extension Act of 1945, the President proceeded to negotiate simultaneously with 22 other countries for the lowering of trade barriers. The negotiating was carried on at Geneva and, although it was conducted on a bilateral basis, the effect was multilateral. The final act, made public in October 1947, is known as the General Agreement on Tariffs and Trade (GATT). It originally provided for trade concessions on approximately 45,000 items and covered about two-thirds of total world trade.

There were further negotiations at Annecy (France) in 1949, at which time 10 additional countries joined the agreement. In 1951, four more countries were admitted at a conference held at Torquay (England). In 1955 Japan was admitted.

Since the Geneva Conference of 1947, 39 couutries have become contracting parties to the agreement. Several countries have withdrawn (China, Lebanon, Liberia, and Syria) so that, on June 30, 1956, there were 35 contracting parties to the agreement.

Since the Trade Agreements Act first became law there has been a steady battle between the protectionist forces, who would take the teeth out of the program, and its proponents who are equally determined to reduce tariffs.

Until 1947, 13 years after the inauguration of the reciprocal trade agreements program, those opposed to tariff liberalization were not able to convince Congress of the necessity of amending the act.

*Restricting the President's power*

The program has long been subjected to the charge that producers who are about to be injured by tariff concessions can obtain no assurance of protection against such injury. Since abrogation of an international agreement is a serious matter, the administration has been reluctant to reopen an entire trade agreement in order to allay the fears of a single industry or group of producers.

As early as 1942 the administration, in response to criticism, but on its own volition, included an escape clause in the trade agreement with Mexico. Under this clause either party to the agreement can suspend or modify any concession if, because of unforeseen circumstances, increased imports threatened serious injury to domestic producers. The administration agreed, in hearings before Congress in 1943, to include an escape clause in all subsequent trade agreements.

In 1947, after the return of the Republican Party to control of Congress, one of the first items on the agenda was modification of the trade agreements program. Following extensive discussion between Senator Millikin, Senator Vandenberg, and Assistant Secretary of State Clayton, the President issued an Executive order stipulating that an escape clause would henceforth be included in every new trade agreement. The purpose of this action was to permit the United States and contracting foreign countries to abrogate parts of any trade agreement which threatened injury to producers in either country.

Instead of rejecting the act in toto, the 80th Congress (in 1948) renewed it, but with several major amendments. The most important of these, the first signficant amendments to the Trade Agreements Act since 1934, was the so-called peril-point provision, which required the Tariff Commission to survey all commodities on which the President proposes to negotiate agreements and to specify the rates of duty below which, in the Commission's judgment, tariffs cannot be lowered without injuring domestic producers. Although the President was permitted to reduce tariffs below these points, he was required, if he did so, to explain in writing to Congress his reasons for such action.

In 1949, Congress repealed the 1948 version of the Trade Agreements Act, including the peril-point amendment, and extended the act in its original form for 2 more years.

The act again came up for congressional review in 1951. This time the administration was not able to overcome the opposition and the act was renewed for 2 years (to June 1953) but with several major amendments. The peril-point provision was restored and, for the first time, an escape-clause provision was written into the act itself.

This version of the act made it more difficult for the President to negotiate tariff reductions. No important trade agreement activity took place under either the act as modified by the 80th Congress or under the Extension Act of 1951.

In 1953, at the request of the new administration, which was not too certain as to what its trade policy was to be, Congress renewed the Trade Agreements Act for 1 year. Meanwhile, it created a Commission on Foreign Economic Policy (which came to be known as the Randall Commission) for the purpose of making a thorough and comprehensive reexamination of the economic foreign policy of the United States.

Congress also provided that, in escape-clause cases, unanimous agreement on any recommendation by any 3 (out of the 6) Tariff Commissioners may be considered by the President as the recommendation of the Commission.

The Randall Commission, which consisted of 5 Senators, 5 Members of the House of Representatives, and 7 public members appointed by the President, was essentially a policy, rather than a research, body. Its purpose was to ascertain the maximum area of agreement that could be obtained among its members with their widely varying attitudes toward international trade and tariffs.

Its recommendations, which were made after only 2 months of deliberation, were exceedingly modest. In the field of foreign-trade policy it recommended, in place of the President's authority to reduce tariffs by 50 percent of their 1945 levels, that he be authorized to reduce them 5 percent a year, below their 1955 levels, over a period of 3 years.

It recommended, further, that the President be empowered (*a*) to reduce tariffs, through international negotiations, by 50 percent of their 1945 levels on commodities imported into the United States in negligible quantities only, and (*b*) to lower tariffs in excess of 50 percent ad valorem to that level, either in the course of international negotiation or on a unilateral basis.

The Randall Commission reported to the President and to Congress in January 1954. In March the President recommended that Congress enact certain of the Commission's proposals, but Congress did not act on the recommendation. Instead, it renewed the existing law for another year, to June 1955.

Debate on the Trade Agreements Extension Act of 1955 was vigorous and prolonged. The President proposed that Congress enact substantially what the Randall Commission had recommended, except that it was made clear that the authority to reduce duties in excess of 50 percent ad valorem, or its equivalent, to that ceiling was to be accomplished only through trade-agreement negotiation and not on a unilateral basis.

The proposals were incorporated in H. R. 1, one of the most controversial of recent tariff bills. It was passed by the House in practically the form the President had requested but, in the Senate, a number of important amendments were added.

The Senate version of the bill became the Trade Agreements Extension Act of 1955. It was much weaker, as a tariff-reducing instrumentality, than either the bill as it passed the House or than the recommendations of the Randall Commission.

As finally passed, the new act which is to expire on June 30, 1958, provides for—

1. Reductions, through trade-agreement negotiation, of 5 percent a year over a period of 3 years, of existing duties, with a proviso that, if any rate is not lowered in the first or second years, the power to reduce the rate by that particular 5 percent is to lapse. (It should be noted that this provision authorizes duty reductions of 5 percent, not 5 percentage points. Thus, a duty of 25 percent can be lowered, not to 10 percent, but to only 21¼ percent.)

2. Reductions, through trade-agreement negotiation, of duties in excess of 50 percent ad valorem to that level over a period of 3 years.

3. No action on the provision recommended by the Randall Commission, that would have given the President power to reduce duties 50 percent below their 1945 levels, on articles imported into the United States in negligible quantities only.

4. Greater ease in obtaining relief under the escape clause. A relative increase in imports may now be deemed to constitute injury if the Tariff Commission finds that such imports have contributed substantially to this result. The term "substantially" however, is not defined. Interpreted narrowly, this provision means than an industry is entitled to relief under the escape clause if it fears injury and is not retaining its previous percentage share of the market, even though the market may be an expanding one.

5. A narrower definition of "domestic industry." For purposes of peril-point and escape-clause action, an industry is now defined

as that portion of a producing organization manufacturing products that are alike, or directly competitive with, imports. Thus, if any domestic producer can show that any item which he produces is in danger of being displaced by imports, he is entitled to relief under the escape clause. In this form, the escape clause is considerably tighter than it was previously. If interpreted narrowly, it can freeze existing patterns of production against import competition.

6. Making public by the Tariff Commission of its findings and recommendations in escape-clause cases at the same time that they are submitted to the President. The effect of this provision is to draw political fire to the White House, while the President is deciding his course of action regarding the recommendation of the Tariff Commission.

7. Restriction of imports whenever the President finds, through the Office of Defense Mobilization, that any article is being imported in such quantity as to threaten, or impair, the national security. In such cases the action of the President is not limited by Congress. He is authorized to take whatever action he deems necessary to adjust imports of the article in question to a level that will not threaten to impair the national security. "National security" is not defined in the law and, as demonstrated with respect to watches, there can be considerable difference of opinion among Government agencies as to what is essential to national security.

From 1934 to 1947, trade agreements were negotiated slowly and methodically, on a country-by-country basis, with generalization of concessions to all countries under the unconditional most-favored-nation policy.

Since 1947 trade agreements have been negotiated more rapidly and on a multilateral basis. Because agreements are now multilateral, the generalization of concessions under the most-favored-nation policy has become less troublesome since countries that would derive benefits from the generalization are already parties to the agreement.[1]

It is significant that the following year Congress began seriously to curtail the power of the President to reduce tariffs.

Since 1947 the administration has been avowedly trying to move consistently along the road of multilateral tariff reduction. At the same time Congress has been equally, if not more, determined to make sure that no domestic producer suffers injury as a result of tariff concessions.

Under the circumstances, it is difficult to say whether the Trade Agreements Act in its present (1957) form is more important as a means for lowering tariffs still further, or because of the escape clause and the defense-essentiality amendment, as a protective measure against import competition.

*Tariff reductions to date*

Tariff duties on almost 90 percent of all commodities subject to duty have been reduced by trade-agreement action during the past 23 years.

---

[1] It is sometimes stated that the United States generalizes tariff concessions only to countries that are members of the General Agreement on Tariffs and Trade. This is not so. Under the unconditional most-favored-nation policy, to which the United States has adhered since 1923, all concessions are extended to all countries regardless of whether they are members of the GATT, provided that they do not discriminate against the commerce of the United States.

Of the 4,818 items listed in the latest edition of schedule A, 4,081 are dutiable. Duties have been reduced on 3,583 items. On only 418 items has there been no change of duty.

Duties have been bound against increase on 74 items, and duties have been increased, by Executive action, on 6. All but 171 of the 737 items on the free list have been bound in that status.

Imports of the 418 items, the duties upon which have not been reduced by trade agreements, amounted to approximately $232 million in 1956, or to approximately 4 percent of total dutiable imports.[2] The fact that these imports account for such a small proportion of total dutiable imports should not be misinterpreted. In some cases, imports are small because the duties are restrictive of imports.

Most of the products upon which duties have not been reduced are those with which imports are competitive, such as certain classes of the following: Olives, feathers, cherries, dates, edible nuts, corduroy, cordage, wool gloves and certain other clothing, Spanish cedar plywood, wallboard, optical glass for spectacles and optical instruments, thumbtacks, pocket knives, synthetic camphor, numerous chemicals (including potassium chlorate, potassium citrate, borax, sodium bromide, chloroform, and terpin hydrate), firecrackers, perfume materials, box-type cameras, phonograph needles, clock parts and movements, hairbrushes, agate buttons, and match splints.

An attempt was made to ascertain whether imports of the products upon which duties have not been reduced have increased less rapidly than those upon which duties have been reduced. It was not feasible to pursue this line of investigation very far, however, because the large number of reclassifications that have been made in connection with trade agreements makes comparison over a period of time impossible.

*Present tariff levels*

In 1953, the United States Tariff Commission compared the ad valorem equivalents of import duties in effect before any trade agreements were signed with those in effect on January 1, 1945, and on January 1, 1953.[3] Tables are presented in various forms so that comparisons are available (1) for total dutiable imports; (2) by broad commodity groups (tariff schedules); (3) for total agricultural and nonagricultural dutiable imports; (4) by rate of duty; (5) by principal dutiable commodities (imports valued at more than $5 million in 1952); and (6) by commodities on which duties were equivalent to more than 45 percent ad valorem. In addition to a comparison of ad valorem equivalents of import duties, the data are broken down according to their agreement status on January 1, 1953.

The technique of applying the effective rate on three different dates to imports during a single year (1952), thereby using a single set of weights, eliminates the effects of price fluctuations and of changes in the composition of imports.

However, when a single set of weights is used (1) no consideration is given to changes in the pattern of imports which may have resulted directly from the reduction in tariff duties; and (2) the effect of

[2] Omitting sugar, the imports of which are limited by quota.

[3] Effect of Trade Agreement Concessions on United States Tariff Levels Based on Imports in 1952, U. S. Tariff Commission, Washington, September 1953. This report is being brought up to date by the Commission. See appendix A.

price on the ad valorem equivalent of specific duties is omitted. A price rise of 100 percent represents a real reduction of 50 percent in the ad valorem percent equivalent of a specific duty, although the rate of duty may have remained unchanged by concession.

The report indicates that the average ad valorem equivalent of duties collected, related to total dutiable imports in 1952, was 24.4 percent, using the rates in effect before any trade-agreement reductions took place. On the basis of rates in effect on January 1, 1953, the ad valorem equivalent was 12.2 percent.

Thus, during the first 19 years of the trade-agreements program the ad valorem of all duties declined by 50 percent, about half of the decrease being accounted for by trade-agreement reductions and half by the general rise in prices during the period.[4]

Ad valorem equivalents fell from 23.7 percent before any agreements to 12.1 percent on January 1, 1953, for metals; from 16.2 to 9.4 percent for agricultural products and provisions; from 36.7 to 22.4 percent for wool; from 10.9 to 4.7 percent for wood; and from 25.1 to 12.4 percent for chemicals.

If subject to rates in effect before any agreement, 32.2 percent of dutiable imports in 1952 would have had ad valorem rates of 10 percent or less compared with 52.3 percent in this category using rates effective January 1, 1953. Although 94 percent of 1952 imports were subject to duties of 30 percent or less with January 1, 1953, rates, only 75 percent of the imports would have fallen into this category with preagreement rates.

*Import quotas*

Tariffs are not the only direct import barriers imposed by the United States. Import quotas, which are applicable to a number of agricultural products, usually are more restrictive than tariffs, as far as the commodities covered are concerned.

The principal absolute[5] import quotas imposed by the United States are provided for legislatively and are applicable to imports of wheat, wheat flour, sugar, long-staple cotton, short-staple cotton, linseed oil, butter, rice and rice products, peanuts, flaxseed, cheese, live cattle, and dressed beef. Most of these products are also subject to tariff charges, which, because of the quota limitations, may be considered as revenue duties.

Also in effect are a number of absolute quotas on imports from the Philippines which are provided for in the Philippine Trade Act of 1946. The commodities affected are rice, cigars, scrap and filler tobacco, coconut oil, buttons of pearl or shell, sugar, and hard-fiber cordage.

Other quantitative limitations are provided for under copyright legislation, and legislation to protect public morals, to control the importation of drugs, to protect patents and trademarks, etc.

*Tariff reductions becoming more difficult*

In the early years of the trade-agreements program it was relatively easy to reduce tariffs, since it was possible to make substantial

[4] The average ad valorem equivalent for dutiable imports was 46.7 percent in 1934, 28.2 percent in 1945, and 12.5 percent in 1951, when based on rates and dutiable imports in those years, respectively.

[5] As distinguished from so-called tariff quotas, the purpose of which is to make possible the liberalization of certain tariff restrictions on limited quantities of imports.

cuts in duties without having to be greatly concerned over competition from imports. In many cases duties were so high that there was considerable excess protection that could be sloughed off without hurting anybody. By "excess protection" is meant higher duties than are necessary to prevent imports from competing with high-cost producers.

Among the higher duties that were reduced, apparently without taking away enough protection to stimulate imports substantially, were:

Nail clippers, the compound duty upon which was cut in half, leaving a duty equivalent to 114 percent ad valorem. Subsequent imports (1952) totaled less than $500.

Blades and handles for low-priced pocketknives, the rate of duty on which was cut in half, leaving a duty equivalent to 110 percent ad valorem. Subsequent imports (1952) totaled approximately $1,000.

Breech-loading rifles, valued at less than $5 each, the compound duty on which was cut in half, leaving a duty with an ad valorem equivalent of 85 percent. Imports in 1952 amounted to $12,000.

Low-priced electric meters, the compound duty on which was cut in half, leaving a duty equivalent to 102 percent. After the reduction imports amounted (in 1952) to $10,000.

Low-priced tobacco pipes, the compound duty on which was cut substantially, leaving a duty the ad valorem equivalent of which was 78 percent. Subsequent imports (1952) amounted to $34,000.

As new trade agreements were made, more and more duties were reduced and it became increasingly difficult to make tariff cuts without intensifying import competition. This is probably the principal reason for the protectionist trend in Congress since the close of World War II.

The amendments that have been added to the Trade Agreements Act since 1947 and the often-repeated assurances by administration officials, evidence an intention to make sure that reductions in tariffs will not be allowed to stimulate imports to a degree that will "injure" any domestic producing interest.

As long as this policy prevails, there appears to be little more that can be done in the way of effectively reducing tariff barriers. This is not to say, however, that there are no longer any tariffs that can be cut. It means that from now on tariff reductions, other than token reductions such as most that have been made since 1955, probably will result in increasing imports. Some of the increases undoubtedly would be judged injurious to certain producers. It is difficult, for example, to conceive of the possibility of increasing imports from low-wage countries, such as Japan, via the present tariff-reducing formula, without injuring certain high-cost producers in the United States.

Yet the stimulation of imports from such countries is of vital importance to the foreign policy interests of the United States. It was in order to resolve this dilemma that David McDonald, president of the United Steelworkers Union and a member of the Randall Commission, in 1954 proposed an adjustment assistance program under which domestic producers would be encouraged to adjust to increased imports when they are in the national interest of the United States.

With relatively minor exceptions, United States tariffs have been reduced about as far as they can be within the "no injury" framework.

Although the United States has been negotiating trade agreements for more than two decades, there are still a number of tariff rates that are indisputably high. Having survived 23 years of trade agreement activity, it is probable that most of them would now be very difficult to reduce. They can be called the "sensitive" items.

The duty on pistols valued at less than $4 each, for example, remains at more than 140 percent. That on cellulose acetate waste is 164 percent, while that on certain types of razors is 158 percent. Ethers and esters containing between 20 and 50 percent alcohol are dutiable at 101 percent.

Over 200 items carrying rates of duty of 50 percent or more are readily identifiable. Some of them are shown in appendix B, together with imports for 1952.[6] In most cases imports are very small. How much larger they would be if duties were to be reduced substantially can only be guessed.

*The escape clause.*

The inclusion of the escape clause in all trade agreements since 1947 undoubtedly has done much to negate the effectiveness of tariff reductions, assuming that the purpose of lowering tariffs is to increase imports and exports.[7]

Eighty-three applications for relief under the clause have been filed with the Tariff Commission. Six have been dismissed at the request of the applicants, 4 were terminated without formal findings, and 6 are pending.

Of the 67 investigations completed by the Commission, 14 resulted in dismissal and 28 in a finding of "no injury." "Injury" was found in 20 cases and in 5 cases the Commission was evenly divided.

Thus, in 25 of the applications filed with the Commission there has been a finding of injury, or an even division of opinion.

The President acted to increase duties in 7 cases (fur-felt hats, hatters' fur, dried figs, cloverseed, watches, bicycles, and flax toweling) but declined to act in 17 cases. One case is still pending.

However, it would be a mistake to conclude, since relief under the escape clause has been obtained in less than 10 percent of the applications filed, that the escape clause is not an important deterrent to imports. The fact that the provision is in the law, and that action can be taken under it, is itself an important deterrent. This is particularly so with respect to manufactured products, the successful marketing of which in the United States requires substantial outlays for advertising and the maintenance of service. As long as there is a probability that success in the American market will precipitate action under the escape clause, there will be hesitancy on the part of foreign producers to introduce new products on the American market.

It is probable that a few domestic producers would be hard hit if imports of the products which they produce were to increase substantially. The question of overriding importance, however, is not whether these few producers have a "right" to continue enjoying in-

---

[6] Because the Tariff Commission no longer makes such information easily available it has been necessary for the author to make these computations himself. There was not sufficient time to ascertain imports for later than 1952. Imports of these items undoubtedly are still small.

[7] Although each contracting party to the General Agreement on Tariffs and Trade reserves the right to invoke the escape clause, it must be remembered that whenever a country invokes the clause with respect to imports which it deems injurious, it runs the risk of retaliation from other countries against products which are important among its exports.

direct subsidy. Of equal, if not greater, importance is the degree to which increased imports will stimulate exports and the degree to which the increased imports will shock the domestic economy. Also, not to be overlooked is the importance of the imports in question, in the light of the international situation, to the foreign policy objectives of the United States.

If the imports are clearly in the national interest the question becomes one of facilitating the adjustment of the economy to them.

"Avoidance of injury" to each and every domestic producer and "adaptation to increased imports" are two quite different, and incompatible, approaches to the problem. The former concentrates entirely upon the short-run interests of domestic producers, whereas the latter takes all aspects of the problem into account. Increasing attention is being given to the latter approach as a substitute for the former.

Generally speaking, those who have reason to fear imports are those who are engaged in lines of production employing a large proportion of labor, relative to machinery. American labor receives relatively high wages because of the great productivity of most American industry. The less fortunately situated industries must pay high wages since they are in competition for labor against more efficient home industries.

Under the law the responsibility of the Tariff Commission, in escape clause cases, pertains solely to the question of injury to domestic producers. It has no official interest in the effects of tariff duties and imports upon consumers, or upon the domestic economy as a whole. Neither does it take into consideration the international economic position of the United States.

On the other hand, in acting upon recommendations of the Commission, the President takes all factors into account. Before accepting or rejecting the Commission's recommendations, the White House seeks the views of various Government departments, including State, Commerce, and Agriculture. The President then acts in accordance with what he believes to be in the national interest in all its aspects.

It is necessary to appreciate this limited jurisdiction of the Tariff Commission in order to understand the reasons why the President has rejected Tariff Commission recommendations for relief under the escape clause in 17 cases. The President is sometimes criticized for not accepting the recommendations of his own Commission. If the interests of domestic producers were all that mattered, there might be some ground for such criticism. As it is, the question of injury to domestic producers is only one of many sides of a complicated problem.

There is much to be said for requiring the Tariff Commission to consider, not only injury to domestic producers, but also the effects of tariff changes and imports upon consumers and upon the economy as a whole. If the powers of the Commission were to be expanded in such fashion it would be necessary to require that appointees to the Commission be persons adequately equipped for the job.

*Tariff changes and United States imports*

The most important single force affecting the size of the foreign trade of the United States is the intensity of economic activity within the country. When the economy is prosperous and the gross national product is growing, exports and imports tend to expand. The converse is true in periods of economic recession.

Compared with many other countries, the foreign trade of the United States is small, relative to the size of the economy. In 1956 exports equaled 4.5 percent, and imports 3 percent, of the gross national product.

Contrary to popular belief, the foreign trade of the United States has been increasing more, rather than less, rapidly than the gross national product.

One of the outstanding statistical facts of the post-World War II period has been the growth of imports. Since 1946 exports and gross national product have expanded at about the same rate (98 percent), whereas imports have grown much more rapidly (160 percent). In part, the comparison reflects the bulge of exports during the war period.

CHART I. *Rates of growth of exports, imports, and gross national product, 1934–56*

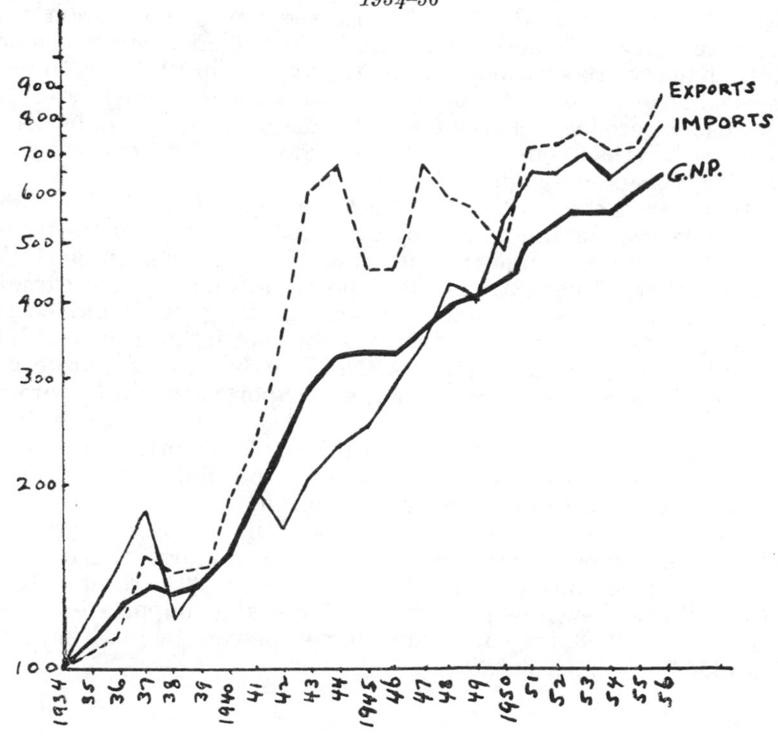


[Logarithmic scale or ratio chart]

TABLE 1.—*Exports, imports, and gross national product, United States, 1934–56*

| Year | Billions of dollars | | | Index numbers | | |
|---|---|---|---|---|---|---|
| | Exports | Imports | Gross national product | Exports | Imports | Gross national product |
| 1934 | 2.1 | 1.6 | 65.0 | 100 | 100 | 100 |
| 1935 | 2.2 | 2.0 | 72.5 | 107 | 125 | 112 |
| 1936 | 2.4 | 2.4 | 82.7 | 115 | 148 | 127 |
| 1937 | 3.3 | 3.0 | 90.8 | 157 | 184 | 140 |
| 1938 | 3.1 | 1.9 | 85.2 | 146 | 119 | 131 |
| 1939 | 3.1 | 2.3 | 91.1 | 149 | 139 | 140 |
| 1940 | 3.9 | 2.5 | 100.6 | 187 | 155 | 155 |
| 1941 | 5.0 | 3.2 | 125.8 | 239 | 197 | 194 |
| 1942 | 8.0 | 2.8 | 159.1 | 381 | 169 | 245 |
| 1943 | 12.8 | 3.4 | 192.5 | 612 | 207 | 296 |
| 1944 | 14.2 | 3.9 | 211.4 | 674 | 237 | 325 |
| 1945 | 9.6 | 4.1 | 213.6 | 456 | 250 | 329 |
| 1946 | 9.5 | 4.8 | 209.2 | 452 | 293 | 322 |
| 1947 | 14.3 | 5.7 | 232.2 | 679 | 345 | 357 |
| 1948 | 12.5 | 7.1 | 257.3 | 597 | 434 | 396 |
| 1949 | 11.9 | 6.6 | 257.3 | 568 | 403 | 396 |
| 1950 | 10.1 | 8.7 | 285.1 | 483 | 534 | 439 |
| 1951 | 14.9 | 10.8 | 328.2 | 709 | 661 | 505 |
| 1952 | 15.0 | 10.7 | 345.4 | 717 | 657 | 531 |
| 1953 | 15.7 | 10.8 | 363.2 | 745 | 659 | 559 |
| 1954 | 15.0 | 10.2 | 361.2 | 713 | 626 | 556 |
| 1955 | 15.4 | 11.3 | 391.7 | 734 | 693 | 603 |
| 1956 | 18.8 | 12.5 | 414.7 | 897 | 764 | 638 |

Over the entire period since the trade-agreements program was inaugurated (1934–56) both exports and imports have increased more rapidly than the gross national product. Exports in 1956 were almost 9 times as large as in 1934, imports almost 8 times as large, and the gross national product between 6 and 7 times as large (all in terms of current, rather than constant, dollars). Since 1937–39 exports have grown 487 percent and imports 421 percent.

By themselves, these observations do not prove that the increased imports have been brought about by tariff reductions under the trade-agreements program. But they most certainly do not support the impression that neither exports nor imports have increased as rapidly as the gross national product. We are speaking, it should be remembered, in terms of rates of increase, and not in terms of absolute magnitudes. Exports and imports are both small, in dollar terms, relative to the gross national product, and exports are still 50 percent larger than imports.

Comparison of the rates of growth of dutiable imports and imports entering free of duty sheds some light upon the significance of tariff reductions under the trade-agreements program.

It is significant that 1956 is the first year in the past 45 years in which dutiable imports have been larger than imports entering free of duty. In 1934, dutiable imports accounted for 39 percent of total imports. Since then, the proportion of dutiable imports has been increasing. In 1953, they accounted for 45 percent of total imports, and in 1956 for 50.2 percent.

TABLE 2.—*Proportion of imports subject to duty, 1934–56*

[In percent]

| Year | Imports for consumption | | Year | Imports for consumption | |
|---|---|---|---|---|---|
| | Dutiable | Duty free | | Dutiable | Duty free |
| 1934 | 39.4 | 60.6 | 1946 | 39.5 | 60.5 |
| 1935 | 40.9 | 59.1 | 1947 | 39.2 | 60.8 |
| 1936 | 42.9 | 57.1 | 1948 | 41.1 | 58.9 |
| 1937 | 41.4 | 58.6 | 1949 | 41.1 | 58.9 |
| 1938 | 39.3 | 60.7 | 1950 | 45.5 | 54.5 |
| 1939 | 38.6 | 61.4 | 1951 | 44.6 | 55.4 |
| 1940 | 35.1 | 64.9 | 1952 | 41.8 | 58.2 |
| 1941 | 37.0 | 63.0 | 1953 | 45.1 | 54.9 |
| 1942 | 36.2 | 63.8 | 1954 | 44.6 | 55.4 |
| 1943 | 35.3 | 64.7 | 1955 | 46.8 | 53.2 |
| 1944 | 30.2 | 69.8 | 1956 | 50.2 | 49.8 |
| 1945 | 33.0 | 67.0 | | | |

The proportion of imports subject to duty since 1934 is shown in table 2. The relative rates of growth of dutiable and free imports have been as follows:

[In percent]

| Period | Increase over the period | |
|---|---|---|
| | Dutiable imports | Free imports |
| 1934 to 1956 | 871 | 526 |
| 1937 to 1939—1956 | 547 | 331 |
| 1946 to 1956 | 232 | 111 |
| 1951 to 1956 | 30 | 4 |

CHART II.—Rates of growth, dutiable and free imports, 1934–56

[Logarithmic scale or ratio chart]

TABLE 3.—*Dutiable and free imports, by years, 1934–56*

| Year | Millions of dollars | | Index numbers | |
|---|---|---|---|---|
| | Dutiable imports | Free imports | Dutiable imports | Free imports |
| 1934 | 644.8 | 991.2 | 100 | 100 |
| 1935 | 832.9 | 1,206.0 | 129 | 122 |
| 1936 | 1,039.0 | 1,384.9 | 161 | 140 |
| 1937 | 1,244.6 | 1,765.2 | 193 | 178 |
| 1938 | 766.9 | 1,182.7 | 119 | 119 |
| 1939 | 878.8 | 1,397.3 | 136 | 141 |
| 1940 | 891.7 | 1,649.0 | 138 | 166 |
| 1941 | 1,191.0 | 2,030.9 | 185 | 205 |
| 1942 | 1,001.7 | 1,767.6 | 155 | 178 |
| 1943 | 1,197.2 | 2,192.7 | 186 | 221 |
| 1944 | 1,169.5 | 2,708.4 | 181 | 273 |
| 1945 | 1,350.8 | 2,724.0 | 209 | 275 |
| 1946 | 1,889.9 | 2,935.0 | 293 | 296 |
| 1947 | 2,211.7 | 3,454.6 | 343 | 349 |
| 1948 | 2,917.5 | 4,174.5 | 452 | 421 |
| 1949 | 2,708.5 | 3,883.2 | 420 | 392 |
| 1950 | 3,976.3 | 4,766.8 | 617 | 481 |
| 1951 | 4,823.9 | 5,993.4 | 748 | 605 |
| 1952 | 4,490.5 | 6,257.0 | 696 | 631 |
| 1953 | 4,859.4 | 5,919.5 | 754 | 597 |
| 1954 | 4,571.6 | 5,667.9 | 709 | 572 |
| 1955 | 5,300.2 | 6,036.6 | 822 | 609 |
| 1956 | 6,270.4 | 6,219.8 | 972 | 628 |

The fact that dutiable imports have been increasing more rapidly than free imports since the inauguration of the trade-agreements program would seem to support the view that reductions of tariffs by trade agreements have been moderately effective.

The figures in the table and in chart II show that the rate of growth of dutiable imports has jumped ahead of the rate of growth of free imports since the close of the war. As observed above, this is also the period of intense trade agreement activity at the Geneva, Annecy, and Torquay Conferences.

*Composition of imports*

Dutiable imports were 184 percent higher in 1956 than in 1947, whereas free imports were only 80 percent higher. Dutiable imports of all major classes of merchandise increased in the 9-year postwar period and imports of all major classes of free imports increased, except manufactured foodstuffs, which declined.

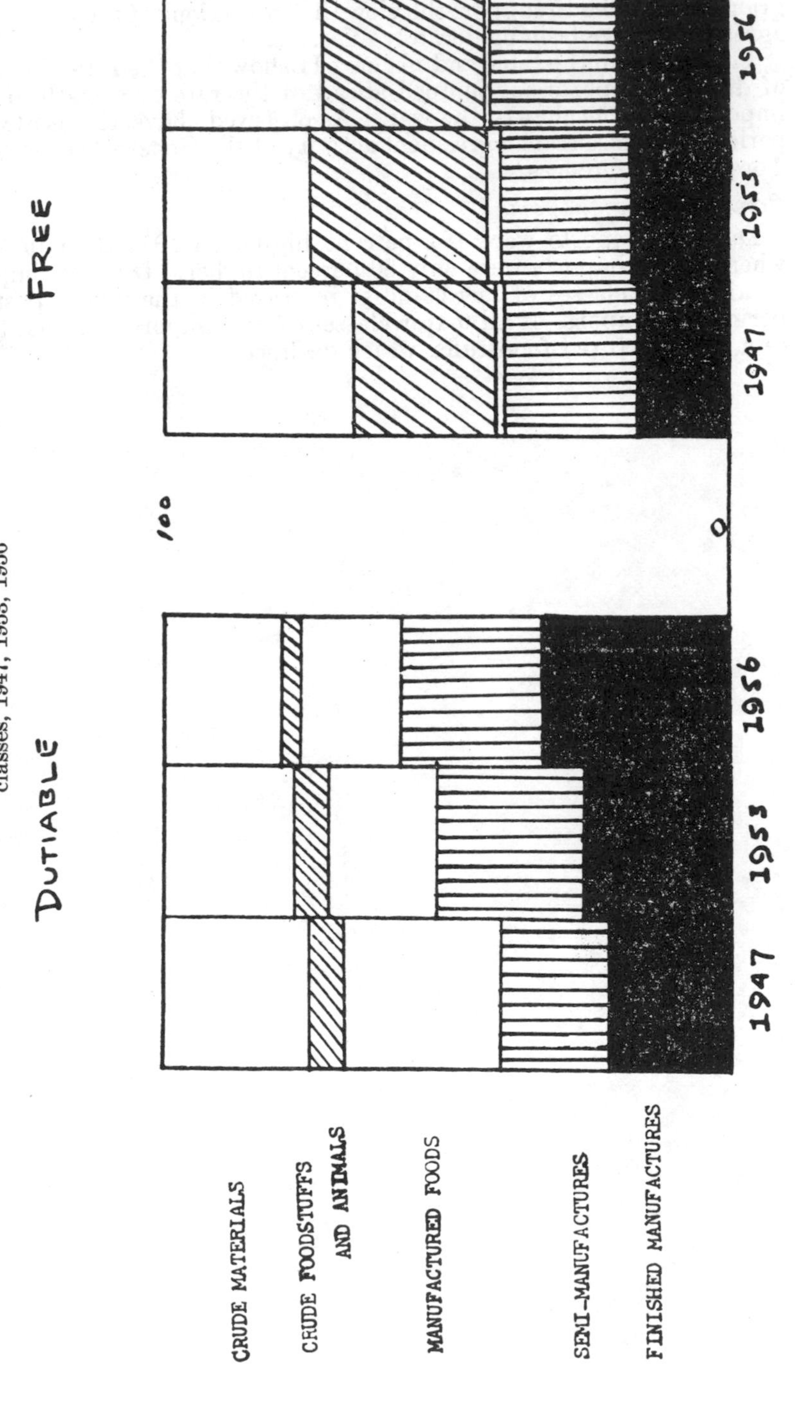


CHART III. Percentage distribution; dutiable and free imports, by economic classes, 1947, 1953, 1956

TABLE 4.—*Imports, dutiable and free, by economic classes, 1947, 1953, 1956*

[Imports in millions of dollars]

| Economic class | Dutiable imports | | | Percentage change, 1947-56 | Free imports | | | Percentage change, 1947-56 |
|---|---|---|---|---|---|---|---|---|
| | 1947 | 1953 | 1956 | | 1947 | 1953 | 1956 | |
| Crude materials | 585 | 1,117 | 1,321 | +125.8 | 1,181 | 1,496 | 1,755 | +48.6 |
| Crude foodstuffs and animals | 138 | 308 | 217 | +57.2 | 879 | 1,877 | 1,818 | +106.8 |
| Manufactured foodstuffs | 617 | 945 | 1,135 | +84.0 | 39 | 163 | 32 | -17.9 |
| Semimanufactures | 420 | 1,272 | 1,564 | +272.4 | 825 | 1,406 | 1,438 | +74.3 |
| Finished manufactures | 452 | 1,217 | 2,034 | +350.0 | 530 | 978 | 1,177 | +122.1 |
| Total | 2,212 | 4,859 | 6,271 | +183.5 | 3,454 | 5,920 | 6,220 | +80.1 |

TABLE 5.—*Percentage distribution, dutiable and free imports, by economic classes, 1947, 1953, 1956*

| Economic class | Dutiable imports | | | Free imports | | |
|---|---|---|---|---|---|---|
| | 1947 | 1953 | 1956 | 1947 | 1953 | 1956 |
| Crude materials | 26.4 | 23.0 | 21.1 | 34.2 | 25.3 | 28.2 |
| Crude foodstuffs and animals | 6.2 | 6.3 | 3.5 | 25.4 | 31.7 | 29.2 |
| Manufactured foodstuffs | 27.9 | 19.4 | 18.1 | 1.1 | 2.8 | .5 |
| Semimanufactures | 19.0 | 26.2 | 24.9 | 23.9 | 23.7 | 23.1 |
| Finished manufactures | 20.4 | 25.0 | 32.4 | 15.3 | 16.5 | 18.9 |
| Total | 100.0 | 100.0 | 100.0 | 100.0 | 100.0 | 100.0 |

The percentage increases were greater in all major classes among the dutiable, than among the free, imports, except crude foodstuffs and animals. The largest increases among the dutiable imports were in finished and semifinished manufactures.

Among the free imports the largest increases were in finished manufactures and crude foodstuffs and animals.

These figures provide some basis for concluding that trade-agreement concessions on manufactured goods are a reason for the substantial increase of dutiable imports in recent years.

Chart III shows the percentage composition of dutiable and free imports in 1947, 1953, and 1956. It shows clearly the increasing proportion of dutiable imports accounted for by finished and semifinished manufactures as well as the lesser relative importance of these classes of goods among the free imports compared with crude foodstuffs and animals and crude materials.

*How restrictive are present tariff rates?*

The arithmetical level of present tariff rates should not be confused with the degree to which they restrict imports. These are two quite different, and often unrelated, concepts.

Since foreign goods that are not able to surmount existing import barriers are excluded from the average altogether, the duties collected on goods actually entering the country are overweighted in the average and the restrictive effects of the tariff are understated. Indeed, if this arithmetical approach is followed to its logical conclusion, the result is a reductio ad absurdum. Up to a certain point, the higher the duties the higher will be the average ad valorem equivalent on actual imports. As the duties become more and more restrictive, however, they result in lower, rather than higher, ad valorem equivalents. If the duties were to exclude all dutiable imports, the only goods entering the country would be those on the free list and the ad valorem equivalent of duties collected would be zero.[8]

The arithmetic fact that duties collected average only about 12.2 percent of the value of all dutiable imports does not shed any light upon the extent to which existing tariffs actually keep foreign-produced goods from entering the country. Many duties are low but that does not necessarily mean that they are not restrictive.

Furthermore, new and often more effective ways of excluding imports have been devised. Quantitative restrictions (quotas), exchange controls, compensating agreements, and other bilateral balancing arrangements—not to mention the complexities of customs formalities and regulations—and such devices as marking regulations, "Buy American" (or "British," etc.) legislation, preferential arrangements among certain countries, have been invoked.

One of the principal purposes of international trade barriers is to protect domestic producers against imports. To concentrate upon a simple comparison of the "heights" of tariff walls is to pay disproportionate attention to only one kind of protection.

In order to judge the restrictiveness of trade barriers, we must determine the extent to which goods would enter the country if those trade barriers did not exist.

A low duty on a certain product might actually be more restrictive of imports than a high duty on some other product. In a purely competitive industry, one that consists of many producers and that cuts across international boundaries, even a slight reduction in a low duty might bring about a substantial percentage increase in imports. This is because, under competition, profit margins tend to be relatively narrow and prices are closely related to marginal costs. An illustration would be the bicycle industry. The duty on bicycles is relatively low (11 to 30 percent). If this duty were drastically reduced, the increase in imports probably would be substantial. Competition between imported and domestically produced bicycles is active, and the fact that the arithmetical "height" of the duty is relatively low does not mean that its removal would have no appreciable effect upon domestic producers.

By way of contrast there are some industries in which imports are not highly competitive with domestic production and in which tariff duties, whether high or low, are not considered of great importance by the producers. In some cases, notably the petroleum industry,

---

[8] Some of the pamphlet material that has appeared purporting to show how low United States tariffs are compared with those of other countries is quite misleading. For example, a recent publication of the American Tariff League presents comparisons, by countries, of the ratio of customs duties collected to the total value of imports in 1937 and 1951. By the simple process of dividing duties collected by the total value of imports in each of these 2 years it is shown that the United States, which in 1937 collected duties amounting to 15.8 percent of the value of total imports was, by 1951, collecting only 5.1 percent. By way of contrast the same kind of computation shows that the United Kingdom, which in 1937 collected 21.3 percent of the value of its total imports, had increased its collections one-fifth by 1951 and was then imposing duties amounting to 25.6 percent of its imports.

The implication is that the United States is now a relatively free-trade country and has decreased its trade restrictions far more (by 68 percent, according to this computation) than have most other countries.

This method is superficially convincing, but basically it is misleading. The fact is that no one really knows (or can know without engaging in a tremendous amount of original research) whether trade restrictions in the United States today are lower or higher than restrictions imposed by other countries or the extent to which they are lower.

domestic producers also produce abroad. Changes in tariffs are important to them only to the extent that they may necessitate shifts in sources of supply. In such cases, production cuts across international boundaries and adapts itself to national trade barriers.

In other cases, costs in the United States are so much lower than costs abroad that the United States clearly is on an export basis. This is the situation with regard to most automobiles. Although some automobiles are imported into the United States, most American-produced cars have been able to undersell other larger cars in world markets.

Another illustration is offered by the steel and cement industries. Here the products are so bulky and transportation costs so high that most domestic production encounters no import competition. For the most part imports penetrate only a short distance inland from seaboard. Consequently, most domestic producers have little reason to fear tariff reductions.

For these reasons, the arithmetical measurement of the degree to which duties have been reduced under the trade-agreements program is not always meaningful. There have been numerous cases where duties have been reduced without any great effect upon imports. An illustration would be cigar-wrapper tobacco, which is the wrapper used to cover the outside of cigars. The domestic product, shade-grown leaf, which competes with imports from Indonesia, is produced in the Connecticut Valley and along the Georgia-Florida boundary under shade provided artificially by the use of cheesecloth. The Tariff Act of 1930 imposed a specific duty on this product which, in 1935, was equivalent to almost 110 percent ad valorem. In the trade agreement with the Netherlands, effective in 1936, this duty was reduced by 35 percent. There was no perceptible increase in imports, however. Such a reduction in duty illustrates a sloughing off of excess protection. The duty that remained after the reduction was sufficient to keep imports from flooding the domestic market. Many other tariff reductions made under the trade-agreements program since 1934 have consisted of such "sloughing off" so that, to some extent at least, tariff reductions that have been made under the program have consisted of token concessions which have not affected materially the restrictive effects of the duties.

*Estimates by experts*

Although there is no way of knowing what economic adjustments will occur if tariffs were to be abolished, further reduced, or temporarily suspended, it is possible to make some informed guesses of the extent to which imports of selected commodities would increase in the event of major tariff reduction. If the guesses are made disinterestedly and in consultation with economic and commodity experts who have spent many years studying the competitive impacts of imports upon domestic production, the method can yield useful results. It stresses practical experience and minimizes purely deductive speculation.

The author of this memorandum attempted to assemble such estimates several years ago.[9] The study was prepared with the full coop-

[9] Piquet, Howard S., Aid, Trade, and the Tariff.

eration of the commodity experts and economists of the United States Tariff Commission and other Government agencies.

It was assumed that all factors, other than the tariff, would remain unchanged, as of the selected base period, 1951.[10] It was also assumed that economic and other conditions that prevailed in 1951 would continue for a period long enough (3 to 5 years) to permit the estimated effects of an assumed temporary general tariff suspension to materialize.

On the basis of these assumptions it was estimated that, in the event of temporary suspension of all tariffs, imports might increase by as much as 17 percent. If import quotas and domestic price supports were also suspended, imports might increase by as much as 25 percent.[11]

Of the $10.8 billion of merchandise imported into the United States in 1951, approximately $6 billion entered free of duty. Broadly speaking, raw materials that are not produced in the United States are admitted into the country free of duty, whereas most foreign products that compete with products made or grown in this country are dutiable. Suspension of tariffs could have little effect upon imports that are not dutiable. Most important among imports entering free of duty are: coffee, natural rubber, newsprint, paper-base stocks, unmanufactured copper, cocoa, tin, vegetable fibers, undressed furs, and fertilizer materials.

Of the $4. 8 billion of dutiable imports in 1951, slightly more than one-half consisted of finished and semifinished manufactured products, over one-third consisted of agricultural products, and the remainder was principally mineral products.

The increase in imports following tariff suspension, as estimated on the basis of summating the individual commodity estimates, would range from a minimum of approximately $800 million to a maximum of $1.8 billion, which would represent an increase of 8 to 17 percent in total imports. In terms of dutiable imports alone, the increase would represent an 18 to 38 percent expansion.

More than 40 percent of the dutiable imports covered by the analysis would not be noticeably affected by tariff suspension. Included in this group are such large imports as: petroleum, cut diamonds, burlap, lumber, nickel, and lead.

---

[10] The initial step in preparing the study was to select commodities that are most important among dutiable United States imports. All commodities imported in the amount of $5 million or more in 1950 were automatically included. To this list were added certain commodities regarding which foreign countries have expressed particular interest in increasing exports to the United States. Also added were commodities appearing on the official list of strategic and critical materials, and finally a few other items in certain commodity groups in order to round out the coverage. The total coverage was 80 percent of all dutiable imports entering the United States in 1951. In order to arrive at the overall estimates, it was assumed that the uncovered 20 percent would exhibit the same pattern of increase as the 80 percent that were covered. If, by any chance, the uncovered 20 percent were to increase considerably more than the 80 percent covered—if, for example, they were to double—the overall estimates of increased imports might be raised to as much as one-fourth.

The published materials of the U. S. Tariff Commission pertaining to the commodities selected were then examined, and this examination was followed by personal conferences with appropriate commodity experts and economists.

Not even the most experienced analyst could pretend to estimate precisely the degree to which imports would be stimulated by tariff suspension. The best that can be hoped for are estimates within relatively wide ranges. Several broad categories of estimated increases were established, therefore, and into them the individual commodities—over 220 of them—were classified.

[11] Not taking into account relative foreign-supply elasticities, although an attempt was made to allow for reasonable changes in United States demand. The year 1951 was marked by inflationary pressures, cold war, and, in general, by conditions characteristic of a sellers' market.

With regard to the other 60 percent (aggregating slightly more than $2 billion) it is estimated that, on the basis of conditions prevailing in 1951, tariff suspension might make possible the following increases in imports:

[In millions of dollars]

| Estimated increase in imports | Imports in 1951 | Estimated increase | |
|---|---|---|---|
| | | Minimum | Maximum |
| Percent: | | | |
| 100 to 300 (or more) | 53 | 53 | 158 |
| 50 to 100 | 807 | 404 | 807 |
| 25 to 50 | 591 | 148 | 296 |
| 10 to 25 | 694 | 69 | 174 |
| Total | 2,145 | 674 | 1,435 |

In terms of percentage increases, the most significant changes probably would be in the textile group, including such items as coarse linen toweling and hemmed linen handkerchiefs, linoleum, certain textile items, such as velveteens and cotton hosiery, woolens and worsteds, and apparel wool, as well as plywood, full-fashioned hosiery knitting machines, bicycles and sewing machines, clocks, optical instruments, toys and dolls.

The commodity groups showing the smallest overall percentage increases in imports would be wood and paper products, vegetable food products and beverages, and metals and metal manufactures.

Among the commodities which would show large percentage increases in imports would be earthenware and chinaware, hand-blown glassware, leather gloves, leather handbags, fur-felt hats, clay tile, clocks, canned tunafish, linen towels, hemmed linen handkerchiefs, scissors and shears, and knives with folding blades. Duties on these commodities in 1951 ranged from a low of 14 percent on certain types of ladies' leather handbags to a high of 184 percent on certain of the lower priced penknives. Other relatively high duties in the group were on clocks (70 to 130 percent), leather gloves (25 to 74 percent), scissors and shears (41 to 84 percent) and certain types of earthenware and chinaware (32 to 66 percent). Imports of most of these commodities amount to less than 10 percent of domestic production. Imports of earthenware and chinaware amount to slightly more than 20 percent of domestic production, and imports of linen towels to slightly less than 40 percent. For the most part, the imports in this group are subject to relatively high duties and are probably significantly restricted by the tariff.

The effects of temporary suspension of tariffs would be different from the effects of their permanent removal. If foreign producers believed that the United States were about to abandon its traditional import restrictions, they probably would expand their production and export facilities, advertise in the American market, and make permanent shifts in their international marketing patterns. If, however, they thought that the American market were to be made more accessible to them for a limited time only, they would be less apt to undertake the cost of a concerted drive to establish themselves permanently in the United States market. They would be more likely temporarily to divert some of their exports from other markets to the United States. It is doubtful that they would be willing to assume the risks of large-scale development programs, including the expenditure of large sums on advertising, if they thought that the penalty of success would be accelerated restrictionism.

Also, American producers, realizing that suspension would be temporary, might be willing to sustain restricted profits, or even to incur losses, for a time by lowering their prices in order to prevent importers from obtaining a strong position in this market. Not many of them, however, would be in a position to do this for any extended length of time.

If the maximum estimated rate of increase is applied to imports in 1956, the temporary suspension of all tariffs (but not import quotas) would indicate an increase in imports of approximately $2.1 billion. If all tariffs were to be removed permanently, rather than temporarily, the increase in imports undoubtedly would be considerably greater, possibly by more than $3 billion.

It is next to impossible to forecast, in any precise way, the probable effects of complete and permanent tariff removal. Staff members of the Treasury Department made an unofficial guess several years ago and concluded that, after the lapse of a few years, imports might increase by as much as $3.5 billion. This figure is almost double the estimates referred to above for temporary suspension.

If the Treasury Department estimate is applied to imports in 1956 it would indicate that imports might increase by over $4 billion in the event of the permanent abolition of all tariffs.

It would be interesting, if time and resources permitted, to repeat these estimates on the basis of conditions prevailing at the present time.[12]

It is probable, however, that the overall conclusions would not be vastly different from what they were 5 years ago. We are still in an inflationary period and, although in terms of dollar valume, the effect of tariff suspension on imports probably would be greater than in 1951, it is not likely that the ratio of total imports to domestic production would be any greater. The forces of inflation affect both imports and domestic production.

*Vulnerability to increased imports*

Estimates such as these involve substantial margins of error and are significant primarily as indicators of orders of magnitude. It seems clear, however, that the increase in imports would not be large enough to present an insuperable problem of adjustment to the United States economy as a whole, even in the short run.

It does not necessarily follow, however, that 1, 2, or 3 billion dollars more of imports a year would injure no one. Averages and aggregates tend to oversimplify and can conceal important details. The purpose of this paper is to show some of the areas of production in

[12] Such a study would be more difficult to make than 5 years ago for the reasons stated below (p. 51).

which increased imports would have the greatest competitive impacts. Import quotas apply only to agricultural products and since their removal, in most cases, would imperil the domestic support programs for the protection of which they are imposed, this discussion is confined to the effects that might follow tariff suspension alone.

Even if all tariffs were to be temporarily suspended, the proportion of the total domestic market that would be supplied by imports would be small, and the area of likely displacement of domestic production would be even smaller.

The great bulk of American industry, agriculture, and mining would not be directly affected by suspension since about 95 percent of the gross national product is consumed at home, and not more than 4 percent of the country's large consumption consists of imported goods. Such large segments of the industrial economy as the steel industry, the construction industry, much of the chemical industry, many of the industries producing machinery and metal products, electrical goods, and automotive equipment as well as the food-processing and clothing industries, and many others, scarcely would be affected by increased imports.

Some of these groups, in fact, would be benefited by the greater ease with which they could acquire certain imported raw materials if tariffs were no longer in effect. Such large producers for export as the automotive industry, producers of many types of industrial machinery, certain producers of chemicals, the petroleum industry, and producers of motion pictures would find their export markets enlarged through the increased purchasing power made available overseas through our increased purchases. Dependence upon exports is particularly great in the agricultural sector of the economy.

Of the $3.8 billion of dutiable imports analyzed almost $1.8 billion consist either of products that are not produced in the United States or of imports which would not increase in the event of tariff suspension. Typical of such products are quebracho tanning extract, handmade oriental-type rugs, hardwood lumber, and synthetic rubber. About $58 million consisted of import specialties which, after duty suspension, would supply 90 percent, or more, of the domestic markets for such products (including castor beans, olive oil, and mica).

Over $104 million would account for less than 1 percent of domestic consumption—including live poultry, cotton yarn, linoleum, and paints—and $450 million consisted of such products as pecans, potatoes, canned tunafish, plywood, and shoes, which, if tariffs were to be suspended, would account for less than 10 percent of the domestic consumption of those products.

In the aggregate, about $2.4 billion of the $3.8 billion of 1951 imports analyzed consisted of products that are not highly competitive with domestic production.

The remaining $1.4 billion consist of imports which, after tariff suspension, would account for between 10 and 90 percent of domestic consumption. This might be referred to as the "area of maximum import competition." This is not to say that all imports in this category would have an immediate injurious impact upon domestic producers, even in the short run, but only that this would be the area in which claims of injury, or of threatened injury, would seem to be most likely to occur.

There also would be many other areas in which there would be keen competition between imports and domestic production outside of the area represented by the 80 percent of dutiable imports covered in the present analysis. In the aggregate, however, such imports would affect a small number of people, or volume of production, particularly on the assumption that the uncovered 20 percent of the picture would not vary greatly from the 80 percent covered.

*Dutiable imports and the domestic market in 1951*[1] *(covers 80 percent of all dutiable imports)*

| | In millions |
|---|---|
| Imports of commodities not produced domestically or imports would not increase in the event of tariff suspension | $1,769.9 |
| Import specialties (imports which would supply 90 percent or more of the domestic market, after suspension) | 58.5 |
| Imports which would supply less than 1 percent of the domestic market | 104.5 |
| Imports which would supply from 1 to 10 percent of the domestic market | 450.1 |
| Subtotal (largely "noncompetitive" imports) | 2,383.0 |
| Imports which would supply between 10 and 90 percent of the domestic market in the event of tariff suspension | 1,414.7 |
| Total imports analyzed | 3,797.7 |

[1] Foreign values, not adjusted to American selling price. Source: Aid, Trade, and the Tariff, p. 43.

Injury is an individual matter and it can sometimes occur even when imports of a product are small in comparison with domestic production. The number of individuals and establishments who would be injured, however, undoubtedly would be small even if all tariffs were to be removed and whatever measures might to taken to facilitate their adjustment to increased imports would not be burdensome upon the economy as a whole.

Producers who probably would be hardest hit by increased imports would be those who use a relatively large proportion of labor in production, those who supply a demand that is inelastic or declining, and those who cannot expand production to meet increased demand as easily as can their foreign competitors. Among the lines of production in which there might be substantial temporary displacement of domestic production by increased imports are the following:

*Imported commodities that probably would supply from 10 to 90 percent of domestic consumption after assumed tariff suspension* [1]

Columns:
(1) Duty (ad valorem equivalent).
(2) Proportion of total consumption supplied by imports after tariff suspension.
(3) Estimated domestic production in 1951 (in thousands).
(4) Imports in 1951 (in thousands).
(5) Estimated increase in imports.

MANUFACTURES

| | (1) | (2) | (3) | (4) | (5) |
|---|---|---|---|---|---|
| | *Percent* | *Percent* | | | *Percent* |
| Knives with folding blades [2] | 33–184 | 14 | $18, 000 | $692 | 100–300 |
| Scissors and shears [2] | 41–84 | 14 | 22, 500 | 892 | 100–300 |
| Leather handbags [2] | 14–25 | 14 | 75, 000 | 2, 961 | 100–300 |
| Linen fire hose [2] | 28 | 13 | 1, 000 | 39 | 100–300 |
| Fur felt hats [2] | 60 | 12 | 75, 000 | 2, 623 | 100–300 |
| Optical instruments | 20–60 | 19 | 50, 000 | 6, 039 | 50–100 |
| Sewing machines | 8–30 | 18 | 170, 000 | 14, 759 | 50–100 |
| Bicycles and parts [2] | 11–15 | 14 | 63, 400 | 5, 013 | 50–100 |
| Musical instruments [2] | 20 | 10 | 175, 000 | 12, 775 | 25–50 |
| Embroidered linen handkerchiefs [2] | 49 | 17 | 8, 500 | 1, 126 | 25–50 |
| Aluminum | 11 | 20 | 296, 560 | [3] 49, 789 | 10–25 |
| Structural steel | 3–8 | 12 | 463, 000 | 44, 340 | 10–25 |
| Leather gloves [2] | 25–74 | 23 | 45, 000 | 3, 050 | 100–300 |
| Earthenware and chinaware: table and artware [2] | 32–66 | 50 | 120, 000 | 30, 237 | 100–300 |
| Coarse linen fabrics [2] | 40 | 61 | 3, 000 | 1, 160 | 100–300 |
| Hemmed linen handkerchiefs [2] | 26 | 36 | 7, 000 | 976 | 100–300 |
| Hand-blown glassware [2] | 39 | 37 | 31, 400 | 4, 468 | 100–300 |
| Sodium nitrite | 75 | 45 | 1, 000 | 203 | 100–300 |
| Optical instrument glass | 50 | 31 | 450 | 77 | 50–100 |
| Naphthenic acids | 10 | 21 | 4, 084 | 553 | 50–100 |
| Levers lace [2] | 32–65 | 38 | 30, 000 | 9, 318 | 50–100 |
| Axminster rugs [2] | 28 | 34 | 45, 000 | 10, 235 | 50–100 |
| Dental and surgical needles [2] | 18–40 | 24 | 1, 000 | 157 | 50–100 |
| Ethyl alcohol | 16 | 28 | 198, 500 | [3] 31, 674 | 25–50 |
| Watches | 37 | 61 | 65, 000 | 61, 489 | 25–50 |
| Wool wearing apparel (knit or crocheted) [2] | 24–41 | 2–79 | 200, 000 | 19, 698 | 25–50 |
| Rayon staple fiber [2] | 17 | 28 | 150, 000 | 38, 512 | 25–50 |
| Motorcycles [2] | 10 | 41 | 9, 083 | 3, 539 | 25–50 |
| Silk fabrics | 25–55 | 64 | 16, 000 | 17, 911 | 25–50 |
| Machine-made Oriental-type rugs | 30 | | (4) | 831 | 10–25 |
| Diamond dies | 17 | | (5) | 431 | 10–25 |
| Crochet needles | 44 | | (5) | 52 | 50–100 |
| Potassium carbonate | 11 | | (5) | 294 | 10–25 |
| Card clothing | 25 | | (5) | 607 | 50–100 |
| Chocolate-making machinery | 15 | | (5) | 470 | 25–50 |
| Aluminum knitting needles | 30 | | (5) | 26 | 50–100 |
| Clay floor and wall tile [2] | 26–41 | 9 | 71, 300 | 1, 749 | 100–300 |
| Woolens and worsteds [2] | 33 | 7 | 1, 085, 000 | 43, 388 | 50–100 |

MINERALS AND MINERAL PRODUCTS

| | (1) | (2) | (3) | (4) | (5) |
|---|---|---|---|---|---|
| Crude barytes [2] | 35 | 17 | $7, 828 | $419 | 100–300 |
| Ferromanganese | 7 | 19 | 122, 346 | [3] 18, 401 | 25–50 |
| Refractory magnesite | 22 | 10 | 15, 000 | 1, 396 | 10–25 |
| Fluorspar | 34 | 33 | 14, 370 | [3] 3, 155 | 50–100 |
| Manganese | 11 | 89 | 7, 100 | [3] 35, 274 | 10–25 |
| Mercury | 16 | 84 | 1, 502 | [3] 4, 403 | 10–25 |
| Bauxite | 8 | 65 | 12, 478 | [3] 13, 943 | 10–25 |
| Zinc | 7 | 29 | 268, 240 | [3] 57, 985 | 10–25 |
| Tungsten | 19 | 47 | 22, 976 | [3] 12, 996 | 10–25 |

AGRICULTURAL PRODUCTS

| | (1) | (2) | (3) | (4) | (5) |
|---|---|---|---|---|---|
| Fresh tomatoes | 23 | 16 | $115, 475 | $13, 668 | 25–50 |
| Rye | 4 | 15 | 32, 857 | 2, 548 | 25–50 |
| Cigar wrapper tobacco | 21 | 11 | 73, 000 | 5, 898 | 25–50 |
| Barley | 5 | 10 | 315, 800 | 19, 650 | 25–50 |
| Clover seed | 7 | 11 | 71, 000 | 7, 170 | 10–25 |
| Apparel wool [2] | 15 | 81 | 260, 000 | 544, 000 | 50–100 |
| Cigar filler tobacco [2] | 13–18 | 34 | 85, 000 | 20, 659 | 50–100 |
| Edible nuts, domestic types (almonds, walnuts, filberts) [2] | 35 | 18–67 | 52, 200 | 9, 200 | 50–100 |
| Green olives, unstuffed | 15 | 84 | 1, 000 | 3, 359 | 25–50 |
| Crude feathers (for beds) | 20 | 36 | 35, 000 | 17, 085 | 10–25 |
| Flower bulbs [2] | 7 | [6] 30 | (5) | 9, 565 | 25–50 |
| Oats [2] | 5 | 5 | 1, 112, 698 | 42, 195 | 25–50 |

**See footnotes at end of table.**

*Imported commodities that probably would supply from 10 to 90 percent of domestic consumption after assumed tariff suspension*[1]—Continued

AGRICULTURAL MANUFACTURES

| | (1) | (2) | (3) | (4) | (5) |
|---|---|---|---|---|---|
| | *Percent* | *Percent* | | | *Percent* |
| Prepared pineapples [2] | 6 | 17 | $65,000 | [3] $3,700 | 25–50 |
| Coconut oil | 4 | 16 | 95,494 | [7] 15 | 25–50 |
| Bovine hides and skins | 5 | 14 | 400,000 | 49,365 | 10–25 |
| Fresh or frozen fish (not fillets) | 2 | 14 | 250,000 | 31,367 | 10–25 |
| Castor oil | 8 | 55 | 26,795 | 18,238 | 50–100 |
| Sardines canned in oil | 15–30 | 48 | 33,998 | 7,058 | 50–100 |
| Fresh or frozen fillets [2] | 9 | 52 | 56,284 | 30,783 | 50–100 |
| Vermouth [2] | 10 | 52 | 10,000 | 4,736 | 50–100 |
| Casein | 9 | 70 | 8,907 | 13,575 | 25–50 |
| Champagne, etc | 24 | 45 | 8,500 | 4,229 | 25–50 |
| Fish or fish liver oils | 5–10 | 72 | 2,579 | 5,433 | 10–25 |
| Wool noils | 10 | 41 | 38,000 | 19,527 | 10–25 |
| Canned beef | 20 | (?) 75 | (4) | 48,803 | 25–50 |

[1] Included also are a few commodities from other groups where displacement of domestic production might occur because of inelastic, or contracting demand.
[2] Some displacement would appear likely.
[3] Dutiable only.
[4] Not available, but small.
[5] Not available.
[6] Estimated.
[7] Taxable only (processing tax).

Source: Piquet, H. S., Aid, Trade and the Tariff.

*Area of potential injury*

In probably not more than 30 of the 72 fields of production listed above would domestic producers be forced to give way in substantial measure to increased imports in the event of temporary tariff suspension. In some cases, producers of some of the commodities would be able to withstand increased foreign competition by introducing new economies of production or by intensifying their sales efforts. In other cases, the demand for the product is probably so inelastic, or contracting to such a degree, as to warrant legitimate fear of increased imports.

These 30 items are indicated by a footnote in the table. Among them are such well-known tariff problems as fur-felt hats, leather gloves and leather handbags, bicycles, motorcycles, apparel wool, woolens and worsteds, clay tile, hand-blown glassware, edible nuts, and fresh or frozen fish fillets.

Imports of these 30 produces totaled $858 million in 1951, which is a small figure compared with the total product of the Nation or with total imports, although it is large compared with total domestic production of the items in question ($4 billion).

The conclusion thus seems warranted that the area of potential injury to domestic producers would be fairly limited, even if all tariffs were suspended.

In the event of complete, but temporary, tariff suspension it is probable that not more than the equivalent of 200,000 workers would be forced to adjust to new lines of production because of inrceased imports.[1] If tariffs were merely to be reduced, particularly on a selective basis, the number of workers who would be forced to adjust would be even smaller. These, of course, are only estimates, but they indicate the order of magnitude of the problem.

[1] Estimated by the Bureau of Labor Statistics on the basis of increases in imports estimated in Aid, Trade, and the Tariff.

The broad policy question that confronts us is whether imports should be further restricted in order to avoid injury to anybody or whether the Nation should decide which new imports are essential and to facilitate adjustment to them. The larger question is whether it is more important to eliminate the necessity of economic adjustment to increased imports, than to undertake the adjustments needed to aid the functioning of a more truly international economy.

*Tariff Commission studies no longer adequate*

In the 1930's, opponents of the trade agreements charged that the administration was keeping trade-agreement negotiations secret. They claimed that it was impossible to find out what was being done.

Notwithstanding subsequent requirements by Congress that the names of members of the Trade Agreements Committee be made public, and that lists of commodities under consideration for tariff concessions be published well in advance of hearings and negotiations, it is more difficult today than it was in the 1930's and early 1940's to ascertain the economic significance of what has been done, even after tariff concessions have been made.

Until the United States started negotiating on a multilateral basis, after World War II, the Tariff Commission used to publish detailed digests of commodity information regarding each product upon which a tariff concession had been granted in any trade agreement. These digests included not only information regarding the tariff treatment of the commodity, but statistics of production, as well as of imports and exports, together with incisive analyses of the competitive impacts of imports upon domestic producers.

Today, this type of information is not being made available to the public. The Tariff Commission now publishes only a list of items included in each agreement, statements of changes made in tariff duties, statistics of imports, and brief comments regarding statistical relationships between imports, exports, and domestic production. In many cases, no production figures are given at all.

The latest Summaries of Tariff Information, which traditionally have been the source of factual information regarding commodities upon which tariffs are significant, have not been published by the Commission since 1948. There is no way, at the present time, for students of the tariff to make an intelligent appraisal of the present status of most commodities.

If the Summaries of Tariff Information were kept current, it would be possible to bring up to date, without too much difficulty, the kind of estimates made in the author's Aid, Trade, and the Tariff. With the paucity of presently available information, it would require about 3 times as much time and effort to make such estimates as it required 5 years ago.

It is also difficult to ascertain, without a large amount of work with materials in the files of the Statistical Division of the Tariff Commission, what the ad valorem equivalents are of current rates of duty. That is why many of the figures in this memorandum are not as up to date as they should be.

The economics work of the Tariff Commission has been greatly curtailed, as far as the public is concerned. What the Commission now publishes, in place of economic analyses, are legalistic summary statements of tariff rates and statistics of imports. It is unfortunate that the Summaries of Tariff Information are not kept up to date and published regularly. After about 4 years, many of them are so out of date that they can be misleading.

*What is a liberal trade policy?*

There probably would be general agreement that the foreign-trade policy of the United States since 1934 has been directed toward trade liberalization. It is not easy, however, to define clearly what is meant by "liberalized trade." Different people use the same term to refer to different concepts.

To some, it means larger exports and larger imports. To those who look upon large and flourishing world trade as beneficial for its own sake, this is a logical meaning. Most such persons would prefer, probably, that foreign trade be conducted with as much freedom as possible, but the essential thing is that there be large world trade. Trade concessions by all countries, on a reciprocal basis, are consistent with this view.

A second, and subtler, view is that not only should there be larger world trade in the aggregate, but the balance between the imports and exports of the dollar area should be altered in favor of larger imports. Such a change, it is maintained, is necessary to bring about balance in the international accounts. To this end, tariffs should be reduced, and as many other trade barriers—such as quotas and licensing arrangements—as possible, should be abolished.

Then, there are those who confine most of their attention to tariff duties, as such. As long as statutory tariff rates are reduced, in trade agreements or otherwise, the more conducive will the environment be for increasing international trade. Those who think this way usually lay great stress upon the importance of nondiscrimination in international trade. To them, such devices as import quotas, exchange controls, clearing agreements, licensing arrangements are evil per se.

Finally, there are those who see in historical and philosophical perspective a more fundamental meaning of liberalized trade. They agree that a large and flourishing world trade is desirable and that imports should increase, relative to exports, but believe that such a circumstance would eventuate if trade were really to be liberalized. They favor the lowering of all tariffs and the abolition of all bilateralism (as opposed to multilateralism) in world trade.

These are the heirs of the doctrines of the classical political economists of the 19th century—Adam Smith, David Ricardo, and John Stuart Mill. These are the true "free traders," using that term with caution and in its pure meaning. Thus used, it is not incorrect to apply the term to more enthusiastic proponents of the trade-agreements program, and quite correct to say that it summarizes the stated trade policy of the United States since 1934.

The term "free trade," it should be observed, has a dual meaning, a fact which has led to considerable confusion in international trade and tariff debate.

In its broader meaning, free trade signifies the absence of all tariffs and discrimination between foreign suppliers. No responsible Government official today would admit that he is a free trader in this sense.

In its purer meaning, free trade signifies merely the absence of discrimination between foreign suppliers, even though moderate tariffs, applicable to all suppliers alike, are imposed. Free trade, in this sense, has been the stated goal of United States trade policy since 1923, when the unconditional most-favored-nation policy was announced by Secretary of State Hughes.

In the 19th century, the logic of a "free trading" world economy was compelling. Under pure competition, as outlined by Adam Smith and his followers, the greatest economic good for the greatest number resulted when each country devoted its energies to lines of activity in which it had the greatest comparative advantage. So well did this system work until the outbreak of World War I that it came to be looked upon as a "natural" arrangement.

Many foreign trade "liberals" are critical of the passive trade policy which was appropriate prior to World War I. Although, for the most part, they favor the establishment of a multilateral trading system eventually, they are critical of relying upon this approach for solutions to problems that confront the country now. They think that today, after two World Wars and profound industrial and economic changes, the 19th century arrangement, instead of being a norm to which we can, and will return, appears for what it really was, a pleasant historical interlude.

Some who are critical of a policy which relies almost exclusively upon reestablishment of a multilateral trading system maintain that, laudable though such an objective is, it is an ineffective way to go about solving today's international economic problems.

As they see it, the foundations upon which the 19th century system of pure competition rested were neither "natural" nor "permanent." The system was made possible, in their view, by the industrial conditions of the period and by the willingness of Great Britain to assume the responsibilities of economic world leadership. It was facilitated by maintenance of the gold standard, the convertibility of the pound sterling through the guardianship of a small group of men in London, the insularity of Great Britain, the nature of her industrial economy and her willingness to enforce peace.

These critics hold that, instead of seeking to reestablish the world economy of the 19th century, the goal of United States policy should be to establish functioning international arrangements among national economies in which negotiated arrangements are substituted for the apparent automaticity of the Old World economy. This they would do through regional arrangements of various kinds, such as the Marshall plan, the OEEC, and international conventions along the lines of those sponsored by the International Labor Organization.

In support of their position they emphasize the following points:

1. The great difference between the position of the United States in mid-20th century and the position of Great Britain in mid-19th century.

In the earlier period Britain's was the leading economy among many, no one of which was far ahead of the others in size and production. Today, the United States is the dominant country in the free world, not so much because of positive political leadership as because of its great economic power.

In the 19th century the British economy was more dependent upon the economies of the rest of the world than they were upon it. The ratio of foreign trade to British national income was high and the pound sterling circulated freely throughout the world.

Today other countries are more dependent upon the United States economy than the United States is dependent upon them. With few exceptions, the United States is not conscious of the need of importing foreign merchandise or of any compelling reason for investing capital abroad. There is little reason to expect, therefore, that the dollar can play a role in the contemporary international economy similar to that played by the pound sterling in the 19th century.

2. The economic adjustment mechanism does not now work with the precision with which it apparently worked even a half-century ago.

Enterprise today is conducted on a much larger scale than it used to be. A relatively small number of companies dominate many important fields of production and economic adjustments tend to be man-made, and administrative, in contrast to adjustments brought about more or less automatically by the forces of the market. Furthermore, production is now so highly specialized that overcapacity threatens in many lines.

In agriculture and labor, also, group action has very largely superseded individual action. Economic adjustments, instead of constituting an automatic equilibrating process, are more aptly described today as the result of negotiation of one kind or another.

In addition to these economic and industrial changes per se is the increasing role played by the state. Governmental intervention in agricultural production and marketing, in population movements through immigration controls, in imposing barriers to international trade and in governmental response to the demands of powerful claimant groups, has made the 20th century far more complex than the 19th.

*Alternative policy choices*

1. The basic problem facing the United States is whether it will continue along a path of international economic cooperation or whether it will return to a policy of greater economic self-containment.

2. One choice within the framework of international cooperation is to continue pressing forward the multilateral trade philosophy of the trade-agreements program. Even though this program has been greatly weakened as an instrument for liberalizing trade, it is still recognizable as a trade-liberalizing instrument. Since 1947 the Presidential power to reduce tariff duties has been greatly curtailed and the escape clause has been strengthened as a barrier to further tariff cuts.

On purely economic grounds there is much to be said for restoring the original trade agreements philosophy, which would involve the repeal, or major modification, of the escape clause.

3. In the belief that tariffs should be reduced in order to stimulate imports, it has been proposed that a program of adjustment assistance be adopted to facilitate the economic adjustments in the domestic economy that would be necessitated in cases where tariff reductions might cause some hardship. Such assistance would be modest in scope and

would consist of increased allowances under the unemployment insurance law, assistance to distressed communities, assistance through the Small Business Administration to companies finding it necessary to adjust to new lines of production, et cetera. Such a program would not be very costly since the displacement effects of tariff reduction are not very great.

The adoption of such a proposal would make it easier to reduce duties in the national interest, since those in positions of responsibility would realize that innocent victims of increased imports would not be called upon to bear the ultimate burden. It would also make it easier for the economy to adjust to lines of production more consistent with the aptitudes of the people and the environment. Unless some such program is adopted, further tariff reductions undoubtedly will result in intensified pressure upon Congress to legislate tariffs and other trade restrictions directly. This is already in evidence by the number of bills that have been introduced seeking to impose absolute import quotas and also by the recent experience with regard to lead and zinc.

4. Another proposal along the same line, but not as comprehensive, would provide that imports be exempted from escape clause action until imports amount to a stated percentage (5 or 10) of domestic production. This proposal has the advantage of being simple, but it has the disadvantage of applying a rigid rule that might not be suitable in all cases.

A variant of this proposal is that all tariff duties be suspended until imports of each commodity reach a stated proportion of domestic production or consumption of that commodity.

Either of these proposals would tend to stimulate imports. Some administrative difficulties might be encountered by virtue of the fact that statistics of production and consumption are often difficult to obtain.

5. A proposal for stimulating imports from low-wage countries, such as Japan and Italy, was made in 1955 by Senator Payne, of Maine. We face a dilemma in that these countries must export to the free world if they are to survive economically and still remain on our side in the world power struggle. Yet, the products that now come from these low-wage countries are among the most troublesome of all imports.

The Senator proposed that the President be empowered to suspend the escape clause and reduce duties on imports of products not currently being imported in appreciable quantities from low-wage countries until such imports reach a specified proportion (say 5 or 10 percent) of domestic production of each of those products. Once imports reach the specified levels, the old rates of duty would be restored and the escape clause machinery would again be available to domestic producers.

This proposal is really an elaboration of the so-called tariff quota device which has been utilized successfully in trade agreements with regard to certain dairy and fishery products. The objective would be to divert imports from lines that hit sensitive spots in the United States economy to lines in which the economy is strong.

6. Another question to which we should be giving attention is the adequacy of reciprocity itself. We often talk as though reciprocity

in the lowering of trade barriers is the only conceivable way whereby we can bring about increased international trade and restore economic balance. As a matter of fact, pursuit of a policy of strict trade reciprocity would be a fairly certain way of seeing to it that we shall not attain international economic viability. The problem today is different from what it was 20 years ago. At that time we were in the midst of depression and economic stagnation and the problem was to increase both exports and imports. Today the problem is primarily to achieve balance between international debits and credits at a high level.

We should be thinking about whether we should supplement the power to negotiate foreign trade agreements with the power to reduce duties unilaterally, in order to make available more dollar exchange to potential purchasers of our goods.

Furthermore, there seems to be little reason why the concept of reciprocity should not be expanded beyond the field of international trade. Why should we not bargain on an across-the-board basis with other countries, giving limited trade concessions in our markets in exchange for concessions from other countries which we feel we need, whether they involve trade or something else? Why should we not utilize trade policy as a bargaining device, for example, to secure actions and commitments on the part of other countries which we deem necessary in the common defense? The objection that this might be construed as dollar diplomacy seems rather farfetched.

## APPENDIX A

*Average ad valorem equivalents of rates of duty in effect on specified dates, by trade-agreement status on Jan. 1, 1953*

| Tariff and trade-agreement status, Jan. 1, 1953 | United States imports, 1952 | | Average ad valorem equivalent based on rates in effect— | | | Reduction in rates from— | |
|---|---|---|---|---|---|---|---|
| | Value | Percent of total dutiable imports | Before any agreements | On Jan. 1, 1945 | On Jan. 1, 1953 | Preagreement to Jan. 1, 1953 | Jan. 1, 1945, to Jan. 1, 1953 |
| | *Million dollars* | | *Percent* | *Percent* | *Percent* | *Percent* | *Percent* |
| Dutiable imports: | | | | | | | |
| Duty reduced | 4,013 | 89.4 | 25.3 | 18.0 | 11.6 | 54 | 36 |
| Duty bound at preagreement rate | 180 | 4.0 | 14.2 | [1] 14.2 | 14.2 | | |
| No concession | 297 | 6.6 | 18.3 | [1] 18.3 | 18.3 | | |
| Total or average dutiable [2] | 4,490 | 100.0 | 24.4 | 17.9 | 12.2 | [3] 50 | [4] 32 |
| Duty free | 6,257 | | | | | | |
| Total dutiable [2] and duty-free imports | 10,747 | | 10.2 | 7.5 | 5.1 | [3] 50 | [4] 32 |

[1] Throughout these tables items not subject to any concession as of Jan. 1, 1953, or with preagreement rates bound, have been considered as subject to these 1953 rates in all periods shown. In fact, a very few of them were subject to reduced rates as of Jan. 1, 1945, but the present treatment does not make any significant difference in the averages.

[2] The figure for total dutiable imports as used in this report ($4,490 million) is based on a tabulation by the U. S. Tariff Commission of official import statistics for individual items. It is about 5/100 of 1 percent larger than the latest available (preliminary) total ($4,488 million) of the U. S. Department of Commerce.

[3] If imports of sugar ($324 million), which are regulated by quota, were excluded from this calculation, the percentage of reduction would be 49 rather than 50.

[4] If imports of sugar, which are regulated by quota, were excluded from this calculation the percentage of reduction would remain unchanged.

Source: U. S. Tariff Commission, Effect of Trade Agreement Concessions on United States Tariff Levels Based on Imports in 1952, Washington, 1953.

APPENDIX B

*Some imports dutiable at 50 percent, or more* [1]

| Tariff paragraph | Product | Duty (ad valorem equivalent) (1957) | Imports (1952) (thousands of dollars) |
|---|---|---|---|
| | | *Percent* | |
| 24 | Ethers and esters, 20 to 50 percent alcohol | 101 | (2) |
| 24 | Flavoring extracts and fruit flavors, containing 20 to 50 percent alcohol | 67 | 12 |
| 24 | Other chemical elements, compounds [3] not specially provided for, 20 to 50 percent alcohol | 104 | (2) |
| 24 | Medicinal preparations, containing over 50 percent alcohol | 84 | 5 |
| 24 | Brewers' yeast (alcoholic) | 50 | (2) |
| 28 | Coal-tar products, flavors, etc., not elsewhere specified | 56 | 104 |
| 28 | Finished coal-tar products, not elsewhere specified | 51 | 6 |
| 28 | Synthetic tanning material | 69 | 6 |
| 31 | Cellulose acetate waste | 164 | (2) |
| 49 | Magnesium oxide (calcined magnesia) | 62 | (2) |
| 81 | Sodium nitrite | 88 | 1 |
| 208 | Unmanufactured mica, valued not over 15 cents per pound (muscovite) | 52 | 25 |
| 212 | Table and kitchen articles of china or porcelain, not decorated | 65 | 157 |
| 212 | Chemical porcelain: plain white | 60 | 1 |
| 212 | Same, decorated or colored | 63 | (2) |
| 218 | Vials for use as containers for perfume, etc., not made by automatic machine | 75 | (2) |
| 227 | Optical glass for use in making lenses for spectacles | 50 | 16 |
| 227 | Same, for optical instruments or equipment | 50 | 67 |
| 228 | Scientific laboratory instruments and parts: colorimeters, etc | 50 | 1 |
| 238 | Watch crystals, other than round | 60 | 7 |
| 309 | Thermostatic metal | 50 | (2) |
| 318 | Fourdrinier wire for use in papermaking machines | 50 | 572 |
| 339 | Gold-plated household utensils | 50 | 14 |
| 346 | Belt buckles, valued under 20 cents per hundred | 52 | 1 |
| 348 | Snap fasteners, mounted on tape | 60 | -------- |
| 348 | Sew-on snap-fasteners, not mounted on tape | 55 | 6 |
| 350 | Dressmakers', and similar, pins | 70 | 6 |
| 354 | Knives with folding blades, valued at 40 to 50 cents per dozen | 90 | 2 |
| 354 | Knives with folding blades, valued 50 cents to $1.25 per dozen | 90 | 3 |
| 354 | Blades, handles, or other parts for knives with folding blades, not over $1.25 per dozen | 111 | 1 |
| 357 | Scissors and shears, not elsewhere specified, valued not over 50 cents per dozen | 84 | 13 |
| 357 | Scissors and shears, valued 50 cents to $1.75 per dozen | 95 | 55 |
| 358 | Razors and parts, 75 cents to $1.50 per dozen | 158 | (2) |
| 364 | Bicycle, and similar, bells | 50 | 6 |
| 365 | Breech-loading rifles, valued not over $5 each | 85 | 12 |
| 365 | Barrels for rifles | 72 | 2 |
| 366 | Pistols, not over $4 each | 142 | 12 |
| 366 | Parts for automatic pistols and revolvers | 53 | 6 |
| 367 | Watches and movements, without jewels, 1.2 inches to 1.5 inches wide | 57 | 537 |
| 367 | Certain watch parts, except jewels, not specially provided for | 55 | 703 |
| 367 | Watches, not over 1 jewel, 1 to 1 11/16 inches wide | 72 | 8 |
| 367 | Watch parts, balance assemblies | 65 | 13 |
| 367 | Watch parts, subassemblies including jewels in assemblies | 86 | 150 |
| 368 | Clocks, under $1.10 each, less than 2 inches wide, not over 4 jewels | 65 | 3 |
| 368 | Same, but over 2 inches wide | 64 | 2 |
| 368 | Clocks and clock movements, not elsewhere specified, not over $1.10 each | 62 | 24 |
| 368 | Clocks, valued $1.10 to $2.25 each over 2 inches wide | 71 | 5 |
| 368 | Other clocks and clock movements, valued $1.10 to $2.25 each | 63 | 51 |
| 368 | Clock assemblies, or subassemblies, not elsewhere specified | 65 | 20 |
| 368 | Electric meters, valued not over $1.10 each | 102 | 10 |
| 368 | Clockwork mechanisms, not elsewhere specified, valued not over $1.10 each | 160 | 1 |
| 368 | Clockwork mechanisms, valued over $10 each | 73 | 122 |
| 397 | Slide fasteners (zippers) valued under 4 cents | 55 | -------- |
| 603 | Scrap tobacco | 103 | 10 |
| 737 | Cherries, sulfured or in brine, without pits | 58 | 673 |
| 741 | Fresh or dried dates, packed in units of under 10 pounds | 61 | 2 |
| 781 | Ground cassia and cassia buds | 64 | (2) |
| 802 | Gin in containers, 1 gallon or more | 77 | 7 |
| 802 | Rum, not elsewhere specified | 69 | 74 |
| 802 | Arrack | 87 | 2 |
| 1107 | Yarns of wool and hair, valued not over 60 cents, pound | 75 | (2) |
| 1109 | Worsteds and woolens, not elsewhere specified, valued under $1.25 per pound (8 to 10 ounces per square yard) | 58 | 4 |
| 1109 | Worsteds, valued under $1.25 per pound | 61–65 | [3] 80 |
| 1111 | Wool blankets, not over $1 per pound (handwoven) | 64 | (2) |
| 1111 | Blankets, handwoven, plain or embroidered, valued $1 to $1.50 per pound | 55 | 6 |
| 1114 | Wool knit outerwear and other wool articles, not specially provided for, valued under $2 | 68 | 1 |
| 1115 | Wool hat bodies, not knit, but blocked; valued under $12 per dozen | 60 | 2 |
| 1115 | Wool hat bodies, not knit or crocheted, not blocked | 77 | 39 |
| 1119 | Tapestries, etc. over 4 ounces per square yard, valued at 80 cents to $1.25 per pound | 63 | (2) |

See footnotes at end of table.

*Some imports dutiable at 50 percent, or more*[1]—Continued

| Tariff paragraph | Product | Duty (ad valorem equivalent) (1957) | Imports (1952) (thousands of dollars) |
|---|---|---|---|
| | | *Percent* | |
| 1209 | Silk handkerchiefs, not over $5 per dozen, hemmed | 53 | 2,083 |
| 1405 | Wet transfer paper containing imprints taken from lithographic plates or stones | 65 | (2) |
| 1406 | Postcards, 12-20/1000 inches thick, less than 35 square inches in diameter, cut or embossed | 56 | (2) |
| 1503 | Beads, other than solid, valued over 5 cents per inch | 60 | (2) |
| 1506 | Hairbrushes, with handles or backs, other than cellulose, valued not over 40 cents each | 55 | 20 |
| 1509 | Pearl buttons (fresh-water) | 85 | 57 |
| 1509 | Pearl buttons (ocean) | 82 | 592 |
| 1513 | Dolls of cellulose, without movable parts | 78 | 7 |
| 1513 | Parts of toys, not specially provided for | 50 | 39 |
| 1515 | Firecrackers, over 1¾ inches long | 100 | 39 |
| 1526 | Hats and caps for women (fur felt) $9 to $12 per dozen | 65 | 445 |
| 1526 | Same, $12 to $15 per dozen | 65 | 454 |
| 1526 | Fur hats, men's and boys', valued $9 to $12 per dozen | 55 | (2) |
| 1526 | Hats, caps of fur, for women, valued $6 to $9 per dozen | 55 | 152 |
| 1526 | Same, valued $9 to $12 per dozen | 65 | 10 |
| 1527 | Jewelry and parts, valued 20 cents to $5 per dozen | 55 | [3] 5,000 |
| 1527 | Cigar and cigar-lighter parts, valued 20 cents to $5 per dozen | 50 | 1,363 |
| 1527 | Cigarette cases | 55 | 5 |
| 1527 | Compacts, powder, vanity cases | 55 | 1 |
| 1529 (a) | Levers lace-machine products, cotton, coarser than 12 point | 65 | 195 |
| 1529 (a) | Levers lace-machine products, silk, coarser than 12 point | 65 | 1,033 |
| 1529 (a) | Hand-made laces, over 2 inches wide | 90 | 25 |
| 1529 (a) | Lace window curtains (other than Nottingham) | 60 | 169 |
| 1529 (a) | Wearing apparel containing embroidery, lace, net, etc | 90 | 27 |
| 1529 (a) | Machine-made lace articles of wool, silk, rayon, or metal thread | 65 | 3 |
| 1529 (a) | Hand-made lace articles of wool, silk, rayon, or metal thread | 50 | (2) |
| 1529 (a) | Hose and half-hose, embroidered, made of cotton, valued under $5 per dozen pair | 60 | (2) |
| 1529 (a) | Wearing apparel, not elsewhere specified, of cotton, wool, silk, rayon, or metal thread | 63 | (2) |
| 1529 (b) | Cotton handkerchiefs, wholly or in part of lace (ornamented) | 93 | (2) |
| 1529 (b) | Cotton handkerchiefs, wholly or in part of lace, valued over 70 cents per dozen | 53 | 364 |
| 1532 | Leather gloves, women's and children's, not trimmed, 14 inches long, lined and hand-seamed | 52 | 2 |
| 1537 | Combs valued at $4.50 or less per gross (cellulose) | 65 | 1 |
| 1542 | Phonograph needles | 58 | 34 |
| 1552 | Tobacco pipes, partly finished, with bowls of briar or other wood or root, valued at $1.20 to $5 per dozen | 56 | 3 |
| 1552 | Pipe bowls, briar, etc., valued at $1.20 to $5 per dozen | 51 | 1 |

[1] Ad valorem duty equivalents shown are for 1957, whereas imports are for 1952. Some of the duties were higher in 1952 than in 1957 and, therefore, were more restrictive of imports. Current ad valorem equivalents are not readily obtainable from presently published Tariff Commission reports and have been derived by the author. Although there may be a few errors of interpretation, it is believed that the figures shown are substantially correct.

[2] Less than $1,000.

[3] Approximate.

# THE SHORT-TERM DOMESTIC ECONOMIC EFFECTS OF REDUCING IMPORT BARRIERS

Walter S. Salant[1]

In this paper, I discuss the short-run domestic consequences of reductions of import barriers, including the dislocations to the domestic economy that they would cause. The paper contains two parts, written so that each may be read independently. The first part, which is an up-to-date version of testimony given in November 1955,[2] takes a general view of the subject. The second part of the paper is narrower in scope but more intensive in treatment. It gives the results of new and detailed estimates of some of the short-term employment effects of reducing import barriers, based on a study I am conducting at the Brookings Institution. The interpretations and conclusions in both parts of the paper are my own and do not necessarily reflect the views of other members of the staff or of the administrative officers of the Institution.

At the outset, it should be emphasized that the short-term effects of changing import barriers are not relevant to the question of what level of barriers is the most desirable in the long run. Such effects are relevant only to the process of adjusting to that level, if it differs from the present level. Short-term effects should not play a dominant or even major role in any broad decision about whether import barriers should be changed. If the Government believes that it is desirable to maintain import barriers at a level different from the existing one, it should not be deterred from attaining the desired level by the fact that the process of transition to it would cause disturbances. A combination of market forces and Government policies directed toward maintaining high levels of employment may be relied upon to prevent most of these dislocations from persisting.

This opinion does not imply, however, that these transitional effects should be ignored. The effects on all individuals may not be temporary. Even if they are, questions of temporary hardship should not be—and in any event will not be—completely disregarded. Therefore, even if the short-term effects are not a major consideration in determining whether the level of import barriers should be changed, they may be a major consideration in the timing and method of changing them and in deciding whether changes should be accompanied by measures to ease the transition. These are the considerations that make this paper relevant to public policy.

---

[1] Mr. Salant is a member of the staff of the Brookings Institution.

[2] Cf. hearings of the Subcommittee on Foreign Economic Policy of the Joint Committee on the Economic Report, published under the title Foreign Economic Policy (84th Cong., 1st sess., p. 230 and following pages) and reprinted by the Brookings Institution as Short-Term Domestic Economic Effects of Reducing Import Barriers (reprint No. 10).

## I. A General View of the Short-Term Effects

In the public discussion of dislocations from reductions of import barriers, some extreme statements have been made by both protectionists and some free traders, especially with regard to the effects upon employment. On the protectionist side, it has been said that a lowering of import barriers would create a major business depression. One speaker said that workers will be thrown out of jobs in industries employing 4 million or 5 million people. (He did not say, however, that 4 million or 5 million people would be thrown out of work.) The adverse effect is often exaggerated and is usually treated as though it is the total net effect. Actually, it is not; offsetting favorable effects upon job opportunities must not be ignored.

On the other hand, some free traders occasionally exaggerate or mislead in the opposite direction. They sometimes mention the beneficial effects of trade liberalization on our exports and on employment in our export industries while failing to mention at the same time the possible adverse effects on the industries that compete with imports. This tends to convey the impression that a reduction of our import barriers can be confidently counted upon to stimulate employment. Others admit that there will be some loss of jobs, but ignore or treat as unimportant the serious human problems that these losses would create.

The wide range covered by statements such as these partly reflects irresponsibility in the use of figures. But I think it also reflects confusion between various concepts of economic effects. It is important, for clear thinking about this subject, to distinguish between several such concepts, all of which are relevant to some policy question but each of which is relevant to a different one.

First, people may have in mind the effects of liberalization on total national production, employment, or profits, resulting from the effects of liberalization on general business conditions. This is the concept of economic effects that is relevant to the question whether liberalization would have a depressing effect on business activity, and, if so, how great the effect would be. To estimate this effect requires estimating the stimulating as well as the depressing effects and striking a balance between them.

Second, people may have in mind the effects only on the industries producing import-competing goods but still considering only the difference between their position if import barriers were not reduced and what their position would be if import barriers were reduced but everything unrelated to these reductions remained exactly the same. An estimate of these effects requires estimating the effect of trade liberalization alone on the industries producing these goods and on their direct and indirect suppliers, without including the effects of other factors unrelated to liberalization that also might be affecting these industries at the same time, such as changes in popular taste, competition from new products, or changes of consumer income resulting from independently caused economic expansion or contraction.

There is a third concept which is also relevant for some purposes: The total change of employment, profits, etc., in an import-competing industry over a period of time, taking into account not only the reduction of import barriers but other developments affecting it. For example, growth of the market would offset the adverse effects; changes in tastes might aggravate them; and technological change might do either. So far as employment is concerned, moreover, whether import liberalization requires the actual discharge of workers in an import-competing industry depends not only on the net effect of the liberalization and other factors, but also on the rate of normal separations in the industry, i. e., turnover due to retirement, death, normal shifting to other industries, and other normal causes. Because of these separations, it is possible to reduce the labor force in an industry without actually firing anyone, simply by failing to replace those who leave in the normal course of events. If the required reduction in the labor force of an industry or firm is sufficiently small, it may be fully accomplished in this way. Thus, if a reduction of import barriers causes employment in the competing domestic industry to be 15 percent less than it would overwise have been but factors unrelated to trade policy are tending to expand such employment by 5 percent in the same period, the actual reduction of employment will be only about 10 percent, and the percentage discharged may be still less.

It is obvious that the net change in employment and the rate of actual discharging in import-competing industries, which depend not only on commercial policy but other factors as well, are more closely related to the human problems of an industry's actual hardship than the first two concepts.

All of these concepts are useful, but they relate to different questions and therefore serve different purposes.

## TOTAL EFFECTS ON THE NATIONAL ECONOMY

I should like first to consider briefly the question of total effects on the national economy. Perhaps the best way to get perspective on this question is to back away from the problem of import barriers and consider for a moment the economy's ability to adjust to dislocations in general, and the factors that influence this ability.

During the past dozen years, the economy has had to adjust to several substantial dislocations of a depressing character. The major dislocation—perhaps the most important to which the American economy has ever been subjected as a result of Government action—was the reduction of war expenditures at the end of World War II. In the short space of 2 years, the Federal Government's purchases of goods and services for national-security purposes fell from $90 billion to about $20 billion.[3] In the first half of 1945, when the higher figure prevailed, the economy was working under forced draft. It was not necessary, therefore, for this entire decrease of expenditure to be offset by increases elsewhere in the economy in order to maintain high levels of employment by peacetime standards. Nevertheless, the increase in other expenditures that was required was a very large one. This increase did take place. As a result, the level of involuntary unemployment was quite low in 1947 and the adjustment was made with surprising ease, when looked at from a national point of view.

[3] The figure for the second quarter of 1947 includes net outflow of Government capital to abroad, which Department of Commerce figures for national product and expenditure include in the net foreign investment component of gross national product.

A second change began in the second quarter of 1947, when the various foreign aid programs of the immediate postwar period began to run out and the Marshall plan had not yet begun. Foreign aid fell by an annual rate of $4.8 billion between the second quarter of 1947 and the second quarter of 1948. This decrease was equivalent to slightly over 2 percent of the gross national production in the second quarter of 1947. Exports fell during the same period by an annual rate of $3.7 billion, which was 1.6 percent of the gross national product in the second quarter of 1947. These percentages would be equivalent to declines of approximately $8 billion or $9 billion now. While the decline was clearly not so great as the massive cut in war expenditures after hostilities ceased, it was substantial. However, it caused no general economic disturbance, and, in fact, was probably not even noticed by anyone who did not study the composition of the national expenditures. During the year when this decline occurred (i.e., between the second quarters of 1947 and 1948), employment and probably also total production rose, and many commodities were in short supply at the time. Domestic demand was unsatisfied and insistent, and this fact prevented any general economic dislocation.

A third major curtailment in a large component of national expenditure began in the second quarter of 1953. At that time, national-security expenditures were running at an annual rate of $53.3 billion, according to the most recently revised figures, and they fell to $41.3 billion in the second quarter of 1955. This decline, amounting to 1¾ percent a year of the GNP at the beginning of the period, was equivalent to one of about $7½ billion a year from present levels. The rate of decline was almost as rapid, on a per annum basis, as the decline in foreign aid during 1947–48, and it was probably reinforced by a tightening of credit. This time the level of economic activity did fall, as is generally known, but a recovery began in the autumn of 1954. Why did economic activity fall then when it did not in 1947–48? Probably in large part because there was less pressure of private demand, even independently of the stricter credit policy, and this in turn probably resulted from the fact that wartime backlogs had been worked off to a much greater extent than they had been in 1947–48. When a rise in other expenditures did occur, business expenditures played a smaller role than in 1947–48, and policy actions such as tax cuts, an easing of housing credit and of general credit conditions, played a greater role.

Two of these major postwar cuts of expenditure failed to create any recession of business activity below normal peacetime levels. The third did cause some, but it was not lasting or deep from the point of view of the economy as a whole.

The first general conclusion to which one is led is that, so far as aggregate effects on the economy as a whole are concerned, a substantial decline in one area of expenditure—of something of the order of 2 percent of GNP or more a year—need not have adverse effects on the general level of prosperity. Whether it does or not depends on whether other demands are rising, either spontaneously or as a result of Government policies.

Although the dislocations caused by these declines were not great when viewed from the point of view of the economy as a whole, they were substantial for many individuals in the places specifically affected, including, of course, management and stockholders as well as labor. The increases in other expenditures that helped sustain the economy as a whole also helped reduce the dislocation or ease the adjustment to it for many firms and individuals. For example, the decline in production of tanks was replaced by the rising production of automobiles in 1946, and these two changes affected the same industry. Thus, even for a specific industry, the dislocation did not necessarily involve economic hardship. (This may be the case in some industries affected by declines in import barriers, as we shall see.) Where demand for labor in particular spots decreased on balance, workers were often able to find jobs elsewhere. I mention this partly to bring out the importance of mobility in the economy, but partly also to point out that mobility is useless unless there is some place to which labor and capital can move.

So far as a reduction of import barriers is concerned, it is sufficient to note at this point that it would take a very substantial reduction to cause an increase of imports of as much as $1 billion a year (as valued in our trade statistics). I do not know anyone who believes that such an increase would be possible under existing law. Even when converted to a domestic port basis, this would be only about one-third of 1 percent of our current gross national product. Moreover, it would give rise to at least some partially offsetting stimuli to exports. Making all allowances for possible reverberations through the economy because of further effects upon the income and spending of people in the industries affected, it is not possible for the effect on the level of total economic activity to be perceptible, let alone substantial. The net effect on the gross national product of the maximum changes possible under the present law would be less, I suspect, than the margin of error in our national income statistics.

This is not the dislocation problem with which people are most seriously concerned, however, and I have discussed it mainly in order to dispose of it. The fact that the effect on our economy as a whole would not be significant does not mean there are no problems. Dislocations would be suffered by specific industries, firms, individuals, and communities which, although not big enough to affect the national economy, are nevertheless the proper concern of Government policymakers.

It may help in identifying the areas of the economy primarily affected to outline briefly the nature and direction of the specific forces that are set in motion by a reduction in import barriers, ignoring other forces that may be at work in the economy at the same time and are independent of such reductions.

The first effect of a reduction in import barriers is to permit foreign products to be sold in the domestic market at a lower price, and to divert domestic purchasers from the domestic to the foreign product to some degree. If, prior to the liberalization, the domestic industry has not been a highly competitive one from a price point of view, it may anticipate this tendency for domestic consumers to shift by meeting the lowered prices at which the foreign goods are offered and bring down its own prices. In that case, the tendency toward the shift of buying from domestic to foreign goods may never become actual. The reduction of barriers will simply result in a reduction of the domestic price and profit margin and may leave unchanged the proportions of foreign and domestic goods that domestic buyers purchase. If the domestic market is sensitive to price reductions, more of both domestic and foreign goods may be purchased.

If the domestic market has been highly competitive in terms of price prior to the reduction of import barriers, it will be more difficult for it to meet the lower prices at which foreign goods may enter after liberalization occurs. The tendency for domestic buying to shift toward the foreign product is then likely to develop into an actual shift. In these cases, there tends to be a decline in employment in the import-competing industries and their suppliers and an increase in imports, expressed in terms of the number of dollars earned by the foreign seller. This is not the end of the chain of effects set up by the reduction of import barriers, however. We must also take into account certain other effects, of which the most important are probably the effects induced by the changes in income of those who are engaged in the import-competing industries and their suppliers, which is a depressing effect, and the effect upon the countries supplying the imports, whose incomes and earnings of dollars are increased, which is a stimulating effect. The latter are concentrated in our export industries. The improvement in foreign countries' balances of payments may also encourage American investors to increase the flow of capital to these countries. If so, there would be additional stimuli again to our export industries.

It is also possible that some of the increase in foreign earnings would be regarded as making possible a reduction of foreign aid and that this would be regarded as permitting a reduction of taxes not otherwise possible. If so, there would be a further stimulus to the extent that taxpayers increased their purchasing.

Reverberations of changes in domestic incomes would be widely dispersed among the different industries of the economy. We may, therefore, concentrate on the import-competing industries and their suppliers and, later, the export industries.

### EFFECTS ON IMPORT-COMPETING INDUSTRIES

I should like to be able to give you some estimates of the effects on employment of some specified reduction of import barriers upon individual import-competing industries and upon the economy as a whole. It is impossible to estimate with much accuracy the effects of a specific program of reductions. We would have to know the nature and magnitude of a great many economic reactions that we do not know, not only in this country but in the rest of the world. In any event, such estimates would not be applicable to other programs of liberalization. I believe it is possible, however, to indicate the orders of magnitude of primary employment effects per million dollars of import increase. By "primary employment effects" I mean employment effects which occur independently of any changes in income, that is, the effects on the number of workers producing the goods with which the additional imports compete, not only in the final stages of their production, but also in the domestic industries supplying goods and services for these final stages, such as raw materials and transportation, and also in the industries which, in turn, supply goods and services to these supplying industries. In the second part of this paper, I give estimates which indicate the great differences in the effects of given amounts of import increases competing with different protected industries. It is not necessary to analyze specific industries very deeply, however, to find a quick way of placing a *maximum* figure on primary employment effects.

*A crude measure of primary employment decreases*

In industries producing goods and in those producing services mainly for commodity-producing industries, the average income originating per person engaged was $5,644 in 1955 and $5,855 in 1956. Among these industries for which separate figures of "income originating" are given, 80 percent or more of the workers and proprietors were in industries in which the average income originating per person exceeded $3,500. In none was the average below $2,600 in 1955 or $2,750 in 1956. (These industry averages would nearly all be higher in 1957.)

This fact makes it possible to develop a crude but simple test to see whether a figure given for the employment effects on import-competing industries and their suppliers of a given increase in imports is at least within the range of reason. (I hasten to add that this method bears no resemblance to the method used to get the results presented in the second part of this paper.) This test consists of adding 30 percent to the assumed increase of imports (which in our trade statistics is based on values at foreign ports) to bring it approximately to a basis of values at domestic ports, and then dividing the resulting figure by the number of workers who are said to be displaced. The result is the implied average value added per worker. If it is below $2,600, the employment estimate is almost certainly unreasonably high.

Thus, if it were said that an increase of imports of $2 billion resulting from a reduction of import barriers would displace 5 million workers in import-competing industries, we can tell at once that the statement is absurd, because it would imply displacement of domestic goods worth about $2.6 billion, and would also imply an average value added per worker of only $520, which is outside the range of possibilities, especially for industries employing 5 million workers.

We can also use the minimum average value added per worker to make a more reasonable estimate of the maximum possible primary employment effect of a given increase of imports due to a reduction of import barriers. Simply raise the import increase by 30 percent and divide by $2,600 or, more simply, divide the import increase by $2,000. This tells us that a $2 billion increase of imports could be equivalent to no more than 1 million workers.

Conversely, if no import figure is given, we can tell, from the number of workers who are said to be displaced by a given proposal, the very minimum increase of imports that this number of workers implies, and consider the reasonableness of the resulting figure. Thus, if it is said that 5 million workers would be displaced, we multiply this by $2,600 per worker and we know at once that this would imply displacement of domestic goods worth $13 billion at the very least. Subtracting 23 percent ($0.30 \div 1.30$) to adjust the domestic port values roughly to the basis of foreign port values, we get $10 billion as the minimum increase in imports that would be required to cause a displacement of 5 million workers in import-competing industries and their suppliers. In short, the minimum implied import increase is the stated primary employment decrease multiplied by $2,000. When it is realized that total United States imports are only about $13 billion and that only about $6 billion are subject to import restrictions of any kind, the improbability of permissible reductions causing an import increase of $10 billion becomes apparent.

There are probably no commodity-supplying industries, even in a highly detailed classification, in which the average income originating per person engaged (which includes proprietors) is below $2,600. One can, therefore, use this low figure confidently, even for liberalizations confined to these industries.

The formula is: Maximum primary employment decrease equals import increase (as valued in trade statistics) divided by $2,000; and conversely: Minimum implied import increase (as valued in trade statistics) equals primary employment decrease multiplied by $2,000.[4]

This rule of thumb makes many crude assumptions, for example, that an increase of imports worth $1 at foreign ports and resulting from a reduction of trade barriers displaces domestic products valued at $1.30. I have tried to allow for the crudity by using figures which are extremely conservative, that is, which give maximum employment effect per dollar of import increase. This rule of thumb does not have any great accuracy but, however crude it may be, it is a great deal less crude than some of the estimates that are often given, even in congressional testimony. It is a very simple rule that may provide a useful and quick check of oral statements.

Please note also that this rule of thumb indicates only a relationship between employment and production. It can, therefore, serve only as a check upon implied relationships between changes in employment and changes in imports due to changes in import barriers. It contributes nothing to answering the question: "How large an increase in imports would result from a given program of reductions in trade barriers?" One has to know the increase of imports in order to judge the order of magnitude of the employment effects. Conversely, one has to have a figure for the primary employment effects in order to deduce the implied increase of imports. One cannot deduce from this implied increase in imports what degree of reduction in trade barriers is implied.

These figures correspond to the second concept of employment effects which I mentioned in the earlier part of my statement. They represent the "primary" employment effects, that is, before taking account of any effects on production caused by changes in income in the import-competing industries or by changes in exports.

*Effects of import competition are not concentrated wholly on import-competing industries in narrow sense.*

It is worth dwelling for a moment on the distinction between what are commonly called the import-competing industries on the one hand, and their direct and indirect suppliers on the other. The term "import-competing industry" is normally used in a narrow sense to refer to the industry that is in the last stage of the process of producing the goods with which the imports compete. This industry, however, may

[4] An explanation of the assumptions underlying this formula is given in addendum A of the first part of this paper.

add little to the final value of the domestic product and may therefore employ only a small proportion of the total number of workers involved in producing the commodity. Most of the final value of the product may be added by other industries from which it purchases component parts or raw materials and most of the workers may be employed in them. These other industries, in turn, may also get supplies from still other industries. In such cases the employment effects in the industry at the last stage in the productive process will not be a large fraction of the total immediate employment effects. This fact should be borne in mind whenever statements are made concerning the effects upon a given import-competing industry.

The point can be illustrated by taking the case of motorcycles and bicycles.[5] If a reduction of import barriers for these commodities were to reduce their domestic output by $1 million and if employment in them and their supplying industries were to fall in the same proportion as output, the gross primary employment decrease (that is, before taking account of increases associated with the process of importation) would be 129 employees. But only about 52 percent of them would be in the motorcycle and bicycle industry. About 24 percent would be in such industries as steelworks and rolling mills, manufacture of tires and inner tubes, internal combustion engines, metal coating and engraving, farm equipment, and even wholesale trade, and the remainder would be scattered through the rest of the economy.

The fact that a substantial portion of employment effects may be direct, that is, in other industries which are immediate or even remote suppliers, is important in connection with such questions as who is hurt and whether the industries hurt are also being injured by other dislocations or are benefiting from offsetting expansionist influences.

EFFECTS ON EXPORT INDUSTRIES

To know the magnitude of the effect upon exports of an initial increase of imports of $1 million for any given commodity, we would have to know the nature and size of many reactions. First, how much do the dollar earnings of foreign countries increase per million dollars initial direct increase in imports? This question arises because a shift of demand from domestic to imported goods reduces production of the competing domestic industry and its suppliers and, insofar as these industries use imported materials, there will be some partially offsetting decrease of other imports. Consequently, the primary increase of imports and the increase of foreign earnings will be somewhat less than $1 million.

Second, will the increase in imports lead the Congress to reduce foreign aid and, if so, how great will the net rise of foreign dollar receipts be?

Third, how much of their increased dollar receipts will foreign countries use to increase their purchases in the United States? Foreign countries have a wide variety of possible responses to those increases of earnings, owing to differences in economic structure, policies, or particular circumstances, for example, their desire for addi-

[5] This is a good case, partly because these two commodities are both protected and bicycles were the subject of an escape-clause action, but mainly because they happen to constitute an entire industry in the interindustry study of the Bureau of Labor Statistics, which is the source of essential data for the illustration. These studies were discontinued in 1953.

tional reserves or the percentage of capacity at which their economies are operating. For our purposes it is sufficient to note that they may use a very substantial portion or perhaps all of the additional export earnings to increase their gold and dollar reserves, to increase their imports from countries other than the United States, or to increase their purchases from the United States. If they use these earnings to increase their gold and dollar reserves, there is no stimulating effect upon United States exports. To the extent that they use them to increase their purchases from other countries, the same questions must be asked about what these other countries do with the proceeds of their increased exports. Insofar as any of the countries uses its additional export proceeds to increase its purchases from the United States, there is an employment increasing effect here which partly offsets the employment decreasing effect of the reduction of import barriers upon our import-competing industries.

I do not feel that it is possible to give reliable estimates of the ratio of increase in exports to the increase in imports arising from liberalization of import barriers. It is possible, however, to say something that probably bears on the question of which export industries would be most affected by whatever increase of exports does in fact occur. If we make the assumption—admittedly a dubious one—that a country would apportion its additional purchases in the same way as its total purchases in 1953, we can get answers to such questions as: Which export industries would be most affected if the additional buying in the United States is done by country A and which if it is done by country B? Does it make much difference what countries do the additional buying?

It is probable that a substantial part of the increased buying would be done by the countries supplying the imports on which barriers are reduced. In that case, which export industries are stimulated would depend in great part upon which import barriers are reduced. With these considerations in mind, the Joint Committee on the Economic Report had tabulated some foreign-trade data which would throw light upon this question. The committee's staff obtained from the Bureau of the Census a tabulation of purchases made in the United States in 1953 by each of 32 countries which are major suppliers of imports now subject to barriers, classified by industries which represent the last stages of fabrication of these exports. In other words, we have a tabulation which enables us to say "Of the total of $580 million of goods which the United Kingdom bought from us in 1953, 14 percent were products of the food grain and feed crop industry, and 18 percent were products of the machinery industry and so on for all of a detailed classification of industries, whereas, in the case of France or India or any of the other countries, the percentage distribution of their purchases from us in 1953 was thus and so." This tabulation shows that there were substantial differences in the pattern of commodity purchases made here by major suppliers of protected imports.[6] It also shows that products of the categories "food grains and feed crops," nonelectrical machinery, chemicals, and transportation equipment were of greatest importance to these countries.[7]

[6] The percentage distribution among industries of United States exports to each of these countries is shown in table 3, addendum B, of my testimony before the Subcommittee on Foreign Economic Policy. Cf. Foreign Economic Policy, cited above in the second footnote, pp. 253–257.

[7] This statement is based on an unweighted average of the percentages of its total purchases which each country devoted to the products of an industry.

To illustrate the possible effects of the differences in the patterns of commodity purchases by various suppliers, let us assume that there is a reduction of protection on two classes of imports, watches and clocks on the one hand, and motorcycles and bicycles on the other, in an amount sufficient to increase the combined dollar earnings of the 3 major suppliers of each class by $1 million, and that this million dollars is distributed among these 3 major suppliers in the same proportion as were their total earnings from sales of these goods to the United States in 1953. Let us assume also that these supplying countries increase their merchandise purchases in the United States by half of the increase in their dollar earnings and that they distribute these additional purchases in the same manner as their total merchandise purchases in 1953. (For simplicity, I ignore the fact that any increase in their purchases from other countries which probably cause these other countries also, to buy more from us.) The table below shows that, on these highly simplified assumptions, the liberalization of watch and clock imports would raise exports of textile mill products by about $43,000 and apparel by about $11,000, whereas that of motorcycle and bicycle imports would raise them by only about $900 and $500, respectively. On the other hand, liberalization of motorcycle and bicycle imports would raise exports of tobacco by $95,000 against only $32,000 resulting from watch and clock liberalization and would raise exports of petroleum and coal products by $30,000 compared with a rise of only about $5,600 from watch and clock liberalization. These differences result mainly from the differences between the patterns of buying in the United States on the part of the United Kingdom, the chief supplier of imported motorcycles and bicycles, and Switzerland, the chief supplier of imports in the watch and clock category.

*Comparative effect on selected industries of additional United States exports resulting from additional United States imports of watches and clocks and of motorcycles and bicycles* [1]

[Figures in thousands of dollars]

| Source of additional dollar earnings and country receiving and spending them | Total additional purchases in United States | Additional exports of selected United States industries | | | | | |
|---|---|---|---|---|---|---|---|
| | | Food grains and feed crops | Tobacco | Textile mill products | Apparel | Petroleum and coal products | Transportation equipment |
| Watches and clocks: | | | | | | | |
| Switzerland | 472.0 | 7.5 | 28.0 | 43.2 | 10.6 | 5.1 | 45.0 |
| West Germany | 26.5 | 5.4 | 3.3 | | | .4 | .2 |
| United Kingdom | 1.5 | .2 | .3 | | | .1 | |
| Total | 500.0 | 13.1 | 31.6 | 43.2 | 10.6 | 5.6 | 45.2 |
| Motorcycles and bicycles: | | | | | | | |
| United Kingdom | 388.0 | 56.1 | 83.8 | .5 | .3 | 28.2 | 3.6 |
| West Germany | 84.0 | 17.0 | 10.4 | .1 | .1 | 1.3 | .6 |
| Italy | 28.0 | 3.1 | .4 | .3 | .1 | .6 | .7 |
| Total | 500.0 | 76.2 | 94.6 | .9 | .5 | 30.1 | 4.9 |

[1] The figures in this table were derived from the assumptions stated in the above paragraph and from the tables referred in footnote 6.

The production, sales, employment, and profit effects of increased exports, of course, will not be confined to the industries at the final stage of fabrication, but will occur partly in their immediate and remote suppliers, just as we found to be the case with import-competing industries. Of course, some industries that supply parts and materials to protected import-competing industries also supply them to export industries. Insofar as the same industries are affected by both, the industry dislocation is reduced.

IMPORT LIBERALIZATION AND GROWTH

Let us now consider what, if anything, can be said about the net effect of import liberalization and expansion of demand required for normal growth, first for the economy as a whole and then for protected import-competing industries.

*Expansion required in the economy as a whole*

Two years ago, I computed the annual expansion of markets required to keep unemployment down to the 1955 percentage of the civilian labor force, using projections of economic growth until 1965 that were made by the Staff of the Joint Committee on the Economic Report.[8] Although the passage of 2 years may affect the required rates of growth slightly, it cannot affect the broad conclusions based on them. I concluded then that markets would have to expand 1.5 percent a year to keep the unemployed percentage of the civilian labor force down to the 1955 level, with output per man-hour and hours of work unchanged. Projected increases in output per man-hour in private industries, if applied to all civilian employment, would require a further market expansion of 2.7 percent a year. Thus it would require an expansion of markets of 4.2 percent a year to prevent the percentage of unemployment from rising above the 1955 level. This expansion is equivalent to $18 billion at the present level of total production. The need for expanded markets, it should be noted, is a problem we face year after year, not just in 1 or 2 years.

The question I want to put is "How much more would markets have to increase if import barriers were reduced than they would if these barriers were not reduced?" I should think it unlikely that import barriers would be reduced in any 1 year enough to increase imports by as much as $500 million a year in terms of foreign-port values or about $650 million at domestic-port values, but let us use this figure in answering the question. Assume also that the increase in exports resulting directly from the increased dollar earnings of foreign countries is only 40 percent of the increase in the foreign value of our imports, i. e., it is only $200 million. This is a conservative figure, especially if one takes account of the possibility that the strengthening of foreign currencies might encourage an expansion of our foreign investment. The net decrease of purchases (in domestic values) would then be $450 million. Now, allowing for secondary effects twice as great as the effects which cause them, which appears generous in view of the existence of built-in stabilizers, the total net decline of markets would be 3 times $450 million or $1,350 million. Stated alternatively, on these assumptions the expansion of markets required to offset the aggregate effects of liberalization would

[8] Computed from data in Potential Economic Growth of the United States During the Next Decade, Joint Committee Print, 83d Cong., 2d sess. (1954), table 1, p. 19.

increase by only $1,350 million, or less than 8 percent, the $18 billion expansion that would be required in any event. This small addition to the necessary expansion would not occur every year but only in the years when the shift of demand from domestic to foreign products took place. I think this overstates the problem for the economy as a whole. Besides assuming a small effect upon exports, this figure makes no allowance for any increase in the amount that consumers spend at given levels of income, despite price reductions and possible increases in the variety of goods available. It should also be noted that it relates to unilateral reductions of import barriers, not to reciprocal reductions.

It seems clear that, from the point of view of its effect upon the economy as a whole, the problem created by a reduction of import barriers could add very little to the normal problem created by growth of the labor force and rising productivity. If we solve the growth problem, the effects of import liberalization on the total economy would not be perceptible.

*Import liberalization and growth in import-competing industries*

It does not follow from this conclusion, of course, that the expansion of markets accompanying normal growth of the economy would necessarily take care of the problems of the industries competing with imports, especially those concentrating on import-competing goods. They might or might not participate in the general expansion of markets.

I should first like to point out, incidentally, that the same thing may be said of the dislocations resulting from increases in output per man-hour due to changes in productive techniques. The average increase in productivity for the economy as a whole is not distributed uniformly over industry but reflects quite substantial reductions of labor requirements per unit of output in some industries and very small reductions or none at all in others. While the commodities most affected by a technical change may not participate much in the general expansion of demand, the employees and capital displaced nevertheless are likely to benefit from such expansion because it increases the alternative employment opportunities available to them. Similarly, if a reduction of import barriers does reduce the sales, production, and employment in an import-competing commodity owing to lack of growth in the demand for it, the resulting dislocation will be less painful for most of the people involved if demand for other commodities is expanding than if it is not, because it is then easier for labor to find other jobs and for capital to find other investment outlets.

Unfortunately, no positive and well-founded generalization can be made, so far as I know, about the extent to which protected import-competing industries (even in the narrow sense) have been participating in general economic growth, although the data necessary for valid generalization are available. It is sometimes said that the import-competing industries are generally characterized by subnormal growth or actual stagnation, but I have never seen the basis for such statements. Of course, many of the import-competing industries have been declining, but the impression that this is true of most of them arises, I suspect, largely from the fact that it is the declining ones (for example, Briar pipes, fur-felt hats, and hat bodies, wool) that have complained most of foreign competition. Even the industries claiming injury from tariff reductions are not all declining industries. The main complaint of the watch industry, for example, has been that they have failed to share sufficiently in the growth of our economy. The chemical industry and the electrical manufacturing industry are also protected import-competing industries, and they can by no means be regarded as laggard in growth. Moreover, if the generalization is doubtful when applied to the industries at the stage of production closest to the competing import, it is much more doubtful when applied to their direct and indirect suppliers, which are in general more diverse and therefore more likely to resemble the economy as a whole. And a substantial part of the total dislocation may be in these supplying industries.

A second question is whether normal separations are low in the import-competing industries so that they will do little to mitigate the dislocations of employment. It is often said that workers in these industries are less mobile than others because they have special skills which are useless elsewhere, or because they are older, and that it is therefore more difficult to move them geographically or to retrain them. I know of no valid statistical basis for this generalization, either. But here again, we may say that, although the mobility of workers in the last stage of fabrication of these goods may be much below the average for the economy as a whole, the mobility of workers in the supply industries is not likely to be.

A third statement sometimes made is that the import-competing industries are either more affected than other industries by other changes now going on in the economy, such as technological change, shifts in demand, etc., or are less able to adjust to them. Whether these other dislocations themselves are greater in the case of these industries than in the case of other industries or not, I believe we do not know. It clearly is true for some industries such as textiles, coal, and woolgrowing, but how about chemicals, electrical manufacturing, or petroleum, which are also protected import-competing industries?

If the question at issue is not the extent of other dislocations to which these industries must adjust, but their difficulty in making the adjustment, then the point reduces to one of growth or mobility, to which I have just referred, or else to unusual inefficiency of these industries in adopting new techniques or altering their products.

SOME POLICY QUESTIONS CONCERNING DISLOCATIONS

What I have said thus far may give the impression that I think the problem of dislocation is not a serious one. That is certainly my opinion so far as the prosperity of the national economy is concerned. I have not intended to imply, however, that there will not be dislocations or that they are not a proper cause for concern. We can be fairly certain that some industries, at least, will suffer dislocations and, in addition, have difficulty in adjusting to them. The fact that others, such as export industries, may receive a stimulus from the same cause may be no consolation to the import-competing industries. This fact clearly does raise policy questions for the Government. I should like to suggest a number of these questions for the subcommittee's consideration.

First, I should like to remind you that dislocations are occurring every day as a result of technological change, shifts in taste, and many other causes. They are a normal part of the economic process. Some of these dislocations involve an almost complete wiping out of demand for a product and may, in some cases, involve an entire community. To illustrate, the Randall Commission heard testimony that the change in public demand from wooden to metal station-wagon bodies caused a serious crisis for the community of Iron Mountain, in the Upper Peninsula of Michigan, because it caused the closing of a Ford Motor Co. plant on which the community was almost wholly dependent. I cite this case to point up the fact that the questions raised by specific industries or plant dislocations are general questions. The problems raised by a reduction of import barriers do not reflect an inherent conflict between the needs of the domestic economy and the needs of international economic policy, but rather the more general conflict between the security of an existing status of an individual or a firm or an industry and any change, whatever its cause.

The fact that specific dislocations occur every day does not of itself imply, however, that Government has no responsibility to avoid or prevent the dislocations that may result from its own acts, such as a reduction of import barriers. Some people argue that it is in the nature of business that it involves risks and that the Government need not be concerned. Others argue, or more often imply, that Government should not take the actions which will result in dislocations. It appears to me that if the Government is convinced that a reduction of import barriers would be desirable and would be in the general interest on other grounds, it ought not to refrain from reducing them merely because somebody would be hurt. At the same time, I believe it clearly has a responsibility to undertake the reduction in a manner that causes the minimum of hardships. It seems to me perfectly feasible to work out a way of protecting the import-competing industries from the worst effects of dislocation without avoiding dislocation itself. The painful effects can be minimized in a number of ways. I believe that it would also be possible to work out schemes to facilitate the adjustment to these dislocations without getting into the difficulties that are involved in proposals to compensate for injury.

A second question, which I believe has not been posed by others is: Exactly what is it that the Government has a responsibility to protect? Here I mean to make the distinction, which I consider important, between the protection of individuals and the protection of particular kinds of productive activity. It appears to me that in the general case, the Government has at most a responsibility to protect the position of individuals, for it is individuals who, in the literal sense, suffer hardship. I say that this is true in the general case because the interests of national defense are an exception; they may require the protection of a particular productive activity, such as the manufacture of a particular type of product.

That this distinction between individuals and productive activity is of some practical significance is illustrated, I believe, by the case of garlic, for which producers sought action under the escape clause a few years ago. If I recall this case correctly, it was found that increased imports attributable to a reduction of import barriers were having an adverse effect upon garlic production. It was also found, however, that virtually all producers of garlilc produced other things and that the production of garlic was only a small part of the total production of most of them. Thus, although the reduction of import barriers on garlic might have a serious adverse effect upon garlic production, it might not do serious injury to any individual. It appears to me that this is exactly the sort of situation that need cause the Government no particular concern. (Let me make it clear that in saying this I am not expressing an opinion about the garlic case—or garlic itself! I am merely using it to illustrate a general point.)

A third question is whether the Government ought to be concerned when only the relative but not the absolute share of a domestic industry in the total market for its product is being reduced. If the absolute level of production and employment in an industry is not shrinking, it is hard to see how any individual is being injured, even though the relative share of the industry in the total market for foreign and domestic products combined is declining. The industry is simply not experiencing the expansion that it would like to have and might have had if barriers had not been reduced. I doubt that this is the sort of injury against which the Government has any duty to give protection.

A fourth general question is how the natural factors helping to minimize the hardships can best be exploited. A number of possible answers to this question are implied in the considerations that I have brought forward in this statement. The factors of normal growth and turnover can be exploited by making reductions gradually. Growth alone can be exploited by selecting reductions which affect, directly or indirectly, industries having rapid growth. Third, mobility can be exploited by making reductions in commodities in which the affected industries are likely to have the highest mobility. This is likely to mean, generally, industries having a relatively youthful labor force, or located in communities where there are other, healthy industries, and similar considerations. Fourth, the reductions can be concentrated on commodities produced by industries which suffer least from other dislocations. Fifth, limited administrative discretion may be given as to the effective dates of the reductions, with legislative instructions as to the factors that should be considered in using this discretion. It might be specified, for example, that the executive branch of the Government should consider the state of inventories of the industry, the condition of its order books, and the general business situation.

Finally, I should like to make the more general suggestion that in setting goals for the expansion of markets for domestic production, we ought not to take into account merely the expected growth of the labor force and the expected increase in output per man-hour. We ought also to include whatever further expansion is required to offset the net employment decreases caused by policies that are regarded as desirable. I have in mind not only net decreases of employment that are expected to result from reductions of import barriers but net decreases of employment that would result from the attainment of any of the accepted goals of economic policy. The expansion of markets should be sufficient to employ people who are now producing goods that we do not want and people who are now producing goods that we could obtain more efficiently in other ways. If we measured it in this way, we would set our sights at levels that facilitate not only the employment of new members of the labor force and the reemployment of those displaced by technological improvement, but also the reemployment of those displaced by policy actions that are regarded as in the general interest.

[Addendum A]

ASSUMPTIONS IMPLIED IN GENERAL FORMULA RELATING IMPORT INCREASES AND PRIMARY EMPLOYMENT DECREASES DUE TO UNILATERAL REDUCTIONS OF IMPORT BARRIERS

*Derivation of formulas in statement*

The formula in the body of the statement for estimating maximum primary employment decreases from given import increases is based on the following more general formula:

Maximum primary employment decrease equals import increase multiplied by average ratio of domestic to foreign port value of imports divided by average income originating per person engaged in affected industries. Conversely, for estimating minimum import increases implied by given primary employment decreases, the more general formula is:

Minimum implied import increase equals primary employment decrease multiplied by average income originating per person engaged in affected industries divided by average ratio of domestic to foreign port value of imports.

In order to provide a rule of thumb for general use, the formula in the text uses 1.30 as the average ratio of domestic to foreign port values. This is a rough upward adjustment of the actual average of 1.19 for 1952 imports (weighted by actual imports). For average income originating per person engaged, it uses $2,600, a round figure below that of every industry in 1955 and 1956 (using the industry classifications given in the Department of Commerce's national income and product statistics for national income and persons engaged). If these figures, 1.30 and $2,600, are inserted in the above formulas, the formulas given in the body of the text are obtained.

For any specific program of import liberalization, a closer approximation would be obtained by using figures for the ratio of domestic to foreign port values and average income per person engaged that are more relevant to the imports and the industries affected by that program. The former ratio requires special tabulations which are not generally available (although one has been made for 1952), but the figure of 1.30 is a reasonable one for general use. The average national income per person engaged in each industry likely to be affected by import competition is shown in table 1 and a frequency distribution of persons engaged among these industries is shown in table 2.

*Assumptions implied in use of the formula*

The formula tends to overstate the primary employment changes associated with a given increase of imports caused by a reduction of trade barriers and, conversely, to understate the import increase required to produce a given primary employment effect. It implies that an additional dollar's worth of imports displaces an equivalent value of domestic goods. A reduction of import barriers, however, causes a fall in price and, in some cases, probably also an increase in the variety of goods from which buyers may choose. It is therefore likely to cause some increase in the total quantity of goods purchased, so that the displacement of domestic goods is not likely to be as great as the increase of imports.

Furthermore, the formula implies that a reduction of $2,600 worth of domestic output eliminates one job. In most cases this overstates employment effects, for two reasons. In 1956, 80 percent of the persons engaged in the industries that could be affected were in industries where the average income originating per person exceeded $3,500; if we eliminate agriculture, where the effects of a decline in demand may not take the form of unemployment, the percentage in industries with averages above $3,500 is 95 percent. In 1957 both of these percentages are undoubtedly higher. Table 1 suggests that for import liberalization programs that do not greatly affect employment in agriculture, apparel, and leather and leather products, a figure of $4,000 or more could be used for average income per person engaged; the figure of $2,600 probably overstates primary employment effects per $1 million of imports by more than 60 percent and understates implied imports per person proportionately.

Moreover, the formula assumes that changes in primary employment are proportional to changes in the value of production that cause it. This contributes to an overstatement of the maximum change of employment because, in many industries, a portion of the labor requirement is largely independent of the volume of production. In some industries this portion is a very large one. In general, therefore, employment varies in smaller proportion than production.

It should also be noted that the assumed value of production of displaced commodities represents the sum of the gross income originating in the industries that produce these commodities, whereas the formula divides this figure of gross value by an average net income originating per person. Gross income originating per person, a conceptually more appropriate figure, would be higher. It would give a lower maximum employment for a given rise of imports and a higher minimum import for a given value of employment.

Finally, the use of averages based on number of persons engaged rather than on number of employees substantially reduces the average income originating per employee in some industries, and thus overstates the effect upon hired workers.

**TABLE 1.**—*National income per person engaged and number of persons engaged, by selected industries, 1955 and 1956* [1]

| Industry | 1955 | | 1956 | |
|---|---|---|---|---|
| | Number of persons engaged | National income per person engaged | Number of persons engaged | National income per person engaged |
| | *Thousands* | | *Thousands* | |
| Farms | 5,175 | $2,971 | 4,986 | $3,050 |
| Agricultural services, forestry, and fisheries | 303 | 2,604 | 318 | 2,752 |
| Metal mining | 107 | 9,290 | 115 | 9,765 |
| Anthracite mining | 33 | 4,212 | 33 | 5,030 |
| Bituminous and other soft coal | 227 | 5,577 | 240 | 6,167 |
| Crude petroleum and natural gas | 332 | 7,009 | 345 | 7,220 |
| Nonmetallic mining | 116 | 6,216 | 125 | 6,320 |
| Food and kindred products | 1,557 | 5,489 | 1,576 | 5,553 |
| Tobacco manufacturers | 101 | 6,772 | 97 | 7,485 |
| Textile-mill products | 1,088 | 3,998 | 1,068 | 4,174 |
| Apparel, etc | 1,240 | 3,247 | 1,247 | 3,499 |
| Lumber and wood products | 759 | 4,130 | 753 | 4,102 |
| Furniture and fixtures | 376 | 4,511 | 387 | 4,765 |
| Paper and allied products | 551 | 6,746 | 568 | 7,035 |
| Printing-publishing, etc | 846 | 5,727 | 873 | 6,017 |
| Chemicals and allied products | 813 | 9,232 | 845 | 9,332 |
| Products of petroleum and coal | 247 | 14,693 | 246 | 15,667 |
| Rubber products | 273 | 6,048 | 273 | 6,709 |
| Leather and leather products | 384 | 3,609 | 380 | 3,770 |
| Stone, clay, and glass products | 560 | 6,693 | 575 | 6,929 |
| Primary metal industries | 1,294 | 7,770 | 1,324 | 8,280 |
| Fabricated metal products | 1,265 | 5,779 | 1,269 | 6,071 |
| Instruments | 317 | 6,341 | 336 | 6,720 |
| Miscellaneous manufacturing | 503 | 4,618 | 515 | 4,911 |
| Machinery, except electrical | 1,605 | 6,449 | 1,737 | 6,991 |
| Electrical machinery | 1,136 | 5,829 | 1,211 | 6,149 |
| Transportation equipment | 938 | 6,206 | 1,021 | 6,416 |
| Automobiles and automobile equipment | 903 | 9,927 | 819 | 8,571 |
| Wholesale trade | 3,035 | 5,956 | 3,193 | 6,097 |
| Banking | 552 | 8,707 | 583 | 9,014 |
| Security and commodity brokers | 78 | 6,103 | 83 | 4,988 |
| Finance, n. e. c | 195 | 6,836 | 211 | 7,038 |
| Insurance carriers | 728 | 4,716 | 760 | 4,480 |
| Insurance agents | 270 | 5,548 | 278 | 5,892 |
| Railroads | 1,197 | 5,774 | 1,185 | 6,122 |
| Highway freight transportation, etc | 795 | 5,531 | 833 | 5,764 |
| Water transportation | 129 | 7,209 | 132 | 7,523 |
| Air transportation | 120 | 6,942 | 135 | 7,000 |
| Pipeline transportation | 26 | 11,846 | 26 | 12,615 |
| Services allied to transportation | 194 | 4,619 | 201 | 4,826 |
| Telephone, telegraph, etc | 752 | 6,387 | 799 | 6,581 |
| Radio broadcasting and television | 74 | 7,959 | 79 | 8,468 |
| Electric and gas utilities | 563 | 10,609 | 573 | 11,136 |
| Local utilities and public services, n. e. c | 34 | 5,206 | 34 | 5,618 |
| Business services, n. e. c | 639 | 5,210 | 698 | 5,367 |
| Legal services | 252 | 6,460 | 259 | 6,579 |
| Engineering and other professional services | 241 | 5,896 | 276 | 6,239 |
| All private industries [2] | 54,473 | 5,221 | 55,971 | 5,386 |

[1] All private industries producing commodities and all those producing services mainly for commodity-producing industries. Private industries excluded are contract construction, real estate, retail trade, local and highway passenger transportation, and all industries classified in the source of the data as service industries, other than "business services not elsewhere classified," legal services, and engineering and other professional services.

[2] Covers all private industries, including those not itemized above.

Source: Number of persons engaged comes from "National Income and Product of the United States, 1956," Survey of Current Business (July 1957), table 28. National income originating in each industry (not shown in above table) comes from table 13 of the same article.

TABLE 2.—*Distribution of selected industries by average national income per person engaged, 1955 and 1956* [1]

| Average national income per person engaged | 1955 | | | 1956 | | |
|---|---|---|---|---|---|---|
| | Number of industries | Number of persons engaged | Percent of total engaged | Number of industries | Number of persons engaged | Percent of total engaged |
| | | *Thousands* | | | *Thousands* | |
| Under $2,500 | 0 | 0 | 0 | 0 | 0 | 0 |
| $2,500 to $3,499 | 3 | [2] 6,718 | 20.4 | 3 | [2] 6,551 | 19.5 |
| $3,500 to $4,499 | 4 | 2,264 | 6.9 | 4 | 2,961 | 8.8 |
| $4,500 to $5,499 | 7 | 4,031 | 12.2 | 6 | 1,917 | 5.7 |
| $5,500 to $6,499 | 17 | 13,343 | 40.5 | 13 | 12,114 | 35.9 |
| $6,500 to $7,499 | 7 | 1,988 | 6.0 | 11 | 5,335 | 15.9 |
| $7,500 to $8,499 | 2 | 1,368 | 4.2 | 3 | 1,535 | 4.6 |
| $8,500 to $9,499 | 3 | 1,472 | 4.5 | 3 | 2,247 | 6.7 |
| $9,500 and over | 4 | 1,739 | 5.3 | 4 | 960 | 2.9 |
| Total | 47 | 32,923 | 100.0 | 47 | 33,620 | 100.0 |
| Total income originating (millions) | | $185,804 | | | $196,835 | |
| Average per person engaged | | 5,644 | | | 5,855 | |

[1] Includes all private industries producing commodities and all those producing services mainly for commodity-producing industries. Private industries excluded are contract construction, real estate, retail trade, local and highway passenger transportation, and all services other than "business services not elsewhere classified," legal services, and engineering and other professional services.
[2] Includes 5,175,000 and 4,986,000 in agriculture in 1955 and 1956, respectively.

Source: Table 1.

## II. Estimates of the Short-Term Effects Upon Employment and Their Distribution Among Industries [9]

In this part of the paper, I present more detailed estimates of the effect of reducing import barriers on domestic employment. I should like to emphasize again the short-term character of these effects.

The estimates presented here are not confined to the direct effects upon employment that are felt in the "liberalized" industry, i. e. the industry making products similar to the liberalized imports. They include the effects upon employment in the industries that supply the liberalized industry, in those that supply these suppliers, and so on throughout the economy.

The estimates also seek to tell us what industries feel these employment effects. That is an important question in connection with any contemplated reductions of import barriers, because the answers to some of the short-term policy problems involved in such reductions depend upon the characteristics of the industries affected—whether they are industries that are growing rapidly or stagnating, whether they have a rapid or slow turnover of employees, whether their labor force consists of workers with specialized skills, of old or young people, etc.

The fact that some employment effects in industries other than the one liberalized are included in the estimates does not mean that these estimates give us all the information we need to appraise even the employment effects of reducing import barriers. The estimates in this paper have some limitations and imply some assumptions which must be explained.

[9] This part of the present paper is based on portions of a study being conducted at the Brookings Institute by the author with the collaboration of Beatrice N. Vaccara.

1. When liberalization causes reductions of domestic output and employment, incomes decrease. These decreases of income are likely to induce decreases of spending and consequently some further reductions of output and employment. The estimates in this paper do not include these secondary changes in employment induced by changes in income.

2. The estimates also do not take into account the changes in employment caused by any increases in exports that can be expected to result from the increases of imports.[10]

3. The estimates refer to employment effects per million dollars of increase in imports, not to the total amount of the effect that would accompany some specified reduction of import barriers.

This point requires fuller explanation.

In order to know how output and employment would be affected by a given reduction of a tariff barrier, we would have to know how much less of the domestically produced goods would be purchased and also how much more of the total product, both domestic and foreign, would be purchased at different, specified lower prices. The amount of these changes depends upon responses to price changes by both domestic and foreign producers and by both domestic and foreign buyers. Unfortunately, little is known about the actual amounts of these responses.[11] Thus, we have no reliable basis for estimating how large a shift of buying from domestic to foreign goods would occur under any specified import liberalization program.

Furthermore, even if we could get or make reliable estimates of the shifts of buying associated with a specified import liberalization program, the estimates of the resulting employment effects would be valid only for that liberalization program, which would be only one out of an infinite number of possible programs.

For these two reasons, I have not tried to estimate the amount of the employment change that would result from any specified liberalization. Instead, the estimates in this paper give the amount of employment change per $1 million shift in buying from domestic to imported goods caused by a reduction of import barriers. In other words, they give the employment change per $1 million increase of imports on the assumption that an increase of $1 million in imports is accompanied by a decrease of $1 million in final purchases of the competing domestic product, when both changes are valued at prices in the United States market before the reduction of import barriers.[12]

[10] Employment effects excluding these secondary effects of domestic income and export changes are referred to as "primary" employment effects.

[11] For a few protected commodities, primarily agricultural, estimates have been made of some of these responses by statistical analysis. Dr. Howard Piquet, in his book, Aid, Trade, and the Tariff (published by Thomas Y. Crowell, New York, 1953), has estimated some of them for a large number of protected commodities after consultation with commodity experts. But, as Dr. Piquet himself says, his estimates are still guesses. It may also be noted that while Dr. Piquet's book gives "guesstimates" of the amount of increase in imports, which is what he was chiefly interested in, it does not give the amount of the decrease in purchases of United States output that is associated with the import increases, which is our first main concern.

[12] Import increases are valued at $1 million in the United States at 1953 prices after payment of 1953 tariff duties, i. e., at 1953 "domestic port values." In order to apply them to a projected million-dollar import increase measured in domestic prices different from those of 1953, e. g., in those of 1957, the estimates presented must be multiplied by the ratio of 1953 to 1957 prices. Thus, if 1957 prices are higher than those of 1953, the employment effect of a million-dollar import increase would be lower, other things being equal, because such an import increase would represent a smaller physical quantity of additional imports in 1957 prices than in 1953 prices.

4. The next point to be noted is the composition of the million-dollar import increases. Separate estimates are given for the effects of import competition with each of 72 industries that had significant protection in the form of barriers against imports in 1953 (and that passed certain other tests designed to reduce the likelihood of error in the results). Thus, there are separate estimates of the effects of $1 million of increases in imports of bicycles and motorcycles, of $1 million of increases in imports of watches and clocks, and so on.

This does not mean, however, that each of the 72 $1 million increases of imports consists of imports of a single homogeneous commodity. It consists of products competing with those of one industry. These industries represent only a two-hundred-fold division of the economy and each one produces more than one, usually a large number of commodities.[13] The import increases in each of the 72 industry cases considered here consist, therefore, of a collection or "basket" of commodities similar to those produced by that domestic industry. For example, the million-dollar increase of imports of "watches and clocks" (one of the most homogeneous of the 72 industries whose liberalization we consider) consists of watches, clocks, and watch cases. The relative share of each protected import in the million-dollar basket of each industry may be regarded as the same as its relative share in the output of the domestic industry in 1953.

To summarize these points, the estimates represent the primary direct and indirect employment change associated with a shift of buying from the output of one domestic industry to corresponding imports when the shift causes a $1 million rise of imports at the original income level and when the associated decrease in domestic output of the liberalized products is also $1 million, both valuations being at 1953 domestic market prices. Thus the estimates are not absolute numbers but ratios, representing employment effects per million 1953 dollars of import increases. It follows from this definition of them that, before they can be used to estimate the employment effects of any proposed program of import liberalization, an estimate of how much imports would increase and how much domestic production would decrease must be obtained from other sources. This means that the information provided is not sufficient, although it is necessary, to answer questions about the primary employment effect of any specified American import liberalization program.

On the other hand, while the estimates do not give all the information required to know the primary employment effects of any given liberalization program, they are applicable to many different liberalization programs, because the results for liberalization in different industries can be combined in any way in order to get estimates of the employment effects of a specific liberalization program.

Finally, before presenting the estimates, it must be emphasized that they involve a number of assumptions besides those already mentioned.[14] Assumptions are unavoidable in estimates such as these. In some cases, there is little choice about these assumptions. For example, because the estimates in this paper seek to identify the indus-

---

[13] The data on interindustry relationships available for making the estimates divide the entire United States economy into 200 industries.

[14] The final study to be published by the Brookings Institution will provide a full explanation of the assumptions and of their empirical or other basis. It will also provide a full explanation of other aspects of the methods and procedures.

tries in which the employment effects occur, they have to be made by an intricate technique that makes certain assumptions about inter-industry relations.[15] This technique assumes that when a domestic industry's output is reduced, it decreases its purchases of the raw materials and the other goods and services it uses in its current production in proportion to the reduction in its output. It also assumes that all the industries supplying these goods and services (with the exception of six agricultural industries) reduce their output by an amount equal to the decline in their sales and that these supplying industries in turn reduce purchases of their supplies when they reduce their output, and so on. These assumptions are the basis for the estimates of the indirect effects on each industry of an initial change of output in one industry.

Where it was possible to choose between alternative assumptions, a considerable effort was made to base the choice upon empirical evidence as to which was the most realistic. Where there was no conclusive empirical basis for choosing between alternative assumptions and where the direction of the effects could be identified, I have deliberately chosen the assumption that involves the greater adverse effect upon employment. This was done in order to be as sure as possible that any error in the estimates is in the direction of overstating rather than understating adverse employment effects and thereby enabling us to be as confident as possible that the results "tell the worst."

The last point may be illustrated by the assumption already mentioned that a million-dollar increase of imports causes a million-dollar decrease in domestic output, measured at prices prevailing before liberalization. If the imported and domestic products sold at the same price before liberalization, this assumption of equal value substitution implies that the corresponding changes in quantities of imports and domestic output are also equal, which implies that the quantity of the product bought from all sources, domestic and foreign combined, remains unchanged when the import barriers are reduced. If the domestic and imported goods sold at the same price before liberalization, therefore, this assumption tends to make the estimates overstate the decrease of domestic output and employment, because a demand response of zero is at one extreme of the range of possible demand responses to a price decline. If buyers really take larger rather than unchanged total quantities when prices fall, then the decrease of domestic output per million dollars of import increase will be less than the estimates assume and the employment decrease will be less than they indicate.

## ESTIMATED PRIMARY EFFECTS ON EMPLOYMENT

The estimated primary effects on employment, for each of the 72 industries whose liberalization was examined, are presented in table 3. Before summarizing what this table shows, let us be clear about what the figures mean.

[15] A crude estimate of the total of these primary direct and indirect employment effects, made by dividing the assumed decrease of domestic output by an average value added to production per man employed, was presented in the first part of this paper. Such a crude calculation provides a satisfactory method of getting the general order of magnitude of primary employment effects, but besides being very rough, it tells nothing about how these effects are distributed among industries.

1. They represent the primary net decreases in domestic employment caused when domestic buying shifts from the protected domestic products of an industry to corresponding imported products. The decreases are net decreases because the process of importation involves some increases of employment and these increases have been subtracted from the decreases.[16]

2. The additional imports represent the quantity that was valued at $1 million in the United States at 1953 prices after payment of 1953 duties.

3. The figures for employment in nonagricultural industries refer to the number of employees, rather than production workers. In agricultural industries they include, in addition to employees in the strict sense, farmers and unpaid farm family workers, although all these workers will be referred to here by the term "employees." The amount of employment effect in an industry represents the number of employees working the number of hours that actually were worked in that industry, generally during 1953, and not full-time equivalent employment, except in the case of agriculture.

We are now in a position to consider what the estimates show. Rather than consider the estimates for each industry separately, we shall consider first the general results, reserving for later discussion both their interpretation and any comment about individual industries that illustrates points of general interest.

*Total primary employment effects*

One of the most striking conclusions to be drawn from the estimates is the great difference in total primary employment decreases resulting from liberalizations of different industries.

These effects range from a minimum of 51 employees for liberalization of the grain-mill-products industry (designated in table 3 as industry No. 24) and an almost equally low figure of 53 employees in the case of the processed-dairy-products industry (No. 22) to a maximum of 214 employees in that of the vegetables and fruits industry (No. 8). The median effect is 114 employees. (The median, the extremes, and also the first and third quartiles, and the range between them, are shown at the bottom of table 3.)

The frequency with which different net decreases occur is shown in chart 1. As this frequency distribution shows, few cases are near the extremes. Out of the 72 cases examined, the total primary employment effect of liberalization in 49 cases, or nearly two-thirds of those examined, is between 80 and 140 employees (using round numbers). Even this range, however, is quite large.

This industries whose liberalization has the smallest total employment effects are, in addition to grain-mill products and processed dairy products, sugar (No. 27), synthetic rubber (No. 51), and primary aluminum (No. 88). Those whose liberalization has the largest effect are, in addition to vegetables and fruits, apparel (No. 34), wood furniture (No. 41), footwear other than rubber (No. 69), and pottery and related products (No. 73).

---

[16] The estimates shown in table 3 differ slightly from those given in Primary Effects on Employment of Shifts in Demand From Domestic to Foreign Products, a paper presented to the Universities-National Bureau Conference on International Economics in April 1956, and to be published in early 1958, because the latter do not include the employment increases in the ocean transportation and other industries participating in the process of importation.

TABLE 3.—*Total primary employment effects and their distribution between "liberalized" and all other industries*[1]—*Number of employees, farmers, and unpaid farm family workers*

| Industry code No. | Liberalized industry | Effect in all industries (number) | Effect in liberalized industry | | Effect in nonliberalized industries | |
|---|---|---|---|---|---|---|
| | | | Number | Percent of total effect | Number | Percent of total effect |
| | | (1) | (2) | (3) | (4) | (5) |
| 1 | Meat animals and products | 92.10 | 74.39 | 80.77 | 17.71 | 19.23 |
| 8 | Vegetables and fruits | 213.95 | 193.63 | 90.50 | 20.32 | 9.50 |
| 13 | Lead and zinc mining | 161.10 | 128.35 | 79.67 | 32.75 | 20.33 |
| 21 | Meatpacking and wholesale poultry | 106.36 | 24.41 | 22.95 | 81.95 | 77.05 |
| 22 | Processed dairy products | 52.66 | 25.49 | 48.40 | 27.17 | 51.60 |
| 24 | Grain mill products | 50.78 | 16.90 | 33.28 | 33.88 | 66.72 |
| 27 | Sugar | 62.37 | 46.17 | 74.03 | 16.20 | 25.97 |
| 28 | Alcoholic beverages | 82.76 | 43.21 | 52.21 | 39.55 | 47.79 |
| 29 | Tobacco manufactures | 69.28 | 42.54 | 61.40 | 26.74 | 38.60 |
| 30 | Spinning, weaving and dyeing | 135.38 | 97.57 | 72.07 | 37.81 | 27.93 |
| 31 | Special textile products | 105.55 | 73.58 | 69.71 | 31.97 | 30.29 |
| 34 | Apparel | 194.19 | 133.87 | 68.94 | 60.32 | 31.06 |
| 35 | House furnishings and other nonapparel | 132.16 | 47.74 | 36.12 | 84.42 | 63.88 |
| 38 | Plywood | 139.07 | 80.92 | 58.19 | 58.15 | 41.81 |
| 40 | Wood containers and cooperage | 159.31 | 93.86 | 58.92 | 65.45 | 41.08 |
| 41 | Wood furniture | 169.88 | 102.75 | 60.48 | 67.13 | 39.52 |
| 45 | Paper and board mills | 83.62 | 39.99 | 47.82 | 43.63 | 52.18 |
| 46 | Converted paper products | 112.15 | 59.62 | 53.16 | 52.53 | 46.84 |
| 49 | Industrial organic chemicals | 75.06 | 35.19 | 46.88 | 39.87 | 53.12 |
| 51 | Synthetic rubber | 62.53 | 19.25 | 30.79 | 43.28 | 69.21 |
| 52 | Synthetic fiber | 90.21 | 55.11 | 61.09 | 35.10 | 38.91 |
| 54 | Drugs and medicines | 118.15 | 52.29 | 44.26 | 65.86 | 55.74 |
| 56 | Paints and allied products | 66.61 | 42.09 | 63.19 | 24.52 | 36.81 |
| 59 | Vegetable oils | 69.36 | 20.58 | 29.67 | 48.78 | 70.33 |
| 61 | Miscellaneous chemical industries | 103.98 | 35.77 | 34.40 | 68.21 | 65.60 |
| 65 | Tires and inner tubes | 91.60 | 44.68 | 48.78 | 46.92 | 51.22 |
| 66 | Miscellaneous rubber products | 116.85 | 76.61 | 65.56 | 40.24 | 34.44 |
| 67 | Leather tanning and finishing | 79.68 | 62.50 | 78.44 | 17.18 | 21.56 |
| 69 | Footwear, except rubber | 178.12 | 132.58 | 74.43 | 45.54 | 25.57 |
| 70 | Glass | 115.05 | 86.73 | 75.38 | 28.32 | 24.62 |
| 73 | Pottery and related products | 189.07 | 163.23 | 86.33 | 25.84 | 13.67 |
| 79.1 | Carbon steel works and rolling mills | 85.05 | 51.36 | 60.39 | 33.69 | 39.61 |
| 79.2 | Alloy steel works and rolling mills, except stainless | 87.71 | 53.75 | 61.28 | 33.96 | 38.72 |
| 79.3 | Stainless steel works and rolling mills | 90.84 | 72.82 | 80.16 | 18.02 | 19.84 |
| 85 | Primary zinc | 94.60 | 36.29 | 38.36 | 58.31 | 61.64 |
| 88 | Primary aluminum, including alumina | 62.33 | 29.95 | 48.05 | 32.38 | 51.95 |
| 89 | Aluminum rolling and drawing | 79.51 | 43.85 | 55.15 | 35.66 | 44.85 |
| 93 | Tin cans and other tinware | 105.89 | 42.12 | 39.78 | 63.77 | 60.22 |
| 94 | Cutlery | 122.47 | 82.61 | 67.45 | 39.86 | 32.55 |
| 95 | Tools and general hardware | 130.18 | 89.16 | 68.49 | 41.02 | 31.51 |
| 103 | Lighting fixtures | 138.36 | 66.70 | 48.21 | 71.66 | 51.79 |
| 105 | Metal barrels, drums, etc | 103.94 | 42.89 | 41.26 | 61.05 | 58.74 |
| 106 | Tubes and foils | 100.09 | 43.95 | 43.91 | 56.14 | 56.09 |
| 116 | Machine tools and metalworkiug machinery | 108.36 | 62.90 | 58.05 | 45.46 | 41.92 |
| 118 | Special industrial machinery | 136.88 | 84.98 | 62.08 | 51.90 | 37.95 |
| 123 | Industrial machinery not elsewhere classified | 123.09 | 55.65 | 45.21 | 67.44 | 54.79 |
| 127 | Ball and roller bearings | 125.39 | 94.46 | 75.33 | 30.93 | 24.67 |
| 131 | Motors and generators | 128.98 | 73.76 | 57.19 | 55.22 | 42.81 |
| 132 | Transformers | 112.85 | 60.50 | 53.61 | 52.35 | 46.39 |
| 133 | Electrical control apparatus | 114.47 | 67.39 | 58.87 | 47.08 | 41.13 |
| 134 | Electrical welding apparatus | 101.93 | 31.11 | 30.52 | 70.82 | 69.48 |
| 135 | Electrical appliances | 133.88 | 52.61 | 39.30 | 81.27 | 60.70 |
| 136 | Insulated wire and cable | 95.64 | 43.91 | 45.91 | 51.73 | 54.09 |
| 138 | Electric lamps | 109.34 | 72.75 | 66.54 | 36.59 | 33.46 |
| 139 | Radio and related products | 154.89 | 80.47 | 51.95 | 74.42 | 48.05 |
| 141 | Communication equipment | 132.39 | 91.95 | 69.45 | 40.44 | 30.55 |
| 142 | Storage batteries | 95.85 | 46.53 | 48.54 | 49.32 | 51.46 |
| 143 | Primary batteries | 118.12 | 80.39 | 68.06 | 37.73 | 31.94 |
| 145.1 | Passenger cars and light trucks | 123.78 | 32.67 | 26.39 | 91.11 | 73.61 |
| 145.2 | Heavy trucks and buses | 113.19 | 32.89 | 29.06 | 80.30 | 70.94 |
| 145.3 | Motor vehicle parts and accessories | 102.92 | 32.82 | 31.89 | 70.10 | 68.11 |
| 148 | Aircraft and parts | 118.44 | 76.31 | 64.43 | 42.13 | 35.57 |
| 152 | Motorcycles and bicycles | 128.05 | 67.66 | 52.84 | 60.39 | 47.16 |
| 154 | Optical, ophthalmic and photo equipment | 127.91 | 83.92 | 65.61 | 43.99 | 34.39 |
| 156 | Watches and clocks | 136.49 | 94.82 | 69.47 | 41.67 | 30.53 |
| 157 | Jewelry and silverware | 136.44 | 90.94 | 66.65 | 45.50 | 33.35 |
| 158 | Musical instruments and parts | 135.02 | 97.43 | 72.16 | 37.59 | 27.84 |

See footnote at end of table

TABLE 3.—*Total primary employment effects and their distribution between "liberalized" and all other industries* [1]—*Number of employees, farmers, and unpaid farm family workers*—Continued

| Industry code No. | Liberalized industry | Effect in all industries (number) | Effect in liberalized industry | | Effect in nonliberalized industries | |
|---|---|---|---|---|---|---|
| | | | Number | Percent of total effect | Number | Percent of total effect |
| | | (1) | (2) | (3) | (4) | (5) |
| 159 | Toys and sporting goods | 157.48 | 100.12 | 63.58 | 57.36 | 36.40 |
| 160 | Office supplies | 128.54 | 87.41 | 68.00 | 41.13 | 32.02 |
| 161 | Plastic products | 121.78 | 77.79 | 63.88 | 43.99 | 36.18 |
| 162 | Cork products | 87.08 | 48.61 | 55.82 | 38.47 | 44.12 |
| 164 | Miscellaneous manufactured products | 154.70 | 77.21 | 49.91 | 77.49 | 50.09 |
| | Median | 113.83 | 62.70 | 58.53 | 43.99 | 41.47 |
| | Minimum | 50.78 | 16.90 | 22.95 | 16.20 | 9.50 |
| | Maximum | 213.95 | 193.63 | 90.50 | 91.11 | 77.05 |
| | 1st quartile | 91.22 | 43.05 | 46.40 | 35.38 | 31.97 |
| | 3d quartile | 133.14 | 84.45 | 68.03 | 60.36 | 53.60 |
| | Interquartile range | 41.92 | 41.40 | 21.63 | 24.98 | 21.63 |

[1] Figures are net decreases of employment resulting from reduction of import barriers, after subtraction of increases associated with the process of importation.

CHART 1.—Frequency distribution of total primary employment effects.

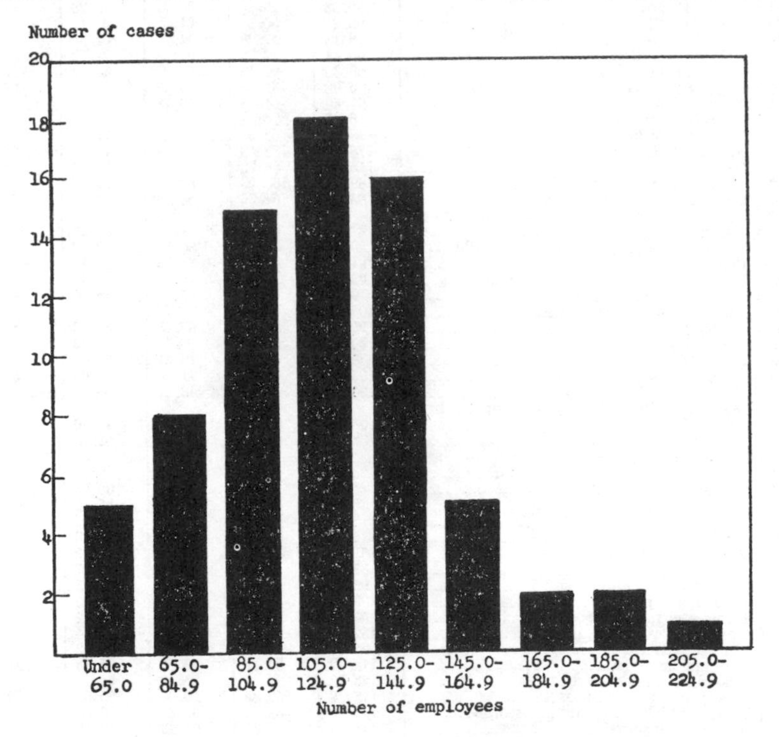


*Reason for wide variation in total primary effects*

What is the main reason for the great differences in the total primary employment effects as we go from case to case? These effects, as presented in table 3, are the net effects of large decreases of employment, resulting from the decline of domestic output in the liberalized industry, offset by increases of employment associated with the process of importation. Since the increases associated with importation are in all but one case very small, we may ignore them and concentrate on the major causes of difference in the gross decreases.

We may conceive of the value of domestic output of the liberalized industry as the sum of value added by many different industries—the liberalized industry, its suppliers, their suppliers and so on. The initial million-dollar decrease in domestic output of a liberalized industry may thus be thought of as the sum of decreases in the value added by itself and by all these other industries. In each industry, moreover, a change in value added is accompanied by a corresponding change of employment, so that for each industry in the economy we may compute a ratio of change in employment to change in value added. Since the decrease in total output of one industry is really just the sum of a large number of decreases in value added in various industries of the economy, the primary decrease of employment in all industries, per million dollars of initial decrease in output of any liberalized industry, is in fact merely a weighted average of the employment changes in each industry per million dollar change in its own value added. (In this average, the employment change in each industry per million dollar change in its own value added is weighted by the value that the industry adds per dollar of initial change in output of the liberalized industry.)

It is obvious from this fact that if the change in employment in an industry, per million-dollar change in its own value added, were the same for all industries in the economy, it would make no difference how much any particular industry contributed to the output of a liberalized industry; the total employment change per initial million-dollar change in the liberalized industry's output would always be the same, no matter what industry is liberalized. It follows, therefore, that differences in the total gross decreases among different cases of liberalization are possible only because the employment changes per million dollars of change in value added do in fact differ among industries.

Given such differences, it is obvious that the total employment change per initial million-dollar change of output in a liberalized industry will depend not only upon (1) the employment change per million dollars of change in value added in each industry, but also upon (2) the change in value added by each industry per dollar of initial change in the output of the liberalized industry, for this determines the weight of each industry in the final result. Since the employment change per million dollar change in value added remains the same for a given industry as we go from case to case, it follows that the difference among the cases reflects the difference in the relative contribution that each industry makes, in terms of value added, to equal initial changes of output of different liberalized industries.

Thus, if the total primary employment decrease from liberalization of a particular industry is high, it means that a large proportion of the value of its output is added in industries that have high employment per million dollars of value added. It does not necessarily mean that the liberalized industry itself has high employment per dollar of value added, for other industries with high employment per dollar of value added may contribute much to the value of its output. It is in fact perfectly possible for the total primary employment decrease to be very large while the liberalized industry itself has very low employment per dollar of value added. That can happen if its own value added constitutes a sufficiently small proportion of the value of its product.

*Distribution of primary employment effects between liberalized and other industries*

The second striking thing about the results is that the proportion of the total primary effect that occurs in the liberalized industry varies greatly from case to case. (The percentage distribution of the total primary effect between the liberalized industry and all other industries is shown in cols. 3 and 5 of table 3.)

It is quite often assumed that the employment effects of liberalization are highly concentrated, if not confined, to the liberalized industry. The estimates show that this is not always the case. The proportion of the total primary effect that occurs in the liberalized industry is in many cases very low. The highest proportion of effect felt in the liberalized industry is 90 percent and occurs in the case of liberalization of vegetables and fruits (No. 8). Liberalization of pottery and related products (No. 73) is a close second, with 86 percent of the total effects of its own liberalization.

The other end of the range may be more surprising. The minimum percentage of effects in the liberalized industry, found in the case of liberalization of the meatpacking and wholesale poultry industry (No. 21), is only 23 percent; in other words, in that case 77 percent of the total primary effect occurs in other industries. For lizeralization of passenger cars and light trucks (No. 145.1), only 26 percent of the effect is felt in that industry, and in the case of heavy trucks and buses (No. 145.2) this "internal" effect is only 29 percent.

In fact, in 26 of the 72 cases, less than half of the effect is felt in the liberalized industry and more than half in others, while in 48 out of the 72 cases the liberalized industry feels less than 65 percent of the effect, more than 35 percent being in other industries. The frequency with which various percentages occur is shown in chart 2.

Consider next the amount of primary employment effects per million dollars in the industry whose protection is reduced, which is shown in column 2 of table 3. The range here is also wide—from a minimum of 17 employees, again in the grain mill products industry (No. 24), to a maximum of 194 employees, again in the vegetables and fruits industry (No. 8). However, for 48 of the 72 cases, or two-thirds of the total number, the effects felt in the liberalized in-

CHART 2.—Frequency distribution of percentages of primary employment effect occurring in liberalized industry.

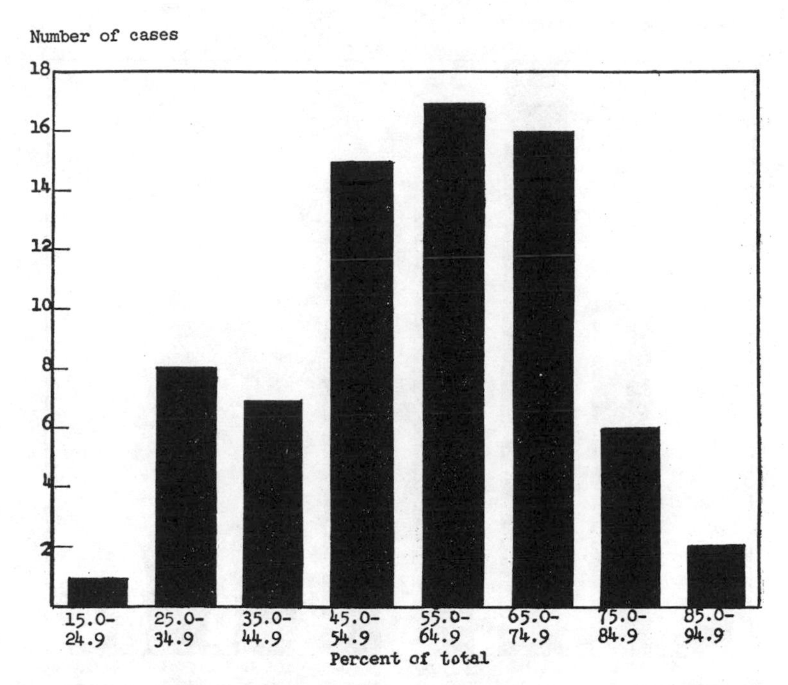


dustry itself are between 45 and 75 employees per million dollars. The frequency of various "internal" effects is shown in chart 3.

The industries at the low end of the range, besides grain mill products, are synthetic rubber (No. 51) with internal effects on 19 employees per million dollars, vegetable oils (No. 59) with internal effects on 21 employees, meatpacking and wholesale poultry (No. 21) with internal effects on 24 employees, and processed dairy products (No. 22) with internal effects on 25 employees.

The industries feeling maximum effects of reduction of their own protection, besides vegetables and fruits, are pottery and related products (No. 73) with internal effects on 163 employees, apparel (No. 34) with 134 employees affected, footwear other than rubber (No. 69) with 133 employees, and lead and zinc mining (No. 13) with 128 employees.

The effect on all industries other than the one for which protection is reduced is shown in column 4 of table 3. It also shows a wide range. The lowest of these "outside" effects, 17 employees, occurs in the case of liberalization in the leather tanning and finishing industry (No. 67). The highest, 91 employees, occurs in liberalization of "passenger cars and light trucks."

CHART 3.—Frequency distribution of amounts of primary employment effect occurring in liberalized industry.

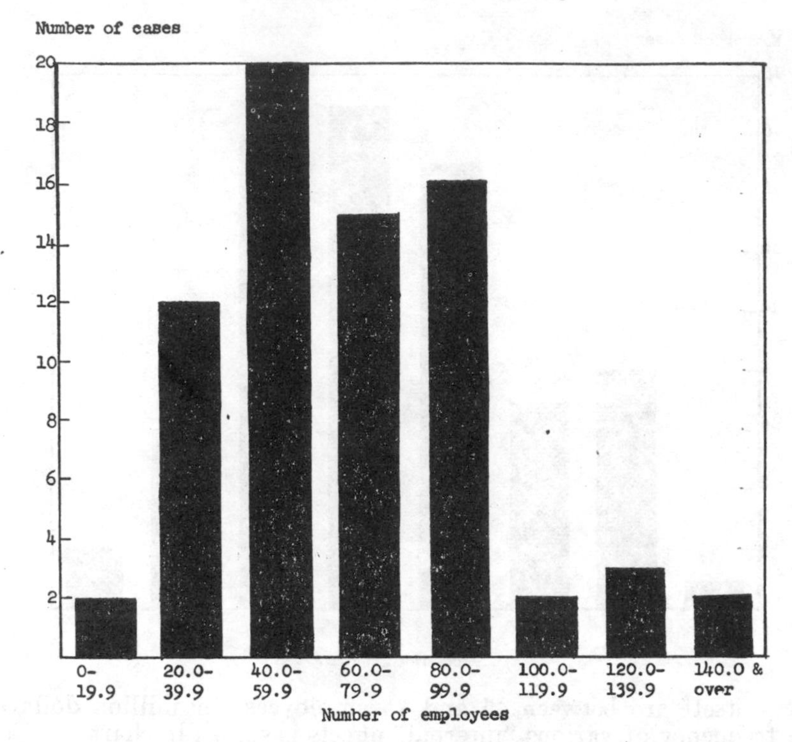


Among the industries at the low end of the range are some whose liberalization has low total effects, which is to be expected, but also two whose liberalization has total effects among the highest of all cases: pottery and related products (No. 73) and vegetables and fruits (No. 8). This reflects the fact that these two industries have not only an unusually high employment per dollar of value added but also an unusually high ratio of value added to value of output, so that their own high employment per dollar of value added has heavy weight in the total.

A comparison of the first, second, and fourth columns of table 3 shows that the large total effect on employment of initial changes in these two industries is the result of large effects in these industries themselves. The "outside" effects of their liberalization, 31 employees in the case of vegetables and fruits and only 26 employees in the case of pottery and related products, are among the smallest outside effects found.

In the case of apparel liberalization, however, while the large total effects result mainly from the large effects in the apparel industry itself, the effects in other industries are also above average—62 employees per million dollars.

The extremely small total primary effects of liberalization of processed dairy products (No. 22) and grain-mill products (No. 24)—53 and 51 employees, respectively—are the result both of small effects in those industries—26 and 17 employees, respectively—and small effects in other industries—27 and 34 employees, respectively.

An interesting contrast is offered by the five industries whose liberalizations have the next lowest total primary employment effects: Sugar (No. 27), tobacco manufactures (No. 29), paints and allied products (No. 56), synthetic rubber (No. 51), and vegetable oils (No. 59). All have total primary employment effects of between 64 and 69 employees. For the first 3 of these industries, the small total effects result from the fact that the outside effects are small—among the smallest found in the 72 cases. In the case of liberalization of synthetic rubber and vegetable oils, on the other hand, the smallness of the total effects results entirely from the fact that internal effects are small—only 19 and 21 employees, respectively; the effects in other industries—45 and 49 employees, respectively—are close to the average for outside effects.

*Distribution of effects among nonliberalized industries*

So far, we have examined the distribution of total primary employment effects only between the liberalized industry and all the nonliberalized industries combined. We may now turn to the distribution of the latter effects among the nonliberalized industries.

It will be recalled that the procedure used to make the estimates provided estimates of the effects in each of the 200 liberalized industries separately. To avoid discussing them in such detail, I have consolidated the 200 industries into 40 industry groups, and shall discuss the primary effects outside the liberalized industry in terms of these 40 groups.

Because a reduction of protection in one industry causes employment effects in nearly all industries of the economy, the effect upon any single industry other than the one liberalized is usually quite small. In nearly every case, a few outside industries feel a significant portion of the outside effects, but this effect is generally not large in relation to the total primary effect. In some cases, however, the outside effects are so concentrated in 1 or 2 industry groups that these groups are considerably affected. In fact, in 2 cases, the effect upon 1 industry group is nearly as great as, or even greater than, the effect on the liberalized industry itself.

The outstanding case of this kind is liberalization of products of the meatpacking and wholesale poultry industry (No. 21). As could easily be guessed, the effects are concentrated in the industries grouped under the heading "agriculture, forestry, and fishing." The effect in this group is 58 "employees" (including, in this industry, farmers and unpaid farm family labor) per million dollars of increase in imports of the products of the meatpacking and wholesale poultry industry. It is hardly surprising that of this amount an effect of 54 employees occurs in the meat and livestock products industry. This effect is more than twice the effect upon the meatpacking and wholesale poultry industry itself, which is only 24 employees.

For liberalization of house furnishings and other nonapparel products (No. 35), the effect on that industry itself is 48 employees. The number of employees affected in spinning, weaving, and dyeing is almost as great—47. This reflects the fact that the "house furnishing and other nonapparel" industry includes so many textile products—

hard-surface floor coverings, coated fabrics, curtains and draperies, and many miscellaneous house furnishings, and also textile bags, and other fabricated textile products. The next most significant outside effect of liberalizing house furnishings and other nonapparel products is found in wholesale and retail trade and is less than 8 employees per million dollars of increase in imports of these products. The remaining 29 employee effects are distributed over the rest of the economy, with less than 3 employees to be found in any 1 of the other 38 industry groups.

In the case of liberalization of vegetable oils (No. 59), with total effects of 69 employees, 21 employees are affected in the vegetable-oil industry, 11 employees in the processed food and alcoholic beverages industry group, and 12 in wholesale and retail trade. The remaining 25 are very widely dispersed.

Other cases in which liberalization has an impact on 1 or 2 outside industry groups that is nearly as great as the effect in the liberalized industry are electrical welding apparatus (No. 134), passenger cars and light trucks (No. 145.1), heavy trucks and buses (No. 145.2), and motor-vehicle parts and accessories (No. 145.3). In the first of these cases the group of nonliberalized industries most affected is electrical machinery and products, where the effect is 20 employees, with the effect in iron and steel and their primary products a poor second.

For liberalization of passenger cars and light trucks, the outside effects are distributed about equally among three industry groups: iron and steel and their primary products; fabricated metal products; and motor vehicles, their parts and accessories. Liberalization of heavy trucks and buses affects both iron and steel and their products and motor vehicles, their parts, and accessories, and also affects fabricated metal products, although by considerably less.

In other cases a noteworthy outside effect occurs in one industry group, even though it is much less than the effect on the liberalized industry itself. Thus, liberalization of plywood (No. 38) and of wood containers and cooperage products (No. 40) would affect 36 and 49 employees, respectively, in the lumber, wood products, and furniture group. In the case of wood containers and cooperage, most of the 49 employees would be in the sawmills, planing, and veneer-mills industry, but in the case of plywood, this industry and the logging industry are about equally affected. For liberalization of primary zinc (No. 85), 28 employees in the metal-mining group would be affected (nearly all, obviously, in the lead and zinc mining industry). For liberalization of tin cans and other tinware (No. 93), 31 employees in the group containing the iron and steel and their primary products industries would be affected. Of these, 26 employees would be in carbon-steel works and rolling mills.

In all but 2 of the 11 cases just discussed, in which there was a concentration of outside effects in 1 or 2 industry groups, the total effect in all the nonliberalized industries was 60 percent or more of the total effect in all industries.

There are 4 other cases that show no concentration of outside effects in 1 or 2 industries, yet have 60 percent or more of the total effect in nonliberalized industries. Thus, for liberalization of grain-mill products (No. 24), the total outside effect is 34 employees per million dollars of import increase, which is 67 percent of the total effect, but in each of the 40 industry groups the effect is less than 5 employees, or less than 10 percent of the total effect.

Similarly, for liberalization of synthetic rubber (No. 51) the outside effect is 44 employees, or 70 percent of the total effect, but it is widely distributed.

A similar dispersion of outside effects is found for liberalization of "miscellaneous chemicals" (No. 61) and electrical appliances (No. 135).

We may now look at the distribution of effects upon the nonliberalized industries in another way. Instead of asking "What industry groups or industries are affected by liberalization of a given industry?" we may ask "Which liberalizations affect a given industry group or industry the most?"

Some industry groups are little affected by liberalization of the products of any of the 72 industries studied. Thus in 13 of the 40 industry groups the outside effects of all of the 72 cases are less than 5 employees per million dollars of import increase of the liberalized products. Another 8 industry groups feel outside effects of 5 or more employees in only 1 of the 72 cases of liberalization. The groups most conspicuously immune from employment effects of liberalization in other industries are tobacco manufactures, apparel, and electric light and power and gas.

The reasons for this immunity are different in the first 2 of these 3 groups than in the last. The products of the tobacco-manufacturing industry go almost entirely to final consumers. The amount that is an input in production of other commodities or services is almost negligible. Employment in tobacco manufacturing is not affected at all in 71 out of the 72 cases of liberalization. The only liberalization that affects it is that of products of the "miscellaneous chemicals" industry. The reason in this case is that nicotine produced by the tobacco-manufacturing industry is used by the miscellaneous chemical products industry in producing insecticides. Even here, the effect is practically zero.

Similarly, the apparel industry is rarely affected at all by liberalization elsewhere; it, too, is not a significant direct or indirect input into any of the liberalized products.

Employment effects upon electric light and power and gas are also negligible in every case of liberalization, but the reason is quite different than in the case of tobacco manufactures and apparel. The output of this industry group is an input for almost every industry, so that its total contribution to the many industries directly and indirectly involved in any case of liberalization could add up to a significant total. Examination of the underlying data shows that this is in fact true; in some cases of liberalization the output effects on this industry group are high. The reason the employment effects are so low is that large changes in output are accompanied by very small changes in employment.

In three other industry groups—instruments, optical and photographic equipment, watches and clocks; auto and other repair services; and other services—the effects of liberalization elsewhere are in no case as high as two employees. In 5 other groups, the effects of liberalization elsewhere are in every case less than 3 employees. In

2 others, they are in every case less than 5 employees. Thus there are 13 industry groups out of 40 that are affected by liberalization elsewhere to the extent of less than 5 employees in all of the 72 cases.

There are, of course, other industry groups in which employment is significantly, even greatly affected by liberalization in 1 or perhaps 2 of the 72 cases examined but very little affected by any of the other cases. This is true of agriculture, forestry and fishing, which is affected to the extent of 58 employees by a shift of buying from domestic to imported products of the meatpacking and wholesale poultry industry but is little affected by such a shift in any other of the 72 cases. Metal mining, too, is vulnerable to liberalization of primary zinc but to none of the other liberalizations examined.

On the other hand, some industry groups are vulnerable to liberalization of the products of many others. The industry group most often affected to the extent of 10 or more employees by liberalization elsewhere is iron and steel and their primary products. It feels effects of that magnitude from liberalization in 11 of the 72 cases. Liberalization of tin cans and other tinware (No. 93) would have the largest effect on it—31 employees per million dollars of import increase. The next largest effect on it—25 employees per million dollars—comes from liberalization of metal barrels, drums, etc. (No. 105). In both cases, the effects within the industry group are highly concentrated on carbon steel works and rolling mills. Liberalization of motor vehicle parts and accessories (No. 145.3) would affect this industry group to the extent of 20 eemployees, but in this case the major effect within the group is felt both in carbon steel works and rolling mills and in iron foundries, with more effect in the latter.

Other industry groups having outside effects of 10 or more employees from 4 or more cases of liberalization elsewhere are spinning, weaving, and dyeing; lumber, wood products, and furniture; fabricated metal products; and machinery other than electrical machinery.

*Employment increases associated with importation*

It has already been pointed out that the estimates given so far represent the net effect on employment in an industry group of (1) the employment decrease associated with a million-dollar shift of buying away from the domestic production of the basket of liberalized commodities, and (2) the employment increase associated with a million-dollar increase in imports of the liberalized products. The latter component of the net figure, i. e., the employment increase, results entirely from increases attributable to the process of importation, for, as will be recalled, employment effects arising from increases of exports are not here taken into account.

The gross domestic employment increases associated with the process of importing amount to a total of 5 or more employees in 8 of the 72 cases. Aside from paints and allied products, where the increase was 24 employees,[15] employment increases of 5 employees or more are found as a result of liberalization of vegetables and fruits, sugar, wood containers and cooperage, carbon steel, alloy steel, stainless steel, and office supplies.

[15] There is no plausible apparent reason why the figure for paints and allied products should be so high and it probably should be disregarded as unrealiable.

As might be expected, these employment increases associated with the process of importation occur mainly in the ocean transportation industry. Nearly all of the 72 cases of liberalization show increases in ocean freight activity. Where no increases are found in this industry, it is generally because the products are imported from Canada and do not come by water. Employment increases also occur frequently in the communications, finances, and business services industry group, which supplies the insurance on ocean shipping, and in the other transportation equipment group, which supplies repair and maintenance services to ocean-going vessels. In almost every other industry group, the increase of employment associated with the process of importation is imperceptible.

Although the employment increases associated with the process of importation are generally small, even for the three industry groups most affected, in some cases of liberalization the small increases of employment exceed the decreases in ocean transportation and in other transportation equipment, so that there is a net increase of employment in these two industry groups.

In general, the estimates of the employment increases associated with the process of importation must be regarded as subject to substantial percentage error. Nevertheless, a closer examination of the estimated effects on the ocean transportation industry is worthwhile because it reveals clearly some of the indirect effects of a shift in demand from domestic production to imports.

In eight cases of liberalization the ocean transportation industry experiences net decreases of employment. At first it may appear incredible that a reduction of import barriers, with its resulting increase of imports, could ever decrease employment in the ocean transportation industry. When we think about the wide ramifications of the initial decrease in domestic output, however, this result is less surprising. A decrease in the domestic production of a commodity whose protection is reduced decreases the use of products needed directly or indirectly in its current production. In some cases, a significant portion of these products is imported. If these output-induced decreases of imports are big enough, they may cause decreases of employment in ocean transportation that equal or even exceed the increases caused by increased imports of the liberalized product itself.

What is involved may be illustrated by liberalization of cork products (No. 62), which involves the only appreciable net decrease of employment in ocean transportation. A reduction of import barriers on cork products would cause a reduction in the domestic use of cork. Since the cork itself is obtained entirely from abroad, it would involve a large decrease of ocean transportation of cork. Moreover, it would also involve decreased use of paper and board mill products, carbon steel, primary copper and other primary metals, large amounts of metal stampings, and other products, which involve some imports. The form in which these materials are imported may be bulky and may involve larger quantities of ocean transportation services than the importation of cork products. This illustrates one factor that may make the employment decreases associated with the process of importation larger than the employment increases associated with it, despite increased imports of the liberalized product itself.

## III

## THE UNITED STATES BALANCE OF INTERNATIONAL PAYMENTS AND ITS RELATION TO FOREIGN-TRADE POLICY

# UNITED STATES BALANCE OF PAYMENTS IN THE POSTWAR PERIOD

United States Department of Commerce

## I. MAJOR CHANGES IN THE UNITED STATES BALANCE OF PAYMENTS SINCE THE WAR

### *1. From the end of the war to the devaluations in 1949*

Following the end of the Second World War, the demand for goods and services by foreign countries, stimulated by monetary inflations during the war and the early postwar period, far exceeded their capacity to produce. The United States Government recognized this situation and provided to those countries which suffered war damages extensive aid directly and through international organizations. Nevertheless, some of these foreign countries had to supplement their current dollar receipts by drawing on gold and dollar reserves which they had accumulated during or before the war. Thus, foreign expenditures in the United States exceeded foreign-dollar receipts by $1.9 billion in 1946, and by about $5.2 billion in 1947 when supplies in the United States became more plentiful. By the middle of 1947, the heavy drain on foreign reserves and the unexpectedly fast exhaustion of credits and other aid provided by the United States Government made necessary a reexamination of the aid requirements, which resulted in the launching of the Marshall plan. At the same time foreign countries took measures to safeguard their remaining gold and dollar reserves, in some instances by reestablishing a balance between their money supply and their output at current prices, and more frequently by tightening their controls over dollar expenditures, or both.

As a result of the combined effect of United States aid, foreign investments by United States enterprises, and investments financed by the foreign countries themselves, considerable progress was made abroad during 1948 and 1949 in restoring productive facilities. This gradually reduced foreign dependence upon goods from the United States and, at the same time, made possible larger imports by the United States.

Foreign expenditures in the United States for goods and services declined after the middle of 1947, while United States expenditures abroad—including imports of goods and services, Government grants and credits, and private investments—increased. Thus, foreign dollar receipts and payments gradually approached a balance, and the rate of liquidation of foreign gold and dollar assets declined from the middle of 1947 through the third quarter of 1948.

During the last quarter of 1948 foreign expenditures here fell below receipts from the United States (including Government aid) which permitted a temporary increase in the gold and liquid dollar assets held by foreign countries in the United States. The foreign dollar position at the end of 1948 was still rather weak, however, and the moderate decline in United States imports which accompanied the relatively minor recession in the United States in 1949 added to other pressures on foreign reserves. In these circumstances, the widely held belief that certain foreign currencies were overvalued led to speculative capital movements which amplified pressures on those currencies and finally resulted in the devaluations in September of 1949.

*2. Recovery of foreign reserves after devaluations*

Since the devaluations had taken place after the restoration of a relatively large part of Europe's capacity to produce, they assisted in improving Europe's balance of payments. Otherwise, the unsatisfied demand in these countries would have made it difficult for exports to rise and imports to decline even if price movements resulting from the devaluations had favored such shifts in the trade. However, a higher production more competitively priced in the rest of the world and the growth of United States business activity which began in the latter part of 1949 initiated a new phase in the postwar history of the balance of payments of the United States. Sparked by the marked decline in the flow of speculative capital to the United States and possibly some return flow following the devaluations, foreign gold and dollar balances started to rise in the fourth quarter of 1949. The rise continued during the first half of 1950 as foreign economies gained further strength, partly as a result of the economic recovery of Germany following the currency reform in that country. During this 9-month period, foreign countries increased their holdings of gold and dollar assets through transactions with the United States by about $1,550,000,000.

*3. The Korean period*

The outbreak of the Korean hostilities at first greatly accelerated the foreign accumulation of gold and dollar reserves. Anticipation of a spread of hostilities raised United States imports sharply in quantity and, because of rising prices, even more in value. It also induced during the first few months of the hostilities a large outflow of capital from the United States, most of which was invested in foreign securities or held abroad in liquid form. These developments, as well as a further rise in domestic business activity which added to the demand for imported materials, and higher military expenditures abroad resulted in a substantial expansion in United States payments to foreign countries during the second half of 1950 and the first 6 months of 1951.

Foreign demand for goods and services from the United States was much slower to rise, however. Thus, during the first 9 months of the Korean conflict, foreign countries added to their gold and dollar holdings about $3.4 billion of the $14.8 billion paid out by the United States. During the second quarter of 1951, however, United States exports advanced sharply in response to the rise in foreign incomes. Although United States payments continued to move up, the amount of dollars retained by the foreign countries declined to about $110 million.

United States exports of goods and services remained high from the middle of 1951 through the first quarter of 1952, although our imports declined both because of the drawing down of stocks accumulated during the first months of the Korean crisis and the drop in import prices from the peaks reached around the middle of 1951. The lag in the movement of foreign expenditures here behind the changes in United States expenditures abroad, which caused foreign gold and dollar balances to rise during the first phase of the Korean period thus resulted in a decline in foreign gold and liquid dollar assets during the 9 months from the middle of 1951 to the end of the first quarter of 1952. Although the decline during these 9 months slightly exceeded $1 billion, it was less than a third of the amount accumulated abroad during the first year of the Korean hostilities. From the outbreak of hostilities to the end of the first quarter of 1952 the balance of payments of foreign countries with the United States thus resulted in a rise in their gold and liquid dollar assets of about $2.5 billion.

*4. The United States recession of 1953–54*

From the second quarter of 1952 until the Suez crisis in the fall of 1956, United States expenditures abroad exceeded foreign expenditures in the United States by about $7½ billion. The resulting rise in foreign gold and dollar assets was relatively large during the first 18 months of that period, when the expansion in United States business activity stimulated United States merchandise imports, and the buildup of our Armed Forces in foreign areas sharply increased United States military expenditures abroad. Government grants in the form of civilian goods and services or of cash, as well as Government credits net of repayments declined during most of 1952 and 1953, but up to the middle of 1953 this decline was more than compensated by a drop in United States exports.

Around the middle of 1953 another business adjustment set in in the United States, lasting approximately 1 year. During this period our merchandise imports fell off and Government grants were also smaller than in the corresponding period a year earlier. However, private investments started to rise around the end of 1953 and offset to some extent the lower dollar outflow from merchandise imports and Government grants. Industrial production abroad continued to rise during this period, but it did not stimulate our exports until the second quarter of 1954, shortly before business activity in the United States started to improve again. As a result of these developments the rate of gold and dollar accumulations by foreign countries declined to $1.7 billion during the year ending in the middle of 1954 from an annual rate of over $2 billion between the second quarter of 1952 and the middle of 1953.

Although somewhat reduced, the $1.7 billion accumulation of foreign reserves was sufficiently high to facilitate a continued expansion of trade between foreign countries and to provide the basis for additional liberalization of restrictions on trade with the United States. The recession in the United States appeared to have had very little adverse effect on the economies of foreign countries in contrast to the recession in 1948–49 which was similar in magnitude and duration. Several major factors were responsible for this difference. First, foreign countries were in a better economic position: their dependence on supplies from the United States was considerably smaller and their reserve position substantially stronger than in the earlier period. Second, United States imports fell less, partly because inventories of imported goods had not been built up during the preceding period of rising business activity and consequently were not reduced when the volume of business declined. Furthermore, the continued rise in foreign demand, offsetting the decline in United States demand, prevented prices of imported raw materials from falling. Third, the decline in foreign dollar receipts merely reduced the rate of reserve accumulations by foreign countries; it did not force them to liquidate their holdings.

*5. The rise in international business between 1954 and the Suez crisis in 1956*

In the fall of 1954 business activity in the United States accelerated again. The rise was quite rapid until the latter part of 1955. During 1956 and the first half of 1957 industrial production in the United States remained more or less at the level reached late in 1955. Although gross national product of the United States continued to advance in 1956, it was at a much slower rate than during the 1954–55 recovery period, and much of this advance was due to rising prices. Industrial production abroad continued the upward trend which, except for a slowdown in 1952, has been uninterrupted since the end of the war. In further contrast to developments in the United States, however, the expansion did not taper off noticeably in 1956 but continued at nearly the same rate as during the 3 preceding years.

These developments affected the balance of payments between the United States and the rest of the world in the following ways.

From the middle of 1954 to the end of 1955, United States payments to foreign countries and United States receipts from abroad inincreased substantially.

During this 1½-year period United States imports of goods and services rose slightly more than United States exports. The rise in merchandise imports coincided with an increase in United States military expenditures abroad. The higher outflow of funds through imports of goods and services, however, was offset in part by a slight decline in Government grants and capital transactions and a somewhat larger decline in the outflow of private capital, particularly of short- and medium-term bank and commercial loans.

The advance in United States exports which usually follows an expansion in foreign business activity was kept down by a larger decline in shipments of cotton. However, the inflow of funds into the United States gradually increased as a result of foreign long-term investments in the United States, and apparently there was also a rise in net receipts from other transactions for which specific data are not available ("Errors and omissions" in the balance of payments tables). Thus, mainly as a result of capital investments, the accumulation of foreign reserves during this period declined, but at the end of 1955 still exceeded $1 billion at an annual rate.

In 1956 the rise in United States imports of goods and services slowed down considerably partly because the expansion in United States business activity leveled off, and partly because military expenditures abroad did not expand further. The outflow of funds from the United States continued to rise, however, because of a very large increase in the outflow of United States capital, both private and Government. The additional capital exports consisted mainly of higher direct investments by American industry in foreign branches and subsidiaries, but new issues of foreign securities in the United States and short-term credits and advances also gained in importance. The rise in direct investments covered a wide variety of industries but was particularly large in the petroleum industry, due to the purchase of a British enterprise by an American company and to extensive payments for exploration rights in Venezuela. The increase in new issues of foreign securities reflected primarily higher capital requirements by local governments in Canada; the rise in the outflow of short-term capital consisted of loans as well as trade credits and was directed mainly to Europe and Latin America.

Government capital movements to foreign countries expanded mostly because of higher sales of agricultural products for foreign currencies. A large portion of these currencies was not utilized during this period with the result that our short-term assets abroad increased accordingly.

The uninterrupted rise in foreign production and investments in 1956, associated in many countries with an intensification of inflationary pressures, and the large capital outflow from the United States contributed to the continued rise in exports of goods and services from the United States. Even before the Suez crisis, United States merchandise exports (other than military) reached an annual rate of $17.5 billion, more than at any previous time. United States incomes on foreign investments advanced to an annual rate of over $2.8 billion during the third quarter of 1956, from $2.5 billion in 1955 and $2.2 billion in 1954. The flow of foreign funds to the United States in 1956 was also augmented by higher foreign investments in the United States through direct investments and foreign purchases of United States securities, and a further rise of net receipts by the United States from unrecorded transactions.

Despite the large rise in foreign expenditures here, foreign countries continued to accumulate gold and liquid dollar assets during the first three quarters of 1956. The rate of such accumulations was, in fact, somewhat higher than in 1955, mainly because of the unprecedented size of the outflow of United States capital, a relatively large part of which took the form of cash transfers. (Uusally a larger part of direct investments is made through the transfer of commodities including capital goods, and services.)

The rise in foreign gold and dollar assets during the first 9 months of 1956 was, however, concentrated among relatively few countries. Some countries had sizable losses.

*6. The Suez crisis*

During the last quarter of 1956 and the first quarter of 1957 foreign expenditures continued to rise sharply while United States expenditures abroad, both for goods and services and for investments, remained at the rate attained around the middle of 1956. As a result, foreign countries as a whole for the first time since the winter of 1951–52 had to draw on their reserves or purchase dollars from the International Monetary Fund.

To a large extent the further rise in foreign purchases here was due to emergency conditions: (1) the need for oil which could not be shipped from the Middle East after the outbreak of hostilities in

Egypt; (2) increased requirements for foodstuffs resulting from exceptionally poor harvests in Europe during the preceding summer; (3) higher demands for United States cotton, partly in order to replenish foreign inventories which had been depleted during the preceding year and to compensate for lower cotton production in other countries. The rise in foreign purchases reflected, however, also the relatively high rate of credit expansion in certain countries, resulting in an increase in their demand in excess of the rise in their capacity to produce and sell, or their ability to obtain capital resources from abroad.

The loss in foreign reserves was further aggravated by a noticeable increase in the movement of private foreign capital to the United States. Part of this was recorded as foreign security purchases here, but a substantial amount escaped statistical recognition and was probably reflected in the large increase in unexplained net receipts in the balance of payments of the United States.

The gradual disappearance of the emergency conditions in the spring of 1957 reduced demand for United States goods and apparently also halted—and possibly even reversed—the flow of private foreign capital to the United States. As a result, the drain on foreign gold and dollar balances eased considerably by the middle of 1957. Several countries which had developed balance of payments difficulties because of an excessively rapid expansion of their demand, however, had to tighten credit or exchange controls and France, in addition, also partially devalued its currency. These measures generally did not become effective before the middle of the year, but may be expected to have some dampening effect on United States exports in the second half of 1957. Assuming that United States imports of goods and services, Government grants and credits, and private investments remain as high as during the first part of the year, foreign countries as a whole should then again be able to balance their transactions with the United States and possibly regain some of the gold and dollars which they had lost between October 1956 and the early spring of 1957.

The balance-of-payments data for the United States thus indicate that, with the exception of the early postwar period and the relatively short interruption in 1951–52, foreign countries as a whole not only were able to meet their obligations in the United States from their current dollar receipts, including United States Government aid, but also were able to accumulate sizable amounts of gold and dollars which strengthened both their official reserves and their private working capital.

In order to evaluate the problems connected with the balance of payments of the United States with the rest of the world it is important, however, to examine the sources of dollars which foreign countries receive and the composition of their expenditures.

## II. THE COMPOSITION OF THE BALANCE OF PAYMENTS IN RECENT YEARS

In 1956 foreign countries received from the United States approximately \$25¾ billion. (This amount does not include grants in the form of military supplies and services amounting to \$2.6 billion.) About half of the \$25¾ billion, or \$12.8 billion, consisted of imports of merchandise; nearly \$4.4 billion came from purchases by our travelers abroad, from private expenditures for transportation, from other services, and from private remittances; about \$3 billion from the net outflow of private capital; the remainder of \$5.6 billion, or nearly 22 percent of all United States expenditures abroad, originated with the United States Government. The latter amount is composed of grants (\$1.7 billion), the net outflow of Government capital (\$0.6 billion), military expenditures abroad (\$2.9 billion), and about \$0.4 billion of miscellaneous administrative expenditures and payments of pensions.

Of the merchandise imports, about 58 percent consisted of industrial supplies and materials, including petroleum and newsprint, and about 25 percent were foodstuffs. Manufactured consumer goods were about 10 percent; and capital equipment, including farm machinery, about 3 percent.

The \$3 billion outflow of private capital included over \$1.8 billion of direct investments, about \$0.3 billion of new foreign security issues less repayments, and about \$0.9 billion consisting mostly of short- and medium-term bank and commercial loans.

Except for the relatively large share of private investments in the total flow of funds to foreign countries, the 1956 distribution among the major categories of United States expenditures was rather typical for recent years, although the total of \$25¾ billion had increased by about \$6 billion since 1954 after having remained nearly stationary at just under \$20 billion between 1952 and 1954.

Merchandise imports declined slightly as a source of foreign dollar receipts from 55 percent during 1952 and 1953 to 52 percent during the following 2 years and to about 50 percent in 1956.

The distribution of imports by the major categories indicated above was relatively stable over the last years, although significant changes occurred if smaller groups or individual commodities are considered.

Imports of foodstuffs fell slightly, from 28.5 percent in 1950–53 to 25 percent in 1956, but imports of manufactured consumer goods and of capital equipment rose, from 9 percent during these years to 13 percent in 1956, as productive capacity abroad expanded and sales techniques improved.

Private service expenditures and remittances rose slowly in importance from about 15.5 percent in 1952 to around 17 percent in 1955 and 1956. The principal factor in the rise was tourist expenditures abroad, which advanced by 50 percent from \$840 million in 1952 to \$1,275 million in 1956.

The outflow of private capital (excluding reinvested earnings of subsidiaries) followed a more erratic course but both in absolute amounts and relative to other dollar expenditures had an upward trend. In 1952, the outflow of private capital was about \$1,160 million and provided nearly 6 percent of foreign dollar receipts, and then declined to \$370 million or less than 2 percent of foreign dollar receipts in 1953. In 1954, about \$1,620 million of United States capital went abroad, contributing over 8 percent of total foreign receipts from the United States, but in the following year it fell to \$1,210 million or 5.5 percent. In 1956, the \$3 billion private-capital outflow accounted for about 11.6 percent of the total outflow of funds from the United States, a record rate both in absolute and in relative terms.

(In addition, about $1 billion was invested abroad from undistributed earnings by foreign subsidiaries of United States corporations.)

The share of Government expenditures in total dollar resources accruing to foreign countries also varied from year to year, but relative to the total dollar flow abroad the tendency was slightly downward. During 1952 and 1953 the Government accounted for about 24.5 percent of total foreign payments, during the 2 following years about 23.5 percent and in 1956 less than 22 percent. Military expenditures were less than $2 billion in 1952 and rose sharply in the early part of the period. In 1955, they amounted to about $2,820 million and in 1956 to $2,910 million. Government grants and the net outflow of Government capital declined from about $2.4 billion in 1952 to $1.5 billion in 1954 but turned upward again and reached $2.3 billion in 1956. The change in direction during the last years was associated principally with the disposal of agricultural surpluses.

Of the total $25¾ billion received in 1956, foreign countries spent here on goods and services about $23.5 billion, invested more than $0.5 billion in branches and subsidiaries of foreign companies located in the United States and in United States securities (other than United States Government securities), and added to their liquid gold and dollar balances about $1.0 billion. The remaining receipts of $700 million consisted most likely of net foreign payments to the United States, which cannot be accounted for from available data.

The $23.5 billion spent here on goods and services includes $17.3 billion for merchandise exported from the United States (excluding military items), about $2.7 billion of dividends, branch profits, and interest on foreign investments and loans by the United States, and $3 billion of United States earnings from transportation services, sales to foreign travelers in the United States, and other miscellaneous transactions.

As with imports, the composition of exports by broad categories also has been rather stable in recent years. In 1950–53, producer's supplies and materials comprised 42.6 percent of total exports, as compared with 42.9 percent in 1956, foodstuffs were 16.2 percent in the earlier period and 16 percent in 1956. Capital and commercial transportation equipment changed from 30 percent to 30.9 percent, and manufactured consumer goods declined slightly from 8 percent to 7.5 percent.

## III. THE SO-CALLED DOLLAR SHORTAGE PROBLEM: DIFFICULTIES OF DEFINITION AND MEASUREMENT

In principle two broad purposes may be distinguished for which foreign countries require dollars: (1) To strengthen their monetary reserves, both official and private, in a form which can be used in international business and which is relatively stable in value, in order to provide a cushion against fluctuations in their international commerce; and (2) to meet their current international obligations to the United States as well as to each other. The need for dollars for this purpose has been greatly increased by the inconvertibilities of other major currencies.

The statistical picture of the United States balance of payments alone does not provide adequate information as to whether foreign countries had sufficient dollar funds to meet their dollar demand. The balance of payments measures the extent to which foreign countries actually met their demand for dollars, from what sources and for what uses, but it does not measure the demand itself. It does not indicate whether residents of foreign countries had purchasing power in local currencies which they would have liked to, but could not, exchange into dollars, or whether foreign import requirements believed to be essential could not be met because foreign dollar receipts or reserves were not sufficiently large.

The balance of payments does, of course, show the amount of Government grants and loans which foreign countries have received, but this does not suffice for the evaluation of the dollar-shortage problem. If such loans and grants had been smaller, most likely exports of United States goods and services (and under certain circumstances the accumulation of foreign reserves) would have been less; if grants and credits had been larger, exports under most circumstances would also have been larger. The size of Government assistance measures only the extent to which foreign countries actually received additional resources. It does not indicate the size or urgency of the foreign requirements for additional imports or reserves, if any, which could not be met from ordinary receipts, nor does it indicate the urgency of the requirements which have been met.

Neither does an excess of foreign dollar expenditures over receipts necessarily measure the extent of a dollar shortage abroad. Only countries which have sufficient reserves can draw them down and thus can have a deficit in their balance of payments. Those countries, which lack reserves, or find it imprudent to use them, have to adjust their foreign expenditures to their current foreign-exchange income, no matter by how much the available foreign exchange falls short of meeting import requirements or import demand. On the other hand a country which has foreign-exchange reserves in excess of what it considers necessary may, up to that amount, spend more abroad than it currently receives without endangering its international liquidity. Also, a country may choose, temporarily, to increase its foreign purchases, in order to take advantage of favorable buying conditions and reduce foreign expenditures in a subsequent period.

Neither does the fact that certain foreign countries did not spend all the dollars they received necessarily indicate that they had more than they needed, because such accumulations are themselves a part of the requirements which have to be met. The accumulation of reserves may not be so high in the scale of requirements as basic foodstuffs, fuels, raw materials, or certain types of capital equipment, but most of the major trading nations in the work have attempted to build up their reserves after they have met what they regarded as their minimum physical needs. In order to accomplish that they have retained restrictions on foreign-exchange expenditures. (Exchange restrictions may, however, also serve other purposes.) As foreign reserves increased, some countries were able to relax restrictions on imports including those from the United States.

Although total foreign holdings of gold and liquid dollar assets increased from the end of 1949 to the third quarter of 1956 somewhat more than in proportion to the value of world trade (excluding United States imports), the distribution of the reserves at the end of that period was not in proportion to the participation of the various countries in world trade, nor in relation to the exposure of their trade to fluctuations. Consequently, many countries including some of those having major shares in world trade consider their reserves more or less inadequate. This applies particularly to the reserves of the sterling area and to those of most of the underdeveloped countries.

The problem of determining or measuring the needs for foreign exchange from actual balance-of-payments data is further complicated for many countries by inflationary credit expansions which usually have a tendency to increase their demand for, and reduce their supply of, foreign exchange and thus enlarge whatever foreign exchange deficit may have existed for other reasons. On the other hand, there are countries which do not maintain foreign-exchange restrictions although their foreign-exchange receipts are less than they believe necessary to meet certain economic goals. In that case the absence of exchange controls indicates that they are not attempting to reach those goals through inflationary expansions of their internal purchasing power or through limitations of their people's freedom to dispose of their incomes according to their own desires.

Criteria used by some countries in judging their foreign exchange shortages, or needs for exchange controls, include the adequacy of their foreign-exchange receipts to meet their minimum physical requirements of goods deemed essential for the health of their population, to maintain their economies at certain levels of operation (as indicated, e. g., by a given percentage of employment) or to achieve a certain rate of economic growth. At best these criteria, however, would indicate for each country only the demand for foreign exchange in general, rather than for dollars specifically. In any event, such criteria cannot be established objectively, but depend upon more or less arbitrary assumptions and judgments regarding the desirability of certain economic goals.

### IV. THE EFFECT OF UNITED STATES TARIFFS AND OTHER IMPORT RESTRICTIONS ON THE BALANCE OF PAYMENTS

Given, that economic aims such as a certain minimum level of employment and welfare, and a minimum rate of economic growth exist in most countries, the size and character of the dollar flow to foreign countries must have a distinct effect upon the methods used in achieving these aims. In the following paragraphs these effects are discussed in general terms.

Countries which cannot offset their imports of goods and services, and the outflow of their capital with sales of goods and services to foreign countries and foreign investments within their own borders initially will find the operation of their economies declining below the level which they want to maintain. In order to remedy this situation, these countries may maintain employment by domestic credit expansion, or restrict their foreign purchases through exchange controls and other devices, stimulate their exports through subsidies, or lower imports and raise exports through devaluations of their currencies.

It would be difficult to evaluate the extent to which United States tariffs actually restrict United States purchases from abroad under various conditions and thus contribute to decisions by foreign countries to adopt such policies. Tariffs are only one of the factors (and not necessarily among the most important ones) contributing to balance-of-payments difficulties in those foreign countries whose sales may potentially be affected by United States import restrictions.

The extent to which foreign countries may feel a shortage of dollars depends not only upon the potential loss of a market for their own products but also upon the importance for their economies of the goods they buy here.

*1. Effects on countries exporting manufactured products*

Countries which are most affected by United States tariffs on manufactured goods purchase in the United States primarily raw and semimanufactured materials, foodstuffs, and a relatively small amount of capital equipment. It may be assumed that the commodities purchased here are essential to the maintenance of the employment volume and the current growth of their economies. Except for the early postwar years when reserves were drawn down, these countries financed their purchases from currently accruing dollar funds, including substantial amounts spent by the United States Government.

In 1956 United States Government expenditures in Europe included about $500 million of (nonmilitary) grants and capital outflows (including the net acquisition of European currencies through the sale of agricultural products) and about $1.7 billion paid out by United States military forces, including funds spent on offshore procurement. Government expenditures in Japan were about $90 million through grants and capital transactions, and about $500 million for military purposes.

If the dollar earnings of these countries do not expand in proportion to their needs for goods supplied by the United States, they may attempt to expand their own production of such goods or obtain them elsewhere. In case such steps are not sufficiently successful, however—and increased purchases in the United States of certain materials, such as coal, during recent years have reflected in part the difficulties of such endeavors—the countries affected would have to increase their efforts to expand their exports. To the extent that tariff or other restrictions prevent them from selling more in the United States, they would have to increase their sales elsewhere (such as in Asia, Africa, Canada, and Latin America) by diverting demand for manufactured goods in these countries from the United States to themselves. Thus, tariffs on manufactured goods may intensify the competition in world markets and affect our exports particularly to less industrialized countries. The increased competition would, of course, require a larger volume of exports by other manufacturing nations in order to pay for the same volume of imports, and thus probably reduce their real income, even if employment and the operation of their economy can be kept at the desired level. Likewise, the increased competition abroad could reduce the earnings from our exports and thus also increase the real costs of imports for the United States.

*2. Effects on countries exporting raw materials and foodstuffs*

A large sector of imported raw materials and foodstuffs are not competitive with United States production and, therefore, not restricted by tariffs and other measures.

Imports of certain foodstuffs and raw materials are restricted in connection with agricultural price-support programs providing for Government loans or purchases and for limitations on domestic production. By such means large quantities of United States output are held off the market and prices are sometimes maintained above those prevailing in international trade. Effects of this kind frequently outweigh the effects of import tariffs, quotas, and fees. Import restrictions associated with restrictions on domestic production and marketing, as, e. g., in the case of sugar, may increase dollar earnings of foreign producers if they can sell here at the higher prices maintained as a result of the support operations although the quantity they may sell is limited.

In many of those cases in which tariffs are levied on a quantitative basis (specific duties), the rise in prices between the prewar and postwar years considerably reduced the ratio of tariffs to the value of the goods. Nevertheless, in those cases in which import restrictions including tariffs reduce the volume of imports below the amount that would be imported without United States Government intervention and at the same time increase the output of United States producers, the higher volume of goods on the world market must be expected to keep world prices lower than they would be otherwise. Since the world market demand for most raw materials is relatively inelastic, lower prices frequently do not stimulate sales in other parts of the world sufficiently to compensate foreign countries producing such materials for a loss in the volume of sales in the United States (or failure of sales in the United States to expand sufficiently to meet their foreign-exchange requirements).

World prices lower than those which would prevail in the absence of United States tariffs and other import restrictions normally result in lower incomes for the producing countries not only from the sales to the United States but also from their sales to other countries, and thus further accentuate their foreign-exchange deficiency.

To maintain employment and incomes, these countries would have to undertake the task of shifting their production to other products, which requires not only appropriate resources but, usually, additional capital. However, countries whose exports consist mainly of raw materials are usually short of capital. Furthermore, it is likely that, even if some capital were available, it would have to be diverted in part to the development of new export industries merely to compensate for reduced sales resulting from United States tariffs, and could not be used for the expansion of these countries' economies, as required to absorb their growing populations and to raise their per capita standard of living.

In order to avoid reductions in standards of living and rates of economic growth, the affected countries would require increased capital resources from the outside world. In the absence of higher capital inflows, they would have to curtail their imports from the United States as well as from elsewhere. Most likely such developments would be accompanied by inflations which would lead to progressively severe import restrictions or currency devaluations.

*3. Effects of United States investments on foreign dollar demand*

The outflow of capital from the United States can be a major factor in helping foreign countries to meet both employment and development aims. This is true to an even larger extent than is indicated by the capital flow as measured in balance of payments statistics. Employment abroad is expanded not only by new funds moving abroad but also through the reinvestment of earnings and, in many instances, of replacement reserves. Furthermore, even if the existing facilities abroad are not enlarged, employment continues as long as these facilities remain in operation. United States investments abroad, in many instances, also provide the raw materials and fuels to other nations, and thus create some of the physical foundation without which the expansion of foreign industries would be greatly hampered.

While direct investments by American industry in foreign branches and subsidiaries comprise most of the private-capital investments, and have the largest and most immediate impact on foreign development, portfolio investments, either directly to foreign countries or through the International Bank and the International Finance Corporation, also have their place in aiding foreign countries in their expansion projects and are thus relieving their foreign-exchange shortages. The same can be said of Government loans and, sometimes, grants. Loans generally pay for the foreign-exchange costs of basic facilities which are usually a prerequisite for the establishment of other investments, and which, in many countries, and for some types even in the United States, are provided by central or local governments.

If the capital export from the United States is limited to amounts which are needed to pay for imported equipment and other goods used in the construction of the new facilities, the immediate balance-of-payments problems of the recipient country may be increased unless the expenses for locally purchased materials and of local labor could be met from local savings. If that is not the case—and most underdeveloped countries have difficulties in increasing saving or even diverting current savings to the new projects—the local costs are usually paid through an expansion of the money supply and thus lead to a deterioration of their foreign-exchange situation. In the long run, it should be expected that foreign investments contribute to the stability of the balance of payments between foreign countries and the United States, but to avoid short-run balance-of-payments difficulties they either have to include funds to meet local costs (such as proceeds from the sale of agricultural surplus goods) or be limited to the point where local capital can be obtained from current savings to meet that portion of the investment which is to be locally financed.

*4. The effects of United States import restrictions on the outflow of United States capital*

The effect of import restrictions by the United States on the outflow of United States capital and, consequently, on the ability of foreign countries to meet their economic-development goals may differ, depending upon the time period under consideration.

When restrictions on foreign sales in the United States reduce foreign dollar incomes, they also will affect adversely United States sales abroad. The short-run effect will be that some of the industries exporting from the United States will attempt to preserve their foreign markets by shifting production behind the tariff and exchange-control walls which foreign countries are likely to keep or possibly even raise. This would stimulate the outflow of capital from the United States, particularly in the manufacturing industries.

United States import restrictions on raw materials, however, would tend to reduce investments in the production of such materials, which would affect mainly the relatively less industrialized countries. Because United States investments abroad in raw-material-producing industries are usually larger than in manufacturing industries, a decline in investments in the former (which includes petroleum and metals) may more than offset an increase in investments in the latter.

In the longer run, however, restrictions on United States imports can be expected to have, also, a dampening effect on United States investments in foreign-manufacturing industries. Tightening of exchange controls abroad may effect the remittances of earnings and the withdrawal of capital, as well as the imports of equipment and component parts necessary for the establishment and conduct of business abroad, and thus discourage the outflow of capital.

Thus, restrictions on imports into the United States can be exepected to affect the foreign-dollar supply not only because foreign countries actually or potentially lose opportunities to sell, but also in some cases because of a lower outflow of capital from the United States. If foreign countries are committed to policies which would provide a certain level of employment or a certain rate of economic development, United States import restrictions are likely to increase the gap between their foreign-exchange requirements and their actual foreign-exchange receipts.

# STRUCTURAL SHIFTS AND RECENT TRENDS IN UNITED STATES TRADE AND PAYMENTS

Fred H. Klopstock and Paul Meek, Federal Reserve Bank of New York [1]

## I. Introduction

The United States is the word's leading trading nation as well as its greatest producer of goods and services. We are the largest external supplier of the world market and the largest market for the products shipped abroad by the rest of the world. Last year our sales of merchandise overseas constituted 19 percent of total world exports; our purchases, 14 percent of world imports. On the score of both exports and imports the United States today is a more important factor in world trade than it was before World War II. This is especially true of our exports which have risen a good deal more rapidly than the exports of other lands.

It has become commonplace to contrast this predominant United States position in world trade with the small proportion of domestic production which is sent to foreign markets. Our imports from foreign countries are said to be of life-and-death importance to their economies while foreign markets are marginal to us since merchandise exports were less than 6 percent of our gross national product last year. The implication frequently drawn from this approach is that our foreign trade is of greater importance to foreign countries than it is to the United States. This, in turn, often leads to the view that it is chiefly foreigners who are interested in the measures we take which affect that trade—foreign aid programs, tariff legislation, quotas on agricultural products, and the like. It cannot be denied that foreigners do have a significant interest in these matters, but this chain of inference appears to go astray when it implies that American interests are not also deeply and directly involved.

The present study undertakes a reappraisal of United States trade and payments in the light of their importance to the functioning of the domestic economy in the belief that this provides the perspective best suited to the examination of policy issues in this field. This review proceeds along two main lines and is concerned solely with the economic issues involved, leaving aside considerations of international politics and national defense that bear on policy formulation. First, an effort is made to depict the shifting structure of our merchandise exports and imports in response to the economic growth and technological advance of the past three decades. Then, the changing pattern of our foreign payments within which merchandise trade takes place is analyzed with particular attention given to the growth of foreign dollar assets in the face of a large United States export surplus.

[1] The views expressed in this study are solely the personal opinions of the authors and are not intended to represent the position of the Federal Reserve Bank of New York on any of the issues or facts treated herein.

The changing commodity composition of our merchandise trade provides a running commentary on the relation between a growing domestic economy and the world beyond our borders. Goods move in response to the pull of high prices, and the flow of goods to and from our shores tends to reflect our standing as a high- or low-cost producer of the items traded, insofar as protective policies at home and abroad have not interfered. This is, of course, the function of foreign trade: to expand the markets of efficient domestic producers, enhancing their productivity in the process, and to supply from outside those commodities which would be more expensive if produced entirely at home.

An examination of United States trade as it has developed since the full employment economy of the late 1920's reveals the important contribution which our foreign trade has made to the shifting of our resources toward their more productive uses and hence to the rise of our real national income. Export markets, for example, have spurred the growth of our capital equipment industries and these, in turn, have paced our economic advance and formed the backbone of our defense potential. Foreign sources of supply have enabled domestic industry to escape the curse of rapidly rising raw material costs which would otherwise have fallen upon them in a number of important cases as low-cost domestic mineral reserves were depleted. The dynamic role of foreign trade in promoting the most efficient uses of domestic human and material resources is perhaps more important to the general welfare in the long run than the domestic income flowing from foreign trade at any particular time.

Our merchandise trade today not only differs markedly in structural composition from bygone days, but it also takes place within a sharply modified pattern of United States transactions in which large export surpluses have existed side by side with increases in foreign holdings of dollar reserves. Government military expenditures abroad, aid, and capital transfers provide an explanation for this development. The magnitude of the export surplus, which has aroused fears of a structural tendency toward a perpetual world dollar shortage, is closely related to the availability of these special types of financing. On closer examination the ties between exports of goods and services and capital and aid outflows are found to be rather close. A substantial flow of exports has moved as the direct embodiment of capital flows and Government financing—for example, the shipment of surplus agricultural commodities and private capital goods. Military expenditures have more directly augmented foreign supplies of freely disposable dollars. Together these special resources have enabled foreign countries to build up their international reserves as well as buy more from us than our own payments to them for our lagging imports would have permitted.

The growth of these foreign assets has been closely linked with a fundamental development on the international financial scene, the rise of the dollar to predominance as an international currency. The strength of the United States economy, its formidable export position, and its highly developed money and capital markets have made the dollar an international "store of value," preferred by some countries even to gold. The postwar accumulation of substantial dollar assets by foreign countries has moved the world economy in the direction of divesting trade from restrictions discriminating against the dollar area by rebuilding international reserves to serve as a more adequate protection against short-term fluctuations. Thus, the dollars made available through private capital flows and Government financing have contributed to the long-run freeing of international trade and payments as well as the current availability of more goods to the rest of the world, our export surplus.

## II. Exports and the United States Economy

Foreign trade helps the people of the United States to achieve a higher standard of living by enabling us to exchange those goods we can produce cheaply for those in which foreigners enjoy a comparative price advantage. This is the central economic fact which must be kept in the forefront of any review of United States foreign trade, its past development and future prospects.

Basically, trade takes place between countries, as between regions within a country, because there are marked differences in the costs of producing any particular item in different areas of the world. If costs were everywhere the same, and everything could be produced everywhere, there would be no international trade. In the real world, of course, costs differ because countries vary widely in their institutions, the numbers and skills of their peoples and the relative abundance of their capital and natural resources; tariffs, subsidies, and the like are also used to change costs and hence price relationships from those springing naturally from different country endowments. Australia and New Zealand are low-cost producers of wool since suitable land is plentiful in relation to population; Switzerland has built up its watchmaking skills until its high quality and low costs have elevated it to a position of world leadership in this field. Trade permits a country to specialize in that range of products in which its constellation of costs give it special advantage and to exchange these products for those goods other countries can make more cheaply.

The real incomes of all trading countries are increased by utilizing their resources fully along the lines indicated by their particular endowment. The fact that frequently it is technically feasible for a country to produce items others make much more cheaply does not ordinarily mean that it is advantageous for it to do so, unless military or other objectives are to take precedence over the raising of real incomes. Natural rubber, for example, can be obtained from guayule bushes grown in the United States, but peacetime production could hardly be justified at the $100-per-pound cost of sizable wartime plantings, so long as tree-grown rubber is selling in the vicinity of 30 cents per pound. Comparative costs are an indispensable element in any consideration of measures affecting the way a country uses its resources.

The foreign trade of a country tends to reflect in its commodity composition the country's cost position vis-a-vis the rest of the world over the whole gamut of items traded. In the absence of government interference its exports consist largely of those goods that can be sold competitively abroad; its imports are chiefly those that would cost considerably more if domestic needs were satisfied entirely from domestic sources. A country's comparative cost position is, of course, not fixed, but varies with changes in economic resources and government policies both at home and abroad. The discovery of large mineral resources abroad may shift the competitive balance sharply in favor of the overseas producer as in the case of petroleum. Technological developments may displace imports and open new export markets—synthetic rubber, for example. Both a rise in world demand for investment goods and in the domestic consumer's appetite for durable goods like automobiles and housing can place a premium on managerial flexibility and agility. Differential rates of inflation may bring rapid realinements in the competitive positions of different countries. Direct government intervention in the form of tariff or quota changes, subsidy programs, tied loans, and the like can move costs toward or away from a realistic economic base.

This study reviews the main trends developing in United States foreign trade over the past three decades with an eye to determining the present areas of competitive advantage and disadvantage of the United States in world trade and to advancing some observations on future prospects. The central conclusion that emerges from this review is that the United States has a very great stake in the continuing expansion of the world economy. The growth of foreign economies since the war has acted as an important stimulus to the United States economy. The expansive effect of foreign markets, substantial as it has been, would have been even larger had our imports, grants and/or investment abroad provided foreigners with more dollars. Rather more important, perhaps, has been the sharp spur given by foreign buying to the rapid expansion of our capital goods industry to its present dominant position with concomitant benefits to our real income, national defense and international competitive position. Our competitive strength, reflected in the recurrence of foreign dollar shortages, has enabled us easily to pay for those industrial raw materials which can now be drawn more cheaply from foreign, rather than domestic sources and for an increasing variety of consumer goods for an expanding population.

The shifts in comparative advantage that have taken place over the past 30 years have improved the position of the American producers of capital goods, and some nonagricultural raw materials, but have weakened that of the producers of some consumer goods and many mineral and agricultural commodities. This differential change has set in motion the process of transferring workers and capital from the constricting fields to expanding ones. It is understandable that this adjustment often causes hardship and uncertainty to those involved, even as the expansion in other areas creates opportunities for both management and labor. Yet, insofar as considerations of raising real incomes rule, it would seem important from the national viewpoint to facilitate the transfer of resources from high-cost industries to the low-cost activities on the frontier of expanding technology. Such a shift should raise rather than lower wages, since a recent study has shown that earnings are higher in export industries than in import-competing ones.[2] The goal of policy would then appear to be to help cushion the adverse impact of the adjustment

---

[2] Irving B. Kravis, Wages and Foreign Trade, Review of Economics and Statistics, February 1956, pp. 14–30.

process on the affected industries and areas without sidetracking it at the expense of large but hidden real costs to the whole economy.

A. EXPORTS IN TODAY'S AMERICAN ECONOMY

Overseas sales provide one of the main pillars undergirding the economic prosperity of the United States, yet our economy is so broadly based and flexible that its strength depends not on this, or any other single, supporting element. This has led emphasis in the past to be laid primarily on how small exports are in relation to our total production. It is quite correct, of course, to say that our record exports of goods and services in 1956 were less than 6 percent of the gross national product, but one wonders whether this way of putting it does not leave the reader feeling that overseas sales are of marginal value to the economy. The impression remains, even if commercial merchandise exports alone are related to the domestic output of movable goods (7.5 percent in 1954). If, perchance, this type of presentation is coupled with a discussion of how important dollar earnings are to foreign countries, it is but a short step to the conclusion that our foreign trade is of considerable benefit to foreigners but of little significance to the United States. Some reemphasis of the important, positive contribution of exports to a healthy and expanding domestic economy would seem in order.

In 1956, the United States sold abroad $17.3 billion of nonmilitary merchandise, and received $6.2 billion in additional payments from overseas investments, transportation, and other salaries. In the first 6 months of 1957, total export receipts, according to preliminary figures, rose to an annual rate of about $26 billion. These figures make it clear that exports are big business. Just how big can be seen by comparing the export sector with other large segments of the economy. Last year, exports of goods and services at $23.5 billion exceeded such personal-consumption expenditures as those for automobiles and parts ($14.6 billion), furniture and other durable household furnishings ($15 billion), and clothing and shoes ($21.6 billion). Exports were somewhat less in 1956 than total private outlays for producers' durable equipment, but were well above nonfarm residential building ($15.3 billion). Total receipts from abroad exceeded by fully $10 billion the net income received by farmers from agriculture ($13.5 billion). Thus, when one sizes up the export market in comparison with large individual domestic markets, one begins to appreciate the importance of foreign sales to domestic producers and our national income.

Employment figures provide another indicator of our stake in foreign markets. In 1952, when our commercial exports were only three-fourths of last year's total, it was officially estimated that 2,150,000 people were employed outside of agriculture and an additional 976,000 in agriculture as a result of export activity.[3] Detailed estimates for the year 1947 show wide variations by industry, with the percentage employed in connection with exports quite small in many consumer industries, fairly high in chemicals (13.1 percent), nonautomotive transportation equipment (11.7), and railway trans-

[3] Commission on Foreign Economic Policy, Staff Papers (Washington, 1954), pp. 373-376.

port (11.3), and quite considerable in such heavy industries as iron and steel (16.6), metalworking machinery (16.5), motors and generators (16.4), and agricultural, mining, and construction machinery (19.2).

This employment distribution points up one key characteristic of the export sector. It does not consist of an easily identifiable industry or group of industries producing solely for overseas markets. Exports are but the foreign sales of industries, nearly all of which produce principally for the domestic market. Partly as a consequence, the role of overseas shipments in boosting domestic income and employment is far less widely comprehended than the appeals of domestic enterprises for protection against competition from low-cost, foreign producers. A considerable number of domestic industries, nonetheless, employ a substantial portion of their existing capacity in production for markets abroad.

The export orientation of industry is particularly marked in two main areas: capital equipment and agricultural staples. Capital-equipment exports accounted for almost one-third of total exports over 1954–56.[4] In 1954, some 60 percent of capital-equipment exports originated in industries selling over 10 percent of their output abroad; almost one-third of these exports came from industries exporting over 20 percent of output. Among the major products enjoying a large proportion of foreign sales in 1954 were tracklaying tractors (47 percent), civilian aircraft (35 percent), motortrucks and buses (20 percent), construction and mining equipment (27 percent), and textile machinery (27 percent). American agriculture depends on foreign markets to absorb a very considerable share of its production of a number of important food and raw-material products. Roughly one-fourth of domestic tobacco and cotton output were sold abroad in the marketing year 1955. About the same share of the production of fats and oils, rice, and wheat found its way into export channels in the same year.

Many other producers have a very sizable dollar stake in foreign markets, even though their dependence is not so great as those just mentioned. An excellent example is provided by the bituminous-coal industry, which earned $745 million last year in shipping 14 percent of its output abroad. Iron and steel exports exceeded $1 billion, while shipments of textile manufactures—over one-third synthetic—amounted to $630 million. Foreign purchases of a wide spectrum of chemical products added $1.2 billion to the sales of the chemical industry.

### B. THE SHIFTING PATTERN OF EXPORTS IN OUR EXPANDING ECONOMY

The export sector has been a dynamic force in the growth of the American economy. Its special importance stems from its key role in the shifting of the country's resources toward their most productive uses—not from the income and employment originating in foreign sales, significant though these are. Foreign demand has enlarged the markets of many domestic industries, and thereby accelerated their achievement of the economies of large-scale production and con-

---

[4] Marie T. Bradshaw, Daniel Roxon, and Max Lechter, Exports and Domestic Business, Survey of Current Business, December 1956, p. 9.

tributed to their advance to the forefront of technological progress. A look backward over the shifting pattern of our export trade is necessary to reveal the inner dynamics of these developments.

The export sector today is far larger than it was in the full-employment economy of 1929. Then exports of both goods and services were $7 billion at 1929 prices whereas by 1956 they had grown to $23.5 billion in current prices. A part of this expansion in foreign sales reflects, of course, the rise in export prices since 1929, but even when this is corrected for, the gain remains impressive. The physical volume of commercial merchandise exports more than doubled between the two dates. Despite this excellent showing, the export sector was a slightly smaller segment of the economy in 1956 than at the end of the twenties. Exports of goods and services dropped from 6.7 percent of the gross national product (total output) in 1929 to 5.4 percent in 1956. This has been partly due to the rising share of our total product derived from private and Government services which do not enter international trade. Yet exports have given ground even in relation to the domestic production of movable goods—i. e., goods which could move in trade between countries. The diminished place of exports in the total picture stems in part from the decline in agricultural exports and in part reflects the dollar-shortage problem whose symptoms are the foreign quotas, tariffs, and exchange restrictions limiting our access to overseas markets, but this must be left aside for the moment. The important thing to note here is that one must look to the qualitative, rather than the merely quantitative, for the special contribution of the export sector to our economic growth over the past 30 years or so.

TABLE I.—*United States export receipts by relative shares, selected periods*

[Percent]

| | 1925–29 | 1935–37 | 1946–49 | 1953–55 | 1956 [1] |
|---|---|---|---|---|---|
| Exports of goods and services (excluding military aid): | | | | | |
| Merchandise | 77 | 74 | 79 | 72 | 75 |
| Investment income | 15 | 15 | 7 | 12 | 12 |
| Other services | 8 | 11 | 14 | 16 | 13 |
| Total | 100 | 100 | 100 | 100 | 100 |

[1] Receipts for miscellaneous, private services have been placed on a net basis to retain comparability with prewar data.

Sources: U. S. Department of Commerce, Balance of Payments of the United States, 1919–53, and Survey of Current Business, various issues.

A review of the period reveals no dramatic shifts in the balance between goods and services in our export receipts from foreign lands. In both 1956 and 1925–29 shipments of commercial merchandise accounted for about three-fourths of the total (table I). This being the case our attention will be directed primarily to the changes in the composition of the goods we ship abroad, the most important component of our export receipts. However, two developments affecting the area of overseas services should be pointed out in passing. First of all, service receipts have been slightly more important in recent years than in the late twenties. This appears to be partly associated with the postwar rise in Government services made available under various aid programs and the requirement that American merchant vessels carry at least half of United States aid shipments. Secondly, there has been a rise in the proportion of service receipts arising from sources other than our investments abroad. Among the factors responsible, in addition to those just mentioned, are increased travel in the United States by tourists from Canada and other nearby lands, larger representational outlays by foreign countries and the new international institutions, and expanded construction activity overseas by American firms. Investment income's share of total receipts declined despite the notable rise in our foreign investments since the war. Presumably this reflects—in part at least—the great postwar shift away from the portfolio investment of the twenties toward direct investment with a consequent lag in the return flow of earnings. Relatively low yields on our postwar Government loans may also have contributed to this decline.

*1. The upsurge in shipments of capital goods*

The special contribution of the export sector to the dynamic growth of the American economy is to be found in the notable rise in the importance of capital equipment in United States exports. Between 1925–29 and 1956 shipments of capital goods—heavy machinery and transportation equipment—grew from 16 to 32 percent of all commercial merchandise exports (table II).[5] Over the same period the only other major shift in commodity composition was the sharp fall in exports of producers' agricultural supplies from 23 to 8 percent of total foreign sales. In both periods producers' nonagricultural supplies were about 35 percent of total exports, food and drugs about 17 percent, and finished consumer goods 8 to 10 percent.

TABLE II.—*Domestic merchandise exports by economic categories, selected periods*

| | Yearly averages | | | | 1956 [1] | |
|---|---|---|---|---|---|---|
| | 1925–29 | | 1930–39 | 1950–53 | Percent | Billion dollars |
| | Billion dollars | Percent | Percent | Percent | | |
| Capital equipment | 0.8 | 15.7 | 20.7 | 30.0 | 31.9 | 5.2 |
| Producers supplies: | | | | | | |
| Agricultural | 1.1 | 22.6 | 19.7 | 11.2 | 7.5 | 1.2 |
| Nonagricultural | 1.7 | 34.8 | 38.1 | 31.4 | 34.4 | 5.6 |
| Food and drugs | .8 | 16.9 | 12.3 | 18.1 | 17.4 | 2.9 |
| Finished consumer goods | .5 | 9.9 | 9.1 | 8.0 | 7.7 | 1.3 |
| Other | | .1 | .1 | 1.3 | 1.1 | .2 |
| Total domestic exports (excluding military aid) | 4.9 | 100.0 | 100.0 | 100.0 | 100.0 | 16.4 |

[1] January–September at annual rate.

Source: Bradshaw, Roxon, and Lechter, Exports and Domestic Business, Survey of Current Business, December 1956, p. 9.

Last year's $5.2 billion in capital equipment exports marked a fivefold increase in dollar volume since 1929 and a sevenfold rise since 1937. This rapidly expanding segment of our export trade thereby outpaced the growth of gross national product which in 1956 was 4 times its 1929 rate and 4½ times its 1937 level. In the 1937—56 period

[5] Bradshaw, Roxon and Lechter, Exports aand Domestic Business, p. 9. The 1956 figures are those of the first 9 months of the year.

overseas shipments of capital equipment scored a faster rate of advance than that closely related bellwether of economic growth, domestic private investment in durable producers' equipment, whose dollar volume has increased almost fivefold in the past two decades to $28.1 billion in 1956.

The conclusion which emerges is clear. Export sales, while in the aggregate lagging gross national product, have acted as an important spur to our capital goods industry whose growth and development lies at the heart of both our economic expansion and our defense potential. By enlarging significantly the domestic market for heavy equipment, exports have facilitated, and in many cases led, the expansion of the economy along lines that represented the most productive use of domestic capital, manpower, and mineral resources. Technological progress in heavy industry has doubtless benefited not only from the larger market but also from the increasing competition in overseas markets of Japanese and western European producers. The real importance of this qualitative contribution of the export sector has not been sufficiently stressed in the past.

A look at the industries producing capital equipment provides a fuller appreciation of the dynamic role played by this particular export sector. An earlier section has already shown how important foreign markets were in 1956 to a number of industries in this field, but here it is appropriate to spotlight those industries in which export sales have increased in importance in recent years, thereby giving an additional boost to growth. Major products for which foreign markets have expanded more rapidly than domestic ones since 1937 include: construction and mining machinery, "specialized" equipment, textile machinery, tractors and agricultural machinery, civilian aircraft, locomotives and railroad freight and passenger cars. Export sales have remained about the same proportion of total sales in the case of electrical machinery (though heavy electrical equipment is more export dependent), internal-combustion engines, and hand tools. Foreign markets have declined in importance for machine tools, trucks, and buses. The pattern of these shifts suggests that export markets tend to serve as an extra reward to technical progress and manufacturing efficiency but that the extra incentive declines in relative importance when foreign producers manage to reduce the competitive gap opened up by United States manufacturers. An important contributory factor to the diminished role of foreign sales in some fields has been the establishment of branch plants abroad by American producers.

The shift in our exports toward higher capital equipment sales has made a direct contribution to producing a higher level of real wages in the United States. Capital goods industries typically pay wages at the upper end of the wage scale and the rapid growth in their foreign markets has meant many more high-paying jobs than would otherwise have been possible. According to a recent study, the high proportion of durable goods (which include capital equipment) in our exports is closely associated with the important finding that United States export industries tend to pay higher wages than those which compete with imports.[6] The higher wage levels are particularly evi-

[6] Irving B. Kravis, op. cit., pp. 14–30.

dent in the main capital equipment industries already reviewed. Average hourly earnings in construction and mining machinery in 1947 (the most recent date for which detailed breakdowns were available) were 11 percent above the average for manufacturing industries other than the main export producers.[7] In textile machinery the margin of superiority was 6 percent, in "specialized" equipment 19 percent, in tractors 17 percent, in motor vehicles (including trucks and buses) 26 percent, in aircraft 18 percent, and in locomotives 27 percent. The favorable margins are about 3 percentage points less if comparison is made with the average hourly wage earnings of 36 leading import-competing industries.

It may appear strange at first glance that high wages should characterize the fastest growing component of our export trade. A little reflection shows that this merely confirms that we are indeed specializing in the products we can produce more cheaply than most of the rest of the world. Wages are high in the capital equipment industries but labor skill, advanced technology and management, and plentiful capital so combine to enhance productivity that the final products can compete with, and in fact undersell, most foreign producers despite the lower hourly wages they pay. This is the way in which foreign trade helps raise real wages in a full employment economy. By enlarging the markets of the most productive industries, it produces an expansion of employment in the higher wage industries raising the general wage level in the process.

*2. The declining importance of agricultural exports*

United States shipments of agricultural products abroad have failed to keep pace over the past three decades with nonagricultural exports. While the latter more than quadrupled in dollar volume between 1925–29 and 1956, agricultural exports did little better than double in rising to $4.2 billion in 1956. This reduced their share in total merchandise exports to 24 percent in 1956 from 39 percent in the earlier period. The poor showing of agricultural sales, in fact, largely accounts, in a statistical sense, for the fall in total exports in relation to gross national product.[8]

Agricultural exports, in failing to keep up with our other foreign sales, continued a trend in evidence at least since 1877–81, when such exports accounted for 80 percent of the total. The recent experience stems chiefly from the fact that the volume of international trade in primary products has been rising less rapidly than trade in manufactures. The United States share of the world export market in agricultural products has indeed risen in the postwar period. In 1953 and 1954 this country provided 16.5 percent of world exports of commodities produced commercially here compared with 11.5 percent in 1934–38, a low period.[9] Even so, the evidence is impressive that our competitive position vis-a-vis foreign producers has deteriorated in recent years. This is clearly indicated by the increasing volume of our agricultural exports being subsidized in one form or another by special Government programs. Some 40 percent of all agricul-

---

[7] All figures drawn from Kravis, op. cit., pp. 17–20. The overall averages are based upon weighting the component industries by man-hours worked in 1947.

[8] Bradshaw, Roxon, and Lechter, Exports and Domestic Business, pp. 8–9.

[9] Interagency Committee on Agricultural Surplus Disposal Prospects of Foreign Disposal of Domestic Agricultural Surpluses (May 1956), p. 27.

tural shipments were moved under such programs in fiscal years 1956 and 1957. The natural result of an effort to maintain the domestic price-support level for many agricultural products above world market prices has been to divert a considerable share of our output from world markets into domestic surplus stocks—except when world demand has been extraordinarily strong, as during the Korean war. Our general position now appears to be that of a supplemental high-priced producer dependent upon special export financing and subsidies—called dumping by our competitors—or upon extraordinary conditions affecting foreign demand.

Upon closer inspection the decline in the importance of agricultural exports is almost entirely due to a falling off in raw material shipments from 23 percent of total exports in 1925–29 to about 8 percent in 1955 and the first three quarters of 1956. This development, in turn, was largely the result of a drastic decline in the volume of cotton and tobacco exports. By the 1954–55 crop-year cotton exports were down to 3.6 million bales compared with 8.8 million in 1924–28; tobacco shipments were 515 million pounds in 1954, down from 611 million in 1926–30. Domestic producers in both instances have lost a substantial part of their overseas markets, partly at least because domestic price supports helped keep world prices at high levels that encouraged an expansion of production abroad. Thus, United States cotton exports, which supplied 43 percent of the outside world's requirements in 1924–28, were a mere 13 percent of non-United States output in 1954–55 because of the doubling of foreign production over the period.[10] Similarly, the stagnation in tobacco exports took place against the backdrop of a 17-percent rise in foreign output over prewar. In both cases domestic producers have become increasingly dependent on the United States market as they have priced themselves out of foreign markets.

The picture is rather different in the case of exports of food products. Here, the expansion in world demand flowing from population growth combined with large-scale United States Government financing has kept exports rising at the same pace as nonagricultural exports as a whole. In 1956 the volume of crude foodstuffs exported was four times the 1929 figure while shipments of manufactured foodstuffs were double those of the earlier year. As foreign producers in general have experienced difficulty in expanding sufficiently to catch up with population growth, the large capacity of the United States has been drawn upon to supply an increasing share of the world's requirements in the postwar period. Thus, United States exports of wheat rose from 21 percent of world exports in 1925–29 to 29 percent in the 1954–55 crop year, shipments of feed grains jumped from 12 to 29 percent, and foreign sales of rice increased from 2 percent to 12 percent of world exports in 1954.[11] The same pattern is to be found in edible fats, oils and oilseeds, cheese, and butter. This increased penetration of world markets was accompanied by greater reliance by domestic food producers on export sales. Wheat exports, for example, advanced to 28 percent of domestic production in 1954–55 from 21 percent in 1925–29. This advance is rather modest but recent shipments represent a spectacular rise over the depressed prewar

[10] Interagency Committee, op. cit., pp. 31–34.
[11] Interagency Committee, op. cit., pp. 30–38.

period—wheat exports being a mere 8 percent of domestic production in 1935–39.

It is difficult to assess the true international competitive position of United States food producers because domestic production controls and price supports obscure the relation between foreign and domestic costs. At the present time our export sales are heavily dependent upon special Government programs which help bridge the gap between artificial domestic prices and world market prices. In the 1955 fiscal year shipments under these programs accounted for 50 percent of all the wheat exported, 31 percent of the cottonseed oil, 20 percent of the feed grains and from 85 to 97 percent of the butter, cheese, and nonfat dry milk. Nevertheless, the amazing progress of American agriculture in mechanizing and raising crop yields leads one to believe that a large segment of it might well be fully competitive on world markets in the absence of special subsidies and production controls. Troublesome surpluses and special export programs are likely to remain, however, as long as the gap between domestic and world prices continues as a result of domestic agricultural programs.

*3. The large and changing market for nonagricultural raw materials*

Nowhere is the shifting world pattern of comparative costs more apparent than in the structure of United States exports of industrial supplies and raw materials (excluding agricultural commodities). Taken as a group such exports have tripled since the last half of the twenties to an annual rate of $5.6 billion in the first 3 quarters of 1956.[12] The group thus accounted for about one-third of all merchandise exports at the end, as at the beginning, of the period, but the main interest centers on the changing commodity composition of the group. Three main trends are discernible: (1) The decline in America's comparative cost advantage in petroleum products; (2) the rise in this country's importance as a marginal supplier to the world's growing industries; and (3) the emergence of new products in which United States producers have outstripped their foreign competitors.

The seemingly insatiable thirst of modern industry for fuel and the exploitation of exceedingly productive oilfields abroad have turned the United States into a net importer of petroleum and its products, the very commodity group for which it was the world's leading exporter but 30 years ago. The rise in foreign production has been so rapid in the postwar period that domestic production, held back by output controls, has declined from its historic prewar two-thirds of world output to less than half in 1956, despite a rise of 150 percent since 1929. More significantly, the markedly higher daily production per well obtained in Venezuela and the Middle East has enabled imported oil to undersell the domestic product and claim a rising share of the market while the domestic industry operates well below capacity. Thus, 1956 exports of crude-oil and petroleum products were only 153 million barrels, a bit below 1929 when they accounted for 11 percent of the total value of exports. Imports, on the other hand, had risen so sharply that in 1956 there were net imports of 313 million barrels of crude oil and 52 million barrels of refined products. Clearly, the cost comparison has moved against domestic producers and through foreign trade the country is holding its fuel costs below what they would otherwise be.

[12] Bradshaw, Roxon, and Lechter, Exports and Domestic Business, p. 9.

The main force continuing to lift our exports of nonagricultural raw materials despite the stagnation of petroleum sales has been the remarkable postwar expansion of the world economy. Although the requirements of our own industrial expansion year after year place heavier demands upon our own mineral resources, the United States still remains the chief source of marginal supplies for a number of important producers' supplies and materials. This has been particularly evident in the last few years when such exports have risen more rapidly than others as European industry, in particular, overreached its local resource base. Between 1953 and 1956 coal exports more than doubled, as did those of iron and steel products and nonferrous metal and ferroalloys. Shipments of metal manufactures, industrial chemicals, and chemical specialties were less spectacular but advanced betwen 35 and 75 percent. In many of these instances the expansion of our sales appears to spring from the possibility of expanding American output as much as, or more than, from an ability to compete pricewise with foreign producers in their home markets. Nevertheless, these overseas sales have made a significant contribution to the prosperity of a number of domestic industries—in the bituminous coal industry, for example, exports accounted for 14 percent of domestic putput in 1956. The importance to these industries of a continuation of economic expansion abroad is evident.

A further stimulus to the buoyancy of our exports of producers' supplies has been provided by the development of many new products by a research-conscious industry. Synthetic rubber is an outstanding case in point, exports rising from practically zero prewar to $97 million in 1956. Synthetic fibers have not only almost eliminated our once-thriving imports of silk but have created an export market which last year absorbed $239 million worth of products. Sales of plastics and synthetic resins amounted to $119 million in 1955 compared with only 8 million in 1937. Most of these developments testify to the tremendous growth and inventiveness of the domestic chemical industry over the past two decades. Exports of chemicals and related products in 1956 were almost 10 times their value in 1936–38, a period in which chemical imports equaled two-thirds of our exports. Here is an area where research, heavy capital investment, and aggressive management seem to have made the United States a strong competitor in foreign markets formerly dominated by German and British companies. It is also of considerable interest that wages in the chemical industry are well above those of nonexport industries. Average hourly earnings in facilities producing organic and inorganic chemicals and plastic materials ranged in 1947 from 13 to 28 percent above the average for manufacturing industries with small export sales.[13]

*4. Shifts in the destination of our exports*

Two main forces can be seen behind the considerable shifts that have occurred in the character and relative importance of our different overseas markets during the past 30 years: (*a*) the vigor of

[13] Kravis, op. cit., pp. 15–18. The 46 export industries treated by Kravis are those with more than $50 million in export sales in either 1947 or 1952. Industries are weighted by the man-hours worked in 1947 in the computation of the average hourly wages for both export and nonexport industries.

economic growth abroad, and (*b*) the all-pervading influence of the dollar shortage in the postwar period.

A decline in Europe's standing, a rise in that of the rest of the world: these are the central facts in the changes wrought by three decades in the relative positions of our foreign markets (table III). Europe in the late twenties and the thirties took almost half of all our exports, today (1956) less than one-third, mostly owing to a decline in exports to the United Kingdom. Canada has become our largest overseas market, accounting for one-quarter of our total sales and Latin America buys only slightly less. Together they now take nearly half our exports whereas in 1925–29 they were responsible for only one-third. Asia and Africa have increased their share slightly since the earlier period so that they now provide outlets for one-fifth of our exports.

TABLE III.—*The geographical pattern of United States trade, 1929 and 1956*

| Area or country | Exports [1] | | | Imports | | |
|---|---|---|---|---|---|---|
| | 1929 percent | 1956 | | 1929 percent | 1956 | |
| | | Percent | Billion dollars | | Percent | Billion dollars |
| Canada | 18.3 | 23.7 | 4.0 | 11.5 | 23.0 | 2.9 |
| Latin America | 18.5 | 23.3 | 3.9 | 25.2 | 31.3 | 3.9 |
| Brazil | 2.1 | 1.7 | .3 | 4.7 | 5.9 | .7 |
| Mexico | 2.6 | 5.0 | .8 | 2.7 | 3.2 | .4 |
| Venezuela | | 4.0 | .7 | 1.2 | 5.5 | .7 |
| Europe | 44.6 | 31.8 | 5.3 | 30.3 | 23.5 | 3.0 |
| Germany | 7.8 | 4.7 | .8 | 5.8 | 3.9 | .5 |
| United Kingdom | 16.1 | 5.4 | .9 | 7.5 | 5.8 | .7 |
| Asia and Oceania | 15.9 | 17.4 | 2.9 | 30.4 | 17.4 | 2.2 |
| Western Asia | .3 | 2.3 | .4 | .8 | 2.4 | 0.3 |
| Japan | 4.9 | 5.3 | .9 | 9.8 | 4.4 | .6 |
| Africa | 2.5 | 3.9 | .9 | 2.5 | 4.7 | .6 |
| Total | 100.0 | 100.0 | 16.8 | 100.0 | 100.0 | 12.6 |

[1] Includes reexports.

Source: U. S. Department of Commerce, Bureau of Census, including data reprinted in the Economic Almanac of 1956 (New York, 1956).

These shifts reflect in considerable measure the varying requirements of economic growth in different areas. The further expansion of the already well developed European economy has pushed raw material demands beyond the domestic resource base. Some 52 percent of our sales to that area in 1955 consisted of producers' supplies and materials, the slowest growing major export group. On the other hand, the less well developed regions depend upon external suppliers for the heavy capital equipment necessary to develop their mineral resources and industrial potential. It is consequently not surprising to learn that capital equipment, the most rapidly growing export category, looms large in our shipments to them—30 to 35 percent in the cases of Canada, Latin America, and Africa—but comprises only a small share (16 percent) of Europe's total.

The present geographic distribution of our exports is linked also with the pattern of dollar disbursements by this country for imports, economic aid, and foreign investments. Here, trade looms large. Our imports from Latin America and Canada have far outpaced those from other areas, the 2 together accounting for 54 percent of total imports in 1956 compared with 37 percent in 1929. Moreover, the Western Hemisphere has taken a large share of American direct investment since the war; in fact, 70 percent of the increase in book value in the 12 years to the end of 1955. It is more than coincidence that our greatest export gains have been made to these two regions where dollar availabilities have been the greatest. At the same time, Europe and Asia supplied only 40 percent of our imports in 1956, down sharply from the 60 percent of 1929. This, in combination with a much stronger American position in Asian markets, once largely supplied from Western Europe, provides an important part of the explanation for the falling share of Europe in our export markets.

Confronted by a shortage of dollars, many countries have found it necessary to maintain controls which discriminate against dollar goods. The same development is very much in evidence in the case of the sterling area. In 1956, it was only half as important as an outlet for our goods as in 1929 (13 percent against 26 percent of our total exports), a development flowing from its reduced role as our supplier (15 percent against 22 percent of imports in 1929) as well as the liquidations of British investments during World War II. Clearly, the accessibility of overseas markets to American producers is closely tied to the accessibility of our markets and investment dollars to the rest of the world.

### C. THE OUTLOOK FOR OUR EXPORTS

The United States has an important stake in the continued growth of the world economy. The trade developments of the past 30 years have made it abundantly clear that the size and nature of our export markets are closely related to the rate and direction of economic expansion abroad. Moreover, they foreshadow the main trends likely to affect our exports well into the future if the present pace of economic advance is maintained.

The economic development of less developed countries is almost certain to be one of the principal factors influencing our exports in the years ahead, barring catastrophic war or a major depression. The benefits of such growth to our export industries are not hypothetical. The almost fivefold expansion of our exports to Canada and Latin America since 1925–29 affords ample evidence of the real gains that can be expected to flow from the further development of these and other regions with high growth potential. Our capital-goods industries, in particular, are likely to find their markets substantially enlarged but the competition more severe from Japanese and European producers. Suppliers of closely related producers' materials like iron and steel are also probably in line for substantial gains. As incomes rise in countries where they are now low and population pressure great, a big impetus may be given to our foreign sales of cotton, tobacco, and some foodstuffs if present-day barriers to the reassertion of our comparative advantage in these products are removed, or if this is not done, large-scale subsidies are continued. Finished consumer goods are likely to remain of minor importance.

A continuation of Europe's economic upsurge will bring somewhat different challenges and opportunities. Europe has already crossed the threshold on which the United States stands—an expansion which overreaches domestic resources successively in field after field. Our most rapidly expanding exports are likely to be those which are in short supply there. Fuel requirements will loom large, and American coal shipments seem destined to rise, at least in the next few years, although competition with petroleum and nuclear energy will affect the permanence of this market. Overseas sources will be called upon for increasing quantities of nonferrous metals and alloys—aluminum, for example. Special products in the capital-goods and chemical fields are likely to be in demand, while marginal supplies of iron and steel products, machinery, and the like are apt to be required in sizable amounts when expansion is rapid. The closer integration at European economics under the plan for a common market should enlarge our markets there to the extent it promotes European economic growth. The rise in Europe's population gives promise of a growing food, cotton, and tobacco market to be served by United States producers if they become competitive again.

The extent to which the main commodity needs for further overseas growth will be translated into tangible United States exports will depend, obviously, on the future availability of dollars to foreigners to make purchases here. The primary producing countries are likely to fare reasonably well on this score if our economy continues its impressive upward climb. Our raw-material and fuel needs will almost certainly expand more rapidly than our domestic capacity to produce them at an economical price, and the outflow of American capital to develop the required supplies seems likely to continue. These developments may, however, increase dollar availabilities chiefly in the Western Hemisphere, Africa, and the Middle East, leaving Asia rather more dependent upon intergovernmental loans and aid. Unlike the primary producing areas, Europe and Japan must obtain a substantial share of the dollars they spend hereby competing with our industry in American or overseas markets. In both, their competition has become increasingly effective in the past 3 or 4 years, and this has led a number of American industries to seek out the crutch of protection at home and special advantage in Government-financed sales abroad. Questions of trade and tariff policy and administration seem destined to turn more and more on the effect of manufactured imports on the national economy.

A very pertinent consideration in the debate which is to be joined on trade and tariff policy is the prospective development of the supply of labor in this country. Peter Drucker, in a provocative essay, has called attention to the labor squeeze to be felt by our economy over the next 2 decades, largely as a result of the low birthrates of the thirties.[14] In this situation, if recent rates of advance in real output and income are to be maintained, the effective labor forces must be increased by automation or other methods of making more efficient

[14] Peter Drucker, America's Next 20 Years (New York), p. 8.

use of existing labor. Foreign trade can play an important role in achieving a more efficient distribution of labor and other resources, if our thinking can be adjusted to the realization that a slowdown in our economic advance is likely to be the penalty should we fail to shift workers toward those industries in which they can be employed to maximum advantage. The task of foreign trade is to indicate, through international differences in comparative costs, the industries in which our labor and other resources can be most effectively utilized. The challenge to the policymaker is to facilitate the actual transfer of resources while ameliorating hardships and dislocations that necessarily follow the shifting fortunes of the affected industries.

### III. United States Imports and Domestic Prosperity

Imports are the other side of the coin of comparative advantage. They embody the real gain to the United States from foreign trade. If the economic forces making for higher domestic real incomes are allowed to operate, our imports will tend to consist of those products and services which others can produce more cheaply than we ourselves. By buying these things, we are able to channel our own manpower, capital, and natural resources into those areas where they can be more efficiently used (i. e., into those products where we enjoy a cost advantage over foreign producers). We thereby maximize the returns the Nation gets from its scarce resources, among which labor is rapidly rising in importance.

The theory is reasonably simple and straightforward: the lower the barriers raised against imports, the more productive will be the use of resources and the higher the real income of the factors, particularly labor which is in short supply in an expanding economy. The practical reality is rather more intractable. In some sections, domestic capital and labor are both already committed to lines of endeavor in which they are unable to meet the competition of foreign producers. The dislocation of foreign production by the war gave domestic industry in a number of cases absolute protection from foreign competition for a decade enabling it to expand capacity well beyond the economic dictates of comparative cost. Marginal producers are the first to feel the brunt of the reentry of foreign competition and their position can be maintained only at the cost of holding prices up artificially through tariffs, quotas or special price-support programs. The upsurge in protectionist sentiment over the past several years indicates that the shelter provided by the dislocation attending wars and rehabilitation is rapidly disappearing.

The plight of the domestic producer hard pressed by foreign competition is one which deserves considerable sympathy. Outside the agricultural field, he is likely to be neither more nor less efficient than other domestic producers in holding down his cost for he is exposed to the domestic competition of his fellows in the same line. In general he is not the inefficient mossback he has sometimes been pictured. His problem in competing with foreign goods may not be one of making the marginal innovations and adjustments required to advance or maintain his domestic competitive standing. He is instead likely to face a situation in which he finds it impossible to meet the price of the foreign producer because the latter operates within a radically different constellation of costs. It is quite natural for the domestic producer to look upon such competition as unfair. He knows he could compete if his wage costs, for example, were to fall to the foreign level of say one-third to one-fourth their present level. Since this is impossible, he would like to see a "scientific" tariff which would raise the foreign producer's price to about the domestic level thereby equalizing costs.

The policymaker is inevitably faced with a dilemma. On the one hand, the national economy stands to benefit directly by switching its resources to industries where it does possess a comparative advantage from those where foreign costs and prices are lower than domestic enterprise can match. We gain from trade when costs differ and to equalize foreign and domestic costs would rob us of the gains in real income which regional specialization makes possible. Moreover, to curtail imports is to limit the expansion of markets for our more productive export industries. There may be much to be said for some special short-term assistance to enable industries, which are exposed to ruinous outside competition, to move into new activities where competitive coexistence is possible. The shifting of men and machines will be, of course, greatly facilitated by the continued expansion of the domestic economy.

This study is not concerned with providing answers to these policy questions but with setting forth developments in our trade and payments necessary to a meaningful discussion of them. The preceding chapter has sketched the changing role of exports in our economy over the past 30 years. The present chapter deals with the changing manner in which these exports have been financed over the same period—i. e., the shifting composition of the dollars made available to foreigners through our imports of goods and services, overseas investment, and grant assistance. Attention is directed principally here to merchandise imports which reflect in considerable measure the changing picture of international price comparisons produced by shifts in comparative cost advantages and in trade and tariff policies. A subsequent chapter takes up the broader implications of our export surplus and foreign dollar gains.

The outstanding feature of the developments traced in this chapter is the failure of our merchandise imports to rise as rapidly as our exports. Between 1929 and 1956 our imports of goods and services rose in value by 200 percent but exports advanced 250 percent; in volume terms merchandise imports rose only by half while exports of goods doubled. The United States Government was the principal factor in bridging the overt dollar gap thus opened, through its military expenditures overseas and its grants and loans to foreign countries. The sluggishness of our imports relative to the exuberance of still unsatisfied foreign demand for our products has stemmed from several factors. Ranking high among these has been the stagnation of imports of raw materials used in the production of nondurable goods, the value of other imports having kept pace with total exports since the late twenties.[15] Principally responsibile for this have been the inroads made by synthetics on the markets for natural fibers. The growth of imports, given continued domestic expansion, appears to depend primarily upon the future course of imports of other industrial raw materials such as newsprint, petroleum, ores and metals, of manu-

[15] Marie T. Bradshaw, Daniel Roxon, and Max Lechter, Imports and Domestic Business, Survey of Current Business, November 1955, p. 17.

factured goods, and foodstuffs. The first two groups have shown rapid growth in recent years; the latter has been held back by domestic quotas. In these instances domestic producers are likely to experience increasing foreign competition and they can be expected to intensify their efforts to obtain special protection with little regard for the broad national benefits to be gained by shifting resources toward more productive uses. The challenge facing the policymaker is to devise means for reducing hardships as they arise without impeding the evolutionary charge of an expanding economy.

### A. IMPORTS AND THE FINANCING OF EXPORTS

United States payments for foreign goods and services have failed to rise over the last three decades as rapidly as our own sales of goods and services to nonresidents. Between 1925–29 and 1956 imports of goods and nonmilitary services rose 200 percent in value to $16.4 billion while exports were advancing some 250 percent.[16] As a consequence, imports last year financed only 71 percent of our exports compared with 83 percent in the last half of the twenties (table IV), Since the rest of the world must make payment for what it buys from us, it is clear that the more rapid advance of exports has been made possible by an increase in the dollars available from other sources.

TABLE IV.—*United States exports and the means of their financing, selected periods*

| | Percent | | | | | Billion dollars |
|---|---|---|---|---|---|---|
| | 1925–29 | 1935–37 | 1946–49 [1] | 1953–55 [1] | 1956 [1] | 1956 |
| Exports of goods and services (excluding military aid) | 100 | 100 | 100 | 100 | 100 | 23.0 |
| Means of financing | 100 | 100 | 100 | 100 | 100 | 23.0 |
| Imports (excluding military expenditures abroad) | 83 | 96 | 48 | 77 | 71 | 16.4 |
| Goods | 65 | 72 | 38 | 61 | 56 | 12.8 |
| Services | 18 | 24 | 10 | 16 | 16 | 3.6 |
| Government financing | | | 41 | 26 | 23 | 5.4 |
| Military expenditures | | | 4 | 15 | 13 | 2.9 |
| Nonmilitary grants | | | 20 | 11 | 8 | 1.8 |
| Loans (net) | | | 17 | 1 | 3 | .6 |
| Private gifts | 5 | 5 | 4 | 3 | 2 | .5 |
| United States private capital (net) | 17 | −10 | 4 | 6 | 13 | 3.0 |
| Foreign capital, gold, errors and omissions | −5 | 9 | 3 | −12 | −10 | −2.2 |

[1] Payments for miscellaneous private services have been placed on a net basis to retain comparability with prewar data.

Source: U. S. Department of Commerce, Balance of Payments of the United States, 1919–53, and Survey of Current Business, various issues.

Aside from goods and service transactions, the United States Government has been the principal source of dollars in the postwar period. In 1956 its disbursements of $5.4 billion "financed" almost a quarter of our exports, whereas in the late twenties the Government's transactions were practically negligible. Government activity

[16] The import figures exclude military expenditures; for 1956, the receipt and payment figures for private miscellaneous services have been netted to preserve comparability with the earlier period.

was rather less important last year than in the recovery years of 1946–49 (when it equaled 40 percent of our overseas sales) but still constituted a very sizable segment of all export financing. Overseas military expenditures growing out of the cold war accounted for a bit more than half of the 1956 outlays, grants, and loans being responsible for the remainder.[17]

Other sources of funds were less important in 1956 than in 1925–29. The outflow of United States private capital, for example, amounted to only 13 percent of exports last year, compared with 17 percent in the earlier period, despite a notable rise which carried it to $3 billion in 1956. Private remittances were down from 5 to 2 percent of export proceeds. A larger share of total foreign dollar receipts were retained, however, as dollar assets—deposits, securities, and direct investments—than in the earlier period.

Several interpretations are possible of the significance of the declining role of imports in the financing of our exports. The basic fact is that the volume of goods and services we now supply to the rest of the world is larger than it would be if Government financing, in particular, were not available. Are exports too large or imports too small? The "tied" nature of some financing may have resulted in the disposal of some goods and services that others would not willingly have purchased. Still, it seems likely that most of the goods foreign countries have obtained through Government financing were desired for their own sake. In general, Government disbursements have simply enabled others to maintain a higher level of dollar expenditures than their dollar earnings would have permitted. Even with these disbursements, a large part of the rest of the world finds it necessary to curb the appetite of its residents for dollar goods by means of special controls. The dollar shortage and discrimination against our products and services can be expected to continue as long as foreign dollar receipts are inadequate to permit the satisfaction of this pent-up foreign demand. In this light, it is our imports that are hobbling our exports. If we could but expand our imports and keep the domestic economy growing, marginal resources could be shifted from their less-productive import-competing uses to the more productive export industries. Why have imports lagged behind exports since the 1920's?

### B. MERCHANDISE IMPORTS OVER THREE DECADES

United States imports have lagged only in a relative sense during the past 30 years. Standing at $12.6 billion in 1956, general imports were almost 3 times their 1929 dollar value. Exports, however, were nearly 3½ times and gross national product 4 times the 1929 level. This relative lag in imports, it is important to note, has not been merely a statistical result of slower increases in import prices. These, in fact, have risen more rapidly than either the domestic price level or the prices we have received for exports. Over the 1929–56 period, imports increased only 52 percent in volume while exports rose 104 percent and gross national product in 1947 prices 123 percent. The relative rise in

[17] As will be noted later, our military expenditures abroad are not entirely governmental in character. They are, however, quasi-governmental in nature, arising from the strategic considerations of the cold war, so that their inclusion gives a more complete picture of the governmental impact on payments than would be obtained by omitting them.

import prices may, in fact, have deterred some purchases and thereby contributed to the sluggishness of imports.[18]

The slower growth of imports has been the resultant of the conflicting forces discernible in the disparate movement of our foreign purchases of four broad groups of commodities. Our purchases of raw materials for use in nondurable goods production have stagnated, but the buying of other industrial raw materials has grown by leaps and bounds. Our consumption of coffee has zoomed but our intake of other goods—mainly other consumer items—has grown much more slowly.

The two buoyant groups—coffee and industrial raw materials (other than those used in nondurable goods production)—have increased their share of total imports from 37 percent in 1923–29 to 56 percent in the first half of 1956; the other 2 groups have correspondingly lost ground.[19]

*1. Raw materials for nondurable goods production lag*

The most drastic shift in our import pattern has taken place in the importation of raw materials for use in the production of nondurable goods (table V). Such imports accounted for fully one-fourth of our overseas commodity purchases in 1923–29, but by 1955 their share was down to 10 percent. Although the dollar value of these purchases was maintained, the volume of goods actually declined about one-third between 1929 and 1955.

TABLE V.—*United States general imports by major end-use categories, selected periods*

| End-use category | Yearly averages | | | | 1955 [1] | |
|---|---|---|---|---|---|---|
| | 1923–29 | | 1930–39 | 1950–54 | | |
| | *Billion dollars* | *Percent* | *Percent* | *Percent* | *Percent* | *Billion dollars* |
| Industrial raw materials | 2.3 | 55 | 52 | 55 | 54 | 6.0 |
| Materials for nondurable goods manufactured | 1.0 | 25 | 20 | 12 | 10 | 1.1 |
| Materials for durable goods manufactured | .9 | 22 | 22 | 28 | 27 | 3.0 |
| Newsprint and paper base stocks | .2 | 5 | 8 | 8 | 8 | .9 |
| Petroleum and products | .1 | 3 | 3 | 7 | 9 | 1.0 |
| Other imports | 1.8 | 45 | 48 | 45 | 46 | 5.0 |
| Coffee | .3 | 7 | 7 | 13 | 12 | 1.3 |
| Other food, beverages and tobacco | .7 | 18 | 22 | 17 | 17 | 1.9 |
| Nonfood consumer goods | .5 | 13 | 11 | 8 | 10 | 1.1 |
| All other imports | .3 | 7 | 8 | 7 | 7 | .8 |
| Total imports | 4.1 | 100 | 100 | 100 | 100 | 11.0 |

[1] January-June at annual rate.

Source: Bradshaw, Roxon and Lechter, Imports and Domestic Business, Survey of Current Business, November 1955, p. 17.

Technological advances have been primarily responsible for the constriction in this particular market although the rise in such im-

[18] A study of the Federal Reserve Bank of New York a few years ago found that price considerations were an important determinant of the level of imports of finished manufacturers, but less significant in the case of other import categories. J. H. Adler, E. R. Schlesinger, and E. van Westerborg, The Pattern of United States Import Trade Since 1923 (New York, May 1952), pp. 45–49.

[19] Bradshaw, Roxon, and Lechter, Imports and Domestic Business, p. 17. This chapter draws substantially upon the reclassifications of trade data and findings presented in this article.

ports would have been held down in any case since textile, apparel, leather, and other nondurable domestic industries have not expanded as rapidly as other manufacturing since the twenties. In some instances technical superiority has ousted the imported product; in other cases it has been the lower cost of mass-produced synthetic items. Synthetic fibers and plastics have made deep inroads into the fiber and leather markets where imports were very important only a few years ago. The development of nylon struck our imports of raw silk almost a death blow. Our silk purchases averaged $368 million annually in 1926–30 when they constituted our largest single import (9 percent of the total); by 1956 they had fallen to $32 million.

In other instances the technological displacement of imports has been less dramatic but the cumulative effect substantial.[20] The increasing use of plastics and light metals as leather substitutes in shoe and luggage manufacture has contributed to the drop in imports of hides and skins. The development of latex-based paints has reduced the demand for drying oils although quota restrictions have also helped curtail imports. The rising popularity of synthetic detergents has kept our large imports of soap fats and oils—copra, coconut oil, palm oil, and the like—from participating in the vigorous growth of the domestic market in soap products. Gum tape and other wrapping materials have displaced imported hard fibers from many uses. Rapid strides in the manufacture of cotton and paper containers have restricted the growth prospects of burlap bagging made from foreign-produced jute. A wide variety of synthetic fibers have cut into the market for carpet wool and have been used in increasing volume in wearing apparel in competition with wool and fur largely purchased abroad.

*2. Imports of other industrial raw materials expands*

While imports of the raw materials used in soft-goods production have sagged, purchases of other industrial raw materials from foreign suppliers have spurted ahead. This group of imports taken as a whole has, in fact, about kept pace with the vigorous growth of the domestic economy, rising by the first half of 1955 to a dollar value ($4.9 billion) 4 times the average of the 1923–29 period.[21] Materials used in durable-goods production constitute the largest component of the group, accounting for some $3 billion of the total in the recent period while the remainder was split almost evenly between newsprint and paper-base stocks, on the one hand, and petroleum and its products, on the other.

Metals and manufactures make up perhaps two-thirds of the imported raw materials used by our durable-goods industries. The particularly rapid growth of this sector of our economy has brought with it increased dependence upon overseas sources of supply as industrial demand has overreached low-cost domestic supplies. The United States in the postwar period has become a net importer of a number of metals for which it was a leading exporter but three decades ago. In 1956 net imports of copper amounted to 319,000 short tons, compared with net exports of 177,000 tons in 1928. There was a net 1956 intake of 743,000 tons of zinc (versus net exports of 37,000 tons

[20] Don D. Humphrey, American Imports (New York, 1955), pp. 259–285.
[21] Bradshaw, Roxon, and Lechter, Imports and Domestic Business, p. 17.

in 1928). The modest import surplus in other commodities has been greatly magnified. Lead imports rose from 33,000 tons in 1928 to 482,000 in 1956; imports of bauxite and crude aluminum made notable gains. Iron ore and concentrates, which did not figure significantly in our foreign trade in the twenties, were imported in the amount of 30 million long tons in 1956.

Considerations of comparative foreign and domestic costs, it is important to point out, have been at the heart of this fundamental shift in the source of our raw materials. As the richest domestic reserves have been depleted, the availability of external supplies have saved the economy the markedly higher costs which the mining of domestic ores of low mineral content would have entailed. The necessary development of foreign ore bodies has been one of the main factors behind United States foreign investment. By the end of 1955 the book value of American investment in controlled mining and petroleum operations abroad was equal to $8 billion. Such enterprises in 1955 accounted for three-fourths of United States imports of crude oil and refined petroleum products, copper, nickel, iron ore, aluminum, lead, and zinc.[22]

Imports have not fully reflected the depletion of our highest grade nonferrous ores, however, because advances in technology have reduced the cost of mining lower quality ores, economized on the use of metals by the development of plastics, and increased the proportion of requirements satisfied by scrap.[23] Even so, the increase in our import bill for nonferrous ores and metals have been impressive, the total rising from $307 million in 1929 to over $1.4 billion in 1956. New techniques have contributed to our import demand in other instances. The increasing importance of alloy steels in total steel output, for example, has caused imports of ferroalloys, ores, and metals to rise from $24 million in 1929 to $271 million in 1956. New methods for processing of domestic taconite reserves have as yet not materially slowed imports of iron ore and concentrates which rose from a mere $8 million in 1929 to $250 million in 1956.

Aside from metals and manufactures, crude rubber and sawmill products are the main types of raw materials used in durable goods production. The first provides another familiar example of the import-saving character of a major innovation, the commercial production of synthetic rubber. Imports of the natural product were still substantial at 714,000 tons in 1955 (versus 632,000 tons in 1929), but the natural product's share of United States consumption was down to 31 percent. Moreover, synthetic rubber exports in 1956 totaled almost $100 million—one-fourth the value of crude rubber imports. Over the same period imports of sawmill products—mainly lumber from nearby Canada—have more than doubled in volume to 3.4 billion board-feet and risen in value from $54 million in 1929 to $306 million in 1956.

The notable rise in raw material imports for durable goods production has been exceeded in percentage terms by the increased influx of newsprint and paper base stocks and of petroleum and its products. The first provides an instance of domestic demand outstripping the physical capacity of the economy to produce a long

[22] Samuel Pizer and Frederick Cutler, Growth of Foreign Investments in the United States and Abroad, Survey of Current Business, August 1956, pp. 19–24.
[23] Humphrey, op. cit., pp. 291–296.

maturing crop; the second involves not the inadequacy of capacity but the competition of low cost oil brought in by American companies operating abroad. The success of Canadian producers in meeting the voracious postwar demand of American publishers has been impressive. The inflow of newsprint was 5.6 million short tons in 1956, almost 2½ times the 1929 figure; woodpulp imports advanced much less rapidly but still amounted to 2.3 million tons in 1956. Since prices also advanced sharply over the period, the value of woodpulp and newsprint imports expanded fourfold to $1 billion last year.

The case of petroleum is similar to that of the nonferrous metals already discussed. American reserves remain substantial, despite the fact that they have supplied over half of all oil consumed in the world to date, but domestic costs are now well above those obtaining in the prolific fields of the Middle East and Venezuela. As a consequence, the domestic price level has attracted a large and growing volume of low-cost oil imports, and the growth of domestic production has been held in check by regulatory bodies, in part motivated by the desire of maintaining prices which will cover higher domestic costs. In 1956, the United States imported 342 million barrels of crude petroleum (equal to 13 percent of domestic production) and 162 million barrels of residual fuel oil (29 percent of domestic consumption). The total import bill for petroleum and petroleum products came to almost $1.3 billion in 1956. Even these figures understate the full impact of the petroleum revolution on our trade, for three decades ago the United States, as noted elsewhere, was a net exporter of petroleum products. Hence, while our imports were rising from 3 to 10 percent of total imports between 1929 and 1956, our petroleum exports were declining from 11 to 4 percent of the total over the period.

*3. Crosscurrents in consumer-goods imports*

The dichotomy evident in our raw-material imports—i. e., with one group sluggish, one dynamic—is found again when our remaining imports are examined. Imports of goods other than raw materials have made up about 45 percent of our total imports over the years. The ability of this group to keep up with imports overall has been entirely due, however, to the expansion of coffee shipments to this country. Between 1923 and 1929 and the first half of 1955, our coffee purchases rose from 7 to 12 percent of total imports, while imports of other products in the group—principally other consumer goods—dropped from 38 to 34 percent of the total.

Coffee is today the largest single import of the United States. Since it is not grown domestically at all, imports have paralleled the rise of domestic consumption unimpeded by protectionist tariffs or quotas. The increases in American real incomes over the last 3 decades has been accompanied by a 50-percent increase in per capita consumption, so that imports doubled in volume between 1929 and last year. Since prices more than doubled between the 2 years, the value of coffee imports advanced to $1.4 billion, almost 5 times the 1929 figure.

Our review of United States imports suggests that it is to the remaining category that attention must be directed for signs of import sluggishness amenable to policy measures. The relative displacement of raw material used in nondurable-goods production has been found to be largely the result of technological developments which yielded products outperforming and/or underselling imported materials.

Imports of other industrial raw materials and coffee have boomed. Hence, hopes for directly stimulating any rise in imports by policy action depend upon finding whether artificial barriers have contributed to the laggard behavior of the remaining one-third of our imports. Foods, beverages, and tobacco (other than coffee) account for about half of the remaining goods at present, and nonfood consumer goods most of the remainder.

Imports of consumer foods other than coffee amounted to $1.9 billion, one-sixth of our imports, in the first half of 1955.[24] The volume of goods imported was, however, about 10 percent less than it had been in 1929. A small part of the items in this group consist of products in which imports supply practically all of domestic consumption as in the case of cocoa, tea, bananas, tropical nuts, and spices. Per capita consumption of most of these noncompetitive imports has remained relatively stable, so that imports have risen with population growth but have not achieved the spectacular rise shown by coffee. Imports of cocoa, for example, undeterred by a strong price advance since 1929, totaled $145 million in 1956, about 3 times the value of imports in the earlier period. As a whole, this group appears to have increased at the same pace as total imports. It has, consequently, lagged behind the rise in exports, but the reasons for this are beyond the scope of official action, apparently rooted in the tastes of the American consumer.

The case of competitive food imports is different. Here, there is little doubt that imports have been kept out by Government measures, many of them the natural consequence of domestic agricultural programs. Sugar provides a striking example of the use of quota restrictions to protect domestic producers absolutely from the outside competition of low-cost sources of supply. Despite an increase of United States consumption by more than one-fourth between 1929 and 1956, imports last year were 7 percent below their earlier volume, the entire increase in consumption having been, in effect, reserved by quotas to domestic producers. Legislation has thus given an artificial stimulus to the growth of domestic industry. This policy has succeeded in maintaining domestic prices generally well above world market prices. The list of other food imports restricted substantially by tariffs and quotas is very impressive: Cattle and dressed beef, butter, cheese, rice products, wheat and wheat flour, and peanuts. It has been estimated, on the basis of 1951 figures, that the suspension of tariffs and quotas on these particular products (including sugar) would increase imports of them by 70 to 150 percent ($350 million to $780 million).[25] The same investigation also compiled a detailed list of agricultural products and manufactures not affected by quotas, for which imports would increase from 10 to 100 percent should tariffs be eliminated. In some of these cases, very low tariffs—2 to 4 percent ad valorem—were found to give substantial protection. These figures, although admittedly imprecise, give some idea of the extent of the barriers that have been erected and maintained in behalf of domestic agricultural producers.

Turning to nonfood, consumer items, one finds that these actually represented a smaller share (10 percent) of total imports in the first

[24] Bradshaw, Roxon, and Lechter, Imports and Domestic Business, p. 17.
[25] Howard S. Piquet, Aid, Trade, and the Tariff (New York, 1953), p. 63.

half of 1955 than in 1923–29 (13 percent). This sluggishness stems, to a very large extent, from the declining importance of textiles and leather goods in the import picture. In the first half of 1955, these items comprised only 3 percent of total imports, compared with 7 percent in 1929.[26] Substantial increases in imports of cotton textiles, for example, took place last year, but the United States remained a net exporter of finished cotton manufactures in an amount of $85 million. Imports of artworks, jewelry, and watches also fell behind the general rise in import activity, amounting to $144 million in 1955, compared with $133 million in 1929. The slow pace exhibited by these imports was more than enough to counterbalance the strong growth of other imports, among which gem diamonds, automobiles, bicycles, sewing machines, and cutlery stand out.

The pertinent question is again whether the relative decline in these imports is due to artificial bariers which might be lowered by official action. There is considerable evidence that tariffs remain an effective deterrent. One cannot, of course, measure the protectiveness of a tariff by its ad valorem height—witness the effective restriction of some imports, already noted, by rates of 2 to 4 percent. High duties, however, do create a presumption of considerable protection even if low duties do not necessarily mean little or no protection. Nonfood consumer items continue to be characterized by high duties despite the considerable reductions achieved under the reciprocal-trade agreements program. This emerges very clearly from Piquet's commodity-by-commodity analysis of the increases in imports which would be produced in 3 to 5 years by the suspension of United States trade restrictions and tariffs under conditions prevailing in 1951. Piquet estimated maximum increases in excess of $10 million for the following products with the ad valorem tariff rates specified: (*a*) increases in imports up to 300 percent—earthenware and chinaware (32 to 66 percent duty), handmade table and art glassware (39 percent duty); (*b*) increases in imports up to 100 percent—woolens and worsteds (33 percent duty), sewing machines (7 to 30 percent duty), boots and shoes (5 to 35 percent duty), axminster rugs (28 percent); (*c*) increases in imports up to 50 percent—watches and parts (37 percent), canned beef (20 percent), whisky (28 percent), automobiles (10 percent), and cotton cloth (23 percent).[27]

This sampling of specific tariff rates points up one important characteristic of our present tariff structure. It is weighted against foreign manufactured products. This means that imports from Europe and Japan as a whole pay a higher rate of duty than do imports from Canada and Latin America which consist to a much greater extent of low-duty raw materials. The decline in the relative importance of western Europe as a supplier of United States imports would appear to be due partly to this fact. High duties still appreciably restrict the entry of many European products. Even so, there appears to have been a very sizable resurgence in Europe's position in the past 5 years. Since 1953 our imports from Europe have risen 27 percent, more than imports from any other major area. The upsurge in sales here of foreign automobiles has been a key feature of this

[26] Bradshaw, Roxon, and Lechter, Imports and Domestic Business, p. 22.
[27] Piquet, op. cit., pp. 38–40.

movement, but it may also indicate that past tariff concessions have finally began to have some effect.

C. THE PROSPECTS FOR UNITED STATES IMPORTS

The future volume and pattern of United States imports is likely to reflect very largely the trends discernible in the recent past provided that the domestic economy continues to expand at something like the recent pace. Economic growth is, of course, basic to the further increase of domestic demand for foreign goods and its continuation seems a reasonable assumption. The extent to which this demand will be allowed to seek supplies freely on the basis of price and delivery considerations will depend upon United States Government policies on tariffs, agricultural price-support programs, and the like. The relative strength of current import trends in future developments will thus be affected by the direction in which policy proceeds and the distance it travels on its chosen course.

There seems little doubt that there is growing dissatisfaction with the reciprocal trade agreements program because it is only within the past 5 years or so that domestic producers have really begun to feel foreign competition. Tariff cutting until recently has been rather painless.[28] In part, this is because United States negotiators have tended to be cautious on "sensitive" items.. More importantly, the high prewar tariff level and the cycle of World War II, reconstruction, Korean war have given most domestic industry almost absolute protection for a quarter of a century. The upsurge of imports of finished manufactures (excluding newsprint and burlap) by 60 percent between 1953 and 1956 suggests, however, that this isolation has ended and that foreign goods are leaping the reduced tariff barriers in substantial volume. The stepped-up pleas for protection this has produced confront the policymaker with the dilemma of deciding whether the national interest requires turning back the clock, halting it, or allowing a liberal trade policy to march on through time.

The issues posed by future trade policy are intimately related to the future growth of the domestic economy. The remarkable expansion of United States production since 1939 has been due in no small measure to the country's ability to expand its effective labor force more rapidly than the population has grown by sopping up unemployment, by attracting more women into the labor force and by using manpower more effectively. Starting today from a full employment base, it is apparent that the United States will not be able in the next 17 years to approach, much less duplicate, the 60 percent rise in nonagricultural employment between 1939 and 1956. The low birthrates of the depression years have already caused additions to the labor force in the 1951–56 period to decline below the number added in the previous 5 years. Current projections of the Department of Commerce indicate that labor-force growth will remain slow at least till 1960 after which the postwar baby boom should lead to a gradual pickup in numbers added.[29] Should college attendance increase spectacularly in the next decade as forecast by Drucker, the labor squeeze

[28] Percy W. Bidwell, What the Tariff Means to American Industries (New York, 1956), pp. 257–260.

[29] U. S. Department of Commerce, Projections of the Labor Force in the United States, 1955 to 1975 (Series P–50, No. 69) (Washington, October 1956).

might be considerably tighter still.[30] In any case, the availability of labor may well prove an important bottleneck obstructing our economic growth in the next several years.

Trade liberalization, even if pursued unilaterally by the United States, could help alleviate the labor shortage by facilitating the shift of workers to areas of higher productivity. In combination with a less restrictive agricultural program it could make possible a further movement of labor out of agriculture (3 million workers moved between 1939 and 1956) while raising the real incomes of those remaining. Within industry, expanded imports could make manpower now in the less productive areas available for the expanding low-cost industries like capital goods already mentioned. Such a movement already appears under way, employment in nondurable goods industries, for example, changing little between 1948 and 1956 while employment in durable goods manufacturing rose over 20 percent.

The actual development of United States imports in an expanding world economy will tend to reflect the interaction of policy measures with the major current trends observed in our review of the changing import pattern: (1) the growing domestic demand for industrial raw materials which can be satisfied more cheaply from abroad because of the depletion of the higher quality reserves of many mineral resources, (2) the steadily rising demand for foodstuffs with the growth of population, (3) the steady growth of domestic consumption of nonfood items, a potential market for foreign suppliers, and (4) the emergence of Europe as an important marginal supplier of industrial goods when domestic investment presses hard on domestic production.

A recent study presents a detailed picture of the substantial further growth in our raw-material imports that can reasonably be expected by 1975.[31] Operating on the conservative assumption that for a specified price range foreign suppliers will supply only the difference between projected domestic consumption and domestic production, the author on the basis of a commodity-by-commodity analysis projects an increase in imports of crude materials and semimanufactures ranging from 87 to 118 percent in 1953 dollars between 1952 and 1975. The author's conservative estimates based on the most likely price indicate that imports are likely to increase sixfold for iron ore; fivefold for petroleum and its products; threefold or so for aluminum, asbestos, and chromite; and substantially for copper, manganese, nickel, oils and oilseeds, zinc, and woodpulp.[32] These demands for fuel and raw materials are likely to prove so compelling in the long run that trade and tariff policy will not long be kept restrictive in the interest of domestic producers where they exist.

The battle of Government policy is likely to be more hotly contested in the case of imported foodstuffs. Coffee, cocoa, tea, and other noncompetitive imports will, of course, be able to flow in as domestic demand rises. Aubrey projects a rise of the order of 80 percent for these commodities by 1975, a considerable gain. The outlook for competitive imports, however, will be heavily affected by the outcome of the rethinking currently going on of the appropriateness of our present domestic agricultural policies in a labor-scarce economy.

[30] Drucker, op. cit., p. 8.
[31] Henry G. Aubrey, United States Imports and World Trade (London, 1957).
[32] Ibid., pp. 32–33.

The course of imports of sugar, butter, beef, cheese, and a host of other raw and processed foodstuffs depends more upon new policies than the growth of domestic demand.

The outlook for imports of finished manufactures likewise depends greatly on the course of United States commercial policy. As has already been pointed out, this is of particular importance to Western Europe and Japan whose exports to us consist primarily of manufactured products. Our review has shown that ad valorem duties still remain quite high on many consumer products. This indicates that there is probably considerable potential saving of domestic labor possible through the importation of a wide variety of labor intensive manufactured products from abroad where labor costs are lower. Past experience with bicycles, watches, automobiles, and textiles shows that foreign suppliers can make a strong competitive effort in the United States market if the product has a strong selling point in distinctive design or price. In other product areas Europe appears to fulfill the role of a marginal supplier called upon when domestic capacity in certain lines cannot keep up with an expansion of demand. This seems to be the explanation behind the rise in imports of steel-mill products to 2.3 million tons in 1953, their decline to 1.2 million tons in the recession year following, and their subsequent rise to 1.8 million tons in 1956. Such imports probably depend more on the level of domestic business activity than tariff levels and serve to re-emphasize the fact that an expanding economy, both at home and abroad, is essential to the growth of international trade and the higher levels of real income it helps make possible.

## IV. The Export Surplus and Foreign Dollar Gains

The transactions of the United States with the rest of the world have been characterized in the postwar period by merchandise trade surpluses far exceeding any recorded before in time of peace. This development, reflecting the extent to which our merchandise exports have outrun our imports, has been reinforced by a substantial rise in our net receipts from commercial services and overseas investments (excluding military expenditures). The resultant large surplus on current account commercial transactions has given rise to much concern that there may be a persistent tendency toward a world dollar shortage.

Paradoxically, foreign countries since 1949 have added steadily to their gold and dollar assets in the face of the large export surplus of the United States. Thus, at the same time they have benefited from a flow of goods and services in excess of that which their current earnings would have enabled them to buy, they have also been able to add to their international reserves. The explanation of this development lies outside the bounds of "normal" commercial transactions. Expenditures by our military forces overseas growing out of the strategic requirements of the cold war have augmented substantially the dollar earnings of foreign countries from more customary sources. Aid transfers and capital outflows have provided not only additional goods but also facilitated the building up of foreign reserves. As these have accumulated, nearly all foreign countries have added substantially to their liquid dollar assets, many of them holding a substantial portion of their total reserves in the United States as earning assets. The postwar increase in foreign dollar holdings has marked the rise of the United States to a predominant position as an international financial center as well as helped provide other countries with the increasing reserve cushion necessary to the continued dismantling of restrictive trade barriers and the further expansion of world trade.

The present chapter is concerned with pointing up the main facets of these two major postwar developments in the pattern of our international transactions: the enlarged export surplus and the growth of foreign reserves. This leads first through a discussion of the nature of the export surplus and its close relation to aid and capital transfers and then to a brief consideration of the buildup of foreign reserves in the postwar period. Finally, some observations are offered on the future course of United States trade and payments.

## A. CURRENT ACCOUNT SURPLUSES AND CASH DEFICITS IN THE UNITED STATES BALANCE OF PAYMENTS

### *1. The coexistence of export surpluses and cash deficits*

The immediate postwar years of 1946–48, in which recovery from war's destruction was launched, were marked by very large United States export surpluses financed in part by heavy drawings on foreign gold and dollar holdings. In the fall of 1949, however, the continuing large current account surpluses began to be accompanied by foreign dollar gains. Over a period extending through the fall of 1956, our balance of payments continued to be marked by both export surpluses and a rise in foreign reserves. In other words, foreign countries as a group were able to add consistently during that period considerable amounts to their dollar holdings here, even though they acquired goods and services from the United States worth much more than their earnings in the United States from the sale of goods and the supply of services. The usual explanation for this apparent paradox is that our aid and capital payments exceeded our export surpluses producing a cash deficit. But this arithmetical exercise obscures more than it explains. A more helpful way of putting it is to emphasize first of all that a very substantial part of our exports did not call for payment by the importing countries. Not only all of our military aid exports, but a large, though indeterminable, part of our "commercial" merchandise exports (as well as some of the services supplied to foreign countries) were paid for by the United States Government under grant or loan programs; an additional part of our exports, especially in the heavy equipment field, reflected direct investments by United States corporations in the form of shipments to their subsidiaries abroad. Moreover, in recent years, the United States Government has been willing to accept payment in foreign currencies rather than in dollars for its sales of agricultural surpluses abroad. This direct financing of our exports by United States official and private institutions in part explains that our balance of payments evidences at the same time an export surplus and a cash deficit.

Of course, our cash deficit is in part the result of dollar cash transfers to foreign countries, some on aid account and others representing the counterpart of investments in exploration rights or of purchases by United States corporations and individuals of foreign bonds and stocks. Bank loans, private remittances and other miscellaneous payments have also helped to swell our cash deficit. But it is well to remember that sizable parts of the dollar amounts shown in our balance of payments under such categories as "grants" or "United States direct investment" do not by any means represent actual dollar transfers to foreign countries. They are not dollar payments to accounts of foreign countries in the narrow sense of the word, but merely accounting offsets for shipments of goods or the provision of services that appear in the export side of the ledger.

Table VI brings together the major accounts of our balance of payments in summary form and rearranged in a manner that puts our international transactions in better perspective for our analysis of recent payments patterns. First of all it breaks down our current account balance into several major segments. It shows the surplus on merchandise account as well as on service account, but sets apart two particularly dynamic and unique types of service transactions, namely military expenditures and receipts and payments on investment income account.[33]

The table brings out the fact the considerable contribution made by our big surplus on investment income to our current account surplus. It also shows that the current account surplus as ordinarily presented in United States balance of payments statements would look even more formidable in the absence of the very large military expenditures by the United States Government and its Armed Forces abroad (line 5). If we deduct these expenditures from our imports of services, the current balance shows a $5.3 billion surplus on "commercial" transactions rather than the $2.8 billion surplus recorded for goods and services as a whole.

TABLE VI.—*Selected items of the United States balance of payments, annual averages*

[In billions of dollars]

| | 1948-50 | 1951-53 | 1954-56 |
|---|---|---|---|
| 1. Merchandise balance (excluding military expenditures) | 3, 970 | 2, 569 | 3, 186 |
| 2. Service balance (excluding military aid) | 386 | 61 | 120 |
| 3. Total | 4, 356 | 2, 630 | 3, 306 |
| 4. Investment income balance | 1, 123 | 1, 475 | 1, 983 |
| 5. Current account balance (excluding military expenditures) | 5, 479 | 4, 104 | 5, 289 |
| 6. Military expenditures | 665 | 1, 921 | 2, 772 |
| 7. Current account balance (including military expenditures) | 4, 814 | 2, 184 | 2, 517 |
| 8. Aid and capital transfers total [1] | −6, 237 | −3, 965 | −4, 547 |
| Of which— | | | |
| 9. Economic grant aid | 4, 125 | 2, 277 | 1, 736 |
| 10. Private remittances and miscellansous transfers | 593 | 558 | 616 |
| 11. Private capital, net | 908 | 865 | 1, 917 |
| 12. Government capital, net | 611 | 265 | 278 |
| 13. Net transfers of gold and dollars | 795 | 1, 355 | 1, 590 |
| 14. Errors and omissions | 628 | 426 | 440 |

[1] Including private remittances and pension payments.

Sources: United States Department of Commerce, Balance of Payments of the United States, 1919–53 (Washington, 1954); Survey of Current Business, June 1956 and March 1957.

[33] Military expenditures are a very unique payments type and deserve to be treated separately in that they are largely of a noncommercial nature. Unlike purchases of most other services, they are only to a small extent determined by price and cost considerations. They are closely associated with our political objectives and activities abroad. Investment income is a very special type of service transaction since it reflects factors that differ from those affecting other types of transactions—such special factors, for example, as the accumulation of investments over many years, rates of return, and the decision to reinvest earnings abroad.

The table further shows that we have reached a considerable measure of balance on service account excluding military expenditures and excluding investment income receipts and payments. This still differs considerably from the prewar situation when we were regularly in deficit with the rest of the world on this account. Another outstanding aspect of our international transactions brought out by the table is the fact that on merchandise account, there has been consistently a huge surplus of several billions of dollars. Actually this surplus has been growing substantially in 1956 and 1957. In the first half of the latter year Suez-induced oil shipments and heavy sales of agricultural surpluses helped boost the trade surplus to an annual rate of about $7.5 billion.

The persistent tendency of the United States to show very sizable surpluses on its merchandise account and at the same time have foreigners acquiring substantial amounts of gold and dollars has intrigued not only balance of payments analysts, but many other members of the economics profession. In numerous books and articles they have addressed themselves to the two separate, though interrelated, questions of whether (1) the continuous trade surplus reflects structural maladjustments of the world economy, in particular a persistent tendency toward United States technological superiority which permits it to outcompete the economies of foreign countries, and whether (2) the continuous cash deficit in our international transactions merely conceals the virtually permanent presence of a so-called dollar shortage or dollar-gap problem. This section does not purport to review this debate,[34] but by pointing up some major features of our payments experience in recent years will attempt to put some of the magnitudes underlying this debate in perspective.

It is first necessary to make mention again of a factor that escapes statistical measurement but that has received a great deal of attention in the past: our trade surplus would have been even larger, and our cash deficit (i. e., the net gains of foreigners) would have been correspondingly smaller, were it not for the fact that an undeterminable amount of potential foreign purchases have been frustrated by discriminatory trade and payments controls abroad. Although there is no way of estimating the magnitude of this suppressed demand for American products, it would appear, however, that it was quite sizable until the early fifties, but has declined sharply in more recent years as foreign production rose and wartime backlogs of demand were worked off. Some of the pent-up demand also was released through a gradual reduction of discriminatory import restrictions against the dollar area. Nevertheless, it is still true that a measure of suppressed demand for dollar products (and services) exists, as the continuance of discriminatory import and payment controls in may areas of the world demonstrates.

The continued existence of a suppressed demand for dollar goods has been used as evidence in support of the view that deep-seated forces of a structural nature are behind the large surpluses in the United States trade account, and that the dollar shortage is merely concealed.

---

[34] See on this: F. Machlup: Dollar Shortage and Disparities in the Growth of Productivity, Scottish Journal of Political Economy, October 1954, p. 250; also Werner Baer; Contemporary Views of the Dollar Problem in Public Policy, A Yearbook of the Graduate School of Public Administration, Harvard University (Cambridge, Mass., 1956).

But large surpluses in our balance of payments do not necessarily indicate the presence of such forces. We must again draw attention to the fact that our exports of goods and, to a lesser extent, of services, on the one hand, and several of the various dollar flow or financing items, on the other, are very closely intertwined. Given the far from adequate reserve position of many countries, it is apparent that a very sizable part of our merchandise exports occurs only because the financing is made available either on a grant basis, through Government loans, or in the form of direct investment by United States corporations equipping their subsidiaries abroad with machinery produced here. Take away the financing and the merchandise (and in some cases service) transaction would not occur. In other words, much of our current account surplus must be laid at the door of our aid and direct investment expenditures.

Our shipments financed by nonmilitary grant aid, much of it so-called defense support, are a case in point. In assessing the contribution made by this economic aid to our export surplus (and to our cash deficit) we really need an answer to the question to what extent foreign-aid recipients would have spent their own dollars for American merchandise in the absence of such aid.[35] No more than very rough guesses are possible in answer to this question.

In some cases, of course, it may be assumed that in the absence of aid grants the foreign country would have drawn on its own resources to acquire the commodities shipped on aid account. In such instances, our aid was actually not responsible for our export surpluses, but had the effect of adding to foreign dollar reserves or limiting a decline of such reserves. In the case of the dollar-poor countries of Asia, such as Korea and the former Indochinese states, to which an increasing proportion of our aid has been directed in recent years, it is clear that our aid was a prerequisite to our exports. In the absence of our aid grants, these countries would have had no choice but to do without the merchandise furnished by us as gifts and to make the necessary and probably painful internal adjustments as best they could. Moreover, there are many other instances, even in countries with more sizable dollar resources where some dollar grant-financed goods have been marginal, and been imported only because payment was not required. This may well be true of a part of our agricultural surplus sales against local currencies. In other cases, our exports have been accepted only because they were tied to other parts of an aid program.[36] A good example is provided by the transportation account on our balance of payments where our exports have benefited by the provision in our aid legislation that 50 percent of Government-financed cargoes be shipped on United States-flag ships.

The degree of interlinkage between capital exports and our merchandise exports is equally difficult to establish, but it is certainly very close. The tie-in between capital and merchandise movements is especially intimate with respect to much of our private direct investment abroad and long-term United States Government credits, which nearly always finance movements of United States merchandise. The rising importance, treated earlier, of capital equipment in our export trade is

[35] See on this Roy F. Harrod: Imbalance of International Payments, IMF Staff Papers, April 1953, p. 6.
[36] See Waltner Lederer: Foreign Aid and the United States Balance of Payments, Social Science, October 1954.

at least partly the result of this linkage. Again the loan recipients ordinarily would not have found the wherewithal to acquire United States goods. Export-Import Bank financing, for instance, has been the prerequisite of many a development project abroad and, in its absence, the shipment of equipment such as heavy machinery to the credit recipient would have not taken place. Similarly, our exports have benefited from direct investments by United States corporations that shipped equipment to their expanding subsidiaries abroad. Such capital transfers do not directly add to dollar holdings abroad. They are entirely reflected in our export account.

It is apparent that our export surplus is due in considerable measure to the special financing provided by aid and capital transfers. It is less clear to what extent this special financing by virtue of its "tied" nature has fostered the export of goods or services that foreigners would not otherwise have bought because of price considerations or because they simply preferred other goods. Some of this has undoubtedly occurred—notably in the case of shipping services already mentioned. Insofar as this has happened, the current account surplus recorded in the balance of payments overstates the surplus which the competitive position of the United States economy would have produced in the absence of the special ties. This overstatement, though it cannot be determined with any precision, may well have amounted to as much as several hundred million dollars annually. Perhaps at least as significant quantitatively has been the effect of special financing on the commodity composition of our exports. In other words, the pattern of shipments is undoubtedly different from that which would have occurred had the financing taken the form of placing freely disposable dollars in the hands of foreign countries. Our various agricultural export programs have doubtless moved more farm commodities than if grants and loans had been provided in equal amounts with their expenditure left entirely to the recipient. In the latter case our capital equipment exports might well have been higher, our agricultural exports somewhat lower.

These considerations lead to the conclusion that the magnitude of the residual dollar shortage is probably rather less than is commonly held because of the tied nature of commodity flows moving as a result of aid programs and our direct investments abroad. The continued existence of systematic discrimination abroad against dollar goods and services, however, stands as a reminder that foreign demand is not lacking for a broad range of American goods. The availability of financing (and reserve inadequacy in many lands) still limits the size of our export market although this is less serious now than a few years ago. To a considerable extent the remaining limitation is one self-imposed by the United States through the maintenance of substantial restrictions against the influx of foreign goods. In other words, foreign restrictions are in large part the counterpart of the barriers we man against foreign competition in our own markets. Our own measures, taken alone, also enlarge the dollar surplus through restricting foreign opportunities to earn through sales here. Even with the qualifications necessary because of the close relation between our exports and aid and capital transfers, it still appears, as argued in the preceding chapter, that exports are not too large but imports are too small.

*2. Aid and capital outflows and the cash deficit*

The close tie-in between capital and aid flows on the one hand and our merchandise and service exports on the other, explains why our surplus on goods and service accounts (excluding investment income) has been as large; it also helps to explain why our cash deficit has been only a fraction of these capital and aid flows. It remains nevertheless somewhat disquieting that throughout the period under review transfers to foreign countries on aid and capital account have been so far in excess of net transfers of gold and dollars to foreign countries. Actually, economic aid alone has been consistently in excess of foreign net gains here. And this has been the case despite the emergence in our service imports of huge military expenditures, an item in our balance of payments that in pre-World War II days was not even recorded. It thus appears that only a relatively small residual of the cash component of our aid and capital transfers has been retained by foreign countries as a group as an addition to their aggregate dollar holdings. The rest of the world as a whole has had to give its current needs for American goods and services precedence over the longer run need for larger international reserves.

A very large proportion of whatever cash transfers we make on aid and capital account is actually absorbed by retransfers to this country on investment-income account. As table VI shows our export surplus on this account is now so substantial that such income payments to this country constitute a major claim on foreign dollar earnings. During the 1949–55 period, our income from investments abroad—even excluding reinvested earnings—has consistently exceeded net outflows of private and Government capital. As a matter of fact, in 1956, United States dollar earnings on direct-investment account alone (as distinct from reinvested earnings of subsidiaries abroad) amounted to almost $2.2 billion. Income on other private investments and on private and Government loans brought total investment income in that year up to almost $2.7 billion. Actually, for some countries sizable proportions of their exports to this country represent shipments to United States corporations by their foreign subsidiaries with the result that a part of the proceeds are often retained by the parent companies as income or a return of capital from their investment. As a consequence the dollar accruals to certain countries derived from exports to this country are below our recorded import values.

It is also well to note that our net capital transfers to foreign countries have been reduced by the gradually increasing repayments of earlier long-term loans by the United States Government. In 1956, such repayments were close to $500 million against a $315 million annual average in the 1948–50 period. In several recent years repayments of long-term loans exceeded new loan disbursements, and such repayments now constitute an important charge against the dollar income of several foreign countries.

There is, of course, a large variety of payments by the United States that contributed to the rise of foreign dollar holdings; on capital account, mention should be made in particular of the amounts derived from the large-scale borrowing by Canadian provincial and municipal governments and also by Canadian corporations in the United States capital market. Such borrowing was particularly active in the period beginning in the summer of 1953 and ending in the spring of 1954 and has again become prominent since the beginning of 1956 as long-term interest rates in Canada rose even faster than in the United States. On the other hand, during several periods in 1954 and 1955, the differential between interest rates in the United States and Canadian capital markets was such that it was no longer advantageous for Canadians to float bonds in the United States capital market. On the contrary it became profitable for Canadians to repatriate bonds and debentures on a large scale. These developments point up the fact that an important sector of our portfolio capital outflow to Canada (which in turn plays a prominent role in our total investments in foreign stocks and bonds) is substantially affected by the relative ease or tightness in the two respective capital markets.

At the same time the experience in the 1953–54 period which was one of more pronounced recession in the United States than in Canada and elsewhere points up another potentially important trend in our payments pattern: In times of economic recession in the United States our capital exports tend to offset, to some extent at least, the effect of declining imports. In such periods foreigners find it profitable to take advantage of lower interest rates in our capital market and American investors become more desirous of putting their funds in markets where rates are more attractive—so long as political and financial conditions there are considered reasonably secure.

Apart from investments in Canadian fixed-interest paying securities, American investors have acquired substantial amounts of the securities issued by the World Bank. Beginning in 1954 several foreign governments, notably Belgium and Australia, were successful in floating bonds in this market.

Throughout the fifties, United States residents have also invested almost continuously and increasingly in Canadian shares. Since 1954, much of this capital outflow has been due to the tax advantages derived by United States investors from investing in diversified mutual investment funds in Canada, the shares of which were distributed solely in this country. Inasmuch as these funds pay no dividends, tax becomes due only on any capital gains at the time of sale. Moreover, in Canada profits to non-resident-owned investment corporations are subject to a tax of only 15 percent.

Other portfolio investments have been sporadic and have consisted mainly of purchases of Dutch and British securities. Especially in 1954, a lively interest of American investors in Dutch-owned and issued shares added substantially to the dollar availabilities of the Netherlands. A similar upsurge occurred in 1955 in the buying of the shares of prominent British corporations, but since then United States interest in European shares, though larger than in earlier postwar years, has been modest.

Apart from these portfolio investments there have also been certain types of direct investments that have substantially benefited the dollar availabilities of foreign countries, quite apart from the many indirect benefits to the dollar-earning capacities associated with such investments abroad. Among the payments that particularly added to foreign dollar assets were the payments by the United States petroleum industry for exploration rights in Venezuela and those reflecting investments in manufacturing industries in Europe and elsewhere.

There is another type of capital movements that has played a prominent role in our payments pattern in recent years and yet is not clearly evident in our balance of payments statements. These are speculative and clandestine capital movements. The former take largely the form of changes in terms of payments in ordinary commercial transactions, the so-called leads and lags, motivated primarily by the desire to profit from anticipated changes in exchange rates. For instance, to take advantage of an appreciation of the currency in which their export bills are denominated, exporters may attempt to defer collection of their outstanding bills, sell on credit rather than against cash or at longer credit terms than previously. While leads and lags are usually self-correcting in time, they have in various periods been exceedingly important, especially for the British dollar position. This was notably true in the period preceding the 1949 devaluation and again in the summer of 1951 and winter of 1956–57 when the sterling area's gold and dollar pool lost substantial amounts of dollars.

Another matter is flight movements of capital, largely those of an illicit nature. To some extent, the trend of these movements is reflected in the "Errors and omissions" item in our balance-of-payments statements which, as shown in table VI, has recorded, on the average, very large credit residuals throughout the period under review here. In times of international tension or financial stress, residents of the countries concerned attempt by various means to transfer funds to American nominees, which the latter then hold for their account. Such transfers are frequently made in a manner that gives rise to a credit residual in our balance of payments. The "Errors and omissions" item reflects, of course, also genuine errors in the computation, or omissions in the reporting, of various items in our balance of payments.[37] But there is little doubt that the acquisition of dollars by foreigners has been larger than shown in table VI and that some of these transfers are concealed in the "Errors and omissions" item in the table.

Apart from capital movements, foreign countries' dollar holdings have benefited also by those aid grants that either took the form of actual cash transfers or of exports of goods or services which the recipient countries would otherwise have acquired out of their own resources. As to actual cash transfers, mention should be made of the fact that in the early years of the Marshall plan a relatively substantial amount of our aid dollars were made available for procurement of goods in third countries; subsequently a very definite trend emerged toward procurement in the United States of Marshall-plan-financed commodities. Our initial capital contribution to the European Payments Union is another instance of dollar cash transfers, and so are the special payments to Turkey, Greece, and other countries to cover their EPU deficits; in more recent years, especially in 1954 and 1955, approximately $1 billion of economic aid took the form of cash payments to several governments in support of their military budgets. Most of these funds went to France to defray costs incurred earlier in the war in Indochina and were of great benefit to that country's dollar position.

[37] See on this Arthur I. Bloomfield: Speculative and Flight Movements of Capital in Postwar International Finance, Princeton Studies in International Finance No. 3 (Princeton, 1954).

*3. The special role of military expenditures*

Among the contributing factors to dollar acquisitions of foreign countries, our so-called military expenditures abroad have been of crucial importance to foreign countries as mentioned before. Military expenditures have, in fact, become one of the most important components in the United States balance of payments. Such spending reflects purchases abroad by the Defense Department under the mutual-security program for transfer to either the producing or third countries; purchases primarily by the United States Army and Air Force for their own operations abroad, such as foods and fuels; purchases for the North Atlantic Treaty Organization construction program; disbursements for services such as transportation and construction of troop housing; and finally, local spending of United States troops and their families stationed in foreign countries. These expenditures are shown as a service item in our balance of payments, but a very sizable part of these payments are of a noncommercial nature in the sense that on the whole they are not motivated by price and cost advantages over United States-produced supplies; they are closely linked to our military-aid activities abroad or the presence of our Armed Forces in foreign countries.

For several countries, these expenditures have made the difference between dollar affluence and penury. Unlike most of our economic aid and a large part of our capital flows to foreign countries, such spending contributes directly to the dollar availabilities of foreign countries. It is true, of course, that military expenditures absorb foreign resources that otherwise would have been available for export or for internal investment and consumption. Yet, in actual practice, such resources could only to a limited extent have been utilized for producing dollar-earning exports or dollar-saving import substitutes. As has been pointed out [38]—

> a large part of these overseas military expenditures are for use of land or buildings for the services of public utilities or for construction which could hardly be exported * * *

Similar considerations apply to local expenditures of American troops abroad.

B. THE MAGNITUDE AND CHARACTERISTICS OF FOREIGN DOLLAR GAINS

Despite the preference the rest of the world has shown in the postwar period for goods rather than gold, foreign countries have nevertheless built up their reserves substantially in recent years. After drawing heavily on their reserves to finance needed imports in the immediate postwar years, foreign countries (excluding international institutions) added some $11.5 billion to their gold and dollar assets over the 1948–56 period through their transactions with the United States.

Through most of the last decade, our balance of payments pattern accommodated not only a very sizable increase in the monetary reserves of foreign countries, but also permitted fairly large increases in the private foreign holdings of short-term dollar balances and United States stocks and bonds. As the following table reveals, fully 60 percent of the dollars transferred to foreign countries during the

[38] United Nations, World Economic Survey, 1955, p. 75.

period 1948–56 ended up in the monetary reserves of foreign countries, including the gold acquired from the United States Treasury. As the dollar holdings of monetary authorities expanded, foreign exchange controllers became increasingly willing not only to lift many of their restrictions on imports from the dollar area, but also to permit the banking and business community to retain some of their dollar acquisitions for the purpose of adding to their working balances and making longer term investments in the United States. The table reveals that traders and other dollar recipients surrendered a decreasing proportion of their dollar accruals to the monetary authorities. Actually in the 1954–56 period almost 50 percent of foreign dollar gains served to increase operating balances and long-term investment holdings of nonofficial institutions.

*Impact of United States international transactions on foreign gold and dollar assets (excluding international institutions)*

| | Gold purchases from U. S Treasury | Increases in short-term dollar assets [1] | | Net purchases, U. S. Treasury notes and bonds | Direct and portfolio investments [2] | Grand total |
|---|---|---|---|---|---|---|
| | | Official | Other | | | |
| 1948–50 | 22 | 1,788 | 479 | [3] 835 | 3 | 3,127 |
| 1951–53 | 695 | 2,047 | 856 | −471 | 513 | 3,640 |
| 1954–56 | 316 | 2,365 | 1,086 | 298 | 1,067 | 5,132 |
| Total | 1,033 | 6,200 | 2,421 | 622 | 1,583 | 11,899 |

[1] In United States banks only.
[2] Other than U. S. Treasury notes and bonds, except for 1948 and 1949.
[3] 1950 only.

The very sizable flow of dollars to the rest of the free world has by no means solved the problem of international reserve adequacy. At close to $30 billion, foreign gold and dollar reserves as a whole are probably adequate in the light of the requirements of foreign countries for the balancing and settling of their international transactions, though this proposition is disputed by some authorities. But international monetary reserves can handly be said to be distributed in relation to needs. For instance, the sterling area's gold and dollar pool, with holdings of no more than about $2.3 billion, is generally regarded as inadequate, considering the key role of the area in the world's trade and payments picture. The gold and dollar reserves of several countries in continental Europe, in Southeastern Asia and Latin America are close to, and in some important cases below, what are generally considered minimum working levels. A very sizable proportion of recent reserve gains has gone into the holdings of countries such as Western Germany, Switzerland, Venezuela, and Canada that already have ample reserves.

The continuing maldistribution of international monetary reserves is a fact of great significance for the international economy. It means that a large number of countries remain ill prepared to weather economic storms that hit their dollar position. Moreover, it means that many countries must take immediate measures to cut down their purchases in this country in case of a sharp contraction of their dollar earnings. Of course, the international distribution of dollar reserves among individual countries is determined not only by the transactions of each country with the United States but also by the transactions among third countries. There are numerous cases where foreign countries have been recipients of very large amounts of dollar aid from the United States and yet lost all or most of these funds to third countries. No amount of aid or favorable trade and financial treatment by the United States of a specific country can by itself correct a tendency of that country to lose its dollar receipts to third countries.

### C. PROSPECTIVE DEVELOPMENTS

*1. The short-run outlook*

The preceding discussion has distinct implications for the future of our balance of payments. To the extent that in the absence of much of our aid and capital outflows, foreign countries would have simply done without the goods that these outflows financed, any reduction in such flows in future years does not necessarily mean a one-for-one cut in foreign dollar earnings. It would, therefore, be misleading to project on the basis of shifts in such flows an equivalent change in foreign dollar holdings and to disregard the effect of such shifts on our export surplus.

At the same time, the fact that aid, capital outflows, and military expenditures have for many years exceeded by a very considerable margin the annual rate of the foreign gold and dollar buildup arising from transactions with the United States points up the fact that the relative dollar affluence of the free world as a whole rests on a rather precarious basis. Assume a stabilization of military expenditures at a somewhat lower level as a result of a sharp reduction of our military commitments abroad, a tendency to go slow with respect to the NATO buildup, further slashes in our economic aid, especially those involving cash payments, and an interest-rate pattern unfavorable to foreign borrowing, and the prospects of the rest of the world for further dollar gains would look poor, indeed.

Little can be said with any assurance about whether such assumptions are at all realistic. Flows of military expenditures and economic aid are essentially items of a political nature on which the economist can hardly say more than what he would like to happen. Much will depend on unpredictable political constellations. But there are some indications that the United States will be forced to continue concerted efforts to strengthen weak economies in countries which either serve as strategic outposts in our struggle to halt the spread of communism or are under the threat of political and economic penetration by Soviet Russia and Communist China. "Extraordinary" has perhaps become the wrong word for a large part of these aid expenditures. Also, so long as the United States Government continues to maintain large military bases in many areas of the world and draws on the economies of these areas for a variety of supplies, and so long as it continues to provide the military forces of foreign countries with armaments, large-scale military expenditures abroad are likely to continue.

One factor of some consequence for the future may well be that international trade in recent years has been strongly influenced by temporary bottlenecks. As domestic capacities, especially in Europe but also in the United States, became fully employed, buyers were forced to turn to foreign sources of supply. In some areas of our own economy, but also in European economies, these bottlenecks may gradually be eliminated. Consequently, Europe's need for American materials and United States demand for European and perhaps Japanese raw materials and finished manufactures may gradually fall back from their present heights.

Concern over payments developments unfavorable to foreign countries has recently gained in strength, largely as the result of the onset of the Suez crisis last fall (but only in part attributable to this crisis). The growing concern has, in turn, rapidly affected adversely the dollar position of numerous countries. Despite drawings on the resources of the International Monetary Fund of $1,159 million, the rest of the world's estimated gold and dollar holdings rose by only about $80 million during the period October 1956 to June 1957. If we deduct the gains of three countries, Germany, Venezuela, and Canada that are well provided with reserves, there would have been a loss of approximately $1.4 billion over and above the increase in liabilities to the International Monetary Fund.

At the time of writing (early August 1957), the decline in foreign dollar availabilities seems to have stopped and the international transactions of the world with the United States appear to be in approximate balance. Of course it is too early to say whether the sizable dollar losses of foreign countries during the winter and spring of 1956–57 were only a temporary phenomenon or foreshadow a definite end to the buildup of foreign gold and dollar holdings. So far as the grand aggregate of foreign holdings is concerned, it is probable that the course over the next few years depends somewhat more upon decisions to be taken in the United States and upon the behavior of our economy, than upon any likelihood of major new developments in the rest of the world—always barring war or major international disturbances. So far as the further redistribution of this grand aggregate among foreign countries is concerned, that is likely to depend primarily upon the domestic performance of the countries themselves, and only secondarily on the nature and direction of steps taken on United States initiative.

*2. Long-term prospects*

It is, of course, impossible to hazard more than some very tentative guesses of the payments pattern of the rest of the world in the longer run. Few of the economic forces operating on our balance of payments are susceptible to precise predictive assessment. One can do little more than discuss some trends that promise to hold. Turning to widely held views of the economic profession, one finds a broad range of views on the future as might well be expected. If it is true that the United States owes its export surplus to our economic predominance, superior competitive strength, our ability quickly to make use of the latest technological developments in our industrial production, then prospects for a lasting and fundamental solution of the world dollar position are decidedly poor. In all likelihood, the United States, owing to its relatively huge research expenditures will continue to spurt ahead in the field of technological innovation.

However, the contention that the great economic strength of the United States must result in a large export surplus in our balance of payments is not universally held by any means. There is much respectable opinion which holds that a more rapid growth in productivity in the United States than elsewhere is unlikely to produce an export surplus here, because—disregarding theoretical refinements—a rise in productivity should be reflected in real income increases which in turn would result in a larger demand for imports and thus in an improvement of the payments position of the rest of the world.[39] And some economists—on the basis of detailed case studies—even deny that productivity in the United States has in the last few decades advanced more rapidly than in other major industrial nations.[40]

In this connection the formation of the European common market and governmental discussion of an associated free trade area must be viewed as an effort to reduce the obstacles to higher productivity and economic growth currently imposed by trade restrictions. The reduction of trade barriers within these regions should lead to greater productive efficiency of European industry in the absence of private arrangements to the contrary. Although in time this could well increase the effectiveness of European competition with American business in third country markets, and, to a lesser extent, in the United States, this country's exports to Europe appear likely to benefit over the long run without being materially impaired over the near term. There may be some shifts in the composition of our exports as a result of the new institutional arrangements but the overall impact appears likely to be small since, as has already been noted, such a large part of our European sales consist of raw materials and foodstuffs which are supplemental in character. The finished manufactures most likely to be affected by tariff changes are already excluded by present barriers to a considerable extent. The evolution of the common market will take place so gradually that the American economy should have little difficulty in adjusting to the new situation as it develops.

Professor Machlup of Johns Hopkins University ventures the opinion that the dollar shortage of nations whose economic circumstances are improving must be attributed to their economic policies rather than to structural elements such as a slower rate of productivity increase than in the United States.[41] Whether economic policies of the rest of the world tend to be favorable to international financial balance remains to be seen. It is only too evident that many governments prefer, for reasons that should not be condemned out of hand, to lose reserves and perhaps adopt discriminatory import restrictions rather than to frustrate or resist economic, social, and political pressures in the direction of rapid economic growth. In other words, the economic environment in which many governments operate today is not conducive to making large temporary sacrifices in terms of employment and real income in favor of maintaining, not to mention building up, gold and dollar reserves. On the contrary this environment with its strong bias toward higher price and wage levels, as well as toward the acceleration of economic growth, makes it extremely

[39] See on this E. M. Bernstein: American Productivity and the Dollar Payments Problem, The Review of Economics and Statistics, May 1955. Also Svend Laursen: Productivity, Wages, and the Balance of Payments, The Review of Economics and Statistics, May 1955.

[40] See G. D. A. MacDougall, Does Productivity Rise Faster in the United States? The Review of Economics and Statistics, May 1956.

[41] See F. Machlup, op. cit.

difficult to maintain internal and external balance in any of the developing economies.

At the same time, there is a great deal of evidence available that effective use of monetary and fiscal policy measures in a favorable external economic climate can succeed in converting dollar deficits into dollar surpluses. This is what has happened in past years quite frequently, and it would be overly pessimistic to argue that we will not witness similar achievements in future years. The formidable task ahead for many governments may be illustrated by the recent estimate of the Organization for European Economic Cooperation, that its member countries must within a few years increase their exports to the dollar area by 40 percent—from $3.8 billion in 1955 to $5.4 billion in 1960 for their current payments with the dollar area to be just in balance.[42]

In the long run, hope that the world will earn enough dollars to pay for its needs must rest on the capacity and willingness of the American economy to absorb substantially larger amounts of goods and services than it does now. Prospects are that our domestic raw material resources will prove increasingly inadequate to cover the needs of an expanding United States industry. This means in the first place that very sizable investments abroad will be required to assure an adequate flow of foreign-produced materials. A large part of these investments can only come from the United States, thereby giving some assurance that capital flows will continue to provide exports that would not otherwise be available to foreign economies. As has already been discussed in the preceding chapter, our growing raw material demands will also gradually expand our exports. Further technological advances may slow down this development but it still appears likely to provide an impressive increase in the flow of dollars made available to foreign suppliers.

The future course of our imports of foodstuffs and manufactured goods promises to depend as much on United States Government policies on trade, tariffs, and agriculture as on the continued growth of the domestic economy. Other things equal, rising consumer incomes here are most likely to generate a continually rising volume of imports. But as has already been noted, it is in this area that this country maintains substantial, though not always prohibitive, barriers to the entry of foreign goods.[43] The actions taken, or not taken, in these policy fields will exert considerable influence in the determination of whether our foreign trade will be balanced at the high level consistent with the most productive use of our resources or at a lower level imposed by the curtailment of dollar availabilities.

---

[42] Organization for European Economic Cooperation, Europe Today and in 1960, II (Paris, 1957), p. 120.

[43] On these points it is worth repeating the findings of a study of the Federal Reserve Bank of New York that United States imports of finished manufactures have been responsive both to advances in real income here and to competitive pricing by foreign suppliers. See Adler Schlesinger, and Van Westerborg, op. cit., pp. 48–49.

# IV

# RECENT DEVELOPMENTS IN THE FOREIGN-TRADE POLICIES OF FOREIGN COUNTRIES IN RELATION TO THE UNITED STATES POLICY

# ANALYSIS OF THE EUROPEAN COMMON-MARKET TREATY AND FREE-TRADE-AREA ARRANGEMENT

United States Department of State

## I. BACKGROUND ON UNITED STATES POLICY REGARDING WESTERN EUROPEAN INTEGRATION

Before World War I Western Europe enjoyed a degree of effective economic coordination despite the large number of separate nations, the diversity of languages, the existence of tariffs with divergent rates, and restrictions on the movement of labor. The international gold standard was nearly universal, quantitative restrictions on trade were few and limited, governmental controls were almost negligible, and there was considerable mobility of capital and business enterprise. Many of the benefits resultant from the absence of controls on trade before 1914 were lost through two world wars and the intervening worldwide depression. At the end of World War II, the world was faced with widespread government controls in the economic sphere, nationally managed monetary systems, a wide prevalence of quantitative restrictions on trade, and a multiplicity of bilateral arrangements.

The general breakdown of the prewar European system in the aftermath of World War II left Europe facing four major problems which leading European statesmen felt could be solved only through unification. These were: (1) How to revive their economies from near collapse, which many attributed not solely to wartime destruction and disruption but also to the stifling effects of narrow markets and rigidly protectionist systems; (2) how to cope with the growing Soviet threat, political and military; (3) how to reintegrate Germany into the European community; and (4) how to find a new basis for restoring Europe to a position of strength. The resulting urge for unification expressed itself in various political, military, and economic moves.

Since 1948 progress in European economic cooperation and integration has been made chiefly through several international organizations: (1) the Organization for European Economic Cooperation (OEEC) and its associated agencies, notably the European Payments Union (EPU) and the European Productivity Agency (EPA); (2) Benelux, the customs union of Belgium, Luxembourg, and the Netherlands, which is seeking to evolve into a full economic union; and (3) the European Coal and Steel Community (CSC), in which Benelux, France, Germany, and Italy are developing a common market in coal, iron, and steel.

### *United States policy*

Since early in the postwar period, the United States Government has encouraged and supported moves toward European integration, bearing in mind that the basic initiatives must come from Europeans themselves. This policy has been based on three main convictions:

(1) That the creation of a new political, economic, and military unit in Western Europe, in alliance with the United States, would contribute decisively to the political cohesion and the economic and military strength of the Atlantic community as a whole;

(2) That the development of common institutions and economic solidarity between Germany and her Western European neighbors would provide an organic basis for attenuating former national rivalries and promoting Franco-German friendship and cooperation;

(3) That the creation of a broad competitive market in Western Europe would build up the economic strength and health of the area as a whole and thus help to remove a major obstacle to development of a multilateral trading system with convertible currencies among the nations of the free world.

The first clear statements of United States policy in this connection came when Secretary Marshall boldly proposed large-scale United States aid to assist European recovery. In a letter to Senator Vandenberg in June 1947, Secretary Marshall stated that—

> the United States welcomes any initiative * * * by the peoples of Europe * * * to insure greater economic cooperation among themselves, to expedite the reconstruction and recovery of the European economy as a whole * * *.

In the first Foreign Assistance Act the Congress declared it to be United States policy to—

> encourage these countries through a joint organization to exert sustained common efforts * * * which will speedily achieve that economic cooperation in Europe which is essential for lasting peace and prosperity * * *

Subsequent steps in trade liberalization and the creation of the EPU were welcomed. In October 1949, ECA Administrator Paul Hoffman, in a speech to the OEEC Council, explicitly offered United States support to European efforts to create a broad single market as a means to restore Europe's standard of living and its competitive position in the world. In addition, the United States greeted as an act of constructive statesmanship the Schuman proposal of May 1950 for the formation of the European Coal-Steel Community.

The Congress has strongly confirmed executive branch support to European integration. This has been most clearly expressed in a section of the annual Mutual Security Act, first inserted in congressional initiative in 1952 and repeated with variations in all subsequent years. This section now reads in part:

> The Congress * * * reaffirms its belief in the necessity of further efforts toward political federation, military integration and economic unification as a means of building strength, establishing security and preserving peace in the North Atlantic area * * *. This act should be so administered as to support concrete measures to promote greater political federation * * * and economic unification in Europe.

Secretary Dulles in December 1955 reaffirmed the hope that the Europeans would go ahead with unity plans; and President Eisenhower stated in a speech at Miami on October 29, 1956:

> Nothing has been more heartening than the recent announcement of two proposals (for a common market and a free-trade area) that would advance further the economic integration of Europe * * *. We shall watch these exciting new developments with the keenest interest. Because, my friends, as Europe grows stronger economically we gain in every way * * *.

In a joint declaration issued in May 1957 by President Eisenhower and Chancellor Adenauer at the conclusion of the German Chancellor's official visit to Washington, gratification was expressed over the significant progress made toward closer economic integration in Europe. Further—

* * * The President expressed the great interest of the United States Government and of the American people in these treaties (European Common Market and Euratom) and his belief that their entry into force will benefit not only the people of Europe, but those of the entire world.

## II. THE EUROPEAN COMMON MARKET

### *Background*

The foreign ministers of the six CSC countries (France, Germany, Belgium, Italy, Luxembourg, and the Netherlands) met at Messina, Sicily, in June 1955 where they accepted the premise that closer political inntegration was a desirable and necessary goal and that political integration could only be achieved concurrently with or following economic integration.

Following a long study by an integovernmental committee, the foreign ministers of the six countries at a meeting in Venice, Italy, May 1956, authorized the drafting of the Euratom and Common Market Treaties. Two groups or experts, working under the general direction of Belgian Foreign Minister Spaak, began work on the treaties on June 26, in Brussels. On March 25, 1957, the treaty establishing the European Economic Community (and a separate treaty for Euratom was signed at Rome by representatives of the six and is now before the various parliaments for ratification.

### *Outline of the treaty*[1]

The proposed European Economic Community creates a customs union among the six countries. Under the terms of the treaty establishing the community, the member states would progressively eliminate tariffs and quantitative restrictions on trade among themselves and would establish a common tariff and commercial policy toward nonmember countries.

The treaty also provides for the elimination of restrictions on the movement of labor and capital among member states, the progressive harmonization of their labor and other social legislation affecting competition among them, the prohibition of restrictive business practices which adversely affect trade among the member states, and the establishment of common institutions designed to achieve the attainment of the treaty objectives. It also provides for the establishment of a fund to facilitate adjustments by labor to the removal of restrictions on trade among the member states and for the creation of an investment bank responsible for financing economic projects within the community which fulfill criteria set forth in the treaty.

A convention annexed to the treaty provides for the economic development, through a special fund, of the dependent overseas territories of the member states of the common market, and for the association of specified overseas countries and territories with the common market.

(*a*) *Tariffs.*—The treaty requires the gradual reduction among the member states of all customs duties and similar charges and their elimi-

[1] A copy of the treaty is attached.

nation by the end of the transition period. As provided in article 8 of the treaty the transition period is to last for 12 years but may be extended to a maximum of 15 years. A definite plan and schedule for the elimination of these duties during the first 2 stages (each stage would be for 4 years with the possible extension of the first stage) is contained in the treaty. The reductions that would still have to be made in the last stage would be made in accordance with a schedule to be agreed upon by the Council of Ministers on the basis of proposals made by the European Commission.

The treaty provides for the establishment of a common external tariff by the member states on imports from outside countries. In the treaty, the Messina countries express their willingness to contribute to the development of international trade and to the reduction of trade barriers through the conclusion of agreements based on reciprocity and mutual advantages. They also declare themselves ready to contribute to the reduction of tariffs below the level they may establish by virtue of the creation of their customs union.

The common external tariff will be derived from a calculation based on the arithmetic average of the duties of the member states. This principle would apply to both agricultural and industrial products. However, the treaty provides for certain exceptions to this general rule.

(*b*) *Quantitative restrictions.*—The treaty provides for the elimination of quantitative restrictions on imports from member states by the end of the transition period. Provision is also made for the prompt conversion of bilateral quotas for imports from member states into so-called global quotas applicable to the trade of all of the members and for annual increases in the quotas. It is estimated that the annual increase in such quotas would result for all practical purposes in the de facto liberalization of most of these products by the end of 10 years. The treaty does not specifically cover the treatment of quantitative restrictions imposed on imports from nonmembers. However, in the preamble to the treaty and in article 110 there is a general expression of desire to contribute to the removal of restrictions on international trade.

To meet problems created by the balance-of-payments difficulties of a member country, the treaty provides for various forms of mutual assistance to that country, including concerted action by the member states in other international organizations, the granting of limited credits to the country in difficulty, and the establishment of transshipment controls when a country in difficulty "* * * maintains or restores quantitative restrictions with respect to third countries."

The treaty does not specify that quantitative restrictions may be imposed by the member state on imports from the other member states in order to solve or to assist in solving its payment problems. However, the European Commission is authorized to grant the member in difficulty the benefit of a conditional escape clause if the mutual assistance measures are not granted by the Council of Ministers or are insufficient. This authorization may be revoked or its conditions modified by the Council acting on the basis of a qualified majority vote.

In the event of a sudden crisis in its balance-of-payments position in which the Council has not been able to act immediately regarding the mutual assistance measures envisaged by the treaty, the member state in difficulties can impose the controls necessary to safeguard its position. These controls are to be no more than necessary to meet the problem. The Council, acting on the recommendations of the European Commission and after consultations with the Monetary Committee, may by a qualified majority vote decide that the interested state must modify, suspend, or eliminate the controls it established.

The treaty also provides for the establishment of a common commercial policy by the end of the transitional period. In accordance with this objective, the member states agree to seek—

* * * as high a degree of uniformity as possible in their liberalization lists in respect of third countries or groups of third countries.

(c) *Agriculture.*—The treaty provides for the inclusion of agriculture and trade in agricultural products in the common market and for the establishment of a common agricultural policy by the member states. The purposes of the common agricultural policy as set forth in the treaty are to ensure the farm population an equitable standard of living, to stabilize the market, to guarantee sources of supply, to ensure reasonable prices for consumers, and to improve the productivity and national development of agricultural production.

The social structure of agriculture and the structural and national inequalities among the different agricultural areas lead to special provisions for the accommodation of agriculture within the common market arrangement. The treaty, however, provides various measures intended to expand the volume of trade between member states. The problem of adjustment for the farm populations is confined to the transition period; the common agricultural policy must be developed by the end of this period. In the interim, to aid the problem of adjustment, the treaty provides for:

(1) Each state would have the right to establish nondiscriminatory minimum prices for imports of certain agricultural commodities and to suspend temporarily or to reduce imports of these commodities from member countries when offered at prices below the fixed minimum. These minimum prices would eventually be formulated on the basis of common criteria. At the end of the transition period a survey would be made of the minimum prices still in effect. The Council, acting on recommendations by the Eureopean Commission, would then establish within the framework of the common agricultural policy the regime to be applied. Thus, prior agreement would have to be reached on the establishment of a common market organization for agriculture. The treaty specified that this common organization is to assume any of the following forms, depending on the product: common rules with respect to competition, compulsory coordination of the various national marketing systems, or a European marketing organization.

(2) Until the national agricultural systems are replaced by any one of the arrangements for a common agricultural policy listed above, the development of agricultural trade among the member states may be assured for some products by the conclusion of long-term multilateral agreements and purchase contracts. These contracts are to be freely negotiated in accordance with certain guidelines laid down in the treaty. In negotiating the quantities covered by the

contracts the trade between the member states in the commodities concerned during the 3 years preceding the entry into force of the treaty is to be taken into account. Provision is to be made for an increase in the quantities "* * * in accordance with the existing needs, *account being taken of traditional trade patterns*" (italic added). The member states are to use all means available to them under their laws, "particularly as regards import policy" to ensure the implementation of the contracts. The prices charged under such agreements are progressively to approach those paid to the domestic producers of the importing country.

(3) If one member country has a national market organization or internal regulations relating to a domestic agricultural commodity which adversely affects the competitive position of a similar commodity in another member country, the other states will impose a special compensatory tax on imports of the commodity concerned from the country maintaining the regulations in question or employ other measures fixed by the European Commission to correct the distortion.

(*d*) *Institutions.*—The responsibility for carrying out the provisions of the treaty would rest to an important extent with a set of common institutions similar to those of the European Coal and Steel Community. These are the Assembly, the Court of Justice, the Council of Ministers, and the Commission.

The Assembly will be composed of representatives of the peoples of the states forming the community. They will be appointed by the parliaments of the six from among their own members.

The Court of Justice will be composed of seven judges and will be concerned with interpreting the treaty. It will review the legality of the decisions of the Council and Commission and give judgment on appeals lodged by a member state.

The Council of Ministers will consist of six members, appointed by each member state and representing the government of the member state. The Council will be responsible for coordinating the general economic policies of member states and will make the major policy decisions of the community.

Except where the treaty provides otherwise, Council decisions are to be taken on the basis of a simple majority vote, i. e., 4 out of 6. When the Council decisions require a qualified majority vote (12 out of 17), the following weighted system of voting is to be employed:

| Country: | Number of votes |
|---|---|
| Germany | 4 |
| Belgium | 2 |
| France | 4 |
| Italy | 4 |
| Luxembourg | 1 |
| Netherlands | 2 |

The Commission will be independent of national governments and would have the day-to-day executive and regulatory responsibilities involved in the functioning of the community. The Commission will be composed of nine members selected for their general competence. In exercising their responsibilities, the members of the Commission would be required to act in the interests of the community as a whole.

During the early period, the Commission's authority would rest to an important extent on the power of initiative assigned to it by the treaty. As the transition period progressed from one stage to the next, the voting arrangements of the Council would make it increasingly difficult for any one state or small minority to block measures looking toward full realization of of the treaty objectives. The relative power of the European Commission, responsible for acting in the general interest, would correspondingly increase. In numerous situations the Council will not be able to act except on the basis of proposals formulated by the European Commission. For example, it is the Commission which will be responsible for formulating recommendations on which the Council will act with respect to the establishment of a common agricultural policy. The Commission will also be responsible for proposing measures to the Council for the coordination of the commercial policies of the member states. Similarly, the Commission will have the right to make proposals for the coordination of the social legislation of the member states and for the elimination of the distortions in competition caused by disparities in legislation and regulations.

The Commission will also supervise the rules designed to assure competition within the common market and may also authorize states to take countermeasures against infractions of the rules, although the authority to remedy the infractions will remain vested in the individual states.

Thus, through the activities of the Commission, the Community increasingly would assume an identity of its own, distinct from that of the nation-states belonging to it. This trend is expected to be accentuated by the provision of the treaty making it impossible for the Council to amend proposals advanced by the Commission under the treaty unless it acts unanimously. Thus, the Council will be under considerable pressure to adopt a Community point of view as represented by the Commission, unless it could agree unanimously on an alternative proposal.

(e) *Movement of capital.*—Provisions are also included in the treaty looking toward the progressive abolition by the member states of restrictions on movements of capital among themselves. By the end of the first stage, at the latest, all restrictions are to be eliminated on current payments connected with the movement of capital, for example, dividends, and interest. The European Commission may suggest to the Council of Ministers measures for the progressive coordination of their exchange policy affecting the movement of capital between the member states and third countries. On such matters the rulings of the Council will require a unanimous vote.

The member states also have agreed not to introduce any new exchange restrictions within the community on movements of capital and on current payments relating to such movements or to intensify the existing regulations. There is also a provision in the treaty permitting exceptions to the rule for the liberalization of capital movements when such liberalization causes serious disturbances in the capital market of a member state.

(f) *Movement of labor.*—Measures which would make possible the free movement of labor are to be formulated by the European Commission. The Commission is to concern itself not only with close cooperation among the national labor agencies but also with the machinery necessary to facilitate the balance of labor supply and demand within the community.

During the transition period all obstacles to the free movement of labor are to be eliminated. In the final stage, the free movement of labor shall include the right of workers to accept any employment which is actually offered without discrimination as to nationality and with due regard where appropriate to the machinery established by the Council of Ministers.

Each of the member states is bound by the treaty not to introduce new restrictions on the exercise of professions within its borders by nationals of other member states. During the first 2 years of the transition period the Commission is to recommend to the Council a general program for the elimination of the existing restrictions within the common market on the exercise of professions. Before the end of the first stage of the transition period the Council is to take action on this program after having consulted the Assembly. The exercise of certain professions within the common market will continue to be subject to the national legislation establishing the qualifications of persons desiring to enter those fields. Legislation and national regulations in the individual member states which regulate the exercise of these professions are to be coordinated at the latest by the end of the transition period.

(*g*) *European Investment Bank.*—The treaty provides for the establishment of a European Investment Bank which will be concerned with financing projects within the six countries for the development of underdeveloped regions, for the modernization or conversion of industries as necessitated by the progressive establishment of the European common market, and for the financing of projects of interest to more than one country which cannot be financed in any other way. The loans may be made either to the member states or to private or public enterprises of the community. The overall total of the bank's loans and guaranties may not exceed 250 percent of its subscribed capital.

The bank's capital will be 1 billion units of account equal to $1 billion. The subscriptions by the member states would be as follows:

| Country: | *Subscription (millions of units of account)* |
|---|---|
| Germany | 300 |
| France | 300 |
| Italy | 240 |
| Belgium | 86.5 |
| Netherlands | 71.5 |
| Luxembourg | 2 |

The treaty provides that each member state will pay in 25 percent of its subscription in regular installments over the first 2½ years. One-quarter of the payments shall consist of gold or convertible currencies and three-quarters shall consist of the national currency of the state. The bank may call for the subscription of the remaining 75 percent as required. The bank will normally meet its borrowing needs on the private capital market.

The Board of Directors of the bank will consist of 12 members: 3 each from Germany, France, and Italy; 2 from Benelux; and 1 from the European Commission. The Board will also consist of 12 alternates. Each director will have one vote. Except where otherwise provided for in the treaty, the Board of Directors will act on the basis of a simple majority. A qualified majority shall consist of eight votes.

(*h*) *European social fund.*—The treaty provides for the establishment of a fund to facilitate the geographical and professional mobility of labor within the community. The amount of the fund is to be provided for in the annual budget of the community. Contributions to the fund are to be made in accordance with the following scale of percentages:

| Country: | *Percentage contribution* |
|---|---|
| Germany | 32.0 |
| Belgium | 8.8 |
| France | 32.0 |
| Italy | 20.0 |
| Luxembourg | .2 |
| Netherlands | 7.0 |
| Total | 100.0 |

The utilization of this fund will require a qualified majority of 67 out of 100 votes. The votes by the 6 countries will be the same as their percentage contributions, except that Belgium will have 8 votes and Luxembourg will have 1.

The fund will be used to cover on a matching basis 50 percent of the expenses of a member state incurred in order to retain and resettle workers and to pay workers temporarily unemployed or on short time because of the conversion of a plant to other production. The payments in each case will be based on evidence that the difficulties of the worker concerned stem from an adjustment arising out of the development of the community.

After the transition period the Council will decide by a majority vote whether part or all of the above assistance should be eliminated and will decide by unanimity whether new activities should be assigned to the fund.

(*i*) *Coordination of social legislation.*—The treaty provides for the member states to cooperate "closely and continuously" in carrying out the coordination of their respective social and economic policies and the alinement of their legislative and administrative arrangements to the extent necessary for the progressive development of the common market.

The treaty provides for such matters as the equalization of wages of men and women for the same types of work, for assuring that social-security benefits will be cumulative regardless of the country in which the work is performed, and for the encouragement of the exchange of young workers through a European program.

(*j*) *Restrictive business practices.*—The treaty forbids any private arrangements which affect trade among the member states and have as their purpose or effect the hindering, restraining, or distorting of competition within the common market. The prohibition is specifically aimed at price fixing, production controls, and the division of markets. Business agreements may be declared valid by the European Commission only when they help "to improve the production or the distribution of goods, or to promote technical or economic progress * * *." However, these agreements must not be more restrictive than is essential for the purpose of the agreement nor give the enterprises concerned the possibility of eliminating competition with respect to a "substantial" part of the products in question. Prohibited agreements may not be invoked before national courts.

"Abusive exploitation" of a dominant economic position in the common market is also prohibited insofar as trade among member states is likely to be adversely affected thereby.

All of the above provisions of the treaty apply, with certain narrow exceptions, to public as well as private enterprises.

Within a period of 3 years after the effective date of the treaty the Council of Ministers, acting unanimously upon the recommendations of the Commission, is to take whatever measures are necessary to apply the foregoing principles. The decision of the Council will require the approval of the Community Assembly.

Until the regulations with respect to competition are established for the community, the right to rule on matters pertaining to the acceptability of business agreements and the exploitation of a dominant position in the common market is reserved to the individual states acting in accordance with their legislation and taking into account the provisions of the treaty against restrictive business practices.

(*k*) *The overseas countries and territories.*—The overseas countries and territories are to be associated with the common market in accordance with the provisions of a separate convention annexed to the treaty. The purpose of the association is to promote the economic and social development of these countries and territories and to establish close economic relations between them and the community as a whole. The convention is for 5 years and the continuance of the arrangements are dependent on the renewal of the convention. The tariff reductions required by the treaty will be carried out to their conclusion whether the convention is renewed or not. Also, the required reduction of quantitative restrictions on imports from the member states will be maintained at the level achieved at the end of the 5 years whether the convention is renewed or not.

An investment fund is provided for in the treaty for the progressive development of these countries and territories. It is fixed for the 5-year period at $581.25 million. The contributions of each of the Messina countries to the fund are the following:

| Country: | *Contribution (millions of dollars)* |
|---|---|
| Germany | 200 |
| Belgium | 70 |
| France | 200 |
| Italy | 40 |
| Luxembourg | 1.25 |
| Netherlands | 70 |

The contributions would not be made in a lump sum but instead in annual increasing amounts as set forth in the convention.

Disbursements from the fund are to be made in accordance with the following table:

| Overseas countries and territories of— | *Investments (millions of dollars)* |
|---|---|
| Belgium | 30 |
| France | 511.25 |
| Italy | 5 |
| Netherlands | 35 |

### III. THE EUROPEAN FREE TRADE AREA

*(a) Background and status of free trade area negotiations*

As a tie-in with the common market, the Secretary General of the OEEC in July 1956 circulated a letter to member countries suggesting the possibility of establishing a "multilateral system of relationships" between the common market countries and any other interested OEEC member countries. Peter Thorneycroft, then president of the United Kingdom Board of Trade, immediately welcomed the proposal on behalf of his government and suggested that discussions take place as soon as possible. The need for such discussions of the problem was already widely felt in the OEEC; the six common market countries, particularly, had long before noted their willingness to seek means to associate with the European Economic Community (common market) any European countries not in a position to become full EEC members. As a result the Council of the OEEC established a special working party (No. 17) to study possible forms and methods of association and to consider as a particular method of association the creation of a free trade area which would include the common market and the OEEC member countries.

Under a free trade area arrangement member countries would remove barriers to trade among themselves, but would retain their individual tariff regimes vis-a-vis outside countries. In this respect a free trade area differs from a customs union which is a more closely integrated type of arrangement typified by the Benelux and by the projected European common market, whereby member states apply a common tariff against outsiders.

Working party 17 submitted its report to the Council on December 26, 1956.[2] Its principal conclusion was that it was technically possible to operate a free trade area in Europe built around the European Economic Community. In arriving at this conclusion, it examined the major problems that would arise, both those of a general nature that would require solution on a political level and those which were of a specific and technical character. In February 1957 the OEEC Council approved this report as the basis for further action.

The following month, representatives of the 17 OEEC countries met in Paris to begin negotiations intended "to determine ways and means on the basis of which there could be brought into being a European free trade area which would, on a multilateral basis, asso- the European common market with other member countries." In order to handle the task the OEEC has established three working parties: One dealing with general problems; the other two to deal with the specific problems of agriculture and the association of the less developed OEEC countries with the projected free trade area.

The United States has been an associated country of the OEEC ever since its inception and participates in OEEC activities at all levels. United States officials attend working party meetings and keep the United States Government fully informed on developments. However, since the United States is not a member of the OEEC and would not be a member of the proposed free trade area, the decisions that are made in the course of working party discussions are the responsibility of the member countries.

---

[2] Report on the Possibility of Creating a Free Trade Area in Europe, OEEC: Paris, France, January 1957.

The working parties pursued their assignments until the end of July when they adjourned for the summer. The negotiators have made good progress in defining and analyzing the problems and in producing suggested solutions to them. The subject is, however, one of great complexity in itself. It is, furthermore, closely connected with the arrangements for establishing the common market provided for in the Treaty of Rome, which has not yet been ratified by all of the six countries involved. Some time must necessarily elapse, therefore, before definite proposals will be available for consideration by the OEEC governments. Meanwhile, the British Chancellor of the Exchequer, Peter Thorneycroft, who has been elected Chairman of the OEEC, is responsible for coordinating the negotiations. He has evaluated the progress achieved and is making arrangements for further discussion among OEEC members this autumn.

Just as the EEC treaty has been submitted to the contracting parties to the General Agreement on Tariffs and Trade, so the free trade area convention, as finally negotiated, will also be subject to GATT review.

(*b*) *Problems in establishing a free trade area*

The problems that confront the OEEC working parties in their attempts to draw up provisions for a free trade area are varied and complex. There are general problems that because of their far-reaching implications will have to be settled on the political level. There are also specific trade problems, some of which can probably be resolved by technical experts. Other trade problems have important political overtones and may require political decisions. All problems are still under negotiation and it would be premature to anticipate what the final settlement will be in each case.

Many of the problems which have arisen in the free trade are negotiations concern the extent to which the free trade area and the common market will be coordinated or "harmonized" with respect to scope, timing and institutional arrangements. As proposed by the United Kingdom, the free trade area would deal primarily with the lowering of regional trade barriers in the narrow sense and would be concerned with broader economic and social issues only as they affect the removal of tariffs and quotas. Some other countries believe that the scope of the free trade area proposal should be expanded to encompass more of the same ground dealt with in the common market treaty and that appropriately strong institutional arrangements should be worked out.

A major problem confronting the negotiators arises from the fact that the common market countries will eventually constitute a customs union with a single tariff regime toward the outside world, while free trade area countries will continue to maintain their individual tariff regimes in regard to nonmember countries. Under these circumstances it might be possible for goods from outside countries to enter the free trade area via low-tariff member countries and then be transshipped free of duty to other member countries, notwithstanding the higher tariffs which may exist in the latter. The chief policy problem arises in determining the extent to which goods from outside the area must be processed or transformed within a member country in order to qualify for duty-free shipment from the country of entry to other countries within the free trade area. For example, it might be possible to determine that the addition of a certain percentage of the original value of the commodities must be added by processing in the importing countries. Other possibilities exist, and no decision has yet been reached.

Another major problem is related to Great Britain's world position. The free trade area negotiations have confronted Great Britain with the problem of reconciling traditional Commonwealth ties with the closer European association which Britain desires. The concrete solution advanced by the British in the free trade area context is the exclusion of foodstuffs, feed, and tobacco. This would assure the maintenance of Commonwealth preferences on these commodities in United Kingdom markets and would have the added effect of assuring continued protection for domestic agriculture in the United Kingdom. Other OEEC countries which are important agricultural exporters have insisted that agricultural products be included in the free trade area arrangement.

Some of the OEEC countries, primarily Greece, Iceland, Ireland, Portugal, and Turkey, are in relatively early stages of economic development, both agricultural and industrial. Not only in their own interests, but in the wider interests of European unity, it has been argued that they should be included within the proposed free trade area. Some of these countries have asked for special treatment on grounds that their "infant industries" will require protection for some years and that they will need financial assistance for long-term development in order to be able to compete with the more advanced countries in a single trading unit. Also, since their exports are largely agricultural, solution of the problem of the less-developed countries is intimately related to solution of the overall agricultural problem in the free trade area. The OEEC has been actively considering the special problems of each of the countries concerned with a view to determining the obligations each should be asked to assume in return for participation in the proposed free trade area.

## IV. THE COMMON MARKET AND THE UNITED STATES

Since the proposed free trade area is still in the early stages of negotiation, this section deals only with common market developments.

It is clear that the welding of six European countries into a common market will have profound worldwide repercussions. A new economic unit composed of 162 million people producing in 1956 goods and services equal to about 32 percent of the gross national product of the United States and accounting in 1956 for 22 percent of free world trade will obviously be an important factor in the world political and economic situation. For the United States, some measure of the importance of the common market can be seen from the fact that in 1956 United States exports to the common market area amounted to $2.9 billion or 17 percent of total United States exports. For example, exports from the United States to the six common market countries accounted for 34 percent of total exports of animal and vegetable fats and oils in the first half of 1956, and 25 percent of metal working machinery exports.

While there can be no doubt that common market developments will affect world trade patterns in the future, it is extremely difficult to predict with any degree of certainty what the effects will be for specific commodity trade or specific countries. Technological, political and social developments, shifts in taste and other factors affecting economic trends becloud any simple cause and effect relationships in international trade and make predictions in this field subject to wide margins of error.

This problem of economic analysis becomes particularly difficult when it involves an unprecedented move toward economic integration which has not yet been put into effect. The common market treaty lays down the basic elements establishing the European Economic Community but, from the very nature of the project, the provisions in a number of areas had to be rather broad. Thus the direction of the interpretation and implementation of the treaty is a significant but incalculable factor in assessing the prospective impact of the common market.

Despite these difficulties of economic analysis it is possible to present some of the factors which will influence the operation of the the common market and its effect upon the United States.

*Removal of internal trade barriers*

One of the basic elements in the formation of a customs union is the elimination of trade barriers within the customs union area. Since trade barriers against the countries outside the area are maintained, the result is to give some immediate advantage to producers within the area with respect to their sales in the area. Competing producers outside the area will have to overcome this advantage to maintain their markets in the customs union area. The degree of advantage to be overcome will depend upon the height of the tariff barrier surrounding the common market area. To permit gradual adjustments and thus minimize economic distress, the tariff changes are scheduled to take place over a 12 to 15 year period.

The expected benefits from the removal of internal trade barriers are increased competition within the area, a shift to lower cost producers and a consequent increase in output and improvement in standards of living within the area. In addition to the requirement for eliminating tariffs and other governmental trade restrictions within the common market, other provisions of the treaty such as those relating to the freer movement of capital and labor, the prohibition of certain restrictive business practices and the establishment of a European investment bank are also designed to foster more rapid economic growth and more efficient production in Europe. These factors in turn are expected to have trade-creating effects both internally and externally. With the increased economic activity in the common market area, increased trade with the outside should take place.

*External trade barriers*

A single external tariff will be established for the common market. As noted above, the height of this tariff will be a significant factor to be overcome in competing with producers located in the common market area. Under the treaty the tariff rates on any particular product will be based upon an averaging process in which some rates will be higher and some lower than the present national rates. In addition, the treaty states that the community is prepared to enter into negotiations with respect to the level of the external tariff. In adopting these provisions, the six were guided by their obligations as contracting parties to the General Agreement on Tariffs and Trade (GATT). The GATT requirements will be discussed below.

It will obviously be in the interest of the United States that the external tariff be as low as possible. Our ability to influence the external tariff will be closely related to the negotiating authority given to the President by the Congress in next year's renewal of the Trade Agreements Act.

There are governmental measures other than tariff which affect imports into the common market area, notably quantitative restrictions maintained for balance-of-payments reasons. Although important restrictions remain, this factor has been mitigated in recent years by the progress achieved in liberalizing restrictions against dollar imports.

The Common Market Treaty does not deal specifically with balance-of-payments restrictions against countries outside the area. It is assumed that the GATT provisions on this point will apply and the form and level of such restrictions will be based on the balance-of-payments situation. On the expectation outlined earlier that the effect of the common market will be to improve the economic situation of the member countries, their external financial situation should improve, thus permitting a further relaxation of restrictions against United States goods.

In any assessment of the effect of the common market on United States exports, important commercial factors such as the unique character of certain United States exports, established United States contacts, and the continued technological progress of American producers would have to be taken into account. These factors, in addition to the highly competitive nature of United States industry and trade, would be important but indeterminate factors.

*Other factors*

There are a number of additional factors which are of particular interest to the United States.

As already noted, special arrangements are contemplated in the treaty for dealing with the problems of agriculture. This is one of the areas where a good deal will depend upon the implementation of the treaty provisions. The aim of these provisions is the development of a competitive and viable agricultural economy. Also, the treaty provides that the agricultural provisions shall be administered with due regard to traditional trade channels. Nevertheless, the provisions for minimum prices and long-term contracts raise special problems which will probably be among the issues in the forthcoming GATT consideration of the Common Market Treaty.

One of the effects of the formation of the common market may be to increase United States investment in Europe. The development of a large, expanding market free from internal barriers should prove more attractive to United States capital.

The Common Market Treaty will be put into effect over a period of 12 to 15 years. In this period United States producers will have an opportunity to adjust to the new trading situation. This gradual approach provides time for any necessary adjustments similar to those being made all the time in the dynamic and competitive free-enterprise economy of the United States.

*GATT consideration of the Common Market Treaty*

An important influence on the development and implementation of the Common Market Treaty is the General Agreement on Tariffs and Trade (GATT) to which all the member states are contracting parties. The GATT contains specific provisions relating to customs unions and represents the major instrument through which the interests of the United States and other countries outside the common market can be safeguarded. Article 234 of the Common Market Treaty provides that the obligations which member states have under prior international agreements (including the GATT) are not affected by the provisions of the treaty.

The General Agreement on Tariffs and Trade recognizes the contribution which a customs union or free-trade area can make to the expansion of international trade and the movement toward a system of multilateral trade. Accordingly, the General Agreement permits a departure from the principle of unconditional most-favored-nation treatment when contracting parties form a customs union or free-trade area. At the same time, however, article XXIV of the GATT establishes certain criteria as a basis for judgment whether a particular set of arrangements is in fact likely to produce a beneficial customs union or free-trade area. Basically, these requirements are (*a*) that trade barriers on substantially all of the trade within the area are to be eliminated and (*b*) that the duties and other regulations of commerce applying to outside countries are not on the whole higher or more restrictive than the general incidence which previously existed in the individual countries.

The contracting parties to the GATT were informed of the progress in developing the Common Market Treaty during the 11th session of the GATT in October 1956. The text of the treaty establishing the European Economic Community was transmitted to the contracting parties after its signature. Subsequently, the Intersessional Committee met in Geneva, at which most of the contracting parties were represented, to establish a procedure for consideration of the treaty. This procedure recognized that considerable preparatory work was necessary to facilitate the effective examination of the treaty by the contracting parties under the relevant provisions of the General Agreement. Substantive discussion with a view to establishing safeguards for outside countries will take place this fall at the 12th session of the GATT.

With respect to the provisions in the Common Market Treaty relating to the elimination of all tariffs, quantitative restrictions and analogous barriers within the area; a "plan and schedule" for the elimination of these barriers to trade; and the covering of "substantially all" trade among member countries, the treaty appears to meet the major tests set forth in article XXIV of the General Agreement. There are, however, certain areas of concern to the United States. A few of these arise directly from the text of the treaty; more from provisions in the treaty which are at this time not fully clear. In any case, a great deal will depend on the spirit and manner in which the treaty is administered.

As noted earlier, one problem of major concern is the level of the common external tariff. A judgment as to its conformity with the standards of article XXIV must await a study of the rates of this tariff when it has been completed and laid before the contracting parties. This should be before the end of the fourth year of the transitional period, when the first changes in external tariffs are scheduled to take place. In cases where the member states have agreed under GATT to keep their tariffs at a certain level, and the common tariff is to be above this level, there will have to be renegotiations with interested contracting parties. Other increases will have to be considered in the light of article XXIV.

As suggested earlier, the agricultural provisions are likely to undergo careful scrutiny in the GATT. Safeguards will be sought to insure that future developments in this area are designed to promote a sound agricultural economy in the member states and to avoid serious danger to the trading interests of other contracting parties.

The provisions of the treaty relating to the association of the overseas territories of the member states represent another area which will be examined carefully in the GATT framework.

## TRADE AND PAYMENTS RESTRICTIONS

United States Department of State

### INTRODUCTION

The subcommittee requested—

> a review and analysis of the special trade and payments restrictions maintained by foreign countries on account of balance-of-payments difficulties or other circumstances usually thought of as more or less exceptional and temporary.

In particular they asked that this report include—

> analysis of the effects of such restrictions on United States exports by types and destinations and also analysis of such liberalization of these restrictions as have occurred and of the prospects for their future liberalization.

Finally the subcommittee desired as much information as possible regarding the operation of these restrictions with respect to the importation of particular commodities from the United States.

Detailed information relating to trade and payments restrictions maintained by foreign countries and the effects of such restrictions upon United States exports is regularly collected and analyzed by the Department of Commerce. Since the information required is available in the Department of Commerce and since the subcommittee has asked the Department of Commerce to supply such information, this report does not include a detailed review and analysis of trade and payments restrictions maintained by foreign countries or an analysis of the effects of such restrictions on United States exports.

However, to supplement the material submitted by the Department of Commerce, with a view to presenting as complete a picture as possible of the role of quantitative restrictions in international trade, particularly in respect to the effect upon United States trade, this report contains some background material and information on the use of trade and payments restrictions and a description of liberalization efforts, particularly as they relate to United States goods, and prospects for further liberalization with respect to dollar goods.

### BACKGROUND

Following World War II a severe disequilibrium of international trade stemming from wartime dislocations and an exceptional demand for imports for reconstruction and consumption resulted in the widespread expansion of the use of trade and payments restrictions. Many countries had exhausted their reserves of foreign exchange during the war and by 1945 had to a great extent lost the means of earning foreign exchange which had enabled them to import prior to the war. Protection of foreign exchange reserves became the primary motivation for maintaining trade and payments restrictions. In this way the flow of imports could be restricted to those commodities deemed most essential to the national welfare.

Most countries recognized, however, that such restrictive measures were not in their long-term interest and subscribed, in principle, to the objective of eliminating trade and payments restrictions when they were no longer necessary for balance-of-payments reasons. This objective was embodied in the General Agreement on Tariffs and Trade and the articles of agreement of the International Monetary Fund. The GATT also recognized other circumstances in which quantitative restrictions might be imposed, such as for economic development purposes, to enforce sanitary regulations, for national security reasons, and in connection with certain types of agricultural limitations. These restrictions were to be nondiscriminatory. Balance-of-payments restrictions, however, could be discriminatory when necessary for financial reasons. At the present time 23 of the 35 contracting parties maintain discriminatory restrictions under provisions of the GATT, two others apply nondiscriminatory restrictions, and the remaining 10 do not apply restrictions for balance-of-payments purposes.

With respect to payments restrictions, article VIII of the IMF agreement states that—

> no member shall, without the approval of the fund, impose restrictions on the making of payments and transfers for current international transactions * * *.

But it also provides in article XIV that—

> in the postwar transitional period members may * * * maintain and adapt to changing circumstances * * * restrictions on payments and transfers for current international transactions.

While there is a natural tendency for vested interests to become attached to the protective barrier resulting from the continued application of trade and payments restrictions, countries belonging to the IMF and adhering to the GATT have maintained their support for the principles of multilateral trade and currency convertibility embodied in these instruments. The practical movement toward these goals has been substantial, particularly in recent years as economic conditions throughout the world have improved. The following section describes the efforts which have been made to promote the movement toward dismantling restrictions on trade and payments.

### ACTIONS TAKEN BY THE UNITED STATES GOVERNMENT TO OBTAIN RELAXATION OF IMPORT RESTRICTIONS ON UNITED STATES GOODS

The United States Government has sought to impress upon other governments the advantages to be derived from reducing barriers to international trade. Although there is general recognition of the desirability of eliminating quantitative restrictions on imports, there has been some hesitancy to take the necessary measures for a variety of reasons, including balance-of-payments difficulties, the lack of convertibility of currencies, fear of the future dollar position, the fear that moving ahead so fast that retrogression may become necessary, and a desire to protect a particular industry. The United States has made particular use of the GATT and the IMF to achieve the desired freeing of trade from excessive restrictions.

The success of the United States efforts is reflected by the substantial progress over the past several years in the relaxation of import restrictions in Western Europe and in other areas of the world. Of the GATT countries in Western Europe, only Turkey, which has serious balance-of-payments problems, has not taken at least a first step to free imports from the United States; France has recently revoked the limited steps she had taken because of serious difficulties regarding her external financial position. For Western Europe, as a whole, dollar liberalization now amounts to 61 percent as compared with 54 percent on January 1, 1956, and 44 percent on September 30, 1954. On an individual basis, examples of a high degree of dollar liberalization of private trade are 99 percent in Greece; 93 percent in Germany; 86 percent in Benelux; and 84 percent in Norway. This compares with no liberalization on January 1, 1953, for all these countries except Belgium, which had a 57-percent liberalization.[3] (See table I.)

There is no quantitative measure available on the extent of dollar liberalization in other areas of the world; however, there has also been progress in these areas. In Africa, the Federation of Rhodesia and Nyasaland has increased the number of products which can be imported freely from any source. The Union of South Africa for several years has not discriminated with respect to source of supply. In the Far East, Ceylon has taken further action to relax import restrictions and to reduce discrimination. With the exception of a few items subject to nominal licensing control, all imports are covered by open general license and can be obtained from any source. New Zealand has increased the list of items which can be imported from any source. Japan has been steadily increasing its foreign-exchange budget and has been widening the scope of the so-called automatic approval system, importation under which is in practice free from quotas. However, there have also been some setbacks in this area. India, for example, has intensified restrictions on imports because of a continuing large drain on her foreign-exchange holdings. In Latin America, some countries have not applied balance-of-payments restrictions, and others have taken steps to relax restrictions on trade. Cuba, the Dominican Republic, Haiti, Nicaragua, and Peru do not have balance-of-payments restrictions on imports. The basic problem of many of the countries in this area is the pressure on the balance of payments arising from internal inflation. Canada, like the United States, does not apply restrictions on imports for balance-of-payments reasons.

The United States Government has utilized the various international forums and bilateral diplomatic representations to obtain the relaxation and removal of quantitative restrictions on imports of United States goods. In the GATT, a series of consultations on import restrictions is taking place this year on the basis of a proposal by the United States. During the first group of these consultations, conducted in June, two countries, Italy and Sweden, announced new measures of dollar liberalization, and Austria and Germany indicated that further steps to liberalize imports from the dollar area would

[3] Dollar liberalization is computed on the basis of private imports in 1953 from the United States and Canada.

be taken in the near future. Norway reported that dollar goods are normally treated as favorably as any other goods. The Netherlands and Greece have stated that, for practical purposes, almost all of dollar and nondollar goods are treated equally by their licensing authorities and that their remaining quantitative import restrictions are negligible.

Under the general agreement countries which substantially intensify restrictions are required to consult with the contracting parties. This affords an opportunity for an exchange of views on the problems created by such action on the exports of other countries as well as those faced by the countries imposing the restrictions. The annual meetings of the contracting parties to the GATT have also been used to discuss on a bilateral basis the various problems created by the maintenance of import restrictions on specific commodities. While recognizing the financial justification for the maintenance of import controls, the United States has sought the alleviation of the hardship which these controls created for United States exporters. In many instances, these discussions resulted in the relaxation of the import restrictions on the products discussed. In some cases, a reexamination of the need for the restrictions was assured. In a few cases, the nonessential character of the product or the availability of adequate supplies from nondollar sources coupled with the difficult external financial position of the country led the consulting country to conclude that it could not at this time relax the particular import restrictions. In every case, however, the full and frank discussion of the reasons for and the effects of the restrictions and the prospect for the elimination led to a better mutual understanding and provided grounds for further joint attention to these restrictions.

The articles of agreement of the International Monetary Fund require member countries which maintain exchange restrictions to consult each year on the further retention of these restrictions. These annual consultations by the International Monetary Fund (IMF) have provided an opportunity for discussion of the economic and financial problems which give rise to restrictive and discriminatory practices and of the possibilities of further relaxation. The decisions reached by the fund are of particular importance because of their impact on the consultations under the general agreement. For example, after the German consultation with the fund in 1957, the GATT Consultations Committee noted that the strong foreign-exchange position of Germany no longer justified the maintenance of restrictions for balance-of-payments reasons. The German Government responded to this by expressing its firm intention to consider the adoption of measures to meet the situation and announced that further liberalization steps would be taken in the near future.

Another international forum where the United States has sought to encourage the liberalization of restrictions on dollar goods has been the Organization for European Economic Cooperation (OEEC). The United States as an associate member of the OEEC has participated over the past several years in the work of that Organization with regard to the relaxation of quantitative restrictions on imports from the dollar area. In this work the OEEC has analyzed the progress achieved in dollar liberalization, the effect of liberalization on the level and geographical composition of imports of member countries, the general economic effects of dollar liberalization, and the prospects for further liberalization. The Organization also examined the economic and commercial policies of the United States and Canada as part of the overall situation influencing the relaxation of restrictions on dollar goods. The exchange of views between OEEC members, the United States, and Canada on the problems of dollar liberalization has contributed to the progress made in recent years. The second report by the OEEC on Liberalization of Europe's Dollar Trade, published in June 1957, recommended that a further review take place during the first half of 1958, and the Council of the OEEC agreed.

Finally, bilateral approaches to foreign governments to impress upon them the importance of further steps to relax their restrictions against United States goods have been undertaken by United States diplomatic officials abroad and by Washington officials. These representations have ranged from discussions on the need for a general forward move to liberalize imports from the United States to a discussion of the desirability of relaxing import restrictions on a particular commodity adversely affected by these restrictions. For example, beginning in the last quarter of 1953 Belgium reduced the amount of United States coal licensed for import from as much as 77,000 tons in 1 month and an average of almost 60,000 tons a month in 1952 to an average of 30,000 tons a month at the end of 1953 and practically none beginning in April 1954. The restrictions were a serious blow to United States coal producers, to whom Belgium was an important market. After discussing the problem with the Belgian Government without any satisfactory result, the United States took the matter to the ninth session (October 1954–March 1955) of the contracting parties to the GATT. The issue was finally resolved through bilateral discussions during that session. Belgium agreed at that time to establish a minimum annual quota for imports of United States coal for consumption in Belgium and since has eliminated virtually all restrictions on such imports. Average monthly exports of coal from the United States to Belgium during the first half of 1957 were over 200,000 tons, valued at more than $2,300,000.

## PROSPECTS FOR FURTHER LIBERALIZATION

The basic factors influencing the further relaxation of restrictions on dollar goods by most countries are their balance-of-payments position and the level of their gold and dollar reserves. Difficulties of a temporary nature may delay progress toward the goal of convertible currencies and multilateral trade free of quantitative import restrictions. However, the advantages to be gained from the removal of these restrictions on imports are generally recognized as are the serious problems raised by unduly prolonging import restrictions. Nevertheless, the extent and timing of further liberalization measures are affected by the external financial position of each country and the special obstacles which may exist. As countries continue to make substantial progress in the liberalization of restrictions on imports, further steps become more difficult. Domestic economic and political factors play an increasingly important role. The problems of removing the protection which has been an incident to import restrictions maintained for balance-of-payments reasons and permitting the adjustment to conditions of competition require additional time in many cases.

Further liberalization of United States imports by the underdeveloped countries presents a number of difficulties. Many of the underdeveloped countries are dependent upon the sales of a few raw materials for their foreign exchange. They are affected by business fluctuations in other countries to a substantially greater extent than industrial countries, and consequently their reserves also tend to vary considerably. In addition, many of the underdeveloped countries are subjected to strong inflationary pressures stemming from their efforts at rapid industrialization, which accelerate the demand for imported goods.

If discrimination and the elimination of restrictions against imports from the dollar area are to be promoted, the countries maintaining the restrictions must be able to feel that United States policies will allow them to earn the necessary dollars to pay for their imports and, where necessary, increase the level of their foreign-exchange reserves. The United States, in its position of economic strength, must continue its liberal trade policy and exercise leadership as well as facilitate the continued growth of the domestic economy. Foreign governments must direct their efforts toward controlling inflationary pressures and making their exports more competitive. Foreign governments generally have recognized the need to take the fundamental remedies necessary to fortify the internal economy by curbing the excessive demands which have created or aggravated balance-of-payments difficulties. Only if governments take the necessary fiscal, monetary, and commercial policy measures can there be progress toward the achievement of the objective of a multilateral system of trade and payments free from quantitative restrictions.

TABLE I.—*Liberalization of private imports from the United States and Canada by western European countries in GATT, 1953–57 (based on private imports in 1953)*

[In percent]

| Country | Jan. 1, 1953 | Jan. 1, 1954 | Jan. 1, 1955 | Jan. 1, 1956 | Dec. 1, 1956 | Aug. 1, 1957 |
|---|---|---|---|---|---|---|
| Austria | 0 | 0 | 0 | 8 | 40 | 40 |
| Belgium-Luxembourg | 57 | 70 | 86 | 86 | 86 | 86 |
| Denmark | 1 | 1 | 38 | 55 | 55 | 55 |
| France | 0 | 0 | 0 | 11 | 11 | 0 |
| Germany | 0 | 24 | 60 | 68 | 90 | 93 |
| Greece | 0 | 90 | 90 | 99 | 99 | 99 |
| Italy | 0 | 10 | 24 | 24 | 39 | 71 |
| Netherlands | 0 | 30 | 86 | 86 | 86 | 86 |
| Norway | 0 | 0 | 0 | 0 | 84 | 84 |
| Sweden | 0 | 0 | 55 | 58 | 68 | [1] 68 |
| Turkey | 0 | 0 | 0 | 0 | 0 | 0 |
| United Kingdom | 7 | 43 | 50 | 56 | 59 | [1] 59 |

[1] This does not include the recently announced dollar-liberalization measures.

# CONTROL REGULATIONS APPLYING TO IMPORTS FROM THE UNITED STATES

United States Department of Commerce

Chairman Boggs' letter of June 1, 1957, to Secretary Weeks asked for information on "* * * the extent to which quantitative restrictions abroad have limited United States exports * * *." The following country statements describe foreign-country controls affecting imports from the United States and comment on the extent to which these controls appear to limit exports. Comment is also made on other aspects of the controls, such as prospects for liberalization.

The statements cover countries that, together, take some 85 percent of United States exports. The countries are:

India
Indonesia
Japan
Republic of Korea
Malaya (Singapore and Federation of Malaya)
Pakistan
Republic of the Philippines
Taiwan
Vietnam
Argentina
Brazil
Chile
Colombia
Cuba
Mexico
Peru
Venezuela
United Kingdom
Belgium-Luxembourg
France
Federal Republic of Germany
Italy
The Netherlands
Spain
Sweden
Switzerland
Yugoslavia
Turkey
Union of South Africa
Australia
Canada

## Control Regulations Applying To Imports From the United States

### INDIA

Import restrictions were first introduced in India in May 1940 as a war measure under the defense of India rules. These controls were continued in effect by the Imports and Exports (Control) Act of 1947 following Indian independence, and by the imports (control) order of 1955. These latter two statutes constitute the legal authority for control of trade. The import regulations issued in pursuance of this authority are administered by the Ministry of Commerce and Consumer Industries, by the Chief Controller of Imports and Exports at New Delhi, and by regional licensing authorties located at Calcutta, Bombay, Madras, Cochin, New Delhi, Pondicherry, Vizagapatnam, and Rajkot.

All merchandise imported into India, except imports on Government account, is subject to license. There are two kinds of licenses: (1) Open general and (2) individual. An open general license is a general permission for any importer to import any commodity on the open general license list, issued by the Government, without quantitative or monetary limitation. No written permit or license is required, although certain procedures must be observed with respect to the remission of foreign exchange. Open general licenses are issued for specified countries or currency areas and goods imported must be shipped within a given time.

All commodities, except those under open general license, require individual licenses. Quantitative limits are applied to many commodities and quotas are generally higher for soft currency area licenses than for licenses covering imports from the dollar area.

For purposes of import licensing, the countries are divided into two main groups: (1) The dollar area (United States, Canada, Philippines, and certain Latin American countries) and (2) soft currency area (all other countries). The import policy of India is based on the country's economic needs, taking into consideration the foreign-exchange resources, and the availability of dollar exchange with respect to purchases from the dollar area. Other considerations are India's economic development plans, industrial requirements, and the protection of domestic industries.

The basic objective of such a policy is to allocate available foreign-exchange funds for imports to the country's best advantage. To achieve this, the Government's foreign-exchange position and economic needs are reviewed periodically, and the import schedules prior to July 1, 1957, were revised and published semiannually (January 1 and July 1) by the Ministry of Commerce and Consumer Industries. In general, foods, capital goods, industrial raw materials, and basic economic essentials are given the highest priority, while luxuries and nonessentials are either prohibited or severely limited. The importation of many commodities is permitted only from soft currency countries. After September 1, 1957, import schedules will coincide with the Indian fiscal year (April 1 to March 31).

Quotas are established for those commodities not on open general license and allocated to "established importers" on the basis of a fixed percentage of imports in any one financial year from a specified basic period, i. e., 1945–52, or even a longer period for certain commodities. "Actual users" are accorded licenses on the basis of current requirements. Individual license applications which do not fall within the criteria laid down for established importers and actual users are for the most part considered on an ad hoc basis.

Historically, the distinction in India's licensing system between the soft-currency area and the dollar area has operated to the detriment of United States exports to India. This distinction is spelled out in detail in that quotas established for many items are applicable for soft-currency-area commodities only, and no provision made for dollar-area imports of like commodities. At the same time, however, quotas for some items are valid equally for imports from both soft and dollar areas.

The extent to which United States exports to India have been discriminated against has varied within recent years reflecting changes made in the semiannual licensing policies. In the period July to December 1956, for instance, increases were accorded to dollar quotas for a number of commodities and permission was given for the validation of imports of some dollar items previously under soft-currency licenses only. Some dollar-area quotas were reduced, however. Specifically, dollar quotas were increased, or established for the first time, on the following items: Machine tools of certain types, electric cooking ranges, table fans, fruits, razor blades, potassium chlorate, pyrotechnic aluminum, cellulose adhesive tape, household hardware, diesel, engines, machinery, ball bearings, and medicinal soap. Quotas were reduced on hacksaw blades, air compressors, aureomycin, spark plugs, dextrose, ammonium chloride, glucose, naphthol dyes, powdered milk, and polystyrene.

For the period January 1957 to June 1957, India, faced with a rapid decline of its foreign-exchange reserves, tightened its import-licensing policy by (1) bringing under quotas 102 items of industrial materials and consumer goods which were formerly licensed liberally, (2) reducing by various amounts quotas on 509 items, e. g., iron and steel manufactures, engineering products, and electrical goods, and (3) abolishing entirely quotas for certain other items, e. g., iron fencing, wood screws of certain types, knitting machines, and cotton ropes. On the liberalization side, (1) the discrimination against dollar goods was substantially reduced by giving holders of soft-currency licenses the option of using at least 50 percent of the face value of the licenses for dollar imports and (2) quotas were increased for 9 items, principally industrial materials and capital goods, and (3) the dollar quotas on machine-work cutters, camphor, lenses, and larger diesel engines were increased.

The decline in India's foreign-exchange reserves continued throughout the January to June 1957 period in part as a result of the utilization of valid import licenses issued in the previous licensing period. As a result, an even tighter licensing policy for the July to September 1957 period was announced by the Indian Government in June 1957. The principal feature of the new policy is the abolition of open general licenses for the July to September 1957 quarter except for a few foodstuffs from Pakistan. Other features of the new policy were: (1) No new licenses for finished goods for the next 3 months (2) licenses for essential raw materials to be issued on an ad hoc basis and (3) imports of capital goods only possible on a deferred payment basis.

Relative liberalization in India's import licensing policy has taken place at various times since 1950. The following periods witnessed some relaxation in licensing restrictions which were advantageous to United States exports: July to December 1950, most of 1951, July to December 1954, all of 1955. Import licensing during 1952–54 was relatively liberal only with respect to essential machinery, industrial raw materials, rice, and foodstuffs.

In summary, discriminatory quantitative restrictions in India's import licensing system have worked to the disadvantage of certain categories of United States exports. While quantitative restrictions invoked by India against United States exports have, by and large, been for balance of payments reasons, there is evidence indicating protection considerations have played a part in the quantitative controls on certain United States exports. The following commodities may be cited as being among the more conspicuous items now facing, or which have faced in the recent past, discriminatory quantitative controls: Fountain pens, apparel and hosiery, leather belting, leather belting preservative, typewriters and parts thereof, sewing machines, automotive vehicles, stationery, and alligator steel belt lacing.

Notwithstanding present quantitative restrictions, United States exports to India have risen steadily over the past 4 years. For instance, data for the year 1956 show exports from the United States to India totaling $267 million compared with $188 million in 1955, $161 million in 1954, and $153 million in 1953. Heavy capital equipment from the United States has been the largest single category of United States exports showing an increase during this period, a trend attributable to India's requirements for such imports for developmental projects under its first 5-year plan. At the same time, exports of United States agricultural products to India will continue under Public Law 480, which calls for shipments of such products in an aggregate value of $360 million during 1956–59. The prospects for future liberalization of restrictions on dollar goods will, in large measure, depend on India's ability to solve its present foreign-exchange difficulties. Assuming that the present situation is ameliorated to the extent that capital goods imports will be permitted in a volume necessary to the success of the second 5-year plan, it is likely that dollar goods will be permitted to participate in this import trade. It is not likely, however, that there will occur a relaxation of restrictions to any substantial degree within the next 12 months. Further, such dollar goods as will be licensed for import into India will only be those which, in the Indian Government's view, will contribute materially to the attainment of the goals of the second 5-year plan.

### INDONESIA

Indonesia has no quantitative import restrictions, nor does it make any distinction by country of origin or currency area in applying trade controls or assessing any of the various charges connected with importations. (In December 1957, as part of the anti-Dutch campaign which broke out in connection with the dispute over West New Guinea, Indonesia threatened cessation of all trade with the Netherlands.) It exercises general exchange controls through licensing procedures and restrictions on imports, primarily for balance-of-payments reasons, but also for other purposes. However, there is no indication of special restrictions or unfair discrimination currently being applied in regard to the importation of particular United States commodities.

Exchange controls have been exercised in Indonesia under numerous different systems since 1940. The general degree of liberalization at any time reflected the country's financial position. Since January 1954, when Indonesia abolished its dollar export certificate system (which had been introduced to stimulate exports to and retard imports from the dollar area, and which during the 2 years in operation had made imports from the United States slightly more expensive), dollar imports have come under the same controls pertaining to all areas of the world.

All regular commercial imports into Indonesia require prior import licenses issued by the Government's exchange authorities. Prior to June 20, 1957, when a broad simplification of the restrictive system was introduced primarily to encourage the export sector, the basic rate for the Indonesian rupiah was 11.40 rupiah per United States dollar. This official rate was applied only to a relatively small group of exchange transactions including the importation of some highly essential imports (principally rice and textiles), which in 1956 represented about 16 percent of the total value of imports. All other imports were divided into 2 broad categories for which importers were obliged to pay additional amounts by means of 2 requirements—payment of import surcharges and surrender of export incentive certificates (issuance of which was tied to the exportation of specific commodities). Applications of recognized importers for foreign-exchange licenses were considered only if the importer presented evidence that he had already paid the full rupiah equivalent of the cost and freight value of the merchandise to be imported plus the price of the required additional import surcharge to an authorized foreign-exchange bank.

Under the most recent revision effective June 20 (details of the implementation are not yet fully available), prior import licenses are still required. However, the previous official rate of 11.40 rupiah is abolished and transactions are taking place in a free certificate exchange market which fluctuates according to the interplay of supply and demand. With the exception of rice, possibly essential textiles, and a few other commodities which will be free of additional import surcharge, all imports are to be divided into priority groupings subject to progressively higher surcharges. The number of multiple effective rates has been cut back from 16 to 6. Prior deposit requirements have also been minimized.

Although less reliance has been placed on bilateralism during the past year, Indonesia remains a party to some 20 bilateral trade agreements with various countries throughout the world. Like many other countries with bilateral agreements, Indonesia has attempted to channelize a larger part of its trade through such agreements in order to live up to commitments thereunder, but the bulk of Indonesia's trade remains on a multilateral basis.

It is difficult to hold much optimism for improved short-term trade prospects in Indonesia in the face of that country's near-bankruptcy in foreign exchange and the political disturbances which continue to preoccupy the Government and hamper seriously the country's economic activity. The fact that United States exports to Indonesia in 1956 were nearly $50 million above the 1955 level was due largely to increased Public Law 480 shipments of food grains and tobacco. This level of trade also reflects the result of Indonesia's general trade liberalization measures instituted during the second half of 1956 but which now have already gone by the board. Indonesia's policy of extreme asterity in buying is reflected in the reduced United States exports to that country in 1957. The decline—to $84 million for the first 9 months of 1957 compared to $93 million for the comparable period of 1956—would have been greater except for continued Public Law 480 shipments. Prospects for sales of other than essential goods anytime soon seem poor as Indonesia will undoubtedly continue to impose severe restrictions on imports of nonessential goods to conserve foreign exchange resources. Moreover, Japanese competition is becoming stronger in the Indonesian market. Trade with Japan is expected to acquire even greater importance when Indonesia and Japan reach an agreement on the terms of reparations payments and credits.

### JAPAN

The Japanese Government compiles semiannually a foreign exchange budget for imports and individual import licenses are granted within the framework of the foreign exchange budget. Commodities programmed for import are divided into two categories: (1) Those importable under the fund allocation (FA) system, and (2) those importable under the automatic approval (AA) system.

Under the FA system of licensing (covering imports of foodstuffs, raw materials, and other essentials), the importer must first obtain from the trade control authorities an allocation of foreign exchange appropriate to the designated sources of the imports. If the allocation is granted, the importer receives an exchange allocation certificate which entitles him to receive import licenses from a foreign exchange bank automatically upon application. Commodities which may be imported without designation of country of origin or currency of settlement are said to be importable under the global quota system. The amount of exchange allocated under the FA system represented 84 percent of the total foreign exchange budget of $2.6 billion allocated for commodity imports in the Japanese fiscal year 1955 ending March 31, 1956. Nearly half (49 percent) of the amount budgeted under the FA system was designated for use under the global quota system in that year and the global system was extended to 60 percent of the FA funds budgeted for the 6-month period ending September 30, 1956.

Under the AA system, licenses for specified commodities from specified areas are issued freely upon application until the total amount appropriated for the system in the exchange budget has been reached. In practice, additional amounts may be provided after the original appropriation is exhausted. There are no quantitative limitations on individual commodities importable under this system. The number of commodities under the automatic approval system in the budget for the first half of fiscal year 1956 (ending September 30, 1956) was 529. As present approximately half the amount programed for AA approvals is allocated to the dollar area.

Import licenses are granted rather freely for essential foodstuffs, basic raw materials and specified machinery and equipment. Licenses for importation of commodities which the Japanese consider to be luxuries or semiluxuries are granted less freely, issuance depending, in general, upon Japan's foreign exchange availabilities.

Japan restricts importation of certain commodities from specified currency areas in an effort to balance trade with each currency area as far as practicable. For trade and payments purposes, Japan designates three major currency areas; the dollar area, the sterling area, and the open-account area. Dollar-area countries include, among others, the United States, Canada, Mexico, Central America and certain South American, European, Asian and African countries. Sterling-area countries include, among others, the United Kingdom and its colonies, Australia, New Zealand, India, Pakistan, Burma, Ceylon, Union of South Africa, West Germany, Sweden, Italy, Thailand, Austria, Denmark, Portugal and Norway. Open-account countries are those with which Japan has concluded bilateral trade arrangements which aim at a balanced trade. Arrangements are made to settle temporary imbalances in either dollars or sterling as designated in the agreement. Open-account countries with which settlement is made in dollars include Brazil, Taiwan, Egypt, Greece, Korea, and Turkey. Roughly, one-half of Japan's total imports in recent years has originated in the dollar area, slightly more than one-fourth in the sterling area, and somewhat less than one-fourth from the open-account area.

United States exports to Japan for the years 1953 through 1956 and 4 months of 1957 have amounted to the following (in millions of dollars): 671; 679; 643; 890; 482 (January to April 1957), constituting about one-third of Japan's total imports. The imbalance in favor of the United States during this 4⅓-year period amounted to $1,650 million. Because of the long standing imbalance in trade with the United States, Japan has followed a fairly consistent policy of allocating dollar funds for the purchase of essential items only. This policy his discouraged many American manufacturers from attempting to develop a market for their products in Japan. Although Japan's import restrictions are designed primarily to prevent depletion of foreign exchange reserves, they undoubtedly have been used as a device to provide protection for many Japanese industries from competition of imported foreign products. Protectionist attitudes are prevalent, particularly in those segments of Japanese industry which depend upon imported raw materials and in those industries which lack modern equipment and production techniques. This includes certain segments of the heavy machinery industry, as well as many consumer goods industries, which would probably have to reduce production if they were exposed to foreign competition resulting from removal of import restrictions. Imports into Japan from the United States which have registered a decline in recent years are automobiles, television receiving sets, fountain pens and mechanical pencils, whisky, raisins and penicillin. It would appear in some cases, that import restrictions may have been imposed as a result of pressures from Japanese manufacturers. In other instances restrictions have resulted from Japan being obliged to import a particular commodity from a country with which Japan had a bilateral trade agreement in exchange for a commodity which Japan wished to export to the other participant in the agreement.

As Japan's balance-of-payments position improved, from late 1954 through 1956, the following measures were taken to reduce import restrictions: (1) The volume of imports was increased considerably; (2) the global quota system, under which choice of sources is left entirely to commercial considerations, was expanded; (3) a policy of abolishing open-account arrangements as far as practicable was adopted.

In January 1957, however, Japan again experienced a balance-of-payments deficit which has continued to the present date (July 1957), and steps will likely be taken to halt the drain on foreign-exchange holdings. No reduction was made in the April to September 1957 import budget, under which $2,236 million was budgeted for commodity imports. Attempts have been made, however, to curtail speculative imports by increasing deposit requirements for importers applying for foreign exchange allocations by restricting credit and raising interest rates. Whether or not the October 1957, to March 1958 import budget will show a continuation of the relaxation of restrictions will depend upon improvement in the balance-of-payments position.

### REPUBLIC OF KOREA

The single most important element in the foreign trade of the Republic of Korea (ROK) over the past decade has been the foreign, primarily United States, aid program. The degree of its significance for Korea's economy and United States exports has increased in recent years. In 1956 foreign-aid imports represented almost 90 percent of total imports, substantially greater than, for example, in 1953, when such imports amounted to 55 percent of the total.

Inasmuch as such an overwhelming proportion of its imports involes aid financing, the trade and exchange laws and regulations of the Korean Government governing trade, in actual practice, affect only a small portion of goods entering the Korean economy. The bulk of United States exports to Korea may be said to be subject to the procurement programs and policies of United States Government agencies. But the ability of United States firms to participate in an increasing portion of Korea's imports is also dependent, as is true in the case of sales to other countries, whether or not trade is financed by United States aid, on the sales ability of United States firms compared with businessmen of other countries, the nature and type of products desired, quality, price, and other commercial considerations. It is noted that, over the years, other things being equal, the ROK Government and people have demonstrated a preference for United States products, and there is no evidence that this is likely to change in the near future. These are some of the benchmarks for any realistic assessment of Korea's trade regulations as they apply to the United States.

Actually, nonaid imports by Korea amounted to $43.2 million in 1956; this was a $39 million drop from the 1955 level. Exports in 1956, although significantly greater than in 1955 aggregated only about $25 million. Merchandise exports over the years have been negligible—amounting on the average not more than 7 to 10 percent of total imports (including aid goods). Even as compared with the modest non-aid imports Korea has not been able to balance its merchandise trade account. In the light of these facts and of Korea's meager foreign exchange resources the ROK Government, although it has maintained a system of trade and exchange controls these have not generally been unduly restrictive against the United States.

On a nonaid basis as well as with respect to total imports, the United States has been Korea's chief supplier. The United States has also been the largest market for Korea in recent years. Korea's nonaid imports from the United States in 1956 amounted to $9.7 million, which was a sharp decline from the $26.2 million in 1955. This large drop was part of the overall reduction from all areas. In 1956 the United States replaced Japan as the No. 1 source for Korean nonaid imports; the United States continued to maintain this position in the first part of 1957.

The ROK Government maintains lists of permitted imports and lists of prohibited and restricted export items. In the case of imports two lists are maintained—the "Ordinary Import List" and the "Special Import List." All other commodities are prohibited import except when specifically approved by the ROK Ministry of Commerce and Industry.

The ordinary import list contains the relativey more essential foodstuffs, raw materials, and industrial goods, which may be imported with any foreign exchange on deposit in the import accounts of the central bank (Bank of Korea) which controls all foreign exchange. It is noted that exporters are required to collect their foreign exchange proceeds in specified currencies and deposit such in foreign exchange accounts maintained in the Bank of Korea. Generally, licenses are not required for the import of items included on this list but specific approval from appropriate Government agencies is necessary in certain cases. The removal of validated import license requirements on these commodities late in 1955 was a form of liberalization but in effect amounted to a greater dependence on foreign exchange control than on licensing control.

Special import items, which include less essential, and in most cases more lucrative materials and products, may be imported into Korea only if they are purchased with foreign exchange proceeds from exports and any other foreign exchange which the Government may designate as "export dollars". Although import licenses as such are not required for the import of special items, many of the approximately 260 commodities included in this list require approval of the appropriate Government agencies. In the special category as well as the ordinary category, foreign exchange controls have the effect of limiting imports.

The latest lists of permissible imports into Korea through private channels for the first half of 1957 cover, under the heading of ordinary, or what are considered very essential commodities, a wide variety of foodstuffs, feedstuffs, and such other agricultural products as livestock and textile raw materials, fuels, forest products, fertilizers, nonferrous and ferrous metals and products, various chemicals, pharmaceuticals, and specified industrial machinery and equipment. The special import list includes products varying from fruits, seeds, sugar, and seasonings to rubber processed goods, paper, cosmetics and perfumes, various electrical products, bicycle parts, office equipment, household sewing machines, electric refrigerators, air conditioners, and a large assortment of other consumers goods. Among the items not included in either of these lists are textile fabrics, automobiles, and television sets. The limitations on permissible imports apply generally to all countries (with more severe restrictions on imports from Japan) and do not generally discriminate against the United States. On the basis of experience in recent years it is clear that the United States is preferred over Japan as a source of supply and that existing limitations are the result of insufficient foreign exchange availabilities rather than any basic desire for protection.

Liberalization has taken place in Korea's import control system over the past several years and more particularly since late 1955 when the rate of exchange was established at 500 hwan to 1 United States dollar. However, such liberalization has been considerably circumscribed by the low level of the country's exchange reserves and export earning ability. In addition to the elimination of basic licensing controls in 1955, the ROK Government has progressively increased the number if items which could be imported. These lists are reviewed twice a year and have been expanded each time since the relaxation of licensing requirements. It would seem safe to assume that this liberalization trend will continue in the future with improvements in its balance-of-payments position. With its limited natural resources and accompanying dearth of export availabilities, it cannot be expected that Korea's private (nonaid) trade will assume such a substantially larger magnitude than the levels of recent years to effect anything more than a continued slow, but nevertheless progressive liberalization over imports. Given the present situation or even moderate improvement, so long as a very substantial portion of the country's resources are channeled into defense and defense related activities, outside aid will likely be necessary to meet its basic import requirements.

### MALAYA (SINGAPORE AND FEDERATION OF MALAYA)

The overall import policies of the Singapore and Federation governments are to grant hard-currency exchange only for goods which are not available from soft-currency areas, particularly the sterling area.

The term "not available," interpreted almost literally as meaning "physically unavailable" at the time of stringent dollar management, has gradually taken on a more liberal connotation in the past few years. At present, it includes goods which are substantially higher in price, obtainable only under unreasonably long delivery terms, qualitatively unsuited for local requirements, or could be less advantageously supplied for other reasons. In addition to this general liberalization in interpretation, the local governments have freed, within the overall limits imposed by affiliation with the sterling bloc, a slowly but steadily growing list from specific import controls, particularly from Japan but also, to a lesser extent, from the dollar area. Partially as a result of this liberalization—but also related to general trade increases—direct imports from the United States in 1956 rose by more than one-third over 1955, from a value of about $24 million to $33 million.

These figures, however, do not represent the full volume of United States exports to Malaya, because they do not include shipments of United States goods by way of Hong Kong, which in 1955 and 1956 amounted to about the same quantities as direct shipments. The "via Hong Kong" procedure, expressly sanctioned in the local governments' Import and Export Guide, provides for licensing of dollar goods of all types which Malayan importers pay for in sterling to middlemen in Hong Kong who, in turn, place the orders with United States exporters. The procedure requires physical shipment of the goods via Hong Kong and establishment there of a new set of documents by Hong Kong middlemen.

It is clearly evident that the restrictions on direct imports of dollar goods to those which are not available from soft-currency areas limit United States exports to Malaya. Although this restrictive treatment appears to be somewhat mitigated by the "via Hong Kong" procedure, analysis shows that even the facilities offered by this latter procedure do not materially alleviate the existing de facto limitation of United States exports. The detour via Hong Kong adds a certain percentage to the landed price of the goods, the amount varying depending on the commodity involved and the Hong Kong rate for United States dollars. In general, the added expense is less burdensome (percentagewise) for finished items than for bulk commodities and, since the major portion of American exports to Malaya consists of manufactured goods, United States exporters are making extensive use of the detour to place goods in the Malayan market which cannot be licensed for direct import. Yet a price reduction of only a few percent—possible if direct import were permitted—could create substantial additional United States sales in the Malayan market, particularly of nonluxury goods.

Further liberalization of direct imports from the United States is considered desirable by the majority of Malayan businessmen and may materialize to some degree, following the Federation's independence on August 31, 1957, and Singapore's at a possible future date. The governments will be able to exercise, through their own currency institutions, greater freedom in determining their foreign-exchange and import policies as independent members of the sterling area. While close economic ties with the United Kingdom will no doubt remain, its predominance in Malay's business life is expected to gradually lessen. Malaya appears determined to play an active, independent role economically in the international family of nations. The Federation has already applied for membership in the International Monetary Fund, the International Bank for Reconstruction and Development, and the International Finance Corporation.

The United States-Malayan trade shows a heavy imbalance in favor of Malaya at a rate of more than 1:4. With its large rubber and tin exports, Malaya is the strongest dollar earner in the sterling bloc, and with independence, the Federation may press for greater use of its earnings for purchases from the United States, its best single customer.

### PAKISTAN

Individual import licenses are required for all private-account imports into Pakistan, irrespective of source, with minor exceptions relating to border trade with neighboring countries. Statements of import-licensing policy, including lists of importable items, are issued to cover 6-month shipping periods (January–June and July–December). Licensable items may be imported from any country in the world; the sole exception to this policy is that separate import quotas for some commodities are reserved for certain countries under bilateral trade-agreement provisions, and licenses for imports against these quotas are issued on a single-country basis. (During the most recent shipping period, January–June 1957, only France qualified for single-country licenses.) The government does not announce the anticipated value of imports, either globally or by commodity group. The import-licensing policy is determined in the light of estimated availabilities of foreign exchange for this purpose. It also takes into account certain special requirements of East Pakistan. In order to control distribution and prices, the government monopolizes imports of wheat, rice, sugar, coal, and chemical fertilizers. These imports are not subject to normal licensing procedures.

In general, the government's policy is to limit, insofar as possible, the importation of nonessential items and to give special preference to industrial requirements. Of the 193 commodities or commodity groups licensable during the January–June 1957 shipping period, 39 were reserved exclusively for industrial consumers (e. g., firebricks, carbon black, leather, crude rubber, raw wool, cotton yarn, nylon yarn, etc.). Items produced domestically in adequate quantity are not licensed for importation. While this policy may, in part, represent protection and encouragement of local industries, this consideration would appear to be secondary to the need to conserve foreign exchange. The value of licenses issued for any particular commodity or group is determined on an ad hoc basis, using the criteria of essentiality or, in a few cases, trade commitments. Utilization of licenses is virtually 100 percent, reflecting the fact that effective demand for imports far exceeds Pakistan's foreign-exchange availabilities.

Licenses to import Public Law 480 surplus agricultural commodities (raw cotton, tobacco, ghee, dried milk, and linseed oil) are valid only for imports from the United States

With regard to imports of food grains, the Pakistan Government favors procurement under Public Law 480 whenever possible in order to conserve foreign exchange. India is the preferred source of coal, as the delivered cost of Indian coal is lower than that of any other foreign coal. Communist China has been a secondary source when sufficient coal has not been available from India. Chemical fertilizers have been purchased from several countries, including the United States, depending on the prices quoted at the time of each transaction.

Pakistan's import controls effectively limit private-account imports from the United States and all other sources. The stringency of these controls is illustrated by the fact that private-account imports in 1956 amounted to only $206.5 million compared with $523.8 million in 1952, when a relatively liberal import system operated (although it discriminated against the dollar area, as explained below). Of the $206.5 million, imports from the United States amounted to $25.8 million, or 12.5 percent. If it were possible at the present time for Pakistan to liberalize imports to the same extent as in 1952 (but without discrimination), and if an effective import demand of roughly $550 million is assumed, then the United States share of Pakistan's private-account imports, on the basis of the 1956 percentage, would be almost $70 million. Nevertheless, this is a purely hypothetical projection in view of the difficult foreign-exchange situation and the need for the Pakistan Government to devote a considerable part of its foreign-exchange reserves to the procurement of food grains from countries other than the United States.

Within the framework of zero liberalization of imports, discrimination against the United States, represented only by single-country licenses on France, is negligible. (During 1956, when France alone qualified for single-country licensing during the first 6 months, private-account imports from France amounted to $9.6 million, or 4.65 percent of total private-account imports. These imports from France were not all necessarily made against single-country licenses, although a breakdown is not available.) The United States in 1956 was free to compete for a minimum of 95.35 percent of Pakistan's private-account import trade.

Emergency procurement of food grains by the Pakistan Government has greatly increased total United States exports to Pakistan, which rose from $54.6 million in 1955 to $137.7 million in 1956. There is no reason to believe that the Pakistan Government will seek to limit imports of United States surplus food grains available under Public Law 480.

Up to 1953, favored by unusually high export prices for jute and cotton during the Korean crisis, Pakistan maintained a liberal import policy, with a large number of items freely importable under open general license from soft-currency sources. A smaller number of commodities was importable from the dollar area, usually under individual import licenses. In 1953, following the collapse of the export boom, all open general licenses were suspended and all imports were brought under individual import-license controls. Discrimination against the dollar area continued, but this was removed in 1955 when licenses were made valid for imports from all countries.

Taking into account the difficult food situation in Pakistan and the limited availability of foreign exchange and foreign aid (from the United States and other countries), there appears to be little prospect for any substantial liberalization of private-account imports within the foreseeable future.

PHILIPPINES

The Philippines does not discriminate as between sources of imports in implementing exchange controls on imports. Unlike most countries, Philippine trade with the world—except for barter transactions which are permitted on a limited scale—is conducted only in United States dollars.

Imports into the Philippines are regulated mainly through exchange controls administered by the Central Bank. The Central Bank establishes a foreign exchange budget prior to the beginning of each semester (January through June, and July through December) which determines the overall availability of foreign exchange for imports during the period. All commodity imports are assigned a priority classification in the Central Bank's statistical classification of (import) commodities based on (1) their essentiality to the economy and (2) their availability from local sources. The classification, in turn, largely determines the relative ease of obtaining foreign exchange for their importation. Certain decontrolled essential commodities, limited largely to particular drugs, foods, and construction materials, may be imported without quantitative limits. Articles listed as unclassified items are virtually banned, since no foreign exchange is generally allocated for their importation.

Three principal objectives, namely, the promotion of rapid economic development (particularly in the industrial area), the protection of domestic industry, and the maintenance of social and economic stability, determine to a large extent the composition of imports. To further the industrialization goal, the Central Bank has pursued a liberal policy in granting foreign exchange for raw materials and replacement parts to keep established industries in continuous operation and for equipment and machinery as well as raw material needs of a growing number of new manufacturing and processing establishments. A gradual shift has taken place in the composition of imports, so that in 1956 capital goods and raw materials accounted for

77 percent (50 percent in 1950) of total imports while consumption goods accounted for the balance of 23 percent (50 percent in 1950).

The protection of domestic industries is realized principally through the reduction or denial of foreign exchange for products which are or may become available in adequate quantity locally. (A considerable number of the larger new manufacturing enterprises in the Philippines are those in which Americans have a majority or at least partial interest or with which technical assistance agreements have been negotiated with American firms.) In addition the new Philippine Tariff and Customs Code which became effective July 1, 1957, establishes rates on goods competitive with domestic products at levels which are clearly protective. Legislation providing price supports has encouraged the local growth of Virginia-type leaf tobacco to a point where United States exports of this product to what was once an important market has vanished. The rapid growth of the textile industry in recent years has led Philippine authorities to drastically curtail foreign exchange availability for many types of cotton textiles, most of which had been imported from the United States. Numerous other articles, mainly consumer goods, have been similarly affected.

To prevent sharp domestic price rises, foreign exchange has continued to be available for certain essential imports, mainly drugs and foods, despite a serious weakening of the country's balance-of-payments position. At the present stage of economic development, the Philippines is still dependent on imports for a number of goods not produced locally. Meanwhile, foreign exchange for goods regarded as nonessential consumer items have been progressively reduced so that they now form only a small proportion of total imports.

Since the United States is by far the largest source of Philippine imports, any tightening of controls tends to affect American suppliers to a greater extent than suppliers in other areas. Imports from the United States rose steadily from 1950 through 1955, except for the year 1951, when a temporary boom related to the Korean war pushed total imports as well as imports from the United States to an unusually high level. Nevertheless, the United States share of total Philippine imports declined during the same period. In 1956, however, imports from the United States dropped substantially, as did total Philippine imports, largely because of sharp reductions of foreign exchange for imports necessitated by balance-of-payments reasons. The United States share of Philippine imports declined from roughly two-thirds of total Philippine imports in 1955 to about three-fifths of total Philippine imports in 1956, while imports from Japan in particular and some European countries, increased both absolutely and percentagewise.

The prospects of maintaining the present level of United States exports to the Philippines in the immediate future have been substantially lessened by the cutback in Central Bank exchange allocations for imports during the second half of 1957, and by a further tightening of exchange controls on imports in December. (In December the bank also temporarily suspended all remittances of profits and dividends.) These actions were taken in order to arrest the steady decline of the country's foreign exchange reserves which now stand at a postwar low, largely because of heavy importation which in part was due to the needs of the Philippine industrialization program. Evasion of exchange controls on both imports and exports apparently also contributed to the exchange loss, but the Philippine Government has recently announced new efforts to prevent such evasion of controls.

On the other hand, import requirements of the Philippines are not expected to diminish, but to increase in the coming years. Reparation deliveries of capital goods from Japan are expected to meet important needs but only in part. Under these conditions the Philippines may very well seek other sources of financing in addition to its reserve, such as available credits from the (United States) Export-Import Bank and increased entry of private foreign capital.

It is believed that some solution to the financing problem will be reached and that the Philippines over the long haul will represent an even bigger market than at present for United States goods. Further changes in the composition of imports are to be expected, with certain consumer goods becoming less important while capital goods and raw material imports increase. Also the growth of local manufacturing will mean, of course, that domestic products will replace those previously imported. The participation of United States exporters in this trade will be aided by the long and friendly political and commercial relations between the two countries, the established channels for trade existing between them, the known preference of Filipinos for American products, and until 1974, the duty preference for United States articles as provided in the Revised United States-Philippines Trade Agreement.

### TAIWAN

All imports into Taiwan not financed by United States aid allocations are subject to control by the allocation of exchange in order to preserve the financial stability of the country. These controls apply in the case of imports from the United States as well.

Controls are exercised by the designation and registration of private traders in order to confine foreign trade activity to reliable and experienced dealers and avoid excessive pressures for speculation. Also, imports considered unessential are banned, and exchange allocations are channeled for the procurement of raw materials for industries and other goods essential for national defense and for the economy, in order to conserve exchange and to protect industries, some of which are public enterprises. In general, priority allocation of exchange is made when proposed imports are raw materials and capital equipment.

The issuance of exchange and import authorizations is the responsibility of the Foreign Exchange and Trade Control Commission (FETCC) which designates the commodities which may be imported, sources from which they may be admitted, and the amount of exchange allocation for each commodity. Bimonthly import quotas are announced by the Commission for the different categories of commodities, and importers may apply only for certain percentages of the total foreign exchange quotas for their imports for each period, and only within one category per budget period.

For control purposes, imports are classified permissible, controlled, suspended, and prohibited. Imports of certain specified luxuries are prohibited, and imports of specified commodities which may be produced locally, or which are in adequate supply are temporarily suspended. Registered importers are classified as traders, industrial end users, and direct end users. Licenses for the importation of industrial raw material are issued for materials needed for production for national defense or essential consumption requirements, or for export. Imports by direct end users which include mines, agricultural establishments, and fishery organizations are restricted to important machinery, productive implements, equipment, vehicles, vessels, or raw materials, seeds, fish fry, and animals for breeding purposes.

Importers of goods for productive enterprises are permitted to finance imports with self-provided exchange when authorization is given by the Foreign Exchange and Trade Control Commission. The same general criteria are applied by the Commission in screening these applications. That is, such imports must be within the approved range. In addition, the Commission must be satisfied that the source of this exchange is valid and proper. The bulk of self-provided exchange originates in Hong Kong where certain funds or income earning enterprises are controlled by Taiwanese.

Application for locally available exchange and import authorizations are submitted to the Bank of Taiwan and then transmitted to the Commission for screening. Upon approval, the bank issues an import license (Registration Certificate of Import), and the holder is then automatically entitled to obtain the foreign exchange from the bank at the time he can submit shipping documents. When application is submitted for an import certificate, the applicant must present the current quotations on the commodities to be imported or a pro forma invoice furnished by the supplier.

ICA-financed imports, which comprised slightly over 40 percent of all imports into Taiwan in 1956, are not subject to these controls. They are controlled, however, in the sense that ICA allocations for procurement are approved within the objectives of the economic development programs which are set up for Taiwan. Under ICA financed commercial to commercial procurement, ICA sets up procurement authorizations for specified commodities in certain amounts. Registered importers then may make application to the Chinese Government for an allocation of such exchange to import the indicated commodity. With the exception of agricultural products which must, under the law, come from the United States, the allocations are made on a worldwide basis, there being no requirement that the commodity be imported from any particular country. It should be noted that in 1956 over 78 percent of all ICA-financed imports were from the United States. Agricultural commodities comprised about 55 percent while other goods, chiefly industrial, made up the balance.

In commercial and project procurement, the interested Government enterprise in Taiwan prepares the specifications and submits them to the Council for United States Aid (CUSA). This agency then consults with J. G. White Engineering Co. (general consulting engineers to CUSA) and a review is made of the specifications. The Central Trust of China, the Government's purchasing agency, then calls for bids. A procurement advisory group, consisting of Central Trust of China, J. G. White Engineering Co., CUSA, and the ICA mission in Taiwan, may be consulted in connection with the award of the contract. In most cases, however, Central Trust makes the award. ICA policy is that United States producers must always have a wholly adequate opportunity to bid on any procurement financed by ICA. It is required that specifications conform to United States standards. There are indications that there have been some departures from this procedure in several countries including Taiwan. ICA has therefore forwarded instructions to ICA missions in all countries urging that the established procurement procedure be strictly observed.

While the import control system may be said to limit imports from the United States, this restriction is in harmony with the overall United States aid policy toward Taiwan which includes among other objectives the promotion of economic and financial stability. Taiwan's unique status requires the maintenance of a substantial defense program which results in a serious drain on its resources. This excessive financial burden coupled with the high cost of carrying on an essential economic development program leaves a gap in Taiwan's foreign exchange earning capacity which forces the adoption of strict controls over the use of exchange for imports and other purposes.

The Taiwan Government regards its import control system as avoiding discrimination in the choice of procurement sources. Commodities may be imported within the system from any country except in those circumstances when a particular currency becomes scarce.

One feature of Taiwan's foreign trade policy brought about by the economics of available markets for its relatively undiversified exports, places an obligation on procurement from Japan. In order to assure an export market for two of its principal crops, Taiwan has found it necessary to enter into a trade and payments agreement with Japan under which the greater part of its sugar and rice are exported to Japan on the basis of barter for various Japanese manufactured goods. The principal items imported into Taiwan from Japan under this arrangement include commercial fertilizers, machinery and tools, and ores, metals, and manufactures.

The United States share in both Chinese and ICA financed imports in 1956, and the position of Japan, which holds second place as a supplier, are shown in the following tabulation:

| | Value | Percent of Total |
|---|---|---|
| Chinese-financed imports, 1956: | | |
| Total | US$113, 109, 043 | |
| From Japan | 64, 361, 726 | 56. 90 |
| From United States | 18, 328, 561 | 16. 20 |
| ICA-financed imports, 1956: | | |
| Total | 80, 587, 173 | |
| From Japan | 5, 919, 650 | 7. 35 |
| From United States | 63, 070, 518 | 78. 26 |
| Chinese- and ICA-financed imports, 1956: | | |
| Total | 193, 696, 216 | |
| From Japan | 70, 281, 376 | 36. 28 |
| From United States | 81, 399, 079 | 42. 02 |

Source: Taiwan Inspectorate General of Customs.

Taiwan's difficult and worsening position with respect to foreign exchange earnings early in 1955 brought about the need to tighten controls. Controls were therefore revised in March 1955 in order to bring about an improved qualitative control over the composition of imports, eliminate speculative imports, and screen import payment allocations.

Little prospect can be seen in the immedite future for a situation in which Taiwan could relax in any degree its measures to select and restrict imports. In addition, although attention is being given to the development of other export crops and additional industrial production for export, Taiwan will continue to be heavily dependent for exchange earnings upon its two main crops—sugar and rice—and it is likely that the barter arrangement with Japan will continue to be in favor in Taiwan.

VIETNAM

All commercial imports into Vietnam are subject to licensing controls in order to conserve foreign exchange and to channel imports into lines of goods considered essential or beneficial to the welfare of the people and the growth and diversification of the economy. A significant secondary objective is to achieve the importation of goods at the lowest landed cost.

Import control regulations and procedures applying to goods shipped under the United States aid program are of primary interest in the Vietnamese market, since more than 95 percent of the total import authorizations granted by the Vietnamese Government in 1956 (amounting to $240 million) were for goods financed by the United States, chiefly under the "commercial import program." Import license applications submitted under this program are examined by the Directoriate General of Foreign Commerce of Vietnam, and are either approved or rejected depending on the availability of exchange for a particular product (as established by annual exchange budgets and supplementary quarterly exchange allocations), the product's essentiality, and the price quoted in the prospective importer's pro-forma invoice. Licenses are not issued for commodities deemed to be luxury or semiluxury products or in competition with domestic articles.

The import controls are nondiscriminatory with respect to country of origin, being based—in line with the general overall ICA policy relating to worldwide procurement—on lowest price. In practice, however, the controls in some instances appear to be de facto limiting with respect to United States exports to Vietnam. Despite the soundness of the principle of worldwide procurement and the high degree of liberalization it automatically implies, undue emphasis in Vietnam on the determination of the competitiveness of like goods primarly from a price standpoint—without adequate consideration of factors such as quality standards, servicing arrangements, and delivery time—is believed to be restricting American participation in the Vietnamese market.

The importance of obtaining all appropriate consideration for United States foods is particularly great at this time, since Vietnam, as a former French colonial area, has only recently been freely open to American products and they are as yet relatively little known in the area. United States aid to Vietnam was channeled through France until 1955, and the last vestige of French preferences under the Vietnamese import control system was only removed in early 1956. Buying habits now being formed will continue after the significance of the American aid program has declined. Moreover, sales now being made, especially in the capital goods line, will have an important bearing on future purchases of spare parts, complementary equipment and machinery, and raw materials for processing.

Both the volume of United States exports and the United States share of trade have increased since the institution of the aid program. In 1954 imports from the United States amounted to $25 million (8 percent of total imports), in 1955, $31 million (12 percent), and in 1956, $60 million (28 percent). Liberalization of trade controls with respect to the United States is not a problem in Vietnam in view of the present supply of dollars available through United Stats aid and the overall lack of discriminatory regulations. It is believed, therefore, that United States trade with the area can be further increased, if United States firms actively investigate and make aggressive sales efforts in the market. Expended sales promotional activities could be aided by a reduction of the excessive stress on price quotations in the administration of worldwide procurement regulations.

### ARGENTINA

Argentina's present system of foreign exchange control dates from the early days of the provisional government in late 1955. Under it, permissible imports are grouped in 3 lists, the first of which includes goods which may be imported at the official rate of exchange (18 pesos to the dollar) with prior exchange authorization or under the quota system. The commodities in this list are those considered most essential to the country's economy.

Certain less essential goods are included in the second list and may be freely imported under automatic license at the free market exchange rate which has been hovering around 40 pesos to the dollar. The third list contains a relatively small number of goods which may be imported with free exchange, plus a surcharge which ranges from 10 to as high as 450 pesos to the dollar, although the great majority of items in this category carry a surcharge of 20 to 40 pesos to the dollar. All goods in the last two lists may be imported by any person registered as an importer without regard to his previous status.

Quite a number of commodities within the three lists are limited as to country or countries of origin, this limitation sometimes being determined by special trade-agreement considerations, and at other times being determined by a desire to limit types of exchange to be used for their importation. This is de facto limiting on the importation of many kinds of commodities of United States origin.

In general, it may be said that the present exchange system represents a considerable liberalization of conditions prevailing during the last years of the Peron administration, although there has recently become evident an increased tendency to restrict certain imports from the dollar area.

A very definite trend toward shifting more and more commodities from the official rate list to the free market list developed during 1956 and some goods not previously importable were added to the latter list or the list of free market rate, plus-surcharge.

In April the Central Bank took a specific measure against certain imports from the dollar area by limiting imports of some 40 commodities to nondollar areas. For the most part, the commodities involved were not significant from the United States viewpoint, but two of them, tinplate and soda ash, were items of importance in our trade. Exporters of tinplate, in particular, were concerned about this development, in view of the fact that Argentina has been probably our principal, traditional market for this product.

A second measure was adopted in May when the importation of machine tools and welding equipment with a unit value of $15,000 or less was likewise limited to nondollar sources, while the importation of a long list of other machine tools and industrial machinery was made contingent upon the granting by the exporter of 8-year credit terms if from the dollar area but only 4-year terms if from the nondollar area.

Officers of United States Government have discussed these two cases and the obvious trend toward limitation of dollar imports with the Minister of Finance in an informal manner. He made it clear that no deliberate discrimination was intended but that dollar balance of payments difficulties made it imperative to limit dollar imports to the most essential goods or to those not readily available from other sources. He said that further restrictions on dollar imports would depend upon whether it might be possible to resolve the difficulties.

Even in the face of these restrictive measures, however, American goods continue to dominate the Argentine market. It seems likely that even though additional commodities may be added to the prohibited list the United States will continue to be Argentina's principal supplier, even though the pattern of dollar imports will obviously change. Imports of United States merchandise of all types amounted to $104.2 million in 1953, to $122.3 million in 1954, to $147.9 million in 1955, the year in which the present system was established, and to $211.8 million in 1956, the first full year of its operation. Thus, despite the fact that United States exporters of certain commodities have seen the Argentine market closed to them, the overall volume of trade has shown a very significant increase since the present exchange system was adopted.

In view of Argentina's known need for substantial expansion in certain industries, notably those of petroleum, electric power, and transportation, and the obsolescence of much of her other industrial equipment, it seems unlikely that any sharp decrease in total imports from the United States will occur. Rather, there will be a changing pattern of imports, with exclusion or limitation of many commodities readily available from nondollar areas, and in earmarking of dollars for the importation of capital equipment.

### BRAZIL

The Brazilian import control system, in effect since October 1953, permits the importation of at least limited quantities of almost any goods desired, on the basis of open bids at public auction for exchange commitment certificates, entitling the holder to apply for an import license covering a shipment to be paid for in a specific currency. For the purpose of the exchange auctions, 5 commodity classifications have been established, based primarily upon the degree of essentiality of the commodity to the national economy. Consideration is also given, however, to providing appropriate protection for domestic industry, with the result that even essential products are placed in the 4th or 5th categories for auction purposes if they are considered to be of a type adequately and satisfactorily produced in Brazil from the standpoint of quantity, quality, and price. The categories have been revised several times since the inauguration of the present system and contain several thousand individual commodity classifications. By virtue of the fact that comparatively limited amounts of foreign exchange are allocated to the 4th and 5th categories, covering less essential and luxury goods, exchange premiums for these categories are high, making it extremely expensive in terms of cruzeiros to import such goods.

The mechanics of the control system are designed to prevent overlicensing of imports and the resultant accumulation of a payments backlog. Varying amounts of exchange certificates for United States dollars and for other currencies are offered at auction, depending upon exchange availabilities, and each currency is auctioned separately. A large proportiton of Brazil's foreign exchange receipts is utilized for Government imports (including wheat), services on loans, and for imports of petroleum and newsprint, both of which are outside the regular auction system.

The effect of Brazil's exchange control system upon individual commodities or commodity groups is difficult to determine with any degree of exactness, because of the complexity of the import category classifications and frequent shifts of commodities from one category to another.

The regulations in force prior to October 1953 involved a so-called positive list of commodities for which licenses would be granted. In this respect the present system under which virtually any product can be imported, provided the Brazilian importer is able and willing to make a sufficiently high auction bid, may be considered less restrictive.

For a considerable period following enactment of the present system, the auction bids or premiums for United States dollar-exchange commitment certificates were generally higher than the bids for certificates in other currencies. As a result, imports from the United States were generally at a competitive disadvantage with those from other countries in terms of cruzeiro costs. More recently the spread between auction premiums for dollar exchange and for other currencies has been substantially narrower. Effective February 1, 1957, revised minimum auction bids were established which had the effect of narrowing still further the spread between the auction premiums for dollars and those for other currencies.

Total allocations of dollar exchange at the exchange auctions (exclusive of petroleum) averaged about $10.3 million per month during 1955 and $15.8 million during 1956, reflecting the substantial increase in dollar offerings in the last 6 months of the year. In January 1957 dollar-exchange allocations amounted to $22.45 million and have since been maintained at approximately that level.

The weighted-average exchange premium for United States dollars in cruzeiros per dollar was 78.46 in 1955, 80.98 in 1956, and 60.85 in January 1957.

The prospects for further liberalization of Brazil's exchange control system, or even of maintaining the present level of dollar offerings at the import exchange auctions, depend to a very large extent upon the market outlook for coffee, which in 1956 accounted for 83.1 percent of total dollar exports. Export shipments during the first 6 months of 1957 have been below those for the comparable period of 1956, with the result that dollar-exchange availabilities have declined by a considerable amount. Shipments of the 1956–57 coffee crop began in July, however, and may be expected to provide a corresponding increase in foreign-exchange receipts.

There are two other developments which may be expected to affect Brazil's import and exchange control regulations. The first of these is a complete revision of the Brazilian import tariff schedule, which would substitute ad valorem duties (generally at a much higher level) for the present specific duties. The tariff revision is to be accompanied by a modification of the exchange control system, under which it is reported that the existing exchange categories would be reduced from 5 to 2.[1] With the increased duties to be assessed against imports, it is expected that the exchange auction premiums will be correspondingly reduced, thereby transferring a large part of the cruzeiro cost of imports from the exchange auctions to the tariff. The overall effect of these changes, although probably not providing a basis for substantially increased imports from the United States, may be expected to result in a somewhat greater degree of flexibility in Brazil's import trade.

## CHILE

Chile's present import control system went into effect in April of 1956 (decree No. 357 of April 3, 1956, published in Diario Oficial No. 23,425, as amended by decree No. 859 of August 9, 1956, published in the Diario Oficial No. 23,526). Under this system, goods that are specified in the above decrees or in subsequent modifications issued by the Ministry of Economy are permitted importation. Those goods that do not appear on these lists are prohibited importation.

Goods permitted entry are subject to a deposit requirement, import duties and surcharges, the usual custom fees and documentation and for certain goods such as foods, drugs, firearms, livestock, etc., the customary health and sanitary regulations. There are no import or exchange licenses required and permitted goods may be imported without quantitative or other restrictions.

The deposit requirement ranges from 5 to 1,500 percent of the value of the import depending on the essentiality of the import. It is made to the Central Bank of Chile, and the deposit is returned when the shipment has been completed. There are nine deposit categories. The percentage requirement for each deposit category is indicated below:

*Deposit requirement, percent of value of the importation*

| Categories: | |
|---|---|
| A | 5 |
| B | 50 |
| C | 100 |
| D | 150 |
| E | 200 |
| F | 400 |
| G | 600 |
| H | 1,000 |
| I | 1,500 |

A certificate indicating payment of the deposit requirement is issued by the central bank and a copy must be presented by the exporter in the exporting country to the Chilean consulate in order to obtain

[1] The revised Brazilian tariff was promulgated on August 14, 1957, at which time the exchange auctions were suspended for a month. Two categories of goods were established on September 6 for the purpose of exchange auctions: "General"—covering essential goods, and "Special"—covering non-essential or luxury products. The first auctions for goods in the "General" category were held on September 10. At this time, however, it is not possible to evaluate the overall effect of these measures upon imports from the United States, although they may be expected to result in a somewhat greater degree of flexibility in Brazil's import trade.

consular authorization of the shipment. In the case of a few goods specified in the decrees, a certificate of necessity from the Ministry of Economy is also required in order to be imported.

Apart from the above restrictions, there are no other significant restrictions on the importation of goods to Chile.

The essentiality of the specific goods to the Chilean economy and the ability of Chilean industry to meet domestic demand have been the principal criteria in determining whether the goods may be included in the list of permitted imports. In general, raw materials and industrial goods deemed essential and those not produced in sufficient quantity domestically are included in the permitted list. Luxury goods and those produced in sufficient supply by the domestic industry are excluded from the list of permitted imports. The present import system has been implemented in an effort to help solve Chile's balance of payments deficit, and is applied without discrimination against the United States or the dollar area.

Prior to the decree of April 3, 1956, Chile had an import control system that was much more restrictive than the present system. Multiple fixed rates of exchange were in effect and applied in accordance with the nature of the product. In addition, the exchange budget established the permitted list of imports, but also featured quantitative limits on the total amount of foreign exchange, and of dollars, that was made available for the importation of a specified product. In addition to these restrictions, numerous bilateral trade and payments agreements entered into by Chile, tended to further discourage imports from the dollar area. These factors tended to decrease the share of the United States in the Chilean market.

Chilean annual data on imports by country of origin, that would permit an assessment of the effect of the new import system, are not yet available. It appears, however, that while Chile's overall imports declined by about 6 percent, imports from the United States will register an increase for the period. The available data for the first 7 months of 1956 show that imports from the United States for the period totaled $108,312,000, representing 45 percent of Chile's total imports of $240,954,000.

Compared to the previous system, the new import system appears to have contributed to an increase in imports from the United States. The present system with its permitted list of imports prohibits the importation of many products, particularly consumer goods and luxury products, but since the Chilean market for the United States products has been largely for raw materials and capital goods the effect of these restrictions are mitigated.

Present import restrictions make no distinction between imports from the dollar area and other imports. In this respect, it represents a liberalization over the prior system, since under the exchange budget the amount of dollars for imports of specified products were prescribed and there was a conscious policy of discouraging imports from the dollar area.

In addition, the numerous bilateral trade and payments agreements entered into tended to further discourage imports from the dollar area. While some of these agreements are still in effect and serve to discourage multilateral trade, there has evolved a new policy oriented toward freer trade.

Prospects for any significant liberalization of the present import system in the near future are not favorable. Chile has been undergoing for some years a period of severe inflation. In the last year strong measures have been taken to check inflation and the present exchange and import system constitutes a major part of the stabilization program. As long as strong inflationary pressures persist it is likely that controls of the type now in force will be used to allocate Chile's limited exchange to those imports deemed essential to the economy.

Copper accounts for about 65 percent of Chile's foreign-exchange earnings. Production has increased but prices have declined considerably since early 1956. During the foreseeable future, prices are likely to remain depressed. Therefore, it is unlikely that further liberalization of the import system can be expected.

On the other hand, the fact that the present import system has worked reasonably well would indicate that there is little reason to expect a tightening of controls at the present time.

COLOMBIA

Colombia has had some import restrictions in effect for many years. Heavy buying after the end of World War II caused the Government to tighten restrictions, but these were relaxed in 1951 when the rise in coffee prices improved Colombia's terms of trade and corrected the balance of payments. These favorable conditions stimulated a greatly increased demand for imported products and caused the volume of imports to rise sharply. United States exports to Colombia, for example, rose from $231 million in 1952 to $343 million in 1954. Colombia's current difficulties began in 1954 when coffee prices dropped somewhat, but there was no corresponding decrease in import demand or in the actual volume of imports. Imports in 1955 and 1956 were at virtually the same level as in 1954. Gold and exchange reserves were reduced seriously and commercial foreign exchange arrearages acccumulated as importers were unable to purchase sufficient foreign exchange to meet their obligations.

The measures taken by the Government to correct the unfavorable balance-of-payments situation were totally inadequate before October 1956. By that time, the imbalance in Colombia's international payments had reached serious proportions and threatened to precipitate an economic crisis which would have profound effects on Colombia's domestic economy.

Severe restrictions were then applied to Colombia's imports and limited internal measures were taken to halt inflation and retard economic expansion. There was still considerable doubt, however, whether the measures taken were sufficient to correct the situation.

The Colombian Government which succeeded to power after the deposition of President Gustavo Rojas Pinilla on May 10, 1957, has undertaken a thorough reform of the country's economic system. In addition to placing severe curbs on further internal economic expansion, the new Government restricted imports further.

On June 18, 1957, the Colombian Government published a list of prohibited imports designed to eliminate the importation of all nonessential goods. The list includes almost all goods of a luxury nature and many basic commodities and manufactured goods produced in Colombia in sufficient quantity to satisfy minimum essential requirements or for which adequate local substitutes are available. Examples of goods included in the prohibited list are dairy products, cereal flours, household appliances, automobiles, tires, clocks and watches, and textiles.

A second list published on the above date consisted of goods which may be imported only upon the approval of each request for an import license by a Government import board. The goods in this list are considered to be essential imports, but the Government will carefully supervise the quantity of imports according to the needs of the importer and general economic conditions. Examples of goods included in this list are cotton, steel bars and shapes, nylon yarn, and internal-combustion engines.

Imports not included in either of the above lists are licensed automatically and are not subject to quantitative restrictions. Goods in this category are mostly highly essential raw materials and manufactured goods which are not produced in Colombia or which are produced in quantities which are manifestly inadequate to supply minimum requirements. Examples of imports in this classification are chemical fertilizers, essential drugs and medicines, and electric motors.

The principal exports of the United States to Colombia in the period 1953–55 are listed below. The value of annual exports in each category was $5 million or more during that period. The present import status of these products is listed in the second column.

| *Principal United States exports to Colombia, 1953–55* | *Present import status* |
|---|---|
| Grains | Wheat, barley, and oats permitted; others prohibited. |
| Cotton manufactures | Almost all types prohibited. |
| Synthetic fibers and products | Only raw fibers permitted. |
| Paper | Only rolls and sheets of unfinished paper permitted. |
| Petroleum products | Permitted. |
| Iron and steel plates and sheets. | Do. |
| Power generators | Do. |
| Household equipment and applances. | Prohibited. |
| Radio and TV apparatus | Do. |
| Industrial engines and turbines. | Permitted. |
| Construction equipment | Generally permitted. |
| Textile machinery | Permitted. |
| Tractors | Do. |
| Trucks and buses | Trucks permitted; buses prohibited. |
| Passenger cars | Prohibited. |
| Medicinals and pharmaceuticals. | Generally permitted. |
| Chemicals | Do. |

Colombian import restrictions have limited imports from the United States for many years but, until October 1956, the effects were not severe. Imports for the first 3 months of 1957, however, were reduced to about 50 percent of imports during the corresponding period of the previous year.

Since import restrictions apply equally to goods from all countries, United States exports to Colombia presumably were reduced in proportion to the decrease in total imports. In 1956, imports from the United States constituted about 62 percent of total Colombian imports.

Prospects that Colombia will be able to relax its import restrictions in the near future are very poor. Although the Government which succeeded to power in May 1957 appears determined to strengthen the economy and liberalize foreign trade, there seems to be little prospect that this can be accomplished in less than 2 or 3 years.

### CUBA

Cuba does not maintain a general system of import controls. There is no general import-licensing system and no exchange controls are maintained on imports insofar as the United States is concerned. However, a few commodities are subject to import licensing or similar controls. These include (1) wheat and wheat flour, (2) rice, (3) dairy products, (4) potatoes, (5) red and kidney beans, and (6) tires and tubes.

The licensing system on imports of wheat and wheat flour was established in Cuba in 1951 on the grounds that it was necessary to the proper administration of Cuba's wheat-quota importations under the International Wheat Agreement. At that time, Cuba's wheat-agreement quota of 202,000 metric tons, wheat equivalent, was divided by Cuban decree into wheat and wheat-flour subquotas; the newly established Burrus Flour Mill, a United States-owned plant, was granted a quota of 80,000 metric tons of wheat and the remaining 122,000 metric tons, wheat equivalent, was allocated for the importation of wheat flour. This distribution remains the same today. Cuba's wheat and wheat-flour requirements approximate the allocation under the International Wheat Agreement. Consequently, all wheat and wheat-flour imports are under license.

Under the provisions of the General Agreement on Tariffs and Trade, Cuba granted a concession to the United States at Geneva in 1947 on rice. An annual low-duty tariff quota was established of 3,250,000 quintales (3,298,500 bags of milled rice of 100 pounds each). It was also agreed that this basic quota would be increased by the Cuban Government by the amount necessary to supply the difference between the estimated Cuban production of rice and the total estimated Cuban consumption in any calendar year. In effect this concession granted a guaranteed basic low-duty tariff quota with the understanding that any additional imports required to meet Cuba's consumption requirements would be added to the low-duty quota. The rice quota of 3,250,000 quintales is on a global basis, but the low-duty rate is applicable to the United States only. The effect of this arrangement has been that all of Cuba's rice imports originate in the United States. In order to administer this concession, the Cuban Government established an import-licensing system on rice. The concession became effective on January 1, 1948, and since that time the Cuban Government has made various changes in the licensing system which have been opposed by the United States rice exporters. The principal changes in the system have been the allocation of the quota on a quarterly basis rather than an annual basis, and the establishment of a requirement that all rice under the quota must be the equivalent of U. S. grades Nos. 1, 2, and 3, containing no more than 30 percent broken grains of not less than one-fourth grain size.

In summary, under the above licensing arrangement, United States exports of rice to Cuba are limited to the basic quota plus any additional amounts which the Cuban Government decides are necessary to meet consumption requirements and cannot be produced in Cuba.

In December 1956, the Cuban Government established controls over the importation of various dairy products which in effect constituted an import licensing system. The resolution making these controls effective states that the controls are designed to prevent any maladjustment that may arise between the national production and the importation and trade in cheese, powdered skim milk, and creams or fats obtained from milk. Importers of butter, powdered skim milk, and cream or fats obtained from milk must obtain a special permit for the removal of import shipments of those products from the Cuban customs. Purchase contracts on these products must be registered, and importers of dairy products must set aside 20 percent of each import shipment for the purpose of having reserve stocks on hand. The reserve requirement for evaporated milk is 10 percent. Evaporated milk and condensed milk are also subject to licensing.

It is too early to determine the impact of the new regulations on American exports to Cuba of these products. However, it would appear that the regulations are designed to protect the domestic industry and if fully enforced would have some detrimental effect on American exports of these items.

In order to avoid overproduction of potatoes in Cuba and to assure reasonable returns to domestic producers, the Cuban Government in January and February of 1955 put into effect regulations restricting domestic production and controlling the importation of seed and table potatoes. An annual quota of 680,000 bags of 100 pounds each for imports of table potatoes and an annual import quota of 175,000 bags of seed potatoes were established. Imports of seed potatoes under the quota are limited to the red variety and table potatoes to the white variety. In administering these total quotas, established potato importers in Cuba were allocated shares based on a historic pattern. Importers are required to register purchases and obtain an authorization for clearance of shipments from the Cuban customs. In recent years, Cuba has had a surplus during the growing season, and the regulations have assisted in avoiding serious disturbances in the market such as existed prior to the establishment of the controls.

In accordance with a Cuban-Chilean commercial agreement, a total of not more than 18,100,000 kilos of red and kidney beans are permitted to enter Cuba at a reduced duty rate each year. The quota year begins April 1. Of this quantity, which has been allocated by countries on a historic pattern, the United States can supply 6,930,000 kilos at the low-duty rate between April 1 and September 30. An import licensing system is maintained to administer the tariff quota arrangement and all imports of red and pink beans are subject to this control.

Imports of tires and tubes are subject to an import permit. The announced reason for the licensing of these items is to maintain better statistical data and thus help to regulate commerce and production in that industry. This system is not exercised at the present time in such a way as to limit imports of tires and tubes from the United States.

It will be noted that import licensing in Cuba is primarily designed to administer trade agreement provisions, or in connection with domestic control arrangements. However, in practice, import licensing has been implemented in such a way as to give maximum protection to domestic producers.

MEXICO

Mexican import control is applied to particular products rather than across the board and has two principal purposes complementing the country's tariff policy: (1) To channel available exchange resources into the acquisition of capital goods, necessary raw materials and other essential items, by discouraging importation of nonessentials and luxuries; and (2) to protect domestic producers. Originally established to protect exchange reserves, in recent years the trend has been to utilize import control increasingly as a protective device, although balance-of-payments considerations are rarely completely submerged because of the country's chronic imbalance on merchandise account.

Under the Mexican system, quantitative import quotas are few and at present seem to apply only to leather shoes, whisky, cigarettes, and unassembled vehicles.

About one-half of Mexico's imports, by value, are subject to prior import licensing by the Mexican Ministry of Economy. The permit system and the import tariff are extremely flexible in administration in order to provide maximum control and protection as necessary. In general, the protection thus afforded is intended to be quite restrictive in its application to imports of products which compete directly or indirectly with Mexican production. Nevertheless, application of this commercial policy is not discriminatory and applies equally to affected products irrespective of origin.

Import control is utilized also in conjunction with the Mexican policy of fostering exportation of hard-to-sell products through barter or other arrangements. To achieve this end, the Government generally permits the importation, in direct compensation, of articles subject to control and for which import permits are not generally granted because of their nonessential or luxury character. The list of hard-to-sell products for which barter deals are approved changes from time to time, and at the present time apparently henequen manufactures and more particularly cotton are the only export items so promoted.

Until recently, most barter deals were single transactions negotiated between Mexican and foreign firms, but subject to the approval of the Mexican National Bank of Foreign Trade. These arrangements do not seem in any tangible way to be discriminatory against United States trade.

Another type of arrangement, i. e., the compensation agreement between countries, e. g., the arrangement entered into between Mexico and France, signed January 9, 1957, at Mexico City, could be considered to be discriminatory against United States trade, depending upon the policies followed by Mexico in its implementation. Under this agreement Mexico agrees to permit the importation from France of various controlled items, including alcoholic beverages, textile products, faience ware, perfumery, paper products, to specified values, the total amounting to US$2 million. France in exchange agrees to permit the importation of various Mexican products including cotton, rice, coffee, oranges, to specified values, likewise totaling US$2 million. Should Mexico in implementation of this agreement, refuse to permit the importation of similar items from the United States, it would seem that discrimination could be charged, though such a charge might be countered with the rebuttal that the United States could have entered into a similar arrangement if it desired.

Still another form of compensation arrangement, in which Mexican import control plays a leading role, is the so-called cotton compensation program initiated in mid-1956. Under this program, Mexico permits the importation of certain products such as assembled and unassembled vehicles, television and radio parts, steel pipes, wines and liquors, firearms, watches, artificial fibers, textiles, fertilizers and insecticides, only when the importer guarantees the exportation of cotton to an equivalent value. This does not involve barter or direct compensation, since the Mexican importer can dispose of the cotton anywhere. While this scheme complicates normal trading practices, it does not place United States exports at any greater disadvantage than those of any other country.

In a sense the barter and compensation policy might be construed as liberalizing certain imports, since, in theory at least, without compensation imports of the particular items are not permitted; in the case of the luxury imports involved, it is undoubtedly true that fewer permits would be granted in the absence of such a program.

The Mexican National Foreign Trade Bank recently reported on 1956 compensation or barter arrangements, stating that there were over 700 individual transactions approved involving trade valued each way at over US$71 million. This is approximately 6.6 percent of total Mexican imports, and 8.3 percent of total exports in that year. According to the report, nearly 90 percent of the value of exports under these arrangements consisted of cotton; over 60 percent of the imports were unassembled automotive vehicles, iron ingots, radio and television receiver components, nylon, whisky, iron and steel sheet, ammonium sulfate, and tinplate.

It is virtually impossible to make a detailed appraisal of the effects of Mexico's import control system and policies on United States exports. Such factors as steadily increasing competition from Mexico's pre-World War II suppliers in Europe, and Japan, credit terms, prices, delivery dates, and other competitive factors in foreign trade, could, and probably do, account as much for certain changes in the United States overall position as a supplier of Mexican imports as does Mexico's import control system. However, there is no doubt that the system as applied severely restricts the market for certain United States products in the luxury or competitive class. Certain general observations can be made, based on United States and Mexican trade statistics.

In recent years the composition of Mexico's imports has shifted markedly from consumer goods to capital equipment, industrial raw materials, component parts, and the like. Thus, while some United States exporters find the Mexican market increasingly restricted, or even closed, the total value of United States exports to Mexico has been rising rapidly, particularly in the past 3 years, although the United States percentage of the market has declined about 8 percent since 1950.

The decline in the United States share of the Mexican market should be viewed in its proper perspective. In 1939 United States goods represented only 66 percent of Mexico's imports, rising during the war and postwar years to 87 to 90 percent of total imports. The decline beginning in 1950 represents the return to a more normal foreign trade pattern.

With the exception of foodstuffs, changes in the general composition of United States exports to Mexico have been small. This is not to say, however, as mentioned above, that particular items within commodity groups have not undergone marked changes. It might be noted, too, that the decline in food imports is more attributable to increased Mexican production through irrigation and improved methods than to protection.

In short, while the Mexican tariff and import licensing systems have served to protect certain Mexican industries (and to conserve or canalize foreign exchange expenditures), thereby restricting the market for selected United States export products, there has been no noticeable restrictive or discriminatory effect on overall United States exports. On the contrary, total United States exports to Mexico have increased.

With the exception of the January 1951 removal of the import prohibition applicable to over 300 classifications of the import tariff (established in 1947 and 1949 for balance of payments reasons) and the placing of many of these items under import control, followed by some relaxation in controls in the early part of 1951, there has been no real liberalization of Mexico's import control system over the past 8 years. On the contrary, the trend over this period has been toward greater utilization of import control for industry protection, although balance of payments considerations have motivated some actions, notably the placing of some 400 tariff classifications under import control in June 1954, following the peso devaluation in April of that year. Nevertheless, since the items affected by the 1954 measure were luxuries or nonessentials, generally competitive directly or indirectly with Mexican products, the correlative protective aspects are obvious.

In view of the avowed and demonstrated protectionist policy of the Mexican Government, prospects for any important relaxation in the import control system seem remote, particularly at the present moment when the country's chronic imbalance on merchandise account is considerably greater than usual.

Mexico is not a member of GATT, has no bilateral trade agreement with the United States, and such commercial or trade agreements as it has negotiated with other countries are of the general, most-favored-nation type; hence, the country has complete freedom of action to modify import duties and controls at will.

## PERU

Apart from the tariff and the quantitative limit on the importation of automobiles, Peru has no restrictions that would limit imports from the United States.

The quantitative restriction on imports of motor vehicles was imposed in 1954 in an effort to check the drain on Peru's foreign exchange reserves. The quota now stands at 8,320 motor vehicles for 1957, of which 4,160 are passenger cars and station wagons and 4,160 are trucks, including pickups and other commercial units. This quota is believed to be adequate to meet the country's normal demands. The quota is distributed among Peru's automobile dealers in accordance with the share of the market held by each make during a base period and it not believed to discriminate toward the United States. Private individuals (noncommercial) are permitted to import motor vehicles outside the established quota but authorization, from the Ministry of Finance and Commerce, is required.

### VENEZUELA

Venezuelan commercial policy has followed a general trend toward providing maximum encouragement to domestic agriculture and industry.

In addition to import duties other types of trade controls are imposed, such as licensing requirements, import quotas, regulations requiring the purchase of specified amounts of local products for each unit imported, import prohibitions, and quarantine laws.

State trading is also employed in products whose price is supported in the domestic market.

The Ministry of Development issues most licenses in accordance with existing laws and the regulations promulgated by other government agencies. In addition, a permit must also be obtained from the Ministry of Agriculture on many agricultural items in order to comply with sanitary regulations.

Pharmaceutical items and food items must be registered with the Ministry of Health before any importation is permitted but once registered do not generally require further licensing or permit. Each shipment of food items containing animal products must have a prior permit.

For some items a government agency may by law be the sole importer for various reasons. The Venezuelan Development Corp. is the sole importer of items for agricultural improvement which are sold to farmers at cost. The Agriculture and Livestock Bank is now the sole importer of agricultural items which are price supported.

A few items which are considered prejudicial to public morality are prohibited, such as gambling devices, opium, and Communist or pornographic literature. Other prohibited items are government monopolies such as war material, or coins and devices for their manufacture, rock salt, and matches. Cigaret papers are a monopoly for controlling the manufacture of cigarets. Pharmaceutical and food items which are not registered are also prohibited.

On some items control measures employed have no effect in limiting imports or may be used to facilitate imports. Infertile eggs, white printing paper, and certain disinfectants are registered for the purpose of being exonerated from the payment of duty. Import licenses applicable to wheat flour are imposed mainly as an accounting device in connection with the International Wheat Agreement. In the case of prefabricated houses a permit is needed solely for the purpose of securing classification as a whole which pays a substantially lower rate of duty than would the component parts.

The government monopoly of items such as cigaret papers and war material cannot be considered to limit trade in these items. Neither can the requirement that pharmaceuticals and food items be registered be considered as a device to limit their importation. The quarantine on uncooked pork which conceivably was unreasonable and detrimental to United States exports was lifted in 1956.

The items (which are mostly agricultural) subject to quotas or requiring a ratio of nationally produced product to that which is imported are for the most part detrimental to United States exports.

Some industrial items such as textiles, tires and tubes, and footwear have received protection at the expense of United States exports.

A trade agreement with the United States, effective December 16, 1939, provided for mutual unconditional most-favored-nation treatment. The 1939 agreement was supplemented and amended by an agreement signed August 28, 1952, and effective October 11 of the same year. This agreement is still in effect.

Under most-favored-nation agreements, these concessions are extended to Belgium, Bolivia, Brazil, Canada, El Salvador, Spain, the United Kingdom, and Italy. Venezuela is not a member of GATT.

The latest agreement covered 60 percent of United States exports to Venezuela by value of 1950 and 90 percent of United States imports. Under the 1939 agreement, only 35 percent of United States exports were included.

Because of demand for protection of local industry Venezuela in 1952 did not find it possible to continue concessions on many items whose local production had increased. Others were kept in the agreement but at import rates calculated to permit development of local production. On some products duty-free treatment was made binding.

Duty concessions on 179 items of United States exports were conceded in the 1952 agreement, as compared with 88 items in the 1939 agreement.

The future prospects for the liberalization of Venezuela's trade restrictions are not good. The broad policy of Venezuela has been to attempt to diversify its economy in order to relieve the country of dependency on oil as a source of foreign exchange, the world demand and price of which may be subject to fluctuations. There is also an indication of national pride in the country's industrial development. Venezuela has also embarked upon a long-range development program for agriculture, improving seed and stock, building dams and irrigation facilities, producing fertilizer from its petro-chemicals, and granting land and liberal credits to settlers on the new lands.

A favorable indication is the possibility of a study sponsored by the Venezuelan Government to formulate a more rational plan for economic development. Development of uneconomic industries may be abandoned or delayed in order to relieve pressures on Venezuela's already very high cost of living.

## UNITED KINGDOM

Since the beginning of World War II, and throughout the postwar period, the United Kingdom has rationed what are considered to be scarce supplies of dollar exchange for what their import licensing authorities believe to be the most essential needs of the British economy.

Under the import licensing policies adopted to carry out this objective, licenses have generally been issued for the import from the United States or other dollar countries of only those goods which the British Board of Trade considers to be essential to the United Kingdom's economy, and for which a suitable substitute is not alternatively available from domestic or other nondollar sources of supply. Since each case is considered on its own merits, there are some exceptions made to this general rule. In the case of an item considered essential, for example, an import license may be granted despite the availability from nondollar sources of a suitable substitute because the American product offers a substantial price advantage or the delivery date is a crucial factor. Licenses are sometimes also issued to import either an essential or nonessential American product when the British importer can demonstrate that the use of such dollar goods would result in an export which could not otherwise have taken place because of the overseas customer's preference for the superior or unique qualities of the United States made item involved.

Under this licensing regime, imports from the United States have been largely restricted to raw materials, basic food and feedstuffs, and industrial equipment and other capital goods. However, special quotas have been established for the import of a considerable number of so-called less essential or consumer goods from the United States. These are described further down.

It is the stated objective of the British Government to move as rapidly as they believe their balance of payments position will allow to reduce their controls on imports from the United States and other dollar countries. The official statements made to this effect recognize the economic benefits, in terms of the cost-price structure and productivity of the British economy, to be derived from permitting producers to choose their raw materials and supplies on the basis of price and quality considerations without reference to the currency which must be paid for such purchases; as well as the desirability of freeing their importers and the Government agencies involved from the burdensome paperwork necessitated by import controls.

Until mid-1955, when the United Kingdom's external finances took a turn for the worse, considerable progress was made toward freeing Britain's dollar imports. The United Kingdom resumed its program of progressive dollar trade liberalization with the announcement this July 3 that import controls are to be removed, effective August 1, on some 500 additional commodities from the dollar area. These additions will increase slightly the estimate made as of January 1, 1957, based on the value of Britain's trade in 1953, that 37 percent of the United Kingdom's imports from the United States are permitted to enter freely.

The main progress in freeing dollar imports was made in the years 1953 and 1954. These earlier liberalization measures were undertaken mainly in connection with the return to private traders about that time of nearly all commodity importing, which since the beginning of World War II had been the business of a number of British Government agencies, including the Ministry of Food, the Ministry of

Supply, and the Board of Trade; and also in conjunction with the reopening in London and Liverpool of long-established commodity exchanges dealing on a worldwide basis with most nonferrous metals, cereals, and cotton.

Again on the basis of United Kingdom's 1953 trade, it is estimated that the percentage of goods which private traders may import freely from the United States rose from 32 percent at end 1954, to 34 percent at end 1955, to 37 percent at end 1956, and will probably be close to 40 percent after August 1, 1957.

The pattern of the United Kingdom's program for dollar trade liberalization is shown in tthe nature of the goods which have been included in the world "open general license" list of items which may be imported from any source, including the dollar area, without license. It is to liberalize in the first instance the raw materials, and semimanufactures as well as the basic foodstuffs and feedstuffs required to keep British industry and agriculture operating efficiently and at capacity. A large number of these items have until now been imported under "open individual licenses" (which do not restrict quantity) or under specific licenses which have in practice been freely issued. The most recent additions to the open general license list fall into the category of what the Board of Trade has described as a "tidying-up operation"; they complete the elimination of controls on the basic raw materials of industry.

As of January 1, 1957, 45 percent of the agricultural products, and 53 percent of the raw materials imported from the United States in 1953 could have entered free of license as compared with 9 percent for manufactured goods. These percentages will also be increased slightly as the result of the latest additions to the world open general license list. Existing restrictions will continue to apply to dollar imports of machinery, fuels, many food items, and most manufactured products. It is reasonable to assume that in any further progressive decontrol of dollar imports, items in the machinery, fuel, and chemicals categories, for example, will have a higher order of priority than most categories of consumer goods.

Among the items on the latest complete open general license list which may be of special interest to United States traders are the following: Nearly all feeding stuffs, grains, and cereals; wheat flour; natural or artificial bladders and casings; lard; molasses; whisky; starches and starch preparations (in bulk, unsweetened); dried beans and peas; various nonferrous metal ores and scrap, and rare earths as well as other minerals; peanuts; cottonseed, peanut, linseed, and soya bean oil; a variety of chemicals and tanning and dyestuffs; most of the inorganic fertilizers; pharmaceutical glands and offals; some cellulose acetate and polyvinyl plastic materials; a variety of hides and skins, including furskins; both hardwood and softwood lumber not further prepared than hewn, sawn, planed, or dressed, including flooring block, staves and caskheads, railroad ties, telegraph, transmission, ladder and scaffold poles, mining timber, boxboards, shingles, and certain other types of siding. Besides chemicals, other manufactured items on this list which may be imported freely from the United States include printing blocks, plates, and cylinders, and impressed flongs and matrices for use in printing processes; refractory or heat insulating bricks, blocks, and other shapes; a wide range of iron and steel (including alloy steel) and nonferrous metal primary forms and shapes, pipes, tubes, and hollow sections, wire and cable; railway rails; solder; nonfiction books; some paper and paperboard; a number of types of fiber building boards; plywood; and wood veneers.

The above-named items and others listed on open general license have been completely decontrolled. There are, in addition, a number of dollar commodities and manufactured goods for which the restrictions on import from the United States have been partially eased. Such items fall into two categories: those on open individual license (for which licenses to import from the United States are required, but issued freely); and a number of others which may be imported from the United States, and in some cases other dollar countries, to the limit of the quotas set up for them.

Most of the items formerly on open individual license for import from the United States have been included in the most recent additions to the open general license list. However, ash and hickory tool handles, raw cotton, and sugar are still in this category.

In the second group for which special import quotas have been established are the following:

Leather, for which a global quota covering all dollar countries of £2 million a year f. o. b. has been established: This represents an increase of about £1¼ million over the complicated quota arrangements previously in effect for leather imports from North America.

Automobiles: An annual quota providing for the import of 650 automobiles from North America has been in effect since 1955. Previous to that time first 6 and then 12 autos per maker (about 150 in all) were permitted to be imported for exhibition at the annual auto show and sale afterward.

Motorcycles, for which an annual quota of 50 has been established for import from the United States effective July 1, 1957.

Periodicals for newsstand sale: Single copies of American magazines and periodicals imported through the mail do not require import licenses. In addition, an annual quota amounting to approximately $850,000 has been in effect providing for the import of United States magazines and periodicals in bulk for newsstand sale. This quota was doubled in 1956.

Canned salmon: The current quota established for imports from North America for year beginning July 1, 1957, is £3.5 million; cost, insurance, and freight, an increase of £0.2 million over both the 1954–55 and 1955–56 periods.

Natural cheeses: Similarly the annual North American quota has been renewed effective July 1, 1957, at the same amount, £1.5 million, as previously.

Apples: Another continuing North American quota is in effect for the import of £1.25 million; cost, insurance, and freight, fresh apples from Canada and the United States. The latest one covers the period November 16 to December 31, 1957.

Honey: An import quota has been set up for honey from all dollar-account countries, except Cuba with whom separate arrangements have been made. The quota amounts to £40,000 f. o. b. for the year beginning July 1, 1957.

British token import plan: The token plan was set up by the British Government in 1946 to afford an opportunity to firms which

22806—58——28

had established a prewar market, built up goodwill and trade contacts in the United Kingdom for products on an approved list of some 200 commodity groups, principally consumer goods, which would not ordinarily be licensed for import from the United States or Canada under the operation of the United Kingdom import licensing criteria, to maintain token quantities of their products on the British market until such time as they could again be imported freely.

Under the plan, the British Government will permit imports in a yearly amount not to exceed 30 percent of the value of the average annual shipments of the specified commodities of each qualified exporter during a base period consisting of the years 1936, 1937, and 1938. The British Government requires appropriate evidence, issued under authority of the United States Government, that manufacturers wishing to take advantage of opportunities under the arrangement did, in fact, make shipments of the commodities to the United Kingdom during the base period. The United States Bureau of Foreign Commerce has agreed to act as certifying agent and issue appropriate certificates, in the form of token quota vouchers, which the exporter forwards to the British importer of his choice for presentation to the British Board of Trade as a basis for obtaining an import license.

Originally designed as a temporary measure for the immediate postwar period, the plan has had to be extended much longer than anticipated. When it became apparent that there were some firms who would otherwise be eligible to participate in the plan on the basis of their prewar exports, but were either unable or not interested in using these quotas, the Department of Commerce was able to obtain the consent of the British Board of Trade to a procedure which the Bureau of Foreign Commerce devised for redistributing these unused quotas.

In all, the plan provides quotas of less than $5.5 million for all of the items involved. These include canned soups and vegetables, cigarettes and smoking tobacco, apparel and footwear, textile piece goods, household electrical appliances, stationery and office supplies, medicinal preparations, toys and sporting goods, and artificial teeth and dental equipment.

### BELGIUM-LUXEMBOURG

Practically all imports from the United States move into the Belgium-Luxembourg Economic Union (BLEU) without any quantitative restrictions. Import licenses are required on a nondiscriminatory basis for a small list of commodities but are issued automatically in the majority of cases. Where commodities are subject to screening, licenses are usually granted for the full amount requested.

A number of agricultural products which are subject to overall quotas or seasonal quotas are of greater concern to the neighboring European countries than to the United States (Belgium-Luxembourg obtained permission, in the form of a waiver, to apply such quotas from the contracting parties of the GATT in 1955). In accordance with the terms of this waiver, these restrictions must gradually be relaxed and completely eliminated in 1962.

Belgium-Luxembourg, in addition, also has reserved the right to control the following industrial commodities: Sand and gravel, coal, carbonic acid, hydrated borax, calcium carbide, trichlorethylene and perchlorethylene, cinematographic film, nitrates, tanned and pretanned leather, wares of porcelain, bottles and flasks, diamonds, silversmith's wares, second-grade tinplate, nylon stockings, automotive vehicles.

For all practical purposes, however, commodities in this group which are of interest to the United States are liberally admitted. Belgium-Luxembourg, as a member of the Benelux Union, has introduced global quotas which apply to the entire Benelux area in connection with the other members of the Customs Union. These quotas apply on the following commodities: Carbon dioxide, methyl chloride, penicillin, wooden packing cases, fishing nets, television sets and chassis thereof, passenger automobiles, chassis for automobiles, coachwork for automobiles, back-pedal brake hubs unbroken peeled and completely polished rice, rice flour, ordinary soap in block and bars, toilet, medicinal and similar soaps, and pipe fittings and flanges of malleable cast iron.

Here, again, the quotas of interest to the United States are ample to protect the United States interest, with the possible exception of penicillin. The quotas will remain valid for 1 year, although the possibility of periodical review is envisaged.

The vast majority of exports from the United States into the BLEU move without any restrictions, and thus the BLEU licensing and/or quota system has no appreciable effect upon exports from the United States. In the majority of cases, the required licenses or declaration licenses are granted automatically. Items under quota, except agricultural items, are most liberally admitted and are, for all practical purposes, treated like nonquota items (coal from the United States is a good example for one of these commodities still under quota). The agricultural items subject to quota restrictions are of greater interest to other European countries than to the United States, and are periodically reviewed by the GATT.

Practically all imports from the dollar area are either liberalized or admitted in most liberal quantities. Although before 1954 there was no formal Belgian dollar-liberalization list, import licenses were granted for a vast number of commodities. On June 1, 1954, the three Benelux countries introduced a common dollar-liberalization list which includes 86 percent of all imports from the dollar area based on 1953 imports. In practice, however, Belgian liberalization is much greater and results in a de facto total liberalization, except for agricultural commodities subject to restrictions under the terms of the waiver. However, even in this small segment Belgium does not discriminate against dollar imports and grants licenses to the dollar area to the same extent as to other areas.

In view of the fact that practically all imports from the United States are unimpeded and also because the Belgian Government desires to retain some standby measures in case of emergencies, it is unlikely that the existing standby controls on dollar imports will be changed to correspond with the actual, almost complete, liberalization status. Also, Belgium is a party to the common market treaty and will not take unilateral liberalization steps before the problems of that treaty have been more closely studied. On the other hand, there is no reason to believe that Belgian import regulations will become more restrictive.

Prior to May 1954 there existed no published list of dollar items which were freely admitted into Belgium-Luxembourg. However, Belgian importers of most United States goods experienced very little difficulty in obtaining licenses prior to that time.

Therefore, comparisons between United States imports prior to and after 1954 do not reflect the influence of Belgian liberalization measures, but may indicate trends in the economic situation.

In May 1954 the Benelux countries published a dollar-liberalization list, referred to above. This list has not been changed until at present. However, 95 to 98 percent of all imports from the dollar area are either formally liberalized or are treated as if they were liberalized.

### FRANCE

Since the end of World War II, controls over imports from the dollar area and other foreign-currency areas have been a feature of French commercial policy. This policy reflects France's need to conserve its foreign-exchange resources by regulating imports. As France's payments position improved during the period 1953–55, there was considerable administrative easing of the import-control system, but the basic system itself was continued. At present, with the recent worsening of France's payments position, licenses are required for all dollar imports, and the French have announced that they plan to reduce both their dollar and nondollar imports considerably. In June 1957 France suspended all import liberalization measures. To restore an equilibrium in its external trade the French Government also introduced a series of important measures in the foreign-trade and exchange-rate fields, including modifications in the exchange-rate system. Since August 11, 1957, the exchange rate of the franc has been effective for all transactions at 420 francs per US$1, corresponding to a 20-percent decrease in the value of the franc.

French trade and exchange controls are administered by the Office des Changes, an agency of the Ministry of Finance and Economic Affairs. Its decisions are reached in consultation with various interministerial committees. Control regulations are published in the Journal Officiel in the form of orders or notices to importers. Applications for import licenses must be made to the Office des Changes. Generally speaking, there are no set rules governing the issuance of import licenses; applications are examined individually, and decisions are made on a case-by-case basis. Among the criteria taken into account in licensing decisions are essentiality, price, and availability of similar items in France or from soft-currency sources. The flexible French import-control system gives the French administrative authorities wide discretionary powers in granting or rejecting import-license applications. A flexible system can result in licenses being denied for reasons that are protectionist, rather than based on balance-of-payments considerations, and, in some instances, protectionist considerations undoubtedly play a part in French licensing decisions. Such cases are difficult to document, however, given France's admitted need to regulate imports for payments reasons.

Under the French export and exchange controls, exporters are generally required to collect foreign-currency proceeds of exports and within 90 days turn them over to the Office des Changes in exchange for francs. As an exception to this general requirement, exporters in some cases are permitted to retain a certain percentage of the foreign currencies earned and to use them to finance imports. The procedures under which such imports not requiring an import license, may be made are as follows:

(*a*) *Ten percent equipment imports.*—Under this procedure, producers of certain specified products destined for export are issued authorizations to import, up to 10 percent of the proceeds of their export transactions, equipment goods and raw materials necessary for the manufacture of the products to be exported. These imports may come from any country if the export proceeds are in United States or Canadian dollars or Swiss francs.

(*b*) *EFAC imports.*—Under the EFAC (exportations-frais accessoires) procedure, generally 15 and in a few cases 10 percent of the export proceeds may be used by the exporter for the import from any source of raw materials, equipment, goods, or merchandise to be used exclusively by the importing enterprise. Imports under EFAC cannot be resold.

As noted above, a principal criterion in French licensing of dollar imports is essentiality. It is usually difficult to obtain import licenses for dollar goods which are considered nonessential. Under these conditions, sales of dollar consumers' goods to France have been substantially restricted by the operation of the French licensing system. United States raw materials and fuels, on the other hand, have been affected relatively little by French import controls, since these items are needed by French industry. Producers' goods and capital equipment for industry have moved from the United States to France in very substantial quantities; in some cases, French licensing controls have prevented the sale of United States equipment similar to that produced in France or in soft-currency areas.

In recent years, despite tight French controls, the value of United States exports to France has been steadily increasing; from $381 million in 1954, United States exports rose to $462 million in 1955, and reached $680 million in 1956. In the first half of 1957, United States exports to France rose even further. On the other hand, United States imports from France amounted to $220 million in 1955 and $223 million in 1956, leaving a considerable disequilibrium in the French trading position with the United States. The high levels at which the French industry has operated in recent years have been reflected in increased requirements of basic raw materials and semifinished products from the United States. France's imports from the United States have reflected French needs for such United States products as wheat (due to the crop failure), corn, oilseeds, tobacco, sulfur, coal, cotton, chemicals, iron and steel, copper, and machinery and electrical equipment. Other important imports from the United States included fruits, plastic materials, rubber and rubber products, synthetic textiles, automobiles, aircraft, optical and scientific instruments. In general, French imports of industrial goods from the United States have shown proportionally little fluctuations. Imports of consumer goods by France from the United States have, however, been extremely limited.

Despite the high levels of United States exports to France in the postwar period, France made little progress toward formal dollar liberalizatiton. All dollar imports remained subject to import licenses until January 1956. On that date, France published a list of commodities which could be freely imported from the United States and other dollar areas. The commodities on this list accounted for 9 percent of France's private imports from the United States (based on 1953 trade figures).

This free list remained in effect until June 18, 1957, when France suspended both its dollar liberalization and its more extensive liberalization lists for the OEEC area. This action grew out of France's increasing financial difficulties. In 1956, for example, France lost almost $800 million of its gold and dollar reserves and this trend continued unabated into 1957. Today France's reserves are less than $1 billion—half of what they were at their postwar highpoint in 1955.

At the present moment, almost all imports into France of dollar goods require individual import licenses. The only exceptions are the very limited imports made with funds retained by French exporters, as described in the system of licensing controls above.

The balance of payments prospects for France are not encouraging. Consequently, it is not anticipated that French imports from the United States will be liberalized in the near future.

The deterioration in France's trade balance seems to be continuing. It is hoped, however, that the recently imposed import restrictions, plus the internal measures being adopted, will reduce the considerable foreign trade disequilibrium. Under the French program, 1957 French imports from the dollar area are to be maintained at the 1955 level—a 30-percent reduction from the 1956 level—but it is too early to say if a cut of this magnitude can be achieved.

## FEDERAL REPUBLIC OF GERMANY

The basic regulations governing the importation of goods into the Federal Republic against payment specify that an import transaction may be carried out only if it falls within the scope of an officially declared import possibility and if a license is issued. Import possibilities are opened either through a foreign trade circular decree or by resolution of the import committee in the form of invitations for import applications in the Federal Gazette. The published notices typically are to the effect that licenses to import particular commodities from certain countries, or areas, will be issued freely until a stated or unstated value limit has been reached, but not after a designated cutoff date.

Import licenses are granted either as general licenses published in the Federal Gazette or as individual licenses issued in writing to the applicant.

By early 1957, all industrial raw materials and most manufactured products were covered by general license, constituting liberalization for imports of these categories.

An individual license is required for any import transaction not covered by a general license.

The small area of total German industrial imports from the United States on private account which are still subject to individual licensing have been made subject to so-called test-tenders which are announced as import possibilities. This system permits the importation of practically any individually licensed industrial commodity in varying quantities and affords the German authorities an opportunity to observe the effect of such imports on the domestic market. These observations often lead to the placing of such items on the liberalization list.

The present degree of import liberalization has reached the point where complaints from American exporters of inability to ship particular industrial products into Germany are few and far between. The isolated cases which have arisen in the recent past have been taken up on an ad hoc basis with the German authorities, resulting in most cases in alleviation or elimination of the import problem.

With the liberalization of 93 percent of German private imports from the dollar area, based on 1953 import statistics, and the licensing of imports of practically all industrial commodities in the remaining 7 percent under the aforementioned test tender program, no clearly defined problem area remains for German imports of dollar industrial goods. Imports of a few selected items where special social or economic considerations are involved will, for the time being, remain subject to control.

The German Government has recently announced that it intends to issue an extension to the present dollar liberalization list in the near future, aiming at the reduction and eventual elimination of the discriminatory gap in the coverage of the present liberalization lists applying to imports from the various currency areas.

German dollar liberalization, based on imports in 1953, has progressed as follows:

| | *Percent* |
|---|---|
| Feb. 17, 1954 | 54.0 |
| Nov. 9, 1954 | 59.0 |
| May 28, 1955 | 68.0 |
| June 19, 1956 | 92.9 |
| May 20, 1957 | 93.4 |

ITALY

For a large number of items originating in the dollar area, validated import licenses are not required. These items appear on a so-called free list. Imports of these products are not subject to any type of screening process and quantitative restrictions are not applied. Products which are not on the free list are subject to examination on a case-by-case basis. Import licenses are approved or rejected for these nonliberalized items according to various criteria including specified quotas, availability of the product within the domestic economy, essentiality, price, terms of bilateral trade agreements between Italy and other countries, and other considerations concerned with the national economy.

The Italian licensing controls are administered by the Ministry of Foreign Trade, to which all import license applications must be submitted. After approval by the Ministry of Foreign Trade, import licenses for dollar imports are issued by the Italian Exchange Office. Holders of valid import licenses can automatically obtain the currency needed to finance their transactions from the Bank of Italy or its authorized agents. Payment of debts resulting from import transactions must be effected not later than 180 days from the date on which the goods were cleared through the Italian customs.

Under the current Italian import control system, a substantial part of the items normally imported from the United States have been formally liberalized and appear on the free list. These products include some foods, most raw materials, and many manufactured goods. In addition, there is another large group of dollar goods which, though not on the formal liberalization list, is quite freely licensed by the Italian Government and is not subject to quantitative controls of any kind. Machinery items form the largest part of this group.

A third group of dollar items is subject to quota limitations which are set annually. In general, the quotas which have been established for these items are small and are considered by the trade as being far below the volume that would normally be imported into Italy. In addition to many agricultural items, quotas have been established for a number of semifinished and manufactured items. Among these are automobiles, pharmaceuticals, tanned leather, tractors, television sets, marine motors, and certain fibers. The quota items are generally those which are produced within Italy or which can be obtained from nondollar sources. Practically all types of goods may be imported freely into Italy from nondollar countries. Consequently, a domestic industry is only protected from competition from imports in those instances where the product is manufactured exclusively in Italy and the United States.

Since restrictive controls over certain United States items have been in effect in Italy for several years, it is difficult to indicate with any accuracy the extent to which the Italian quota system has restricted United States exports. Even with the elimination of such controls, the United States would face stiff competition in most fields from Italian and other western European producers. Although in some instances dollar import quotas have not been fully utilized, this is probably due to a lack of interest by Italian importers caused by the small size of the quota rather than an indication that the market for the American product has been reduced. In general, however, there is a definite demand for practically all quota items considerably in excess of the amounts now permitted entry into Italy.

Total United States exports to Italy have shown large increases in recent years; such increases have been largely due to Italian demands for United States coal, scrap, and metals, and for manufactured goods not produced in Italy or Western Europe. The establishment of dollar quotas has represented a step toward liberalization in a number of cases where hardly any dollar imports were permitted prior to the setting up of quotas.

By a ministerial decree dated June 22, 1957, the Italian Government further expanded its trade liberalization measures toward the dollar area. As a result, Italy has now attained a liberalization percentage of 71 percent, based on imports from the dollar area in 1953. On the basis of 1956 trade, the Italian free list covers almost 80 percent of its dollar imports. Among the new items which have been recently liberalized are cotton, wool, coffee, textile machinery, certain steel items, agricultural machinery, and certain types of industrial machinery.

Since the liberalization measures taken in June 1957 represent a substantial move toward the elimination of trade restrictions, it is not expected that Italy will undertake additional steps in the immediate future. It is possible, however, that quotas established for certain products which have not been affected by the most recent liberalization step may be increased in some instances.

The Italian Government recognizes that it should progressively eliminate quantitative import restrictions in order to strengthen the competitive position of the Italian economy. Its producers have been advised of the temporary nature of current restrictions and have been urged to take steps to prepare themselves for the competitive situation which will exist when it becomes possible for Italy to abolish its restrictions designed to protect its balance of payments. The Italian trade imbalance with the dollar area has been offset by tourism receipts, emigrant remittances, offshore procurement earnings and other invisible receipts. Unless there is an unforeseen deterioration in Italy's payments position, it is expected that Italy will continue to work toward the progressive relaxation of restrictions on goods originating in the dollar area.

Italy's first stop toward dollar liberalization was taken in August 1954, when it established a dollar free list covering 24 percent of dollar imports (based on 1953 trade). This list was composed mainly of raw materials, with a few manufactured items. Among the freed products were waxes, coal, crude petroleum oils, asbestos, certain chemicals, paper pulp, iron and nonferrous ores, nonferrous metals and their alloys, and carbon black. On March 29, 1956, 87 additional items in the Italian statistical nonmenclature were added to the free list, increasing the percentage of liberalized items to 40 percent of the 1953 dollar imports. Among the new items were some foods and a number of manufactured goods, including certain types of textile machinery, machine tools, office machinery, and some precision instruments and apparatus. The latest liberalization measures, adopted in June 1957, increased the coverage of freed items to 71 percent of 1953 dollar imports by including additional raw materials, such as cotton, and by expanding the list of manufactured goods, particularly in the machinery sector.

### THE NETHERLANDS

Practically all imports from the dollar area enter the Netherlands without restrictions, although they are subject to the issuance of individual licenses. The majority of dollar commodities have been liberalized, and licenses are granted automatically. A small number of commodities is still subject to screening before licenses are granted, but licenses are issued, ordinarily, up to the amount requested. There are a very few items in this latter group which are still under quota, but they are relatively of little trade interest to the United States. This is evidenced by the almost complete absence of complaints on the part of the United States business and agriculture in regard to exports to the Netherlands.

Information on the above-mentioned items still under Netherlands quotas is not available. However, the Netherlands, together with Belgium-Luxembourg, its partners in the Benelux Customs Union, has introduced so-called Benelux global quotas, which pertain to importation from all sources into the Benelux Union. The following commodities are subject to such Benelux quotas: Carbon dioxide, methyl chloride, penicillin, wooden packing cases, fishing nets, television sets and chassis thereof, passenger automobiles, chassis for automobiles, coachwork for automobiles, and back-pedal brake hubs, peeled rice, and certain soaps.

These quotas are generally very ample to permit a normal flow of trade. They are valid for 1 year, although a periodical review is envisaged.

Under the Netherlands system, exports from the United States enter the country with hardly any limitations. Licenses are granted automatically for the majority of dollar exports and, in the few cases in which applications are screened, licenses are usually fully granted. The items under unilateral Netherlands quotas apparently are of no trade interest to the United States, as evidenced by the absence of business complaints. The Benelux global quotas also are generally of little interest to the United States. On items in which a United States trade interest is involved, the Benelux quotas are ample to take care of United States interests with possibly 1 or 2 exceptions.

Only 2 percent of dollar exports to the Netherlands are subject to possible limitations, although even in these cases the licenses issued are usually satisfactory. Ninety-eight percent of imports from the dollar area are either completely liberalized or licenses are granted, after screening, up to the amount desired.

In view of the almost complete absence of restrictions on dollar imports, it is unlikely that further liberalization steps may be expected in the near future. Still, the Netherlands Government has indicated that the existing regime of controls is a transitional one, and has expressed its intent of gradually enlarging the few remaining quotas with an eventual view of eliminating such restrictive measures completely. However, the Netherlands dollar reserves have somewhat deteriorated over the past year, and the declining trend still continues.

Furthermore, the Netherlands is a party to the common market, and it is not expected that she will take unilateral liberalization steps at present before the intricate problems of the common-market treaty have been more closely studied. On the other hand, it is also unlikely that the Netherlands will institute new restrictive measures in regard to dollar imports. In conclusion, it may be said that the continuation of the present Netherlands system seems to be satisfactory to United States exporters.

While liberalization of imports from the OEEC countries began in October 1949 and was gradually expanded, the first partial Netherlands liberalization list, vis-a-vis the dollar area, was published in October 1953 and concerned mostly raw materials and producers' goods. This list was materially expanded on May 31, 1954, and appeared in the form of a common Benelux list, which at that time encompassed 86 percent of all imports from the United States on the basis of 1953. This list has not been changed since.

In addition to the figure of 86 percent, which applies to commodities under automatic licensing, another 12 percent of all imports from the United States is now licensed up to the amounts requested, thus bringing the effective liberalization percentage to 98 percent.

## SPAIN

Imports into Spain of all goods from all countries are subject to license and exchange control by the Ministry of Commerce. This system has been in effect since 1937.

In general, specific regulations regarding quantitative restrictions on imports are not published. Each application for an import license is usually considered on an individual basis, in accordance with the appraisal of the Ministry of Commerce of the most urgent needs of the Spanish economy and other criteria, such as the availability of similar products of domestic manufacture, prices or terms available from other countries, and trade-agreement commitments.

Spain's chronic shortage of foreign exchange has limited imports from the United States to the more essential products, such as cotton, raw materials, and machinery of various kinds, and will probably continue to do so for some time to come.

There has been no formal liberalization of dollar imports, nor is any likely in the near future.

The Minister of Commerce in the Spanish Cabinet has on various occasions placed emphasis on the need to orient Spanish foreign trade policy toward greater liberalization. However, aside from a simplification of the multiple-foreign-exchange-rate system, no Government action has been taken along this line. It is too early to say what effect the new foreign-exchange rate system will have on foreign trade, although first reactions were generally favorable.

United Statesexports to Spain in 1956 were valued at $253.6 million, an increase of 65 percent over the $153.5 million recorded in 1955. Almost two-thirds of the 1956 exports, however, represented shipments under the defense-support program and the Public Law 480 program for the disposal of agricultural surpluses.

## SWEDEN

Sweden's general import-license controls, which were established in 1947, for balance-of-payments reasons have been successively relaxed since October 1, 1954, so that the import-license requirements have been removed for over 80 percent of Sweden's private import trade with the United States. For most commodities that remain subject to import control, the licenses are issued on a liberal basis. On July 1, 1957, such important agricultural products as wheat, rye, corn, wheat and rye flour, smoked and salted horsemeat, soybeans, sugar, sirup, molasses, and certain fats and oils were added to the dollar-import free list.

In order for a commodity on the dollar-import free list to enter Sweden without a license: (1) The country of origin must be considered as part of the dollar area; (2) the country of purchase (i. e., the country in which the commodity has been purchased or dispatched to Sweden, whether direct or via a third country, whether for sale or for any other purpose) must be a country belonging to the dollar area, a country or area of the European Payments Union, or Finland, Indonesia, or Yugoslavia; and (3) in settling payment for the commodity, provisions governing the settlement of payments between Sweden and relevant country of purchase shall apply. However, payment for a commodity purchased from a country belonging to the dollar area which is not the country of origin may be settled alternatively, direct with the country of origin.

Some commodities are on a transit-dollar list. To import commodities on this list: (1) They must originate in the dollar area, and (2) payment must be made by the Swedish importer either in so-called transit dollars obtainable from commercial banks at a small premium or through triangular transactions with non-dollar-area countries. (Transit dollars are dollar exchange which Swedish commercial banks are authorized to obtain from abroad at a premium price.)

In order to import goods not on any import-free list, the Swedish importer must make application to the State Agricultural Board for agricultural products, fertilizer, and food, and to the State Trade and Industry Commission for all other products. An import license is usually valid for 6 months, and foreign exchange is granted to pay for and import goods provided the license is properly registered with the Foreign Exchange Control Office or commercial bank authorized to handle foreign exchange.

Dollar-area commodities still subject to general import license include such items as apples and pears, dairy products, eggs, honey, raw tobacco, alcoholic beverages, coal and coke, crude petroleum, fuel oil, gasoline and kerosene, finished textiles, precious metals, automobiles and parts for assembly, and ships.

In general, import licenses are granted liberally for such commodities as raw tobacco, alcoholic beverages, coal and petroleum, automobiles and parts for assembly.

Restrictions on the importation of apples and pears are seasonal in character and apply to such fruit from all sources. These seasonal restrictions are maintained in connection with Swedish agricultural policy and are maintained for the protection of domestic production. The same conditions may be said to apply to dairy products, eggs, and honey.

Raw tobacco is imported by the State tobacco monopoly and imports are governed primarily by the price and quality of the tobacco.

Commodities subject to transit dollar regulations include fresh citrus fruit, grapes, coffee and coffee substitutes, tobacco products, crude copper, lead, tin, zinc, and airplanes.

With a high percentage of Swedish imports liberalized or granted liberal treatment under the license regulations it is difficult to evaluate the limiting effects of licensing.

Although Sweden has an announced policy of relaxing import regulations as rapidly as conditions permit, it is probably that a hard core of controlled commodities will be retained for a while. Control of automobiles may be continued for bargaining purposes, control of fuels for the purpose of influencing the direction of trade, and controls in the field of agriculture and textiles for protection of domestic production.

Sweden's first move toward dollar liberalization was taken October 1, 1954, when a wide range of commodities was placed on the dollar import free list. Even prior to this time many commodities in the field of machinery, chemicals, and such items as tobacco and cotton were licensed on a liberal basis. The dollar import free list has been expanded on several occasions since then with the most significant expansion being made at the time of the issuance of the new cumulative import free list on July 1, 1956.

In announcing the establishment of the dollar import free list on October 1, 1954, the Swedish Government indicated that one of its objectives was to increase competition in order to reduce costs and prices thereby preparing the way to facilitate any move toward convertibility.

## SWITZERLAND

Practically all imports into Switzerland regardless of country of origin are completely free of import restrictions. Although licenses are required in some instances, they are granted automatically in almost all cases. Certain agricultural products and a very few industrial commodities which are subject to quota restrictions are either of no particular interest to the trade of the United States or, in the few cases where a United States trade interest exists, the quotas are sufficient to allow for reasonable exports from the United States.

Generally speaking, imports into Switzerland from the United States move completely unhindered. The few commodities under quota, apart from certain agricultural products, are the following: Trucks with a carrying capacity of more than 3,000 kilograms; trolley buses, omnibuses, and other buses with a seating capacity of more than 20 persons, as well as films and agricultural tractors.

The few above-mentioned Swiss controls have no appreciable effect on exports from the United States. The Swiss quotas on agricultural products concern mainly items of interest not so much to the United States as to neighboring European countries. The restrictions on the importation of trucks and buses is based on military considerations in order to have standardized types of auxiliary military transportation and not to be dependent on spare parts from abroad in an emergency. The ample quota on films has not been taken up in recent years.

Since the end of the war imports from the dollar area have moved freely into Switzerland. In the majority of cases these imports took place without the formality of import licenses. Wherever licenses were required they were generally granted up to the amount desired. Consequently, a description of Swiss liberalization measures vis-a-vis the dollar area would be meaningless, since it would only show the relationship of items entering without licenses or under automatic license. The distinction between completely free items and items under license is only important insofar as Switzerland wishes to retain the legal possibility to screen imports in case of emergency.

Since exports from the United States for all practical purposes move into Switzerland without any restrictions further liberalization of dollar imports is hardly possible. The liberalization of agricultural products which is of main concern to neighboring European countries is still under active consideration and may possibly have a mildly stimulating effect on a few United States products.

Referring to the above description of Swiss controls percentage figures of Swiss liberalization would only indicate the relationship between completely free commodities and commodities which move freely although under automatic license or under ample quotas. On September 24, 1956, 91.3 percent of all Swiss imports were completely free of import formalities, except for the usual customs procedures.

## YUGOSLAVIA

The Yugoslav import-licensing system was abolished in January 1954. At present all Yugoslav commercial enterprises in principle are authorized to import any type of goods from any source, without restriction; import licenses are not required. Since Yugoslav commercial enterprises are registered by the state, however, and since the National Bank of Yugoslavia is the sole seller of foreign exchange, purchases by Yugoslav enterprises in practice conform very closely to the pattern of the Yugoslav Government's import program. This means that almost all Yugoslav current foreign purchases consist of commodities considered essential by the Yugoslav authorities.

With very limited exceptions, the foreign currency to pay for imports may be obtained by authorized foreign traders from the National Bank in 2 ways: (1) as part of an allocation to a given group of importers at fixed settlement rates (allocated at special meetings of foreign-exchange centers); and (2) to a more limited extent, from bidding on the free market; i. e., at regular meetings of the foreign-exchange centers. Certain types of enterprises are permitted to retain foreign exchange realized through their activities but the use of such retentions for commodity trade is negligible.

A system of multiple foreign-exchange rates results from a series of export and import coefficients applied to the fixed settlement rates based on the foreign values at the Yugoslav border. The size of the coefficients varies for each commodity in accordance with the Yugoslav Government's desire to discharge a given commodity's import or encourage its export and to adjust the disparity between external and internal prices.

Import and export coefficients are fixed by administrative organs designated by the Federal Executive Council on the recommendation of the Foreign Trade Board.

For commodity imports and invisible imports there are 19 coefficients, ranging from 0.6 to 3.

For commodity exports and invisible exports there are 16 coefficients, ranging from 0.5 to 2.

While export payments and most commercial import transactions take place at the fixed settlement rates multiplied by coefficients, special arrangements are made for calculating charges on certain categories of imports. Government imports of such essential foodstuffs as wheat and fats are effected at the official rate of 300 dinars per dollar, and no coefficient is applied; but the importing agency pays to (or receives from) the Government an additional amount equivalent to the difference between the landed cost and the domestic price. Other essential food items are imported at the fixed settlement rate multiplied by a "revaluation factor" to be determined.

Faced with recurrent balance-of-payments difficulties and acute dollar shortage, the Yugoslav Government has been using its scarce dollar resources to purchase in the United States primarily goods considered essential for the operation of the Yugoslav economy.

There are no special import regulations affecting specific commodities. In general, the policy has been to import from the dollar area only indispensable products.

Yugoslavia has not liberalized imports from the United States. In view of Yugoslavia's extremely limited dollar resources, imports from the United States have been limited to capital goods and machinery necessary for Yugoslav's industrialization program. Furthermore, as long as the Yugoslav foreign-trade position remains unfavorable, it is unlikely that dollar imports will be liberalized.

## TURKEY

Imports into Turkey have been subject to various kinds and degrees of control since 1929. Controls were relaxed for a brief period after World War II due to a wartime accumulation of foreign exchange and in the 1950–52 period when liberalization of imports from member countries of the European Payments Union (EPU) was in effect. The liberalization program covered about 63 percent of Turkish imports from EPU countries and was attended by a rapid increase in imports, especially of capital goods for development purposes. The excess of imports over exports was so great during this period and by mid-1952 the trade deficit reached such critical proportions that the Government enacted restrictions on liberalized imports which were tantamount to cancelation of liberalization. Liberalization was officially suspended in late 1953.

Over the past 3 years the shortage of foreign exchange has caused a restriction in imports far beyond that intended in the control system. Thus licenses have not been issued for items on the import lists even though the country is in dire need of such commodities.

Turkey's controls on imports are contained in a document known as the Foreign Trade Regime which is issued periodically. The latest Regime was issued in September 1953 and consists of Decree No. 4–1360 and implementing regulations, plus several other decrees and regulations dealing with specific phases of Turkish foreign trade. Controls on foreign exchange are contained in Decree No. 14 on the Protection of the Value of Turkish Currency, dated September 15, 1955. These decrees, with amendments, give the Government very broad powers over Turkish foreign trade with the purpose of assuring that the limited amount of foreign exchange available is utilized to the country's best interest and of directing the flow of exports in such a way as to prevent the loss of scarce commodities and to generate foreign exchange in credits to Turkey's advantage. Administration of these regulations is by the Ministry of Commerce, the Union of Chambers of Commerce and Industry, the Central Bank, and the Ministry of Finance.

The Foreign Trade Regime of September 1953 established six lists of commodities, with lists I and II covering exports and the remainder imports. List III was originally intended to itemize products which could be imported without an import license from EPU countries (i. e., under EPU liberalization) and with an import license from non-EPU countries. However, list III has never been made effective insofar as liberalization is concerned and the products on list III are treated as though they were on list IV, the general import list, for which an import license must be obtained before importation is allowed. Generally lists III and IV include the historical Turkish imports needed but not available in Turkey, such as raw materials, industrial and agricultural machinery and equipment, spare parts, and essential and semiessential consumer items not available in Turkey. List V contains products for which import licenses will be issued only in cases where there is an exceptional need. List VI includes commodities which may be imported on long-term credits, i. e., 1 year or more. The latter list has been widely utilized by Turkish importers since it has been the one which has offered the widest amount of governmental approval during the last 2 or 3 years.

To be eligible to import goods into Turkey, an importer must be registered with his local chamber of commerce and industry from which he receives an "importer's permit." Importers file applications for import licenses with the Central Bank which collates the information submitted by applicants and forwards their applications to the Ministry of Commerce. The Ministry analyzes the requests in light of Turkey's requirements and refers the applications to the Foreign Exchange Committee which approves or disapproves requests in light of the availability of exchange and other demands. Applications filed with the Central Bank must be accompanied by a deposit of 10 percent of the amount requested. Deposits are refunded if the application is denied.

Manufacturers file applications for their needs through their local chamber of commerce which examines the application and forwards it to the Union of Chambers in Ankara for submission to the Ministry of Commerce. Manufacturers deposit 10 percent of the amount of the application only if the application is approved. In all cases the decision of the Foreign Exchange Committee is communicated through the Ministry of Commerce to the Central Bank and then to the applicant.

Payment for imports into Turkey may be affected by letter of credit, by sight or time drafts, or on a deferred basis.

Turkey's controls prohibit import of most food and agricultural products and most luxury items. Turkey is self-sufficient in food products and produces a diversified line of agricultural products and, therefore, does not need agricultural imports except in emergencies. Over the past 7 years, 1950–56, about 80 percent of Turkey's imports have consisted of capital goods, raw materials, and essential equipment. Consumer goods have accounted for less than 20 percent of the 7-year total.

In general, the traditional United States exports to Turkey are on the approved import list. Such exports include various types of industrial machinery and equipment, electrical machinery and equipment, motor vehicles and parts and accessories, tractors, chemicals, tinplate, tires and tubes, and various other manufactured goods. Several United States food companies have complained about Turkish prohibitions on food imports and the tobacco industry feels strongly that Turkey should allow imports of cigarettes which are also prohibited imports.

While the control system certainly has some limiting effects on United States exports to Turkey, such controls have been of secondary importance to the exchange problem and have not been a hindrance of major import in United States trade with Turkey.

Turkey has not introduced any measures for dollar liberalization nor are any such measures in prospect. The extent of the current liberalization of dollar trade is not measureable since there is no base period of uncontrolled dollar trade and because the liberality of the control system has not been fully tested due to severe restrictions on dollar and other imports because of the exchange crisis.

Despite the control system and the exchange crisis, United States exports to Turkey have consistently increased since 1950. However, this increase has been due entirely to exports financed by foreign aid funds and to export of agricultural commodities under Public Law 480. The latter products have been required by Turkey to compensate for short grain crops caused by drought and to help meet internal requirements which have been increasing due to a rise in living standards. In the past several years most United States exports to Turkey have been financed through some form of aid or credit. United

States exports to Turkey in millions of dollars in the 1950–56 period are as follows:

| Year | Millions of dollars |
|---|---|
| 1950 | 58. 9 |
| 1951 | 60. 8 |
| 1952 | 63. 3 |
| 1953 | 64. 5 |
| 1954 | 79. 3 |
| 1955 | 96. 0 |
| 1956 | 109. 0 |

Turkey's foreign exchange shortage, particularly her dollar problem, does not promise to improve over the next few years. In fact, the situation may become even more critical before any improvement is possible. There are no signs that Turkey can increase her dollar earnings substantially in the immediate future although in the long run such an increase is possible in the minerals category. On the other hand, should oil be discovered in Turkey in sufficient quantities by any of the 14 companies engaged in exploration activity, Turkey could effect a large savings in imports of petroleum products which are supplied mostly by United States oil companies from Middle East supplies but payable in dollars. Imports of petroleum products consume roughly two-thirds to three-quarters of Turkey's total dollar export income which ranges from $60 million to $80 million per year.

The demand for United States products in Turkey is excellent and far outstrips available exchange. There is no doubt that Turkish control authorities would approve import licenses for these products if exchange were available. In this regard, licenses for goods on long-term credits appear to be approved almost automatically, but United States firms in practically all cases will not risk extension of credit in view of the exchange situation and outlook.

### UNION OF SOUTH AFRICA

The current import control system in the Union of South Africa dates back to November 1948 when, because of balance-of-payments difficulties, the Union considered it necessary to reimpose restrictions on imports that had been dropped at the end of World War II. Originally applying only to dollar imports, the control system was subsequently extended to all imports of any origin, although different rules governed imports from dollar and nondollar sources.

Since January 1954, important modifications have been made in the control system which have had the effect of removing discrimination against dollar imports and of generally easing import curbs. These developments have reflected an official policy of "selective relaxation and decontrol" in consonance with more favorable trends in the Union's balance of payments.

The current South African control system operates through the mechanism of licensing and exchange allocations to importers. Salient features of the system are as follows:

(1) Imports from all countries (except for decontrolled items) are subject to license, valid for imports from any country, including the United States.

All importers are registered with the Director of Imports and Exports, according to the various categories of goods, such as consumer goods, capital goods, and industrial raw materials. Importers are required to file with the Government, as required by Government notices issued from time to time, detailed returns concerning the volume and value of import transactions during given periods for the various classes of goods.

On the basis of such data, periodic permit (exchange) allocations to importers for various goods categories are made. The Government usually determines at the beginning of each calendar year the total amount of exchange which may be expended for all imports and for broad component categories of goods (e. g., capital equipment; consumer goods; raw materials, consumable stores, and maintenance spares for industrial needs). Such calculations are based, in turn, on the expected foreign exchange receipts and general balance-of-payments position of the country and relative need for goods categories during the licensing period.

Each permit indicates the general category of goods to be imported (i. e., consumer goods, industrial raw materials, etc.) and the f. o. b. cost of the goods authorized, the amount being expressed in South African currency units. Once the permit has been issued to an importer, the actual release of foreign exchange becomes a formality; however, foreign exchange can be issued to an importer only by a bank authorized by the Government to deal in foreign exchange and only up to the amount authorized by the permit. Thus in effect, each import permit represents a specific exchange allocation or quota.

(2) Special commodity listings are maintained, revised from time to time, which either are wholly decontrolled and require no license (free and exempted list) or practically decontrolled in the sense that no exchange quota applies except for the formality of applying for a special license which is routinely granted.

(3) Likewise certain commodities which are in short supply are given exchange quota bonuses in order to encourage imports of these items rather than other items regarded as being in plentiful supply.

(4) Special "industry allocations" of exchange are given certain industries (as the automobile assembly industry) to meet their specific requirements for imported goods used in the industry.

Since 1954, modifications made have tended to substantially liberalize controls. Nondiscriminatory licensing was established in January 1954; thereafter, modification has been of two types: (1) expanded exchange allocations, (2) liberalization of commodity listings which had been subject to special licensing requirements.

Prior to 1956, a lengthy list of consumer goods were restricted to a greater extent than other goods in that importers had to surrender £2 of their regular exchange quota licenses for every £1 in special exchange quota licenses to be granted for imports on the restricted list (regular licenses were issued automatically and importers desiring to import restricted list goods had to apply for special licenses).

In 1956, by various official notices, this conversion ratio was reduced to £1 for £1, so that importers need only apply for a special license to import "restricted list" goods with no exchange quota loss.

In April 1957, further concessions were announced which have the effect of increasing exchange quotas for consumer goods and removing existing exchange quota restrictions for imports of selected items. It is estimated that these latest changes will permit, during 1957, an increase of some £30 million or 6 percent in total imports into South Africa above the 1956 level.

The Union of South Africa consistently has been the major market in Africa for the United States since World War II, and in 1948 it actually held the distinction of being the eighth largest customer of the United States taking no less than $492 million worth of goods. Rigid import curbs imposed by South Africa at the end of 1948, which favored soft currency sources as opposed to dollar suppliers, reduced the value of United States exports in the following year by half. Trade had little opportunity to expand until June 1954 when South Africa removed discrimination against dollar imports and officially embarked on a policy of trade liberalization. As result United States exports to South Africa rose to $260,618,000 in 1955, compared with $225,918,000 in 1954 and $207,357,000 in 1953.

This growth record is significant, but the United States has not increased its share of the South African market proportionately with those of other competing suppliers. For example, in 1955 South Africa allowed about $100 million worth of additional imports through expanded exchange allocations to importers; the United States absorbed less than one-third of this amount, the bulk going to the United Kingdom and Germany. Similarly, United States export data for 1956 show United States exports to the Union increased by only $400,000 to a total of $261 million; yet South African trade data show total imports into that country rose by almost $39 million.

It appears, therefore that within the limits imposed by import exchange allocations foreign competition in the South African market has become the basic factor influencing the level of United States exports to the Union.

The Union of South Africa represents a growing market for diversified goods and services, and most economic indicators in the country point to sustained development in transportation power generation, and productive activities in agriculture, mining, and industry.

In 1956 economic growth, as reflected in national income estimates, proceeded at a slower rate than in 1955, but the general economic situation has remained favorable. Despite a reduced flow of foreign capital into South Africa, the country's balance-of-payments position in 1956 showed improvement as a result of expanded export earnings, primarily from gold and uranium production. Available data for 1957 indicate continuation of these favorable trends.

Barring unforeseen difficulties, the Union's relatively buoyant economy should make possible continued liberalization of import controls. Indeed, stated Government policy is to aim at complete abolition of such controls, and some officials have indicated it may prove possible to achieve this objective next year. Whether controls can be lifted entirely during 1958 will depend on the future course of the country's external financial position, but continuation of the present policy of trade-control liberalization seems assured.

In these circumstances, the South African market offers expanded promise to American exporters, provided exporters can counter the competitiveness of other foreign aggressive suppliers of that market.

AUSTRALIA

Australia has maintained rigid control over imports from the United States since the establishment of the customs import licensing regulations in December 1939. The method used in restricting imports from the United States has continued practically unchanged for several years. Importers in Australia are required to obtain import licenses in advance of shipment and applications for licenses are considered administratively on their merits in each case. Under this procedure, licenses are generally approved only for highly essential goods which are not available from domestic production or from nondollar sources. In some cases, price, quality, and time of delivery may have some bearing on the approval of licenses.

The rigidity of Australian control of imports from the United States is determined largely by the dollar balance of payments position from year to year. In recent years Australia has had deficits in trade with the United States. The only exception was in the fiscal year 1950–51 when, due to exceptionally high wool prices, Australia had a substantial surplus in trade with the United States.

With the exception of a quota for motor vehicles, based on imports in 1936 and reduced from time to time, no quotas are fixed or announced in advance for imports from the United States. Having to await the administrative decisions on licensing puts American manufacturers and exporters to a great disadvantage in comparison with most nondollar countries which are given advance information as to quotas or licensing treatment to be applied.

The Australian Government set an encouraging precedent in October 1955 by establishing a special "all countries budget" for certain essential commodities including titanium dioxide, sulfur, paper pulp, cotton, aluminum, nickel, copper, ferrous alloys, leaf tobacco, hops, hog casings, crude asbestos fiber, and newsprint. Quarterly import allocations are made for these products and holders of import licenses are permitted to purchase from any country regardless of currency considerations. The Minister of Customs at that time stated that this innovation would enable purchase from the best and cheapest source of supply and would be of value in international trading relations since exporting countries would be able to compete on more even terms and would not feel at a disadvantage by discrimination in import licensing.

The United States has been a leading or important supplier of some of these products to Australia, especially sulfur, cotton, tobacco, hops, and hog casings. This "all countries budget" licensing provision represents practically the only instance where the Australians have shown a tendency to ease the licensing discrimination against imports from the United States.

In the period 1950–56 the IBRD made several loans to Australia, totaling over $300 million, to finance the purchase of capital goods and equipment for the following development programs: (*a*) Agriculture and forestry; (*b*) electric power; road transport; (*c*) railways; (*d*) air transport; (*e*) mining; and (*f*) basic industries. These loans have enabled Australia to license freely and increase imports from the United States of capital goods and various types of equipment authorized for purchase in the loan agreements. Also, the loans have helped to offset Australia's normal dollar deficits in trade with the United States.

With the principal exceptions of the establishment of the "all countries budget" in October 1955, and the licensing of goods supplied under the provisions of the IBRD loan agreements, Australia has not made any substantial relaxation on imports from the United States for several years. In fact, Australia reduced the overall level of licensing imports from the United States by 12½ percent in October 1955. Any other relaxation on intensification of dollar restrictions that may have been made have resulted from the case-by-case administrative consideration of applications for licenses. The specific results in such cases are not generally known until annual trade statistics are published by Australia.

The prospects for general liberalization by Australia of restrictions on imports from the United States depend largely on the trend in its dollar balance of trade position. Increased United States imports of Australian nonferrous minerals and metals, and possibly wool, are anticipated. Unless Australia is able to earn more dollars by a substantial increase in exports to the United States, or unless the major currencies become fully convertible, it is unlikely that any significant relaxation of dollar import restrictions will be made.

### CANADA

Canada has had no quantitative import restrictions for balance of payments reasons since 1950. Imports are free of control except in a few instances as follows:

*Prohibited (generically and permanently)*

Oleomargarine, butter substitutes, and spreads, because some Provinces with large dairy interest prohibit production and sale. No estimate of United States trade banned can be made. However, Canadian consumption in 1956 amounted to 125 million pounds, all of local production.

Second-hand automobiles and motor vehicles of all kinds manufactured prior to the year in which importation is sought. Purpose is protection of Canada's smaller domestic market against what would undoubtedly be large import from the United States. Longstanding restriction predating GATT.

Secondhand aircraft: Same as automobiles but regardless of the year of manufacture.

*Imports regulated by permit*

Butter except for personal use of importer and not exceeding $5:

Because the Canadian market is price supported and there is a (Dominion Government) stockpile. Control dates from 1951.

Inasmuch as the Canadian supported price is usually lower than the United States (supported) price, there has been for many years only an inconsequential import into Canada. The trend is toward increased Canadian consumption of dairy products but it is not possible to predict that import regulations will not continue into the foreseeable future.

Cheese (cheddar):

Because the Canadian market is price-supported and there is a (Dominion Government) stockpile. Control inaugurated May 28, 1957, to divert a threatened increased import from third countries and it was indicated no permits would be granted for 1 year. United States export of cheddar cheese to Canada in 1956 amounted to 17,970 pounds.

Butter oil and any other form of butterfat containing 55 percent or more of butterfat. Because the Canadian market is price supported. Import control effective from November 13, 1957. Recent sharp increases in imports of butter oil have tended to interfere with the price-support program for butter and butterfat. Import restrictions were therefore deemed necessary.

Dried skim milk:

Complete embargo from September 23, 1957, to May 31, 1958, except on imports for personal use of importer and his household and not exceeding $5 in value. Controls imposed because Canadian market is price supported.

Turkeys and fowl:

Complete embargo, effective from July 17, 1957, on turkeys and on class of birds known technically as "fowl" but not including shipments not exceeding (*a*) 1 turkey and 4 fowl for each noncommercial importation, (*b*) purebred turkeys and fowl for improvement of stock, (*c*) turkey poults, and (*d*) turkeys and fowl in jars or cans of 10 pounds or less. Canada has inaugurated price supports on turkeys and fowl.

Wheat, oats and barley, and products containing more than 25 percent of these grains by weight, including wheat, wheat flour, cake mixes, batter mixes, cakes, breakfast foods, cereals, macaroni, spaghetti, vermicelli, noodles, animal and poultry feeds, wheat starch, wheat malt. No import permit is required for manufactured bread or biscuits.

In aid of pooled marketing of the grains which is a monopoly of the Canadian Wheat Board, the Board has had since 1940 authority to regulate imports by permit. Inasmuch as Canada is a large and quality producer and exporter of these grains, the import has never been large and there is no indication that licensing policy has had any particular effect on imports. Recently, however, the Board announced it would refuse to issue permits for the processed products, especially cake and pie mixes, and pet food. The United States 1956 export of cake and pie mixes was valued at $171,000. Canadian imports of "dog food and pet stockfood" from the United States in 1956 were valued at Can$211,000, including presumably some items not covered by the restriction.

Radioactive and fissionable materials, isotopes, and any equipment which may be used for the production, use, or application of atomic energy:

This is a regulatory rather than a competitive kind of control which does not affect trade. No statistics are available except for radioactive isotopes and radium emanation salts of which United States exports to Canada in 1956 were valued at $144,000.

Natural gas:

Pending the construction of Canadian pipelines for the transmission of domestic fuel resources eastward, Canadian imports of natural gas have increased sharply from 6 billion cubic feet in 1952 to 15.7 billion cubic feet in 1957, but it is expected (and in fact agreed upon with United States suppliers) that imports will be curtailed, beginning in 1958, when Alberta gas becomes available to Toronto and Montreal.

*Prognosis*

These restrictions seem likely to remain in force for the foreseeable future. In view of their paucity and character, however, it can be said that they are of little consequence in Canadian-United States trade which has increased sharply mainly, but not wholly, in producer goods required by the country's rapid industrial expansion.

*Limitation of trade by antidumping provisions of the tariff*

Outside the field of quantitative restrictions per se, there are some instances of limitation of trade by application of the antidumping provisions of the tariff on the ground of abnormally low price which injures Canadian producers. Minimum fixed values now affect cut flowers and strawberries, the former since 1951 and the latter since June 14, 1957, effective for 6 months. Not all but only the lower priced import is vulnerable and there is no statistical measure of the extent to which importers are inhibited from purchasing goods offered below the set figure. Both products are trade agreement items.

A less definite limitation may be extended, at the discretion of Canadian Customs, to any manufactured goods on which the market price has declined, as the result of the advance of the season or the marketing period, to levels that do not reflect the "normal" price. In the market recession of late 1953 and early 1954, a variety of consumer goods was reported struck by antidumping duties incident to this regulation but inasmuch as the effect was to discourage importers from purchasing reduced price goods, no statistics of actual effect in trade can be compiled.

*Limitation of alcoholic beverage imports by provincial monopolies*

The Provinces have a monopoly of the sale of alcoholic beverages and a provincial license is necessary to admit shipments. Most are willing to give hotels and clubs permits to import for private stock but will not carry United States products in their own stores allegedly because of the small demand. Ontario has recently admitted United States beer for distribution in competition with Canadian beer but the high rate of taxation (for revenue) is apparently a deterrent to general export promotion. The extent to which trade is inhibited is therefore indeterminate.

*Limitation by various standards*

Allegations have been made from time to time to the effect that certain trade is limited by special requirements having a protectionist effect. Thus, fresh fruits and canned goods may be imported only in specified size containers, not always identical with United States domestic market practice. These are Federal specifications over and above quality and sanitary standards.

Provincial regulations and Federal home-loan regulations require electrical apparatus to pass Canadian quality standards certification which entails the payment of substantial fees and the opening of manufacturing processes to inspection.

# IMPLICATIONS FOR UNITED STATES TRADE POLICY OF THE EUROPEAN COMMON MARKET AND FREE TRADE AREA

Miriam Camps [1]

It is now clear that 6 European countries will establish a customs union over a 12- to 15-year period and highly probable that a number of others, of whom the United Kingdom is the most important, will during the same period establish a free trade area in which the customs union will participate. It is the purpose of this paper to summarize the main implications of these developments for the United States and to suggest the type of legislation that seems now to be required if the United States is to regain its position of leadership in the trade field and to be able to exert a constructive influence on these European developments.

*Present status of the common market and the free trade area plans*

The six countries of the European Coal and Steel Community (France, the German Federal Republic, Italy, Belgium, Luxembourg, and the Netherlands) signed at Rome on March 25, 1957, a treaty establishing a European Economic Community. Ratification of the treaty was approved this summer by the French Assembly, the German Parliament, and the lower house of the Italian Parliament. With these hurdles cleared there is every reason to suppose that the ratification process in the six countries will be completed during the autumn.

The treaty provides for the gradual establishment over a 12- to 15-year period of a common market among the signatory powers. As conceived by the six, the common market is first of all a customs union: when fully in effect no tariffs, quantitative restrictions or other barriers to trade will exist among the participating countries and the same tariff rates will be applied by all six countries to countries outside the common market.[2] But in addition to committing the countries concerned to the progressive establishment of a full customs union the treaty takes them a long way down the road of economic union. It provides for the progressive abolition of obstacles to the free movement of persons, services, and capital among the countries of the community; the establishment of a common transport policy, the abolition of agreements, mergers or concerted practices among firms that are likely to affect trade among member states and that have as their object or result the prevention, restriction, or distortion of the free play of competition within the common market; the elimination of those forms of state aid that distort competition (insofar as they affect trade between member states); the coordination

[1] Mrs. Camps was formerly Chief Economic Officer, European Regional Affairs, United States Department of State.

[2] When the customs union is fully in effect the external tariff rates will, in general, be the arithmetic average of the rates existing on January 1, 1957.

of economic policies and the harmonization of national laws insofar as required by the common market; the creation of a European Social Fund to assist in the retraining, resettlement, etc., of workers; and the creation of a European Investment Bank. The treaty provides that the common market shall extend to agriculture and to trade in agricultural products but the specific provisions relating to agriculture envisage a managed rather than a free market for many products, although common "community" action will take the place of national regulations. Finally, the treaty provides for the association of specified overseas possessions of the six with the community, thus giving the colonies free access to the markets of the area as a whole.

An elaborate timetable for the establishment of the common market is provided, but the basic schedule is a transitional period of 12 years divided into three 4-year stages. During each stage certain aspects of the common market are required to be brought into operation. Since the core of the plan is the creation of a customs union, the timing is most precisely provided in the case of the removal of tariffs, the elimination of quantitative restrictions, and the establishment of the common external tariff to which the implementation of the other aspects of the treaty is geared. The possibility that the first period may have to be extended from 4 to 6 years is provided for and, by a unanimous decision of the Council of Ministers, the later stages may be extended or curtailed but in no case may the transitional period be extended to more than 15 years from the date of the entry into force of the treaty. Generally speaking, as the transitional period proceeds more and more decisions are to be taken either by the European Commission or by the Council of Ministers acting by less than unanimity.[3] For ease of reference the main essentials of the plan for the progressive establishment of the customs union have been summarized in appendix A annexed to this paper. It is anticipated that the first reduction in duties will take place on January 1, 1959.

The proposal for a free trade area is still under negotiation and no detailed plan has yet been published. The Organization for European Economic Cooperation (OEEC) has been responsible for the examination of the idea and the formulation of specific proposals. In February 1957 a report[4] prepared by an OEEC committee which had been charged with studying the technical feasibility of a free trade area between the six and the other OEEC countries was considered by the OEEC Council meeting at ministerial level and the decision taken—

> to enter into negotiations in order to determine ways and means on the basis of which there could be brought into being a European free trade area, which would, on a multilateral basis, associate the European common market with other member countries of the Organization, and to prepare necessary instruments.[5]

Since then three special committees have been meeting to consider (i) technical problems relating to the freeing of trade; (ii) the problem of agriculture; and (iii) the problem of the less developed countries who wish to participate but who may not be able to remove barriers as rapidly as the more developed countries. Although it was

[3] The institutions of the community are described on p. 8 below.
[4] OEEC. Report on the Possibility of Creating a Free Trade Area in Europe, Paris, January 1957.
[5] OEEC, press release A(57) 7, February 13, 1957.

originally planned that the ministers should meet again in July, their session was postponed, principally to avoid prejudicing the consideration of the common market treaty by the French Assembly. The present plan is to hold an OEEC Council meeting (at the ministerial level) in October, but at the time of writing it is unclear whether the informal negotiations which have now begun among the countries concerned will have reached a point where important substantive decisions can be taken or whether the meeting will be largely procedural. Because of the fluid state of developments there is a danger that anything written now will be out of date by the time this question is considered by the subcommittee. It may, nevertheless, be useful to summarize the current state of planning and the assumptions as to the final form of the free trade area that underlie the recommendations at the end of the paper.

Shortly before the February OECC Council meeting, the British Government issued as a white paper the memorandum it had circulated to the other members of the OEEC giving its views on the scheme. It strongly endorsed the idea of creating a European free trade area for industrial goods but stated categorically that foodstuffs [6] must be excluded from the free trade area. The British insistence that agriculture should be excluded has met with strong opposition from a number of countries, in particular France, the Netherlands, and Denmark, and it seems clear that various arrangements will have to be made for those agricultural commodities that figure prominently in intra-European trade. These might take the form of British guaranties to the European countries that their existing share of the British market would not be curtailed by Government action and, perhaps, by modifications in certain British tariffs or seasonal quotas on, for example, various horticultural products. The British are also at odds with the French over the treatment of colonies: the terms of the association of the colonial territories with the common market mean that produce from the colonies of the six will enter the common market area duty free, whereas, the produce of British colonies will be subject to duty and even in some cases to new or higher duties than heretofore. This will create particular problems for Britain's West Indian and African colonies (and certain members of the Commonwealth, e. g., Ghana) but the possible solution of assuring British colonial produce free entry by including the colonies in the free trade area is opposed by the British Government. This would in any case have the undesirable effect of accentuating the difficulties of other producers of colonial products such as Brazil. There will undoubtedly be considerable pressure on the six to keep any tariffs on colonial produce low and perhaps to grant tariff-free quotas to traditional suppliers.

Problems have also arisen on the subjects to be included in the treaty establishing a free trade area, that is whether it should contain commitments on greater freedom of movement for capital and labor, harmonization of social and economic policies and the establishment of a social fund and investment fund similar to those included in the treaty establishing the common market. Here again, the main division of opinion is between the British (and the Scandinavians and Swiss) who

[6] "Foodstuffs" is defined as covering chapters 1 to 24 of the Brussels nomenclature. These include food, drink, tobacco, and feeding stuffs.

wish to keep the free trade area fairly narrowly confined to trade questions and the French (and Italians) who would like it to cover most if not all of the subjects included in the common market treaty. Finally, there are differences on technical questions having to do with the definition of origin. A significant proportion of intra-European trade consists of "mixed" products, that is goods incorporating raw materials, semimanufactures or components of outside origin partly or wholly processed in the area. Agreement has yet to be reached on the criteria to be adopted for judging whether a "mixed" product is deemed to "originate within the area" and thus be accorded duty free treatment when exported to another participating country. Although technical in nature this is an important point for, as the OEEC report made clear, the system adopted will determine the scope of the free trade area:

> If a narrow definition is adopted, whereby products incorporating only a very small proportion of raw materials imported from abroad are regarded as not originating within the area, the volume of trade covered by the duty-free provisions will be more restricted. On the other hand, on the basis of a very broad definition whereby products incorporating only a very small proportion of materials or processing added within the area are recognized as originating therein, nearly all the goods traded between member countries would become duty free.[7]

The French have recently been arguing for definitions which would result in a severely restricted area. However, it seems unlikely that either the British or most of the most of the other potential participants will be willing to accede to the French views on this point and that reasonably generous definitional standards will, in the end, be adopted.

Although there have been no official reports published since the OEEC report of last February, it is generally assumed that the scheme adopted by the countries of the free trade area for the progressive reduction and eventual elimination of tariffs and for the progressive enlargement and eventual elimination of quantitative restrictions will be closely patterned on that of the common market and phased in the same way. In the free trade area there is, of course, no question of the establishment of a common external tariff.[8] The highly sensitive point of whether, and if so, on what conditions, quantitative restrictions may be reimposed is still being debated. But again it seems probable that the rules of the free trade area will be similar to those of the common market, that is, that prior consultation is desirable but that in the event of a sudden crisis in the balance of payments a country may act first and consult afterward.[9] Although there has been no formal decision, it is generally assumed that the OEEC will provide the institutional framework for the free trade area. How drastically its structure will have to be altered to assume these new responsibilities depends in part on the answers to the questions still under negotiation such as the functions to be included in the free

---

[7] OEEC, report cited, p. 33.

[8] The essential difference between a customs union and a free trade area is that in the former the participating countries have common external tariff rates and that in the latter each country maintains separate rates for third countries. Some consideration has been given to having common external rates as a matter of convenience among the free trade area countries where there is no great difference in existing rates, but this would be the exception rather than the rule.

[9] In the common market treaty the council voting by a specified majority may decide that the state concerned must amend, suspend, or abolish the measures taken in an emergency.

trade treaty and the countries to be included in the scheme.[10] Again the British and the French are the chief protagonists, the former advocating minor and the latter major changes in the OEEC's structure. It seems probable that, as foreshadowed in the white paper, the British will agree to some modification of the unanimity procedures of the OEEC but resist the establishment of any body with as much independent power as the European Commission.

*Implications for the United States of these new European trading arrangements*

If the common market treaty and the free trade area scheme are initiated according to plan the result will be that from January 1, 1959, about half of the world's trade will come within the purview of institutions to which the United States does not belong[11] and will be conducted in accordance with rules that we have had little part in shaping. It means that from that time until 1974 trade among 17 countries (assuming participation by all the OEEC countries) will be progressively freed from restriction and that at the end of the period trade within the area will, normally, be free from any form of trade restriction. Six important trading nations will not only have common tariffs on their trade with third countries, but will have gone a considerable distance toward full economic union. And even the broader group may well have been driven by the pressures arising from a freer market to a much closer system of economic cooperation than is now foreseen. In the short term these developments may have various unfavorable effects on the United States, but the impact on the total United States economy would be minor. Although both groups have stated that their intention is to reduce barriers on trade among themselves, but not to raise them against third countries, the degree of discrimination against third countries is of course frequently intensified in the process of removing barriers among the participants. For example, if the French now have a 20-percent duty on, say, sewing machines applicable to both United States and German sewing machines and are importing roughly the same number from each country, one would assume that as the duty on German machines is reduced more German machines would be sold in the French market and the existing rate on United States sewing machines would become a more important barrier to trade than it had been previously. Furthermore, although the new rates will not, in general, be above the average of existing rates, it is a complicated calculation whether the United States stands to gain more from the lowering of some of the existing high rates than it loses from the raising of some of the existing low rates.

The creation of a large area within which trade is relatively free may also tend to prolong the period of the discriminatory use of quantitative import restrictions. Although in the last few years the OEEC countries have made impressive progress in eliminating quotas on trade with the dollar area, it would not be surprising if this process slacked off in the early stages of the creation of the common market and the free trade area. The natural tendency of most governments

[10] The extent and nature of the participation of the less developed countries (Portugal, Greece, Turkey, Iceland, and Ireland) of the OEEC is still undecided.

[11] The United States and Canada are associated with the work of the OEEC but are not full members and are not bound by the commitments in the OEEC convention.

may well be to delay any further liberalization of dollar trade until the domestic effects of the new measures of intra-European liberalization are somewhat clearer. Finally, both arrangements, if they live up to expectations, should improve the competitive position in third markets of important United States competitors and tend to stimulate intra-area trade. Initially at least this increase in intra-European trade would probably be to some extent at the expense of other countries.

In the longer term the common market and linked free-trade area should tend to have more favorable effects on the United States; total trade as well as intraregional trade should increase and the stronger competitive position of the European countries should lead to the ending of discrimination.

Despite the probable short-term economic disadvantages for the United States, the Government has warmly welcomed the decision of the six to form a common market. Although the free-trade-area negotiations have not yet proceeded to the point where it has been necessary for the United States to adopt a formal position, it is generally assumed to favor its formation. There are persuasive reasons for encouraging both developments that clearly outweigh any short-term economic disadvantages. United States encouragement of the customs union and the free-trade area rests fundamentally on the belief that a strong, prosperous, and more unified Western Europe is in the best interest of the United States and that these projected developments will contribute to that end. The record of the Congress since the early days of the Marshall plan has clearly advocated the encouragement of strength and unity in Western Europe as a prime objective of United States policy; the arguments supporting this view need no reiteration here. But this does not of course require us to give blind support to any scheme put forward as a means to these ends. On the contrary, the United States has a direct and legitimate interest in doing what it can to see that these new arrangements are set up and evolve in such a way that they, in fact, contribute to strengthening the economies of Western Europe and that the inevitable discrimination against the United States and other countries outside the area is held to a minimum.[12]

The common market treaty as it emerged from a year of hard bargaining among the six countries is in many respects a more timid document than the Spaak report[13] on which it was based. There are more opportunities for slowing down the rate of liberalization, more safeguards to protect weak industries from the effects of competition and more special provisions to take care of the special economic and political problems of the member countries, particularly France. Much of this watering down was inevitable in the process of transforming a general plan into a binding treaty requiring parliamentary ratification. But it must nevertheless increase the concern of third countries. The treaty as it now stands makes possible the creation

[12] The United States has a genuine interest in seeing that these new trade groups do not cause avoidable hardship to countries other than the United States, as well as to ourselves. Although this may seem to be a peripheral concern, it can assume considerable importance in particular cases. For example, if trade between Western Europe and Japan is made more difficult by these new developments, the problem of adjustment to Japan's growing exports becomes more acute for the United States.

[13] Comité Intergouvernemental créé par la Conférence de Messine, Rapport des Chefs de Délégation aux Ministres des Affaires Etrangères, Brussels, April 21, 1956.

of a genuine free market capable of profiting from the increased opportunities for specialization and economies of scale in production and marketing. But the treaty does not make inevitable the creation of a freer and more competitive market. A great deal will depend on decisions which will be taken as the transitional period proceeds whether the result is a freer and more dynamic European economy progressively integrated with world markets or simply a more highly managed European market with more effective barriers to trade with the outside world. Similar dangers are inherent in the free-trade-area scheme, although the British dependence on world trade creates a stronger presumption that the interests of third countries will be borne in mind and the British preference for loose institutional arrangements, although in some respects tending to make the efficient functioning of the free-trade area more difficult, is probably a safeguard against a highly managed market.

Two things would seem to be required if the United States is to have any real impact on the way these two schemes evolve. First the proposed Organization for Trade Cooperation should be established on a firm basis as soon as possible and with unqualified United States participation and support. Second, the administration must be given bargaining power in the form of new authority to reduce tariffs. The reasoning underlying these two recommendations is developed further below.

*Importance of the Organization for Trade Cooperation*

The implementation of the treaty establishing the European Economic Community is entrusted to a council composed of representatives of member states, each government appointing one of its ministers to it; a commission composed of nine members chosen for their general competence and responsible to the community rather than national governments; and assembly; and a court of justice. The council and the commission together form the "executive." As in the case of the Coal and Steel Community certain powers normally exercised by national governments have been transferred by treaty to these new institutions. This transfer of power goes beyond the limitation on the independent exercise of power, which most countries accept when they become members of many international organizations. Although there will be less transfer of power from national governments to the central institutions in the case of the European Economic Community that there was in the Coal and Steel Community [14] it is clear from the treaty that the community will regard itself as a new entity which will deal directly with the governments of third countries on matters within its competence rather than through the intermediary of the governments of the member states. The United States will presumably establish a mission to the new community as it has done to the Coal and Steel Community, but it is probably fair to say that although useful in many ways to the Coal and Steel Community and to ourselves, the United States mission has had little effect on how the Coal and Steel Community has developed. This is no fault of the United States mission but inherent in the situa-

[14] The European Economic Community Treaty of course covers a much wider range of economic activity than does the Coal and Steel Community but the procedure for reaching decisions gives a more prominent role to the Council of Ministers, i. e., the governments, in the case of the European Economic Community.

tion, since the institutions of the community are charged with implementing a treaty to which the United States is not a party. The six countries and the United States are, however, both bound by the obligations in the General Agreement on Tariffs and Trade and the common market treaty specifically recognizes these obligations. The commitments in the general agreement are ones which will encourage the common market and the free-trade area to keep discrimination against third countries to a minimum and to ease discriminatory measures as circumstances permit. The proposed Organization for Trade Cooperation would therefore seem to be the logical focal point for discussions of trade questions among the six, the countries of the free-trade area, the United States, and those other countries that will be most affected by these developments.

Until a few months ago, it looked as though the meetings of the contracting parties to the GATT would gradually lose importance unless the United States took action on the OTC and thus put the organizational arrangements for the GATT on a more durable basis. Today the outlook has changed. Increasingly the countries outside the common market are looking to the meetings of the contracting parties as the logical place to discuss questions of common concern. Continued United States inaction on the OTC is therefore unlikely to kill the general agreement or to prevent the member countries from meeting and transacting business, but, by leaving the United States delegation in an ambiguous position, it cannot fail to make it more difficult for the United States to influence developments. Furthermore, the present makeshift organizational arrangements are inadequate to deal with the almost continuous sessions which may well now be required.

If the OTC is to be really effective, it is also important that it should not be unduly circumscribed in the subjects it can discuss. One of the principal reasons for the success of the OEEC trade liberalization scheme has been that, although the basic obligations in the code have been fairly narrowly confined to the removal of quantitative restrictions, there has been acceptance of the fact that quantitative restrictions on trade cannot reasonably be discussed in a vacuum and that fiscal and monetary problems as well as tariffs and other protectionist devices enter into a country's decision as to what action it can take and therefore are properly subjects for discussion and explanation. A similar latitude must be given the OTC, although there is probably no need to broaden the field of direct competence foreseen for it. The common market (and the free trade area, to a lesser extent) will be concerned with all problems related, however tangentially, to trade. This does not mean that the OTC need have powers in all these fields but it does mean that it needs latitude to discuss whatever the countries concerned feel is germane to the development of mutually beneficial trade relations. The OTC should not be thought of as a tribunal before which the countries of the customs union and the free trade area are arraigned to justify themselves at intervals. At times overtones of this kind have been present during the review by the contracting parties of the waiver from the GATT obligations granted to the Schuman Plan countries: the discussions have been least rewarding when the high authority of the Coal and Steel Community has been in the position of justifying its stewardship before an obviously suspicious body and most useful when there has been a sense of give and take on both sides. The kind of organizational arrangement required is one which will ensure a continuing close relationship between the United States and the European groups with both sides recognizing that they are under obligations as to the broad pattern of their trading relationships. Problems should be fully and informally discussed before they come to a head, not simply "handled" once they have become the subject of complaint and countervailing action.

*Importance of new bargaining power*

The second thing that would seem to be required if the United States is to have an influence on the evolution of these new trading arrangements is for the United States to have something to offer in the trade field. During the discussion of trade policy that accompanied the Randall Commission investigations and again during the investigations made by this subcommittee, considerable evidence has been produced to suggest that United States tariffs in themselves (with minor exceptions) are not the greatest problem for the foreign exporter; that a more important impediment to an increase in imports is the lack of certainty surrounding United States tariff policy—in particular the uncertainty provided by the possibility of recourse to the escape clause or (more recently) to the defense provisions of the Trade Agreements Act, the delays and doubts surrounding customs classification, and the fact that the basic legislation is renewed for such short periods of time that the entire policy is in almost perpetual jeopardy. The more progress that can be made in giving stability to existing concessions and predictability to United States policy the better. For example, a statute of limitations might be applied to the escape clause in the Trade Agreements Extension Act or concessions might be enacted into law after a waiting period during which time changes would be possible. But, though important, these are essentially negative concessions to other countries. Some authority to make further reductions in tariff rates is also desirable, both in order to obtain reciprocal reductions from the European countries and on the broader ground of having something positive with which to encourage the kind of developments we believe to be important.

Reciprocity has in the past frequently been an almost meaningless concept. It may become less so when the complex with which the United States is bargaining concessions consists of 6 highly industrialized countries with a total population of 160 million. Furthermore, although the countries of the free trade area (as distinct from the customs union) will retain their individual tariff schedules for goods imported from third countries the existence of the free trade area will tend to make the third-country tariffs of its members relatively more important and therefore concessions more attractive to the United States and other countries. Reciprocity should not, however, be thought of simply in terms of seeking to match advantages through item-by-item tariff reductions. If a mutually advantageous trading relationship is to be developed between the United States and the customs union free-trade area, latitude to do two things would seem to be desirable. The first is to reduce tariffs on an across-the-board basis rather than as at present only on a product-by-product basis.

The second is to recognize more explicitly than has been the case in the past that reciprocity may be compounded of many things, not simply of tariff reductions.

Since the Torquay conference of the contracting parties to the GATT in 1950–51, there has been considerable feeling among the member countries that the technique of product-by-product tariff bargaining is of increasingly limited usefulness and that new techniques are required. The low tariff countries in Europe were the first advocates of the need for a new approach. The rebinding of an already low tariff (frequently all they had to offer) was proving to be a poor bargaining counter in negotiations with high-tariff countries and the pressure on them in the OEEC to reduce quantitative restrictions (on which some of the low tariff countries traditionally relied for protection) accentuated their interest in finding some means of obtaining the reduction of the tariffs of their principal European trading partners. The original Benelux proposal was directed to the problem of high European tariffs; as an alternative, the French Government suggested a scheme of broader scope which would apply to all countries and thus got around a major obstacle to a purely European plan—i. e., the obligation in accordance with the most-favored-nation commitment in the GATT to extend "European" tariff reductions to non-European countries. The French plan was refined and improved by the contracting parties over a period of 2 years and at the eighth session in October 1953 it was reported by a group of experts to be "technically feasible" and was submitted to governments for their views. As described in the GATT document, the principal features of the plan are that—

> Each government participating in the plan would undertake to reduce the average incidence of its customs tariff in a base year by 30 percent, in stages of 10 percent in each of 3 successive years. Governments would not be required to reduce every tariff rate by this amount, for within certain limits they would be free to choose the items on which to make reductions. The reductions would, however, have to be distributed throughout the tariff and not concentrated in any one part of it, thus insuring that the benefits would accrue to all supplying countries even to one whose interest might be limited to products of a certain class. In order to achieve that object the tariff would be divided into sectors covering broad categories of related products, such as primary foods, products of the chemical industry, etc., and the 30 percent reduction would be applied to each sector. * * *
>
> Reduction by 30 percent is the general rule, but less than that is required of countries having comparatively low duties. This would be accomplished by the establishment of a demarcation line and, below that, a floor for each sector. A country whose average duty incidence in any sector was below the demarcation line would be required to make less than the 30-percent reduction, and if the incidence was below the floor rate no reduction at all would be required. * * *
>
> * * * Each participating government would undertake the further obligation to reduce all duties which exceed certain upper limits.[15]

As the GATT document makes clear, the concept of reciprocity or mutual advantage remains, but it is measured not by offsetting specific concessions obtained and granted but by the overall reductions made by all countries in accordance with common standards. In addition, the plan requires effort roughly proportionate to a country's tariff level—that is, larger percentage reductions for high tariff countries.

[15] Contracting Parties to the General Agreement on Tariffs and Trade, A New Proposal for the Reduction of Customs Tariffs, Geneva, January 1954.

In the common market plan, both the procedure for the elimination of tariffs between participating countries and the harmonizing of rates to form a common external tariff are based on the principle of applying automatic, across-the-board percentage changes to existing tariff rates. As indicated above, the free trade area will adopt a similar system for reducing tariffs within the area. The fact that so many tariff reductions will in the future be made on an across-the-board basis may strengthen the pressure for a general adoption of some variant of this approach. Across-the-board cuts, particularly if coupled with some flexibility, might make the domestic problem of special interest groups less intractable; first, because it is at least psychologically less painful to be part of a process that is comprehensive in its impact, and second, because any genuine trouble spots can frequently be accommodated while at the same time satisfying the general goals of reduction.[16]

Legislative leeway to negotiate an across-the-board tariff reduction plan would require at a minimum a rewritten and greatly narrowed peril-point provision and probably its total elimination. This is not the place for an extensive discussion of the philosophy and problems underlying the peril-point provision. But if the United States wishes to regain leadership and strengthen free world commitments to nondiscrimination and a competitive economic system, it will find itself in a defensive position so long as the peril-point provision in its present form remains on the books. American encouragement of the customs union and the free trade area has been based in large part on the belief that a wide area of competition is indispensable to a vigorous and healthy economic society. Most American enterprise professes to be dedicated to the same principle. The common market proposal, it is true, is shot through with safeguards, but the basic philosophy is still that trade barriers must be removed and those who cannot survive the process be helped to adapt to the new situation. American influence is understandably diminished to the extent that the United States finds this principle too radical for home consumption.

---

## APPENDIX A [1]

### THE EUROPEAN ECONOMIC COMMUNITY TREATY

#### SUMMARY OF TARIFF AND QUOTA PROVISIONS

*Institutions*

1. The tasks of the community will be carried out by an Assembly, a Council, a Commission, and a Court of Justice.
2. The Council and the Commission will be assisted by an Economic and Social Consultative Committee.

*Timetable*

1. The common market will be established progressively over a transitional period of 12 years divided into 3 stages each of 4 years.

---

[16] Further discussion of this approach is contained in appendix B to this memorandum. "Across-the-board," although a convenient shorthand phrase, is something of a misnomer, particularly because it is used to describe not only the situation—as in the formation of the customs union—where all tariffs are progressively reduced, but also the proposal in the French plan which aimed at a general reduction of the overall incidence of tariffs. Under the latter plan, individual tariffs could be left at their existing rates, provided the average reduction for each of the agreed tariff groups was achieved. (The French plan also contained an additional commitment on the reduction—to agreed ceilings— of exceptionally high tariffs.)

[1] Appendix A is from Freer Trade in Europe, pp. 30–31, prepared by the British Treasury.

2. Before passing on to the second stage the Council must decide whether the objectives set down for attainment during the first stage have been achieved.

3. The second and third stages cannot be prolonged or shortened save by unanimous decision of the Council.

4. In any case, the period of transition may not be longer than a total of 15 years. At the end of the period of transition all the rules and regulations for the common market must come into effect.

*The customs union*

1. Customs duties will be progressively eliminated in respect of trade between the member states. Taking the duties actually applied on January 1, 1957, as base, duties must be reduced by stages according to the following timetable:

(*a*) 1 year after entry into force of the treaty;
(*b*) 2½ years after entry into force of the treaty;
(*c*) 4 years after entry into force of the treaty;
(*d*) 18 months after the beginning of the second stage;
(*e*) 3 years after the beginning of the second stage;
(*f*) 4 years after the beginning of the second stage.

2. On the first occasion each duty must be reduced by 10 percent. On each subsequent occasion the overall incidence of the tariff must be reduced by 10 percent, individual rates in excess of 30 percent must be reduced by at least 10 percent and other rates by at least 5 percent.

3. The remaining reductions required to abolish tariffs altogether will be made during the third stage in accordance with a timetable to be decided by the Council. Any special difficulties of member governments in complying with these provisions will be settled by the Council.

4. Export taxes on trade within the common market must be abolished by the end of the first stage.

5. Revenue duties must be abolished in the same way as other import duties but they may be replaced by internal taxes which do not discriminate against imports.

*The common external tariff*

1. Apart from specific exceptions, the common external tariff will be the arithmetic mean of the tariffs of the various members on January 1, 1957. The common tariff may not exceed:

(*a*) 3 percent for most raw materials;
(*b*) 10 percent for most semimanufactured goods;
(*c*) 15 or 25 percent for certain chemicals. (For certain chemicals tariffs of less than 3 percent will be considered to be tariffs of 12 percent for the calculation of the common tariff.)

2. For a specified list of products the tariff will be fixed by negotiation and not by calculation. Some of these negotiations are completed but most are still to come.

3. The common tariff will be introduced successively at the end of the three stages. Thirty percent of the difference above or below the common tariff will be removed at the end of the first stage, 30 percent at the end of the second stage. But if the national tariff is not more than 15 percent greater or less than the common tariff, the common tariff will be introduced at the end of the first stage.

4. No change may be made in the common tariff save by unanimous decision of the Council. The Council may, however, by majority vote modify for a period of not more than 6 months and for not more than 20 percent. A member may also be authorized to suspend any part or the whole of the tariff on agricultural products.

*Quantitative restrictions*

1. In general quantitative restrictions on imports between members are prohibited.

2. There must be no intensification as between members of existing quantitative restrictions which are to be progressively eliminated in the course of the transitional period.

3. A year after the treaty comes into force all bilateral quotas are to be converted into global quotas available without discrimination to all other members.

4. The total value of quotas is to be increased by 20 percent compound annually with a minimum of 10 percent for each individual product.

5. For every product a minimum quota of 3 percent of domestic production must be established a year after the treaty's signature, to be increased to 4 percent after 2 years, 5 percent after 3 years, and thereafter annually by at least 15 percent. If there is no domestic production the Commission will fix an appropriate quota.

6. At the end of 10 years all quotas must be at least equal to 20 percent of domestic production.

7. Quotas representing more than 20 percent of domestic production need not be increased by the minimum of 10 percent annually, provided that quotas are increased by 20 percent overall and the Council by a majority vote on the Commission's recommendation approve.

8. The Commission shall determine how and when restrictions equivalent to quantitative restrictions shall be removed.

9. The above arrangements can be altered by decision of the Council on the Commission's recommendation.

10. Quantitative restrictions on exports as between members are prohibited. Existing restrictions must be removed not later than the end of the first stage.

---

## Appendix B

### Further Comment on the Across-the-Board Approach to Tariff Reduction

The only specific plan for an across-the-board negotiation that has been fully developed is the so-called French plan which is described in detail in the GATT document, A New Proposal for the Reduction of Customs Tariffs, Geneva, 1954. There are various alternative arrangements that might well be explored. For example, there might be advantages in dividing the tariff schedule into broad groups by height of tariff, rather than by type of commodity as the GATT document suggests. This would probably be technically easier.

One of the purposes of the GATT plan, or any variant, would be to get away from item-by-item bargaining. An across-the-board approach would quickly degenerate into an item-by-item negotiation if, in carrying it out, each country were free to bargain on what tariffs other countries included in their across-the-board cuts and to accept or reject them. It is, therefore, necessary to have an automatic plan of tariff reduction which, once the ground rules have been agreed, is not subject to further bargaining.

The ground rules might, for example, set the end objective of an overall 50-percent reduction in the average incidence of the countries' customs tariff in, say, 7 years, coupling this with commitments as to the percentage level of reduction to be made in each tariff group in each year. The countries participating in the plan could then count on a final performance by each country which was roughly comparable and a rate of progress which was similar. But individual countries would have the possibility of determining, within certain limits, which tariffs they would reduce, which they would lower first, and which they would reduce more than 50 percent and which less. A tighter arrangement might couple a minimum requirement to reduce every tariff by, say 15 percent, with a commitment on an overall average reduction by 50 percent. (The figures used are illustrative only and are not recommendations.)

The advantage of dividing the tariff schedules into groups, either by height of tariff or by type of commodity, is, of course, to give some guaranty that tariff reductions will be widely spread and not concentrated on a few items, while at the same time retaining to the individual country a measure of flexibility in deciding which tariffs to reduce.

The various procedures which have been discussed by the six countries planning to form a common market, as well as the GATT discussions on the French plan, suggest a number of ways an across-the-board plan might be devised. On the basis of these discussions it seems clear that such an approach is technically feasible.

# QUANTITATIVE IMPORT RESTRICTIONS AND UNITED STATES FOREIGN TRADE POLICY[1]

Raymond F. Mikesell, professor of economics, University of Oregon

## I. TRADE AND PAYMENTS RESTRICTIONS ABROAD

There are no satisfactory measures for comparing the degree of restriction on world trade resulting from direct import and foreign exchange controls with that arising from tariffs. Certainly during the decade before 1950 tariffs played a relatively minor role in impeding world trade as compared with direct quantitative controls. But since 1950, trade and exchange liberalization, particularly by the countries of Western Europe, has greatly increased the significance of tariffs as barriers to trade. Direct trade controls and bilateralism continue to play the major role in limiting imports in the majority of the less developed countries, and in South America multiple exchange rates have been more important than tariffs as a protectionist device.

Foreign exchange and direct import restrictions[2] are employed both as a device for protecting domestic producers against import competition and for protecting the country's foreign exchange position. During and following World War II most countries adopted comprehensive exchange and import controls (hereafter referred to as quantitative import controls) principally for balance of payments reasons. They also established state import monopolies for a number of basic commodities, such as food, raw materials, and fuel, as a part of their general system of rationing and allocation controls during the war and postwar reconstruction periods. In the immediate postwar period when nearly everything was in short supply, protection of domestic producers was a minor factor in determining import policies. But as time went on there was a tendency to impose the severest restrictions on those industrial and agricultural commodities which were being produced in reasonably adequate quantities at home while permitting other commodities to be imported more freely. In this way the protection of domestic industry and agriculture, which before the war was usually (but not always) secured by protective tariffs, became intermingled with protection of the balance of payments. Thus countries tend to justify their quantitative import restrictions on balance of payments grounds but often design their system of restrictions to provide maximum protection for domestic producers.

---

[1] This paper was prepared in July 1957 at the request of the Subcommittee on Foreign Trade Policy, Committee on Ways and Means, U. S. House of Representatives.

[2] In most countries the system of foreign exchange controls is closely bound up with import quotas and licensing. The usual practice is to sell foreign exchange only to holders of import licenses or, if certain commodities are not subject to licensing or quota controls, to sell foreign exchange without limit specifically for the importation of such commodities. Where countries have multiple exchange rate systems, the cost of the foreign exchange in terms of the local currency varies with the type of commodity to be imported.

*Discriminatory restrictions*

Most countries outside of the dollar area—that group of countries encompassed by North America, northern South America, the Caribbean Republics, the Philippines, and Liberia—not only have quantitive restrictions which they justify on balance of payments grounds, but these restrictions discriminate between sources of supply. The most common type of discrimination is that in favor of nondollar as against dollar sources of supply. But there is also discrimination in favor of certain regional groupings such as the members of the Organization for European Economic Cooperation or, in the case of certain commodities, preference is given to imports from individual countries under bilateral trade agreements. However, as we shall discuss later on, bilateralism, except in trade between free world and Soviet bloc countries, has been on the decline; but regional preferential arrangements appear to be in the ascendency.

The practice of discriminating against dollar sources of supply—which, though declining, is still widespread—had its origin in the immediate postwar period. At the end of the war many countries were faced with serious shortages of the commodities necessary to maintain even their low wartime levels of living and to restore the productive capacity of their economies. Exportable surpluses of many of the things they needed were available only in Western Hemisphere countries which demanded dollars, or currencies convertible into dollars, for their exports. But the supply of dollars from exports and other sources was low relative to the unusually heavy demand brought about by the wartime dislocations. Countries like France were reluctant to make purchases with dollars in the Netherlands or Italy because the dollars were needed to buy the most essential goods available only in the dollar area.

In order to encourage trade among themselves, nondollar countries negotiated bilateral trade and payments agreements which provided for the acceptance of currencies which were not convertible into dollars or even other nondollar currencies. Thus there grew up the distinction between hard currency countries and soft currency countries. Dollar countries were of course hard currency areas but some of the nondollar countries like Belgium and Switzerland also had relatively hard currencies. Hard currencies were in relatively short supply and the dollar was, of course, shortest of all; hence the dollar shortage.

*The dollar shortage*

The concept of the dollar shortage is quite significant because even today it is used as a justification for discriminatory quantitative restrictions again United States exports. In one sense the dollar shortage has not existed throughout the postwar period. Since the end of World War II the United States has made available through imports, foreign loans, and military expenditures abroad—not to mention the enormous flow of grant aid—a large and increasing supply of dollar purchasing power. And since 1949 to the end of 1956 foreign countries have been able to add to their gold and dollar holdings about $11 billion through transactions with the United States alone.

We may contrast the postwar situation with that of the 1929–32 period during which the annual supply of dollars made available to the rest of the world through our imports of goods and services and foreign investments was cut to less than one-third of the 1928–29 average. This was brought about by the severe United States depression and the sharp rise in import duties imposed by the Smoot-Hawley Tariff Act of 1930. The world economy could not readily adjust to this reduction in the supply of international means of payment. There followed not only a precipitous fall in world trade but a widespread adoption of exchange controls, quotas, and high tariff rates, many of which were discriminatory against the United States. While the term had not yet been invented, this was indeed a period of dollar shortage brought on in large measure by the domestic and foreign economic policies of the United States.

The large United States export surpluses have sometimes been cited as evidence of the existence of a dollar shortage. This is by no means an indication of a condition of disequilibrium since export surpluses are often financed by capital movements or by military or economic assistance. The period 1946–49 can be characterized as one of severe structural disequilibrium resulting from wartime dislocations, the low level of production of foodstuffs and basic raw materials outside the Western Hemisphere, and the great demand for materials and equipment for the reconstruction of productive capacities. There was certainly a shortage of resources and capital which was reflected in a heavy demand for dollars.

But by 1950 this situation had modified considerably. Alternative sources of supply for most of the basic commodities became available outside the dollar area. The rest of the world began to rebuild their gold and dollar reserves after the currency devaluations of September 1949 and have continued to increase them in every year since 1949. Dollar and nondollar prices became more competitive and world trade was being gradually freed from the shackles of bilateral balancing and state trading.

By 1953 most Western European countries had worked off the excess liquidity in their economies and had largely gotten rid of rationing and price and allocation controls. Monetary and fiscal policy had been substituted for direct controls over the internal economy and to an increasing degree over the balance of payments as well. A number of countries achieved impressive trade surpluses and foreign countries as a group increased their gold and dollar holdings from $15.8 billion at the end of 1949 to $29.4 billion at the end of 1956,[3] 80 percent of which was accumulated through transactions with the United States. The leading currencies of Western Europe, including the pound sterling, the deutschemark, and the belga, are selling in free dollar markets at only 1 or 2 percent below their official dollar values, and the Canadian dollar has soared to a 5-cent premium.

However one may choose to characterize the situation in the immediate postwar period—and I personally think that the term "dollar shortage" is inappropriate when applied even to the 1946–49 period—there is certainly no dollar shortage today in any but the most naive sense of the term. Of course most of us in the United States have fewer dollars than we would like to spend or perhaps fewer than we think we need to spend. It is also true that many

[3] Includes official gold and total short-term dollar holdings and holdings of U. S. Government securities. Source: Federal Reserve Bulletin.

countries have a tendency toward balance-of-payments deficits in the sense that their residents and governmental agencies want to buy more from abroad than they earn in foreign exchange. But this is not a dollar shortage; it is an excessive demand for free foreign exchange of all kinds—dollars, sterling, deutschemarks, Swiss francs, belga, and other international currencies.

The United States has paid out more dollars to the rest of the world in the form of imports of goods and services, foreign investment, military expenditures abroad and gifts than it has absorbed in exchange for its exports of goods and services in every year since 1949. In a sense this country has had a rather substantial dollar deficit, largely as a consequence of its economic and military programs abroad. The rest of the world has been able substantially to strengthen its international reserve position while at the same time expanding its productive capacities and improving its competitive position in world markets. The strong and growing demand for United States imports and the large outflow of capital have contributed to the stability of international markets and have helped to provide an ample supply of international liquidity for a growing world trade. Certainly not since 1914—and perhaps never before—have the basic external conditions for international equilibrium and currency convertibility been so favorable as they are today. Dollar shortage should be regarded as a myth; it is only a cloak used to cover up the fallacies of governmental policymakers.

I have dwelt so long on the dollar shortage issue because it goes to the heart of the problem of discrimination against dollar goods. It is also used to justify bilateral discrimination and avoiding the use of freely transferable currencies in financing trade, although in such cases the argument must be couched in terms of a general shortage of international exchange media. The rejection of the dollar shortage myth means the rejection of the argument for discrimination on balance-of-payments grounds. But before going on with the implications of this proposition we shall consider the current status of quantitative restrictions in the rest of the world.

*Current status of quantitative import restrictions imposed by foreign countries*

The vast majority of the countries of the world accounting for the bulk of the world's trade outside of the United States impose quantitative trade or exchange controls on a substantial proportion of their imports.[4] While this has been true throughout the postwar period there has been a considerable relaxation in the degree of restriction imposed by a number of countries in recent years and an increase in the number of countries which have removed all or nearly all quantitative import restrictions. Also significant is the fact that the degree of discrimination against imports from the United States and other dollar countries has been markedly reduced in the past few years.

The countries which impose either no restrictions or relatively mild restrictions on United States imports fall into three groups:

1. A group of Western Hemisphere countries including Canada, Chile, Costa Rica, Cuba, Dominican Republic, El Salvador, Guate-

[4] See "Summary of Foreign Control Regulation Applying to Imports From the United States", Foreign Commerce Weekly, December 3, 1956, pp. 7–8.

mala, Haiti, Honduras, Mexico, Nicaragua, Panama, Peru and Venezuela. (Several of these Latin American countries have multiple exchange rate systems which involve penalty rates on certain types of imports, however.)

2. A group of western European countries, including Belgium-Luxembourg, West Germany, Greece, Netherlands, Norway and Switzerland, which have removed quantitative restrictions on 80 percent or more of their private imports from the United States.

3. A miscellaneous group of countries including Afghanistan, Ceylon, Hong Kong, Lebanon, Liberia, and Thailand.

In the case of a number of the countries included in the above list the degree of dollar-import liberalization has been achieved in the past 2 or 3 years. Several other countries, including the Union of South Africa and Pakistan, have largely eliminated discrimination between dollar and nondollar imports. Several European countries, including Britain, Italy, Sweden, and Denmark, have reduced substantially the degree of discrimination against dollar imports.

For the OEEC countries as a group, overall liberalization of dollar imports based on private imports from the United States and Canada in 1953 was raised from 54 percent on January 1, 1956, to 61 percent on January 1, 1957.[5] This compares with 89 percent for overall liberalization of trade from quantitative restrictions for intra-OEEC trade. As of April 1957 all OEEC countries except Denmark, France, Iceland, Norway, and Turkey had achieved an overall intra-OEEC country trade liberalization of over 90 percent of their private trade.[6] Countries with a relatively high degree of dollar-import liberalization as a percentage of private trade include Belgium-Luxembourg (87 percent), Greece (99 percent), Germany (92 percent), Italy (71 percent), Netherlands (87 percent), Norway (83 percent), Sweden (68 percent), Switzerland (98 percent), and the United Kingdom[7] (59 percent). Certain of these countries, including Belgium-Luxembourg, Greece, Germany, Netherlands, and Switzerland, treat imports from dollar and nondollar sources on virtually equal terms.

In spite of recent progress toward the elimination of discrimination against dollar goods, a substantial amount of such discrimination remains. There is still a considerable gap between the degree of liberalization of intra-OEEC country trade and the liberalization of dollar trade by these countries, although that gap has been considerably narrowed during 1956 and 1957.[8] In some cases the OEEC countries have liberalized their imports from all nondollar sources on the same basis as they have liberalized from OEEC country sources.

Discrimination against dollar imports also arises from the use of bilateral trade and payments agreements. Although western Euro-

[5] On the basis of total imports, including governmental imports, the percentage of dollar-import liberalization was only 54 as of January 1, 1957.

[6] France temporarily suspended import-trade liberalization in June 1957 as a consequence of a severe foreign exchange drain.

[7] Britain has announced a further liberalization of dollar imports, effective August 1957. Liberalization percentages are based on private imports in 1948 (1949 for Germany, 1952 for Austria, and 1955 for Benelux).

[8] Under the OEEC code of trade liberalization adopted in 1949, the OEEC countries have been gradually freeing their trade with one another from quantitative restrictions. The present liberalization goal, to be achieved by the end of 1957, is an overall liberalization of 90 percent of private trade (based on 1948 trade) and at least 75 percent for each of 3 categories of imports, namely, foodstuffs, raw materials, and manufactures.

pean countries have greatly reduced the number of their restrictive bilateral trade and payments agreements (except possibly with the Soviet bloc countries), a number of Latin American and Asiatic countries continue to organize a large part of their trade on this basis.

## II. CURRENT DEVELOPMENTS IN PAYMENTS ARRANGEMENTS

Much of the recent progress in the field of trade liberalization has been made possible by a broadening of the area of transferability of the major nondollar currencies. Before 1950 most trade between nondollar countries was financed by means of bilateral-payments agreements. This meant that trade had to be rigidly controlled so as to achieve a bilateral trade balance. The European Payments Union made it possible for a group of countries, including both the OEEC members and the countries and territories associated with them in the same currency areas, to finance trade among themselves multilaterally. This multilateral-payments system paved the way for the liberalization of trade among a group of countries and territories accounting for some 40 percent of the world's trade.

Since 1950 the transferability of the major currencies has been extended beyond the EPU area. In March 1954 the pound sterling, which had already been transferable over a wide area, became transferable for financing current trade throughout the nondollar world. There are also free dollar markets for transferable account sterling although such sterling cannot legally be used to finance trade directly between a dollar area country and the sterling area.

Western Germany has also established a nonresident deutschemark account which is transferable throughout a large part of the nondollar world and available for financing current trade between Germany and most nondollar countries. Like Britain, Germany has terminated all of her restrictive bilateral payments agreements. More recently Belgium-Luxembourg, Italy, the Netherlands, and Sweden have established transferable currency areas for their currencies which include not only Western Europe but a number of Latin American, Middle East and Asian countries as well. For example, the transferable Dutch guilder area comprises the EPU countries (except Turkey), Afghanistan, Brazil, Chile, Ethiopia, Finland, Iran, Lebanon, Saudi Arabia, Sudan, Syria, Tangier, Thailand, Uruguay, and Yemen. Sweden's transferable kroner area includes Argentina, Japan, and Uruguay as well as most of the EPU countries.

Recently a number of EPU countries have negotiated multilateral payments agreements with the two principal nondollar countries of Latin America, Argentina and Brazil. The agreement with Brazil, known as the Hague Club, involves Austria, Belgium-Luxembourg, France, Germany, Italy, the Netherlands and the United Kingdom on the European side. The so-called Paris Club agreement with Argentina involves Austria, Belgium-Luxembourg, Denmark, France, Germany, Italy, Netherlands, Norway, Sweden, Switzerland, and the United Kingdom. Under both of these agreements the Latin American partner is permitted to use any of the currencies of the European partners which it receives from its exports for making payments to any of the European partners in financing its trade. This multilateral agreement replaces a number of bilateral payments agreements which these countries previously had with European countries and obviates the necessity of bilateral bargaining. The arrangement has also made possible a substantial liberalization of trade between Argentina and Brazil on the one hand and the European partners on the other.

*Impact of trade and payments arrangements on United States exports*

What has been the effect of these payments developments upon United States trade? Before the establishment of the EPU, fears were expressed that the arrangement would lead to the creation of a more or less permanent soft-currency bloc and the perpetuation of discrimination against dollar imports. Similar anxieties have been expressed with respect to the Hague Club and Paris Club arrangements. This question has an important bearing on the possible effects of the proposed European common market and free-trade area and on the attitude which the United States should take toward them.

A consideration of the impact on the United States of the EPU and other arrangements for broadening the area of multilateral currency transfers requires a comparison, not between limited multilateralism and full convertibility into dollars, but between bilateralism and limited transferability. Before there could be a substantial degree of liberalization of dollar imports, the OEEC countries had to get rid of bilateralism. It was far easier for them to move from bilateralism to multilateralism within the EPU area and partial convertibility into gold, than from bilateralism directly into full convertibility into gold and dollars. By first trading among themselves on a more competitive basis in freer European markets the OEEC countries were put in a better position to compete in dollar markets. Much the same discipline is required for maintaining equilibrium within the EPU area without quantitative trade restrictions as is required for maintaining overall equilibrium without quantitative restrictions. By and large the European countries have turned to monetary and fiscal policies as the primary means of balancing their international accounts as opposed to quantitative trade and exchange controls.

The large expansion of intra-OEEC country trade made possible by the EPU, and the improved competitive position of Western Europe, has greatly strengthened Western European currencies. Gold and dollar holdings have doubled since 1949 and the major transferable currencies such as sterling, the deutschemark and the Dutch guilder sell in the dollar markets of New York and Switzerland at discounts of from 1 to 2 percent of their official dollar values.

The fact that major EPU currencies can be sold for dollars at relatively small discounts and the fact that EPU deficits must be settled by a 75 percent payment in gold and the remainder in the form of credits means that there is relatively little incentive to discriminate against dollar imports in favor of imports payable in EPU currencies. This applies to countries outside of Europe that are trading with EPU currencies as well as to the OEEC countries themselves.

An examination of the trade statistics provides no evidence that the establishment of the EPU and the OEEC code of trade liberalization or of the Hague and Paris Clubs have adversely affected United States exports. United States commercial exports to Western Europe in 1956 were nearly 80 percent above the level of 1950 in spite of the sharp decrease in economic aid. Only a small percentage of Western

Europe's dollar trade was free from quantitive restriction in 1950 as against over 60 percent in the first half of 1957. Moreover, in spite of the high degree of intra-OEEC trade liberalization, there is less discrimination against dollar imports today than in 1950.

Nor has the Hague Club, inaugurated in August 1955, or the Paris Club, inaugurated in July 1956, appeared to have had an adverse effect on United States exports to Brazil or Argentina. United States exports to Brazil increased 22 percent in 1956 over 1955 and the United States share of the Brazilian import market rose from 23.6 to 29.2 percent. During the second half of 1956 United States exports to Argentina rose sharply over the first half and for the entire year 1956 the United States supplied 20 percent of Argentina's total imports as against 13 percent for the previous year.

*The relationship of the GATT and the International Monetary Fund to quantitative restrictions*

An important objective of both the International Monetary Fund and the General Agreement on Tariffs and Trade is the elimination of quantitative restrictions on current trade. The existing restrictions tend to arise from two major sources. First, a number of countries follow internal economic policies which result in a condition of chronic disequilibrium which necessitates the use of various types of restrictions and multiple-exchange rate systems in order to avoid a foreign exchange drain. While the Monetary Fund can assist countries which are in temporary disequilibrium and are taking steps to correct its causes, little can be done in the case of countries which persist in disequilibrium policies.

A second source of quantitative restrictions has arisen from the fact that the major international currencies have not been convertible or that certain countries have insisted on trading under bilateral trade and payments agreements. It is difficult for a few countries by themselves to trade on a fully multilateral basis and demand convertible currencies for their exports if the countries which form their principal markets are discriminating against goods for which dollar payment is required or seek to trade on a bilateral basis. Hence a country may be forced to adopt discriminatory controls and to trade with inconvertible currencies if it is to maintain its customary markets. Thus, for example, the officials of several western European governments have indicated that their currencies will become convertible the very day after the pound sterling is made fully convertible.

As has already been stated, it is my view that there is no longer a need for bilateralism or for discriminatory trade and currency controls. But their elimination is in many cases a matter of concerted action. Through their annual consultations with members, both the GATT and the Monetary Fund are seeking to reduce the degree of discrimination against dollar goods and to eliminate bilateralism. During the course of the GATT consultations with 8 western European countries in June 1957, pledges were received from all of them that they would ease the remaining restrictions on their imports as their financial position improves, and 5 of them—Austria, Germany, Italy, Norway, and Sweden, announced additional liberalization measures. Much of the credit for the progress of European dollar liberalization must also be given to the work of United States representatives in the OEEC.

While the GATT and the Monetary Fund provide important forums for consultation, persuasion, and for the airing of complaints on matters concerning the use of trade and exchange controls which impede commerce, it is important to realize their limitations. There are first of all a number of exceptions to the rules regarding the use of quantitative trade restrictions. Under the GATT rules, for example, a member country may maintain import restrictions to avoid a loss of reserves or to increase its reserves if they are below an adequate level. Both the GATT and the Monetary Fund Agreement provide for a postwar transitional period of indefinite duration during which members are permitted to retain their quantitative restrictions. In the case of the GATT, transitional arrangements apply only to discriminatory restrictions. However, annual consultations are held by both organizations for the purpose of determining the need for continuing existing restrictions.

Finally, it must be recognized that these international institutions have little power to discipline members even in cases where a direct violation of the agreement is involved. This also applies to the United States whose actions have at times been regarded by other countries as having been in contravention of certain GATT obligations.

## III. PREFERENTIAL TRADING ARRANGEMENTS

The advantages of a broad free trading area for achieving increased productivity and higher living standards have been well recognized both in the United States and abroad. One of the long-run objectives of the Marshall program was the economic integration of Western Europe and the creation of a common European market like that which exists among our 48 States has been strongly advocated by a number of leading European statesmen throughout the postwar period. This movement has already taken concrete form in the establishment of the European Coal and Steel Community providing for a common market and supranational regulation of the coal and steel industries of six European countries—Belgium, France, West Germany, Italy, Luxembourg, and the Netherlands. These same six countries have negotiated a treaty for the establishment of a European Economic Community. The treaty provides for the gradual establishment of a common market for goods and services over the next 12 to 15 years and a common customs tariff and commercial policy toward countries outside of the community. This treaty which was signed in March 1957 is now in the process of ratification by the governments of the six member countries and there is every prospect that it will be brought into being.

Still in the preliminary discusison stage is the proposed European free-trade area which would include the United Kingdom along with the six European Community countries plus such other OEEC countries as may want to joint. Under the free-trade area, as proposed by the British Government, trade in industrial products and raw materials would gradually be freed of all tariffs and quantitative restrictions within the area but each member, including the European community as a group, would determine its own tariffs and commercial policy with the outside world.

Interest in the creation of regional common markets or free-trade areas is not confined to the countries of Western Europe. Five Central American countries have negotiated a treaty for a free-trade area and at the seventh session of the Economic Commission for Latin America, held in La Paz, Bolivia, in May 1957, a resolution was passed endorsing the principle of regional common markets for Latin America.

A comprehensive review of the European Economic Community and other current proposals for the creation of customs unions or free-trade areas [9] is not possible within the limitations of this paper. I shall therefore confine my discussion to certain aspects of the European Economic Community which have special implications for the United States.

First of all it must be recognized that by their very nature these arrangements will result in increased discrimination against United States exports. Tariffs within the European Economic Community and the wider free-trade area (with the possible exception of those on foodstuffs) are to be gradually abolished while United States goods will be subject to a common tariff in the case of the European community and individual member tariffs in the case of other members of the free-trade area. Moreover, quantitative restrictions are to be abolished on trade within both the European Community and the free-trade area, while some quantitative restrictions may remain against United States goods.

Fears have been expressed that the European regional trade proposals may result in the creation of a highly discriminatory trading bloc which will seek to avoid competition from United States exports, and that the progress toward the restoration of a multilateral trading system will be arrested. It has been argued both in the United States and abroad that Western Europe will have to deliberalize trade with the outside and to maintain a high tariff wall in order to protect the French balance of payments which has been threatened by high costs and an overvalued exchange rate. (The French franc underwent de facto devaluation in August 1957.) Such fears have in fact been expressed by a number of Belgian, Dutch, and German economists and government officials.

But there is another way of looking at these proposed regional trading arrangements and their probable outcome. If the French are forced to compete with Germany and Benelux on a free-trade basis and without the aid of export subsidies and tax rebates, will not France be forced to adopt policies which will enable her to compete with the rest of the world on a nondiscriminatory basis? Moreover, may not the gains in real incomes from an expanded intra-European trade increase the demand for United States products so as to more than offset any diversion of trade arising from tariff discrimination? Also may not the improved competitive position of Western Europe enable these countries to eliminate most of the remaining quantitative restrictions on their imports from the outside world? Finally may not the United States be able to reduce the degree of tariff discrimination by negotiating reciprocal tariff reductions with the European Economic Community? The answer to this

[9] A customs union provides for a common tariff and common commercial policy vis-a-vis the outside world, while under a free-trade area each member country maintains its own external tariff system and commercial policy with respect to trade with countries outside of the area.

last question of course may depend more upon United States policy than upon European commercial policy.

There is good reason for optimism in considering these questions. The majority of the countries which make up the Community of Six appear to be dedicated to the principles of free enterprise and to freedom of trade and payments, including currency convertibility. There is certainly no enthusiasm in Germany or in Benelux for the creation of a high-cost, discriminatory trading bloc. The Germans or the Dutch are not interested in sacrificing the gains from an expanded trade in order to maintain an overvalued French franc.

Certainly, there is nothing in the experience of the OEEC trade-liberalization program or of the Coal and Steel Community which suggests that United States exports will be adversely affected by a further reduction of the barriers to intra-European trade. In fact, the evidence is all to the contrary.

*Relationship of regional trading arrangements to the GATT*

A fundamental principle of the General Agreement on Tariffs and Trade is that of nondiscriminatory or unconditional most-favored-nation treatment in the administration of tariffs. Certain preferences existing at the time the agreement was formulated in 1947 were permitted to continue, although margins of preference could not be increased without the consent of the contracting parties. Among the preferential systems specifically exempted in the GATT are the British Commonwealth preferences and those involving Cuba and the United States.

The GATT does recognize, however, the right of a group of countries to form a customs union or a free-trade area or to adopt preferential tariff arrangements while in the process of establishing a customs union or free-trade area. Article XXIV of the GATT sets forth certain basic criteria for an exception from the rules requiring most-favored nation treatment (article I) for countries announcing their intention to form a customs union or free-trade area:

(*a*) The duties or other regulations of commerce imposed at the institution of such area or union shall not, on the whole, be higher or more restrictive than the general incidence of the duties and regulations applicable in the constituent territories prior to the formation of such union or area or the adoption of an interim agreement leading to its formation.

(*b*) Any interim agreement for the formation of a customs union or free-trade area—

shall include a plan and schedule for the formation of such a customs union or of such a free-trade area within a reasonable length of time.

(*c*) Duties and other restrictive regulations of commerce are eliminated with respect to substantially all the trade between the territories of the customs union or free-trade area in products originating in such territories.

(*d*) The contracting parties may, by a two-thirds majority, approve proposals which do not fully comply with these requirements—

provided that such proposals lead to the formation of a customs union or a free-trade area in the sense of this article.

In addition to the possibility noted in paragraph (*d*) of the approval of a proposal which departs from the conditions described in paragraphs (*a*), (*b*), and (*c*) above, article XXV 5 (a) of the general agreement contains a general waiver clause whereby the contracting parties may waive any obligation imposed by the agreement—

provided that any such decision shall be approved by a two-thirds majority of the votes cast and that such majority shall comprise more than half of the contracting parties.

The contracting parties have the right to review any plan and schedule included in the interim agreement for the formation of a customs union or a free-trade area to determine whether or not the agreement is likely to result in the formation of such a union or area within a reasonable period of time.

The contracting parties have approved interim agreements for a customs union in the case of the Union of South Africa and Southern Rhodesia, and a free-trade area in the case of Nicaragua and El Salvador. At the 11th session of the GATT in October-November 1956, the contracting parties approved a proposed interim arrangement looking toward the establishment of a free-trade area among Nicaragua and four countries not contracting parties to the GATT, namely, El Salvador, Costa Rica, Guatemala, and Honduras. Under the proposed arrangement, tariffs and other restrictions would be eliminated on substantially all trade among these states within 10 years after the draft Central American Free-Trade and Economic Integration Treaty enters into force. As is the case with other interim arrangements looking toward the establishment of a customs union or a free-trade area, which have been approved by the GATT, Nicaragua agreed to submit a definite plan and schedule to the contracting parties and to make an annual report on the progress made in eliminating tariffs and other restrictions.

The contracting parties have granted a waiver for the establishment of tariff preferences contrary to article I (provision on most-favored nation treatment) in a number of cases not involving a free-trade area, some of which involve the trade of less developed countries. These cases include (1) a waiver for the establishment of the European Coal and Steel Community, (2) special customs treatment for Italian imports from Libya, (3) special customs treatment for Australian imports from Papua-New Guinea, and (4) a waiver to permit the United Kingdom to assist industrial development in its dependent overseas territories.

At the seventh session of the contracting parties to the GATT in 1952, the member states of the European Coal and Steel Community were granted a waiver from the obligation which would normally require that the products of all contracting parties receive most-favored-nation treatment, to permit them to form a common market in coal and steel products. The waiver was granted in recognition of the fact that the creation of the common market would be of economic benefit not only to members of the Coal and Steel Community but also to other members as a consequence of the increased productivity and larger incomes and world trade of the members of the community. The common market for coal and steel was analogous to a free-trade area as regards the limited range of commodities which was included. While the conditions of the waiver require the eventual removal of all restrictions on commerce in these commodities, certain exceptions to the duty-free treatment were permitted for a limited transitional period. The waiver also stated that—

the member states propose to harmonize their customs duties and other trade regulations applicable to coal and steel products originating in the territories of other contracting parties to the general agreement, upon a basis which shall be lower and less restrictive than the general incidence of the duties and regulations of commerce now applicable * * *

This harmonization is to be carried out by 1958. It is also significant that the common market in coal and steel products is under the direction of a high authority having supranational powers considered necessary for the integration of the national industries in these fields, including those relating to investment, taxation, prices, business practices, the raising of capital, labor policies, transportation rates, etc.

The Treaty for the Establishment of a European Economic Community of six nations is, for the most part, in conformity with the GATT criteria for treatment as a customs union. The treaty provides for the gradual removal of all governmental barriers to the flow of trade among members, and for a common commercial policy for the six members. A common tariff structure applicable to imports from outside the community is to be put into operation during the transition period. For individual members some rates will be raised and others lowered to the common duty levels, but the overall average, in conformity with the GATT requirement, is to be no higher than the overall average of rates prevailing before the establishment of the community. Special preferential arrangements for the dependent overseas territories of the members are also provided for in the treaty.[10] While the Economic Community proposal may require certain waivers from the GATT, particularly as regards the treatment of the dependent overseas territories, the treaty does not appear to depart substantially from the conditions for the customs-union exceptions to the most-favored-nation rules set forth under article XXIV of the general agreement.

The European free-trade-area proposal, as presently envisaged, involves certain radical departures from the article XXIV requirements. The major departure lies in the proposed exclusion of foodstuffs from the free-trade area. Britain feels that she must continue to give preferential treatment to foodstuffs coming from the dependent overseas territories and the independent Commonwealth countries. This would be impossible if Britain joined a free-trade area with other European countries in which tariffs on foodstuffs were removed. The limitation of the free-trade area to trade in manufactures and raw materials would certainly require a GATT waiver and the interim agreement for the transitional period for both the free-trade area and the Economic Community would require GATT review and approval. The transition period in the case of both proposals would be at least 12 years and probably longer.

The European Economic Community provides for a common foreign trade policy after the transition period, including the joint negotiation of tariffs and quotas, import liberalization, and antidumping and

[10] Exports from the dependent overseas territories to the community would be treated the same as exports from the metropolitan territories, but exports from any member to the dependent overseas territories would receive as favorable treatment as those of the mother country.

export subsidy measures. However, according to article 104 of the treaty, each member state agrees to—

pursue the economic policy necessary to insure the equilibrium of its overall balance of payments and to maintain confidence in its currency * * * [11]

While individual member states may in a period of balance-of-payments crisis take measures to protect their foreign exchange position, there appears to be no obligation on the part of other members to intensify their quantitative trade controls in order to assist other members in balance-of-payments difficulties. On the other hand, the treaty clearly contemplates an eventual unification of trade policy, including "the standardization of measures of liberalization" (art. 113). Article 110 states, however, that member states intend to contribute—

* * * to the harmonious development of world trade, the progressive abolition of restrictions on international trade, and the lowering of tariff barriers.

## IV. QUANTITATIVE RESTRICTIONS ON UNITED STATES IMPORTS

Since the United States does not employ exchange controls or other measures designed to protect its balance of payments, quantitative import restrictions are employed principally for the protection of domestic producers and for national-security reasons. At the time of writing, mandatory import quotas are confined to certain agricultural commodities. Section 22 of the Agricultural Adjustment Act provides that quantitative import restrictions or import fees shall be established whenever the President determines that imports are materially interfering, or are practically certain to interfere, with any domestic agricultural programs operated by the Department of Agriculture. Absolute quotas are also imposed on sugar imports under the Sugar Act and on cordage from the Philippines under the United States-Philippine trade agreement.

The President has the power, under section 7 of the Trade Agreements Act of 1955, to impose quotas or additional duties on imports of any commodity which, upon advice of the Director of the Office of Defense Mobilization, the President believes "is being imported into the United States in such quantities as to threaten to impair the national security." While mandatory import restrictions have not, at the time of writing, been imposed under this provision, the petroleum industry has been asked to restrict imports of petroleum voluntarily.

I shall refrain from dealing, except superficially, with quantitative import restrictions imposed either for national-security reasons or for avoiding interference with domestic agricultural support programs. As to the former, I am in agreement with the recommendation of the Randall Commission report, which was stated as follows:

The Commission recommends that tariffs or other import restrictions on raw materials should be determined on economic grounds. Upon a finding by the Executive that it is necessary on solely military grounds to assure a strictly domestic source of supply, the Commission recommends that the purpose should be accomplished by other means, the cost of which should be borne in the defense budget.[12]

---

[11] "Treaty establishing the European Economic Community" (provisional translation prepared in mimeo by the Information Service of the European Coal and Steel Community, Washington, D. C., May 1957).

[12] "Report to the President and to the Congress", Commission on Foreign Economic Policy, January 1954, p. 41.

I also believe that careful consideration should be given to the conclusions of the Subcommittee on Foreign Economic Policy of the Joint Committee on the Economic Report, which were embodied in a report of July 1956 entitled "Defense Essentiality and Foreign Economic Policy." The determination of requirements for a mobilization base is exceedingly complex, and the protection of our national security calls for considerations which go far beyond even this broad and complex problem. Finally, there is the problem of how to accomplish a given mobilization objective at the lowest cost to the public, including that forgotten man, the consumer. Too often, I fear, national-defense interest is a cloak for special interest.

Our special restrictions on agricultural commodities are a logical counterpart of a system maintaining the prices of agricultural commodities above world prices. High domestic support prices for various farm products often attract abnormal quantities of imports or price commodities we normally export out of foreign markets. This means we must insulate our domestic markets from foreign competition, and subsidize or give away our farm products in order to retain our foreign markets. The special restrictions on agricultural imports are certainly harmful to our exports, including exports of agricultural commodities, and greatly weaken the efforts of United States representatives in the GATT and elsewhere for reducing quantitative restrictions abroad. The fact that the United States had to ask for and receive a waiver from the GATT with respect to certain GATT rules which are inconsistent with the operation of section 22 of the Agricultural Adjustment Act surely weakens our bargaining position with respect to other matters. Perhaps, in fairness to the United States, it should be said that many other countries, including most Western European nations, have import quotas and other special protection on agricultural commodities which they produce.

I want to turn now to the general question of the use of quotas as a protectionist device. Legislation for imposing quotas is being suggested for a number of commodities such as textiles, bicycles, and watches. So-called voluntary export controls have been imposed on Japanese exporters of textiles to the United States under threat of the imposition of mandatory import quotas by the United States.

It will not be possible in this paper to deal with the entire problem of protection. This discussion will, therefore, be confined to the domestic and international implications of the use of quotas as against tariffs for providing protection to domestic industry. On the domestic side, there are two basic disadvantages arising from the use of quotas. First, it gives a windfall profit to the importers, since they are able to sell at the higher domestic price induced by the quota restrictions on supply while continuing to buy abroad at the same or perhaps a lower price than before.[13] The substitution of a tariff would permit the Government to capture this windfall.

The second argument against the use of a quota lies in its inflexibility. Once quotas are fixed, competitive advantage, as between domestic and foreign producers, no longer operates to determine the

[13] The reduction of demand in the foreign market caused by the United States import restriction may lead to a fall in the foreign price.

share of the market. Moreover, if quotas are fixed by law, they are not subject to negotiation under the trade-agreements program.

These considerations raise certain fundamental issues as to the purpose of protection from import competition. Should public policy be directed toward giving a domestic industry a permanent share of the domestic market insulated from foreign competition and from the necessity of reducing costs and improving quality? Or should public policy in this field be directed toward avoiding serious injury from a sudden influx of imports, and of providing time, along with the economic incentive, to domestic industries to adjust to a new, competitive situation? If the latter is the objective of public policy, the ideal instrument would appear to be a flexible tariff rather than a rigid quota.

Ideally, all protective tariffs should be gradually reduced, either under a reciprocal agreement with other countries to cut all tariffs by a certain percentage each year or by reciprocal negotiations covering individual items as under the present trade-agreements program. In the event of serious injury caused, say, by sudden influx of imports of a particular commodity, the tariff rate might be raised to provide time for adjustment, but with the provision of an automatic decrease in the rate each successive year thereafter. Raising the tariff rate as a means of dealing with serious injury would, of course, necessitate renegotiating certain tariff concessions with other members of the GATT, just as is done at present under the escape-clause provision.

Turning to the international implications of the use of quotas as against tariffs, we must recognize that a general use of quotas for protection of domestic industry would almost certainly wreck the trade-agreements program as now constituted. A general use of quotas for this purpose clearly violates the letter and the spirit of the GATT and, indeed, is completely inconsistent with the principles of reciprocal tariff bargaining. A widespread adoption of protective quotas would very likely result in a complete collapse of the complex and interdependent structure of tariff concessions built up within the GATT framework over the past 10 years.

*International implications of an extension of the use of quota restrictions by the United States*

An extensive use of import quotas as a protectionist device would most certainly be fatal to the trade-agreements program. Moreover, if nations are free to impose quantitative restrictions on imports whenever they want to give added protection to the domestic industry, the whole basis for tariff bargaining disappears. This principle cannot be compromised by saying that, since most countries have employed quantitative import restrictions throughout the postwar period, the United States should be permitted to employ them. Countries employing quantitative restrictions have, for the most part, been in balance-of-payments disequilibrium during the postwar period, and under the GATT rules they had the right to employ restrictions. As already noted, a great deal of progress has been made in the elimination of import restrictions, and several western European countries are virtually free of such restrictions except for agricultural imports. A decision on the part of the United States Government to extend the use of import quotas to nonagricultural commodities for purposes of protecting industry would most certainly reverse the trend away from their use abroad. This might very well mean that the western European countries would not only intensify their efforts to create a common market and free-trade area, but would erect a permanent wall of discriminatory restrictions against the United States. In addition, a collapse of the negotiated tariff structure which would probably accompany the termination of GATT might well result in a broad use of preferential tariff duties which discriminate against United States imports.

A reversal of the recent trend toward the liberalization of international trade and payments would undoubtedly result in a loss of real income both at home and abroad. It might of course be argued that the American exporters and the American consumers can afford to pay this additional cost so that profits and employment in the textile or bicycle or violin factories will not be reduced. Yet as a matter of public policy, it does not seem desirable to subsidize less efficient industries at the expense of production and employment in our export industries.

But while the direct cost of this subsidy to the American public may be small, the indirect cost to our foreign policy interests may be very great. Just in the past few years the Sino-Soviet bloc has discovered the political and economic advantages of an expanded trade with the free world. Between 1953 and 1956 this trade increased by over 80 percent in value terms and is continuing to increase. The bulk of this trade with the Soviet bloc countries, nearly 70 percent, is under bilateral trade agreements. The bloc countries prefer planned trade and seek or organize their trade on a Government-controlled, barter basis, as opposed to multilateral trade conducted by private enterprise. It is important that the United States endeavor to show the free world by its example that countries have more to gain by selling in free markets with a minimum of governmental controls. United States Government control of our import trade for the benefit of special business interests would certainly be contrary to this principle.

American leadership in the field of international economic cooperation bears a close relationship to our leadership and influence in the political sphere. If we adopt autarchic and isolationist policies in the field of foreign trade our foreign relations are bound to suffer. Moreover, the principles of free enterprise and competition which we so freely preach to the rest of the world are not confined within national boundaries. There has been a new birth of economic liberalism, of faith in free enterprise and unshackled commerce in the world, especially in Western Europe. If we are to win the ideological war with the Communist front, America, of all countries, must not turn its back on this movement.

## V. ALTERNATIVE COURSES FOR UNITED STATES TRADE POLICY

Until a few years ago the United States maintained a position of leadership in the field of international trade policy. This country was the moving spirit behind the negotiation of the proposed charter for the International Trade Organization, the GATT, and the International Monetary Fund, and our Government played a major role in the creation of the European Payments Union and the negotiation of the OEEC code of European trade liberalization. Following the recommendation of the Randall Commission of February 1954, the United States played a leading role in drafting the agreement on the Organization for Trade Cooperation, which is designed to provide a more effective administration for the General Agreement on Tariffs and Trade.

In recent years United States leadership in the field of international trade policy has waned. First there was the failure of the Congress to accept the ITO charter in 1950. In 1951 the trade agreements program was weakened by the inclusion of mandatory peril point and escape-clause procedures, and since that time Congress has broadened the concept of injury so as to open the door for escape-clause action in cases where the industries as a whole may be quite profitable. Several important escape-clause decisions resulting in a withdrawal of tariff concessions, including the bicycle case decision of August 1955 and the watch case decision of July 1954, have shaken the confidence of foreign countries in the stability of our tariff structure. Moreover, the very small amount of additional tariff bargaining authority given to the President in the 1955 act has greatly retarded the movement toward lower tariff levels achieved through multilateral bargaining. Finally the failure thus far of the Congress to take action on the OTC has raised serious doubts abroad as to the interest of the United States in a continuation of the reciprocal trade agreements program.

While the trade agreements program under United States leadership has definitely lost its momentum, three important developments have taken place: First, the de facto interconvertibility of the world's major currencies and the virtual elimination of any justification for trade discrimination on balance-of-payments grounds; second, the movement toward regional trading systems in Western Europe and elsewhere; third, the strong bid for world trade by the Sino-Soviet bloc, and the likelihood of this trade continuing to increase in absolute as well as relative volume in the future.

What alternative courses are open to the United States in the light of these developments and what are the implications of these alternatives?

First, the United States could abandon the trade agreements program. By denouncing its bilateral trade agreements and withdrawing from the GATT it would be free to employ quantitative import restrictions or adjust upward tariffs on commodities already subject to agreement.

While the consequences of such a course cannot be predicted with accuracy, it is most likely that the dollar import liberalization movement would be brought to a halt and probably reversed. Efforts to create a European common market and free-trade area would be intensified but without continued progress toward the removal of quantitative restrictions on dollar goods, the European regional trading system might well become a permanent area of trade discrimination against the United States.

A general use of quantitative import controls by the United States and the elimination of the GATT as an instrument of consultation would very likely reverse the present trend away from bilateralism.

Finally, lack of confidence in the stability of United States markets would make countries more willing to trade with the Sino-Soviet bloc on the basis of trade and clearing agreements.

A second possible course for the United States is one of simply holding on to the gains already achieved under the trade-agreements program but without seeking to extend these gains by any substantial reduction in United States tariffs on a reciprocal basis. Under this course the Congress might renew the Trade Agreements Act but without significantly enlarging the power of the President to adjust tariff duties.

It is difficult to say what the outcome of such a course would be. Clearly the trade-agreements program would lose whatever momentum it has left and the GATT as an instrument of trade liberalization would inevitably lose much of its force. This would be especially true if the Congress failed to ratify the Organization for Trade Cooperation even though it renewed the Trade Agreements Act in much its present form. Without an active international trade organization enthusiastically supported by the power and prestige of the United States, the outcome of this second course may be little different from the likely outcome of the first course as described above.

A third alternative course is one designed to recapture the leadership of the United States in the international trade field and to mobilize the movements toward regional trade liberalization for the liberalization of trade on a free-world basis. The elements of such a course are suggested as follows:

First, the United States would support the common market and free-trade-area proposals in Western Europe, except for any provision which may be inconsistent with the principles of nondiscrimination in the use of trade quotas and the eventual elimination of all quantitative restrictions against dollar goods.

Second, the United States would join the Organization for Trade Cooperation and announce its intention to negotiate substantial reductions in tariff rates through the OTC and GATT machinery. This would, of course, require that the President be given considerably increased authority to reduce United States tariff duties, say by 50 percent from their present levels. The United States would also need to avoid the use of quantitative restrictions on imports as a protective device, at least for nonagricultural commodities.

Finally, it is suggested that if the United States is to mobilize and to lead the strong forces now working for regional common markets in the direction of free-world trade liberalization, it should announce a long-term goal toward which we believe the free world should be moving. I shall not attempt to suggest how this goal should be formulated except to say that as an ideal it should be bold and dramatic. But let us suppose that the Congress were to pass a resolution to the effect that the long-range goal of the United States was the creation of a free trading area for the free world, to be achieved gradually over the next 20 or 25 years by mutual tariff reductions and the elimination of all quantitative restrictions. Such an announcement would not only help reestablish this country's leadership and influence in international trade cooperation, but would give a tremendous boost to the champions of free enterprise throughout the world. There could be no more dramatic and effective answer to Mr. Khrushchev's challenge to democracy and economic freedom.

# IMPLICATIONS OF THE EUROPEAN COMMON MARKET AND FREE TRADE AREA PROJECT FOR UNITED STATES FOREIGN ECONOMIC POLICY

Gottfried Haberler, professor of economics, Harvard University

At the time of writing (July 1957), the agreement on the common market has not yet been ratified. I shall not speculate on the chances of early ratification. I shall, rather, assume that the agreement has been ratified.

But even if it is duly signed and ratified, and if the first steps for its implementation are being taken, we cannot be sure that the project will be carried out to its intended end—the complete elimination of intra-European trade barriers and establishment of a common tariff against the outside world.

For reasons which I shall discuss presently, it makes a great deal of difference, not only for the members of the group but also for the United States and other outsiders, whether the project is fully carried out, or whether it gets stuck in an intermediate position with intra-European barriers reduced (but not entirely eliminated) and no common tariff established.

I shall first discuss the implications of a complete European customs union, that is to say, of the common market when fully carried out; secondly, of an incomplete customs union, that is to say, of the common market incompletely realized; and, thirdly, some problems raised by the free-trade area.

## 1. COMPLETE CUSTOMS UNION

In my opinion, there can be no doubt that the creation of a completely free market will greatly benefit the six participating European countries. This has been repeatedly acknowledged by those responsible for United States foreign policy. They have consistently urged the Europeans to create a large free market in order to strengthen their economies and make them more viable without financial support from the United States.

It follows that the United States must welcome the common-market project even though it implies tariff discrimination against imports from the United States. Such discrimination is, indeed, implicit in the scheme, because in each of the six countries products from any other will enter free of duty, while competing American products will be subject to the common tariff of the union. It does not necessarily follow, however, that the total volume of United States exports to the common market will decline. It may well rise. This will be the case, if the creation of the common market strongly stimulates the European economy and if the common tariff is kept at a reasonable level. It is here that the United States and other countries are most vitally and legitimately interested.

According to the GATT agreement, the six European countries have the right to establish a customs union without laying themselves open to claims on the strength of most-favored-nation principle. But GATT also lays down the rule that the common tariff of a customs union must not be higher than the average tariff on the various members. The common market agreement provides that the common tariff shall be the arithmetic mean of the national tariffs of the participating countries in force on January 1, 1957—the highest level permitted by GATT. There are supplementary rules fixing maximum common tariffs on certain specified commodities, and there are rules of procedure for the implementation and for altering the common tariff.

This arrangement means that United States exports to the Benelux countries and Germany, which now have low tariffs, will pay higher duties after the common market has gone into effect, while exports to France and Italy, whose tariffs are higher than those of the countries just mentioned, will pay less than now.

Although there are fairly precise rules governing the common tariff, there will certainly be room for argument and negotiation. The United States and other outsiders should insist that the common tariff be as low as possible. This problem ought to be discussed before the forum of the GATT.

Moreover, these will not be problems which require a once-for-all solution. It will become a lasting task, for the reason that the transition to the common market will last many years and that, after it has been fully established, trade negotiations will have to be held with the new organization.

It is extremely important for our export interests that the GATT machinery be maintained and strengthened. It is before GATT that United States and the interests of other outsiders (e. g., those of the other American states and of Japan) can be best defended. It would, therefore, be most desirable if the United States could join the proposed OTC which will provide GATT with a much-needed Secretariat, putting it into a better position to perform its duty as a watchdog to forestall undue tariff discrimination against United States and other imports from the outsider into the European common market.

### 2. INCOMPLETE CUSTOMS UNION

An incomplete customs union is one where the trade barriers between the members are only reduced, but not entirely abolished. The European common market is intended to be a complete customs union, but during the period of transition, which will last 12 to 15 years, it will be incomplete, because intra-European tariffs will be reduced only gradually. Moreover, there is the possibility that the scheme will get stuck in the middle of the transition or that the transition will be prolonged indefinitely and thus the common market transformed into an incomplete customs union.

An incomplete customs union involves less discrimination against outsiders than a complete customs union. The same is true of a preferential tariff regime, as, for example, the so-called imperial preferences between the members of the British Commonwealth. The United States, nevertheless, always took the position that customs unions are permitted, while preferential regimes are to be outlawed. This position has also been incorporated into the GATT agreement.[1]

This differentiation between preferential regimes and customs unions has been much criticized, but it has a sound economic basis. In order to explain, I must introduce the distinction between trade-creating and trade-diverting tariff reductions. If a tariff is reduced for all imports (general tariff reduction), it always creates more trade. If a duty is reduced only preferentially for imports from certain countries, but not from others (preferential tariff reduction), it may only divert trade or there may be a mixture of trade diversion and trade creation.

Take the case of a pure trade diversion. Suppose that in a European country, duties for the import of European automobiles are abolished while the duty on American cars remains and that total imports remain the same. In that case, import trade is diverted from the United States to a European country. If total imports increase, then we have trade diversion plus trade creation.

Now, it is easy to see that trade diversion does not carry the same economic advantages in shifting demand from costly to cheaper sources of supply. On the contrary, it diverts trade to more expensive, less efficient sources of supply. If, under a uniform tariff, United States automobiles were bought, the reason was that they were cheaper or more suitable for their users than European automobiles. If, now, demand is artificially diverted to European cars which could not stand up under equal (nondiscriminating) treatment to American competition, we get an inefficient redistribution of production.

Now, in the case of a complete customs union, trade creation and trade diversion come along together. The same is true in the case of an across-the-board, preferential tariff reduction and incomplete customs union. In the case of a complete customs union, we can be pretty sure that the favorable effects of trade creation will outweigh the unfavorable effects of trade diversion.

However, if the preferential tariff reductions are made selectively and the customs union is shot through with exceptions, the chances are that primarily trade-diverting tariff reductions are made for the simple reason that domestic industries will put up fierce resistance, when total imports threaten to increase while their resistance will be less, if only a diversion of imports is to be expected.

A predominantly trade-diverting customs union would not improve the economic position of its members. It will also hurt the outsiders. If trade creation predominates the productive power of the member economies will be strengthened and in that case it is possible (although not necessary) that in the end also the outsiders (such as the United States) will gain in the event that the increased income of the members of the union leads to larger overall imports.

It follows from this analysis that it is in the interest of the United States (as well as that of other outsiders) that the European common market should be as complete and across the board as possible. By "across the board" I mean that import duties and other impediments to trade should be uniformly reduced and not selectively.

---

[1] The GATT agreement, however, makes exceptions for the preferences which existed when it came into force, with the proviso that the existing preference margins must not be increased. They have, in fact, been substantially reduced over the years.

On the whole the common market agreement as it stands does correspond to these postulates. United States policy should therefore exert its influence in such a way that the plan is carried out according to the present plans and not be riddled by exceptions and escape clauses. In particular we should see to it that purely trade-diverting measures are avoided. The United States can insist on that with clear conscience because trade diversion hurts not only countries outside the proposed union but also the true interests of the members of the union themselves.

### 3. FREE TRADE ZONE

While the six original members of the common market are planning a complete customs union, other European countries, Great Britain among them, are considering joining the common market in the form of a free trade zone or area. The distinguishing feature of the free trade zone is that its members maintain their own tariff against imports from the outside while abolishing trade barriers for imports from the other members countries.

As compared with the customs union approach the free trade area approach has the advantage that it is unnecessary for the members of the group to agree on a common tariff. From the point of view of the outsiders, such as the United States, this has the advantage that the low tariff members of the free trade area maintain their low tariff and the disadvantage that the high tariff members maintain their high tariff. Only a detailed study of the patterns of trade plus a knowledge of the structure of the common tariff could reveal whether for the United States or other outsiders the free trade area or customs union would be preferable on balance.

As compared with a complete customs union the free trade area has the great disadvantage that complete customs control on intrazonal trade must be maintained in order to prevent imports into the high tariff members via low tariff members from the outside world. It will be necessary to introduce a complicated system of controls of origin. How much value added to imported raw materials or semifinished goods is sufficient to qualify the finished product for being treated as originating in the processing country? If a country produces certain commodities and imports the same commodity (or a close substitute), can it be prevented from exporting duty free its whole domestic production?

These and similar questions posed formidable administrative problems which concern primarily the members of the free trade area. But the solution of these problems will inevitably affect imports into the free trade zone from the outsider and thus become a legitimate concern of outsiders such as the United States.

The complete customs union is a simpler, more clean-cut form of economic integration than the free trade area. But in practice the difference will not be great, because, during the lengthy period of transition and perhaps forever, the customs union will not be complete and will therefore require intra-European customs inspection and rules of origin.

Hence the free trade zone approach will confront the United States and other outsiders with the same type of problems as the customs union approach. We should insist that the methods adopted are across the board and not selective; that is to say, that intra-European tariffs are reduced by uniform percentages and that purely trade-diverting and hence grossly discriminatory, and even for the member countries useless, tariff reductions be avoided.

If the United States insists on these points, basing its claims on the relevant provisions in the GATT agreement and bilateral commercial treaties containing most-favored-nation clauses, it will not only protect its own legitimate export interests, as well as those of other countries outside the common market, but will also serve the true interests of the members of the common market.

### CONCLUDING REMARK

A much better solution for all nations, members of the common market and the free-trade zone as well as others, than the proposed European or any other regional free-trade area or customs union, would be a truly multilateral policy of freer trade. A general reduction of tariffs, generalized by the operation of the unconditional most-favored-nations principle, excluding any kind of discrimination would be the ideal solution.

The United States is, however, in a poor position to urge that approach on other countries and to persuade them to adopt that approach in preference to their regional free-trade projects. We could do that with a good conscience and chance of success only if we were prepared to make substantial concessions in our tariff; that is to say, if we were prepared to reduce some of our import duties in exchange for similar reductions in tariff and of other impediments to trade elsewhere.

If we are not willing to reduce our tariffs substantially, we cannot object to other countries going ahead on a regional and therefore discriminatory basis. All we can do is to insist that other countries comply with the spirit and the letter of the GATT provisions on common market and free-trade area. This insistence will remain a continuing task, not a once-for-all job. It is therefore essential for the protection of our legitimate export interests that the GATT machinery be strengthened. It follows that the United States should join the proposed OTC which will provide GATT with a much-needed efficient secretariat.

# NOTES ON TRADE LIBERALIZATION AND REGIONALISM

Robert Triffin, professor of economics, Yale University

1. There can be no doubt that the widespread use of quantitative trade and exchange restrictions abroad in postwar years has often thwarted and nullified—or even more than nullified—the tariff concessions granted to the United States under reciprocal trade agreements. It is highly tempting to conclude from this observation that we should extend our tariff bargaining process to apply to nontariff trade restrictions and indeed to other forms of impediment to international trade.

2. Before accepting this conclusion, however, we must be clear as to:

(*a*) the real impact of foreign restrictions and other foreign and United States policies upon our exports;

(*b*) the actual leverage of international negotiations and agreements upon a country's policy.

3. Paradoxical as it may sound, foreign restrictions and discrimination against United States goods have a far lesser impact on our overall export levels than is usually imagined. The level of our merchandise and services exports is, indeed, primarily determined by our own dollar expenditures abroad and cannot exceed for long the amount of such expenditures except for relatively small additions financed by foreign gold sales or disinvestment of previously accumulated dollar assets. Such gold sales and disinvestments financed a modest 7 percent of our exports in the early postwar years (1946–49). In the following 7 years, foreign countries retained about 9 percent of their current dollar earnings in order to reconstitute their depleted gold and dollar assets. The bulk of this, however, took the form of a net inflow of foreign capital to the United States ($10 billion), and only $2 billion was withdrawn in the form of gold purchases from the United States, as compared to the $4.5 billion of foreign gold sales to the United States in the years 1946–49.

Over the whole 11-year period 1946–56, our exports of goods and services ($196 billion) absorobed 97 percent of our expenditures abroad ($204 billion), the difference ($8 billion) being added to foreign countries' gold and dollar assets.

4. Our overall export levels had never before been so high, indeed, as they were maintained throughout the postwar years, in spite of generalized restrictions and discrimination abroad against all transactions involving payment in scarce dollars. Our merchandise exports have progressed, in dollar terms, from a postwar low of 3 times their 1938 level in 1946 to nearly 6 times in 1956. In volume terms—correcting for price increases—they have ranged from a low of 1.75 times prewar in 1950 to more than 2½ times prewar in 1956.

*Financing of United States exports of goods and services, 1946–56*

| | In billions of United States dollars | | | | | | In percent of United States exports | | | | |
|---|---|---|---|---|---|---|---|---|---|---|---|
| | United States expenditures abroad | | | | Foreign gold sales and dollar disinvestment | United States exports of goods and services [3] | United States expenditures | | | | Foreign gold sales and dollar disinvestment |
| | Current account [1] | Private capital [2] | Economic aid and Government capital | Total | | | Current account | Private capital | Foreign aid | Total | |
| | (a) | (b) | (c) | (d=a+b+c) | (e) | (f=d+e) | (g) | (h) | (i) | (j=g+h+i) | (k=100−j) |
| Years: | | | | | | | | | | | |
| 1946 | 7.6 | 0.2 | 5.3 | 13.1 | 1.6 | 14.7 | 52 | 1 | 36 | 89 | 11 |
| 1947 | 8.9 | .1 | 8.9 | 17.8 | 1.9 | 19.7 | 45 | 1 | 45 | 90 | 10 |
| 1948 | 10.9 | −.1 | 4.8 | 15.6 | 1.2 | 16.8 | 65 | −1 | 29 | 93 | 7 |
| 1949 | 10.3 | −.2 | 5.6 | 15.7 | .1 | 15.8 | 65 | −1 | 35 | 100 | 1 |
| 1950 | 12.6 | 1.2 | 3.6 | 17.6 | −3.7 | 13.9 | 91 | 9 | 26 | 127 | −27 |
| 1951 | 15.6 | .6 | 3.2 | 19.3 | −.5 | 18.8 | 83 | 3 | 17 | 103 | −3 |
| 1952 | 16.3 | .6 | 2.4 | 19.3 | −1.2 | 18.1 | 90 | 3 | 13 | 107 | −7 |
| 1953 | 17.3 | .1 | 2.0 | 19.4 | −2.3 | 17.1 | 101 | ---------- | 12 | 114 | −13 |
| 1954 | 16.7 | 1.4 | 1.6 | 19.7 | −1.8 | 17.9 | 93 | 8 | 9 | 110 | −10 |
| 1955 | 18.5 | .7 | 2.2 | 21.4 | −1.5 | 19.9 | 93 | 4 | 11 | 107 | −7 |
| 1956 | 20.4 | 2.1 | 2.3 | 24.9 | −1.5 | 23.4 | 88 | 9 | 10 | 107 | −6 |
| Yearly average: | | | | | | | | | | | |
| 1946–49 | 9.4 | ---------- | 6.2 | 15.6 | 1.2 | 16.8 | 56 | ---------- | 37 | 93 | 7 |
| 1950–53 | 15.5 | .6 | 2.8 | 18.9 | −1.9 | 17.0 | 91 | 4 | 17 | 112 | −12 |
| 1954–56 | 18.6 | 1.4 | 2.0 | 22.0 | −1.6 | 20.4 | 91 | 7 | 10 | 108 | −8 |

[1] Imports of goods and services, private remittances, pensions, and other transfers.
[2] Including errors and omissions.
[3] Excluding military transfers under aid programs.

Source: Survey of Current Business.

In the years 1946–49, however, 37 percent of our exports of goods and services were financed by our foreign-aid programs. This percentage declined gradually in the following years down to an almost stable level of 10 percent in 1954–56. This is very nearly compensated by the current increase in gold and dollar assets of foreign countries taken as a group, 98 percent of our exports being currently financed in fact by foreign sales to the United States and net foreign investments of private United States capital. Some Asian countries, however, remain heavily dependent on our aid—for obvious reasons related to military and political conditions—while continental Western Europe—with the main exception of France—was, at least until recently, adding far more to its gold and dollar assets than the tapering-off amounts of economic aid still directed to that area.

Broadly speaking, high and rapidly growing—by more than 31 percent over the last 2 years—export levels are now financed overwhelmingly—up to 98 percent in 1954–56—by our expanding levels of imports (91 percent) and of private capital exports (7 percent).

5. One may well ask, therefore, what is the actual significance to us of foreign restrictions and discrimination against dollar goods. Several aspects of the problem should be considered in turn.

(*a*) Foreign restrictions often constitute, to a large extent, a mere offset to abnormal levels of import demand arising from current or past inflationary trends which the country would be unable to finance in any case. The lifting of restrictions would not expand imports, as it would require the simultaneous adoption of other alternative measures—anti-inflationary policies or exchange rate readjustments—necessary to keep the country's foreign expenditures within the limits of the foreign exchange available for their financing. To this extent, foreign restrictions do not substantially affect the overall level of American exports.[1] Their main impact upon us derives from the fact that foreign countries may then influence the composition of their imports in accordance with some administrative criteria of essentiality rather than allow this composition to be determined by market forces in a free economy. This may, of course, introduce some disturbances in our markets, benefiting some of our producers at the expense of others.

(*b*) Foreign restrictions, however, tend to decrease—although as already indicated to a much lesser extent than usually imagined—the overall level of our exports.

The main reason for this is that the resort to restrictions—in preference to alternative policies of balance-of-payment readjustment—does nothing to correct the depressive effect of internal inflation upon the country's exports, and may, in addition, discourage capital imports and stimulate capital flight. Moreover, the substitution of domestic production for prohibited imports—or of costlier imports for cheaper imports under discriminatory restrictions—adds an upward push to domestic costs and reduces further the country's competitiveness in export markets. These disadvantages, however, bear far more heavily on the restricting country itself than on its trade partners and competitors. The persistent trend for its exports to decline under such policies sets a limit to the practicable use of restrictions. An ex-

[1] The current high level of French restrictions, for instance, has not prevented a 50-percent increase in French imports from the United States in 1956 over 1955.

cessive postponement of more fundamental measures of readjustment would, in the end, dry up exports far below the level necessary for the financing of imports essential to the maintenance of production and economic activity.

Foreign restrictions will also reduce our export levels insofar as they are used in order to accumulate or reconstitute foreign countries' gold and dollar reserves. While some international agreements might legitimately aim at preventing abuses in this respect, this has never been a serious problem for us in the past, and would be unlikely to become one in the future if it were not for the total inadequacy of current levels of gold production to supply a satisfactory rate of growth of international reserves. This difficulty has been met in recent years by an unprecedented growth of our short-term dollar liabilities, at a rate of $1 billion to $2 billion a year. These dollar balances have exactly doubled over the last 7 years, passing from $8.2 billion at the end of 1949 to $16.4 billion at the end of 1956. A full discussion of this problem and of its implications, however, far transcends the scope of this paper and bears only a distant relation to the question of foreign restrictions which we are here discussing.

6. The maintenance of high and growing export levels by the United States depends primarily:

(*a*) On our own willingness to import goods and services from abroad, and to export American capital either through foreign aid or through private loans and investments. Our willingness to import is, by far, the most significant factor in the present and highly satisfactory state of our export activities. It is, in turn, dependent on the preservation of high and growing levels of activity at home and on the continuation and expansion of liberal trading policies by this country.

(*b*) On the ability of foreign countries to provide high and growing levels of exports at competitive prices and to attract United States capital. This, in turn, is closely related to the maintenance of high levels of activity and growth abroad, but is also dependent on the pursuit of noninflationary policies or on the willingness to offset the failure of such policies through exchange-rate readjustments rather than through restrictions and discrimination. Our concern about other countries' restrictions is, therefore, justified, but should not make us forget the far greater impact of our own policies upon our export levels.

7. Our own influence upon other countries' policies, through bilateral or international negotiations and agreements, should be based on a realistic appraisal of the desirable and feasible objectives and techniques of such agreements.

The objectives of international cooperation among independent countries should minimize, rather than maximize, at the outset the interference of international organizations with the national process of policymaking, and respect a clear ordering of priorities inspired both by the urgency and feasibility of such interference. It would, for instance, be utopian at this stage to expect international commitments and jurisdiction to be able to preclude any and all failings of national leadership in a democratic society to preserve and enforce ideal norms of internal economic and monetary policy. Devaluation or restrictions may, therefore, become inescapable at times to correct persistent deficits in a country's balance of payments. International agreements should beware of any procedural rules and regulations that would discourage the first of these alternatives at the cost of encouraging the latter.

A total ban on all restrictions—tantamount to free trade—would, however, also be utopian at this stage. The most urgent and feasible goal of international economic policy in this respect should be the elimination of bilateralism in world trade and payments. This would restore the essential characteristic of 19th century convertibility, i. e., the maintenace of competition among exporters in all third markets, and would not be incompatible with a certain measure of protection to national producers within each country's own boundaries.

The second goal of international trade and monetary agreements should be the gradual relaxation of existing restrictions, including quantitative trade and exchange restrictions as well as customs duties. These various techniques of restriction are indeed largely interchangeable, and any piecemeal attack might be useless, or worse than useless, if the ban on some restrictions merely leads to a tightening of the others. We may well have put the cart before the horse when negotiating painfully the lowering and consolidation of tariff duties before obtaining parallel commitments with respect to trade and exchange controls.

In correcting this error and broadening the scope of trade negotiations to encompass all forms of restrictions, we should, however, keep in mind the impossibility of rigidly enforcing comprehensive commitments of this sort, as long as all participating countries are not fully agreed on the alternative measures that will be taken to cushion, finance, or correct serious disequilibria in their balance of payments. The remedies to be applied will almost unavoidably have to vary with the circumstances of each case, and may have to take into account political and administrative factors limiting the actual acceptability and feasibility of strictly rational economic solutions to the problem. These considerations make it well-nigh impossible to agree in advance on clearly defined rules and commitments, and indispensable to preserve a wide latitude for negotiations on escape clauses, stabilization credits, readjustment programs, and so forth. They also suggest that the mutual understanding and effective cooperation that can be elicited in such negotiations is likely to vary in inverse ratio to the number and heterogeneity of the participating countries in the agreement. Regional agreements among highly interdependent countries can, for this reason, define far more ambitious aims and require a correspondingly greater degree of mutual cooperation and assistance than worldwide agreements among a vast number of countries having little or no familiarity with one another's problems and policies.

8. Regional and worldwide forms of cooperation have each a role to play in harmonizing national policy decisions in an economically interdependent world. These roles should be viewed as complementary and mutually supporting rather than as antagonistic to one another.

Various arguments, however, have been marshaled up against this conclusion.

The first is that regional agreements promote discrimination against nonmember countries. This danger is certainly real, and has led a number of economists to prefer nondiscriminatory restrictions to discriminatory liberalization, and to oppose all kinds of preferential agreements up to and including partial customs unions. A full discussion of these arguments would far exceed the scope of this paper. Let us merely observe here that the liberalization of intra-European trade and payments, while admittedly discriminatory at the outset, was instrumental in reintroducing competitive forces over a vast trading area. The consequent improvement of Europe's competitive position has been followed by a gradual extension to nonmembers of the liberalization measures initially accepted only on a reciprocal basis among the participating countries themselves.[2] Intra-OEEC exports and imports nearly doubled in value between 1950 and 1956, but OEEC imports from the rest of the world also increased by more than 60 percent in spite of the near elimination of foreign aid financing, and OEEC exports rose by 78 percent to the rest of the world, and 130 percent to the dollar area. This spectacular recovery of exports should do much to dispel earlier fears that European integration would develop into a sheltered, soft-currency area increasingly isolated from world trade, and particularly from United States competition. The last 2 years have witnessed a particularly rapid rate of progress in the removal of European dollar restrictions and discrimination and an expansion of more than 60 percent in imports from the United States.

A second argument against regional integration is the danger of a division of the world into a few, powerful autarchic blocs, even more threatening than national protectionism to world trade, prosperity, and peace. This fear, however, ignores the fact that there exist few, if any, areas outside Western Europe where intraregional trade would constitute more than a minor fraction of the participating countries' total trade. The EPU and the dollar area together account for nearly 85 percent of total world trade and absorb nearly 75 percent of other countries' exports. The maintenance of multilateral trade and payments rules by the EPU and dollar area countries would leave little or no room or incentives for bilateralism and discrimination by others. It would indeed resurrect an international trade and payments system comparable in many ways to that of the 19th century gold standard, which rested essentially on the maintenance of convertibility policies by the United States and the European countries—together with their monetary areas—but did not preclude varying degrees of trade restriction and protectionism by individual countries, and of exchange rate instability in Latin America and Asia. Similar limitations on any ideal pattern of international economic institutions are likely to remain with us as long as political and administrative difficulties make it utopian to contemplate a merger of national sovereignties into an effective world government.

Finally, we cannot forget the political implications of European economic integration for the strengthening of the free world. A weak and divided Europe would constitute a permanent danger to world peace—as it has in the past—and present a most tempting prey for outside aggression. A united Europe on the other hand, would eliminate the traditional sources of past world wars and become a formidable deterrent to potential attacks against the West.

---

[2] Germany, for instance, has just announced the expansion of its dollar liberalization measures to more than 93 percent of its imports from the United States.

9. The above considerations justify, in my opinion, the constant support given by the United States since the war to the movement toward economic and political integration in Europe. Some of the immediate and long-run implications of European integration, however, are yet to be taken into account if our own policies are to become fully consistent in this respect, and to derive from it the maximum possible benefits for us as well as for others.

First of all, we must accept less grudgingly than we have done in the past the unavoidable discriminatory features of the preferential trade or payments arrangements inseparable from such integration. These have never been questioned in relation to a full merger of political sovereignties, nor generally objected to in relation to a complete customs union. They have, on the other hand, elicited considerable opposition in many quarters against partial or progressive steps unaccompanied by firm commitments to a relatively rapid and total abolition of all trade barriers among the participating countries. We should realize that excessive rigidity in this respect might be tantamount to blocking altogether feasible progress toward highly desirable and fundamental objectives.

On the other hand, we and other countries will have a vital interest in stimulating the adoption by an integrated Europe of as liberal trading policies as possible toward the outside world. Our bargaining power in trade negotiations and our cooperation in worldwide agreements such as the IMF, GATT, and the proposed OTC should be directed toward that aim. As already suggested above, however, our ambitions in this respect will have to be tailored to the feasibility of the policy commitments and harmonization indispensable for the practical acceptability and implementation of the sacrifices of sovereignty implicit in such agreements.

Close cooperation within the Atlantic Alliance between Europe, the United States and Canada would create a most promising framework for economic stability and growth throughout the world. This should be a prime objective of American economic policy, but is likely to depend far more on a permanent willingness to search and negotiate solutions for the new problems that may emerge than on rigid, once-and-for-all commitments implying a much larger renunciation of sovereignty than either we or our partners would be willing to contemplate at this time. This is particularly true in our case, as specific preferential agreements with Europe alone might risk embittering our relations with other parts of the free world essential to our security and to the fulfillment of the broader objectives of our international policy.

# V

# TRADE-AGREEMENTS LEGISLATION AND ADMINISTRATION

# PROPOSALS FOR LEGISLATIVE REFORM OF THE TRADE AGREEMENTS ACT

Richard N. Gardner, associate professor of law, Columbia University Law School

The primary purpose of American trade policy should be the prosperity and security of the United States. With these broad aims in view, we must overhaul and strengthen the Trade Agreements Act when it comes up for renewal in 1958.

When the Trade Agreements Act was first adopted, it met a very real need. Up to that time, tariffmaking in the United States was almost entirely done by Congress. This system was—to use the expression of Senator Vandenberg—an "atrocity." Congressmen had neither the time nor the information necessary to fix individual tariff rates. They were often the victims of irresistible protectionist demands from an influential minority of constituents. The Trade Agreements Act sought to improve this situation by delegating substantial tariffmaking powers to the Executive. Thus, it marked an important step forward toward the efficient regulation of our foreign trade.

That was in 1934. Since then, revolutionary changes have taken place in the political and economic position of the United States in world affairs. The act has not been altered to take account of these changes. On the contrary, it has been subjected to periodic amendments which have moved against, rather than with, the current of world events. If the act was a step forward in 1934, it is no longer adequate in 1958.

The deficiencies of the present act can be summarized under four heads: (1) Its stated purpose, (2) the powers delegated to the President, (3) the injury concept, (4) the defense concept. In the following pages I shall try to give examples of the need for legislative reform under each of these topics.

## I. THE PURPOSE OF THE ACT

The Trade Agreements Act (19 U. S. C. 1351 et seq.) begins with the following language:

> For the purpose of expanding foreign markets for the products of the United States (as a means of assisting in establishing and maintaining a better relationship among various branches of American agriculture, industry, mining, and commerce) by regulating the admission of foreign goods into the United States in accordance with the characteristics and needs of various branches of American production so that foreign markets will be made available to those branches of American production which require and are capable of developing such outlets by affording corresponding market opportunities for foreign products in the United States, the President, whenever he finds as a fact that any existing duties or other import restrictions of the United States or any foreign country are unduly burdening and restricting the foreign trade of the United States and that the purpose above-declared will be promoted by the means hereinafter specified, is authorized from time to time * * *.

This is a pretty complicated piece of legal language, but its basic significance seems clear enough, particularly when it is read against the historical background of congressional debate. The overriding purpose of the act is to expand American exports. This is to be done with a view to the ultimate objective of improving unsatisfactory domestic United States economic conditions. (One must remember that the act was passed in 1934 in the midst of the great depression.) The means of increasing American exports is the offering of "corresponding market opportunities" for the products of other countries in the United States, but—and this is a very important "but"—the admission of such foreign products is to take place in accordance with the "needs" of domestic American producers. The background of legislative debate makes it very clear that this qualification amounts to a guaranty of continued protection for domestic industry. On numerous occasions, in 1934 and subsequently, the administration promised publicly that, in the process of expanding American exports, imports into the United States would not be increased to the point where they caused injury to American producers.

The logic of this formula was very dubious even in 1934. According to economic analysis, domestic employment and economic activity can be increased by an increase in the export surplus; they cannot be increased significantly by an increase in exports balanced by an equivalent increase in imports. The main benefit from a truly reciprocal expansion of trade (which is the purported objective of the Trade Agreements Act) is an increase in real income. Moreover, it is not clear how American exports can be significantly expanded on a reciprocal basis when imports into the United States may not be increased to the point where they displace American producers.

At this point someone may ask: Why all this fuss about the statement of purpose? Is it not just so much nice language, quite irrelevant to practical questions of law and policy? The answer is no, for at least three reasons.

First, the statement of purpose is the standard for executive action. The administrators of the act are empowered to make trade agreements and changes in American tariffs only when these will contribute directly to the limited objective described above. In specific terms, this means that the Executive cannot make unilateral reductions in the American tariff or even any change at all which may injure an American producer. One might almost say the administrators of the act are required to make a maximum of tariff changes with a minimum of practical results.

The statement of purpose is important also as a standard for congressional appraisal. The present statement makes the whole program vulnerable to protectionist criticism. Since the tariff concessions given us by other countries are frequently nullified by the maintenance of direct controls such as quotas, exchange restrictions, and the like, the critics can argue, with a certain amount of justice, that the program has failed to achieve its stated objective of increasing American exports.

Finally, the statement of purpose is important as a standard for public education. So long as the purpose of the act is inadequately conceived, the public will not be told its real interest in freer trade. Slowly but surely, long-term support for the policy will be progressively undermined.

If a new statement of purpose is required, what should it contain? Surely, at the very least, it should make reference to the following interests:

First, there is the interest of the American consumer. The act should recognize frankly that one of the major purposes is to provide the American consumer with products he cannot obtain at home, or which he can only obtain at home in inferior quality or at greater cost.

It is seldom realized how far the United States has moved from self-sufficiency. We now import about one-tenth of our raw-material requirements. Already we are largely or wholly dependent on imports for such vital materials as asbestos, coffee, chromite, industrial diamonds, manganese, nickel, tea, tin, tungsten, and wool. Authoritative studies warn us that this tendency will greatly increase in the years ahead.

Obviously, our interest as consumers is not confined to imports of products we cannot obtain at home or which are essential to our existence. We are interested also in products such as bicycles, wines and spirits, kitchenware, gloves, cheese, handmade glass, maraschino cherries, garlic—things we could do without if necessary but whose presence make life a good deal more agreeable. To be sure, we could produce all of these products at home if we had to. But in each of these cases the cost would be much greater than if we acquired them from countries more efficient in their production.

At this point someone may raise the familiar argument that imports must be restricted in order to "protect" the American worker against "cheap foreign labor." Later on we shall deal squarely with this argument, using recent estimates of the actual labor displacement which substantial tariff reduction would involve. Here let us only recall the obvious point that the rational end of economic policy is not just full employment but full and productive employment. If we seek to protect the present occupation of every worker who might be displaced by foreign competition we may achieve full employment—but it will be full employment of large numbers of people producing inferior products at ridiculous costs. This reductio ad absurdum of the protectionist philosophy was effectively satirized in the following petition drafted a century ago by the Frenchman Frederic Bastiat:

*To the Chamber of Deputies:*

We are subjected to the intolerable competition of a foreign rival, who enjoys such superior facilities for the production of light that he can inundate our national market at reduced price. This rival is no other than the sun. Our petition is to pass a law shutting up all windows, openings, and fissures through which the light of the sun is used to penetrate our dwellings, to the prejudice of the profitable produce we have been enabled to bestow on the country.

(Signed) CANDLE STICK MAKERS.

The interest of the consumer in freer trade has other important aspects. Imports, for example, can play an important role in curbing inflation. In recent years we have found ourselves in a situation aptly characterized as one in which "too much money has been chasing too few goods." As long as this continues an increase in imports (not matched by an increase in exports) can provide an antidote to inflation by adding to the stock of goods moving against the existing money supply. Quite apart from this point, imports have the additional advantage of providing a competitive stimulus to American industry.

In so doing they help to assure the consumer of lower prices and the fastest possible technical advance.

The second major interest in trade policy which should be reflected in the statement of purpose is the interest of the American taxpayer. Since the end of the Second World War the United States has enjoyed an export surplus of some $60 billion. To put it more crudely, we have enjoyed the privilege of selling abroad $60 billion more than we have bought in return and we have financed the difference with private loans and foreign aid.

This way of doing business, far from dying out, is actually on the increase again. In 1955, American exports of goods and services (ex cluding military items) were $19.9 billion, imports $17.9 billion. In 1956, exports rose to $23.4 billion, imports to $19.7 billion. Thus exports rose more than imports in both absolute and relative terms and our export surplus (exclusive of military assistance) rose from $2 billion to $3.7 billion.

Let us recall for a moment just what this means. When the United States sends goods and services abroad in excess of goods and services purchased abroad, the balance can be financed through foreign aid, the export of capital, or the purchase of gold from other countries. When private investors export capital, however, they do so in the anticipation of returning at least some of the profits of that investment to this country and ultimately the original investment itself. When the United States takes gold from other countries this in no way adds to the stock of goods and services available to American consumers, unless the United States at some time uses this gold to purchase goods abroad. In either case the United States in the long run can obtain real payment for its capital exports and its gold purchases only by importing more goods and services.

What then are the alternatives of future policy? One possibility is to maintain the huge export surplus, which must ultimately be financed by foreign aid. But most Americans, even if they regard foreign aid as a necessary element in our foreign policy, do not regard its indefinite maintenance on the present scale as either possible or desirable. Thus, we have no alternative but to move toward a balancing of our exports and imports, either by allowing our exports to fall, or by allowing our imports to rise.

There are obvious reasons why we do not wish our exports to fall. This would have serious consequences for important countries of the world which are heavily dependent on large quantities of American goods. It would also cause serious dislocations in our own economy. A substantial share of the American labor force derives its employment directly from foreign trade. Exports alone account for a larger share of our national product than such key factors in our prosperity as consumer purchases of automobiles or nonfarm housing construction. Obviously our best alternative is to allow imports to rise. To be sure, this is an obvious point. Yet it is something that those responsible for the framing of American trade policy have not yet been willing to face.

The third major interest which should be expressed in the statement of purpose is the interest of American investors. I have in mind here both the obligations owed to the American Government and the obligations owed to our private citizens and corporations who have made investments abroad. These investments cannot be serviced or repaid except out of dollars supplied by aid or trade from the United States. Moreover, only through a more satisfactory balancing of American exports and imports can we achieve that removal of restrictions on dollar exchange and the purchase of American products which is considered so important by our foreign investors.

The fourth major interest which should be expressed in the Trade Agreements Act is the interest of American foreign policy. It has been aptly remarked that "foreign policy begins at home." Recently this point was stated as follows by a former United States Ambassador to Russia:

> We seem to have a feeling that because such things as tariffs and immigration rules, crop subsidies, security procedures, and race relations are technically domestic matters, we can go ahead and do whatever we want to about them without taking seriously into account the feelings of other people. This is precisely where we make our mistake.

Applying this to trade policy, we may consider the case of the Swiss watch imports into the United States, which amounted to $79 million a year or about one five-thousandth of our national product. When we restricted this trade in 1954 we dealt a serious blow to an industry which employed 1 in every 10 workers in Switzerland and which accounted for one-half of Swiss exports to the United States. It is no wonder that our relations with Switzerland are still embittered as a result.

Examples like this could be multiplied. We are constantly involved in the paradox of giving vast amounts of assistance to restore the productive capacity of other countries while undermining their ability to support themselves by selling their production in world markets. Thus a foreign policy which is based on the restoration of these countries as prosperous and stable partners in the free world is frustrated by a trade policy which destroys their capacity to do so. Clearly we must achieve a harmony of our political and economic policies—or pay a very heavy price. The statement of purpose of the act should contain a clear recognition of this fact.

A fifth interest which should be reflected in the statement of purpose is that of American security. The link between security and trade appears in a number of ways. I have already referred to the fact that in the years ahead we will be increasingly dependent on foreign supplies of essential raw materials. We should also note that if we wish to maintain strategic controls on the shipment of western goods to Communist countries we must provide alternative outlets for the products of our allies in the United States. If we fail to do so, the economic and political contribution of these countries to western defense is very likely to slip away.

A dramatic illustration of this danger recently occurred in the case of Iceland. In 1951 that country exported virtually nothing to the Soviet Union or its satellites. It made its territory available for an airbase of great importance to our global security. Then the New England fishing industry, which employs several thousand workers, stepped up its campaign to restrict the imports of fish. Iceland, 97 percent of whose export trade consists of this product, reacted with a major change in policy. By 1955 that country was sending 28 percent of its exports to the Soviet Union and taking 22 percent of its imports from the Soviet in return. Gradually the new Soviet role in the island began to make itself felt. In the middle of 1956 the

Icelandic Parliament announced that it wished to close our airbase and remove American troops from Iceland's soil. Thus did policies of protection for a few thousand workers threaten the security of the Nation as a whole.

The conclusion of the foregoing analysis seems clear. Some 160 million Americans—as consumers, taxpayers, investors, and citizens vitally concerned with their foreign policy and security—have a direct interest in trade policy. The various aspects of this interest should find expression in the Trade Agreements Act.

Here is the first need for legislative reform. The Supreme Court of the United States has held that Congress may not delegate its tariff-making or other powers unless it lays down an "intelligible principle" to guide the Executive in the use of those powers. (See, e. g., *Hampton* v. *U. S.*, 276 U. S. 394 (1928).) As was made clear last year in a report of the Association of the Bar of the City of New York, the courts have been very liberal in upholding delegations of power, particularly in the field of foreign affairs. There is no reason to think that the various purposes of trade policy set forth above cannot be incorporated in a formula that will satisfy the "intelligible principle" standard. The devising of such a formula should have high priority on the legislative calendar of the 85th Congress.

## II. THE DELEGATED POWERS

Let us turn now from the question of purpose to the question of powers. The authority granted by Congress to the President is very carefully defined and is subject to a number of important restrictions. The act authorizes the President to "enter into foreign-trade agreements" and to "proclaim such modifications of existing duties and other import restrictions" as are appropriate to carry out these agreements.

The first problem here is the precise nature of the delegated power. The President is authorized to "enter into foreign-trade agreements." This may be thought to be a somewhat superfluous "delegation" of power, since the President, by virtue of his office, already has inherent authority to reach certain agreements with foreign countries in the field of trade. A score of executive agreements concluded by the President in the field of commerce and navigation in the past 150 years bear witness to this fact. But Congress is concerned lest the President, operating under his inherent authority and under the express delegation in the Trade Agreements Act, should conclude far-reaching agreements which will commit the United States to major changes in its domestic economic arrangements. This concern was reflected in the hearings held in 1956 before the House Ways and Means Committee on the proposed Organization for Trade Cooperation. It is reflected also in the disclaimer written into recent renewals of the Trade Agreements Act which states that such renewals—

> shall not be construed to represent or indicate the approval or disapproval by the Congress of the executive agreement known as the General Agreement on Tariffs and Trade.

The Association of the Bar of the City of New York has taken the position, based on a report of its committee on international law, that our participation in the multilateral trade agreement known as GATT is within the scope of the President's power. A revision of the Trade

Agreements Act should affirm this constitutional position and should also endorse American participation in GATT as a matter of policy. This could be accomplished simply by replacing the existing disclaimer in the act with an affirmation that American participation in GATT is a desirable exercise of the President's power.

Once this were done it might be desirable to remove the congressional fear that the President might accept amendments greatly expanding the scope of GATT or enter into some new species of commitment under liberal construction of his delegated powers. Accordingly, an attempt could be made to spell out the kind of agreements which Congress does and does not wish the President to make in the trade field. There are certain matters which the Congress is apparently unwilling to have included by the President in an executive agreement—for example, obligations on full employment, restrictive business practices, commodity stabilization, and foreign investment. The inclusion of these items in the charter of the International Trade Organization contributed to the demise of that ill-fated institution. GATT excludes all of these subjects and covers only what might be described as matters of commercial policy proper—restrictions laid by governments to the flow of goods. The definition of the agreements which the President is authorized to make could be drafted in these terms.

In the process of defining the subject of the President's power, we are led to consideration of a second problem. The President is authorized to alter United States laws pursuant only to the conclusion of a trade agreement. This means that even if changes in American tariffs or other trade laws are required in the national interest the President is powerless to make them unless he goes through the long and complicated process of negotiating an international agreement. The origin of this requirement is obviously the desire for "reciprocity"—the concern that we should not "give away something for nothing."

As some of my earlier statements may have already suggested, the reciprocity concept simply does not meet the facts of life in the world today. So long as we have a huge export surplus, unilateral reductions in our tariffs and other restrictions may be clearly desirable. Even without an export surplus, unilateral reductions in our restrictions may benefit our citizens. There is no reason why the President should be barred from lowering tariffs until he can get concessions from other countries—concessions which may be nominal in character or inconsistent with the interests of both parties to the trade agreement. The act should be amended, accordingly, to permit the President to make changes in American tariffs and other trade barriers without requiring similar changes from other countries. At the very least, he should be empowered to make such changes in return for different kinds of concessions from other countries—that is, economic or political commitments quite outside the tariff and trade field.

A third problem with respect to the powers of the President relates to their quantitative limits. The renewal of the act in 1955 authorized the President to reduce existing tariff rates by 5 percent a year over a 3-year period. It continued the prohibition of the original act against the transfer of an article from the dutiable to the free list. Thus the President is now authorized, to take an example, to reduce an ad valorem tariff rate of 50 percent to 47½ percent in any 1 year.

This is hardly a very handsome benefit to offer a foreign country, particularly when one considers the still formidable height of most American tariffs and the difficulties and hazards facing foreign producers in reaching the American market. Moreover, at the very time Congress gave the President these niggardly powers the Soviet leaders embarked on an ambitious program of economic penetration, offering long-term contracts for the purchase of large quantities of goods from non-Communist countries. Sending the President into trade competition with the Communists under these circumstances is rather like sending a boy with a popgun to fight a Soviet tank.

If the objectives of the Trade Agreements Act are to be implemented effectively, the maximum permissible tariff reduction must be substantially enlarged. Such quantitative limits as are retained in the act should not be aimed at maintaining uneconomic producers, but only at providing a transitional period in which the movement from protection to competition can be made without undue dislocation and can be spread over a period of years.

A final problem with respect to the President's powers is the question of duration. The delegation of authority to the President has been for extremely short terms—3-year periods from 1934 to 1943, followed by varying terms necessitating renewals in 1945, 1948, 1951, 1953, 1954, and 1955. This system puts a great burden on the proponents of liberal trade, and facilitates the incorporation of crippling amendments. In addition, it causes great anxiety and uncertainty abroad about the stability of American tariff rates and the future of American trade policy.

Consideration should be given to placing the delegation to the President on a permanent basis. In other words, the President would have the powers until such time as the Congress wished to withdraw them. This would place the burden on the opponents of trade cooperation to show why the President's powers should be withdrawn, rather than (as at present) on the proponents to show why they should be maintained.

There is one technical difficulty involved in this suggestion. Having delegated its powers by majority vote of both Houses, the Congress might find legislation withdrawing those powers frustrated by a Presidential veto. Thus it would need a two-thirds vote to recover powers which a majority vote had given away. This problem might be met, however, by drafting the act so that the powers are delegated to the President until such time as the Congress, by joint resolution, shall declare them to be withdrawn.

If this proposal were rejected and the fixed-term system retained, the length of the term could at least be extended beyond the 3-year period—for example, to 5 or 10 years. Equally important, the period of delegation could be devised so that it would not expire in an election year—a time when issues of trade policy are usually obscured by short-term political considerations and seldom resolved in the national interest.

The implementation of these various alternatives for expanding the President's tariff-making powers provides the second need for legislative reform.

III. THE INJURY CONCEPT

Let us turn now to the concept of injury. This is embodied in the peril-point and escape-clause provisions of the Trade Agreements Act which provide, in effect, that tariff concessions shall not be made or maintained when they cause or threaten serious injury to an American industry.

The injury concept has been the object of vigorous criticism by numerous official commissions here at home and by Government and business leaders abroad who complain bitterly that it penalizes a foreign businessman for success in the American market and undermines the attempt of our allies to pay their way in world trade.

Recently the various national affiliates of the International Chamber of Commerce were asked to list foreign economic policies of the United States which they regarded as particularly disadvantageous and troublesome. Two-thirds of the respondents listed the escape clause. The Japanese complained that it "looms as a towering threat to free international trade," the Dutch that it "sows the seeds of self-destruction in any success in the sphere of exports." The British noted—

> that it is the likelihood of action under it and the uncertainty as to what will be the import duty that is the grave handicap to trade.

The Italian Embassy in Washington has warned:

> If the United States * * * makes increasing recourse to peril level or escape clauses and adopts restrictive measures with respect to the very items of foreign imports which stand to benefit by conventional tariff rates and other concessions * * * the whole policy of trade liberalization, while honored in principle, becomes disregarded and inoperative in practice.

These are strong words—too strong, some might argue—in view of the historical record. After all, the injury concept has been in the Trade Agreements Act from the very beginning. Why, after all these years, has it become the subject of such intensive controversy? The explanation is twofold. First, it is only in recent years that tariff reduction has begun to have a significant effect in increasing American imports. Second, the injury concept has now grown from a concept stated only obliquely in the statement of purpose to a stringent requirement crystallized in Executive orders and amendments to the act itself.

This new expression of the injury concept has brought unfortunate consequences in procedure and substantive interpretation. On the procedural side, the Tariff Commission—by nature a protectionist-minded body concerned only with the interests of American producers—has replaced the broadly constituted interdepartmental committee in the executive branch which used to administer the injury role. To make matters worse, the Commission, which once had the power to dismiss applications for escape-clause relief when these were clearly insufficient (and which used this power to dismiss 10 of the first 23 applications on their face), is now required to issue a report on every application for protection, no matter how specious or frivolous it may be.

Moreover, the Tariff Commission has never placed any limitation on the renewal of applications by unsuccessful claimants. Thus, to take one example, we have just witnessed the fourth application for relief from the spring-clothespin industry. This kind of procedure may provide a windfall in fees for lawyers representing American producers in customs and tariff matters. But the cost and uncertainty involved in such a lengthy and, perhaps, indefinite struggle is enough to discourage most importers and foreign businessmen. To appreciate the injustice of these arrangements one need only imagine a Civil Practice Act with no provision for summary judgment and no rule of res adjudicata.

The substantive side of the injury question presents many fascinating legal aspects, of which I will mention only two. The first is the definition of the term "injury." In the early escape-clause cases (spring clothespins, ground-fish fillets, canned tuna, and bonito) the Tariff Commission refused to find injury in the absence of a decline in the absolute position (sales, profits, employment, etc.) of the domestic American industry. This interpretation is now open to considerable doubt. In the second Swiss Watch case 3 of the 6 Commissioners found injury to exist merely because of the relative decline in the sales of the domestic industry; i. e., because United States producers enjoyed a smaller share of the total market. Since the increased market for watches in the United States was largely due to the ability of Swiss producers to market an excellent product within the means of a large new group of low-income consumers, these Commissioners were deciding in effect that the domestic industry was losing a market it never had. Obviously this tendency to find injury even in the absence of any signs of actual loss on the part of American producers makes the injury concept a much more serious obstacle to the future growth of international trade.

A second important question on the substantive side is the definition of industry. It is bad enough that, from the very beginning, the term was held applicable even to a single American firm (such as the producer of violins in the Midwest who was recently granted escape-clause relief by the Tariff Commission). But it has now been extended by formal amendment of the act to embace not only the single producer but a portion or subdivision of a producing organization. This sanctifies the Tariff Commission decision which found injury to the garlic industry even though the 3 or 4 American farmers producing garlic grew other crops as well and could easily have avoided injury to themselves by replacing garlic with these other crops.

The saving factor in the midst of all these unfavorable developments has been the area of Presidential discretion. On several occasions the President has refused to follow a Tariff Commission recommendation that a tariff concession should be withdrawn. He has based his action in these cases on the permissive character of a phrase in the Trade Agreements Act which states that the President "may" make such adjustments (raising tariffs or imposing quotas) as are found necessary by the Commission.

Unfortunately, however, the precise nature of the President's authority is not beyond controversy. The permissive word "may" has been linked with an earlier paragraph of the act which provides flatly that no tariff rate (or other customs treatment) "shall" be permitted to continue in effect if injury results. Some have read these two parts of the act together and concluded that the President has the power to disregard Tariff Commission recommendations only where he disagrees with its finding of injury. According to this theory the President has no power to disregard a recommendation for protective relief simply because he feels that the interests of producers injured by imports are less important than other American interests furthered by maintaining them.

It is significant that in every instance where he has disregarded a Tariff Commission recommendation the President, even while invoking the national interest, has been careful to question the finding of injury. Clearly we should clarify the authority of the President to disregard recommendations of the Tariff Commission solely on the basis of the national interest as a whole.

In the preceding remarks I have suggested a number of changes in the administration and interpretation of the injury concept. These changes should be regarded as the minimum objectives of law reform in this field. But we ought to ask ourselves whether we should not also alter our present system of escape clause relief. By raising tariffs or imposing quotas without limit of time we now encourage the indefinite maintenance of protected business activities—no matter how inefficient or uneconomic these may be. We do little or nothing to encourage producers, workers, and communities affected by imports to adjust to a more efficient pattern of production.

We ought to consider a new system of escape clause relief under which a finding of "injury" to an "industry" (the terms being defined more narrowly than at present in accordance with my earlier observations) would be the occasion for a temporary tariff increase coupled with a temporary program of Government aid, mainly from existing sources. The sole purpose of the Government aid would be to assist the producers, workers, and communities to adjust to more efficient lines of production. Part of the tariff increase would be removed automatically each year, and no increase at all would be maintained if producers, workers, and communities were not carrying out a satisfactory adjustment program.

Such a proposal is sometimes regarded as wildly impractical until reference is made to the actual magnitude of the adjustment involved. Protectionist propaganda has created a widespread impression that the elimination of the injury concept coupled with significant tariff reductions would disrupt the American economy with a flood of products from "cheap foreign labor". This is utter nonsense. In most cases American producers are in a strong competitive position vis-a-vis their foreign counterparts because the greater productivity per man-hour of the American worker far offsets his higher money wages and also because American producers have access to better research facilities and more effective services such as banking, transportation, and advertising. Expert studies have estimated that the complete elimination of tariffs (much more drastic than the program suggested here) would result in increased imports of $0.8–$1.8 billion over 3 to 5 years involving a displacement of 96,000 to 203,000 American workers. This is obviously insignificant when compared to our gross national production of over $400 billion a year and our total working force of approximately 63 million. Indeed, the displacement from imports suggested here is much less than that resulting every year from causes within the domestic economy—changes in technology, consumer tastes, and the like. The majority of the workers displaced by these domestic causes quickly find new employment in other lines of production and there is no reason to believe that this would not also be true of most of the workers displaced by an increase in imports.

Naturally the overall figures given above understate the impact of increased imports on particular lines of production. The industries which would be most affected by additional imports are by and large already characterized by low wages and low profits. Generally they face a stagnant or at least a declining domestic market. The latest statistics suggest that, even with respect to these industries, the damage resulting from imports has been greatly exaggerated. The following, for example, are estimates of the percentage of the labor force of particular industries which would be displaced by the complete elimination of American tariffs: textile mill products (1.2 percent); chemicals and allied products (0.4 percent); leather and leather products (0.9 percent); food and kindred products (0.4 percent); stone, clay, and glass products (4.7 percent).

Once we remove the bugaboo of a vast disruption of the American economy, we can proceed to rational analysis of escape clause relief. We are a nation which has learned to accept change as a condition of progress. We do not give anyone a vested right in the status quo. No businessman or worker can go to court or to a Government commission to ask for protection simply because the greater efficiency of an American competitor is threatening his livelihood. Why should he be able to do so simply because the competitor happens to live abroad?

Our present system of escape-clause relief is not simply at odds with our competitive philosophy—it is inconsistent with the very purposes of the Trade Agreements Act. It is simply impossible to reconcile the various interests cited earlier—those of consumers, taxpayers, investors, foreign policy, and security—with a rule which forbids any injury to American producers. Let us face up to the fact in trade policy as in other fields that we cannot have our cake and eat it too—that we cannot enjoy significant advantages from trade without displacing some domestic American producers. If the gains from freer trade greatly exceed the cost—and every serious study of the problem suggests that they do—we have no rational alternative but to accept the consequences.

This brings us to the case for temporary Government assistance. The gains from freer trade will be shared by the Nation as a whole. Why should the costs, however much smaller, be borne alone by a few producers, workers, and communities? The sharing of the costs as well as the gains would provide a net advantage for everyone.

At first glance this approach might seem inconsistent with our earlier criticism of vested rights in the status quo. But the costs which would be shared here are the costs of adjustment to a new state of affairs—not the costs of staying in the same place. It is appropriate that citizens who have made decisions on the basis of a protectionist policy should be assisted to adjust to the consequences of its abondonment. Moreover—and this is the most practical argument—acceptance of an adjustment program will cut the ground from under much of the political opposition to freer trade.

Outlines of a program for injured producers, workers, and communities have already been suggested in Government and private reports. The staff papers of the Randall Commission suggested Government assistance in the form of loans and technical aid to businesses and communities; moving allowances, retraining services, and expanded unemployment compensation for workers. Since it is hard to isolate economic difficulties due to tariff reductions from the difficulties due to other factors, assistance could not be given for tariff adjustment alone. It would have to be available for adjustment generally. But main reliance could be placed on existing Federal (and State) programs. These could be expanded at comparatively moderate cost to handle the gradual adjustment which would accompany the temporary and tapering form of escape-clause relief.

### IV. THE DEFENSE CONCEPT

The defense concept is embodied in recent amendments to the Trade Agreements Act under which the President must withdraw or refrain from making tariff concessions which may injure an industry considered important to the national security.

These amendments charge the Director of the Office of Defense Mobilization with the duty of advising the President on the security implications of trade policy. Accordingly this Office may become a busier center than the Tariff Commission for the hearing of applications for protection. Lobbyists specializing in trade matters are quickly adapting themselves and are now talking about "minimum defense requirements" and "maintaining the mobilization base" instead of "share of the market" and "declining profit margins." A host of industries not satisfied with the relief they have achieved under the injury concept are claiming to be vital to our war potential. These include the producers of thermometers, watches, wooden boats—and according to some reports—clothespins and dehydrated garlic.

It is becoming increasingly apparent that the defense amendment is dangerously subject to abuse. A notorious example of the danger here was presented in the second Swiss watch case. Although it had no authority and no experience for passing on the question, the Tariff Commission found the watch industry to be essential to our defense and gave this as one reason for its recommendation of escape-clause relief. Subsequently, however, the Department of Defense declared that manufacturers outside the watch industry could produce the time fuse and safety devices neeeded for mobilization and that special protection of the watch industry was not required. This conclusion was also reached after a special investigation of the question by a congressional committee.

Surely the time has come to reconsider the assumptions which prompted the passage of the defense amendment. Does tariff protection of "essential industries" really augment our national security? To begin with, we have to ask ourselves for what kind of war we are preparing. If, as we have been told· it is to be an atomic holocaust decided within a few days or weeks, the outcome will be determined by our stock of military hardware and striking power in being at that moment—not by our capacity to produce material in the long run. If, on the other hand, it is to be a war like the one in Korea or like the Second World War, we are not going to be cut off from our most important overseas supplies. There is not much point in self-sufficiency under either of these alternatives.

Even if it could be shown that the United States is likely to be deprived of foreign supplies of a strategic item whose production is required for some period of time—this would not provide a conclusive argument for protection. One of the basic lessons learned in the Second World War, in the United States, Germany, and other countries, was that an industrialized economy can overcome what seems to be serious deficiencies in skills and materials by the imaginative substitution of other resources. This experience contradicts the assertion that our domestic watch industry is the only source of machinery and workmen for the production of timepieces required in a future war.

If we wish to assist certain producing organizations considered important to our military strength, trade restriction is a poor device for doing so. It removes the spur to efficiency and technological advance. It protects the inefficient producers as well as the efficient, those well located from a strategic point of view as well as those who are badly located. Moreover, a single does of trade restriction seldom proves to be sufficient. We need only witness the new attempt of the watch industry for new measures of relief under the defense amendments. Like a drug addict, the protected industry seems driven to return for more and more.

Far from enhancing, the defense concept may actually be undermining our security. It opens a way by which we may stimulate the uneconomic production of every possible article that could prove useful in a future emergency. This will speed the exhaustion of domestic raw materials and reduce the flexibility and rate of growth of the American economy. By reducing the capacity of other countries to buy American goods, it will also undermine the export industries which by nature are of greater significance in war production than the smaller scale and less mechanized industries requiring protection from foreign competition.

Perhaps most important, the use of trade restrictions as an instrument of defense is inconsistent with the coalition strategy which is at the heart of our political and military planning. In a direct way, it undermines the economic and political position of friendly governments. We maintain air bases in such far-flung countries as the United Kingdom, Pakistan, and Japan. When we restrict the trade of these countries on defense grounds, we are sacrificing present security for illusory security in the long run. As a Supreme Court Justice said recently in another connection: "Surely, this is to burn the house to roast the pig."

The relations of national defense and trade policy involves some very difficult problems. These remarks are intended to suggest only that the defense concept does not belong in the Trade Agreements Act. Perhaps there are instances in which a program of special assistance to domestic producers can be justified on national defense grounds. If so, the considerations outlined above suggest that such assistance will be more likely to achieve its purpose if it is supplied by direct subsidies rather than by tariff protection. Unlike the tariff, the subsidy is an open means of assistance whose cost can readily be calculated. It can be used with comparatively greater precision. To define the circumstances and the procedures for the granting of such assistance poses the fourth need for legislative reform.

## V. CONCLUSION

The Trade Agreements Act was a step in the right direction in 1934. But it has been weakened by subsequent amendments until its potentialities for trade obstruction are as great as its potentialities for trade promotion. Some of its original provisions have been rendered obsolete by world events. It needs to be revamped and strengthened if it is to serve the two main aims of trade policy—the prosperity and security of the United States.

# THE TRADE AGREEMENTS LEGISLATION

## *Its Intent, and an Evaluation of Its Administration*

**Eugene L. Stewart,[1] Steptoe & Johnson, Washington, D. C.**

### Introduction

This paper, submitted at the invitation of the subcommittee's chairman, will consider the scope of the authority delegated to the Executive by the Trade Agreements Act, and the standards and procedures governing the use of that authority. It will also evaluate the administration of the act in the light of these criteria.

It has been remarked in the press of late that opposition to the trade-agreements program is finding wider support in the Congress. The current distress of United States producers resulting from increased import competition from the industrially resurgent nations of Western Europe and from Japan is said to be the cause for this congressional concern.

An assessment of any supposed shortcoming of the trade-agreements program should not consist merely of a review of the philosophical arguments for and against the program. The philosophical dispute will always exist and will be resolved from time to time more on the basis of the mood of the people of the United States than on any other factor. That mood will change as changes occur in the emphasis which the people place upon the right of individuals to engage in business activity in which direct labor represents a high proportion of the unit cost. If this right is to be recognized, governmental policy will be required to maintain some semblance of equality of opportunity vis-a-vis foreign competition. This is the same kind of "fairness" which presently underlies minimum wage and hour requirements for those engaging in interstate commerce in the United States.

The philosophical problem aside, it would seem quite appropriate for the Congress to examine the actual use which is being made by the Executive of the trade agreements authority to determine—

(*a*) Whether it exceeds the actual scope of the delegated power contained in the Trade Agreements Act; and

(*b*) Whether the use is conditioned upon a proper observance by the Executive of the procedural safeguards which Congress has specified.

### I. The Scope of the President's Power Under the Trade Agreements Act

Delegated power presupposes the definition of lawful objects for its use as well as understandable limits which mark out the quantum

[1] The invaluable assistance of Karl E. Bakke of Steptoe & Johnson is gratefully acknowledged.

of power delegated. In a consideration of the actual scope of the President's authority under the Trade Agreements Act, therefore, it will be appropriate to consider first the particular objectives for which Congress provided the power, and second the limitations which Congress placed upon the use of the power even for the attainment of such objects.

A. THE OBJECT OR PURPOSE OF THE TRADE AGREEMENTS ACT

As adopted in 1934, the act described the expansion of foreign markets for the products of the United States through the trade agreement authority—

(as a means of assisting in the present emergency in restoring the American standard of living, in overcoming domestic unemployment and the present economic depression, in increasing the purchasing power of the American public, and in establishing and maintaining a better relationship among various branches of American agriculture, industry, mining, and commerce) * * *.[2]

At the time this legislation was being considered, the world was in the throes of one of the most acute general depressions of modern times. Accompanying, and to a considerable extent contributing to this distress was an alarming shrinkage of world trade. Although many causal factors were responsible for such a state of affairs, a major one was felt to be the almost universal existence of high-trade barriers, built up by commercial nations in a—

frenzied effort to gain a so-called favorable balance of trade by shutting out foreign goods in disregard of the inevitable effect upon those branches of production which depend upon a world market.[3]

Not only had most countries erected ever-mounting tariff barriers, but quantitative import restrictions, state monopolies, and governmental control over foreign exchange were common features of this incipient economic impasse.[4]

In the United States some 10 million wage earners were idle,[5] and the country was faced with the specter of industrial collapse and growing agricultural surplus. Although drastic measures were introduced to restore some semblance of order to the domestic scene, it was readily perceived that steps also had to be taken with regard to participation in world commerce: in the period between 1929 and 1933 our share of the international export trade had dropped from 15.61 percent to 12.39 percent in volume, and from $5.24 billion to $1.67 billion in value.[6]

It was recognized that many of our industries and farm operations depended to a considerable extent on foreign markets for their prosperity, while still others were indirectly affected in varying degrees.[7] In order to round out the recovery program, revival of such markets was felt to be essential. The proposed legislation was conceived with the purpose in mind of enabling the United States to win back lost export markets as an essential part of the recovery program. This facet of the legislation's purpose is indicated by the following colloquy between Representative Cooper (Tennessee) and Secretary of

[2] Sec. 1, Public Law 316, 73d Cong.
[3] H. Rept. 1000, 73d Cong., 2d sess., p. 2.
[4] Ibid.
[5] Congressional Record, 73d Cong., 2d sess., p. 10079.
[6] Congressional Record, 73d Cong., 2d sess., pp. 5618, 5658.
[7] Congressional Record, 73d Cong., 2d sess., p. 5623.

State Cordell Hull during the hearings before the House Ways and Means Committee:[8]

Mr. COOPER. Mr. Secretary, is this a fair statement of the purpose to be accomplished by the pending bill now under consideration by this committee? During the last year we have enacted legislation recommended by the administration conferring upon the President broad discretionary authority affecting business affairs of this country, and this bill simply carries forward and confers upon the executive branch of the Government the same type of broad discretionary authority with reference to international trade.

Mr. HULL. Yes. * * *

Mr. COOPER. And * * * it is a very vital and essential part of the present recovery program of the administration?

Mr. HULL. Absolutely.

At another point, Secretary Hull stated emphatically that furtherance of the recovery program was the basic purpose of the measure and said:[9]

[O]therwise I do not think there would have been the slightest disposition to propose such a measure.

The new legislation was to contribute to the recovery program by making possible an expansion in the exports of United States products. Secretary Hull told the Senate Finance Committee:[10]

A vast and ever-increasing foreign trade is easily within the grasp of this country, unless we fritter away the opportunity. It is a first step in such an undertaking that the proposed bill is offered.

The only way that any progress could be made toward this objective was through the mechanism of agreements with other countries for the mutual reduction of the tariffs which were preventing the desired access to foreign markets. The House Ways and Means Committee, in reporting the trade agreements bill, stated:[11]

The difficulties resulting from such a network of barriers can be successfully overcome only by agreements between governments.

It added:[12]

If the United States is to compete successfully with other countries to regain a fair share of foreign trade, it is necessary that the United States should create machinery whereby it can bargain successfully for such trade.

This finding by the committee was in accord with President Roosevelt's message to Congress describing this need:[13]

Other governments are to an ever-increasing extent winning their share of international trade by negotiated, reciprocal trade agreements. If American agricultural and industrial interests are to retain their deserved place in this trade, the American Government must be in a position to bargain for that place with other governments by rapid and decisive negotiation based on a carefully considered program, and to grant with discernment corresponding opportunities in the American market for foreign products supplementary to our own.

The expansion of United States foreign trade through the use of trade agreements was by no means viewed as an end in itself. Rather, the new machinery was explicitly created for the purpose of reviving the failing commerce of the United States to promote domestic prosperity. Thus, in the Senate debates, Senator Robinson, of Arkansas, stated:[14]

---

[8] House hearings, pp. 22–23.
[9] House hearings, pp. 12, 23.
[10] Senate hearings, p. 6.
[11] H. Rept. 1000, 73d Cong., 2d sess., p. 2.
[12] Ibid., p. 5.
[13] Ibid., p. 5.
[14] Congressional Record, 73d Cong., 2d sess., p. 10193.

The purpose of the pending measure—its outstanding, dominating, and controlling purpose—is to revive the failing commerce of the United States. * * *

Secretary Hull, in testifying before the House committee, made it clear that the primary and paramount purpose of the proposed legislation was to promote our domestic prosperity.[15] Specifically, this purpose was to be served by making it possible, in President Roosevelt's words, for the important branches of agriculture and industry with mass production methods to "find expanded opportunities and productive capacity in foreign markets and * * * thereby be spared, in part at least, the heartbreaking readjustments that must be necessary if the shrinkage of American commerce remains permanent."[16]

This was viewed essentially as a problem of disposing of the surplus production of American agriculture and industry. Secretary Hull, in testifying before the House committee, viewed the function of the new authority as one of supplementing—

our most impregnable domestic markets with a substantial and gradually expanding foreign market for our more burdensome surpluses.[17]

The Ways and Means Committee report found that:[18]

If the United States is to regain prosperity and not sacrifice large and important agricultural and commercial interests which give employment to millions of the workers of the country, it must sell certain of its surplus products abroad.

Not only was it felt that the measure would afford a "much-needed market for our troublesome agricultural surpluses,[19] but industrial "surplus," once the recovery program took effect, would also effectively lend itself to this program.[20]

As originally enacted, therefore, the trade-agreements authority was very clearly limited in its purpose to assisting in the recovery of the United States economy from the subnormal levels to which it had sunk during the depression by securing foreign markets for the surplus production of American agriculture and industry.

This limited purpose of the original act is also shown by the understanding which both its sponsors and the Congress held of its emergency nature. The proposed legislation was frankly characterized by Secretary Hull as being an "emergency remedy for emergency conditions,"[21] a fact which was clearly spelled out in the bill itself by virtue of an amendment made by the Senate Finance Committee. The committee report said:[22]

In order to emphasize the emergency character of the bill, the first amendment adopted by the committee inserts in subsection (a) after the words "as a means of assisting" the words "in the present emergency," so as to make this language applicable to all the objectives set forth in that part of subsection (a) enclosed within the parentheses.

The parenthetical reference alluded to read, in its final form:[23]

as a means of assisting in the present emergency in restoring the American standard of living, in overcoming domestic unemployment and the present economic depression, in increasing the purchasing power of the American public, and in establishing and maintaining a better relationship among various branches of American agriculture, industry, mining, and commerce.

[15] House hearings, p. 12.
[16] H. Rept. 1000, 73d Cong., 2d sess., p. 11.
[17] Senate hearings, p. 5.
[18] H. Rept. 1000, 73d Cong., 2d sess., p. 11.
[19] Congressional Record, 73d Cong., 2d sess., p. 5370.
[20] Id., pp. 5432, 5433.
[21] Senate hearings, p. 4.
[22] S. Rept. 871, 73d Cong., 2d sess., p. 1.
[23] Sec. 1, Public Law 316, 73d Cong.

It was felt to be absolutely essential that the President be permitted to embark upon international negotiations with vigor and dispatch; but at the same time the administration was willing to concede that once the immediate problem had been resolved, a more moderate approach could be considered. According to Secretary Hull: [24]

> There will be ample time and opportunity after the crisis shall have been met and passed * * * for a thorough review, reexamination, and discussion of any and all methods, policies, plans, and programs that may have been placed in operation during the panic periods in a desperate endeavor to curb, control, and cure such conditions.

The authority desired by the administration was said by Secretary Hull to be "special and temporary." [25] This sentiment no doubt played a substantial role in securing support for the measure, and its advocates were careful to emphasize this fundamental concept. During the Senate debate on the bill, Senator Walsh of Massachusetts, a member of the Senate Finance Committee, stated: [26]

> "* * * with the President's seeking to bring about recovery in this country by means which he believes will be helpful, he should be entrusted *temporarily*, in view of the conditions of the world, in view of the trade barriers that have been erected all over the world, in view of the discrimination against our products, in view of the decline in exports, with the power proposed to be given to him by the pending bill. I see nothing inconsistent with a position in opposition to a general policy of Executive control of tariffs and favoring a *temporary* policy, during this period of distress, during this period of depression, entrusting him with the authority by negotiation to improve, if he can, conditions and giving him an opportunity to undertake negotiations, designed to improve by this method our declining export business. * * *
>
> * * * * * * *
>
> Further, there is an entire difference between a permanent policy and a *temporary* policy. * * * we would not permit the President * * * under normal conditions and circumstances to enjoy the power we propose here. [Emphasis added.]

This concept was echoed by Senator Robinson of Arkansas, who said: [27]

> This proposed legislation does not contemplate a *permanent* policy in tariff making different from that which has prevailed throughout the past. [Emphasis added.]

Further indicative of the limited purpose of the program is the fact that the power of the President to negotiate trade agreements was explicitly limited by the bill to a period of 3 years. That such a limiting provision was not devoid of material significance can be seen from a statement made by Senator George, of Georgia: [28]

> * * * we may treat these conditions as extraordinary; * * * [opponents of the bill] may have confidence in the integrity and courage of the legislative branch of the Government * * * to discontinue this extraordinary power * * * at the time fixed * * * if, happily, the extraordinary conditions which now seem to justify its use shall have ceased to exist.

*Change in the object or purpose of the Trade Agreements Act*

Because the Trade Agreements Act, as adopted in 1934, was limited in duration to a period of 3 years, it was necessary for the Congress to consider extension of the act as that period came to an end. The

---

[24] House hearings, p. 6.
[25] Senate hearings, p. 7.
[26] Congressional Record, 73d Cong., 2d sess., p. 10189.
[27] Ibid., p. 10193.
[28] Congressional Record, 73d Cong., 2d sess., p. 10078.

Congress decided to extend the act, and hence the authority of the President to enter into trade agreements, for an additional, limited period. When that extension of the term of the act neared an end, the Congress again decided to grant an extension. In this manner, by a series of acts extending the term of the original Trade Agreements Act, the Congress has had occasion to review the purpose and objectives of the trade-agreements program.

In the course of its consideration of the various extensions of the Trade Agreements Act, the Congress has been presented by representatives of the executive department with new reasons justifying the continuation of the President's trade-agreements authority. Though the wording of the basic authority delegated in the act itself has remained substantially unchanged, the acceptance by the Congress of the new rationale for the act, as evidenced by committee reports and debates on the various bills, has served to bring about a change from the original purposes of the act.

Since the purpose and objects for which the trade-agreements authority is currently in effect have an important bearing on the validity of the actions taken by the Executive in the use of that authority, it is essential to any consideration of the present scope of the power delegated to the President in the trade agreements legislation to analyze the exact nature of these changes.

Though the continued existence of an emergency in domestic agriculture and industry was still advanced as the principal purpose for the extension of the act in 1937, a new rationale was also advanced and accepted by the Congress. In a letter to the chairman of the Ways and Means Committee, President Roosevelt, after stressing the importance of an extension of the act to a continuation of economic recovery, introduced a new justification for the program in these words:[29]

> *The development of liberalized trade practices has another effect, which transcends in importance* even the material benefits conferred by trade improvement. Economic strife, resulting from inordinate or discriminatory trade barriers, is one of the most fruitful sources of political animosity and military conflict. A policy designed to reduce excessive trade barriers and to establish *equality of trade rights is a powerful instrument of economic appeasement and stability. It thus serves to strengthen the foundations of world peace.* [Emphasis added.]

The Secretary of State also referred to this new justification for the program in his testimony before the House Ways and Means Committee. In reporting the bill, the committee expressed its approval of the new basis as follows:[30]

> The committee finds itself in full agreement with the Secretary's view that failure to go forward with the program at this critical juncture in international affairs would retard our march toward full recovery and employment and would seriously undermine the economic forces which are tending to strengthen the foundations of peace. * * *

Three years later, the Congress was called upon to consider a second extension of the Trade Agreements Act. World War II had broken out in Europe, and the part which the trade-agreements authority might play in the strengthening of the peace after the war loomed

[29] H. Rept. 166, 75th Cong. (1937), p. 2.
[30] Id., p. 3.

large in the attention of the Executive and the Congress. President Roosevelt, in urging the extension of the act, stated:[31]

> But what is more important, *the Trade Agreements Act should be extended as an indispensable part of the foundation of any stable and durable peace.* * * * the United States must use its influence to open up the trade channels of the world *in order that no nation need feel compelled in later days to seek by force of arms what it can well gain by peaceful conference.* For this purpose we need the Trade Agreements Act even more than when it was passed [Emphasis added.]

The Secretary of State, in testimony before the House committee, stated that the trade agreements then in effect were of inestimable value in defending United States export trade from the inroads of wartime controls and dislocations. He indicated that the action of Congress in extending the act would have "an enormous influence upon the problems of economic reconstruction" when "hostilities have ceased," when "the establishment of sound international trade relations will be an essential problem * * *."[32]

The House Ways and Means Committee concurred in the views of the President and the Secretary of State. It said that failure to extend the Trade Agreements Act would, among other things[33]—

> serve notice to the world that our country had *abandoned its position of leadership* as a peace-loving nation *in the effort to reestablish* the basic and essential economic *foundations of an enduring peace.* [Emphasis added.]

While the major discussion in the committee's report was concerned with the benefits of the program to the domestic economy, there was a positive acceptance by the committee of the importance of the program to the foundations of a stable peace as a justification for the extension.[34]

This new purpose was also accepted by the Senate Finance Committee as a justification for the program. It stated that it was "impressed with the profound significance attaching to the enactment of this legislation" as set forth in the following testimony of Secretary of State Cordell Hull:[35]

> * * *. Unless we continue to maintain our position of leadership in the promotion of liberal trade policies, unless we continue to urge upon others the need of adopting such policies as the basis of postwar economic reconstruction, the future will be dark, indeed. * * *

The next occasion for the extension of the act arose in 1943 in the midst of United States preoccupation with its own role as a combatant in World War II. The justification for the program found in its assumed effect on the establishment of the peace following World War II, already advanced in the two preceding extensions, was retained. A new and different objective was also declared. The United States economy was operating at unprecedented levels with the greatly expanded capacity of both industry and agriculture. The disposition of the surplus production of this enlarged capacity following World War II was viewed by the House Ways and Means Committee as an independent basis for warranting the extension of the Trade Agreements Act. The committee reported:[36]

---

[31] H. Rept. 1594, 76th Cong. (1940), p. 2.
[32] Id., p. 2.
[33] Id., p. 3.
[34] Id., pp. 3, 42.
[35] S. Rept. 1297, 76th Cong. (1940).
[36] H. Rept. 409, 78th Cong. (1943), pp. 10, 11.

From the point of view of sound policy, there are two broad considerations. In the first place, *if we are to maintain and raise our standard of living we must adopt a policy which fosters the fullest possible utilization of our incomparable productive capacity.* * * * When this war is over *our producers will need broader market opportunities than ever before* * * *.

* * * * * * *

In the second place, *we must pursue international commercial policies which give some hope of providing an economic basis for building an enduring peace.* * * * The Trade Agreements Act represents a policy of positive international economic cooperation and it has come to be so regarded in the eyes of the other nations. * * *

If the Trade Agreements Act policy is sound from the point of view of both our domestic and international interests, it is essential that it be carried out effectively. * * * [Emphasis added.]

Whereas the recovery program of the 1930's had provided the blueprint for the Trade Agreements Act of 1934, a new blueprint for the recovery of the free nations of the world from the tragedy of World War II became the guide for the extension of the trade-agreements program commencing in 1943. This new guide was the Atlantic Charter with its affirmation of the right of all nations to access on equal terms to the trade and raw materials of the world. This relationship is made plain by Secretary Hull's testimony to the House Ways and Means Committee, which was quoted approvingly in the committee's report: [37]

Important as was the trade-agreements program in the past, important as it has been and will be from a broader point of view, it will be more significant than ever, from the viewpoint of our own material interest, when the present fighting stops. * * * Foreign markets will be very important to us * * *.

* * * * * * *

As we look into the future, it is [the] theme of international cooperation that should be uppermost in our minds, if we really want to make sure that another world conflict is not to be ahead of us after we win the war.

* * * * * * *

Of the various necessary fields of international collaboration one of the most essential is the field of economic life. * * * That is why *it is so essential, in the words of the Atlantic Charter, to bring about the fullest collaboration between all nations in the economic field with the object of securing for all, improved labor standards, economic advancement, and social security.*

This objective, and the balance of the charter, have now been endorsed by all of the United Nations: * * * [Emphasis added.]

The committee accepted the extension of the trade-agreements program as necessary on grounds which relegated its contribution to American prosperity to an inferior position to the establishment of peace: [38]

It is desirable to continue in existence *this tested and sound instrument* of *international cooperation,* in the interest both of *unity in the war effort,* of a *secure peace hereafter,* and of *American prosperity.* [Emphasis added.]

When the Congress extended the Trade Agreements Act in 1945, the report of the House Ways and Means Committee contained language prophetic of the objective which was to be stated in the General Agreement on Tariffs and Trade and the charter for an International Trade Organization. The committee said that the following were included among the objectives of the law: [39]

---

[37] Id., p. 12; see also id., p. 24.
[38] Id., p. 54.
[39] H. Rept. 3240, 79th Cong. (1945), p. 3.

(4) To contribute thereby to an increase of production, employment, consumption, and general prosperity in the United States and foreign countries, and to raising levels of living and material welfare in this country and abroad; and

(5) By the whole process to contribute to making more solid and enduring the partnership of the United Nations on which security and peace depend.

The objective numbered 4 above is comparable to the following objectives of the Habana Charter for an International Trade Organization:[40]

1. To assure a large and steadily growing volume of real income and effective demand, to increase the production, consumption and exchange of goods, and thus to contribute to a balanced and expanding world economy.

* * * * * * *

3. To further the enjoyment by all countries, on equal terms, of access to the markets, products, and productive facilities which are needed for their economic prosperity and development.

The preamble of the General Agreement on Tariffs and Trade, as adopted in 1947, provides:[41]

Recognizing that their relations in the field of trade and economic endeavor should be conducted with a view to raising standards of living, insuring full employment and a large and steadily growing volume of real income and effective demand, developing the full use of the resources of the world and expanding the production and exchange of goods. * * *

Considering the limited purpose for which the Trade Agreements Act was enacted in 1934, it is interesting to note in one of President Roosevelt's last messages to Congress before his death the following statement in reference to Secretary Hull's trade agreements program:[42]

Under him *the reciprocal trade-agreement program represented a sustained effort to reduce the barriers which the nations of the world maintained against each other's trade. If the economic foundations of the peace are to be* as *secure* as the political foundations, it is clear that *this effort must be continued* vigorously and effectively. [Emphasis added.]

The committee also quoted with approval a communication from Cordell Hull declaring that the trade agreements program was one of—

the essential prerequisites to economic prosperity and to maintaining and improving standards of living in our own and in all countries.

Significantly, Mr. Hull added that:[43]

*Its purpose has always been—and must continue to be—to bring about a reduction or elimination, on a reciprocal basis of mutual benefit, of excessive barriers to trade which impair the well-being of all countries.* * * * [Emphasis added.]

That the committee fully realized the completely new purpose and objectives of the trade agreements authority is evident from its comment that Mr. William L. Clayton, then Assistant Secretary of State in charge of economic matters, "presented the case [for enactment of the extension] so well that it is useful to quote from it in some detail." The portion of Mr. Clayton's testimony quoted in the committee report includes the following:[44]

---

[40] Department of State Publication 3206, Commercial Policy Series 114 (1948), p. 29.
[41] GATT—Basic Instruments and Selected Documents, vol. 1, Geneva (1952), p. 13.
[42] Id., p. 15.
[43] Id., p. 16.
[44] Id., p. 19.

I believe that all of us would profit from an effort to look at this bill, not in terms of what we thought about reciprocal trade agreements in 1934, 1937, 1940, and 1943, but as a new instrument for use in the world of tomorrow. For it is, in fact, a new instrument—made so not by new language but by a new world. Those who judge the trade-agreements program solely in the context of its prewar operation are likely to miss the new and portentous meaning of this idea.

* * * * * * *

In the years before the war the trade-agreements program was an instrument for defense against an epidemic of destructive and demoralizing trade warfare. Today, with the end of the great holocaust finally within sight, this *same instrument is transformed into a powerful device for shaping a better world.—This, I believe, is the new meaning of the trade-agreements program as it comes before the Congress for its fourth renewal.* [Emphasis added.]

The Ways and Means Committee also emphasized another of the newer objectives of the act as justification for the extension. This was the importance of the trade agreements program to a disposal in the postwar period of the surplus production of the greatly expanded capacity of the American agricultural and industrial economy: [45]

*After this war the productive capacity* of the United States *will be greater than it has ever been.* A substantial part of this greatly enlarged *productive capacity will be devoted to the output of products*—including heavy capital equipment and major agricultural crops—*far in excess of the quantities that can be consumed within the United States* * * *. At the same time, there will be an unparalleled demand for these surpluses in foreign countries * * *.

But these *large exports cannot continue* indefinitely * * * *unless the United States is prepared to facilitate larger imports* through a moderation of its existing tariffs. To do this, and at the same time to obtain the necessary assurance that foreign countries will not maintain, or establish in the future, burdensome restrictions on our exports, *an effective program for the reduction of trade barriers is essential.* [Emphasis added.]

In the debate on the 1945 extension bill in the House of Representatives, Congressman Doughton, then chairman of the Ways and Means Committee, indicated quite clearly that the trade agreements authority under the extension bill was intended to place the United States in a position of leadership "in a world organized on a policy and program of cooperation both politically and economically." He also referred to the objective of the act in making available markets for the surplus products of the United States.[46] Any possibility that the act was to be regarded any longer as being temporary in nature was eliminated by Mr. Doughton's statement in the debate that the legislation, "by its nature and success, has become the key arch in our postwar economic policy." [47]

This shift in the scope of the act is emphasized by the fact that those who were opposed to the extension of the trade agreements program were alert to recognize that the justification for its continuation had shifted from the original temporary or emergency nature of the law to a rather permanent part of the foreign policy of the United States.[48]

---

[45] Id., p. 38.
[46] Congressional Record, May 22, 1945, p. 4872.
[47] Id., p. 4874.
[48] See, for example, the remarks of the following Republican members of the Ways and Means Committee: Congressman Woodruff of Michigan, Congressional Record, May 24 and 25, p. 5007; Congressman Jenkins of Ohio, id., pp. 5027–5028; Congressman Gearhardt of California, id., p. 5041; Congressman Carlson of Kansas, id., p. 5052; Congressman Curtis of Nebraska, id., pp. 5068–5069.

The interpretation which the Executive placed upon the sweep of the power conferred by the trade agreements legislation during the immediate postwar period is shown by President Truman's message to Congress on the 1948 extension bill. Referring to the General Agreement on Tariffs and Trade, President Truman declared that the agreement was "a landmark in international economic relations." A continuation of the authority of the Trade Agreements Act was stated by him to be necessary to enable the United States to play its part in extending GATT's "intensive effort to reduce barriers to trade" to still other countries. He also stated that the trade-agreements authority would be needed to enable the United States in concert with other nations to carry out the International Trade Organization Charter.[49]

Though the chilled reception of the Congress to the proposed charter for an International Trade Organization subsequently resulted in the plan for that comprehensive world organization to die aborning, President Truman's remarks to the Congress, referred to above, are significant in that they reflect a considered evaluation by the executive department of the Government of the somewhat permanent necessity for the trade-agreements authority to carry out an intensive program for the reduction of trade barriers for the purpose of strengthening the peace and security of the free world, raising the standard of living of the peoples of the world, and other rather general objectives which appear quite remote to the limited scope so carefully placed upon the authority delegated by Congress in 1934.

Significantly, though the Republican Party was in control of the Congress which extended the Trade Agreements Act in 1948, the Congress did not indicate any disagreement with the changed purpose and objective of the Trade Agreements Act which had been made evident in earlier extensions, and which were referred to in President Truman's message, set forth in the committee report. While the 80th Congress revised the preparatory procedure to be followed in connection with the trade-agreement negotiations, it failed to disaffirm the new and broadened objectives of the trade-agreements program itself.

The 1948 extension was for but 1 year. With the earlier temporary or emergency scope of the trade-agreements authority by now rather clearly repudiated, it is not surprising that in the 1949 extension the Congress amended the text of the Trade Agreements Act to delete the clause in the preamble which since 1934 had indicated that the purpose of the act was to assist "in the present emergency, etc." [50]

As if to emphasize the widespread acceptance in the Congress of the change in purpose implied by the deletion, the report of the House Ways and Means Committee stated that none of the amendments made to the act by the 1949 extension was "controversial." [51]

That report contained other evidence of a recognition of the sweep of the authority which had been claimed for the Executive under the extension acts by President Truman's message in 1948. Thus the report declared that "the greatest achievement of the trade-agreements program to date is the conclusion of the General Agreement on

[49] H. Rept. 2009, 80th Cong. (1948), p. 7 (minority views).
[50] Sec. 4, Public Law 307, 81st Cong.
[51] H. Rept. 19, 81st Cong. (1949), p. 2.

Tariffs and Trade, negotiated at Geneva in 1947." [52] Elsewhere the committee suggested that an extension of the authority provided for "the strongest and most effective program available to expand international trade." [53]

It has been said by many thoughtful students of the trade agreements program that the regulation of imports is properly considered a part of the domestic policy of the United States. In the 1949 extension, however, the House Ways and Means Committee accepted the contention that the program is part of the foreign policy of the United States. Thus, the committee reported— [54]

"*It is our earnest conviction that peace, freedom, and world trade are inseparable, and that the foreign relations of the United States, political and economic, are indivisible.* * * *.

"*Continued expansion of trade and commerce among free nations is an essential corollary to our foreign assistance program. Failure to enact H. R. 1211 would be the subordination of American leadership in world economic affairs* to the special interests of a few domestic producers.

"*The Reciprocal Trade Act,* in our opinion, *is the keystone of our bipartisan foreign economic policy* * * *" [Italic added.]

In the 1951 extension, the House Ways and Means Committee again affirmed its view that the trade agreements program is "broad in scope." [55] Indeed, so broadly was the scope of the act viewed that the committee described the extension as an affirmation of the determination of the United States "to continue to participate in the cooperative effort to expand world trade." The program was likened to one of "the tools of peace." [56] The committee agreed with the Secretary of State who had testified that the trade agreements program is a way in which the United States—

can *assure* the peoples of the free world *that economic expansion and rising living standards for all countries is still the goal of the United States.*[57] [Italic added.]

The Senate Finance Committee, in reporting the 1951 extension, cast some doubt upon whether the Congress could any longer fairly be said as viewing the General Agreement on Tariffs and Trade as a major achievement in the use of the trade-agreements authority. The committee referred to the fact that in its report on the 1948 and 1949 extensions it had endeavored to make clear that the extensions "would not be construed as approval or disapproval of the General Agreements on Tariffs and Trade." [58] In order to give the comments which it then made "the unquestionable force of law," the committee inserted a provision to that effect in the bill.

The readiness of the committee to insert a caveat to the effect that its extension of the Trade Agreements Act did not constitute approval of GATT offers a marked contrast to its failure and that of the Congress to insert any caveat to the effect that its action in extending the Trade Agreements Act should not be construed as approval of the scope of the power or objectives of the act claimed by the Executive directly in the testimony and communications presented to the legislative committees of the Congress. In these circumstances it is

[52] Id., p. 2.
[53] Id., p. 7.
[54] Id., p. 9.
[55] H. Rept. 14, 82d Cong. (1951), p. 2.
[56] Id., p. 6.
[57] Id., p. 6.
[58] S. Rept. 299, 82d Cong. (1951), p. 7 .

difficult not to conclude that the Congress has intentionally accepted the change in purpose and objectives of the act which are described above.

The 1-year extension of the Trade Agreements Act in 1953 brought forth nothing significant so far as a change in the policy of the act. President Eisenhower's letter to Congress in connection with foreign trade policy echoed sentiments developed in earlier years emphasizing the asserted importance of the trade-agreements program to cooperative action among free nations to achieve the highest possible level of trade for the sake of the economic strength and security of the free world.[59]

The 1954 extension was enacted in the face of testimony by Assistant Secretary of State Morton that the extension would permit the President—

> to improve Japan's trading prospects in the world, an essential element to stability in the whole Far Eastern situation.[60]

It is impossible to reconcile such a statement with any concept of a purpose or objective of the act other than a general international economic program as distinct from a program addressed primarily to the interests of the domestic economy of the United States.

The enactment of H. R. 1 in 1955 in the context built up by the Randall Commission served mainly to reaffirm the broadest scope for the purposes and objectives of the act. The report of the House Ways and Means Committee referred approvingly to testimony by the Secretary of State that failure "to rededicate our Nation to liberalized trade policies * * * would have grave consequences." The testimony of the Secretary of Defense was relied upon by the committee as indicating that the trade-agreements program was now "an important measure in strengthening our common defense against Communist aggression."[61] The Senate Finance Committee's report stressed the importance of the trade-agreements program to "an ever-growing surplus of the products of our farms and factories which must find markets abroad."[62] A sense of permanence in the program is perhaps suggested by the committee's observation that—

> the importance of the trade-agreements program as a factor for expanded world trade has come to be accepted by the leading free nations of the world.[63]

The foregoing review of the developments in the assertion of changed purposes and objectives of the Trade Agreements Act and a rather uniform acceptance of these suggested changes by the committees of Congress as justification for the repeated extension of the trade-agreements program lead to no other conclusion but that the scope of the act's purpose and objectives has indeed materially changed from those carefully delineated by the Congress when the act was passed in 1934. Whether or not one would be prepared, as an academic matter, to agree at this juncture that the act presently has a scope which reaches the purposes and objectives claimed for it by the Executive, it must be admitted that the Congress itself has placed its stamp of approval upon a concept of the trade-agreements program embracing the following points:

---

[59] H. Rept. 521, 83d Cong. (1953), p. 2.
[60] H. Rept. 1777, 83d Cong. (1954), p. 2.
[61] H. Rept. 50, 84th Cong. (1955), pp. 6–8.
[62] S. Rept. 232, 84th Cong. (1955), p. 1.
[63] Ibid.

1. The delegation by Congress of power to the President to enter into trade agreements is not premised upon the existence of emergency conditions of a temporary nature.

2. The purpose of the trade-agreements authority is broadly conceived to permit the President to exercise in behalf of the United States leadership in the establishment of international trade relations which will result in:

(*a*) A reduction of trade barriers.

(*b*) An expansion in the levels of international trade.

(*c*) Strengthening the economies of the free nations of the world.

(*d*) Adding to the military strength of the free nations to resist Communist aggression.

3. The purpose of the trade-agreements program is no longer merely to secure a reduction in trade barriers of foreign countries to accommodate the need of surplus American agricultural or industrial products for foreign markets.

### B. LIMITATIONS UPON THE EXECUTIVE'S USE OF THE TRADE-AGREEMENTS AUTHORITY

Because of the nature of the problems involved in negotiating trade agreements with other countries, the Congress concluded that the responsibility for action should be placed upon the President rather than retained by the Congress. In its report on the 1934 act, the House Ways and Means Committee stated:[64]

> The very nature of international negotiations required that it should be in the hands of the Executive; and to meet international conditions where foreign [E]xecutives are being clothed with even greater and greater power to effectuate speedy trade agreements, the United States, if it is to regain its lost proportion of world trade, must repose similar confidence in its President.

In the course of the House debate on the bill, it was also pointed out that no legislative body could effectively negotiate reciprocal trade agreements, and that, in order to accomplish the desired result, Congress must decide upon a policy to be pursued and then delegate the authority to effectuate it.[65]

It was not intended, however, that the President should have plenary power. The report of the Ways and Means Committee stated in unequivocal terms that Congress intended to retain exclusive control over the policy considerations underlying this legislation:[66]

> The proposed bill * * * does not remove from Congress its control of policy which must underlie every tariff adjustment. Although the exigencies of present-day conditions require that more and more of the details be left to Presidential determination, the Congress must and always will declare the policy to which the Executive gives effect.

This language is in no way surprising, because it is a fundamental truism of our constitutional form of government that Congress alone may formulate legislative policy; the Executive is limited to actions which will carry out this policy, and, where latitude of action is allowed, an "intelligible standard" of conduct must be declared by Congress. In other words, the Executive may, at best, merely "fill up the details" of the framework of legislative policy laid down by Congress. *Hampton* v. *United States* (276 U. S. 394 (1928)).

---

[64] H. Rept. 1000, 73d Cong., 2d sess., p. 14.
[65] Congressional Record, 73d Cong., 2d sess., p. 5652.
[66] H. Rept. 1000, 73d Cong., 2d sess., p. 14.

This concept was recognized with respect to the basis upon which trade-agreements negotiations were to be conducted, as revealed by both House and Senate debate on the subject. Representative Sisson, of New York, said:[67]

> * * * we retain the power here in Congress; we delegate the administration of the power; we, with respect to certain broad vital policies affecting this Nation and other nations, determine and legislate a policy; we properly empower and direct the President to administer the details of such policy.

Representative Vinson, of Kentucky, a member of the House Ways and Means Committee, said:[68]

> The language of the pending bill, in the first part of section 1, * * * [is] a legislative expression of conditions, purposes, and intent. It is a very vital part of the bill itself. * * *
>
> * * * * * * *
>
> This language sets forth not only the purposes which the Congress hopes and intends to obtain by the passage of this legislation, but it also constitutes a direction to the President * * * in the use of the powers conferred upon him. * * * The yardstick or formula is prescribed. The Executive is vested with the power to execute the formula established. * * *

The authority to be granted the President by the proposed legislation was likened to the flexible tariff provision in the Tariff Act of 1930. Senator Borah, of Idaho, said:[69]

> The President is required to find certain facts, and, when these facts are found, he is given the same power that was granted in the flexible-tariff case * * *.

Referring to a provision in the McKinley Tariff Act which permitted the President to suspend the duty-free privilege of certain imported articles when the exporting country imposed duties on United States products which he deemed to be "reciprocally unequal and unreasonable," which was sustained by the Supreme Court in the case of *Field* v. *Clark* (143 U. S. 649), Senator George, of Georgia, stated:[70]

> * * * it cannot be said, as a matter of law, that the determination of when duties are "reciprocally unequal and unreasonable" is more a matter of precise fact than the determination of when duties "are as a fact * * * unduly burdening and restricting the foreign trade of the United States."

It is readily apparent from the foregoing analysis of the legislative history of the 1934 act that the Congress specifically intended to limit the President's exercise of the authority conferred in the act to those instances in which he could find as a fact that the criteria specified in the act were satisfied. These guiding principles are contained in section 1 of the act, which can be segmented for ready analysis as follows:

> For the purpose of expanding foreign markets for the products of the United States * * *,
>
> By regulating the admission of foreign goods into the United States in accordance with the characteristics and needs of various branches of American production,
>
> So that foreign markets will be made available to those branches of American production which require and are capable of developing such outlets.
>
> By affording corresponding market opportunities for foreign products in the United States,
>
> The President, whenever he finds as a fact that any existing duties or other import restrictions of the United States or any foreign country are unduly bur-

---

[67] Congressional Record, 73d Cong., 2d sess., p. 5656.
[68] Congressional Record, 73d Cong., 2d sess., pp. 5781, 5790.
[69] Congressional Record, 73d Cong., 2d sess., p. 9010.
[70] Congressional Record, 73d Cong., 2d sess., p. 10077.

dening and restricting the foreign trade of the United States, and that the purpose above-declared will be promoted by the means hereinafter specified, is authorized from time to time—

(1) to enter into foreign trade agreements * * *; and

(2) to proclaim such modifications of existing duties and other import restrictions * * * as are required or appropriate to carry out any foreign trade agreement that the President has entered into hereunder.

The language of the section itself clearly indicates that each element, as set out above, is intended as an essential prerequisite which must apply before the President is empowered to act. This intention was also established by the legislative history of the 1934 act. During the Senate debates, Senator George of Georgia stated:[71]

What are the limitations upon the Executive in his bargaining? First, he cannot change the basic tariff rates more than 50 percent up or down; second, he can make only such modifications or other action as is required to carry out trade agreements; only to this extent can he make any change in the tariff law; thirdly, no agreement can be made except for the purposes set out in the bill and in harmony with the basic principle thereof quoted above ["regulating the admission of foreign goods into the United States in accordance with the characteristics and needs of various branches of American production so that foreign markets will be made available to those branches of American production which require and are capable of developing such outlets by affording corresponding market opportunities for foreign products in the United States"]. Finally, before the President can exercise any power under the bill he must find as a fact that any existing duties or other import restrictions * * * are unduly burdening and restricting the foreign trade of the United States and that the purpose above declared will be promoted.

Senator George's statement indicates the intention of the Congress that all of the qualifications recited in section 1 of the act were to be respected by the President as policy guidelines which must be satisfied before trade agreement action was authorized. The importance of each of these limitations upon the power of the President to act under the trade agreements authority is emphasized in the report of the House Ways and Means Committee on the 1945 extension. There the committee summarized the relationship of all of the policy guidelines stated in the act, as follows:[72]

This authority is granted "for the purpose of expanding foreign markets for the products of the United States." It is to be exercised only if the President finds as a fact that any existing duties or other import restrictions of the United States or any foreign country are unduly burdening and restricting the foreign trade of the United States.

It is to be exercised by regulating the admission of foreign goods into the United States in accordance with the characteristics and needs of various branches of American production so that foreign markets will be made available to those branches of American production which require and are capable of developing such outlets * * *.

Before any trade agreement can be entered into, the President must seek information and advice with respect thereto from the United States Tariff Commission, the Departments of State, Agriculture, and Commerce, and from such other sources as he may deem appropriate; and in each case reasonable public notice of the intention to negotiate an agreement must be given in order that any interested person may have an opportunity to present his views.

Other evidence concerning the intention of the Congress respecting each of these qualifications strengthens this conclusion:

*Avoidance of injury to domestic industries*

In inserting the phrase, "by regulating the admission of foreign goods into the United States in accordance with the characteristics

---

[71] Congressional Record, 73d Cong., 2d sess., p. 10077.
[72] H. Rept. 594, 79th Cong. (1945), p. 4.

and needs of various branches of American production," Congress intended to direct the use of the President's authority in a manner which would avoid causing injury to domestic industries. The House Ways and Means Committee stated in its report that "the authority which [the trade agreements bill] would delegate to the President must be very carefully exercised so as not to injure manufacturers or domestic producers." The committee referred to President Roosevelt's message to Congress, quoting him as follows: [73]

The exercise of the authority which I propose must be carefully weighed in the light of the latest information so as to give assurance that no sound and important American interests will be injuriously disturbed. The adjustment of our foreign trade relations must rest on the premise of undertaking to benefit and not to injure such interests. In a time of difficulty and unemployment such as this, the highest consideration of the position of the different branches of American production is required.

Secretary of State Cordell Hull's testimony before the committee was quoted in part in the committee report where he assured that—[74]

it can be stated with emphasis that each trade agreement undertaken would be considered with care and caution, and only after the fullest consideration of all pertinent information. Nothing would be done blindly or hastily.

The committee did not content itself with these direct expressions of assurance that domestic industries would not be injured nor their needs lightly considered in the use of this new authority. It undertook to deny that the new authority would be used to destroy even small or "inefficient" domestic industries, stating: [75]

It has been assumed by some that following such a tariff bargaining program as proposed in H. R. 8687 would seek to eliminate or destroy small industries or industries inefficiently conducted. One of the members of this committee, questioning the Secretary of Agriculture upon this point, said:

"We can at least protest in behalf of the people we represent if you are endeavoring to put them out of business in industry or agriculture, either one."

The Secretary of Agriculture, protesting against such an interpreation of the proposed program, replied:

"It seems to me, sir, that the essence of the 'new deal,' if I may be permitted to say it, is to take account of human rights. It would seem to me also that a man of the character of the President in administering powers of this sort would not be so inhuman as to retire in any barbarous way, such as you seem to contemplate, inefficient industries."

Secretary Hull characterized the anticipated effect as being one which would "bring to our domestic situation the full stability and the business prosperity that our people are entitled to have." [76] He also said that commodities would be selected which would form the basis of a mutually profitable interchange so that the "American people will be helped." [77] To the same effect is the following colloquy between Representative McCormack of Massachusetts and Secretary Hull: [78]

Mr. McCormack. In addition to the foreign trade, the purposes are also to preserve the American standard of living and assure adequate protection to American industry, consisting of a foreign trade policy which would be for the general welfare of our people.

---

[73] H. Rept. 1000, 73d Cong., 2d sess., p. 13.
[74] H. Rept. 1000, 73d Cong., 2d sess., p. 13.
[75] Id., pp. 13, 14.
[76] House hearings, p. 18.
[77] Id., p. 24.
[78] Id., p. 13.

Mr. HULL. The whole purpose, of course, is to further primarily our domestic prosperity; * * *.

Secretary Hull also said:[79]

But in any event, whatever our Government may do in negotiating reciprocal trade agreements, it will first see to it that they are mutually profitable and that they are not negotiated in a way that would result in injury or hurt to our own country.

The same tenor of thought is revealed in expressions of purpose found elsewhere in this paper. A considerable amount of skepticism was displayed, both in the House and the Senate, over whether the program could be administered without adverse effect upon some segment of the economy. Typical of the statements made by the skeptics was the one voiced by Representative Boileau, of Wisconsin:[80]

In considering this legislation from any angle, it must be evident that if we are to enter into any trade agreements and give an advantage to some particular industry, some other American industry is going to be hurt; * * *.

Some support for this fear was lent by Secretary of Agriculture Henry A. Wallace, who told the House Ways and Means Committee:[81]

For my own part, I believe it is important for the Congress to realize that high tariffs cause unemployment just as surely as low tariffs, perhaps even more certainly. It is just a question of where the unemployment is to be. In the case of high tariffs, unduly high tariffs, the unemployment is in the efficient industries which have been able to produce goods for the export markets. In the case of the low tariffs, the unemployment would tend to be in the inefficient industries which are exposed to competition from abroad. * * *

In order to calm these doubts, the proponents of the legislation took pains to make clear the philosophy by which administration of the proposed legislation would be guided.

The House Ways and Means Committee quoted with approval the President's message, which stipulated:[82]

If American agricultural and industrial interests are to retain their deserved place in [international] trade, the American Government must be in a position to bargain for that place with other governments for rapid and decisive negotiation based on a carefully considered program, and to grant *with discernment* corresponding opportunities in the American market for *foreign products supplementary to our own.* [Emphasis added.]

This position was amplified by Secretary Hull in his testimony before the committee:[83]

It should be kept in mind that American labor at good wages produces the billions of commodities we export, while our imports chiefly comprise commodities *we do not produce in this country at all or in sufficient quantities*, with the result that American labor is helped rather than hurt by most of our imports. [Emphasis added.]

Secretary of Commerce Daniel C. Roper told the House Ways and Means Committee:[84]

* * * it is the intention of this bill to bring about the sale abroad of products which a great many of our people are engaged in producing and to let in only such products as are now excluded or burdened with excessive duties without contributing materially to the employment of many of our people. * * * [We] will be able in our treaty negotiations to control the character of the imports

[79] Id., p. 23.
[80] Congressional Record, 73d Cong., 2d sess., p. 5456.
[81] House hearings, p. 45.
[82] H. Rept. 1000, 73d Cong., 2d sess., p. 5.
[83] House hearings, 73d Cong., 2d sess., p. 4.
[84] House hearings, p. 64.

which we will receive in payment so that they will not belong to classes of products where foreign competition would result in serious loss to the established industries of the Nation.

Representative Ford of California said flatly:[85]

If the plan involved the lowering of tariffs on competitive products from abroad, whereby established American industries might suffer, we would none of us be for it. Neither would the President * * *.

In summary, the words of Chairman Doughton are significant:[86]

[The President] has predicated this whole bill upon the solid foundation that no essential American industry shall be crippled. Its sole purpose is to benefit and alleviate American industry by creating a wider market and bringing about an improvement in the welfare of all the people.

A policy of avoidance of injury to domestic industry in the administration of the trade-agreements program has remained uppermost in the minds of the Congress. In the 1945 extension of the act, the Ways and Means Committee stated that it was an objective of the law, among other things, to reduce such American tariff rates—

as are disclosed after careful and informed investigation to be capable of reduction without serious damage to any important domestic interest.[87]

The committee discussed various provisions which had been included in trade agreements "for the purpose of assuring that no serious injury will be caused to any domestic industry."[88] It referred approvingly to the—

extreme care which the President and the trade agreements organizations have taken in protecting the interests of American producers.[89]

During the debate in the House on the 1945 extension, Chairman Doughton of the Ways and Means Committe, in stating an objective of the extension, clearly indicated that the trade-agreement authority would remain subject to the limitation that its use should not injure any domestic industry. He said:[90]

In this new postwar situation we need to indicate, in a positive manner that we are sincere in our efforts to work out with foreign nations, *as far as can be done without injury to any substantial domestic industry,* a sound approach to the solution of some of our economic problems. [Emphasis added.]

Congressman Camp of Georgia, a member of the Ways and Means Committee, also stated in the debate that—

the objective of the Trade Agreements Act is to successfully build up our foreign trade without injury to American producers * * *.[91]

President Truman's message to the Congress urging extension of the Trade Agreements Act in 1948 expressed the Executive understanding that his use of the trade-agreements authority was conditioned upon an avoidance of serious injury to domestic industry. He stated:[92]

In addition, the interests of domestic producers are carefully protected in the negotiation of each trade agreement. I assured the Congress when the Reciprocal Trade Agreements Act was last extended in 1945, that domestic producers

[85] Congressional Record, 73d Cong., 2d sess., p. 5652.
[86] Congressional Record, March 26, 1934, p. 5261.
[87] H. Rept. 594, 79th Cong. (1945), p. 3.
[88] Id., p. 8.
[89] Ibid.
[90] Congressional Record, May 22, 1945, p. 4874.
[91] Congressional Record, May 25, 1945, p. 5075.
[92] H. Rept. 2009, 80th Cong. (1948), p. 7.

would be safeguarded in the process of expanding trade. That commitment has been kept. It will continue to be kept.

At the same time, the Senate Finance Committee sounded a stern warning to emphasize the impatience of the Congress with any failure on the part of the Executive to respect the policy guideline in the act of avoiding injury to domestic producers. The committee's report stated: [93]

From progressively widening sources your committee hears complaints that domestic producers who require protection against injurious competition from imports do not receive adequate consideration in trade-agreement negotiations. There is much feeling that fully justifiable needs for tariffs adequate to safeguard the well-being of our domestic economy are being subordinated to extraneous, and perhaps overvalued, diplomatic objectives. There is considerable evidence that advice to the President against injurious tariff reductions and concessions is diluted and obscured in a maze of executive committees not primarily concerned with safeguarding our domestic producers against injury.

* * * * * *

The bill provides a procedure designed to lessen these doubts in the future by requiring that the President shall give focused attention to the injury test. This procedure for focused attention by the President to the injury test merely gives statutory expression to the repeated Presidential assurances that in the conduct of the trade-agreements program domestic producers would be protected from injury.

The 80th Congress in the 1948 extension of the Trade Agreements Act added the peril-point procedure, referred to in the Senate Finance Committee report quoted above. This precautionary provision, which had been adopted to strengthen the policy already expressed in the act of avoiding serious injury to domestic industries in the trade-agreements program, was repealed in the 1949 extension. There was, however, no intention that the repeal of the peril-point procedure would affect in any way the policy expressed in the basic trade-agreements legislation of regulating the exercise of the trade-agreements authority so as to avoid serious injury to domestic industries. This was made clear in the 1951 extension when both the peril-point and escape-clause remedies were incorporated into the trade-agreements law. The report of the House Ways and Means Committee stated that the procedures which were being followed in the administration of the act—

*provide for tailoring concessions to meet the particular situation of particular products so as to combine the maximum opportunity for imports with avoidance of injury to domestic interests.*[94] [Italics added.]

Though the House committee declined to accept the peril-point amendment (the amendment was added during the debate in the House after the bill was reported by the committee), the comment just quoted indicates its adherence to the basic policy of the act of avoiding serious injury to domestic producers.

In the most recent extension of the act in 1955, there was no indication of a departure from adherence to this policy. In fact, the Senate Finance Committee in reporting H. R. 1 referred to—

the need for a planned and well-organized program so that trade expansion can be obtained without serious injury to any segment of our economy.

The committee quoted approvingly President Eisenhower's statement that—

[93] S. Rept. 1558, 80th Cong. (1948), p. 3.
[94] H. Rept. 14, 82d Cong. (1951), p. 2.

Changes which would result in the threat of serious injury to industry or general reduction in employment would not strengthen the economy of this country or the free world.[95]

*Bargaining for the reciprocal exchange of concessions*

The intention underlying the clause contained in section 1 of the 1934 act—

so that foreign markets will be made available to those branches of American production which require and are capable of developing such outlets by affording corresponding market opportunities for foreign products in the United States—

was graphically characterized in the Senate debate on the 1934 act by Senator Gore, of Oklahoma, a member of the Senate Finance Committee:[96]

If we desire to sell our surplus goods abroad we must buy the surplus of the foreigner in the foreign markets. What we produce and do not need we must exchange for what others produce and do not need. We must exchange what we have and do not want for what we want and do not have. * * *

It has come to pass that we must prevail upon the foreigner to relax his restrictions against our exports, and in order to do that we may be obliged to relax our restrictions against his exports to this country. The barriers that have gone up together may have to come down—barrier for barrier.

Senator Vandenberg, of Michigan, in expressing reservations about the bargaining mechanism of the bill, pointed out that the foreign countries with whom we intended to negotiate were anticipating that reduction of their restrictions would be the inevitable outcome of these dealings, and were preparing themselves accordingly:[97]

European countries have learned that the way to bargain is to put their rates up in the hope that they can bargain them back down. * * *

This practice, he observed, put the United States at a real disadvantage in any program premised on reciprocal concessions:[98]

* * * it is the considered policy of European countries to increase their rates on the threshold of a contemplated bargain for the purpose of ultimately reducing the rates without loss in respect to an indicated commodity.

* * * * * * *

Mr. President, we Americans have no padding upon which we can fall when we undertake to enter the international market place and seek one of of these so-called bargains. Other countries have already provided themselves with the padding * * *. We have no padding. When we fall, we fall with a dull sickening thud upon the hard floor of reality. We have no cushion. When they fall, they fall upon the padding which they have created for this precise purpose. * * *

Though the Senator's statements indicate that he felt that very little actual progress would be made so far as eliminating the barriers to United States exports was concerned, his remarks do reflect an awareness that the policy of the Trade Agreements Act called for the use of concessions on United States tariffs in bargaining for the reduction of foreign-trade barriers. There is other evidence of an understanding that the policy of the act in this regard was to secure measure-for-measure reductions of trade barriers. Congressman West, of Ohio, a member of the Ways and Means Committee, said our lost trade would be regained through the vehicle of "equivalent and commen-

[95] S. Rept. 232, 84th Cong. (1955), p. 2.
[96] Congressional Record, 73d Cong., 2d sess., p. 10357.
[97] Congressional Record, 73d Cong., 2d sess., p. 9803.
[98] Id., pp. 9800–9801.

surate concessions for obtaining increased opportunities for marketing of our products." [99] To the same effect was a comment by Senator George, of Georgia: [1]

> * * * the bill under consideration is * * *. Firstly, a policy of tariff bargaining * * * which authorizes the President to negotiate "commercial agreements in which reciprocal and equivalent concessions may be secured. * * *"

In this connection, the net effect hoped for from these trade concessions was repeatedly explained as being "mutually profitable" and for "mutual benefit." Secretary Hull told the House Ways and Means Committee: [2]

> The entire policy as proposed by the pending House bill would rest upon trade relationships that would be mutually and equally profitable both to our own and other countries. * * *

Again, he said: [3]

> * * * we will, with the utmost care and pains, single out only those commodities where it would be a reasonable and practical thing, and a thoroughly profitable arrangement.

In view of these statements, a use of the authority which would merely secure adherence to the status quo by foreign countries to whom the United States grants reductions in duty cannot be regarded as coming within the intention of Congress.

*The finding of fact that import restrictions are unduly burdening the foreign trade of the United States and that the act's purposes will be promoted by entering into a particular trade agreement*

There is very strong evidence that the Congress was expressing a deliberate intent when it inserted in section 1 of the 1934 act the clause—

> whenever [the President] finds as a fact that any existing duties or other import restrictions of the United States or any foreign country are unduly burdening and restricting the foreign trade of the United States and that the purpose above declared will be promoted by the means hereinafter specified.

The bill as originally introduced in the House did not require the President to find as a fact that existing restrictions were unduly burdening. This requirement was added by amendment in the Senate, and the following statement was made with regard thereto in the report of the Senate Finance Committee: [4]

> The committee has inserted the words "as a fact" following the words in subsection (a) "the President, whenever he finds." This is to make clear that Congress under the proposed bill is establishing a policy and directing the Executive to act in accordance with the congressional policy only when he finds as a fact that existing duties or other import restrictions are unduly burdening and restricting the foreign trade of the United States. * * *.

The committee was at pains to make it clear that Presidential action was dependent upon findings of fact of both the restrictive effect of duties and the furtherance of the policy of the act which could be achieved by a trade-agreement concession. It said, [5]

> The House bill makes the action of the President dependent upon his finding either that existing duties or import restrictions are unduly burdening and

---

[99] Congressional Record, 73d Cong., 2d sess., p. 5621.
[1] Id., p. 10072.
[2] House hearings, p. 13.
[3] Id., p. 29.
[4] S. Rept. 871, 73d Cong., 2d sess., pp. 1–2.
[5] S. Rept. 871, 73d Cong., 2d sess., p. 2.

restricting the foreign trade of the United States or that such action will promote the purpose set forth. In order to require a finding by the President on both of these points, the word "for" has been changed to "and."

In view of these two amendments it is unmistakably clear that the "findings of fact" which the act makes a condition precedent to the exercise of the trade-agreements authority by the President was to be no mere idle ceremony. Rather, the finding was regarded as being of great importance by the Congress. Certainly the care and attention which was devoted by the committees to the refinement of the legislative language calling for the twin findings of burdensome restrictions and promotion of the purposes of the act do not contemplate an administration of the act which *assumes* the existence of both facts whenever a trade agreement is under consideration.

This review of the legislative history pertaining to the policy criteria specified in section 1 of the Trade Agreements Act as enacted in 1934 strongly indicates that the Congress specifically and carefully intended that the delegated authority would be used by the President only in a carefully defined set of circumstances. These circumstances exist only when, after an investigation, he can find as a fact that specific tariff or customs provisions of the United States or a foreign country are definitely retarding the foreign commerce of the United States, and where he can find that a reduction of these barriers to trade would serve the purpose of the act of strengthening the domestic economy of the United States by expanding its exports of the products affected. In addition, the circumstances appropriate for action exist only where—

(1) a reduction can be made without causing serious injury to domestic producers; and

(2) bargaining would achieve an exchange of tariff concessions by the United States and a foreign country in which the products of each country, requiring and seeking markets in the other, would be provided such market opportunities.

### C. PROCEDURAL REQUIREMENTS FOR THE USE OF THE TRADE AGREEMENTS AUTHORITY

The act and the legislative history reveal the intention of Congress concerning procedural facets of the use of the Executive's trade agreements authority.

*Preparation for trade agreement negotiations*

The preparatory phase of negotiating such reciprocal trade agreements was envisioned by Secretary Hull, in his testimony before the House Ways and Means Committee on the 1934 act, as being a careful selection by each country of those commodities which it felt other countries would be willing to purchase and which could be used advantageously in bargaining for the commodities of those other countries.[6] Secretary Hull indicated, however, that a high degree of caution would be exercised in negotiating to insure that any concessions made would have a favorable net impact upon the economy as a whole.[7]

[6] House hearings, p. 27.
[7] Id., p. 24.

In making these particular arrangements, if they have any effect pertaining to our production, transportation, and distribution situation, that effect would be taken into consideration; and all phases would be given the most careful consideration so that we would finally ascertain the given commodities on which we could base our arrangements that would be mutually profitable and not hurtful.

The Secretary was careful to stress, both to the House Ways and Means Committee and to the Senate Finance Committee, that [8]—

* * * it can be stated with emphasis that each trade agreement undertaken would be considered with care and caution, and only after the fullest consideration of all pertinent information. Nothing would be done blindly or hastily.

While it was recognized that the President personally could not possibly be the factfinding agency for such a determination,[9] reassurance was given both by Secretary Hull and by the chairman of the House Ways and Means Committee, Congressman Doughton, of North Carolina, that all competent Government agencies and facilities would be enlisted in arriving at the conclusion that a particular commodity could be used advantageously as a trading item without causing an adverse effect upon the domestic economy.[10]

While not specifically stated in the act, it would appear that the procedure envisioned by the framers of the legislation is the selection by careful analysis on the part of Government agencies of commodities which would lend themselves to give-and-take bargaining, which commodities would then serve as the basis for negotiating with foreign countries, the ultimate concessions depending upon which of the commodities the foreign country desired and the extent to which favorable concessions could be secured. This procedure is implicit in a statement made by Secretary Hull before the House Ways and Means Committee: [11]

* * * each government that may be so disposed should sit down and ascertain whether it has a commodity that others can afford profitably to purchase, and whenever two countries find commodities that might be exchanged with mutual profit, then in that way they may increase trade between them * * *.

Although there was nothing in the bill which would require the President to base his decision as to what commodities would be used for bargaining on the findings and/or advice of responsible Government agencies, this was one of the facets of the proposed legislation which was taken on faith. Senator Barkley of Kentucky said: [12]

* * * it is inconceivable that he would arrive at any agreement without taking advantage of all the information of all the departments of the Government * * *.

The act itself simply provided in section 4 that before concluding a trade agreement "the President shall seek information and advice with respect thereto from the United States Tariff Commission, the Departments of State, Agriculture, and Commerce [by amendment this passage now reads 'from the United States Tariff Commission, from the Departments of State, Agriculture, and Commerce, from the National Military Establishment'] and from such other sources as he may deem appropriate."

[8] Id., p. 13; Senate hearings, p. 7.
[9] Congressional Record, 83d Cong., 2d sess., p. 5261.
[10] Senate hearings, p. 7; Congressional Record, 73d Cong., 2d sess., p. 5261.
[11] House hearings, p. 27.
[12] Congressional Record, 73d Cong., 2d sess., p. 10199.

In the 1945 extension, the House Ways and Means Committee cited Secretary Hull's assurances concerning careful preparations for trade agreement negotiations, as follows:[13]

Neither the original act nor your bill contemplates any indiscriminate slashing of tariffs. When your bill has been adopted the act will still contain all the provisions that it has always contained for full consultation, before action, among the departments of the Government that know the most about commercial questions, and for public hearings at which any citizen may submit facts and arguments * * *

The committee itself referred approvingly to the fact that the extension bill would preserve without change the "thorough and carefully safeguarded procedures, which have been developed through years of experience."[14]

*Public notice*

Section 4 of the 1934 act states that before any trade agreement is concluded with any foreign government—

reasonable public notice of the intention to negotiate an agreement with such government or instrumentality shall be given in order that any interested person may have an opportunity to present his views to the President, or such agency as the President may designate * * *.

The bill as originally presented to the House made no provision that public notice of pending or existing negotiations be given. When asked about this omission, Secretary Hull indicated that it was deliberate and that the administration was vigorously opposed to such a provision for two reasons: (1) It might "tip our hand"; and (2) it would impede speedy negotiations. The bill passed the House without any real issue being made of the subject, but in the Senate a determined campaign was launched to secure the addition of a clause requiring public notice. It became readily apparent to proponents of the measure that compromise was the better part of politics, and accordingly such a clause was written into the bill. The report of the Senate Finance Committee said:[15]

In order to protect American producers and manufacturers, who may fear hasty or ill-considered action without their being given a chance to present their views, section 4 was added providing for public notice to be given.

In discussing the measure on the floor of the Senate, the following statements were made by Senator Borah of Idaho:[16]

Referring * * * to section 4, it says:

"Before any foreign-trade agreement is concluded with any foreign government." That contemplates that a trade agreement with a foreign country has been under consideration, but has not yet been concluded. * * * That is, in a measure the minds of the parties will have met; and then, before the agreement shall have been concluded, the President will take counsel of whomever he desires to hear from.

[A]s a practical proposition, when we begin to negotiate * * * we will not advertise in the United States that we are contemplating a negotiation * * *. We will first meet with [the foreign country] and in a measure we will meet [their] minds * * *. After we have done so, before the matter is concluded, the parties at home will be given an opportunity to be heard. That, in my judgment, will be the practical working of the bill. * * *

---

[13] H. Rept. 594, 79th Cong. (1945), p. 16.
[14] Id., p. 7.
[15] S. Rept. 871, 73d Cong., 2d sess., p. 3.
[16] Congressional Record, 73d Cong., 2d sess., pp. 8995, 8996.

The reason for such an approach as this was revealed by a statement made by Senator Harrison, of Mississippi:[17]

* * * naturally, there would be no need to serve notice that we contemplated doing a certain thing and have a lot of people come in and protest, and so forth, or give their advice, unless the other country had been sounded out as to whether or not they would even listen to some kind of proposal. * * *

When the bill, as amended, was reported back to the House, some question arose as to the form which the public notice would take, leading to the following colloquy between Congressman Snell, of New York, and Congressman Doughton, of North Carolina, chairman of the House Ways and Means Committee and the bills sponsor:[18]

Mr. SNELL. Does the gentleman understand by that language that * * * they would definitely state in the announcement that it was on * * * [a particular] product, or would it simply refer to a general trade agreement * * *?

Mr. DOUGHTON. The details, of course, would have to be made known on inquiry; but when it is suggested that a trade agreement will be negotiated with the government of any country, that gives notice. It is generally known what commodities as to which that country would be interested in entering into an agreement.

Mr. SNELL. But when we consider a country that sends a great many different kinds of imports into this country, it seems to me it would be very indefinite. * * *

Apparently sensing the merit of this contention, Chairman Doughton replied:[19]

I may say * * * I have not the slightest doubt that the President will give due notice to any individual or corporation that may be affected or might be interested in any trade agreement he proposes to negotiate. * * *

Having secured an opening, Congressman Snell pressed his advantage:[20]

* * * it is the opinion of the chairman of the committee that at least the probabilities are that the administration will tell the country the articles which they propose to consider for trade agreements?

Chairman Doughton, judiciously retreating, said:[21]

I would not want to go that far. * * *

* * * * * * *

This is my individual opinion. * * *

It is rather generally understood that a major purpose of the hearings conducted by the Committee for Reciprocity Information, which functions as the President's agent under section 4 of the act, is to provide domestic producers with an opportunity to inform the Government agencies represented on the Committee of the problems which would be created for them if the tariff were reduced on imported products which were competitive with their production. When the Congress enacted the peril-point procedure, first in the 1948 extension act, and then subsequently in the 1951 extension act, doubt was expressed in some quarters as to whether the hearings of the Committee for Reciprocity Information were any longer necessary. Since the Tariff Commission made an investigation, including public hearings, of the effect of the proposed tariff reductions on domestic products,

---

[17] Congressional Record, 73d Cong., 2d sess., p. 8995.
[18] Id., p. 10628.
[19] Congressional Record, 73d Cong., 2d sess., p. 10628.
[20] Ibid.
[21] Ibid.

it was suggested that the hearings by the Committee for Reciprocity Information were a needless duplication. The Congress itself understood that the separate CRI hearings were necessary in any event—

in order that a segment of the American economy can have an opportunity to be heard. This segment is vastly larger than the one which appears at the Tariff Commission hearing. It consists of people interested in exports; it consists of people who are interested in better international relations; it consists of consumers; it consists of a predominant part of labor; it consists of a large share of the farmers.[22]

*Conduct of the negotiations*

As revealed by the testimony and debates during consideration of the 1934 act, it is clear that the proponents of the bill envisioned the conduct of the negotiations which the President would be authorized to make as being bilateral negotiations with the principal supplier of one or a few commodities with respect to those particular commodities.

To be sure, the bill was unspecific about this bilateral concept of negotiations; the language was (and is) that the President may "enter into foreign-trade agreements with foreign governments," and some concern was expressed by Senator Steiwer, of Oregon, in the Senate debate on the bill, that such broad language would vest the President with authority to go way beyond the bilateral-agreement concept:[23]

* * * he may, if he chooses, enter into 1 agreement with 1 government; he may enter into 2 agreements with 2 governments; he may enter into 1 agreement with many governments; he may enter into a number of agreements with governments in combination. There is no restraint upon the President with respect to that matter; * * *.

To this statement, Senator Borah, of Idaho, replied:[24]

I cannot help but believe that * * * was the design of the framers of the bill. Otherwise, the President would be greatly embarrassed in dealing with the subject. I think it was the design to give the President complete power over the subject.

However, since this colloquy flies directly in the face of the express statements of Secretary Hull, the "father" of the bill, that bilateral negotiations were the contemplated manner of exercising the power to be given, it would seem that little or no weight should be accorded Senator Borah's comments.

The bilateral character of the anticipated negotiations was stressed by Secretary Hull in his testimony before the House Ways and Means Committee:[25]

If it is once agreed that a normal amount of trade among nations is a vital and necessary factor in the restoration of full and stable prosperity, the conclusion seems clear that the proposed policy of *bilateral trade agreements* offers virtually the only feasible and practical step in this direction. [Emphasis added.]

Again:[26]

Nothing would be done blindly or hastily. The economic situation in every country has been so thoroughly dislocated and disorganized that the people affected must exercise patience while their respective governments go forward with such remedial undertakings as the proposed bilateral bargaining arrangements.

---

[22] H. Rept. 19, 81st Cong. (1949), pp. 4–7.
[23] Congressional Record, 73d Cong., 2d sess., p. 10201.
[24] Congressional Record, 73d Cong., 2d sess., p. 10202.
[25] House hearings, p. 2.
[26] Id., p. 4.

Also, in explaining the manner in which the negotiations would be handled, Secretary Hull said that each country would sit down and ascertain whether it has a commodity that others can afford profitably to purchase, and then "wherever *two countries* find commodities that might be exchanged with mutual profit" the negotiations would be pursued with regard to reciprocal concessions.[27] [Emphasis added.] Furthermore, in the House debate, Congressman West, of Ohio, said, in emphasizing the need for this legislation:[28]

> * * * unless some method of this character of dealing specifically *with individual nations* with respect to particular commodities * * * there is absolutely no way of meeting the problem * * *. [Emphasis added.]

In conducting the bilateral negotiations, it was also intended that the contract would be primarily with those countries which were the principal suppliers of one or more commodities, according to Secretary Hull.[29]

The House Ways and Means Committee stated its understanding that the authority to negotiate trade-agreement concessions would be so limited, as follows:[30]

> A survey of the situation indicates that almost every important commercial country is the principal supplier of certain articles to the United States. The reciprocity agreements will deal primarily with the articles of which the other parties to them are, respectively, the principal supplier to this country. The result is that, from the point of view of both sound policy and political procedure, the rule of equality should prevail.

This was also brought out in a colloquy between Congressman Treadway of Massachusetts and Secretary Hull:[31]

> Mr. TREADWAY. Wherever was the principal source of importation, you would negotiate in that country * * *?
>
> Mr. HULL. Yes, that is correct * * *.

In discussing further the mechanics of the negotiations, Secretary Hull made it clear that the area of negotiating was to be limited. At one point he said:[32]

> * * * our purpose is to make a beginning by picking out one item very carefully here, another commodity over there very carefully * * *.

On another occasion, he said:[33]

> As I have already said, the whole world is in a hard knot so far as its economic international affairs are concerned. We want to see if that condition cannot be attacked in some way and liberalized before so many nations get choked to death. This is a limited method, operated by singling out a leading commodity we buy from one country and ascertaining whether we can enter into * * * arrangements that would be equally profitable to us and the other countries.

This concept of limited scope was also propounded by Congressman West.

From the foregoing it is clear that the administration, speaking through the man who fathered the legislation, was seeking—and intended to use—only such power as was necessary to negotiate bilateral agreements with regard to a limited field of commodities, conducted

[27] House hearings, p. 27.
[28] Congressional Record, 83d Cong.,2d sess., p. 5624.
[29] House hearings, p. 10.
[30] H. Rept. 1000, 73d Cong., 2d sess., p. 15.
[31] House hearings, p. 14.
[32] Id., p. 24.
[33] Id., p. 15.

between our Excutive and representatives of the country which was the principal supplier of each commodity.

The bilateral nature of the trade-agreement negotiations which were authorized was stressed further in the 1943 extension act. The House Ways and Means Committee in its report discussed the administration of the act as a bilateral undertaking: [34]

When it has been determined to attempt negotiation of a trade agreement with any country * * *. The notice names the country * * *. Upon the announcement * * * that a trade agreement is to be negotiated with a particular country * * *.

## II. Major Deviations in the Trade Agreements Program From the Scope of the Delegated Authority

This section of the paper will examine the extent to which use of the trade-agreements power appears to exceed the lawful scope of the authority delegated by Congress. It will also consider the extent to which the limitations placed upon the use of the trade agreements authority by the policy criteria in section 1 of the 1934 act have been exceeded.

Because of the major differences in the scope of the program during the postwar or GATT era as compared with the bilateral trade agreements of the prewar period, only the postwar agreements and negotiations will be considered.

### A. THE OBJECT OR PURPOSE OF THE POSTWAR AGREEMENTS

In November 1946 the State Department and the President announced preparations for simultaneous trade agreement negotiations with 18 foreign nations. The President issued a statement for the purpose of calling attention to "the true significance of these negotiations, for us and for the world." He said: [35]

They are not solely trade bargains. They are that; but they are much more. They are central to the structure of international economic cooperation under the United Nations. They are necessary to achieve the objectives of the Atlantic Charter and of article VII of our mutual-aid agreements. They are necessary to strengthen and support the foundations of the International Monetary Fund and the International Bank for Reconstruction and Development and to pave the way for the kind of economic world envisaged in the Suggested Charter for an International Trade Organization.

The State Department's announcement described the proposed negotiations as "a further important step in the program of international economic collaboration begun with the Atlantic Charter." It said further that the negotiations were one of the principal means by which the nations then meeting in London to study a suggested charter for an International Trade Organization could supplement "general rules for international commercial and trade relations" such as those set forth in the charter by specific action to reduce or eliminate "barriers to trade." [36]

As is well known, the negotiations held at Geneva in 1947 pursuant to the preparations which were announced in November 1946 cul-

[34] H. Rept. 409, 78th Cong. (1943), p. 9.
[35] Press release, the White House, November 9, 1946.
[36] Department of State press release No. 782, November 9, 1946.

minated in the provisional execution of the General Agreement on Tariffs and Trade in which 23 countries were contracting parties. At a second round of negotiations held at Annecy, France, in 1949, 10 additional countries were accepted as members of GATT.

It is apparent from the above-quoted statements that the essential purpose of the trade-agreement negotiations proposed in 1946 which culminated in GATT was to forge a link in the chain of international organizations which in their totality were viewed at the time as an important structure for international cooperation in the preservation of peace in the postwar era.

The fact that congressional approval was given to other key parts of this structure, such as the International Monetary Fund and the International Bank for Reconstruction and Development, merely emphasizes the unusual nature of GATT as an international organization whose creation was attempted by the United States solely through the Executive's power under the Trade Agreements Act.

It can hardly be said that the immediate object of the negotiations was to promote the export trade of the United States. In late 1946 and for at least several years thereafter the exports of the United States were carried to unprecedented levels by the urgent demand for materials of every category for use in rebuilding the war-devastated countries of Europe and the Far East.

What seems to have happened to the executive department's concept of the scope of the trade-agreement power is this: During the latter part of the war and in the immediate postwar period persons in the executive department were occupied with bold policies of international economic cooperation which, from their point of view, would offer the best possible climate for the establishment of an enduring peace.[37]

These matters were also the concern of the Congress and were exhaustively considered by the Colmer committee.[38] That committee and the executive department seem independently to have concluded that an international conference leading to the cooperation of the nations of the free world in a reduction of trade barriers would be most desirable. It is not apparent, however, that the Colmer committee considered that such a vast undertaking could be carried out under the President's authority under the Trade Agreements Act.[39] Its final report referred to the proposed International Trade Organization as an acceptance by the executive department of the committee's suggestions for the creation of an international conference for a general reduction in trade barriers. From the fact that the nature of the proposed charter for an ITO and the common understanding of its proponents and the Congress was that congressional approval would be required before any such instrumentality could be brought to life, as well as from the fact that the Colmer committee's separate discussion of the advisability of an extension of the Trade Agreements Act seems not related to the establishment of the International Trade Organization, it is fair to conclude that in that commitee's view the Trade Agreements Act was not an instrument for the creation of the international economic order then thought desirable.[40]

[37] Wilcox, A Charter for World Trade (1949), p. 23.
[38] House Special Committee on Postwar Economic Policy and Planning, 79th Cong.
[39] H. Rept. 541, 79th Cong. (1945), pp. 37–40.
[40] H. Rept. 2729, 79th Cong. (1946), pp. 85–87.

In the context of these developments, it seems fair to conclude that the State Department did intend the multilateral negotiations at Geneva in 1947 to be a part though not necessarily a definitive part of the unfolding of the plan for a comprehensive assault upon international economic problems. Its concern then was more predominately related to the creation of the desired facade of international organizations than to any more limited practical objectives such as increasing export markets for products of the United States.

When its timetable for the postwar erection of massive international organizations to bring permanent order into international economic problems was frustrated by the reluctance of the Congress to authorize United States participation in the proposed International Trade Organization, the Department was left in the position of making the best use of the General Agreement on Tariffs and Trade as a substitute instrument of international economic cooperation. This is reflected in the State Department's announcement in April 1950, of the intention to undertake a new round of tariff concessions under GATT at Torquay. Noting that with the nations which were expected to take part in those negotiations, the GATT membership would account for some four-fifths of the world's international commerce, the Department's announcement stated:[41]

> The accession of new countries to the general agreement in the forthcoming negotiations will result in a wider acceptance, by additional trading nations, of the commercial principles upon which the United States economic foreign policy is based. These principles include reduction of unnecessary governmental interference with foreign trade, progressive abolition of discriminatory trade practices, and opportunity for multilateral expansion of foreign trade as a means of raising living standards throughout the world.
>
> It is the belief of the United States that general acceptance of these principles will help solve the problems involved in United States foreign-assistance programs and the "dollar gap" by helping foreign countries to improve their economies, increase their production, and to pay with their own goods and services for United States products which they would like to buy and which United States producers would like to sell abroad. The Torquay conference will thus represent another step in the advancement of the entire economic foreign program of the United States.

The use of the trade agreements authority to secure adherence by the nations of the free world to the commercial principles which had been transferred from the charter for an International Trade Organization to the General Agreement on Tariffs and Trade as a "step in the advancement of the entire economic foreign program of the United States," would seem to transcend the scope of the authority delegated by the Congress. This is so notwithstanding the change in the purpose and objects of the act which took place in the postwar period, as described in section I–A of this paper. It is one thing for the Congress to place trade agreement authority in the hands of the President so that through reciprocal bargaining export markets for products of the United States can be promoted while providing foreign countries with profitable markets in the United States for their products—all with the ultimate objective in mind of strengthening the economies of the nations of the free world as a peace and security measure. It is quite another thing for the Executive to use that authority as a means to bring the nations of the free world into a

[41] Department of State Publication 3819, Commercial Policy Series 126, p. 2.

quasi-international organization whose major benefits were consciously regarded by the United States as the code of "commercial principles" which it would administer rather than the actual increase in trade which could be expected to flow from the tariff concessions exchanged.

This aspect of the Torquay negotiations is emphasized by the State Department's release analyzing the Torquay Protocol to GATT, which stated in part as follows: [42]

> The success of the conference will also be measured by the fact that, when all the countries now in the process of joining the agreement have become parties to it, a total of 38 countries will be bound by a single set of standards regulating the use of tariffs, limiting the use of quotas, internal taxes and restrictions on imports, and providing for all a forum for the adjustment of trade problems of mutual concern.

An even more sweeping claim of power by the Executive under the Trade Agreements Act is illustrated by the negotiations in early 1955 under GATT "for the benefit of Japan." The State Department's release announcing the executive department's intention to enter into such negotiations states that the purposes of the conference was—

> tariff negotiations looking to Japan's full accession to the general agreement, thus enlarging her trade possibilities with other countries as well as with the United States.[43]

As if to underscore the objective of the negotiations, the Department stated that—

> The President has given high priority to expanding of Japan's trading opportunities because of Japan's vital importance to free world mutual security.[44]

The dominant purpose of the negotiations, to strengthen Japan, was further emphasized by the acknowledgment in the release that the list of articles proposed for consideration in the negotiations contained many articles which are of primary interest to countries other than Japan. These were to be used by the United States to purchase concessions for Japan from other countries with whom Japan wished to trade. Thus, the announcement stated: [45]

> For these articles consideration will be given to possible concessions under circumstances where these other countries are also negotiating with Japan under the general agreement and where a concession by the United States would broaden the overall results of the multilateral negotiations through the triangular exchange of benefits.
>
> In addition, because of the extensive and time-consuming nature of the procedures for getting information on possible concessions, there are a relatively few articles of interest primarily to countries which may decide to negotiate with Japan though they have not yet done so. As a general rule no concessions would be made on such products if the country having a primary interest does not complete its negotiations with Japan.

If these statements were not sufficient to establish conclusively that the Executive's purpose in using the trade-agreements authority in the 1955 negotiations was to strengthen Japan's economy as distinct from expanding export markets for United State products, all doubt was removed by the State Department's supplemental announcement in February 1955 advising of additional items which would be considered for possible concessions in the negotiations for the benefit of Japan. This announcement stated: [46]

---

[42] Department of State Publication 4209, Commercial Policy Series 135 (1951), p. 1.
[43] Department of State Publication 5653, Commercial Policy Series 145 (1954), p. i.
[44] Ibid.
[45] Id., p. ii.
[46] Supplemental Notice, Interdepartmental Trade Agreements Organization, February 21, 1955, p. i.

The need for considering additional items in the negotiations involving Japan arises primarily out of developments that have taken place since last November. In some cases, study has indicated serious weaknesses in the bargaining position of the United States in negotiating with some of the third countries that have planned all along to negotiate with Japan and with which the United States may consequently wish to carry on supplemental negotiations to expand benefits to Japan. In others, countries that had previously no firm plans to negotiate have now decided to undertake such negotiations.

When the negotiations had been concluded, the State Department's Analysis of Protocol for Japan's Accession to GATT described the event as "a significant forward step in the reintegration of Japan into the community of the free world" which "marks a notable achievement in the President's foreign economic program, and a fulfillment of arrangements undertaken last year when the 1-year extension of the Trade Agreements Act was sought and obtained." [47] The announcement undertook to explain that Japanese participation in GATT "will help United States interests in a variety of ways." These are described as follows: [48]

Expansion of Japan's foreign trade, which participation in the general agreement will promote, is essential if Japan is to have a sound self-sustaining economy capable of providing adequate living standards for the Japanese people. By offering Japan expanded trade opportunities, participation in the general agrement also will give the Japanese people a concrete basis for continuing their alinement with the free world, thus lessening the danger of enforced Japanese dependence on Communist-dominated areas of the mainland of Asia.

One need not disagree that the objectives referred to above are laudable in order to raise the question as to whether they cannot reasonably be said to lie outside of the scope of the purposes for which the Congress has delegated trade-agreement authority to the Executive. The objects of the Trade Agreements Act have, indeed, been changed from the temporary emergency objectives of the 1934 act to the present purposes of expanding the export and import trade of the United States as a means of strengthening the nations of the free world and thus serving the cause of peace and security. There is as yet no indication, however, that the Congress intended that trade agreement concessions be granted by the United States for the promotion of trade between other countries as distinct from the foreign commerce of the United States with other countries. Since the former had a predominant place in the purpose of the negotiations for the benefit of Japan in 1955, it would appear that in this instance also the President exceeded the proper scope of his authority.

*Unilateral concessions to compensate for escape-clause action*

Under the caption, "Avoidance of injury to domestic industries" in section I–B above, it has been seen that the Congress intended that the use of the trade-agreements authority be limited in order to avoid causing injury to domestic producers. To make explicit the logical corollary to that principle, the Congress in the 1951 extension act provided in section 6 (a) that no concession shall be permitted to continue in effect when it has caused actual or threatened serious injury to domestic producers. The escape-clause procedure, initially established in the Mexican trade agreement in 1942,[49] was a procedural

[47] Department of State Publication 5881, Commercial Policy Series 150 (1955), p. 1.
[48] Ibid.
[49] H. Doc. 328, 82d Cong. (1952), p. 4, note 3.

safeguard to insure that the United States would have the freedom to correct injury which might result from a trade-agreement concession without requiring the termination of the entire trade agreement.

Though the escape-clause procedure has been invoked in 83 instances, recommendations of the Tariff Commission for relief have reached the President in only 26 cases. Of these the President has invoked the escape clause and withdrawn the offending concession in whole or part in only 7 instances.[50]

The Executive has been disposed to grant "compensatory" tariff concessions to the countries deemed to be affected by the withdrawal of the concessions involved in certain of these escape-clause actions. In February 1955 the State Department announced negotiations to compensate Switzerland for the partial withdrawal of the tariff concessions granted on watch movements in the trade agreement with Switzerland. The announcement stated that the escape clause—

> obligates the country taking such action to consult at the request of the other country regarding appropriate measures which would maintain the general level of reciprocal and mutually advantageous concessions in the agreement.[51]

The pertinent portion of the Swiss trade agreement states that the country invoking the escape clause shall afford the other government which is a party to the agreement—

> an opportunity to consult with it in respect of the proposed action and with respect to such compensatory modifications of the trade agreement as may be deemed appropriate, to the extent practicable maintaining the general level of reciprocal and mutually advantageous concessions in the agreement. If agreement between the two Governments is not reached as a result of such consultation, the Government which proposes to take the action under paragraph 1 shall, nevertheless, be free to do so and, if such action is taken, the other Government shall be free, not later than 90 days after the action has been taken and on 30 days' written notice, to suspend the application to the trade of the government taking action under paragraph 1 of substantially equivalent obligations or concessions under said trade agreement.[52]

In view of the unmistakable legislative policy of the United States with respect to the avoidance of injury in trade-agreement negotiations, it is highly questionable that the Executive has the actual authority to interpret the above clause in a manner which would constitute an obligation on the part of the United States to grant compensatory concessions for the withdrawal, in whole or part, of a concession which resulted in serious injury to domestic producers. Furthermore, the premises upon which the negotiations for compensatory concessions proceed appear to be highly questionable. The State Department's analysis of the supplementary trade agreement entered into between the United States and Switzerland in 1955 states that United States imports from Switzerland of the watch movements affected by the withdrawal of the concession were valued at an annual average value of $56.8 million during the 5-year period 1950–54.[53] New concessions were granted to Switzerland covering items for which United States imports in 1954 were valued at $10 million.[54] The withdrawal of the tariff concessions became effective in July

[50] U. S. Tariff Commission, "Investigations Under the Escape Clause" (August 1957), pp. 6–9.
[51] Notice, Interdepartmental Trade Agreements Organization, Feb. 21, 1955, p. 1.
[52] H. Doc. 328, 82d Cong. (1952), p. 10.
[53] Department of State Publication 5880, Commercial Policy Series 149 (1955), p. 1.
[54] Id., p. 2.

1954.[55] The value of United States imports of watch movements in 1956, however, amounted to $57.3 million.[56] Virtually all of the imports came from Switzerland. It is apparent, therefore, that notwithstanding the increase by the United States in the tariff on watch movements to correct the serious injury caused the domestic watch industry, the value of imports from Switzerland has not dropped below the 1950–54 average. There is, therefore, no justification for the "compensation" granted to Switzerland. This is especially true where the value of United States imports of watch movements from Switzerland at or about the time the trade agreement was entered into was less than $6 million a year.[57]

If the policy limitations specified in section 1 of the 1934 act (sec. 350 (a) of the Tariff Act of 1930, as amended) forbidding a reduction of duties which would cause injury to a domestic industry are observed, there is no proper basis for an agreement on the part of the United States that would condition in any way its right to withdraw a concession which violated this principle. On the other hand, any other concessions which are granted under the authority of the Trade Agreements Act would themselves have to qualify under the limiting criteria specified in the Trade Agreements Act, including notably the requirement that concessions be granted in exchange for equivalent concessions secured from another country. It is no justification for the unilateral grant of compensatory concessions that the United States agreed, in entering into the Swiss trade agreement, that it would consider compensating the Swiss if it withdrew a concession, since by definition the concession which would be withdrawn is a concession which either should not have been granted in the first place or which, at least, could not be allowed to remain in effect once it became apparent that the policy of the law with regard to injury was being violated.[58]

Nor is there justification for such compensatory concessions on the ground that the United States regularly receives compensation from other countries which withdraw concessions under article XXVIII of GATT. That article is not an escape clause premised upon the limits in the authority of the withdrawing country to act, as is the case with the United States escape clause. Rather, article XXVIII involves a categorical right in a country to withdraw a concession at the end of the period in which the GATT concessions are bound against modification or withdrawal. The article itself obliges the withdrawing party by agreement with affected parties to endeavor to maintain a general level of concessions not less favorable than that provided for in the agreement. There is no comparable obligation under the escape clause and there is an implied prohibition of such compensatory action, under section 6 of the Trade Agreements Extension Act of 1951 and under the Trade Agreements Act itself, as shown in the above discussion.

---

[55] Id., p. 1

[56] Bureau of Census, Quarterly Summary of the Foreign Commerce of the United States (January–December 1956), p. 30.

[57] U. S. Tariff Commission, Summaries of Tariff Information (1949), vol. 3, pt. 3, p. 216.

[58] Similar action to grant compensatory concessions to affected countries was taken by the United States in both the case of bicycles and linen toweling. The negotiations to compensate for the increase on the duty on bicycles took place under GATT at Geneva in 1956, while those to compensate for the action on linen toweling were concluded in Washington in July 1956.

The United States has also granted compensatory concessions in other circumstances, as where the Congress enacts into law an increase in the tariff applicable to an item otherwise subject to the General Agreement on Tariffs and Trade.[59] It is open to question whether the Trade Agreement Act permits the executive department of the Government to undertake, as in GATT (arts. II, XXII, and XXIII), to commit the United States, directly or indirectly, to grant unilateral concessions in the event that later action by the Congress should affect concessions which have been granted at an earlier date. The principal objection again is that the power to grant tariff concessions in trade agreements is expressly contingent upon the satisfaction of all of the policy limitations spelled out in the Trade Agreements Act. When the United States unilaterally grants a tariff reduction, none of these criteria are called into operation.

It is not an answer to this problem to say that compensation in such circumstances is not unilateral action by the United States because the United States receives in exchange for the compensation an undertaking by the other country not to retaliate by the withdrawal of concessions which it had previously granted the United States. Even if an agreement not to retaliate can be equated to the granting of a concession so as to make it possible to say that the grant of compensatory concessions by the United States would be a reciprocal exchange of concessions, the deficiency in the President's power is not entirely cured. The power to grant a concession is conditioned not alone upon the receipt by the United States of a reciprocal concession, but upon other criteria as well. While the President might conceivably be able to agree in advance that he would grant compensatory concessions in order to prevent a retaliatory withdrawal of concessions by another country, he does not have it within his power to agree that the other policy considerations spelled out in the Trade Agreements Act, which are also a condition precedent to his authority, would be operative.

### B. FAILURE TO OBSERVE THE LIMITATIONS UPON THE EXECUTIVE'S TRADE AGREEMENTS AUTHORITY

Contemporary use of the trade-agreements authority is limited almost entirely to the operations of the United States under the General Agreement on Tariffs and Trade. An analysis of the acts of the United States in the name of the trade-agreement authority necessarily depends, therefore, upon an examination of the actions which the United States has taken or in which it has acquiesced as a member of the contracting parties of GATT.

*Avoidance of injury*

The Tariff Commission in 26 escape-clause cases has forwarded a recommendation to the President for the withdrawal of the trade-agreement concession on the ground that increased imports resulting from the concessions had caused or threatened serious injury to a domestic industry. In 17 of these cases the President has refused to

[59] See, e. g., agreements compensating Canada in re Public Law 689, 83d Cong., and the Benelux countries in re Public Law 479, 83d Cong., both entered into at Geneva on June 8, 1955. State Department press release No. 331, June 9, 1955.

invoke the escape clause (2 cases are pending and the President increased the tariff in 7 cases). In 16 of the 17 cases in which the President refused to act, the offending concession was granted by the United States under the General Agreement on Tariffs and Trade.[60] Regardless of whether or not the President's failure to place the Tariff Commission's recommendations into effect was a permissible exercise of his discretion in the national interest, the fact remains that a responsible agency, after a full investigation, found in each instance that a concession had been granted by the United States under GATT which had resulted in serious injury to a domestic industry. In each of these cases the policy criteria contained in the Trade Agreements Act which limits the power of the President to grant a concession where it would cause serious injury have therefore been exceeded.

It may be argued that in view of the many thousands of concessions which the United States has granted under the general agreement, the relatively small number of injury findings by the Tariff Commission is an indication of care on the part of the President in the exercise of his authority.

It is difficult to ascertain the actual degree of care which is exercised by the executive department in the selection of items for consideration in proposed negotiations so as to avoid the possibility of causing serious injury to domestic producers. The enactment of the peril-point procedure in 1948 and its reenactment in 1951 would seem to represent a judgment by the Congress itself that adequate consideration was not being given by those in the executive department charged with the responsibility for preparing for trade-agreement negotiations.

The House Ways and Means Committee, in reporting the 1951 extension bill, indicated that the small number of escape-clause proceedings which had then been filed (20) was an indication of—

> the care with which the authority given to the President to reduce the tariffs by the Trade Agreements Act has been administered.[61]

As the committee noted, the escape clause had been in effect since 1943, but a formal procedure for its invocation by domestic producers was not established until Executive Order 9832 dated February 25, 1947. The 20 cases referred to by the committee during the 8 years that the escape clause had then been in effect must be contrasted with the 63 cases which were filed subsequent to the time of the committee's report in 1951 to the present.

At one time, though during the GATT era, there was an indication "that calculated risks affecting domestic producers" were taken in the preparations for trade-agreement negotiations.[62] Little or no specific information is available as to the manner in which persons in the executive department, charged with the preparation of the list of

---

[60] The President declined to invoke the escape clause in the following cases (involving GATT concessions): Garlic (July 21, 1952); tobacco pipes and bowls (November 10, 1953); scissors and shears (May 11, 1954); groundfish fillets (second investigation) (July 2, 1954); lead and zinc (August 20, 1954); handmade blown glassware (September 9, 1954); spring clothespins (third investigation) (November 20, 1954); screen-printed silk scarves (December 23, 1954); wood screws (third investigation) (December 23, 1954); fluorspar, acid grade (second investigation) (March 20, 1956); para-aminosalicylic acid and salts thereof (August 10, 1956); ferrocerium (lighter flints) (November 13, 1956); groundfish fillets (third investigation) (December 10, 1956); velveteen fabrics (January 22, 1957); straight pins (second investigation) (Mar. 29, 1957); violins and violas (March 30, 1957).

[61] H. Rept. 14, 82d Cong., (1951), p. 2.

[62] S. Rept. 1558, 80th Cong. (1948), p. 3.

items for negotiation, give effect to the criteria which the Trade Agreements Act imposes by way of limitation upon the exercise of the President's authority. Perhaps the most complete description of the procedure followed is the memorandum and testimony of Carl D. Corse, of the State Department, in hearings before the Subcommittee on Customs, Tariffs, and Reciprocal Trade Agreements of the House Committee on Ways and Means last year.[63] That description may be summarized as follows:

1. President decides to negotiate.
2. Trade Agreements Committee appoints "country subcommittees" (specialists on trade with the country involved).
3. Country subcommittees study data in Government files and reports of commodity experts from Tariff Commission and Departments of Commerce and Agriculture, and pick items of which United States is principal exporter to X and of which X is principal exporter to United States. (Special export items may also be included.)
4. List is submitted to Trade Agreements Committee along with supporting data.
5. Trade Agreements Committee reviews list, scrutinizes supporting data for each item, makes modifications, and sends list to President. (There may be communication back and forth with country subcommittee re adding or removing offers or requests.)
6. President decides whether to negotiate and, if so, which items will be negotiated.
7. President sends list to Tariff Commission for peril-point proceeding. Public notice of intent to negotiate; list published (each item).
8. Committee for Reciprocity Information announces hearing.
9. Committee for Reciprocity Information hearing:
    (*a*) Written memo required in advance;
    (*b*) Analyzed by Government experts before hearing; and
    (*c*) Request for comments re concessions to be asked.
10. Informal conferences and discussions with interested private parties.
11. Peril-point hearings by Tariff Commission.
12. Copies of briefs furnished to members of the Trade Agreements Committee, country subcommittees, and others interested in hearings before hearing.
13. All transcripts, briefs, etc., available to negotiators.
14. After hearing, the information elicited is given to country subcommittees, which study it along with briefs, studies, and material in Government files. May recommend supplemental list on basis of recommendations made at hearing.
15. Country subcommittees decide whether concession should be granted and, if so, of what nature.
16. The study is presented to the Trade Agreements Committee, which reviews it item by item, getting information from the country subcommittees and Government experts as well as studies on hand and results of the CRI and Tariff Commission hearings, and approves, modifies, or rejects. Things considered—
    (*a*) Relation of imports to domestic production;
    (*b*) Is the comparable domestic industry on a net export basis;

[63] Hearings, 84th Cong. (1956), pt. 2, pp. 1068 et seq.

(*c*) Size and diversity of domestic industry;

(*d*) National-security aspects; consultation with Office of Defense Mobilization;

(*e*) Are wages of industry in principal exporting country substandard (result of Randall Commission recommendation);

(*f*) Possibility of concession on only part of tariff category under consideration;

(*g*) Possibility of using quotas and other devices;

(*h*) Are our offers adequate or out of line re concessions we may reasonably expect;

(*i*) Would a concession to X jeopardize chances for future negotiation with Y, which also is an important source of the product;

(*j*) What is the status of the domestic industry—healthy;

(*k*) Is the item subject to section 22 of the Agricultural Adjustment Act;

(*l*) Are the contemplated concessions well balanced; and

(*m*) Peril-point findings.

17. The Trade Agreements Committee recommendations go to the President.

18. The President reviews the report, especially recommendations below peril point and those not unanimous, and gives O. K.

19. Negotiators are representatives of the Departments of State, Commerce, Agriculture, and sometimes Treasury, and of the Tariff Commission (advisory only).

20. Negotiators are authorized to make concessions as recommended if they can get concessions requested.

21. Negotiators report to Trade Agreements Committee if they feel departure from original limits of authority is desirable.

22. Trade Agreements Committee considers the request, and if merited refers the request to the President with its recommendation.

23. The President makes a decision and the negotiators proceed accordingly.

24. If additional items are involved, must have publication, hearings, peril-point determination, etc.

25. When negotiations are complete, they are integrated into a single document, which is reviewed by the Trade Agreements Committee and referred to the President, who approves them and his representative signs.

It is not apparent from the above procedure that any specific attention is given to the possibility that an item under consideration might cause injury to a domestic industry until after the preliminary list is published and has been made the subject of hearings. Step 16 suggests, though hardly conclusively, in topics (*a*), (*c*), and (*j*), that some general consideration may be given to factors which have a bearing on the question of injury. Topic (*m*), the peril-point findings of the Tariff Commission, represents the Tariff Commission's judgment on whether or not there would be injury. This, while an important supplementary safeguard, is not an adequate substitute for the direct consideration and exercise of judgment on the question of injury by the executive department personnel themselves. This is so because, within the executive department, a series of country subcommittees go over the items to be proposed for consideration for a more extensive period of time than the Tariff Commission, and with fewer products to consider. The Tariff Commission is forced to make its investigation, including public hearings, on the entire list within the space of 120 days. In the GATT area, the entire list commonly consists of many hundreds of tariff paragraph provisions and thousands of statistical classifications of commodities. The strangeness of the procedure, the inability of many business organizations to know that a concession is under consideration which would affect their products—all combine to prevent the Tariff Commission's peril-point findings, though helpful, from being a definitive determination that a reduction can be made without causing injury.

A crucial consideration in an understanding of whether or not the above preparatory procedure sufficiently encompasses the limiting criteria of avoiding injury to domestic producers is the composition of the country subcommittees. It is said that these are staffed by persons in the various executive departments who are experts in the trade and commerce of the country in question. Such persons would not seem to offer the best possibility of applying an informed judgment on the question of possible injury to a domestic industry. In the 1955 and 1956 trade-agreement negotiations of GATT, it appears that experts in the characteristics and needs of domestic industries were given an opportunity to express a viewpoint to the country subcommittees during the preparatory stage of the negotiations. The country subcommittees themselves, however, appeared to retain the final voice and, therefore, applied the basic judgment as to whether or not a concession on particular articles would be likely to result in injury to the domestic producers.

The seeming paucity of informed judgment from the domestic producers' viewpoint during the preparatory stage is underscored by the fact that the Tariff Commission, in supplying data to the country subcommittees, appears to be limited to a résumé of import data bearing on the articles for which particular countries are the principal producers. The Tariff Commission contains probably the greatest single body of expert judgment on domestic industry matters of any agency of the Government (though the Business and Defense Services Administration of the Department of Commerce has acquired a commendable degree of expertise in these matters also). To limit the Tariff Commission during the preparatory stage to the submission of statistical summaries bearing solely on the quantum of import trade in principal products exported by the countries under consideration is an unfortunate waste of the abilities of that agency at a stage of the preparations where their judgment would appear to be of key importance.

It is not a sufficient answer to this deficiency in the mode of action which apparently has been adopted by the Executive to point to the membership on the country subcommittees of a representative of the Tariff Commission. Considering that the range of products with which a country subcommittee may be occupied would involve many different domestic industries, it is not seen how the participation of the Tariff Commission through advisory membership on the country subcommittees could supply the type of informed evaluation which should be exercised in the preparation of the preliminary list so as to keep items off the list which would be likely to result in injury to domestic producers if a concession were granted. It is not evident, in any event, that the country subcommittees give any significant consideration to the injury-potential aspect of the matter at any time during the preparations which culminate in the publication of the preliminary list.

*Bargaining for a reciprocal exchange of concessions to expand market opportunities*

The nature of the concessions which can be put into effect by the President under the trade-agreement authority is described in the act as including not only modifications of existing duties and other import restrictions, but also such continuance for such minimum period of existing customs or excise treatment as is required or appropriate to carry out a trade agreement. This language is the basis for United States action in binding an existing rate of duty or in binding the existing treatment of an item on the free list as a concession which may be offered in trade-agreement negotiations. Very little light is thrown on the particular meaning of this language in the legislative history of the Trade Agreements Act. Taking into view the historical context in which the act was origially adopted, it is reasonable to postulate that the Congress wished to give the President freedom to promise a foreign country that the United States would continue unchanged an existing favorable treatment of imports from that country if the foreign country would reduce an unduly burdensome duty which was restricting exports from the United States.

There is support for this view in the legislative history of the Trade Agreements Act, as developed in section I–B of this paper. Senator Vandenberg's reference to the practice of foreign countries putting the rates up prior to negotiations in the hope that they can bargain them back down would suggest that the Congress had in mind that, among other means, the President would carry out bargaining by promising to hold the United States duty at a particular level in order to secure the reduction of a foreign duty. Normally, however, the legislative history referred to shows that Congress intended the concessions exchanged to be mutually profitable to the parties to the agreement. Though the objectives and purposes of the act appear to have changed in the 23 years of its existence, the means and technique to be employed in achieving the purposes have remained the same. It is reasonably inferable from the legislative history that Congress specifically intended that action by the United States under the trade-agreements authority, where otherwise appropriate, would be reasonably calculated to result in an expansion of the exports of the United States to the country concerned. This result would be achieved by requiring each concession by the United States to be bought or paid for by an equivalent concession.

Contrary to this intention, the United States has, to an increasing extent, acceped various types of bindings of existing customs treatment as concessions which authorize the reduction of United States duties. In the 1956 negotiations at Geneva under GATT, a type of action considerably more remote from an actual reduction in duty than a mere binding was accepted as a concession. This was the agreement by a country not to raise a duty above a specified, higher level.[64] The very high proportion of the concessions received by the

[64] U. S. Tariff Commission, Operation of the Trade Agreements Program, Ninth Report (1957), p. 92.

United States which are in the form of bindings strongly suggests that the expansion in United States exports which can be expected as a result of the concessions will be much smaller than the volume of items exchanged would otherwise indicate.[65]

The United States appears to follow this practice because of a rule of the contracting parties [66] rather than the exercise of the Executive's judgment on the merits in each case. This emphasizes the conclusion, forced by the State Department's description of the procedure, that the Trade Agreements Act's requirement of a "finding of fact" that existing duties are "unduly burdensome" and that the agreed concessions will further the purposes of the act is treated as a mere formality. This certainly was not the intention of the Congress in specifying the requirement for those findings of fact.

The following table shows the number of bindings compared with actual reductions in duty accepted by the United States as concessions in the 1956 negotiations under GATT:

*Nature of concessions obtained by the United States*

| From | Reductions in duty | Bindings | Remarks |
|---|---|---|---|
| Austria | 19 | 6 | |
| Benelux | 16 | 25 | Novel "concessions" included in the bargains received by the United States were 3 reductions in legal rates for items in which duties had temporarily been suspended, a binding of the existing rates of duty on 3 items which had previously been bound under GATT to other countries and to which treatment the United States was entitled under the most-favored-nation clause of the agreement, and 1 item where it was agreed not to increase the duty above a specified level. |
| Canada | 69 | 48 | Canada also transferred 15 items to the free list, but it increased rates of duty on 3 items, transferred 2 more from the free list to the dutiable list, and increased the current rate of duty on 5 of the items for which it lowered the GATT rate. |
| Chile | 22 | 1 | The basic duty was also reduced on 1 item which now enters duty-free. |
| Cuba | 5 | ------- | |
| Denmark | 3 | 17 | |
| Dominican Republic | 10 | 8 | |
| Finland | 13 | 10 | 2 items transferred to the free list. |
| France | 16 | 7 | |
| West Germany | 55 | 71 | Germany has statutory rates and "effective" rates. This table is based on a comparison of the concession granted and the effective rate. The statutory rate was reduced on 12 items currently entering free of duty. Two items transferred to the free list. Duty on 16 items was increased over a lower currently effective rate. Through the High Authority of the European Coal and Steel Community Germany granted the United States an additional 6 concessions in the form of reductions in duty. |
| Haiti | 9 | 1 | |
| Italy | 38 | 29 | Italy also bound 7 items above the temporary rates of duty and eliminated the temporary rates on 2 items. |
| Japan | 47 | 25 | |
| Norway | 10 | 8 | 1 item transferred to the free list. |
| Peru | 9 | -------- | 2 items were reduced from 11.667 to 11.5 percent; 7 items were reduced from 13.667 to 12.5 percent. |
| Sweden | 10 | 9 | 3 items transferred to the free list. |
| Turkey | 20 | 5 | |
| United Kingdom | 66 | 8 | |

There is another major fallacy in the interpretation which the executive department places upon the policy criteria specified in the act calling for an exchange of concessions—

[65] U. S. Tariff Commission, Operation of the Trade Agreements Program, Ninth Report (1957), ch. 3, pp. 109 et seq.; Department of State Publication 6348, Commercial Policy Series 158, pp. 8 et seq.

[66] H. Doc. 93, 85th Cong. (1957), p. 20.

so that foreign markets will be made available to those branches of American production which require and are capable of developing such outlets by affording corresponding market opportunities for foreign products in the United States.

The State Department values the concessions for bargaining purposes by taking the value of United States exports of the products on which concessions are offered by a foreign country and comparing it with the value of United States imports of the products on which the United States proposes to offer concessions to that foreign country. The process seems to consist entirely of adding or subtracting items measured by their import and export values until a rough balance in terms of value of trade is achieved.[67] The State Department traditionally describes the concessions given and obtained in terms of the value of the exports and imports of the commodities to which the concessions apply.[68]

It is puzzling to relate this approach to the concept of a reciprocal exchange of concessions to one of the clear and abiding purposes of the Trade Agreements Act, described in section I of this paper, of making available foreign markets for branches of American production which require and are capable of developing such markets by granting corresponding market opportunities to foreign producers. The thought which seems to be contained in the statutory language is that the bargaining power of the trade-agreements authority will be used to open up market opportunities which do not exist at the time the negotiations take place so that American producers who require such outlets for their surplus production and who are capable of taking advantage of the commercial opportunities thus presented will be able to increase their exports. Indeed, the meaning of this language seems to have been summed up succinctly by Senator Gore, of Oklahoma, a member of the Senate Finance Committee during the debate on the 1934 act, when he stated:[69]

We must exchange what we have and do not want for what we want and do not have. * * * We must prevail upon the foreigner to relax his restrictions against our exports and in order to do that we may be obliged to relax our restrictions against his exports to this country.

If a substantial volume of trade between the United States and a foreign country is taking place, as evidenced by imports and exports significant in value, it would seem that there is little or at least less occasion to secure a reduction in the tariff which each country maintains on the products concerned than if the authority of the act were to be turned toward a reduction of tariffs on those items where there was little or no volume of trade because the tariff (in the language of the Trade Agreements Act) was "unduly burdening or restricting" commerce in the product.

In short, the meaning of the Trade Agreements Act and the intended use which the Congress had in mind would seem more to liken the President's authority to a scalpel which would be used to carve away with precision those unnecessary obstructions to the bloodstream of

---

[67] See memorandum submitted by Carl Corse, hearings, Subcommittee on Customs, etc., House Ways and Means Committee, 83d Cong. (1956), pt. 2, p. 1079.

[68] See, for example, Department of State Publication 6348, Commercial Policy Series 158 (1956), p. 1.

[69] Congressional Record, 73d Cong., 2d sess., p. 10357.

commerce which prevented circulation at all, than as an administration of a stimulant to secure some temporary burst of extraordinary activity in a normally functioning system.

Certainly the number of articles which have been placed into negotiations by the United States in the GATT sessions belie any concentration by the Executive on a selective process which would place into bargaining only those requests and offers which relate to trade barriers in fact "unduly burdening or restricting the foreign commerce of the United States." In 1947, the United States list included nearly 2,000 import classifications. At Torquay in 1950 the United States list embraced nearly 2,800 statistical classifications of imports. Even the more limited negotiations for the benefit of Japan resulted in a United States list containing some 600 statistical classifications, while the Geneva negotiations in 1956 covered more than 1,000 import classifications.

If, as it clearly appears from the above analysis, the Executive considers that actions or affirmations by a foreign government resulting in no change in the customs treatment accorded United States exports may appropriately be accepted in exchange for United States concessions, how can a prime policy criterion of the act limiting the use of the trade-agreements authority to occasions which would provide market opportunities for United States producers who require them be satisfied? There is no possible answer to this question which can validate the use to which the trade-agreements authority has been placed in the negotiations under GATT.

*Discriminatory practices against United States trade*

The initial exchange of concessions is not an end to the matter of trade-agreement administration. The policy of the Trade Agreements Act requires—

> That the President shall, as soon as practicable, suspend the application [of trade-agreements concessions] to articles the growth, produce, or manufacture of any country because of its discriminatory treatment of American commerce or because of other acts (including the operations of international cartels) or policies which in his opinion tend to defeat the purpose of this section.

Though the above provision appears as a proviso to the most-favored-nation section of the Trade Agreements Act,[70] the principle expressed requiring the withdrawal of the benefits of trade-agreement concessions from countries which discriminate against United States commerce should be as fully applicable to discrimination practiced by the country to which the concession was granted as to other countries who enjoy the most-favored-nation benefit of United States concessions.

It would seem to follow from the very nature of the limitations imposed upon the President's right to extend concessions that any action by a foreign country, as a recipient of the concession, which has the effect of nullifying the concession granted to the United States should require the withdrawal by the United States of the concession which it made in that exchange.

There are, unfortunately, many instances in which the United States has tolerated discriminatory action against its commerce by a

[70] Sec. 350 (a) (4) of the Tariff Act of 1930, as amended, Public Law 86, 84th Cong.

member of the General Agreement on Tariffs and Trade or seemingly acquiesced in the discrimination as a result of some action or principle contained in GATT rather than obeying the mandate of the statutory principle quoted above. For example, the First Annual Report of the President on the Trade Agreements Program,[71] in describing the "complaints" procedure of GATT, states that under that procedure—

the United States can bring a case against the country imposing unwarranted restrictions on United States trade and can seek a recommendation from the Contracting Parties for action that will help to obtain a relaxation or removal of those restrictions.[72]

Such a procedure is contrary to the no-discrimination proviso in the most-favored-nation section of the Trade Agreements Act. If, as is frequently asserted by the executive department, GATT was executed by the United States under the authority of the Trade Agreements Act, it cannot properly involve the United States in a procedure which prevents it from obeying any categorical directives contained in the Trade Agreements Act.

The position of the United States with regard to the widespread acceptance of bindings of existing customs treatment as a concession in negotiations under GATT may also have resulted from the collective decision of the contracting parties to GATT rather than an independent judgment by the United States representatives as to the requirements of our Trade Agreements Act under which they were assuming to act. It appears that the contracting parties adopted a negotiating rule which was used at the various GATT sessions providing that the binding of an existing low rate of duty should be considered as equivalent to the reduction of a high rate of duty.[73]

There are several things wrong with the adherence by the United States to such a rule. It obviously takes away from the President the discretion which the Trade Agreements Act requires him to exercise in evaluating concessions offered in trade-agreement negotiations both from their suitability to accomplish the purposes of the act and from the point of view of their conformance to the limiting principles set forth in the act.

An agreement by the United States through adherence to article XII of GATT to tolerate discrimination against United States exports in the form of quantitative restrictions imposed ostensibly for balance-of-payments reasons, is another example of action contrary to the requirements of the Trade Agreements Act. It is not a sufficient answer to this objection to point to the problems faced by foreign countries in controlling inflation. If the discrimination practiced against United States exports would oblige the United States under the terms and spirit of the Trade Agreements Act to withdraw concessions previously granted relating to the items on which the discrimination is practiced, or to suspend most-favored-nation benefits to the discriminating country, the mandate of the statute should not be set aside by an Executive judgment as to the merits of the foreign country's action.

In many instances the quantitative restrictions which are imposed against United States exports nullify the benefit of the concessions which the United States bargained for in granting United States

[71] H. Doc. 93, 85th Cong. (1957).
[72] Id., p. 7.
[73] Id., p. 20.

tariff reductions under the Trade Agreements Act. Of the 43 countries with which the United States had trade agreements in force during the period 1955–56, 27 restrict imports for balance of payments reasons and discriminate between sources of supply.[74] Since the effect of these restrictions is directly contrary to the benefits which the Trade Agreements Act is intended to secure for the export trade of the United States, it is difficult to see how the action of the United States in participating in GATT with its acceptance of the use of restrictions for balance-of-payments reasons can be defended as being within the scope of the act.[75]

When the executive department has been challenged in the past as to the authority of the President to execute a multilateral agreement, such as GATT, containing general commercial policy rules applicable by their terms to the entire foreign commerce of its nation members, the explanation is offered that these provisions are authorized under the Trade Agreements Act because they are appropriate or necessary to protect the value of the concessions which have been secured by the United States through trade-agreement bargaining. Such an answer proves too much, however, because many of the provisions of GATT clearly apply to articles which are not the subject of concessions, or they transcend any rational relationship to the mere protection of the benefit of those concessions.

The Government's dilemma regarding section 104 of the Defense Production Act and section 22 of the Agricultural Adjustment Act is a case in point. Commencing with the sixth session of the contracting parties of GATT in 1951, continuous pressure has been applied against the United States to repeal section 104 and to conform the scope of section 22 to the permissible limits of action set forth in article XII of GATT.[76] Section 104 expired by its own terms, but section 22 continues very much in force. At the ninth session of the contracting parties the United States finally succeeded in securing a waiver which would permit it to apply section 22 without being held to be inconsistent with "its obligations" under the general agreement.[77]

The exact nature of the conflict of section 22 with GATT consists in the possibility of an import fee being imposed on an agricultural product whose tariff has been reduced or bound by a concession granted under GATT; or the imposition of an import quota where corresponding restrictions are not imposed on the domestic production of the agricultural product concerned.

Quotas imposed by the United States under section 22 on imports of cheese and other dairy products have called forth the principal complaint. The report of the chairman of the United States delegation to the ninth session of GATT states that the waiver (and other desired United States action) was granted because the other nations who are members of GATT—

> recognized that wholeheated participation of the United States was essential to the continued successful operation of the general agreement.[78]

---

[74] U. S. Tariff Commission, Operation of the Trade Agreements Program, ninth report (1957), p. 231.

[75] The initiative of the United States in securing the current consultations with GATT members on the need for their continuing trade restrictions for balance-of-payments reasons, while commendable, emphasizes the relative acquiescence by the United States in discrimination under GATT. GATT Press Release 332 and State Department Press Release 403, July 1, 1957.

[76] Id., p. 31.

[77] Id., p. 55.

[78] Id., p. 90.

Some additional light is thrown upon the position of the executive department in extricating itself from the dilemma created by the direct conflict between United States domestic law (sec. 22) and the principles of GATT to which they have assumed to commit the United States under authority of the Trade Agreements Act. The Executive Secretary of GATT, in an address delivered in December 1956, referred to this dilemma and the action taken on the United States request for a waiver, as follows: [79]

> The United States Government is acutely aware of this as a United States domestic problem. It is also acutely aware that it creates serious external problems as well. The domestic support program makes it necessary for the United States to impose restrictions on imports from third countries and thus **it puts the United States in a position of not being able to carry out a consistent international economic policy.** The United States has been in the forefront of the countries which, mainly through the GATT, have fought for the restoration of a multilateral trading system. At the same time, the policy of agricultural import restrictions cuts across this general direction of United States policy and weakens its position in international discussions on these matters. The United States is, therefore, extremely sensitive to the political pressures which bear upon its policy in relation to agricultural imports. *In order to take account of these difficulties and in order to put the United States in a position to go to Congress and seek the ratification of the Agreement on the Organization for Trade Cooperation, the contracting parties found it necessary to give the United States a waiver leaving the United States free, so far as GATT is concerned, to take measures affecting agricultural imports which are necessary to give effect to the domestic price-support program.* [Emphasis added.]

It is evident that the United States received a waiver because the members of GATT came to believe that refusal to yield on the point would jeopardize the chances for favorable action by an aroused Congress on United States participation in OTC.

It may be appropriate for a trade agreement to contain provisions defining the rights of the parties if one or the other takes an action which is inconsistent with a concession granted. It is quite a different thing for a party such as the United States to commit itself to rules of conduct for foreign trade in the course of exchanging concessions dealing with a segment of its foreign trade which would prevent the legislative authority of the country from exercising its constitutional prerogatives to establish national policy with reference to particular foreign trade problems. It simply passes belief that the executive department of the Government really believes that the general rules of commercial policy contained in GATT go no further than are required to protect the value of the concessions granted in GATT.[80] Congress simply cannot be held to have intended in delegating the trade-agreements authority to permit the Executive to make commitments in the name of the United States in the area of policy itself to an extent which precludes congressional action in those areas. It is well to bear in mind the unequivocal statement by the House Ways and Means Committee in reporting the trade-agreements bill in 1934: [81]

> The proposed bill * * * does not remove from Congress its control of policy which must underlie every tariff adjustment. Although the exigencies of

[79] Address by Mr. Eric Wyndham White, Executive Secretary of GATT, at the Graduate Institute of International Studies, Geneva (1956), pp. 14, 15.

[80] But see comment by the Chairman of the United States Delegation to the ninth session of GATT: "In the manner of a bilateral agreement, the General Agreement * * * includes certain general provisions designed to restrict the use of nontariff barriers to trade which could nullify or impair the expected benefits of these concessions" (H. Doc. 93, 85th Cong. (1957), p. 59).

[81] H. Rept. 1000, 73d Cong., 2d sess., p. 14.

**present-day conditions require that more and more of the details be left to Presidential determination, the Congress must and always will declare the policy to which the Executive gives effect.**

If, as the above statement of the committee indicates, the Congress intended in passing the 1934 act to retain control over the policy to which the Executive gives effect, it is indeed anomalous to consider the present dilemma of the United States in which the commitments made by the Executive in the policy area (such as the use of import quotas on agricultural products) is interpreted by an agency (the contracting parties) to whom the Executive is contractually bound as prevailing by its own force over the policy enunciated by the Congress in statutes such as section 22.

A similar dilemma is involved in the provisions of GATT which prohibit a member country from paying export subsidies without prior consultation with the contracting parties affected. There can be no way in which payment of an export subsidy by the United States on agricultural products could be deemed to impair the value of a concession granted by the United States to a foreign country for the importation of its products into the United States. It is difficult, therefore, to make a case for the inclusion of such a provision in a trade agreement even if commercial rules can validly be placed into effect under the trade-agreements authority to the extent necessary to protect the value of the concessions exchanged in the trade agreement. This question has nothing to do with whether or not it is objectively desirable that general rules of commercial conduct for the orderly expansion of world trade be administered by an international organization for the benefit that that would have in strengthening the economies of the participating nations. The point involved here is that the Trade Agreements Act does not provide the authority under which such a code of general rules and such an international organization can be created so far as United States participation is concerned.

One should not lose sight of the fact that for better or worse GATT in operation, so far as the United States is concerned, represents our trade-agreements program in action. When the contracting parties take an action such as the grant of a waiver which relieved the United Kingdom from its commitment against increasing margins of preference over those in existence when concessions were exchanged, it is equivalent to action by the United States itself to the same effect. But the Trade Agreements Act directs the President to suspend the benefit of concessions to countries which discriminate against American commerce. There can be no doubt that the increase in a preference in behalf of a commonwealth country discriminates against the United States. It is not necessary that the discrimination be solely against the United States for the mandate of the statute to apply.

The United States appears similarly to have given up freedom to act to eliminate discriminatory practices against its trade by the removal or threatened removal of benefits of trade-agreement concessions in the case of the recently imposed French tax on automobiles. The tax falls principally upon American automobiles and impairs the benefit of a concession on automobiles granted to the United States by France.[82] The French delegate to GATT has declined to accept a

[82] H. Doc. 93, 85th Cong. (1957), p. 222.

United States complaint concerning the tax. Meanwhile, the United States has effectively hampered its freedom of action by asking the Intersessional Committee of GATT to examine the complaint. It is not intended to suggest here that the Trade Agreements Act requires the immediate unilateral withdrawal or suspension of the benefit of trade-agreement concessions to a country discriminating against its trade. But there is considerable difficulty in reconciling the direct action called for by the Trade Agreements Act in cases of discrimination, and the direct remedies for the termination of the trade agreement or the withdrawal of the concession which was granted to France in exchange for the concession on automobiles,[83] with the indirect and remote possibility for action which is made contingent upon the judgment of the Intersessional Committee and contracting parties to whom the matter must ultimately be referred under the GATT procedures.

If there is any difficulty connected with deciding whether certain of the general commercial rules contained in GATT have any relation to an appropriate measure to protect the value of concessions received by the United States, there can be no question at all that the matter of discrimination in transport insurance is completely outside of the scope of such a provision. Yet the contracting parties to GATT at the eighth session reached the conclusion that the question of discriminatory transport insurance laws and regulations appeared pertinent to the aims of GATT.[84] The mere fact that a practice has an impact on trade in goods generally is no justification for regarding it as within the scope of the authority granted the Executive in the Trade Agreements Act. Because concessions exchanged under the authority of the act relate indirectly to trade in the products affected by discrimination in transport insurance, it is not a sufficient basis for regulating the practice as an appropriate or necessary provision to protect the benefit of the particular concessions received. Where the authority to incorporate rules pertaining to the administration of the trade touched by the concessions exchanged must be worked out on the basis of an inference, as is certainly the situation under the Trade Agreements Act, there must be a limit to the breadth of the provisions which the delegated authority is stretched to cover. Particularly is this so where, as in the Trade Agreements Act, the Congress has indicated that it, and not the Executive, retains control over the policies underlying the use of the authority.

Another example of a provision in GATT which is binding upon the United States and its member countries is article XX's prohibition on the adoption or enforcement by any country of measures pursuant to intergovernmental commodity agreements other than those which conform to the principles approved by the Economic and Social Council of the United Nations. Again, it is simply impossible to trace any source of authority for agreement by the United States to such a provision from the Trade Agreements Act. A GATT working party on commodity problems secured the adoption of a resolution at the 11th session of the contracting parties setting forth ways in which the contracting parties might enter into discussions of commodity problems and obligating contracting parties to consult with respect to commodity problems.[85] Though it appears that the United States delega-

[83] See sec. 350 (a) (4) and (5) of the Tariff Act of 1930, as amended.
[84] H. Doc. 93, 85th Cong. (1957), p. 43.
[85] Id., p. 236.

tion was opposed to any change in the provisions of the general agreement, this merely serves to highlight the fact that the United States has placed itself in a position in GATT where the judgment and discretion of the President, applied within the permissible area of action defined in the Trade Agreements Act, is not the determinant of the decisions which will be made affecting United States trade.

Our Government is in a similar dilemma with respect to proposals that GATT be amended to include a prohibition of restrictive business practices which might adversely affect international trade, with a commitment on the part of member nations to consult upon request and to take appropriate measures to eliminate the harmful effect of such practices.

## Conclusion

The Trade Agreements Act originally was intended as an emergency measure to assist in the recovery effort of the depression era. Its objective was to strengthen the economy of the United States through a reciprocal reduction of trade barriers to secure export markets for the surplus production of American farms and industries.

Under the impact of the United States role of leadership in attempting to establish and protect peace and the collective security of the free nations, the Congress has changed the purpose and objective of the Trade Agreements Act. It now recognizes the contribution which this reduction of trade barriers makes to the economic strength and security of the free-world community.

Today, as in 1934, the authority of the act is to be used under the policy guidelines which define the extent and circumstances under which concessions can be granted by the United States. These include the avoidance of injury to domestic industries, the reciprocal creation of needed market opportunities in the United States and in the countries with whom the United States is bargaining, and a direction of attention to tariff and import provisions which unduly burden the foreign commerce of the United States. The enjoyment of benefits conferred in United States trade agreements is subject today, as in 1934, to a rule of nondiscrimination.

The administration of the act by the Executive appears to place primary emphasis upon a systematic attainment of the changed objective of strengthening the economies and security of the nations of the free world without special regard to a strict observance of the limitations which remain in the policy guidelines set forth in the act.

By changing the purposes and objects of the act while retaining unchanged the policly guidelines for use of the authority, Congress either intended that the extent to which the new purposes could be realized would be governed by action conforming to the original policy limitations; or, on the other hand, it intended that the meaning of the policy limitations be changed wherever they would tend to limit an optimum realization of the new purposes in strengthening the economic foundations of international peace and security.

Because of the nature of the policy limitations which necessarily inhere in delegations of authority by the Congress, a reassessment is in order, either of the present purposes of the act, or of the policy guidelines provided for the use of the authority of the act.

If Congress intends the Executive to be able to exercise leadership with a minimum of restraint in acting to create international economic strength and security, the reassessment should result in a revision of the policy guidelines for the use of the delegated authority.

If, on the other hand, Congress intends that the policy guidelines presently expressed in the act are to remain the criteria for Executive action in the use of the delegated authority, then clarification is required to eliminate and guard against future recurrence of actions taken in excess of the delegated authority.

# ANALYSIS OF EXECUTIVE DOMINATION OVER TARIFF AND TRADE ADMINISTRATION

O. R. Strackbein, chairman, the Nationwide Committee of Industry, Agriculture, and Labor on Import-Export Policy

Ordinarily, an inquiry into the administration of a law or a program concerns itself with questions of cost, efficiency, waste, and so forth, or with organizational features of such administration. In the latter case, the inquiry will seek to throw light on the appropriateness of the organizational structure to its functions and objectives. There are well-known techniques for testing administrative deficiencies in these various directions.

In the case of trade-agreements legislation, the principal need for an inquiry into the question of its administration arises from an entirely different source. It is not a question of waste or efficiency or structural defects, much as these matters might deserve attention. It is a more basic question, with much farther reaching implications than the one of mechanics of administration. This is the question of basic authority and its analysis in point of origin and its course in recent years.

It is, indeed, a constitutional question, but not an academic one. Most of the great controversy over the trade-agreements program in recent years has revolved about this question.

Why?

Because it is a question of substantive importance. The rights of citizens—not merely abstract rights, but the very contents that give meaning to rights—are involved. To say that something is a constitutional question is often an invitation to sterile debate, but we may be sure that the questions to which the Constitution addresses itself were not sterile ones when the document was written. They were live questions. They were fullblooded and full of meaning. In some aspects, some of these questions later became dormant because no issues revolved about them for long periods of time. As a people, we lost much of our appreciation of the principles that underlay the settlements that were reached in writing the Constitution.

In recent years, in the sphere of tariffs and trade, as from time to time in other fields, particular aspects of our organic law have come once more to glow with the very essence of meaning. As is usually the case, the meaning became clearest and most vital to those whose interests were most closely implicated. It is seldom the beneficiary of an alleged infraction of the rules who calls for a halt of the game and a decision on the facts. Indeed, the beneficiary is usually strongly anti-inclined and characteristically seeks to minimize the issue, often to the point of arguing heatedly that no issue exists.

This has been the experience under the trade-agreements program. Its beneficiaries have studiously denied or brushed off what is basically wrong with its administration. The overriding issue is the shift from

Congress to the executive branch of the authority to regulate the foreign commerce of the United States and to modify the tariff.

When the Constitution was written, both the authority to regulate the foreign commerce of the United States and the power to establish tariff rates were expressly and unmistakably put upon the shoulders of the Congress.

For this there was a sound reason that was well understood at the time, and it is a mistake to overlook or ignore it today. The Congress is the most responsive of the three branches of our Government to the electorate. The Constitution makers saw to it that the subjects over which in their judgment, the people should retain closest control were placed under the control of Congress, such as taxation, money, appropriations, war, and commerce. It should be noted that these are fields of operation in which a shift of authority to the Executive could readily lead to legislative atrophy and, therefore, loss of control by the electorate.

The reason that moved the Constitution makers is as good today as it was 170 years ago. If experience should lead, on a sufficiently broad scale, to the conclusion that authority was unwisely bestowed upon Congress in any one of the fields defined in the Constitution, a constitutional amendment should be proposed to change the Constitution . One such proposal might suggest shifting the power over the tariff and the regulation of foreign commerce to the President. However, no such suggestion has been made. No one has seriously proposed that the congressional powers over the national activities revolving about tariffs and trade should, by amendment, be transferred to the Executive.

Nevertheless, the attempt has been made, and is, indeed, still underway, to effect an actual transfer of such powers without a constitutional amendment. It is this persistent, relentless, and protean effort that has drawn the fire of those whose interests are jeopardized and who see in the drain away of congressional authority the creation and fill-up of a reservoir of power in the Executive wherein the voice of the electorate could easily be drowned.

The feeling is strong that the producers of domestic products, including the workers, who are injured or stand to be injured by import competition no longer enjoy a fair opportunity of having their difficulties entertained and remedied. The reason for this serious deterioration of their position goes to the very shift of power referred to above.

As more and more industries began to feel the effects of the tariff reductions executed by the President through the medium of trade agreements, and as one after another industry tested the successive reassuring Presidential statements that no domestic industry was to be jeopardized, and pondered repeated State Department protestations that all duty reductions were made only after adequate hearings and careful examination of the facts, and found both the Presidential assurances and State Department protestations misleading, it soon became apparent that a qualitative change in our constitutional system, as it relates to the regulation of foreign commerce, had taken place.

This feeling culminated in vain legislative efforts to give clear guidance to the executive branch through amendments to the Trade Agreements Act, to section 22 of the Agricultural Adjustment Act and some other laws. Congress had become aware of the growing dissatisfaction with the system of foreign trade regulation that had been initiated with the Trade Agreements Act of 1934, but more particularly as it was modified and given startling new direction in 1947 when the General Agreement on Tariffs and Trade was negotiated. First there was enacted the so-called peril-point legislation in 1948. The purpose of this was to give the United States Tariff Commission, an agency of Congress, a hand in guiding the executive in the negotiation of trade agreement concessions. Subsequently, in 1951, the so-called escape clause was written into the Trade Agreements Extension Act. The purpose was to provide a sure remedy against injury.

However, as successive escape clause cases were processed through the Tariff Commission and it became increasingly clear that the President, dating from 1951, was rejecting a vast majority of the Tariff Commission cases, including unanimous decisions (tobacco pipes, silk scarves, lead and zinc, ferrocerium, groundfish fillets, velveteen fabrics), it became obvious that the State Department, as principal administrator of our foreign relations, had effectively superseded the Congress as the branch of the Government that regulated our foreign commerce and administered tariff adjustments.

This represented a transformation of power executed within Washington, D. C., without referendum, constitutional amendment or recourse to any of the known and recognized democratic processes. It represented a coup as surely as a bloodless stroke of arms; and it made a dead letter of all trade legislation so long as the latter did not in fact bring back to Congress its constitutional authority.

The right of petition has been vitiated. That our Government was a representative one had in the field of tariffs and trade all but lost its meaning.

It became a wholly frustrating experience, with few exceptions, for industry and labor groups seeking relief from oppressive import competition, to make representations to their elected Representatives, to exhaust their supposed legislative remedies or to take their troubles to the executive departments that had to all intents and purposes replaced the Congress

The elected officials were powerless. They had in one way or another been dispossessed of their authority. This now lay elsewhere, diffused in various executive departments, offices and agencies and therefore became as difficult to identify and piece together as the scattered and broken bones of a prehistoric missing link. Thus there was substituted for the responsiveness of the legislator the elusiveness, the finely split but interlocking irresponsibilities and sublime helplessness of the bureaucrat who is caught in the mesh of a policy that he himself perhaps helped fashion and would not in any case change if he could.

It became clear that under the circumstances such officials had only one characteristic recourse and that was knowingly to offer fair words and sympathy to petitioning groups who sought their help; for the bureaucrat knew that he could not extricate himself from the policy mesh in which he found himself entangled even if in some improbable event he disagreed with it.

Therefore, unless the petitioning group had a problem the solution of which could be found to lie within the lines of the general policy to which the executive was committed, the bureaucrat was in fact helpless, unless indeed he aspired to a martyr's crown. Since there was no wish frontally to offend the people who appealed to him, lest slow political erosion set in, the bureaucrat made a show of sincere regret and offered a number of suggestions that he probably knew to be wholly sterile. This could be calculated to have the practical value of keeping the petitioners occupied for another 6 months until they dimly learned the complicated truth. Depending upon the bureaucrat's resourcefulness on the one hand and the degree of patience and faith of the petitioners on the other, this cat-and-mouse game might be good for 2 or 3 or 4 years.

The bureaucrat's supreme hope was that in the meantime the pressing group would have gone broke, become cynically disillusioned or that fate had been good to them and helped them out of their difficulty.

The upshot is that the concentration of what is a legislative responsibility in the hands of the executive is in fact delivering powei to those who cannot exercise it equitably except by accident or coincidence and can use it only as an instrument in furtherance of an executive policy. Only when the petitioner's request fits into the policy can he hope for relief—unless he is sufficiently powerful to bargain against the life of the policy itself. This latter, as it happens, is the case in rare instances and calls for accommodation of politically powerful or strategic groups even at the cost of outright inconsistency with policy. The cynical effect is thus compounded.

Under these circumstances there is an inevitable flight from equalhanded justice into the arms of favoritism and political expediency. Examples of this have not been unknown in recent years in the executive administration of the trade-agreements program. Perhaps the most flagrant case lay in forcing upon Japan a so-called voluntary limitation of cotton textile exports to the United States.

The clear outlines of both bureaucratic objectives and ambitions as well as helplessness showed through this transaction.

Imports of Japanese textiles had greatly aroused the fears of New England and Southeastern States over the grave threat to the domestic mills posed by the low-wage type of competition that confronted them. Employment in the textile and garment industry as a whole was well over 2 million workers. Congressional representation in the affected States could therefore easily hold the balance of power in the closely contested tariff and trade issue as a whole.

This confronted the executive branch with a most disconcerting problem. Accommodation of the textile industry by imposing import quotas could only be accomplished at the expense of violating the general trade policy to which the executive was dedicated. Failure to make the accommodation, on the other hand, could produce 1 of 2 results, or both, neither of which was acceptable.

Congress, as it appeared, in responding to the persistent representations of the domestic textile industry, gave distinct evidence of determination to extend legislative relief. If this were not immediately forthcoming, as well it might not, the textile forces would in a natural combination with other groups have become a threat to the whole program of trade agreements. Moreover, if they came to look to Congress for a remedy or to the implementatin of laws already on the statute books, such as section 22 or the escape clause, the State Department's generally dominant position in the field of tariffs and trade would have suffered a mortal blow. Therefore, in order to preserve its grip the State Department must block any such consummation.

Under these circumstances the fiction that Japan might "voluntarily" restrict her exports of cotton textiles to us made a strong appeal to the executive officials concerned, especially since it was clear that we could compel Japan to be "voluntary." Even though quota limitations were severely frowned upon by the State Department and in fact had been banned, with some exceptions, in the General Agreement on Tariffs and Trade (GATT) with State Department initiative and strong support, the cotton-textile competition from Japan was a situation that must be met. The choice between a violation of the fundamental principles of GATT and serious loss of face and prestige by the State Department left little doubt about the outcome. Japan was pressed into announcing a "voluntary" export limitation on her cotton-textile shipments to the United States. This was outside the law and was duly interpreted officially as not representing an agreement. Therefore the "arrangement" could not be regarded as a violation of GATT. It had from the State Department's point of view the supreme merit of neatly bypassing Congress and all laws passed by Congress to apply to precisely such situations, and thus leaving the textile industry beholden to the executive rather than the legislative branch.

Here was an example of the very kind of action under executive control to which the strongest objection is registered. It showed (1) that responsiveness by the executive is reserved to the powerful on a basis that is not equally available to all groups that find themselves in the same circumstance; (2) that the executive branch is willful and if permitted to do so, will make accommodations to special interests in a manner that excludes public hearings, prescribed procedures, and the rule of law; and (3) that the State Department and the executive will violate their own most firmly avowed principles in order to retain their power.

Other repeated experiences with executive administration of the trade-agreements program have deeply convinced the successively frustrated participants that, under the escape clause or other instrumentalities, such as section 22 of the Agricultural Adjustment Act or the national-security clause, an industry or branch of agriculture will not be extended relief from injurious import competition on the basis of the facts of the case and the criteria set forth in law but will be judged, either favorably or unfavorably, but generally unfavorably, by factors that are nowhere set forth in any written law.

The conclusion became inevitable that the doctrine of the divine right of kings as a means of placing grievances beyond the reach of a remedy at law was no less offensive in repression than the alienation of the powers of Congress and delivering them to the executive. The destruction of responsiveness where responsiveness is the essence of democratic control is a backward step that must rank on a level with doctrines that justify autocratic power.

The assumption invoked in support of the executive administration of the trade-agreements program must be that the people of the United States are not competent to regulate their foreign commerce through Congress. Otherwise we must conclude that the State Department's insistence upon retention of the power that it has accumulated since 1934 when the Trade Agreements Act was first passed arises purely from lust for power. This, to be sure, is not an unheard-of source of ambition. The tendency toward tyrannical power lies near enough to the surface in the human breast to break out when the opportunity arrives. All that may be needed is some dogma that attracts fanatical support, such as free trade and global economic planning, with a backing of parties in interest, such as export industries and import groups. From there it is easy to proceed on the principle that the end justifies the means and that all opposition, such as protectionism in this case, is heresy.

Whatever the source or explanation of the executive domination that has become so obstrusively obvious to all who encounter it in tariff and trade administration, it is to them a stubborn and unwelcome reality. Congress itself must share some of the guilt because of its willingness to step aside and entrust to the Executive certain delegated powers without so much as a requirement of an accounting until it was too late. The only justification for an inquiry into the origin of the development about which so much venom has been generated lies in the hope that by this route the objectionable condition may the more surely be eradicated.

If there be any remaining doubt about the reality of the constitutional issue involved in the administration of the trade-agreements program it can readily be dispelled. It is only necessary to say that those who have gone against the camouflaged executive barriers in futile quests for relief find an unfailing mark of identification in anyone who belittles or brushes aside the issue of executive usurpation of congressional power. Either he is a layman far removed from and untutored in the tariff and trade issue and perhaps bored by constitutional questions or he is a party in interest and a beneficiary, direct or indirect, of the State Department policy. In the latter event he characteristically invokes the national interest, peace, and the brotherhood of man as his bedfellows.

It is precisely because there was no coup d'etat or any other visible seizure of power by the Executive in this case that the usurpations of the Executive went largely unnoticed and the decline and atrophy of Congress attracted so little attention from those who are not parties in interest. There was no declaration of intent, no proclamation of the imminent ouster of Congress from its constitutional function. It happened as if by stealth or by seizure of successive windfall advantages by those who were on the lookout for empires to build and philosophies to enthrone, such as were not lacking in the Department of State.

The usurpation made its way largely through loopholes, and prospered and grew through congressional inattention. When, as already pointed out, Congress awoke sufficiently to the danger to lead it to enact what was regarded as remedial legislation, the Executive power had already waxed sufficiently self-confident to respond with a combination of duplicity, evasion, and defiance. (See hearings before the

Committee on Finance, United States Senate, 81st Cong., February and March 1949.) This attitude was later to ripen into one bordering on an arrogance born of security and then, as self-assurance began to crumble, it was to take on the color of desperation.

The self-assurance came from the rise of internationalism as a domestic political force and its use as justification for executive domination in the field of tariffs and trade. The Communist menace became the favorite tool of the rationalizers. The United States must walk on its toes in tariff matters lest we offend one or more of the friendly countries that enjoy an export market in this country.

The Executive duly began to make international relations the ultimate criterion of his disposal of Tariff Commission recommendations under the escape clause. This was the infinite opening through which every congressional enactment on tariffs and trade could be scuttled. It was also the opening through which congressional authority was sent down the drain.

That is why Executive domination over tariff administration is the uppermost issue today in the formulation of foreign trade policy by Congress.

Now, let us fill in some of the gaps. Let us see what were the forces that combined to bring about the result. Let us trace the devious path to the composite objective; and let us inquire into the makeup of the strange caravan that pushed toward its mecca.

First we must recognize that the drive toward free trade did not come from any single source. It came from several sources, some of them from widely separated segments of the political spectrum.

There were the philosophical seers and intellectual malcontents who saw in free trade and worldwide economic planning the hope of delivering mankind from many of its ancient and chronic ailments. This group provided the idealistic ferment around which others of a less finely spun philosophy could rally.

Agricultural groups, agonizing under the weight of surpluses and oppressively low prices, but as varied as cotton farmers of Mississippi, wheatgrowers of the Dakotas, and hog farmers of Iowa, were among those attracted by the grand vision. They had a reason, a very practical one. They wanted to ship more of their crops and products abroad. It needed no idealism to spur them on.

Then there were tobacco planters, applegrowers, and other farm-surplus victims who became natural allies. The song they all learned to sing under the hypnotism of the State Department baton was that we must buy in order to sell or conversely that if they wished to sell more abroad others among us must import more. It was a catchy tune; and the chorus was eagerly joined by such unlikely partners as the large mass-production industries and the CIO unions organized in them (automobiles, steel, electrical equipment, packinghouses). Later came the bing international oil companies. The ideals had taken on real muscle.

The wedding ceremony was blessed by the international bankers while the metropolitan press, eternally thankful that newsprint had been triply bound on the free list in sundry trade agreements, sang the praises of the Hull program, with few exceptions, from one end of the land to the other.

It was a formidable combination even before it was eagerly embraced by the League of Women Voters.

The program that was so variously supported naturally gained great political momentum and, inevitably, began to suffer from the disease that so often afflicts lopsided majorities. This is the disease of self-righteousness, smugness, and contempt for opposite views. Protectionism was duly desecrated and buried as the symbol of a bygone age, as has been done other times with other policies only to see them exhumed later and given new life.

However, the top seers in the official hierarchy sensed the tide that runs in human affairs and set about making their victory secure and permanent.

The means and procedures employed to assure such permanency deserve very close attention.

Obviously if the control over tariffs and trade should continue to reside in Congress no one could guarantee that the next Congress or the one after that or any future Congress would not modify, reverse, or shatter the grand plan. It was equally clear then that Congress must be eluded and bypassed and then so thoroughly overwhelmed with weighty counterconsiderations to self-assertion that when it sought again to reassert itself it would find itself paralyzed.

It was not even necessary that this be done consciously through premeditated steps. The logic of the situation was impulsion enough. This was that the State Department could not accomplish its purpose if Congress were free to intrude at any time with contrary policies upon the scene; and that was exactly what might be expected if the branch of the Government that is most responsive to the people were given its head.

If, now, the free-trade and global planning policies that had been adopted, to some extent, at least, with the consent of the Congress then sitting, could be embedded in a formidable international agreement, such policies would hold against the changing tides of sentiment in the country. In order thereafter to change the policies, it would no longer be enough to produce a mere change of sentiment in Congress. Congress would be faced with something that it had not contemplated when it gave to the Executive the power to enter into trade agreements. It would find its freedom hedged by the force of international commitments made by the State Department in pursuance of its own uninhibited interpretation of the powers delegated by Congress.

If Congress objected that the State Department had gone too far, such objection would still not remove the foreign obligations that had in the meantime been assumed by the Department. Moreover, the State Department could argue that the delegated power was, indeed, broad enough to empower it to make the commitments that it had undertaken. Where would the Congress be then? It might kick furiously and voice deep resentment. The Members would have the privilege of milling around like wild horses in a corral, while noting the ropes around the necks of their leaders.

Thus it was that the State Department initiated and, over a period of 3 years (1945–48), negotiated the charter for an International Trade Organization, known as the ITO. This was a highly ambitious, as well as an involved and complex, document that would have brought our tariff and trade administration into the vortex of the United Nations.

Under the prodding of the Senate Finance Committee, the State Department conceded that the charter should be brought before Congress, but it was not willing to say that so far-reaching an agreement should be given the status of a treaty. In the end, the instrument was sent to Congress as an Executive agreement under a resolution that called for approval by both Houses. Thus, a majority vote would suffice, as against a two-thirds-vote majority, had it been submitted as a treaty.

To date, no criteria have been developed by which to classify an agreement as a treaty or as something of a different category. The State Department saw this loophole and utilized it, without an effective challenge from Congress.

Nevertheless, Congress withheld its approval from the signed charter. The supporting resolution, after a hearing before the House Committee on Foreign Affairs in 1950, died in the committee without a formal report. The President subsequently withdrew the charter, and the ITO died a-borning.

This congressional action gave some evidence of the legislative displeasure over the lengths to which the State Department had run with the delegated powers.

In the meantime, however, the Department had also negotiated the General Agreement on Tariffs and Trade (1947), known as GATT. This agreement had incorporated many of the ITO provisions, but fell somewhat short of the global economic ambitions of the latter.

The State Department, having witnessed the legislative fate of the ITO, refused to send GATT to Congress for approval. Again there was no explanation that differentiated between a treaty, such as the general agreement could have been interpreted to be, and an executive agreement, such as the ITO was acknowledged to be, and something else that the general agreement was, in fact, interpreted by the Department as being. In this great void, where nothing was seemingly defined, the State Department made its own determinations and followed its own counsel. It had an open field.

The general agreement, be it a treaty, an executive agreement, or something else, was converted, hocus-pocus, without submission to Congress, into an operating organization and began functioning as GATT. How to convert an agreement into an administrative organization required powers of transmutation that the State Department could hardly have found had it not by this time evolved a quite definite plan of evading Congress and establishing its own free-wheeling franchise. Obviously, the Department was intent by this time on staying as far away from Congress as it could.

The only grip left to Congress was the Trade Agreements Act itself. This never was permanent legislation so far as the delegation of power was concerned. On no occasion had the Congress extended the delegation of authority to the President to enter into trade agreements, and under which the State Department operated, for a period of more than 3 years. On occasion the act was extended only 1 or 2 years. Even this tenuous grip was more than the State Department could abide, for the Department had not finally clinched its own control. In fact, a few shadows began to darken the previously sunny skies.

It became apparent after the failure of the ITO Charter that the sentiment in Congress was growing less and less favorable to the State Department stewardship of the delegated congressional powers. Not only did Congress enact the escape clause (1951), as already mentioned, and otherwise amend the Trade Agreements Act, but the heavy majorities by which the President's authority had previously been extended had begun to melt away. In 2 successive years the act was renewed for only 1-year periods (1953 and 1954).

Obviously, the halcyon days of the free-trade ascendancy were over. The need for compromise began to impress the forces that were in support of GATT and Executive control over our foreign trade. This was the atmosphere in which the Randall Commission, composed of congressional and public members, studied the trade program and formulated recommendations in 1954.

The outcome of this study reflected the mood of compromise, and the final report represented a rather cautious endorsement of the trade-agreements program. It was accompanied by a biting minority report. The principal fruit-bearing recommendation was a revision of GATT to be undertaken in its ninth session. Superficially, it appeared as a retreat from the Executive domination of the preceding 20 years.

However, when the GATT revision was completed in March 1955, the hand of the Department of State again became most visible. Very cleverly concealed in the revision and in the new proposals that were offered was unmistakable evidence that the ideas and plans of 1945 were still alive, unabashed by the fate of the ITO and the multiple signs of the restive mood of Congress.

In a show of contriteness, it was announced that the organizational features of the revised GATT would be sent to Congress for approval. This was undoubtedly the tribute that was to be offered to Congress, and was designed to answer the complaints against bypassing of that body. The revised trade rules, on the other hand, would simply become a part of the general agreement as soon as they were ratified by a sufficient number of the member countries. This distinction represented a maneuver that could be deceptive while appearing to be uncommonly generous, coming as it did from the State Department.

Parenthetically, it should be noted that the State Department, as representing the Executive, once more determined unilaterally what was regarded as subject to approval by Congress and what was to take effect without submission. No criteria were set forth to justify the distinction, and the area remains wholly unilluminated. The State Department continued as the sole and unchallenged arbiter.

It is important to note what the State Department offered to Congress and what it reserved to the jurisdiction of the Executive. This will throw further light on the Department's view of who's who in tariff and trade regulation.

The organizational features of the revised GATT were chosen for submission to Congress, and, indeed, were duly forwarded. These, be it noted, did not touch the substance of the general agreement. On the other hand, the revised trade rules that did embody the very substance of the agreement (that is, GATT) were to be withheld and, indeed, were withheld.

It turned out that the organizational features took the form of a further agreement to establish the Organization for Trade Cooperation, which has become known as the OTC.

In sending the OTC proposal to Congress, the Executive, in fact, overplayed its hand. It did so by minimizing the powers that would be exercised by the new organization, and generally describing it as a bloodless entity. It could readily be concluded, from all these disavowals of power to be lodged in the OTC, that its establishment would be a wholly trivial act; that OTC was not needed; and that it was an insult to Congress to offer to it such an empty shell while keeping the trade rules of GATT itself, which the OTC was to administer, well out of reach.

Here, again, was evidence that the Executive continued to adhere to the notion that it was safe to entrust to Congress the harmless and simple features of our foreign-trade operations but not the part that really counted. For example, among the trade rules of GATT are the provisions that renounce the establishment and maintenance of import quotas, govern the bases of customs valuation, and so forth. These, it should be emphasized, are of the very essence of commerce regulation; and yet it is precisely these substantive provisions that the State Department will not entrust to congressional review.

However, the belittling of the powers of the OTC was in reality a stance consciously assumed to obtain congressional approval. While it is true that the OTC would be an administrative agency, and while the articles of agreement which provide for its organizational structure, functions, and so forth, do not contain the trade rules of GATT, the fact is that OTC would undertake to give full effect to the objectives and purposes of GATT. This being the case, congressional approval of the OTC would be tantamount to approval of GATT, including the trade rules.

Having advertised the OTC as an innocent organization given largely to consultations and housekeeping functions and under this guise hoping to obtain congressional endorsement of United States membership in it, it needs little shrewdness to see that the State Department would, should it succeed, have gained approval by remote control of what it has steadfastly withheld from Congress for fear of defeat. It would have gained back-door approval of the substantive aspects of GATT while exposing only the organizational features to scrutiny and possible rejection.

As evidence of State Department awareness of what it is up to, we need only to consider the extent of the apparent dilution of the OTC resolution since its introduction into Congress. This dilution took the form of amendments to which the Department has assented and was no doubt offered to render the legislation more palatable and to improve its chance of adoption. These amendments come close, on superficial examination, to throwing the baby out with the wash. If appearances reflected reality it would be most difficult to justify State Department acquiescence. However, two reflections will clarify the mystery.

The first is that, as just described, approval of the OTC would carry the congressional blessings of the Department's aims in the field of tariffs and trade and above all of its stewardship of delegated authority under which it has been working. This would be a coup indeed and the Department could well afford to throw the OTC out with the wash in order to win such a victory.

The second is that the amendments and reservations added to the OTC bill to oil its passage through Congress are purely unilateral and therefore superficial. They change not one word or comma in the articles of agreement controlling the OTC, signed in Geneva in 1955. No reservations or amendments adopted by one of the contracting parties changes the contractual obligations assumed all around. Other member countries would not be bound to recognize our strictures. This fact would make of these amendments and reservations excellent targets for other countries; and the State Department could connive at frittering the amendments away. To believe that the Department would not be capable of doing so would be naive indeed. It would be worse; it would be culpable negligence and foolhardy.

This brief account of the means and procedures employed by the State Department and other promoters of the executive tariff and trade policy to assure the permanent divorcement of Congress from its constitutional authority and its lodgment in the executive must suffice. The gambit is clear enough. The bait of the mousetrap has reached a sufficient degree of maturity to make its presence known.

For the skeptical, however, i. e., those who believe that the facts as related above with respect to State Department design and practice merely rest on inferences and that contrary deductions could properly be made with equal plausibility, let one more piece of evidence speak for itself. This will be in the form of article XXVIII of GATT.

Stripped of its complicated phraseology, article XXVIII provides that any member of GATT may withdraw a previous concession (e. g., in the form of a tariff increase) for any reason at all, provided only that the matter be negotiated with the contracting party to which the concession was initially granted. In other words, the concessions were not to be regarded as strictly binding on the members. Article XXVIII represented recognition of the right of self-determination or of sovereignty in control of the tariff and regulation of foreign commerce.

If a country found that it had struck a bad bargain in granting a concession (e. g., a duty reduction) it could on its own initiative undertake to correct the mistake through renegotiation by simply announcing the fact.

This freedom at least comports with a degree of self-reliance that should go hand in hand with national self-determination—a principle to which the State Department scrupulously pays repeated homage on the world stage.

Strange then that the Department has been a willing partner if not a leader in the successive postponement, totaling 10 years, of the date on which article XXVIII is to take effect. Indeed a provision in the latest postponement called for future automatic postponement at the end of specified periods. This is yet to take effect.

Here is the paradox: the State Department flatly denies that the authority of Congress has been abridged or set aside by the Department's administration of its delegated authority. It maintains that Congress is still free to legislate as it sees fit. Why is it necessary then to postpone the effective date of article XXVIII which would do no more than unbind the hands of the United States (as well as other GATT members)? Why postpone the effective date of something that would do no more than recognize a freedom that the State Department contends already exists?

Obviously the State Department in fact agreed to a binding of the United States in GATT and means to see that the binding holds. That explains the Department's opposition to article XXVIII. This is the same as assuming that Congress should abide by the Department's commitment and accordingly stand mute. The net of it is that the freedom of Congress as visualized by the State Department is thus limited to the precious right to dishonor this country's signed agreement before the whole world.

If the State Department is as free in making international trade commitments as its own interpretation decrees, obviously Congress has only one of two alternatives this side of revoking the delegation of power. It could indeed betray its trust, forget its constitutional authority and responsibility, and leave the field to the State Department. That would please the Department. Or it could exercise its freedom and legislate as it saw fit regardless of any State Department commitments.

The first alternative would represent abject abdication by Congress. That would be intolerable. The second would leave the executive branch in possession of the weapon of coercion that it has used so persistently, and this would be equally intolerable. At best it would bedevil our international relations by having two foreign-trade spokesmen in this country, one legislative and one executive, possibly at odds with each other, to the immeasurable confusion of other countries.

The policy of postponing the effective date of article XXIII shows clearly where the State Department stands, notwithstanding all disavowals. A submissive Congress would greatly ease its task.

We have now come to the real question. What is wrong with Executive domination of our foreign trade? Let us assume that the State Department would say what it has not yet been bold enough to say: "We admit the allegation. What of it?"

On the negative side the answer has in great part already been given. The repeated experience of the domestic industries and producing groups in failing to obtain relief from injury under the administrative remedies provided by law has led to the conclusion that the State Department dominancy has stood in the way and still stands in the way. It has inhibited the constitutional procedures that would assure the proper degree of responsiveness of the Government to its citizens and substituted a system that from its nature cannot respond equitably.

Against this negative indictment might be set the pragmatic question of how much better the interests in question would be served if the Executive domination were broken.

The answer must address itself to two facets of the practical question. One part must be addressed to the aggrieved interests concerned; that is, whether they would fare better under the restored congressional power. The other part must be addressed to the interests of opposing elements; that is, whether they in turn would fare better or worse if the Executive dominance in this field were broken.

If a determination can be made in these two aspects, the final judgment must then be made on the relative balance of the opposing interests. The question would finally resolve itself into one of the comparative importance of the two claims.

This is not to say that the final answer with respect to public policy must conform to the pragmatic test, since much more may be at stake, such as the breakdown of our constitutional system. Nevertheless, an inquiry such as the present one will be greatly concerned with the practical aspects of policy and its administration.

It is a regrettable fact that we lack conclusive data that would permit a final answer. One of the fields in which our information falls short is that of employment in the production of products for export, on one hand, and the displacement of workers caused by imports on the other. Worse yet, we have no sure way of determining the indirect effects of exports and imports, either as reinforcing or canceling each other in their helpful or injurious effect upon our economy.

Do competitive imports hurt domestic producers more than exports help them or other elements of the economy? If a higher volume of competitive imports is necessary to stimulate exports, would the supposed benefits to exporters offset or more than offset the harm done to other domestic producers?

Should the beneficial effects of exports merely offset the harm inflicted on others, national policy could hardly justify the harmful transaction on the grounds that it helped the exporters unless certain beneficial byproducts could be added, such as a contribution to the peace of the world, lower consumer prices, facilitation of diplomatic operations, and so forth.

Unfortunately these questions can also not be answered with finality; and it is certain that directly conflicting testimony would come from the opposing interests. For example, it can be said that competitive trade as distinguished from complementary trade notoriously fails to make friends and, on the contrary, may stir up bitter rivalry.

There is one point, however, about the very persistence of foreign trade that may be taken for granted. Evidently there is a monetary advantage both in selling abroad and in buying. Otherwise the channels of trade would narrow down and sooner or later would close. It also seems safe to say that in purchasing our total imports compared with the sale of our total commercial exports we are buying more man-hours of labor than we are selling. This would be counted as a consumer advantage and one of the real bases of foreign trade.

Yet there may be some real question, on the other hand, whether an added price is not being paid above the merely monetary cost in many of our low-cost foreign purchases. Our economy has been bolstered and cushioned by many laws that unquestionably increase our cost of production. Competitively we have been made more vulnerable to imports than would be the case if we still operated in a free market. This is most surely true in the field of basic farm prices and industrial wages, both of which have virtually been taken out of competition by legislative interference.

Under these circumstances it is no longer possible to know whether competitive imports flow because foreign producers really outdo us in a genuine economic sense or whether the flow owes its impetus to artificial competitive advantages. Insofar as foreign producers enjoy a competitive advantage that is derived largely from the mere fact that we support our farm prices or that we pay higher wages than those prevailing in other countries, it is clear that their advantage is not of the kind contemplated by the classical free-trade philosophy. Moreover, since our own producers are no longer able because of various legislative enactments to enjoy any great degree of competitive flexibility, they are placed at an unfair disadvantage by tariff reductions that expose them to competition of a lower level not fettered to the same degree.

It is unfortunate, indeed, that so many of the questions that go to the heart of the controversy cannot be answered by reference to factual data. That very fact perhaps explains why the tariff issue has so long been a political issue in this country. Where mathematical or scientific certainty cannot be established, differences of opinion will flourish and generally reflect diversity of interest. Policy determinations must be resolved on incomplete data and through judgments that in great part must stand on their own feet. Ultimate proof in support of the position of either side is lacking.

It is in this setting that executive control takes away the interplay of forces that we look to in our system to assure a fair chance for all concerned. What the exponents of executive control say in effect is that Congress in policy matters cannot be trusted to "stay put" precisely because it has its ears to the ground. Yet it is for the very reason that Congress does listen to the voters that we can have a governnment of the people, by the people, for the people.

Those who prefer executive control of foreign trade are perhaps in the position of riding a good horse that happens to be going their way. The rigidity of executive control suits them for the simple reason that the current executive policy happens to express their own particular current interest. Since executive control promises greater continuity and in fact strives for permanency it represents the best bet in sight. Other times and on other questions these ardent supporters of executive power might be in a different mood.

It might, of course, as readily be said that the supporters of congressional as opposed to executive control see in legislative control a good horse going in their own particular direction; and that they too might be singing a different song were the executive policy arrayed on their side of the issue instead of the opposite side. This may be granted without destroying the integrity of their present advocacy even if this advocacy is a matter of self-interest. The point is that under congressional control no one can hope to snatch a temporary advantage and make it permanent by putting it beyond reach of due democratic process.

In the ebb and flow of economic tides and the permutation of advantages that go with them, it will always come about that a program or line of action that may have looked good to the people of this country yesterday may today confront us with a strangely unwelcome aspect. If the particular program is based on legislation, the people can adapt themselves to the changed conditions, but only so long as the legislative channels are kept open. The turn of those who had been ill favored by the existing tide may now at long last present itself. They who have been waiting are entitled to have their chance and this they can grasp only if the means of doing so have not been taken from them or perhaps even destroyed.

Those, on the other hand, who had been favored by what had been borne in upon the preceding tide, if they would be fair and if they would be true to the rules of the game that underlie our form of government, must be willing to take their own chances along with everyone else when the tide changes. They are not entitled to depend for the extension and perpetuation of their good fortune upon a device calculated to stop all future ebb and flow of the tide.

It is therefore precisely because there is no final answer to the question of tariff and trade policy that it would be repugnant to the rules of the game and at the same time unwise to accept and insulate one particular policy against change by delivering it to executive control; and that is what has been happening and that is what is now under challenge in the tariff and trade controversy.

The force of this conclusion is reinforced by the experience with executive procedures that were devised to carry out the executive administration of the trade agreements program. Widespread complaints have come from the domestic industries that have from time to time appeared before the Committee for Reciprocity Information. As trade agreement after trade agreement was subsequently proclaimed it became clear, or so it was alleged, that the hearings were meaningless, and that they were an expense, a waste of time, and an offense against good faith.

Yet, on reflection, it seems clear that the system of procedures actually adopted by the executive was indeed in keeping with the exigencies of executive control. It is the function of the executive to execute, not to debate and take votes. In the Trade Agreements Act certain powers were delegated to the executive, rightly or wrongly. The executive undertook to carry out the expressed policies, not to fritter them away. Therefore, procedures were set up with the very purpose of preventing dissipation of the policy. After all the executive is not a parliament.

On further reflection it becomes clear that even the trade-agreement procedures in the long run were in any event of little moment, and mere window dressing at best, because in the end the President could backstop any throws that seemed to him to be heading outside the policy limits. This was particularly true after 1951 when Congress passed the escape-clause amendment to the Trade Agreements Act with the very purpose of tightening the delegated power. The escape clause was the final test of whether an injured industry could obtain a remedy.

Here again the executive practice of overruling the Tariff Commission, on one pretext or another, showed that the President and his executive staff regarded executive control as an instrument of policy to be used as the executive saw fit. No interested party had any rights. These rights were effectively surrendered when the Congress delegated authority to the executive. The only possible means of influencing the final decision therefore must rest with such "influence," almost surely political, as the interested parties could muster. Otherwise the decision was made in conformity with the dictates of the executive's pleasure.

Under this self-serving construction the executive power saw nothing incongruous in its practice of herding up new facts in addition to those provided by the Tariff Commission, and considering them in camera or with private groups but without exposing such new or supplementary data to the hearings process or challenge by the opposition. The permissive feature of the law under which the President had discretion not to accept the Commission's recommendation was thus used as a door to walk away from any semblance of a tie to congressional power. The President has claimed the right to invoke considerations that do not appear in the law to support his rejection of Tariff Commission recommendations; and has done so repeatedly. This means that the criteria laid down in the law become inoperative once a recommendation leaves the portals of the Commission. Since the Tariff Commission itself is an agency created by Congress to carry out certain aspects of tariff administration, the authority of Congress also collapses once the Commission has finished its findings and recommendation. The result is that Congress has so far lost its authority in this field that the right of petition by aggrieved citizens as guaranteed in the Constitution has in turn also lost its meaning.

What we have witnessed in the executive administration of the trade-agreements program is tantamount to the well-known suspension of constitutional guaranties as practiced in unstable countries where the democratic processes are not yet well rooted. What has happened under the Trade Agreements Act, as extended and amended, since 1934 offers an object lesson to Congress. It shows clearly that it is a mistake to delegate powers to the executive unless they are very clearly and sharply defined. It also shows that in order to regain its own power to regulate foreign commerce and to adjust the tariff Congress must break the elaborate coils fashioned by the State Department for congressional strangulation.

If, indeed, these coils are not stripped away any further legislation designed specifically to restore the power of Congress will be predestined to futility on the day of its passage.

The foregoing brief review of the administrative and procedural aspects of the trade agreements program must suffice. Documentary evidence can be supplied in abundance. Several recommendations are offered for correction of the unjustifiable trends that have been described:

1. Determine the distinction between (*a*) a treaty, (*b*) an executive agreement subject to congressional approval, and (*c*) an executive agreement made in pursuance of delegated authority and not subject to congressional approval.

In this controversial field the State Department alone cannot be relied upon for a satisfactory answer. The temptation to offer a self-serving classification of agreements would be too great. At stake is the separation of powers, and the executive branch could hardly be relied upon for an impartial response. A thorough study of the subject is imperative if this twilight area is to be illuminated for establishment of procedures that answer to the Constitution.

2. Withdraw H. R. 6630, which proposes approval of the OTC, pending the clarification called for in the preceding recommendation. Thereafter offer a bill for approval only if the articles of agreement of the OTC are revised in such manner that approval of them by Congress (*a*) will not impair or abridge the constitutional authority

of Congress to regulate the foreign commerce and to adjust the tariff of the United States, and (*b*) will not lead to embarrassment of Congress by opening the way to international executive commitments that may be used by the Executive to coerce Congress.

Surely there are legitimate methods by which the regulation of our foreign commerce and the adjustment of our tariffs can be correlated with the executive conduct of our foreign affairs without violating the Constitution or doing violence to the substantial guaranties contained in that document.

This goes to the heart of the complaint outlined in this paper. Such correlation does not call for either congressional abdication or transfer of authority to the Executive under such broad terms that the Executive can contrive the elimination of Congress from its ligitimate field of control. It does call for an advisory liaison between the Executive, i. e., the State Department, and the Congress, but the freedom of Congress to accept or reject any advice that might be tendered must be recognized as the ruling principle of the relationship.

3. Eliminate the Presidential veto over Tariff Commission findings under the escape clause and section 22 of the Agricultural Adjustment Act. Instead, send such findings to Congress under a 60-day deadline after expiration of which they will become effective unless either House of Congress prior to that time has rejected them by majority vote.

Elimination of the Presidential veto is vital to the restoration of congressional power. To retain this veto would be to foredoom all other efforts to break the Executive domination. It is this power of final review that enables the State Department, through the President, to frustrate the responsiveness of Congress to the people. It is this final power that makes a mockery of all intermediate procedures, such as conscientious hearings and investigations. It is also this final power that enforces the executive policy as distinguished from the legislative and puts all interested parties, the industries, the workers, the farmers, the owners of mines, plants, or mills into the palm of the Executive's hands and at the mercy of his predilections and those of his advisers. Lastly, it is this final power that destroys the equal treatment, under law, of large and small alike, that we have come to regard as the guarantor of equity.

4. Build an expert professional staff as adjuncts of the House Ways and Means Committee and the Senate Finance Committee to provide expert surveillance of tariff and trade legislation, commensurate with the congressional responsibility.

The need for competent committee assistance has been widely acknowledged as an outgrowth of the tremendous legislative burden that has fallen upon congressional committee members. Certainly the two committees vested with the responsibility of tariff and trade legislation are no exception. Their burden of work needs no detailing to impress its reality. A beginning has been made toward the direction of this recommendation.

5. Review the functions of the Tariff Commission with a view to its conversion into a true arm of the Congress. To this end define more sharply the criteria and guidelines of the various enactments entrusted to its quasi-judicial administration.

To reshape the Commission so that it will have the dignity and standing which should go with its very establishment, and to take it out of the present status as an executive undergrowth, it should be changed from an evenly numbered agency to one of an odd number, preferably 7 or 9. The evenly divided setup is either meaningless or a frustrating device that can paralyze, as it has been known to do, the very function the Commission was set up to perform.

Also the wholly meaningless bipartisanship of the Commission should be abolished. At best this device represents an invitation to horse trading to prevent a deadlock; at worst it offers a cynical refuge for raw executive political maneuvering. Party affiliation as such lost its meaning in the field of tariffs and trade years ago. Bipartisanship is therefore no barrier whatever against packing the Commission with like-minded members. It is as vestigial as the appendix and should come out.

6. Make a thorough study of the direct and indirect effects of imports and exports on employment and wages. The relative productivity of workers in particular industries here and in countries that export to us should also be determined where the necessary facts can be obtained.

As pointed out above, the lack of definitive information on the effects of imports and exports on employment and wages is a great drawback to policy determination.

# FOREIGN TRADE POLICY AND ITS ADMINISTRATION

Morris S. Rosenthal, senior councilor, National Council of American Importers, Inc.

Before going into specific suggestions on foreign trade policy, I should like to point out that it is essential to resolve the basic problem as to whether or not all segments of industry, mining, and agriculture, and individual companies or producers have an inherent right to tariff protection. In my testimony before your subcommittee on September 26, 1956, I posed these fundamental questions:

Should we, as a matter of national policy, adopt the principle of the inherent right to protection against imports, when we can buy certain goods abroad at lower prices and in many cases of better quality or of different type or style? Or, should our national policy be one of selective protection and aim only to protect industries essential to our economic welfare or to national security? Should we not recognize that there may well be companies and industries and segments of agriculture for which protection cannot be justified, and that they, therefore, might have to change to other fields of economic endeavor because they cannot successfully compete with imports from abroad? Should we protect everyone, or should we decide we need not make and grow everything ourselves? To what extent should we admit foreign competition to our vast markets?

In that testimony I stressed that our tariff system and structure should be based on the overall national interest, which may be defined as the greatest good for the greatest number. In general business terms, it may be said to be the greatest amount of capital invested and used in American agriculture and industry, and the greatest number of people gainfully employed in factories, in offices, on farms, in mines, and so forth. If we have lower tariffs, people in other countries will be able to sell more in our markets. With the dollars they get they will be able to buy more of the goods we produce, mine, and manufacture. As a result of this greater exchange of goods, our country as a whole will benefit and prosper. More capital will be invested and more people will have jobs, even though some industries or some companies are compelled to change their production, and even though some workers must change jobs and the kind of work they are doing. This has been true as a result of the many and substantial technological changes that have come about in American life over the years, and no one would say that such progress should have been limited or retarded. After all, the tariff is in the nature of a subsidy and any subsidy should be used wisely and well, and employed to the extent needed by our overall national economic welfare, our defense program, and the changed conditions that affect them.

The National Council of American Importers has for a great many years, with the help of its various technical committees, given careful thought to foreign-trade policy and questions affecting United States import trade. I should, therefore, like to present a series of specific suggestions for consideration by your subcommittee:

I. RECIPROCAL TRADE AGREEMENTS PROGRAM

The Reciprocal Trade Agreements Extension Act of 1955 will expire on June 30, 1958, and the Congress will have under consideration a further extension of that important act. We would suggest:

1. *New expiration date.*—The reciprocal trade agreements program is a proven mechanism for the reciprocal reduction of trade barriers and should now be given a definite status. We feel that the act should be made permanent. As in all other laws, the Congress may amend the act from time to time as needed. At the very least, the act should be extended for 11 years to June 30, 1969, so that the expiration of the act will fall in a year following a presidential election.

2. *Bargaining power.*—The bargaining power authorized in the present act should be increased and made more flexible. Specifically, we would suggest:

(*a*) The President should be authorized to decrease rates of duty which are higher than 25 percent ad valorem (or its equivalent) to 25 percent ad valorem (or its equivalent).

(*b*) The President should be authorized to reduce rates that are less than 25 percent ad valorem (or its equivalent) by 25 percent of such rates.

(*c*) As a new type of concession in negotiating reciprocal trade agreements, the President should be further authorized to guarantee that the rate of duty on selected commodities will be status-bound against an increase for a fixed period of 3 to 5 years. It is true that several trade agreements include the binding of existing rates of duty, but these items are not exempt from escape-clause action, quotas, and other restrictions which may be imposed any time after the conclusion of the agreement. Thus, they are not actually duty status-bound for a definite period, as we now suggest. The binding of dutiable articles against an increase in rates or new restrictions for a definite period would provide an element of stability that is so much needed in our international trade relations. Of course, it is assumed that imported articles which have in the past offered substantial competition to sensitive domestic industries would not be subject to status-bound dutiable treatment.

3. *Escape clause.*—The escape clause frustrates the basic purpose of the act. It should be substantially revised in the following respects:

(*a*) Its principal criteria should be based on the overall national economic welfare and the needs of our Nation's security program.

(*b*) The authority under which tariff concessions may be withdrawn or suspended should be strictly limited to actual emergency cases, in which the domestic industry entitled to added protection is confronted, because of previously unforeseen situations, with the actual necessity of making too rapid adjustments to avoid serious loss of capital, or a rapid decrease in employment.

(*c*) When the escape clause is used for such a specific reason, the tariff should not be increased above the rate of duty that was in effect prior to the last reduction made under the authority of the act. Specifically, section 7 (a) of the Trade Agreements Extension Act of 1951, as amended, should be changed to substitute the words—

> It [the Tariff Commission] shall recommend to the President the withdrawal or suspension of the last concession granted, in whole or in part—

for the words—

> It shall recommend to the President the withdrawal or modification of the concession, its suspension, in whole or in part, or the establishment of import quotas.

The word "modification" in the present escape-clause provisions has been interpreted by the Tariff Commission to permit recommendations to the President of increases in duty rates beyond the preagreement rate by as much as 50 percent above the rate that existed on January 1, 1945. In a few cases, where the January 1, 1945, rate, was the same as the original 1930 rate, the recommendation under the escape-clause procedure has been for a 50-percent increase in the Hawley-Smoot tariff rate. It should be made clear that the purpose of the escape clause, when invoked, is to restore the degree of tariff protection to the level which existed before it was lowered through trade-agreement procedures. The original purpose of the escape clause was to deal with special cases where the reduction of a particular rate of duty resulted in an unexpectedly large inflow of imports that might threaten serious injury to a domestic industry, and to provide a method to remedy such unforeseen situations by restoring the previous protective rate. It certainly was not intended to be used as a tariff-raising device to establish rates of duty in excess of those in effect before a trade agreement was undertaken. The authority in the present escape clause to establish import quotas goes far beyond the original purpose of the escape clause.

(*d*) The Tariff Commission should be granted discretion with respect to instituting an investigation upon application of any interested party. Specifically, section 7 (a) of the Trade Agreements Extension Act of 1951, as amended, should be changed to substitute the words "when in the judgment of the Commission there is a good and sufficient reason therefor, upon application of any interested party" for the words "upon application of any interested party."

(*e*) Said section 7 (a) should be further amended to provide that interested parties making repeated applications for relief be required to establish a prima facie case of substantially changed competitive conditions in all instances where the Tariff Commission has previously conducted a formal investigation and has made findings of no injury with respect to a certain commodity.

(*f*) The escape clause (sec. 7 (a) of the act) should contain a definition of the word "injury." Our suggestion for such a definition is:

> The word "injury," for the purpose of this section, shall mean a steady decline, over a representative period, in the sales volume, in the working force employed, and the profits of an industry economically and efficiently operated in the United States, directly caused by a rising trend of competitive imports which are similar in material, use, quality, texture, grade, and other physical characteristics, thus giving rise to a situation whereby such domestic industry is confronted with the actual necessity of making too rapid adjustments to

avoid serious loss of capital: *Provided, however*, That such decline in sales, working force employed, and profits is not due, wholly or in part, to technological developments, style or fashion changes, or to other factors not related to said import competition.

(*g*) The definition of "industry" in the present act is unsatisfactory, and has led to the use of the escape clause by one lone producer who admitted that its production methods had not been changed in over 50 years (Linen Toweling case). There should be substituted a definition of the term "the domestic industry producing like or directly competitive products," as used in section 7 (a) of the act, to mean all of the producers in the United States producing such competitive products. The basic objective of the escape clause is to prevent serious injury or the likelihood of serious injury to an American industry, and not to a special group of inefficient producers, and surely not to a single company.

(*h*) Any increase resulting from action under the escape clause should be made effective for a specific period of time that is calculated to be adequate to permit domestic capital and labor to make the necessary adjustments to the competitive situation. United States importers should have the right to apply for a review of the escape-clause action at any time prior to the expiration of the specified period of time if they can present evidence that the adjustments to the competitive situation appear to have been made by domestic capital and labor.

4. *Peril points.*—Section 3 of the Trade Agreements Extension Act of 1951 should be repealed. From our observation, all agencies of Government that have responsibilities in connection with trade agreements have shown an understanding of the problem and concern for our economic welfare. They can well be trusted as a group to think in terms of so-called peril points, and to act wisely. If, however, the Congress decides that peril points are still needed, they should be established in the future by the Interdepartmental Committee on Trade Agreements, rather than by the Tariff Commission alone. The Tariff Commission is represented on the Committee for Reciprocity Information, and when that committee holds public hearings in preparation for trade agreement negotiations, it is necessary for the Tariff Commission to hold separate hearings (usually at the same time) in connection with the establishment of peril points. Such procedure is an unnecessary duplication which the elimination of the peril point procedure would correct.

5. *Defense essentiality.*—Section 2 (b) of the act authorizes, in vague terms, the President to take "such action as he deems necessary to adjust the imports" for the protection of American industries essential to national security. There is a need for defining in exact terms what constitutes an industry or a company within it that is essential for our security program. This section of the act should also provide exact procedures to be followed by the Office of Defense Mobilization in reaching considered determinations, including notices of and access to all complaints filed by domestic industries; provisions for public hearings with full opportunity for interested parties to present their views; publication of all recommendations by the ODM to the President; and a suitable grace period before any new restrictions imposed upon imports shall become effective.

6. *Initial trade agreements period.*—Concessions granted as a result of new trade agreements concluded should go into effect for an initial period of 5 years rather than for 3 years as in the past. A greater degree of certainty that an agreement will not be disturbed would thus be provided. Of course, the existing provisions for earlier termination in unforeseen emergency situations, or by mutual consent, would still be in effect under the General Agreement on Tariffs and Trade, and by the specific terms of our trade agreements.

7. *Grace period.*—In all cases where there is an increase in the existing rate of duty, or where there is a new or changed restriction of any kind upon imports, there should be a suitable period provided for the importers involved to adjust their affairs to the new situation. A minimum period of 90 days is suggested.

## II. PROPOSED ORGANIZATION FOR TRADE COOPERATION

The Congress should approve the bill, H. R. 6630, authorizing the President to accept membership on behalf of the United States in the proposed Organization for Trade Cooperation, and at the same time section 10 of the Trade Agreements Extension Act of 1951, and all similar provisions in other existing laws which state, in effect, that such legislation shall not indicate the approval or disapproval by the Congress of the executive agreement known as the General Agreement on Tariffs and Trade should be repealed. The General Agreement on Tariffs and Trade, negotiated in 1947, has proven its worth as a most effective international arrangement for the progressive reduction of trade barriers during the difficult postwar period and as a successful medium for the friendly settlement of trade disputes between nations. The GATT promises to become of particular importance as an international forum for the discussion and settlement of questions that are bound to arise as a result of the formation of the common market in Europe, as well as common markets that may be established in the coming years in other areas of the world. The notion that the GATT is merely an international agency with power to cut tariffs to the disadvantage of domestic industries and that United States participation in the agreement is contrary to the Constitution and therefore illegal has been advanced from time to time by protectionists in and out of the Congress. These questions should be settled once and for all by the approval of H. R. 6630 with a clear-cut statement that the GATT is an appropriate executive agreement negotiated under the authority of the Reciprocal Trade Agreements Act to carry out the stated purpose of that act by multilateral negotiations for the reciprocal reduction of trade barriers, rather than the less effective bilateral method employed earlier in the history of the act. In this connection, it should be noted that our negotiators have been able to obtain important concessions from participating countries which are not the principal suppliers of the imported commodity under consideration. United States exporters have thus benefited.

## III. REGULATION OF IMPORTS BY QUOTAS

The use of quotas for the restrictive control of any imported commodity should be entirely discontinued as a national policy. Quotas are designed for a protective purpose similar to tariffs, but they are worse because if consumer demand grows, there can be no increase in imports as even a tariff allows except by a specific administrative action. Quotas imply the assignment of shares of the market and this inevitably means that choices must be made between countries of supply and individual traders. In addition, the imposition of quotas invites retaliatory measures by foreign countries. At the present time, there are various types of quotas imposed on imports. Among these are:

1. *Absolute quotas.*—Under section 22 of the Agricultural Adjustment Act, absolute quotas have been established on certain types of cheese, peanuts, butter and butter substitutes, rye and rye flour, wheat and wheat flour, cotton waste, long-staple raw cotton and certain short-staple raw cotton. Such absolute quotas limit the quantity that may be imported in a calendar year, or other specified period, to a fixed amount. The administration of such absolute quotas leads to forms of regimentation of trade, the fostering of monopolies and the opportunity for favoritism, all of which are alien to the American system of private enterprise and freedom from Government controls. Such absolute quotas also tend to discriminate against small-business men engaged in the import trade who cannot afford to store large quantities of overquota merchandise in bonded warehouses or foreign-trade zones in order to make quick withdrawals at the time a new quota period begins.

2. *Quotas related to tariff rates.*—In negotiating trade agreements in the past, some imported products have been subject to an arrangement whereby the rate of duty is reduced for a given quantity and imports that exceed the specific quantity in a given period are dutiable at a higher rate. Several examples of this will be found in the Geneva agreement, effective January 1, 1948, with respect to certain kinds of cattle, whole milk and cream, walnuts, white or Irish potatoes and certain kinds of fresh or frozen fish. While it is true that if such limitations had not been set it might not have been possible for our negotiators to grant any concession at all and perhaps this type of quota arrangements is least objectionable, we still feel that any restriction of imports by quotas is fundamentally unsound, and weakens our position when we wish to object to quotas imposed against United States exports by other countries.

3. *Quotas related to domestic consumption.*—Another variation of the quota system is the establishment of a reduced duty rate as a result of a trade agreement limiting imports to a certain percentage of the domestic production in a given period and to assess a much higher rate of duty on imports that exceed that limit. This situation exists at present with reference to woolen fabrics, imported in excess of 5 percent of the average domestic production during the 3 immediately preceding calendar years, and also to canned tunafish in brine in excess of 20 percent of the United States pack of canned tunafish during the immediately preceding calendar year. The limitation for wool fabrics was established during the negotiations at Geneva in 1947, and there is no provision for periodic consideration of the limit set at that time. This particular situation illustrates the need for a review from time to time of arbitrary restrictions in the light of changed market conditions, and also for omitting from the quota count specialties of a noncompetitive type.

4. *So-called voluntary quotas.*—This type of quota is established either by the exporting country, as in the case of Japanese cotton textiles, or by the United States, as in the case of crude oil, as a result of a threat that more severe import restrictions will be imposed either by the Congress or by the administration unless imports are limited on a voluntary basis.

We object to all forms of quotas, as we strongly feel that when protection of domestic producers is required in the national interest, it should be afforded entirely by tariffs designed to equalize any advantage foreign producers may have in our markets, and we reject completely the idea that resort to quota controls is ever justified.

### IV. NEW PROCEDURE FOR MODIFYING EXCESSIVE RATES OF DUTY

The Tariff Act should be amended to insert a new provision authorizing the President to proclaim a 50-percent reduction in any rate of duty which is found unduly restrictive or which constitutes an unwarranted barrier to the imports of any commodity. While considerable progress has been made under the Trade Agreements Act toward the reduction of excessive rates of duty on imports, there are still many commodities where the existing rate is unnecessarily high. There is no present administrative procedure whereby an importer may apply for a reduction in a rate of duty that is excessive, except where an item is under consideration in trade-agreement negotiations or under section 336 of the Tariff Act of 1930. Section 336 is now of very limited application, and is not a very practical procedure in any case. We suggest the President be authorized to reduce any existing rate of duty by not more than 50 percent of such rate where the Tariff Commission, after due investigation, finds that the existing rate is unduly restrictive, constitutes an unwarranted barrier to imports, or is unnecessarily high. Such investigation should be undertaken by the Tariff Commission upon the request of the President, upon resolution of either House of Congress, upon resolution of either the Committee on Finance of the Senate or the Committee on Ways and Means of the House of Representatives, upon its own motion, or when in the judgment of the Commission there is a good and sufficient reason therefor, upon application of any interested party.

### V. TRANSFER TO THE FREE LIST

A new provision should be inserted in the Tariff Act authorizing the President to transfer to the free list imported commodities which are not produced at all in the United States, or which are commercially produced in this country only in small or insignificant annual volume. Very recently, the Congress has recognized the validity of this idea by approving bills to provide for temporary suspension of duty on such commodities as casein, istle or Tampico fiber, and certain tanning extracts. There are many other imported commodities required by our domestic industries which are not available, or only available in insignificant quantities from domestic sources. The Tariff Commission should be charged with the preparation of a preliminary list of all such imported commodities, and public hearings should be held to enable all interested parties to make representations about any articles for which a duty-free status is proposed. The Commission should then submit to the Congress a final list of such articles, and we would suggest that the Congress then authorize their transfer to the free list for the benefit of the domestic industries concerned, either for a 3-year trial period or permanently. As an alternative, the Congress might authorize the President to transfer any article on the final list to the free list as a concession in connection with trade-agreement negotiations to be undertaken in the future.

### VI. INTERNAL TAXES

The proposal made in the closing days of the 1st session of the 85th Congress to suspend the present duties on lead and zinc, and to substitute in their place an internal revenue tax on a sliding scale according to average market prices in the United States is contrary to the well-established concept of tariff protection by appropriate rates of duty under the Tariff Act. It is also contrary to the generally accepted principles in the conduct of international trade that internal taxes should not be applied in such a manner as to afford special protection to domestic production. The principle is sound that once imported products have cleared customs at a port of entry they should not be subject to discriminatory internal taxes which are different from those levied on domestic products.

### VII. BUY-AMERICAN LEGISLATION

The so-called buy-American legislation should be promptly repealed by the Congress. The public interest and economy in Government operations should be the controlling factors in our Federal procurement policies. It is clear that the economic depression and widespread unemployment in the United States which originally gave rise to this type of legislation have long ceased to exist. The act tends to stimulate extreme nationalists to cry "Buy American" and so generates hostility among consumers against goods that are produced abroad, and also creates an emotional fear of international trade.

### VIII. ANTIDUMPING ACT

In the closing days of the 1957 session of the 85th Congress, the House of Representatives approved a bill, H. R. 6006, to amend certain provisions of the Antidumping Act. In its report on this bill, Report No. 1261, the Committee on Ways and Means made it clear that this bill did not undertake to make any changes in the basic policy objectives of the act. The report noted that during the public hearings on H. R. 6006 suggestions were advanced for amendments to the act to provide for a statutory definition of "fair value," "injury," and "industry"; judicial review of the determinations of the Treasury Department and of the Tariff Commission; Presidential review of dumping findings, and so forth. Our views on the proposals in H. R. 6006 were presented to the Committee on Ways and Means at the public hearings held on July 30, 1957, by Harry S. Radcliffe, executive vice president of our organization. In that testimony it was suggested that the act be amended in the following respects:

1. That section 205 of the act be changed to substitute world market prices for "foreign market value." This would mean that where foreign merchandise is sold to the United States at less than the average prices at which such or similar merchandise is sold for export to third countries, such sales to the United States, with due allowances for all differences in circumstances of sale, would be considered at "less than fair value."

2. That the term "less than fair value" should be specifically defined to relate to deliberate or predatory dumping, and to exclude from consideration sales by foreign producers to United States importers made in good faith at prices necessitated by normal competitive conditions and circumstances in our domestic market.

3. That there should be a precise statutory definition for the term "injured or likely to be injured." The definition we suggested is the same as that we propose in this memorandum for the escape clause.

4. That there should be a precise definition for the term "an industry in the United States" to mean all of the producers in the United States producing articles like or directly competitive with the imported merchandise under consideration.

5. A provision requiring the Treasury Department to give all interested parties an opportunity to be heard on the question of fair value before a determination is made, and that any finding that an imported article is being sold at less than fair value should be subject to judicial review in the United States Customs Court.

6. A specific provision requiring public hearings before the Tariff Commission on the question of injury with notice of such hearings to interested parties.

7. Any finding by the Tariff Commission of injury or likelihood of injury in dumping cases should be subject to review by the President.

8. That the retroactive period of 120 days should be reduced to a period of 30 days.

9. That the Antidumping Act should apply to dutiable merchandise only.

### IX. A BASIC TARIFF ACT

Our basic tariff act is the Tariff Act of 1930, which has been amended many times during the past 27 years. There is a real need for the codification of all our laws relating to the tariff into a new tariff law which is to be the basic tariff statute. We suggest that, as soon as possible after the Congress acts on the tariff classification report which the Tariff Commission is now preparing, a new tariff law should be enacted which, among other things, should provide that the Antidumping Act of 1921, as amended, be incorporated as a part of that law.

# VI

# QUANTITATIVE REGULATION OF IMPORTS—ADVANTAGES AND DISADVANTAGES—UNITED STATES AND FOREIGN EXPERIENCE

# TARIFF POLICY AND THE ESCAPE CLAUSE

Don D. Humphrey, professor at Duke University

The American trade-agreements program has accomplished much that is constructive. But it has become stalled in recent years as the Congress was reluctant to grant authority for substantial further reduction of tariffs and has invited the President to use the escape clause more generously.

The purpose of tariff reduction is to expand mutually beneficial trade. Expansion of trade means both exports and imports. In its present form the escape clause is not fully consistent with this objective because it provides that if lower duties accomplish their ostensible purpose, mutually beneficial trade may be destroyed by again restricting imports.

Actually, the escape clause has been invoked so rarely that the restrictive effect from its actual use has been small. If the world were assured that the escape clause would be used as sparingly in the future as in the past, it would not seriously impair our foreign-trade policy. But, under its present provisions, there can be no assurance that trade will not be restricted for the next 10 or 20 years. A major objection to the escape clause is the uncertainty that it creates.

Development of an American market for manfactured imports may entail considerable costs in expanding plant and adapting production to serve the tastes and specifications of American buyers, in developing sales organizations, and in stocking warehouses. Foreign producers are discouraged from risking this investment and from trying to expand their American markets by the express threat that, if they are successful, their trade maye be restricted by the American Government in its endeavor to avoid serious injury to domestic producers of similar products. This policy leaves out of account half of the picture; it fails to recognize that domestic producers of exports are injured by restrictions on American imports.

On the other hand, domestic producers who feel threatened by foreign competition may well feel that the escape clause offers little hope of relief. On a basis of the historical record, the chance of obtaining protection under the escape clause would seem to be quite small. Moreover, higher duties imposed under the escape clause may not always actually reduce imports. Once the costs of adapting production and developing an American market are already incurred, imports may continue at least for a time despite higher duties.

## THE PRESIDENT'S RESPONSIBILITIES

The President's responsibilities place him in the rather awkward position that he has rejected more often than he has accepted the Tariff Commission's recommendations to invoke the escape clause. This is clearly an undesirable situation. In declining to invoke the escape clause, the President has brought into account the following considerations (which are beyond the responsibilities of the Tariff Commission as provided by the Congress):

1. The effect on American export markets.
2. The implication with respect to foreign policy.
3. Protection of American consumers.
4. Compensating reductions to foreign countries whose exports would be restricted by the escape clause.

These considerations are of the highest importance and some of them should be taken into account by the Congress when it lays down the criteria for action under the escape-clause proceedings. Present policy is that no segment of domestic industry, however small, shall be seriously injured as a result of tariff concessions. The possible effects of extensive use of the escape clause in this form are so serious that the President may well be justified in using, as he has, the discretion granted him. It is wise to continue granting him some discretion in this matter; but it would improve the process of government in escape-clause proceedings if the criteria of serious injury were modified and clarified. The many split decisions of the Tariff Commission indicate that the present tests of serious injury are difficult to apply objectively.

THE TEST OF SERIOUS INJURY

Most industries produce many different products. Often the same industry produces commodities protected by tariffs and, at the same time, enjoys expanding export markets in other commodities. Where lower tariffs successfully expand both imports and exports within the same industry, the industry can adjust to freer trade by changes in the composition of its output. If such an industry as a whole is healthy and expanding, it ought not to be eligible for relief under the escape clause. The so-called fragmentation amendment should be repealed because it tends to encourage expansion of domestic production in those lines that employ resources less productively at the expense of competing lines that employ resources more productively.

The defect in our present policy is that the escape-clause and peril-point amendments concentrate attention exclusively on domestic production of those commodities which may be seriously affected by competitive imports, and neglect the damaging effect of tariff restrictions on domestic production of exports. To protect one segment of home industry is certain to damage another. Domestically produced commodities that depend on tariff protection can be obtained more cheaply by importing them in exchange for exports. The gain from trade is derived from exchanging exports for imports. Workers and capital are more productively employed in producing exports than in producing import-competing commodities that require tariff protection. For this reason, the Nation benefits from freer trade which expands the more productive industries, and loses from protection which expands the less productive import-competing lines of production.

Since tariffs restrict imports and exports alike, and, conversely, freer trade expands both imports and exports, the basic policy issue is which line of domestic production shall be encouraged—the more productive or the less productive. The tariff and escape-clause problem is best viewed as a struggle for expansion between segments of domestic industry that compete for labor and capital. The test of serious injury should include the production-expanding effects of increased exports as well as the production-contracting effects of increased imports.

The peril-point amendment should be repealed because it fails to take account of the production-expanding effects of exports that are created by imports.

The first and overriding principle to guide our policy is this: Healthy, growing indutries have no legitimate claim to tariff protection in order to attract workers and expand employment at the expense of competing American industries that would otherwise employ these same resources to produce goods of greater value. Industries with expanding trends of employment should not be eligible for relief under the escape clause and tariff protection for such industries can be gradually reduced without serious injury. If this policy were adopted, a lenient attitude could be taken toward use of the escape clause for industries that show a trend toward declining employment or stagnation.

Imports are only one of several causes of contraction in domestic production, and they are most serious when an industry is already beset with other disclocations such as domestic competition from new products, changes in consumer taste, techological displacement of workers and other changes in our dynamic economy. Even though imports are not the principal cause of declining employment, it seems only fair to consider such an industry eligible for relief under the escape clause if increased imports "contribute sustantially" toward causing serious injury. The escape clause should be used primarily as a reprieve to allow an industry more time to adjust. Insofar as tariff reduction is the cause of unemployment in declining industries, skilled workers who do not find alternative employment may be allowed to finish their working lives in the industries for which they have special training. Similarly, owners of industrial plants are entitled to a generation in which to deplete their fixed investment and find more favorable opportunities for reinvestment.

As a matter of equity, it seems unfair to further reduce the tariffs of declining and stagnant industries until the protection of those industries that show pronounced growth has been substantially eliminated. I would hope that the Congress would authorize the President to reduce tariffs by 5 percent annually for 5 years on the commodities produced by industries that show pronounced growth. While it is impossible to predict which industries would benefit most from this policy, it is obvious that the peoples of other countries will buy more American goods if we permit them to earn more dollars by selling more freely in the American market. Our concern should be that the total effect of such a program will be too small, rather than that it will be too large, because the direct economic benefits depend on the amount of trade that is created.

Over the period of 23 years since the trade-agreements program was begun, this committee has heard many thousands of pages of testimony. It would be enlightening if the committee's staff could review this record and compare the testimony with the subsequent record of employment, production, and profits of the protected industries themselves. The record will show, I believe, that those who feared serious injury from lower tariffs have, in the event, been proved wrong more often than right.

The reduction of average realized duties by about 75 percent since 1934 has produced no flood of imports compared with the expansion of domestic production in the protected industries as a whole. And often the exports of protected industries have increased as much or more than competitive imports. The apprehension created by tariff reduction appears to be more disturbing than the actual damage suffered in the event. It is also relevant to note that the producers of exports who benefit from freer trade are often less articulate in presenting their case to the Congress than the producers of import-competing commodities who fear injury from tariff reduction. In part, this is because it is impossible to predict which exports will expand as a result of increased imports. But, with notable exceptions, it is also more difficult than it may appear to predict which industries will be seriously injured. All the evidence is that support for freer trade is stronger in the business community than when the trade-agreements program was begun. This may be due in part to the underestimate of the effects of tariff reduction on the expansion of exports.

The only way our exports can be sold abroad is for the United States to import from other countries or to lend them dollars. Thus, the exceptions to the rule that imports create exports are that other countries may use the proceeds of their dollar exports to pay their debts to us, or to increase their dollar reserves. Clearly, our interest dictates that we import enough to enable other countries to pay their debts. Our interest is also served by other countries acquiring adequate dollar reserves for use in emergencies. Such reserves are essential in order to eliminate discrimination against American exports and to restore the convertibility of currencies. A second use of dollar reserves is to enable other countries to maintain their imports of American commodities during periods, such as 1954, when we bought less from them owing to a recession in our national income. To the extent that other countries delay spending their dollar earnings to tide them over an American recession, it has a stabilizing effect on American production and employment.

## ADMINISTRATION OF IMPORT QUOTAS BY THE BUREAU OF CUSTOMS

United States Treasury Department

TREASURY DEPARTMENT,
OFFICE OF THE SECRETARY,
*Washington, August 23, 1957.*

Hon. HALE BOGGS,
*Chairman, Subcommittee on Foreign Trade Policy,*
*Committee on Ways and Means,*
*House of Representatives, Washington, D. C.*

DEAR MR. BOGGS: This is in response to your request of May 31, 1957, for a review of our experience with the regulation of imports by quotas, and our views on certain problems incident to the administration of these quotas.

I am attaching for your use a summary of the import quotas which are now administered by the Bureau of Customs of the Treasury Department, together with a statement of the procedures followed in carrying on this work. As you may know, the responsibility of the Bureau in this field is purely administrative; it has no policymaking functions.

The only quotas which are allocated and administered on a country basis are those where this is so specified by the Presidential proclamation establishing the quotas. Therefore, the Bureau is confronted with allocation problems only in those cases where entries filed at the same time cover a total quantity in excess of a particular quota. In such instances the quota, or the portion of the quota involved, is apportioned on an equitable basis against the amount covered by the pertinent entries.

With the exception of the quotas which are applied to certain imports from the Philippines and the tariff quotas on woolen fabrics, certain ground fish, and tunafish, the quota controls now in effect are applied entirely to agricultural products. I believe you will wish to rely upon the executive departments most closely concerned and familiar with the appropriate domestic industries to indicate the circumstances which have made such controls appropriate.

With regard to country allocations, which are applicable only in the case of certain agricultural commodities, it is our understanding that the Department of Agriculture will cover the considerations which have led to their imposition in that Department's submission to you.

In the past, the application of quota controls has not necessitated the elaboration of commodity classifications because the Presidential proclamations have been framed in tariff terms. Were this policy modified, however, it might well have that effect. Our experience does not indicate that the concentration of import trade in the hands of a few concerns would affect the ease of administering quota controls, although it might influence the volume of work entailed.

The administration of import quotas does impose an additional burden on the Bureau of Customs, the cost of which is difficult to measure. This cost would, of course, increase if the use of quota controls were increased.

On the broader question of policy, quantitative import restrictions have long been opposed by the United States as a general instrument of commercial policy, and the President has on several occasions confirmed this opposition. The Treasury is in accord with this general position. However, in certain special cases, such as where we are engaged in domestic price-support programs, the more definitive control over imports which quotas afford may provide more certain means of limiting the financial burdens of the domestic programs.

I hope you may find these materials and views of assistance in your work.

Sincerely,

W. RANDOLPH BURGESS,
*Acting Secretary.*

The import quotas administered by the Bureau of Customs fall into two principal classes: (1) Tariff-rate quotas and (2) absolute quotas.

Certain of both classes of quotas apply only to Philippine commodities. The tariff-rate quotas are all global, and all of the absolute quotas are also global except those applying to short-staple cotton (less than 1⅛ inch staple) and to cotton waste, wheat and wheat flour, and rye, rye flour, and rye meal. The country allocations under the cotton and cotton-waste quotas are provided for in Presidential Proclamation No. 2351 of September 5, 1939; those under the wheat and wheat flour quotas in Presidential Proclamation No. 2489 of May 28, 1941; those under the rye quota in Presidential Proclamation No. 3189 of June 27, 1957.

Tariff-rate quotas place no quantitative limitation upon the amount of the product that may be imported, but quantities in excess of the stipulated quota are subject to higher duties. Imports from Iron Curtain countries are not entitled to modified-duty rates under these quotas. Absolute quotas, in contrast, impose specific limits beyond which no entries are permitted during a quota period.

Attached are exhibits containing a list of the commodities subject to import quotas administered by the Bureau of Customs, together with a recent set of Treasury Department press releases showing the current amount of each quota, the country allocations specified in the pertinent presidential proclamation, and other material. These press releases are prepared periodically by the Bureau of Customs and made available to the public. Information is also enclosed showing the dates when quota limitations became applicable under presidential proclamations issued pursuant to section 350, Tariff Act of 1930, as amended, and section 22 of the Agricultural Adjustment Act, as amended. In addition, there are tables giving the annual quota and quantity entered during recent years for each item under quota, together with the source of imports for some of them.

All of the tariff-rate quotas, as shown in column 1 of exhibit 1, and in exhibit 2, with the exception of the peanut-oil quota, were established by Presidential proclamations issued pursuant to section 350 of the Tariff Act of 1930, as amended (act of June 12, 1934, 19 U. S. C. 1351). The quota on peanut oil was established by Presidential Proclamation No. 3019 of June 8, 1953, issued under section 22 of the Agricultural Adjustment Act of 1933, approved May 12, 1933, as amended (7 U. S. C. 624). This latter proclamation also established quotas on certain dairy products, which are administered by the Department of Agriculture.

The tariff-rate quota on alsike clover seed represents the only quota established through escape-clause action under section 7 (c) of the Trade Agreements Extension Act of 1951, (Public Law 50, 82d Cong., approved June 16, 1951). The tariff-rate quota on tuna fish (Presidential Proclamation No. 3128 of March 16, 1956) and that on woolen fabrics (Presidential Proclamation No. 3160 of September 28, 1956) were established following the invocation by the President of the reservations contained in items 718 (b) and 1108 of the General Agreement on Tariffs and Trade, as supplemented.

All of the absolute quotas, as listed in column 2 of exhibit 1, and described in greater detail in exhibits 2, 3 and 4, were established by Presidential proclamations issued pursuant to section 22 of the Agricultural Adjustment Act of 1933, approved May 12, 1933, as amended (7 U. S. C. 624).

The quotas on Philippine commodities,as listed in column 3 of exhibit 1, and exhibit 5, are provided for in article II of the Philippine Trade Agreement, Presidential Proclamation of October 26, 1955, issued pursuant to the Philippine Trade Agreement Revision Act of 1955 (Public Law 196, 84th Congress, approved August 1, 1955). This agreement applies to Philippine merchandise entered on or after January 1, 1956.

The quotas on Philippine buttons, cigars, coconut oil, and tobacco (exhibit 5) are duty-free for the calendar years 1956 through 1958, and represent 95 percent of the respective base amounts set forth in article II, paragraph 2, of the Philippine Trade Agreement. Article II, paragraph 2, sets forth the base amounts on which the duty-free quota on each of these commodities is to be computed during each 3-year portion of the period beginning January 1, 1956, and ending December 31, 1973, both dates inclusive. Any such Philippine article entered during a calendar year in excess of the duty-free quota for that year is subject to the same tariff treatment as like merchandise from any other foreign country (including Cuba). As of January 1, 1974, no duty-free treatment will be accorded any of these articles.

The absolute quotas on cordage (Philippine articles and other products) and on sugars (Philippine articles) for each calendar year during the period beginning January 1, 1956, and ending December 31, 1973, will be the same as stated in exhibit 5, unless, as provided in article II, the Congress of the United States sees fit to increase the sugar allocations to the Philippines. Duties are assessable on these commodities in the fractional amounts specified in article I of the Philippine Trade Agreement Revision Act of 1955. During the period January 1 through July 3, 1974, the quotas on cordage and sugars will be one-half of the respective quantities stated in exhibit 5. Imports of these commodities during this period will be dutiable at the full rates.

In the administration of tariff-rate quotas, the quota status of a commodity cannot be determined in advance of its entry. The Bureau of Customs, therefore, ordinarily assesses the quota rates of duty on such commodities until such time as it is determined that the quota is nearing completion. All collectors of customs are then instructed to require the deposit of estimated duties at the full rate and to report the time of official acceptance of each entry. A final determination is made by the Customs Bureau of the date and time when the quota is filled, and all collectors are advised of this fact so that the proper rates of duty may be assessed.

Many of the commodities subject to absolute quotas are presented for entry in such volume at the opening of the yearly quota that the quota is filled at that time. Ordinarily, the Bureau is aware of the possibility that the quota may be filled at or shortly after the opening of the quota period. In such circumstances, customs officers are directed to make special arrangements whereby all importers are afforded equal opportunity for the simultaneous presentation of entries at a given moment of time on the opening day of the quota period. Advance notice of the arrangement is usually given through the medium of a press release. When the quantity for which entries are filed at the opening of the quota period exceeds the quota, a proration among the various entries is made in order to insure equitable distribution. If the quota is not filled at the opening moment of the period, subsequent entries are treated in the order of their presentation.

On the administrative side, the principal burden of quota controls has been the cost entailed. Such problems as have been encountered have been confined chiefly to efforts on the part of some importers to circumvent existing control procedures. Little difficulty has been experienced, however, in meeting these situations promptly through appropriate corrective measures.

EXHIBIT 1

*Commodities subject to import quotas aadministered by the Commissioner of Customs*

| Tariff-rate quotas | Absolute quotas | Philippine quotas |
|---|---|---|
| Alsike clover seed. | Cotton, harsh or rough, having a staple less than ¾-inch.[1] | Absolute quotas: |
| Cream, fresh or sour. | Cotton (other than linters) having a staple of less than 1⅛-inch, other than harsh or rough less than ¾-inch. | Philippine cordage [yarns, twines (including binding twine described in par. 1622 of the Tariff Act of 1930, as amended), cords, cordage, rope, and cable, tarred or untarred, wholly or in chief value of manila (abaca) or other hard fiber]. |
| Whole milk, fresh or sour. | Cotton (other than linters) having a staple length of 1⅛-inch or more.[1] | Philippine sugar, refined and unrefined. |
| Cattle, weighing less than 200 pounds each. | Cotton card strips made from cotton of less than 1 3/16-inch staple length, comber waste, lap waste, sliver waste, and roving waste, whether or not manufactured or otherwise advanced in value. | Tariff-rate quotas: |
| Cattle, weighing 700 pounds or more each (other than dairy cows). | Peanuts, whether shelled, not shelled, blanched, salted, prepared, or preserved (including roasted peanuts, but not including peanut butter).[1] | Philippine buttons of pearl or shell. |
| Fish, fresh or frozen, filleted, etc., cod, haddock, hake, pollock, cusk, and rosefish. | Rye, rye flour, and rye meal. | Philippine cigars (exclusive of cigarettes, cheroots of all kinds, and paper cigars and cigarettes, including wrappers). |
| Tuna fish, classifiable under par. 718 (b), Tariff Act, as modified. | Wheat, fit for human consumption. | Philippine coconut oil. |
| White or Irish potatoes: | Wheat flour, semolina, crushed or cracked wheat, and similar wheat products (not including products unfit for human consumption). | Philippine scrap tobacco, and stemmed and unstemmed filler tobacco. |
| Certified seed. | Butter substitutes, including butter oil, containing 45 percent or more butterfat, and classifiable under par. 709, Tariff Act, as modified.[1] | |
| Other than certified seed. | | |
| Walnuts, shelled, blanched, roasted, and prepared or preserved (not including walnut paste). | | |
| Peanut oil. | | |
| Worsted and woolen fabrics. | | |

[1] These absolute quotas are global; therefore the products involved may be entered thereunder without regard to the country of origin. There are allocations by country involved in the other absolute quotas.

EXHIBIT 2

The Bureau of Customs announced today preliminary figures showing the imports for consumption of the commodities listed below within quota limitations from the beginning of the quota periods to June 29, 1957, inclusive, as follows:

| Commodity | Period | Quantity | Unit of quantity | Imports as of June 29, 1957 |
|---|---|---|---|---|
| Tariff-rate quotas: | | | | |
| Cream, fresh or sour | Calendar year | 1,500,000 | Gallon | 195 |
| Whole milk, fresh or sour | do | 3,000,000 | do | 427 |
| Cattle, less than 200 pounds each | 12 months from Apr. 1, 1957. | 200,000 | Head | 10,879 |
| Cattle, 700 pounds or more each (other than dairy cows). | Apr. 1, 1957, to June 30, 1957. | 120,000 | do | 17,956 |
| Fish, fresh or frozen, filleted, etc., cod, haddock, hake, pollock, cusk, and rosefish. | Calendar year | 37,375,636 | Pound | (1 2) |
| Tuna fish | do | 44,528,533 | do | 17,654,752 |
| White or Irish potatoes: | | | | |
| Certified seed | 12 months from Sept. 15, 1956. | 150,000,000 | do | 111,912,085 |
| Other | do | 60,000,000 | do | 34,507,861 |
| Walnuts | Calendar year | 5,000,000 | do | 1,354,926 |
| Alsike clover seed | 12 months from July 1, 1956. | 2,500,000 | do | 235,814 |
| Peanut oil | do | 80,000,000 | do | |
| Woolen fabrics | Calendar year | 14,000,000 | do | 11,165,940 |
| Absolute quotas: | | | | |
| Peanuts, shelled, unshelled, blanched, salted, prepared, or preserved (including roasted peanuts, but not peanut butter). | 12 months from Aug. 1, 1956. | 1,709,000 | do | (2) |
| Rye, rye flour, and rye meal | 12 months from July 1, 1957: | | | |
| | Canada | 182,280,000 | do | [3] 174,960,031 |
| | Other countries | 3,720,000 | do | |
| Butter substitutes, including butter oil, containing 45 percent or more butterfat. | Calendar year | 1,800,000 | do | (2) |

[1] Imports for consumption at quota rate limited to 18,687,818 pounds during the 1st 6 months of calendar year.
[2] Quota filled.
[3] Imports through July 9, 1957.

EXHIBIT 3

**Preliminary data on imports for consumption of cotton and cotton waste chargeable to the quotas established by the President's proclamation of September 5, 1939, as amended.**

*Cotton (other than linters)*

[In pounds]

| Country of origin | Established quota | Imports |
|---|---|---|
| Cotton under 1⅛ inches other than rough or harsh under ¾ inch, imports Sept. 20, 1956, to July 10, 1957: | | |
| Egypt and the Anglo-Egyptian Sudan | 783,816 | |
| Peru | 247,952 | |
| British India | 2,003,483 | 124,060 |
| China | 1,370,791 | |
| Mexico | 8,883,259 | 8,883,259 |
| Brazil | 618,723 | 600,000 |
| Union of Soviet Socialist Republics | 475,124 | |
| Argentina | 5,203 | |
| Haiti | 237 | |
| Ecuador | 9,333 | |
| Honduras | 752 | |
| Paraguay | 871 | |
| Colombia | 124 | |
| Iraq | 195 | |
| British East Africa | 2,240 | |
| Netherlands East Indies | 71,388 | |
| Barbados | | |
| Other British West Indies [1] | 21,321 | |
| Nigeria | 5,377 | |
| Other British West Africa [2] | 16,004 | |
| Other French Africa [3] | 689 | |
| Algeria and Tunisia | | |
| Cotton, harsh or rough, of less than ¾ inch, imports Sept. 20, 1956, to June 29, 1957 | [4] 70,000,000 | 8,223,371 |
| Cotton 1⅛ inches or more, imports Aug. 1, 1956, to June 29, 1957, inclusive | [4] 45,656,420 | 21,137,549 |

[1] Other than Barbados, Bermuda, Jamaica, Trinidad, and Tobago.
[2] Other than Gold Coast and Nigeria.
[3] Other than Algeria, Tunisia, and Madagascar.
[4] Global.

*Cotton wastes*

[In pounds]

Cotton card strips made from cotton having a staple of less than 1$\frac{3}{16}$ inches in length, comber waste, lap waste, sliver waste, and roving waste, whether or not manufactured or otherwise advanced in value: *Provided, however*, That not more than 33⅓ percent of the quotas shall be filled by cotton wastes other than comber wastes made from cottons of 1$\frac{3}{16}$ inches or more in staple length in the case of the following countries: United Kingdom, France, Netherlands, Switzerland, Belgium, Germany, and Italy:

| Country of origin | Established total quota | Total imports, Sept. 20, 1956, to July 10, 1957 | Established 33⅓ percent of total quota | Imports, Sept. 20, 1956, to July 10, 1957 [1] |
|---|---|---|---|---|
| United Kingdom | 4,323,457 | 95,562 | 1,441,152 | 95,562 |
| Canada | 239,690 | 239,690 | | |
| France | 227,420 | | 75,807 | |
| British India | 69,627 | 69,627 | | |
| Netherlands | 68,240 | | 22,747 | |
| Switzerland | 44,388 | | 14,796 | |
| Belgium | 38,559 | | 12,853 | |
| Japan | 341,535 | | | |
| China | 17,322 | | | |
| Egypt | 8,135 | | | |
| Cuba | 6,544 | | | |
| Germany | 76,329 | 22,775 | 25,443 | 22,775 |
| Italy | 21,263 | | 7,088 | |
| Total | 5,482,509 | 427,654 | 1,599,886 | 118,337 |

[1] Included in total imports, col. 2.

Source: Prepared in the Bureau of Customs.

EXHIBIT 4

The Bureau of Customs announced today preliminary figures showing the quantities of wheat and wheat flour authorized to be entered, or withdrawn from warehouse, for consumption under the import quotas established in the President's proclamation of May 28, 1941, as modified by the President's proclamation of April 13, 1942, for the 12 months commencing May 29, 1957, as follows:

| Country of origin | Wheat | | Wheat flour, semolina, crushed or cracked wheat, and similar wheat products | |
|---|---|---|---|---|
| | Established quota | Imports, May 29, 1957, to June 10, 1957 | Established quota | Imports May 29, 1957, to June 10, 1957 |
| | *Bushels* | *Bushels* | *Pounds* | *Pounds* |
| Canada | 795,000 | 795,000 | 3,815,000 | 3,815,000 |
| China | | | 24,000 | |
| Hungary | | | 13,000 | |
| Hong Kong | | | 13,000 | |
| Japan | | | 8,000 | |
| United Kingdom | 100 | | 75,000 | |
| Australia | | | 1,000 | |
| Germany | 100 | | 5,000 | |
| Syria | 100 | | 5,000 | |
| New Zealand | | | 1,000 | |
| Chile | | | 1,000 | |
| Netherlands | 100 | | 1,000 | |
| Argentina | 2,000 | | 14,000 | |
| Italy | 100 | | 2,000 | |
| Cuba | | | 12,000 | |
| France | 1,000 | | 1,000 | |
| Greece | | | 1,000 | |
| Mexico | 100 | | 1,000 | |
| Panama | | | 1,000 | |
| Uruguay | | | 1,000 | |
| Poland and Danzig | | | 1,000 | |
| Sweden | | | 1,000 | |
| Yugoslavia | | | 1,000 | |
| Norway | | | 1,000 | |
| Canary Islands | | | 1,000 | |
| Rumania | 1,000 | | | |
| Guatemala | 100 | | | |
| Brazil | 100 | | | |
| Union of Soviet Socialist Republics | 100 | | | |
| Belgium | 100 | | | |
| Total | 800,000 | 795,000 | 4,000,000 | 3,815,000 |

EXHIBIT 5

The Bureau of Customs announced today the following preliminary figures showing the imports for consumption from January 1, 1957, to June 29, 1957, inclusive, of commodities for which quotas were established pursuant to the Philippine Trade Agreement Revision Act of 1955:

| Commodity | Established annual quota quantity | Unit of quantity | Imports as of June 29, 1957 |
|---|---|---|---|
| Buttons | 807,500 | Gross | 361,448 |
| Cigars | 190,000,000 | Number | 2,052,322 |
| Coconut oil | 425,600,000 | Pound | 84,052,259 |
| Cordage | 6,000,000 | do | 2,643,078 |
| Sugars: | | | |
| Refined | 1,904,000,000 | do | 22,275,756 |
| Unrefined | | | 1,205,307,991 |
| Tobacco | 6,175,000 | do | 2,153,343 |

***Tariff rate quotas proclaimed by President under sec. 350, Tariff Act of 1930, as amended (19 U. S. C. 1351)***

| Commodity | Date limitations effective | References |
|---|---|---|
| Cream, fresh or sour (par. 707, T. A.) | Jan. 1, 1936 | Pres. Proc. of Dec. 2, 1935 (T. D. 48033, Canadian Trade Agreement). Pres. Proc. 2761A of Dec. 16, 1947 (GATT), (T. D. 51802). |
| Whole milk, fresh or sour (par. 707, T. A.). | Jan. 1, 1939 | Pres. Proc. of Nov. 25, 1938 (T. D. 49752, Canadian Trade Agreement). Pres. Proc. 2761A of Dec. 16, 1947 (GATT), (T. D. 51802). |
| Fish, fresh or frozen, filleted, skinned, boned, etc., n. s. p. f.: cod, haddock, hake, pollock, cusk, and rosefish (par. 717 (b), T. A.). | do | (See references on milk.) |
| Irish or white potatoes: | | |
| Certified seed (par. 771, T. A.) | Jan. 1, 1936 | Pres. Proc. of Dec. 2, 1935 (T. D. 48033). Pres. Proc. 2761A of Dec. 16, 1947, GATT. Pres. Proc. 3184 of May 16, 1957 (T. D. 54406). |
| Other than certified seed (par. 771, T. A.). | Jan. 1, 1939 | Pres. Proc. of Nov. 25, 1938 (T. D. 49752). Pres. Proc. 2761A of Dec. 16, 1947, GATT. Pres. Proc. 3184 of May 16, 1957 (T. D. 54406). |
| Cattle, 700 pounds or more each (other than dairy cows) (par. 701, T. A.). | Jan. 1, 1936 | *Pres. Proc. of Dec. 2, 1935 (T. D. 48033). |
| Cattle, less than 200 pounds each (par. 701, T. A.). | Jan. 1, 1939 | *Pres. Proc. of Nov. 25, 1938 (T. D. 49752). *Quota limitations on both classes of cattle discontinued Jan. 31, 1943, by Pres. Proc. of Dec. 28, 1942 (T. D. 50797). *Quota provisions on both classes of cattle in GATT (T. D. 51802) became effective Apr. 1, 1953, Pres. Proc. 3007 of Mar. 2, 1953 (T. D. 53213). |
| Walnuts of all kinds, except unshelled, and walnut paste (par. 760, T. A.). | May 22, 1948 | Pres. Proc. 2761A of Dec. 16, 1947, GATT. Pres. Proc. of May 4, 1948 (T. D. 51909). Pres. Proc. 2908 of Oct. 12, 1950 (T. D. 52587). |
| Alsike clover seed (par. 763, T. A.) | July 1, 1954 | Pres. Proc. 3187 of June 24, 1957 (T. D. 54397). |
| Tuna fish (par. 718 (b), T. A.) | Apr. 16, 1956 | Pres. Proc. 3128 of Mar. 16, 1956 (T. D. 54051). |
| Woolen and worsted fabrics (par. 1108 and 1109 (a), T. A.). | Oct. 1, 1956 | Pres. Proc. 3160 of Sept. 28, 1956 (T. D. 54212). |

Abbreviations: Pres. Proc., Presidential proclamation; T. D., Treasury Decision; T. A., Tariff Act of 1930; GATT, General Agreement on Tariffs and Trade.

***Quota proclaimed by President under sec. 22, Agricultural Adjustment Act, as amended (7 U. S. C. 624)***

| Commodity | Date limitations effective | Reference |
|---|---|---|
| Peanut oil | July 1, 1953 | Pres. Proc. No. 3019 of June 8, 1953. |

*Absolute quotas proclaimed by President under sec. 22, Agricultural Adjustment Act, as amended (7 U. S. C. 624)*

| Commodity | Date limitations effective | References |
|---|---|---|
| Cotton of less than 1⅛ inches in staple length (other than harsh or rough cotton of less than ¾ inch in staple length, and other than linters).[1] | Sept. 20, 1939 | Pres. Proc. 2351 of Sept. 5, 1939 [1] (T. D. 49956) as amended by Pres. Proc. 2715 of Feb. 1, 1947 (T. D. 51624). |
| Cotton of 1⅛ inches or more (other than linters). | -----do------- | Pres. Proc. 2351 of Sept. 5, 1939 (T. D. 49956) as amended by Pres. Proc. 2560 of June 29, 1942 (T. D. 50681) and Pres. Proc. 2856 of Sept. 3, 1949 (T. D. 52311) and Pres. Proc. 3145 of June 29, 1956 (T. D. 54134) (global quota). |
| Harsh or rough cotton of less than ¾ inch in staple length. | Sept. 20, 1946 | Pres. Proc. 2715 of Feb. 1, 1947 (T. D. 51624) (global quota). |
| Cotton waste: [1] Cotton card strips made from cotton having a staple of less than 1³⁄₁₆ inches in length, comber waste, lap, sliver, and roving waste, whether or not manufactured or otherwise advanced in value. | Sept. 20, 1939 | Pres. Proc. 2351 of Sept. 5, 1939 (T. D. 49956) as amended by Pres. Proc. 2544 of Mar. 31, 1942 (T. D. 50603). |
| Wheat, not including any commodity unfit for human consumption. | May 29, 1941 | Pres. Proc. No. 2489 of May 28, 1941 (T. D. 50404), as amended by Pres. Proc. No. 2550 of Apr. 13, 1942 (T. D. 50609). (Pres. Proc. No. 2489 allocates to specific countries; like products from foreign countries not enumerated in the Proclamation inadmissible, under terms of the Proclamation.) |
| Wheat flour, semolina, crushed or cracked wheat and similar wheat products, not including any commodity unfit for human consumption. | -----do------- | |
| Peanuts, shelled, unshelled, blanched, salted, prepared, or preserved (including roasted peanuts, but not peanut butter). | July 1, 1953 | Pres. Proc. 3019 of June 8, 1953 (T. D. 53289). Pres. Proc. 3025 of June 30, 1953 (T. D. 53289). as amended by Pres. Proc. 3095 of May 16, 1955 (T. D. 53808) (global quota). See also Pres. Proc. 3084 of Mar. 9, 1955 (T. D. 53755) and Pres. Proc. 3152 of Aug. 29, 1956 (T. D. 54180). |
| Rye, rye flour, and rye meal----------- | Mar. 31, 1954 | Pres. Proc. of Mar. 31, 1954 (T. D. 53470). Pres. Proc. 3101 of June 29, 1955 (T. D. 53838).[2] Pres. Proc. 3189 of June 27, 1957 (T. D. 54394).[2] |
| Butter substitutes, including butter oil, containing 45 percent or more of butterfat and classifiable under par. 709 of the Tariff Act of 1930, as amended. | Jan. 1, 1957 | Pres. Proc. No. 3178 of Apr. 15, 1957 (T. D. 54345) (global quota). |

[1] Pres. Proc. 2351 allocates the quotas on short staple cotton (staple length of less than 1⅛ inches) and on cotton wastes to specific countries, and provides that no such cotton or cotton wastes produced in any country not listed in the proclamation may be released for consumption in the United States.

[2] Proclamations 3101 and 3189 provide a quota of 186,000,000 pounds for each 12-month period beginning July 1, 1955, 1956, 1957, and 1958, on an allocated basis—182,280,000 pounds to Canada and 3,720,000 pounds to "other foreign countries."

*Imports for consumption of tariff-rate quota commodities during periods indicated*

| Commodity and quota period | Annual quota | Quantity entered | Remarks |
|---|---|---|---|
| Cream fresh or sour: | | | |
| Calendar year: | *Gallons* | *Gallons* | |
| 1952 | 1,500,000 | 1,114 | |
| 1953 | 1,500,000 | 1,104 | |
| 1954 | 1,500,000 | 825 | |
| 1955 | 1,500,000 | 765 | |
| 1956 | 1,500,000 | 707 | |
| 1957 | 1,500,000 | | |
| Entered Jan. 2 to June 30, 1957 | | 195 | |
| Whole milk, fresh or sour: | | | |
| Calendar year: | | | |
| 1952 | 3,000,000 | 23,414 | |
| 1953 | 3,000,000 | 13,146 | |
| 1954 | 3,000,000 | 52,563 | |
| 1955 | 3,000,000 | 4,286 | |
| 1956 | 3,000,000 | 2,032 | |
| 1957 | 3,000,000 | | |
| Entered Jan. 2 to June 30, 1957 | | 437 | |
| Walnuts, shelled, blanched, roasted, and prepared or preserved (not including walnut paste): | | | |
| Calendar year: | *Pounds* | *Pounds* | |
| 1952 | 5,000,000 | 6,315,996 | Quota filled Sept. 26, 1952. |
| 1953 | 5,000,000 | 7,281,605 | Quota filled Aug. 7, 1953. |
| 1954 | 5,000,000 | [1] 7,150,118 | Quota filled Aug. 19, 1954. |
| 1955 | 5,000,000 | [1] 8,705,323 | Quota filled June 29, 1955. |
| 1956 | 5,000,000 | [1] 11,403,435 | Quota filled Mar. 7, 1956. |
| 1957 | 5,000,000 | | |
| Entered Jan. 2 to June 30, 1957 | | 1,354,926 | |
| Tuna fish, par. 718 (b): | | | |
| Apr. 16 to Dec. 31, 1956 | 28,757,393 | 27,783,267 | Quota limitations effective Apr. 16, 1956. |
| Calendar year 1957 | 44,528,533 | | |
| Entered Jan. 2 to June 30, 1957 | | 17,794,207 | Preliminary. |
| Alsike cloverseed: | | | |
| July 1, 1954, to June 30, 1955 | 1,500,000 | [1] 2,308,882 | Quota limitations effective July 1, 1954. |
| July 1, 1955, to June 30, 1956 | 2,500,000 | [1] 3,487,019 | Quota filled Oct. 22, 1955. |
| July 1, 1956, to June 30, 1957 | 2,500,000 | 235,814 | Quota filled Sept. 27, 1954. |
| Worsted and woolen fabrics: | | | |
| Oct. 1 to Dec. 31, 1956 | 3,500,000 | 3,269,487 | Quota limitations effective Oct. 1, 1956. |
| Calendar year 1957 | 14,000,000 | | |
| Entered Jan. 2 to June 30, 1957 | | 11,163,541 | Preliminary. |
| Peanut oil: | | | |
| July 1, 1953, to June 30, 1954 | 80,000,000 | 1,529.820 | |
| July 1, 1954, to June 30, 1955 | 80,000,000 | 26,037,536 | |
| July 1, 1955, to June 30, 1956 | 80,000,000 | 11,100,727 | |
| July 1, 1956, to June 30, 1957 | 80,000,000 | 0 | |
| Certified seed potatoes: | | | |
| Sept. 15, 1952, to Sept. 14, 1953 | 150,000,000 | 114,224,233 | |
| Sept. 15, 1953, to Sept. 14, 1954 | 150,000,000 | 100,578,047 | |
| Sept. 15, 1954, to Sept. 14, 1955 | 150,000,000 | 79,674,270 | |
| Sept. 15, 1955, to Sept. 14, 1956 | 150,000,000 | 139,892,180 | |
| Sept. 15, 1956, to Sept. 14, 1957 | 150,000,000 | | |
| Entered Sept. 15, 1956, to July 13, 1957 | | 111.912.085 | |
| Other than certified seed: | | | |
| Sept. 15, 1952, to Sept. 14, 1953 | 798,900,000 | 84,529,736 | |
| Sept. 15, 1953, to Sept. 14, 1954 | 60,000,000 | [2] 77,290,420 | Quota filled Feb. 18, 1954. |
| Sept. 15, 1954, to Sept. 14, 1955 | 329,100,000 | 16,600,003 | |
| Sept. 15, 1955, to Sept. 14, 1956 | 60,000,000 | [2] 111,376,537 | Quota filled Mar. 19, 1956. |
| Sept. 15, 1956, to Sept. 14, 1957 | 60,000,000 | | |
| Entered Sept. 15, 1956, to July 13, 1957 | | 34,891,316 | |
| Cattle, less than 200 pounds each: | *Head* | *Head* | |
| Apr. 1, 1953, to Mar. 31, 1954 | 200,000 | 4,654 | Quota limitations effective Apr. 1, 1953. |
| Apr. 1, 1954, to Mar. 31, 1955 | 200,000 | 5,129 | |
| Apr. 1, 1955, to Mar. 31, 1956 | 200,000 | 5,886 | |
| Apr. 1, 1956, to Mar. 31, 1957 | 200,000 | 9,401 | |
| Apr. 1, 1957, to Mar. 31, 1958 | 200,000 | | |
| Entered Apr. 1, to June 30, 1957 | | 10,879 | |
| Cattle, 700 pounds or more each (other than dairy cows): [3] | | | |
| Apr. 1, 1953, to Mar. 31, 1954 | 400,000 | 39,734 | |
| Apr. 1, 1954, to Mar. 31, 1955 | 400,000 | 90,449 | |
| Apr. 1, 1955, to Mar. 31, 1956 | 400,000 | 26,538 | |
| Apr. 1, 1956, to Mar. 31, 1957 | 400,000 | 21,956 | |
| Apr. 1, 1957, to Mar. 31, 1958 | 400,000 | | |
| Entered Apr. 1, to June 30, 1957 | | 17,959 | |

**See footnotes at end of table.**

*Imports for consumption of tariff-rate quota commodities during periods indicated*—Continued

| Commodity and quota period | Annual quota | Quantity entered | Remarks |
|---|---|---|---|
| | *Gallons* | *Gallons* | |
| Fish, fresh, or frozen, filleted, skinned, boned, sliced, etc.: Cod, haddock, hake, pollock, cusk, and rosefish: | | | |
| Calendar year 1952 (quarterly quota 7,868,027 pounds): | *Pounds* | *Pounds* | |
| 1st quarter | 7,868,027 | 31,022,123 | Quota filled Jan. 18, 1952. |
| 2d quarter | 7,868,027 | 22,180,250 | Quota filled Apr. 21, 1952. |
| 3d quarter | 7,868,027 | 26,179,349 | Quota filled July 14, 1952. |
| 4th quarter | 7,868,027 | 28,626,473 | Quota filled Oct. 1, 1952. |
| Total | 31,472,108 | 108,008,195 | |
| Calendar year 1953 (quarterly quota 8,486,572[4] pounds): | | | |
| 1st quarter | 8,466,572 | 23,376,064 | Quota filled Feb. 2, 1953. |
| 2d quarter | 8,466,572 | 20,202,401 | Quota filled May 4, 1953. |
| 3d quarter | 8,466,572 | 23,120,913 | Quota filled July 23, 1953. |
| 4th quarter | [4] 8,466,571 | 24,871,834 | Quota filled Oct. 15, 1953. |
| Total | 33,866,287 | 91,571,212 | |
| Calendar year 1954 (quarterly qouta 8,487,597 [4] pounds): | | | |
| 1st quarter | 8,487,597 | 29,087,187 | Quota filled Jan. 20, 1954. |
| 2d quarter | 8,487,597 | 32,713,939 | Quota filled Apr. 19, 1954. |
| 3d quarter | 8,487,597 | 43,206,417 | Quota filled July 6, 1954. |
| 4th quarter | [4] 8,487,595 | 32,617,189 | Quota filled Oct. 14, 1954. |
| Total | 33,950,386 | 137,624,732 | |
| Calendar year 1955 (quarterly quota 8,858,156[4] pounds): | | | |
| 1st quarter | 8,858,156 | 36,165,587 | Quota filled Jan. 24, 1955. |
| 2d quarter | 8,858,156 | 26,506,790 | Quota filled Apr. 21, 1955. |
| 3d quarter | 8,858,156 | 35,156,364 | Quota filled July 18, 1955. |
| 4th quarter | 8,858,156 | 32,239,005 | Quota filled Oct. 7, 1955. |
| Total | 35,432,624 | 130,067,746 | |
| Calendar year 1956 (quarterly quota 8,799,144 [1] pounds): | | | |
| 1st quarter | 8,799,144 | 38,123,353 | Quota filled Jan. 19, 1956. |
| 2d quarter | 8,799,144 | 28,277,572 | Quota filled Apr. 20, 1956. |
| 3d quarter | 8,799,144 | 36,344,996 | Quota filled July 10, 1956. |
| 4th quarter | [4] 8,799,143 | 35,873,913 | Quota filled Oct. 1, 1956. |
| Total | 35,196,575 | 138,708,834 | |
| Calendar year 1957 (quarterly quota 9,343,909 pounds): | | | |
| 1st quarter | 9,343,909 | 35,237,353 | Quota filled Jan. 2, 1957. |
| 2d quarter | 9,343,909 | [4] 31,242,118 | Quota filled Apr. 17, 1957. |
| Total [4] | 18,687,818 | [4] 66,479,471 | |

[1] Census import figures.
[2] Census import figures September through August.
[3] Quota administered on quarterly basis. Pres. Proc. of Mar. 2, 1953 provides (1) that not more than 400,000 head of such cattle may be entered during the quota year at the modified duty rate of 1½ cents per pound; (2) that not more than 120,000 head may be entered at this rate in any 3-month period beginning Apr. 1, July 1, Oct. 1, or Jan. 1.
[4] Preliminary.

*Imports for consumption of absolute quota commodities during periods indicated*

| Commodity and quota period | Annual quota (number of pounds) | Number of pounds entered | Remarks |
|---|---|---|---|
| Rye, rye flour, and rye meal: | | | |
| Mar. 31 to June 30, 1954 | 31,000,000 | 31,000,000 | Limitations effective Mar. 31, 1954, quota filled Apr. 16, 1954. |
| July 1, 1954, to June 30, 1955 | 186,000,000 | 186,000,000 | Quota filled Aug. 25, 1954. |
| July 1, 1955, to June 30, 1956 | (186,000,000) | | |
| Canada | 182,280,000 | 182,280,000 | Quota filled Jan. 12, 1956. |
| Other countries | 3,720,000 | 0 | |
| July 1, 1956, to June 30, 1957 | (186,000,000) | | |
| Canada | 182,280,000 | 182,276,116 | |
| Other countries | 3,720,000 | 0 | |
| July 1, 1957, to June 30, 1958 | (186,000,000) | | |
| Canada | 182,280,000 | 182,280,000 | Quota filled July 19, 1957. |
| Other countries (as of July 19) | 3,720,000 | 0 | |
| Butter substitutes, including butter oil, containing 45 percent or more butterfat and classifiable under par. 709, T. A., as modified: Calendar year 1957. | 1,800,000 | 1,800,000 | Quota filled May 24, 1957. |
| Peanuts, shelled, unshelled, blanched, roasted, prepared, or preserved (including roasted peanuts, but not including peanut butter): | | | |
| July 1, 1953, to June 30, 1954 | 1,709,000 | 9,265 | |
| July 1, 1954, to June 30, 1955 | 1,709,000 | 1,709,000 | Quota filled Nov. 16, 1954. |
| Mar. 9 to June 30, 1955 [1] | 51,000,000 | 26,650,492 | Entered Mar. 9 to May 14, 1955.[1] |
| Aug. 1, 1955, to July 31, 1956 | 1,709,000 | 1,709,000 | Quota filled Dec. 20, 1955. |
| Aug. 1, 1956, to July 31, 1957 [2] | 1,709,000 | 1,709,000 | Quota filled Aug. 1, 1956. |

[1] Pres. Proc. No. 3084 of Mar. 9, 1955, further modified Pres. Proc. No. 3019 of June 8, 1953, to permit entry, or withdrawal, for consumption from Mar. 9 through June 30, 1955, of not more than 51,000,000 pounds of peanuts, shelled, blanched, salted, prepared, or preserved (including roasted peanuts, but not including unshelled peanuts or peanut butter), of sizes averaging in representative samples not more than 40 kernels per ounce, subject to a fee of 2 cents per pound but not more than 50 per centum ad valorem, the fee to be in addition to any other duties on such peanuts.

Pres. Proc. No. 3095 of May 16, 1955, further amended and modified Pres. Proc. No. 3019 of June 8, 1953, so as to—

(1) extend the then current quota period through July 31, 1955;

(2) permit an unlimited additional quantity of shelled peanuts of all sizes to be entered, or withdrawn, for consumption from May 16 through July 31, 1955, subject to a fee of 2 cents per pound, but not more than 50 per centum ad valorem; and

(3) establish thereafter as the quota year for peanuts the 12-month period beginning August 1 in any year.

[2] Pres. Proc. No. 3152 of Aug. 29, 1956, further modified Proc. No. 3019 so as to permit an unlimited quantity of shelled peanuts of the Virginia type, of sizes averaging in representative samples not more than 40 kernels per ounce, to be entered, or withdrawn, for consumption during the period beginning Aug. 30 and ending at the close of business on Sept. 10, 1956, subject to a fee of 7 cents per pound, but not more than 50 per centum ad valorem. These peanuts were not reported for quota purposes, but information received from collectors showed 2,202,740 pounds of such peanuts were entered in the prescribed period.

Preliminary data on imports for consumption of cotton and cotton waste chargeable to the quotas established by the President's proclamation of September 5, 1939, as amended.

*Cotton (other than linters)*

[In pounds]

| Country of origin | Established quota | Imports |
|---|---|---|
| Cotton under 1⅛ inches, other than rough or harsh under ¾ inch, imports Sept. 20, 1956, to July 10, 1957: | | |
| Egypt and the Anglo-Egyptian Sudan | 783, 816 | |
| Peru | 247, 952 | |
| British India | 2, 003, 483 | 124, 060 |
| China | 1, 370, 791 | |
| Mexico | 8, 883, 259 | 8, 883, 259 |
| Brazil | 618, 723 | 600, 000 |
| Union of Soviet Socialist Republics | 475, 124 | |
| Argentina | 5, 203 | |
| Haiti | 237 | |
| Ecuador | 9, 333 | |
| Honduras | 752 | |
| Paraguay | 871 | |
| Colombia | 124 | |
| Iraq | 195 | |
| British East Africa | 2, 240 | |
| Netherlands East Indies | 71, 388 | |
| Barbados | | |
| Other British West Indies [1] | 21, 321 | |
| Nigeria | 5, 377 | |
| Other British West Africa [2] | 16, 004 | |
| Other French Africa [3] | 689 | |
| Algeria and Tunisia | | |
| Cotton, harsh or rough, of less than ¾ inch, imports Sept. 20, 1956, to June 29, 1957 | [4] 70, 000, 000 | 8, 223, 371 |
| Cotton 1⅛ inches or more, imports Aug. 1, 1956, to June 29, 1957, inclusive | [4] 45, 656, 420 | 21, 137, 549 |

[1] Other than Barbados, Bermuda, Jamaica, Trinidad, and Tobago.
[2] Other than Gold Coast and Nigeria.
[3] Other than Algeria, Tunisia, and Madagascar.
[4] Global.

*Cotton wastes*

[In pounds]

Cotton card strips made from cotton having a staple of less than 1³⁄₁₆ inches in length, comber waste, lap waste, sliver waste, and roving waste, whether or not manufactured or otherwise advanced in value: *Provided, however*, That not more than 33⅓ percent of the quotas shall be filled by cotton wastes other than comber wastes made from cottons of 1³⁄₁₆ inches or more in staple length in the case of the following countries: United Kingdom, France, Netherlands, Switzerland, Belgium, Germany, and Italy:

| Country of origin | Established total quota | Total imports, Sept. 20, 1956, to July 10, 1957 | Established 33⅓ percent of total quota | Imports, Sept. 20, 1956, to July 10, 1957 [1] |
|---|---|---|---|---|
| United Kingdom | 4, 323, 457 | 95, 562 | 1, 441, 152 | 95, 562 |
| Canada | 239, 690 | 239, 690 | | |
| France | 227, 420 | | 75, 807 | |
| British India | 69, 627 | 69, 627 | | |
| Netherlands | 68, 240 | | 22, 747 | |
| Switzerland | 44, 388 | | 14, 796 | |
| Belgium | 38, 559 | | 12, 853 | |
| Japan | 341, 535 | | | |
| China | 17, 322 | | | |
| Egypt | 8, 135 | | | |
| Cuba | 6, 544 | | | |
| Germany | 76, 329 | 22, 775 | 25, 443 | 22, 775 |
| Italy | 21, 263 | | 7, 088 | |
| Total | 5, 482, 509 | 427, 654 | 1, 599, 886 | 118, 337 |

[1] Included in total imports, col. 2.

Source: Prepared in the Bureau of Customs.

**Data on imports for consumption of cotton and cotton waste charged to the quotas established by the President's proclamation of September 5, 1939, as amended.**

*Cotton (other than linters)*

[In pounds]

| Country of origin | Established quota | Imports |
|---|---|---|
| Cotton under 1⅛ inches other than rough or harsh under ¾ inch, imports Sept. 20, 1955 to Sept. 19, 1956, inclusive: | | |
| Egypt and the Anglo-Egyptian Sudan | 783,816 | |
| Peru | 247,952 | 25,180 |
| British India | 2,003,483 | 358,883 |
| China | 1,370,791 | |
| Mexico | 8,883,259 | 8,883,259 |
| Brazil | 618,723 | 618,723 |
| Union of Soviet Socialist Republics | 475,124 | 322,197 |
| Argentina | 5,203 | |
| Haiti | 237 | |
| Ecuador | 9,333 | |
| Honduras | 752 | |
| Paraguay | 871 | |
| Colombia | 124 | |
| Iraq | 195 | |
| British East Africa | 2,240 | |
| Netherlands East Indies | 71,388 | |
| Barbados | | |
| Other British West Indies [1] | 21,321 | |
| Nigeria | 5,377 | |
| Other British West Africa [2] | 16,004 | |
| Other French Africa [3] | 689 | |
| Algeria and Tunisia | | |
| Cotton, harsh or rough, of less than ¾ inch, imports Sept. 20, 1955 to Sept. 19, 1956, inclusive | [4] 70,000,000 | 12,554,412 |
| Cotton 1⅛ inches or more, but less than 1¹¹⁄₁₆ inches (Feb. 1, 1956 to May 27, 1956) cotton 1⅛ inches or more (May 28, 1956 to July 31, 1956) imports Feb. 1, 1956 to July 31, 1956: | | |
| Interim quota [5] | [4] 22,828,210 | [6] 16,658,488 |
| Egypt | | [6] 14,278,330 |
| Peru | | 2,380,158 |

[1] Other than Barbados, Bermuda, Jamaica, Trinidad, and Tobago.
[2] Other than Gold Coast and Nigeria.
[3] Other than Algeria, Tunisia, and Madagascar.
[4] Global.
[5] Presidential Proclamation 3145, of June 29, 1956.
[6] All cotton entered under interim quota had staple length of 1⅛ inches or more but less than 1¹¹⁄₁₆ inches.

*Cotton wastes*

Cotton card strips made from cotton having a staple of less than 1$\frac{3}{16}$ inches in length, comber waste, lap waste, sliver waste, and roving waste, whether or not manufactured or otherwise advanced in value: *Provided, however,* That not more than 33$\frac{1}{3}$ percent of the quotas shall be filled by cotton wastes other than comber wastes made from cottons of 1$\frac{3}{16}$ inches or more in staple length in the case of the following countries: United Kingdom, France, Netherlands, Switzerland, Belgium, Germany, and Italy:

[In pounds]

| Country of origin | Established total quota | Total imports Sept. 20, 1955, to Sept. 19, 1956 | Established 33$\frac{1}{3}$ percent of total quota | Imports[1] Sept. 20, 1955, to Sept. 19, 1956 |
|---|---|---|---|---|
| United Kingdom | 4,323,457 | 946,576 | 1,441,152 | 946,576 |
| Canada | 239,690 | 239,690 | | |
| France | 227,420 | 68,287 | 75,807 | 68,287 |
| British India | 69,627 | 57,637 | | |
| Netherlands | 68,240 | | 22,747 | |
| Switzerland | 44,388 | | 14,796 | |
| Belgium | 38,559 | | 12,853 | |
| Japan | 341,535 | | | |
| China | 17,322 | | | |
| Egypt | 8,135 | | | |
| Cuba | 6,544 | | | |
| Germany | 76,329 | 25,443 | 25,443 | 25,443 |
| Italy | 21,263 | 7,039 | 7,088 | 7,039 |
| Total | 5,482,509 | 1,344,672 | 1,599,886 | 1,047,345 |

[1] Included in total imports, col. 2.

Source: Prepared in the Bureau of Customs.

Data on imports for consumption of cotton and cotton waste charged to the quotas established by the President's proclamation of September 5, 1939, as amended.

### *Cotton (other than linters)*

[In pounds]

| Country of origin | Established quota | Imports |
|---|---|---|
| Cotton under 1⅛ inches other than rough or harsh under ¾ inch, imports Sept. 20, 1954, to Sept. 19, 1955, inclusive: | | |
| Egypt and the Anglo-Egyptian Sudan | 783,816 | |
| Peru | 247,952 | 5,931 |
| British India | 2,003,483 | 214,953 |
| China | 1,370,791 | |
| Mexico | 8,883,259 | 8,883,259 |
| Brazil | 618,723 | 618,723 |
| Union of Soviet Socialist Republics | 475,124 | 411,813 |
| Argentina | 5,203 | |
| Haiti | 237 | |
| Ecuador | 9,333 | |
| Honduras | 752 | |
| Paraguay | 871 | |
| Colombia | 124 | |
| Iraq | 195 | |
| British East Africa | 2,240 | |
| Netherlands East Indies | 71,388 | |
| Barbados | | |
| Other British West Indies [1] | 21,321 | |
| Nigeria | 5,377 | |
| Other British West Africa [2] | 16,004 | |
| Other French Africa [3] | 689 | |
| Algeria and Tunisia | | |
| Cotton, harsh or rough, of less than ¾ inch, imports Sept. 20, 1954, to Sept. 19, 1955, inclusive | [4] 70,000,000 | 13,264,231 |
| Cotton 1⅛ inches or more, but less than 1<sup></sup>11/16 inches, imports Feb. 1, 1955, to Jan. 31, 1956 | 45,656,420 | 45,656,420 |
| Egypt | | 40,788,846 |
| Peru | | 4,340,546 |
| Mexico | | 527,024 |
| British India | | 4 |

[1] Other than Barbados, Bermuda, Jamaica, Trinidad, and Tobago.
[2] Other than Gold Coast and Nigeria.
[3] Other than Algeria, Tunisia, and Madagascar.
[4] Global.

### *Cotton wastes*

Cotton card strips made from cotton having a staple of less than 1 3/16 inches in length, comber waste, lap waste, sliver waste, and roving waste, whether or not manufactured or otherwise advanced in value: *Provided, however*, That not more than 33⅓ percent of the quotas shall be filled by cotton wastes other than comber wastes made from cottons of 1 3/16 inches or more in staple length in the case of the following countries: United Kingdom, France, Netherlands, Switzerland, Belgium, Germany, and Italy:

[In pounds]

| Country of origin | Established total quota | Total imports Sept. 20, 1954, to Sept. 19, 1955 | Established 33⅓ percent of total quota | Imports Sept. 20, 1954 to Sept. 19, 1955 [1] |
|---|---|---|---|---|
| United Kingdom | 4,323,457 | 1,441,152 | 1,441,152 | 1,441,152 |
| Canada | 239,690 | 238,346 | | |
| France | 227,420 | 72,721 | 75,807 | 72,721 |
| British India | 69,627 | 67,894 | | |
| Netherlands | 68,240 | 20,382 | 22,747 | 20,382 |
| Switzerland | 44,388 | | 14,796 | |
| Belgium | 38,559 | | 12,853 | |
| Japan | 341,535 | | | |
| China | 17,322 | | | |
| Egypt | 8,135 | | | |
| Cuba | 6,544 | | | |
| Germany | 76,329 | 24,390 | 25,443 | 24,390 |
| Italy | 21,263 | 6,627 | 7,088 | 6,627 |
| Total | 5,482,509 | 1,871,512 | 1,599,886 | 1,565,272 |

[1] Included in total imports, col. 2.

Source: Prepared in the Bureau of Customs.

**Data on imports for consumption of cotton and cotton waste charged to the quotas established by the President's proclamation of September 5, 1939, as amended.**

***Cotton (other than linters)***

[In pounds]

| Country of origin | Established quota | Imports |
|---|---|---|
| Cotton under 1⅛ inches other than rough or harsh under ¾ inch, imports, Sept. 20, 1953, to Sept. 19, 1954, inclusive: | | |
| Egypt and the Anglo-Egyptian Sudan | 783,816 | |
| Peru | 247,952 | 50,357 |
| British India | 2,003,483 | 33,968 |
| China | 1,370,791 | |
| Mexico | 8,883,259 | 6,339,207 |
| Brazil | 618,723 | 618,723 |
| Union of Soviet Socialist Republics | 475,124 | 431,975 |
| Argentina | 5,203 | |
| Haiti | 237 | |
| Ecuador | 9,333 | |
| Honduras | 752 | |
| Paraguay | 871 | |
| Colombia | 124 | |
| Iraq | 195 | |
| British East Africa | 2,240 | |
| Netherlands East Indies | 71,388 | |
| Barbados | | |
| Other British West Indies [1] | 21,321 | |
| Nigeria | 5,377 | |
| Other British West Africa [2] | 16,004 | |
| Other French Africa [3] | 689 | |
| Algeria and Tunisia | | |
| Cotton, harsh or rough, of less than ¾ inch, imports, Sept. 20, 1953, to Sept. 19, 1954, inclusive | [4] 70,000,000 | 12,806,952 |
| Cotton 1⅛ inches or more, but less than 1 11/16 inches, imports, Feb. 1, 1954, to Jan. 31, 1955 | [4] 45,656,420 | 41,041,666 |
| Egypt | | 39,518,998 |
| Peru | | 1,508,761 |
| British West Indies | | 13,395 |
| Mexico | | 512 |

[1] Other than Barbados, Bermuda, Jamaica, Trinidad, and Tobago.
[2] Other than Gold Coast and Nigeria.
[3] Other than Algeria, Tunisia, and Madagascar.
[4] Global.

*Cotton wastes*

Cotton card strips made from cotton having a staple of less than 1$\frac{3}{16}$ inches in length, comber waste, lap waste, sliver waste, and roving waste, whether or not manufactured or otherwise advanced in value: *Provided, however*, That not more than 33$\frac{1}{3}$ percent of the quotas shall be filled by cotton wastes other than comber wastes made from cottons of 1$\frac{3}{16}$ inches or more in staple length in the case of the following countries: United Kingdom, France, Netherlands, Switzerland, Belgium, Germany, and Italy:

[In pounds]

| Country of origin | Established total quota | Total imports Sept. 20, 1953, to Sept. 19, 1954 | Established 33⅓ percent of total quota | Imports Sept. 20, 1953, to Sept. 19, 1954 [1] |
|---|---|---|---|---|
| United Kingdom | 4,323,457 | 914,896 | 1,441,152 | 824,529 |
| Canada | 239,690 | 239,690 | | |
| France | 227,420 | | 75,807 | |
| British India | 69,627 | 69,408 | | |
| Netherlands | 68,240 | 16,668 | 22,747 | 16,668 |
| Switzerland | 44,388 | | 14,796 | |
| Belgium | 38,559 | 1,099 | 12,853 | 1,099 |
| Japan | 341,535 | | | |
| China | 17,322 | | | |
| Egypt | 8,135 | | | |
| Cuba | 6,544 | 6,544 | | |
| Germany | 76,329 | 23,940 | 25,443 | 23,940 |
| Italy | 21,263 | 7,088 | 7,088 | 7,088 |
| Total | 5,482,509 | 1,279,333 | 1,599,886 | 873,324 |

[1] Included in total imports, col. 2.

Source: Prepared in the Bureau of Customs.

Data on imports for consumption of cotton and cotton waste charged to the quotas established by the President's proclamation of September 5, 1939, as amended.

*Cotton (other than linters)*

[In pounds]

| Country of origin | Established quota | Imports |
|---|---|---|
| Cotton under 1⅛ inches other than rough or harsh under ¾ inch, imports Sept. 20, 1952 to Sept. 19, 1953, inclusive: | | |
| Egypt and the Anglo-Egyptian Sudan | 783,816 | |
| Peru | 247,952 | 53,664 |
| British India | 2,003,483 | |
| China | 1,370,791 | |
| Mexico | 8,883,259 | 8,883,259 |
| Brazil | 618,723 | 550,127 |
| Union of Soviet Socialist Republics | 475,124 | |
| Argentina | 5,203 | 1,382 |
| Haiti | 237 | |
| Ecuador | 9,333 | |
| Honduras | 752 | |
| Paraguay | 871 | |
| Colombia | 124 | |
| Iraq | 195 | |
| British East Africa | 2,240 | |
| Netherlands East Indies | 71,388 | |
| Barbados | | |
| Other British West Indies [1] | 21,321 | |
| Nigeria | 5,377 | |
| Other British West Africa [2] | 16,004 | |
| Other French Africa [3] | 689 | |
| Algeria and Tunisia | | |
| Cotton, harsh or rough, of less than ¾ inch, imports Sept. 20, 1952 to Sept. 19, 1953, inclusive | [4] 70,000,000 | 22,481,999 |
| Cotton 1⅛ inches or more but less than 1 11/16 inches, imports Feb. 1, 1953 to Jan. 31, 1954 inclusive | [4] 45,656,420 | 45,656,420 |
| Egypt | | 43,379,556 |
| Peru | | 2,209,565 |
| Mexico | | 67,299 |

[1] Other than Barbados, Bermuda, Jamaica, Trinidad, and Tobago.
[2] Other than Gold Coast and Nigeria.
[3] Other than Algeria, Tunisia, and Madagascar.
[4] Global.

*Cotton wastes*

Cotton card strips made from cotton having a staple of less than 1 3/16 inches in length, comber waste, lap waste, sliver waste, and roving waste, whether or not manufactured or otherwise advanced in value: *Provided, however*, That not more than 33⅓ percent of the quotas shall be filled by cotton wastes other than comber wastes made from cottons of 1 3/16 inches or more in staple length in the case of the following countries: United Kingdom, France, Netherlands, Switzerland, Belgium, Germany, and Italy:

[In pounds]

| Country of origin | Established total quota | Total imports Sept. 20, 1952, to Sept. 19, 1953 | Established 33⅓ percent of total quota | Imports Sept. 20, 1952, to Sept. 19, 1953 [1] |
|---|---|---|---|---|
| United Kingdom | 4,323,457 | 167,354 | 1,441,152 | 166,747 |
| Canada | 239,690 | 239,495 | | |
| France | 227,420 | 13,032 | 75,807 | 13,032 |
| British India | 69,627 | 66,004 | | |
| Netherlands | 68,240 | 15,715 | 22,747 | 15,715 |
| Switzerland | 44,388 | | 14,796 | |
| Belgium | 38,559 | 12,853 | 12,853 | 12,853 |
| Japan | 341,535 | | | |
| China | 17,322 | | | |
| Egypt | 8,135 | | | |
| Cuba | 6,544 | | | |
| Germany | 76,329 | 24,618 | 25,443 | 24,618 |
| Italy | 21,263 | 6,430 | 7,088 | 6,430 |
| Total | 5,482,509 | 545,501 | 1,599,886 | 239,395 |

[1] Included in total imports, col. 2.

Source: Prepared in the Bureau of Customs.

Data on imports for consumption of cotton and cotton waste charged to the quotas established by the President's proclamation of September 5, 1939, as amended.

*Cotton (other than linters)*

[In pounds]

| Country of origin | Established quota | Imports |
|---|---|---|
| Cotton under 1⅛ inches other than rough or harsh under ¾-inch, imports Sept. 20, 1951, to Sept. 19, 1952, inclusive: | | |
| Egypt and the Anglo-Egyptian Sudan | 783, 816 | |
| Peru | 247, 952 | 40, 185 |
| British India | 2, 003, 483 | |
| China | 1, 370, 791 | |
| Mexico | 8, 883, 259 | [1] 8, 542, 602 |
| Brazil | 618, 723 | 142, 837 |
| Union of Soviet Socialist Republics | 475, 124 | |
| Argentina | 5, 203 | |
| Haiti | 237 | |
| Ecuador | 9, 333 | |
| Honduras | 752 | |
| Paraguay | 871 | |
| Colombia | 124 | |
| Iraq | 195 | |
| British East Africa | 2, 240 | |
| Netherlands East Indies | 71, 388 | |
| Barbados | | |
| Other British West Indies [2] | 21, 321 | |
| Nigeria | 5, 377 | |
| Other British West Africa [3] | 16, 004 | |
| Other French Africa [4] | 689 | |
| Algeria and Tunisia | | |
| Cotton, harsh or rough, of less than ¾-inch, imports Sept. 20, 1951, to Sept. 19, 1952, inclusive | [5] 70, 000, 000 | 7, 123, 128 |
| Cotton 1⅛ inches or more but less than 1$^{11}/_{16}$ inches, imports Feb. 1, 1952, to Jan. 31, 1953 | [5] 45, 656, 420 | 45, 656, 420 |
| Egypt | | 40, 775, 298 |
| Peru | | 2, 995, 871 |
| Mexico | | 1, 885, 251 |

[1] Quota officially filled Jan. 20, 1952, but certain cotton was found to be long staple and so deleted. Deletions and adjustments so reduced quantity charged this quota was officially reopened. Quota was filled only to extent shown.

[2] Other than Barbados, Bermuda, Jamaica, Trinidad, and Tobago.

[3] Other than Gold Coast and Nigeria.

[4] Other than Algeria, Tunisia, and Madagascar.

[5] Global.

*Cotton wastes*

[In pounds]

Cotton card strips made from cotton having a staple of less than 1$\frac{3}{16}$ inches in length, comber waste, lap waste, sliver waste, and roving waste, whether or not manufactured or otherwise advanced in value: *Provided, however*, That not more than 33$\frac{1}{3}$ percent of the quotas shall be filled by cotton wastes other than comber wastes made from cottons of 1$\frac{3}{16}$ inches or more in staple length in the case of the following countries: United Kingdom, France, Netherlands, Switzerland, Belgium, Germany, and Italy:

| Country of origin | Established total quota | Total imports Sept. 20, 1951, to Sept. 19, 1952 | Established 33$\frac{1}{3}$ percent of total quota | Imports Sept. 20, 1951 to Sept. 19, 1952[1] |
|---|---|---|---|---|
| United Kingdom | 4,323,457 | 441,647 | 1,441,152 | 441,647 |
| Canada | 239,690 | 233,803 | | |
| France | 227,420 | | 75,807 | |
| British India | 69,627 | 69,627 | | |
| Netherlands | 68,240 | | 22,747 | |
| Switzerland | 44,388 | | 14,796 | |
| Belgium | 38,559 | | 12,853 | |
| Japan | 341,535 | | | |
| China | 17,322 | | | |
| Egypt | 8,135 | | | |
| Cuba | 6,544 | | | |
| Germany | 76,329 | 24,890 | 25,443 | 24,890 |
| Italy | 21,263 | 7,049 | 7,088 | 7,049 |
| Total | 5,482,509 | 777,016 | 1,599,886 | 473,586 |

[1] Included in total imports, col. 2.

Source: Prepared in the Bureau of Customs.

The Bureau of Customs announced today preliminary figures showing the quantities of wheat and wheat flour authorized to be entered, or withdrawn from warehouse, for consumption under the import quotas established in the President's proclamation of May 28, 1941, as modified by the President's proclamation of April 13, 1942, for the 12 months commencing May 29, 1957, as follows:

| Country of origin | Wheat | | Wheat flour, semolina, crushed or cracked wheat, and similar wheat products | |
|---|---|---|---|---|
| | Established quota | Imports, May 29, 1957, to June 30, 1957 | Established quota | Imports, May 29, 1957, to June 30, 1957 |
| | *Bushels* | *Bushels* | *Pounds* | *Pounds* |
| Canada | 795,000 | 795,000 | 3,815,000 | 3,815,000 |
| China | | | 24,000 | |
| Hungary | | | 13,000 | |
| Hong Kong | | | 13,000 | |
| Japan | | | 8,000 | |
| United Kingdom | 100 | | 75,000 | |
| Australia | | | 1,000 | |
| Germany | 100 | | 5,000 | |
| Syria | 100 | | 5,000 | |
| New Zealand | | | 1,000 | |
| Chile | | | 1,000 | |
| Netherlands | 100 | | 1,000 | |
| Argentina | 2,000 | | 14,000 | |
| Italy | 100 | | 2,000 | |
| Cuba | | | 12,000 | |
| France | 1,000 | | 1,000 | |
| Greece | | | 1,000 | |
| Mexico | 100 | | 1,000 | |
| Panama | | | 1,000 | |
| Uruguay | | | 1,000 | |
| Poland and Danzig | | | 1,000 | |
| Sweden | | | 1,000 | |
| Yugoslavia | | | 1,000 | |
| Norway | | | 1,000 | |
| Canary Islands | | | 1,000 | |
| Rumania | 1,000 | | | |
| Guatemala | 100 | | | |
| Brazil | 100 | | | |
| Union of Soviet Socialist Republics | 100 | | | |
| Belgium | 100 | | | |
| Total | 800,000 | 795,000 | 4,000,000 | 3,815,000 |

The Bureau of Customs announced today figures showing the quantities of wheat and wheat flour authorized to be entered, or withdrawn from warehouse, for consumption under the import quotas established in the President's proclamation of May 28, 1941, as modified by the President's proclamation of April 13, 1942, for the 12 months commencing May 29, 1956, as follows:

| Country of origin | Wheat | | Wheat flour, semolina, crushed or cracked wheat, and similar wheat products | |
|---|---|---|---|---|
| | Established quota | Imports May 29, 1956, to May 28, 1957 | Established quota | Imports May 29, 1956, to May 28, 1957 |
| | *Bushels* | *Bushels* | *Pounds* | *Pounds* |
| Canada | 795,000 | 795,000 | 3,815,000 | 3,815,000 |
| China | | | 24,000 | |
| Hungary | | | 13,000 | |
| Hong Kong | | | 13,000 | |
| Japan | | | 8,000 | |
| United Kingdom | 100 | | 75,000 | |
| Australia | | | 1,000 | 695 |
| Germany | 100 | | 5,000 | |
| Syria | 100 | | 5,000 | |
| New Zealand | | | 1,000 | |
| Chile | | | 1,000 | 1,000 |
| Netherlands | 100 | | 1,000 | |
| Argentina | 2,000 | | 14,000 | |
| Italy | 100 | | 2,000 | |
| Cuba | | | 12,000 | |
| France | 1,000 | | 1,000 | |
| Greece | | | 1,000 | |
| Mexico | 100 | | 1,000 | |
| Panama | | | 1,000 | |
| Uruguay | | | 1,000 | |
| Poland and Danzig | | | 1,000 | |
| Sweden | | | 1,000 | |
| Yugoslavia | | | 1,000 | |
| Norway | | | 1,000 | |
| Canary Islands | | | 1,000 | |
| Rumania | 1,000 | | | |
| Guatemala | 100 | | | |
| Brazil | 100 | | | |
| Union of Soviet Socialist Republics | 100 | | | |
| Belgium | 100 | | | |
| Total | 800,000 | 795,000 | 4,000,000 | 3,816,695 |

The Bureau of Customs announced today figures showing the quantities of wheat and wheat flour authorized to be entered, or withdrawn from warehouse, for consumption under the import quotas established in the President's proclamation of May 28, 1941, as modified by the President's proclamation of April 13, 1942, for the 12 months commencing May 29, 1955, as follows:

| Country of origin | Wheat | | Wheat flour, semolina, crushed or cracked wheat, and similar wheat products | |
|---|---|---|---|---|
| | Established quota | Imports May 29, 1955, to May 28, 1956 | Established quota | Imports May 29, 1955, to May 28, 1956 |
| | *Bushels* | *Bushels* | *Pounds* | *Pounds* |
| Canada | 795, 000 | 795, 000 | 3, 815, 000 | 3, 815, 000 |
| China | | | 24, 000 | |
| Hungary | | | 13, 000 | |
| Hong Kong | | | 13, 000 | |
| Japan | | | 8, 000 | |
| United Kingdom | 100 | | 75, 000 | |
| Australia | | | 1, 000 | |
| Germany | 100 | | 5, 000 | 2, 550 |
| Syria | 100 | | 5, 000 | |
| New Zealand | | | 1, 000 | |
| Chile | | | 1, 000 | |
| Netherlands | 100 | | 1, 000 | |
| Argentina | 2, 000 | | 14, 000 | 100 |
| Italy | 100 | | 2, 000 | 1, 000 |
| Cuba | | | 12, 000 | |
| France | 1, 000 | | 1, 000 | |
| Greece | | | 1, 000 | |
| Mexico | 100 | | 1, 000 | |
| Panama | | | 1, 000 | |
| Uruguay | | | 1, 000 | |
| Poland and Danzig | | | 1, 000 | |
| Sweden | | | 1, 000 | |
| Yugoslavia | | | 1, 000 | |
| Norway | | | 1, 000 | |
| Canary Islands | | | 1, 000 | |
| Rumania | 1, 000 | | | |
| Guatemala | 100 | | | |
| Brazil | 100 | | | |
| Union of Soviet Socialist Republics | 100 | | | |
| Belgium | 100 | | | |
| Total | 800, 000 | 795, 000 | 4, 000, 000 | 3, 818, 650 |

The Bureau of Customs announced today figures showing the quantities of wheat and wheat flour authorized to be entered, or withdrawn from warehouse, for consumption under the import quotas established in the President's proclamation of May 28, 1941, as modified by the President's proclamation of April 13, 1942, for the 12 months commencing May 29, 1954, as follows:

| Country of origin | Wheat | | Wheat flour, semolina, crushed or cracked wheat, and similar wheat products | |
|---|---|---|---|---|
| | Established quota | Imports May 29, 1954, to May 28, 1955 | Established quota | Imports May 29, 1954, to May 28, 1955 |
| | *Bushels* | *Bushels* | *Pounds* | *Pounds* |
| Canada | 795,000 | 795,000 | 3,815,000 | 3,815,000 |
| China | | | 24,000 | |
| Hungary | | | 13,000 | |
| Hong Kong | | | 13,000 | |
| Japan | | | 8,000 | |
| United Kingdom | 100 | | 75,000 | 70 |
| Australia | | | 1,000 | |
| Germany | 100 | | 5,000 | |
| Syria | 100 | | 5,000 | 5,000 |
| New Zealand | | | 1,000 | |
| Chile | | | 1,000 | |
| Netherlands | 100 | | 1,000 | |
| Argentina | 2,000 | | 14,000 | |
| Italy | 100 | | 2,000 | 2,000 |
| Cuba | | | 12,000 | |
| France | 1,000 | | 1,000 | |
| Greece | | | 1,000 | |
| Mexico | 100 | | 1,000 | |
| Panama | | | 1,000 | |
| Uruguay | | | 1,000 | |
| Poland and Danzig | | | 1,000 | |
| Sweden | | | 1,000 | |
| Yugoslavia | | | 1,000 | |
| Norway | | | 1,000 | |
| Canary Islands | | | 1,000 | |
| Rumania | 1,000 | | | |
| Guatemala | 100 | | | |
| Brazil | 100 | | | |
| Union of Soviet Socialist Republics | 100 | | | |
| Belgium | 100 | | | |
| Total | 800,000 | 795,000 | 4,000,000 | 3,822,070 |

**The Bureau of Customs announced today figures showing the quantities of wheat and wheat flour authorized to be entered, or withdrawn from warehouse, for consumption under the import quotas established in the President's proclamation of May 28, 1941, as modified by the President's proclamation of April 13, 1942, for the 12 months commencing May 29, 1953, as follows:**

| Country of origin | Wheat | | Wheat flour, semolina, crushed or cracked wheat, and similar wheat products | |
|---|---|---|---|---|
| | Established quota | Imports May 29, 1953, to May 28, 1954 | Established quota | Imports May 29, 1953, to May 28, 1954 |
| | *Bushels* | *Bushels* | *Pounds* | *Pounds* |
| Canada | 795,000 | 795,000 | 3,815,000 | 3,815,000 |
| China | ---------- | ---------- | 24,000 | ---------- |
| Hungary | ---------- | ---------- | 13,000 | ---------- |
| Hong Kong | ---------- | ---------- | 13,000 | ---------- |
| Japan | ---------- | ---------- | 8,000 | ---------- |
| United Kingdom | 100 | 34 | 75,000 | 140 |
| Australia | ---------- | ---------- | 1,000 | ---------- |
| Germany | 100 | 46 | 5,000 | 100 |
| Syria | 100 | ---------- | 5,000 | ---------- |
| New Zealand | ---------- | ---------- | 1,000 | ---------- |
| Chile | ---------- | ---------- | 1,000 | ---------- |
| Netherlands | 100 | ---------- | 1,000 | ---------- |
| Argentina | 2,000 | ---------- | 14,000 | ---------- |
| Italy | 100 | ---------- | 2,000 | ---------- |
| Cuba | ---------- | ---------- | 12,000 | ---------- |
| France | 1,000 | ---------- | 1,000 | ---------- |
| Greece | ---------- | ---------- | 1,000 | ---------- |
| Mexico | 100 | ---------- | 1,000 | ---------- |
| Panama | ---------- | ---------- | 1,000 | ---------- |
| Uruguay | ---------- | ---------- | 1,000 | ---------- |
| Poland and Danzig | ---------- | ---------- | 1,000 | ---------- |
| Sweden | ---------- | ---------- | 1,000 | ---------- |
| Yugoslavia | ---------- | ---------- | 1,000 | ---------- |
| Norway | ---------- | ---------- | 1,000 | ---------- |
| Canary Islands | ---------- | ---------- | 1,000 | ---------- |
| Rumania | 1,000 | ---------- | ---------- | ---------- |
| Guatemala | 100 | ---------- | ---------- | ---------- |
| Brazil | 100 | ---------- | ---------- | ---------- |
| Union of Soviet Socialist Republics | 100 | ---------- | ---------- | ---------- |
| Belgium | 100 | ---------- | ---------- | ---------- |
| Total | 800,000 | 795,080 | 4,000,000 | 3,815,240 |

The Bureau of Customs announced today figures showing the quantities of wheat and wheat flour authorized to be entered, or withdrawn from warehouse, for consumption under the import quotas established in the President's proclamation of May 28, 1941, as modified by the President's proclamation of April 13, 1942, for the 12 months commencing May 29, 1952, as follows:

| Country of origin | Wheat | | Wheat flour, semolina, crushed or cracked wheat, and similar wheat products | |
|---|---|---|---|---|
| | Established quota | Imports May 29, 1952, to May 28, 1953 | Established quota | Imports May 29, 1952, to May 28, 1953 |
| | *Bushels* | *Bushels* | *Pounds* | *Pounds* |
| Canada | 795, 000 | 794, 576 | 3, 815, 000 | 3, 815, 000 |
| China | | | 24, 000 | |
| Hungary | | | 13, 000 | |
| Hong Kong | | | 13, 000 | |
| Japan | | | 8, 000 | |
| United Kingdom | 100 | | 75, 000 | 44 |
| Australia | | | 1, 000 | |
| Germany | 100 | | 5, 000 | |
| Syria | 100 | | 5, 000 | |
| New Zealand | | | 1, 000 | |
| Chile | | | 1, 000 | |
| Netherlands | 100 | | 1, 000 | |
| Argentina | 2, 000 | | 14, 000 | |
| Italy | 100 | | 2, 000 | |
| Cuba | | | 12, 000 | |
| France | 1, 000 | | 1, 000 | |
| Greece | | | 1, 000 | |
| Mexico | 100 | | 1, 000 | |
| Panama | | | 1, 000 | |
| Uruguay | | | 1, 000 | |
| Poland and Danzig | | | 1, 000 | |
| Sweden | | | 1, 000 | |
| Yugoslavia | | | 1, 000 | |
| Norway | | | 1, 000 | |
| Canary Islands | | | 1, 000 | |
| Rumania | 1, 000 | | | |
| Guatemala | 100 | | | |
| Brazil | 100 | | | |
| Union of Soviet Socialist Republics | 100 | | | |
| Belgium | 100 | | | |
| Total | 800, 000 | 794, 576 | 4, 000, 000 | 3, 815, 044 |

# JAPANESE PROGRAM FOR REGULATION OF EXPORTS OF COTTON TEXTILES TO THE UNITED STATES

United States Department of Commerce

### 1. BACKGROUND

On January 16, 1957, the Japanese Government announced a 5-year voluntary program for the control of cotton textile exports to the United States. This program was developed after many months of discussions between United States and Japanese officials which were aimed at finding a sound and reasonable solution for the problems which had arisen as a result of the substantial increase in shipments of low-priced Japanese cotton textiles to the United States. The stated purposes of the Japanese program were to effect orderly marketing of Japanese cotton textiles in the United States, to avoid excessive concentrations, and to achieve broader diversification of such shipments.

In their program, the Japanese set an overall annual ceiling of 235 million square yards for export to the United States of cotton fabrics and cotton-manufactured goods. Ceilings were established for five major groups of cotton manufactures and for a number of specific items, such as ginghams, velveteens, blouses, shirts, brassieres, pillow cases, dish towels, etc. Provision was also made for consultation between the two Governments, should new areas of concentration of imports develop in the field of cotton textiles. Attachment 1 is a press release which summarizes the program.

The voluntary action by the Japanese Government was the culmination of a series of efforts by both Governments to meet the special problems faced by the domestic textile industry in a manner consistent with the basic foreign trade policy of the United States, and with the maintenance of close and friendly relations with Japan. As a result of the program and the discussions leading to it, "escape clause" actions on blouses and ginghams filed with the Tariff Commission under section 7 (a) of the Trade Agreements Extension Act of 1951, as amended, were withdrawn. Also the recommendation of the Tariff Commission for a sharp increase in velveteen-import duties was not accepted by the President.

### 2. IMPLEMENTATION—UNITED STATES

Both the Japanese and the United States Governments have adopted new measures to help the control program work. The United States, as of July 1, 1957, revised completely its statistical classification of cotton textile imports.[1] With this new classification and the import

[1] This revised classification is described in Statistical Requirements for Reporting Imports of Cotton Manufacturers—Supplement to Schedule A. Statistical Classification of Commodities Imported into the United States, Bureau of Census, U. S. Department of Commerce.

procedures agreed upon between Commerce and Treasury, a more precise identification of cotton textile imports will be possible. More detailed and useful data on imports of cotton textiles from all countries will be published monthly. These will show, among other things, United States imports of the items for which the Japanese have assigned specific quotas. A procedure has been arranged under which customs appraisers will verify the accuracy of importers' classification of cotton textiles. This should reduce the differences between Japanese export statistics and United States import statistics. Customs will also endeavor to identify all cases in which unauthorized transshipment is suspected. Information about certain of these cases will be passed on to the Japanese Government for appropriate remedial action. The Census Bureau will also undertake a comparison and reconciliation of Japanese export and United States import statistics. This should provide further indication of the degree of success of the program.

Attachment 2 is the Secretary of Commerce's announcement of the program.

Attachment 3 is the revised Statistical Requirements for Reporting Imports of Cotton Manufactures.

### 3. IMPLEMENTATION—JAPAN

For their part, the Japanese have instituted a comprehensive export licensing system which operates and is enforced both on the governmental level and also on the trade association level. A principal purpose of the licensing system, aside from limiting shipments of cotton goods to the quantities set forth in the program, is to prevent unauthorized transshipments to the United States. For the type of goods which are likely to be consumed in the United States, the sailing route of the vessel, the financial arrangements, and import policy of reported country of destination are checked. Also, in some cases a delivery verification certificate is required to be filed with the Government. Violators of the regulations may be refused further export allocations.

### 4. TRENDS OF SHIPMENTS UNDER THE PROGRAM

As of August 1, 1957, statistics of trade during 1957 are available only for the first 5 months of the year. The revised United States import classification became effective as of July 1, so that data for the first half of the year are not as detailed as they will be in the future. However, it is clear from the available data that United States imports of cotton products from Japan for the period January through May 1957 were substantially below imports during the comparable period of 1956.

On an overall basis, United States imports of cotton textiles from Japan are reported at $29 million for the first 5 months of 1957 compared with $41 million in the same period of 1956, a drop of 30 percent. Imports of cotton cloth during January–May 1957 were more than 50 percent below the rate in the same period of 1956 and well below the annual rate permitted by the quotas. In the apparel group, imports of sport and dress shirts and of knit T shirts and gloves are running below the annual rate which the Japanese quotas would allow.

Tables 1 and 2 provide a tabular summary of the statistics available as of August 1, 1957.

### 5. CHANGES IN QUOTAS

On July 9, 1957, the Japanese Embassy advised that the Japanese Government had decided to take advantage of the provision in the program which states, "within the overall annual total, the limit for any group may be exceeded by not more than 10 percent." The Japanese propose to reduce group I, cloth, by 6.2 percent, to increase group II, certain made-up goods, and group III, woven apparel, by 6 percent each, and to increase group V, miscellaneous, by 10 percent. These shifts are consistent with the program.

In summary, the changes are as follows:

[Million square yards]

| | As of Jan. 16, 1957 | As of July 9, 1957 |
|---|---|---|
| Group I—Cotton cloth | 113.0 | 106.0 |
| Group II—Made-up goods | 30.0 | 31.8 |
| Group III—Woven apparel | 71.0 | 75.3 |
| Group IV—Knit goods | 12.0 | 12.0 |
| Group V—Miscellaneous cotton textiles | 9.0 | 9.9 |
| Total | 235.0 | 235.0 |

### 6. EVALUATION

It is still far too early to attempt any comprehensive evaluation of the Japanese program on exports of cotton textiles. All indications are that Japanese authorities are doing their utmost to make the program a success. It may be anticipated that efforts will probably be made by some trading firms on both sides of the ocean to circumvent the program by unauthorized transshipments. In those few cases that have come to light thus far, the Japanese have moved promptly to take remedial measures. The Japanese have also been appreciative of suggestions and information relating to the program which have from time to time been passed on to them.

From the data available for the first 5 months, it would appear that the flow of Japanese cotton-textile imports has been stabilized, particularly with respect to the several items in which imports in 1955 and 1956 had been heavily concentrated.

The response of most segments of the domestic textile industry to the Japanese program has been favorable, and the great concern about import competition has been substantially alleviated. No new major problems of cotton-textile import competition have arisen in 1957. There has been a sizable increase in the rate of export of locally produced low-priced shirts from Hong Kong to the United States. The Japanese have been concerned about this because of a feeling that Hong Kong may be seeking to capitalize on the Japanese control, and because these shipments might be viewed as a Japanese effort to evade the control program. As a consequence, the Japanese are reported to be screening carefully and limiting shipments to Hong Kong of fabrics which might be used in the manufacture of shirts in Hong Kong for the American market.

22806—58——41

### 7. APPLICATION OF "VOLUNTARY CONTROLS" APPROACH TO OTHER SITUATIONS

In many ways the situation with respect to cotton textiles may be regarded as exceptional. The discussions with Japan which led to the voluntary control program were preceded by the institution of escape-clause investigations on imports of several cotton products including ginghams, velveteens, blouses, and pillowcases. Other domestic textile producers also discussed with the Tariff Commission the filing of requests for action on other kinds of textile products. In addition, Senate Resolution 236, pending in 1956, would have directed the Tariff Commission to make an escape-clause investigation with respect to the entire textile industry. The Tariff Commission, in commenting on the resolution, indicated that it would not be feasible for the Commission, within the 9-month period provided by statute, to complete the numerous investigations that the resolution would have required. The Congress recognized the validity of this point and modified the resolution to direct the Tariff Commission to give priority to escape-clause investigations relating to textiles.

The cotton-textile industry is extremely complex and produces thousands of closely interrelated products. Many of these different products are made in the same establishments with the same machinery by workers with the same skills. Consequently shifts in the production of individual textile items can be made with comparative ease. By the same token, because of these interrelationships the impact of heavy imports of a particular textile product could have repercussions on the price structure and competitive position of a large number of related products.

Another factor in the textile situation is its place in the economic and political relations between the United States and Japan. In recent years, Japan has been the principal foreign market for United States raw cotton. In terms of dollar value, Japanese imports of raw cotton from the United States were more than double the United States imports of cotton textiles from Japan. Cotton textiles have, on the other hand, constituted Japan's most important export to the United States. The possibility of successive imposition of import restrictions on a wide range of products under the escape-clause procedure and a disruption of its trade with the United States was a matter of grave concern to Japan. The Japanese Government decided therefore that it would be desirable to take steps to promote a more orderly and diversified development of trade in cotton textiles between the United States and Japan. Because of the various interests involved, it was natural that the Japanese Government should discuss with United States officials the program of voluntary controls which it was developing.

Thus it may be seen that voluntary restriction by foreign countries of their exports to the United States should be regarded as exceptional. Otherwise, many industries concerned about import competition would request that foreign restraints be sought on the products of concern to them. This would set aside the orderly procedures established by the Congress and jeopardize our trade policy.

Our trade agreements legislation recognizes in the escape clause that there may be cases where increased imports as a result of trade agreement concessions might cause or threaten serious injury to a domestic industry. An equitable procedure has been established to deal with situations involving the possibility of serious injury, and we should rely primarily on that procedure.

TABLE 1.—*United States imports from Japan of cotton-textile products for certain items subject to Japanese quota control*[1]

| Commodity | Unit | Japanese annual export quota 1957 [2] | United States imports [3] | | |
|---|---|---|---|---|---|
| | | | Year 1956 | January-May 1956 | January May 1957 |
| Total cotton semifinished and finished manufactures. | Million dollars | | 85 | 41 | 29 |
| Cotton cloth (including velveteens) | Thousand square yards | 113,000 | 149,841 | 82,112 | 40,087 |
| Velveteens | do | 2,500 | 6,898 | 2,308 | 124 |
| Handkerchiefs | Thousand dozen | 1,200 | 1,895 | 666 | 689 |
| Table damask | Thousand dollars | 3,720 | 4,895 | 1,551 | 1,336 |
| Sport shirts | Thousand dozen | 750 | 1,181 | 469 | 204 |
| Dress shirts | do | 300 | | | |
| Knit gloves and mittens | do | 450 | 476 | 185 | 189 |
| Floor coverings | Thousand square yards | | 3,744 | 1,747 | 1,429 |

[1] The revision of cotton textile import classifications effective July 1, 1957, will make available import data in terms closely comparable to items covered by the Japanese program.
[2] As established Jan. 16, 1957.
[3] United States imports will show some variation from Japanese export data because of shipping time, etc.
Source: Department of Commerce, Bureau of Foreign Commerce.

TABLE 2.—*Shipment of cotton products to the United States from Japan*

| Commodity | Unit | Japanese annual quota, 1957 [1] | Shipments, January–May 1957 |
|---|---|---|---|
| Group I: | | | |
| Gingham | Thousand square yards | 35,000 | 9,716 |
| Velveteen | do | 2,500 | 118 |
| Sheeting | do | 75,500 | 8,151 |
| Shirting (80 by 80) | do | | 0 |
| Other shirting | do | | 1,079 |
| Poplin | do | | 3,064 |
| Twill, sateen | do | | 8 |
| Yarn-dyed fabrics | do | | 3,827 |
| Others | do | | 2,107 |
| Total | | 113,000 | 28,070 |
| All combed | | 26,000 | 4,699 |
| Group II: | | | |
| Pillow cases | Thousand dozens | 400 | 130 |
| Dish towels | do | 800 | 297 |
| Table damask | Thousand dollars | 3,720 | 1,032 |
| Handkerchiefs | Thousand dozens | 1,200 | 451 |
| Others | Thousand pounds | 1,875 | 476 |
| Group III: | | | |
| Blouses | Thousand dozens | 1,500 | 734 |
| Sport shirts | do | 750 | 180 |
| Dress and work shirts | do | 300 | 37 |
| Brassieres | do | 600 | 275 |
| Trousers | do | 600 | 280 |
| Others | Thousand pounds | 2,321 | 718 |
| Group IV: | | | |
| T-shirts | Thousand dozens | 500 | 85 |
| Gloves and mittens | do | 450 | 145 |
| Others | Thousand pounds | 1,477 | 521 |
| Group V: | | | |
| Miscellaneous | do | (2) | 592 |
| Floor covering | Thousand square yards | (2) | 1,181 |

[1] As established Jan. 16, 1957.
[2] Quota for group V is not broken down. It is 9,000,000 square yards (1,965,522 pounds) in total.

Source: Prepared by Department of Commerce from Japanese Government reports.

[Attachment 1]

UNITED STATES DEPARTMENT OF COMMERCE, OFFICE OF THE SECRETARY

[Advance for release at 4 p. m. e. s. t., Wednesday, January 16, 1957]

(The following news release is being issued by the Departments of State, Commerce, and Agriculture.)

JAPANESE TEXTILES

The United States Government was informed today by the Government of Japan, in a note from the Ambassador of Japan to the Secretary of State, concerning the details of the Japanese program for the control of exports of cotton textiles to the United States.

This program, effective as of January 1, 1957, has a 5-year duration. The details were developed pursuant to a note submitted to the United States Government by the Government of Japan on September 27, 1956.

The new program places an annual overall ceiling of 235 million square yards on the export of all types of Japanese cotton cloth and cotton manufactures to the United States, with specific ceilings on many items.

The Departments of State, Commerce, and Agriculture issued the following joint statement commenting on the new Japanese program:

"The action taken by Japan is a major step forward in the development of orderly and mutually beneficial trade between the United States and Japan. It is a contructive measure aimed at forestalling possible future injury to the United States cotton-textile industry. It recognizes the problem faced by various segments of the domestic industry, and meets this problem through the voluntary exercise of restraint on exports of cotton textiles to the American market.

"The program demonstrates an understanding by Japan of the importance of the orderly marketing of an item as significant to the economies of both countries as cotton textiles. It not only provides an overall limit on the total volume of cotton-textile exports to the United States, but perhaps even more important, it sets a pattern for the diversification of these exports over the entire area of cotton-textile manufactures. Under this program, it should be possible to avoid situations such as those which developed during 1955 and 1956 in blouses, velveteens, and ginghams.

"The Japanese action provides a basis for the expansion of 2-way trade between the United States and Japan in an atmosphere of the friendliest cooperation between the 2 nations, such as that which has characterized the economic and political relations between the 2 countries over the last decade.

"For the United States cotton-textile industry, the Japanese program should provide a basis on which it can look forward to the future with the confidence and the knowledge that import competition from Japan will follow an orderly pattern.

"Officials of the several interested United States Government departments had the opportunity to hold a series of constructive discussions with representatives of the Japanese Government. Such discussions may be held from time to time, as needed, during the course of the program."

The overall ceiling for the export of cotton manufactures to the United States announced by the Japanese Government is 235 million square yards. Within this ceiling, the limit for cotton cloth is 113 million yards; the limits for woven and knit apparel total 83 million yards; and the limits for household goods and miscellaneous items total 39 million yards.

The cloth ceiling of 113 million square yards compares with a ceiling of 150 million square yards in 1956. Individual ceilings are specified for velveteens, ginghams, and high-grade (combed) cotton fabrics. The export limit for velveteen is 2.5 million square yards for each of the first 2 years. The export limit for gingham is 35 million square yards for each of the first 2 years. With respect to the remaining 75.5 million yards for "all other fabrics" a limit for high-grade (combed) cotton fabrics of 26 million square yards is established.

In the other groups covering cotton made-up goods, individual annual ceilings have been established for pillowcases, dish towels, handkerchiefs, table damask, blouses, sport shirts, dress and work shirts, brassieres and other body supporting garments, men's and boys' T-shirts, and gloves and mittens.

The program also provides for Japanese cotton-textile exports to the United States to be distributed equally by quarters as far as practicable and as necessary to meet seasonal demands. The Japanese Government will also take all feasible steps to prevent transshipments to the United States through third countries.

The Japanese program has been developed in an effort to meet the problems which arose in 1955 when exports of Japanese textiles to the United States increased sharply. These exports were heavily concentrated with respect to certain commodities such as blouses, velveteens, and ginghams. Not only were the domestic producers of these items affected, but the entire textile industry became concerned because of the impact on the price structure of the industry and the uncertainty as to where other concentration of Japanese exports might hit.

The concern of the textile industry was expressed in a number of escape clause petitions filed with the Tariff Commission, and in requests to the Congress and to the executive branch for action to establish quotas on imports of textiles.

More than a year ago the executive branch of the United States Government began an extensive study of the problem with a view to finding a resolution which would provide appropriate safeguards for the domestic industry within the framework of established United States foreign-trade policy.

One phase of the executive branch action involved factfinding and frequent consultation with representative United States cotton-textile and apparel manufacturers.

A second phase involved a series of discussions with representatives of the Japanese Government, aimed at exploring constructively measures which might alleviate the situation, and at conveying to the Japanese Government a better appreciation of the nature of the American market and the desirability of a program of orderly marketing and sound merchandising.

On December 21, 1955, the Government of Japan announced a program for the voluntary control of exports of cotton goods to the United States in 1956. On May 16, 1956, the Japanese Government advised the United States officially of the details of the program and of its intention to exercise similar controls for 1957.

On September 27, 1956, the Japanese Government advised the United States as to the principles on which Japan intended to base its control of cotton-textile exports to the United States for 1957 and subsequent years. This note set forth the principles of diversification of exports and avoidance of excessive concentration of exports in any particular period or on any particular item. The 5-year program now established represents the actual implementation of these principles.

---

[Attachment 2]

UNITED STATES DEPARTMENT OF COMMERCE, OFFICE OF THE SECRETARY

[Advance release for Monday a. m.'s, May 27, 1957]

SECRETARY WEEKS ANNOUNCES IMPROVEMENT IN COTTON-TEXTILE IMPORT STATISTICS

Secretary of Commerce Sinclair Weeks announced today that the United States will collect and publish more detailed statistics of cotton-textile imports from all countries commencing July 1, 1957.

"This action is a step forward in the efforts which the Government is making to keep the business community and the public better informed about the volume of cotton-textile imports and their relationship to the domestic textile situation," Secretary Weeks said.

That the United States would move to obtain fuller information on the volume of cotton-textile imports was indicated early this year after the Japanese Government announced its 5-year program for control of cotton-textile shipments to the United States.

The new statistics will be in terms of a revised and modernized classification which has been developed because of the great interest in imports of cotton textiles. This interest has been stimulated by the increased volume of such imports during the past 2 years.

To provide for continuity, the Bureau of the Census of the Department of Commerce will continue to publish monthly import statistics for cotton textiles on the present basis. In addition, Census will publish monthly statistics summarized on the revised basis.

The new statistics on the revised basis will provide, for example, for separation of a number of apparel items now combined in the statistics. For some apparel items there will be a further breakdown by material of which made (gingham, corduroy, poplin, etc.). For cotton cloth, distinctions will be made by material and by whether the yarn was carded or combed.

Obtaining and publishing cotton-textile import statistics on both the present basis and the revised basis will be accomplished by requiring importers to furnish Census with figures in accordance with a new reporting manual, Statistical Requirements for Reporting Imports of Cotton Manufactures. Importers will provide detailed information which can be summarized into each of the two series of statistics which will be available for July and subsequent months.

The Department of Commerce and the Treasury Department's Bureau of Customs are issuing proposed regulations simultaneously to require that the more detailed descriptions be shown on the import entry form and also on an annex to the customs invoice for cotton textiles. The entry form is ordinarily prepared by the importer or customs broker, the invoice by the foreign supplier.

As part of the program for obtaining more complete and accurate data, special efforts will be made at the time of clearance of the merchandise through customs to verify the origin of United States cotton-textile imports and to identify instances in which the original destination has been changed.

The revised reporting requirement covers the entire range of cotton manufactures, including yarn, fabric, woven and knit garments, and household goods made of cotton or in chief value cotton. A new commodity-numbering system will be employed in which the letter "X" will precede all numbers.

Secretary Weeks added that domestic production statistics of textile and apparel items are also being reviewed.

# THE REGULATION OF IMPORTS BY QUOTAS

**O. R. Strackbein, chairman, the Nationwide Committee of Industry, Agriculture, and Labor on Import-Export Policy**

The tariff has been the principal means employed by the United States throughout its history for the protection of its industry from foreign competition in the home market. Until recent years the tariff was relied on almost exclusively as our instrument of protection. In more recent times, import quotas have been used as a supplementary device to protect certain agricultural products.

The aim of this paper is to examine the relative merits of the tariff and the quota as means of regulating import competition.

The protective tariff as distinguished from a tariff for revenue only may serve one or more related purposes.

First and foremost stands the aim to reduce the impact of competitive imports by increasing their landed cost. A duty levied on imports may result in reducing the quantity of the goods that otherwise would flow into the country or in raising the price of the goods that do enter. If the quantity of imports falls off because of the tariff, the domestic manufacturers will presumably be able to sell more of their own output. If the price of imported goods is increased because of the tariff but the volume of the inflow is not reduced, the pressure on the prices obtained by domestic producers nevertheless is lessened and domestic production becomes or remains more profitable.

The tariff may serve other purposes, depending upon its flexibility. It may be used to encourage manufacturing industry by providing low rates of duty or none at all on raw materials or semifinished goods and higher ones on finished products. It may be used to encourage particular industries, such as those of strategic importance to the national defense.

In the past and to some extent today the tariff was and is also used by trading nations to favor imports from some countries over others or to discourage imports from particular countries. The use of the tariff as a flexible instrument for discriminatory purposes was more widespread in the past than it is today. Many countries had 2 or 3 levels of tariffs for the very purpose of discrimination—sometimes for bargaining purposes, other times for retaliation, and then again at times for preferential treatment of members of an empire or other close political association.

In recent years, particularly since the signing of the General Agreement on Tariffs and Trade in 1947, the tariff as such has been made much less flexible through wider acceptance of the most-favored-nation clause and the general principle of nondiscrimination. Even the preferential tariff, such as the British imperial preferential system, based on special political and economic relations, has been condemned and substantially reduced.

This is not at all to say that discrimination has been eliminated from world trade. Where the tariff has lost much of its flexibility in this respect other methods of controlling the flow of trade, both inward and outward, have more than filled its previous office. Exchange controls, import and export licenses, multiple-exchange rates, bilateral-trade agreements, import quotas, and other means have been used very extensively to direct both the volume and the origin and destination of trade.

The United States, in sharp contrast with most of the other leading trading nations, has continued to rely, for the most part, and with respect to industrial products, exclusively, on the tariff as its principal protective instrument. It is also faced with the fact that some of the important trading nations do not adhere as we do to the unconditional most-favored-nation clause. As a result, this country lacks the flexibility enjoyed by other countries in their protective devices.

These facts, among others, have done much to bring the tariff under closer scrutiny in the United States in recent years. The tariff's failure to fit particularly serious competitive situations has been revealed as a glaring weakness as imports of one product after another have since 1948 eaten into our market at will, gaining an ever-increasing share of the whole. Some of these circumstances came to light in escape-clause cases before the United States Tariff Commission.

The revival of Japan in particular as a source of imports, together with the sharper competitive impact of goods coming from that and similar areas, showed up the tariff as a frail protective instrument indeed, limited as its flexibility has been by the strictures of the escape clause and our adherence to the unconditional most-favored-nation clause.

There may be a wide gap, for example, between the prices on the same goods coming from different countries. A given tariff rate, say one of 25 percent might be suitable with respect to the goods coming from some countries but wholly inadequate when these goods come from other parts of the world. A rate as high as 100 or 200 percent might be necessary in such cases to provide the same braking power as the 25-percent rate in the other cases.

Yet any given tariff rate under the most-favored-nation clause and the principle of nondiscrimination must be applied to the same goods coming from all countries without distinction. This fact, on the other hand, has made the tariff almost useless as a protective instrument with respect to many products. If the higher rate of duty (100 or 200 percent) were applied under the circumstances cited above, our market would be delivered to the countries shipping at the lowest cost. The higher cost countries would be excluded. If, on the other hand, a low tariff were used, the low-cost countries would still enjoy a competitive margin and could elbow the higher cost ones out of the way, as has been happening in recent years.

Contrary to some economic theories, high cost of goods does not necessarily arise from relative inefficiency. It may and often does arise from unequal social legislation that imposes higher cost burdens on producers in one country than those borne by their competitors in other countries. This fact often places the higher standard countries at a relative disadvantage.

The failure of the tariff, when used without other props, is therefore not of concern to the United States alone. Other countries have seen themselves superseded in our market by cheaper imports from third areas; and the end is not yet. This gives them an interest in any system, such as the import quota, which might help preserve their share of our market.

Quite aside from the unequal braking power of the tariff when employed by itself, it has other deficiencies. One of these defects, namely, rigidity in relation to market conditions, was partially overcome when we adopted seasonal rates on fresh vegetables, in recognition of an uneven seasonal relation between supply and demand; but other weaknesses remain.

Specific rates, based as they are on some measurement of quantity, for example, do not respond to the changes in price levels that occur over a period of time. Exclusive of the tariff reductions made under the trade agreements program, the protective incidence of our specific duty rates have fallen as much since 1934 as prices on our imports have risen. No compensation has been provided by the United States to offset this shrinkage although other countries have in many cases raised their rates in keeping with the rise in prices.

Purely ad valorem rates, on the other hand, offer least protection precisely where and when prices of imports are low and can do the most damage. This defect has already been mentioned as arising when the same imports come respectively from lower and higher standard countries. It shows itself just as disastrously when the general price level itself has fallen and imports aggravate an already bad surplus situation. The ad valorem rate is then at its weakest. The compound rate, consisting of a combination of the ad valorem and specific rate, has been adopted in some instances to overcome this weakness; but widespread reductions in both the specific and the ad valorem rates in compound rates have largely nullified the intent of the compound system.

Undoubtedly the greatest failure of the tariff, used alone, is encountered when a surplus position has developed on a broad front and a buyer's market threatens a recession or a depression.

It is on such occasions that a more flexible instrument is needed. Protection of industry and labor and of the economy as a whole from competitive imports is never more important than in times of surplus accumulation. Even without the problem of imports domestic industries have great difficulty in adjusting to a buyer's market, i. e., an overstocked condition. However, their hope of doing so is greatly enhanced if they can control the supply of goods. This they can often accomplish on the domestic front by cutting back production.

If under these circumstances imports remain out of control their unimpeded flow can wreck all the efforts of domestic producers to make the necessary adjustment of supply to demand. A single, fixed tariff rate is then of little or no avail. What is needed is an instrument that is responsive to the needs of the occasion. Such an instrument would serve the double purpose of protecting not only a given industry but the economy in general.

An import quota, either alone or in combination with the tariff, lends itself to the requirements of a flexible instrument. It can be designed to meet the usually foreseeable situations and at the same time may be provided with provisions for emergency adjustments. An example of such adjustability is found in the sugar quota established under the Sugar Act. The annual quota can be opened for revision when circumstances of consumption or supply demonstrate that the estimate on which the quota was initially based was in error. The quota can then be adjusted in a short time, by upward or downward revision.

The need for a flexible instrument is not usually appreciated in fair economic weather. Under stable conditions the stability of a fixed tariff rate is indeed highly esteemed. Yet a quota system can be devised to provide equally stable treatment of imports. A flexible implement need of course not be flexed when there is no occasion for a change in treatment. The very fact, however, that it can be used to ward off trouble should it threaten, is conducive to continuation of stability. In this respect an import quota system would introduce a measure of confidence in the future similar to the confidence in the money supply introduced under the Federal Reserve System.

Such a stabilizing influence and such a prop to confidence would be of immeasurable value to domestic production and employment because of its effect on planning forward commitments and expansion proposals. If the trend of imports is such that grave doubt is cast upon the future market for the domestic product, confidence cannot thrive. Planning then labors under a severe handicap. A damper falls upon plants to expand plant capacity; and outlays for development and promotion fall under a spell of fear. Such an atmosphere is essentially the atmosphere of panic, of negative behavior and eventual defeat. It is wholly contrary to the needs of an expanding economy.

Even in the postwar years of vast economic expansion in this country there have been several occasions when doubts began to arise about the future course of business. On each such occasion several industries have faced difficult import competition and the elements of a recession were present in sufficient degree to cause considerable concern. However, the uneven front of our economy possibly saved the day. As one industry or trade receded another moved forward. In the end the forward momentum prevailed; but not so surely that it could not be said that the situation had been delicate.

Obviously, since imports and exports represent only a small share of our total national product, they are not the most important factor in determining the general economic trend; but in a delicate situation they may exert enough influence to tip the balance. It is therefore important that they be brought under effective control. Of the two, the trend of imports will exert a greater influence than the trend of exports.

A decline in exports has not nearly the panic-impelling power as an increase in imports. Control of imports should therefore give us the greater concern.

The reason is that imports much more than exports confront the domestic producer with an unknown potential for trouble that is not only unpredictable but is wholly beyond his control. If imports have been increasing and particularly if they have been capturing a larger share of the domestic market nothing but gloom meets the outlook. Obviously the competitive advantage lies with the imports or they would not have gained so much ground.

Very well: What to do?

Every effort must, of course, be made under such circumstances by domestic producers to assess the relative competitive situation as it affects sales of imports versus the domestic product. This means an analysis of costs, kind of product, distribution methods and all other factors, such as advertising, that have a bearing on comparative competitive standing. One difficulty that explains some of the fear of imports under such circumstances is that it is not easy to arrive at an answer to some of these questions because the imports come from other countries, and in many instances the competitive factors that determine their market advantages or limitations in this country are a closed book to our domestic producers.

Often, of course, it is known in gross why the foreign product has succeeded in displacing its domestic rival: the reason may be nothing more than a distinct price advantage. To market a product of equal quality at a competitive price the domestic producer would find that his labor and material costs are too high. Yet these are quite inflexible factors, more or less fixed or determined by law. Price supports of basic farm products, minimum wage laws, obligatory collective bargaining, etc., have virtually destroyed his competitive resources.

If the domestic industry is a small one, composed of a number of competing producers, a running battle with imports is almost certainly a losing engagement. The funds necessary for research and development, product improvement, promotional activity, so badly needed, will probably not be available or if on hand will be needed in the struggle itself.

The natural reaction of domestic producers, faced with an overstock of high-priced goods, when confronted with an increasing tide of imports, is to curtail production in order to reduce inventory losses and, if possible, to adjust to the new situation. This means laying off employees or putting the force on a short workweek. In any case, it means unemployment and shrinking payrolls. Of course, even such steps may not succeed so long as imports remain free to come in at the same rate or even a higher one. Should such a situation become widespread the danger to the economy as a whole would be obvious.

Now, say some scholarly economists, such beleaguered domestic producers should give up and go into the production of different goods, goods in which foreign competition is not so keen; or, say others, the Government should lend assistance in the form of loans, subsidies, training of workers in new occupations or similar support, so that the previous field of production may be surrendered to imports.

These suggestions usually rest on 1 of 2 assumptions, or a combination of both. The first is that a domestic industry that cannot compet with imports ipso facto convicts itself of inefficiency. The other is that for the sake of a larger volume of foreign trade, of which imports represent one-half of the equation, some domestic industries must give way to the national interest, especially as this may be determined by the exigencies of a general foreign trade policy.

Neither of these assumptions can be credited if we keep in mind, first, that inability to compete with imports is not of itself proof of inefficiency, since obligations of the kind already mentioned, imposed by law, may be and probably are the cause of inability to compete;

and, second, that the sacrifice of a domestic industry not only cannot be justified in behalf of a national policy that may itself be faulty, either in its conception or execution, but is abhorrent to a sense of justice and national self-respect. There is no clear cause-and-effect relationship, for example, between increasing imports of some product that is not essential to the national defense, and the success of any sound foreign policy. A policy that suggests such a relationship is more likely to be at fault itself.

It would be more compelling to say that any legitimate American industry is entitled to continue its existence in this country if it can supply a product that the consumer demands, at prices the consumer is ready and willing to pay and high enough to return a reasonable profit. It must be assumed, of course, that such an industry is in compliance with the laws of the land in respect of minimum wages, maximum hours, taxes, social security, etc. so that such relatively high costs as may burden its production from these sources are inescapable and not the result of poor management. This test would properly cut through the foggy uncertainties of the theory of comparative costs and dispose of the unavailing calculus of the academic economists.

If entitlement of this kind is recognized the next question would naturally be how best to assure continuance in existence of a domestic industry so far as it might be jeopardized by import competition.

This brings us back to the question of the best form of protection. We have noted the weaknesses of the tariff by itself and also the superiority of the import quota to the tariff, especially in point of flexibility. There now remain some questions about the most suitable form of quota.

If we keep in mind the purposes of an import quota system as indicated in the preceding pages, we find that it should be designed, either by itself or in combination with the tariff: (1) to afford protection against undue encroachment of imports on the domestic market without introducing unnecessary rigidity into the trend of trade; (2) to introduce greater certainty into planning, scheduling, and pricing in domestic production so that development of products, renewal or expansion of plant and equipment, and greater employment may proceed in an atmosphere of greater confidence in the future, freed from the panic-potential of import competition; (3) to provide for sharing of the domestic market with imports under conditions that make it possible for domestic producers to live with the type of competition involved; and (4) to assure a maximum of trade by setting up an orderly system of fair competition in place of a chaotic and disruptive operation in the name of a liberal trade policy.

An import quota involves a limitation of the quantity of imports, and by this very fact hits at the source of injury from import competition. At the same time, however, it may strike at the very heart of trade. That is reason enough for proceeding with care in the establishment of quotas.

By puttiug a ceiling on imports, either absolute or approximate, the import quota deprives import competition of its most objectionable feature, namely, the creation of uncertainty and, therefore, the destruction of confidence, as described above. Ridding those of our producers and industries who are faced with severe or potentially severe import competition of this disruptive factor would be of inestimable value; and would be justified so long as the limitation was neither too severe nor so inflexible as to freeze particular trade patterns against change.

One of the merits of the flexible import quota, either by itself or in combiuation with the tariff, is its adaptability to a great diversity of circumstances. For example, in combination with the tariff a quota may be shaped so that a predetermined share of domestic consumption could be accorded free entry in the form of imports. This might be 5 percent, 10 percent, 25 percent, 50 percent, or any other share. Beyond that level a tariff could be levied for the purpose of limiting additional imports. Because of the uncertainty of the braking power of particular tariff rates, a secondary but higher rate could be provided for imports beyond a second specified level. This rate might be fixed at a considerably higher level than the first rate in order to insure an adequate braking effect.

It would, of course, not be necessary to admit free of duty imports representing any particular share of the market; but there can be little question that many industries would consider a tariff-free volume of imports with either an absolute quota or with a tariff barrier as described above more conducive to business activity than a low tariff rate applicable to all imports but without a quota limitation. An exception to this preference might be encountered if imports have already captured a high share of the market. Under those circumstances, duty-free imports, even if backstopped by a quota device, might have too much influence on prices. To overcome this objection, a relatively low duty might be applied to imports representing a predetermined share of the market, followed by a higher rate beyond that level.

A tariff quota would in all instances be preferable to an absolute quota if a suitable tariff rate or combination of rates could be determined. This follows from the greater ease of administration of a tariff quota. Also, a tariff quota does not close the market absolutely. Goods may still come in so long as they can surmount the limiting tariff barrier.

Objections are often raised against import quotas as a means of regulating foreign trade on the grounds that quotas are too restrictive and tend to put trade into a straitjacket. Unquestionably, import quotas could be used, as they have been, to produce precisely these effects. That fact, however, does not condemn quotas as such for the simple reason that their use need not produce such results, and indeed can be designed to avoid them. Condemnation of quotas cannot be justified by pointing to the undesirable consequences of their misuse. As well, condemn all food because its use can be abused.

The establishment of import quotas should not be proposed as a substitute for the tariff. It should be regarded as a supplementary device in those instances in which the tariff alone does not meet the exigencies of forward planning of production, the mapping of expansion proposals, and orderly marketing, etc.

Therefore, quotas should be studied in relation to individual products or industries and the conditions of competition encountered. Instead of reviewing our tariff system in general, regardless of any requests for a change, it would be preferable to proceed on application of interested parties, as is the general practice under the escape clause of the Trade Agreements Act and as was the usual practice under the cost-of-production provision of section 336 of the Tariff Act of 1930. There is no call for a general upward revision of the tariff, but there is an urgent need for supplementing the tariff with flexible quota provisions and in some instances for substituting absolute but flexible quotas for the tariff.

Each case, however, should rest on its own merit.

What is called for therefore is enabling legislation that would empower an agency of the Congress, such as the United States Tariff Commission, to impose an import quota either in combination with the tariff or separately, in accordance with guidelines set forth in the legislation.

Such guidelines should set forth the trend of imports that in terms of the share of the domestic market supplied by such imports, would create a presumption of injury and therefore entitlement to a quota.

Next, the legislation should set forth the limits of the quota in relation to the import trend of any particular product. Assuming that entitlement was established to the satisfaction of the Tariff Commission, for example, the Commission should by reference to the legislation be able to determine the upper and lower limits of the particular quota that would be called for in terms of percentage of the domestic market.

It would, of course, also be necessary to set forth the method of calculating the tentative or estimated annual or seasonal quota, since a flexible quota, geared to domestic consumption of the product, must necessarily be tentative until a final estimate could be established for the year in course to which the quota was being applied. Ordinarily, such a final estimate could be made in September or before the beginning of the fourth quarter of the year.

Because any estimate might be upset by unforeseen events and in order to shape the quota so that it would most effectively perform its function, provisions should be incorporated into the basic law to make both emergency or short-range and long-range adjustments.

In order to meet a sudden shortage in the domestic supply, resulting in a falling inventory and rising prices, provision should be made for reopening the quota and increasing the permissible import volume until such time as the condition were corrected. On the other hand, should a domestic oversupply develop, either because of excessive production (bumper crops, an unusually abundant run of fish, a rich mineral discovery) or because of a fall in demand (a crisis heralding a recession or depression), the power to reopen the quota for a reduction in the volume of imports should also be established. In other words, imports would be called upon to carry a part of the burden of readjustment instead of being left free to wreak havoc by nullifying efforts of domestic producers to curtail their output.

The law itself should again set forth the deviations from normal that would call for the type of short-range adjustment just described.

The short-range adjustment provision, however, would not be sufficient to meet the need for flexibility. A provision for long-range flexibility woud therefore be necessary. Again, the law should lay down the conditions for invoking such a provision.

The purpose would be to avoid freezing the trade pattern of a given time and to allow for change and growth. Application would be made to the Tariff Commission by any interested party alleging, for example, that the domestic industry was failing to meet the needs of the market, as in the case of a raw material used by a domestic manufacturing industry, and that the import quota should be liberalized; and the Commission would hear the plea, gather evidence from the pertinent sources and render a decision. Again, importers or users of foreign products might allege that a larger volume of imports could be absorbed without doing serious injury to the domestic producers of the like or similar product. This plea would be taken to the Tariff Commission.

Thus the usual complaint that import quotas tend to stifle trade and prevent its growth could be overcome by shaping the quota system with the necessary degree of responsiveness to the needs of commerce and industry.

Other countries, that is, those exporting to us, often have a great interest in this market. Flexibility in the quota system should make room for countries to begin exporting to this country even though they had not done so in the past. This could be done by providing a tentative set-aside of a small percentage of the annual quota for this purpose.

Other provisions for flexibility could be established; and other provisions to meet other needs of commerce, both foreign and domestic, could be incorporated into the basic legislation. For example, encouragement of rising labor standards abroad could be written into the law by offering a quota bonus to any foreign industry producing a given product upon satisfactory proof that it had substantially narrowed the wage gap between its previous wage level and that prevailing in the United States.

Indeed, the potentials of the import quota in terms of flexibility and responsiveness to the conditions and requirements of a maximum of trade with other countries are far superior to a tariff rate used by itself. Economic disruption and distress attributable to import competition, in the form of unemployment, upset prices, mounting surpluses and loss of confidence, need not be regarded as a necessary and unadvoidable accompaniment of foreign trade. The import quota, properly prepared legislatively and intelligently administered, could be the savior of a liberal trade policy.

# THE USE OF QUOTAS FOR THE REGULATION OF IMPORTS

Gottfried Haberler, professor of economics, Harvard University

It has been the policy of the United States Government for many years to discourage other countries from the use of quotas. The reason for the American opposition to quotas and other quantitative restrictions on trade has not only been the fact that American exports have been greatly hampered during the postwar period by the application of quotas and other quantitative import restrictions on the part of foreign countries. There are broader, in a sense ideological but nevertheless compelling reasons for the rejection, in principle, of quantitative trade restrictions, especially quotas, by American foreign economic policy.

It can be said without exaggeration that the widespread use of quotas is incompatible with the principles of the free-enterprise economy. While tariffs, at least if used in moderate doses, do not interfere with the operation of the free-enterprise economy and the market mechanism of demand and supply on which the free competition enterprise economy is based, the use of quotas requires the substitution of government fiat for the anonymous forces of the market. Suppose we wish for any reason whatever to reduce imports of any commodity below the actual level. This can be done either by introducing an import duty (or by raising an existing duty) or by imposing a quota.

If the tariff method is used all the Government has to do is to collect the duty on imports at the border. The forces of the market, demand and supply still determine the precise volume of imports and who is to do the importing, and so forth. After imposition of the duty the price of the dutiable commodity will be higher inside the country than in the exporting country—the difference over and above transportation costs in the broad sense going to the Public Treasury as duty.

If, on the other hand, the quota method is used for the restriction of imports, there will be also created a price difference. The price inside the country which restricts imports will rise above the level in the exporting country (plus transportation cost). But in this case the price difference goes not to the Government but to those individuals or firms who are allowed to import. Importing becomes in this case the source of easy, unearned incomes. Many people will try to rush imports until the quota is exhausted. To prevent a disorderly scramble for the limited amounts which may be imported, the authorities charged with the administration of the import control must have resort to rationing and allocation. That is to say, a governmental agency must decide who is to be allowed to import. The granting of import licenses bestows financial favors upon the receiver of the license.

The usual procedure is to issue the import permits according to previous imports. Different importers receive import licenses in proportion to the volume of their imports during an earlier representative period.

It is easy to see, and experience in foreign countries which have used the quota system on a large scale has confirmed this expectation many times, that this is not a satisfactory arrangement. It creates vested interests, produces the appearance of unearned windfalls, and gives rise to favoritism and corruption. The longer the system lasts, the less representative the base period, the more arbitrary the allocation of import permits. The importing business ceases to be a commercial pursuit where efficiency and resourcefulness of the businessman counts, but becomes a sinecure depending on the chance of past events and on arbitrary bureaucratic decisions. It especially hampers the growth of new firms and of dynamic, innovating old ones because they have not had the previous imports which would entitle them to receive import licenses for foreign machinery, tools, and so forth. This has been the experience of France, a country long addicted to the use of quotas. There the quota system has greatly contributed to the stifling of competition and retardation of growth which the French economy would need so badly.

In view of these obvious disadvantages of the quota method which fly in the face of the American tradition of free enterprise and competition—why it is then that so frequently the demand is raised to substitute quotas for tariffs? The principal reason for the widespread use of quotas in foreign countries has been that import restrictions are used as a means for equilibrating the balance of payment. Many countries suffer from balance-of-payment deficits, primarily because they pursue inflationary policies. Since they are unwilling or unable to stop inflation and to depreciate their overvalued currencies, they are forced to restrict imports drastically. And tariffs are rightly or wrongly regarded as too slow and unprecise in their operation for that particular purpose.

These considerations do, of course, not apply to the United States. Why is it, then, that even in the United States the call is now frequently heard for the use of quotas instead of tariffs as a means to reducing imports?

It is understandable that protectionist interests who are afraid of foreign competition prefer quota to tariff protection. Tariff protection leaves the quantity of imports variable. If costs at home rise as compared with costs abroad, imports will rise despite an existing tariff. If foreign countries, in order to correct a fundamental disequilibrium in their balance of payments, depreciate their currency in accordance with the provisions of the charter of the International Monetary Fund, their exports to the United States will rise despite an existing tariff.

All that is excluded by a quota. In other words quotas provide a more powerful protection from foreign competition than tariffs do by putting a rigid ceiling on the volume of imports.

There is, however, one exception to the rule that quotas provide stronger protection than tariffs, which is rarely mentioned: Suppose domestic demand for a particular commodity shrinks. Then imports will fall and from a certain point on, an unchanged quota will become ineffective. In that case the domestic industry loses all protection (unless the quota is changed) while a tariff still provides some protection, because the shrunken imports are still subject to duty.

There are other reasons why protectionists prefer quotas to tariffs. Quotas are financially more attractive, because it is the importer who receives the price difference between the domestic and foreign market, and not the Public Treasury as in the case of tariffs. The beneficiaries of these windfalls, that is, the receivers of the import licenses, will, of course, not always or perhaps even rarely, be the protected interests themselves, but rather middlemen (dealers) or in some cases the final users of the imported commodities; the latter will be the case, if the imported commodity is not a finished consumer good but raw materials, semifinished goods, or machinery. In all these cases the opposition of the dealers or users of the commodities in question against the restrictions of imports will be lessened, if, as a compensation for lower imports, they receive the fat windfall profits connected with the granting of the import licenses. The quota system thus provides a method to bribe and silence the natural opposition to import restrictions. The quota system thus creates an unnatural and unholy alliance and conspiracy of vested interests in import restrictions, and restraints of trade consisting of the protected industries themselves and of dealers and users of the imported commodity—a conspiracy at the expense of the final consumer of the imported commodity or the final consumption goods into which the imported commodity enters as a cost item. Another victim of this conspiracy is the Public Treasury which loses the receipts from import duties and public morality which sooner or later must suffer from the necessity of creating a bureaucratic apparatus for the distribution of lucrative import licenses.

Some—but not all—disadvantages of the quota system would disappear, if the import licenses were sold in free competitive auctions to the highest bidder. In the case of standardized products this should be quite easy to arrange. Unearned profits would be taken out of the system and would make it less attractive to special interests and incidentally provide an income for the Public Treasury. The auction system would, however, not eliminate the disadvantage of the quota system which consists of the fact that it makes imports rigid, that it eliminates healthy foreign competition and, if applied over a wide range of imports, reduces the adaptability of the balance of payments, making it difficult for foreign countries to acquire the dollars they need for paying for American exports, and thus increases the demand for American foreign aid in the form of grants or loans to foreign countries.

I cannot see any justification for using quotas in preference to tariffs. Anyone who understands their working and believes in the American system of free enterprise, competition, and absence of bureaucratic intervention and meddling must shun the quota system like the plague.

There is surely no reason why imports from Japan should be treated differently than imports from anywhere else or why imports of agricultural products should be dealt with in a different manner than other imports.

Tariff quotas are less objectionable than absolute import quotas, because they do not freeze imports but make them only more expensive when they go beyond the quota level. But tariff quotas, like absolute import quotas, give rise to unearned windfall profits to those who are lucky enough to get in on the ground floor. If the basic quota which is allowed to come in duty-free or at a low duty (compared with amounts exceeding the basic quota) is small, compared with the volume of import, it will be necessary for the authorities to allocate permits to would-be importers, according to some principles, just as in the case of absolute import quotas. The granting of such import licenses is, again, equivalent to giving a cash bonus or subsidy, with the same undesirable consequences as in the case of absolute import quotas.

What holds of quotas, holds also of other types of quantitative import restrictions, such as exchange control, which is practiced by many foreign countries.

### SUMMARY AND CONCLUSIONS

Quantitative import restrictions in general and quotas in particular are a much less desirable method of import control than tariffs.

On the international level, if applied by the United States, they freeze imports and reduce the adaptability of the balance of payments. They make it more difficult for foreign countries to earn the dollars which they need to pay for American exports. They thus increase the demand for foreign aid. Moreover, if the United States uses quotas in its import policy, it weakens and contradicts the American attempts at persuading other countries to desist from using quantitative import restrictions which hamper, and discriminate against, American exports.

On the domestic level, quotas are in glaring contradiction to the American system of free enterprise and competition. They lead to a proliferation of bureaucratic controls and inject elements of planning, rationing, and allocation into the market mechanism. The granting of import licenses is equivalent to giving a cash bonus or subsidy, with all the dangers of corruption and favoritism inherent in such a system of distributing public money. It creates vested interests, not only in the protected industries (this a tariff does, too) but also among importers who are the beneficiaries of the import licenses, to the detriment of the free-enterprise system and at the expense of the consumer and the Public Treasury.

Tariff quotas are only a little less objectionable than absolute import quotas.

I thus reach the conclusion that the quota system should not be allowed a place in American foreign economic policy.

# VII

# FOREIGN TRADE POLICY AND NATIONAL SECURITY—THE NATIONAL SECURITY AMENDMENTS

## REPORT TO SUBCOMMITTEE ON FOREIGN TRADE POLICY

**Executive Office of the President, Office of Defense Mobilization**

*The national-security amendments.*—The Congress of the United States has expressed its concern with the national-security aspects of foreign-trade policy by the enactment of the so-called national-security amendments which authorize the President to avoid or to prevent any impairment of the domestic mobilization base resulting from imports of foreign articles. There is general agreement that the terms "national defense" and "national security" employed by the Congress in the national-security amendments (Public Law 464, 83d Cong., and Public Law 86, 84th Cong.) definitely include as a standard of action consideration of the probable results, if any, of the impact of imports on a domestic industry or a segment thereof determined to be essential to defense mobilization in time of war.

The 1954 amendment stated the authority of the President to limit trade-agreements negotiations to cases in which the duty reduction would not threaten domestic production needed for defense mobilization. It did not give any new trade-controlling power to the President.

However, section 7 of the Trade Agreements Extension Act of 1955 involved the grant of additional trade-controlling authority to the President and is, by far, the more important of the two national-security amendments. It reads as follows:

> In order to further the policy and purpose of this section, whenever the Director of the Office of Defense Mobilization has reason to believe that any article is being imported into the United States in such quantities as to threaten to impair the national security, he shall so advise the President, and, if the President agrees that there is reason for such belief, the President shall cause an immediate investigation to be made to determine the facts. If, on the basis of such investigation, and the report to him of the findings and recommendations made in connection therewith, the President finds that the article is being imported into the United States in such quantities as to threaten to impair the national security, he shall take such actions as he deems necessary to adjust the imports of such article to a level that will not threaten to impair the national security.

While this section does not prescribe the specific actions which the President would be authorized to take, congressional discussion of the legislation indicated that the imposition of new or increased tariff duties on imports and the establishment of import quotas were authorized by the language adopted. The section has also been construed to authorize the President to urge upon importers in the United States such voluntary import limitations as he deems appropriate or advisable. The President's action must, however, be such—

> as he deems necessary to adjust the imports of such article to a level that will not threaten to impair the national security.

Since whatever action the President might take in any given case under this section would be taken after the receipt of advice from the Director of the Office of Defense Mobilization, it is important to understand the exact function of the Director and the procedures employed to perform that function.

*The function of the Director of the Office of Defense Mobilization.*—The function of the Director of the Office of Defense Mobilization under the 1955 amendment is solely and entirely to "advise the President," and then only whenever he—

> has reason to believe that any article is being imported into the United States in such quantities as to threaten to impair the national security.

The statute under which the Office of Defense Mobilization proceeds does not require that public hearings be held. Nor is the function which the statute gives the Director such a function as under general principles of administrative law would call for notice and opportunity to be heard for the persons affected. Nevertheless, the Director has made it a practice to hold public hearings whenever domestic industries petition the Office of Defense Mobilization for relief, and it appears that such hearings would provide an effective means of acquiring useful information and viewpoints.

Thus, the primary purpose for holding public hearings under the national security amendment of 1955 is to assure the marshaling of all the facts in order to aid and assist the Director of the Office of Defense Mobilization in determining whether or not he has reason to believe that a threat exists. Therefore, the public hearings granted by the Director are not held as a matter of right, are not adversary in nature, are not determinative of contentions between the parties, but are intended to yield information and to advance investigation of the relevant facts. However, once a public hearing is decided upon, then representatives of both the importers and domestic producers or manufacturers, and other interested parties—such as representatives of labor—are provided sufficient time and equal opportunity to be heard and to present their contentions and facts, and are extended the privilege of submitting supplemental arguments or briefs.

The information obtained through public hearings is studied, analyzed, and coordinated with other facts at hand and on file with the Office of Defense Mobilization. Other agencies of the Government familiar with the subject matter and possessing information, expert advice, and experience concerning any of the cases are consulted to obtain their views and knowledge. The information and advice developed by this procedure enables the Director to consider all domestic factors concerning a petitioning industry, our relationships with friendly countries and allies of the free world, and the effects of restrictions on imports upon United States exports. The net result of this process assists the Director in arriving at a judgment concerning a petition, and serves as the foundation upon which he bases his reason to believe, if such is the case, that any article is being imported into the United States in such quantities as to threaten to impair the national security.

*Problems of administration of the 1955 National Security Amendment.*—Attention is drawn to several aspects of the 1955 amendment respecting its interpretations and administration. The section can be so interpreted by parties of interest as to become a substitute for the escape clause and thus provide another vehicle for domestic industries to use in seeking protection from competitive imports. The essential function of the Tariff Commission under the escape clause is the determination of injury from imports. Therefore, the escape clause provides a means for restricting imports in such cases whether or not the injured industry is essential to the national security. Section 7, on the other hand, provides a means for relief only in cases where imports threaten the national security by impairing or inhibiting the creation of essential productive capacity, required skills, or other factors important in times of emergency.

A question of procedure has arisen in relation to the administration of the national security amendment. If the major function of the Director of the Office of Defense Mobilization is to ascertain what industrial capacity is essential to defense mobilization and to determine whether that capacity is adequate to meet the defense mobilization demands which may be placed on it in time of emergency, then, it has been asked, Is not this responsibility a continuing one for the Office of Defense Mobilization rather than one on which judgment should be rendered only in response to requests from domestic industries that regard themselves as being essential to the defense mobilization base? That responsibility is a continuing one, of course, and the Government is armed with various forms of assistance other than that authorized by section 7 which are used to expand productive capacity in appropriate cases. It might be thought the Director of the Office of Defense Mobilization, in order to determine whether imports are threatening the national security, could meet the problem by determining in advance each and every domestic industry which is considered essential to the national security. The difficulty is that most industries, in some degree, produce items needed in time of war but the capacity necessary to produce the essential portion of the total production of the items varies extensively from industry to industry.

One of the problems in arriving at conclusions regarding petitions filed under the national security amendment is the length of time required for processing cases. Specific data to support a petition are not always readily available in industry or in any one place in the Government. The nature of a case often requires checking with several Government agencies and extensive compilation of data. Even after the facts concerning a petition are available, it is a difficult task to measure possible impacts upon the complex mobilization base. Consequently, to arrive at a reasonable and just disposition of a petition has sometimes required what could appear to the public to be an excessive period of time.

Another problem in administering the national security amendment is the difficulty of reaching really final solutions. The dynamics of trade and commerce in the setting of rapid domestic and international developments impose a requirement upon the Office of Defense Mobilization that some cases be reopened periodically upon request of the petitioners. Such inevitable requests for review or reconsideration increase the workload on the limited staff available for handling cases.

In effect, the very nature of the national security amendment is such as to produce these particular kinds of administrative problems.

*The President's actions under the national security amendments*—Once the Director of the Office of Defense Mobilization advises the President that he has reason to believe that imports are threatening to impair the national security, the President, if he agrees that there is reason for such belief, causes an investigation to be made to determine the facts. If, on the basis of such investigation, and the report to him of the findings and recommendations made in connection therewith, the President finds that the article is being imported in such quantities as to threaten to impair the national security, he is to take such action as he deems necessary to adjust the imports to a level that will not threaten to impair the national security.

On April 23, 1957, the Director of the Office of Defense Mobilization advised the President, pursuant to section 7 of the Trade Agreements Extension Act of 1955, that he had reason to believe that crude oil was being imported into the United States in such quantities as to threaten to impair the national security . The President, in a reply dated April 25, 1957, agreed, on the basis of then available information, that there was reason for the belief and caused an investigation to be made to determine the facts as required by section 7 of the act. The President requested the Director of the Office of Defense Mobilization to examine carefully, while this investigation was going on, the possibility that oil imports might effectively be limited by individual voluntary action of the importing companies. It seemed to the President there would be advantages in adjusting imports in that fashion if it were practicable to do so. The President stated that it would be important for him to know whether an adjustment of the imports could be accomplished voluntarily, or whether other measures may be necessary, if the finding and recommendations resulting from the investigation which he caused to be made resulted in his determining that an impairment of the national security was in fact threatened.

On June 26, 1957, the President appointed a Special Cabinet Committee to investigate crude-oil imports, with a request that it report its findings and recommendations at the earliest practicable date. Later the Commitee submitted its report and, on July 29, 1957, the President approved the recommendations of the Committee and ordered them to be put into effect.

The Committee found that increased volume of crude-oil imports and the proposed imports for the latter half of 1957 threatened to impair the national security and that this threat, under existing conditions, required a limitation on imports. The Committee recommended that unless the importing companies complied voluntarily with the import limitation plan set forth by the Committee, the President find that there is a threat to the national security within the meaning of section 7 of the Trade Agreements Extension Act of 1955. The Committee was continued in active status, pending the outcome of the voluntary program.

*Current status of petitions.*—As of August 31, 1957, the Office of Defense Mobilization had been requested to consider 14 petitions for restrictions upon imports under the national security amendment. The status of these requests for investigation under section 7, Public Law 86, 84th Congress, is shown on the attached list.

The petitions for photographic shutters and for stencil silk were withdrawn by action of the submitting industry group.

The petition for fluorspar was canceled at the request of the petitioners after the Office of Defense Mobilization had scheduled a public hearing. This action was taken to allow time for the industry to evaluate the effects of the Government-purchase program authorized by Public Law 733, 84th Congress, which legislation was passed before the date scheduled for the fluorspar hearing. At the time of cancellation of the hearing, it was agreed that the industry association would be permitted to request a new hearing date upon 6 weeks' advance notice to the Office of Defense Mobilization.

The Felt Association requested the postponement of action on their wool-felt petition pending the results of their escape-clause action before the United States Tariff Commission.

Action on the petition for wooden boats has been delayed because of the petitioning association's difficulty in obtaining information from its members. The association agreed to revise and supplement its petition at a later date.

In the case of the petitions for analytical balances and clinical fever thermometers, the respective petitioning association and guild agreed to restudy their petition and supporting data with members of their industry. In May 1957 both petitioners notified the Office of Defense Mobilization of their continuing interest and intent to file supplementary data for their respective petition. Such data have not been filed as of August 30, 1957.

A public hearing was held by the Office of Defense Mobilization on January 7–9, 1957, to hear arguments for and against the petitions of the clock, pin-lever watch, timer, and jeweled watch industries. The material obtained on these cases has been under active study with the cooperation of the United States Tariff Commission, the Department of Labor, the Department of Defense, and the Business and Defense Services Administration (Commerce). A decision on these petitions is anticipated in the near future.

A public hearing was held on October 22–24, 1956, in connection with the petition regarding imports of oil. After study of the problem, the Director of the Office of Defense Mobilization on April 23, 1957, certified to the President that he had reason to believe that imports of crude oil were threatening to impair the national security within the meaning of section 7 of Public Law 86, 84th Congress.

A public hearing was held on September 11–12, 1956, on the petition regarding imports of hard fiber cordage and twine. On March 7, 1957, the Office of Defense Mobilization rendered a negative decision, regarding the cordage petition, finding that imports of hard fiber farm and industrial twines were not threatening to impair the national security within the meaning of section 7 of Public Law 86, 84th Congress. On July 1, 1957, the Cordage Institute on behalf of its industry members requested reconsideration of this decision. After a preliminary examination of the brief submitted with the request, the Cordage Institute and other interested parties were notified on August 20, 1957, that a further study including a review of the March 7, 1957, decision had been ordered.

A public hearing was held on June 3–4, 1957, in connection with the petition on imports of wool textiles. The information submitted for this case is under current study.

Petitions regarding imports of fine-mesh wire cloth and dental burs were filed during May 1957, and the processing of these cases has been started. On August 28, 1957, the American Dental Trade Association withdrew its petition regarding imports of dental burs.

*Status of requests for investigation under sec. 7, Public Law 86, Aug. 31, 1957*

| Industry | Presented by— | Date of action |
|---|---|---|
| Analytical balances | Scientific Apparatus Makers Association, 20 North Wacker Dr., Chicago, Ill. | Filed, Feb. 6, 1956. Restudy by association July 27, 1956. Refiled May 24, 1957. |
| Burs, dental | American Dental Trade Association, 1010 Vermont Ave. NW., Washington, D. C. | Filed, May 22, 1957. Withdrawn Aug. 28, 1957. |
| Clocks, pin-lever watches and timers. | Clock and Watch Manufacturers Association of America, Inc., 1625 K St. NW., Washington, D. C. | Filed, Apr. 18, 1956. Hearing held Jan. 7 and 9, 1957. |
| Cordage (hard fiber cordage and twine). | Cordage Institute, 350 Madison Ave., New York, N. Y. | Filed, July 12, 1955. Hearing held, Sept. 11 and 12, 1956. Negative decision, Mar. 7, 1957. Decision appealed, July 1, 1957. Restudy ordered, Aug. 20, 1957. |
| Fine mesh wire cloth | The Industrial Wire Cloth Institute, 75 West St., New York, N. Y. | Filed, May 6, 1957. |
| Fluorspar | Committee representing American Fluorspar Producers, care of Clyde Flynn, attorney, Elizabethtown, Ill. | Filed, June 21, 1955. Hearing scheduled Nov. 12, 1956. Canceled by petitioners, Nov. 1, 1956. |
| Oil | Independent Petroleum Association of America, 1110 Ring Building, Washington, D. C. | Filed Aug. 7, 1956. Hearings held Oct. 22 and 24, 1956. Referred to President, Apr. 23, 1957. |
| Photographic shutters | Wollensak Optical Co., 850 Hudson Ave., Rochester, N. Y. | Filed Feb. 24, 1956. Withdrawn Apr. 17, 1956. |
| Stencil silk | Albert Goode Bedin, Inc., 437 Fifth Ave., New York, N. Y. | Filed Nov. 2, 1955. Withdrawn Apr 5, 1956. |
| Thermometers, clinical fever. | Americal Clinical Thermometer Guild, 110 East 42d St., New York, N. Y. | Filed Jan. 13, 1956. Restudy by Guild July 24, 1956. Refiled May 24, 1957. |
| Watches, jeweled | American Watch Manufacturers Association, Inc., 1100 Shoreham Building, Washington, D. C. | Filed Dec. 29, 1955. Hearings held Jan. 7 and 9, 1957. |
| Wooden boats | American Boat Builders & Repairers Association, Inc., 2382 Grand Concourse, New York, N. Y. | Filed Sept. 14, 1956. Petition to be revised by association Dec. 4, 1956. |
| Wool felt | The Felt Association, 75 West St., New York, N. Y. | Filed Apr. 20, 1956. Postponement requested by association May 27, 1957. |
| Wool textiles | National Association of Wool Manufacturers, 386 4th Ave., New York, N. Y. | Filed Mar. 14, 1956. Hearings held June 3 and 4, 1957. |

# IMPORT RESTRICTIONS AND NATIONAL SECURITY: A PROBLEM IN AMERICAN POLICY

Klaus Knorr, Center of International Studies, Princeton University

When extending the trade-agreements authority in 1954 and 1955, the Congress enacted amendments directing the President to use his control over imports, delegated to him by the Congress, in order to prevent the industrial-mobilization base of the United States from being weakened. According to section 2 of the Trade Agreements Extension Act of 1954, import duties should not be cut on any article if the President finds "that such reduction would threaten domestic production needed for projected national-defense requirements." Section 7 of the Trade Agreements Extension Act of 1955 grants to the President the authority to impose new tariff duties, or to increase existing ones, or to impose import quotas, if he finds that an article "is being imported into the United States in such quantities as to threaten to impair the national security. * * *"

To seek protection from foreign competition on the grounds of national security has, of course, been a long-established tradition in the United States as well as in other countries. The above laws reflect the considerations underlying this practice. The weight of defense considerations in public policy is indeed obvious. Unfortunately, the defense argument for tariff protection is for this very reason peculiarly subject to abuses. Since few people want to go on record as slighting national security, arguments for protection on security grounds are always in danger of not receiving hard-headed scrutiny, and of not meeting the full range of countervailing arguments. General statements in regard to policy may sound unexceptionable but fail to give useful instrumental guidance. One might say, for example, that security demands must be given their full due if the security of the United States rests seriously and demonstrably on the limitation of particular imports; and that imports should go unrestricted on this ground if the country's security is not seriously and demonstrably affected by foreign competition. The trouble with this statement lies, on the one hand, in the difficulty of defining "seriously" and "demonstrably" in the absence of valid criteria for judging the "defense essentiality" of a particular commodity or industry, and, on the other hand, in the disposition to give national security the benefit of the doubt when neither proponents nor opponents of a specific act of import restriction are able to prove their case. In order to permit policy to be informed by a reasonable degree of wisdom, it is therefore necessary to push back as far as possible the obscurities surrounding the concept and test of defense essentiality; and, to the extent that any industries meet this test, to evaluate the relative benefit and disadvantage of various protective measures.

### I. THE MOBILIZATION BASE

Advocacy of the protection of war-important industries rests squarely on the idea of the industrial-mobilization base—that is, of a rich conglomerate of industries that, in the event of emergency, can be quickly converted to all war-essential production. Even if entire industries or firms cannot be so converted, particular components of their resources, e. g., skilled manpower, may be drawn readily into wartime production. In the light of experience gained in the First and Second World Wars, the concept of the mobilization base has seemed to make sense. However, past experience should guide the policymaker only to the extent that future wars will resemble past wars; and it is exactly on this score that the concept, as used in current tariff discussion, now appears completely outmoded.

The last two world wars were prolonged wars of attrition. Thus, during World War II there was time to mobilize war potential, to convert the automobile industry, the watch industry, the chemical industry, and hundreds of other industries to defense production; and all these industries deserved to be considered as war essential. But it is now utterly improbable that the United States will be engaged once again in hostilities of this kind.

### II. THE NATURE OF PROBABLE WAR

It is, of course, difficult to predict the shape of future wars with any high degree of dependability. However, the recent changes that have taken place in the technology of warfare, in American defense planning, and in the complexion of international politics sharply narrow down the range of possibilities, the extraordinary revolution in the technology of war being the most momentous of these innovations. In view of these conditions, the most likely types of hostilities in which the United States might become involved are all-out thermonuclear war and limited war.

Military experts agree that, in the event of unlimited war with thermonuclear weapons—at present possible only between the United States and the U. S. S. R.—the decisive blows will be dealt right at the start, within a matter of days or a few weeks. The main purpose of our strategic air force is to deter such a war altogether by being ready to inflict, at a moment's notice, instantaneous and unprecedented destruction on any aggressor. This power to deter, and to wage all-out war should it break out, rests entirely on military force in being before the outset of hostilities. If there should be any second phase in such a war—the phase of the broken-backed war—it must likewise be fought by means of forces available at the start, because the United States itself will immediately suffer immense destruction of its population and its capacity to produce. Present estimates of civilian casualties range in the tens of millions and it is assumed that more than one-third of our productive capacity will be knocked out and more than another third paralyzed for a considerable period of time. Under these circumstances, any mobilization base will be irrelevant once war is precipitated. For one thing, there will be no time to convert it to wartime production; for another, this "base" will be nearly ruined or at least crippled.

Limited war is war limited in the theater of operations, in war aims, and possibly in the application of weapons. It may be a brushfire operation or an operation on the scale of the Korean war; it will certainly not involve the home territories of the United States and Soviet Russia as theaters of hostilities. It must be limited in war aims, because anything but moderate objectives would turn a limited war into all-out thermonuclear war. Whether it would be limited to the use of nonnuclear weapons depends on a number of circumstances but, except for police actions against small countries, becomes less and less likely, since the United States no longer possesses a great enough nonnuclear capacity to fight such "conventional" actions with any prospect of success. The defense policy which the United States has pursued during the last few years has diminished the chance of anything but minor actions being fought with prenuclear armament.

It is in the nature of limited war that it will not require a major war effort on the part of the United States. The premium placed on timely and quick action calls again for main reliance on ready forces. If limited war should reach a relatively large scale and turn out to be protracted, additional forces might have to be mobilized and additional military equipment produced. Yet no substantial conversion of peacetime industries is anticipated. What is expected is some expansion in the output of firms normally producing military items. To the very limited extent that there might be any mobilization of industrial potential, it would take place almost entirely in the armament industries and their immediate suppliers. This was the experience during the Korean war which, for a limited war, was a sizable engagement.

The probable dimensions of limited war also imply that, for the most part, the channels of international trade will remain open except for the areas involved in combat. This is a prospect militating against any need to make the United States less dependent on foreign supplies in order to be better prepared for limited war. It stands to reason that North America—including Canada, Mexico, and the Caribbean—can be regarded, for practical purposes, as a unit whose parts will surely remain accessible to one another in limited-war situations. It is very unlikely that limited war would involve South America and Africa south of the Sahara. For reasons indicated below, Western Europe will hardly become the scene of limited war transcending border skrimishes; and it is not very probable that all the rest of the world will be visited by limited war at one and the same time.

If this is the reasonable expectation, limited war at any one time will hardly disrupt American trade with more than the Middle East or some areas in south Asia, southeastern Asia, or the Far East. With the exception of oil, the United States is not at present importantly dependent on the supplies of any one of these areas, or even of all of them together. Even in the case of the Middle East, the United States itself can make do with oil supplies from the Western Hemisphere. The real problem presented by a disruption of oil exports from the Arab world arises from the dependence of Western Europe on this area, and hence on the United States should Middle Eastern supplies be cut off. Yet, as the Suez crisis demonstrated, this is not at present an insoluble matter, provided some rationing of consumption is initiated in time. In the long run, this special problem might become aggravated if the United States comes to rely less on domestic and more on Arabian oil. This long-run prospect raises the question of whether the United States should not, by one means or another, assure a sufficient rate of oil exploration in the continental United States. The sufficiency of the rate, however, would have to be determined in the light of the petroleum potential of Canada and the area surrounding the Caribbean as well as that of the United States itself.

Regarding limited war, then—or, better, regarding the risk that limited war might reach a fairly large scale and be prolonged—the conclusion is that there may be a few selected industries which the United States will want to maintain at a capacity larger than needed in peacetime. Oil and some armament industries, such as aircraft, would be the likely candidates. Even for this very special mobilization base, possibly excepting oil, the extra margin of capacity to be maintained need not be very large. With defense expenditures running at between $30 billion and $40 billion a year, the industries producing military hardware and the industries supplying them with materials and components have attained considerable capacity. In this respect, the United States is now better prepared for limited war than it was at the time of Communist aggression in Korea, when United States defense expenditures had been at a relatively very low rate for several years.

If we wish to insure that civilian supplies will stay at nearly normal levels in the event of a sizable limited war, some stockpiles of scarce raw materials might be maintained as well, not so much because limited war is likely to interfere with customary trade channels as because any war scare engenders a worldwide desire to build up inventories of raw materials and hence leads to shortages and high prices. However, what is needed along these lines, in principle, is not the strategic stockpile which this country is maintaining as present. The idea of this stockpile is based on the obsolete concept of preparing a mobilization base for a protracted and large-scale war of attrition. Stockpile goals prescribing several years' normal supply underscore this intent. Rather, the new need is for smaller stockpiles to be used in the event of war scares and limited engagements. What is needed, furthermore, in preparation for limited war, is provision for prompt action to confine inflationary pressures.

To be sure limited war is not as easily defined as all-out thermonuclear hostilities, for it may take different forms and assume different scales dependent on locality, the identity and number of opponents, and a host of other variable circumstances. Nevertheless, a protracted and massive war of attrition with or without full resort to nuclear weapons—a war of the World War II variety—is extremly unlikely. Speculation on the possibility of such a war is usually confined to a conflict in Western Europe, but chances of such a war occurring in this area are slight for several reasons. First, a Soviet invasion of Western Europe would involve on either side war aims so important that neither would be likely, under presure, to forego victory by limiting itself to nonnuclear arms. Second, neither the western European nations nor the United States are prepared to fight a massive nonnuclear war of attrition. The ground forces planned by NATO are intended only as a shield to be used in conjunction with the sword—that is, SAC and the British Bomber Command. NATO ground forces actually in existence or available fall short of this plan. They constitute hardly more than a trip wire. Confronted with a massive Soviet invasion, NATO would have no choice, therefore, except to surrender or to effect a nuclear riposte. Third, if the U. S. S. R. were to advance on Western Europe without simultaneously unleashing its thermonuclear striking force against the United States, while there is a strong risk that the United States would retaliate against any westward interruption of the Red army by throwing SAC into action, the Kremlin would lose to the United States the advantage of striking the first blow. This advantage the Soviet Union is unlikely to forego. In short, anything but a very limited, nibbling operation on the part of the Soviet bloc in Western Europe seems at present, and for the foreseeable future, bound to end up in unlimited war.

Proponents of import restrictions for the sake of protecting the mobilization base of the United States are apt to retort: How do we know for sure that a war of attrition is extremely unlikely? Who can prove that this is so? Certainty is, of course, rare regarding future events, and it is impossible in this case. But we can be reasonably sure. The fact is that our national defense effort, for which we have been paying between $30 billion and $40 billion per annum for a number of years, is squarely based on the reasonable nature of the estimate presented in this paper. At immense cost, the United States is preparing itself for all-out thermonuclear war and, to a lesser extent, for limited hostilities. The United States is definitely not preparing itself militarily for waging a large nonnuclear war of attrition. Whoever advocates import restrictions for the purpose of protecting the mobilization base should first challenge the direction of the American defense effort. If it still makes sense to protect war-essential industries against foreign competition, then the Pentagon's strategy is crucially at fault. The two policies are not complementary. They are in conflict. They cannot both be right. We should either regard our military planners as wholly incompetent or in general, stop talking about tariff protection for defense-essential industries.

Proponents of the mobilization base may furthermore contend that what seems reasonable in the present situation and for the foreseeable future may turn out to be inadequate in the more remote future. However, there are only two fundamental changes conceivable now that might drastically alter the future conditions of warfare and defense. One is a technological innovation in the field of arms—new bombs, bomb carriers, and perhaps new defenses against planes and missiles—which is unlikely to bring back massive and prolonged nonnuclear war. The other fundamental change might take place as a result of disarmament or international armament control. Here two relevant conditions are uppermost even at this early juncture. First, it is not in the interest of the United States to agree to complete nuclear disarmament, because stocks of finished thermonuclear weapons can be concealed by a country determined to evade armament controls. Unless a foolproof system of detection as well as inspection can be discovered, the United States will insist on retaining a reprisal capacity of last resort. Second, it is not in the interest of the United States to agree to far-reaching nuclear disarmament without concurrent disarmament of "conventional" (i. e., prenuclear) forces. For these reasons, it again seems improbable that there is any future for world war III.

Despite the foregoing arguments, anyone pressing for protective import duties for defense reasons may yet persist on the grounds that, improbable as American involvement in a prolonged and massive war of attrition may be, we cannot be certain, and we should be prepared against even unlikely contingencies. However, preparations for defense are costly. As will be argued below, even tariff duties are a real expense to the Nation. Although, in the face of uncertainty, a country would be pennywise and pound foolish to prepare against only one eventuality, no country, no matter how rich, can afford to protect itself against all contingencies. To do so would not only be detrimental to the American standard of living but also, in the long run, diminish this country's economic capacity for defense. Instead of preparing against all possible threats, it is, therefore, necessary to make choices and to compromise. These choices must be based on three considerations: (*a*) The relative probability of each threat; (*b*) the relative seriousness with which national security would be compromised if a threat, not prepared against, should eventuate; and (*c*) the relative costs of protection against different threats.

Applying these criteria, it appears that the threat of a large-scale war of attrition should be accepted without protective provision being made. The threat of such a war is highly improbable; and the consequences of this unlikely contingency actually becoming reality would hardly be deadly. For one thing, the American economy constitutes the richest national mobilization base in the world, even without special limitations on imports for security reasons. The relative slowness of industrial mobilization during World War II resulted only to a very minor extent from any incompleteness of this base of industries normally geared to producing peacetime goods. The delay occurred primarily because direct armament industries were relatively small and because, for administrative and political reasons, it proved difficult to convert peacetime industries quickly into wartime industries. Second, the terrific thermonuclear punch of SAC would deter any aggressor from pressing too far any advantage he might have in massive, but still limited, war.

### III. CAPACITY FOR RECUPERATION

Should the United States prepare itself to recover as expeditiously as possible from the destruction caused by a thermonuclear onslaught, and should import restrictions in peacetime be considered for this purpose? The reasonable answer to the second part of this question is in the negative. Suppose a certain industry were maintained at a certain peacetime capacity by means of tariff protection. In the event of a nuclear attack on the United States, this industry might be largely wiped out, or its sources of supply might be destroyed, or there might be no transport for its raw materials and fuel, or there might be little demand for its product, or its labor might be needed urgently for other employment. This sort of fate is in store for many industries and numerous enterprises if the United States is devastated. Since the patterns of attack, destruction, and paralysis cannot be foreseen, it makes no sense to foster artificially a certain industrial structure which will be inevitably fragmentized in the event of all-out war.

Moreover, the industries, skills, and tools in most urgent demand in a disaster economy are largely those which do not meet international competition in peacetime. Most urgently needed will be the construction industry, transportation, repair, and other services, the industries producing building materials, etc. If advance preparations are to be made, they should—in addition to planning for efficient government and communications to facilitate recovery—chiefly take the form of stocks of goods ready for use, e. g., food, medical supplies, and construction, transport, and repair equipment. Oil fields, and coal and other mines may largely escape destruction, although some of these may be contaminated by fallout. To employ import restrictions for maintaining such natural-resource industries at a level affording self-sufficiency in peacetime will not bolster the country's potential for recuperation. For a long time after a thermonuclear attack, only a small proportion of normal output will be able to be transported, and only a small proportion will be needed, because a large proportion of the country's plants for refining oil and using coal and other minerals will be ruined or crippled, because the country's population will be diminished, and because the standard of living of the survivors will be only a shadow of what it was in the prewar period.

### IV. SUSTAINING A LARGE DEFENSE EFFORT IN PEACETIME

The grave military threat posed by the U. S. S. R., the new emphasis on mobilized rather than potential military strength, and the rapid obsolescence of military equipment resulting from accelerated development of ever more effective arms and weapons systems have imposed a large defense budget on the United States. During the last 5 years, defense expenditures have averaged about one-tenth of the gross national product. Even at these huge costs, this country has been compelled to compromise between the requirements of national security and the Nation's willingness to pay for defense. Strategic airpower has logically been the first claimant on available resources, while the capacity to fight conventionally with prenuclear arms has been sharply reduced and little has been done for civil defense. According to numerous critics, provisions for defense against limited or unlimited war are seriously deficient. There is, indeed, no foreseeable chance at present of permitting the Nation's defense effort to be materially pared. If anything, the pressure may operate in the opposite direction. Only effective international disarmament or a profound and dependable change in Russian behavior could bring relief, but it would be unrealistic to expect either in the near future.

In all probability, therefore, the United States will have to continue living with very large defense outlays. Whatever their actual level, the greater the growth of the national income, the more easily and readily they will be borne. A high rate of economic growth is consequently a prime constituent of defense potential. There are many relevant conditions of rapid economic growth in the United

States, but business competition, both domestic and foreign, is certainly one condition of long-run growth.

Market forces remain a healthy instrument for encouraging the efficient and weeding out the inefficient use of productive resources, for stimulating innovation, and for preserving the high degree of flexibility and resilience which is the property of a progressive national economy. Interference with international competition is to be rejected on these grounds, for tariff protection tends to support industries which are relatively inefficient and unenterprising, and which lack adaptability to changing business opportunities. Any request for import restrictions for the sake of national security must meet this objection, along with several others.

### V. AN INTERALLIED MOBILIZATION BASE?

Suggestions have been made occasionally that, since the United States is the kingpin of a collective-security system, notaly NATO, a sound mobilization base should be fostered on an interallied rather than on a national basis. This proposal might be taken to imply that any interference with foreign competition required by this objective should not apply to interallied trade. Indeed, it could be argued on this basis that present import restrictions among the Allies should be done away with.

It is clear, however, that such proposals for an interallied mobilization base are outmoded for the same military reasons as those for a national mobilization base. The mobilization base is useless in full-fledged nuclear war and—as an artificial creation—it is hardly necessary for conducting limited war. As pointed out above, the sole exception arises with respect to Western Europe's dependence on Middle Eastern petroleum. The success with which the Suez crisis was weathered suggests that, at present at any rate, no advance interallied preparations are needed to cope with similar emergencies resulting from limited war. It is a situation, however, that bears watching and may call for advance planning as western dependence on Arab oil increases. In general, interruptions of international trade engendered by limited war should not induce vital supply crises which emergency cooperation by the Allied Nations, and perhaps moderate emergency stocks of scarce materials, could not solve.

### VI. CRITERIA FOR IDENTIFYING WAR-ESSENTIAL INDUSTRIES

Policymakers who, on the one hand, still think in terms of an industrial mobilization base as a major means of preparedness for war and who, on the other hand, wish to kep tariff protection on these grounds within reasonable bounds are naturally perplexed by the problem of discovering valid general criteria for selecting appropriate industries. Even in retrospect, it would be an appalling, if not a hopeless, undertaking to pick the American industries that should have received protection prior to World War II in order to bolster the United States economy for that particular war. To begin with, it would be technically difficult to define industries and markets from the viewpoint of defense essentiality as much as it is difficult to define industries and markets for monopoly investigations or any other purpose. Waiving this problem, it would be hard, in most cases, to ascertain the degree to which slowness in expanding the output of defense items was the outcome of a small production capacity for peacetime products or of a host of other factors, such as general shortages of raw materials, parts, and labor or the vagaries of military-production planning. It would be impossible to determine to what degree tariff protection of some of these industries would have increased their capacity or would have diminished the capacity of other industries equally or more important in the defense economy.

All these obstacles are necessarily aggravated when it comes to analyzing the problem, without benefit of hindsight, in relation to future war emergencies. In the light of recent economic and technological changes, past experience would be a treacherous guide for the future. As argued above, technological and military innovations have been so revolutionary since the last war that the problem is largely irrelevant today and can be dismissed as a major one. If the contingency of limited war should require the maintenance of more production capacity than is needed for peacetime purposes, the industries concerned will be the direct armament producers and perhaps a few supplying industries. It is furthermore possible, as President Eisenhower has officially declared, that the domestic oil-producing industry merits close attention from this point of view. On the other hand, it is most unlikely that the American watch industry, for example, requires tariff protection for defense reasons.

Of course, the problem of discovering general criteria for selecting industries for special measures remains, in principle, as intractable as ever. Provided it has been decided—and this is in itself a difficult decision to make—that the United States should at any one time maintain, say, an aircraft or missile manufacturing capacity of such-and-such a volume, careful input-output analysis could yield reasonably accurate data on the current shortfall in the capacity of these industries and the subsidiary industries supplying components. However, since most of these industries also produce for civilian customers, the question immediately arises of how much and how speedily production for the civilian market could be suspended in a limited war emergency. This is in large part a political question and therefore hard to answer in advance. Next, estimates are needed of how much and how rapidly existing capacity could be expanded in a time of emergency. Then it would be necessary to decide the extent to which the relevant parts of the industry concerned are kept by foreign competition from expanding their capacity. Finally, the computations and estimates would have to be remade frequently as military and industrial conditions change.

Yet, under the circumstances described in this paper, the problem is perhaps less forbidding in practice than it at first seems. Although this author did not have the resources to investigate the industries concerned, he surmises that most of them (aircraft, missiles, nuclear equipment, etc.) do not actually suffer from foreign competition. In nearly all of the cases in which foreign competition is a significant factor, the industries concerned will be supplying a substantial civilian market and hence already command an output capacity that can be diverted to military production. Since limited war would not ordinarily require an output capacity greatly in excess of current defense production, this reserve capacity should suffice in virtually all instances.

To make the series of calculations and decision described above will be no mean undertaking. Even though there will be few conclusions indicating the need for special measures, the number of cases to be examined will inevitably be larger. The crucial decision, of course, concerns the level of output capacity which would be desirable in the event that limited war turned out to be relatively demanding of men and arms. The important point in this respect, too, is that the United States must be ready to run certain risks, as it is now doing in all aspects of its defense effort. Three considerations must be remembered in this connection: First, as long as SAC retains its deterrent power, only limited objectives will be at stake in limited war. Second, the chances are that United States and Soviet forces will not be directly pitted against one another, for both countries are aware of the risk inherent in such a situation that limited war might precipitate full-fledged thermonuclear war. Third, the maintenance of ready forces and supplies for conducting limited operations at a reasonably substantial level should permit the United States, and its allies, to stop limited aggression promptly in its tracks and, perhaps, deter it altogether. As already observed, the very maintenance of sufficient mobilized forces for this purpose should insure automatically the maintenance of a substantial manufacturing base specific to the needs of limited war.

When it comes to ascertaining whether this manufacturing base is marginally large enough in all its parts, allowing for reasonable risks, the factors to be considered are obviously so complex, and some of them so intangible, that there can be no resort to a mechanical formula. The task is one of judging calculated risks from case to case.

One further point needs to be made. If there are any instances in which the capacity of an industry that would be important in limited war is now inadequate and in which the industry is subject to keen foreign competition, the initiative for special measures of one kind or another, and even the initiative for exploring the question, should come from Government officials charged with defense policy. Initiatives from the industry concerned should be regarded as irrelevant, and should be ignored. Such industries are hardly in a position to explore the complex defense situation from which defense essentiality arises, and their claims for tariff protection for security reasons must always be suspected of special pleading under false colors.

### VII. IMPORT RESTRICTIONS AS A MEANS OF POLICY

If it is found imperative for reasons of defense to increase the output capacity of an industry beyond its current peacetime volume, the remedy, of course, is not necessarily to be found in import restrictions, whether tariffs or quotas. The problem is to adopt the remedy giving the best result at the lowest price. The result is best when the remedy brings about quickly and maintains the required increase in capacity. The price to be considered involves a variety of disadvantages.

Regarding results, the effect of new or increased tariff duties on the output and output capacity of the protected industry is difficult to predict, because the protected industry might, at least to some extent, raise prices rather than production, and because foreign producers might be able and willing to cut prices. Import quotas will reduce imports to a specified amount, but they cannot prescribe the response of the protected industry. Moreover, import quotas are difficult to administer, requiring a considerable bureaucracy for the purpose.

Regarding disadvantages, five major ones deserve mention. First, and, as stated above, in view of the large defense budgets which the United States might be prepared to support for an indefinite period of time, the highest possible rate of American economic growth is desirable. Import restrictions tend to retard such growth. They serve to maintain inefficient producers and to reduce the incentive of efficient producers to be innovating and enterprising. Even for defense reasons, the United States needs not only a particular capacity in a particular industry, and this is much more important, but also maximum productivity throughout its entire industrial structure.

Second, from a defense point of view, it would be desirable to obtain expanded capacity in efficient firms, and in firms with locations that are suitable for defense reasons. Import restrictions, however, are likely to maintain output capacity in inefficient firms and in firms in strategically vulnerable locations.

Third, import restrictions will harm foreign exporting countries and, hence, are liable to alienate our friends and weaken the economies of our allies and of neutral countries. Again, these effects are undesirable from the viewpoint of national security.

Fourth, if foreign countries earn fewer dollars as a result of American import barriers, they will, in the long run, buy fewer American exports; and they may, in fact, retaliate against the United States by increasing their import restrictions against American goods and services. One effect to be anticipated, therefore, is a shrinking of markets for American export industries which, in many cases, are defense-essential industries.

Fifth, while the United States Treasury collects revenue from import tariffs, the consumer is likely to be forced to pay higher prices for the protected goods. While this is undesirable in itself, the concealed form of the subsidy—a subsidy paid by the American consumer to the protected industry—also makes it likely that the case for limiting imports is not given careful consideration and is not properly reviewed over time.

It is apparent that these weighty disadvantages of import restrictions—and they are nearly all disadvantages precisely from the point of view of national defense—make them singularly costly as a means of policy. While it is obviously hazardous to generalize, there are probably only a few cases in which such restrictions might yield a net benefit for defense purposes.

Direct assistance in the form of direct subsidies or tax concessions will be preferable in most cases. If it enhances the competitive power of domestic industries against foreign exporters, direct assistance will also, of course, entail the third and fourth disadvantages attributed above to import restrictions. It is also true that direct assistance raises administrative difficulties which import duties do not. But it should be realized that the administrative burden arises precisely from the use of a precision tool rather than a haphazard method. Direct assistance can be channeled to relatively efficient firms in desired locations, and it can be adapted to the precise increment in output and output capacity which is wanted. Moreover, involving as it does the use of public funds, it is more likely to be used sparingly and for good reasons. The objection is also raised that direct assistance—for example, tax concessions—raise problems of equity because they give advantages to some businesses and not to others. Though this is true, two points are relevant. Tariff protection for some industries and not for others also raises the question of equity. Furthermore, direct assistance can be administered so that the advantage given to a firm or industry is roughly no more than compensation for investment, production, or employment practices which are inefficient on commercial grounds.

When the above considerations are applied to the defense needs discussed in this paper, the problem becomes, fortunately, a rather minor one. It has been concluded that very few industries will require capacity-increasing measures in order to prepare the United States for fighting limited wars; and it has been assumed that most of the likely candidates for such measures are not held back by foreign competition. To the extent that foreign competition is an insignificant factor, direct assistance is clearly the only appropriate remedy. To the very limited extent that foreign competition is a factor, the weight of the argument in general favors direct assistance as against import restriction. The applicability of general principles, to be sure, must be reviewed in the light of the specific circumstances of each actual case. It is not impossible that, in an exceptional case, resort to import restrictions may on balance yield better results than direct assistance.

## VIII. LARGER ASPECTS OF NATIONAL SECURITY

The United States is interested not only in preparing itself for future war emergencies but also in seeing other countries prepared as well as possible against military aggression by Communist countries. Furthermore, it is generally understood by now that the security of the United States is threatened not only by possible military aggression but also by aggressive policies short of war. This country must be ready to meet the efforts of the Sino-Soviet bloc to expand Communist control by means of political, economic, and ideological pressures and attractions. It is therefore American policy to work for stability and strength in the entire non-Communist world so that its members will not be subverted by the cold-war policies of the Communist states.

The foreign trade policy of the United States must, among other goals, also serve these wider considerations of national security. There is no need to belabor the point. Obviously, curtailing the access of foreign goods to the vast American market can only have harmful effects—that is, effects harmful to the security of the United States—on this score. Being hospitable to foreign economic competition befits the role of leadership which this country has assumed as the wealthiest and most powerful nation in the non-Communist world. This is the positive aspect of the matter. And there is the negative aspect that this country should be most reluctant to take action which will injure the national economies of other non-Communist countries, and thereby impair their military and political as well as their economic viability.

## IX. CONCLUDING REMARK

The problem of arriving at a rational answer to the question of import restrictions on behalf of national security ultimately concerns the general public understanding of the issues involved. For one thing, the arguments presented in this paper are fairly complicated. For another, the entire analysis must perforce proceed in terms of probabilities rather than absolute certainties. If he is sufficiently determined, the person unwilling to be persuaded is always able to refuse being convinced. Such determination may arise from the specific and countervailing interests of industries desirous of tariff protection. The Congressman who understands the problem as presented here may be unable to act on his understanding. His chief role is, after all, to represent his constituents; and, to the extent that they are even aware of having an interest in this matter, the majority of these constituents may be impelled by contrary interests or may be predisposed in favor of tariff protection on general, though fallacious or dubious, grounds. The main prerequisite for rational policy is therefore a determined attempt by the Nation's leaders to increase the general public understanding of the problem.

## THE NATIONAL SECURITY AS AFFECTED BY THE IMPORTING OF POWER PRODUCING EQUIPMENT

Philip D. Reed, chairman of the board, General Electric Co.

SUMMARY

I

The national security amendment's effectiveness is limited if it is regarded as a mere device for protecting domestic industry from the impact of foreign competition.

The amendment proceeds from the premise that importation of certain critical articles can in itself threaten to impair the national security. If the amendment is to serve its purpose it is essential that such articles be identified. In establishing the identity of these critical articles the health of the domestic industry producing them is one of the factors to be considered. One should also consider:

1. The strategic significance of the articles themselves.
2. The purpose served by the articles.
3. The effect of the articles on the ability of the industrial mobilization base to respond to any challenge which it may encounter.
4. Their effect on the mobilization base if such articles are not delivered when promised.
5. The effect on the mobilization base if such articles cannot be promptly and adequately serviced or maintained by foreign suppliers due to international conditions over which we do not have control.

Measured by such criteria heavy electrical equipment is demonstrably vital to the Nation's security, and the extent to which Federal and non-Federal governmental agencies should import such equipment is a proper matter for consideration.

II

The design, manufacture, and installation of such equipment frequently involves 5- to 10-year time intervals. There can be no assurance that the ability of a foreign producer to make delivery will not be impaired by international events, or that such foreign producer will be able to service such equipment after its installation.

III

A major breakdown of foreign heavy electrical equipment cannot be repaired as expeditiously as can domestic equipment. Foreign suppliers do not maintain substantial service facilities in this country. Due to extensive differences in design, materials, and tools, foreign equipment cannot be readily serviced by domestic manufacturers.

IV

Each time foreign heavy electrical equipment is ordered for our electrical generation and distribution system the system is weakened to the extent that such equipment after delivery cannot be serviced or repaired under conditions approximating the efficiency with which domestic equipment can be serviced and repaired.

V

Under the Buy American Act, current procurement policies of the Federal Government as they relate to heavy electrical equipment place too much emphasis on price and too little emphasis on the strategic significance of such equipment. The current procedure does not provide for a true evaluation of the effect of imported equipment on the industrial mobilization base.

---

## I. The "National Security Amendment" of the Trade Agreements Extension Act of 1955 Is Directed Against the "Articles" Which Threaten To Impair the National Security

The national security amendment, as its name implies, was adopted for the purpose of protecting our security interests against certain imports. Experience to date does not convince us that this legislation has been completely effective as a means of protecting the national security. Under this law the President can impose new or increased tariff duties on imports without any limitation as to their level, or he can impose an import quota, so as to reduce imports to such levels as he deems appropriate. Under the national security amendment the only limitation on the President's authority over imports is that his action must be such "as he deems necessary to adjust the imports of such articles to a level that will not threaten to impair the national security."

Some persons have interpreted the national security amendment to mean that the President is obligated to act only in situations where he deems it necessary to do so in order to protect industries essential to the Nation's industrial mobilization base.

We submit that the legislation is intended to provide the President with a broader power, and an obligation. He is obligated to act whenever he finds that an "article is being imported into the United States in such quantities as to threaten to impair the national security."

Impairment of the national security and impairment of a domestic industry essential to the industrial mobilization base of the Nation are not synonymous concepts. Obviously, impairment of a domestic industry essential to the mobilization base involves an impairment of the national security. What must be equally well understood, however, is the fact that the national security may be impaired, through imports, notwithstanding an assumed healthy condition of the domestic industry producing products similar to the imported products.

The extent to which the complexity of this problem may not be fully appreciated is perhaps manifested by the administration of the national security amendment The Director of the Office of Defense Mobilization has the responsibility to determine whether imports are impairing the national security. However, it appears that the Director of ODM does not investigate threats to the national security as a result of imports except where domestic industries appeal to his office for relief It would seem desirable to regard the term "national security" as somewhat more inclusive than a synonym for protection of domestic industry.

National security certainly includes the health of domestic industry essential to the mobilization base. It also, of course, includes our overall foreign policy relations—the effect of our actions on the economies of nations allied with us, and the impact of import restrictions on our own exports.

In addition, we submit, national security requires an objective appraisal and evaluation of the strategic importance of certain "articles." In making this evaluation, certain contingencies must be given realistic consideration. We refer specifically to the situation which the Nation would face in the event of war.

No one can predict whether or not this Nation will become involved in a major war, nor can one say when such a war might occur. Nevertheless, prudence dictates certain assumptions in the event of war:

1. Electric power-producing products are of a critical defense nature, inherently essential to our ability to prepare for and our ability to survive any war.
2. The Nation's domestic territory is not immune from attack.
3. Electric power-producing sites are logical strategic targets for attack or sabotage.
4. If hostilities occur, no foreign nation will be able to deliver substantial quantities of power-producing products.
5. Replacement and repair of destroyed or damaged equipment will be essential to survival and will have to come from domestic facilities.
6. Time will be of the essence.

If these premises are supportable, certain conclusions inevitably emerge. National security requires a plentitude of at least five factors in connection with such products:

(*a*) Adequacy of supply.
(*b*) Excellence of quality.
(*c*) Supply of skilled workers trained in the art.
(*d*) Adequacy of domestic research and development facilities.
(*e*) Facilities, equipment designs, and know-how for rapid repair and replacement.

The strategic products which are the source of our concern may be generally described as follows:

1. Large generating equipment (both hydroelectric and thermal): These equipments are so completely tailormade that seldom are units for any two plants built alike.
2. Transformers: Virtually all transformers of foreign design differ materially from those of domestic origin.
3. Switchgear, circuit breakers: This product is normally custom-built to suit the particular requirements of a specific installation. It consists of an assemblage of myriad components, including subassemblies of complicated relays, meters, instruments, regulators, and control devices.

The above-listed types of heavy electrical equipment are vital to this Nation's security—so vital that special standards and procedures should be adopted in regard to their acquisition by both Federal and non-Federal governmental agencies.

In the final analysis, the single most important physical factor in national defense is industrial production. This production is totally dependent on a uninterrupted flow of vast quantities of electrical power—power which is produced, transmitted, and distributed by heavy electrical equipment. World War II demonstrated the magnitude of the burden which this equipment must endure during an all-out mobilization of the industrial base. Failure of such equipment to perform up to expectations would be disastrous.

The extent to which the Nation is handicapping its ability to respond to an emergency is graphically illustrated on the map, marked "Exhibit I," which is attached hereto. This map shows a number of the installations of foreign equipment which have been made an integral part of our electrical energy generation and distribution complex within the last 5 years.

This foreign equipment cannot be serviced with anything approximating the speed and efficiency with which domestic equipment can be serviced in a time of national peril.

## II. The Logistics of Obtaining Repair and Maintenance Service From Foreign Suppliers

In order to appreciate fully the difficulty of repairing, maintaining or rebuilding such equipment it is necessary to know something about the time and design factors in making the original installations of such equipment.

For instance, let us consider the equipment that is specially designed for a large hydroelectric project, the kind of projects which are being installed on our major rivers. The construction of such projects usually involves a time interval of from 5 to 10 years. The advance planning and design work may require several additional years before construction begins. Furthermore, the design, manufacture, and installation of the electrical equipment must be coordinated with the construction schedule of the entire project.

For example, we initiated preliminary design work on electrical equipment for the Columbia River, McNary Dam project, in 1943. Bids were taken on the first generators in November 1948. We supplied and installed the first 12 generators which were scheduled for completion in June 1956—13 years after the initiation of preliminary design work.

We are currently supplying 14 generators for the Dalles Dam, Columbia River, Oreg. Preliminary design work on these generators was initiated in 1951. Bids were taken on the first 8 generators in October 1954 and the scheduled completion date for these generators is May 1959. The 6 additional generators were bid December 1956 and their scheduled completion date is November 1960. Present plans contemplate the addition, at a later date, of 8 more units to complete the installation.

Consideration of the time involved in constructing such facilities and the high degree of coordination required compels one to speculate about the wisdom of entertaining foreign bids on such projects.

Awards to foreign manufacturers calling for delivery several years in the future require an assumption that such foreign manufacturers' nation and this Nation will avoid becoming involved in any international hostilities which will interfere with completion and delivery of the equipment. The dynamic quality of world events challenges the prudence of such assumption.

If the equipment is not delivered an alternative source of supply is not immediately available. For example, a single generator may embody 3 million pounds of material and 550,000 man-hours of labor, and must be designed and built for a specific installation. When one considers that the design and erection of the basic structure into which a specific generator is to be installed is coordinated with and is complementary to the generator, it is apparent that obtaining substitute equipment would present problems of the first magnitude.

If a foreign supplier is unable to make delivery, the consequent loss of electrical power needed for utilization of the industrial base cannot be measured in dollars.

The hazard involved in purchasing such equipment from foreign manufacturers also manifests itself after it has been installed. All suppliers of such complicated electrical apparatus encounter occasional troubles or failures of equipment. This is not surprising in view of the rapid development of the art and the required increases in sizes and ratings of such equipment.

It appears to us, however, that there have been an unusual number of such difficulties with foreign equipment in the last year or two when related to the total number of foreign units installed. Whether or not the number of such difficulties is unusual is not, however, as significant as the complexity of the problem encountered when such difficulties arise.

Three illustrative cases listed below demonstrate the nature of the difficulties to which we refer:

1. The Elin Company of Austria supplied a 50,000 kilovolt-ampere 3-phase transformer to Bonneville Power Administration for installation near McNary Dam during 1955–56. We have been advised that this transformer suffered an insulation failure about July 1956. Because Elin had no service facilities in this country, the unit was reportedly shipped to an aluminum plant in Spokane, Wash., for repairs. It then developed that Elin was unable to provide facilities for retesting the unit in the United States, so it was shipped back to Austria for testing. Tests were conducted in early 1957 and the unit failed again under impulse test. The transformer has been scheduled for another rebuild and retest later in 1957. It is apparently still in Austria.

2. Two generators for the McNary Dam provided by the English Electric Co. reveal a similar story. These two 73,684 kilovolt-ampere generators were reported to have undergone tests during August-September 1956 which indicated failure to meet specified temperature guaranties. Thereupon the units were disassembled and rebuilt with smaller airgap and other design changes, but as of April 1957 Electrical World reported that the generators still had not met guaranties and were still not accepted by the Corps of Engineers.

3. The English Electric Co. supplied the Corps of Engineers for Chief Joseph Dam, Columbia River, Wash., 10 103,300 kilovolt-am-

pere power transformers. These units were awarded in 1953 and installed about 1955–56. A failure of one of these units was reported in May 1956. It appears that this was an insulation failure between high- and low-voltage windings. Damage was quite extensive and the unit was reportedly sent to Canada for repairs. In order to determine the cause of the weakness another 103,300 kilovolt-ampere unit was reportedly removed from Chief Joseph Dam and returned to the manufacturer's plant in England for examination. The unit repaired in Canada was returned to service and failed again. After this second failure, we are advised the unit was returned to England for rebuilding. It is possible that all 10 units will be returned to England for rebuilding.

Fortunately, incidents of the type referred to have not been further complicated by any outbreak of major hostilities. As a consequence of this coincidence perhaps the loss can be measured in terms of time and dollars. It could not be so measured in time of war.

The long-time bet that there will be no outbreak of hostilities which will interfere with future deliveries of vital components of hydroelectric projects is being made by both Federal and non-Federal governmental agencies. For example, the Public Utility District of Grant County, Wash., is building a hydroelectric project on the Columbia River at Priest Rapids. The English Electric Co. is supplying eight 83,000-kilovolt-ampere generators and the accompanying power transformers and hydraulic turbines. Construction started in 1956 and is scheduled for completion within about 5 years. These large units are custom designed to the specific hydraulic conditions of the Priest Rapids development. Each generator will require some 50 freight carloads for shipment and the hydraulic turbines and transformers are in proportion. Should war intervene, delivery would no doubt be impossible. We could be deprived of a power facility that otherwise would be delivering 600,000 kilowatts of electric power—enough power to supply an average industrial community of 500,000 people. Should major trouble develop in the generators, transformers, or turbines, the manufacturer's lack of service facilities in this country could result in the kind of expense and delay incurred by returning the equipment to England for servicing. In peacetime this would be possible; in case of war it would be impracticable, even if possible.

### III. Reasons Why Foreign Equipment Cannot Be Readily Serviced

The differences between the ability of foreign and domestic producers to service and maintain their respective equipment is manifest. For example, the American industry maintains a field staff of over 3,000 service engineers and over 5,000 service technicians located widely throughout the United States. These are in addition to the research, development, and design engineering staffs. The geographical coverage is such that within a few hours practically every important power generating station can be reached. Supporting this service are manufacturing plants in many cities, well-equipped repair shops are located in every important center with warehouses for parts, complete products, and materials. The personnel which supervise and perform this fieldwork are highly trained, and have skilled and intimate knowledge of the domestic equipment. The introduction of foreign equipment frustrates the effectiveness of this remarkable maintenance and repair corps by reason of the complete lack of design information, drawings, tools, parts, and processes required for servicing.

Heavy electrical equipment is completely tailormade for each specific installation and has no counterpart anywhere else in the world. Such equipment may give 25 to 50 years of service; replacement of parts and breakdowns may occur even under normal conditions. When this happens to foreign-built equipment, spare parts are not usually available in this country, nor can they be readily and quickly fabricated here. A major breakdown of a foreign-built generator simply cannot be remedied in anything remotely approaching the same time in which a domestic-built generator can be repaired.

The difficulty that a domestic manufacturer or service agency would encounter in servicing or repairing foreign-built equipment arises from differences in standards, fundamental differences in designs and materials, unavailability of drawings and specifications, different units of measurement in foreign-built equipment, and the greater use by foreign manufacturers of hand labor to fit specific parts into given equipment. Because of the custom-built nature of such equipment it has not been economical or necessary in the case of equipment supplied by domestic manufacturers to provide many spare replacement parts. Domestic manufacturers of heavy electrical equipment keep on file complete drawings and design information for each of the units produced. In case of failure of a machine supplied by a domestic manufacturer, one of the manufocturer's experienced service engineers, who are located throughout the country, can reach any domestic installation in a matter of hours. This experienced engineer can inspect the damage, telephone his factory, and review the circumstances with experienced design engineers and decide what must be done to repair the machine. Required replacement parts can be ordered at that time and their fabrication can start immediately.

In case of a breakdown of a machine supplied by a foreign manufacturer such service is not possible. In the first place foreign manufacturers do not maintain extensive service organizations in the United States, nor do they maintain complete records and drawings for their machines, except at their headquarters. In the event of a serious failure of a machine supplied by a foreign manufacturer, even in peacetime, it might be necessary to get a specialist from foreign headquarters to inspect the damage to determine what must be done. It might be possible for the specialist with the assistance of his design engineers to arrange for the repair by service organizations in the United States. Ordinarily, however, this would not be the procedure since it would take as long or longer for domestic organizations to make the tools and jigs or to procure nonstandard sizes of material as it would to ship material from the foreign manufacturer. Thus even in peacetime the difference between service by a domestic organization and a foreign manufacturer might easily be several weeks or months.

In the event of war a foreign manufacturer would be unable to deliver such parts and might be unable to offer any assistance either in

22806—58——44

the form of engineering advice or drawings. In this circumstance if the equipment supplied by a foreign manufacturer were to be repaired by a domestic manufacturer, it would be necessary for the engineering specialist of a domestic manufacturer to disassemble the machine to the point where it would be possible to measure the parts, make the necessary drawings, make the tools, dies, and jigs for manufacturing such parts, and procure materials that might not be standard in the United States, or adapt such materials as are normally used in this country before one could even begin to make the replacement parts. From the time that the diagnosis and tools are completed the repair of foreign-built equipment would proceed at about the same rate as similar domestic work.

If the machine breakdown were a winding failure in a waterwheel generator the time for inspection of the machine, preparation of drawings, production of tools, and procurement of material would be at least several months. There are cases on record during World War II in which United States manufacturers were called upon to repair equipment supplied by foreign manufacturers in Mexico and South American countries. It took 1 year to obtain the necessary information and preparation of drawings and tools for winding failures. The seriousness of this time barrier in a hostile situation is patent.

Most transformers of foreign design are considerably different than those of domestic origin. Such differences involve the core, winding, insulation, tank, and accessories. Frequently the wire sizes and core steel thicknesses vary from standard domestic dimensions. If drawings and manufacturing information are not available, a disabled transformer would have to be sent to a factory for disassembly so that each component could be analyzed, so that drawings could be made and manufacturing information obtained for fabricating replacement parts. It has been estimated that a major repair schedule on a foreign transformer would require 2 to 3 times as many man-hours of work as a similar repair on a domestic transformer. Furthermore, if a standard stock replacement is compared to a special adaptation for a foreign transformer, the man-hour ratio may rise to 10 or more.

Given the fact that there are domestic producers which can do the job—expeditiously in the case of their own equipment, and considerably less so where it is of foreign design—the real question is, How much time is it intelligent for the Nation to assume it will have to lose in the event of an emergency? To what extent can the Nation safely gamble with delay? We sincerely believe that the national security requires power-producing electrical equipment to be capable of replacement or repair in the minimum amount of time. This should be axiomatic.

## IV. The Nature of Our Choice and Considerations Which Should Guide Us

Ultimately this problem is one of choosing between two factors in the national interest. Which is more important—an electrical distribution and generation system, every vital component of which can be serviced, repaired, rebuilt, and installed under optimum conditions; or a system, numerous components of which cannot be so treated under anything approximating optimum conditions? Jeopardizing our basic power supply seems a very high price to pay for whatever beneficial effects might accrue to the economies of the foreign nations which supply such equipment. This is especially true in view of the well-recognized shortages of such equipment in the very nations from whom we are making some of our purchases. It is by no means clear that the dollar balances accruing to these countries through the sale of this equipment are an unmixed blessing in view of the shortages of such equipment to service their own industrial bases. Patently, measurement of this consideration is the prerogative of the nations concerned; however, it does not follow that in our own interest we should not give consideration to the possibility that their sources of power may be improved more rapidly if we take action to terminate the diversion of such equipment from them.

Whether foreign equipment is purchased by a Federal or a non-Federal agency is not important in relation to a national security problem. The risk is the same. It is within the power of the Congress and of the Executive to eliminate this risk to the national security. The Buy American Act is applicable to the Federal agencies and the national security amendment is a vehicle for reaching the procurement practices of both Federal and non-Federal agencies.

To obviate any misunderstanding, we think it is important that our views be placed in proper perspective. Exhibit II shows the estimated purchases of foreign electrical equipment, listed by purchasers and listed by product for the years 1953 through 1956.

The percentage of increase between 1953 and 1956 is in itself significant, as is the spectacular increase of 1956 over 1955. The dollar amounts of these purchases are of no great significance in the total import-export picture. In fact, to attach significance to these dollar amounts is to miss the point.

The dollar amounts are so small that it is somewhat shocking that we should risk crippling ourselves in a time of national stress by continuing to import into our electrical generation and distribution system a series of key components which can be serviced and kept in operation only by overcoming conditions of maximum complexity.

It would appear that consideration should be given to the following factors:

1. The defense essentiality of an uninterrupted flow of electrical power.

2. The fact that even under normal conditions such equipment requires repair and replacement of parts.

3. The fact that in a period of international hostility such repairs and replacements must come from domestic sources.

4. The fact that neither domestic nor foreign sources could possibly replace or repair foreign-built equipment as efficiently or expeditiously as domestic producers could service domestic equipment.

5. The fact that domestic and foreign equipment are not "like materials" because, while the American electrical industry provides continued and easily available maintenance and repair service for domestically built equipment, such service is not and cannot be provided for foreign-built equipment. This difference is real, though not measurable in dollars.

6. Whether the national security can best be protected by legislation preventing the purchase of such equipment by Government agencies or whether the matter should be left to the discretion of the Executive is a proper matter for consideration by this subcommittee. In this connection it should be of interest that the British attitude is manifested in a report of a Parliamentary Committee of Inquiry set up to investigate the electric supply industry. It was brought out that the Central Electricity Authority, the Government agency in charge of the generation and transmission of electricity, regarded it as "unwise for the electricity supply industry to be dependent upon foreign manufacturers for spares and maintenance," and hence has refused "to go abroad for heavy electrical plant" (Report of the Committee of Inquiry into the Electricity Supply Industry (January 1956), pp. 114–115).

It is possible that British experience with hot wars has predisposed them to a realism in this respect which has eluded us.

V. THE CURRENT PROCUREMENT POLICIES OF THE FEDERAL AGENCIES EMPHASIZE PRICE IN AN AREA WHERE PRICE SHOULD BE SECONDARY TO THE NATIONAL SECURITY

The strategic quality and national defense essentiality of these products has been recognized by the Government in applying the Renegotiation Act. A large part of the Federal Government purchases of such equipment are made by the Corps of Engineers, Department of Defense. Such purchases are subject to the Renegotiation Act.

Congress has frequently recognized vital defense considerations when it authorized construction, operation, and maintenance of major river projects. Legislation has frequently referred to the generation of hydroelectric power for the national defense.

The President's Executive order of December 17, 1954, relating to the Buy American Act takes cognizance of the national security problem. Section 3 provides:

> Nothing in this order shall affect the authority or responsibility of an executive agency—
>
> (*d*) to reject any bid or offer for materials of foreign origin if such rejection is necessary to protect essential national security interests after receiving advice with respect thereto from the President or from any officer of the Government designated by the President to furnish such advice.

The Director of ODM has been designated as the officer—

> to furnish advice to executive agencies with respect to the rejection of bids or offers to furnish materials of foreign origin upon the ground that such rejection is *necessary* to protect essential national security interests. [Emphasis added.]

However, the President further advised the Director of ODM:

> It is my conviction that exceptions under this provision of the Executive order should be made *only* upon *a clear showing* that the payment of a greater differential than the order provides for is *justified* by considerations of national security. [Emphasis supplied.]

With this charter the Director of ODM has been unwilling to proceed on anything but a case-by-case basis in reference to procurement of these vital defense materials.

Unfortunately a case-by-case approach is not an effective way to determine whether or not the national security is impaired, threatened, or protected. If each potential purchase of heavy electrical equipment is considered in isolation from all the other purchases—past and future—then the effect of the particular purchase on the national security is never brought into perspective. Using such an approach it is difficult to find that rejection of one particular purchase is "*necessary* to protect essential national security interests." It is doubtful whether such an approach assures any protection to the national security. Even if we assume that each such purchase is considered in relation to all the foreign installations already ordered or in place, what criteria can the Director of ODM use to determine whether the particular purchase should or should not be made. In other words, at what point does he by some occult means recognize that a particular purchase *must* be rejected because it is "*necessary* to protect essential national security interests." As noted above, the British avoid this problem with a realistic overall recommendation so far as such equipment is concerned.

It is undoubtedly true that everything is not black or white; it is equally true that everything is not gray. Determining the dominant shade requires looking at the whole picture. We respectfully suggest that an informed decision in relation to this matter can be arrived at only by looking at the vital role which this equipment plays in the national-security picture.

Exhibit I gives some indication of the amount of foreign equipment in place today. This map shows where much of the foreign equipment that has been ordered in the last 5 years has been or will be installed. This equipment is being made an integral part of our electrical systems. Most of the equipment shown was purchased by Federal agencies. A few purchases by other bodies are also shown but we have only limited information on the total extent of such purchases.

The information revealed by this map should be considered in the light of certain other related information. The United States Corps of Engineers, the Bonneville Power Administration, and the Bureau of Reclamation have been receiving foreign bids for about 5 years. During the 5-year period these agencies have been receiving foreign bids many new projects have been under construction in the Missouri River Basin with purchasing done by the Corps of Engineers and the Bureau of Reclamation. This accounts for the high concentration of foreign equipment in this area. Unless restrictions are placed on the purchase of foreign equipment, we can expect similar situations to develop in other areas, with a higher content of foreign equipment throughout the country. For instance, TVA did not start considering foreign bids until 1954 but already has placed a considerable volume of foreign orders. The inability of foreign manufacturers to service, repair, or rebuild that equipment in the event of war is obvious. The fact that domestic manufacturers cannot service, repair, or rebuild this equipment, except by an agonizing expenditure of essential time is undisputed. The necessity of an efficient electrical generation and distribution system to serve the industrial base needs no elaboration. All considerations of enemy action aside, such equipments, foreign and domestic will require periodic repairs. Foreign components which may have to be replaced by domestic equipment or rebuilt or repaired by domestic equipment or rebuilt or repaired by domestic producers constitute a *threat* to the national security to the extent that such replacements, repairs, or rebuilding require inordinately longer to consummate than would be the case with domestic equipment.

It appears to us that section 7 of the Trade Agreements Extension Act of 1955 recognizes the possible strategic significance of certain articles. It states:

> In order to further the policy and purpose of this section whenever the Director of the Office of Defense Mobilization has reason to believe that any *article* is being imported into the United States in such quantities as to threaten to impair the national security, he shall so advise the President, and if the President agrees that there is reason for such belief, the President shall cause an immediate investigation to be made to determine the facts. If, on the basis of such investigation, and the report to him of the findings and recommendations made in connection therewith, the President finds that the *article* is being imported into the United States in such quantities as to *threaten* to impair the national security, he shall take such action as he deems necessary to adjust the imports of such article to a level that will not threaten to impair the national security. [Emphasis supplied.]

It is notable that the thrust of this legislation is in an entirely different direction from that of the Buy American Act as applied pursuant to the President's Executive order of December 17, 1954. The national-security amendment deals with the importation of any "article * * * in such quantities as to *threaten* to impair the national security." The legislative language indicates that importation of some "articles" can, under some circumstances, constitute a "threat," or forewarning of an impairment to the national security.

This concept is different from the one embraced by the Buy American Act and the President's Executive order which deals with the rejection of bids or offers of material "if such is *necessary* to protect essential national-security interests." The national-security amendment would seem to require the President to act if importations "threaten" impairment of the national security, yet we find that under the Executive order the Government buys on price unless the Director of ODM finds that an exception on a specific acquisition should be made because of a "*clear showing* that the payment of a greater differential * * * is *justified* by considerations of national security" or "is *necessary* to protect essential national-security interests." There is a substantial difference in the quantum of proof and the kind of proof which should compel action under the two acts. To make a clear showing that a specific foreign generator must be rejected because it is "*necessary* to protect essential national-security interests" is very different from determining that the continued importation of foreign generators, transformers, switchgear and steam turbines above a particular rating "*threatens* to impair the national security."

It may well be true that it would be possible for a particular fact finder to come to the same conclusion in either case. It does not follow, however, that the national-security-amendment approach should go unutilized and that no proceedings should be instituted pursuant to it. If nothing else, a proceeding pursuant to the national-security amendment would at least provide an inquiry into the whole problem as distinguished from the case-by-case approach currently utilized under the Buy American Act.

Unfortunately, our interpretation of the security amendment is not unanimously shared. As indicated at the outset, some persons believe that the national-security amendment is simply a device for protection of domestic industry; we feel that the Congress was concerned with maintaining the integrity of the entire industrial mobilization base. We respectfully suggest that this subcommittee should give consideration to clarifying the congressional intent in this respect. Furthermore, we urge recognition of the fact that some articles are of such strategic significance that their continued importation is contrary to the best interests of national security. At least there should be an established procedure for determining the validity of this contention. Furthermore, we do not believe that as a condition precedent to invoking such procedure it should be necessary for the domestic industry producing such products to allege that it is threatened with destruction from foreign competition.

Foreign manufacturers can undersell domestic producers of heavy electrical equipment. The tremendous wage differential of the foreign manufacturers of this equipment permits them to furnish it at prices lower than those of domestic manufacturers. The fact remains that whether in the long run these items constitute a bargain to the Nation has not been adequately explored. The workmen involved in this industry are in the nature of master craftsmen whose peak efficiency can be achieved only after years of training and experience. There is no possibility in the foreseeable future of replacing these craftsmen with mechanized operations, because each piece of power-producing equipment is a special custom-built item. The items are not adaptable to mass production. It is inevitable that in the absence of sufficient employment opportunities the special skills which these workers have developed will be lost as they turn to other less exacting jobs either in or outside of the electrical industry. Possible dissipation of this magnificent asset as a direct result of depressed wages by our standards is not in the national interest. Such dissipation is by no means inconceivable if price is to be the dominant basis upon which such equipment is acquired.

EXHIBIT I

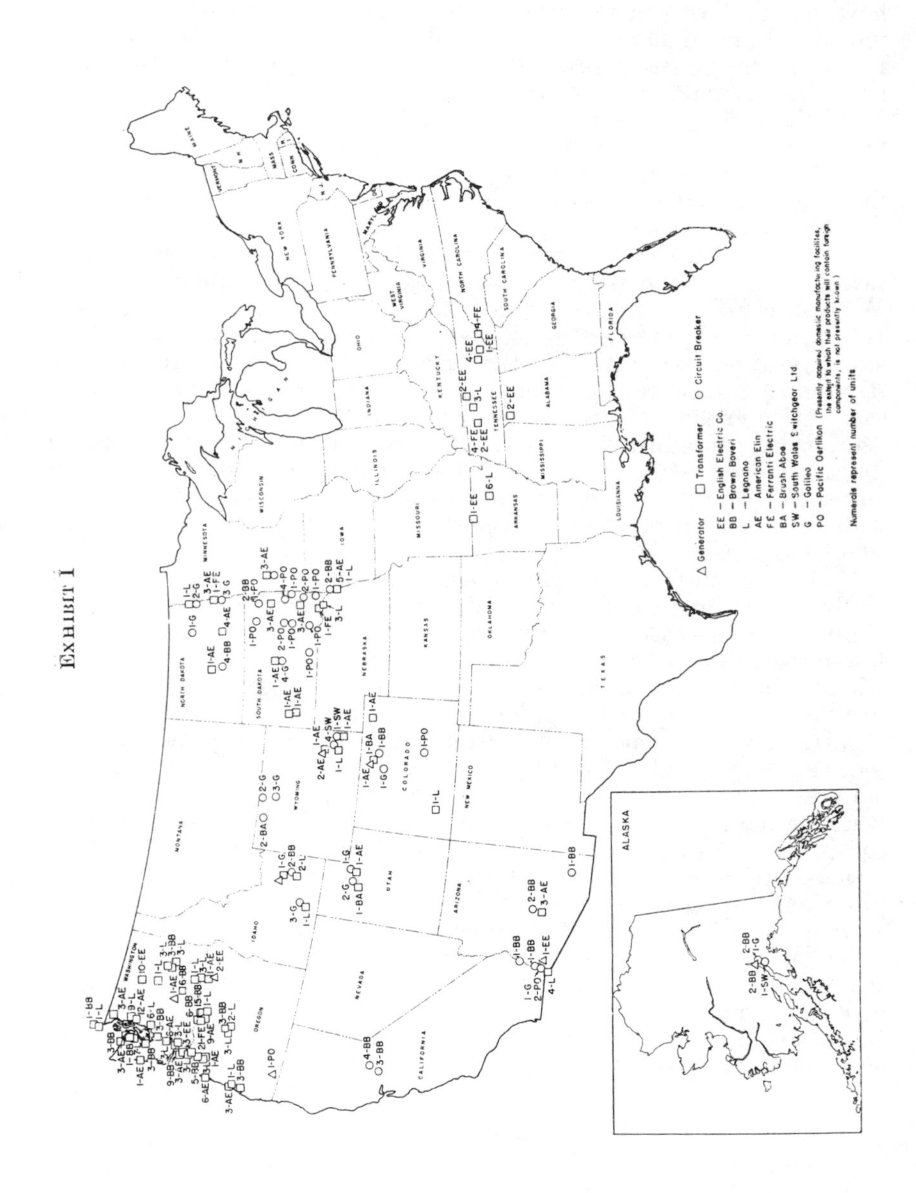

Δ Generator □ Transformer ○ Circuit Breaker
EE — English Electric Co.
BB — Brown Boveri
L — Legnano
AE — American Elin
FE — Ferranti Electric
BA — Brush Aboe
SW — South Wales Switchgear Ltd.
G — Galileo
PO — Pacific Oerlikon (Presently acquired domestic manufacturing facilities, the extent to which their products will contain foreign components, is not presently known.)
Numerals represent number of units
ALASKA

EXHIBIT II

*Estimated purchases of foreign electrical equipment*

LIST OF PURCHASER

| | Amount awarded | | | |
|---|---|---|---|---|
| | 1953 | 1954 | 1955 | 1956 |
| TVA | 0 | 0 | $462, 160 | $3, 076, 530 |
| Corps of Engineers | $6, 595, 516 | $137, 351 | 183, 688 | 2, 059, 140 |
| Bonneville Power Administration | 965, 265 | 188, 678 | 305, 891 | 1, 749, 344 |
| Bureau of Reclamation | 2, 722, 675 | 1, 145, 035 | 1, 195, 198 | 1, 597, 058 |
| Municipal, State, and public utility district | 330, 670 | 8, 700 | 3, 247, 205 | 13, 519, 617 |
| Utilities, investor-owned | (1) | 358, 000 | 44, 625 | 620, 000 |
| Total | 10, 614, 126 | 1, 837, 764 | 5, 438, 767 | 22, 621, 689 |

LISTED BY PRODUCTS

| | 1953 | 1954 | 1955 | 1956 |
|---|---|---|---|---|
| Hydrogenerators | $5, 629, 298 | 0 | 0 | $12, 287, 065 |
| Transformers and allied products | 4, 092, 402 | $1, 360, 347 | $4, 620, 100 | 9, 214, 797 |
| Switchgear | 765, 241 | 431, 751 | 217, 456 | 946, 452 |
| Turbine generators | 0 | 0 | 350, 000 | 0 |
| Instrument transformers | 127, 185 | 45, 666 | 251, 211 | 173, 375 |
| Total | 10, 614, 126 | 1, 837, 764 | 5, 438, 767 | 22, 621, 689 |

[1] No record.

# VIII

# FOREIGN TRADE POLICY IN RELATION TO UNITED STATES AGRICULTURE

# SPECIAL REGULATION ON UNITED STATES IMPORTS OF AGRICULTURAL PRODUCTS

United States Department of Agriculture

DEPARTMENT OF AGRICULTURE,
*Washington, D. C., September 6, 1957.*

Hon. HALE BOGGS,
*Chairman, Subcommittee on Foreign Trade Policy,*
*Committee on Ways and Means, House of Representatives.*

DEAR CONGRESSMAN BOGGS: This is in further reply to your letter of June 18, 1957, requesting the Department of Agriculture to provide a review of its experience with respect to two of the items of the subcommittee's study program; namely, item (3) "Analysis of the Regulation of Imports by Quotas" and item (4) e, "Protection of Programs of the Department of Agriculture From Import Interference."

Quotas and tariff quotas as well as other quantitative restrictions are currently imposed on imports of agricultural commodities and products thereof under several different authorities. These authorities include (1) section 22 of the Agricultural Adjustment Act, as amended; (2) section 7 of the Trade Agreements Extension Act of 1951, as amended; (3) section 350 of the Tariff Act of 1930, as amended; and (4) the Sugar Act of 1948, as amended. Brief factual analyses of quotas, tariff quotas and other quantitative restrictions on agricultural products under these authorities are attached.

Each of these authorities has a different specific objective. The purpose of section 22 is to provide a means of controlling imports when they render or tend to render ineffective or materially interfere with price support or other programs of the Department of Agriculture. The objective of the section 7 escape-clause actions is to prevent or remedy serious injury from imports which might result from unforeseen developments following a tariff concession. The purpose of tariff quotas under section 350 is to put a limit on imports at the concession rate in order to safeguard domestic producers or for other reasons. The aim of the Sugar Act is to achieve prices which will fairly and equitably maintain and protect the domestic sugar industry and at the same time will not be excessive to consumers.

The powers to establish and allocate quotas (including tariff quotas) provided by these authorities, except under the Sugar Act, are exercised by the President after consideration and review of the pertinent facts by several agencies. For example, the steps involved in section 22 cases are: (1) an investigation and determination by the Secretary of Agriculture, (2) a finding by the President that a Tariff Commission investigation is warranted, (3) an investigation by the Tariff Commission including a public hearing, (4) a finding and recommendation by the Tariff Commission to the President, (5) agency views as may be requested by the President, and (6) action by the President. Procedures under the Sugar Act are described in the attached analysis of the regulation of sugar imports by quota. The various areas of analysis suggested by the committee, insofar as they relate to sugar controls, are dealt with for the most part by a recital of actual experience before and since institution of the quota system.

The considerations bearing on the appropriateness of a quota, tariff quota, or additional fee depend on the elements of the specific case. Under section 22 procedures each individual case is studied in detail and the final decision as to the appropriate action is made by the President. It has in general been found that fees would not as effectively protect the domestic programs as quotas. In some cases, however, such as currenly for flaxseed (including linseed oil), fees have been used to prevent interference with the program by imports.

In the case of section 22 actions, the appropriateness of the action appears to have been determined primarily on its anticipated effectiveness in removing the interference caused by imports. We are not aware of any instance where quotas were applied because of features of the trade agreements program which limited the duties or import fees that might be appropriately imposed by executive action.

In a number of cases, the quotas proclaimed under section 22 have been allocated among supplying countries. Country allocations for long-staple cotton, short-staple cotton, and cotton waste were made pursuant to the requirements of the provisions of section 22 at the time the quotas were proclaimed. This requirement was eliminated in 1940. However, the country allocations have been continued except for long-staple cotton, which was put on a global basis in 1942 at the request of Peru after negotiating a reduction in the duty. The country allocations on wheat, rye, and their products, though not necessary to protect the Department's programs, serve to provide equitable treatment to the foreign supplying countries by protecting their historical share in the United States market. The wheat and wheat-product quotas were allocated on a country basis when initially established in 1941. The quota initially established for rye was a global quota. The annual quotas in effect since July 1, 1955, however, have been allocated to supplying countries. In the case of both wheat and rye the allocation is based on a historical supplier position.

The import controls imposed on certain dairy products is the only instance where the quotas are allotted to domestic importers by means of licenses as well as allocated among supplying countries. The Presidential proclamation delegated the issuance of licenses to the Secretary of Agriculture in order to insure the equitable distribution of the quotas among the importers and users. The adoption of a licensing system in this instance appears to be less a matter of essential control for the purpose of the act than an effort to prevent distortion of established patterns of trade. It recognizes that the cheeses under control are specialty products, the trade in which has been developed over the years. The historic marketing structure developed by the domestic users of the imported cheeses is maintained and protected under the licensing system.

The experience to date under section 22, therefore, indicates that allocations of the total quota among individual supplying countries or among importers has been in consideration of trade interests of the traditional supplying countries and of the importers rather than for the purpose of mitigating the adverse effects of imports on the domestic programs.

The effect of quotas, tariff quotas, and fees pursuant to section 22 on the operation of competition cannot be considered independently of the agricultural programs they are intended to protect. Legislative enactments authorize the Department of Agriculture to operate programs designed to support farm income and stabilize prices of farm products. Three of these programs pertinent to this discussion are (1) the general price-support program, (2) section 32 programs, and (3) market agreement and order programs.

1. *General price support programs.*—Under these programs the Department attempts to establish a floor under the price of the commodity being supported by making loans, purchase agreements, or actually purchasing any lot of the supported commodity which will meet specified eligibility requirements at the announced support level. In the case of wool, payments are made under the incentive-payment program authorized by the National Wool Act.

Price supports are mandatory for corn, wheat, cotton (upland and extra long staple), rice, tobacco, and peanuts—the so-called basic commodities. Support is also mandatory within certain price limits for tung nuts, honey, milk, and butterfat—the designated nonbasic commodities—and for wool and mohair. On all other commodities price support is discretionary with the Secretary. In 1957 such discretionary support programs were in effect for barley, sorghum grain, oats, rye, cottonseed, flaxseed, soybeans, dry edible beans, and gum naval stores.

2. *Section 32 programs.*—Under authority of section 32 of the act of August 24, 1935, an amount equal to 30 percent of the customs receipts is made available to the Secretary of Agriculture. These funds are used principally to assist in the marketing of perishable agricultural commodities through (*a*) payments to encourage exports; (*b*) purchase of the surplus and its donation to nonprofit schools, charitable institutions, and public or private welfare agencies to assist needy persons; or (*c*) payments to encourage domestic consumption of commodities by diverting them to new or different uses. Such assistance is, of course, limited by the availability of outlets for the surplus. In the past, there have been purchases for distribution to nonprofit schools, charitable institutions, and public or private welfare agencies, and subsidy payments. These programs have given valuable price assistance to some commodities. In many cases it is the only type of price assistance which is feasible for these commodities.

Surplus commodities acquired in fiscal year 1957 included rice, dry edible beans, shelled eggs, cabbage, plums, lard, pork and pork products, beef, turkeys, butter, cheese, nonfat dry milk, wheat flour, and cornmeal. Export payments were made on fresh and processed citrus fruit and frozen poultry meat. The only diversion-payment programs that year were for dates, figs, and Irish potatoes.

3. *Marketing agreement and order programs.*—Under the Agricultural Marketing Agreement Act of 1937, as amended, the Department seeks to establish and maintain such orderly marketing conditions for certain relatively perishable commodities as will establish adequate producer prices. In 1957 programs under this act were in effect for milk, certain fruits, vegetables, and tree nuts; and anti-hog-cholera serum and hog-cholera virus. Milk order programs provide for the classification of milk on the basis of use, and for the establishment of minimum prices that must be paid producers for the milk going into various uses. For commodities other than milk, the marketing agreement and order programs seek to achieve the objectives of the act in a variety of ways, such as by regulating the quantity that may be marketed, by regulating the grade and quality, and by establishing reserve pools. These programs do not involve Government loans or purchases under support prices but leave the marketing of the commodities to commercial channels. The extent to which producers attain the price or income goal, therefore, depends upon the effective regulation of the supply in the domestic market in accordance with the demand forthcoming in this market.

*Interference by imports*

Imports may materially interfere with the operation of a USDA program. Imports may become available, or may be expected to become available, at landed costs below the level of a United States support price or in such quantities or under such conditions as to make a program ineffective.

Interference from imports becomes particularly serious if the domestic price-support level is substantially above the world market price even after allowance for the customs duties and transportation. In such cases imports are unduly attracted to the United States from other countries. Unless, in such cases, imports are restricted, the United States agricultural price-support program would either become ineffective, or it would have to be expanded from a domestic program to a worldwide support program. United States agricultural programs are not, however, financially able to, nor should they be expected to, support prices on a worldwide basis. The huge acquisitions resulting from a price floor on an international scale (with no control over world production of the quantities that could be imported) could result in an excessive cost leading to the discontinuance of the price-support programs, or to a further cutback in domestic production, or a reduction in the price-support level, or a combination of these.

Imports can interfere with the achievement of the objectives of marketing agreements and orders even though the effects are not as obvious as under price support. Under a marketing agreement and order program a plan is developed which generally limits the volume to be marketed domestically in order to obtain a certain price objective. Imports tend to be attracted by the higher price. If they turn out to be larger than planned, it becomes more difficult, if not impossible, to achieve the price objective. To compensate for these larger imports, more of the domestic production must be withheld as surplus or else growers obtain lower prices. In any case they will receive smaller total returns.

Similarly, unrestricted imports can undo the effects of section 32 surplus removal operations. If imports increase by the amount of the surplus that the section 32 operation removes, the effects of the section 32 operation thus are nullified.

*Protection of programs*

Section 22 of the Agricultural Adjustment Act is a recognition of the fact that, in such ways as outlined above, imports may render or tend to render ineffective or materially interfere with price support or other programs of the United States Department of Agriculture.

Section 22 provides for the imposition of import quotas or import fees on any article or articles whenever the President determines that such articles are being or are practically certain to be imported in such quantities and under such conditions as to render or tend to render ineffective or materially interfere with any price support or other program operated by the Department of Agriculture. Restrictions on imports currently applied under the provisions of this act are described in attachment B.

The legal relationship between section 22 and trade agreements is discussed in your subcommittee's recent report. As pointed out in that discussion, Congress has specifically provided that no international agreement shall be applied in a manner not consistent with the terms of section 22. The contracting parties to the GATT have granted a waiver to the United States so that the import restrictions, whether quotas or additional fees, required by section 22 are not considered as being in violation of GATT.

Although section 22 has been in effect since 1935 it has been necessary to apply restrictions thereunder in relatively few cases. Attachment B reveals that currently there are only six commodities or groups of commodities subject to section 22 controls. For many commodities these quotas have not significantly reduced the imports below the amounts that had been imported before the quotas were put into effect. These quotas are always related to imports in a historical period. Further, under the provisions of section 22 import restrictions are to be modified or withdrawn whenever changed circumstances permit.

In conclusion, section 22 has been effectively implemented to prevent imports from materially interfering with agricultural programs designed to support farm income. At the same time every effort has been made to implement them in a way that minimizes interference with the trade-agreements program to expand international trade.

Further, United States agricultural programs have not prevented reciprocal tariff concessions under the trade-agreements program to facilitate trade. In this connection, it might be noted that tariffs on dutiable agricultural imports are now substantially lower than they were in the prewar period as the result of price changes and of reductions under the reciprocal trade-agreements program.

United States agriculture has achieved significant benefits under our reciprocal trade-agreements program. As the result of the reduction of tariffs and other trade barriers abroad restrictions which would have otherwise affected the sale of American farm products have been reduced or eliminated. Also, reductions in United States tariffs have enabled foreign countries to increase their dollar earnings and thereby have bolstered the market for United States farm products. In calendar year 1956, about 80 percent of our agricultural exports went to countries with which we had trade agreements, and about 60 percent of that trade was in products on which the United States had received tariff concessions.

We trust that the foregoing information and the views expressed herein will assist the subcommittee in its study. We will be glad to cooperate further in this work.

Sincerely yours,

DON PAARLBERG,
*Assistant Secretary.*

[Attachment A]

## ANALYSIS OF REGULATION OF SUGAR IMPORTS BY QUOTA

### LEGISLATION

The importation of foreign produced and the marketing of domestically produced sugar is regulated under the Sugar Act of 1948, as amended in 1956. The preamble of the act states that its purpose is "to regulate commerce among the several States, with the Territories and possessions of the United States, and with foreign countries; to protect the welfare of consumers of sugar and of those engaged in the domestic sugar-producing industry; to promote the export trade of the United States; and for other purposes." Stated more directly the act is designed to maintain a healthy domestic sugar industry of limited size, related to the level of domestic consumption; to assure adequate sugar supplies to consumers at reasonable prices; and to promote our general export trade. This program is designed to fit the conditions applying to sugar, a commodity of which the United States is a large importer.

The act prescribes seven principal mechanisms for accomplishing its objectives: (1) The determination each year of the quantity of sugar needed to supply the Nation's requirements at prices reasonable to consumers and fair to producers; (2) the division of the United States sugar market among the domestic and foreign supplying areas by the use of quotas; (3) the allotment of domestic quotas among the various processors in each area; (4) the adjustment of production in each domestic area to the established quotas; (5) a tax on all direct-consumption (refined) sugar manufactured in the United States or imported from abroad; (6) benefit payments to domestic growers who comply with stated conditions; and (7) the equitable division of sugar returns among processors, growers, and farmworkers.

### CONDITIONS PRECEDING SPECIAL SUGAR LEGISLATION

*Tariff for revenue*

In 1789 the United States as a new nation, seeking means of supporting its Government, imposed the first tariff on raw sugar,[1] to help raise revenue. At that time and through most of the next century, import duties and domestic excise taxes were the major source of Government receipts. The sugar "tariff for revenue" yielded close to 20 percent of all import duties. This duty remained on sugar continuously until 1890, holding at about 2½ cents a pound during most of the period but ranging from 1 to 3½ cents a pound.

Although the purpose of the first sugar tariff was to produce money for the Treasury, it also provided considerable market protection to sugarcane growers in Louisiana after that area became a United States Territory in 1803. The Louisiana industry had reached significant size by 1830. Then later, the same protection was granted to Hawaii under the terms of the reciprocal treaty of 1876 between the United States and what was then the Kingdom of Hawaii. Under the agreement Hawaiian sugar was admitted duty free. With this market advantage, and a climate ideally suited to growing sugarcane, Hawaii rapidly expanded sugar production. By the 1890's, the production of sugar had become Hawaii's most important industry—dependent principally on market outlets in this country for its prosperity.

*The sugar bounty, 1890–94*

In 1890, with a surplus in the Treasury, the need to maintain a sugar tariff to produce a revenue was no longer pressing and the duty, then 2¼ cents a pound, was repealed. The placing of sugar on the free list reduced its cost to consumers, but removed tariff protection to domestic producers. Protection, however, was continued in the form of a 2-cent bounty on each pound of sugar domestically produced.

The removal of the tariff and the inauguration of the bounty had an important effect in two producing areas—Hawaii and Cuba. Production in Cuba was stimulated when the removal of the tariff further opened the United States market. On the other hand, Hawaii was hurt badly when it lost its preferred position in the American market as a result of the discontinuance of the sugar duty. (By treaty since

[1] The tariff discussions in this paper will be confined to the tariff on raw sugar only since most of the sugar imported is in raw form. Historically refined sugar tariffs have been higher than raw sugar tariffs.

1876, Hawaiian producers had enjoyed tariff protection along with domestic producers.) The price of Hawaiian sugar fell sharply. General unrest followed, leading to revolt against the monarchy of Queen Liliuokalani and the establishment of the Republic of Hawaii in 1894.

*Tariff for protection, 1894 to 1934*

In 1894, the bounty system was discontinued and a new tariff levied on sugar. However, the primary purpose of the new tariff was not to produce revenue, as was formerly the case, but to protect the domestic industry, which had reached significant size under the first tariff and the bounty. An additional motive was to return Hawaii to its preferred status in our market.

The second sugar-tariff program remained in force from 1894 to 1934. The history of the sugar industry during that period is a sequence of stable earnings, wild prosperity, severe but short-lived depression, temporary recovery, and prolonged depression, in that order.

As a result of the Spanish-American War, three potentially heavy sugar-producing areas were added to the areas receiving protection in our market. Free trade was extended to our new possessions, Puerto Rico and the Philippine Islands, and a preferred status was granted to Cuba. Puerto Rico received free-trade status in 1901. Tariff aid was given more gradually to the Philippines, but by 1913 Philippine sugar was granted unlimited free entry. Cuba was granted a 20-percent tariff preferential under the convention of commercial reciprocity of 1902.

Production expanded rapidly in these areas with the granting of protection. Cuba and Puerto Rico, like Hawaii, became specialized one-crop areas directly dependent upon the continuation of our protective policy for the livelihood of their people. Sugar also became a mainstay of the Philippine economy.

Our beet industry, which got its start under the "tariff for revenue" and the bounty system, also flourished with tariff protection. By the time of World War I, the beet area was supplying almost one-fifth of the sugar market in this country.

At the turn of the century, slightly more than half of our sugar came from foreign countries other than Cuba. But by 1913 the increase in sugar supplies in the continental United States, in our Territories, and in Cuba pushed practically all other foreign sugar from our market.

In World War I, the Government placed rigid controls on sugar distribution and on prices of refined sugar. In addition, a price guaranty was placed on Cuban sugar and domestic sugar beets to encourage production. The beet areas did not respond to wartime price incentives except to maintain production, but Cuba, where sugar offered the principal means of participating in wartime expansion, greatly increased its production. The high prices immediately after the war, however, did cause the beet area to expand its output.

After World War I, with the lifting of controls and the prospect of short supplies, sugar became one of the speculative leaders in the worldwide inflationary boom of 1920. The world price of raw sugar reached a monthly average peak of more than 19 cents a pound in

May 1920. The bubble soon burst, and the price of world sugar dropped to an average of less than 5 cents a pound in December 1920. The depression in world sugar lasted through most of 1922. Toward the end of the year, however, sugar prices began to advance and by 1923 reached a second, but much lower, postwar peak of slightly more than 6.5 cents a pound and ranged between 5 and 6 cents a pound for more than a year.

Many believed that the sugar industry, both in this country and generally throughout the world, had recovered its prewar order and prosperity. Americans, especially, showed their confidence in the future of sugar by pouring large sums of money into Cuban sugar production.

But the international sugar industry was in for a rude shock. World sugar production began outstripping world demand in 1925. Surpluses accumulated and prices dropped below 1922 levels. The trend in world production continued upward, even in the face of mounting surpluses and unprofitable prices. This was partly because of artificial stimulation of beet-sugar production in countries which had historically imported sugar but which desired to become self-sufficient. In addition, there were tremendous improvements in methods of cultivating and processing sugarcane during the 1920's and early 1930's. Except for a slight upturn in 1927, world sugar prices did not improve between 1925 and 1928. In 1929, prices began to decline once more. The situation worsened each year from 1929 to the bottom of the general depression.

The depression in world sugar, in both the early and late 1920's, was felt by domestic producers as well as by producers in the large exporting countries, as United States prices generally moved with world prices. In 1921, the United States price was lower than at any time since 1916, and Congress raised the sugar tariffs. The duty on sugar from Cuba, our principal foreign competitor, was increased in 1921 from 1 to 1.60 cents a pound, and in 1922 to 1.7648 cents a pound. The duty on other foreign sugar was also increased each time, so that the Cuban tariff preferential was maintained.

As the world price was firm, these increased duties solved the immediate price problems of domestic producers. In fact, when the world price strengthened in 1923 and 1924, consumers complained that the tariffs were forcing the United States price too high.

When the world depression in sugar became serious in the late 1920's, Congress was asked for still higher tariffs to offset world price reductions. As a result, in 1930 the duty on Cuban sugar was raised to 2 cents a pound and the duty on other foreign sugar was raised to 2.5 cents. However, the bottom was falling out of the world sugar market. By May 1932 the world price of raw sugar dropped to less than 1 cent a pound. The United States price followed the world price downward, reaching the depression low of less than 3 cents a pound in 1932—the 2-cent duty on Cuban sugar plus the world price and the cost of freight from Cuba.

Although the domestic sugar price was quite low compared with prices in previous years, the duty did hold the price at an irreducible minimum—a guaranty that other agricultural industries did not have. The duty-paid price actually permitted production to increase in Puerto Rico, the Philippine Islands, and the beet area.

The increase in production in the beet area was not due to the fact that returns from sugar were high at the going price but, primarily, to the fact that competing crops promised even lower returns at that time. Technological progress and the efforts to offset income loss resulting from low prices by increased output caused production to climb in the islands.

*Developing the present program*

It was generally agreed that domestic producers needed higher prices if they were to realize fair returns. On the surface, at least, the tariff promised to give sufficient protection to our sugar producers if it were raised high enough. But, in the severe depression years of 1932 and 1933, it become clear from two important standpoints that further increases in the tariff would not be a good solution to the sugar problem.

First, the stimulus of high tariff protection was already causing overproduction in certain domestic areas, thus offsetting the price benefits of the protection. It was apparent that if the tariff were raised enough to afford adequate returns to the highest cost producers low cost production would have been excessively stimulated and our market further crowded.

Second, there was ample evidence that our 2-cent tariff on Cuban sugar was causing severe suffering of the Cuban people and that its continuation or increase would bring further hardship. Cuba's depression became extreme after 1929 when the downturn in world sugar prices grew sharper and the protective tariffs in the various importing countries, including the traditional buyer, the United States, were increased to help maintain returns to domestic producers. These high tariffs not only forced the Cuban price down to less than 1 cent a pound but also encouraged production in importing countries, thereby further reducing demand for Cuban sugar. As a consequence, Cuba was compelled to cut production substantially. The one crop on which Cuba's livelihood primarily depended was almost unsalable. Reduced production plus a record low price spelled economic distress and political unrest.

During the early months of 1933, the United States Tariff Commission made a careful appraisal of the prevailing sugar situation and recommended a program emphasizing supply controls rather than the traditional tariff method of assistance. In a letter to the President of the United States, dated April 11, 1933, the Chairman of the Commission outlined the failure of the tariff to solve the sugar problem. His letter pointed out that the price had declined to disaster levels for both American and Cuban producers; that both the domestic industry and that of Cuba required price relief; that prices should be raised by limiting, through a quota system, the supply of sugar offered for sale in this country; and that if some type of quota system were instituted by this country, the duty on Cuban sugar might be reduced to help restore the purchasing power of Cuba.

The first attempt to develop a new sugar program was made in 1933 by representatives of the sugar industry under the authority of the Agricultural Adjustment Act. This attempt resulted in a plan which was submitted to the Secretary of Agriculture for approval.

Although the proposed plan was rejected, the Government used it as a starting point and drafted a new set of proposals. These proposals were recommended by the President to Congress for legislative action in early 1934. On May 9, of that year, Congress enacted the Jones-Costigan Act which included most of the President's recommendations. Succeeding sugar legislation has carried forward the basic philosophy underlying the Jones-Costigan Act.

## HOW THE PROGRAM WORKS

Since original enactment, sugar legislation has been reenacted, amended or extended a number of times. The Sugar Act of 1948 was last amended in 1956 and its life extends through 1960. The seven principal mechanisms for accomplishing the objectives of the legislation mentioned earlier have been retained. A brief description of these features follows.

### *Determining the sugar needs of consumers*

Every December, the Secretary of Agriculture determines how much sugar will be needed in the continental United States during the following calendar year. The initial determination has been revised during the course of every post-war year. Typically, the revisions have provided for the marketing of additional quantities of sugar, as the need became evident; but in a few instances a reduction in sugar requirements has been determined. The Secretary's actions are guided by statutory criteria. Separate requirements determinations for Hawaii and Puerto Rico are also issued.

### *Establishing quotas to domestic and foreign producing areas*

Each area is assigned a quota representing its share of the requirements determination. Domestic areas have minimum quotas totaling 4,444,000 tons at any level of requirements and in addition receive 55 percent of all increases in requirements above 8,350,000 tons. The first increments in the share of the domestic areas are distributed among them on the priority basis specified in the Sugar Act. The following table shows the approximate percentage division of changes in total quota requirements when consumption requirements exceed 8,691,818 short tons, raw value. That is the level at which the priority increases in domestic quotas would be filled and 55 percent of the increases above that quantity are prorated to domestic areas on the basis of their quotas at that point. Changes in quotas of foreign countries other than the Republic of the Philippines would be on the percentage basis shown when requirements exceed 8,350,000 tons. Changes for Nicaragua, Haiti, Netherlands, China (Formosa), Panama, and Costa Rica may vary slightly from the percentages shown since 1.03 percent of the total change is prorated to these countries on the basis of their 1951–54 average entries.

| | Short tons, raw value | | Percentage changes in quotas in excess of basic levels |
|---|---|---|---|
| | Quotas when total quotas are 8,350,000 | Quotas of domestic areas when total quotas are 8,691,818 | |
| | (1) | (2) | (3) |
| Domestic areas: | | | |
| Domestic beet sugar | 1,800,000 | 1,884,975 | 22.382 |
| Mainland cane sugar | 500,000 | 580,025 | 6.887 |
| Hawaii | 1,052,000 | 1,052,000 | 12.492 |
| Puerto Rico | 1,080,000 | 1,100,000 | 13.061 |
| Virgin Islands | 12,000 | 15,000 | .178 |
| Total domestic | 4,444,000 | 4,632,000 | 55.000 |
| Foreign areas: | | | |
| Philippines | 980,000 | | 0 |
| Cuba | 2,808,960 | | 29,590 |
| Full-duty countries | 117,040 | | 15.410 |
| Peru | 50,062 | | 4.330 |
| Dominican Republic | 29,482 | | 4.950 |
| Mexico | 11,259 | | 5.100 |
| Nicaragua | 8,001 | | .574 |
| Haiti | 4,820 | | .209 |
| Netherlands | 3,000 | | .070 |
| China (Formosa) | 3,000 | | .059 |
| Panama | 3,000 | | .059 |
| Costa Rica | 3,000 | | .059 |
| Canada | 631 | | 0 |
| United Kingdom | 516 | | 0 |
| Belgium | 182 | | 0 |
| British Guiana | 84 | | 0 |
| Hong Kong | 3 | | 0 |
| Total foreign | 3,906,000 | | 45.000 |
| Grand total | 8,350,000 | | 100.000 |

When an area is not expected to fill its quota, a deficit is declared and reallotted to other areas by statutory procedures. In spite of a deficit declaration, an area may market its full quota or any part thereof.

Only a portion of the important offshore foreign and domestic quotas may be entered in the form of direct-consumption sugar (generally refined sugar). This amounts to roughly one-tenth of the total of such quotas. In addition to crystalline sugar quotas, Cuba may enter about 33,500 tons of sugar in liquid form, the Dominican Republic about 3,500 tons, and the British West Indies about 1,300 tons, each year. These statutory restrictions serve to protect the mainland cane-sugar-refining industry.

*Establishing marketing allotments*

To assure the orderly marketing and equitable sharing among marketers of each area quota, the Secretary of Agriculture is authorized to allot quotas among marketers or importers. Allotment orders currently are in effect for the marketing of the beet-sugar and mainland cane-sugar quotas. Statutory criteria are applied in the establishment of these allotments. In most years the Puerto Rican quota also is allotted. Hawaiian sugar is marketed by a Capper-Volstead cooperative. Virgin Islands sugar is marketed by a Government corporation. Consequently, no marketing allotment orders have been necessary in these two offshore areas. The Department has never undertaken to allot quotas for imports from foreign countries.

*Production adjustment*

The act also authorizes the Secretary to divide the market among individual farms in the domestic areas. Each area is permitted to produce a sufficient amount of sugar to fill its prospective quota and to have a normal carryover. That amount is divided among farms. The proportionate share of each farm may be expressed in acres, tons of sugar beets or sugarcane, or in tons of sugar. Proportionate shares are assigned on the basis of past production and of ability to produce. A special clause in the law provides for the protection of the interests of new producers and of small producers. Sugar used for livestock feed may be exempt from quotas and may be processed from beets or cane grown in excess of proportionate shares.

### BENEFIT PAYMENTS AND EQUITABLE DIVISION OF RETURNS

Growers who meet conditions specified in the act receive Government payments. The base rate of payment is 80 cents per 100 pounds of commercially recoverable sugar. This rate is scaled down for farms which produce in excess of 350 tons of sugar and declines to a minimum of 30 cents per 100 pounds on that portion of the farm's total production in excess of 30,000 tons. To be eligible for these payments a grower must not exceed the proportionate share for his farm; must refrain from employing child labor; must pay fair wages to agricultural labor; and, if he is also a processor who buys beets or cane from other growers, he must pay a fair price to other growers for beets or cane. Fair wages and prices are determined by the Secretary. Fair wage and price determinations assure the equitable division of returns among the processors, growers, and farmworkers.

### THE EXCISE TAX

The manufacture of sugar is taxed at the rate of 50 cents per hundredweight of sugar, raw value. A compensatory import tax is levied on the importation of direct-consumption sugar. Since the tax is levied on foreign as well as domestic sugar but benefit payments accrue only to domestic producers, an annual net revenue of almost $20 million to the Treasury tends to result, even though the average payment rate is about 69 cents per hundredweight sugar, raw value.

### SOME ACCOMPLISHMENTS OF THE SUGAR ACT

The Jones-Costigan Sugar Act of 1934 and the Sugar Act of 1937 constituted the major means by which our domestic-sugar industry and the sugar industry of Cuba were brought from severe economic depression to full recovery. Similarly, other sugar-supplying countries have benefited. During the war the payment provisions under the Sugar Act helped to maintain domestic production in the face of rising costs and controlled sugar prices. Since the war, the Sugar Act of 1948 has largely stabilized domestic sugar prices despite extreme variation in world prices (fig. 1). Limitation of domestic as well as foreign sugar marketings in the United States to the level of the Secretary's requirements determination has tended to stabilize the domestic market and to establish the price of raw sugar at a level which is usually but not always in excess of the comparable world-market price. The average monthly value of raw sugar in Cuba destined to the United States has varied between 4.25 and 5.72 cents per pound since 1948, a range of only 1.34 cents, while the corresponding price of sugar destined to the world market has fluctuated between 3.10 and 7.41 cents, a range of 4.31 cents per pound. The price equivalent of sugar destined to the United States averaged 1.03 cents above the price of sugar destined for the world market from 1948 to 1956. However, during the Korean crisis in 1950 and 1951 and in 1957 with international tension and world shortage, the world price has been the higher. For the 4 years 1953 through 1956, the quota premium averaged 1.84 cents per pound (fig. 1).

With the quota system as the major price-protection mechanism for the domestic sugar industry, it has been possible to reduce the tariff on Cuban sugar from 2 cents per pound, the Smoot-Hawley Tariff Act rate which was in effect at the time the Jones-Costigan Act was enacted, to the present level of 0.50 cent which has been effective since 1948. Similarly, the full duty rate was reduced from 2.50 cents per pound to 0.625 cent per pound.

One of the major achievements of our sugar legislation is the assistance given to our export trade through strengthening the purchasing power of Cuba, the Philippines, and our other foreign sugar suppliers. In 1933, Cuban producers received 1.1 cents per pound of raw sugar, free alongside ship, for shipments to the United States; in 1956, they received 5.1 cents per pound.

In amending the Sugar Act, the Congress in 1951 and again in 1956, increased the quotas for full-duty countries with history of supplying this country. These increases as well as the restored increases made for domestic areas came from increases in the growth of the United States market, practically all of which (98.64 percent) had accrued to Cuba under the original Sugar Act of 1948. The full-duty countries as a whole had a quota of only 1.36 percent of our sugar requirements in excess of fixed domestic and Philippine quotas under the original 1948 act. That quota was raised to 4 percent in 1951, approximately three times the former level.

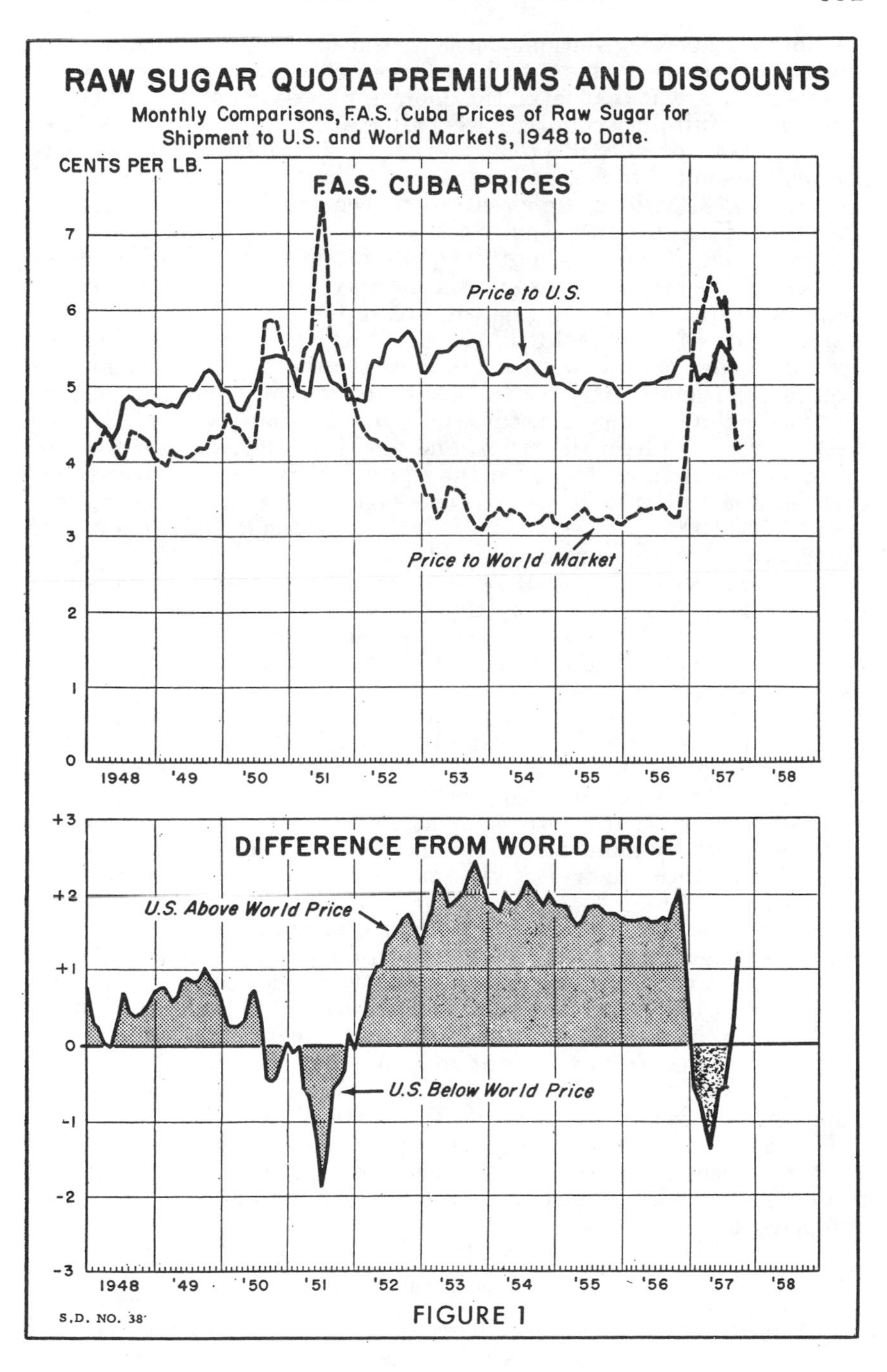
RAW SUGAR QUOTA PREMIUMS AND DISCOUNTS
Monthly Comparisons, F.A.S. Cuba Prices of Raw Sugar for Shipment to U.S. and World Markets, 1948 to Date.
CENTS PER LB.
F.A.S. CUBA PRICES
Price to U.S.
Price to World Market
7
6
5
4
3
2
1
0
1948
'49
'50
'51
'52
'53
'54
'55
'56
'57
'58
DIFFERENCE FROM WORLD PRICE
U.S. Above World Price
U.S. Below World Price
+3
+2
+1
0
-1
-2
-3
S.D. NO. 38

FIGURE 1

Under the 1956 legislation, the 4-percent quota was left intact for total sugar requirements up to 8,350,000 short tons, raw value. When requirements are at that level, the quota for those countries is 117,040 tons. These full-duty countries were allotted 15.41 percent of requirements in excess of 8,350,000 tons. As of the end of July, requirements for 1957 amounted to 9,300,000 tons; accordingly, those countries had a quota of 263,435 tons, which is 7.66 percent of the combined quotas of Cuba and the full-duty countries.

Throughout the operation of the quota program, requirements have been established so that consumers are always assured of ample sugar supplies. (Quotas were suspended during the World War II sugar-scarcity period from April 1942 to 1947.) At least 98 pounds of sugar, raw value, per capita, were made available each year through the requirements determination. In most years, well over 100 pounds were provided. But consumers' needs required particular attention in 1950, 1951 (during the Korean crisis), and again in 1957, when the world market price of sugar exceeded the equivalent value of Cuban sugar destined for the United States. The sugar-requirements determination of 9,300,000 tons, issued on July 5, 1957, made 108.6 pounds of sugar, raw value, per capita, available.

From 1933 through mid-1957, the general price level as measured by the Wholesale Price Index (Bureau of Labor Statistics) has risen 125 percent while the wholesale price of refined sugar at New York has risen 100 percent. The average retail price throughout the country has likewise doubled.

The sugar program which imposes area quotas, marketing allotments to processors and individual farm allotments (proportionate shares) might be expected to slow down economic adjustments. The fact appears to be, however, that it has facilitated long-term planning and reduced the hazard to investment. It is a further fact that enormous productivity gains have been made in the domestic-sugar industry. For instance, sugar-beet yield per harvested acre increased from 11.4 tons in 1931–33 to 16.4 tons in 1954–56, a 44-percent increase. Labor requirements for producing sugar crops in terms of man-hours per ton of sugar have been almost halved during the last 10 years.

The raw cane-sugar processing margin in all domestic areas increased from 1.54 cents per pound in 1937–39 to 2.61 cents in 1953–55, a 70-percent increase and during the same period the net refining margin increased from 0.85 cent to 1.46 cents, a 72 percent increase compared with the 111-percent increase which occurred during the same period in general price level (Wholesale Price Index).

Returns to growers per unit of sugar in the domestic areas increased by 104 percent from 1937–39 to 1953–55. During the same period minimum wages of workers in cane and beet fields increased about 226 percent.

---

[Attachment B]

## Import Controls Under Section 22 of the Agricultural Adjustment Act, as Amended

### AUTHORITY

Section 22 of the Agricultural Adjustment Act, as amended, authorizes the President to impose additional fees or quotas on the importation of commodities when he finds such importation tends to render ineffective or materially interfere with any price support or other program relating to agricultural commodities undertaken by the Department of Agriculture. The additional fees may not exceed 50 percent ad valorem, and the quotas proclaimed may not be less than 50 percent of the quantity imported during a previous representative period, as determined by the President.

It is specifically provided that no trade agreement or other international agreement entered into at any time by the United States may be applied in a manner inconsistent with the requirements of section 22.

Actions under section 22 are initiated in the Department of Agriculture. The Secretary of Agriculture, on his own initiative, or upon application of any interested person, conducts a preliminary investigation. If, on the basis of such investigation, he has reason to believe that any products are being or are practically certain to be imported in such quantities and under such conditions as to materially interfere with a program of the Department, the Secretary so advises the President. If the President agrees there is reason for such belief, he directs the Tariff Commission to conduct an investigation. Upon such direction, the Tariff Commission is required to make an immediate investigation, including a public hearing, and to make a report and recommendation to the President. The views of the Department of Agriculture are presented at the public hearing. Any decisions of the President as to the facts under section 22 are final.

Special procedures are provided for use in emergency conditions due to the perishability of any agricultural commodity. Upon report to the President and the Tariff Commission by the Secretary of Agriculture that due to the perishability of the commodity a condition exists requiring emergency treatment, the Tariff Commission must make an immediate investigation and submit appropriate recommendations to the President. The Commission's report and the President's decision must be made not more than 25 calendar days after the case is submitted to the Tariff Commission. The President may, however, take action without awaiting the report of the Commission.

Provision is also made for the President to take immediate action without awaiting the recommendations of the Tariff Commission whenever the Secretary determines and reports to him with regard to any article or articles that a condition exists requiring emergency treatment. Any such action by the President continues in effect pending the report and recommendations of the Tariff Commission and action thereon by the President.

## ACTION TAKEN

Import controls under section 22 are in effect for six commodities or groups of commodities at the present time: cotton, wheat, and wheat products, certain dairy products, flaxseed and linseed oil, peanuts and peanut oil, and rye. Two of these actions, on cotton and on wheat and wheat products, have been in effect for many years. The other four are relatively recent. Import controls on oats, barley, and certain edible tree nuts have recently been in effect, but were not continued beyond September 30, 1955. Except for rye these controls are of a continuing nature. This means they continue automatically from year to year until modified or terminated by the President because of changed circumstances. Controls on rye are on a 2-year basis and expire June 30, 1959, unless renewed in some form by the President following an investigation by the Tariff Commission. Imports of wheat, flaxseed, and rye certified or registered and approved for planting purposes, pursuant to the Federal Seed Act, are not subject to quota. However, imports for such purposes in quantities of over 100 bushels require permits from the Department of Agriculture. Imports of wheat and wheat flour for experimental purposes are not subject to quota; however, imports in quantities of more than 10 pounds require a permit from the Department of Agriculture. Wheat and wheat flour which are classified as unfit for human consumption are not subject to the import quota. The commodities now under control and the dates on which the original controls were imposed are discussed below.

*1. Cotton*

Controls have been in effect on long-staple and short-staple cotton and on cotton waste since September 20, 1939, and on harsh or rough cotton since September 20, 1946. In recent years, supplemental quotas were issued for certain types of long-staple cotton. The current quotas are the same as those imposed initially. In 2 cases they are total global quotas and in the other 2 cases individual country quotas are provided. Annual quotas are currently in effect, as follows:

(*a*) Global quotas:

| Article | Quota | Quota period |
|---|---|---|
| | *Pounds* | |
| Long-staple cotton (1⅛ inches or longer) | 45, 656, 420 | Aug. 1–July 31. |
| Harsh or rough cotton (under ¾ inch) | 70, 000, 000 | Sept. 20–Sept. 19. |

(*b*) Country quotas:

| Article | Quota (total for all countries) | Quota period |
|---|---|---|
| | *Pounds* | |
| Short-staple cotton | 14, 516, 882 | Sept. 20–Sept. 19. |
| Cotton waste (card strips made from cotton under 1³⁄₁₆ inches, comber waste, lap waste, sliver waste, roving waste). | [1] 5, 482, 509 | Do. |

[1] However, not more than 33⅓ percent shall be filled by cotton wastes other than comber waste made from cottons of 1³⁄₁₆ inches or more in staple length in the case of certain countries.

(*c*) The quotas compare with average imports during the statutory representative period as follows:

| Article | Representative period | Average imports during representative periods | Present quota |
|---|---|---|---|
| | | *Pounds* | *Pounds* |
| Long-staple cotton (1⅛ inches or longer) | July 1, 1928–June 30, 1933 | 68, 085, 885 | 45, 656, 420 |
| Harsh or rough cotton (under ¾ inch) | Jan. 1, 1929–Dec. 31, 1933 | 33, 390, 000 | 70, 000, 000 |
| Cotton waste | July 1, 1928–June 30, 1933 | [1] | 5, 482, 509 |
| Short-staple cotton | do | 15, 504, 403 | 14, 516, 882 |

[1] Not available. The annual average imports of 23,173,884 pounds during the representative period includes receipts of nonquota wastes.

(*d*) Imports for the periods indicated compare with the quotas as follows:

| | Period | Quotas | Imports |
|---|---|---|---|
| COTTON | | | |
| | | *Pounds* | *Pounds* |
| Staple less than 1⅛ inches | 1953-54 | 14,516,882 | 7,833,000 |
| | 1954-55 | 14,516,882 | 10,516,882 |
| | 1955-56 | 14,516,882 | 10,208,000 |
| Imports through Aug. 12, 1957 | 1956-57 | 14,516,882 | 9,607,319 |
| Staple of 1⅛ inches or more | 1953-54 | 45,656,420 | 45,656,000 |
| | 1954-55 | 45,656,420 | 45,656,000 |
| | 1955-56 | 45,656,420 | 45,656,000 |
| Extra quota, Feb. 1 to July 31, 1956 | 1956 | 22,828,210 | 15,850,000 |
| | 1956-57 | 45,656,420 | 45,656,000 |
| Cotton waste | 1953-54 | 5,482,509 | 1,252,000 |
| | 1954-55 | 5,482,509 | 1,482,509 |
| | 1955-56 | 5,482,509 | 1,342,270 |
| Imports through Aug. 12, 1957 | 1956-57 | 5,482,509 | 427,654 |
| Harsh staple of less than ¾ inches | 1953-54 | 70,000,000 | 12,429,000 |
| | 1954-55 | 70,000,000 | 13,439,000 |
| | 1955-56 | 70,000,000 | 12,554,000 |
| Imports through Aug. 3, 1957 | 1956-57 | 70,000,000 | 9,330,476 |

*2. Wheat and wheat products*

Quotas were instituted on May 29, 1941. Wheat and wheat flour classed as "unfit for human consumption," wheat for experimental purposes, and certified or registered seed wheat approved for planting pursuant to the Federal Seed Act, are not subject to the quota. Since this adoption in 1941 the basic quotas have not been changed, although certain exemptions were granted during World War II.

Separate quotas by country are currently in effect totaling:

| Article | Quota | Quota period |
|---|---|---|
| Wheat ... bushels | 800,000 | May 29-May 28. |
| Wheat products ... pounds | 4,000,000 | Do. |

These quotas compare with the average imports during the statutory "representative period," January 1, 1929 to December 31, 1933, as follows:

| | Quota | Average imports |
|---|---|---|
| Wheat ... bushels | 800,000 | 25,923 |
| Wheat products ... pounds | 4,000,000 | 237,137 |

Imports for the periods indicated compare with the quotas as follows:

| | Period | Quota | Imports |
|---|---|---|---|
| | | *Bushels* | *Bushels* |
| Wheat | 1953-54 | 800,000 | 795,080 |
| | 1954-55 | 800,000 | 795,000 |
| | 1955-56 | 800,000 | 795,000 |
| | 1956-57 | 800,000 | 795,000 |
| | | *Pounds* | *Pounds* |
| Wheat flour | 1953-54 | 4,000,000 | 3,815,240 |
| | 1954-55 | 4,000,000 | 3,822,000 |
| | 1955-56 | 4,000,000 | 3,818,650 |
| | 1956-57 | 4,000,000 | 3,815,000 |

*3. Certain dairy products*

Controls under section 22 became initially effective July 1, 1953. Total annual quotas are established for the period July 1 through June 30 for all the dairy products as listed below. The Department of Agriculture issues import licenses to individual importers, apportioning these quotas generally on the basis of the proportionate share of total imports imported by each individual importer during a representative base period when no restrictions were in effect. Such licenses are issued, to the fullest extent practicable, so as to assure supplying countries of equitable shares of the quotas.

Current total quotas are the same as those initially imposed. They are all for the annual period July 1 to June 30.

| | Annual quota, pounds |
|---|---|
| (a) Butter | 707,000 |
| (b) Dried whole milk | 7,000 |
| (c) Dried buttermilk | 496,000 |
| (d) Dried cream | 500 |
| (e) Dried skimmed milk | 1,807,000 |
| (f) Malted milk, and compounds or mixtures of or substitutes for milk or cream | 6,000 |
| (g) Cheddar cheese and cheese and substitutes containing or processed from Cheddar | 2,780,100 |
| (h) Edam and Gouda cheese | 4,600,200 |
| (j) Italian type cheese, made from cow's milk, in original loaves (Romano made from cow's milk, Reggiano, Parmesano, Provolone, Provolette, and Sbrinz) | 9,200,100 |

Effective April 15, 1957, a quota was instituted on butter substitutes, including butter oil, containing 45 percent or more of butterfat, at 1,800,000 pounds for calendar year 1957. For subsequent calendar-year periods, the quota is 1,200,000 pounds. On August 7, 1957, an embargo was placed on imports of all articles containing more than 45 percent or more of butterfat, except those articles already subject to quotas, cheeses, evaporated and condensed milk, and products imported in retail packages.

| | Annual quota, pounds |
|---|---|
| (a) Butter substitutes, including butter oil, containing 45 percent or more butterfat | 1,200,000 |
| (b) Articles containing 45 percent or more of butterfat, except those articles already subject to quotas, cheeses, evaporated and condensed milk, and products imported in retail packages | 0 |

The comparison of quotas with representative period imports are:

| Commodity | Representative period | Average imports during representative periods | Quota |
|---|---|---|---|
| | | Pounds | Pounds |
| Blue-mold cheese | 1948-50 | 2,066,000 | 4,167,000 |
| Cheddar cheese | 1948-50 | 5,490,262 | 2,780,100 |
| Edam and Gouda cheese | 1948-50 | 1,831,085 | 4,600,200 |
| Italian types of cheeses | 1948-50 | 8,121,987 | 9,200,100 |
| Butter | 1930-34 | 1,411,525 | 707,000 |
| Dried cream | 1948-50 | (1) | 500 |
| Dried whole milk | 1948-50 | 13,055 | 7,000 |
| Dried skimmed milk | 1948-50 | 3,613,279 | 1,807,000 |
| Dried buttermilk | 1948-50 | 991,283 | 496,000 |
| Malted milk | 1948-50 | 11,418 | 6,000 |
| Butter oil | 1956 | 1,800,000 | 1,800,000 |

[1] Less than 500.

Imports during each quota year since controls were instituted compare with the quotas as follows:

| Commodity | Period | Quota | Imports |
|---|---|---|---|
| | | *Pounds* | *Pounds* |
| Blue-mold cheese | 1953-54 | 4,167,000 | 3,464,863 |
| | 1954-55 | 4,167,000 | 3,372,984 |
| | 1955-56 | 4,167,000 | 3,876,503 |
| | 1956-57 | 4,167,000 | 3,832,154 |
| Cheddar cheese | 1953-54 | 2,780,100 | 2,685,964 |
| | 1954-55 | 2,780,100 | 2,440,098 |
| | 1955-56 | 2,780,100 | 2,649,336 |
| | 1956-57 | 2,780,100 | 2,646,565 |
| Edam and Gouda cheese | 1953-54 | 4,000,200 | 4,378,890 |
| | 1954-55 | 4,600,200 | 4,452,945 |
| | 1955-56 | 4,600,200 | 4,377,495 |
| | 1956-57 | 4,600,200 | 4,373,146 |
| Italian types of cheeses | 1953-54 | 9,200,100 | 8,218,537 |
| | 1954-55 | 9,200,100 | 6,952,057 |
| | 1955-56 | 9,200,100 | 7,245,816 |
| | 1956-57 | 9,200,100 | 8,154,284 |
| Butter | 1953-54 | 707,000 | 669,731 |
| | 1954-55 | 707,000 | 622,367 |
| | 1955-56 | 707,000 | 665,772 |
| | 1956-57 | 707,000 | 618,777 |
| Dried cream | 1953-54 | 500 | 0 |
| | 1954-55 | 500 | 0 |
| | 1955-56 | 500 | 0 |
| | 1956-57 | 500 | 0 |
| Dried whole milk | 1953-54 | 7,000 | 4,332 |
| | 1954-55 | 7,000 | 5,300 |
| | 1955-56 | 7,000 | 5,900 |
| | 1956-57 | 7,000 | 5,900 |
| Dried skimmed milk | 1953-54 | 1,807,000 | 447,800 |
| | 1954-55 | 1,807,000 | 1,520,220 |
| | 1955-56 | 1,807,000 | 1,807,000 |
| | 1956-57 | 1,807,000 | 1,578,286 |
| Dried buttermilk | 1953-54 | 496,000 | 489,980 |
| | 1954-55 | 496,000 | 495,306 |
| | 1955-56 | 496,000 | 158,360 |
| | 1956-57 | 496,000 | 108,416 |
| Malted milk | 1953-54 | 6,000 | 5,768 |
| | 1954-55 | 6,000 | 5,992 |
| | 1955-56 | 6,000 | 5,992 |
| | 1956-57 | 6,000 | 530 |
| Butter oil | 1957 | 1,800,000 | 1,800,000 |

### 4. *Flaxseed and linseed oil*

Controls under section 22 were initially effective July 1, 1953. Current limitations are the same as those initially imposed.

| | *Percent ad valorem* |
|---|---|
| (a) Flaxseed (except flaxseed approved for planting pursuant to the Federal Seed Act) | 50 |
| (b) Linseed oil, and combination and mixtures in chief value of such oil | 50 |

Imports since the application of the additional fee have been:

| Period | Flaxseed | Linseed oil |
|---|---|---|
| | *Bushels* | *Pounds* |
| 1953-54 | 22,000 | 0 |
| 1954-55 | (1) | 500 |
| 1955-56 | 1,000 | 0 |
| 1956-57 (11 months) | 722 | (1) |

[1] Less than 500.

*5. Peanuts and peanut oil*

Limitations pursuant to section 22 were initially instituted July 1, 1953. Current controls are the same as those initially imposed.

| | |
|---|---|
| (*a*) Peanuts, whether shelled, not shelled, blanched, salted, prepared or preserved (including roasted peanuts, but not including peanut butter). | 1,709,000 pounds (aggregate during period August 1–July 31, quantity). Peanuts in the shell charged against this quota on basis of 75 pounds for each 100 pounds of in-shell peanuts. |
| (*b*) Peanut oil | Ad valorem fee of 25 percent on imports in excess of 80,000,000 pounds during any one period—July 1–June 30. |

The quota for peanuts is one-half the average quantity, 3,417,812 pounds, imported during the representative period 1936–39.

Imports during the periods indicated were as follows:

| Commodity | Period | Quota | Imports |
|---|---|---|---|
| | | *Pounds* | *Pounds* |
| Peanuts, shelled, unshelled blanched, roasted, prepared, or preserved (including roasted peanuts, but not including peanut butter). | 1953–54 | 1, 709, 000 | 9, 265 |
| | 1954–55 | 1, 709, 000 | 1, 709, 000 |
| | 1955 | [1] 51, 000, 000 | 26, 650, 492 |
| | 1955–56 | 1, 709, 000 | 1, 709, 000 |
| | 1956–57 [2] | 1, 709, 000 | 1, 709, 000 |
| Peanut oil | 1953–54 | 80. 000, 000 | 1, 529, 820 |
| | 1954–55 | 80, 000, 000 | 26, 037, 536 |
| | 1955–56 | 80, 000, 000 | 11, 100, 727 |
| | 1965–57 | 80, 000, 000 | 0 |

[1] Extra quota of shelled, blanched, salted, prepared, or preserved peanuts, in sizes averaging not more than 40 kernels per ounce, at a fee of 2 cents per pound but not more than 50 percent ad valorem.

[2] An unlimited quantity of Virginia type, or sizes not more than 40 kernels to the ounce, was permitted import during the period Aug. 30–Sept. 10, 1956, at a fee of 7 cents per pound, but not more than 50 percent ad valorem. Imports were reported at 2,200,000 pounds during the prescribed period.

*6. Rye, rye flour, and meal*

Controls became initially effective March 31, 1954, on imports of rye, rye flour, and rye meal. Certified or registered seed approved for planting pursuant to the Federal Seed Act is not subject to the quota. Current limitations are the same as those initially imposed and expire on June 30, 1959, unless renewed in some form by the President.

Current controls are in terms of pounds.

| Country | Quota | Quota period |
|---|---|---|
| | *Pounds* | |
| Canada | 182, 280, 000 | July 1 to June 30. |
| Other countries | 3, 720, 000 | |
| Total | [1] 186, 000, 000 | |

[1] About 3.3 million bushels of 56 pounds each, of which not more than 15,000 may be rye flour and rye meal.

During the representative period 1950–53, 185,759,365 pounds of rye were imported. Imports under the quota have been as follows:

| Commodity | Period | Quota | Imports |
|---|---|---|---|
| | | *Pounds* | *Pounds* |
| Rye, rye flour and meal | 1953–54 | [1] 31, 000, 000 | 31, 000, 000 |
| | 1954–55 | 186, 000, 000 | 186, 000, 000 |
| | 1955–56 | 186, 000, 000 | 182, 280, 000 |
| | 1956–57 | 186, 000, 000 | 174, 960, 031 |

[1] Partial-year quota from Mar. 31, 1954, when controls became effective, through marketing year ending June 30, 1954; of the quota, no more than 2,500 pounds could be rye flour or meal.

[Attachment C]

## Tariff Quotas Under Section 350 of the Tariff Act of 1930, as Amended (Agricultural Products Only)

Under the Reciprocal Trade Agreements Program, the United States has in a number of instances granted concessions to other countries in the form of so-called tariff quotas. These are reductions in duty on a specified volume of imports, additional imports being subject to a higher rate of duty. The general purpose of such tariff quotas has not been to put a limit upon the imports but rather to limit the increase in imports resulting from a duty concession in order to safeguard domestic producers. Tariff quotas are the result of negotiations with the specific countries involved, and are preceded by a review in the Trade Agreements Committee on which the various departments are represented.

At the present time tariff quotas are in effect for the following agricultural commodities or products thereof:

1. Cattle (under 200 pounds or 700 pounds and over, excluding dairy cattle)
2. Whole milk, fresh or sour
3. Cream, fresh or sour
4. Butter
5. Walnuts
6. Certified seed potatoes
7. Table stock potatoes

A brief résumé of some of the principal provisions and other considerations relative to these quotas follows:

| Tariff par. No. | | Rates of duty per pound |
|---|---|---|
| 701 | Cattle: | |
| | Under 200 pounds: | *Cents* |
| | Quota of 200,000 head, year beginning Apr. 1 | 1.5 |
| | Over quota | 2.5 |
| | 700 pounds and over, excluding dairy cattle: | |
| | Quota of 400,000 head, year beginning Apr. 1, but not more than 120,000 head in any 3-month period, beginning Apr. 1, July 1, Oct. 1 and Jan. 1 | 1.5 |
| | Over quota | 2.5 |

These tariff quotas are provided for in the General Agreement on Tariffs and Trade (GATT) (January 1, 1948) but have not always been in effect. Under the terms of a proviso in the GATT they were to remain suspended "until the President, after termination of the unlimited national emergency proclaimed on May 7, 1951, shall have proclaimed that the abnormal situation in respect of cattle and meats has terminated." Tariff quotas on these classes of cattle were also included in the 1936 and 1939 trade agreements with Canada, and in the trade agreement with Mexico signed in 1943. Under this last agreement the quotas were suspended under the same emergency proviso later incorporated in the GATT. There had been no effective tariff quotas since 1943, and the duty rate of 1½ cents per pound was applied to all imports of these classes of cattle from that date until April 1, 1953, when the tariff quotas became effective. Since that date imports compared with the quotas as follows:

22806—58——46

| | Annual quota (head) | Quantity entered (head) |
|---|---|---|
| Cattle, less than 200 pounds each: | | |
| Apr. 1, 1953 to Mar. 31, 1954 | 200,000 | 4,654 |
| Apr. 1, 1954 to Mar. 31, 1955 | 200,000 | 5,129 |
| Apr. 1, 1955 to Mar. 31, 1956 | 200,000 | 5,886 |
| Apr. 1, 1956 to Mar. 31, 1957 | 200,000 | 9,401 |
| Apr. 1, 1957 to Mar. 31, 1958 | 200,000 | |
| Entered Apr. 1 to June 30, 1957 | | 10,879 |
| Cattle,[1] 700 pounds or more each (other than dairy cows): | | |
| Apr. 1, 1953 to Mar. 31, 1954 | 400,000 | 39,734 |
| Apr. 1, 1954 to Mar. 31, 1955 | 400,000 | 90,449 |
| Apr. 1, 1955 to Mar. 31, 1956 | 400,000 | 26,538 |
| Apr. 1, 1956 to Mar. 31, 1957 | 400,000 | 21,956 |
| Apr. 1, 1957 to Mar. 31, 1958 | 400,000 | |
| Entered Apr. 1 to June 30, 1957 | | 17,959 |

[1] Quota administered on quarterly basis. Presidential proclamation of Mar. 2, 1953 provides (1) that not more than 400,000 head of such cattle may be entered during the quota year at the modified duty rate of 1½ cents per pound; (2) that not more than 120,000 head may be entered at this rate in any 3-month period beginning Apr. 1, June 1, Oct. 1, or Jan. 1.

It might be noted that under the Mexican agreement a tariff quota was also set up for medium weight cattle (200 pounds or more but less than 700 pounds) under which 400,000 head could enter annually at 1½ cents per pound, with an overquota rate of 2½ cents. These quotas, too, were suspended under the emergency proviso. Since they were not subsequently included in the GATT, and since the Mexican agreement was terminated in 1951, all imports of this class are again dutiable at 2½ cents per pound, with no provision for a future quota.

| Tariff par. No. | | Rates of duty per gallon |
|---|---|---|
| | | *Cents* |
| 707 | Whole milk, fresh or sour: | |
| | Quota of 3,000,000 gallons, calendar year | 2.0 |
| | Over quota | 6.5 |
| 707 | Cream, fresh or sour: | |
| | Quota of 1,500,000 gallons, calendar year | 15.0 |
| | Over quota | 56.6 |

These tariff quotas were included in the GATT.

Tariff quotas in the same amounts, but at higher rates of duty, were provided for in earlier trade agreements with Canada, which were superseded by GATT.

Imports of fresh whole milk and cream are very small compared with the quotas. Imports during calendar year 1952 and subsequently are as follows:

| | Annual quota | Quantity entered |
|---|---|---|
| Cream, fresh or sour: | *Gallons* | *Gallons* |
| Calendar year: | | |
| 1952 | 1,500,000 | 1,114 |
| 1953 | 1,500,000 | 1,104 |
| 1954 | 1,500,000 | 825 |
| 1955 | 1,500,000 | 765 |
| 1956 | 1,500,000 | 707 |
| 1957 | 1,500,000 | |
| Entered ½, June 30, 1957 | | 195 |
| Whole milk, fresh or sour: | | |
| Calendar year: | | |
| 1952 | 3,000,000 | 23,414 |
| 1953 | 3,000,000 | 13,146 |
| 1954 | 3,000,000 | 52,563 |
| 1955 | 3,000,000 | 4,286 |
| 1956 | 3,000,000 | 2,032 |
| 1957 | 3,000,000 | |
| Entered ½, June 30, 1957 | | 437 |

| Tariff par. No. | | Rates of duty per pound |
|---|---|---|
| 709 | Butter: | |
| | Nov. 1 to Mar. 31: | *Cents* |
| | 50 million pounds | 7 |
| | Over quota | 14 |
| | Apr. 1 to July 15 and July 16 to Oct. 31: | |
| | 5 million pounds in each period | 7 |
| | Over quota | 14 |

It may be noted that while imports from Cuba under the quota are also charged the rate of 7 cents per pound, the overquota rate for Cuba is only 11.2 cents per pound.

The November to March quota was negotiated in 1947, and the quotas for April to October in 1949, both under GATT.

United States import controls over butter, in effect since the beginning of World War II, have virtually kept out all imports. Currently and since July 1, 1953, imports are limited to an annual absolute quota of 707,000 pounds under section 22 of the Agricultural Adjustment Act, as amended.

| Tariff par. No. | | Rates of duty, per pound |
|---|---|---|
| 760 | Walnuts, shelled, blanched, roasted, and prepared or preserved (excluding paste): | |
| | Calendar year quota of 5,000,000 pounds (shelled walnuts imported count against quota although dutiable at 15 cents per pound; see comment below) | *Cents* 7.5 |
| | Over quota | 15.0 |

One tariff quota covering the two tariff categories (shelled walnuts and blanched, roasted, prepared, or preserved walnuts excluding walnut paste) was originally negotiated in Geneva under GATT in 1947. However, when China withdrew from GATT in 1950, the duty on the shelled walnuts within the quota reverted to its former higher level. Thus, the unusual situation came about that shelled walnuts imported count against the quota although they pay the full rate of duty. In recent years total imports have been as follows:

| | Annual quota | Quantity entered | Quota filled |
|---|---|---|---|
| Walnuts, shelled, blanched, roasted and prepared or preserved (not including walnut paste): | *Pounds* | *Pounds* | |
| Calendar year 1952 | 5,000,000 | 6,315,996 | Sept. 26, 1952 |
| Calendar year 1953 | 5,000,000 | 7,281,605 | Aug. 7, 1953 |
| Calendar year 1954 | 5,000,000 | [1] 7,150,118 | Aug. 19, 1954 |
| Calendar year 1955 | 5,000,000 | [1] 8,705,323 | June 29, 1955 |
| Calendar year 1956 | 5,000,000 | [1] 11,403,435 | Mar. 7, 1956 |
| Calendar year 1957 | 5,000,000 | | |
| Entered Jan. 2 to June 30, 1957 | | 1,354,926 | |

[1] Census import figures

| Tariff par. No. | | Rates of duty, per pound |
|---|---|---|
| 771 | White or Irish potatoes: | |
| | Certified seed: | |
| | Quota of 1,900,000 bushels of 60 pounds each, year beginning Sept. 15, 1957 | *Cents* 0.375 |
| | Over quota | .75 |
| | Table stock, not product of Cuba: | |
| | Minimum quota of 600,000 bushels of 60 pounds each per year beginning Sept. 15, 1957. Quota to be increased by amount by which the Sept. 1 crop estimate is less than 350,000,000 bushels. Cuban potatoes not counted against quota | .375 |
| | Over quota | .75 |

Until its modification this year the quota provisions, which are incorporated in GATT were essentially the same as those in the 1939 trade agreement with Canada except for an increase in the low-duty quota on certified seed from 1½ to 2½ million bushels, and except for a reduction in the quota duty for table stock which had been 0.60 cents from December through February under the old agreement. Under the 1936 trade agreement with Canada there was a low-duty quota of 750,000 bushels for certified potatoes only. Canada recently withdrew and modified its concession to the United States by raising the import duty on potatoes. In compensation for such action the United States by action effective September 15, 1957, reduced the tariff quota on seed potatoes from 2.5 million bushels to 1.9 million bushels and the minimum-tariff quota on table stock from 1 million bushels to 600,000 bushels.

In general, until 1944 potato imports were well below quota levels. But with wartime production incentives and postwar price-support programs creating an attractive market in the United States imports of both seed and table stock potatoes have overrun the low-duty quotas by substantial amounts since that year.

The curtailment of price support in 1950–51 together with the high yields and consequent abundant domestic supplies in that year, resulted in low prices and a decline in imports, although considerable amounts entered at the over-quota rates. In 1951–52 price support was removed and production declined sharply, but although prices as a result were high, the Canadians, because of a short crop were not able to take advantage of the market. Hence, for the first time in recent years imports fell below the low-duty quota. Imports of certified seed potatoes in that year amounted to only 1.3 million bushels compared with the quota of 2.5 million, while table stock imports were less than the minimum quota figure of 1 million bushels. The actual quota in that year was set at 4 million bushels, in accordance with the provision of the trade agreement whereby the quota is increased by the amount by which the September production estimate falls below the figure of 350 million bushels. Recent imports are as follows:

| Commodity and quota period | Annual quota | Quantity entered |
|---|---|---|
| | *Pounds* | *Pounds* |
| Certified seed potatoes: | | |
| Sept. 15, 1952 to Sept. 14, 1953 | 150,000,000 | 114,224,233 |
| Sept. 15, 1953 to Sept. 14, 1954 | 150,000,000 | 100,578,047 |
| Sept. 15, 1954 to Sept. 14, 1955 | 150,000,000 | 79,674,270 |
| Sept. 15, 1955 to Sept. 14, 1956 | 150,000,000 | 139,892,180 |
| Sept. 15, 1956 to Sept. 14, 1957 | 150,000,000 | |
| Entered Sept. 15, 1956 to July 13, 1957 | | 111,912,085 |
| Other than certified seed: | | |
| Sept. 15, 1952 to Sept. 14, 1953 | 798,900,000 | 84,529,736 |
| Sept. 15, 1953 to Sept. 14, 1954 | 60,000,000 | [1] [2] 77,290,420 |
| Sept. 15, 1954 to Sept. 14, 1955 | 329,100,000 | 16,600,003 |
| Sept. 15, 1955 to Sept. 14, 1956 | 60,000,000 | [1] [3] 111,376,537 |
| Sept. 15, 1956 to Sept. 14, 1957 | 60,000,000 | |
| Entered Sept. 15, 1956 to July 13, 1957 | | 34,891,316 |

[1] Census import figures, September through August.
[2] Quota filled Feb. 18, 1954.
[3] Quota filled Mar. 19, 1954.

[Attachment D]

## Actions Under Escape Clause Provisions of Trade Agreements (Agricultural Products Only)

### 1. AUTHORITY

Section 7 of the Trade Agreements Extension Act of 1951 lays down procedures and specifies the factors to be considered for the withdrawal or modification of trade concessions when such concessions result in or threaten serious injury to the domestic industry. These provisions formalized and liberalized procedures existing under Executive Order 10082 dated October 5, 1949. In this legislation the Tariff Commission was deprived of the power to turn down appeals for relief without a regular investigation and a detailed list of factors to be considered in an investigation was included.

Section 7 states in part that any product on which a concession has been granted under a trade agreement is "* * * as a result, in whole or in part, of the duty or other customs treatment reflecting such concession, being imported in such increased quantities, either actual or relative, as to cause or threaten serious injury to the domestic industry producing like or directly competitive products, it (the Tariff Commission) shall recommend to the President the withdrawal or modification of the concession, its suspension in whole or in part, or the establishment of import quotas, to the extent and for the time necessary to prevent or remedy such injury. * * * The President may make such adjustments in the rates of duty, impose such quotas, or make such other modifications as are found and reported by the Commission to be necessary to prevent or remedy serious injury to the respective domestic industry."

Section 7 actions are taken by the President and are preceded by (1) an investigation including a public hearing, by the Tariff Commission; (2) a finding and recommendation by the Tariff Commission to the President; and (3) receipt of agency views as may be requested by the President.

2. ACTION TAKEN

Prior to the passage of this section 7, there were four inquiries on agricultural commodities undertaken under the provisions of Executive Orders 10004, dated October 5, 1948, and 10082, dated October 5, 1949. These were on marrons, hops, narcissus bulbs, and beef and veal, fresh, chilled, or frozen. Under the Executive orders the Tariff Commission had the power to turn down appeals without a complete investigation. All four actions were dismissed after preliminary inquiry.

Since the passage of section 7 the United States Tariff Commission has received applications concerning the following agricultural products: blue-mold cheese, garlic, dried figs, cherries (candied, crystallized, or glace), mustard seeds, alsike clover seed, ground chicory, coconuts, and red fescue seed.

The Tariff Commission recommended modification of concessions on garlic, dried figs, and alsike clover seed. The President rejected modification of the concession on garlic.

The Tariff Commission unanimously recommended that the duty on dried figs be raised. In a proclamation dated August 16, 1952, the President modified the concession on dried figs. The duty on dried figs was raised from 2½ cents per pound to 4½ cents per pound; the duty on figs fresh or in brine remained 2½ cents per pound.

On May 21, 1954, the Tariff Commission recommended the modification of the concession on alsike clover seed to permit the assessment of a duty of 4 cents per pound on the first 1.5 million pounds of alsike clover seed entered for consumption in any year and the assessment of a duty of 6 cents per pound on such seed entered in excess of 1.5 million pounds. By Proclamation No. 3059 dated June 30, 1954, the President established for 1 year only a tariff quota of 1.5 million pounds dutiable at the trade agreement rate of 2 cents per pound with imports in excess of that quantity subject to a duty of 6 cents per pound.

On April 28, 1955, the Commission reported to the President its findings that it is necessary to continue beyond June 30, 1955, an annual tariff quota on alsike clover seed and that the annual quota should be 2.5 million pounds subject to duty at the agreement rate of 2 cents per pound with imports in excess of that quantity during any quota year to be subject to a duty of 6 cents a pound. By Proclamation No. 3100 dated June 29, 1955, it is provided that during each of the 12-month periods beginning July 1, 1955, and July 1, 1956, not more than 2.5 million pounds of alsike clover seed entered for consumption shall be dutiable at 2 cents per pound and that all seed entered in excess of that amount shall be dutiable at the rate of 6 cents per pound.

In its report of May 8, 1957, the Commission recommended an extension of a 2.5-million-pound tariff quota. On June 24, 1957, the President proclaimed a tariff quota of 3 million pounds for a 2-year period.

In 1954–55 when the tariff quota was 1.5 million pounds, 2.3 million pounds were entered. The quota was filled by September 27, 1954. In the quota year 1955–56 when the tariff quota was 2.5 million pounds,

3.5 million pounds were entered, exceeding the quota by 1 million pounds. The quota was filled on October 22, 1955. In the quota year 1956–57 imports totaled only 0.3 million pounds, owing to the very small production in Canada caused by severe frost damage to the crop.

*Use of quotas in escape clause actions*

Dried figs and alsike clover seed are the only agriculture products on which escape clause action has been taken. In both cases it was found that modification of the tariff rate would afford adequate remedy for the injury caused by increased imports resulting from the tariff concessions.

# AGRICULTURAL PRICE POLICY AND INTERNATIONAL TRADE

D. Gale Johnson, professor of economics, University of Chicago

An appraisal of the interrelations and inconsistencies between international trade policy and agricultural price policy in the United States appropriately may begin with a description and analysis of the farm price programs. Such a beginning is justified because the major steps to eliminate some of the inconsistencies between farm price and international trade programs must start with the farm-price programs. This position does not rest upon the presumption that nothing can be done through international economic measures to heal the breach between trade and agricultural policies. Instead, two other premises are uppermost. First, the present farm price policies are basically inimical to the long-run interests of American farm people, as well as to the general level of productivity in the United States. Second, the price and other policies that can be designed to meet the most important economic objectives of American farm people would not require a significant interference with the expansion of international trade as a means of gaining the advantages of international specialization.

But before examining agricultural price policy and international trade policy, it is pertinent to consider the linkage that exists between domestic and international markets for agricultural products. If the United States were neither an important exporter nor importer of agricultural products, its actions in the farm-price field would have little significance to international trade policies.

## I. UNITED STATES TRADE IN AGRICULTURAL PRODUCTS

The United States is in a rather unique position of being a major exporter of both manufactured and agricultural products and a major importer of agricultural products and raw materials. As a result, our farm programs as well as our trade policies can and do have a significant influence on the total world movement and prices of agricultural products.

Although there are great variations in the year-to-year value and quantity of our agricultural imports and exports, United States trade in many farm goods is an important part of the world trade in such products. As an importer, the United States in recent years has been taking about one-fifth of the world's exports in sugar and from 15 to 30 percent of the wool—the two major products for which we are an important producer and importer. As an exporter, this country plays an even greater role, having accounted during the period 1949–52 for the following percentages of total world exports: wheat, 30 to 55 percent; cotton, 30 to 45 percent; tobacco, 35 to 40 percent; rice, 10 to 13 percent; lard, 75 to 90 percent; tallow, 60 to 80 percent; and all fats and oils, 17 to 19 percent. In the years 1955 and 1956 the situation was much the same. United States exports were the following percentages of world exports: wheat, 30 and 46 percent; cotton, 24 and 38 percent; tobacco, 39 and 36 percent; rice, 10 and 16 percent; lard, 81 and 81 percent; tallow, 79 and 78 percent; cottonseed and oil, 80 and 74 percent; and soybeans and oil, 71 and 81 percent.

There are several different ways of depicting the importance to the United States farmer of his export markets and of the changes in their importance over time; perhaps the most significant for present purposes is the ratio of the value of exports to cash farm income. As table I shows, this ratio in recent years has been well below that of the twenties, but exports still account for about 10 percent of the farmer's total cash receipts.

TABLE I.—*United States agricultural exports and total cash farm income, 1910–53* [1]

[Exports as percentage of cash farm receipts]

| Period: | |
|---|---|
| 1910–14 | 17.5 |
| 1925–29 | 17.3 |
| 1930–34 | 12.9 |
| 1935–39 | 9.4 |
| 1946 | 12.9 |
| 1947 | 13.1 |
| 1948 | 11.5 |
| 1949 | 12.8 |
| 1950 | 10.0 |
| 1951 | 12.2 |
| 1952 | 10.5 |
| 1953 | 9.1 |
| 1954 | 10.1 |
| 1955 | 10.7 |
| 1956 | 13.4 |

[1] Sources: 1910–50 U. S. Department of Agriculture, United States Farm Products in Foreign Trade, Statistical Bulletin No. 112, Washington, D. C., 1953, p. 11. The data for 1951 to date were derived from publications of the Department of Agriculture, Foreign Agricultural Trade of the United States, Statistical Report for Calendar Year 1956, June 1957, p. 16, and The Farm Income Situation, July 1957, p. 28.

These overall statistics hide the even greater dependence of several farm commodities upon foreign markets. During 1949–51, more than a third of all our wheat, cotton, and rice were exported; and approximately one-quarter of our soybeans, tobacco, rye, grain sorghums, lard, tallow, field peas, and hops were sent abroad. In 1956, a year of record agricultural exports—

> Exports in relation to United States output were 59 percent for cotton, 54 percent for wheat, and 83 percent for rice. Also, 49 percent for rye, 45 percent for tallow and grease, 35 percent for soybeans and oil, 23 percent for tobacco and dry edible peas, and 22 percent for lard.[1]

It should be noted that the large volume and relative importance of exports in 1956 was the result, to a significant extent, of governmental programs to encourage agricultural exports. Furthermore, in several cases, the exports were made from accumulated stocks rather than from current production.

Looked at in still another way, in recent years the value of agricultural exports has accounted for some 20 to 25 percent of the total of United States commodity exports. Imports of products of agri-

[1] Foreign Agricultural Service, U. S. Department of Agriculture, Foreign Agricultural Trade Digest, July 1957, pp. 2 and 5.

cultural origin have bulked even larger in our total trade, constituting about a third to two-fifths of our total commodity imports. However, about 60 percent of these agricultural imports are not competitive with domestic agriculture, including as they do such commodities as coffee, crude rubber, copra, bananas, tea, spices, and wool for carpets.

Sketchy as these few data are, there can be no doubt that the United States has in the past and does at present play a significant role in international trade in agricultural products and that important linkages exist between the international and the domestic market for such goods.

## II. A SHORT HISTORY OF FARM PRICE PROGRAMS, 1933–57

Although the Federal Farm Board was engaged in certain price-supporting operations as early as September 1929, the beginning of the present farm-price programs was in 1933 when the Agricultural Adjustment Act was passed and the Commodity Credit Corporation was created. The Corporation immediately offered nonrecourse loans to producers of cotton and corn and they have been available every year since that time. The first cotton loan was at 10 cents a pound, although the market price had just previously been around 6 cents. The first corn-loan rate was set at 45 cents a bushel, only moderately above the market price at the time the loan was announced. The first wheat loans were not made until 1938—the small crops of 1933, 1934, 1935, and 1936 having resulted in relatively favorable wheat prices—but they too have since been continuously available. Tobacco producers have also enjoyed a price-support loan program since the midthirties. In addition, many other commodities, such as rye, oats, barley, wool, flaxseed, dried milk, butter, soybeans, cheese, honey, and mohair, have had their prices supported through the use of nonrecourse loans or direct Government purchases.

The nonrecourse feature of these loans means simply that the Commodity Credit Corporation cannot collect the amount of money borrowed by a farmer, unless the farmer wishes to repay. The farmer in obtaining such a loan has two alternatives: (1) He may deliver the farm product which served as a security for the loan, or (2) he may pay the amount borrowed. Thus, if the market price exceeds the loan value the farmer will redeem the farm product used as a security for the loan by paying the Corporation the amount borrowed. However, if the market price is below the loan value, he will deliver the product to the Corporation. The nonrecourse loan is only one, albeit the most important, of a number of methods used to influence the level of market prices. Efforts have been made to restrict supply through acreage allotments, marketing quotas, grade and quality regulation, and actual destruction of output. In addition, steps have been taken to increase demand through distribution of farm products at low cost, or free, to individuals on relief and to certain types of institutions such as schools and homes for the aged and the indigent. During the late thirties and early forties, the food-stamp plan was tried as a means of expanding demand through a two-price plan available to certain segments of the population, primarily persons on relief.

But efforts to control supply or to expand demand are relatively blunt instruments. The output of farm products is not entirely within the control of man—with no apparent change in acreage planted or seeded, the amount of fertilizer applied, or the production practices followed, output of an individual crop may vary by 20 to 50 percent from one year to another. This is why direct methods of price influence have become an important and significant part of the farm program. The nonrecourse loan and Government storage programs represent direct means of assuring a given price, if sufficient storage space is available. Though other methods of direct price maintenance have been used, such as purchase operations, the loan and storage operations have been the mainstay of the farm price support program.

Formally, the objective of these programs is price parity. But the definition of parity and the extent of attainment of that objective has not remained unchanged over the past two decades. The concept of parity originally expressed in the Agricultural Adjustment Act of 1933 was a very simple notion (even though there is either one too many or one too few commas):

> * * * prices to farmers at a level that will give agricultural commodities a purchasing power with respect to articles that farmers buy, equivalent to the purchasing power of agricultural commodities in the base period.

The base period for all agricultural commodities except tobacco was August 1909 to July 1914; that for tobacco was the 10 years starting with August 1919.

In 1935 the sentence structure was straightened out, and, in addition, certain adjustments in the definition of parity were introduced. Prior to 1935 purchasing power of the prices farmers received was defined solely in terms of prices paid by farmers for products used in production or consumed by the household. In 1935 "interest payments per acre on farm indebtedness secured by real estate and tax-payments per acre on farm real estate" were added. That year the index of prices paid was 125; the addition of the other two factors increased the overall index to 130. Thus the change in definition increased parity prices by 4 percent. However, by 1942 the rise in prices paid so outstripped the change in mortgage interest and taxes that the inclusion of the latter reduced parity prices. In fact, in 1948 the prices paid index was 264 while the combined index used in calculating parity prices was only 250.

The next major changes in the calculation of parity prices came in 1948 and 1949, when, for the first time, farm-wage rates were included in the calculation of parity prices. The inclusion of wage rates would have resulted in a very significant increase in parity prices (about 6 percent in 1948) but a concurrent revision of the whole index reduced the net effect of the change to about 3.5 percent for 1948. Although there is no question but that the intent of these changes in the calculation of parity prices was to raise the level of parity prices, their net effect (including the statistical revisions) often has been to leave the parity prices unchanged. If the parity prices were calculated on July 15, 1957, by the method used from 1933 to 1935, the prices-paid index would be 298; the index now in use for most commodities is 295. The best laid plans of mice and men often go astray.

There was another change in the calculation of parity prices, however, that has had a substantial impact. In the Agricultural Act of

1948 a new method of determining parity prices was enacted. This method was not designed to change the average level of parity prices; its purpose was to modify the relative parity prices of the various farm commodities. It was recognized that the previous methods of calculating parity prices of each commodity had resulted in serious distortions of relative farm prices. Not only did the relative prices which prevailed in the 1910–14 period fail to represent current demand and supply relationships, but over the years many other base periods were used as parity prices were calculated for an ever-increasing number of commodities. In fact, in 1949, only about one-third of the farm commodities for which parity prices were calculated were based entirely on the 1910–14 base periods. The remainder involved various base periods for the interwar period. The 1948 revision specified that the relative parity prices were to be based on actual relative market prices for the 10 preceding years. Thus farm products whose market prices were lagging behind the general level of farm prices would have their parity prices lowered.

This revision of parity prices was recognized by most agricultural economists as a decided improvement. But from a political viewpoint, the new parity formula had the basic disadvantage of lowering parity prices for a number of politically important crops, namely, cotton, wheat, corn, and peanuts. As a result, in 1949 Congress legislated that for the 4 years beginning January 1, 1950 (when the new parity prices were to be effective), the parity price would be the higher of the old or the new parity for the so-called basic commodities (cotton, wheat, rice, corn, peanuts, and tobacco). This provision was later extended until December 31, 1955. It so happened that the new parity formula increased the parity prices of all important livestock and livestock products, except poultry and eggs; some of the increases were quite substantial, 35 percent for beef cattle, for example. The parity price for wheat, on the other hand, as of January 15, 1954, would have been reduced from $2.48 to $2.13 a bushel by the change in formula. Cotton prices would have been reduced by only little more than a cent a pound while corn prices would have been reduced by 19 cents a bushel (about 11 percent). There is no question that the current large stocks of wheat and corn would now be appreciably smaller if the lower parity prices had been in effect since 1950, and even the 1.2 cents reduction in the price of cotton would not have been without some influence.

This short discussion of the development of the parity-price calculations is intended primarily to indicate the capriciousness of the general approach to the concept. But there is another important facet of parity price as an objective, or as a standard for price support, that warrants notice. This is the question of the relation between the support level and full parity. The original Agricultural Adjustment Act did not specify the level of price support as a percentage of parity. The first loans for corn and cotton were established at approximately 70 percent of parity. In the Agricultural Adjustment Act of 1938, it was specified that loan rates for corn, wheat, and cotton should range between 52 and 75 percent of parity, relatively modest objectives on the whole. For the years 1938, 1939, and 1940, corn loan rates were at 70 to 75 percent of parity and those for cotton and wheat were at 52 to 57 percent. In early 1941 the level of price supports for corn, wheat, cotton, and tobacco was increased to 85 percent and, later that year, the same level of support was extended to the so-called nonbasic products, the purpose being to encourage increased production. The price-support legislation was modified in October 1942, in two ways. First, the price-support levels were increased to 90 percent of parity, and, second, price supports for all basic commodities, and for nonbasic commodities for which the Secretary of Agriculture had found price supports necessary to achieve increased production, were to be maintained at 90 percent of parity for 2 years following the close of the war. Except for the changes in the parity formula described earlier, price supports were generally unchanged with respect to parity level from 1942 through 1954. With respect to certain products, however, the Secretary of Agriculture had some discretion in setting loan rates.

Since 1955, when the flexible price-support provisions of the Agricultural Act of 1949 were allowed to become effective, price supports on wheat and corn, as well as several other commodities, have been established at lower levels, both absolutely and as a percent of effective parity. The presumed advantage of the flexible price-support provision was that the level of price supports would reflect the accumulation of stocks as a result of price-support operations. However, there has not been much flexibility in price-support levels for three main reasons. First, the range of permitted variation in price supports has been rather limited. Second, large stocks of some farm products have been set aside as emergency reserves and the emergency reserves are not included in the determination of the minimum level of price supports. Third, when stocks are reduced through large-scale export dumping, the level of price supports may be increased even though current production is substantially in excess of current normal demand at the price-support level.

At the present time, it may be noted, there seems to be less willingness to experiment with different methods of price support than was true 15 years ago. Today major reliance is placed upon purchases and loans, with acreage restrictions being imposed when the former result in stocks that become difficult to manage. But in the thirties it was fairly generally accepted that some income transfers might be made through techniques other than price supports. Two illustrations may be given. During 1935 and 1936 direct price payments were made to producers on each pound of cotton sold as a means of encouraging farmers to sell their cotton rather than to place it under loan. The loan rate was set at 10 cents a pound, but farmers were paid the difference between the actual market price and 12 cents a pound, up to a maximum of 2 cents a pound. The Agricultural Adjustment Act of 1938 included a provision for parity payments which was designed to supplement price supports and to bring the return to the farmer up to 75 percent of parity. Such payments, totaling $967 million, were made in 1939 through 1942.

A general overall view of the price support and related activities from 1933 to the present would note the following points: During the last 24 years attempts to regulate production (if one excludes tobacco) were made in only 11 years. Most agricultural economists would agree that the methods used to limit output have been relatively ineffective, having been accompanied by positive incentives to increase production. Not only were price supports maintained at relatively profitable levels and direct payments made to producers, but many of the activities associated with the farm programs have been effective means of increasing output by inducing or aiding farmers to adopt improved production techniques.

As of May 31, 1957, the Commodity Credit Corporation had a total investment of $7,645,075,000 in farm commodities. A year earlier the investment was $8,500,534,000. The decline in the value of the inventory was due primarily to a significant reduction in the quantity of cotton held by the CCC—a reduction of about 4 million bales in inventory or under loan. The reduction in cotton stocks was the result of a large export subsidy on cotton, a matter to which we will return later. During the same year, the CCC's holdings of corn increased, while those of wheat declined by about 15 percent.

There have been two previous occasions when the stocks of price-supported commodities rose to burdensome levels. In both cases—1942 and 1950—wars intervened to rescue the farm price-support programs.

Since 1951 farm-operator incomes have been declining (except for a small upturn this year), while CCC stocks and the costs of price support, disposal operations, and other features of the farm programs have been increasing. While the facts will not be known for some years to come, it is probable that the net costs of Government programs for agriculture have ranged between a quarter and a third of the amount of farm-operator income for the past 3 years.

### III. THE INCONSISTENT ELEMENTS

The above sketch of farm price-support programs does not indicate specifically the elements of inconsistency between those programs and the objective of freer foreign trade. The basic source of conflict is not hard to determine. Many of the support prices are for products for which the United States is either an exporter or an importer. In either case an effective price support in the American market soon presents serious and obvious problems. If the price support is for a product that is exported and that price support has any influence in increasing domestic prices, exports decline and domestic stocks rise. This loss of foreign markets may be of major importance to some sectors of the farm community and may, indeed, prevent the United States from taking full advantage of its real comparative cost advantages. If the price support is for an imported product, the domestic price support attracts increased imports, as illustrated a few years ago by the relatively large imports of oats from Canada, and may create significant strains on our relations with friendly governments if, as was done in the case of oats, measures are taken to limit such imports.

In the first 4 or 5 years of the development of farm programs under the New Deal, the role given to price supports was secondary to other aspects of the programs. It was generally believed that the adjustment features of the programs—restrictions on acreages, transfer of land from one product to another, payments directly to farmers, and creation of orderly markets—were more important than the nonrecourse loans. As a result, the first uses of restrictions on imports were not envisioned as an adjunct to price supports, but as a means of retaining to farmers any benefits that might accrue to them from making certain adjustments. The first restriction on imports was made in 1934 in connection with the sugar program, which did not include a price-support or commodity-loan provision. The first general legislative approval for import restrictions was enacted in 1935 as an amendment to the Agricultural Adjustment Act of 1933. This amendment allowed restrictions (import quotas) only for commodities for which there was an adjustment program under the act. Section 22, as this authority became generally known, was soon extended to include programs operated under the Soil Conservation Act of 1937 and the Marketing Agreements Act. Authority was also granted to impose, in addition to import quotas, import fees up to 50 percent ad valorem and to impose either in connection with any program using section 32 funds (see below).

Until 1941 import quotas were established under section 22 only for wheat and cotton. These quotas are still in effect. During the war numerous restrictions were placed on imports, primarily to aid the administration of various schemes for the international allocation of relatively scarce agricultural products. Some imports, such as butter, were prohibited entirely.

At the end of the war spokesmen for certain farming interests argued that the provisions for action under section 22 authority were too restrictive. Many of the price-support operations were not conducted under authority granted in the various acts referred to above. As a result, section 22 authority was extended to any program undertaken by the Department of Agriculture.

It should be noted that until recently the executive branch of the Government has used the authority under section 22 with considerable restraint. The only new section 22 action from the end of the war through mid-1953 was the imposition of import fees on almonds; the quotas on wheat and cotton were continued, however. Under authority given in the Second War Powers Act, the importation of butter, flaxseed, linseed oil, peanuts, peanut oil, and rice and rice products were prohibited. These controls were continued until July 1, 1951, and the following month the Secretary of Agriculture was given broader authority to restrict imports by section 104, as amended, of the Defense Production Act of 1950. While action under section 22 is essentially discretionary with the President, the conditions laid down in section 104 were such as to leave the Secretary of Agriculture little room for discretion. For a specified list of products, no imports were permitted if the Secretary determined that imports would (*a*) impair or reduce domestic production, or (*b*) interfere with the orderly domestic marketing or storing of the commodity, or (*c*) result in any unnecessary burden or expenditure under any Government price-support program. Imports of butter, nonfat dried milk solids, peanuts, peanut oil, flaxseed, linseed oil, and rice were prohibited and quantitative restrictions were placed on cheese.

The restrictions on the imports of cheese came at a rather unpropitious time, since the United States, under the Economic Cooperation Administration, had been encouraging certain countries, especially France, Italy, and the Scandinavian countries to expand production of cheese for the American market. Canada was also displeased, to put it lightly, at the reduction in access to the American market.

In mid-1953 Congress let section 104 lapse, but it agreed to do so only after President Eisenhower had stated that he would impose essentially the same restrictions on imports of the affected fats and oils under the authority of section 22, and other administration spokesmen had promised that they would make section 22 more "effective" than it had been in the past. Furthermore, Congress amended the Trade Agreements Act in mid-1953 so as to provide that the President, in an emergency, could impose section 22 restrictions immediately; that is, without awaiting the recommendations of the Tariff Commission.

The relative arbitrariness of section 104, together with the changes made in 1950 and 1951 which permitted section 22 action to be taken regardless of the provision of any trade agreement or other international agreement, indicated the nature and significance of the schism between trade and agricultural policy. It is apparent that there is a strong tendency for many Members of Congress, particularly those holding influential positions on the agricultural committees, to hold the position that no interference is to be allowed with any action affecting domestic agricultural interests or programs. International trade is a necessary evil, but an evil that must be controlled and restricted whenever possible.

Section 22 quotas have been applied in recent years primarily to cotton, wheat, oats, barley, rye, butter, dried milk products, cheese, and peanuts. With the decline in grain prices in recent years, the quotas on oats and barley are ineffective. It should be noted that, in the absence of price-support programs, the cotton and wheat quotas would also be ineffective because the United States would be on a net export basis for these two crops. Section 22 quotas are, with little question, providing significant protection for the dairy industry and perhaps also for peanuts.

Import fees have been imposed, pursuant to section 22, on linseed oil, flaxseed, peanut oil, shelled almonds, and filberts. These fees have had a significant effect upon the level of imports of these products. The commodities on which import fees are levied are ones which we would import in some volume if no protection were afforded.

It is worthy of note that the value of all agricultural imports has declined in recent years. The peak level of agricultural imports was reached in 1951, when the value was $5,166 million. In 1956 the value of agricultural imports was $3,948 million.[2] In value terms most of the decline was in imports competitive with products produced in the United States. Such imports amounted to $2,319 million in 1951 and $1,553 million in 1956.[3] However, I do not want to imply that restrictive trade practices were responsible for all or even a major part of the decline. Much of the decline was the result of lower prices of agricultural products in the United which had the twofold effect of reducing the value of products actually imported and of reducing the incentive of exporting to the United States. The quantity of supplementary imports declined by about 15 percent between 1951 and 1956.

[2] Foreign Agricultural Trade of the United States, statistical report for calender year 1955 and 1956.
[3] Id.

While the value of our imports of agricultural products was substantially less in 1956 than in 1951, the value of agricultural exports in 1956 was slightly greater than in 1951. The record level of agricultural exports in 1956 was due to what constituted the greatest export dumping and subsidy program that the world has known. Agricultural exports in 1956 exceeded 1955 by 30 percent. In delineating the factors responsible for the increase, the Department of Agriculture states:[4]

Some of the gains in agricultural exports arose from the prosperous conditions abroad. Another contributing factor notably for cotton and grains, was Government export programs which helped overcome problems of pricing and dollar shortage. In 1956, 41 percent of United States farm exports ($1.7 billion) was shipped to foreign countries without an expenditure of dollars on their part; of the 59 percent that was sold for dollars, about one-fifth moved at prices below those in the United States market.

The above quotation implies that something more than 50 percent of our agricultural exports in 1956 were directly affected by governmental programs.

Since 1921 the United States has had antidumping or countervailing duties as a means of counteracting the effect of export subsidies or dumping by foreign producers or nations.[5] In spite of our own attitudes and legislative and executive actions on export subsidies and dumping by others, section 12 of the Agricultural Adjustment Act of 1933 authorized export subsidies for certain agricultural products. Section 32 of Public Law 370, 75th Congress, authorized the Secretary of Agriculture to use up to 30 percent of the gross customs receipts of the United States to expand domestic demand and to encourage the exportation of farm products. The latter provision obviously allowed export subsidies or export dumping.

Excluding war and postwar grants of agricultural products, large-scale subsidization of agricultural exports did not start until 1949 when, under the International Wheat Agreement, export subsidies were paid on wheat. Most of our recent export-subsidy programs have not been paid for from section 32 funds. The costs of the wheat-export subsidies under International Wheat Agreement, for example, are met by direct appropriation, while the cotton-export-subsidy program has been authorized by title II of the Soil Bank Act. The other main legislative authorizations for various types of foreign surplus disposal are Public Law 480 and the Mutual Security Act. Public Law 480 permits a wide range of activities, generally inconsistent with the conduct of international trade by private enterprise. These include sale of products for foreign currencies not convertible into

[4] The Demand and Price Situation, DPS–26, February 1957, p. 12.

[5] The following is a quotation from the report of the Committee on Ways and Means on United States customs, tariff, and trade agreement laws and their administration, by the Subcommittee on Customs, Tariffs, and Reciprocal Trade Agreements (U. S. Government Printing Office, Washington, 1957): "Commercial dumping and Government subsidization of exports are closely related matters affecting international trade. The net effect of these practices is to reduce the price of commodities in the importing country below the price those commodities command in the exporting country. Low prices are generally desirable from the point of view of the importing country. However, where lower prices on imports involve unfair and injurious competition to domestic producers, it has long been the policy of the United States Government to impose antidumping duties or countervailing duties.

"Dumping consists of unfair international price discrimination in which goods are exported to one market at lower prices than those prevailing in the home market or in other export markets. These lower prices may be the result of the granting of an export subsidy by the Government of the exporting country. In such a case, the importing country may resort either to antidumping or to countervailing duties in order to protect its domestic producers of competitive products." (P.91)

dollars at fixed exchange rates, donations, special arrangements for famine and other urgent relief, and direct barter.

As a consequence of the various measures and programs, over half of our agricultural exports in 1956 were directly handled and subsidized by the United States Government. Countries other than the United States—Canada, for example—are having difficulties with their agriculture. Our aggressive actions in expanding agricultural exports make it much more difficult for smaller and less wealthy economists to find profitable outlets for their agricultural products.

The basis of the complaint of other nations concerning our export subsidies on farm products can be stated as follows. American farmers receive prices substantially above world market prices for many agricultural products, especially wheat and cotton. These high prices encourage farmers to increase production. While various efforts have been made to reduce production of farm products in the United States, these efforts have been of little consequence, as evidenced by the steady increase in farm production in recent years. Not only have support prices increased farm production in the United States, but these prices restrict consumption in the largest single market in the world. Consequently, the quantity of farm products that are available for export is increased in two ways: First, by increasing production and, second, by reducing domestic consumption.

To summarize, our present farm programs result in conflicts with a liberal trade program. This conflict results from the necessity to impose import quotas or other restrictions as a means of insulating domestic from world market prices and to use export subsidies as a means of disposing of surpluses accumulated when support prices are above the level that would equate demand and supply. Import quotas tend to restrict the dollars that foreign countries can earn by selling to the United States market, while export subsidies reduce the markets available to competing exporters.

## IV. APPRAISAL OF THE FARM PROGRAMS

Advocates of the use of import quotas and export subsidies are sincere in their belief that these programs are necessary for the economic health of American agriculture. Such a belief has as a basis 1 or 2 different propositions. First, many segments of American agriculture cannot compete with imports from the rest of the world. Second, price supports as high or higher than those now in effect are necessary if American farmers are to have a satisfactory income.

It is obvious that if restrictions on imports of agricultural products were removed, the output of some farm products would decline. this is certainly true of wool, sugar, certain nut crops, and butter and cheese.[6] However, it must be remembered that a general liberalization of trade would result in increased agricultural exports from the United States.[7]

[6] See D. Gale Johnson, Trade and Agriculture (John Wiley & Sons, New York, 1950), pp. 50–53, for an effort to indicate the effect of freer trade upon the output of United States agricultural products. I concluded that on balance the increase in demand for United States agricultural exports due to a larger volume of trade would be about equal to the decline in demand for United States farm products that would result from eliminating import barriers in the United States.

[7] This statement assumes that we are starting from a relatively normal situation, namely, one in which there are no export subsidies. I do not wish to imply that in a free-trade situation that agricultural exports would be at the same level as now prevails with our producers of competitive products." (P. 91.)

The first of the propositions is not a logically correct statement. It would be logically correct if it stated as follows:

Many segments of American agriculture cannot produce farm products at the price at which these products are available in world markets and at the same time pay to land, labor, and capital the same return as is obtained in the production of other farm or nonfarm products in our own economy.

The producers of beet sugar in Colorado do not compete with the producers of sugar in Cuba, but instead must compete with the rest of United States agriculture and industry for the labor, land, and capital required for the production of sugar. It is incorrect to argue that the low absolute wages paid to sugar workers in Cuba gives sugar producers in Cuba an advantage relative to the sugar producers in Colorado. If this position were correct, it would not be possible for the United States to export large quantities of lard to Cuba since the absolute returns to workers producing hogs in Cuba are low as well.

The second proposition, namely that price supports as high or higher than those now in effect are necessary if American farmers are to have a satisfactory income, deserves more extended comment. If this proposition is valid, then it will be necessary to have large governmental intervention in American agriculture. But it does not necessarily follow that this intervention must take a form that will require extensive use of import quotas and export subsidies. An alternative farm program is presented in the next section of this paper. This program, which is designed to maintain an efficient agriculture and a satisfactory level of income to farm people, would not require import quotas or export subsidies. At this point, I would like to consider the general issue of the gains that American farmers have achieved, if any, from the farm programs that we have had for the past quarter of a century.

I do not believe that American farmers have received any long-run income gains from the price-support programs and the related subsidy payments that have been made since 1933.[8]

There are three main reasons why our past farm programs have not been effective in increasing the average incomes of American farm families:

1. Contrary to original expectations, the farm programs have tended to increase farm output in the United States.

2. Unless entry into agriculture is controlled, which has not been done, there is no reason to expect that returns to mobile resources (labor and capital) would be increased by increasing the prices of farm products.

3. In some cases, the effects of the farm programs have been to increase production in other parts of the world.

Since 1929 there has been a significant increase in the output of farm products; 1956 farm output was 52 percent greater than in 1929. During the same period output per unit of input increased by about

[8] For the fiscal years 1932 through 1955, the total net cost programs primarily for stabilization of farm prices and incomes, programs primarily for conservation of resources, and Government procurement of agricultural commodities for forgein-aid programs was $19,760 million. Since that time costs have probably been in excess of $4 billion. For estimates of costs for 1932–55, see F. D. Stocker, Governmental Cost in Agriculture (Agricultural Research Service, USDA, ARS 43–28, May 1956), p. 25.

40 percent.[9] The increase in technical efficiency (the rise in the ratio of output to input) has meant that fewer resources, especially labor, has been required to produce any given volume of output.

There are several reasons for attributing at least part of the increase in technical efficiency (the rise in the ratio of output to input) to the farm programs. For one thing, where attempts were made to restrict the output of farm products by rationing land, farmers tried out methods of substituting other inputs for land and discovered that these methods of production were profitable even when the land input was not rationed. In addition, most of American agriculture was short on capital by the midthirties as a consequence of disinvestment during the first part of the decade. The rate of investment in agriculture was increased sharply in the late thirties, in part, because of the large direct payments to farmers. Certain of the farm programs, particularly the soil-conservation efforts, constituted a large-scale extension or education program, with a feature that other educational activities lacked—namely, money to give to farmers. Finally, price supports by reducing uncertainty undoubtedly acted to induce farmers to try out new methods of production and to expend more on current inputs requiring cash expenditures.

While a large part of the increased output of farm products has probably been the result of increased efficiency in production, it is also true that price supports at levels above what market prices would have been otherwise, have induced farmers to increase their output or to fail to reduce output when supply was exceeding demand at the price support. This has surely been true in the cases of wheat and cotton.

I do not want to leave the impression that I would criticize our farm programs because they have resulted in greater technical efficiency in agriculture; in fact, the gains in technical efficiency have been of great significance to the American economy. But the increase in output per unit of input and the increases in output induced by higher prices have meant that farmers were prevented from realizing any long-run income gains from the programs. Given the competitive character of agriculture and the low price elasticity of demand, the end result has been, with the possible exception of tobacco, that farm products have been available to consumers at prices as low, if not lower, than what would have prevailed in the absence of the farm programs.[10]

Unless entry into agriculture is controlled, there is no reason to believe that returns to mobile resources would be increased by increasing the price of farm output. Any higher returns, in the short run, will induce greater employment in agriculture and thus tend to drive

[9] The construction of the indexes of output and input are described in U. S. Department of Agriculture, Farm Production Practices, Costs and Returns, Statistical Bulletin No. 83, Washington, D. C., October 1949, pp. 7 and 74. However, the estimate of inputs used in the text differs from that published in the above reference since the price weights used here in the quantity index of inputs were averages for 1946–48 and the labor input was based on estimates made by the Bureau of Census.

[10] I am not saying that specific instances cannot be found in which the price paid by consumers for some farm product has been increased by price supports and surplus disposal operations. What I am saying is that the effects of the farm programs over an extended period of time has been to increase farm output and thus to increase the total supply of food and fiber available to consumers. The effect of the greater output is to depress prices and price supports, which directly affect considerably less than have tended only to delay the downward adjustment of prices. Though I would have great difficulty proving the following statement; namely, that if there had been no price supports for the past decade farm prices might now average between 90 and 100 percent of parity rather than less than 85 percent of parity, I believe that there is considerable basis for such a conclusion.

down returns to the old level. Agriculture is particularly vulnerable to this kind of adjustment because there is a normal or usual outflow of labor from agriculture to nonagriculture. Labor employment can increase quickly through the process of slowing down the outflow In addition, given the price policies of firms supplying such inputs to agriculture as machinery and fuel, the supply functions of many current inputs and short-term investment items are almost perfectly elastic, at least in the short run. These and other influences mean that any income gains will be realized by the most immobile resource; namely, land. If price supports are effective in increasing the value of farm marketing through time, it means that new entrants into agriculture will be faced with higher land prices and their net return on a dollar invested would be no greater than if the price-support program had not been in effect. Thus, most of the gains go to the owners of land during the early years of the price-support program. It is true, of course, that persons who inherit farmland do gain in the sense that the value of the asset would be greater than would otherwise have been the case. But it is doubtful if it is an appropriate objective of national policy to increase the incomes of those who inherit their land.

I do not want to place too much emphasis upon the effect of American price supports upon the output of foreign areas. I believe that it has been of significance in increasing the output of tobacco in Africa and of cotton in Mexico and Africa. The wheat expansion that has occurred can probably be explained by the relatively high wheat prices throughout the world from 1945 through 1952. However, whatever expansion of output has occurred as a result of our price supports makes it more difficult to find profitable export outlets for our farm products.

American agriculture has a high degree of flexibility. It was this flexibility that permitted large increases in output during World War II. But it was this same flexibility that largely negated the efforts to restrict farm output in the late thirties, in the early forties and again in recent years and will probably defeat the same methods when tried in the future. There is, therefore, little likelihood that acreage limitations will be capable of reducing or even stabilizing stocks of farm commodities.

In the early part of 1954 I said—

> Unless the United States embarks upon extensive export dumping devices, the present price-support program may fall from its own weight.[11]

It was obvious at that time that the price-support program was in the process of accumulating vast quantities of cotton, wheat, corn, and other farm products and that efforts to restrict our output by acreage controls would be of little avail. I believed that the continued accumulation of farm commodities would result in a general reappraisal of farm price supports, unless we engaged in extensive export dumping. While there is undoubtedly greater recognition now of the difficulties involved in relatively high-level price supports and increasing evidence of their ineffectiveness in increasing farm incomes, our farm program is still very much the same as it was several years

[11] D. Gale Johnson, Agricultural Price Policy and International Trade, Essays in International Finance, No. 19, June 1954 (Princeton University).

ago. Rather than turning to more effective measures for a solution for our farm difficulties, we have engaged in export dumping on an unprecedented scale. There is more than a little merit in the argument of our foreign critics that what we have tried to do is to export our farm problem.

### V. A SUGGESTED FARM PRICE POLICY

The proposals which President Eisenhower made to Congress in January 1954, included two major features. The first was that the basic provisions of the Agricultural Act of 1949 be allowed to become effective: The variable price schedules in January 1955, and the modernized parity the following year. The second was the proposal to insulate from the market a large part of the existing Government-held surpluses by creating an emergency reserve, together with a provision that might make it possible to use the variable price schedule for the basic crops and to rely less upon the use of acreage allotments and marketing quotas. The President's proposals were certainly a step in the right direction in reducing the area of conflict between trade and agricultural policy and in eventually reducing price-support levels from their then unrealistic levels.

But the task of reconciling agriculture and trade policies required a sharper break with past price policies than was involved in the President's proposals.[12] An obvious way out would be to discontinue all price supports. But this is not only unlikely for sheer political reasons; it also might not represent the optimum policy for the United States. A strong case can be made, however, for a policy of forward prices that would aid farmers in making their production plans, reduce risk and uncertainty confronting farmers, and provide some protection against the incidence of depression. In essence, a forward price policy involves estimates of the market prices that would equilibrate supply and demand. These estimates would be made by a governmental agency and announced in advance of the time important production decisions have to be made. In order to reduce and transfer uncertainty, the Government would guarantee price returns equal to some major fraction, say 90 percent, of the estimated price.[13]

During periods of full employment such a price policy would not be designed to influence the level of farm prices. The objective would be to present farmers with as accurate forecasts as possible of anticipated prices prior to the time most production decisions are made. Except when the estimates of anticipated prices were in error, no price-supporting operations would occur. However, there are some circumstances in which the price estimates will be in error; namely, for products whose output cannot be predicted with a fair degree of accuracy. This includes most of the farm crops since their actual yield does not depend entirely upon the inputs controlled by man. Because of the low-price elasticity of demand for most farm crops, a large yield

[12] The actual changes made in the farm program were much less than requested by the President. Farm price supports in 1955 were only slightly lower than in 1954 for corn and wheat and were even slightly higher for cotton. Of the major crops, there has been a significant reduction in the price support for corn only and the corn situation has failed to improve significantly mainly because of the use of diverted acres in cotton and wheat areas for the production of feed grains.

[13] For details, see my Forward Prices for Agriculture (Chicago, 1947) and Trade and Agriculture, A Study of Inconsistent Policies (New York, 1950), especially pp. 92–125.

usually results in a substantial reduction in the gross income from the crop.

There are two main ways of handling the price variability that would result from yield variations. For the storable crops (corn, wheat, cotton, tobacco, rice, and many feed grains) the Government could adopt a storage program that would reduce market offerings from large crops and increase market supplies when crops are small. If the objective of the storage policy were to stabilize use of the products rather than to stabilize prices, the storage program would not be consistent with relatively free trade in the major exported and imported farm products.

For the crops which cannot be stored except at high cost, the forward prices should be not a single price, but a schedule of prices that would approximately stabilize total revenue. The forward price would be an estimate of prices if yield were average; the schedule would translate the expected total revenue from an average crop into a series of prices for relevant yields.

In addition to the two techniques described above, it would be essential that the method used to guarantee the farmers the forward price when expectations were in error not interfere with the flow of the commodity into domestic and international trade. Major reliance should be placed upon direct payments to producers if the forward price were higher than actual market price. Thus markets would be allowed to clear, except as it was desirable to add to stocks from a relatively large output of a storable crop.

During a depression, if one should occur, it would be advisable to establish forward prices at a level above that which would be an estimate of market prices. This procedure would have several advantages. First, it would mean that the treatment of agricultural producers would be, roughly, comparable to the treatment of other groups in the economy. Second, the policy would constitute an additional means of preventing the cumulative destruction of purchasing power that normally occurs during the downturn of the cycle. There can be no doubt that price-support operations during 1949 and again during late 1953 were of value in maintaining money income in the economy and in preventing a greater decline in economic activity. Third, the maintenance of a relatively high level of income in agriculture would serve to maintain employment in certain rather volatile sectors of the economy, particularly in farm machinery.

The means for meeting the price commitments should be the same as during a full-employment period. Storage programs should be continued to partially offset output variations, though no attempt should be made to offset the decline in demand by increasing stocks during the depression. The techniques used in establishing the forward-price levels during a depression would probably have to be somewhat arbitrary. Certain guidelines might be established, however. Relative farm-product prices should not depart far from the relationship in the immediately preceding full-employment period, and, further, the absolute level of forward prices should reflect a downward drift in prices paid by farmers. Further, it would be reasonable to permit some decline in real farm income in order that farmers not be given a preferred income position during the depression. However, the decline in real income should be fairly moderate—

perhaps 15 to 20 percent—if the program is to have the advantages referred to above. It should be added that the proposal for forward prices during a depression is not intended as a substitute for an integrated monetary and fiscal policy for the stabilization of employment at high levels. It is suggested as one element in a broad-gaged attack upon the prevention of a cumulative downswing, and would be relatively impotent in a serious downswing if concerted activity were not used in other directions.

The price proposals suggested here are not intended to result in an income transfer to farm people during full-employment periods. It was argued earlier that such income transfers are not likely to have any significant, long-run effect upon the return to labor engaged in agriculture. In addition, the short-run transfers tend to go, primarily, to the highest income groups in agriculture. The proposal is made in the present form, not because it is argued that there is no problem of low incomes in agriculture, but rather that price policy is an ineffective means of contribution to the solution of such problems.

There are a large number of farm families, perhaps a million or more, who now realize less from the employment of their labor in agriculture than could be obtained if the same labor were employed elsewhere. There has been, and continues to be, a large transfer of labor force from agricultural to nonagricultural employments. But this transfer has not been rapid enough to bring real returns to comparable labor in agricultural and nonagricultural pursuits into approximate equality. During the past decade large changes have occurred in agriculture on this score. In the late thirties it was true for almost the whole of the United States that the returns to farm labor were substantially below the returns to comparable and employed nonfarm labor. Admittedly, the high level of unemployment that prevailed in the nonfarm sector as late as early 1941 makes comparisons of this sort questionable, but it is worthy of note that, by the end of World War II, most of the differences in labor returns had disappeared, except for the Southern States, most of Missouri, and an area immediately north of the Ohio River. Transfer of labor out of agriculture in the nonsouthern areas has continued, and the income differential sufficient to induce the movement is a relatively small one. However, in the South (and the other areas noted), the income differential that is associated with the current rate of outmovement is a very large one, of the order of $500 to $1,000 a year of labor.

There is little evidence that farm price policy has contributed or can contribute anything to narrowing this difference. It seems reasonable to argue that more information, and more accurate information, about alternative employment opportunities would help to increase the rate of labor transfer. Direct assistance to movement, such as locating jobs prior to movement, loans or grants to pay the cost of moving and to cover living expenses prior to the first paycheck, and assistance in locating housing might have a substantial impact. In the longer run, improvng the qualty of primary and secondary education in the low-income, agricultural areas might have the most substantial impact of all.

It may well be that the present excess of resources, especially labor, is so great that much more spectacular steps are required to reduce the resources engaged in agriculture. Many farm people in the more prosperous agricultural areas are now receiving lower incomes than people of the same skill and talents receive in the rest of the economy. While the decline in the income of farm operators since 1948 has been offset by the increase in income from nonagricultural resources, the income of the rest of the working force has increased substantially since then.[14]

But it is clear that the movement of people off farms will have to be substantially greater in the next few years than the large movement of the last 5 years if our farm people are to have satisfactory incomes. The program outlined above, if it had been put into effect several years ago, might have been adequate to meet needs of the next few years. But at the present time, consideration should perhaps be given to a proposal called homesteads in reverse that has been made by my colleague, Prof. T. W. Schultz.

Professor Schultz describes his proposal as follows:[15]

> One important way would be to offer, say, $5,000, to any farm family now operating a farm, giving all of its time to farming, and producing not less than $2,500 of products—to help the family to acquire a home in some other sector of the economy where the family wants to live and work, provided the family stays at the new location not less than 5 years. These grants would be "homesteads in reverse."

Even if a million farm families chose to accept such a payment, the cost of the program would not be more than what we have spent on farm programs during the past 30 months. The advantage of Schultz' proposal is that it would make a basic contribution to the solution of our farm problem, while the expenditures on the present types of programs seem to be making the situation worse.

### VI. THE PROBLEMS OF TRANSITION

There have been times in the past when it would not have been at all difficult to change from the then current price-support programs to one such as that outlined above, assuming agreements as to the desirability of the change. But such is not the case today. The large stocks of many farm commodities that exist at present, or will exist in the near future, constitute a real barrier to any modification of farm-price programs. It these stocks were abruptly released and placed upon the market, price decines of 25 to 50 percent could be expected in many instances. It would take from 1 to 2 years before current demand for consumption and production once again became the dominant price determining considerations.

So drastic a readjustment in prices would mean the political doom of any new price program. This was recognized by President Eisenhower in his proposal to establish a special emergency reserve of farm products. This reserve was to be sterilized, and withdrawals made only under special conditions, such as in case of war or to meet emergency situations arising in friendly nations.[16] While the justi-

---

[14] A change to the price program described above would have to be accompanied by some form of income supplementation as a means of preventing a drastic, short-run decline in farm incomes. Some aspects of this problem are discussed briefly in the next section.

[15] T. W. Schultz, Homesteads in Reverse, Farm Policy Forum, summer 1956, pp. 14–15.

[16] However, the main effect of the reserve has been to result in higher support prices for some products than would have been established otherwise, given the other features of the price-support legislation and the extensive foreign surplus-disposal operations.

fication for establishing a stockpile of farm products on the grounds of military necessity rests on somewhat dubious grounds if we were starting from scratch, so to speak, there may be some merit in trying to create some virtue out of past and present vices. The large stocks of farm products which existed in 1941 and again in 1950 reduced somewhat the difficulties of the transition to a war economy. And it might be argued that if we were to be subjected to aerial attack in another war, the value of appropriately dispersed food reserves might be substantial. But, in trying to make virtue out of vice, we should not forget the costs of such a program. Ignoring the costs of the commodities themselves, it costs between 15 and 20 cents per year per bushel to store wheat and corn, for example. Thus, to store for a decade a billion bushels, which are readily available, would cost between $1.5 billion and $2 billion. This is a large total cost in some absolute sense, but some perspective may be gained by comparing it with one's estimate of total defense expenditures for the same span of time.

However, the present stocks of several farm commodities are much larger than can be justified as an emergency reserve. Some reduction of the size of these stocks is required if current supply and demand conditions are to be accurately reflected in market prices. As a result, a program might be adopted of reducing the size of the stocks to the desired level over a period of approximately 3 years. During that period, the level of price supports might be kept near their present levels, but market prices should be allowed to be free of direct governmental intervention. The producers should then be paid the difference between the support price and the market price. A procedure similar to this is now being followed for wool, and other examples have been noted earlier. By the end of the transition period, some effort should be made to establish the support prices at a level that would equate the amount produced and the amount consumed if the stock liquidation were not occurring.

## VII. CONCLUSION [17]

During the past two decades, our efforts to achieve greater liberalization of international trade frequently have been accommodated to the actual or presumed needs of our agricultural price-support pro-

---

[17] It has not been possible in a short essay to discuss all the issues relevant to the interrelations and inconsistencies between international trade and agricultural policy. Two important omissions may be noted—problems arising from price instability in internationally traded products, and the implications of our efforts to aid certain areas of the world in their economic development. The omission of the second—aid to economic development in low-income countries—may be justified on the ground that the changes in comparative advantage that may result cannot be predicted at this time. In any case, such changes as may occur in the demand for American farm products—either in a favorable or unfavorable direction—will be spread over a sufficient period of time to permit gradual adjustments.

The first omission is more serious, however, and can be justified, if at all, only on the grounds that we know so little about the possibility of reducing the erratic, short-run instability of prices of many internationally traded goods. Reference may be made to the price behavior of wool and jute during 1950, 1951, and 1952. Wool prices increased more than 150 percent between the first half of 1950 and the first quarter of 1951, and then declined by 60 percent by the third quarter of 1951. Jute prices increased by more than 150 percent between the second half of 1950 and the second quarter of 1951, and then declined by 75 percent by the third quarter of 1952. These violent changes resulted, primarily, from variations in the willingness to hold inventories, and, in the case of jute, from the response of producers to the very high price in mid-1951.

It may be noted that the proposals outlined in section V would go some distance in minimizing the effects of this type of price variability upon the plans made by farmers and upon their incomes. The forward prices would serve as guides for production planning, and the guaranties implicit in the proposals would at least moderate the effects on income of drastic downturns in prices that occur at times.

grams. While the trade restrictions and export subsidization have had the effect of protecting and expanding American farm output, and thus creating some inefficiency in the use of our resources, perhaps the most important consequence has been the picture of American indecision and inconsistency that we have created in the minds of our friends and allies. Our vacillation between freeing and restricting trade has certainly cast doubts upon both our sincerity and our ability to carry forward constructive international economic policies.

Most of the adjustments that are required for consistency in our trade and agricultural policies require modification of the farm price policies. The current price policies require various forms of interferences with trade in order that specific price programs can operate without the accumulation of exceptionally large stocks or requiring large expenditures from the Treasury. However, at the present time even with the absolute prohibition of some imports (butter, for example) and large export subsidies on others (wheat), stocks of many farm commodities have become so large as to create significant problems of management.

The required modification of the farm price policies would not be damaging to the income position of labor employed in agriculture, for the past and present farm programs have not had any significant influence on labor incomes in agriculture. In most of American agriculture the level of labor incomes is dependent primarily upon the availability of jobs in the nonfarm sector and upon the relative ease of changing from farm to nonfarm jobs, not upon the level of farm price supports.

# PROBLEMS OF DOMESTIC AGRICULTURE AND GOVERNMENTAL AGRICULTURAL POLICIES IN RELATION TO OUR TARIFF AND FOREIGN TRADE POLICY

**Ernest T. Baughman, assistant vice president, Federal Reserve Bank of Chicago**

It seems appropriate to state briefly the basic objective of our foreign policy and the purpose of international trade before proceeding to a consideration of problems of domestic agriculture and governmental agricultural policies in relation to our basic international economic and trade policy.

## FOREIGN POLICY

The foreign policy of the United States is aimed basically at improving our security and well-being. And this is the aim of our economic and trade policies, also. It would be folly, indeed, to follow international trade policies which were inconsistent with the basic aim of our foreign policy (which includes, in addition to economic and trade policy, our military, political, and social relations with other countries). Similarly, if domestic policies are inconsistent with our foreign-trade policy, we find ourselves in an awkward situation wherein one hand tends to undo what the other accomplishes. This paper is directed, in part, to a consideration of some of the cause-and-effect relations of domestic agricultural policies to foreign-trade policy and related problems.

## ROLE OF TRADE

The prosperity of the United States has been built largely on specialization. The advantages to be gained from each person doing the job he knows best—farmer, merchant, mechanic, lawyer, doctor, etc.—are obvious. But individual specialization is of no purpose unless combined with its Siamese twin, trade. (And the benefits of trade are independent of any differences in levels of income of the individual producers.)

Quite obvious, also, are the advantages of specialization by region. Many commodities cannot be produced outside their usual areas except at a considerable increase in cost and a very considerable list not at all. Well-known mining, agricultural, and industrial areas have emerged as a result of the regional differences in soil, climate, location, and other factors. But, as with occupational specialization, there is little object in specializing by region unless there is an exchange of the results of such specialization. While this is perfectly obvious within a community and between geographical regions within a nation which is accustomed to free trade within its borders, it seems to be much less obvious as between nations. Nevertheless, it should be obvious that international trade merely permits the widespread realization of the benefits of specialization. (And, as with trading between individuals in the same area, or different areas within a nation, the benefits of trade are independent of the income levels of the individuals whose products are traded.)

The need for trade—domestic and international—grows out of the immobility of resources. Land, labor, and capital have varying degrees of mobility between areas, and between nations, ranging from zero for land to a very high degree of mobility for short-term capital. The movement of goods and services is the most effective substitute available for the movement of the factors of production and, in fact, is essential to the provision of that abundance which adds up to an American standard of living.

Man's desire for a rising level of real income is sufficient reason to justify his interest in achieving a rising efficiency in the utilization of resources. But for the major part of two decades now there has been another prime reason. Our military strength depends heavily upon the strength of the supporting economy. Economic strength, in turn, depends upon efficient use of human and other resources. And, impressive as it is, the resources of the United States alone could prove inadequate to insure our security. It is deemed essential, therefore, that the resources of the free world be utilized with maximum efficiency. And efficiency would be reduced greatly if each nation were to attempt to build exclusively on its own resources. Furthermore, there is a strong tendency for military and political interests to be alined with trade channels.

Thus, the problems of domestic agriculture and governmental agricultural policies must be considered against a backdrop of a foreign policy which aims basically at improving our security and well-being. Insofar as our domestic agricultural policies contribute to an efficient utilization of resources and to amicable relations with other countries, they make a positive contribution to our foreign-policy aims; insofar as they detract from these goals, their contribution is negative. The problem is to find ways to accentuate the positive while achieving desirable domestic objectives.

## PROBLEMS OF DOMESTIC AGRICULTURE

The basic problem of United States agriculture is that too many resources, especially manpower, are engaged in the production of agricultural commodities. The result has been an output of agricultural commodities in excess of that which can be sold at prices deemed reasonable. The resulting returns to many farmers for their labor and capital have been substantially below the average returns to comparable labor and capital engaged in many other pursuits.

But this situation is not new. The output of agricultural commodities in the United States has tended in the direction of surplus since the early 1920's. Technological developments which make possible increased output per acre, per man-hour, and per animal have permitted increased output with fewer workers. In most years supplies of a number of commodities have exceeded the amounts markets would absorb at what were considered "fair" prices.

Sporadic relief from burdensome supply situations was provided by severe and widespread drought in the middle thirties, the onset of World War II, the foreign-aid programs in the late forties, and the outbreak of hostilities in Korea. However, each of these gave fresh stimulus to expanding production and some brought forth programs for enlarging carryovers, e. g., the ever-normal granary in the 1930's and the 1954 set-asides. Since 1954 attention has focused on programs to expand disposition of surpluses, particularly in foreign markets, and on programs to further curb current output.

Government price-support programs have been an important feature of our domestic farm policy, beginning about 1929. During the 1930's, both domestic and foreign demand were weak. Support programs were intended to raise farm prices and incomes from their depression lows.

Following outbreak of World War II, domestic and foreign demand strengthened and support prices were no longer needed to raise market prices, but were used to provide incentives to farmers to engage in all-out production without fear of market collapse. Price supports, which previously had been at lower levels, were raised to 90 percent of parity on a wide range of farm commodities, but, nevertheless, remained largely inoperative through the war and early postwar years as market prices were held above support prices by the large wartime and "reconstruction" demands, financed in part through a variety of foreign-aid programs.

Price supports have been continued at levels which have encouraged farmers to maintain or expand production even though foreign demand declined as agricultural production in Western Europe and other areas recovered. As world market prices declined below domestic support prices, large stocks were acquired by the Commodity Credit Corporation. Despite the development of programs to curb output, expand domestic consumption, and increase exports, surpluses have persisted. These conditions—of excess supplies and heavy dependence on Government assistance—can be expected to continue at least until such time as the amount of resources utilized in the production of agricultural commodities is adjusted to the required level.

Resource adjustment has been taking place, but not fast enough to bring the agricultural situation into balance. The farm population has been declining and the farm labor force has declined even faster. But the transfer of workers out of agriculture and into nonagricultural pursuits has not yet proved adequate to offset the effects of the fast pace of improvement in farm technology, the relatively high rural birth rates, and the relatively inflexible price supports and inelastic demand for agricultural commodities.

The problem is not entirely one of farm population and work force. Farmers have continued a high rate of new investment which has had the result of expanding capacity even after the exceptional demands of war and reconstruction had passed. A slowing, for a time at least, of the rate of new capital investment that is primarily of the output-expanding type would prove helpful. (New investment which is primarily cost reducing should prove desirable, if accompanied with flexible prices, as it tends to strengthen the competitive position of the lower cost producers.)

### CONFLICTS WITH INTERNATIONAL ECONOMIC POLICY

Domestic agricultural price policies come into conflict with our aims to achieve an efficient utilization of the resources of the United States and the "free world" at several points. Once a specific set of support prices has been established as a domestic goal the support program comes into conflict with our international goals whenever the world price falls below prices in domestic markets. In this situation our commodities are priced out of world markets. The United States becomes a residual supplier, that is, exports only the amount desired at the support price after other countries have disposed of their salable supplies. Domestic supplies in excess of this amount are acquired by CCC and as these stocks increase in size they become an unsettling factor in both domestic and world markets. Farmers, private traders, and governments alike expect that the stocks will be moved into consumption at some time, but there is uncertainty as to both the probable time and price.

Furthermore, a United States policy of maintaining a support price, for a commodity in which we provide a substantial proportion of world exports, above the price which would prevail in a "free" market, and exporting only the amount that can be sold at that price, provides a price umbrella for producers in other countries as well as in the United States. This promotes new investment as farmers in both the United States and other countries respond to the attractive price. However, output in the United States may be restrained under these supply conditions by acreage allotments, marketing quotas, or other measures. To the extent that such measures are effective, United States exports are replaced by increased output in other countries.

Finally, domestic prices, supported above world prices, tend to attract imports. Thus, while domestic products are priced too high to compete effectively in world markets and United States farmers are restrained from making a full and efficient utilization of their resources, imports may be attracted in increasing volume. If allowed to enter, they increase domestic stocks and add to the difficulties and cost of making the support program effective. This leads to demands for added restrictions on imports; objections may arise to allowing imports to share at all in the supported market.

As surpluses increase and production curbs begin to "pinch," interest often turns to exports as providing a possible solution for domestic agricultural problems. Subsidies and other special export programs may be utilized in an effort to achieve a larger volume of exports. However, the sale of commodities below domestic prices often is viewed by producers in other countries as providing unfair competition and may lead to retaliatory action. The United States, for example, has provided authority for countervailing duties in instances of this sort (sec. 201 of the Anti-Dumping Act, 1921, and sec. 303 of the Tariff Act of 1930). Nor is the adverse reaction limited to countries which receive the subsidized exports. Other countries which export the same or similar goods may feel that the subsidized exports encroach upon their markets. The result can be a proliferation of threats and retaliatory actions as individual nations take steps intended to insulate their own producers from the "unfair" competition of other countries.

It is quite obvious that the end result of such actions could easily be a maze of trade restrictions which preclude consumers in each nation from realizing the full benefits of specialization and maximum efficiency in the use of human and natural resources. But this alone is not the worst feature of the conflicts between domestic agricultural policy and our foreign policy goal, namely, to improve the security and well-being of the United States.

The United States is the largest and strongest by far of the "free" nations and is in a relatively favorable position insofar as its dependence upon trade. The wide range of resources found within its borders is extremely rare. Reflecting this broad and diversified economic base, the foreign trade of the United States is relatively small as compared with its gross production. Nevertheless, exports are vital to many industries and we are wholly or partially dependent on imports for many essential items (coffee, tea, cocoa, sugar, wool, newsprint, natural rubber, copper, tin, lead, mica, industrial diamonds, chromite, manganest ore, and other items).

This is in sharp contrast with nations which have a narrow economic base. For the more specialized a nation's resources the greater is its dependence on international trade for improvement of living standards. It is understandable, therefore, that such nations will view with grave concern any actions which restrict their ability to sell the limited types of goods produced and from which they must necessarily earn exchange with which to purchase needed imports. This difference in relative importance of foreign trade to the economic welfare of different countries is an important factor which we cannot overlook in the conduct of our international economic policies.

As the leader of the "free world" forces, our actions necessarily speak louder than our words. And while we have subscribed to the view that the interests of the United States and the "free" world will be served best by a relatively free multilateral trade and convertible currencies, as indicated by our leadership in the reciprocal trade agreements program and our active participation or endorsement of a number of other programs, we have found it necessary to undertake restrictive measures in support of our domestic agricultural program.

Other nations, typically, are much more sensitive to such actions than is the United States. American discussions of import restrictions on wool, tuna, cheese, or any of a long list of commodities, while barely known outside of the producer groups immediately concerned, are front page news in other countries which depend heavily upon exports of the particular commodity. An atmosphere charged with threats and counterthreats to the economic well-being of nations is hardly conducive to the maintenance of strong military, political, and ideological loyalties.

## DO WE WANT TO EXPORT?

Although exports, overall, account for only about 8 percent of United States total production of movable goods, the proportion is much larger for many commodities. Agricultural products produced on about 1 harvested acre out of 10 have been exported in recent years. In the 1955 marketing year the following percentages of production of selected commodities were exported: Tallow, 42 percent; flue-cured tobacco, 37; wheat and flour, 36; milled rice, 34; prunes, 30; soybeans and soybean oil, 29; lard, 21; cotton, 16; barley, 11; oranges and tangerines, 7. Furthermore, the volume represented by even a relatively small proportion of total output often can have an important effect on the profit margins and economic health of individual industries.

But United States exporters, quite naturally, wish to receive payment, and in dollars. Buyers of United States exports obtain dollars largely by exporting to the United States. Additional dollars may be obtained from loans, grants, liquidation of investments, payment for services, etc. But there is no international currency. Sooner or later we must be paid in terms of imports of goods or services. Hence, if we want to sell abroad, and receive payment, we must stand ready to accept imports. A policy of holding a tight rein on imports by means of tariffs and other restrictions is inconsistent with a policy of seeking expanded exports.

### ECONOMIC DEVELOPMENT

Another facet of our international economic policy has been that of aiding and encouraging the maximum development of underdeveloped, friendly nations. Substantial amounts of assistance have been provided, both material and technical. Our objectives have been to assist such nations to raise their real income, to strengthen their ability to defend themselves from aggression, and to provide an economic environment conducive to the development of stable governments. Most underdeveloped areas are heavily dependent on exports of raw materials and semifinished goods to finance the capital goods required for effective utilization of their natural and human resources. Furthermore, there is every indication that the United States will require increasing amounts of imports of raw materials to provide the input for its expanding industrial complex.

To the extent that our resources can be utilized more efficiently by importing raw materials and producing manufactured goods for export, it clearly is to the mutual benefit of the underdeveloped areas and the United States that our domestic policies be formulated so as to encourage that kind of adjustment in utilization of resources. Such adjustments are not encouraged by policies which, for example, provide domestic price support above world price levels for wheat and subsidize the export of wheat in large volume. Similarly, such adjustments are not encouraged by policies which subsidize the use of domestic resources for the production of sugar and wool and restrict imports of such commodities from areas which are better adapted to their production and, incidentally, heavily dependent on their export to finance imports needed for consumption and economic development. Possibly the greatest assistance that the developed nations could be to the underdeveloped nations would be to move aggressively in the direction of freer international trade. And, since much of our trade is multilateral rather than bilateral, it would be to the benefit of the United States that any such move be undertaken jointly, as through the international trade agreement program and the GATT.

### POLICY ISSUES

The basic argument of this paper is that each feature of our international trade and domestic policies should always be considered against the background of how it fits into our national aim, and therefore the aim of our foreign policy, of improving the security and wellbeing of the United States.

*Price support*

Sociological considerations may make it imperative to provide Government assistance to buoy up agricultural income (although this is not established beyond question in prolonged periods of full employment and rapid economic expansion, overall. But such assistance need not be in the form of price supports which encourage increased output and interfere with the movement of commodities into domestic consumption and export. Many of the difficulties arising out of agricultural price supports in recent years, as these programs affect trade, are a direct result of the attempts to utilize support programs to raise farm income rather than as a stabilizing device. As noted above, price supports above world price levels stimulate production and interfere with trade. In exporting countries, supplies over and above domestic requirements can only be sold by means of export subsidies, sometimes direct and sometimes concealed as in some two-price systems. These subsidies inevitably put economically weak exporting countries at a disadvantage in relation to economically strong countries. In importing countries support levels above world prices lead to increased obstacles to world trade, usually in the form of quotas or variable exchange rates or alternatively heavy calls upon the Treasury and the taxpayer when price guaranties are implemented by such means as supplementary payments.

Supported prices. if used at all, should be utilized primarily as a stabilizing device, not primarily as a device to raise income, and should be held as near as possible to the level of prices in world markets. They can provide protection against large and sudden falls in prices, but even at these levels must retain a large degree of flexibility if they are to avoid substantial interference with the movement of commodities into consumption at home and abroad. Price supports should be modified so as to encourage a gradual reduction of high cost, uneconomic production of agricultural commodities, and to speed up the transfer of manpower from low-income agricultural areas to urban occupation. If, during the transition period, programs are needed to support farmers' incomes, primary emphasis should be placed on measures other than price supports. Furthermore, support programs should be so designed as to permit the greatest possible flexibility of agricultural production in response to consumer demand so as to achieve the most efficient use of agricultural and other resources and minimize the costs of the support program to the community.

There is an evident tendency to view our domestic price-support programs as paramount to our foreign policy and to underrate the tremendous stake which the United States has in effective international cooperation to maintain the peace and to build a successful mutual-security program to protect the free world. To make our foreign aid and development programs fully effective in strengthening the economies of overseas countries and to enable them to earn the dollar exchange they need to buy commodities from us, we have urged them to increase their productivity, to integrate their production more effectively, to adapt themselves to exporting and to remove or reduce some of their trade barriers to imports. These are compelling reasons why the United States as the leader of the free world forces should make every possible effort to minimize conflicts between domestic agricultural programs and our foreign economic policy.

*Reciprocal trade agreements*

Available evidence indicates that the reciprocal trade agreements program has served farmers and other residents of the United States very well. The program has helped to reduce existing trade barriers and to deter the development of new ones. This has been accomplished largely by centering tariff bargaining in the international arena where the interests of both exporters and importers of individual commodities are considered simultaneously and where interest may be focused on the multilateral characteristics of trade for a variety of commodities. Consistent with the objective of our foreign policy aim of improving the security and well-being of the United States, the authority for the reciprocal trade agreements program should be continued and broadened in the interest of increasing the efficiency of resource utilizations in the free world and expanding the markets for United States goods. Any lesser action would almost certainly touch off a wave of nationalism and protectionism which could seriously hinder the efforts of the free world to develop an effective mutual-security program.

*Export subsidies*

Over 40 percent of the $3.1 billion of agricultural commodities shipped abroad in fiscal 1954–55 was aided by one or more Government programs to facilitate exports, according to a study made for the Interagency Committee on Agricultural Surplus Disposal. The percentage probably has been higher in subsequent years. A substantial portion of the Government-assisted exports ($787 million estimated export value) were subsidized in the sense that they were sold for export at prices below domestic market prices. The export subsidies are of several types and are provided under several authorities. In general, they have the effect of providing assistance to United States farmers from the Treasury in their competitive struggle for foreign markets. It is understandable that this is viewed as unfair competition in the eyes of many farmers in other countries and can lead to efforts to obtain the imposition of additional trade barriers and offsetting subsidies. Thus, export subsidies should be utilized with great restraint. Reliance on export subsidies provides prima facie evidence that resources are not being put to their most efficient use. Domestic consumers are discriminated against in the sense that commodities are made available more cheaply to consumers in other countries, and this is a policy of questionable merit except possibly as a part of a foreign-aid program. Furthermore, subsidized exports inevitably tend to strengthen dependence upon Government and weaken dependence on private initiative in the development and conduct of international trade.

Possibly export subsidies should be authorized for any individual commodity for only a limited number of years and in decreasing amounts so as to encourage domestic adjustment in production; possibly greater emphasis should be placed on domestic disposal of surpluses and smaller amounts of funds utilized to subsidize exports; in the interest of minimizing dissension and possible retaliation by other countries, possibly export subsidies should be utilized only for commodities for which international agreements are in effect; possibly export subsidies should be gradually reduced and eventually eliminated as a major device for bridging (and thereby maintaining) the gap between domestic prices and world prices for agricultural commodities. As a trading device we have generally considered the use of export subsidies to be inconsistent with our objective of a relatively free multilateral trade but in our efforts to export larger amounts of surplus agricultural commodities we have been relying on export subsidies to an increasing extent.

*Section 22*

Section 22 of the Agricultural Adjustment Act provides that when the President determines that imports are materially interfering or are practically certain to materially interfere with any domestic agricultural program operated by the Department of Agriculture, he shall impose such additional fees or import quotas as he determines are necessary to prevent such interference. Additional import fees up to 50 percent ad valorem may be imposed under section 22, and import quotas may be established in amounts not less than 50 percent of the quantities imported during a previous representative period.

If domestic prices of agricultural commodities are to be supported above world levels, and the supported price is not to be extended to world supplies, some type of restriction on imports obviously is needed. Nevertheless, rigid restrictions on the volume of commodities that may enter the United States is inconsistent with our general trade objectives. A basic adjustment of our agricultural programs could eliminate the need for import quotas and strengthen the position of this country when it raises objections to the use of quantitative restrictions on imports of United States goods by other nations. In the absence of such action, section 22 should be revised so that it will interfere as little as possible with our leadership of the free world toward the goal of a relatively free multilateral trade and convertibility of currencies. Frequently overlooked is the large size of the United States market relative to that of other countries and relative to the amount of their exports of most commodities. Reducing or shutting off imports which may provide only a small part of our consumption of a commodity can have serious consequences to an exporting country which depends heavily on sales of that commodity for its dollar exchange.

Possibly the interests of friendly countries should receive greater consideration than is provided in section 22 in the establishment of import quotas or additional fees. Although interested parties are usually consulted before action is taken under section 22, the act probably should require it, consistent with our sponsorship of cooperative actions. Since section 22 is intended to protect domestic programs its import restrictions possibly should be applicable only to those imports induced by the domestic programs—that the imposition of an import quota should be at a level that permits imports equal to 100 percent of these imported in some representative base period prior to the agricultural program concerned, or that some minimum volume of imports should be permitted, as for example, equal to the percentage of the domestic consumption which was provided by imports in some representative base period. In general, quotas probably should lean in the direction of liberality in view of their inherent repressive effect on trade. As a minimum, United States policy relative to import quotas, and similar quantitative limitations on imports should not move further away from the principles established in the reciprocal trade agreements program and the GATT, and preferably should move in the direction of increased compatibility with them; namely, to minimize the use of quantitative restrictions on imports. However, the basic problem is that price supports are established without due consideration of world market prices and this impedes efforts toward removal of trade barriers.

*Foreign currency sales*

A very substantial volume of agricultural commodities has been exported under programs authorizing sale for foreign currencies. The cost, and the impact on other countries, of a foreign currency sales program are not easy to determine. The transaction assumes the nature of a gift when the foreign currency is made available to the country government for uses beneficial to it and without repayment obligation; it assumes the nature of a loan when the currency is available to the country government for uses beneficial to it but with an obligation to repay; it assumes the nature of barter if the currency is for the use of the United States in lieu of dollar purchases; and finally, to the extent that a country prefers to allocate local currency rather than dollars to the procurement of commodities and the uses of the local currency are restricted, the transaction assumes the characteristics of a special price deal and may become an instrument for compensating for import restrictions and exchange controls.

Probably it is fair to say that most countries which export the same or similar commodities as are exported by the United States for foreign currencies view the transactions under our programs as special price deals involving varying amounts of subsidy. Numerous objections have been lodged with our Department of State. On the other hand, countries which have benefited substantially from the programs have shown favorable reactions.

The programs are an outgrowth of domestic price-support programs and the large stocks acquired by CCC. A number of the trade practices followed under these programs are inconsistent with our foreign trade goals. We have generally considered bilateral government trading, sales for export at prices below domestic prices, linking sales under preferential conditions with sales under normal market terms, settlement in blocked currencies as restrictive practices which are inconsistent with the development of an expanding international trade based on an efficient utilization of resources.

Sales for foreign currencies, and other subsidized export programs, tend to displace exports for dollars and can be expected gradually to assume greater importance in the foreign trade of the United States if permitted to expand. Several studies of the possible uses of surplus agricultural commodities have concluded that the best opportunities for increasing exports without risking substantial displacement of United States exports for dollars or of usual exports of friendly countries exist in the low-income, low-consumption areas. Exports at special prices, for foreign currencies, grants for relief feeding, etc., should be directed largely to such areas, and under arrangements which assure that they will, in fact, result in increased consumption in those areas. It is possible also for agricultural surpluses to provide some contribution to programs designed to accelerate capital development in underdeveloped areas. The United States would appear to be well advised to direct its special export programs, to the extent that they are to be used to help relieve the surpluses generated by our domestic programs, primarily to the export of commodities to the low-consumption, underdeveloped areas. The financial returns to the United States would be small, especially in the short run but the cost in terms of deterioration of economic relations with other friendly nations would be minimized. And it is quite possible that the orientation of special exports to these areas would prove even more effective in the building of permanent markets than sales for foreign currencies to high-consumption areas.

*Summary*

Domestic agricultural programs which conflict with our foreign policy aim of improving the well-being and security of the United States should be subjected to critical review. A relatively free, multilateral international trade and convertibility of currencies is consistent with a domestic economy organized primarily on the basis of competitive private enterprises. That type of world trade will enable private United States exporters and importers to participate effectively. The alternative is to move progressively in the direction of an increasing dependence on state trading in which an efficient utilization of resources often becomes a secondary consideration, and a form of trading in which governments having highly centralized control of their domestic economies can conduct more effectively than the government of a country in which economic decisions rest largely in private hands and are made largely in response to competitive markets.

Price-support programs which attempt to maintain a domestic level of prices above the world level inevitably will be in conflict with a goal of a relatively free international trade. This should be recognized openly. Also, such price-support programs tend to interfere with the most efficient allocation of resources and provide a heavy financial drain on the Treasury, thereby contributing to inflationary pressures in periods of full employment and high economic activity. Furthermore, it is not necessary that the desired assistance to agriculture be provided by means of price supports set independent of world market prices. The desired supplements to farm income can be provided by other means. Finally, the benefits of competitive market prices, domestic and international, are so great that domestic agricultural programs which interfere materially with such prices should be adopted only under the most compelling emergencies and then after consultation with other interested governments which may help to provide a mutually acceptable solution to the basic economic or security problem.

The United States cannot escape her position of responsibility in shaping the course of economic policy in the free world. Individual features of our domestic and foreign economic policies should be considered against this backdrop. In the absence of forthright moves to adjust domestic price policies to the realities of international markets and a rational utilization of resources within and between countries there is little opportunity to make progress toward a resolution of the policy conflicts which have developed.

## AMERICAN AGRICULTURE AND FOREIGN TRADE POLICY

**The American Farm Bureau Federation, John C. Lynn, legislative director**

The American Farm Bureau Federation appreciates this opportunity to contribute to the study being made by the Subcommittee on Foreign Trade Policy of the Ways and Means Committee.

Pursuant to a letter from Chairman Boggs, we are limiting our comments primarily to (1) the importance of export markets to American farmers, (2) the questions of conflict that may be involved between the objectives of our tariff and foreign trade policies and domestic price support and adjustment programs, (3) a discussion of section 22 of the Agricultural Adjustment Act, and (4) brief mention of the trade agrements program and its importance to agriculture.

*How important are export markets to American farmers?*

American agriculture has a vital interest in the maintenance and expansion of our foreign trade outlets. Farmers know their prosperity is closely linked to the maintenance of a high level of agricultural exports.

The maintenance of a high level of exports is of great importance, not only to the producers of export crops but also to the producers of all other agricultural commodities. We have been exporting in recent years the production from some 50 million acres of cropland. If we lose our export outlets and find it necessary to take out of production the millions of acres of cropland now devoted to the production of commodities for export, this land undoubtedly will be shifted to the production of another commodity such as dairy products, beef cattle, fruits and vegetables, poultry and poultry products. This increased production within the United States would expand the supply of these commodities, and consequently reduce the price and income of these producers.

We sincerely believe in freer international trade. We believe that such trade among nations not only raises the level of living of people involved, but likewise is a cohesive force for peace. Farm Bureau believes there is more to be gained by continued efforts to reduce quotas and other restrictive trade devices than there is in efforts to arbitrarily divide by agreements of one kind and another the smaller markets resulting from such restrictions.

Insofar as United States policy relating to international trade is concerned, we believe it should be designed to promote trade with other nations on a fair basis and at a high level.

The progress being made in expanding exports of agricultural commodities is very encouraging. Agricultural exports in 1953 were at a level of only $2.8 billion. This was increased only slightly in 1954 and 1955. In fiscal year 1956 we exported $3.5 billion of agricultural commodities but in the fiscal year ending June 30, 1957, agricultural exports reached an alltime high—$4,724 million as follows:

*Agricultural exports, fiscal year 1957*

[Millions of dollars]

| Commodity | Total exports | Exports under Government programs [1] | Outside of programs | Percentage under Government programs |
|---|---|---|---|---|
| Grains and feeds | 1,600 | 980 | 620 | 61 |
| Cotton | 1,115 | 525 | 580 | 47 |
| Livestock products (dairy) | 700 | 240 | 460 | 34 |
| Vegetable oil and oil seeds | 455 | 135 | 320 | 30 |
| Fruits and vegetables | 363 | 25 | 338 | 7 |
| Tobacco | 340 | 30 | 310 | 9 |
| Other | 151 | 10 | 141 | 7 |
| Total | 4,724 | 1,945 | 2,779 | 41 |

[1] Programs: Public Law 480 all titles, Mutual Security, 402, Export-Import Bank loans (only $70,000,000).

Source: USDA estimates.

While these gains are encouraging, the picture may look brighter than it actually is, since it is estimated that about 70 percent of our agricultural exports were made possible by direct or indirect Government subsidy programs. We would make it clear that we are not condemning these interim programs that have enabled us to increase our agricultural exports; however, it is imperative that American agriculture not become overdependent on these types of sales. Our export market must be developed through commercial channels for dollars whenever and wherever possible.

*Domestic agricultural policies and foreign trade*

Wisely conceived and properly administered price-support programs can help facilitate opportunity for farm families to earn high net incomes. But price supports at levels determined by Government without regard to supply and demand relationships operate to reduce net farm incomes. Whenever political solutions to essentially economic problems are sought, everyone should analyze carefully the possible adverse consequences. History records that there are many. Any price-support program, to be of benefit, must complement our free-choice production and distribution system.

In addition to the adverse effects of unsound Government price policies, there are many other obstacles to a healthy expansion of international trade in agricultural commodities. Among them are (*a*) the scarcity of dollars in several countries (this limits their ability to buy our exports), (*b*) import restrictions, either in the form of quantitative restrictions or dollar allocations, (*c*) currency manipulation and exchange controls. The effect of these and other Government policies, both in and outside the United States makes it necessary to have programs designed to overcome to the maximum extent possible these deterrents to increased trade.

The Agricultural Trade and Development Act (Public Law 480) was a program designed to tap the nondollar market. This program has been extremely successful in expanding agricultural exports. However, farm bureau considers Public Law 480 and similar programs as temporary. We hope that effective steps will be taken to adjust the United States agricultural production plan to effective market demand and avoid the accumulation of large surplus stocks in Government warehouses. Until we begin to approach this objective, it will be necessary to rely to some extent on Public Law 480 and other export subsidy programs, if we are to export at a high level and keep down burdensome surpluses.

Certainly no one in the United States has less responsibility than the American Farm Bureau Federation for the continuation in peacetime of the high, fixed, wartime support prices for certain agricultural commodities that contributed so much to creating these surpluses. Since 1947 we have consistently and aggressively worked to evolve price-support and adjustment programs designed to protect and expand markets, thereby serving the real interests of farmers and the general public.

*What is a fair basis on which to conduct international trade?*

As stated before, farm bureau believes that international trade should be on a fair basis and at a high level. Application of this principle to United States Government price policies has particular significance to the American farmer and to friendly nations throughout the world.

We agree that it is not fair on a continuing basis to subsidize the production of surpluses of our export crops through policies which require Government surplus disposal programs to market the commodity. That is why we have insisted that so-called "surplus disposal" programs should be temporary. We are not interested in their becoming "a way of life."

That is why we have insisted that Government price policies on "supported" commodities should be consistent with production objectives. We should keep in mind that the 6 so-called basic commodities having price supports, about which we have heard much discussion, account for less than 25 percent of United States cash farm receipts and that commodities accounting for over 50 percent of cash farm receipts have no Government price supports.

This objective of conducting international trade in farm products on a "fair basis" cannot be attained by proposals to assure producers a relatively high price for that portion of a crop sold domestically—or for a part of that portion of the crop sold domestically as in the case the "three price" wheat proposal which has been under discussion for some time in the United States.

United States feed grain and livestock producers are as frightened by the possibility of this sort of "economic dumping" on a permanent basis in the domestic market as are the producers in other wheat exporting countries who have analyzed its implications to them.

What is the real test of "fairness" so far as the production and export sales policy of any government with respect to price-supported agricultural commodities?

Is such test whether the supported commodity is sold for export at a price not lower than the price at which the production of the commodity was induced by government programs? Such programs include loans, purchases, blend price arrived at by multiple price schemes, payments (incentive payments, deficiency payments, compensatory payments, production payments, etc.) and other similar devices.

We would like to reaffirm our belief that production payments and similar devices are undesirable (1) as a substitute for price supports or (2) as a method of bringing income to agriculture or (3) as a method for increasing international trade. In fact, we believe if such governmental devices were to be put in operation, it will lead to less income for farmers and serious disruption in international trade in agricultural commodities.

*The need for section 22*

The subcommittee specifically asked for comments on section 22.

Section 22 originally was enacted in 1935 as an amendment to the Agricultural Adjustment Act of 1933. It has since been amended and reenacted on a number of occasions. In brief, section 22 authorizes the imposition of import quotas or fees whenever increased imports threaten to materially interfere with the operation of certain domestic programs designed to increase the prices and incomes received by producers.

In the opinion of the American Farm Bureau Federation some authority to restrict the imports of farm products is necessary and desirable as long as it is a national policy to attempt to raise the domestic prices of farm commodities above the world level. Unless such authority is retained on the statute books and effectively used when necessary, any domestic program which successfully raised farm prices above the world level would attract a flood of imports.

This in effect would force United States domestic programs to undertake the burden of supporting world prices. The inevitable result would be to nullify the effects of domestic programs, or to impose an intolerable burden on the United States Treasury.

The marketing agreement programs which attempt to improve prices by regulating marketings could be rendered completely ineffective by increased imports. Where prices are supported by loan or purchase programs, increased imports almost inevitably mean that the Government must take over a larger percentage of the domestic production.

In extreme cases imports could take over the entire United States market and force the entire United States production into the hands of the Commodity Credit Corporation. Wheat is an example of a commodity where this could happen if it were not for the quotas that have been imposed under the authority of section 22. Authority to restrict imports is also necessary to prevent the reimportation of surplus products exported at reduced prices, or in exchange for foreign currencies.

While the Farm Bureau has supported the use of section 22 as a measure for the protection of domestic programs, we have opposed its use when the real objective has been to impose trade barriers rather than to protect domestic programs.

Section 22 contains a number of safeguards designed to prevent abuse. Import fees may not be imposed at a rate in excess of 50 percent ad valorem. Imports may not be limited by quota to less than 50 percent of the quantity of a commodity that was imported during a representative period. These provisions are intended to prevent section 22 from being used to completely embargo imports, and to permit the continued importation of products that might be expected to come in in the absence of a domestic support program.

Another safeguard against abuse is to be found in the fact that groups desiring import restrictions must present convincing evidence to administrative authorities that imports are a threat to domestic programs before action can be taken under section 22.

While foreign countries naturally dislike any action that reduces their ability to sell in the United States, the orderly procedure provided in section 22 is more acceptable to other countries than arbitrary actions imposed without a careful study of the circumstances of individual cases. For example, there has been much less foreign resentment against the import quotas imposed on dairy products under section 22 than there was against the quotas imposed under section 104 of the Defense Production Act a few years ago. The difference is that section 104 quotas were imposed in an arbitrary fashion rather than by the orderly procedure that is required under section 22.

It must be conceded that quotas and import fees imposed under section 22 are an interference with international trade, and that such restrictions make it more difficult to build the export markets that are badly needed for farm products. The fault, however, lies with domestic price support policies and not with section 22, itself. While the authority provided by section 22 will be needed as long as we maintain domestic price support programs, the extent to which this authority must be used depends on the level at which we attempt to support domestic agricultural prices.

The chief administrative problem encountered under section 22 appears to be the time required to obtain action. This is a very serious problem in the case of marketing agreement programs for perishable commodities. Many such commodities have a short marketing season. Unless action can be taken quickly when increased imports threaten to nullify the effects of a marketing agreement program, producers may suffer irreparable damage.

From time to time we have suggested both legislative and administrative action, designed to overcome some of the administrative problems connected with section 22. We believe that some progress has been made in this connection.

*Reciprocal Trade Agreements Act*

Even though consideration of the Reciprocal Trade Agreements Act will be the subject of future hearings by the Ways and Means Committee, Farm Bureau believes that this act must be extended in 1958 as a real instrument for the implementation of a sound foreign trade policy. We will, of course, present in more detail our policies dealing with the trade agreements program following the annual meeting in December 1957 of the official elected voting delegates from the 48 State farm bureaus and Puerto Rico.

We believe the work of this subcommittee will be very benefical to the policymakers, both in and out of government, as consideration is given these vital programs dealing with domestic and foreign economic policies.

# FULL PARITY FAMILY FARM INCOME PROTECTION PROGRAM—A UNITED STATES FARM, FOOD, AND FIBER POLICY THAT MAKES INTERNATIONAL GOOD SENSE

James G. Patton, president, National Farmers Union

The existing sliding scale farm price support philosophy and the law of the Federal Government seriously interfers with the conduct of an intelligent and desirable foreign economy policy. Moreover, the existing foreign economic policy of our Nation is neither as intelligent nor as effective as it ought to be and could be if less official solicitude were spent to preserve vast monopolist international cartels and more concern were exercised for the coordinated economic development of democratic nations in the interests of all their citizens.

*Farmers have direct interest in foreign economic policy*

National Farmers Union is a member of the International Federation of Agricultural Producers, an organization made up of national farm organizations of many countries of the free world. As president of National Farmers Union of the United States, I am vice president and a member of the executive committee of that organization. IFAP, for all of its 10 years, has taken an active interest in improved farm life and increased consumer purchasing power throughout the free world in an expanding free economy.

For many years, also, as president of National Farmers Union, I was a member of the public advisory boards of Economic Cooperation Administration, Mutual Security Administration, and Foreign Operations Administration. National Farmers Union members have served as members of United States delegations to all of the early meetings leading up to the establishment of Food and Agriculture Organization and of the United Nations and many of their subsequent meetings.

As a result of this intimate participation in these programs we in National Farmers Union have gained and maintained an active and informed interest in all phases of United States foreign economic policy, trade policies as well as programs of technical assistance and economic development. State and National officials and staff members of Farmers Union have played active roles in the development and conduct of our Nation's foreign trade policies and programs of technical assistance and foreign economic development.

Our participation in these affairs has been grounded upon the direct and manifest interest in them on the part of Farmers Union members and farmers generally, both as citizens and as farmers.

*Farmers' interest in foreign affairs*

Farmers' basic interest in foreign affairs, economic and political, is grounded upon their deep-seated desire for peace. Farmers are convinced that a permanent peace will be easier of attainment in a world where living standards are rising, where economic growth rather than stagnation gives a basis for hope to replace the feeling of hopelessness generated by generations of chronic poverty.

Farmers everywhere, including American farmers also, deeply feel the Biblical injunction to "love thy neighbor." American farmers want farmers all over the world and people generally to enjoy and be able to earn a better life and better living.

Moreover, American farmers know that they themselves can earn better livings if people in other nations can earn the purchasing power required to buy the commodities we produce. And it is good sense for us to buy from other nations the things they can produce to a better advantage than we can. Farmers in America are benefited by economic growth in other democratic nations as well as in our own.

For those reasons, National Farmers Union has strongly supported all United States efforts to promote, encourage, facilitate, and assist economic development and growth in the democratic nations of the world.

*Need a democratic World Economic Union*

We have said that we are convinced that these aims could best be obtained by the early establishment of a democratic World Economic Union, composed of nations that would subscribe to the kinds of democratic rights and privileges set forth in the United States Constitution and Bill of Rights. Such an economic union of democratic nations, we feel, could develop and operate the economic development and trade promotion programs that would contribute most to a rapid integration and growth of free world economies.

Until such time as a democratic World Economic Union can be established and put into operation, we are convinced that the policies of the United States, operating through foreign economic agencies and the United Nations and the specialized agencies, such as Food and Agriculture Organization, should be adapted to coincide as nearly as possible with the kind of economic program for the free world as would be adopted by its representative governing body if such an economic union were in existence.

We feel that the largest possible proportion of our foreign economic programs should be implemented through agencies of the United Nations. Further, we are convinced that those parts of these programs that cannot under current conditions be best administered through the U. N. should be carried out as fully as possible through the voluntary private foreign relief organizations such as CARE, registered for that purpose with Foreign Operations Administration. This has two advantages, we feel. First, it helps overcome the appearance, as well as the actuality, of economic imperialism. Second, we are convinced that we can be more fully assured that the people in other nations who need our economic help most will be more likely to receive it if such programs are administered through private relief organizations than by government-to-government procedures.

*Why communism will fail*

The Soviet system is likely to break up because it refuses to recognize the facts of life about family farming. This fact provides a great challenge to America, both domestically and in our foreign economic programs. To quote an article appearing in Harper's magazine:

> Perhaps the most dangerous enemy of communism is the stoic, passive peasant in Eastern Germany, Poland, the Soviet Union itself, China, and Northern Vietnam. * * * The passive figure of the peasant, trapped in totalitarianism, is joined as a potential mortal enemy of communism by the farmers of the free world—notably in the underdeveloped areas and perhaps most notably, at the moment, by the awakening of the Indian peasant.

AGRICULTURAL LAND REFORM

This challenge has been the basis of the deep interest and strong efforts of National Farmers Union to insist that a central part of United States foreign economic programs should be to promote agricultural land reform in all its phases—secure land tenure, adequate farm-production income programs, development of farmers' purchasing, marketing, and service cooperatives, adequate family farm credit facilities, organization and growth of free farm organizations, and the like.

The desire of the agricultural producers of the world to become substantial family farmers with secure tenure and decent incomes can be a strong moving force for expansion of democracy and the basis for a secure peace.

We feel that agricultural land reform has never been given the important place it deserves in our foreign policy. Further, we feel that emphasis upon it has been reduced markedly in the last 5 years. We look on this lessening of emphasis upon agricultural land reform as an adverse and dangerous development in United States foreign economic policy.

If time permitted, we would cite in detail the examples where successful, United States-assisted agricultural land reforms have had most desirable results—to mention a few, South Korea, Japan, Iran, the Philippines. We think that subsequent events have proved the tragic blunder that the United States made in failing to follow a similar policy in Egypt.

WHICH WAY?

In exercise of its economic world leadership, the United States can take either of two routes: the road to scarcity or the road to abundance.

Faced with the problems of tariffs, low productivity, dollar shortages, embargoes, and other problems restricting sale of United States farm products in other countries, the United States can take the road of abundance or the road of scarcity.

There are two kinds of scarcity roads:

1. Economic isolation or go it alone; and
2. Exclusive reliance upon cartel-dominated free trade.

*The go-it-alone road to scarcity and chaos*

The United States can go it alone: American markets for American goods; hold out competing imports; give up foreign markets for United States production.

The United States farmer would have to shift 50 million acres now producing wheat, cotton, tobacco, rice, corn, soybeans, apples, and other commodities into production of something else that could be sold in the United States.

A large segment of United States industrial production would have to shut down, lay off workers, reduce consumer demand in the United States for farm commodities for lack of raw materials and lack of foreign markets.

United States farmers' cost of production and consumers' cost of living would rise owing to our not being able to buy imported goods.

The entire free-world (including United States) production and living standards would be reduced. "Stomach communism" in many areas of the world would be promoted. A fortress America would become inevitable.

If we want this, if we want to go it alone, it can be done with preclusive protective embargoes and tariffs against imports; expansion of "Buy American" policies; refusal to support U. N. and FAO; and stopping United States economic aid to nations of the free world.

*The cartel-dominated road to scarcity and chaos*

The other road to scarcity is to rely exclusively upon cartel-dominated, so-called free international trade.

We can do this by repealing our tariffs, abolishing our embargoes against competing imports, such as sugar, wool, feed grains, barley, and dairy products; stopping United States economic aid to other countries; abolishing the United States Export-Import Bank, the International Wheat Agreement, pulling out of World Bank and International Monetary Fund, refuse to implement reciprocal trade agreements, repeal section 22, and the escape clause.

International trade would then be dominated by international private cartels—huge international trade monopolies. Only the farmers and other raw material producers of the world would fully enjoy the fruits of competition.

Foreign countries could not be expected to greatly reduce their government restrictions on trade and currency exchanges. United States producers would be set free in an administered-price market dominated by foreign government regulation and international private cartels. Selling prices received by United States producers would be uncertain and artificially low. Buying prices paid by United States consumers would be uncertain and artificially high.

The world price of farm commodities and other raw materials such as tin, rubber, and iron ore would fluctuate greatly from month to month and year to year. This would discourage productive investments and retard free-world economic expansion.

Neither of these scarcity roads is the right road.

*Road to abundance and peace*

The road to abundance is through negotiated international regulation of expanded international exchange of materials—greater international economic cooperation and coordination, preferably through international agreements and agencies comprised of many nations.

These include negotiation and establishment of (1) a world economic development agency; (2) additional international commodity agreements such as the International Wheat Agreement for each and every raw material that enters importantly into international trade; (3) renewal of reciprocal trade agreement; (4) ratification of an international trade agency truly consistent with these principles; and (5) the proposed International Food and Raw Materials Reserve.

If these things are done, this would—

(*a*) Encourage investments;

(*b*) Stabilize markets;

(*c*) Promote increased production in all countries;

(*d*) Reduce, and ultimately eliminate, famines, chronic undernutrition, low living standards; and

(*e*) Make possible the use of abundant food supplies to aid in establishment in the lesser developed area of the world a system of public school for every child.

Serious gaps now exist in present United States laws and international agreements.

There is no provision for international handling of interrelated financial and commodity market problems.

Thus, the United States with 7 percent of world's people, 30 percent of world's resources, but 70 percent of world's manufacturing output is using up resources very rapidly and does not have a stabilized source of supply.

While raw materials producing nations are still subject to wild ups and downs in world raw materials markets and monetary exchanges.

It is our considered and mature opinion that these gaps must be closed. We are convinced they can be closed to the great benefit both of the United States and all the other democratic free nations of the world. We are also convinced that this is the only type of foreign economy that is consistent with an expanding full employment domestic economy, with the attainment of the needs and aspirations of United States family farmers, and most conducive to national security.

*Sliding scale farm program a handicap*

The sliding scale farm price and income policy now being operated by the Federal Government is a detriment and a handicap to an intelligent and effective foreign economic policy. Exclusive reliance for farm-income protection on market price propping not only serves as an artificial suction to draw in unneeded imports and thus invites and requires the imposition of tariffs and import quotas. The exclusive use of market-price propping of sliding-scale farm price supports may also build up in Government ownership a stock of commodities beyond the need for an adequate national safety reserve. When this happens and such stocks are put into a special set-aside as has been done, for special foreign disposition of the dumping variety instead of being insulated as should have been done, these stocks become a burden on, and threat to, trade and economic development all over the free world.

We are convinced that our domestic farm income-protection program can and should be made fully consistent with the internationally planned abundance type of foreign economic policy.

The full parity family farm income protection program, the adoption of which is urged by National Farmers Union, is of this nature.

FULL PARITY FAMILY INCOME PROTECTION PROGRAM

The following is a brief outline of the major phases of the full parity family farm income protection program that we feel is fully consistent with a desirable foreign economic policy.

I. Fair trade for farmers:

(a) Enactment of mandatory income protection for family-farm production of all farm commodities giving farm families the opportunity to earn income reflecting full parity with nonfarm segments of the population, by use of production payments as well as loans, purchase agreements, and purchases as methods of support.

(b) Revitalize and expand Federal crop insurance program.

II. Expanding human use and demand for farm commodities:

(a) Domestic consumption expansion.

(b) Expanded exports.

III. Keeping supply marketing in balance with augmented demand:

(a) Establish conservation acreage reserve.

(b) Revise and extend marketing quotas.

(c) Marketing agreements and orders.

IV. Establishment of a yardstick family farm loan agency.

*Fair trade for farmers*

Almost all family farms today are commercial farms. They must buy a very large part of the machinery and supplies used for farm operation and for modern family living, about 89 percent as an average. They sell a very large part of what they produce, more than 90 percent on the average. The terms they trade on makes a big difference in the standard of living the family is able to earn.

The prices of things that farmers buy, both production and family living items, are retail prices like the prices all consumers pay. These retail prices, and the wholesale prices behind them, are administered prices—prices set by manufacturers, money-market bankers, railroad companies, and others, on the basis of their ability to withhold supply to maintain the set price. Experince has shown that these prices paid by farmers and consumers rise fast enough in periods of inflation. However, experience has also shown that the prices paid by farmers for things and services they must buy from nonfarmers do not drop very much even in periods of economic stagnation. This is because manufacturers and the others protected by tariffs and corporation laws and Government commissions, can hold down protection and maintain price, partly because of the small number of firms in each industry. They can do so profitably because overhead fixed costs are a small proportion of total costs thus enabling them to make large cuts in costs as a result of reduced production.

On the other hand, there are about 3½ million farmers selling in competition with each other. None of them controls a significantly large enough share of the total market to raise prices received by withholding supplies from the market. Nor have they been able successfully to band together voluntarily to do so. Moreover, unlike the industrialist, a farmers' fixed costs are a very high proportion of total costs. He cannot reduce costs much by curtailing production. Operating alone the only out for the individual farmer is to produce more as long as he can to raise gross income by increasing volume of sales. In competing with each other to do so in the past year by obtaining more land, farmers have bid up land values in the face of falling income. The increased supply resulting from 3 million farmers each doing this causes a very large drop in prices received by farmers. The nature of demand for food and clothing is such that a small percentage increase in supply or decrease in demand will cause a six-times greater percentage drop in prices received by farmers.

Coupled with these adverse terms of trade for farmers is the tendency for improved farm technology to cause farm production to increase faster than population and improving diets even if special Governmental consumption-expanding measures are put into effect.

The net result of farmers' adverse terms of trade is chronic farm economic depression when farmers are not protected from the forces of the so-called free market. The indication of recent history is that even in a relatively full employment economy farm-family incomes will drop continuously about 5 percent per year in the absence of fully adequate specific governmental farm income protection programs. This drop will continue until such time as farm families exhaust a substantial portion of their assets and net worth, until they are living in utter poverty and have worn out their capital equipment and exhausted their soil and water resources. History as well as current statistical estimates indicate the bottom of the free market sliding scale is a parity ratio somewhere between 50 and 60 percent of parity.

Experience has shown the only solid protection available to even up farmer bargaining power and the only way that farmers can obtain fair terms of trade is to make use of programs of the Federal Government—

To increase demand and markets through direct action programs;

To establish farm parity income program to protect farm income against adverse terms of trade; and

To enable farmers to keep the volume of marketed farm products in reasonable balance with augmented demand.

*Income protection for farmers*

National Farmers Union continues to urge the enactment of laws requiring the Government to use production payments and price-support loans, purchase agreements, and purchases in workable combinations to maintain the returns per unit of commodity of the family-farm production of all farm-produced commodities at 100 percent of a fair parity.

*Parity.*—Parity for any farm commodity should be figured as the return per unit of the commodity that would give farm families who produce it an opportunity to earn the equivalent income and purchasing power that can be earned by people in other occupations in an expanding full employment economy.

*Family farm volume protected.*—Individual farm family would be eligible to obtain payments and price-support protection on their sales only up to the maximum size of a family farm.

*Methods of support.*—Price-supporting Government purchases of commodities would be used only where required to relieve temporary seasonal market gluts and where either the commodity can be economically stored from year to year or where noncommercial outlets are in sight for the commodities purchased. Price-supporting purchase agreements and nonrecourse price-support loans would be used to even out seasonal patterns in prices, prevent gluts at harvest time, and to maintain orderly marketing and market stability. Price-supporting Government purchases would also be used where needed to develop and maintain the Nation's safety reserve, strategic stockpile, or ever-normal storehouse of food and fiber commodities. But primary reliance for farm-income support would be placed upon use of compensatory production payments direct to farmers to make up the margin by which market prices received by producers of that commodity were below the parity level for that commodity.

*Crop and livestock insurance.*—Farm commodity income-support programs protect against unfair economic hazards resulting from their weak bargaining power in the market. They do not help at all in case the crop is a failure because of drought, flood, insects, or other natural disaster or there are livestock losses from natural causes.

To fill this need, National Farmers Union urged adoption and rapid expansion of the Federal crop-insurance program. Its provisions should be expanded to farm livestock. The fundamental idea of this program is that Americans never do sit idly by as their neighbors in another part of the country are subjected to great loss and destruction due to natural causes. Billions of dollars of relief funds in past years have been expended to overcome the suffering due to drought and such after they happened. The idea of crop insurance is that the people in the Nation by paying the administrative and experimental costs of such a program enable farmers through the annual payment of premiums to insure themselves against the income loss due to natural hazards, and thus reduce the future need for special disaster relief expenditures.

*Expanding full employment economy*

National Farmers Union was one of the original sponsors of the Employment Act of 1946. We are convinced the domestic market demand for farm products resulting from increasing farm productivity can be maintained only in an expanding full employment economy. The economic history of the Nation shows that over the 45 years, for which statistical data are available, farm-family incomes fall in any year when the total national economy grows by less than 10 percent above the previous year. Except in years when total national economic growth is 10 percent or more per year, the terms of trade are against farmers for the reasons discussed in the previous section.

Therefore, National Farmers Union continues to support all policies and programs such as: interest rate reduction; increased personal income-tax exemptions, expanded school, hospital, highways, hydroelectric and irrigation dam construction and other public works; higher minimum wages; more nearly adequate social security protection for unemployed, disabled and retired citizens; and protection of rights of organization and collective bargaining of those who work for employers.

With a national annual economic growth rate of about 6 percent, industrial unemployment would be reduced to a fractional minimum and consumers purchasing power for farm and other products would be at a maximum consistent with a stabilized price level. This would mean that increasing demand for farm products would lack only about 1 percent per year in keeping up with increasing farm productivity and net farm income would drop only 3 percent per year. Recognizing that economic growth as rapid as 10 percent a year might bring inflation yet knowing that a slower growth rate means falling farm income, National Farmers Union continues to urge adoption of special governmental consumption-expanding programs and a fully adequate farm income-protection program as well as maintenance of a national economic growth are of 6 percent per year.

*Expanding domestic consumption and market demand*

Effective advertising and merchandising of farm-produced commodities are of some value in expanding domestic markets for farm products. But they cannot be relied upon to bring about any very large expansion in the total United States demand for all food and fiber. The Nation's leading economists are agreed that the only way to very greatly increase consumer demand for food and fiber is through increased purchasing power of groups of consumers that do not now have sufficient buying power to buy the food and clothing they need and want.

*Special consumption expanding programs.*—The largest untapped market for farm products is made up of the unemployed, the dependent widows and children, permanently handicapped and disabled, the aged, and other low-income consumers. These people, with incomes from private and governmental sources of less than $1,000 per person per year, simply do not have enough purchasing power to maintain all the needs of life and still spend as much for food and clothing as they want and need for adequate standards. These people want to buy more. They will accept commodities provided through direct Government distribution, but they would prefer to be able to buy them at regular stores like anybody else.

To make this possible, and bring about a vast increase in United States consumption of food commodities, National Farmers Union continues to urge—

Adoption of a nationwide food allotment stamp plan;

Expansion to all schools of the national school-lunch program now serving less than one-third of the schools;

Improvement and expansion of the fluid milk for schoolchildren program to provide free at least 2 half-pints of milk per child per day and pay local school district administrative costs;

Adoption of improved Federal standards and inspection of perishable farm commodities in terminal, as well as shipping, markets with adequate Federal financing;

Adequate nutrition standards for the Armed Forces and veterans' hospitals, penal institutions, hospitals, and other public and private nonprofit agencies by means of commodity donation or food subsidies; and

Adoption of a credit program to encourage modernization and improvement of perishable farm commodity terminal markets.

Adequately financed, the programs listed on the preceding page would keep consumer demand in a full-employment economy increasing as rapidly in the next few years as farm production.

*Expanding foreign consumption and market demand for United States farm commodities*

Many United States-produced farm commodities, up to 10 percent of total production, must, in normal years, find a market outside our national boundaries. This market can and should be expanded. Additional agricultural attachés and improved advertising and merchandising will help some. But, just as in the case of the domestic market, the really big increases in market demand for United States-produced farm commodities can come only from increased purchasing power in foreign countries, or from United States Government purchases designed for foreign shipment. We are convinced that this total can be raised from the current annual export sales of about $3 billion to at least $4.5 billion by the combined and coordinated use by our Nation of the following (and we will be protecting our farmers at the same time, by intelligent methods, rather than restrictive ones, against the ill effects of imports that compete with United States farm products):

Negotiation and establishment of additional international commodity agreements for all raw materials that enter importantly into international trade, similar to the International Wheat Agreement, which will bring into agreement all of the importing nations as well as all of the exporting nations for each commodity.

Negotiation and establishment of an international food and raw-materials reserve or clearinghouse to stabilize supplies, relieve famines and stabilize prices of all food and other raw-material commodities that enter importantly into international trade.

Continuation of the Agricultural Trade Development and Assistance Act to provide for $3 billion per year of donations and sales for soft currencies of United States farm commodities and expand the purposes for which donated commodities and loans of soft currency may be used in include establishment and operation of systems of universal, free, general and vocational education in nations of the free world where such do not now exist.

Continuation and intelligent expansion of the point 4 program of United States aid to economic development of other free nations in a way that will increase coordinated economic growth of the nations of the free world.

Continuation of the reciprocal trade agreements providing for worldwide tariff reductions and customs simplification.

Inauguration of full parity compensatory production payment methods as primary reliance in supporting farmers' returns on farm commodities, some of the supply of which are either imported or exported, as part of a nationwide program of trade adjustment aids to United States industries, communities, workers, and farmers injured by tariff reductions and elimination of import quotas.

*International food and raw-materials reserve*

Probably the most persistent, most disturbing, and most perplexing of modern economic problems is the human suffering and relative stagnation enforced upon producers of raw materials by the extreme ups and downs in the prices of raw materials and, consequently, in their realized and expected incomes. The problem is serious in all the more highly developed nations. It is even more seriously present and damaging in the lesser developed nations.

Wide swings in raw-material prices present prospective investors in raw-material development, whether persons, firms, or States, with a very large range of variation in expectations as to returns that can be earned by opening up and developing an augmented raw-material supply. This condition is one of great risks where at any moment not only might part of the investment be rendered valueless but earnable returns may even fail to cover day-to-day operating costs and the entire enterprise will have to be shut down with attendant loss of income and human suffering.

Faced with such great uncertainty in expectations, both States and individuals are hesitant to open up or expand enterprises that are currently profitable but which may at any time dip drastically below the break-even line through no fault of the enterprise management itself. The multiplication of this kind of situation throughout farming and all other raw materials industries puts a very severe damper upon the rate of economic development in these industries.

This slowing down of the rate of expansion in raw-material industries not only reduces the supply of such materials to meet human needs and to fuel manufacturing and other secondary industries; it also holds down the purchasing power of persons and firms on the raw-materials sector, and thus cuts down on sales, scale of operation, and, consequently, of income and purchasing power of the industrial and service segments of the economy. Consequently, the entire economy idles along at a lower rate of production and expansion than should or needs to be the case. In the more highly industrialized nations, the symptoms are seen in chronically depressed industries, like farming and coal mining in the United States. Among the lesser industrialized nations, a drop in raw-material prices can bring an entire nation dangerously close to bankruptcy and can directly cause a widespread drop in personal income and standards of living of the entire population.

It is only natural that the economic segments and nations involved in these debilitating circumstances would take evasive and protective action, just as an intelligent bomber pilot takes evasive action from destructive antiaircraft fire.

Such protective or evasive action, when taken unilaterally by different nations, helps to solve the problems caused by fluctuating raw-material prices only at the cost of reducing the magnitude of international exchange of commodities, and thus results in the loss by each and all nations of the advantages of specialization. Everybody in all nations has less real income and a lower standard of living than they might otherwise be able to attain.

Through the administrative machinery of an international food and raw-materials reserve, the stabilized prices of each different raw material that enters importantly into international trade would be negotiated and agreed upon. The reserve would thereafter stand ready at all times to buy any raw-material commodity offered it at the agreed-upon stabilized price, and would stand ready to sell such commodities on the agreed-upon stabilized price.

The industry of advanced nations is chewing up basic resources at a tremendous and rising rate. For example, the United States, which has 7 percent of the world's population and 30 percent of the world's natural resources, accounts for 70 percent of the world's manufactured goods. The United States is using up its resources base at a very rapid rate, and very much faster than the rest of the world. To be secure in our rising living standards and to retain the resource base for an expanding economy, we must assure ourselves a stabilized source of supply of the raw materials for our manufacturing industry. The same situation is true in other industrial nations, such as the United Kingdom, France, Germany, and Japan. The thought-provoking details for different commodities were thoroughly considered in the Paley report of several years ago.

Highly industrialized nations could depend entirely upon private industrial concerns to make long-term contracts with raw-material producers in other lands, and this should be done. But it can only be successfully and securely accomplished under the protection and encouragement by governments and international economic accords.

These latter, conceivably, could be done exclusively through bilateral arrangements between the United States and foreign nations, one nation at a time, one commodity at a time. However, no supplier, private enterprise, or state, wants to become dependent exclusively on 1 buyer, nor does any importing nation or industrialist want to become dependent upon only 1 seller.

Through the international food and raw-materials reserve, exporting nations can obtain assured, long-term, stabilized markets, and importing nations can obtain an assured, long-term, ample supply at stabilized prices of imports on terms that will not injure domestic producers who must sell their commodities in competition with imports.

The international food and raw-materials reserve would operate in coordination with the International Monetary Fund and the World Bank. Many of the national restrictions we now have that hold down greater international exchange of commodities are caused by the desire of nations to preserve their monetary position in different currencies are caused by the desire of nations to preserve their monetary position in different currencies, particularly dollars and pounds sterling. The international food and raw-materials reserve would completely eliminate this problem by operating in terms of all currencies on the basis of internationally agreed-upon, official exchange rates.

*Permanent peace depends on international institutions that will promote more rapid economic growth*

The international food and raw-materials resolution has been before Congress for 4 years. It was passed by the Senate in 1956 as a part of the mutual-security bill, but was lost in conference by a close vote. The concepts involved in the resolution have their roots in the still unsolved problems of extreme human need, starvation, economic stagnation, and poverty throughout the world in the midst of surpluses of raw materials that cannot be sold at prices that will return an adequate, stable income to producers.

The geneses of the ideas are found in the efforts of National Farmers Union of the United States to work out a solution to the farmer's income problem. Recommendations presented 10 years ago to the International Federation of Agricultural Producers by National Farmers

Union representatives were fully considered and favorably acted upon by this international, private, farm organization, among whose members are all the national farm organizations of the United States.

The international food and raw-materials resolution, as passed by the Senate, does not, itself, establish an international agency. The resolution merely calls upon the President to undertake negotiations with other nations to that end. Any agreements reached would, of course, be subject to review and ratification by the Senate of the United States, and appropriation of any needed capital and other funds would have to be fully considered by both Houses.

The international food and raw-materials reserve will help solve many of our Nation's most difficult problems of both domestic and foreign policy. It will make a major contribution toward permanent peace by facilitating a more rapid rate of economic expansion. Its operation will stabilize world raw-material markets. It will put abundant production to work.

INTERNATIONAL COOPERATION AND PLANNING

The proposal for the establishment of an international raw-materials reserve to cover petroleum, iron ore, tin, rubber, and other raw materials, as well as food and fiber, is not new. An international food-reserve resolution was introduced in 1956 by Senator Murray and 23 other Senators and by Congressman Metcalf.

World food board idea was proposed immediately after World War II by Lord John Boyd Orr, first Director General of Food and Agriculture Organization.

An international commodity clearance house was proposed by Committee of Exports of FAO and IFAP, but was never ratified by the governments.

The United States is already embarked upon a small and timid program to make use of abundant United States farm production to further the aims of the United States foreign policy on a unilateral and bilateral basis through—

(*a*) Agricultural Trade Development and Assistance Act.

(*b*) Title I, Agricultural Act of 1954 (Public Law 690).

(*c*) "Farm product" amendment to Mutual Security (foreign aid) Act provides for donations and safes up to $300 million in this fiscal year.

(*d*) Section 416 of the Agricultural Act of 1954, as amended in 1954 authorizes CCC to sell stocks at "competitive world prices and pay repackaging costs and transportation from present location to shipping port."

(*e*) Section 202 of the Agricultural Act of 1956 directs the Commodity Credit Corporation to exercise its powers and authorities to encourage the sale, for export at competitive world prices, of its stocks of extra-long-staple cotton.

(*f*) Section 32, enacted in 1938, allows up to 30 percent of tariff revenues to finance foreign sales of United States farm products. The Agricultural Act of 1956 authorizes an appropriation, beginning July 1, 1956, of not over $500 million to supplement operations under section 32 of Public Law 320. Of this amount only one-half may be used for one commodity or the products thereof.

This program has an excellent aim. The major trouble with it is that which has already been revealed by the extreme slowness with which the program was put into operation. In actual practice, even this unilateral United States program can be carried out only by international negotiation, seldom bilateral but usually requiring consideration for side effect upon third and fourth parties. How much better if an international institution were available to operate this essentially good program.

The United States must intensify its efforts to assist in the development of a coordinated program of aid to relieve hunger and suffering, and to promote expansion and strengthening of the national economies of the democratic nations in ways that will not destroy the principle of self-determination of peoples. The United States should help these nations to develop economic conditions that will—

(*a*) Create an international community of economic effort for common purposes, avoiding the extremes of either forcing unwanted policies on others as a condition of our help, or of undertaking action ourselves in the absence of appropriate efforts in in the countries that participate.

(*b*) Promote material well-being and allow employment, production, trade, and investment in ways that will enrich human life and eliminate economic weaknesses that threaten political stability and inevitable totalitarian imperialism.

(*c*) Afford all democratic nations increasing opportunities for economic growth and improving standards of living in ways which will operate so that economic gains are distributed equitably within countries.

(*d*) Attract peoples and governments toward the democratic system of political freedom.

To attain these objectives, we support continued international economic negotiation, increased United States contributions to the specialized agencies, such as the Food and Agriculture Organization, and expansion of United States foreign economic assistance and of the program by which our advanced technological knowledge is made available to other nations to assist them to increase the efficiency of production and marketing and to improve the agricultural land-tenure systems, eliminate colonialism, and reform their economic and social structures.

The operations of an international food and raw-materials reserve would generate the purchasing power and stabilize international markets in a manner that would greatly facilitate more rapid economic development in the free world.

An international food and raw-materials reserve would greatly strengthen the operations of our point 4 laws.

The Mutual Security Authorization and Appropriation Acts provide, with some changes in means and emphasis, in 1957, a small amount of funds for loans and grants to other nations to facilitate economic development and expansion and to send United States experts to foreign countries to provide technical assistance or know-how.

The United States appropriations to FAO and other specialized U. N. agencies and limited United States contribution to expanded technical assistance program of the U. N. are needed and have been approved by Congress with increasing support.

With an operating food and raw materials reserve, these funds would go a lot further because, first, they would be augmented by the loans available from sale of buffer stocks. The stabilized international markets would greatly reduce the risks of price fluctuations and thus raise expectations sufficiently to really speed up investment in resource development.

Emphasis has been centered too much on engineering and production techniques and largely shifted away from institutional reform.

Attention to organization and development of farmers cooperatives and farm credit agencies has been continued but at a reduced scope. Work on land-tenure improvement and setting up free private farm organizations has largely been curtailed or eliminated.

Our Nation must recapture leadership in this vital field. We need to enlist the cooperation of other economically strong nations, preferably under auspices of international organizations.

The proposed international food and raw materials reserve is a necessary supplement to the technical assistance programs of the United Nations, the World Bank, and other specialized agencies.

*Other measures*

In addition to restoring a larger scope to our point 4 programs and establishing an international food and raw materials reserve or world food bank, National Farmers Union urges:

Continued operation and improvement of the International Wheat Agreement, the International Sugar Agreement, and additional international commodity agreements for all commodities that enter importantly into international trade. Such agreements should include net-importing as well as net-exporting nations and the pricing arrangements should be based upon an international parity or general price index.

Expansion of Agricultural Trade Development and Assistance Act, to increase scope of program and expand authorization to include establishment of systems of universal free education in nations that do not have them.

Make greater use of the authorities provided in the Reciprocal Trade Agreements Act.

Enact legislation to establish a program of trade-adjustment aids to United States industries, workers, communities, and farmers injured by reductions in tariffs and import restrictions. This can be accomplished with respect to farmers by legislation to provide 100 percent of parity income protection primarily by means of production payments. Such action would entail expansion of this type program to include milk and its products and other farm commodities provided in United States and sold in competition with imports as well as wool and sugar for which partially adequate payment programs are in operation.

Participation of the United States in establishment of a free world economic development agency of the type proposed as the United Nations Special Fund for Economic Development (SUNFED). What is needed is a vast expansion of the type of work done by the Export-Import Bank and the World Monetary Fund, with greater emphasis on economic growth and less upon short-term repayment ability.

United States appropriations of economic and technical assistance to other democratic nations and for cultural exchange, such as the Fulbright program should be greatly expanded with as much as feasible of such aid extended through the instrumentalities of the United Nations and the specialized agencies such as Food and Agriculture Organization.

We are convinced that if existing sliding scale foreign economic policy were reversed to move in the directions indicated this would in itself further the prospects of peace as well as increase the demand for United States farm products. We are convinced that such foreign economic policies are a basic part of an intelligent and desirable full parity family farm income protection program that should also include:

Fair trade for farmers:

Enactment of mandatory farm income protection for family farm production of all commodities at full income parity, using production payments in workable combinations with price-supporting purchase agreements loans and purchases.

Revitalize and expand Federal crop-insurance program.

Expanding human use and demand for farm commodities:

Expanding full-employment economy.

National food allotment or stamp plan.

Expand school-lunch program to all schools.

Federal-financing of 2 half-pints of milk per schoolchild per day.

Credit program to encourage improvement of terminal markets for perishable farm commodities.

Better terminal market inspection of perishables.

Provide more nearly adequate nutrition standards for public institutions.

Keeping supply marketed in balance with augmented demand:

Continue conservation acreage reserve.

Revise and extend marketing quotas.

Provide for additional marketing agreements and orders.

Establishment of a "yardstick" family farm loan agency.

IX

# FOREIGN TRADE POLICY IN RELATION TO WAGES AND EMPLOYMENT—PROBLEMS OF ADJUSTMENT

# EMPLOYMENT, WAGES, AND FOREIGN TRADE

**United States Department of Labor, Bureau of Labor Statistics, September 1957**

This memorandum is designed to bring together available information relating to international trade and domestic employment, the quantitative effects of such trade in relation to other factors affecting wages and employment, and the relationship between wage rates, labor productivity, and the movement of international trade.

## INTERNATIONAL TRADE AND DOMESTIC EMPLOYMENT

The most recent analysis of the effects of United States foreign trade upon domestic employment was made by the Department of Labor for the Commisison on Foreign Economic Policy (the Randall Commission) and was published in the staff papers of that Commission. This study indicated that in 1952 approximately 4¼ million workers in the United States owed their jobs either to making goods for export, processing imported raw materials and semimanufactured goods, or transporting and distributing imported commodities.[1] On the basis of the growth in foreign trade which has occurred since 1952, the Department now estimates that in 1956, this number had increased to about 4½ million workers:

*United States employment attributable to foreign trade in 1956*

| | |
|---|---|
| 1. Exports: | |
| Nonagricultural workers | 2,516,000 |
| Agricultural workers | 602,000 |
| 2. Imports: | |
| Transportation and distribution | 524,000 |
| Processing imported materials | 858,000 |
| Total | 4,500,000 |

A comparison of the components of the 1956 estimate with that for 1952 indicates that there was an increase of over 360,000 workers in making manufactured goods for export and over 130,000 workers in handling and processing of imports. This total gain of almost half a million workers has been partially offset by a drop of 265,000 agricultural workers, leaving a net gain of approximately 225,000 jobs in the 4-year period. The decrease in agricultural employment reflects both the increase in productivity of farm labor and the shifts in the pattern of agricultural exports among individual commodities.

The estimate of 4½ million jobs generated by our foreign trade is, of course, not a complete statement of the effect of foreign trade on domestic employment. It must be recognized, of course, that some jobs are "displaced" by competitive imports, always keeping in mind that exports must be paid for, in the long run, by imports.

[1] Staff papers of the Commission on Foreign Economic Policy, U. S. Government Printing Office, February 1954, pp. 373–374. As originally published, the estimate was 4.4 million workers, but the estimate of agricultural workers was later revised.

In its budget request for the current fiscal year, the Department of Labor included funds to carry out the necessary statistical work and analyses to obtain an accurate indication of this "displacement." The work, as planned, called for detailed studies of employment changes in individual industries affected by import competition and the determination of the employment losses which could be charged to imports. The House Appropriations Committee recommended that funds be made available for this project, but the final approved appropriations for the Department did not permit undertaking this work. As a result, we are not in a position to submit a concrete estimate of the number of American workers who may have been displaced at any time by competitive imports. In the absence of such concrete estimates it is, however, possible to make some crude estimates which will throw some light on this matter.

If we assume that all of the United States dutiable imports in 1956 could have been made by American workers, then these imports would have required the full-time services of approximately 1 million workers.[2]

This figure is obviously much too high for a variety of reasons, none of which can be numerically evaluated at this time. Some of these reasons are:

(1) Some dutiable imports have a particular appeal because of special characteristics impossible to duplicate here, such as "native style" handwork, and do not replace American workers.

(2) Some dutiable imports are used in later stages of processing and are not producible in the United States due to a lack of the basic raw material.

(3) In some instances where imports are considerably lower-priced than United States products, they may find customers in a market which had not and could not be tapped by American production.

Perhaps a somewhat more realistic method is to consider the employment history of the industries which have filed escape-clause petitions for tariff relief.

Between April 1948 and March 1957, 74 applications for escape-clause action had been filed with and acted upon by the Tariff Commission. In 49 cases the Commission either (*a*) found so little evidence of injury caused by imports that the application was terminated or dismissed after only a preliminary investigation or (*b*) after making a full investigation decided that the affected product was not suffering from import competition and that no tariff relief was justified. Twenty-five reports (involving only twenty-three commodities since two commodities were the subject of more than one report in this period) were sent to the President with at least half the Commission recommending Presidential action modifying the tariff.

During the postwar period, 1947–56, according to data included in the Tariff Commission reports, the peak employment in the plants producing these 23 commodities was 113,000 workers. At the low point for each individual industry, total employment in the plants producing these commodities was 85,000 workers, a drop of 28,000 workers. (See table 1.) This decline, of course, cannot be attributed

---

[2] This estimate is made by taking the declared value of all dutiable imports, raising this value by 25 percent to cover the costs of insurance and freight and duty, and then dividing the adjusted total by average output per United States worker.

wholly to imports. In some instances the lowest employment coincided with a year of domestic recession rather than with a peak in imports; in other instances there is strong reason for believing that at least some share of the decline was the result of competition from other domestic products or resulted from changes in consumer preferences. On the other hand, it is recognized that these cases do not encompass all types of complaints or all cases of displacement, but in a field where facts are hard to establish, this source of information should not be overlooked.

TABLE 1.—*Estimate of total employment*[1] *involved in escape-clause cases in which the Tariff Commission recommended presidential action*

| Commodity | Highest employment[2] | Lowest employment[2] | Net decrease |
|---|---|---|---|
| I-A. Tariff action by President | 36,000 | 26,000 | 10,000 |
| I-B. Nontariff action[3] | 45,000 | 35,000 | 10,000 |
| Total | 81,000 | 61,000 | 20,000 |
| II. Rejected by President: | | | |
| A. Action recommended by Commission majority | 13,000 | 9,000 | 4,000 |
| B. Commission divided evenly | 19,000 | 15,000 | 4,000 |
| Total | 32,000 | 24,000 | 8,000 |
| Grand total | 113,000 | 85,000 | 28,000 |

[1] Total employment in plants producing the commodity. The general period covered is 1946–56, but the entire period is not used for each commodity. Unless otherwise indicated, employment data are based on Tariff Commission reports, and the period is determined by the data shown in these reports (both original and supplementary). No commodity is counted more than once (i. e., watches and fish).

[2] Highest and lowest refer to that portion of the 1946–56 period for which data are available in the Tariff Commission reports.

[3] Velveteen and lead-zinc.

Displacement, of course, does not necessarily mean unemployment for the individual worker. The worker may take another job within the same plant, shift to another plant, or, in some instances retire voluntarily. Other studies of worker displacement for all types of reasons, indicate that, in general, workers do shift jobs and find new jobs.

Some workers, of course, do encounter significant difficulty in shifting jobs within an economy, but a great many shifts take place regularly without major adjustment difficulties. Over 3 million persons, on the average, enter the labor force each month and almost the same number of persons leave. In addition to this large volume of shifts into and out of the labor force, about 800,000 persons in the labor force go from jobs into unemployment status and vice versa. Manufacturers reported almost 600,000 hires a month in 1956 and about the same number of separations. Almost half of the separations were due to workers being laid off their jobs for a variety of reasons. (See table 2.[3])

The unemployed, currently about 3 million, is an everchanging group of individuals. Each month one-third to one-half of them find jobs or leave the work force and they are replaced by about the same number of new job seekers. As a result, the long-term unemployed—

[3] Since these turnover data are based on establishment reports covering every day in the month, workers who shift from one plant to another in the same month are counted as a separation in one plant and a hire in the other plant.

those who have been looking for work for over 26 weeks—comprise only 5 to 10 percent of the unemployed at any one time.

TABLE 2.—*Monthly accessions and separations in manufacturing industries, annual averages: 1947–56*

| Year | Monthly average turnover rate (percent) | Average monthly turnover (thousands) |
|---|---|---|
| Total accessions: | | |
| 1947 | 5.1 | 780 |
| 1948 | 4.4 | 674 |
| 1949 | 3.5 | 496 |
| 1950 | 4.4 | 659 |
| 1951 | 4.4 | 709 |
| 1952 | 4.4 | 719 |
| 1953 | 3.9 | 672 |
| 1954 | 3.0 | 480 |
| 1955 | 3.7 | 613 |
| 1956 | 3.4 | 575 |
| Total separations: | | |
| 1947 | 4.8 | 734 |
| 1948 | 4.6 | 705 |
| 1949 | 4.3 | 610 |
| 1950 | 3.5 | 524 |
| 1951 | 4.4 | 709 |
| Total separations—Con. | | |
| 1952 | 4.1 | 670 |
| 1953 | 4.3 | 741 |
| 1954 | 3.5 | 560 |
| 1955 | 3.3 | 547 |
| 1956 | 3.5 | 592 |
| Quits: | | |
| 1947 | 3.4 | 520 |
| 1948 | 2.8 | 429 |
| 1949 | 1.5 | 213 |
| 1950 | 1.9 | 284 |
| 1951 | 2.4 | 386 |
| 1952 | 2.3 | 376 |
| 1953 | 2.3 | 396 |
| 1954 | 1.1 | 176 |
| 1955 | 1.6 | 265 |
| 1956 | 1.6 | 270 |

Source: U. S. Bureau of Labor Statistics.

In the past 10 years total employment in the United States has increased by nearly 7 million despite declines in employment in a number of important industries and increased productivity per worker throughout almost the entire economy.

The reason that employment has expanded in the face of individual industry declines and large increases in productivity is the tremendous increase in the total output of all United States industries. With output per man-hour in the private nonfarm sector of the economy increasing by about 3 percent per year, an annual average of almost 1.5 million workers (including self-employed and unpaid family workers) would have been displaced, despite a slight decline in weekly hours of work if total output had not increased during the postwar years 1947–56. Actually, output did increase by 44 percent during the period, and employment increased by about 16 percent between 1947 and 1956.

WAGE DIFFERENCES AND FOREIGN TRADE

Marked differences in monetary wage levels such as exist between the United States and most other countries are frequently cited as "unfair competition" and an obstacle to lowering tariffs.[4] It should be noted that this problem is not limited to the United States but has also risen in the case of the formation of the Benelux Customs Union and the European Common Market, among others.

The objections arising from wage level differences usually are based on the assumption that monetary wage rate differences accurately

[4] In any consideration of wage level differences between the United States and foreign countries, it must always be kept in mind that the available statistics, particularly on foreign wages, do not adequately measure all types of payments for labor made by the producer. Many of the payments not directly related to time on the job are comparatively high in foreign countries where social security and related "fringe benefit" programs generally entail costs far greater, relative to basic wages, than in the United States.

reflect differences in either unit labor costs or unit total costs of production. The relationship of wage levels to unit labor costs depends upon the productivity of labor (or the labor input per unit of product). The relationship of wage levels to total costs depends not only on the ratio of wages to unit labor costs but also the ratio of unit labor costs to total costs. This involves all the other factors of production, particularly capital and natural resource proportions, as well as the technical methods employed in production.

It cannot be concluded that the United States is at a disadvantage in foreign trade because United States wage levels are uniformly considerably higher than those of other countries. The fact that the United States is the ranking export nation of the world, competing successfully in most items in all markets from which its products are not restricted because of exchange problems, is ample evidence that high wage levels in and of themselves are not a deterrent to competition in international markets. Proper evaluation of the comparative level of wages and their effects on the flow of foreign trade requires not only a careful definition of the elements included in "wages," but also the addition of information on productivity, and the role of all the other factors of production. The output of an economy and, therefore, the income of its population, reflects the health, training, and skill of its labor force, entrepreneurial abilities, and its stock of capital including natural resources.

Consideration of differences in monetary wages among individual countries, and among industries within each country, is further complicated because of differences in the nature and method of financing fringe benefits or payments not directly related to time on the job. If the customs of a country are such that the costs of fringe benefits are largely borne from general taxation, the absolute level of monetary wages will be different from the case where fringe benefits are financed by direct taxes upon the employer, with these taxes approximately proportionate to payrolls. For example, in Great Britain social-security programs are largely financed by general taxation whereas in France this program is mainly financed by taxes on the employer proportionate to his payroll. A still different level would be expected if the fringe benefits were derived by direct taxes on or contributions by the worker. The range of variability in the direct cost to the employer of these benefits under different types of financing can be approximated from some limited studies of European experience which have been made by the ILO and OEEC. Studies made by these organizations indicate that within Europe direct charges to the employer range up to more than 100 percent of basic wages with the average charge well above that of the United States. All studies indicate that, as one would expect these costs tend to vary inversely by country with the level of basic wages.

Finally, comparisons of differences in wage levels among countries must take into account the general economic situation in each country—for example, is one of the countries under inflationary pressures, or suffering from balance-of-payment problems? Comparisons of wage levels between countries can only be made statistically by converting their different monetary units into some common unit. Normally, this is done by using exchange rates as the conversion factor, but this procedure has many defects. Two of the more important of these defects are: (1) Exchange rates may not reflect the differences in the economic situations of the countries as a result of such factors as exchange controls, quotas, and prohibitive tariffs; (2) exchange rates are determined by a comparison of prices of internationally traded goods and the real purchasing power of the wages in each country may be largely determined by the prices of domestic goods. A more complete description of this problem will be found in the work of Gilbert and Kravis.[5]

Thus, the major qualifications on using differences in wages as an explanation of the flow of international trade fall into three main categories: (1) Technical differences among countries in the definition of wages; (2) the fact that wages are not necessarily associated with unit labor costs; (3) the relationship of each country's wage level to its general economic situation.

The problem of measuring international differences in productivity in a way which can be utilized to evaluate the significance of differences in wage levels among countries is extremely difficult, particularly with respect to the availability of reliable data. Appendix 1 to this report describes the major work which has been done in this field, the problems encountered, and the limitations of the results. However, utilizing available data from the United Nations,[6] it is possible to make some approximate adjustments for productivity differences by taking account of per capita national product in the countries being analyzed.

The total national product of any country reflects (*a*) its total population; (*b*) participation of that population in the labor force and the distribution of the labor force among different types of endeavor; (*c*) the natural resources of that country; (*d*) the country's stock of capital, in the broadest sense; and (*e*) the general level of productivity in that country. If we take into account these differences in per capita national product in comparing wage differentials among the major trading nations of the free world, we get the results shown in chart I. The procedure followed in preparing this chart has been to express all data in terms of United States dollars, converted at official exchange rates. The vertical axis of the chart represents average hourly wages in manufacturing in each country; the horizontal axis, per capita national product. Wherever data permitted, two points have been plotted for each country's wage level: (1) The basic wage, or average hourly earnings figure, in manufacturing, and (2) the basic age adjusted for fringe benefits or social charges paid by producers. The fact that the points for each country tend to fall along a line which could be drawn between the comparative point for the United States and the zero point on the chart would appear to indicate that wage differences among these specific nations are generally related to their differences in national productivity.

The general level of nonagricultural wages in these countries appears to be closely related to the country's overall economic position, stage of development, and the distribution of its labor force among industry, service, and agriculture.

[5] Milton Gilbert and Irving Kravis, An International Comparison of National Products and the Purchasing Power of Currencies. Organization for European Economic Cooperation, Paris, France, chs. I and VI.
[6] United Nations Publications, Series H.

The problems which exist in the comparison of general wage levels are compounded when an attempt is made to compare differences in wage levels between specific industries in different countries. However, there do appear to be logical grounds for making internal comparisons between industries within a single country to see whether or not the wage levels in its export industries are below some national standard. The Commission on Foreign Economic Policy in its report to the President stated that:

1. American industry should not be subject to unfair labor standards competition that was in fact unfair.
2. Mere differences in wage rates did not constitute an indication of unfairness.
3. The clearest case of unfair wages was one in which the competing industry had standards that were unfair when judged in the light of standards in the economy involved.

This concept has been adopted by the President and has been applied in the trade-agreements process.

This same general type of comparison made for national wage levels—that is adjusting for differences in national income—can also be made for individual export industries. In this case, however, it is necessary not only to reimpose all the limitations involved in comparisons of general wage levels, but also to consider some additional factors which apply to individual industries. Basically these additional factors center around the stage of development of the individual industry and the extent to which any gains in productivity within the industry have been incorporated in wage increases or in price decreases. In this case the procedure followed has been that of comparing the wage levels in the individual exporting industries for each of nine countries with the average wage level in all manufactures in that country. These data shown in tables 3 and 4 are extremely crude in that they were based upon the information available for each country and usually cover a wide range of products. Professor Kravis' work on the United States patterns has clearly indicated that our export industries on the average tend to be our higher wage industries.[7] This may well be the case in other countries, but thus far there has been inadequate analysis of this question.

Many qualifications of the data shown in these tables are required (appendix 2). The data should be adjusted for differences in industry practices, fringe benefits and social charge payments, historical relationships among wage levels in different industries, and the role of collective bargaining in establishing the wage level of an industry, and so forth. In short, it would appear that analysis of interindustry differences both within and between nations requires both additional general data and individual case studies. The Assistant Secretary of Labor for International Labor Affairs, in his position as the United States Government representative on the Governing Body of the International Labor Organization, has formally proposed that the ILO begin a program of pilot studies in this area. If this program is initiated and successfully carried out we may, at a future date, have material which will permit detailed analyses of industries and throw more light on the entire problem of the relationship of wage levels to international trade.

[7] Review of Economics and Statistics, vol. XXXVIII, No. 1, February 1956.

TABLE 3a.—*Belgium and United States wage levels as percent of all-manufacturing average, selected industries*

| Belgium | | United States | |
|---|---|---|---|
| Industry | Percent | Percent | Industry |
| Textiles | 87 | 73 | Textile mill products. |
| Nonmetallic minerals; glass | 96 | 112 | Flat glass; glass and glassware, pressed or blown. |
| Art and precision | 97 | 84 | Jewelry and findings. |
| Fabrication of articles from common metals (not elsewhere specified). | 95 | 104 | Fabricated metal products. |
| Melting, casting, rolling, forging, extracting metal. | 120 | 119 | Primary metal industries. |
| Fabrication of machines, including electrical and transportation (excluding ship repairing). | 102 | 107 | Machinery (excluding electrical); and electrical machinery. |
| All manufacturing | 100 | 100 | All manufacturing. |

TABLE 3b.—*Canada and United States wage levels as percent of all-manufacturing average, selected industries*

| Canada | | United States | |
|---|---|---|---|
| Industry | Percent | Percent | Industry |
| Meat products | 104 | 102 | Meat products. |
| Grain mill products | 93 | 94 | Grain mill products. |
| Metal mining, other | 131 | 123 | Iron mining. |
| Mining—fuels; oil and natural gas | 129 | 125 | Petroleum and natural-gas production. |
| Distilled and malt liquors | 113 | 108 | Beverages. |
| Saw and planing mills | 93 | 89 | Sawmills and planing mills. |
| Pulp and paper mills | 123 | 104 | Pulp, paper and paperboard mills. |
| Agricultural implements | 112 | 110 | Agricultural machinery and tractors. |
| Aircraft and parts | 114 | 115 | Aircraft and parts. |
| Nonferrous metal smelting and refining | 123 | 112 | Primary smelting and refining—nonferrous metals. |
| Chemical products | 106 | 107 | Chemicals and allied products. |
| All manufacturing | 100 | 100 | All manufacturing. |

TABLE 3c.—*France and United States wage levels as percent of all-manufacturing average, selected industries*

| France | | United States | |
|---|---|---|---|
| Industry | Percent | Percent | Industry |
| Agricultural and food industries | 87 | 92 | Food and kindred products. |
| Chemicals and rubber | 90 | 108 | Chemicals and allied products; rubber products. |
| Hides and leather | 98 | 75 | Leather and leather products. |
| Textiles | 97 | 73 | Textile mill products. |
| Glass, clay, construction materials | 89 | 99 | Stone, clay, and glass products. |
| Production of metals | 81 | 119 | Primary metal industries. |
| Initial processing of metals | 97 | 127 | Blast furnaces, steel works, rolling mills. |
| Apparel and other products from similar materials. | 94 | 73 | Apparel and finished textile products. |
| All manufacturing and trade | 100 | 100 | All manufacturing. |

TABLE 3d.—*Germany and United States wage levels as percent of all-manufacturing average, selected industries*

| Germany | | United States | |
|---|---|---|---|
| Industry | Percent | Percent | Industry |
| Food industry | 79 | 92 | Food and kindred products. |
| Brewing | 106 | 131 | Malt liquors. |
| Chemical | 102 | 107 | Chemicals and allied products. |
| Iron industry | 134 | 122 | Blast furnaces, steel works, rolling mills; iron and steel foundries. |
| Nonferrous metals | 115 | 112 | Nonferrous metals: Primary smelting and refining; secondary smelting and refining; rolling, drawing, alloying; nonferrous foundries. |
| Ceramics | 85 | 96 | Pottery and related products. |
| Glass | 94 | 112 | Glass and glassware; flat glass. |
| Metal fabrications: | | | |
| Iron, steel, tin and metal products | 102 | 104 | Fabricated metal products. |
| Machine construction | 113 | 112 | Machinery (excluding electrical). |
| Ship construction | 115 | 114 | Ship and boat building and repair. |
| Road and air transport and equipment. | 121 | 117 | Automobiles; aircraft and parts. |
| Electrotechnical and equipment | 98 | 100 | Electrical machinery. |
| Precision machinery and optical equipment. | 96 | 102 | Instrument and related products. |
| All manufacturing | 100 | 100 | All manufacturing. |

TABLE 3e.—*Great Britain and United States wage levels as percent of all-manufacturing average, selected industries*

| Great Britain | | United States | |
|---|---|---|---|
| Industry | Percent | Percent | Industry |
| Cocoa, chocolate, and sugar confectionery | 82 | 78 | Confectionery and related products. |
| Other drink industries | 80 | 106 | Distilled, rectified, blended liquors. |
| Rayon, nylon, etc., production | 105 | 98 | Synthetic fibers. |
| Chemicals and allied trades | 103 | 107 | Chemicals and allied products. |
| Leather (tanning and dressing), fellmongery. | 98 | 94 | Leather: tanned, curried, finished. |
| Woolen and worsted | 82 | 79 | Woolen and worsted. |
| Glass (other than containers) | 107 | 139 | Flat glass. |
| China and earthenware | 83 | 96 | Pottery and related products. |
| Jewelry, plate and refining of precious metals. | 95 | 90 | Jewelry, silverware, plated ware. |
| Iron and steel tubes | 117 | 128 | Blast furnaces, steel works (excluding electrometallurgical). |
| Nonferrous metals: smelting, rolling, etc. | 118 | 112 | Nonferrous metals: Primary smelting and refining; secondary smelting and refining; rolling, drawing, and alloying. |
| Engineering, shipbuilding, and electrical goods. | 108 | 108 | Ship and boat building and repair; machinery (nonelectrical); electrical machinery; ordnance and accessories. |
| Manufacture of motor vehicles and cycles | 135 | 118 | Automobiles, other transportation equipment. |
| Manufacture and repair of aircraft | 123 | 115 | Aircraft and parts. |
| Clothing | 77 | 73 | Apparel; footwear. |
| All manufacturing | 100 | 100 | All manufacturing. |

TABLE 3f.—*Italy and United States wage levels as percent of all-manufacturing average, selected industries*

| Italy | | United States | |
|---|---|---|---|
| Industry | Percent | Percent | Industry |
| Canned meats, fish, vegetables | 84 | 79 | Canning and preserving. |
| Silk: Spinning | 66 | 68 | Yarn and thread mills. |
| Cotton; silk weaving; synthetics | 81 | 69 | Broadwoven fabric—cotton, silk, synthetic fiber. |
| Wool | 88 | 79 | Woolen and worsted. |
| Knitwear and hosiery | 69 | 72 | Knitting mills. |
| Hats | 81 | 82 | Hats (excluding cloth and millinery). |
| Sawmills; wood products | 72 | 88 | Lumber and wood; furniture and fixtures. |
| Metallurgy | 134 | 119 | Primary metal industries. |
| Machinery and electrical apparatus | 106 | 107 | Machinery (except electrical); electrical machinery. |
| Construction of cycles | 88 | 98 | Other transportation equipment. |
| Construction of automobiles and aircraft | 138 | 117 | Automobiles; aircraft and parts. |
| Pottery | 88 | 96 | Pottery and related products. |
| Glass | 106 | 112 | Glass and glassware; flat glass. |
| Chemicals and pharmaceuticals | 109 | 107 | Chemicals and allied products. |
| All manufacturing industries | 100 | 100 | All manufacturing. |

TABLE 3g.—*Japan and United States wage levels as percent of all-manufacturing average, selected industries*

| Japan | | United States | |
|---|---|---|---|
| Industry | Percent | Percent | Industry |
| Food and kindred products | 90 | 92 | Food and kindred products. |
| Lumber and wood products | 74 | 89 | Lumber and wood products. |
| Chemical and related industries | 126 | 107 | Chemical and allied products. |
| Textile mill products | 58 | 73 | Textile mill products. |
| Stone, clay, and glass products | 105 | 99 | Stone, clay, and glass products. |
| Primary metal industries | 153 | 119 | Primary metal industries. |
| Fabricated metal products | 100 | 104 | Fabricated metal products. |
| Machinery | 110 | 112 | Machinery (excluding electrical). |
| Transportation equipment | 137 | 114 | Ship and boat building and repairing. |
| Apparel and other finished products | 53 | 73 | Apparel and other finished textile products. |
| Medical and scientific instruments, photo and optical, watches and clocks. | 105 | 102 | Instruments and related products. |
| All manufacturing | 100 | 100 | All manufacturing. |

TABLE 3h.—*Netherlands and United States wage levels as percent of all-manufacturing average, selected industries*

| Netherlands | | United States | |
|---|---|---|---|
| Industry | Percent | Percent | Industry |
| Slaughtering, preparation and preservation of meat. | 97 | 102 | Meat. |
| Manufacture of cocoa, chocolate, sugar confectionery. | 95 | 78 | Confectionery and related products. |
| Pharmaceuticals and dressings | 95 | 98 | Drugs and medicines. |
| Textiles | 103 | 73 | Textile mill products. |
| Metal industry, air, road transport equipment. | 100 | 107 | Machinery (excluding electrical); and electrical machinery. |
| Shipbuilding and repair | 110 | 114 | Ship and boat building and repair. |
| All manufacturing | 100 | 100 | All manufacturing. |

TABLE 3i.—*Switzerland and United States wage levels as percent of all-manufacturing average, selected industries*

| Switzerland | | United States | |
|---|---|---|---|
| Industry | Percent | Percent | Industry |
| Clothing and wearing apparel | 100 | 73 | Apparel and other finished textile products; and footwear. |
| Textiles | 96 | 73 | Textile mill products. |
| Metals and machinery | 99 | 107 | Machinery (except electrical); electrical machinery. |
| Watches and jewelry | 116 | 91 | Watches and clocks. |
| All manufacturing, trade, private transport. | 100 | 100 | All manufacturing. |

TABLE 4a.—*Belgium and United States wage comparisons for selected industries*

| Belgium, male production workers | | United States, all production workers | |
|---|---|---|---|
| Industry | Daily earnings,[1] 3d quarter 1956 | Hourly earnings, 1956 average | Industry |
| | *United States cents* | *Cents* | |
| Textiles | 376 | 145 | Textile mill products. |
| Nonmetallic minerals: Glass | 418 | 221 | Flat glass; glass and glassware. |
| Art and precision | 422 | 166 | Jewelry and findings. |
| Fabrication of articles from common metals (not elsewhere specified). | 414 | 207 | Fabricated metal products. |
| Melting, casting, rolling, forging, extracting metal. | 521 | 236 | Primary metal industries. |
| Fabrication of machines, including electrical and transportation (excluding ship repairing). | 443 | 212 | Machinery (excluding electrical); and electrical machinery. |
| All manufacturing industries | 434 | 198 | All manufacturing. |

[1] Converted at exchange rate; 1 Belgian franc equals 2 United States cents. No information available on hours worked.

TABLE 4b.—*Canada and United States wage comparisons for selected industries*

| Canada, all production workers | | United States, all production workers | |
|---|---|---|---|
| Industry | Hourly earnings,[1] May 1957 | Hourly earnings, 1956 average | Industry |
| | *United States cents* | *Cents* | |
| Meat products | 173 | 202 | Meat products. |
| Grain mill products | 155 | 187 | Grain mill products. |
| Metal mining, other | 218 | 243 | Iron mining. |
| Mining; fuels; oil and natural gas | 215 | 248 | Petroleum and natural gas production |
| Distilled and malt liquors | 189 | 213 | Beverages. |
| Saw and planing mills | 156 | 177 | Sawmills and planing mills. |
| Pulp and paper mills | 206 | 206 | Pulp, paper and paperboard mills. |
| Agricultural implements | 187 | 217 | Agricultural machinery and tractors. |
| Aircraft and parts | 190 | 228 | Aircraft and parts. |
| Nonferrous metal smelting and refining | 205 | 222 | Primary smelting and refining—nonferrous metals. |
| Chemical products | 177 | 211 | Chemicals and allied products. |
| All manufacturing | 167 | 198 | All manufacturing. |

[1] Converted at exchange rate, 1 Canadian cent equals 1.0465 United States cents.

TABLE 4c.—*France and United States wage comparisons for selected industries*

| France,[1] skilled male production workers | | United States, all production workers | |
|---|---|---|---|
| Industry | Hourly basic wage rates,[2] (Apr. 1, 1957) | Hourly earnings, 1956 average | Industry |
| | *United States cents* | *Cents* | |
| Agricultural and food industries | 55 | 183 | Food and kindred products. |
| Chemicals and rubber | 57 | 213 | Chemicals and allied products; rubber products. |
| Hides and leather | 62 | 149 | Leather and leather products. |
| Textiles | 61 | 145 | Textile mill products. |
| Glass, clay, construction materials | 56 | 196 | Stone, clay, and glass products. |
| Production of metals | 51 | 236 | Primary metal industries. |
| Initial processing of metals | 61 | 252 | Blast furnaces, steel works, rolling mills. |
| Apparel and other products from similar materials. | 59 | 145 | Apparel and finished textile products. |
| All manufacturing and trade | 63 | 198 | All manufacturing.[3] |

[1] Data represent Paris area except for production of metals which represents rates paid in the highest wage zone outside Paris.
[2] Converted at exchange rate, 1 French franc equals 0.2857 of 1 United States cent.
[3] Data not available to calculate average for all manufacturing and trade.

TABLE 4d.—*Germany and United States wage comparisons for selected industries*

| Germany, all production workers | | United States, all production workers | |
|---|---|---|---|
| Industry | Gross hourly earnings, November 1956 [1] | Hourly earnings, 1956 average | Industry |
| | *United States cents* | *Cents* | |
| Food industry | 37 | 183 | Food and kindred products. |
| Brewing | 50 | 259 | Malt liquors. |
| Chemicals | 48 | 211 | Chemicals and allied products. |
| Iron industry | 63 | 241 | Blast furnaces, steelworks, rolling mills; iron and steel foundries. |
| Nonferrous metals | 54 | 221 | Nonferrous metals: Primary smelting and refining; secondary smelting and refining; rolling, drawing, alloying; nonferrous foundries. |
| Ceramics | 40 | 191 | Pottery and related products. |
| Glass | 44 | 221 | Flat glass; glass and glassware. |
| Metal fabrications: | | | |
| Iron, steel, tin and metal products | 48 | 207 | Fabricated metal products. |
| Machine construction | 53 | 221 | Machinery (excluding electrical). |
| Ship construction | 54 | 225 | Ship and boat building and repairing. |
| Road and air transport and equipment. | 57 | 232 | Automobiles; aircraft and parts. |
| Electrotechnical and equipment | 46 | 198 | Electrical machinery. |
| Precision machinery and optical equipment. | 45 | 201 | Instruments and related products. |
| All manufacturing | 47 | 198 | All manufacturing. |

[1] Converted at exchange rate, 1 German mark equals 23.81 United States cents.

**TABLE 4e.**—*Great Britain and United States wage comparisons for selected industries*

| Great Britain, all production workers | | United States, all production workers | |
|---|---|---|---|
| Industry | Hourly earnings,[1] October 1956 | Hourly earnings, 1956 average | Industry |
| | *United States cents* | *Cents* | |
| Cocoa, chocolate, and sugar confectionery. | 49 | 155 | Confectionery and related products. |
| Other drink industries | 48 | 210 | Distilled, rectified, blended liquors. |
| Rayon, nylon, etc., production | 63 | 195 | Synthetic fibers. |
| Chemicals and allied trades | 62 | 211 | Chemicals and allied products. |
| Leather (tanning and dressing), fellmongery. | 59 | 187 | Leather: Tanned, curried, finished. |
| Woolen and worsted | 49 | 157 | Woolen and worsted. |
| Glass (other than containers) | 64 | 275 | Flat glass. |
| China and earthenware | 50 | 191 | Pottery and related products. |
| Jewelry, plate and refining of precious metals. | 57 | 178 | Jewelry, silverware, plated ware. |
| Iron and steel tubes | 70 | 253 | Blast furnaces, steel works (excluding electrometallurgical). |
| Nonferrous metals: Smelting, rolling, etc. | 71 | 222 | Nonferrous metals: Primary smelting and refining; secondary smelting and refining; rolling, drawing and alloying. |
| Engineering, shipbuilding and electrical goods. | 65 | 213 | Ship and boat building and repair; machinery (nonelectrical); electrical machinery; ordnance and accessories. |
| Manufacture of motor vehicles and cycles. | 81 | 234 | Autos; other transportation equipment. |
| Manufacture and repair of aircraft | 74 | 228 | Aircraft and parts. |
| Clothing | 46 | 145 | Apparel; footwear. |
| All manufacturing | 60 | 198 | All manufacturing. |

[1] Converted at exchange rate, 1 British penny equals 1.167 United States cents.

**TABLE 4f.**—*Italy and United States wage comparisons for selected industries*

| Italy, all production workers | | United States, all production workers | |
|---|---|---|---|
| Industry | Hourly basic wages,[1] June 1956 | Hourly earnings, 1956 average | Industry |
| | *United States cents* | *Cents* | |
| Canned meats, fish, vegetables | 27 | 157 | Canning and preserving. |
| Silk: spinning | 21 | 134 | Yarn and thread mills. |
| Cotton; silk weaving; synthetics | 26 | 137 | Broadwoven fabric—Cotton, silk, synthetic fiber. |
| Wool | 28 | 157 | Woolen and worsted. |
| Knitwear and hosiery | 22 | 142 | Knitting mills. |
| Hats | 26 | 163 | Hats (excluding cloth and millinery). |
| Sawmills; wood products | 23 | 174 | Lumber and wood; furniture and fixtures. |
| Metallurgy | 43 | 236 | Primary metal industries. |
| Machinery and electrical apparatus | 34 | 212 | Machinery (except electrical); electrical machinery. |
| Construction of cycles | 28 | 193 | Other transportation equipment. |
| Construction of automobiles and aircraft. | 44 | 232 | Automobiles; aircraft and parts. |
| Pottery | 28 | 191 | Pottery and related products. |
| Glass | 34 | 221 | Flat glass; glass and glassware. |
| Chemical and pharmaceuticals | 35 | 211 | Chemicals and allied products. |
| All manufacturing industries | 32 | 198 | All manufacturing. |

[1] Converted at exchange rate, 1 Italian lira equals 0.16 of 1 United States cent.

TABLE 4g.—*Japan and United States wage comparisons for selected industries*

| Japan, all production workers | | United States, all production workers | |
|---|---|---|---|
| Industry | Hourly earnings,[1] April 1957 | Hourly earnings, 1956 average | Industry |
| | *United States cents* | *Cents* | |
| Food and kindred products | 17 | 183 | Food and kindred products. |
| Lumber and wood products | 14 | 176 | Lumber and wood products. |
| Chemical and related industries | 24 | 211 | Chemical and allied products. |
| Textile mill products | 11 | 145 | Textile mill products. |
| Stone, clay, and glass products | 20 | 196 | Stone, clay, and glass products. |
| Primary metal industries | 29 | 236 | Primary metal industries. |
| Fabricated metal products | 19 | 207 | Fabricated metal products. |
| Machinery | 21 | 221 | Machinery (excluding electrical). |
| Transportation equipment | 26 | 225 | Ship and boat building and repairing. |
| Apparel and other finished products | 10 | 145 | Apparel and other finished textile products. |
| Medical and scientific instruments, photo and optical, watches and clocks. | 20 | 201 | Instruments and related products. |
| All manufacturing | 19 | 198 | All manufacturing. |

[1] Converted at exchange rate, 1 yen equals 0.2778 of 1 United States cent.

TABLE 4h.—*Netherlands and United States wage comparisons for selected industries*

| Netherlands, male production workers | | United States, all production workers | |
|---|---|---|---|
| Industry | Hourly earnings,[1] October 1955 | Hourly earnings, 1956 average | Industry |
| | *United States cents* | *Cents* | |
| Slaughtering, preparation, and preservation of meat. | 38 | 202 | Meat. |
| Manufacture of cocoa, chocolate, sugar confectionery. | 37 | 155 | Confectionery and related products. |
| Pharmaceuticals and dressings | 37 | 193 | Drugs and medicines. |
| Textiles | 40 | 145 | Textile mill products. |
| Metal industry, air, road transport equipment. | 39 | 212 | Machinery (excluding electrical); and electrical machinery. |
| Shipbuilding and repair | 43 | 225 | Ship and boat building and repair. |
| All manufacturing | 39 | 198 | All manufacturing. |

[1] Converted at exchange rate, 1 guilder equals 26.32 United States cents.

**TABLE 4i.—*Switzerland and United States wage comparisons for selected industries***

| Switzerland, male production workers | | United States, all production workers | |
|---|---|---|---|
| Industry | Hourly earnings,[1] October 1955 | Hourly earnings, 1956 average | Industry |
| | *United States cents* | *Cents* | |
| Clothing and wearing apparel | 76 | 145 | Apparel and other finished textile products; and footwear. |
| Textiles | 73 | 145 | Textile mill products. |
| Metals and machinery | 75 | 212 | Machinery (except electrical); electrical machinery. |
| Watches and jewelry | 88 | 181 | Watches and clocks. |
| All manufacturing, trade, private transport. | 76 | 198 | All manufacturing.[2] |

[1] Converted at exchange rate, 1 Swiss franc equals 23.27 United States cents.
[2] Data not available for calculation of average for all manufacturing, trade and transport.

## APPENDIX I

### INTERNATIONAL COMPARISONS OF PRODUCTIVITY

Postwar interest has led to a number of attempts at measurement of the levels and rates of growth of productivity in different countries. Attention has been directed to all three types of measures: Individual plant comparisons, physical productivity in groups of industries, and overall gross national product measures. All the studies stress the difficulties involved in making international comparisons and the tentative nature of the conclusions to be drawn.

Among the problems are: Lack of output and man-hour data for many countries; comparability between output and man-hour data; nonhomogeneity of product between countries; differences in the structure and degree of integration of firms in different countries; valuation of services in each country; and conversion of values of output or expenditure into standard currencies.

It is not surprising that such studies as have been made are studded with words of caution concerning the conclusions. These range from Rostas' 1948 warning that his figures "can at best give only an aproximate picture of the position" to the footnote to the table in the eighth OEEC report published in 1957 that "the very tentative nature of these calculations must be stressed." These strictures should be kept in mind in appraising the summary of material that follows:

#### *1. Manufacturing*

The United States and England, long the most industrially advanced of the nations and for both of which are available relatively large amounts of data, are the subjects of one of the earliest and one of the latest of the studies.

(*a*) Dr. L. Rostas' study of the prewar (1935–39) relationship of the productivity of the manufacturing sector in the United States and the United Kingdom was based on an analysis of the physical output of 33 comparable industries accounting for two-fifths and one-half, respectively of the net output of manufacturing in the 2 countries. He concluded that the United States physical output per man-hour was 2.8 times that of the United Kingdom. He also indicates, on the basis of admittedly meager statistics, that a United States advantage of varying degrees was also present in the nonmanufacturing sector.

(b) Mr. Frankel in his study, based on 1947 census data for the United States and 1948 census data for the United Kingdom found only 30 reasonably homogeneous industries constituting only 13 and 16 percent of value added in manufacturing in the United States and the United Kingdom. In only one of these and in one subgroup of another, did the physical output per man-hour of the United Kingdom exceed that of the United States. No weighted average is shown but the United States/United Kingdom ratio ranges from 1 to 5.

*2. Gross national product*

Physical measures have the same shortcoming for economic analysis in international comparison as within the domestic economy and, as a result, there has been a great deal of interest in making comparisons on a net product basis. Among the factors affecting the gross national product type measure are the relative importance of high and low value-added-per-man-hour industries, the proportion of the population employed and relative importance of income from foreign investments.

Unfortunately no comparison of the levels of gross national product per man-hour are published. Most of the work in this field has been directed to obtaining comparable estimates of GNP which involves difficult conceptual problems as well as the currency conversion difficulty. Gilbert and Kravis have, however, developed some estimates of per capita GNP in selected European countries relative to the United States.

*3. Rate of change*

The relative position of the United States and other countries as to the levels of productivity is influenced by the rates of growth in productivity in these countries. The rates of increase in productivity in the United States and other countries in the world in the 20th century was investigated by MacDougall. After a lengthy presentation of historical statistics covering almost all the developed countries he concluded that, contrary to the commonly held impression, the output of food, raw materials and manufactures per head of population "have increased no faster in the United States than in the rest of the world as a whole in peacetime years * * *" and further than this conclusion "seemed to be largely unaffected if output were reckoned per man-hour since there is no clear evidence that leisure had increased faster in the United States than elsewhere."

A great deal of the pre-1939 data presented by MacDougall is based on the estimates by Colin Clark. These show that during the period 1924–39 the average annual rate of increase in real national product per man-hour worked for the United States was 1.8, a rate below 10 other nations in Europe, Africa, and Asia.

Additional data on movements of output per man-hour are presented by OEEC to indicate the relative progress of member countries. In the sixth report, however, the United States is included in a comparison which indicates that United States productivity has increased faster since prewar than any member country but that a large part of the difference has been due to the influence of the war. There are indications in the eighth OEEC report, however, that the year-to-year changes in output per man-hour in manufacturing from 1952 to 1956 in some member countries have equaled or exceeded those in the United States.

*4. Reasons for differences*

Many factors influence the productivity levels of different countries but there is scant statistical evidence for confirming the relationship between individual factors and the level of productivity. Furthermore the relative importance of the factors will vary among countries depending upon the composition of the country's output.

Among the factors frequently cited as contributing to the growth of United States productivity are availability of natural resources, size of market, size of plant, capital investment per worker, standardization of product, specialization of labor, managerial organization, and social attitudes toward competition and technical innovation. These factors are not easily separable since the existence of some follows from the others.

In Mr. Frankel's study he attempted to relate the few of these factors that are measurable to the differences in the United States and United Kingdom productivity by industry, market size, plant size, and equipment differences. It was his conclusion that while all of these contribute to the United States advantages in productivity there is no clear-cut relationship between each of these factors and productivity for the individual industries included in the study. That is, the industries for which the United States/United Kingdom ratio of productivity were highest were not necessarily those with the greatest United States/United Kingdom difference in plant size, market size or equipment.

The less tangible factors of organization and attitude have been emphasized by many writers including the members of the United Kingdom productivity teams that visited the United States after the war.

## Appendix II

## Wage or Average Earnings Statistics and Nonwage Labor Costs, Selected Countries

### BELGIUM

The statistics present average gross earnings of production workers employed in manufacturing industries. They include payments in kind, paid holidays, profit shares, and bonuses. The averages are presented separately for male and for female workers.

The averages are computed from data on total payments made to workers covered by the social-security system and on the total number of "days remunerated" as supplied by employers at the end of each quarter to the National Social Security Office. Such reporting is required by law. Counted as a "day remunerated" is any day or part day for which the worker is paid. The daily earnings reported do not represent workdays of a uniform length, therefore. [Due to the lack of statistics on hours actually worked, it is not possible to adjust for these differences.]

Nonwage costs are estimated to add approximately 25 to 30 percent to average earnings. Over two-thirds of these additional costs represent employer contributions to the social insurances and family allowance payments. Payments for days not worked account for the remainder.

### CANADA

The statistics report average gross earnings of full- and part-time production workers, including apprentices and working foremen paid on the same basis as production workers. Piece rates, incentive pay, and special payments like cost-of-living allowances which are made at regular and frequent intervals are included in the averages. Excluded are the value of payments in kind and any bonuses which may be paid at infrequent intervals.

The averages are calculated from data on gross wages paid and on total hours paid for, including hours credited to workers on leave with pay, as this information is supplied by establishments employing 15 persons or more.

Additional nonwage costs to the employer are low. Payments for days not worked are included in the averages as published, while family allowances, old-age pensions, and health programs are financed, not by taxes levied specifically for those programs, but through general taxation.

### FRANCE

The statistics present average wage rates paid production workers 18 years of age and over. Any bonuses which are applicable alike to all workers in a given establishment are included. The averages are given separately for men and for women workers in each of 5 wage zones and 5 skill groups; no averages covering both sexes, or the entire country, or all skill groups are computed.

The data are assembled at the close of each quarter by the Ministry of Labor and Social Security by means of questionnaires sent to all privately operated establishments employing more than 50 workers and to about one-half of those with from 10 to 50 workers. Excluded from coverage are enterprises in the nationalized sector of the economy, many of which are large and relatively high-wage establishments. Somewhat more than two-thirds of all production workers are represented in the statistics.

At infrequent intervals, the Ministry of Labor and Social Security assembles information on the relationship between average earnings and the wage rates reported in its quarterly surveys. Principally because the standard workweek is 40 hours and most plants regularly operate on an overtime basis, the premium payments which are not included in the official wage statistics represent an important element in most workers' take-home pay. In October 1955 average earnings were reported to range from a low of 4 percent above average wage rates in the case of workers in the apparel industry, to a high of 34 percent for chemical and rubber industry workers.

The employer's nonwage costs represent an additional expenditure amounting to from 40 to 45 percent of the amounts paid out in wages. One-third of these additional expenditures take the form of special bonuses and payments for time not worked. Most of the remainder represents payroll taxes and employer contributions to finance the social insurances and family allowances. A small amount, not exceeding 3 or 4 percent of wages, finances supplementary services and benefits relating principally to health and recreation.

GERMANY (FEDERAL REPUBLIC)

The statistics report gross earnings of production workers of all ages. Included in the averages are bonuses and family allowances. Not included are profit shares, reimbursement for tools, uniforms, travel, ètc., and payments in kind.

The averages are based on data relative to total wages paid and total hours paid for, including paid holidays and vacations. All establishments are required by law to submit this information, on request, to local statistical services which in turn forward it to the Federal Statistical Office. The sample from which such information is requested 4 times a year consists of establishments employing 10 or more persons, and covers well over 90 percent of all production workers employed in industry and construction.

Since the earnings statistics include family allowance payments and since they are averaged from data on hours which include paid leave, some 10 percent of the employer's nonwage costs are included in figures reported. Additional nonwage costs, representing social-insurance assessments and fringe benefits afforded workers on a voluntary basis, amount to about 25 or 30 percent of earnings.

UNITED KINGDOM

The official statistics give average gross hourly earnings of manual workers in manufacturing industries. They include overtime, premiums, bonuses, etc., paid to minors as well as to adult workers. Home workers are not covered.

The averages are calculated from information on total man-hours worked and total wages paid which is submitted semiannually to the Ministry of Labor by manufacturing establishments. For the most part, the firms from which this information is requested 4 times a year consists of establishments employing 10 or more persons, and covers well over 90 percent of all production workers employed in industry and construction.

Nonwage costs incumbent on employers in manufacturing industries approximate 10 to 15 percent of the amounts paid out in wages. Half or more of these additional costs represent payments for time not worked on holidays and during vacations. Employer assessments to help finance the social-security system are relatively low compared to assessments in other European countries, principally because much of this program is financed through general taxation rather than through employer contributions earmarked for this purpose.

ITALY

The statistics represent average wage rates paid production workers of both sexes and all ages. Included are cost-of-living allowances and payments in kind.

The averages are computed from information which the local offices of the Ministry of Labor and Social Security assemble by questionnaire. In the case of one-third of the industries covered the surveys include all operating establishments; for the remainder only those establishments employing at least 10 production workers are included. Altogether, approximately 55 percent of all production workers employed in Italian industry are covered. Questionnaire returns are checked each month by inspectors of the Ministry of Labor who investigate a random 3-percent sample.

The relationship between average wage rates and total costs to the employer for each man-hour worked may vary greatly from one month to another because of the incidence of paid holidays and vacations and the practice of periodically paying very substantial bonuses. Prorated over the course of a year, employer costs which are not directly associated with time spent on the job have been calculated to equal between 65 and 70 percent of the amounts expended in the form of basic wages. Special bonuses and the cost of paid holidays and vacations make up somewhat more than one-fourth of these additional payments, and employer assessments for social security, family allowances and related programs account for nearly three-fourths.

### JAPAN

The statistics present average monthly gross earnings of manufacturing production workers employed either on a permanent basis or else for at least 18 days in each of the 2 preceding months. Included in the averages are overtime pay, incentive pay, premiums, bonuses, and, in most instances, family allowances. Any payments in kind that may be made are not taken into consideration. The earnings of foremen, supervisors, and similar classifications are not included.

The data are compiled from replies to questionnaires sent each month by the Ministry of Labor to a sample of industrial firms. The sample is made up, for the most part, of firms employing 30 or more workers, but to the extent that it may be necessary to enlarge it in order to obtain data for 50 percent of all production workers in the country, it may include smaller establishments as well. [Data on hours worked which are assembled in the same way have been used to reduce to hourly averages the statistics on monthly earnings which are reported in the official series.]

Fringe benefits which are not reflected in the averages for each month are substantial. The largest single item is a bonus paid at mid-year and again in December or January; averaged for all private firms and governmental institutions, the semiannual bonuses total somewhat more than 2 months' pay per worker per year. In addition workers receive pay for generous amounts of leave for sickness, vacations, holidays, and contingencies like marriage, maternity, deaths of relatives, voting. Those employed in large cities may receive special area allowances to offset higher living costs. Many large industrial firms normally furnish housing for a substantial number of their employees. An assessment amounting to 2.5 percent of payrolls is paid by employers to help finance social insurances. Altogether, these nonwage payments which the employer makes have been estimated to amount to from 35 to 50 percent of base wages.

### NETHERLANDS

The statistics present average gross hourly earnings of adult production workers, including working foremen and related workers like maintenance and delivery personnel. Excluded are administrative and sales personnel, and employees whose functions are exclusively supervisory. The averages are presented separately for male and for female workers.

The hourly averages are computed from data on total wage payments and on total hours worked during 1 week in October of each year, as reported to the Central Bureau of Statistics by questionnaire. In most industries, only large and medium-sized establishments are surveyed in this fashion; in a few, where small enterprises occupy an important place, establishments employing 10 or fewer workers are included as well.

Nonwage costs to the employer not reflected in these statistics amount to about 35 percent of the payroll. About half of these additional expenditures represent employer contributions to family allowance funds and to social insurances. The remainder represents payment for vacations and holidays not worked, plus a payroll tax of about 4 percent.

### SWITZERLAND

The statistics give average gross hourly earnings of industrial production workers. They cover all types of payments made to workers, including family allowances and payments in kind. Averages are presented separately for 4 groups of workers: Skilled adult males, semiskilled, and unskilled adult males, adult female workers, and young workers under 18 years of age.

The averages are computed annually for one pay period each October, on the basis of information on total payments made and total hours worked which is assembled by the Government by means of questionnaires. An attempt is made to obtain complete coverage of all manufacturing establishments.

Family allowance payments comprise less than 1.5 percent of the earnings figures. Other nonwage costs incumbent on the employer but not reflected in the earnings statistics equal about 10 percent of the amounts paid out in wages. Of this, approximately 6 percent covers the cost of paid holidays and vacations, and the remainder represents social-insurance assessments.

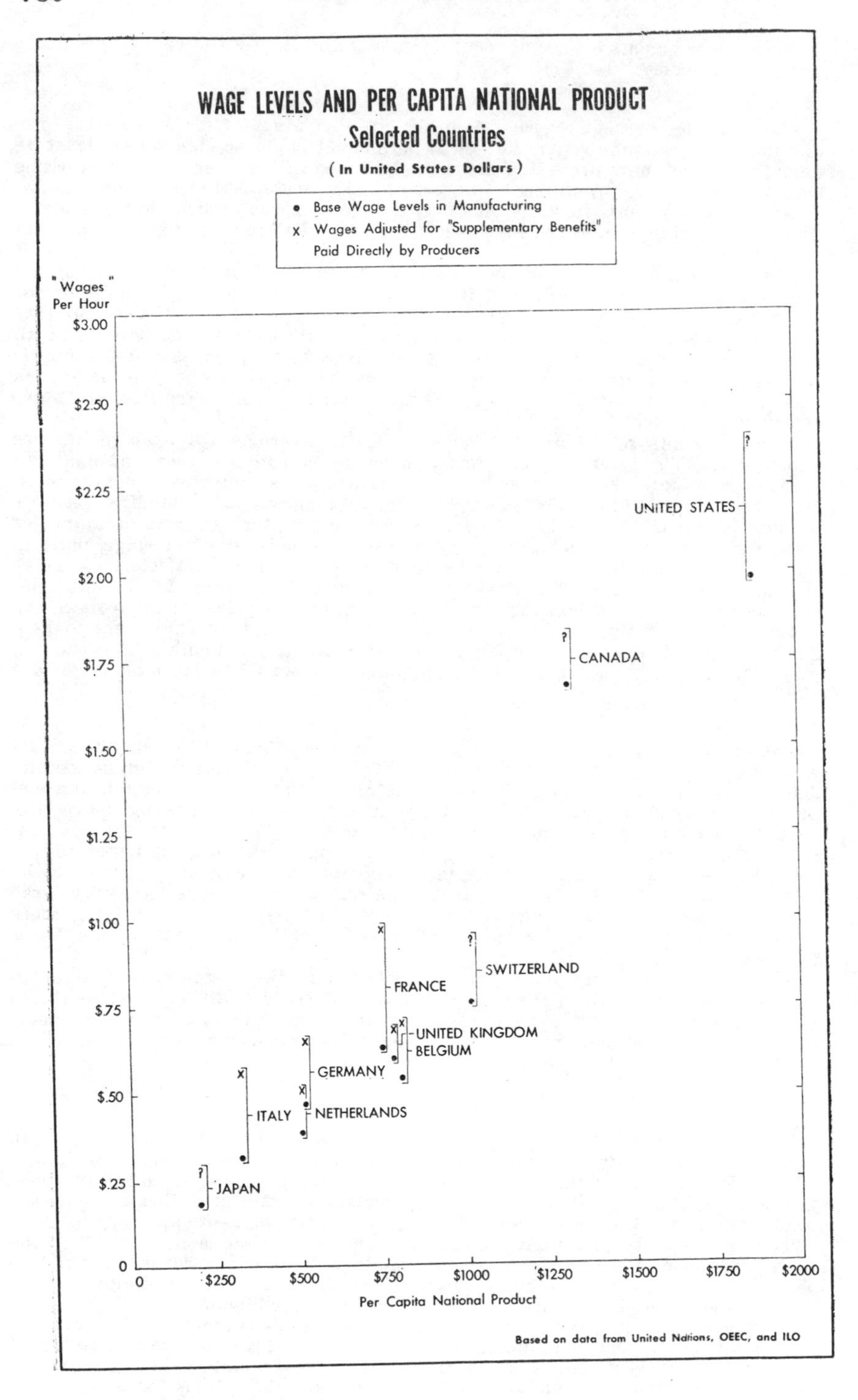
WAGE LEVELS AND PER CAPITA NATIONAL PRODUCT
Selected Countries
( In United States Dollars )
• Base Wage Levels in Manufacturing
x Wages Adjusted for "Supplementary Benefits" Paid Directly by Producers
"Wages" Per Hour
$3.00
$2.50
$2.25
$2.00
$1.75
$1.50
$1.25
$1.00
$.75
$.50
$.25
0
UNITED STATES
CANADA
SWITZERLAND
FRANCE
UNITED KINGDOM
BELGIUM
GERMANY
NETHERLANDS
ITALY
JAPAN
0
$250
$500
$750
$1000
$1250
$1500
$1750
$2000
Per Capita National Product
Based on data from United Nations, OEEC, and ILO

## PROBLEMS OF ADJUSTMENT FOR AMERICAN INDUSTRY IN THE LIGHT OF UNITED STATES FOREIGN TRADE POLICY

Stanley H. Ruttenberg, director of research, American Federation of Labor and Congress of Industrial Organizations

America is at a crossroads in its tariff and trade policy. It is now nearly a quarter of a century since the enactment of the Reciprocal Trade Act of 1934. The reciprocal trade program has been the vehicle for a considerable reduction of the barriers to commerce between the United States and other nations.

We can certainly view the experience of the past 25 years with considerable satisfaction. But while a look at the past is valuable for an assessment of historical achievements, what is much more essential today is a long, hard look into the future of America's tariff and trade policy. A thoroughgoing reappraisal of requirements and prospects in this field is especially necessary at this time in view of the impending expiration in 1958 of the 3-year extension of the reciprocal trade program.

In considering the future of American tariff and trade policy, we must face up to the actual facts which confront us. At the outset, let me frankly state that unless we are prepared to meet the realities of the situation—political and psychological, as well as economic—it is almost certain that the forward movement toward liberalization of trade which we have witnessed during the past 25 years will cease. Instead, we will probably see the erection of ever higher barriers against international trade and the gradual constriction of the economy of the free world.

Economic theorizing, no matter how logical or airtight the theories may be, will not assure the continuance of a liberal trade policy. Like most other economists, I tend to agree with the traditional "comparative advantage" theory of international trade. However, candor compels me to state that this is a theory to which most economists have adhered for generations; yet, by and large, it has had very little appeal either to the general public or to the political leaders who determine economic policy.

Mere theories, however valid, will not be enough to stem the onslaught of the growing protectionist forces in this country. These forces must be met on their own ground with a practical program which takes account of the very factors which have strengthened the drive toward protectionism.

I would point to two factors in particular. The first is the disparity between wages and labor standards in the United States and in other countries. Our tariff and trade policy must contribute to the gradual narrowing of this gap by focusing on the necessity to improve labor standards in exporting countries.

The second major factor is our failure to provide any avenue of adjustment to industries affected by import competition except the raising of tariff duties. It is imperative that we begin to provide assistance to the workers and employers in these industries to permit them without undue hardship to move into other industries and areas. We should not be forced to keep out foreign goods simply to permit American industries, long past the peak of their efficiency, to stay in business.

I am convinced that a liberal trade policy can be developed which will take account of these factors and thereby win the support of the American people. Let me briefly outline what I regard as the essential elements of such a program. In order to reverse the recent trend toward injection of ever tighter protectionist features in our tariff procedures and policies, I would suggest three specific steps:

1. Removal of mathematical limitations on United States tariff negotiators to permit them to lower tariff duties to actual peril points.
2. Modification of the escape-clause procedure in two respects:
   (*a*) Reduction or suspension of tariff duties on certain items accompanied by closing of the escape-clause route until imports reach a specified percentage of United States consumption.
   (*b*) As an alternative to increasing tariff duties in an escape-clause action, authorization of an adjustment program to provide Government assistance to workers, employers, and communities adversely affected by import competition.
3. Promotion of fair labor standards in exporting countries as a key element of fair competition in international trade.

In the ensuing sections, I shall develop these suggestions in greater detail.

BACKGROUND FACTORS

Before turning to some specific recommendations for consideration in developing tariff and trade policy, let me briefly outline a few salient factors which provide the background for whatever action may be taken in this field. I must frankly state that each of these factors enhances rather than reduces the complexity of the problems we face.

I am quite convinced that there are still ample opportunities for further reduction in tariff duties without serious impact on American industry and labor. Still, the very fact that the reciprocal trade program is now nearly 25-years-old means that such opportunities for completely noninjurious tariff reductions are becoming decidedly more limited. This is particularly true for many of the items on which other countries particularly desire tariff reductions.

Nevertheless, our ability in recent negotiations to reduce duties on large numbers of items without reaching the peril points on those items indicates that further lowering of duties on many items is still possible. However, by and large, our negotiators have chosen for tariff concessions, items on which there would be the least serious impact. This simply means that future negotiations, if conducted on the same basis as in the past and without the introduction of any mitigating factors, would become increasingly difficult.

A second factor which must be considered in any realistic appraisal of tariff and trade policy is the widespread misunderstanding of both the facts of our trade position and the character of our tariff and trade policy. This misinformation has engendered a very vigorous opposition to our current policy and to any steps toward removal of restrictions on trade.

While the impact of imports on a few specific industries cannot be minimized, the fact still remains that we have a large export balance and the volume of competitive imports has actually had a minimal effect on the economy as a whole. Far too few people seem to realize that trade is a two-way street. We are dependent on other countries for certain articles, principally raw materials, which we do not produce at all or produce in insufficient quantity for our requirements. But, as is evidenced by our continuing export balance, our sales abroad more than match our imports from other countries. Obviously, this is a situation which cannot continue indefinitely.

We could conceivably reduce our exports, but this would simply mean a contraction in our domestic economy. Moreover, it would deprive other countries of our products which they want and need. Foreign aid in the form of economic loans, grants, and military assistance is another way of permitting us to maintain a continuing export balance, but the contraction of the foreign-aid program, particularly to the more industrially developed countries, has limited that possibility for providing other countries with the funds to buy our products. The remaining alternative, therefore, is expansion of opportunities for foreign countries to sell their products to us as the only means by which they can, in turn, obtain the dollars they must have to buy our products. Our own economic interest, therefore, calls for a gradual expansion of imports.

Much more important, however, is the close tieup between our tariff and trade policy as one important facet of our overall foreign policy and the security of our own Nation and the entire free world. The markets which we provide other nations are needed to strengthen their economies and to permit them to import from us the machinery, equipment, agricultural commodities, and other items they must obtain to permit advancement of their own economies. If they cannot find markets for their products in the United States, they may be tempted to seek them behind the Iron Curtain. It is obviously, therefore, in our own national interest to seek to expand our trade with the other nations of the free world. We can ignore this fundamental requirement only at our own peril.

A third important consideration is the potential impact of the European Common Market. The United States has welcomed the organization of the ECM as a significant contribution to the development of economic cooperation of the European nations and integration of the European economy which we have been encouraging since the end of World War II. I intend to discuss this problem in some detail. At this point, I merely want to emphasize that the establishment of a free-trade area in Western Europe may have serious repercussions on our trade with that area. It will, therefore, be essential that our tariff and trade policy be sufficiently flexible to permit us to meet the problems that may develop in a manner which is to the mutual advantage of the United States and the nations of Western Europe which have joined together in the European Common Market.

IMPLICATIONS OF CURRENT TARIFF AND TRADE POLICY

Before the enactment of the Reciprocal Trade Act of 1934, United States tariff policy was predominantly protectionist. Protectionism perhaps reached its zenith in the Smoot-Hawley Tariff Act which preceded the Reciprocal Trade Act. Increasing emphasis on (1) mathematical limitations on tariff reduction, (2) peril points, and (3) escape-clause procedure more and more favors the protectionist approach. We seem to be returning to a policy which tends to place the interests of import-resisting industries paramount in our tariff and trade policy

The reason for this is not hard to find. The trade interests of exporting industries and firms tend to be diverse and marginal to their primary interest in the domestic market. On the other hand, the concern with tariff and trade policy of companies and industries most affected by the competition of foreign imports is quite specific and bulks large in their total business outlook. The result is that those whose interest lies in restricting imports tend to be united, vociferous, and militant. Export interests are much less vocal, and the broad interest of the consumer in getting the best value for his money is hardly expressed at all in the development of tariff and trade policy.

As a result, the one objective which seems to be at the core of our tariff and trade policy over and above all other considerations is absolute 100 percent assurance of noninjury to domestic industry. All other considerations, however essential to the economic and political interests of the Nation as a whole, are relegated to a secondary position. Moreover, restriction on imports, through imposition of tariffs, quotas, or both, seems to be the only means we have considered for guaranteeing noninjury to domestic producers.

In theory, one justification for continued high tariffs against the importation of items which have the largest competitive impact on domestic industry is protection of American employers and American workers against adverse competitive effects stemming from unduly low wages and labor standards in the foreign industries. In practice, however, the industries most affected by import competition tend to be among those with relatively low wages. This is because these have tended to be low-productivity industries by American standards and therefore least able to withstand the impact of foreign competition.

Moreover, we have done virtually nothing to improve labor standards in exporting countries. This should be an important objective in our tariff and trade policy. Yet, until we do so, we will fail to assure American workers and employers in competing domestic industries that they will not be the victims of unfair competition based on substandard wages and working conditions in foreign countries.

EUROPEAN COMMON MARKET

At this writing, the treaties establishing the European Common Market have been or will soon be ratified by the parliaments of the 6 member nations—France, Germany, Italy, and the 3 Benelux countries, Belgium, the Netherlands, and Luxembourg. There are many complex ramifications of the European Common Market for American tariff and trade policy, including the implications involved in the gradual equalization among the member nations of ECM of their tariffs against imports of nonmember countries, including the United States. Perhaps the most important change, however, is the creation of a free-trade area among the member nations of the ECM and probably in time also among an even larger group of nations, including Great Britain, the Scandinavian countries, Austria, Switzerland, and perhaps eventually all western European countries.

The United States has welcomed the organization of the ECM and indeed has done everything possible to foster it. As the financial editor of the Manchester Guardian has put it:

> The American decision to give Europe a large amount of money to get on its feet again, and the American insistence that the distribution of this aid should be decided by a joint European organization (OEEC), galvanized all the tentative European yearnings toward integration.

Our enthusiasm for the development of the ECM in the European free-trade area should in no way be tempered by a sober appraisal of the effects it may have on the American economy. A complete appraisal would require an industry-by-industry and product-by-product analysis. Such a study should certainly be made as soon as possible. Even without such a detailed study, however, it can certainly be stated that our exports to the free-trade area are likely to be seriously affected. United States exporting industries will have to clear tariff barriers while their competitors located in the free-trade area countries will have the advantage of being able to export to other countries in the free-trade area without any tariff duties being imposed against them. Clearly, United States exporters will be operating under a severe competitive disadvantage.

More than 16 percent of United States exports in 1955–56 were to the 6 ECM countries and more than 29 percent to the countries of the potential free-trade area. The jobs of about 500,000 workers depended on exports to the ECM area and 900,000 if the non-ECM countries in the free-trade area are considered.[1] This is obviously a sizable proportion of the labor force. Therefore, it is essential that we do everything possible to preserve our export markets in the European free-trade area.

It may be worth while to put this problem in its proper perspective by comparing the impact on employment of exports to the free-trade area on the one hand and competitive imports on the other. As I have indicated, some 900,000 workers depend for their jobs on exports to the European free-trade area. It has been estimated that if all tariff duties were temporarily suspended, total displacement of American workers might range from somewhat less than 200,000 to slightly more than 400,000.[2] This means that potential displacement from total tariff suspension is from one-fourth to one-half the potential displacement from loss of export markets to the European free-trade area.

Of course, nobody is seriously suggesting total suspension of tariffs. What these figures do suggest, however, is the importance of developing our tariff and trade policy so that we can effectively meet this very real threat to our export markets. In a later section, I shall indicate my suggestions for liberalizing our tariff policy so as to be able to

[1] Based on estimates of total number of workers dependent on exports given in Staff Papers Presented to the Commission on Foreign Economic Policy, February 1954, p. 373.
[2] See op. cit., p. 381.

effectively meet this situation. Whether or not these specific ideas are considered, it cannot be stressed too strongly that this new factor in the international trade scene must be given full weight in the debate which will take place next year on extension of the reciprocal trade program.

NEED FOR RECOGNITION OF LABOR STANDARDS IN TRADE POLICY

We should concentrate on the European Common Market development not solely as a potential source of difficult problems but also as an effort which may throw considerable light on our own policy considerations here in the United States. We may have much to learn from the ECM experience, because the removal of tariff barriers between these nations is forcing them to really face up to the problems involved in international economic competition.

One important area of concern in the ECM nations is whether removal of tariff barriers will give an unfair competitive advantage to a country with a lower level of wages and labor standards and, if it will, what can be done about it. The ECM countries have recognized that fair competition in international trade requires fair labor standards in export industries.

This is a principle long advocated by organized labor in the United States which has been given at least some official recognition in recent years. Thus, in its January 1954 report, the President's Commission on Foreign Economic Policy (Randall Commission) stated:

> The clearest case of unfair competition is one in which the workers on a particular commodity are paid wages well below accepted standards in the exporting country. In such cases, *our negotiators should simply make clear that no tariff concessions will be granted on products made by workers receiving wages which are substandard in the exporting country.* [Commission's emphasis.]

During the tariff negotiations between the United States and Japan in 1955, explicit recognition was given for the first time in the framework of a tariff conference to the importance of fair labor standards as an objective in tariff negotiations. At the conclusion of that conference, the head of the Japanese delegation formally stated to the chairman of the United States delegation:

> In connection with the recently concluded tariff negotiations sponsored by the contracting parties involving Japan, it is the foremost concern of the Japanese Government that wage standards and practices be maintained at fair levels in industries, including export industries, of Japan.

The ECM nations, however, have gone further than mere statement of principles. They have taken limited but significant steps toward what they term "harmonization" of labor standards. Specifically, they have provided that during the first stage of the transitional period, expected to be about 4 years, member states must put into effect the principle of equal wages for men and women and must also develop uniform vacation practices. The purpose is clearly to begin, at any rate, to develop a common pattern of fair and equalized labor standards.

As yet, ECM has not extended this idea to the most significant aspect of labor standards, the wage level. Here it is clear that fair competition in international trade requires that the level of wages must be related to productivity. Of course, it cannot be expected that the wages in the United States and, let us say, in Italy will or can be equalized. By and large, the level of efficiency is so much greater in United States industries than in Italy that the Italian firms cannot begin to pay the same wages as their American competitors. Moreover, the Italian firms attempting to sell in the United States market have to meet transportation and other costs which their American competitors selling in their own domestic market do not have to bear. However, the principle suggested in the Randall Commission report that only wages "which are substandard in the exporting country" would be an indication of substandard labor conditions may not be appropriate in all cases.

Unfortunately, we do not yet have the facts which would permit one to lay down a hard and fast policy in this area. I would strongly urge both our own Government agencies, such as the Bureau of Labor Statistics, and such international agencies as the ILO to begin to collect information on comparative labor standards in countries competing in international trade. Nevertheless, even if we do not have precise facts, we do know that the existence of unfair labor standards in some industries in exporting countries has tended to hold back efforts to obtain a liberal trade policy not only in the United States but in other countries as well.

Let me emphasize that attention must be focused on the problem of unfair labor standards in international trade, not to provide a basis for countries with higher labor standards to restrict trade, but in order to secure an improvement of the labor standards in exporting countries as a means of equalizing competition in international trade. I am convinced that if this problem is approached properly—that is, with due regard for differences in productivity as well as differences in size of market, transportation costs, and other relevant factors—relatively few instances will be found in which genuinely unfair labor standards have contributed to unfair competition in international trade.

Nevertheless, some such cases do exist and can be found. The question is: How can they be identified and what steps can be taken to mitigate them? With respect to the problem of unfair labor standards in international trade, I have already suggested that the Randall Commission test of wages "which are substandard in the exporting country" may not always suffice.

It is quite conceivable that employers in a particular industry might be paying wages which were high as compared with other industries in their country and yet have an unfair advantage over foreign competitors. This would be the case if the wages paid, while relatively high for that country, might still fail to reflect the level of productivity of the industry. In other words, one way of determining whether unfair wages are resulting in unfair competition in international trade is to compare the level of wages as against the level of productivity in the firms in the competing countries.

However, in making this comparison, account must also be taken of additional unavoidable costs in the exporting industries, such as costs of transportation, marketing, availability of raw materials, and the like. The test, therefore, should be whether the differential in total unit costs can be traced solely to differentials in labor costs. Only in such a situation are there grounds for suspecting that the superior position of the firms in the exporting industry rests on the existence of unfair labor standards.

This is one possible approach to the identification of unfair labor standards in international trade. Its effectiveness would depend in large measure on the feasibility of obtaining the relevant data in the two countries relating to wages and social charges (fringe benefits), productivity, and the various elements of nonlabor cost. Obviously, the availability of such data will vary from country to country and to some extent, from industry to industry.

Another approach might be to determine whether the exporting country, and particularly the specific industry involved in that country, was or was not meeting internationally accepted labor standards. Generally speaking, these are the standards which have been set forth in the conventions and recommendations of the ILO. The difficulty with this approach is that as yet, the ILO has not developed an internationally accepted policy with respect to the most important aspect of unfair labor standards—substandard wages. Thus, while the test of adherence to ILO standards is appropriate as far as it goes, it does not meet the major issue.

The practical difficulties of obtaining adequate data in what might be called the labor standard differential approach and the inadequacy of the ILO standards adopted thus far lead to the pragmatic conclusion that even though the Randall Commission formula may prove to be inadequate in some cases, from the point of view of effectiveness, combined with feasibility, it may in most cases be the best test available for determining the existence of unfair labor standards. Nevertheless, it would be a mistake to be bound by the Randall Commission standard because in the last analysis, it may not measure the ability to pay the exporting industry. Therefore, we would do well not to tie policy in this area rigidly to the Randall Commission standard. Rather, we should attempt to improve our data for identifying unfair labor standards in international trade to include instances where unfair labor standards are suspected in industries even though such standards may not be substandard in the exporting country.

Turning to the second question, namely, how do we mitigate unfair labor standards in international trade where they are identified, let me emphasize again that we cannot accomplish this objective by restricting imports. Clearly, the exporting countries cannot correct unfair labor standards if we restrict their markets. On the contrary, this can only have the effect of reducing their productivity and their earnings and forcing them, in all probability, to reduce labor standards still further rather than to raise them.

It is for this reason that the Randall Commission's recommendation that "no tariff concessions * * * be granted on products made by workers receiving wages which are substandard in the exporting country," if carried out literally would be self-defeating. The best interest of our own country and countries seeking to export to us will be served if our efforts are directed toward the twofold objective of expanding trade and raising labor standards in exporting countries.

If this is the objective we are seeking, then our course should be to make tariff concessions in accordance with a liberal trade policy, but for those items made in industries where there are unfair labor standards in the exporting countries, our concessions should be for a limited period and their continuing effect should be conditional upon sincere efforts in the exporting country to eliminate unfair labor standards. Such efforts will be enhanced by the economic opportunities afforded by the expanded market opened to the exporting countries, which would provide the earnings necessary to increase productivity and thereby improve labor standards. At the end of the stated time period, if such efforts have been made—efforts which in the context of the economic framework of the competing firms in two countries would tend to narrow unwarranted differentials and labor costs—the concessions would continue in force. Failure of the exporting country to take steps to eliminate unfair labor standards would be grounds for withdrawal of the concession. However, it would clearly be in the interest of the exporting country, even if no other internal political or humanitarian consideration were involved, to raise its labor standards and thereby maintain its export market.

Thus far, I have discussed an essentially bilateral approach to the problem of unfair labor standards in international trade. However, as I have already indicated, this is a problem which faces not just the United States but many other countries also. Therefore, it is a problem which can be met most effectively on the international level, perhaps through the cooperation of the ILO and the GATT.

I have already indicated that as yet the ILO has not adopted policies which would clearly identify the most significant instances of unfair labor standards in international trade. The AFL-CIO Executive Council has urged the ILO to make a thorough study of the question and to develop suggestions which would minimize the effect of labor-standard differentials on trade. It might be appropriate for the ILO to adopt a general policy, in the form of either a recommendation or a convention, under which the countries of the world would agree to eliminate substandard labor conditions which contribute to unfair competition in international trade. Machinery might then be established under which an aggrieved country or group of workers or employees within a country might request the ILO to investigate in a specific situation whether or not unfair labor standards existed in a particular exporting industry. An affirmative finding by the ILO might then provide grounds for the affected country to utilize the complaint machinery of the GATT to invoke international attention to request correction of the unfair labor standards as a condition for continuance of previously agreed-upon tariff concessions.

In this connection, I would strongly recommend that United States representatives to the GATT continue to seek acceptance in the GATT of the clause the United States informally proposed in 1953 which would help to correct unfair labor standards in international trade. Indeed, the clause itself went beyond, and in my opinion, is therefore superior to, the Randall Commission formula because it identifies as unfair labor conditions "the maintenance of labor conditions below those which the productivity of the industry and the economy at large would justify." The proposed clause was as follows:

The Contracting Parties recognize (1) that all countries have a common interest in the achievement and maintenance of fair labor standards related to productivity, and thus in the improvement of wages and working conditions as productivity may permit, and (2) that unfair labor conditions (i. e., the maintenance of labor conditions below those which the productivity of the industry and the economy at large would justify), particularly in production for export, may create difficulties in international trade which nullify or impair benefits under this Agreement. In matters relating to labor standards that may be referred to the Contracting Parties under Article XXIII they shall consult with the International Labour Organization.

Whatever specific techniques are worked out, it is important that the principle that fair labor standards are essential to the assurance of fair competition in international trade should be advanced and supported by the United States. We can do this by adopting a firm policy under which tariff concessions would be made conditional on efforts to establish and maintain fair labor standards in the exporting industries. Specific techniques for accomplishing this objective can and should be developed, but I would urge that specific recognition be given to this principle in the legislation which I hope will be enacted next year extending the reciprocal trade program. We should also seek to obtain acceptance of this principle on the international level in both the ILO and the GATT.

Development of fair labor standards in international trade is a highly desirable objective. It will benefit workers and employers in the United States because it will assure them that they will not be faced by unfair competition from foreign imports based on unduly low wages and labor standards in the exporting country. It will thereby tend to allay opposition to trade liberalization from those who feel that unfair competition from abroad based on substandard wages is depriving American workers and employers of jobs and economic opportunities.

Promotion of fair-labor standards in international trade would also contribute significantly to advancement of living standards and economic growth in the exporting countries. They will find as we have found in America that maintenance of decent wages and decent labor standards promotes domestic purchasing power, industrial productivity, and sound economic growth.

NEXT STEPS IN TRADE LIBERALIZATION

Establishment of the principle of fair labor standards in international trade is essential to continued progress toward removal of trade barriers. Assuming that effective action will be taken both by the United States, and through United States initiative on the international level, toward this objective, the key question for us is what further contribution can the United States make toward trade liberalization? As I have emphasized in an earlier section, this question has become all the more important because of the impending removal of tariff barriers among the countries of the European Common Market and the free-trade area.

Rather than advance precise formula for tariff reduction, I should like to indicate two possible approaches which might be considered, both of which I believe deserve careful study. Incidentally, the suggestions I shall make are not necessarily mutually exclusive.

One possibility would be for the Congress to authorize United States tariff negotiators to lower tariff duties to the actual peril points. If the peril points are sound, there is no reason to anticipate injury to American firms if tariff duties are not reduced below peril-point levels. Mathematical limitations placed on tariff negotiators which authorize a maximum percent of reduction actually mean that most tariff duties are held considerably above their peril points.

The only difficulty with this suggestion for reduction of tariff duties to actual peril points might be that here and there peril points might be estimated inaccurately and that a particular duty might be established at too low a level. It is extremely doubtful that this would happen in more than a very few instances. My personal observations of United States tariff negotiations as a public adviser have convinced me that our representatives bend over backward to protect American interests. Nevertheless, the possibility exists that in a few instances an unduly low peril point might be determined.

The answer, however, is not to hamstring all negotiations in order to meet this occasional problem. This problem must be met by developing an effective program of adjustment which will protect the welfare of those who may be adversely affected. I shall indicate the requirements of such a program in the following section.

A second possibility would be the institution of a program of limited tariff suspensions, an idea which has been advanced by Howard Piquet in his book, Aid, Trade, and the Tariff. The idea here would be that legislation should be enacted which would set forth that for certain items tariffs would be reduced or suspended and that escape-clause actions would be barred until imports exceeded a specified percentage of United States consumption. This would give foreign exporters the assurance they now lack that they could attempt to meet a known proportion of United States demand without fear of retaliatory action. Thus, an element of certainty would be injected into the international trade situation which is now missing.

This would obviously be advantageous to the foreign exporting firms, but it would also have very real advantages for us. Let us take the case of Japan, for example, on which so much attention has been focused in recent years. Japanese exporters are now concentrating on such items as textiles, apparel, and other soft goods requiring relatively little investment in plant and machinery, development of sales outlets in the United States, and other heavy long-term outlays. This means that Japanese firms in these soft-goods industries probably would not suffer a huge loss on their investment in export markets if exports to the United States were to be cut off or drastically curtailed. Nevertheless, because the Japanese must export in order to import the commodities without which their island economy would founder, they will continue to do everything possible to maintain their exports of soft goods to the United States.

Japanese manufacturers of machinery, metals, and other hard goods cannot afford to take such a risk. For them to develop an export market would necessitate large investment in plant and machinery and development of effective sales outlets in the United States. Such investments simply will not be made unless there is reasonable assurance of a continuing export market. The result has been that Japanese exports have been concentrated in the soft-goods area and have consequently had their heaviest impact on a relatively small sector of American industry; a sector, incidentally, which is least able to bear the brunt of import competition. However, if Japanese hard-goods manufacturers could be assured that they could try for a given percentage of the American market without reprisal, this might distribute the impact of Japanese exports more evenly on the American economy. It would also encourage diversification of the Japanese economy and thereby promote economic growth in Japan.

I have used Japan as an example, but of course, the same principles should apply in our trade policy as a whole. The dollar shortage has been a worldwide problem which has had serious economic repercussions. We have to face the fact that as the richest and most industrialized nation in the world we must be willing to provide a market for the products of other nations. I cannot emphasize too strongly that for the United States especially, trade must be a two-way street.

Let me hasten to add that I am not prepared to make specific recommendations as to the specific items where we might appropriately reduce or suspend tariffs (and obviously reduction might be appropriate in some cases and suspension in others) and provide an escape-clause waiver until imports reach a certain share of our domestic market. A delineation of the policy I am suggesting in terms of specific items and rates would require detailed facts on our present tariff structure and its effects both at home and abroad which are not now available. I would urge that the Tariff Commission and other appropriate executive agencies begin to make such studies at once on an industry-by-industry basis so that we will be able to assess in advance the probable impact of the policy I am recommending or, for that matter, any other policy that may be proposed. The failure of the Tariff Commission in recent years to keep up such studies has created a tremendous void in the facts we must have if we are to develop an effective tariff and trade policy geared to the realities of our own and the world economy.

Again, we cannot be certain that adoption of such a policy will not adversely affect some American firms and their employees, especially those whose business might be diverted to the exporting countries within the preimposed limitation. With the escape-clause route barred to them for redress, some other mechanism must be developed to meet their problem. The answer, I am convinced, must be an effective adjustment program.

## ADJUSTMENT PROGRAM

An effective adjustment program is an alternative to the escape clause and other types of protections which result in raising rather than lowering tariff barriers. It represents an effort to meet the problems resulting from import competition without resorting to measures which restrict rather than liberalize international trade.

The need for an adjustment program rests on two fundamental principles: (1) Tariff policy should not be so restrictive that tariffs must be maintained at or raised to unduly high levels in every situation where the domestic industry cannot maintain levels of activity without such a high tariff; but (2) the entire burden of the impact of increased imports must not be placed on the firms and workers adversely affected by tariff reductions. If tariff reduction is part of a national policy required in the best interests of the Nation as a whole, then no one group should be expected to pay the price of that policy. It is a cost which should be borne, insofar as possible, by the Nation as a whole.

I have already indicated that the total conceivable impact of import competition even if all tariffs were to be temporarily suspended would be exceedingly small. In all, some 200,000 to 400,000 workers might be affected, of whom only about one-third are in nonfarm employment. Clearly, therefore, the scope of the adjustment program could be quite limited, but this in no way detracts from the need for establishing it.

The basic feature of an adjustment program would authorize the President, where the Tariff Commission finds injury resulting from the impact of import competition, to provide certain types of governmental assistance to communities, workers, and employers adversely affected by such import competition. This would provide the President in such cases with an alternative other than the presently available ones of raising the duty or imposing a quota. Such a program might include:

For workers:

(*a*) Supplementary unemployment compensation benefits.

(*b*) Earlier retirement and eligibility for receipts of old-age and survivors' insurance.

(*c*) Retraining for new job opportunities.

(*d*) If necessay, transportation for entire families to new areas of employment.

For industrial enterprises:

(*a*) Loans for the adjustment to economic conditions resulting from trade policies.

(*b*) Technical information, market research and other forms of information and advice from Government departments and agencies to assist in developing more efficient production methods as well as new lines of production.

(*c*) Accelerated amortization to permit development of new or different lines of production by a business enterprise affected by import competition.

For communities:

(*a*) Loans to communities and industrial development corporations similar to those available to business enterprises.

(*b*) Technical information, market research and other forms of information and advice for developing a more balanced and diversified economy in the community.

This type of program was recommended in the report of the Commission on Foreign Economic Policy (Randall Commission) by President David J. McDonald of the United Steelworkers of America who was a public member of that Commission.

While his recommendation was not accepted, some members of the Commission thought that it deserved serious consideration. In a comment included in the text of the report, Prof. John H. Williams of Harvard University, with Mr. Jesse W. Tapp concurring, said:

I could not subscribe, without much further study, to the details of Mr. McDonald's statement, but I do sympathize with its general intent. As the report points out, however, it is part of a much broader problem, which I think deserves serious study by the administration.

Mr. John Hay Whitney, another member of the Commission, stated:

While not concurring with the program of labor adjustment outlined in Mr. McDonald's statement, I do recognize the principle of governmental assistance for adjustment to changed economic conditions involving hardship on individual workers.

Prof. Jacob Viner, a well-known economist and authority on trade policy, commented as follows on Mr. McDonald's proposal:

This is an interesting proposal, although the idea of compensating for the damage done by legislative reform or change is not new. According to some historians, the abolition of slavery in the British Empire came a generation sooner than it would have otherwise because the Government gave generous compensation. Similarly the British temperance movement in the 1870's and 1880's was able to reduce the opposition because the Government reduced the number of liquor licenses by buying up those it regarded as in excess at a fair appraisal of their market value before the new legislation. The lesson I draw from this is that one of the arguments for compensation is not merely the equity of it but also that it makes reform possible by diminishing opposition.

Subsequent to Mr. McDonald's recommendation to the Commission on Foreign Economic Policy, bills have been introduced by Representatives Eberharter (Democrat, Pennsylvania) and Williams (Democrat, New Jersey), and Senator Kennedy (Democrat, Massachusetts), designed to assist workers, industrial enterprises and communities to adjust to the problems created by increased imports. These bills would authorize specific action to establish and implement the type of program which has been summarized above.

In this area as in the field of labor standards, the countries which have joined together in the European Common Market have already taken specific action. They have provided for a European fund for the retraining and relocation of workers. This fund will be financed by contributions from the member nations and written into the general budget of the program. It will cover 50 percent of the amounts that each member state devotes to the productive reemployment of workers whose jobs are eliminated as a result of trade liberalization. The fund is expected to help meet the cost of retraining, relocation allowances, or compensation for part-time unemployment in cases of conversion of firms from one type of production to another. The experience of the ECM should be closely watched as we develop programs to meet our own needs.

## CONCLUSION

I have attempted in the foregoing sections to indicate some of the major issues which ought to be considered in the further development of our tariff and trade policy. My comments have been predicated on the conviction that reduction of barriers to trade and expansion of international trade are in the best interests of our own country and will advance the welfare and strengthen the security of the entire free world.

Yet, mere recognition of the desirability of a liberal trade policy will not assure its adoption. Indeed, I have reluctantly come to the conclusion that a liberal trade policy for America is doomed unless we face up realistically to the serious problems which such a policy entails. Among the most important such questions are the need to establish fair labor standards as a requirement for fair competition in international trade and the need to establish a program of adjustment to mitigate the impact of import competition. Both programs, I am sure, would significanly contribute to a greater public understanding of and public support for a liberal trade policy.

## THE LOW-FOREIGN-WAGE ARGUMENT FOR PROTECTION

Irving B. Kravis, professor of economics, University of Pennsylvania

Throughout the year, one of the main themes of those seeking more protection or opposing measures that might reduce protection has been the claim that domestic producers are confronted with unfair competition from foreign firms owing to the very low wage levels that prevail abroad. In the Ways and Means Committee hearings on H. R. 1 a year or two ago, for example, the low-foreign-wage argument was employed in connection with chemicals, hats, handbags, pins, electrical porcelain, watches, glass, textiles, and agricultural products, among others. Sometimes protection against cheap, foreign labor is held to be justified on the basis of equity in competition. The Government, apparently, is expected to maintain fair competition or, at least, to rule out or offset this particular source of unfairness. In other instances, the avowed justification of protection is not so much the interest of the producers as those of the workers. Foreign wages, it is pointed out, are often far below the minimum wage established by United States law. Unrestricted competition will, therefore, undermine the standard of living of American workers (sic).

In appraising the low-wage arguments for protection, I will first set forth the facts about comparative wage levels in the United States and other countries. Secondly, I will try to assess the role of wage differences in international competition. The question here will be: Are relative wage differences, generally, the decisive factor in determining what goods a country will export and import? Finally, I will discuss the policy implications of my findings, with due attention to specific cases where wage differences may, in fact, be responsible for trade patterns.

### COMPARATIVE WAGES

#### *International differences in wage levels*

Perhaps a good starting point is to ask ourselves how large a difference in wage levels might normally be expected between the United States and other countries. The wage level of each country depends, in the long run, upon the productivity of its labor force. Therefore, the total output of goods and services per worker should provide an indicator of the international differences in wages that will tend to exist. Internationally comparable figures on output per worker are not readily available, but data for a closely related alternative measure, output per capita, exist ready made in a United Nations source (see table 1).[1] The rankings of the countries and the general magni-

[1] The many technical difficulties limiting the reliability of international income and product comparisons cannot be discussed here, but it should be mentioned that the United Nations method is particularly vulnerable to criticism, since it is based on the conversion of the national income of each country to dollars at official rates of exchange. Because the official rates tend to place a premium on dollars—i. e., to understate the relative purchasing power of nondollar currency—the national income of foreign countries is generally made to appear smaller, relative to the United States income, than it really is. For comparisons of welfare, therefore, the United Nations figures for most foreign countries would be subject to substantial upward revision. For our purposes, on the other hand, conversions at the official exchange rates have more to recommend them. From the standpoint of competition in the domestic markets of the United States and in third markets, the wages, other costs, and prices of other countries should be translated into dollars at the rates of exchange which are effective in international trade.

tude of the output differences vis-a-vis the United States will differ but little from those on a per worker basis, since the proportion of the population engaged in the labor force tends to be similar from one country to another.

Examination of the table indicates that the per capita production of commodities and services in most countries of Western Europe during the period 1952–54 was in the range of 20 to 50 percent of United States output per capita. The per capita product of Japan was only 10 percent of the United States level. Aside from exceptional cases, such as the very rapid postwar recovery of Germany, these relationships among countries are unlikely to change rapidly in a short span of years, and 1957 data would probably show a very similar picture.

TABLE 1.—*Output per capita, selected countries, net national product, 1952–54*

| | United States dollars | Index | | United States dollars | Index |
|---|---|---|---|---|---|
| United States | 1,870 | 100 | France | 740 | 40 |
| Canada | 1,310 | 70 | Germany | 510 | 27 |
| Switzerland | 1,010 | 54 | Netherlands | 500 | 27 |
| Sweden | 950 | 51 | Austria | 370 | 20 |
| Luxembourg | 890 | 48 | Italy | 310 | 17 |
| Belgium | 800 | 43 | Japan | 190 | 10 |
| United Kingdom | 780 | 42 | India | 60 | 3 |

Source: Per capita national product of 55 countries, 1952–54, Statistical Papers, Series E, No. 4, United Nations, 1957.

Given these low per capita outputs, even in the most advanced foreign countries, we may expect to find corresponding low outputs and incomes for workers in foreign manufacturing. Some illustrations selected on the basis of readily available data are as follows:

| | Index of net product (1952–54) (United States=100) | Hourly earnings in manufacturing (1954) | |
|---|---|---|---|
| | | In United States cents | Index (United States=100) |
| | (1) | (2) | (3) |
| United States | 100 | 181 | 100 |
| Canada | 70 | 141 | 78 |
| Sweden | 51 | 76 | 42 |
| United Kingdom | 42 | 52 | 29 |
| France | 40 | 38 | 21 |
| Germany | 27 | 40 | 22 |
| Italy | 17 | 28 | 15 |

Sources: Col. 1: Table 1; col. 2: Bulletin of Statistics, United Nations; col. 3: Derived from col. 2.

The expectation of low foreign manufacturing earnings is more than confirmed. Except for Canada, foreign hourly earnings in manufacturing appear to be further below those of the United States (col. 3) than seems warranted by the differences in the overall incomes or products per capita (col. 1). A large part of the gap between the two indexes would be closed, however, if the hourly earnings figures could be adjusted so as to take into account supplements to wages such as paid vacations, family allowances, pensions, and the like, which tend to form a larger share of labor cost in Europe than in the United States. In France and Italy, for example, wage supplements in 1952 were equivalent to 42 and 67 percent, respectively, of direct wage payments as compared to only 16 percent in the United States in 1951.[2]

Taking all factors into account, then, the general level of foreign wages does not appear to be unduly low in terms of overall levels of productivity prevailing abroad. With current average hourly earnings in United States manufacturing running a little over $2, hourly earnings in the vicinity of 20 cents in Japan and 40 cents to $1 in Western Europe will not afford the typical foreign industry an unfair competitive advantage, or, indeed, a competitive advantage of any type, fair or unfair.

*Effect of domestice wage spreads among different industries*

Account must be taken, however, of the spread of wages in different industries around the national average. Owing to interindustry differences in wages within each country, the possibility still remains that while the average foreign industry may not enjoy an advantage from low wages, those that are actually successful exporters may. This raises the question of whether exports to the American and other markets are based on wages that are substandard in terms of prevailing wages in the country of origin. (We ignore, for the moment, the relation of wages to productivity, and concentrate on the probable range of variation in the ratio of foreign to United States wages.)

A first step in examining these issues is to determine what are "normal" wage spreads. Are wages in a particular industry "substandard" if they are only half the national average? One-third? Two-thirds? An exhaustive analysis of the idea of "substandard" wages is obviously beyond the scope of this paper. It does not seem unreasonable, however, to start with the assumption that there are no manufacturing industries in the United States today which pay average wages that are "substandard" in American terms, and to examine the wage spreads that exist among manufacturing industries in this country as a reference base for evaluating the spreads of other nations.

Among the 20 major categories of manufacturing industries of the United States (i. e., census 2-digit industries), the higest earnings are a little less than twice the lowest, and among the some 400 minor categories (i. e., census 4-digit industries) the highest earnings are a little more than twice the lowest. Examination of data for Canada, the United Kingdom, and Sweden suggests that this spread is typical for industrialized western countries. Interindustry wage spreads in Japan are somewhat larger with the highest wages being closer to three times the lowest. This, incidentally, is a marked change from the 1930's when Japanese textile wages were only a fifth or sixth of wages in the heavy industries instead of half or a third as they are now.[3] Wage spreads this large might compel further investigation of the substandard wage issue, but, fortunately, it seems highly probable that current interindustry wage spreads in foreign countries that produce the bulk of our competitive imports—including Japan—are

---

[2] M. Rothbaum, National Wage-Structure Comparisons, in G. W. Taylor and F. C. Pierson (editors), New Concepts in Wage Determination (1957), p. 316.

[3] Miyohei Shinohara, A Survey of Japanese Literature on Japanese Economic Growth, Department of Economics, Stanford University (processed), January 1957, p. 38.

not much greater than those of the United States. Indeed, some may be smaller. Wages that are substandard by foreign standards are therefore unlikely to be a major issue in trade and tariff policy.[4]

Nevertheless, the existence of domestic wage spreads of this size can conceivably increase very greatly the gap between United States and foreign wages in a particular industry. If it is assumed that in both countries earnings in the highest wage industry are twice those of the lowest wage industry and that the all-industry average is midway between the wages of the two extreme industries, the foreign-United States wage ratio for a particular industry can fall to as low as half of the foreign-United States ratio for the general level of wages. We may imagine, for example, that the "sky hook" industry is the highest wage industry in the United States and the lowest wage industry in the foreign source of supply, say England, and that the "widget" industry occupies the opposite position in the wage structure in each country. Starting from an all (manufacturing) industry average of $2 in the United States, the illustration works out as follows:

*Average hourly earnings*

| | All manufacturing | Sky hooks | Widgets |
|---|---|---|---|
| United States | $2.00 | [1] $2.67 | [2] $1.34 |
| United Kingdom | [3] .58 | [2] .39 | [1] .77 |
| United Kingdom-United States ratio | .29 | .14 | .57 |

[1] 1.33 times the all manufacturing earnings.
[2] 0.67 times the all manufacturing earnings.
[3] 29 percent of United States wage of $2. See text table, p. 3.

The implication is that the relation of foreign to United States wages may vary over a very wide range indeed from one industry to another. If in some industries the foreign-United States wage ratio may be half of the ratio for the general level of wages, and in others, twice the ratio for the general level, the variation from one industry to another could be as much as fourfold.

*International similarity of interindustry wage structures*

Actually, however, our illustration was based on the assumption that an industry which pays relatively high wages in one country pays relatvely low wages in another. If the identity of the high-wage industries tends to be the same in different countries, the international wage ratios for particular industries will tend to conform more closely to the average ratio for all industries (such as those shown in the text table on p. 4).

Although the question has never been investigated thoroughly, there is accumulating evidence that wage structures tend to be similar in different countries.[5] In general, the newer, more rapidly growing, less

[4] The Randall Commission recommended, and many people would agree, that tariff concessions should not be granted on products made by workers receiving wages that are substandard in the exporting country. (Commission on Foreign Economic Policy, Report to the President and the Congress, January 1954, p. 62.)

[5] Taussig surmised that this was the case many years ago. See his International Trade, 1927, pp. 55–60. For more recent evidence, see S. Lebergott, Wage Structures, Review of Economic Statistics, vol. 29 (November 1947), pp. 2[illegible]–285; Economic Commission for Europe, Changes in the Structure of Wages in European Countries, Economic Bulletin for Europe, vol. 2, No. 2 (second quarter, 1950), pp. 53–56; I. Kravis, Availability and Other Influences on the Commodity Composition of Trade, Journal of Political Economy, vol. 64 (April 1956), pp. 144–145; L. G. Reynolds and C. H. Taft, The Evolution of Wage Structure, 1956, pp. 355–357; and M. Rothbaum, op. cit., pp. 310–312.

competitive, and larger scale industries such as metals, machinery, petroleum refining, and chemicals tend to pay higher wages in all countries than the older, less rapidly growing, smaller scale and more competitive industries such as food, textiles, and apparel. Many illustrations could be given of the international similarity in the ordinal rankings of industries according to wage levels. One example involves 48 manufacturing industries in the United States and Great Britain which were selected by another student and for a different purpose.[6] The industries accounted for 41 percent of net manufacturing output in the United States and 48 percent in Great Britain. When the industries of each country are arrayed in order of annual wages paid to production workers, the rankings of the industries in the two countries are highly correlated. The coefficient of rank correlation is 0.79. This is very close to the result I reported to your subcommittee last year when I compared 20 Japanese and American industries and almost identical with results obtained by Rothbaum for comparisons among France, Italy, and the United States.[7] An earlier study by Lebergott concluded that—

> * * * for the years surveyed the United States pattern of (manufacturing) earnings is almost identical with the Canadian and the British, much like the Swiss or Swedish pattern, and is surprisingly similar to the Russian.[8]

The international similarity in wage structures has been noted also in several recent studies of the United Nations and its specialized agencies. A report by the International Labor Office, for example, has this to say:

> * * * though there are rather substantial differences in interindustrial patterns of wages, particularly as between agriculture and industry, there is also a definite general similarity among the various national wage patterns. For example, in all countries agricultural money wages are lower than wages in industry and in practically all cases wages in mining, quarrying, metals, and engineering are substantially higher than in textiles and other light industries."[9]

The way in which these similarities in wage structure operate to narrow the range within which the international wage ratios for different industries fall is well illustrated by the 48 British and American manufacturing industries mentioned earlier. United Kingdom annual earnings of production workers range from 24 percent of those of American production workers in the case of the automotive and cardboard box industries to 41.5 percent in the furniture and upholstery industry. (The average for all 48 industries is 31 percent.) Thus the highest ratio is less than twice the lowest, rather than four times.

We may summarize our findings about comparative wage levels as follows:

1. With levels of per capita production and income only 10 percent that of the United States in Japan and 20 to 50 percent of the United

[6] See reference to the work of Lawrence B. Krause in footnote 10. The industries are listed in the appendix.
[7] Op. cit., p. 311.
[8] Op. cit., p. 274.
[9] Social Aspects of European Economic Cooperation, Studies and Reports, N. S. No. 46 (1956), p. 34.

States in Western Europe, we may expect to find correspondingly low outputs and incomes for foreign workers in manufacturing.

2. It follows that when hourly earnings are around $2 in United States manufacturing as at present, hourly earnings in the neighborhood of 20 cents in Japan and 40 cents to $1 in Western Europe will merely reflect the productivity of the typical industry relative to that of the United States rather than confer any special competitive advantages on the foreign industry.

3. Since in each country wages for some industries are lower than the national average while others are higher, attention must be paid to international wage differences for particular industries as well as for industries in general. However, the ordinal ranking of industries appears to be similar in different countries, so that while some foreign-United States wage ratios will be higher and others lower than those indicated in the overall averages of the preceding paragraphs, the extent of the deviations will be relatively small. In one comparison of 48 British and American manufacturing industries, for example, the ratio of British to United States annual earnings ranged from 24 to 41.5 percent.

### THE ROLE OF WAGE DIFFERENCES IN INTERNATIONAL COMPETITION

The relatively narrow range of variation in international wage ratios implies either that (1) trade patterns are very sensitive to differences in wages or (2) wage differences play only a limited role in explaining the commodity composition of trade.

What conditions are required for the first of these alternatives to be true? The answer is that wage differences must be a good guide to cost differences, for success or failure in competition depends directly upon costs. There is, however, no particular reason for expecting that time wages (wages per hour or per annum) will be good indicators of cost differences even for the labor component of total cost. Indeed in the study of the 48 British and American industries there was almost a zero correlation between the ratios of British to American wages and the ratios of British to American labor costs (the coefficient of rank correlation was 0.07).[10] *Relative wages were thus a complete failure as a guide to relative labor cost.*

A good test of the bearing of relative wages in the 48 British and American industries upon international competition is provided by the relationship of the relative wages to relative exports of the two countries to third markets. The third market test is an effective one

[10] The labor-cost ratios and also the export ratios referred to subsequently were taken from a doctoral dissertation by Lawrence B. Krause entitled "Current Balance of Payments Problems of Industrial Countries: An Empirical Study," Harvard University, July 1957. This source was used because it offered a reconciliation of export and production statistics for both countries. Mr. Krause selected 52 industries from approximately 140 given in the summary tables of the British census of production. His criteria of selection were (1) both the United States and Great Britain must export the product of the industry to third markets, and (2) the classifications pertaining to the product in the two countries' export statistics and to the industry making the product in the production statistics must be readily reconcilable. The present writer added annual earnings data to Mr. Krause's information about exports and production, using the 1947 Census of Manufactures for the United States and the 1948 Census of Production for Great Britain (sources used by Mr. Krause also). Four industries included in Mr. Krause's analysis were omitted because the writer was uncertain how the reconciliation of British and American production data had been achieved. Mr. Krause's measure of relative labor cost, the ratio between Great Britain and the United States of the wage bill to net output, was used here. Thus what is referred to in the text as "labor cost" is really the wage component of labor cost. The 48 industries are shown in the appendix.

because the two countries enter third markets, it may be presumed, on a more equal basis with respect to trade obstacles than each enters the other's home market. The ratio of British to American exports to third markets was not correlated with the ratio of British to American wages, although it was correlated with the ratio of British to American labor costs.[11] That is, relatively low labor costs rather than relatively low wages determined which country exported more of a particular good to third markets. *Relative wages were thus a complete failure as a guide to an advantageous position in international competition.*

In evaluating the proposition that low wages generally provide the basis for successful competition in international markets, it is relevant also to consider the wage levels that characterize American import-competing industries and export industries. If wage structures were not similar and if low wages were in fact the determining influence, there would be some tendency for the leading export industries in each country to be found among the low-wage industries. For the United States, at least, the opposite is true as I showed in my testimony before this subcommittee last year.[12] Not only are American export industries relatively high-wage industries, but American manufacturing industries which are most vulnerable to import competition tend to pay wages below the average for United States manufacturing as a whole. (However, increasing reliance on foreign sources for minerals means that imports are shifting more toward higher wage industries, especially petroleum and other mining.)

If wage structures in different countries tend to be similar, it follows that American imports which tend to be competitive with the domesic output of low-wage industries must be produced by industries which pay wages that are low in terms of the foreign country's pay scale. However, this in itself would not confer a competitive advantage upon foreign producers unless low wages were accompanied by low labor and total costs. But while low wages, like low prices for other inputs, improve the international competitive position of an industry, given the level of labor productivity, we have seen that low wages are not systematically correlated with export success. Hence, one cannot say that in general international trade results from differences in relative wage levels.

## POLICY IMPLICATIONS

The only sense in which low wages aid the competitive position of an industry occurs when wages are low relative to labor productivity as compared to the relationship in other countries. Such will be the case, of course, whenever an industry has low labor costs as compared to its foreign competition. This situation thus characterizes American export industries such as automobiles and steel and foreign export industries such as English bicycle and Japanese textile manufacturing. Low wages in this restricted sense—i. e., relative to productivity—undoubtedly constitute an important influence upon trade patterns.

The policy issue is thus how to deal with particular situations in which foreign labor costs are lower than those at home. We have seen that such low costs cannot generally be ascribed to low wages per se,

[11] Spearman's coefficient of rank correlation for exports and wages was 0.18; for exports and labor cost it was 0.52. A coefficient as high as 0.18 could easily be obtained by chance alone, but there is less than 1 chance in 1,000 that a coefficient of 0.52 would have been obtained through the operation of purely random factors.

[12] Hearings on the Administration and Operation of Customs and Tariff Laws and the Trade Agreements Program, 84th Cong., 2d sess., pp. 297 ff.

because the whole structure of foreign wages is very low compared to American standards and because it is a combination of wages and productivity rather than low wages alone or even low wages primarily that enables a foreign country to achieve labor costs in a particular industry that are lower than those in the comparable American industry.

The very root of the gain from international trade lies in the fact that, owing to natural or cultural differences, certain industries will be able to produce at relatively lower costs in one country, while others will be able to produce at lower costs in some other part of the world. American producers confronted with the natural or acquired advantage of foreign industries often feel (quite rightly) that they are facing unequal odds and (more questionably) that they have the right to Government help in order to equalize the odds. Thus a Pennsylvania oil producer whose wells produce less than 1 barrel a day feels that it is "unfair" to have to compete with the wells of the Middle East that produce 5,000 barrels a day, and so, in a sense, it is. A large chemical company and a well-known glass company contend that competition from abroad is "unfair" because the low level of foreign costs enables foreign producers to capture American markets; and, in a sporting sense of the term "fair," they are right.

But surely no sound policy can be based on the principle of eradicating all economic advantages possessed by any contestant and reducing economic competition to a sports contest in which appropriate handicaps are assigned to all entrants. By this criterion laws should be passed excluding beautiful women from the stage and screen and handsome and intelligent men from Congress. In each case those favored by nature have an "unfair" advantage over others who are eager for an equal chance of success.

The oft-advocated policy of "equalizing competition" amounts to just this kind of nonsense. It would require us to throw away talents and advantages that are to be found in foreign production and thus to lose the gains that are available from international trade, just as excluding beautiful women from the stage and intelligent men from Congress would cause us to lose the benefits of their particular advantages. Matters would be made worse, of course, if foreign countries began to exclude American autos and steel on the same ground of "unfair" competitive advantage.

Does this mean that the claim for continued or even increased protection of every industry should be swept aside? Not necessarily. What it does mean is that claims for protection on the ground of "unfair" wage competition should be viewed with great skepticism. Indeed, they should be ignored unless the claimant can prove that some extraordinary wage or other situation exists.

In my opinion, the major consideration upon which claims for protection should turn is the extent and cost of the dislocations that would be entailed in the American economy were protection withheld. These costs, of course, must be weighed against the long-run gains to the United States—both political and economic—of a freer trade policy.

Our wage structure is safe from foreign competition. Indeed, the expansion of our imports would probably bring an expansion in our export industries, and this would involve the shift of workers into higher-wage industries and thus improve our labor-income structure.

APPENDIX

*48 British and American industries*

| | Great Britain minimum list heading | United States standard industrial classification |
|---|---|---|
| 1. Woolens and worsted | 112 | 221. |
| 2. Earthenware and china | 21 | 326. |
| 3. Wallpaper | 181 | 2693. |
| 4. Electrical wire and cable (insulated) | 71 | 3631. |
| 5. Umbrellas | 99 (8) part; 147 (4) | 3995. |
| 6. Musical instruments | 103 | 3663; 393. |
| 7. Toys and games | 193 (1) | 3941; 3942. |
| 8. Confectionary products | 156 | 207. |
| 9. Brushes and brooms | 192 | 3981. |
| 10. Asbestos | 129 (1); 199 (3) part | 3292. |
| 11. Rope and twine | 117 | 2298. |
| 12. Stationery and paper bags | 183 | 265; 266; 2691; 2694. |
| 13. Hats, caps, and millery, all types, cloth, leather or fur excluding knitted and rubber. | 143 | 228 (except 2284); 2326; 2351; 2381; 2382. |
| 14. Brass manufactures | 95 | 3361. |
| 15. Office supplies | 194 | 395. |
| 16. Paints and varnishes | 34 | 2851. |
| 17. Leather goods | 131 | 3161; 317; 319. |
| 18. Cotton yarn | 110 | 2224. |
| 19. Blast furnace products | 40 | 3311. |
| 20. Leather tanning, belting | 130 (1) | 3111; 3121. |
| 21. Hardware, metal products | 94; 99 (1, 2, 3, and 7) | 3411; 3429; 3442; 3491; 3492; 346 (except 3463, and 3467); 2514; 2552. |
| 22. Textile machinery | 56 | 3552. |
| 23. Mechanical engineering (general) | 52, 53, 55, 57 (part); 69:1–6, 9–12. | 3443; 351; 3522; 353; 355; 356 (except 3565); 357; 358 (except 3552 and 3555); 3593. |
| 24. Cotton cloth | 111 | 2233. |
| 25. Toilet preparations | 32 (2) | 2893. |
| 26. Hand tools | 90 (1) | 342 (except 3421 and 3429). |
| 27. Cutlery | 90 (2) | 3421. |
| 28. Glass other than containers | 22 | 3411; 3229; 3231. |
| 29. Abrasives | 29 (1) | 3291. |
| 30. Polishes | 35 (2) part; 199 (3) part. | 2842. |
| 31. Jewelry | 102 part | 391. |
| 32. Wire and wire manufactures | 93 | 3392; 348. |
| 33. Nonferrous metals | 49 | 333; 3341; 335. |
| 34. Tobacco products | 169 | 21. |
| 35. Batteries | 75 | 3691; 3692. |
| 36. Motor vehicles and cycles | 80; 83 (part) | 371; 375; 3521; 3565; 3943. |
| 37. Cardboard boxes | 182 | 267. |
| 38. Rubber manufactures | 190 | 30 except 3031. |
| 39. Fertilizers, insecticides, etc | 31 (2) | 287; 2897. |
| 40. Sporting apparatus | 193 (2) | 3949. |
| 41. Furniture and upholstery | 171 (2) | 251 (except 2514); 252 (except 2522); 2531. |
| 42. Coke and byproducts | 30 | 293. |
| 43. Scientific and photo goods | 100; 199 (2) | 38 except 387. |
| 44. Electrical engineering (general) | 70, 79 (part) | 361 (except 3611 and 3612); 364. |
| 45. Machine tools | 54 | 3541. |
| 46. Radio and tele-com-products | 72; 73; 74 | 365; 366 (except 3663). |
| 47. Drugs and pharmaceuticals | 32 (1); 31 (4) part | 283. |
| 48. Glass containers | 23 | 3221. |

Sources: For selection of industries, see text footnote 10.
Great Britain Board of Trade Censuses of Production for 1950, 1949, and 1948, summary tables, pt. I (H. M. Stationery Office, 1953).
Great Britain Central Statistical Office, Standard Industrial Classification, (H. M. Stationery Office, 1948).
U. S. Bureau of the Census, Census of Manufactures: 1947 (Government Printing Office, 1950).
U. S. Bureau of the Budget, Standard Industrial Classification, November 1945.

# LABOR STANDARDS IN RELATION TO FOREIGN TRADE POLICY

N. Arnold Tolles, professor of economics, New York State School of Industrial and Labor Relations, Cornell University

## INTRODUCTION

This memorandum, submitted in response to an invitation by the Subcommittee on Foreign Trade Policy of the Committee on Ways and Means of the United States House of Representatives, provides three proposals for revision of United States policy toward imported goods which compete with the products of American labor. These proposals are based on some underlying logic which needs to be set out frankly in advance of the specific proposals.

## I. ANALYSIS OF THE FOREIGN-TRADE PROBLEM

1. In the United States, as in every other country, the economic welfare of the buyers of goods can be promoted best by unrestricted freedom of international commerce. Freedom of trade within the vast area of the United States has been vital to the great development of our country. Freedom of international trade benefits the buyers of goods in just the same way as it has benefited the American people. Hence, there is a prima facie case for unrestricted international trade, in the interests of the buyers. Since the American working people constitute the overwhelming majority of buyers, both in numbers and in the volume of purchases, the general interest of workers, as consumers of goods, is in unrestricted international trade.

2. The interests of buyers are normally supported by the interests of those producers who expect to sell goods abroad. The greater the volume of sales by foreign producers, the greater will be the dollar purchasing power which can be used by foreigners to buy the products of American industry. However, American exports can be financed by American loans and gifts as well as by the proceeds of the sales of foreign goods to this country. The large volume of United States Government loans and grants to foreign countries, since 1940, has weakened the interest of American exporters in the admission of imported goods into the United States. Hence, the buyer interest in freer international trade is not as strongly supported as it was before 1940 by the producer interest of the American exporting industries. The American exporting industries have been having little trouble in finding foreign markets because the United States Government has been furnishing the loans and grants which have made it possible for the buyers in foreign countries to buy American exported goods. Thus we are in danger of submitting to unreasonable restrictions on imports because the buyer interests in freer imports may not be supported, as strongly as in the past, by the exporter interests.

3. Before we come to the basic labor-standards argument for restriction of imports into the United States, it may be well to consider each of the types of argument for tariff quota restriction of imports which have appeared in recent years. Restriction of imports has been claimed to be necessary for four reasons:

(1) In the interest of national defense.

(2) In the interest of protecting the value of a nation's currency.

(3) In the interest of using unemployed labor and resources.

(4) In the interest of protecting domestic producers against "unfair competition."

The first three of these arguments can be considered very briefly. The fourth argument is the principal subject of this memorandum.

4. The defense argument for protection against imports lies outside the area of the ordinary economist. In essence, this argument is to the effect that certain key industries, even if they are high-cost producers, should be maintained because their existence would be essential to the winning of a future war. Thus it is argued that any such key industry should not be allowed to decline or disappear because of the availability of cheaper imports. In a few special cases, this argument for restriction of trade may be persuasive, depending on the logistic assumptions which are accepted. The danger is that this argument for restriction of imports may serve as a mere cloak for those producers who find competition to be unpleasant. Fortunately, the economy of the United States provides very few cases of industries which are both essential to national defense and at the same time in danger of disappearing because of the competition of foreign goods. It is to be hoped that the relatively few cases now pending before the Office of Defense Mobilization will receive careful review to distinguish between truly urgent needs for protection against imports in clear cases of defense needs and those cases where in the defense argument is subordinate to the self-interest of the particular producers.

5. The currency argument for import restriction has been that a nation must restrict purchases from abroad to protect the value of its currency. Many foreign countries have based their import restrictions on the ground that these restrictions were necessary to restrict the outflow of payments and thus maintain the official international value of the currency in question. It is questionable whether the solution to a net outflow of money from any country can be corrected by import restrictions. Fortunately, again, the United States is not in the position of suffering from any lack of international demand for United States dollars. Thus we may short-circuit the academic arguments as to whether the exchange level or the price and wage levels should be adjusted. In the foreseeable future, there is simply no cause for United States restriction of imports on the ground that such a measure is necessary to protect the international value of the United States dollar.

6. The depression argument for import restriction has been based on the belief that idle domestic capital and labor may be put to use if competitive foreign goods are excluded. In a period of deep and general business depression there may be an exception to the general "law of comparative advantage" simply because the labor and capital used in the domestic industry which is relieved of foreign competi-

tion may not be taken away from use in more advantageous kinds of production, but may be drawn from the pool of unused resources. It should be noticed that this argument for exclusion of imports assumes that other countries will not also increase their trade barriers. If every country were equally prompt in shutting off imports to alleviate depressions, there would be a loss to all from the construction of trade and no net gain to any country. Regardless of this "beggar thy neighbor" consideration, the depression argument has little application to the condition of the United States. The United States Government is committed to a policy of promoting full employment, and it has shown its actual ability to carry out such a policy since World War II. There have been temporary lapses from full employment, but a policy of import restriction can hardly be used to correct short-lived conditions of business depression.

7. The most important current argument for import restriction is based on the interests of competing domestic producers. This producer argument for import restriction is firmly embedded in the foreign-trade policy of the United States. It restricts both any reciprocal lowering of international trade restrictions and also the continuation of any existing level of tariff rates or other import admissions. Negotiations of trade agreements is limited by the peril-point clause in the Reciprocal Trade Act, which requires that the Tariff Commission should not object to any contemplated lessening of import restriction on any commodity under negotiation. Objection can block any reciprocal trade negotiation if the Tariff Commission believes that the resulting increase in imports might threaten serious injury to any American industry which would be competing with the expected imports of foreign goods. Furthermore, any reciprocal trade agreement which already has been concluded may be abrogated at any time by means of the escape clause. Under the escape-clause provision, an American producer may complain to the Tariff Commission that the competition of foreign imports threatens serious injury to some domestic industry. If the Tariff Commission finds that any such serious injury is threatened, it is required to recommend to the President of the United States that import duties be increased or that import quotas be imposed. The President has not always implemented the recommendations of the Tariff Commission. Whatever the eventual outcome of an escape-clause case, its effect is to disrupt the orderly conduct of international trade. If any foreign producer has too much success in selling goods on the American market under the established rules of the game, the rules may be changed at any time if it is judged that the competing goods from abroad threaten the interests of some American producers.

8. Serious attention needs to be given to the interests of American producers—workers, managers, and investors—in any future foreign trade policy of the United States, as has been given in existing foreign trade policy. It is not sufficient to say that the buyers of goods would benefit from unrestricted international trade. The buyer argument assumes that all the buyers will have the same purchasing power, regardless of what is done about foreign trade. Actually, all wage earners and all but that tiny fraction of American citizens who enjoy assured fixed incomes, obtain their incomes as a result of their oppor-

tunities to contribute to the production of saleable goods and services. The particular American worker, manager, farmer, or investor whose money income has been reduced because of the competition of foreign goods cannot be expected to be interested in the fact that he might save 1 or 2 percent on his purchases from whatever income he may have left. Those who favor freer international trade must face the problems—especially the problems of labor—of those whose incomes may be reduced or eliminated as the result of the competition of imported goods.

9. There are two producer arguments against unrestricted imports:

(*a*) That the domestic producers are injured thereby.

(*b*) That the injury results from what is called "unfair" competition.

It is important to examine the cause and nature of the alleged injury, especially the injury to workers, and to examine closely the alleged unfairness of the foreign competition.

10. The injury of imports to competing domestic producers arises from the fact that most modern production techniques require the commitment, in advance of sales, of both capital and labor to specific types of production. Let us, first, consider the commitments of capital. It is true, that if imported goods are cheaper than those which the domsetic producers can supply that means that the domestic capital would be better used in some other type of production. But to say that domestic capital should be used elsewhere does not solve the problem for the particular producer of goods. At any one time, a very small proportion of the capital of a producing enterprise will consist of liquid funds which might be used in one type of production or another. Most of the capital will consist of particular buildings, machines and stocks of materials which can only have value if they can be used to provide salable goods. If it turns out that the investment should have been made in the production of, say, guided missiles instead of stockings, this will be of small comfort to those who have sought to earn an income by producing stockings. There is no known way of converting stocking frames into machines for the production of guided missiles. If the stocking producer could realize the depreciated value of his plant and thus reinvest in the required type of machine-tool production for the missiles, all would be well. The ordinary economist could rub his hands and reflect on the fact that foreign imports of cheaper stockings had caused the Americans to turn their energies to industries of greater comparative advantage, to the benefit of everyone.

Unfortunately, the facts of life are a little more complicated. Capital which is already invested in particular producing facilities is not, for long periods, available for investment in other industries of greater compartive advantage. Hence, a great flood of cheaper goods from abroad does cause real injury to the interests of domestic producers. The cheaper goods certainly benefit the domestic buyers. The fact that the goods may be obtained more cheaply from abroad may be an indication that domestic producers should turn to other lines of production. Actually, however, the domestic producers should not shift their lines of production—in their own interests—unless their revenues are less than their average variable costs. At that point, nothing at all will be realized on the past investments of fixed capital.

It may be argued that the availability of lower priced imports proves that the past savings as devoted to the investment in the particular production facilities were economically wasteful. However, the proof of that fact comes too late to prevent even the wisest management from avoiding the loss of expected earnings on a capital investment which was most advantageously committed at the time of the decision to employ the particular production facilities. Thus the producer argument for restriction of imports, to avoid serious injury, has a real basis in the facts of production—however damaging import restrictions may be to the overall interests of domestic buyers.

11. The injury to particular workers from cheaper competing imports is somewhat different in character from the injury to investors and managers, but the injury to workers is more serious because the workers generally have smaller financial reserves than the investors or managers of enterprises. Only a very few workers derive their incomes from financial investments in the enterprises where they are employed. However, most of the employed American workers are as much tied to their respective places of employment, as a source of income, as are their employers. The ordinary American employed worker who loses his job, for whatever reason, will have little income or accummulated resources unless and until he finds another job. When after a time, he finds a substitute job, he will probably earn less than he did in his former job. If then, a worker loses his source of income because his employer can no longer compete with foreign imports, that worker is almost certain to face a serious economic injury. What is even more galling to the individual worker is that the company which employed him may continue with only a minor reduction in earnings whereas he may be, until he manages to find another job, without any income at all.

12. Of course, the competition of producers within the United States results in much more extensive economic injury to both investors and workers in unsuccessful enterprises than the injury that is caused by foreign competition. The objection to unrestricted imports would not be persuasive on the mere ground that serious injury results to particular producers. However, the various economic injuries are objected to on the further ground that the foreign competition is "unfair competition." It may be admitted that any competition from an unfamiliar source is likely to be regarded as "unfair" by anyone who suffers from the competition. However, there is some substance to the claim of American competitors with imported goods that they are subject to unfair competition. Within the United States, the Federal Government has the power, and has used its power, to enforce certain minimum standards of fair competition. Among American competitors in interstate markets, some common rules of the competitive game have been provided by the antitrust laws, the food and drug laws, the Federal Trade Commission Act, the Fair Labor Standards Act, and many factory and sanitary acts. By contrast, the United States Government has no direct power to compel foreign producers to abide by conditions of market competition which are considered to be "fair" in this country. Hence many domestic producers believe that they should be protected against the competition of imported goods which are cheap for buyers because, as alleged, the goods are produced under conditions which are unfairly competitive.

13. What is meant by the contention that imported goods are unfairly competitive? Obviously, cheapness cannot be unfair to the buyers, no matter what the reasons for the cheapness. Any unfairness must be in relation to the competing producers. American producers can hardly complain that their foreign competitors have an unfair advantage over them as regards the supply of capital or the quality of management. It is generally acknowledged that American enterprises have access to larger and cheaper supplies of capital and better managerial ability than do enterprises in any other country in the world. Occasionally American producers do ask for protection on the ground that foreigners enjoy an unfair advantage because they can use richer natural resources. Excluding considerations of national defense, this is the weakest of all justifications for protection. If some other country has richer sources of some mineral or the soil and climate that is superior to ours for the growing of certain crops, it is futile to waste American labor and capital on the relatively poor natural resources. Imports of products that are cheap because of better natural resources have the effect of conserving the American natural resources by making use of the natural resources of the foreign country. Hence, American producers cannot complain that foreign competition is unfair because of differences in the supplies of capital, managerial ability, or natural resources between the United States and other countries.

14. The contention that foreign competition is "unfair competition" is, in fact, usually based on the fact that foreign wages are lower than American wages. Why, it is asked, should an American employer be required to compete with foreign employers who hire labor at only a fraction of the cost per hour of labor which the American employers must pay? Within the United States a producer is already protected against gross unfairness of this kind in a number of ways. The workers, within the country, are free to move from low-wage to high-wage employment. Industries, likewise, are free to move from high-wage to low-wage areas. Moreover, minimum wage and other minimum labor-standard legislation serves to reduce the impact of competition which is based on low wages. Also, the pressure of labor union demands works to get rid of low-wage competition within the country. As between countries, however, these equalizing forces are lacking or are very feeble. Labor and capital are much less free to move to take advantage of their best opportunities. There is no direct way for the American Government to enforce labor standards on foreign producers and labor-union pressures toward equalization of labor standards between countries are obviously weaker than are these pressures within a single country.

15. The argument that low foreign wages make possible unfair competition with domestic producers must, in spite of what has just been said, be examined critically. The mere fact that foreign wages are comparatively low is not sufficient, by itself, to prove that the foreign competition is unfair. We must make a basic distinction between low costs per hour of labor and low costs of labor per unit of product. Unit labor cost depends not only on the hourly wage (and other costs per hour of employing labor) but also on what is produced per hour of labor. In general, foreign wages are below American wages because foreigners produce smaller quantities of goods of

marketable value per hour of labor than do Americans. The most important reason for both the lower productivity and the lower wages is that foreign workers in general do not have the advantages of as large a quantity of the other factors of production as do American workers. Thus it is probable that industrial workers in India must work with less than $100 worth of capital per worker while American industrial workers have the advantage of working with about 50 times as much capital per worker. Clearly, the American workers will produce a much greater quantity of valuable goods per hour of labor and consequently the American employers can afford to incur much higher costs per hour of employed labor without having high labor costs per dollar of sales. Because of all kinds of contrasts between countries, the wage-paying ability of employers is certain to be different in these various countries. Competition of foreign producers is not unfair to American producers if the foreign producers are paying as much as they can afford to pay per hour of labor.

16. While lower wages abroad are not unfair, in general, it is quite possible that low wages may be the basis of unfair competition in particular cases. The general tendency of wages to be related to the value of product per hour of labor does not, by any means, require that every employer will pay labor as much as he could afford to pay. A particular employer in a foreign country may use production techniques which are as efficient as those of the competitive American producers and thus get as much, or nearly as much, salable value product from each hour of labor as does the American competitor. Such a foreign employer could afford to incur nearly as high a cost per hour of employed labor as the American employer. Nevertheless, this foreign employer may be able to pay much less per hour of labor than the American employer is required to pay. How much an individual employer finds it necessary to pay per hour of employed labor depends on conditions in his own country which may be quite different than conditions in the United States. The foreign workers may not be able to move to the places of employment where they might earn the most. The particular foreign wages may be much less than the employer could afford to pay because of the desperate competition of unemployed workers. The foreign workers may not be represented by any labor union or the union may be weak or inefficient with the result that the foreign employer may be under no such pressure as that faced by his American competitor to pay as much for labor as he can afford to pay. And the foreign government may exercise much less effective pressure than the American Government to bring wages (and fringe benefits) into line with what the various employers can afford in cost per hour of employer labor.

17. The practical test of whether low-wage foreign competition is unfair is to be found in a comparison of wages, not between countries, but within each country. It is to be expected that the level of wages will be low in countries where the produce per man-hour is low. The question to be answered is whether the producer of goods which are to be sent to the United States is paying wages that are comparable to those paid in the country where he is located or whether he is competing with American producers with the unfair advantage of paying wages which are substandard in the country of origin. By the

word "wages" is meant, of course, all of the costs of employing a worker including the costs of fringe benefits as well as payments which are currently received by the workers. This was the standard of judgment which was wisely proposed by the Randall Commission. After stating that mere (intercountry) differences in wage rates did not constitute an indication of unfairness, the Commission went on to say that:

> The clearest case of unfair wages is one in which the competing [foreign] industry has standards that are unfair when judged in the light of the standards of the foreign economy involved.

The basis of distinguishing between low wages in general and unfairly low wages in particular cases is quite consistent with the general theory of the comparative advantage of international trade. The general theory presumes that all wages are in harmony with the productivity of labor in each country. As far as that is the case, the freest international trade will provide a net economic gain to each of the countries involved in trade, because it will cause the producers in each country to specialize in those types of production for which each country has the greatest comparative advantage. The case is quite different when cheap goods are offered in international trade on the basis of wages which are substandard in the country of origin. The latter type of competition is unfair because the low wages of the exporter are out of line with true comparative advantage. The workers who are being paid less than their economic value are, in effect, subsidizing the exports and at the same time causing injury to the enterprises and workers of the country which receives the low-cost goods.

18. The substandard test of foreign wages is necessarily a rough, practical test. It is possible, for example, that some of the highest paid workers in a foreign country may receive substandard wages in the sense that they are being paid much less than the marginal revenue product which their labor makes possible. However, such cases provide a less clear cause for complaint by the competing producers in the importing country. An industry or a company which is a wage leader is, at least, helping to set an improved labor standard, whereas those who pay the lowest wages tend to undermine or to set limits to the improvement of labor standards both in their own countries and (when they are exporters) also throughout the world. If wages which are substandard in the country of production could be raised so as to be roughly in line with wages for other comparable work in that country, the chief legitimate basis for complaint against admitting imported goods would be removed.

19. The actual measurement of comparative wages involves some technical problems. Those who shut their eyes to complaints of low-wage, unfair competition can produce several examples of such technical difficulties. One of these difficulties is that of the varying fringe benefits which constitute a cost of employing labor, even though these benefits do not constitute wages in the traditional sense. Recent work of the International Labor Organization has done much to clarify this problem. It is now possible to relate the cost of the various fringe benefits to the direct wages paid in each of the major exporting countries of the world. Another difficulty arises from the fact that the workers in some foreign countries are willing to work for low current

wages in order to gain other advantages such as improved chances of marriage. This problem of wage measurement is as old as 1776, at which time Adam Smith noted the various nonwage advantages and disadvantages of various employments. A third technical problem arises when the various employers in an industry located in some foreign country all pay the same wages but employ some special group of workers who are prevented from seeking employment in the more productive industries of that country. If one presumes that any such isolated group of foreign workers could not obtain any income elsewhere, one can raise the tricky question as to whether their wages are truly substandard—however far below the wages of other comparable workers these wages may be. A fourth technical problem arises from the fact that the skill mix is different in different industries. Hence it may not be sufficient to look at the mere average wages in a plant on industry, in comparison with average wages in other industries. It may be necessary to consider the wages in more precisely comparable jobs in the exporting industry and in other industries which use similar human material. The long-continued research work of the United States Bureau of Labor Statistics has provided techniques for comparing wages for similar work in different industries and these techniques might well be applied whenever the question of substandard wages might arise.

It may be admitted that decisions as to whether a foreign producer is or is not paying substandard wages in the context of his own country cannot be made entirely by the operation of a calculating machine. Some expert judgments would be required. However, those judgments could be based on information which would be as good or better than the information which is now used by the Tariff Commission to decide as to whether an import duty should be raised or lowered and, if so, by how much.

## II. THREE POPOSALS FOR THE REFORM OF AMERICAN FOREIGN TRADE POLICY

### *Relation of the proposals to the foregoing analysis*

20. The foregoing analysis suggests the general direction of possible reforms in United States trade policy which would aim at increased international trade as a means of raising living standards. It seems clear that the United States needs to admit a larger volume of imports and to be cautious about imposing any further import restrictions. However, this objective can hardly be attained by a mere repeating of classical free-trade doctrine. More attention needs to be paid to the practical problems which are faced by domestic enterprises and workers which have to make adjustments as a result of competitive imports from abroad. More attention also needs to be paid to the widespread conviction that low foreign wages lead to "unfair competition" with domestic enterprises. More effort should be exerted to insure that the undoubted benefits of international trade are actually used to improve the lot of workers, both in the United States and in other countries.

21. The three proposals which follow provide suggestions for changes in United States policy to make liberalized trade both palatable and constructive. Any one of these reforms, it is believed, would improve the present situation. They are independent proposals in

the sense that any one of them might be adopted without the others. While no attempt is made to work out the necessary legal details, some attention is paid to the practical ways by which each of the proposed forms might be implemented.

22. Basic to all the proposals is the presumption that the Reciprocal Trade Act will be extended, as it should be, when it comes up for renewal in 1958. It would be both tragic and damaging to the interest of the United States if the reciprocal trade policy were abandoned. It would be tragic because other countries, which face more difficult trade problems than those of the United States would hardly fail to restrict trade further if the United States abandoned what liberal trade policy it now has. The resulting wave of protectionism would certainly damage the world markets for American goods. Already serious questions are being raised as to the effect on American enterprises of the recently established European common market. While the leading countries of continental Europe have agreed to a gradual reduction in the trade barriers between themselves, their future common policy toward the outside world, and toward the United States in particular, is quite uncertain. The common market might provide greatly improved opportunities for American enterprises if liberal policies toward external trade were followed. At the same time, the common market countries, taken together, would have much greater economic power than in the past to restrict trade with the United States if they chose to do so. Abandonment or weakening of American reciprocal trade policies would certainly encourage the protectionists in Europe.

23. Underlying the three following proposals is the presumption that the United States Government will retain some form of the peril-point and escape-clause procedures when the Reciprocal Trade Act is extended. These limitations on the liberalization of international trade are opposed by the doctrinaire advocates of free trade. However, these limitations are now so deeply embedded in United States policy that it seems unlikely that they will be abandoned completely. The two clauses do, indeed, serve in a crude way to meet the problems of adjustment by American producers to the impact of increased foreign competition. The trouble is that the understandable problem of short-run shifting of labor and resources from one line of production to another is now mixed up with the granting of indefinitely continuing protection to the domestic industry, without any incentive whatever to induce the American producers to shift to production for which this country has a greater comparative advantage than in competitive production of goods which could be obtained more cheaply from abroad.

24. Even if the peril point and escape clause is retained, it does not follow that this kind of restriction on freer trade should operate as in the past. In the recent past, the Tariff Commission has been compelled by law to find that any shifting of labor and capital out of any line of production which foreigners can provide more cheaply in important volume constitutes a "serious injury" to the American industry. In fact, there may be no injury at all if the employers are able to shift from one particular product to another and if the workers are able to obtain equally remunerative employment in some particular type of production. Apart from the three proposals, to be

presented hereinafter, serious thought should be given to what is meant by an "industry" which is supposed to be injured. Actual injury must be felt by real persons, whether these persons are investors, managers, or workers. One cannot "injure" a product. If import restrictions are to be justified and relaxation of import restrictions are to be resisted on the ground that they cause serious injury, the Tariff Commission ought to be compelled to find that serious injury is threatened to real persons, over and above the usual competitive risks of production and employment.

If none of the following proposals is accepted, then the application of the concept of "serious injury" ought to be revised. However, it is believed that any one or all of the following proposals will enable the United States better to reconcile the interests of buyers, in this country and throughout the world, with the legitimate interests of producers in being protected from the injury of imports from other countries.

*Proposal I. Graduated decreases in import restrictions.*

25. The simplest of the three proposals made herein is that any future restrictions on imports should be imposed under terms which would provide automatic decreases in the protective effect over a stated period of time in each case. As applied to reductions in trade barriers, the parallel policy might be to apply the reductions gradually over time. Suppose, for example, an escape-clause case under which the Tariff Commission would, at present, recommend the raising of a tariff duty from 10 to 20 percent. Under the proposed reform, the Commission might recommend the 20-percent duty for 1 year only, to be followed by a 15-percent duty during the second year, a 10-percent duty the third year, 5 percent the fourth year and free entry after 4 years from the effective date of the new regulation. Similarly, in a case where the Tariff Commission would not find that a proposed reduction in a duty as a result of reciprocal trade negotiations would imperil a domestic industry, the reformed policy would allow the Commission to recommend that the reduction be provided in annual installments instead of all at once. The same policy might be applied to the operation of any import quotas (although it is to be hoped that in the future quota restrictions may be avoided). Instead of fixing a single, permanent quota, it would be better to establish a series of stipulated increases in the quota, ending with an unlimited quota after some stated period of time.

26. The proposed change in foreign-trade legislation would be a simple one. All that would be necessary would be an amendment to present legislation to authorize the Tariff Commission to recommend and the President to impose by executive order, multiple graduated downward rates of duty or multiple graduated upward amounts of import quotas. It would not be desirable or necessary to stipulate in the basic legislation the precise rate of graduation or any simple period of time under which the graduation of duties or quotas should occur.

27. This proposal deals with one of the basically valid objections of domestic investors, managers, and workers to increased imports. It is true, as has been pointed out, that both management and labor need time to adjust themselves to the competition of increased imports.

Any sudden flood of cheaper goods from abroad, may, indeed, cause serious injury to the competing domestic producers. American producers will gain from their access to the cheaper or superior foreign goods. In the longrun, the American economy will gain as a result of the concentration of its efforts on those kinds of production for which the United States has the greatest comparative advantages. But the process of achieving the longrun gain involves a shortrun loss to the particular producers which face the new market competition. The object of the proposed reform is to reconcile the general, longrun interest with the particular, shortrun interest. This objective would be achieved by forcing American labor and management to shift to more economical types of production or to increase their competitive efficiency while giving these domestic producers a reasonable period of time to make the desired adjustment.

28. While simple in form, this proposal would meet the varying needs of different specific cases. Unlike a general and across-the-board formula for graduated tariff reductions, the proposed policy would allow different periods and different rates of withdrawal of protection to fit each specific circumstance. In one case it might be feasible to allow free imports after, say, 2 years. In another case as much as a 10-year period of declining protection might be required. The extent of the protection should be as little as would avoid really serious injury to domestic producers as individuals and the lapse of time before unrestricted imports should be authorized to be as short as would allow each specific industry to adjust itself to the foreign competition in each case. An appropriate declaration of policy might aid the Tariff Commission in carrying out this intention.

29. A possible weakness of Proposal I is that its actual operation would depend on the quality of judgment of the executive agencies. If the information and ability of the members of the Tariff Commission and the Presidential advisers were poor, the revised procedure would not insure any different result than at present. However, the option of enacting graduated declining degrees of protection to domestic producers should encourage the exercise of sharper judgments on foreign trade policy than those of the recent past. Once the executive agencies were offered the challenge of deciding on how much protection was needed for how long to avoid serious injury to domestic competitors, they might examine particular situations more closely than they do at present. The existing peril-point and escape-clause procedures invite decisions in favor of import restriction whenever any kind of case for a threat of serious injury can be put forward by any domestic producer. The proposed revision of policy would put the question differently to the executive agencies. The question would be what would be the minimum amount of protection and the minimum time of adjustment that would be required in each case to avoid serious injury to domestic producers while requiring them to meet the conditions of world competition in the long run. Under these conditions, it might be expected that restriction of imports could be reduced much more than at present, precisely because the temporary protection might be combined with the forcing of a long-run adjustment.

30. The vital importance of a prestated declining rate of protection should be strongly emphasized. One of the evils of even the most justifiable of import restrictions is that these restrictions tend to become permanent. Behind the trade barrier an inefficient or uneconomical producer may continue indefinitely, without any need to change the nature of his operations. Only after long periods is it possible for the Government to review the case of the protected domestic producer, and when his situation is reviewed it may be that he needs protection as much as before, because he has relied on this continued protection and has done little to improve his competitive position. On the other hand, both domestic producers and foreign competitors deserve more assurance of the future than is provided by present procedures. At present an American enterprise cannot know when a change of governmental policy may result in a sudden loss of markets. Likewise, as has been mentioned, the foreign producer can never know when his very success in selling goods on the American market may lead to governmental restriction of his selling opportunity. Modern production and selling operations must be based on private long-term planning. The efficient producer can adjust his production, selling, and employment schedules, provided only that he can know what the "rules of the game" will be by the time his long-term plan materializes. This proposed reform of United States tariff procedure would improve the necessary basis for business planning, at home and abroad, while limiting protection to the minimum amount that was necessary in each case to avoid serious short-run injury to American producers.

*Proposal II. Government assistance to adjustment*

31. An alternative, or possibly a supplement, to automatic decreases in protection, might be a policy of compensating the American producers who suffered serious injury because of increased imports from abroad. Instead of recommending increased import restrictions or resisting a reduction in such restrictions, it would be better if the Tariff Commission certified such cases for special adjustment grants and/or loans by the United States Government. In stead of shoring up the position of domestic producers by increased or continued restriction of imports, the Government might better pay the cost to help to meet part of the injury from liberalized international trade. This kind of governmental assistance would help to meet the specific problems of American producers, while encouraging the growth of international trade.

32. This second proposal would be much less costly to the American economy as a whole than a policy of protection against any imports which might threaten serious injury to an American industry. A common situation is one in which an inefficient American company (A) required protection against imports if its whole operation or some part of it is to be continued, while at the time other American enterprises in the industry (say B and C) are fully capable of meeting the foreign competition without serious injury to their economic interests. One of the evils of protectionist policy is that it shores up the high price to purchasers that may be required to avoid serious injury to company A and thereby exacts higher-than-necessary costs to American consumers while providing excessive profits to companies

B and C. The situation here described is not imaginary but it is typical of both the largest and the smallest of American industries.

33. The essence of this second proposal is that any specific serious injury from increased imports should be covered, in part, by the United States Government, when this serious injury was determined to be the result of relaxation of import restrictions. By these means it would be possible to reduce the present restrictions on imports to the United States and to also face up to future cases where foreign imports might cause serious injury to certain American interests—not by restricting imports but by overcoming the problem of injury to the particular American interests which might suffer from the import competition.

34. A good precedent for this second proposal is provided in the arrangements for the new European Common Market. An integral part of this recent international agreement consisted of a common adjustment fund, to be used to assist the particular producers which might be injured by this plan of reducing trade barriers. The continental Europeans have evidently concluded that the gains of unrestricted international trade justify the indemnifying of the losses of those particular producers who may be injured by the reduction of trade barriers.

35. Various methods of compensating the injured American interests might be contemplated. First priority should be given to the wage earners in the industry which may be injured by the competition of increased imports. These wage earners have smaller reserves and more restricted opportunities than do the investors or managers of American enterprises. One feasible plan would be to increase the amount and duration of unemployment benefits of workers in any industry which might be certified (by the Tariff Commission or another appropriate agency) as being threatened by loss of earning opportunity because of competitive imports.

Admittedly, it is difficult to provide an acceptable basis for indemnifying the owners and managers of invested capital in a company which is faced with serious injury because of increased imports. There are obvious problems connected with the determination of the true depreciated value of invested capital and the extent of the potential decrease in the value and earning power of that capital as a result of any prospective increase in imported goods. However, the United States Government might well provide some practical offsets to the short-run injury to investors and managers in the form of accelerated depreciation (for income-tax purposes) in the form of longer periods of carryback of past business losses (again for income tax purposes) and in the form of low-interest or guaranteed loans to enterprises which might be certified as facing serious injury because of increased imports. Both the method of income tax allowances and the method of low-interest loans have been used by the United States Government in similar, and no more justified cases, than in the case of the enterprise which faces this kind of immediate need for adjustment in the interest of the general economic welfare.

*Proposal III. Import restrictions confined to cases of substandard wages*

36. The third proposed reform is that any finding of serious injury to domestic producers should be coupled with a required finding that

the foreign exporting industry was paying substandard wages in the country of origin of the imports. According to this proposal, it would not be sufficient for the Tariff Commission to find that imports threatened "serious injury" or that a proposed relaxation of import restrictions might imperil an American industry. It would be further required that the Tariff Commission should find that the wages (together with associated costs of employing labor) of those who were sending goods to the United States were substandard costs of employing labor in the country of origin. Only after such a finding could the Tariff Commission recommend increased import duties or quota restrictions on imports and only after such a finding could the Commission object to a negotiated reciprocal reduction of import restrictions on any commodity.

37. The logic of this third proposal follows that of the Randall Commission, and has been developed in the foregoing analysis. Briefly stated, this logic is based on the proposition that the only valid basis for claiming a condition of unfair competition is a condition wherein the foreign producers are paying wages that are substandard in relation to the wages (and other costs of employing labor) in their own country. We have seen that the mere fact that the wages in some foreign country are below those paid in the United States does not prove that the foreign competition is unfair. However, we have also seen that it is quite possible in particular cases for a foreign exporter to pay substandard wages, as compared with wages in his own country. In the latter case, the producer of goods which were imported into the United States might be legitimately charged with wage dumping of these exported goods.

38. This third proposal for reform proceeds on the basis that international trade, like domestic trade, will, naturally, cause serious injury to particular producers from time to time. It is not the mere fact of mere economic injury, but the possibility that the injury is based on substandard wages, which justifies protection of domestic producers from foreign competition. Only when the wages (and associated costs of employing labor) are abnormally low, in comparison with other wages in the country of origin, is import restriction justified on the basis that the market competition is unfair.

39. To enact this third type of reform, the basic legislation need only require that the Tariff Commission find a condition of substandard wages in the country or countries of origin before recommending that imports be restricted or before the reciprocal negotiation of relaxed restrictions should be prohibited.

40. To implement the third proposal, realistically, it would be desirable that the Tariff Commission develop information on wage structures in foreign countries which is not now available. For this purpose, it is also proposed that the regular executive channels should be required to notify the International Labor Office and each of the countries involved whenever either an escape clause or a peril-point action of the United States is contemplated. This official notification should be accompanied by a request for any relevant information or views on the matter in question within 9 months of the time of notification. The text of any report, by the ILO or by the countries involved, should be admitted as a basis for argument before the Tariff Commission or any other executive agency involved

in the raising or lowering of restrictions on imports into the United States.

41. The suggested procedures under this third proposal would delay both the reduction and the increase of import restrictions. Neither of these results would be bad, since they would serve to make possible a gradual and orderly adjustment of American commercial operations to proposed changes in American foreign-trade regulations. More important, however, would be the consequence that it would be possible to separate the justified from the unjustified complaints that low foreign wages constitute unfair competition with American enterprises. Gradually, it would become clear that imports from a generally low-wage country should be admitted, and that American enterprises should adjust themselves to this competitive requirement of the improvement of the general economic welfare. Gradually, also, the cases would be identified in which import restrictions might be justified to protect American employers and workers from the low-wage dumping of those occasional foreign producers who provided substandard conditions of labor in relation to what had been proven to be possible in their own respective countries.

42. The suggested procedure, though novel, is believed to be administratively feasible. There might, indeed, be many technical problems in arriving at a judgment as to whether certain exporting companies or certain foreign exporting industries did or did not pay substandard wages (and related benefits) in comparison with other employers in the exporting country. However difficult these problems might be, they would be no more perplexing than those already faced by the Tariff Commission in judging whether an American industry would be seriously injured by a proposed relaxation of trade barriers or whether prospective imports under existing arrangements threaten serious injury to some American industry. Surely, a foreign country might be considered to be entitled to report any facts it has to present before the United States changes its rules to restrict the sales of its citizens to the United States. Similarly, American enterprises have a right to know whether wage costs of prospective foreign competitors are truly substandard before they are faced with the competition of low-priced imports as a result of a new reciprocal-trade negotiation. As for the more technical problems, the United States Bureauof Labor Statistics has had long experience in measuring inter-industry wage differences, and the International Labor Office has recently completed international studies of the costs of fringe benfits in relation to direct wages. Finally, it should be noted that the interpretation of any factual reports on foreign wages would be subject to argument by the parties, and would be left to the final judgment of the duly authorized executive agency, presumably the Tariff Commission. The proposed procedure is no more complex than is the inherent international economic problem which is involved in any reduction or increase in import restrictions.

43. A possible indirect result of Proposal III might be an encouragement to the raising of labor standards in foreign countries, within the limits of what was practical in each industry and country. Once it had been reported that American action on trade regulation would depend on a finding as to the wage relationship within some foreign

country, pressures would develop in that foreign country to raise the labor standards of the industry involved to the limit of what was practicable in the circumstances. One result might be the enactment of a minimum-wage law in the foreign country or the improvement of labor standards under an existing minimum-wage law. Regardless of any governmental action, the reporting of an international substandard-wage problem should provide substantial encouragement to the representatives of the foreign workers involved in any such cases to press for such improvements in labor standards as might be feasible in the particular situation. Not only would such measures encourage the raising of wages in low-wage industries of foreign countries, but in some cases the very procedure might make the further protection of American enterprises unnecessary. It would be futile to dismantle an American industry in the interests of free trade, if some practical wage increase in some particular wages in a foreign country would later be shown to have made the abolition of the American industry unnecessary. The very delay might well serve to avoid many temporary dislocations in production while putting pressure on foreign competitors to raise wages to the limit of their ability to do so.

# X

# UNITED STATES COTTON AND COTTON TEXTILES IN RELATION TO INTERNATIONAL TRADE

# UNITED STATES COTTON AND FOREIGN TRADE POLICY

John C. White, Counsel, American Cotton Shippers Association

AMERICAN COTTON SHIPPERS ASSOCIATION,
*Memphis, Tenn., August 27, 1957.*

Hon. HALE BOGGS,
*Chairman, Subcommittee on Foreign Trade Policy, House Committee on Ways and Means, Washington, D. C.*

DEAR MR. CHAIRMAN: The American Cotton Shippers Association, whose individual members are actively engaged in the merchandising of cotton to foreign and domestic mills, has continually recognized the vital importance of a high level of two-way international trade to the prosperity of the cotton industry.

United States cotton must find a foreign market for at least one-third of the minimum crop which our producers can tolerate. Otherwise higher producer costs and prices lose the domestic market as well to synthetic fibers. No substantial element in the cotton industry believes that cotton can be produced profitably for the domestic market alone. Though the domestic market is larger at present, foreign countries with much lower per capita consumption present even greater opportunity for expansion.

Whether the foreign market for United States cotton will expand depends upon several factors:

(1) Our cotton must be sold a a price competitive with foreign fibers, natural and synthetic;

(2) The economic level of the foreign consuming countries must continue to rise;

(3) The foreign importing countries must be able to earn the dollars necessary to pay for United States cotton.

Present statutes seem to assure, at least so long as the CCC has cotton, that United States cotton will be priced more competitively in world markets. Factors too numerous to mention, in addition to our own economic programs, will affect the second. But we can see no way to get away from the fact that foreign consuming countries must earn the required dollars primarily from their own exports either to the United States for dollars, or to other countries for dollars which they in turn must earn by exports to the United States. Dollars earned from tourism, and like sources, are important, but obviously insufficient even with large government grants, which are temporary, or loans which must be repaid.

Every cotton exporting firm has had to become familiar with the difficulties his foreign customers face in getting dollars to pay for the cotton ordered, and every customs duty or import quota effectively reduces the available dollars, and the exports of either cotton or some other United States products.

As suggested, the enclosed paper is directed specifically to the importance of export markets to United States cotton; to the relation of the price support and other Department of Agriculture cotton programs to the need for quota restrictions on imports of raw cotton; to the need for equivalent subsidization of textiles if raw cotton exports are subsidized; and to the need for subsidization of exports or some other method of maintaining a two-price system for cotton.

Convinced that the high tariff rates contained in the Smoot-Hawley Act were an important cause of the loss of exports and decline in price of raw cotton, this association originally believed and urged that Congress should directly reduce United States tariff rates and remove quotas on an annual percentage basis that would give protected industries time to adjust their operations. Before congressional action was taken, however, foreign countermoves, tariffs, quotas, and exchange restrictions became so prevalent that it became apparent that more than unilateral tariff reductions were required if multilateral international trade essential to a high level of United States exports, and to world prosperity itself, was to be restored. The Reciprocal Trade Agreements Act was an effective instrument designed to meet this general problem and has been of the greatest benefit in effecting reduction of foreign trade barriers as well as those imposed by the United States. The General Agreement on Tariffs and Trade is an obvious and useful development, and we have been disappointed that the Congress has not approved the Organization for Trade Cooperation, which would make it still more useful to United States exporters confronting foreign trade barriers. Fortunately, raw cotton meets few specific barriers, other than lack of dollars, but its products meet constant and ever-changing barriers, as do other American manufactures.

Unless foreign trade programs which provide a high level of international trade are continued and improved by Congress, it is our belief that continued costs, artificial aids, subsidies, and financing will be required for cotton, and that these would be little more than crutches to a hopelessly restricted industry.

We appreciate the opportunity of placing this material before you, and you may be assured we shall be glad to cooperate in any further study of a problem so important to the future of the cotton industry of the United States and the many people dependent upon it.

Yours very truly,

JOHN C. WHITE, *Counsel.*

## PRESERVATION OF ITS EXPORT MARKET IS ESSENTIAL TO THE FUTURE PROSPECTS OF THE UNITED STATES COTTON INDUSTRY

The export market has been, and is, of the greatest importance to the cotton industry in the United States.

| | Production (bales) | Value of crop, including seed | Exports (bales) | Domestic consumption (bales) |
|---|---|---|---|---|
| 1947 | 11,857,000 | $2,294,751,000 | 1,968,000 | 9,354,000 |
| 1948 | 14,868,000 | 2,660,513,000 | 4,748,000 | 7,795,000 |
| 1949 | 16,128,000 | 2,589,446,000 | 5,769,000 | 8,851,000 |
| 1950 | 10,014,000 | 2,360,118,000 | 4,117,000 | 10,509,000 |
| 1951 | 15,148,000 | 3,305,506,000 | 5,515,000 | 9,196,000 |
| 1952 | 15,139,000 | 3,048,590,000 | 3,048,000 | 9,461,000 |
| 1953 | 16,465,000 | 3,009,920,000 | 3,760,000 | 8,576,000 |
| 1954 | 13,696,000 | 2,645,264,000 | 3,445,000 | 8,851,000 |
| 1955 | 14,721,000 | 2,648,292,000 | 2,229,000 | 9,202,000 |
| 1956 | 13,310,000 | 2,401,187,000 | 7,600,000 | 8,700,000 |

The effects of the United States attempt to maintain its domestic fixed prices for export are shown in the exports for 1952 through 1955. The declining exports were also shown in the buildup of the carryover from 2.3 million bales on August 1, 1951, to 14½ million on August 1, 1956.

During the 10-year period ending with 1956, exports of raw cotton averaged approximately 4.3 million bales and domestic consumption 9 million. Loss of the export one-third value of the crop would cost producers some $800 million a year, or even more. There is every expectation that exports can be maintained at 5 million bales, as a minimum, if we do not try to maintain artificially high world prices and if the importing countries can earn the necessary dollars to pay for the cotton.

Not only is the preservation of its historical export market essential to the continuance of a profitable production of cotton in the United States. Foreign markets offer a much greater possibility of expanding the sale of United States cotton than does the domestic market. Figures as to the per capita consumption of cotton in the United States and in foreign countries were given in the Cotton Situation for July 1957, as follows:

TABLE 12.—*Consumption of cotton, in pounds, per capita, United States and rest of the world*

| Year | United States [1] | Foreign countries [2] |
|---|---|---|
| 1938 | 22.5 | 5.4 |
| 1948 | 30.4 | 4.3 |
| 1949 | 25.7 | 4.5 |
| 1950 | 30.9 | 4.3 |
| 1951 | 31.5 | 4.7 |
| 1952 | 28.5 | 4.7 |
| 1953 | 27.9 | 5.0 |
| 1954 | 25.4 | 5.3 |
| 1955 | 26.5 | 5.4 |

[1] USDA data.
[2] FAO data.

TABLE 13.—*Foreign cotton consumption, in pounds per capita, by geographic area, 1938 and 1948–55*

| Year | Africa | Oceania | Central and South America | Asia, except China | China | Western Europe | Eastern Europe and U. S. S. R. | Canada |
|---|---|---|---|---|---|---|---|---|
| 1938 | 2.5 | 8.4 | 6.3 | 4.8 | 3.5 | 8.8 | 6.9 | 13.7 |
| 1948 | 2.6 | 10.1 | 6.8 | 3.2 | 2.9 | 8.2 | 4.5 | 17.1 |
| 1949 | 2.7 | 11.2 | 6.6 | 3.3 | 2.9 | 8.4 | 5.5 | 17.6 |
| 1950 | 2.6 | 9.6 | 6.5 | 3.0 | 2.3 | 9.5 | 5.6 | 17.9 |
| 1951 | 2.8 | 11.4 | 6.5 | 3.3 | 3.0 | 9.9 | 5.9 | 20.0 |
| 1952 | 2.9 | 11.5 | 6.3 | 3.9 | 3.2 | 8.7 | 6.5 | 15.4 |
| 1953 | 3.0 | 5.3 | 6.0 | 4.1 | 3.4 | 8.4 | 8.7 | 16.5 |
| 1954 | 3.3 | 10.5 | 6.4 | 4.3 | 2.9 | 9.6 | 9.0 | 13.4 |
| 1955 | 3.1 | 11.0 | 6.8 | 4.4 | 2.7 | 9.9 | 9.2 | 15.1 |

The Cotton Situation points out, too, that the average consumption of rayon and acetate was only 1.5 pounds in 1955. The importance of an expanding level of economic activity is shown by the following statement:

Per capita consumption of cotton and rayon has increased the greatest in the areas where economic activity has expanded most rapidly. In Europe, although the consumption of rayon per person has expanded somewhat more rapidly than consumption of cotton, expanded economic activity has caused the consumption of both to increase. In Asia, economic activity has been at a relatively low level and use of both rayon and cotton has remained small.

A recent calculation presented by the American Farm Bureau to the House Committee on Agriculture shows the yield per harvested acre during the last 10 years increased from 254.1 pounds in 1945 to 407.6 pounds in 1956.

The bureau stated, moreover, that:

If the trends of recent years continue, we will be averaging at least a bale per acre and possibly more in a relatively few years.

And, finally, it predicted:

Rising yields mean that further acreage cuts are inevitable unless we can expand our markets. Acreage already has been cut substantially, and many people feel that this year's national allotment of about 17.6 million acres is too small for a healthy cotton economy. If present trends continue, we may have to reduce production to 10 million acres or even less within the next 10 years.

If, in addition to the effects of the increasing yield per acre, there should be a loss of the foreign market, it is plain that the acreage devoted to cotton would be reduced substantially below the 10 million-acre figure.

Virtually every cotton area is reflecting the greatest discontent with the present 17.6 million acres, and the cost of production is higher as a result of the acreage restraints already imposed. Both higher gross income and lower per-bale costs are dependent upon the retention and expansion of our cotton-export markets.

According to the New York Cotton Exchange Service Bureau, United States cotton exports for the period August through June 1957, which means the first 11 months of the season, were as follows:

| | *Thousands of bales* |
|---|---|
| Great Britain | 943 |
| Belgium | 312 |
| Denmark | 22 |
| France | 407 |
| German, Federal Republic | 967 |
| Greece | 21 |
| Holland | 245 |
| Italy | 653 |
| Norway | 19 |
| Poland | 2 |
| Portugal | 84 |
| Spain | 165 |
| Sweden | 99 |
| Switzerland | 113 |
| Yugoslavia | 135 |
| Other European countries | 83 |
| Japan | 1,978 |
| China (Formosa) | 123 |
| India | 283 |
| Canada | 339 |
| South America, etc | 182 |
| Total | 7,175 |

Total exports for the season are now estimated at 7.6 million but are not yet distributed by countries.

A glance at the above table of United States exports shows that in the case of most foreign countries offering a market for United States cotton a significant dollar-exchange problem exists. In some, cotton is so essential a raw material that its financing will be provided at the expense of other imports. In others, such as France, Italy and India, Public Law 480 [1] or ICA aid has been necessary for even essential requirements. Japan, which as the above table shows, has been the largest customer, for United States cotton, has borrowed some $115 million from the Export-Import Bank to finance its takings this season, and has postponed purchases of dollar cotton which it would otherwise have made, except for its concern over its reduced dollar holdings. With few exceptions the foreign customers of the United States cotton still face difficulties in earning dollars to pay for the cotton they can use.

---

[1] To the extent those represent loans the problem of earning the necessary dollar exchange is only postponed. To the extent they represent grants, it must be assumed such financing will not be continued indefinitely, so that unless United States markets are to decline, the importing country must replace such grants with its own foreign-exchange earnings.

## COTTON IMPORT QUOTAS ARE NEEDED ONLY TO PROTECT THE SUBSIDIZING EXPORT SALES PROGRAM

Insofar as price-support programs for upland cotton are concerned, import quotas have been of minor significance. Mexican and other competitive foreign cotton kept out of the United States by quotas moved to export markets in Europe and the Far East to which, otherwise, United States cotton would have moved. The chief effect was to give foreign mills an advantage in access to particular qualities less available in the United States crop.

With a heavily subsidized export sales program in effect, of course, the quotas are essential since otherwise foreign cotton would move to the United States where the CCC loan program is maintaining cotton prices some 6 cents a pound over the price at which it is selling for export.

The situation as to extra-long-staple cotton is different. The United States has for many years been an importer rather than exporter of extra-long-staple cotton. The cotton produced here was less satisfactory to our mills and its production considerably more costly than upland cotton. There were times, therefore, when the only way to force domestic mills to use United States extra-long-staple cotton at the support price was to limit imports. The situation here, too, has changed. The extra long staple now being produced is far better and quite acceptable to the mills, and the producers have deliberately adopted a pricing policy which makes the cotton competitive with foreign extra long staple, particularly since the Communist bloc started taking large quantities of Egyptian cotton. The result is that imports are far below the permissible quota. Some such United States cotton has been sold for export but not upon a subsidized basis. It would appear, therefore, that at present the import quotas on extra-long-staple cotton are serving no purpose,[2] and those on upland cotton serve only to protect the subsidizing export-sales policy.

## COTTON TEXTILE EXPORTS ARE ENTITLED TO EQUIVALENT SUBSIDIES

So long as CCC is selling raw cotton for export at prices substantially below the domestic market price, it is plain that the United States textile exporter must receive an equivalent subsidy or be unable to meet the competition of a foreign mill buying subsidized raw cotton. With raw cotton amounting to 55 percent of the cost of manufacturing gray cotton cloth, as the American Cotton Manufacturers Institute states, 6 cents a pound would represent an initial 3.3-cent disadvantage.

Since the cotton products export program was put into effect in August 1956 through June 1957 payments of $12.9 million have been made on exports of 181.2 million pounds of products.

This same disadvantage is imposed upon the domestic manufacturer who sells in the United States market in competition with products made abroad from United States cotton or other raw material the price of which is controlled by our export-sales price. The Japanese agreement affords some protection against excessive imports, but there

[2] The CCC recently filled the existing quota with cotton from the stockpile, and if it continues to follow this course it may effectively limit imports during the period of liquidation of the stockpile.

is nothing to offset this cost disadvantage which our cotton program creates. This unfair treatment cannot be continued indefinitely and furnishes another reason for opposing two-price programs.

AN EXPANDING MARKET, BOTH FOREIGN AND DOMESTIC, AND NOT SUBSIDIZATION OF SOME OTHER METHOD OF MAINTAINING A TWO-PRICE SYSTEM, IS WHAT RAW COTTON MUST HAVE

Experience has thoroughly demonstrated that an export market for United States cotton cannot be maintained at a price level dictated by an unrealistic, theoretical formula. In spite of all the special financing available exports during 1955–56 were reduced to a low of 2,215,000 bales, while foreign production of both cotton and artificial fiber expanded many times. Congress has directed that CCC stock be sold at competitive prices, though this has involved losses of some $60 a bale. As a result exports during 1956–57 are now estimated at 7.6 million bales. Of course, foreign anticipation of an abandonment of the attempt to maintain export sale prices at the domestic level contributed to the disparity but it is now generally conceded that the United States must sell cotton at a competitive world level.

Substantial cotton groups, including producers, mills, as well as merchants, believe we are facing a similiar problem within the United States. Here, almost alone in the free world there was a decline in consumption during 1956–57. From 9,210,000 bales in 1955–56 United States consumption declined to 8,700,000 bales. In other countries it rose from 19.3 million bales to 20.7 million.

Mr. Charles Cannon, testifying for the American Cotton Manufacturers Institute recently told the House Committee on Agriculture that:

> On the domestic front cotton has failed completely to share in the broadly expanding markets that are present as a result of population gains and the enormous increase in consumer spending. In fact, we haven't even held our own in the increased fiber market. Since World War II, consumption of cotton and man-made fiber has increased by the equivalent of 3 million bales. The annual rate of domestic consumption of paper, translated to cotton equivalent, amounts to 2½ million bales; jute, hemp, etc., amounts to 1½ million bales; and the trend is sharply upward in all cases except cotton's. The trend of cotton consumption actually has been downward during this period—from 9.8 million bales in 1946 and 9.5 million in 1947 to probably 8.7 million during the current crop year which ends in July.

And he went on to say:

> The result is that cotton has lost at a double-barreled rate. In the first place, we are losing our share of the total fiber market. On the other hand, since 1948 consumer spending has increased 28 percent, but spending for textile products has increased only 4 percent. So in addition to losing the battle of the fibers, we are also losing the battle to retain our historic share of the consumer dollar.

In the face of this analysis, with which virtually every element in the cotton industry agrees, there are very few who believe that a program of maintaining an artificially high level of domestic prices while selling abroad at a lower price offers any long-term benefits to the cotton industry.

There are additional objections to any such plan. It injures the United States futures markets since they become less useful for hedging purposes. It requires the use of either a direct subsidy, a sale for export at a loss, or some other device which we regard as unfair methods of exportation or encouraging production for exportation, when practiced by others.

Opinions differ among producers and within the cotton trades as to the justification for any form of subsidy to cotton producers but more and more are recognizing that the attempt to accomplish it by maintaining theoretically calculated prices is self-defeating in both foreign and domestic markets. Expanding markets at lower prices offer greater returns than continually contracting markets at an arbitrarily fixed support price, particularly as mechanization and new cultural practices permit lower cost production.

A recent study prepared by the Department of Agriculture at the request of the Senate Committee on Agricultual Appropriations states that:

> In general, there has been a sharp decrease in inputs per bale and they were 30 percent less in 1955 than in 1945.

The quantity of inputs—i. e., land, labor, fertilizer, planting seed, ginning, power, machinery, irrigation, and other items—used for cotton production decreased at an average rate of 3 percent per year during this period.

With such declining inputs per bale possible, and with the expanded market which has resulted from reducing the export price some 6 cents a pound below the domestic price, while domestic consumption at the supported price has declined, it is quite possible that not subsidization but freedom to meet its competition in both domestic and foreign markets is what cotton needs from an economic viewpoint.

Dr. M. K. Horne, Jr., chief economist of the National Cotton Council, had this to say about the possible total market for cotton:

> This record of recent years still leaves open the real possibility that the basic trend of our total market may turn either down or up. There is overwhelming evidence that it will trend downward if we leave it to drift, or that it will trend strongly upward if we push hard enough on the things that can make cotton consumption expand in this country and all over the world and that will keep competitive production from expanding too fast. It is not a farfetched dream but a genuine possibility, even by conservative estimate, that in 5 years' time our normal domestic market could be up to 11 million bales and our exports to 9 million, with a total of 20 million bales and pointed on upwards. We are living in a dynamic economic world where that is altogether possible. When we think of all the pains and inefficiencies of trying to adjust our great industry's production to a declining or a static market, it is certainly hard to see any way to a sound future unless we have the programs that will really make that market grow.

# FOREIGN TRADE POLICY: THE COTTON TEXTILE CASE

R. Buford Brandis, chief economist, American Cotton Manufacturers Institute, Inc.

Of all the major United States industries, none is more clearly caught between the millstones of foreign-trade policy on the one hand and agricultural policy on the other than is the cotton textile industry. The reason is simple: the industry processes a price-supported agricultural commodity, the cost of which constitutes more than half of its basic manufacturing costs. This basic raw material of the industry is available more cheaply to cotton textile manufacturers outside the United States.

According to the United States Department of Agriculture, in the crop year just closed on July 31, 1957, raw cotton constituted 54.3 percent of the total cost of manufacturing basic cotton cloth in the United States. The world market price of United States-grown raw cotton is now about 20 percent below the price in the United States, as a result of the Government's cotton export program.

On June 27, 1957, there was filed with the House Committee on Agriculture on behalf of the American Cotton Manufacturers Institute, a statement of fundamentals regarding United States Government cotton policy which represents the industry's thinking on the agricultural aspect of its problem. A copy of this statement is attached.

To understand completely the cost differentials which pose such a terrific problem of foreign competition for the United States textile industry, the other costs apart from raw-cotton costs must, of course, be taken into account. Next to raw cotton, the largest part of the total cost of producing cotton cloth in the gray is labor. In the past 10 years, the average hourly earnings in the textile mill products industry have increased by 44 percent—from $1.04 to $1.50, according to the United States Department of Labor. In the broad woven fabric mill section of the industry, the figure is now up to $1.45. Over the past 10 years, hours worked per week have not varied greatly and have averaged about 39.

The cost of new machinery, as reflected in basic spinning equipment, has risen some 60 percent since the late 1940's. Production per man-hour rose from about 15.3 yards in 1950 to 17.9 yards in 1954. The continuing decline in spindleage—down from 23 million to 21 million in the past 5 years—has also contributed no doubt to some increase in the average productivity by eliminating older equipment. While exact productivity measurements are, of course, difficult to make in any industry, it is apparent that the rise in costs in recent years in the cotton textile industry has been only partially offset by increases in productivity.

In addition, it must be remembered that advances in productivity have been going on at the same time in overseas textile industries, financed in some instances by United States Government funds. The net result clearly is a serious worsening in the international competitive position of the United States industry.

This is reflected in both a decline in exports and an increase in imports in recent years. In 1952, for instance, United States exports of cotton cloth totaled 761.6 million square yards. In 1956 this had declined to 511.6 million square yards. In the same 2 years, imports of cotton cloth were 35 million and 188 million square yards, respectively. Expressed another way, in 1952 United States imports of cotton cloth were 4.6 percent of United States exports of cotton cloth, but by 1956 imports amounted to 36.7 percent of exports. Of course, there are substantial imports of manufactured cotton textile items in addition to cloth. To get a total measure one must rely upon dollar figures which, generally speaking, understate the import side because the dollar valuations are based on foreign price levels. Nevertheless, according to United States Census data, United States exports of cotton manufactures declined from $312 million value in 1952 to $239 million in 1956. In the same period the dollar valuation of imports rose from $59 million to $154 million, or from 19 to 64.5 percent of exports.

When the present raw cotton export program was begun on August 1, 1956, the Government at the same time, as a matter of equity, established an export equalization fee program for cotton manufactures in export trade. This fee is paid to the United States cotton textile exporter by the Government on the basis of a formula designed to equalize the cost of United States raw cotton in the exported item with the cotton cost enjoyed by an overseas manufacturer of the same item.

Of course, this fee applies to export business only. The 20 percent cotton cost differential in favor of the overseas manufacture, already referred to, is not offset on that 95 percent of the United States cotton textile business which is transacted within the United States. True, there is a tariff payable on imports of cotton manufacturers, but the already low rates were cut drastically in 1955 and no compensatory duties were imposed when the raw cotton export price was lowered. The fact that imports were increasing rapidly before the cotton export program was instituted and prior to the latest reduction in tariff, clearly indicates that overseas manufacturers are in a position on the average to bring most of their new cotton cost advantage over the tariff to compete for the domestic market.

While it is true that the man-made fibers have been competing increasingly with cotton in this country since World War II, it is also true that they have been growing even more rapidly overseas. Between 1946 and 1956 manmade fiber consumption in the United States increased 81 percent; during the same period of time manmade fiber production overseas increased 562 percent. In the crop year just ended, United States cotton consumption was 11 percent below its level in the first postwar crop year; in contrast, cotton consumption by overseas industries rose 70 percent between 1946 and 1956.

Between 1955 and 1956 in the United States per capita consumption of cotton and manmade fibers both declined—cotton from 26.5 pounds per capita to 26 and manmade fibers from 11.2 to 10 pounds. Perhaps most significantly of all, total per capita fiber consumption in the United States has declined from 40.6 pounds in 1946 to 36 pounds in 1956, according to the United States Department of Agriculture.

Here, then, is an industry in no shape to sustain increased import competition. Over the past 5 years after-tax profits in the textile mill products industry, whether figured on equity or sales, have averaged no more than half the rates for manufacturing industry as a whole. For July 1957, the latest available month, the United States Bureau of Labor Statistics has reported that the Wholesale Price Index of textiles and apparel products is 5 percent below the pre-Korean average. For comparison, in July the all-commodity Wholesale Price Index was 26 percent above the 1947–49 average.

So far, the grinding of the millstones of trade policy and agricultural policy, respectively, upon the deteriorating position of the United States cotton textile industry, has been most dramatically reflected in the Japanese import situation, now happily alleviated. The current increases in imports from Hong Kong, particularly of apparel items, may be heralding a new problem of major proportions and bear careful scrutiny.

So far as the Japanese situation itself is concerned, the facts may be briefly reviewed because they are well known. The rapid rise in Japanese cotton textile and apparel exports to the United States beginning late in 1954 were sharply accelerated after the 1955 United States tariff concessions took effect. Finally, with Japanese-manufactured items constituting three-quarters of total cotton-textile imports, friendly discussions between the United States and Japanese Governments were followed by the imposition of voluntary export controls on cotton textile shipments to the United States market by the Japanese Government for a 5-year period beginning January 1, 1957.

The Japanese have established an export ceiling of 235 million square yards annually with this total broken down into various subcategories to assure greater diversification of shipments, thus spreading the import impact so as to avoid excessive concentration on particular product markets.

The Japanese industry is apparently cooperating fully with its Government's program and, in the first half of 1957, textile imports from Japan have been running below the comparable period of 1956; seasonal increases in textile imports usually occur during the fall months, of course.

Remembering that the Japanese program naturally applies only to that country's cotton-textile shipments to the United States market, and is itself limited to a 5-year period, it is clear that foreign-trade problems remain to be faced by the United States textile industry. When it is recalled, for instance, that the textile wage rate in India is substantially below that in Japan and that, in addition, India grows is own raw cotton, which is available to the domestic industry at a price lower than that paid by overseas mills, the possibility of rapid and dangerous import developments in the future is clear. Nor is the problem limited to Asia; in Europe also there are strong textile industries enjoying substantially cheaper cotton and labor costs.

The textile industry is one of the largest in this country. Together with the related apparel industry, it employs 1 out of every 7 workers in manufacturing today. Furthermore, it is typically located in smaller communities where loss of industrial payroll can be catastrophic. Beyond these economic reasons for preserving a healthy textile industry in the United States, there is the overriding consideration of national defense. The World War II Quartermaster General of the Army has stated that in that conflict textiles were second only to steel in military importance.

STATEMENT OF FUNDAMENTALS REGARDING UNITED STATES GOVERNMENT COTTON POLICY BY AMERICAN COTTON MANUFACTURERS INSTITUTE, INC., JUNE 27, 1957

The American Cotton Manufacturers Institute has refrained, in past years, from taking a position on specific proposals for Government cotton policy.

We believe the determination of cotton policy should rest with the producers of cotton.

We continue to adhere to this belief but, at the same time, feel that our experience in processing the raw material and merchandising its products should be considered with regard to certain fundamentals which must be a part of any successful long-range program for cotton.

It should be made clear, at the outset, that the cotton manufacturing industry is not seeking "cheap" cotton. Contrarily, the record shows that the industry has enjoyed good earnings when cotton prices were at high levels. The industry is interested in competitively priced cotton; otherwise, its cotton products cannot be priced competitively.

As manufacturers, we like cotton. Our heritage is closely geared to a cotton economy.

We have hundreds of thousands of employees who share with us a stake in the future of the product.

We have billions of dollars invested in plants and equipment; over the years we want to invest billions more.

We are not satisfied with a stagnant rate of cotton consumption in a period of rapid population increase when practically everything else the public uses is enjoying a vast upswing in consumption.

It seems clearly indicated that consumption of textile fibers and/or textile substitute materials will increase, both in this country and abroad. The question is whether a fair share of the increase will go to cotton or whether cotton policy will force us, as the primary processors, and the consuming public, away from cotton and toward cotton's competition.

The ability of cotton to compete is directly related to the soundness of Government policy. The continued use of emergency palliatives may bolster the situation temporarily, but such expedients fail completely to generate the expansion process. There is urgent need for a positive and courageous course of action on the part of both Government and the entire raw-cotton industry.

TWO COURSES OPEN

**The United States cotton industry, from the farmer through the final processor, stands at a point of determination regarding a course for the future.**

**One course leads very shortly to consumption by our domestic mills of around 8 million bales and an insecure export market for perhaps 3 million to 5 million—for a total offtake of 11 million to 13 million bales—with a downward trend. This course would tend to make it impossible to price cotton's products competitively and, accordingly, lessen interest in cotton's future.**

**The other course leads shortly to domestic consumption of 11 million to 12 million bales and an export market for 5 million to 7 million or more—for a total offtake of 16 million to 19 million bales—with an upward trend. This course would lead to a renewed confidence on the part of the domestic consumer and the investment of hundreds of millions of dollars each year in the processes necessary to keep the product competitive.**

THE FUNDAMENTALS

With the foregoing background and an unlimited interest in the subject, it is our considered judgment that for our whole industry to be vigorously alive and growing any permanent policy for cotton must involve these fundamentals:

1. An immediate and significant increase in cotton acreage above the 17½ million acres that was allotted this year, and which likely will be allotted in 1958 under present law. The efficiency of the cotton farmer, the ginner, and, in fact, the whole raw-cotton industry is bound to suffer under such an acreage restriction.

2. A clear-cut procedure for improving the net-income position of the cotton farmer. Unless this result is obtained, no cotton program can succeed over the years.

3. The one-price system, with the price realistically geared to competitive factors, including foreign-grown cottons and other important competing materials. Obviously, price alone will not determine cotton's ability to compete. But without a competitive price cotton cannot compete, regardless of how favorable all the other factors may become.

(Two experiences of the past year have demonstrated in an almost sensational manner the influence of price on consumption. First, when the export price was made competitive, foreign sales of American cotton skyrocketed beyond even the most optimistic predictions. The second experience involves the impact of price on a domestic market. When farsighted western cotton producers and the Congress teamed up to make competitive the extra-long-staple cotton produced in this country, offtake again exceeded the most enthusiastic predictions and the extra-long-staple-producing industry was given a new birth.)

We are positively convinced that a competitive price for all cotton in the domestic market will have just as sensational a result.

4. The objective of encouraging cotton to move through normal trade channels, rather than through Government hands. Whenever cotton is forced through Government hands, efficiency is reduced and costs increase.

5. A sizable reduction in the enormous cost of the present program and a clear objective for further reductions in the years ahead. There are signs that neither the Congress nor the public will tolerate a continuation of the present high cost of the cotton program. On the other hand, there is certainly justification for a Government outlay that is geared to a realistic program of self-help for the cotton farmer, particularly one that in the beginning represents a substantial reduction below current costs.

6. The exclusion of any form of processing tax on the manufactured product. It is completely fallacious to assume that any product can be helped by being taxed. It is not possible to equalize the competitive disadvantage that would be created for cotton products by taxing the whole wide range of materials with which cotton competes. Furthermore, the whole American business system and the public rebel at the concept of taxing one product for the benefit of another.

CONCLUSION

Given a program involving the above fundamentals, the American cotton-textile industry with all the enthusiasm and determination at its command pledges itself to a program of vigorous product improvement, market expansion, and increased consumption of cotton. We reemphasize our deep conviction that the results will exceed expectations.

# AMERICAN COTTON-TEXTILE INDUSTRY AND FOREIGN-TRADE POLICY

Textile Workers Union of America, research department,
Solomon Barkin, director

American foreign-trade policy must be tested by its impact on the cotton textile industry. This is the most important single manufacturing industry to be affected by such policy. If this policy is likely to produce undesirable results for this industry, it should not be adopted. An analysis is, therefore, necessary of the relation of imports to the future of the American cotton textile industry to help define a positive and constructive national trade policy.

## A. AMERICAN TRADE POLICY SHOULD PROTECT THE COTTON TEXTILE INDUSTRY

The industry is beset by many problems which it is tackling with varying degrees of intensity and success. These existed prior to the appearance of recent threats of Japanese imports. They are domestic in character and arise from interfiber and interproduct competition and from the struggle among various items for the consumer dollar. Though these basic problems existed before the current import question reared its head, their solution will become more difficult, if not impossible, if the plight of the industry is aggravated by the demoralizing effect such imports will have upon the industry. We believe, therefore, that this country needs a more restrictive policy on textile imports than is assumed by the present legislation and the administration.

### 1. EMPLOYMENT ADJUSTMENT DIFFICULT FOR TEXTILE WORKERS

The free traders who have dismissed or minimized the likely impact of imports upon domestic employment and activity cannot justifiably maintain such a position with respect to the cotton textile industry. Our experience in 1955–56 is too alive to be denied. The sharp upsurge in imports seriously affected a number of branches and, when associated with a domestic drop in activity, compounded these difficulties. Textile employment has been shrinking in most areas and the displaced workers have had great difficulties in finding jobs. A large proportion of those displaced have suffered long periods of unemployment and many are now permanently out of the labor market. Many textile communities where mill closings have occurred have been classified as distressed for several years and continue to suffer from chronic unemployment despite the high level of national employment. A number of underdeveloped areas which never did have a sufficient number of jobs for its employable population have also experienced mill closings and their numbers of unemployed and underemployed have increased.

These displacements are largely due to domestic developments. Would the free traders compound these problems through the flood of new imports which would close additional mills and reduce textile employment even more rapidly than has been experienced to date?

The Congress has not yet adopted legislation to assure the distressed and underdeveloped communities the aid needed for their rehabilitation and economic recovery. The national platforms of both parties and both presidential candidates in the 1956 elections endorsed the principle of such legislation. But the present administration endorsed principles for a bill which would have given feeble support for these activities and the Senate bill, on which hearings were held, still has not been acted upon by the subcommittee to which it was assigned. In view of the failure to help workers and communities adversely affected by internal economic adjustments, it behooves us to insist that no action be taken with respect to international trade policy which will further aggravate the lot of these people.

Adherents of lower tariff rates have also urged strongly upon the Congress and the people that the necessary adjustments to changes in employment will ultimately take place. They have argued this position as have those who have tried to assure us that technological displacements will be taken care of by the usual processes of economic growth. Both groups, however, overlook the serious adjustments required of the individual in effecting both or either of these changes. They blind themselves to the large pockets of chronically unemployed. In the case of technological displacement, the trade-union movement is harnessing its economic strength both to obtain the requisite severance pay and the shorter workweek to solve the problems created by the rising level of productivity and to assure more balanced growth in our economy. No such cushions exist for the distress caused by mill closings resulting from competitive imports. One reason for this contrast is that concerns in the latter category are generally in a poor economic condition due, in part, to the pressure of imports. They are less capable financially to provide these benefits.

To date, no analysis has adequately established that there is an easy adjustment in employment, even on a national basis, to reductions in employment resulting from rising imports. Many have hypothesized that the numbers injured would be few, but no one has proved that they are absorbed.

The processes of economic growth, even under the favorable circumstances we have witnessed during the last few years, are, moreover, unlikely to provide jobs in sufficient volume to balance the losses resulting from displacements in import-affected industries such as textiles.

A current analysis of the import problem, made under the auspices of the Twentieth Century Fund by Don H. Humphrey, concludes:

Even an inflationary rate of expansion failed to eliminate underemployment and relative deflation in the leading import industry.

He explains that—

under a full head of prosperity steam, growth industries erupt in inflation before the excess resources are completely drawn out of agriculture and the relatively stagnant industries, particularly in the South. Here lies the root of the difficulty. The expansion of demand is directed chiefly at the growth industries and, in part, escapes in inflation before reaching the stagnant import industries which are relatively deflated.

If there is to be an easy adjustment—

domestic production in the durable goods and services must expand more rapidly than they have. Otherwise, the labor which would be displaced by additional imports will not be absorbed.

Inflation, administered prices and investment bottlenecks bring high prices which dissipate consumer demand before resources are "shifted from the relatively stagnant industries to growth industries."[1] In our economy, with the prevalence of semimonopolistic price practices, it is unrealistic to expect the realization of the free trader's dreams. The growth industries do not expand adequately nor, of course, concurrently to offer job opportunities to the displaced. Our current experience is adequate proof of this conclusion.

Workers in industries beset by domestic difficulties, particularly those which are large and localized and in one-industry areas, as is the textile industry, or in areas where underemployment already prevails are unlikely to find new employment if competitive interests eliminate their jobs. The textile industry, as we shall show, falls into this category and, therefore, invites the greatest caution in the development of foreign policy. However the concept of injury may be defined, the consensus of opinion is that the cotton and other divisions of the textile industry are afflicted by domestic difficulties which have caused serious contraction of capacity and employment. Employees displaced from such mills will find it difficult to obtain new employment even in periods of greatest prosperity.

### 2. FINANCIAL REVERSES HAVE BEEN WIDESPREAD

Many textile investors have also been adversely affected by these industrial reverses. Mills have been liquidated and enterprises abandoned. New capital has been difficult to attract. Nevertheless, there is a group of highly profitable corporations, particularly among those who have cultivated special products, developed advantageous merchandising practices, and maintained technically advanced mills. Smaller mills and those considered marginal often continue to operate without investing new funds, pursuing a vigorous search for new markets, or modernizing productive machinery or processes. Other operators have escaped from their entrepreneurial responsibilities by selling their corporations with their attendant tax-loss positions to financially profitable interests frequently possessing little knowledge of the textile industry. The latter have utilized the loss carryover position to their own advantage. The continuing low profit level in the industry has discouraged many operators and enterprises.

The addition of any new factors which will further aggravate the lot of specific mills, as resulted from the flood of ginghams, velveteens, and other specialties in 1955–56, cannot but depress management and discourage positive, expansion attitudes so necessary to surmount the problems confronting the industry. A rise in imports will discourage industrialists from undertaking the constructive job of finding the keys to further modernization, new markets, and overall growth.

[1] Don D. Humphrey, American Imports (New York: Twentieth Century Fund, 1955), p. 472.

To allay any fear that the removal of competitive foreign pressures might diminish the drive for technical, managerial, and product advances in the domestic textile industry, we shall demonstrate in a subsequent section of our statement that the American cotton textile industry is probably in the forefront of all other national textile industries and is being prodded by the vast advances of other American industries, rising labor costs, and the dynamic domestic market to undertake the tremendous changes necessary for its ultimate revitalization. In fact, the rate of increase in productivity in this country in this industry probably vastly outdistances that in any other country.

### 3. AMERICAN NATIONAL INTERESTS DICTATE MAINTENANCE OF A VIRILE TEXTILE INDUSTRY

Not only are we convinced that any policy which adversely affects the industry is unwise because of the current difficulties of adjustment experienced by workers and communities confronted with mill closings and the financial reverses of an impressive number of mills, but we also believe that the industry is essential to the American economy and should not be forced to contract beyond the limits set by internal competitive forces now at work. They are serious and challenging and have taken and are likely to take a substantial toll unless the industry bestirs itself to find new markets and regain many it has lost.

A domestic textile industry is essential to the American economy. Textiles provide a basic need in the life of the people. They are the essential materials for clothing, many household needs and considerable amounts of industrial production. To be fully useful the industry should be responsive to the American way of life and be prepared to promote new fabrics and ideas which will express our special needs in dress. There are plentiful illustrations of the industry's competencies.

The American textile producers have innovated in most diverse fields, producing fabrics and effects for which there have been no previous precedents. Where the textile weaver and knitter have been backward, the chemical companies have been available to introduce new finishes and dyes which have broadened the appeals and merits of these fabrics.

The American cotton textile industry succeeded in making the many attractive women's cotton fabrics which have reigned supreme for many years in the women's wardrobe supplanting the rayon fabrics which dominated the same field during the thirties. Similarly, one may refer to the more recent fabric innovations which have come with the upgrading of work clothes from the old denims and chambrays to the twills and other sport clothing fabrics. New fabrics are being developed to enable the American housewife to use her home laundry equipment with a minimum of effort. Good-looking utilitarian fabrics were introduced to satisfy the new needs of the new suburbanite.

These are not innovations which could be satisfied by the foreign producer. There must be a native industry eager at all times to respond to the varying impulses and pressures of a dynamic society.

Not only are the foreign producers not prepared for these new products, but their primary usefulness will be limited to the production of the staple items, which we may add, are an ever-shrinking proportion of the industry's total output. Furthermore, their specialty products are more than likely to be responsive to their own national way of life which is hardly fitting for our people on a permanent basis. Part of the cost of having these advantages is, of course, the obvious need of maintaining an industry producing the full range of products so that it is constantly meeting the widest variety of needs in the various markets. Short-run advantages must not be pressed to the point of incurring long-term setbacks.

In reviewing the great need for a domestic textile industry, we must not overlook the essential military needs. During the last war, 18 billion yards of cotton fabrics were produced for military use. Not only were we able to supply our own needs, but we furnished fabrics to other countries which had been overrun or had substantial parts of their industries destroyed or had diverted their manpower to the production of other more immediately necessary military requirements.

American industry also needs a domestic textile industry to be ever ready to supply it with its fabric needs. The process of introducing new industrial uses for fabrics is a long and arduous one. It requires intimate knowledge of textile properties and industrial needs. Experiment and trial precede the final applications. There must be close cooperation among the salesmen and representatives from immediately accessible mills, ready to play their part in developing new potentials.

We believe firmly that the United States, with the largest textile industry in the world, cannot be dependent upon other countries. However much they may be prepared to supply specific fabrics at any one time, their supply must be irregular and reliance upon them is impossible and undesirable.

Besides being essential to the national development, it is worthy of note that the prices of cotton textiles are among those which have been least inflated in the postwar years. To provide an index of the price of cotton textiles, we shall consider the trends of cotton manufacturing margins, for example, the difference at the wholesale level between the sales price for cotton cloth and the cost of the raw cotton contained therein. According to the United States Department of Agriculture, which publishes mill manufacturing margins based on 17 representative fabrics, cotton cloth costs in the United States have been remarkably stable during the past 6 years. The average mill margin for the 1956–57 crop year (12 months ended July 1957) was 28.72 cents per pound, compared to 29.62 cents in the previous year and 29.08 cents in the 1951–52 crop year. During this period, the Bureau of Labor Statistics Index of Wholesale Prices for Industrial Commodities increased by 9.4 percent (from 113.9 to 124.6).

The Congress and the executive branch of the United States Government have accepted the principle that foreign imports should not seriously injure an American industry. Tariff reductions granted under the Reciprocal Trade Agreements Act had fairly well observed this principle insofar as cotton textile products are concerned. A whole series of concessions have been granted, beginning with the bilateral agreements preceding the war which culminated in the agreement with the United Kingdom in 1939. Postwar tariff concessions have been negotiated on a multilateral basis. The resulting rates were, of course, applicable to all nations entitled to the most-favored-nation agreements. Despite the many concessions and reductions which brought the ad valorem equivalent rates (based on imports in 1952) from 37.6 percent before the institution of the reciprocal trade agreements program to 30 percent on January 1, 1945, and to 21.8 percent on January 1, 1953, and to a lower level at the present time, the actual level of imports was most modest until 1955.[2] The volume remained below 75 million square yards through 1954. Most of these were specialty fabrics which did not challenge the industry as a whole.

The import problem only became serious with the appearance of Japanese products after the benefits of the most-favored-nation treatment were extended to it in September 1955. Then it was that the insufficiency of the present rate structure became evident. And it must be remembered that the tariff schedule had not been intended to injure the American industry and it would not do so as long as the foreign sources were those with whom the rates had been negotiated and for whom they were designed. But when Japan was granted the benefit of these rates, its producers were able to capitalize on them and gain a considerable foothold in this market since the rates were not negotiated with an intention to meet the threat from Japan.

This country is now confronted with a dilemma of having been saddled with rates intended specifically to adjust the competitive positions between the American cotton-textile industry and those of foreign countries to keep the volume of imports at a modest level. Such imports would not be truly injurious. But now we are faced with the intrusion of an unexpected factor. The present tariff-rate structure and our agreements with other countries were not shaped for such an occurrence, except for the general overriding provisions within the agreements providing for an escape clause in case of injury. Certainly the American people are entitled to and may appropriately employ this provision to cope with this unexpected and completely novel competitive circumstance created by the appearance of a new foreign source not anticipated in the original rates. Having assumed the obligation and recognized the desirability of maintaining this industry in the national interest, the United States Government is entitled to protect the industry in this new situation.

The preservation of the American industry is desirable also from the point of view of the vast investment which our economy has made in the growth and distribution of raw cotton. In the crop year 1956–57, the United States produced 13.1 million bales of cotton of a world total of 38 million. Even under the unusually favorable circumstances created by the governmental policy of selling American cotton abroad below the domestic price, domestic consumption of 8.7 million bales absorbed two-thirds of the domestic output. In the previous years the ratio was even higher. The American raw-cotton producers and distributors are dependent upon the maintenance of the domestic industry for their own survival. They will ultimately lose out to other countries if the share of the domestic crop consumed by American mills continues to decline. It is more than likely that these foreign countries will tend to encourage, insofar as possible,

[2] U. S. Tariff Commission, "Effect of Trade Agreement Concessions on United States Tariff Levels Based on Imports in 1952" (Washington, D. C.: U. S. Government Printing Office).

their own raw-cotton growers and thereby further limit the market for the American farmer. The shrinkage in the size of the American cotton-textile industry will be the beginning of a cycle which will spell more trouble for the cottongrower.

#### 4. THE INTERNATIONAL TEXTILE INDUSTRY WOULD BENEFIT FROM THE MAINTENANCE OF A VIRILE AMERICAN COTTON TEXTILE INDUSTRY

The major argument of the proponents of freer trade is that the reduction in the tariff rates would result in the specialization of nations in the industries in which they would have comparatively the greatest advantage. This position has, of course, been found deficient insofar as the underdeveloped countries are concerned. Their interest is to promote their development and to assure the most efficient use of the available labor supply and land largely in the face of an existing shortage of capital or industrial experience. In some instances, such as Canada and Australia, they have brought new peoples to their countries. To gain these objectives, it is often desirable to protect their infant industries. This was our American experience. This same approach is now being duplicated by other nations.

Another circumstance in which we have found this same practical rationale for protection is the one in which an industry is undergoing a marked transformation. To allow it the time in which to reorganize and revamp its organization so as to be in a position thereafter to meet the threat of foreign competition, the Government protects it during the transition. The vast changes now being effected in the textile industry indicate that it is entitled to protection from injury for this reason.

There is another more long-term justification for the protection of a domestic industry for the benefit of the entire consuming world. It arises from the fact that while the American cotton-textile industry is not comparatively the lowest cost producer, it is, nevertheless, the most efficient industry. This high level of productivity has been the result of many factors to which reference has already been made. They are the relatively higher wages in comparison to other countries, a dynamic and advanced industrial environment, the great emphasis on the use of capital, and an intense competition for the consumer dollar. These have impelled the more aggressive companies to utilize their profits, garnered particularly during periods of unusual demand, for the modernization of their plants. Because of the close proximity of the highly efficient newer industries, the managements are more quickly adopting the advanced practices that prevail in other industries.

Mill layouts have been recently improved almost universally. Control systems are being applied at an impressive rate. While extensive laboratories are yet uncommon, they are no longer rare. In fact, some companies have established extensive research facilities of their own. New equipment is being introduced at a very high rate.

The result of these advances is that the American textile industry has become an international showplace. Other countries compare their effectiveness with that prevailing in this country. Their representatives come here to study the practices and operations. Recent descriptions of the Russian textile industry confirm this same attitude. They tend to measure their accomplishments with our own operations.

The discouragement and elimination of the American industry would, therefore, constitute a setback for the remainder of the world. There would no longer be available a hard-driving and aggressive lead country which could set the pace for the other nations. The rate of development would be slowed up for the cotton industries the world over. With the reduction in the incentive for improvement which would occur in the lower wage and poorer countries, they would be less inclined to press for advances and all nations would, therefore, suffer.

We contend that the short-run economic advantage which would accrue to the public from the slightly lower prices of imported merchandise coming primarily from the Asiatic countries would not be long sustained. In time the slow pace of technological advance would result in comparatively higher costs, and therefore, place this industry even farther behind in the competitive struggle for the consumer's dollar. To enable these countries to progress, it is necessary to maintain the industry in our country and permit it to operate safely. Schumpeter, in his consideration of the influence of a protective tariff in the United States, observed that—

> Whatever we may think about this (protection) from other standpoints, in a rapidly progressive country, it will have the effect of accelerating the pace of that progress by propelling investment and making it easier to face risks.[3]

Moreover, it would be unfortunate if the potential foreign suppliers of this market were encouraged to expand their capacity. It is a basic observation that the volume of world trade in cotton textile necessarily has and will decline. There are many reasons for this trend. The outstanding cause is that the traditional importing countries are developing their own domestic industries and will, therefore, become more and more self-sufficient. A country like India, which has been a market for world textiles before the war, has now become a large net exporter. It would, therefore, be unwise for these countries to use scarce capital to expand their textile capacity. All countries with existing cotton-textile industries are likely to find it wisest to divert their capital to other purposes since their industries are being increasingly oriented to their domestic market. Relatively greater benefits will accrue from investments in other industries than in a textile operation intended for the expansion of exports.

### 5. EXPANSION OF IMPORTS IS DEPENDENT UPON DOMESTIC NEEDS, ECONOMIC GROWTH, AND FULL EMPLOYMENT

No statement analyzing the problems of a particular industry, even one as important as textiles, can overlook the questions confronting our country in the field of international trade. Foreign countries do want our goods and services and they must have some form of payment for these purchases. In part these will be covered by an increasing volume of personal travel to foreign countries and loans to and investments made in foreign countries. But what place is there for the acceptance of merchandise?

[3] J. A. Schumpeter, Influence of Protective Tariffs on Industrial Development in the United States, proceedings, Academy of Political Science, May 1948.

Every analysis of the likely effect of the complete elimination of all tariffs indicates how modest the consequential rise in imports would be. One analysis indicates that of 1951 imports of $10.8 billion, $6 billion were duty-free and $4.8 billion were dutiable. Of the latter, $1.8 billion could not be substantially affected by tariff reductions.

As a result, the impact of lower duties would depend upon the elasticity of consumption in the remaining volume of $3 billion. About half of the potential increase in imports would be in agricultural products. Many of the remaining imports are products of older, nondurable goods industries, including textiles.[4]

This study definitely indicates that the potential rise in imports resulting from tariff reductions would be modest. The impact of such minor increase, however, would be most serious upon the affected sectors of our economy and would require major shifts and economic expansion to absorb the displaced persons. In this area, as we have pointed out, our record to date has not been too impressive, particularly when viewed from the experience of the textile worker. The same conclusion would be reached if this issue were viewed in terms of other similarly affected industries.

It is neither the tariff structure nor the administrative procedures adopted by our customs officials which are the limiting factor on the volume of imports. Rather, it is the nature of our economic and technical development. We have become more efficient and therefore more self-sufficient and less reliant upon goods from abroad. As a result, we are importing fewer and fewer manufactured goods.

The proportion of imports to our gross national product has been consistently declining. Equally significant, the proportion of semiprocessed materials of our total imports has been increasing. Dr. Humphrey, in his study, concludes that during the past 25 years, the aggregate increase in the value of imports of 8 commodities has about equaled the total increase in imports. The 12 commodities imported in the largest volume (by value) accounted for 64 percent of the total imports in 1952 compared with only 43 percent in 1929. The items we have been importing are, in order of value: coffee, nonferrous materials, newsprint and woodpulp, petroleum and products, manufactured wool, machinery and vehicles, watches and clocks, and industrial diamonds. These imports will probably grow in importance as American corporations expand their holdings of mines and oil wells abroad.

Analysis of the factors determining our volume of consumption of these and similar commodities indicates their dependence upon the level of domestic economic activity. Should our economic growth continue unbroken by major recessions, our consumption of these commodities will grow and the volume of imports rise. In this connection, the major concern is industry's resourcefulness, which may well develop synthetic or domestic substitutes for these raw materials. Already, wool is threatened by synthetic fibers and natural industrial diamonds by synthetic ones. However, the major reliance for the growth in imports must be placed upon the maintenance of an expanding and relatively stable economy.

[4] Humphrey, op. cit., p. 412.

As a political slogan, the cry "Trade, not aid" may be proved useful to attract votes. But it hardly has proved to be a viable and realistic principle upon which to build American foreign policy. Advocates of this form of fiscal retrenchment have had to change their position; in fact, they have become vigorous proponents of foreign assistance programs. Recent expansion of American investments abroad has helped maintain the balance of trade. The type of imports which will substantially pay for our volume of exports will be the semiprocessed materials required by our vast industrial system. In view of the minor contribution which lower tariff rates would make to our import-export balance, it is particularly important that we be most selective in the reductions we make, so that the injury to domestic industries may be minimized and our national interest not be sacrificed.

## B. The American Cotton Textile Industry

The cotton textile industry of the United States has historically been oriented toward supplying the needs of the domestic market. Exports, which averaged 5 percent of domestic production in the past 5 years, have been declining steadily and are likely to continue to shrink as underdeveloped countries expand textile production and the major exporting countries (Japan, India, and European nations) press for higher exports to offset their trade deficits.

Domestic demand for cotton goods has lagged behind the great growth in the Nation's consumption of goods and services since 1951. Indeed, the modest rise in the quantity of cotton goods available for domestic consumption (from 10.7 billion square yards in 1951 to 11.2 billion in 1956) did not keep pace with the increase in population so there was actually a decline in per capita consumption during this period.

The fourfold increase in imports of cotton cloth since 1951 has seriously aggravated the difficulties faced by the cotton textile industry in meeting the problems of a stagnant domestic market, declining foreign markets, excess capacity, style shifts, and the competition of synthetic textiles and other substitute products. Imports from Japan, which comprised virtually the entire increase in foreign-made cotton goods entering the American market, have been particularly unstabilizing since their effects were not confined to the particular sections of the market in which they were concentrated. As a result of the interrelated character of cotton textiles and the sag in demand in early 1956 these imports initiated a series of chain-reaction effects which weakened cotton goods prices and depressed the entire trade.

The "voluntary" restrictions imposed by the Japanese cotton textile industry on shipments to the United States since January 1957 have not been in effect for a long enough period for a conclusive evaluation of their effectiveness to be made. But the experience during the first half of 1957, which will be reviewed later in our statement, suggests that they have to date limited imports within the bounds prescribed by the policy. In this period, when the industry has been experiencing a slump for entirely domestic reasons, the restriction on imports has prevented even greater demoralization than now exists. As our description of the experience indicates, while this expedient is serving temporarily we do not believe that this improvised system of quotas represents a satisfactory long-term solution. We urge the American executive and legislative departments forthrightly to consider the problem and to adopt a definite system of Government-fixed quotas for textile imports to prevent the threat of further injury to the cotton textile industry.

A full understanding of the nature and impact of import competition in the cotton textile industry requires a study of the industry's position in the domestic and world markets for cotton goods, an evaluation of the forces affecting supply and demand at home and abroad, and the influence of the United States Government price-support and cotton export programs. Within the framework of such a study, we believe that means of expanding the market for cotton textiles can be found which will inure to the benefit of the American cotton textile industry and at the same time promote a foreign trade policy in the public interest.

### 1. DEPENDENCE OF AMERICAN INDUSTRY ON DOMESTIC MARKET

The cotton textile industry of the United States is a major industry. As of 1954, there were 1,549 establishments, employing 421,052 persons in this industry, distributed in the following divisions:

| Division [1] | Plants | Employees |
|---|---|---|
| Yarn mills, cotton system [2] | 357 | 85,275 |
| Thread mills | 97 | 13,908 |
| Narrow-fabric mills | 513 | 25.676 |
| Broad-woven fabric mills | 582 | 296,193 |
| Total | 1,549 | 421,052 |

[1] Includes mills producing yarn, thread, or fabric from silk or synthetic fibers where primary products are predominantly cotton.
[2] Includes yarn mills, silk system.

Source: U. S. Bureau of the Census.

The production of the cotton textile industry includes yarn, tire-cord and tire-fabric thread and narrow fabric (12 inches or narrower) as well as broad-woven fabric. Since the issues of foreign-trade policy relate primarily to broad-woven fabrics, this paper will concern itself exclusively with this division of the industry. It may be noted that cotton system yarn mills are substantially affected by conditions in the broad-woven fabric market since they supply yarn to broad-woven fabric mills as well as to others.

#### (a) *Historic importance of domestic market*

Unlike the industries in other major cotton manufacturing countries, the United States cotton textile industry has produced predominantly for the domestic market. In 1956, United States exports of 512 million square yards comprised 4.5 percent of total production. By contrast, the corresponding ratio of exports to domestic production for the other major producing countries were as follows:

| | *Percent* |
|---|---|
| Japan | 38 |
| United Kingdom | 29 |
| India | 14 |

Source: International Cotton Advisory Committee.

The dependence of the United States industry upon domestic sales has been characteristic of the industry throughout its history. Except for 1947, when exports were inflated by the world shortage of textiles following World War II, the quantity of American cotton goods shipped abroad has comprised less than 10 percent of production in every year during the past 30 years.

The United States industry is adapted to the task of serving the peculiar needs of the domestic market. This market requires a wide variety of fabrics for use in myriad products for apparel, household, and industrial purposes. It needs large orders of standard-quality goods to serve the enormous mass market which is peculiar to the United States. It also requires relatively small quantities of the numerous specialty fabrics which lend spice to the American wardrobe and housefurnishings. Speed and flexibility are essential to meet the frequent shifts in style and fashion. Imagination and ingenuity are required to devise new constructions and to engineer fabrics for particular end uses. Technological innovation and alertness are essential to increase efficiency and produce high-quality goods at a cost which will promote sales in a competitive market. A skilled work force is required to maintain and operate automatic machinery and make the frequent adjustments necessary to meet changing demands.

These qualities have been developed by the American textile industry in the course of its concentration upon serving the domestic market.

(*b*) *The trend of exports is downward*

United States exports of cotton broad-woven fabrics have been declining steadily since 1951 (table I). After reaching a record of 1,480 million square yards in 1947 as a result of the worldwide shortage following the war, exports fell sharply during the next 3 years as the textile industries of Europe and Asia made great recovery strides. After a partial recovery in 1951, when 802 million square yards were exported, foreign shipments have declined steadily during the past 5 years. Exports in 1956 totaled 512 million yards, a postwar low, and amounted to 4.5 percent of domestic production.

This decline is a reflection of the secular trend toward greater self-sufficiency among underdeveloped countries. Textiles have been a convenient starting point in the industrialization of many areas, particularly those which produce cotton. As a result, the volume of international trade in cotton cloth has been falling steeply while world production has increased substantially over the past 40 years:

[Thousands of metric tons]

| | 1913 | 1938 | 1953 | 1955 |
|---|---|---|---|---|
| Free-world production | 2,553 | 2,930 | 3,446 | 3,525 |
| Free-world exports | 983 | 608 | 505 | 510 |
| Percent exported | 39 | 21 | 15 | 14 |

Source: 1913–38, International Federation of Cotton & Allied Textile Industries; 1953–55, International Cotton Advisory Committee.

At the same time as the cotton-textile industry was growing in underdeveloped countries, Japan emerged as a major exporter. In

1933, Japan displaced the United Kingdom as the world's leading exporter of cotton cloth. The destruction of the bulk of Japan's cotton-textile industry during the war was followed by a postwar rebuilding program, which resulted in the development of a completely modern productive plant capable of producing 4 billion square yards of cloth per year. Japan's exports have risen sharply in the past 4 years, displacing United States goods in several markets.

*Exports of cotton cloth*

[Millions of square yards]

| Destination | United States | | | Japan | | |
|---|---|---|---|---|---|---|
| | 1952 | 1956 | Change | 1952 | 1956 | Change |
| Canada | 200 | 192 | −8 | 1 | 16 | +15 |
| El Salvador | 12 | 5 | −7 | 1 | 12 | +11 |
| Indonesia | 77 | 14 | −63 | 127 | 139 | +12 |
| Philippines | 95 | 67 | −28 | 4 | 60 | +56 |
| Thailand | 21 | 4 | −17 | 41 | 79 | +38 |
| Union of South Africa | 27 | 25 | −2 | 11 | 20 | +8 |
| All countries | 762 | 512 | −250 | 758 | 1, 262 | +504 |

Source: United States, Bureau of the Census; Japan, Institute of Textile Trade Research and Statistics.

As a result of the rebuilding of the Japanese textile industry, she has recaptured her position as the leading exporter of cotton cloth. India, which was a large importer of cotton goods before the war, has become the second largest exporter, shipping 740 million yards overseas in 1956. The modernization program currently underway in the Indian textile industry will, no doubt, strengthen its position in the world market. These two countries ranked first and second among the nations of the free world as volume exporters, with the United States a lagging third, and Great Britain fourth.

With the textile industries in underdeveloped areas continuing to grow and the low-cost producers in Japan and India strengthening their position through expansion and modernization, the export markets for United States cloth are bound to shrink further. The two major markets, Canada and the Philippines, are definitely shifting to the Japanese export orbit (exhibit I). The American cotton-textile industry must look to domestic demand for its survival.

(*c*) *The continuing threat of imports*

Imports of cotton cloth have risen sharply in recent years. In 1956, imports of "countable cotton cloths"[5] aggregated 188,248,000 square yards, an increase of 41 percent over the 1955 volume. This marked gain culminated a rise which started in 1952, when imports totaled 36,337,000 (table II).

Imports of countable cotton cloths have been concentrated in a few types of fabric, particularly in 1955–56, when Japanese exporters flooded the American market with ginghams and other box-loom fabrics. While domestic production of these types comprised 2.6 percent of all cotton broad-woven fabrics produced in the United States in 1955, imports of ginghams and related fabrics amounted to 28.8

[5] Countable cotton cloths are those whose threads have to be counted in ascertaining the average yarn number on which the progressive rates of duty are based under tariff pars. 904 (for cloths made wholly of cotton) and 905 (for cloths in chief value of cotton but containing silk or rayon).

percent of all countable cotton cloths imported. In 1956, Japanese shipments of ginghams to the United States of 72,430,000 square yards comprised 59 percent of that country's total cotton-goods exports to the United States. In addition, large quantities of gingham have been made up into blouses and shirts for export to this country.

Imports of cotton cloths other than countable cloth, which include filled or coated fabric, tapestries, and other jacquard-figured upholstery cloths, pile fabrics, table damask, and blanket cloth, and jacquard-figured napped cloths have also been increasing in recent years. The most notable instance of this rise has been in velveteen fabrics. These are cotton fabrics in which filling yarns are cut to form a pile. Imports increased from 5,600 square yards in 1946 to 8,325,000 in 1956, when they were twice as great as domestic production (table III). The bulk of the imported velveteens comes from Japan, which accounted for 83 percent of the total in 1956. Most of the balance comes from Italy.

While the primary impact of imports has been concentrated on the markets for the particular types of fabric involved, the repercussions are felt throughout the industry. Claudius Murchison, former economic adviser to the American Cotton Manufacturers Institute, has described this process as follows: [6]

> Imports which concentrate on a given product group naturally force curtailment of American production in that group, both because of increased foreign supply and because of the attendant collapse of prices.
>
> Domestic mills thus shorn of their market in one product group have no choice but to crowd into another. In doing this, they create new conditions of overproduction and force still another shifting of product lines. This process of adjustment and readjustment continues until it has permeated the entire industry. With each step there remains behind some residue of loss. When the entire sequence is finished, the net overall result is a loss of active spindles just about equivalent to the number which had to make the initial adjustment.
>
> It is a method of adjustment which is dictated by the law of survival. In the final analysis, the effect is to distribute group loss over the industry as a whole, financially and physically.
>
> With expanding imports of cotton goods, there is no such thing as confining industry damage to the points of original impact.

Shipments of cotton cloth from Japan assumed serious proportions in 1955, when that country was admitted to the General Agreement on Tariffs and Trade and became eligible for the benefits of the most-favored-nation tariff rates. Japanese shipments to the United States increased from 48.6 million square yards in 1954 to 140.3 million yards in 1955; the latter figure includes approximately 25 million yards which were subsequently transhipped to Indonesia.

In December 1955 the Japanese Textile Export Council, representing the Government and the textile industry, imposed the following quotas on exports to the United States for 1956:

> 150 million square yards of cotton cloth, including 70 million yards of gingham, 5 million yards of velveteen and 20 million yards of print cloth;
>
> 2½ million dozen blouses.

While exports to the United States in 1956 did not reach the total cloth quota, shipments of ginghams and velveteens exceeded the subquotas for these cloths and substantial shipments of made-up goods, woven apparel and knit goods brought exports to the equivalent of

---

[6] Claudius Murchison, The Cotton Textile Industry and Foreign Economic Policy (1954), p. 16.

approximately 250 million square yards of cotton cloth. Shipments of ginghams amounted to 72 million yards; velevteens, 5 million yards; all cotton cloths, 122 million yards.

In January 1957, the Japanese Government announced the adoption of a 5-year export quota program which set limitations for two dozen categories of fabrics and finished cotton products with an overall limit of 235 million square yards of textiles and apparel per year. The quota on cotton cloth is 113 million square yards, which includes 35 million yards of gingham and 2.5 million yards of velveteen, (exhibit II).

Data on shipments in the first half of 1957 indicates that the quotas have been effective in limiting exports so far but the peak months for shipments come in the latter half of the year so it is not yet possible to make a conclusive finding.

Shipments of cotton cloth to the United States in the first half of 1957 totaled 31 million square yards, including 10 million yards of gingham. Shipments of made-up goods, woven apparel, knit goods and miscellaneous cotton textiles reached proportions which indicate that the quotas for these products will generally be filled by the end of the year (table IV).

The Japanese quota program presents numerous administrative problems which make its enforcement difficult. Responsibility for administering the program is in the hands of the Japan Textile Products Exports Association, which is a nongovernmental agency. Complaints have been reported about various devices being used to evade the quotas. The Daily News Record of July 25, 1957 publishes reports from Tokyo and Osaka to the effect that investigations are underway into complaints about transshipment of cotton blouses via Switzerland and Panama, ginghams via England, Holland, and Israel, and velveteens via Holland. Exports of gingham from these countries in the first 5 months of 1957 totaled over 2 million yards compared with 700,000 yards in all of 1956.

Another means of circumventing the Japanese quotas on shipments to the United States is indicated by the fact that Japanese exports of cotton cloth to Hong Kong has risen sharply and this has been followed by a large increase in Hong Kong exports of cotton shirts to the United States. Thus, Japanese cloth shipments to Hong Kong jumped from 61 million square yards in 1955 to 138 million yards in 1956; Hong Kong exports of cotton shirts to the United States rose from 38,000 dozen in all of 1956 to 91,000 dozen in the first 5 months of 1957. The annual rate of shirt shipments from Hong Kong in May 1957 was 582,000 dozen.

It is currently reported that the Japan Textile Products Exports Association has developed an export certification procedure to prevent or minimize transshipment. Each cargo of velveteen and gingham, the fabrics on which the procedure has been applied, is to be accompanied by a customs clearance certificate which must be certified in the country of destination and returned to the council within 2 months of the loading date. The exporter must post a bond of 5 percent of the value of the cargo, which is forfeited if he fails to submit the proper customs clearance. The United States Customs Bureau is to inform Japan concerning any imports which lack this certification. Japanese exporters have also restricted exports of many cotton fabrics to Hong Kong because of this transshipment procedure. The Japanese Government, through its Ministry of International Trade and

Industry, is to investigate all exports to foreign countries exceeding 1956 levels. The United States Customs Bureau reports that since July 1 it has been keeping a close check on textile imports to spot transshipments. When such transshipped goods are discovered, the Census Bureau is notified so that the items can be counted correctly against the Japanese quota. But the procedures are unlikely to be foolproof.

In the absence of United States Government quotas on imports of cotton cloth and products the American textile industry is at the mercy of foreign producers and foreign American traders pursuing policies in their own self-interest.

The problem of the threat of imports is, of course, not restricted to Japan, though it is now one of most serious to the American market. Other countries are greatly in need of new outlets for their production and would like to gain access to the American consumer. Countries like the United Kingdom, France, and Italy as well as Japan have suffered major losses in export trade compared with prewar standards, and could use the American market to cushion these blows and those which lie ahead of them. New exporters are also appearing as the native cotton-textile industry begins to expand. The particularly outstanding postwar exporter is India. Another country seeking such markets is Brazil, which finds its own domestic market inadequate to absorb its huge output. All countries are vying for the shrinking export market and therefore are ready to exploit any opening which may be available, even if it is only on a temporary basis.

### 2. CONTRACTION OF THE DOMESTIC INDUSTRY

The cotton-textile industry of the United States has been suffering from an excess of capacity since the midtwenties. The extension of three-shift operations and the expansion in consumption of rayon led to the scrapping of one-third of the cotton-spinning spindles in place between 1925 and 1939 (from 37.9 to 25.3 million, respectively). By the end of 1945, the number of spindles in place had declined to 23.8 million.

#### (a) *Decline in plant and equipment*

The industry has continued to contract since the war. Cotton spindles in place totaled 21.2 million at the end of July 1957, a decline of 11 percent from the end of 1945. The number of looms in cotton mills dropped from 412,200 at the end of 1945 to 360,100 at the end of 1956, a drop of 13 percent. These declines in equipment have resulted largely from the liquidation of plants. From 1946 through August 1957, 327 cotton and synthetic textile mills were closed permanently, displacing 88,120 employees (table V). The period since 1953 has been particularly disastrous, witnessing the demise of 139 mills, with 39,270 employees, in 3 years and 8 months.

Another measure of the shrinkage is provided by the United States Census of Manufactures, which reports a decline of 69 in the number of establishments in the industry from 1947 to 1954 and a decrease in employment of 73,000 persons or 15 percent. The declines occurred in the yarn and broad-woven fabric mills. In the former, the number of mills dropped by 117 and employment by 32,000. While the nominal number of plants in the broad-woven fabric industry increased by 7, employment dropped by 20,000.

| Division [1] | Establishments | | Employment | |
|---|---|---|---|---|
| | 1947 | 1954 | 1947 | 1954 |
| | | | *Thousands* | *Thousands* |
| Yarn mills, cotton system [2] | 474 | 357 | 121 | 85 |
| Thread mills | 89 | 97 | 15 | 14 |
| Narrow fabric mills | 480 | 513 | 28 | 26 |
| Broad-woven fabric mills | 575 | 582 | 330 | 296 |
| Total | 1,618 | 1,549 | 494 | 421 |

[1] Includes mills producing yarn, thread, or fabric from silk or synthetic fibers where primary products are predominantly cotton.
[2] Includes yarn mills, silk system.

Source: United States Census of Manufactures.

Available data on cotton textile employment indicate the marked decline which has occurred since the war. According to the census of manufactures, employment fell from 494,000 in 1947 to 421,000 in 1954, a drop of 15 percent. As of mid-1957 we estimate employment at 394,000, a decline of 100,000 or 20 percent in the past 10 years (table VI).

Workers in all parts of the country have suffered from the wave of mill liquidations in this period. The regional distribution of mill closings in the cotton-rayon division in the first 8 months of 1957 has been as follows:

| Region | Number of plants | Number of employees |
|---|---|---|
| New England | 5 | 2,470 |
| Middle Atlantic | 8 | 1,150 |
| South | 7 | 3,100 |
| Total | 20 | 6,720 |

(*b*) *Regional impact*

Each of these major textile regions has suffered substantial reductions in total textile employment. Between February 1951 and June 1957, New England lost 139,000 textile jobs; the Middle Atlantic States, 105,000 jobs; and the South, 68,000 jobs. As a result, the latest compilation of "areas of substantial labor surplus" by the Bureau of Employment Security of the United States Department of Labor, covering May 1957, includes 18 textile areas, listed below:

New England:
- Fall River, Mass.[7]
- Lawrence, Mass.[7]
- Lowell, Mass.[7]
- Providence, R. I.[7]
- Danielson, Conn.
- Biddleford-Sanford, Maine
- North Adams, Mass.

Middle Atlantic:
- Scranton, Pa.[7]
- Wilkes-Barre-Hazleton, Pa.[7]
- Berwick-Bloomsburg, Pa.
- Sunbury-Shamokin-Mount Carmel, Pa.

South:
- Asheville, N. C.[7]
- Fayetteville, N. C.
- Kinston, N. C.
- Rocky Mount, N. C.
- Shelby-Kings Mountain, N. C.
- Waynesville, N. C.
- Radford-Pulaski, Va.

[7] Major area.

The critical fact about the above communities is that most of them have remained distressed for long periods of time. When they lost a major textile mill, they became chronically distressed. They have in the past been one-industry towns, having had no other major employments. The workers have had only one-industry association. The economies have been completely dependent upon one or a group of employers. Few of the industries were locally owned. There was no substantial middle-class or independent enterprises within them. The small-business man had had little opportunity to develop new undertakings since the textile mill owners dominated the community. The absence of experience with new enterprise and the lack of local capital make recovery difficult if not impossible. Recovery tends, therefore, to be greatly delayed.

The workers have borne the full burden of suffering imposed by mill liquidations. Many of these plants had been in operation for generations and the workers had devoted their entire adult lives, as their fathers and grandfathers had before them, to working in the mills. Thousands of textile workers have been forced out of the labor market because of the pervading hopelessness of finding a job. Unemployment benefits have frequently been exhausted as alternative employment opportunities were not available in the area.

The impact of unemployment has been particularly onerous on older persons, whose age has barred them from finding new employment.[8]

Two major cotton textile centers which have been extremely hard hit by the industry's decline are Fall River and New Bedford, Mass. These neighboring communities had supported 34 cotton mills in 1945, which had provided jobs for 25,000 workers. At present, there are only 19 cotton mills left with 6,500 workers employed. The toll has been particularly great among New Bedford's cotton mills, with 9 of the town's 14 plants being liquidated and employment dropping from 15,000 to 2,800 since the war.

*(c) Structural changes*

Significant structural changes have taken place during this period. Cotton yarn mills have suffered a 37-percent reduction in employment since 1947, when a considerable portion of their output went into tire cord and fabric; synthetic yarns have since absorbed the bulk of this market. This development caused considerable distress in small towns in the South, particularly in those States which had substantial concentrations of yarn mills. The impact of the decline in this division is indicated by the distribution of cotton yarn mill employment in the Southern States as reported in the Census of Manufacturers:

| State | Employment [1] | | Percent change |
|---|---|---|---|
| | 1947 | 1954 | |
| Alabama [2] | 10,056 | 7,057 | −30 |
| Georgia | 28,895 | 16,845 | −42 |
| North Carolina [2] | 60,132 | 51,653 | −14 |
| South Carolina | (3) | 4,852 | (3) |
| Tennessee | 2,371 | 2,152 | −9 |

[1] Including tire cord and tire fabric mills.
[2] Including thread mills.
[3] Not available.

[8] William H. Miernyk, Interindustry Labor Mobility, Boston, 1955.

The largest part of the loss in employment in the cotton broad-woven fabric mills occurred in the New England and other Northern States. But among the southern cotton textile States, Alabama showed a marked reduction in employment amounting to about 8 percent (from 32,345 to 27,532). Drops of less than 2,000 employees took place in South Carolina (from 103,965 to 102,790), Tennessee (from 6,676 to 5,058), and Virginia (from 20,685 to 19,118). Increases took place in North Carolina (from 68,481 to 69,280) and Georgia (from 50,393 to 52,140).

(*d*) *Decline in cotton consumption*

United States mill consumption of cotton has been declining since World War II (table VII). The downward trend which started in 1947 was interrupted by the boom caused by the Korean war but it has been resumed since 1953. Consumption of 4,339 million pounds in 1956 represents a decrease of 10 percent over the past 10 years.

On a per capita basis, the decline has been even steeper, the 23.7 pounds consumed per person in 1956 being 17 percent below the 1946 level. In spite of the vast gains in American living standards over the past 30 years, per capita consumption of cotton has been lower in the past few years than in the middle twenties. The average rate of per capita consumption was 22.9 pounds in the period 1954–56 compared to 23.8 pounds in 1925–27.

(*e*) *Stable cotton fabric production and consumption*

In the face of the marked contraction in the industry's plant, equipment, and labor force since the war, the volume of cotton broad-woven fabric production and consumption has been maintained at a fairly stable level. With the exception of 1949, production has fluctuated between 10½ and 11½ billion square yards a year during the past decade (table I). The total yardage available for domestic consumption has tended to rise slightly (as exports declined and imports increased) but the concomitant growth in the population has kept per capita consumption in the narrow range between 66 and 67 yards in most years since the war (table VIII). Deviations from this level occurred in years of marked recession (1949, 1952, and 1954) and in the Korean war boom (1950–51).

The ability of the industry to maintain the level of its output in spite of the sharp reduction in its capacity and employment is the result of the great gains in productivity which have been achieved in the past decade. While precise quantitative data are not available, the profusion of evidence available on improved efficiency and technological innovation during the postwar period clearly indicate that the cotton textile industry has kept pace with the gains in productivity recorded by the most progressive American industries (exhibit II).

Available data from the United States Bureau of the Census indicate that the cotton and synthetic-textile industry has spent an average of $162 million a year for new plants and equipment since 1947 (table IX). These vast expenditures have been used to renovate the industry's capacity and modernize its operations. More than half of the equipment in use is of postwar design. As a result of the industry's technological innovation and modern methods of operation, it is the most efficient textile industry in the world.

*(f) Market lost by cotton*

The inability of the cotton-textile industry to expand its domestic market in line with the postwar growth in the Nation's population and the tremendous rise in the American standard of living has been due to a complex of forces operating on the American scene. One set of factors which has tended to restrict cotton consumption is embodied in the decline of the proportion of consumer expenditures accounted for by apparel. The ratio of apparel expenditures has declined steadily since 1946, with a ratio of 10.3 percent; by 1956 it had dropped to 6.7 percent (table X).

This marked shift in consumer living habits resulted from the huge backlog of demand for durable goods and housing which developed during the thirties and World War II; the claims imposed on future incomes by credit extended to purchase durable goods and housing; the trend to suburban living; the growing proportion of households headed by older people; the increasing proportion of new homeowners and the relative increase in the population of the West.[9]

(1) *Losses to other fibers.*—The competition of manmade fibers in end uses traditionally served by cotton has caused considerable dislocation in the cotton-textile industry. Before the war cotton accounted for more than 80 percent of total mill consumption of textile fibers in the United States. By 1945 cotton's share had declined to 75.5 percent and it has decreased steadily during the past 12 years (table XI). In 1956, cotton accounted for 66.9 percent of the total; while rayon and acetate, which had absorbed 12.9 percent of the market in 1945, jumped to 18.5 percent. The newer manmade fibers (dacron, orlon, dynel, nylon, etc) which are all postwar products except for nylon, rose from 0.8 percent of the total in 1945 to 7.5 percent in 1956.

The incursion of the manmade fibers into cotton textile markets has been particularly effective in the following end uses. [10]

(*a*) Tire cords and fabric: This market had been cotton's largest single end use before the war, when cotton had the field virtually to itself. Expansion of rayon tire cord and fabric production capacity during the war led to the gradual displacement of cotton. By 1949, production of the rayon product exceeded cotton in this field and, by 1955, 87 percent of the fiber consumed in this end-use was manmade.

(*b*) Men's separate trousers: The share of the separate trouser market accounted for by cotton declined from 65 percent in 1937 to 8 percent in 1953 as a result of the expansion in the use of manmade fibers, which accounted for 61 percent of the totals in 1953.

(*c*) Sport shirts: Cotton's share of this market declined from over 96 percent in 1937 to 55 percent in 1953, when manmade fibers accounted for 36 percent.

(*d*) Women's coats: Cotton's position as the second most important fiber in this market (with wool as the major one) was taken over by manmade fibers, which increased their share from 5 percent in 1937 to 8 percent in 1953 while cotton's share dropped from 9 to 1 percent.

---

[9] Textile Organon, Textile Economics Bureau, August 1957, pp. 121–123.

[10] Data on end-use consumption of textile fibers are from Textile Economics Bureau and National Cotton Council.

(*e*) Blankets: Cotton's share of this market declined from 80 percent in 1937 to 46 percent in 1952 while the proportion accounted for by manmade fibers rose from less than 1 to 28 percent.

(*f*) Curtains: From 93 percent of the fabric curtain market in 1937, cotton's share dropped to 64 percent in 1952 while manmade fibers raised their portion of the total from 7 to 36 percent.

(*g*) Men's gloves (dress and semidress): Cotton's share of this market dropped from 74 percent in 1937 to 39 percent in 1952, when manmade fibers accounted for 17 percent. An expansion in wool use in this field from 26 percent in 1937 to 44 percent in 1952 was a major factor in the decline of cotton.

(*h*) Women's underwear and nightwear: Cotton's share of the woven and knit products in this field declined sharply as manmade fibers expanded, except for woven underwear, in which cotton increased its share:

[Percent of total fiber consumption]

| | Cotton | | Manmade | | | Cotton | | Manmade | |
|---|---|---|---|---|---|---|---|---|---|
| | 1937 | 1952 | 1937 | 1952 | | 1937 | 1952 | 1937 | 1952 |
| Underwear: | | | | | Nightwear: | | | | |
| Woven | 27 | 43 | 64 | 57 | Woven | 84 | 67 | 12 | 33 |
| Knit | 54 | 20 | 43 | 80 | Knit | 67 | 11 | 31 | 88 |

(*i*) Auto seat covers: Cotton had supplied all the fiber used in this market before the war; in 1952, manmade fibers accounted for 73 percent and cotton 27 percent.

(*j*) Filter fabrics: Cotton's share declined from 100 to 41 percent between 1937 and 1952, when manmade fibers absorbed 26 percent of the total.

(2) *Losses to other products.*—The demand for cotton textiles has been severely constricted by the substitution of plastic, paper products, and nonwoven fabrics in many end-uses since the war.

(*a*) Plastics:

Apparel uses: Plastic products have made considerable inroads into the market for textiles in rainwear, aprons, sport jackets, and footwear. Approximately 10 million pounds of calendered vinyl film were consumed in the fabrication of rainwear in 1953; consumption of textile fibers for rainwear amounted to 12 million pounds. The continued growth in acceptance of film rainwear, particularly for women's wear, has no doubt resulted in plastics surpassing textiles in this field in 1956.

Plastic film has absorbed a large part of the women's apron market and has also expanded rapidly in the industrial apron field. Consumption of vinyl film in these enduses increased from 1½ to 3 million pounds between 1953 and 1956. Textile fibers used in making women's aprons, smocks, and pinafores amounted to 13 million pounds in 1953.

An indication of the growing importance of plastics in the footwear field is furnished by the expansion of playshoe production (other than rubber soled, canvas top) from 31.8 million pairs in 1947 to 74.7 million pairs in 1954. Plastic playshoes generally require less fabric than regular leather shoes. Clear plastic rain boots for women are currently displacing the rubber and cloth footwear formerly used for this purpose.

A new type of plastic foam has recently been developed which has potentialities for the displacement of interlinings in coats. Formulations of urethane have been produced which are reported to have superior insulating qualities combined with extreme light weight. While the principal use to which this product has been put so far is as a substitute for foam rubber, it is entering the interlining market this fall and may displace worsted, horsehair, and cotton interlining.

Household uses: Plastic materials have displaced textile products in a large number of household uses. Consumption of vinyl film and sheeting in principal household end uses in 1956 was as follows:

| End use: | *Consumption (millions of pounds)* |
|---|---|
| Upholstery (including transportation) | 42 |
| Draperies, bedspreads, kitchen and bathroom curtains | 14 |
| Closet accessories | 7 |
| Shower curtains | 8½ |
| Table covers | 3½ |
| Appliance covers | 2½ |
| Furniture covers | 3½ |

Analysis of available data on manufacturers' shipments of specific household products reveals the prevailing trend toward plastics at the expense of textiles:

Draperies: In 1947 cotton draperies accounted for 47.5 percent of the total; by 1954, this proportion had declined to 35.7 percent and the bulk of the noncotton draperies (60 percent) was made of plastics.

Window curtains (excluding lace): In 1947 cotton curtains comprised 83.8 percent of the total and by 1954 cotton curtains' share had dropped to 39.2 percent, with plastics jumping to 12.8 percent (principally bathroom curtains).

Shower bath curtains: In the 1930's virtually all shower curtains were made of cotton; in 1955, only 2 percent were cotton, having been largely displaced by unsupported plastic film.

Molded garden hose: Plastic hose, introduced since the war, accounted for 68.4 percent of the total shipped in 1954 and has continued to expand in this market, displacing rubber hose, which included layers of cotton cloth; the plastic products use no cloth.

Industrial uses: Plastics have made major inroads into traditional textile markets in the automotive, tape, electrical insulation, and tent fields. These incursions have resulted in substantial declines in production of the types of cloth formerly used for these purposes.

Consumption of textile fibers in automobile upholstery, sidewalls, headlining, and sheeting declined from 86.4 million pounds in 1949 to 79.2 million pounds in 1953. Vinyl chloride resins consumed in the production of passenger cars increased from less than 4 million pounds to more than 16 million pounds in this period. Further gains at the expense of textile fibers have been scored by plastics in this market as new-car styling has favored the sporty appearance which plastics can provide at lower cost than textile fabrics. In 1955 it is estimated that more than 23 million pounds of vinyl chloride resins were consumed in the production of passenger cars.

The automobile seat-cover market has been largely captured by plastics and plastic combinations, which accounted for 78.4 percent of total shipments in 1954. It is estimated that 11 million pounds of vinyl resins were consumed in this end product in 1956.

In the pressure-senstive tape field, tape with plastic backing has come to dominate the market, accounting for 56.8 percent of total shipments in 1954 compared to 6.9 percent for tape with cloth backing.

Textiles have lost considerable ground in the electrical insulation field. In 1947, cambric-insulated power wire and cable accounted for 20.9 percent of the value of shipments in this market. By 1954 the proportion had declined to 8 percent and further declines have occurred since then as rubber and plastic insulation have grown in importance. Further indication of the declining role played by textiles in this field is evident in data on consumption of cotton by end use, which show a decline from 152,000 bales in 1947 to 104,000 bales in 1955.

It is anticipated that textiles will lose a substantial part of the tent market as military requirements for lighter weight tents make cotton duck obsolete for this purpose. Experiments are being conducted by the Army with paper and film laminates for this purpose. This will mean the loss of the bulk of the tent market for cotton, which absorbed 60,000 bales of cotton in 1955.

(*b*) *Paper:* Paper products have displaced textiles in one major market (packaging) and in several other fields. The primary advantage of paper over textiles in these end-uses has been in cost but in a number of cases paper has offered qualities which textiles could not match, e. g., the sanitary advantages of facial tissues, bibs, towels and diapers that are disposed of after a single usage.

*Packaging:* With the development of the multiwalled paper sack in 1924, a great new market was opened up for paper products at the expense of cotton and burlap bags. This sack, a 3- to 5-ply kraft paper product, is strong enough to hold materials up to 100 pounds. It can be made moisture- and gas-proof to serve some purposes better than a textile bag. For shipment of bulky commodities such as cement, fertilizer and chemicals, this type of sack has other advantages over the cotton or burlap bag. Losses from sifting and from residues clinging to the bag when it is emptied are often greater for textile bags than for paper. The development of automatic, high-speed packaging machines also favors the paper bag over the textile bag.

The extent to which paper has displaced textiles in the packaging field is indicated by the following tabulation of production from 1947 to 1956:

| Year | Textile bags | | | Paper shipping sacks (1947-55=100) |
|---|---|---|---|---|
| | Cotton | Burlap | Total | |
| | *Millions* | *Millions* | *Millions* | |
| 1947 | 857 | 623 | 1,480 | 79 |
| 1948 | 737 | 525 | 1,262 | 83 |
| 1949 | 760 | 465 | 1,225 | 75 |
| 1950 | 667 | 442 | 1,109 | 101 |
| 1951 | 655 | 305 | 960 | 117 |
| 1952 | 577 | 487 | 1,064 | 98 |
| 1953 | 504 | 479 | 983 | 109 |
| 1954 | 477 | 466 | 943 | 117 |
| 1955 | 421 | 486 | 907 | 123 |
| 1956 | 360 | 519 | 879 | 127 |
| Percent change, 1947-56 | −58 | −17 | −41 | 61 |

As a result of the growth in the use of paper bags, the quantity of cotton consumed in bagging declined from 483,960 bales in 1947, when this use accounted for 5 percent of cotton consumption, to 221,340 bales in 1955, only 2 percent of total cotton consumption. In 1947, bags were the second largest end-use consumers of cotton in the United States. In 1955, bags were 10th on the list of cotton-consuming uses.

Facial tissues: Paper handkerchiefs and facial tissues have cut deeply into the cloth-handkerchief market, particularly since the war. In 1939, 51,000 tons of facial-tissue stock was produced. By 1947 the volume of facial-tissue shipments had risen to 131,000 tons, and, in 1954, to 165,000 tons.

Napkins: Production of paper napkin stock increased from 70,000 tons in 1939 to 103,000 in 1947 and 178,000 in 1954 as the paper product largely displaced cloth napkins in public eating places as well as in homes.

Towels: Paper towels have taken over the bulk of the market for toweling in public washrooms as a result of their advantage over cotton in making available low-cost sanitary products for one-service use without the necessity of laundering. Paper towels are also used in homes, chiefly in the kitchen.

Production of paper-toweling stock increased from 129,000 tons in 1939 to 206,000 in 1947 and to 319,000 tons in 1954, a boost of 55 percent over the 1947 output and 147 percent over the prewar level. Cotton consumption in toweling in 1954 amounted to 323,000 bales, only 6 percent over the 1947 volume and 17 percent over the prewar rate.

Miscellaneous paper products: Paper products have been developed for a host of other end uses which are competitive with textiles. Substantial inroads have also been made into the following traditionally textile markets: Sanitary napkins, window shades, draperies, mats, bookbinding, automobile-seat covers, diapers, bibs, doilies, and dust mops.

Paper also has great potentialities in the apparel market, if current experiments with nonwoven paper fabrics are successful. The Kimberly-Clark Corp., of Neenah, Wis., has developed a fabric composed of a cross-laid web of fiber bonded by an adhesive, and laminated between two layers of high wet-strength paper. This fabric is reported to be capable of achieving a high resistance to fire and water, and can be printed and textured with processes used on paper. It is expected to achieve particular importance in apparel uses in which sanitation is a determining factor, such as uniforms for nurses and doctors, coveralls for workers in atomic-energy plants, etc.

(*c*) Nonwoven fabrics: American manufacturers started experimenting with the production of nonwoven fabrics at the end of World War II and are rapidly developing products which promise to displace knitted and woven fabrics in many significant end uses. Nonwoven fabrics are a mat of fibers held together with a bonding agent. Production amounted to 25 million pounds in 1953, and it is estimated to have exceeded 50 million pounds in 1955, with expansion going on at a rate which is expected to double output every 3 years until the midsixties.

In the apparel market, nonwoven fabrics have won considerable acceptance in interlinings, and have also been used for skirts, dresses, petticoats, tapes, and ribbons.

Household uses include dishcloths, filling for comforters, napkins, towels, wiping cloths, and draperies.

Industrial applications have been developed for nonwoven fabrics in filter cloths, mats, casket linings, and surgical masks. These fabrics are also used as backing for vinyl sheeting, particularly in automobile uses, including upholstery, door paneling, scuff pads, and seat bolsters. The fabric is combined with the sheeting by coating on a calender, electronic welding, quilting, or laminating. The nonwoven fabric provides strength and support to the exterior vinyl sheet, adding thickness to the sheet, increasing tear resistance, and retaining the soft, pliable hand normally found in an unsupported sheet.

(*g*) *Predominance of internal factors*

It is evident from the above that the contraction of the industry since the war has been a product of several forces impinging upon the demand for cotton textiles. The primary influence has been the decline in domestic demand, which has traditionally accounted for the overwhelming proportion of the total demand for the industry's products. The concurrent decline in foreign demand for fabrics has reinforced the depressing effects of the drop in domestic demand. Consequently, the American cotton-textile industry has been in the poorest possible position to absorb an additional competitive burden. The sharp increase in imports during 1955–56 served to aggravate the industry's distress, making its adjustment to the problems of contracting demand more difficult.

The problems of adjustment have also been accentuated from the supply side. The growing productivity of the industry as a result of technological improvements in machinery, new methods, and better plant layouts has served to augment the industry's capacity to produce at a time when demand was not growing. Moreover, the extension of 3-shift operations throughout the industry and the prevalence of the 6-day-per-week work schedule added further to the potential supply of cotton textiles.

### 3. GOVERNMENT COTTON PROGRAMS HAVE MADE INDUSTRY'S ADJUSTMENT MORE DIFFICULT

The United States Government conducts a series of programs designed to support the price of American cotton and to promote disposal of surplus cotton abroad. These programs have had the following effects:

(*a*) Domestic cotton prices have been maintained from 5 to 7 cents a pound higher than the world price. These higher prices have handicapped raw cotton in its competition with synthetic fibers, particularly rayon, and have, no doubt, limited its market and the opportunities for uses in other products.

(*b*) Surplus American cotton has been sold to foreign mills at prices 5 to 7 cents a pound less than the cost to United States mills. As of August 15, 1957, the Commodity Credit Corporation had sold 7.7 million bales of cotton for export at world prices since August 1, 1956. Congress has passed legislation permitting the sale of another large volume in the new crop year.

The difference between the domestic and world price constitutes a subsidy which the United States Government offers to foreign mills in competition with American mills. While domestic mills producing for export receive export payments to compensate them for the difference in cotton prices, domestic production for the United States market is not eligible for compensatory payments. The subsidy at most has permitted American producers to hold onto their current foreign market. Domestic producers are now particularly vulnerable to competition from foreign mills whose purchase of cotton is subsidized by the United States Government. If the current voluntary quota system had not been invoked by Japan, this differential in raw-material cost would have played havoc with the domestic industry.

4. SOLUTION OF INDUSTRY'S PROBLEMS MUST COME THROUGH EXPANDING MARKETS

The basic challenge the American cotton-textile industry must meet is its need to expand markets for its products. Much has been done to produce new fabrics for existing uses, but only modest efforts have been directed to the creation of new outlets. If this problem is to be solved successfully, the industry will have to devote sufficient resources and imagination to the study of consumer preferences and potentialities and our evolving pattern of living; to research for the development of new industrial uses; to the engineering of fabrics and finishes to provide the qualities which could expand cotton-textile consumption; and to the promotion of sales on a sound and expanding basis.

The domestic industry cannot expect to obtain such new ideas and fabrics from foreign sources. They are geared to meet the particular needs of their own domestic markets. The peculiarities of the American market, with its mass base, high-quality standards, and frequent style changes, require special treatment.

The American cotton-textile industry must look to its own resources for the research, development, and promotion of new and expanded uses which are essential to a growing market. Only a virile, optimistic, and secure industry can fulfill these responsibilities.

Substantial progress has been achieved in developing new finishes which have enlarged the use of cotton fabrics in many end uses. Thus, cotton dresses for street and formal wear increased from 7 percent of the total market in 1937 to 28 percent in 1953, and in 1956 comprised more than 35 percent of the total. Cotton sport shirts, which had declined to 42 percent of the total in 1951, rebounded to 75 percent in 1956. Cotton's share of the women's woven blouse, waist, and shirt market expanded from 26 percent in 1937 to 51 percent in 1953 and to 65 percent in 1955.

There is some promise that the apparel industries could absorb a higher volume of textiles, but the textile industry must apply itself to cultivate this market before alternative consumer products beat it in the competition for the consumer's dollar. A recent study by the E. I. du Pont de Nemours & Co. textile-fibers department concludes that—

> given a reasonably prosperous peacetime economy, in the next 5 to 10 years, clothing expenditures will, on the average, keep pace with increases in income, i. e., a 1-percent increase in consumer disposable income will generate a 1-percent increase in the demand for clothing expenditures.

The analyst properly cautions that this promise will be realized only if—

**all branches of the apparel industry, through imaginative and aggressive merchandising, exploit this favorable economic environment for clothing.**

Previous studies have pointed out the fact that part of the challenge is that "families own more clothing than has been generally assumed." If the consumer is encouraged to substitute new items of clothing for old ones, a truly aggressive and creative promotional task is required. The industry has recently formed agencies for advertising clothing needs, but these are too modest in their objectives really to do the full job.

The textile industry serves a wider market than merely apparel uses. It is primarily a service industry, trying to get other processors to employ its products. To be successful, it cannot rest on its oars and assume that the processors of it products will forever remain attached to textiles. The textile industry has lost markets, and will lose additional ones if it does not adopt an aggressive attitude of promoting the use of its products. It must broaden its services to and knowledge of the apparel, household furnishing, construction, and other industries in order to discern, develop, and promote new uses. Unfortunately, the cotton-textile industry has hardly made a beginning in this direction.

#### 5. WAGE DIFFERENTIALS ARE MOST MARKED AMONG THE VARIOUS NATIONAL TEXTILE INDUSTRIES

The wage levels prevailing among the various textile industries differ markedly, with the American scale standing on top, though it rates low on the United States ladder of wage payments and fringe benefits. These differences in wages explain why it is possible for countries like Japan to overcome the relatively higher American efficiency. Even at that, Japan is not able to compete with the present schedule of tariff rates on many types of cotton-textile products.

We are compiling, and hope to have available for the December panel discussions, a compendium of wage information which will provide a measure of the differential levels of wages and hours and, where possible, fringe benefits.

It must be noted, however, that in various countries other costs, including the cost of borrowing money, are very high, so that the overall production costs are considerably above the levels suggested by their prevailing wage levels.

### C. Legislative Proposals

The above analysis unfolded the steps needed to be undertaken to revitalize and protect the industry. First and foremost, there is need for an industry agency devoted to the study and development of markets and products. There are many prototypes for this work in such industries as paper, wool felt, and synthetic yarn. What the cotton-textile industry requires is the leadership, the determination, and the spirit of cooperation necessary for its own promotion. Some realization of these elementary requisites to growth is discernible within the industry, but the individualism and suspicion permeating the producers has prevented significant action from being taken. But, of course, this step is beyond the purview of the present committee.

As relates to foreign economic policy, two issues must be considered. First is the problem of the 2-price system of cotton, which handicaps the American cotton-textile industry to the extent of 5 to 7 cents per pound. Moreover, this higher price curtails some uses of cotton, and inhibits the exploitation of cotton products in new markets. Many proposals are now before the House Agriculture Committee on how to resolve this dilemma. We believe that there should be one price for all cotton users, and that production payments should be paid to farmers for the share of the cotton crop consumed in the domestic market. The cost of these payments should be covered by the Treasury rather than by any levy on consumption. We are attaching our analysis and position on this problem (exhibit III).

The most important issue relating to the problem of imports is how we shall deal with cotton-textile imports. The present administration has finally recognized the importance of preventing further injury to this industry. However, instead of proceeding through the normal administrative process of invoking the escape clause or the national-security amendments or supporting the various legislative proposals considered by Congress, the administration appealed to the Japanese Government to apply voluntary quotas upon its exports, particularly since its regulatory system already provided for such controls. This voluntary quota system has been operating with moderate effectiveness despite the problems it has created. Nevertheless, it cannot be envisaged as a permanent solution to the problem of cotton-textile imports.

There are various disadvantages to the present system. Some are inherent in a voluntary program which is dependent upon the exporting nation. Changes in government officials and policy may reduce the value of these voluntary restraints. While the threat of cotton-textile imports comes primarily, if not exclusively, from Japan, new exporting nations may arise. They may be India or China, through the use of the Hong Kong market. We shall not be prepared to deal with these crises under our present laws. The transshipment problems are obviously difficult to deal with, and no system of policing will be able to track down every act of evasion. Ultimately, therefore, we shall have to develop our own system of control.

One aspect of the current system of voluntary quotas which requires further comment is that its very informality as relates to the negotiations prevents full participation by the various interested parties. While the representatives of American manufacturers were consulted in the elaboration of the program, the trade unions were rebuffed on the several occasions that they proposed that they be consulted. If secret diplomacy allows for the inclusion of employers in the process of negotiations, it seems to us that worker representatives are equally entitled to participate.

There are alternative courses available to this Nation to establish an effective system of import control. Escape clauses are provided in all of our bilateral trade agreements and in the GATT regulations. Since the current tariff system was the result of negotiations with countries other than Japan, it is more than appropriate that a revision shall be made in view of the accession of Japan to the privileges of GATT.

In formulating controls, various approaches may be followed. We should, of course, prefer to have an outright quota system on imports which would resemble the system applied by the Japanese, but in our case would be applied against all imports. Another course would be to follow the plan adopted for the woolen and worsted industry, which provides for an escalation in rates for imports exceeding a defined level.

We urge the committee to recommend the adoption of a positive system of American regulation of cotton-textile imports.

TABLE I.—*United States production and exports of cotton broad-woven fabrics, 1946–56*

[Millions of square yards]

| Year | Production | Exports | Percent exported | Year | Production | Exports | Percent exported |
|---|---|---|---|---|---|---|---|
| 1946 | 10, 171 | 775 | 7. 6 | 1952 | 10, 593 | 762 | 7. 2 |
| 1947 | 11, 083 | 1, 480 | 13. 4 | 1953 | 11, 333 | 621 | 5. 5 |
| 1948 | 10, 863 | 939 | 8. 6 | 1954 | 10, 892 | 605 | 5. 6 |
| 1949 | 9, 392 | 880 | 9. 4 | 1955 | 11, 319 | 543 | 4. 8 |
| 1950 | 11, 207 | 559 | 5. 0 | 1956 | [1] 11, 400 | 512 | 4. 5 |
| 1951 | 11, 415 | 802 | 7. 0 | | | | |

[1] Estimated.

Sources: Production, Association of Cotton Textile Merchants of New York; exports, U. S. Bureau of the Census.

TABLE II.—*Imports of countable cotton cloths, 1946–56*

[Imports for consumption in thousands of square yards]

| Year | | Year—Continued | |
|---|---|---|---|
| 1946 | 43, 758 | 1952 | 36, 337 |
| 1947 | 15, 962 | 1953 | 64, 300 |
| 1948 | 31, 749 | 1954 | 73, 484 |
| 1949 | 19, 743 | 1955 | 133, 252 |
| 1950 | 47, 799 | 1956 | 188, 248 |
| 1951 | 45, 779 | | |

Source: U. S. Bureau of the Census.

TABLE III.—*Imports and domestic sales of cotton velveteens, 1946–56*

| Year | Imports | Domestic sales | Ratio of imports to domestic sales [1] | Year | Imports | Domestic sales | Ratio of imports to domestic sales [1] |
|---|---|---|---|---|---|---|---|
| | *Sq. yds.* | *Sq. yds.* | *Percent* | | *Sq. yds.* | *Sq. yds.* | *Percent* |
| 1946 | 6, 000 | 3, 390, 000 | 0. 2 | 1952 | 1, 741, 000 | 7, 531, 000 | 23. 1 |
| 1947 | 14, 000 | 4, 328, 000 | . 3 | 1953 | 2, 732, 000 | 6, 752, 000 | 40. 5 |
| 1948 | 62, 000 | 4, 865, 000 | 1. 3 | 1954 | 5, 157, 000 | 5, 459, 000 | 94. 5 |
| 1949 | 403, 000 | 4, 435, 000 | 9. 1 | 1955 | 8, 600, 000 | 4, 184, 000 | 205. 6 |
| 1950 | 1, 861, 000 | 6, 681, 000 | 27. 9 | 1956 | 8, 325, 000 | (2) | [3] 196. 2 |
| 1951 | 2, 677, 000 | 7, 660, 000 | 34. 9 | | | | |

[1] Calculated on the unrounded figures.
[2] Not available.
[3] Based on data for 1st 3 months.

Source: Imports, U. S. Bureau of the Census; domestic sales, U. S. Tariff Commission.

TABLE IV.—*Japanese quotas and shipments of specified cotton-textile products, 1957*

[Thousands of dozens]

| Item | 1957 quota | 1st half shipments | Item | 1957 quota | 1st half shipments |
|---|---|---|---|---|---|
| Plain pillowcases | 400 | 155 | Brassieres | 600 | 336 |
| Dish towels | 800 | 395 | Shorts, pedal pushers, and other trousers | 600 | 340 |
| Handkerchiefs | 1,200 | 600 | T-shirts | 500 | 98 |
| Blouses | 1,500 | 908 | Gloves | 450 | 177 |
| Sportshirts | 750 | 401 | | | |
| Dress and work shirts | 300 | 72 | | | |

Source: Japan Textile Products Exports Association.

TABLE V.—*Liquidation of cotton-textile mills in the United States,*[1] *1946–57*

| Year | Number of mills | Number of employees | Year | Number of mills | Number of employees |
|---|---|---|---|---|---|
| 1946 | 4 | 300 | 1933 | 28 | 7,750 |
| 1947 | 13 | 5,500 | 1954 | 38 | 12,600 |
| 1948 | 26 | 9,300 | 1955 | 46 | 10,850 |
| 1949 | 36 | 9,000 | 1956 | 35 | 9,100 |
| 1950 | 24 | 2,600 | 1957: January–August | 20 | 6,720 |
| 1951 | 28 | 5,600 | | | |
| 1952 | 29 | 8,800 | Total, 1946 through August 1957 | 327 | 88,120 |

[1] Including synthetic textile mills.

Source: Textile Workers Union of America Research Department.

TABLE VI.—*Employment in cotton-textile mills, 1947, 1954, 1957*

| Division | 1947 | 1954 | 1957 (June) | Percent change, 1947–June 1957 |
|---|---|---|---|---|
| Yarn mills, cotton system | 121,400 | 85,300 | 76,000 | −37 |
| Thread mills | 14,700 | 13,900 | 13,000 | −1 |
| Narrow-fabric mills | 28,100 | 25,700 | 25,000 | −1 |
| Broad-woven fabric mills | 330,200 | 296,200 | 280,000 | −15 |
| Total | 494,400 | 421,100 | 394,000 | −20 |

Sources: 1947, 1954—U. S. Bureau of the Census; 1957 (June)—Estimated on the basis of U. S. Bureau of Labor Statistics data.

TABLE VII.—*Cotton consumption in the United States, 1946–56*

| Year | Mill consumption | Per capita civilian consumption[1] | Year | Mill consumption | Per capita civilian consumption[1] |
|---|---|---|---|---|---|
| | *Pounds* | *Pounds* | | *Pounds* | *Pounds* |
| 1946 | 4,803,000,000 | 28.5 | 1952 | 4,437,000,000 | 23.3 |
| 1947 | 4,668,000,000 | 24.5 | 1953 | 4,521,000,000 | 24.2 |
| 1948 | 4,461,000,000 | 24.9 | 1954 | 4,125,000,000 | 21.7 |
| 1949 | 3,838,000,000 | 21.0 | 1955 | 4,384,000,000 | 23.2 |
| 1950 | 4,680,000,000 | 26.8 | 1956 | 4,339,000,000 | 23.7 |
| 1951 | 4,847,000,000 | 25.3 | | | |

[1] Based on mill consumption, with the following adjustments: Deduction of spinnable waste; addition of imported manufactures; deduction of exported manufactures; deduction of military uses in excess of 5 percent of mill use.

Source: Textile Economics Bureau.

**TABLE VIII.—*Cotton broad woven fabrics available for domestic consumption, total and per capita, 1946–56***

| Year | Total consumption | Population | Per capita consumption |
|---|---|---|---|
| | *Millions of square yards* | *Millions* | *Square yards* |
| 1946 | 9,440 | 141.4 | 66.77 |
| 1947 | 9,619 | 144.1 | 66.74 |
| 1948 | 9,956 | 146.6 | 67.90 |
| 1949 | 8,531 | 149.2 | 57.18 |
| 1950 | 10,696 | 151.7 | 70.51 |
| 1951 | 10,659 | 154.4 | 69.05 |
| 1952 | 9,868 | 157.0 | 62.84 |
| 1953 | 10,776 | 159.6 | 67.50 |
| 1954 | 10,361 | 162.4 | 63.79 |
| 1955 | 10,910 | 165.3 | 66.01 |
| 1956 | [1] 11,176 | 168.2 | 66.45 |

[1] Partly estimated.

Source: Association of Cotton Textile Merchants of New York.

**TABLE IX.—*Expenditures for new plant and equipment by cotton and synthetic textile mills in operation, 1947–54***

[Thousands of dollars]

| Year | Yarn and thread mills | Broad-woven fabric mills | Narrow fabric mills | Total, excluding narrow fabric mills |
|---|---|---|---|---|
| 1947 | $36,647 | $121,653 | $5,670 | $158,300 |
| 1948 | | | (1) | (1) |
| 1949 | 26,907 | 161,682 | (1) | 188,589 |
| 1950 | 27,316 | 151,346 | (1) | 178,662 |
| 1951 | 36,986 | 177,914 | (1) | 214,900 |
| 1952 | 33,038 | 120,162 | 3,534 | 153,200 |
| 1953 | 23,210 | 84,985 | 6,076 | 108,195 |
| 1954 | 30,255 | 68,195 | 4,802 | 98,450 |
| Annual average expenditure | | | [2] 5,020 | [3] 157,185 |

[1] Not available.
[2] Based on data for 4 years.
[3] Based on data for 7 years.

Source: U. S. Bureau of the Census.

**TABLE X.—*Consumer expenditures for apparel as a percent of total consumer expenditures, 1946–56***

[Dollar amounts in billions]

| Year | Apparel [1] | Total | Percent for apparel | Year | Apparel [1] | Total | Percent for apparel |
|---|---|---|---|---|---|---|---|
| 1946 | $15.1 | $146.6 | 10.3 | 1952 | $16.6 | $218.3 | 7.6 |
| 1947 | 15.6 | 165.0 | 9.5 | 1953 | 16.4 | 230.5 | 7.1 |
| 1948 | 16.4 | 177.6 | 9.3 | 1954 | 16.1 | 236.6 | 6.8 |
| 1949 | 15.4 | 180.6 | 8.5 | 1955 | 16.8 | 254.4 | 6.6 |
| 1950 | 15.2 | 194.0 | 7.8 | 1956 | 17.8 | 267.2 | 6.7 |
| 1951 | 16.1 | 208.3 | 7.7 | | | | |

[1] Clothing and accessories, except footwear.

Source: U. S. Department of Commerce.

TABLE XI.—*Percentage distribution of United States mill consumption of specified fibers, 1945–56*

| Year | Cotton | Manmade fibers | | Wool | Silk | Total |
|---|---|---|---|---|---|---|
| | | Rayon and acetate | Other | | | |
| 1945 | 75.5 | 12.9 | 0.8 | 10.8 | | 100.0 |
| 1946 | 74.2 | 13.5 | .8 | 11.4 | 0.1 | 100.0 |
| 1947 | 72.8 | 15.4 | .8 | 11.0 | | 100.0 |
| 1948 | 69.8 | 18.0 | 1.1 | 11.0 | .1 | 100.0 |
| 1949 | 70.5 | 18.3 | 1.7 | 9.4 | .1 | 100.0 |
| 1950 | 68.5 | 19.8 | 2.1 | 9.5 | .1 | 100.0 |
| 1951 | 71.1 | 18.7 | 2.9 | 7.2 | .1 | 100.0 |
| 1952 | 69.5 | 19.0 | 3.9 | 7.5 | .1 | 100.0 |
| 1953 | 69.2 | 18.7 | 4.3 | 7.7 | .1 | 100.0 |
| 1954 | 68.7 | 19.2 | 5.5 | 6.5 | .1 | 100.0 |
| 1955 | 65.7 | 21.3 | 6.5 | 6.4 | .1 | 100.0 |
| 1956 | 66.9 | 18.5 | 7.5 | 7.0 | .1 | 100.0 |

Source: Textile Economics Bureau.

## EXHIBIT I

### COTTON TEXTILE IMPORTS OF CANADA AND THE PHILIPPINES

#### CANADA

The Canadian market has been a significant postwar outlet for American textiles which have displaced British textiles. The United States has been the dominant exporter throughout the postwar years largely because of style and price advantages. In 1951 the volume of United States shipments reached a total of 215 million square yards. In 1956 they dropped to 194 million. During this same period the volume of imports from other countries, exclusive of Great Britain, rose substantially. The major growing sources were India, which exported 20 million yards to Canada in 1956, and Japan with 16 million yards. The total imports from countries other than the United States and Great Britain amounted to 55.4 million yards in 1956 which compares with the previous high of 39 million yards in 1955 and 38 million yards in 1950. In other postwar years the volume has been much lower. Complaints against the growing imports of Japanese and Indian cotton textiles and finished goods have been mounting in Canada.

A current survey of the Canadian cotton textile industry comments as follows:

"Many United States mills are attempting to reduce inventories by shipping goods to Canada at what is described as 'very shaky prices.' * * * Japan, too, is taking advantage of the Canadian market. Made-up flannel shirts for men and boys are coming into this country in large volume. Also Japanese flannel piece goods for linings for jeans. In the industrial field more cheap pocketings for the work-clothing trade and cotton duck are being shipped here from India." [11]

The rise in exports from Japan has been very steep: 1954, 2.1 million square yards; 1955, 13.8 million square yards; and 1956, 16.1 million square yards.

#### THE PHILIPPINES

The Philippine market has historically been second to Canada as an outlet for American cotton cloth. United States shipments to the Philippines totaled 121 million square yards in 1954. However, exports were cut to 100 million yards in 1955 and 67 million yards in 1956. This marked decline resulted from the imposition of import license restrictions by the Philippine Government, the application of import duties on United States merchandise for the first time, and the sharp rise in shipments from Japan. Using barter deals, Japan was able to increase exports from 4 million square yards in 1952 to 60 million yards in 1956.

A current report announces that despite the restrictions imposed on Japanese imports, the Cabinet approved applications of 11 firms and individual importers to open letters of credit representing the value of their unused balances with respect to barter permits for the export of logs in exchange for cotton textiles.

[11] Canadian Textile Journal, August 23, 1957, p. 21.

## Exhibit II

### Productivity Trends in the Cotton-Textile Industry

Man-hour productivity in the cotton-goods industry rose most impressively during the years 1919–39. During this 20-year period, the total rise was 64 percent, according to the United States Bureau of Labor Statistics. The average annual rise was 2.6 percent. Detailed overall industry data have not been released for the subsequent period because of the changes in the industrial classifications followed by the Census Bureau and the Bureau of Labor Statistics. We must, therefore, rely on reports on various segments of the industry to provide us with an insight into the rate of change in productivity.

Several reports are available on the man-hours required to produce printcloths. According to the Bureau of Labor Statistics the technology prevailing in 1910 required 328 man-hours to produce 1,000 pounds of printcloth. By 1936 the requirements had been reduced to 216 man-hours.[12] A Bureau of Labor Statistics survey for 1951 indicates that the 5 printcloth plants which it surveyed reported a range extending from 140 to 203 man-hours per 1,000 pounds.[13] The three middle plants reported requirements of 176, 184, and 186 man-hours. In 1954, a new printcloth plant was built in Greenwood, S. C., by Greenwood Mills with the most modern machinery and layout in the industry. It reported that it would require 143 man-hours per 1,000 pounds in 1956. The Whitin Machine Works in its latest review of the productivity of a modern mill, laid out 95 man-hours as the requirement per 1,000 pounds of printcloth.

The Bureau of Labor Statistics survey for 1910 indicates that the prevailing technology in that year would require 256 man-hours for 1,000 pounds of narrow sheeting. By 1936 it had dropped to 162 man-hours. In 1951 the Bureau of Labor Statistics surveyed 7 mills and found that the man-hour requirements ranged from 107 to 172 man-hours per 1,000 pounds. They ranked as follows: 107, 126, 136, 141, 150, 150, and 172.

A recent report on the Harriet and Henderson Mills, Henderson, N. C., provides additional information on changes in narrow sheeting productivity. Its modernization program began in 1938; by 1939, man-hours output had risen by 33 percent. By 1942, it had risen by 86 percent and by 1954, 118 percent.

Data reported by the Graniteville Co. for its plants in Graniteville, Vancluse, and Warrenville, S. C., and Augusta, Ga., which produce drills and twills, show a decline in man-hour requirements from an average of 171 in 1945 to an average of 111 in 1954. Output per man-hour increased by 54 percent during this period, or an average of 4.6 percent per year.

The remaining available information relates to the yarn sector of the industry. The Harriet No. 2 cotton-yarn mill in Henderson, N. C., which produces ply yarns for weaving, began its modernization production in 1938. Man-hour productivity rose by 33 percent in 1939, 82 percent by 1942, and 124 percent by 1954.

The Whitin Machine Works reports that the modernization of a 20,000-spindle combed cotton knitting-yarn mill would reduce costs by 36 percent from 15.24 to 9.62 cents per pound. Most of the reduction would be effected through lower labor costs. This item would be cut from 14.3 to 6.2 cents per pound or by 57 percent. The labor complement would be reduced from 217 to 124 persons or by 43 percent. The man-hour output would be increased from 8.5 pounds to 15 pounds per man-hour.

The American Textile Machinery Association reports that a modernization program in a carded-yarn mill of 30,336 spindles would effect an increase in output per man-hour from 4.94 to 9 pounds, or 82 percent. A similar program in another carded-yarn mill of 34,704 spindles would raise output from 4.72 pounds per man-hour to 7.63 pounds or 62 percent.

The same source indicates that the modernization of a combed broadcloth mill would effect a reduction in manpower per shift from 70 to 43 employees or 63 percent.

---

[12] Effects of Mechanical Changes in the Cotton-Textile Industry, 1910 to 1936 (serial No. R612).

[13] Case Study Data on Productivity and Factory Performance: Coarse Cotton Gray Goods (BLS Rept. No. 16).

## Exhibit III

## TWUA Position on Raw Cotton Prices

### I. GENERAL POSITION OF THE TEXTILE WORKERS UNION OF AMERICA

TWUA's position is that it is in the best interests of the American consumer, the cotton textile workers, the cotton textile industry, the cotton-growing industry, and the Government, that (*a*) a single-price system—the world price of cotton—replace the present two-price system which establishes a higher price for domestic than for foreign cotton, and (*b*) that farmers receive compensatory production payments equal to the difference between the market price and protected price of cotton.

### II. THE PRESENT CRISIS IN RAW COTTON

The crisis was precipitated by a number of different factors:

(*a*) The existence of a program for the sale of cotton held by the Commodity Credit Corporation on the world market at world prices, 5 to 7 cents a pound below current support prices and domestic spot-market prices. The CCC will have sold about 7.7 million bales for export between August 1, 1956, and August 15, 1957, and will sell an additional 2.9 million bales for export between August 16, 1957, and August 1, 1958. As a result, the accumulated stockpile has been substantially lowered and will continue to contract.

This program was fostered not only by the low prices charged by the CCC but also by the financial help provided by Export-Import Bank loans, the International Cooperation Administration, and titles I and II of Public Law 480.

(*b*) The cotton products export program, which compensates exporters of processed cotton goods, has resulted in the payment of $12,388,000 in differential payments in the period from August 1, 1956, through June 21, 1957, and has raised total exports slightly above previous years' levels.

The differential payment equals the difference between domestic and foreign prices of raw cotton; it is, therefore, a measure of the disadvantage suffered by American cotton textile producers in competition with foreign manufacturers.

(*c*) The current high level of raw cotton exports has helped reestablish America's position in the free world cotton market but, at the same time, it has substantially reduced the American carryover to about 11.6 million bales, 3 million bales below that of August 1, 1956. As for the new crop, it is expected that the acreage devoted to cotton will be the lowest in 80 years; upland cotton in cultivation on July 1, 1957, totaled 14¼ million acres, compared to 16.8 million on July 1, 1956. The allotment was 17.6 million acres but 3 million were placed in the acreage reserve program under the soil bank provision. Raw cotton production in the 1957 crop year (August 1, 1957 to July 31, 1958) is currently estimated at 11.3 million bales as compared with 13.3 million last year. This drop in cotton production will leave a small margin out of the current supply for exports. There is, therefore, some concern about the adequacy of the cotton supply. With output declining and exports continuing at high levels under the export subsidy programs, domestic cotton prices may tend to rise and thereby place the domestic textile industry under a greater competitive disadvantage.

(*d*) The relative position of cotton in total fiber consumption in the United States has been constantly dropping, with its share diverted to synthetic fibers. This trend has recently aroused the concern of the manufacturers and the raw cotton interests who see a need for lowering cotton prices to meet this competition.

(*e*) The cotton middlemen (particularly the brokers, merchants, and ginners, compressors, shippers, and warehousemen) have begun to complain that, with so much cotton bought and handled by the Government, especially in the case of exports, they are losing out on the business.

(*f*) Raw cotton cultivation costs have dropped measurably because of the mechanization of many processes, increased use of irrigated lands and of fertilizers, and the growth in the size of farms. Many farmers, particularly the big ones, are able to make substantial profits at much lower prices than the support level and even the world price.

(*g*) The rising cost of living has made the public more sensitive to the cost of the support program and there has been considerable concern about high prices. Those doubting the value of these programs have become more articulate as the present price-support program with its acreage limitation and soil-bank payment provisions has not solved the farm problem. Scandalous practices and irrational payments are being uncovered.

(*h*) The present administration has been unfriendly to the high price-support programs, preferring flexible price suports. With the failure of the soil-bank program, it has renewed its interest in flexible price programs with the hope of moving toward a completely free price market.

(*i*) These developments are worrying the agricultural groups who are concerned lest the price-support programs lost out under the impact of the economy wave. They have, therefore, become more sympathetic to the idea of such compensatory production payments as the program in effect in the woolgrowing industry.

(*j*) Local merchants oppose the soil-bank program, because the soil retirement, though maintaining the farmers' income, has reduced local business.

### III. ALTERNATIVE POSITIONS

A number of plans which seek to meet the present cotton crisis have been proposed in Congress.

(*a*) *Continuance of the current plan.*—Under this program, national acreage allotment will continue; under the sliding provisions, the support price of 77 percent of parity (32.74 cents) may be raised to about 85 percent of parity.

(*b*) *Free market prices with no compensatory payments.*—The administration would prefer to support prices at a level which would eliminate all surplus (about 24 cents a pound) and maintain current marketing quotas. Farmers would not be paid any compensatory payments.

(*c*) *Lower support prices and more acreage.*—One bill (S. 2273), sponsored by the Farm Bureau, would give farmers a choice between the current program and a plan for 75-percent support prices with a 20-percent rise in acreage allotment.

(*d*) *Loans and compliance payments.*—The Poage bill (H. R. 877) provides for loans at 75 percent of parity plus compliance payments up to 90 percent of parity with a limit on payments to a single farmer of $10,000.

(*e*) *Two-price system.*—H. R. 7816 would give farmers 90 percent of parity on their share of the domestic market and the world price for export. The domestic market quota would be limited to seven-tenths of the present acreage allotment.

(*f*) *Two-price system plus processing tax.*—H. R. 7836 would provide producers full parity of income (38 to 48 cents a pound) on domestic allotment, equaling two-thirds of present allotments, and world price for exported cotton, with financing provided by a tax on all processors of cotton and synthetics.

### IV. TEXTILE WORKERS UNION POSITION: WORLD PRICE PLUS COMPENSATORY PAYMENTS TO FARMERS

TWUA believes that the present situation is intolerable from the point of view of the textile workers, the textile industry and the consumer. We are in favor of protecting the farmer but believe that the present approach will, in the long run, provide no solution to the cotton problem. Maintenance of the current high cost of cotton will only discourage expansion of cotton usage and thereby aggravate the problems of surplus accumulation. The wide gap between foreign and domestic prices makes the domestic textile industry vulnerable to outside competition. With Federal Government unwilling to provide direct controls on imports, the cotton price program will lead to the strangulation of the domestic textile industry.

We, therefore, propose the following program:

(*a*) A single price, determined on the open market, for raw cotton, to equalize domestic and world prices.

(*b*) Compensatory production payments to farmers, equal to the difference between the price received and the support price for that portion of the crop used for domestic consumption or that produced under a defined marketing program.

(*c*) Maximum production payments of $10,000 to any single enterprise; under present price-support levels, this would mean payments for approximately 400 bales.

(*d*) We have also proposed that, pending the adoption of this program, support be given to the Smith bill (S. 314), which would authorize the Secretary of Agriculture to make available to American textile manufacturers of cotton products for export the "surplus cotton owned by the Commodity Credit Corporation at such prices as the Secretary determines will allow the United States cotton textile industry to regain the level of exports of cotton products maintained by it during the period 1947 through 1952" and to meet competition from foreign imports.

We see the following advantages to the various affected interests under this program:

(*a*) *Textile worker.*—Lower prices for cotton would permit the industry to push the product into new uses and to expand markets. A 20 or 25 percent reduction in raw cotton costs would also permit an increase in wages, since labor costs on medium count fabrics represent about 40 percent of the current raw material cost.

(*b*) *Consumer.*—Prices of cotton products would be substantially reduced at at time when all other prices are being increased.

(*c*) *Cotton farmer.*—His interests would be safeguarded, since he would be compensated directly for the cotton he produces under the protected program. The limitation on payments to any one farmer would insure the protection which the family farmer needs. The large mechanized farmer, already producing cotton at costs below the world price, is making money thereon. The industry would be able to hold its world markets.

(*d*) *The Government.*—It would be freed from all the responsibilities of cotton purchase and marketing, and be able to disband its complicated administrative structures. There would be a saving in actual outlays by the Government, depending on the plan, variously estimated as running up to $100 million a year.

# THE COTTON TEXTILE INDUSTRY AND AMERICAN TRADE POLICY

Seymour E. Harris, chairman, department of economics, Harvard University

## SUMMARY

### 1. GENERAL TRADE POLICY

Tariff policy vis-a-vis textiles depends in part upon general tariff policy. The more the pressure toward free trade, the greater the pressure is likely to be, all other things being equal, toward reduced tariffs on textiles. I am not discussing tariff policy in general in this paper. But it should pointed out that in the past the greatest emphasis has been put on reduced tariffs as a means of increasing our foreign trade. The assumption is that if we import more we export more. In more recent years, and especially since World War I, a much greater emphasis has been put upon other aspects of foreign trade; namely, dollar shortage. A crude estimate suggests that dollar shortage in the last 40 years or so has been of the order of about $125 billion. Foreigners can obtain more dollars by selling us more goods, by taking away our export markets, or by obtaining loans or grants from the United States through official or private sources.

An appropriate policy for the United States would be one that would use all three methods as a means of solving the problem of dollar shortage. In the last 40 years the largest contribution has come from loans and gifts, and particularly gifts of the United States Government. This is quite appropriate since the problem of dollar shortage is partly an economic and partly a political problem, and the burden should to some extent be put upon all the people and not excessively upon the weak industries which would suffer as a result of excessive imports.

Also, in recent years there has been a tendency for foreign countries to capture our export markets. This has been true in textiles as in many other fields. Their problems have been eased to some extent by the large rise of imports, and this rise has been partly the result of a freer trade policy, but more largely the result of the rising income in this country.

Despite the frequent view expressed that the American policy is a highly protectionist one, the facts are that abroad the tendency toward restrictive trade is much greater than in the United States. Since 1933 there have been significant reductions in our tariff levels, but abroad there has been a tendency for increased quotas, the use of foreign exchange, and many other protectionist devices.

### 2. THE TEXTILE INDUSTRY

Over the last 50 years textiles has been one of the slowest growing of all United States Census industries. In recent years the industry has tended to lose jobs even as the country was increasing its jobs by substantial numbers. This experience of the textile industry is the result partly of a change in the pending pattern of the American consumer; partly the result of great technological revolutions that have affected the textile industry and have tended to result in larger output per man-hour of work. The distress in the industry is measured much more by the reduction in the number of employees than in the number of yards of cloth turned out for the use of textiles in other areas. This decline in textiles can also be related to certain Federal policies and notably the tendency of the Federal Government to encourage purchases of houses and consumer durable goods through liberal credit policies.

In the years 1939 to 1955 textile employment declined by 13 percent the country over, whereas in the same period employment in all manufacturing rose by 64 percent, or a relative loss for textiles of almost one-half. These facts certainly suggest a case for special treatment of textiles in trade policy. In other words, insofar as the Government finds it necessary, given its economic and political objectives, to introduce freer trade policies, it should be especially careful not to put the brunt of such adjustments on weak industries like textiles.

The measure of the decline in textiles is also suggested by the figures in the two recent censuses. Employment in all textiles fell by 17 percent from 1947 to 1954, and in woolens and worsteds by 49 percent. The loss of man-hours of work was 22 percent and 52 percent, respectively. Investments declined by 39 percent and 62 percent, respectively.

Another indication of the weakness of the textile industry is given by the average weekly wage. An industry that has trouble in selling its goods and maintaining its employment tends to have lower wages than all industries. In 1939 weekly wages in textiles averaged 71 percent of the national manufacturing level, 83 percent in 1947, 71 percent in September 1956, and 70 percent in May 1957.

The level of employment in the textile industry is an important matter. In considering this industry, we should, however, also take into account North-South competition. The competition of the South makes the problem of the textile industry a much more serious one in the Northeast. Not only does the Northeast have to worry about foreign competition, but it has to worry even more over southern competition. In setting its wages in the North the textile industry has to worry about the wage level in the South. If wages are set too high, then the industry is lost to the South. If they are not set high enough, industry does not maintain its necessary number of workers for a high employment economy.

Profit figures also suggest the weakness of the textile industry. The SEC studies reveal much lower profits in textiles than in all manufacturing. We also find in a study of numerous textile mills that the profit level is much below the general average and that it is about one-half as high in New England as it is in the South. In fact, in 3 years for 12 large New England firms, we found profits averaging only about 1.4 percent. These are profits in relation to sales.

In part the difficulties of the industry may be laid to the fact that it is still a highly competitive industry. The largest firm in the industry ranks 70th in the Nation in the amount of sales. It had $515 million in sales in a recent year and also 50,000 employees. But these sales accounted for but 4 percent of the $12.4 billion of sales of General Motors. Whereas the 500 leading manufacturing firms account for more than 50 percent of factory employment, the 19 textile firms in the top 500 accounted for about 25 percent of textile employment.

Another feature of the textile industry relates to the fact that it tends to be squeezed from both ends. Agricultural policies tend to result in higher prices for raw materials and therefore a decline in competitive position vis-a-vis other consumer goods as well as competitive position vis-a-vis foreign nations. At the other end, the apparel industry tends to squeeze the textile industry. Though this industry is broken up into even smaller units than textiles, apparels have been able to hold their own in the economy much more effectively than textiles. Thus textile employment as a total of all employment fell from 3½ percent in 1929 to 2 percent in 1955, or a reduction of 40 percent. In apparel the percentage was 7.4 in 1929 and 7.4 in 1955.

### 3. AN EXAMPLE: THE TEXTILE INDUSTRY IN RHODE ISLAND

Because Rhode Island has the highest concentration of textiles in the Northeast, I have taken the trouble to present some facts concerning that State. The trouble seems to be that with such a heavy concentration of textiles and with the textile industry declining the country over and especially in New England, Rhode Island suffers especially from this particular development. The population of Rhode Island does not rise as rapidly as that for the whole country, but the rise is certainly substantial. From 1946 to 1956 the population rose about 60,000 and about 25,000 jobs might have been expected additional. Actually, the number of new jobs was only 2,000. This suggests that with the unsatisfactory development in textiles and with new industries not coming in in sufficient numbers, the trouble was reflected not in a substantial rise of unemployment, but in a very large desertion of the labor market. From 1929 to 1954 the old-line industries, inclusive of food, apparel, etc., provided 6,000 jobs, or a rise of one-half. But what about the rapidly growing industries? These industries include paper and pulp, chemicals, rubber, metals, machinery (exclusive of electrical machinery), electrical machinery, and transportation equipment. In all of these industries where the growth has been great, Rhode Island was able to add only 5,000 jobs. The rise was substantial, but small compared to most of the rest of the country—an increase of 14 percent from 34,500 to 39,500. This was a small increase compared to the loss of 40,000 textile jobs. In 6 important industries, inclusive of textiles, Rhode Island in these 25 years, had she obtained the 1.17 percent of her share of manufacturing jobs in 1929, would have added almost 30,000 jobs. In these 6 industries, paper, primary metals, stone, clay and glass, chemicals, textile, and rubber, she lost 35,000 jobs. Her net loss was therefore 65,000 jobs, more than 20 percent of all her jobs—for she had lost 35,000 jobs when she should have gained 30,000.

A number of tables presented here reveal the fact that Rhode Island would have been in a position roughly equal to that of other New England States had she not been so dependent upon the textile industry, which has suffered such severe losses in recent years. In 1947, 44 percent of her manufacturing employment was in textiles as compared to 28 percent in New Hampshire, 24 percent in Maine, 17 percent in Massachusetts, 14 percent in Vermont, and 10 percent in Connecticut. Yet, though she suffered much more than the other States in New England, her loss of textiles was not significantly out of line. As a matter of fact, Massachusetts had a decline of 45 percent, but Massachusetts was saved by electronics. Rhode Island's decline was 41 percent, and Connecticut's 37 percent. Connecticut, of course, was helped greatly by the rise of jobs in transportation equipment.

#### 4. FURTHER CONSIDERATIONS OF THE INDUSTRY AS A WHOLE

Even in these 7 years between the 2 censuses, textile employment declined relatively by about 25 percent. A related industry—the apparel industry—however, increased its employment by 11 percent, even as employment in textiles was declining by 17 percent. Apparently the American public was prepared to spend a larger part of its income for processing of textiles, but was not prepared to maintain a textile industry in its earlier condition. The growth and decline of the industry vary greatly by subindustries. New England has suffered greatly in the last generation in relation to the South. As a matter of fact, by 1955 New England had only 8.5 percent of cotton production and the Middle Atlantic States only 0.8 percent, whereas the South had more than 90 percent. Even in woolen and worsteds, the New England share had dropped to about 50 percent by 1955 as compared to about two-thirds in 1947; the Middle Atlantic output was down to 10½ percent; and southern output up to 32 percent. The South also had a substantial lead in silk and synthetics. The advantage of the South over the years has been a substantial differential in wages. This differential has been largely eliminated in cotton and is being reduced in other areas as well. It is not equally clear that all labor costs have been reduced correspondingly, relatively speaking, in the North. Adjustment of workloads proceeds much more expeditiously than was true before in New England. Gradually, as the South becomes industrialized more and more, the pressure for higher wages will increase. It should be pointed out, however, that the South has additional advantages: proximity to raw material, cheap power, a more friendly attitude on the part of government, and relatively newer machinery. In local government there are certain tax differentials which, of course, should be set against a less favorable provisioning of services.

#### 5. TRADE AND TEXTILES

In the early years of the postwar, the American textile producer benefited greatly from a large rise of exports as compared to prewar. But once the older manufacturers began to recapture their export trade the situation deteriorated. This decline in export markets has been a serious matter for the American textile industry, coming as it did with other difficulties. It is, of course, still true that exports are larger than imports, and it is also true that Japan, one of our most serious competitors, still buys more cotton from us than they sell us cotton textiles. But the industry has been greatly disturbed by the rise of imports from $82 million in 1953 to $159 million in 1955 and still further increases in 1956. With investments low and great fear concerning the future of Japanese competition, the effect of these large imports has been an unwillingness to expand. In particular fields, the situation has been especially serious, for example, in velveteen, gingham, and blouses. In velveteen, imports in 1 year were more than twice domestic sales. On all criteria, whether sales, production, prices, ratio of imports to domestic production, the situation in the cotton velveteen market was serious for American producers. Industry had sustained a substantial net operating loss during the last 2 years, according to the United States Tariff Commission.

In the fall of 1956, the United States Government and the Japanese Government had agreed on a so-called quota, that is, a voluntary quota. The Japanese agreed to introduce specific ceilings where the rise of imports had been particularly troublesome and had also agreed to keep their exports to the United States down to a reasonable level in relation to earlier years. The attitude of the textile industry has been that Japanese competition was serious and particularly with the low wages and relatively favorable technical methods, and that in these circumstances a weak industry should not be asked to contribute excessively to the solution of the Japanese dollar problem.

In order to assure fair distribution of the burden, a large part should be put upon the taxpayer and also other countries should contribute toward the solution of the Japanese problem as has this country. It would also be helpful if Japan would diversify her exports more and particularly in the textile area. Better control of inflation and imports of luxuries would also help solve the Japanese dollar problem. It is a long time since economists have argued that the proper policy is to destroy the weak and save the strong. In the last generation we have learned how to help the weak in many matters.

In determining trade policy the United States Government should take into account the effect of other policies upon a particular industry or a particular region. If, as a result of agricultural policies, development of resources in other parts of the country, and in general through its tax-collection and spending programs, the Government helps other industries and regions at the expense of the Northeast, then to that extent tariff policy should take into account these other policies. In other words, the Government should have a well integrated policy which is fair to all regions and all industries.

In view of the increased difficulties of the Japanese in the last year as reflected in the loss of reserves, the Japanese will be inclined to insist once more on a growth of their export markets. Obviously, the United States has a great interest in assuring a relatively stable economic situation for Japan. It is to be hoped, however, that this burden will not be distributed unfairly among the relevant interests. We should do everything possible to encourage Japanese trade with Asia and particularly with southeast Asia where possible foreign loans and Government grants should be made available.

We should also point out that as the American income rises imports correspond. The most effective help that could be given to Japan would be continued growth in this country, and with this growth a corresponding rise of imports which do not, therefore, have unfortunate effects on our own industries. A rise of imports, however, that result from excessively liberal trade policies is another matter. In the past the largest rise of imports has come with the increased income.

6. THE ESCAPE CLAUSE

The escape clause has not been of much use to the textile industry and in part because the industry consists of so many different parts and the Tariff Commission has been unwilling to deal with the industry as a whole through the use of the escape clause. Perhaps another reason why the escape clause has not been of much use to the textile industry is that it has not been a very serious factor in all American industry. On the whole, the cases that have come up have not covered a substantial part of foreign trade. Furthermore, the Tariff Commission has turned down many applications and has been responsible for long delays. On top of that, the President, wherever he could possibly do so, has turned down recommendations of the Tariff Commission in favor of higher tariffs or quotas. Indeed, the President has the responsibility to take into account the overall economic and political situation and therefore may go beyond the recommendations or the criteria used by the Tariff Commission. It may well be, however, that because of the amendments of 1955 the escape clause will play a larger part in the determination of trade. This remains to be seen. From the experience of recent years it is quite clear that the escape clause has not been a large factor. It is also clear to this writer that it is important to have this kind of a provision in our tariff administration. Otherwise, civil servants who negotiate tariff concessions may well make excessive concessions and may do serious damage to American industries. A good example of this is the agreement that was made under the Geneva protocol that resulted in a substantial decline in the tariff on woolens and a very large reduction of employment over a period of 8 years. I am not assuming that the tariff was the only factor in the situation.

7. TEXTILES AND AGRICULTURAL POLICY

Ever since 1933 the governmental policy directed at keeping the price of cotton up has, of course, had an adverse effect on the textile industry. The early legislation involved a processing tax which was to be put upon the textile industry. In addition, the reduced output of cotton with the resultant higher prices would, of course, have an unfavorable effect on an industry which competes with foreign producers of textiles and also competes with other products. In the early New Deal days, the result of the processing tax was a loss of consumption of about 2 million bales, or roughly about one-third of the total consumption of that year. This figure might be a little high because it does not allow for the reduced exports associated with the higher cotton prices in this country.

On the basis of estimates made by Government econometricians we can conclude that in these early years the actual consumption of cotton in the United States was about 10 percent less than it otherwise would have been. This does not, of course, include the effect of the processing tax which would further cut cotton consumption. The net effect was a reduction of consumption of about 17 percent. On the basis of various estimates of the relationship between price rises and consumption of cotton, we may estimate that employment in the textile industry in 1934 was cut by 15 or 20 percent, or in other words, affected adversely from 115,000 to 150,000 workers. In the later thirties the Government continued its policy of restriction of output and this, of course, had adverse effects on the textile industry. From 1937 to 1940 it has been estimated that prices would have averaged about one-third less than the average price which actually prevailed, and therefore consumption of cotton would have been 8.2 million bales instead of 7.5 million bales a year, that is, consumption at home.

During the war period and probably right through 1951 the effects of the support program were not serious in the cotton industry. Prices were generally above the support level. But in the early 1950's trouble began to confront the Government again with the accumulation of large surpluses and the CCC had to increase its holdings year by year. In the last few years the Government has helped to solve this problem by dumping large supplies of cotton abroad to our competitors at prices substantially below the American price. The various aid programs also contributed to improving the competitive position of farmers by making large supplies of cotton available under these programs.

For example, in August 1955, Broach, Bijay, fine cotton in the Bombay market, was worth 24.2 cents per pound, export tax included, while roughly equivalent quality of American cotton middling fifteen-sixteenth inch was worth 34.9 cents at New Orleans, a difference of 10.7 cents.

In the 1956–57 marketing year about 7 million bales would be exported from this country in contrast with 2.2 millions in the previous 12 months. The policy after that is supposedly to be the same as in the marketing year 1956–57.

If American mills were able to buy American cotton at the price it was offered to foreigners, consumption in this country would be about 5 percent or about a half a million bales greater. This loss of 5 percent in business may be a serious factor for textile firms in a precarious position. In fact, on the basis of more recent estimates, and the relationship between prices and consumption, the loss may be as much as 8 percent.

The important issue for the textile industry is really the question of who pays the bill of supporting the income of the cotton farmer. We would suggest that it would be more equitable to put the burden on all the country and not merely on the textile producer, who is already in a serious condition. Hence we are opposed to the certificate plan or a processing tax which would be put upon the textile mills. In wool, we now have an income program.

## 8. WOOLENS

In woolens, under 1954 legislation, the Government now supports the price of wool and puts the burden properly on the taxpayer. The industry at long last confronted with the increased competition of manmade fabrics is protesting against any trade policies that raise the price of raw wool.

In cottons, also, the pressure is increasing to keep the price down and compensate the farmer through larger output and markets, and, insofar as this is inadequate, to put an increased burden on the taxpayer rather than on the processor. For both cotton producers and the textile industry, there are advantages in lower prices for cotton.

The contrast in financial cost is given by the following. Under an income program the Government would have to pay $45 a bale for each bale of cotton consumed. Consumption at the free market price would be 10.7 million bales. Hence the amount involved would be $480 million, that is, 10.7 times 45. The cost of the CCC-type program would obviously be the cost of buying the amount of cotton that must be taken off the market to raise the price to 90 percent of parity, or $160 a bale. This would be 10.7 minus 9.41 million bales times $160, or $208 million. Hence the cost to the Government would be over half as great if the Government were to raise the price by destroying 1.3 million bales than if it were to let the price fall and make up the difference through a special payment to farmers. When by taking 4 percent of the cotton supply off the market the price rises 10 percent, it is obvious that a relatively inexpensive way for the Government to support the price is by holding some of the crop off the market.

But what are the costs to the consumer is also a matter of some importance. Under the income payment program consumers would pay $115 a bale for 10.7 million bales, or a total of $1.2 billion. Under the CCC restriction of supply programs consumers would pay $160 a bale for 9.4 million bales, or $1.5 billion. That is to say, the consumers pay $300 million less for 1.3 million bales more of cotton under the income plan.

Relative burdens are suggested by the following: Under the income-payment plan, the Government spends $480 million and consumers spend $1.22 billion, or $1.7 billion in all. With the price-support program, the Government spends $200 million and consumers $1.5 billion, the total again $1.7 billion.

### 9. TRENDS IN WORLD TEXTILE PRODUCTION

In general, output rose relative to all output from 1938 to 1947, but declined from 1947 to 1956. The underdeveloped countries gained at the expense of the developed countries, notably in spinning. The gains in woolens and weaving were not notable. In general, woolens experienced larger losses than cottons. Despite large losses of woolens in this country, absolute and relative, and in cottons, especially relative, the United States remained the most advanced country in technology. The same could not be said for the United Kingdom. Underdeveloped countries, with late starts, frequently have much more modern machinery than developed countries.

### 10. PROBLEM OF SUBSTITUTING FOR BUSINESS LOST

The committee raised the issue of transfers of production to replace lost markets. In textiles, this is not easy. Particularly in the finer cotton and worsted mills, adjustments are difficult. Often they are not possible; when possible, the increased costs may make them impractical. In an industry that is highly competitive, with investment money difficult to obtain, with declines of output widely spread, with profits low, and with diversification or movement into nontextile areas not successful or practical as a rule—the possibilities of shifts do not offer much hope.

## The Cotton Textile Industry and the American Trade Policy

### SECTION I. GENERAL TRADE POLICY

In this paper I am concerned primarily with the tariff policy vis-a-vis textiles. Obviously, the more the country tends toward free trade, the greater the pressures that are likely to be put on the textile industry. Therefore, I would hope that the Government would move cautiously in the direction of free trade or freer trade. There may even be periods when the argument may be strong for increasing the tariffs on textiles. Such occasions occurred, for example, in relation to the Geneva protocol of 1948, when, as a result, in part, of greatly reduced tariffs, the amount of employment in the woolen industry dropped by roughly one-half. Again, the large relative rise of textile imports from Japan raised serious problems in 1955 and 1956 and required some unusual measures to reassure American textile producers, and thus encouraged them to move ahead on their plans for expansion or maintenance of their present capital outlays.

As I have noted, I am not going into the general problem of what the appropriate tariff policy should be for the United States in general. I would like to emphasize, however, that there are two crucial problems involved. One is the problem of how much trade this country wants. Most of our tariff discussions have been in terms of trying to reduce our tariffs in order to make it possible to import more and, therefore, to export more. But in recent years a second problem has become of some importance, namely, the problem of equilibrium in the dollar market. In other words, there have been dollar shortages, and foreigners have not been able to obtain enough dollars to purchase the goods and services that they seem to require in this country. This problem, of course, is related to the adverse effects of war, hot and cold. In fact, I have estimated that, over a period of about 40 years, the dollar shortage has been of the order of something like $125 billion. Foreigners have obtained these dollars in part by borrowing from this country and not repaying, in part by sending us gold, and in part by gifts and loans of various kinds by this Government. Obviously, the greater the shortage of dollars, the greater the pressure to reduce tariffs on American goods, because reduced tariffs are supposed to provide foreigners with the adequate supply of dollars to purchase our goods.

If a rise of imports does not solve the problem, then the country has to have recourse to a reduction of its exports in other markets, or else make available to foreigners dollars through loans or grants. As one looks over American economic history of the last 40 years, it is quite clear that the largest contribution has come from loans and gifts, and particularly gifts of the United States Government.

The tendency to make dollars available through loans and gifts by the American Government can be justified to some extent because of the fact that the dollar shortage problem is a political as well as an economic one. It is the responsibility, in part, of the American people to solve this problem, and, insofar as it is their problem, it is appropriate that the United States Government should make dollars available through the process of taxation.

In the last few years the countries short of dollars have increasingly tended to capture our markets abroad. This, to some extent, has helped solve the general problem. It is much easier for a foreign nation to capture our market abroad than at home. The explanation of this fact is, in part, that competition is much more severe in our own markets than it is abroad, and, in part, that in order to penetrate our market foreigners have to build up their position in this country through large public relations and advertising campaigns. Fearful that the United States Government may change its policies, there are very few corporations abroad that are ready to take these chances. Furthermore, the costs of distribution and other services are so high in this country that even a substantial reduction of tariffs will not result in a very large reduction of prices for the American consumer because the major part of the final price arises not from the export price but rather from all the services that go into marketing the commodity in the American market.

While we are on the subject of general trade policy, it is well to point out that, on the whole, in the last generation the United States, much more than most countries abroad, has moved in the direction of free trade. One has but to consider the many quotas, the frequent use of exchange control, and other protectionist devices abroad to realize that protectionism has become a much more favored policy in foreign countries than in the United States. One may often justify these policies abroad because of the scarcity of dollars. But one must also say that part of the difficulties of exportation of foreign countries result from excessive tariffs, quotas, and exchange control which, in turn, tend to make these countries independent of foreign competition and also to bring about low degrees of productivity.

Indeed, in some countries in recent years these tendencies have been stopped to some extent. This is particularly true of Germany and some of the other countries that have not experienced such serious shortage of dollars. But even the official publication of the Office of Economic Cooperation, which represents the western European countries, has noted that many of the concessions made in accepting American goods have been those which do not put any great burden on the competitors to American goods in these countries. In other words, restrictions tend to be removed where they do not really count for very much.

## SECTION II. THE TEXTILE INDUSTRY

In order to understand our trade policy in textiles, one must also consider the special features of our textile industry.

First, we must realize that textiles in the last 50 years has been one of the slowest growing industries. In fact, over a number of years the textile industry has tended to lose jobs in years when the country was increasing its total number of jobs. Why has the textile industry had this unusual experience? One factor clearly is changes of taste. The country seems to be able to get along with relatively less clothing, and also the great technological revolutions that have struck the textile industry in recent years have tended to make it possible to produce a given amount of textiles with declining numbers of man-hours of work. The result is that the decline of the textile industry is measured much more effectively by the number of employees than by the number of yards of cloth turned out. As a matter of fact, over a period of about 25 years, the total amount of textile employment has not greatly changed the country over (see below), but the total amount of production per man-hour has approximately doubled. Second, the troubles of the textile industry can be related also to certain Federal policies. For example, the lift that the Federal Government has given to the housing and consumer credit markets has had considerable effect upon the textile industry. By making it much easier to buy homes, automobiles, and television sets, the American consumer increasingly diverts his dollars into these markets and tends to withdraw his dollars from the clothing market.

It is not surprising therefore that in the light of this fact and increased productivity that in the 16 years 1939–55, employment in textiles declined by 13 percent, whereas in the same period employment in all manufacturing rose by 64 percent. This is a relative loss in textiles of almost one-half, and certainly suggests the difficulties of the industry and perhaps also establishes a case for special treatment in trade policy. What I am saying here, in fact, is that there are important issues that the Government takes inadequate account of in determining its tariff policy. Given a desire for reduction of tariffs, the Government still has to decide who is to take the brunt of the adjustment. An industry that has trouble in maintaining its employment should certainly not be sacrificed in order to further the general principles of a liberal trade policy.

It is also well to remember that the incidence of this decline of employment varies a great deal. For example, in woolens and worsteds, the decline from 1947 to 1954 was no less than 49 percent. An indication of what has happened to the textile industry is given by a comparison of the two latest censuses, 1947 and 1954.

*Percentage change, several variables, 1947–54, in various textile groups*

| | All textiles | Woolens and worsteds | Subindustry with largest gain |
|---|---|---|---|
| Employment | −17.1 | −49.4 | [1]+3.8 |
| Man-hours | −22.1 | −51.8 | [2]+40.7 |
| Payrolls | +5.2 | −34.4 | [2]+36.8 |
| Value added | −10.9 | −43.7 | +36.5 |
| Investment | −38.6 | −62.0 | [3]+14.3 |

[1] Finishing textiles, except wool.
[2] Miscellaneous.
[3] Carpets and rugs.

This table shows that on the basis of employment the industry has lost 17 percent of its jobs; on the basis of man-hours of work, 22 percent; on the basis of value added, 11 percent; on the basis of investment, 39 percent. The increase of payrolls of 5 percent is accounted for in large part by the inflation of this period, as is to some extent the relatively small reduction in value added.

Perhaps as good an indication of what is happening to an industry is its wage level. For in an industry having trouble wages tend to be below the average. Weekly wages average 71 percent of the national manufacturing average of 1939, 83 percent in 1947, and 71 percent in September 1956, and also 70 percent in May 1957.

Among the factors accounting for low wages in textiles are the following: Heavy concentration of output in the South where wages are low and trade unionism weak; the strong or growing industries competing for the consumer dollar; the more rapid growth of industries where automation is more strongly entrenched; the large proportion of female labor; the age of the industry; and the competition of foreign low-priced labor.

A third factor that should be taken into account in considering the textile industry is the competition between North and South. In general, the industry is a weak industry, and this is suggested by the low wages. This is also suggested by the declining employment. But if the industry is weak generally, it is doubly weak in the Northeast. In the Northeast, the industry has to face the competition of highly productive industries that pay high wages. If it meets that competition its costs rise to such an extent that the loss of employment to the South grows rapidly. Hence the trade union leaders and management have to work out a solution which allows the textile worker to be paid a lower wage than all workers in the Northeast, and yet not so low a wage that the workers will be lost to the textile industry in a period of full or overfull employment. If wages go up too much, the industry loses jobs to the South. If they do not go up far enough, the result is that the industry loses its necessary workers. It is difficult to draw the fine balance that is necessary in order to achieve competition with the South, and yet to keep workers in the industry.

Another indication of the state of an industry is given by its profits. For example, net profits from sales by all manufacturing industries were 10 percent in the first quarter of 1956, and 9.5 percent in the first quarter of 1957. In textiles, the respective percentages were 6.1 percent and 4.8 percent.

In relation to the stockholders' equity, the profits before income tax in the first quarter of 1956 were 23.8 percent for all manufacturing, and 22.5 percent for the first quarter of 1957. The same figures reveal a profit of 13.7 percent for textiles before Federal income taxes in the first quarter of 1956, and 10.1 percent in the first quarter of 1957.

These figures are from a quarterly financial report from manufacturing corporations of the FTC and SPC. In a special study which I made, I found that in 1953–54 and 1955, the profits in relation to sales for 12 New England firms were 1.6 percent, 1.1 percent, and 1.6 percent, respectively, in the years 1953, 1954, and 1955; for 29 southern firms, the figures were 4 percent, 2.3 percent, and 3.3 percent. These are certainly not high profits.

Another feature of the textile industry is that it is still a relatively highly competitive industry. For example, recently the largest firm in the industry ranked 70th in the Nation in the amount of sales and had $515 million in sales, $510 million in assets, $16.4 million net profit, and 50,000 employees. Sales accounted for but 4 percent of the $12.4 billion of sales of General Motors. Whereas the 500 leading manufacturing firms accounted for more than 50 percent of factory employment, the 19 textile firms in the top 500 accounted for about 25 percent of textile employment. Obviously, the more competition the greater the tendency for price cutting, and therefore adverse effects on both profits and investments. Investments in the textile industry are far below the general level of the American industry.

Another peculiarity of the textile industry is the fact that it tends to be squeezed from both ends. For example, the agricultural policies tend to result in higher prices for the raw materials which form such an important part of the final cost of the product. This, of course, tends to result in a weaker competitive position, vis-a-vis the foreign nations, and also vis-a-vis the producers of competing commodities. At the other end, it is interesting that, despite the fact that the apparel industry is broken up into even smaller units than textiles, apparels have been able to hold their own in the economy much more effectively than textiles. For example, textiles accounted for 3½ percent of total employment in 1929, and only 2 percent in 1955, or a reduction of about 40 percent, relatively speaking. In apparel, the percentage was 7.4 in 1929 and 7.4 in 1955.

### SECTION III. AN EXAMPLE: THE TEXTILE INDUSTRY IN RHODE ISLAND

A good example of what the decline of textiles, and particularly in the weaker areas, does to an economy is suggested by the experience of Rhode Island where textiles have been such an important part of the total amount of employment.

From 1930 to 1955, Rhode Island's population rose from 650,000 to 817,000, or by 167,000. That means, therefore, a demand for 65,000 additional jobs, but from 1929 to 1954, Rhode Island lost 40,000 textile jobs. Dependence on industries that have been weak in the Nation, and even weaker in New England, is the greatest source of concern to those responsible for the Rhode Island economy.

Where does Rhode Island obtain the necessary jobs? In the older industries, inclusive of food, apparel, printing, lumber, and furniture, leather and stone, glass and clay, the State added more than 6,000 jobs from 1929 to 1954, with the rise averaging one-half. But the base was not large enough to provide many additional jobs. Even apparel with a gain of 250 percent yielded only 3,300 more jobs. These are the industries that grow slowly. Their expansion of income from 1929 to 1953 was but a little more than one-half of that for all manufacturing.

What about the rapidly growing industries? In paper and pulp, chemicals, rubber, metals, machinery, exclusive of electrical, electrical machinery, transportation equipment—in all these industries where the growth has been great, Rhode Island was able to add only 5,000 jobs. In general, the rise was substantial, but small compared to growth in the South, the Middle West, and the Far West, and the loss of jobs in textiles. The percentage rise of jobs in Rhode Island in these 8 categories was 14 percent, from 34,500 to 39,500. The large gains were in metals, electrical machinery, and transportation equipment. In chemicals, there was a 13 percent loss from 1929 to 1953; in rubber a 10 percent loss; in machinery, except electrical, a 14 percent loss.

The expensive sources of power are a handicap when a State is looking for new employment to take the place of old ones lost. For example, in Rhode Island in 6 industries where power was of some importance, paper, primary metals, stone, clay, and glass, chemicals, textiles, and rubber; had Rhode Island obtained the 1.17 percent per share of manufacturing jobs in 1929, she would have added almost

30,000. Actually she lost 34,600 jobs. Her net loss was 65,000 jobs, more than 20 percent of all her jobs.

In the last 10 years Rhode Island added about 60,000 population. She should have added roughly 25,000 jobs. Actually, the net increase in jobs was but 2,000. This seems to suggest that although unemployment did not rise during this period, there was really a substantial loss because large numbers of the population deserted the labor market in a period when obtaining new jobs was not easy.

These figures, as well as the study that was made by Miernyk, suggest the difficulties confronting a region, and especially an older region, when it loses jobs because of the weakness of the textile industry and the intense competition of another region for the limited number of jobs available. In determining tariff policy, the authorities in Washington must take such factors into account. It is clear that even the unemployment figures, and certainly unemployment has been relatively high in Rhode Island, do not tell the whole story.

I also enclose a number of tables which emphasize the peculiar problems faced by States that are heavily dependent on the textile industry. Table I shows that the largest rise of employment in New England for 1947–56 was for Connecticut, with 16.8 percent rise of nonagricultural employment. The rise for Massachusetts was 8.4 percent, and for Rhode Island 0.7 percent.

Table II shows that of manufacturing employment Rhode Island had by far the worst record, with a decline of 16.2 percent. Massachusetts with a decline of 1.7 percent can be thankful for the large gains in electronics. Connecticut with a gain of 4.5 percent can be grateful for the many additional jobs in transportation equipment. But Rhode Island had no such good fortune.

Table III shows quite clearly the reasons for the Rhode Island difficulty. It is the heavy concentration of textiles. Note that Rhode Island has 43.6 percent of her manufacturing jobs in textiles and she is one of the most heavily concentrated manufacturing areas in the country. The corresponding figures for Massachusetts are 17.2 percent and for Connecticut 9.9 percent, and the next highest figure to Rhode Island is New Hampshire with 28 percent.

Yet the loss of jobs in textiles for Rhode Island in the years 1947–56 was not out of line with the rest of New England. As a matter of fact, Vermont had a substantially larger decline as did Massachusetts. But the 41 percent decline of textile jobs for Rhode Island was a much more serious matter than the declines in the other States.

Table V reveals the change in jobs exclusive of textiles, that is, the change in all manufacturing employment except textiles. Here it will be noted that Rhode Island did not do as well as any other State, but the differences are much smaller than when the total picture is examined.

Connecticut has had the best record probably in New England. But table VI shows that if textiles and aircraft are removed from the totals for manufacturing employment, there is an actual decline of 11 percent in manufacturing jobs for 1947–56 in Connecticut. The next table, No. VII, reveals that the 44,000 rise of employment in transportation equipment was, of course, the crucial factor in the important gains made by Connecticut. No other manufacturing industry yielded as much as 4,000 additional jobs and 8 industries actually lost jobs.

TABLE I.—*Total nonagricultural employment, New England States, 1956 and 1947*

| | 1956 | 1947 | Percent rise |
|---|---|---|---|
| | *Thousands* | *Thousands* | 8.4 |
| Massachusetts | 1,844.5 | 1,702.2 | .7 |
| Rhode Island | 295.0 | 292.9 | 16.8 |
| Connecticut | 903.8 | 773.8 | 7.5 |
| Maine | 281.7 | 262.0 | 9.5 |
| New Hampshire | 182.5 | 166.7 | 6.5 |
| Vermont | 105.0 | 98.6 | |

Source: U. S. Department of Labor, Bureau of Labor Statistics.

TABLE II.—*Manufacturing employment, New England States, 1956–1947*

| | 1956 | 1947 | Percent change |
|---|---|---|---|
| | *Thousands* | *Thousands* | −1.7 |
| Massachusetts | 710.6 | 722.8 | −16.2 |
| Rhode Island | 127.8 | 152.5 | 4.5 |
| Connecticut | 434.0 | 415.5 | −3.8 |
| Maine | 110.1 | 114.5 | −.1 |
| New Hampshire | 82.7 | 82.8 | −3.0 |
| Vermont | 38.6 | 39.8 | |

Source: U. S. Department of Labor, Bureau of Labor Statistics.

TABLE III.—*Degree of concentration in textile employment in 1947*

[Percent of manufacturing employment]

| | |
|---|---|
| Massachusetts | 17.2 |
| Rhode Island | 43.6 |
| Connecticut | 9.9 |
| Maine | 24.4 |
| New Hampshire | 28.0 |
| Vermont | 13.8 |

Source: U. S. Department of Labor, Bureau of Labor Statistics.

TABLE IV.—*Textile employment, New England States, 1956–1947*

| | 1956 | 1947 | Percent change |
|---|---|---|---|
| | *Thousands* | *Thousands* | −45.2 |
| Massachusetts | 68.4 | 124.9 | −40.8 |
| Rhode Island | 39.5 | 66.7 | −36.8 |
| Connecticut | 25.9 | 41.0 | −36.4 |
| Maine | 17.8 | 28.0 | −41.0 |
| New Hampshire | 13.7 | 23.2 | −50.9 |
| Vermont | 2.7 | 5.5 | |

TABLE IV–A.—*Percent decline arrayed by States, 1947–56*

| | |
|---|---|
| Vermont | 50.9 |
| Massachusetts | 45.2 |
| New Hampshire | 41.0 |
| Rhode Island | 40.8 |
| Connecticut | 36.8 |
| Maine | 36.4 |

Source: U. S. Department of Labor, Bureau of Labor Statistics.

TABLE V.—*Manufacturing employment for all industries except textiles, New England States, 1956–1947*

| | 1956 | 1947 | Percent change |
|---|---|---|---|
| | *Teousands* | *Thousands* | |
| Massachusetts | 642.2 | 597.9 | 7.4 |
| Rhode Island | 88.3 | 85.8 | 2.9 |
| Connecticut | 408.1 | 374.5 | 6.3 |
| Maine | 92.3 | 86.5 | 6.7 |
| New Hampshire | 69.0 | 59.6 | 15.7 |
| Vermont | 35.9 | 34.3 | 4.7 |

TABLE V–A.—*Percent gain over 1947*

| States arrayed: | *Percent* |
|---|---|
| New Hampshire | 15.7 |
| Massachusetts | 7.4 |
| Maine | 6.7 |
| Connecticut | 6.3 |
| Vermont | 4.7 |
| Rhode Island | 2.9 |

Source: U. S. Department of Labor, Bureau of Labor Statistics.

TABLE VI.—*Connecticut manufacturing employment, 1947–56*

| | 1956 | 1947 | Change in jobs |
|---|---|---|---|
| | *Thousands* | *Taousands* | |
| Total manufacturing | 434.0 | 415.5 | |
| Less textiles | 25.9 | 41.0 | |
| Total | 408.1 | 374.5 | +6.3 |
| Aircraft | 74.7 | 30.4 | |
| Manufacturing employment less textiles and aircraft | 333.4 | 344.1 | −10.7 |

Source: U. S. Department of Labor, Bureau of Labor Statistics.

TABLE VII.—*Connecticut manufacturing employment showing influence of transportation equipment industry, 1956–1947*

| | 1956 | 1947 |
|---|---|---|
| Total manufacturing employment | 434.0 | 415.5 |
| Transportation equipment | 74.7 | 30.4 |
| Manufacturing less transportation equipment | 359.3 | 385.1 |

*Details of Connecticut manufacturing employment changes, 1956 and 1947*

[Change in number of jobs. In thousands]

| | | | |
|---|---|---|---|
| Ordnance | −0.5 | Food | +1.3 |
| Primary metals | −3.8 | Textiles | −15.1 |
| Fabricated metals | −6.4 | Apparel | −1.4 |
| Nonelectrical machinery | −3.6 | Furniture and wood | +1.3 |
| Electrical equipment | −5.0 | Paper | +0.9 |
| Transportation equipment | +44.3 | Printing and publishing | +3.8 |
| Instruments and clocks | +0.7 | Chemicals | +2.1 |
| Silverware | −2.6 | Rubber | +2.6 |
| Miscellaneous metallic | −0.5 | Miscellaneous nonmetallic | +0.5 |

Source: U. S. Department of Labor, Bureau of Labor Statistics.

SECTION IV. FURTHER CONSIDERATION OF THE INDUSTRY AS A WHOLE

But let us return to the national industry. Like most industries, the fortunes of the industry vary in different subindustries. For example, from 1947–54 the number of employees dropped from 1,203,000 to 1,022,000 or a drop of 17.1 percent. In other words, in 1954 employment was 82.9 percent of 1947 employment. The greatest losses of jobs were, of course, in woolens and worsteds, where the decline was from 180,000 to 91,000 or a decline of almost one-half.

In contrast, in textile finishing, except wool, there was an actual increase from 69,000 to 70,000 jobs. Other subindustries that fared relatively well were knitting mills with a reduction from 231,000 to 220,000 or a reduction to 94.2 percent of the 1947 level. With the building boom and refurnishing, carpets and rugs stood up reasonably well, with a decline of only 6,000 from a 57,000 level or a little more than 10 percent. As might be expected, hats did not experience a prosperous situation. The decline was from 21,000 to 13,000 or almost 38 percent. Miscellaneous textile goods experienced a loss of jobs at 2,000 or roughly 3½ percent. In this category there were actual increases for felt goods, padding, and upholstery filling, and textile goods not otherwise classified. Broadwoven fabrics declined from 455,000 to 375,000 jobs, or a loss of 17.6 percent.

From almost 15 percent of total employment in the textile industry woolen and worsted manufactures declined to approximately 9 percent in 1954.

*Related industries, United States total*

| Industry | Employment (thousands) | Payrolls (millions) | Production workers (thousands) | Production workers payrolls (millions) | Value added (millions) | Man-hours (millions) | Change value added per man-hour | Capital expenditure (millions) |
|---|---|---|---|---|---|---|---|---|
| All industries: | | | | | | | | |
| 1947 | 14, 294 | $39, 690 | 11, 916 | $30, 242 | $74, 426 | 24, 303 | | $6, 004 |
| 1954 | 16, 135 | $66, 011 | 12, 397 | $44, 631 | $116, 001 | 24, 459 | | $7, 757 |
| 1954 as percent of 1947 | 112. 9 | 166. 3 | 104. 0 | 147. 6 | 15. 9 | 100. 6 | 155. 0 | 129. 2 |
| Textile industry: | | | | | | | | |
| 1947 | 1, 233 | $2, 836 | 1, 147 | $2, 499 | $5, 341 | 2, 308 | | $368 |
| 1954 | 1, 022 | $2, 985 | 932 | $2, 485 | $4, 672 | 1, 797 | | $226 |
| 1954 as percent of 1947 | 82. 9 | 105. 3 | 81. 3 | 99. 4 | 87. 5 | 77. 9 | 112. 3 | 61. 4 |
| Apparel industry: | | | | | | | | |
| 1947 | 1, 082 | $2, 527 | 973 | $2, 015 | $4, 443 | 1, 811 | | $84 |
| 1954 | 1, 197 | $3, 211 | 1, 077 | $2, 530 | $5, 033 | 1, 907 | | $78 |
| 1954 as percent of 1947 | 110. 6 | 127. 1 | 110. 7 | 125. 6 | 113. 3 | 105. 3 | 107. 6 | 92. 9 |
| Textile machinery industry: | | | | | | | | |
| 1947 | 54 | $158 | 45 | $126 | $256 | 99 | | $14 |
| 1954 | 37 | $146 | 28 | $99 | $217 | 56 | | $9 |
| 1954 as percent of 1947 | 68. 5 | 92. 4 | 62. 2 | 78. 6 | 84. 8 | 56. 6 | 149. 8 | 64. 3 |

The above table indicates the general history of this industry in between the last two censuses. For example, it is clear that the textile industry has suffered greatly in relation to all industries. Its employment declined *relatively* by about 25 percent in the short period of 7 years. In contrast, a related industry, the apparel industry, increased its employment by 11 percent, even as employment in textiles was declining by 17 percent. Apparently, the American public was prepared to spend a larger part of its income for processing of textiles, but was not prepared to maintain the textile industry in its earlier condition. Obviously, if the textile industry suffers losses, this is likely to be reflected in related industries. This is quite clear from the experience of the textile-machinery industry, which also experienced a reduction of jobs by 17,000, or almost one-third.

The prospects for the future are well suggested by the capital expenditures. In all industries there was a rise in 1954 over 1947 of 29 percent. In apparels there was a decline of 8 percent; in textiles a decline of 39 percent; and in textile machinery a decline of 36 percent.

## SECTION V. THE REGIONAL PROBLEM

It is clear from what has gone before that the industry has been suffering losses. But, of course, these losses are much more serious when one region suffers as a result of the competition of newer industrial areas.

What has happened to the regional distribution of the industry is evident from a table below, which gives the percent of distribution of cotton, wool, and synthetic broad-woven fabrics, by regions, 1955.

*Percentage distribution of cotton, wool, and synthetic broad-woven fabrics, by region, 1955*

| Region | Cotton | Woolen and worsted [1] | Silk and synthetic | Total |
|---|---|---|---|---|
| New England | 8.5 | 50.5 | 18.7 | 11.6 |
| Middle Atlantic | .8 | 10.5 | 8.9 | 2.6 |
| South | 90.6 | 31.7 | 72.3 | 85.5 |
| Far West } North Central } | .1 | 1.7 | .1 | .2 |
| North Central | | 5.6 | | |

[1] Except woven felts.

Source: Computed from U. S. Bureau of the Census, Broad Woven Goods: Geographic Summary for 1955, Facts for Industry Series M–22–T.

It will be noted, for example, that New England had but 8.5 percent of the output of cotton goods in 1955. This compares with approximately 80 percent early in the century. The South has virtually taken over this industry, with 90.6 percent of total output.

In woolen and worsteds, the South now has almost 32 percent of total output, whereas at the end of the war she was an unimportant producer. New England, with about two-thirds of output in 1947, is now down to 50 percent, and the Middle Atlantic States account for 10½ percent. In silk and synthetics, the South is also in the lead, though not nearly as much as in cotton. For the whole industry, the output in New England accounts for 11.6 percent of cotton, wool, and synthetic broad-woven fabrics, as compared to 85 percent for the South and only 2½ percent for the Middle Atlantic States.

The Middle Atlantic States have suffered almost as much as New England, but, because textiles were less important in their economy, results have not been quite so disastrous.

The gain to the South ought to be explained by various factors. First, of course, has been a large differential in wages, which has largely been eliminated in the last few years. It is not clear, however, that labor costs are equal, North and South. The labor costs are related not only to wages paid but also to output per man-hour. Although it is true in New England the problems of adjusting workloads have been largely solved, it is nevertheless true that the South, with relatively newer machinery, and starting fresh in many instances, and with a labor group coming fresh off the farms and unaccustomed to substantial wages—the South tends to produce at lower unit costs than the North.

Gradually, as the South becomes industrialized more and more the pressure for higher wages will increase. In many of the advanced industries, there is very little differential in wages between North and South, and processes are often similar. The time may not be far off when labor costs between North and South may be roughly equal.

But the South has other advantages. Proximity to raw materials is an advantage, to some extent, though not a very important one. Power is cheaper, and this is not a large factor in the textile industry, but it is of some importance. Tax differentials are of some significance, though generally State taxes in textile States are not lower in the South than they are in New England. In the local taxation, however, there generally are advantages for the South. One of these advantages results from the fact that textiles are more largely produced in smaller communities, where both property taxes are lower and services are not available as they are in the North. It is probably also true that, on the whole, government is more friendly to the textile industry in the South than in the North. This is an advantage, however, which has been greatly reduced as northern governments have increasingly realized the importance of southern competition and the need for presenting a more friendly attitude toward industry in order to compete with the South.

Another advantage that the South has is the recourse to tax exemption from Federal income taxes as a means of luring industry to the South. The southern municipality often issues a bond, builds the plant, offers the plant to northern management, and with a proviso that the plant will ultimately be sold to the northern management at a small price. In the meanwhile, the northern management has only to pay a modest rent. This is made possible by the low rates of interest at which southern communities can sell their bonds when they are tax exempt. It should be pointed out, however, that since the value of the tax-exempt securities is considerably less than it used to be because the market has largely been saturated, this advantage is becoming less important. There also has been considerable opposition from investment bankers against communities that misuse the tax-exemption privilege to build plants and lure northern management to the South.

## SECTION VI. TRADE AND TEXTILES

Since the prewar period exports of textiles have tended to increase, at least in the early postwar years textile exports were at a very high level. In fact they have been higher than imports during the postwar period. For this reason many have contended that the textile industry should not be concerned about a reduction of tariffs or other liberalization of trade because they still gain more from exports than they lose from imports.

But we should be clear on one point. This point is that the industry, and particularly in New England, has been suffering serious effects from the decline of jobs and markets. In the last few years the export market has been largely lost, in part as a result of the renewal of competition from old competitors. But whatever the cause, even though it is true that exports are still larger than imports, the point is that the decline of the export market along with other factors weakening the industry and particularly in New England have tended to aggravate the general situation in the textile industry.

Along the same lines it has often been said that the United States should not be concerned over Japanese competition in textiles. The argument has been, for example, that Japan sells us cotton textiles using about 150,000 bales of cotton and purchases from us about 800,000 bales; that the Japanese purchase about $120 million of cotton from this country and sell us only $60 million of cotton textiles. In purchasing around $400 million of agricultural products in 1954 and 1955 from this country, Japan proved to be our best customer of these products. It should be added, however, that to a considerable degree the purchases are financed by the American taxpayer.

Certain aspects of the textile trade particularly concern the textile industry. For example, the rise of imports from $82 million in 1953 to $95 million in 1954, $159 million in 1955, and still further increases in 1956 troubled the industry. Undoubtedly in an industry where investments are low and prospects do not seem to be great a very large increase of imports, especially from a country with very low wages, is likely to have a very serious effect on investment and employment. This is true even if to some extent the management in the industry were excessively concerned about Japanese competition.

Another factor that concerned the industry was the tendency of Japan to move into higher count yarns. In velveteens imports from Japan rose from 1.7 million yards in 1939 to 2.1 million yards in 1950–52 and to 8.6 million yards in 1955. In the last year imports were 206 percent of domestic sales.

The United States Tariff Commission has well summarized the issues in the following. This is from the tariff report on cotton velveteen fabrics, 1956, page 30:

> The data given in the preceding sections of this report show that domestic sales and production of both plain- and twill-back velveteens have declined drastically in recent years; that imports of both types of velveteens have increased substantially and continuously in the same period; that the ratio of imports to domestic production has increased greatly and the share of the domestic market that is supplied by domestic production has declined correspondingly; that inventories of finished veleveteens in the hands of producers have been growing; that employment in the production of velveteens in the United States has declined sharply; that total wages paid production and related workers engaged in the production of velveteens were more than 50 percent smaller in 1955 than in 1951 and that hourly earnings of the workers have decreased; that prices of domestic velveteens have declined considerably in recent years and that prices of Japanese velveteens in the domestic market are

much lower than the prices of similiar domestic fabrics; and that the domestic industry considered as a whole, has sustained a net operating loss during the past 2 years. The Commission finds that the domestic industry producing velveteens is being seriously injured and that the increasing imports of velveteens have contributed substantially toward causing such injury.

As is usual in this kind of competition, the domestic manufacturers tended to emphasize the low wages in Japan and in other nations competing with the United States. But in addition, much was made of the introduction of relatively new machinery and of newest techniques by Japan. The combination of low wages and late techniques made Japanese competition formidable. The Japanese, on the other hand, tended to stress the noncompetitive nature of their products, the difficulty of preparing to sell in a rather unstable market like ours, and the abnormal nature of the spectacular rise of imports in early 1956. Though they admitted that their exports would have to rise in order to provide an adequate supply of foreign currencies, the Japanese nevertheless set modest goals for the total rise of exports of textiles. Their proposed rise of exports from 1954 to 1960 was cotton textiles, from 1 billion yards in 1954 to 1.3 billion yards in 1960; spun rayon fabrics in 1960, 686 million yards, a gain of about 60 percent; raw silk, 140,000 bales, a gain of over 50 percent.

In order to deal with the problem of Japanese imports, all kinds of approaches were suggested by those interested in the industry. A proposal to deal with the problem by an application of the escape clause for all cotton textiles was ruled out by the Tariff Commission as not being practical. The Japanese introduced a so-called voluntary quota in 1955, and in the fall of 1956, under great pressure from the United States Government, another quota was introduced. The supporters of the industry tried, though unsuccessfully, to introduce a unilateral quota as a rider to important legislation, first under the farm bill and then under the foreign aid bill. In both instances the measure was lost by just a few votes in the Senate.

The State Department was strongly opposed to a unilateral quota. This would have been a new attack in the field of manufactured goods. In agriculture it was deemed necessary to impose quotas in order to assure the success of price support measures. According to the State Department, the introduction of quotas on imports of manufactured goods would have been a serious blow to our general trade and economic policy and would have greatly weakened our position with our friends abroad.

The agreement during the latter part of 1956 provided for an initial overall ceiling for Japanese exports of cotton cloth and cotton apparel on the basis of trade in 1955. Where there had been serious rises the Japanese agreed to introduce specific ceilings, for example, in the case the velveteens and ginghams. The Japanese agreed also to try to distribute their exports evenly over the year.

The Japanese problem is part of the overall issue of how to deal with a weak industry. It has seemed to us that on the whole the United States Government has not allocated or distributed its tariff liberalization among industries and regions in the most equitable manner. For example, we would argue that where a region is gaining economic strength relatively and absolutely that region should be able to absorb a larger part of the cost of trade liberalization. We would contend that in the rapidly growing industries like chemicals, electrical machinery, rubber, transportation equipment and the like, the tariffs could easily be cut without the industry seriously feeling the effects. Increased imports would be absorbed out of a rising market.

Again we stress the point that an excessive burden should not be put on the weak industries that have to compete with imports. We would argue that the export industries which have been subsidized to the extent of over $100 billion since 1913 should bear a significant part of the burden. They are generally the strong and growing industries. That means that the adjustment in the dollar position of foreign countries should to a larger extent be made by losses of foreign markets by our export industries. Furthermore, insofar as the taxpayer bears his fair share of the total cost of adjustment in the dollar market, to that extent the export industries would continue to be able to penetrate foreign markets. Hence it seems to us that in a general way we should depend more upon foreign grants, aids, and loans, and also on the loss of export markets and to a smaller extent on increased imports. Insofar as there are increased imports as a result of tariff policy, the burden should more largely be put on the growing and dynamic industries.

The old classical theory that you always hit the weak and save and encourage the strong is not one that checks well with modern economic policy. In the last generation we have learned how to help the weak in many matters. We do not tend to destroy the weak but rather to help them survive. In our economic policies we have introduced all kinds of controls and interference on the part of the Government. This is true in social security, in agricultural policy, and in the development of our resources. In a similar way in dealing with foreign trade we should take into account the relative strength and weaknesses of those who are going to be affected by new policies. What is more, insofar as some industries and regions are injured by the economic policies of the Federal Government other than trade policy, to this extent trade policy should take into account the effects of these other policies. I have in mind in particular the many policies which tend to deprive the Northeast of cash and build up other areas that compete with the Northeast for its industries. Many of these policies are justified and we have no objection to them. We do however feel that when segments of the industry in the Northeast experience difficulties these should be taken into account in determining our trade and related policies.

In this connection the Japanese situation is germane. In the years since the end of the war we have poured large amounts of dollars into the Japanese economy, first through foreign aid, and more recently through expenditures on military installations and of military and civil personnel. By providing Japan dollars in this manner we have enabled that country to build up again a healthy economy and to meet its most essential needs for imports of food and raw materials.

With the large reduction in foreign aid, the problems for the Japanese have become more serious. Added to this, there has been some tendency in Japan in the postwar period to indulge excessively in importation of luxuries and in inflation, though in the last year or two the Japanese have tended to correct their inflationary trends. Up until a year ago they were able to increase their reserves in a rather striking manner, at least in the last few years. But in 1956–57 there are again signs of inflation and excessive imports.

In such a situation the Japanese are inclined once more to demand an expansion of their exports. Since textiles play a large part in their economy, and since these textiles are competitive with ours both at home and abroad, we are very much concerned with the large textile exports of Japan. In effect New England tends to pay an excessive part of the costs of solving the Japanese problem through large expansion of imports into the American market.

In order to take account of the requirements of our foreign policy as well as the need of a fair distribution of the burden, I would suggest the following attack on the Japanese problem. First, other countries should share with the United States the inundation of Japanese exports. In the past many European countries have refused to make the concessions that the United States has made. In some instances their behavior is justified by the difficulties in their foreign exchange position, but not in all instances. Second, the Japanese should be urged to diversify their exports in the textile area as well as in their economy generally. Third, there should be more attention paid to the possibility of foreign loans to the Japanese, which might temporarily ease their position and might make it possible for them to develop new industries. Fourth, everything possible should be done to encourage the Japanese to trade with Asia. We realize there are still many serious difficulties in this connection, and we are aware of the unwillingness of the Communists to deal or trade with the Japanese. But insofar as trade with Asia is possible, the Japanese should be given every encouragement. This after all has been her main major source of exports.

On pages 118–125 of the report to the Committee on Ways and Means on United States customs, tariffs, and trade agreements, laws and their administration, the Ways and Means Subcommittee has dealt very effectively with the Japanese problem. It is to be noted that the committee hopes for an increase of trade between Japan and southeast Asia. The committee is well aware of the inflationary dangers in Japan during 1956–57. Inflation not only brings about a rise of imports but also tends to absorb large supplies of commodities that might otherwise have been exported.

Another problem that might arise in the Japanese case would result from any tendency toward demobilization or reduction of armament expenditures. Should foreign aid be cut as military expenditures are reduced, this would also raise serious problems for Japan. It is therefore important for her to find foreign markets, to scrutinize her imports very carefully and to obtain as much capital abroad as possible. Our only reservation to the excellent statement by the Ways and Means Committee is that too much of the burden should not be put on textiles and too much should not be expected of the United States.

We should point out however that a large rise in imports is possible. In fact over the years the largest rises of imports have come not as a result of tariff policy but as a result of the rise of income. This does not mean that tariff policy does not effect imports, though frequently less than many believe, but rather that the major force determining the level of imports is the level of national income in the country. From the years 1933 to 1939 imports into the United States rose by $900 million. This was a period during which large cuts were made in tariffs and national income rose by $35 billion. But from 1939 to 1953 when tariffs were cut as they had been in the earlier period, imports rose by 9.6 billions. In this period gross product had risen by $278 billion. In the later period the increase of imports was 10 to 11 times that of the earlier period, and that of income 8 times. Over the years from 1919 to 1953, a total of 35 years, the relative movements of imports and income failed to be in the same direction only in 3 years.

### SECTION VII. THE ESCAPE CLAUSE

It is clear to most economists that an escape clause is a necessary part of tariff policy. Since our tariff concessions are made through negotiation by public servants, in collaboration with public servants of other countries, it is clear that there must be some review of the action taken by these negotiators on the part of the American Government. Otherwise it would be possible for civil servants to destroy an industry without any right of appeal. Under the escape clause the President, upon recommendation of the Tariff Commission, may increase tariffs by as much as 50 percent above the 1945 level and if necessary impose quotas. But it is assumed, of course, that injury is shown in such cases. The relevant criteria are the following:

> If as a result of unforeseen developments of the effect of the obligations incurred by a contracting party under this agrreement, including tariff concessions, any product that is being imported into the territory of that contracting party in such increased quantities and under such conditions as to cause or threaten serious injury to domestic producers in that territory of like or directly competitive products, the contracting party shall be free, in respect of such product, and to the extent and for such time as may be necessary to prevent or remedy such injury, to suspend the obligation in whole or in part, or to withdraw or modify the concession.
>
> In arriving at a determination of the foregoing procedure the Tariff Commission, without excluding other factors, shall take into account a downward trend of production, employment, prices, profits, or wages in a domestic industry concerned, or a decline in sales, an increase in imports, either actual or relative to domestic production, a higher or growing inventory, or a decline in the proportion of the domestic market supplied by domestic producers.

This quoted passage suggests many of the problems that arise in interpreting the escape clause. As a matter of fact, the 1955 legislation further amended the law and made it clear, for example—

> that the domestic industry producing like or directly competitive products shall be construed to mean that portion or subdivision of the producing organization manufacturing, assembling, processing, extracting, growing or otherwise producing like or directly competitive products in commercial quantities.

This amendment of course tends to result in a more narrow interpretation of the domestic industry concerned. Therefore, if some particular part of the operations of a manufacture or industry are affected adversely, this may allow treatment under the escape clause.

In refusing to accept the recommendations of the Tariff Commission in 1953, when that Commission proposed relief for the watch industry, the President emphasized the point—

that the shared doctrine goes much further. In fact, it finds that serious injury exists when the domestic industry fails to gain something it never had, even though the industry may be prospering by all the customary standards of levels of production, profits, wages, and employment. This is the doctrine on which the claim of injury by three Commissioners seems to be based.

In other words, what the President was saying was, here was a prosperous industry which was producing more watches in a period when imports expanded. He could not see why relief was necessary if the industry was producing more watches than ever even though imports accounted for a larger part of the total market. Similarly, he could not find cause for relief in the garlic case because most of the producers produced garlic along with other products and garlic was a small part of the total output.

In the ground fish fillets case, the President in 1954 refused to grant concessions. His position was that this was an industry that was now getting into the new fish-stick business and would soon be out of its difficulties and that he did not wish—

to hamper and limit the development of the market for the product and jeopardize the present prospects for the increase in per capita consumption of fish, which was the real solution of the industry's problem.

In a clarifying amendment in 1955, the Congress ruled that imports need not be the sole cause of injury in order to obtain relief; but they must be an important cause.

One of the points about which there has been much discussion is the rights of the President in these matters. There are some who hold the President should have no discretion if injury is shown. But the general view seems to be the President is responsible for foreign policy, and foreign policy is tied to the issues of free trade and protection; and that if this country becomes too protectionist this would affect adversely our general international position. Whatever the rights of the President, the tendency has been in recent years for the President to turn down recommendations of the Tariff Commission for relief under the escape clause. As the excellent report of the Committee on Ways and Means points out, of 22 proposals to grant relief by the Tariff Commission, the President accepted only 5, rejected 14, and made smaller concessions in 2.

Of 19 investigations on the escape clause during the year ended June 30, 1952, only 1 concession was made. The investigations did not cover a large amount of trade: motorcycles and parts, screws, spring clothespins, garlic, cherries, (candied, crystallized or glace), bonito (canned in oil, etc.), tobacco pipes, and tobacco pipe bowls of wood or root, pregnant mare's urine, dried figs.

Professor Kravis covered a period ending 1953 and found there were 51 escape-clause cases. The Tariff Commission had decided 40 cases and recommended the President act in 8 cases but the President invoked the escape clause in only 3 instances and requested further study in 2 cases. Only about 10 percent of imports in 1951 were involved in these cases—with whiskys, spirits, crude petroleum and its products, beef and veal, aluminum and its alloys, lead, and watches accounting for 9 percent.

Even the year ending June 30, 1955, 14 new escape-clause proceedings were instituted and 13 were completed. Most of these did not cover important amounts of trade. The exceptions were hardwood, plywood, lead and zinc, bicycles, watches, and fresh or frozen ground fish filets. The President approved increased restrictions in only two instances, alsike clover seed and bicycles.

It is clear that those who wanted relief under the escape clause have not received much help. It may, however, be different as a result of the 1955 amendment.

What is the significance of the escape clause for the textile industry? On the whole the relief so far rendered by the escape clause has not been serious. This is an industry in which prices tend to fall, profits are certainly unsatisfactory, employment and production have been declining. On all these criteria, there would be a case for relief. Certainly in some segments of the industry the rise of imports has been a substantial factor. But since much of these imports have come from Japan, the possibility of raising tariffs by 50 percent has not been adequate to solve this problem. Hence, the quota in 1956.

Those who oppose the escape clause are inclined to argue that the remedies under the escape clause should be used with great discretion, and that they should be used only in defense industries, and where the damage done over a short period is very severe. The relief should only be temporary. This theory is based on the assumption that where injury is done it is possible to move resources into other parts of the industry or into other industries. But where there is heavy concentration of production in one firm or one place, such relief is not easily achieved. In the Japanese experience, for example, the excessive imports of Japanese goods would jeopardize the oldest textile firm in New England. Indeed, shift from cotton to synthetics, and particularly to rayon, helped many textile firms over the years. But the possibility of shifting to another field of production is not great today. First, because there is not adequate capital to make the shifts, and secondly, because in general textiles are experiencing declines, though at varying rates of decline.

Perhaps the most dramatic experience of this kind relates to the concessions made under the Geneva protocol of almost 10 years ago. Undoubtedly, had the negotiators anticipated a decline of employment in the woolen and worsted industry of 50 percent in the next 8 years, they would not have been so generous in making these concessions. This is not to say that the decline in the output of woolens and worsteds was the result exclusively or even primarily of the traiff concessions. But there can be little doubt but that tariff concessions were an important item. Under the Geneva protocol it was stipulated that protection would be offered to the domestic producers should imports exceed a designated proportion of domestic output. After long deliberations it was agreed that tariffs would be increased by a given percentage once imports exceeded 5 percent of domestic production. This restriction, however, has to be reapplied each year and becomes effective only once the 5-percent limit has been reached. Certain problems of measurement of the imports, as well as domestic production, make this a rather difficult provision to administer.

Although the escape clause can often be of some use in such instances as velveteens, for example, although another way out was found for this item, on the whole the escape clause has not been of great use to the textile industry. One reason for this are the long delays. A second reason is that the difficulties affect the whole industry and cannot easily be treated by individual small segments. Perhaps the best solution would be to deal with this problem primarily through an attack on the whole industry. At these investigations it should be made clear that the further concessions would very seriously injure the whole textile industry. It is hard to think of a major industry that has experienced, say, a 50-percent decline in output as has the woolen and worsted industry and yet has been subject to tariff concessions.

In other words, the negotiators should take into account the general condition of the industry. In fact the situation may be so serious that even an increase in tariffs may be called for.

## SECTION VIII. TEXTILES AND AGRICULTURAL POLICY

One of the reasons for the difficult position of the cotton textile industry over the last generation has been Federal agricultural policy. That policy has had the worthwhile objective of improving the economic status of the agricultural farmer. Indeed, in the early years of the depression, the farmer suffered a severe setback which the Government could not afford to allow to continue untreated.

But the fact is that the early processing tax, the reduction of output of cotton through marketing quotas and production control, the resultant rise in the price of cotton and the reduction of consumption of cotton, the stimulus given thereby to foreign production of cotton, and also the production of competing synthetics—all of these tended to cut down the consumption of cotton on the American market and to damage the position of the American cotton textile industry.

A much better solution of these problems would have been an income payment to the farmer. In this case the greater burden would have been put on the taxpayer and a smaller burden on the consumer of cotton in the American textile industry. This would have been a much more equitable attack on the problem, since of course the problem of helping the farmer should be one that should be put on the Nation, not merely upon one segment of the American economy. That the United States Government should strike the textile industry at one and the same time, first by increasing the prices of the raw materials that they need, and secondly, by increasing foreign competition through reduction of tariffs, seems to be a rather unfair approach to an industry that is having its share of adjustment problems.

In 1933 this process of injuring the textile industry began. The Government introduced a 4.2 cents processing tax upon the cotton manufacturer and also provided for reduction of planting. The farmers were to plow under 11 billion acres, or about 25 percent of the amount planted. The price of cotton, which had been 18 cents a pound in 1928, 9 cents in 1930, and 5½ cents in 1932, now rose to 10 cents. The farmer was allowed to put his 1933 cotton on loan with the Commodity Credit Corporation, at 10 cents a pound. If the price rose above 10 cents a pound, the farmer, of course, would get the difference. Otherwise, the farmer could keep his loan money. In 1934–35, through improved production controls, the price of cotton stayed above the loan level of 10 cents, but in January 1936 the Supreme Court declared the processing tax and other parts of the AAA program unconstitutional.

The cotton-textile industry was affected by these programs in part by the need of absorbing part of the cost of the processing tax and partly by the effects on prices of reduced production of raw cotton.

It has been estimated by experts that the 10 percent increase in the price of cotton will cause a 2.3 percent reduction in consumption. Hence, the processing tax might be held to account for a reduction of cotton consumption in domestic mills by about 420,000 bales, or around 8 percent in the early days of the New Deal. A comparison of annual production from 1928–29 to 1932 of 14.6 million bales with a production of 11.1 million bales from 1933–34 to 1935–36 suggests crudely the proportions of reduction of output associated with the new control policies. On the basis of the proportion of cotton consumed at home and abroad this would mean a loss of consumption of 1.6 million bales as compared to the current consumption of 5.5 million bales. Inclusive of the effects of the processing tax, this would mean a loss of consumption of 2 million bales. This, however, is only a rough figure, and perhaps it is excessive because it does not allow for the reduced exports associated with the higher cotton prices in this country. Furthermore, the fact that the Government kept the price of cotton up may have contributed toward a rise of output. If this country had produced the share of world output for 1933–34 through 1935–36 that it had for 1920–21 to 1932–33, this country would have produced 14 million bales instead of 11 million bales. Again correcting for the amounts exported, this suggests a reduction of consumption in this country of 1.3 million bales, or a decline in the business of the American textile mills by about 30 percent. This, again, can only be the roughest kind of estimate.

A number of Government econometricians have attempted to study the effects of the AAA program on farm income and farm prices. For example, the Richards study suggests the average cotton price in 1933–34 if there had been no program would have been 6.4 cents per pound. Another writer, Cooper, came to essentially the same conclusion: 7 cents per pound. The actual price was 10.2 cents. Assuming that these estimates are roughly accurate, I conclude that the consumption of cotton in the United States would have risen from its actual level of 5.7 million bales by 0.6 million bales. Inclusive of the effect of processing tax, it appears the Government policy decreased the consumption of cotton just less than a million bales or about 17 percent in 1933–34. In this and the following year, it is estimated that consumption would have been a million bales greater without Government interference or a difference of just over 20 percent. Some other evidence is suggested by the amount of consumption in the United States and abroad. If one compares 1925–33 with the years August 1933 through July 1935, one finds that foreign consumption rose about 10 percent and United States consumption dropped about 12 percent. This is, of course, an oversimplification of the problem which suggests a relative decline for the United States of about 20 percent. For one must take into account varying business conditions in Europe and the United States and it is probably true that recovery was greater in some of the European countries than in the United States.

These various estimates suggest at least that the Governments agricultural policy may have cut consumption of cotton textiles in this country by more than 15 percent. All the techniques yield a reduction of at least 15 percent. In 1934 the cotton-textile industry employed 765,000 workers. If there had been no price-support program of the AAA type, presumably the employment in the textile industry would have been greater by 15 to 20 percent, that is, 115,000 to 150,000 more workers would have been employed. A rise of these proportions could have a considerable effect on the profitability of a large proportion of the American textile firms.

We do not argue that the processing tax was necessarily absorbed by the textile manufacturers. The major effect was through reduced output and higher prices and reduced consumption. In fact, in the 2½ years the processing tax was in effect, the average difference between the selling price of gray cloths and the market price of the raw cotton used in these cloths was 16.8 cents per pound. The first 6 months after the invalidation of the tax the spread averaged 12.4 cents. The tax was 4.2 cents, so the mill margin fell by a trifle more than the amount of the tax. During the harvest years of 1930 to 1932, inclusive, however, the mill margin as a percentage of the price of cotton cloth for 17 constructions averaged 57 percent. But from August 1933 through July 1935 the mill margin averaged 52 percent when the tax is excluded. From 1936 until the war mill margins averaged 56 percent of the price of cotton cloth.

In *United States* v. *Butler*, commonly known as the Hoosac Mills case, the Supreme Court on January 6, 1936, declared the New Deal agricultural program unconstitutional. But the Government got around this decision by tying the program to conservation and also, of course, dispensing with the processing tax. By early 1937 favorable prices resulted in large reductions in CCC stocks, but by the latter part of 1938 stocks were once more up to 7 million bales. The price had fallen from 12 cents to 9 cents, the loan rate. As a result of the large 1937 harvest, the Government introduced more stringent forms of production control, inclusive of marketing quotas. With a large 1938 crop, by August 1, 1939, the Government's stock had risen to the phenomenal level of 11 million bales. Undoubtedly in the years 1937 through 1940 farmers' income rose as a result of Government operations, and the volume of business for textile manufacturers was reduced. It was, however, difficult to estimate the precise effects on price. Nevertheless, Benedict and Stine estimated that the price for 1937 through 1940 would have averaged about 6 cents had there been no price program, or about one-third less than the average of the price which actually prevailed. On the basis of earlier estimates of elasticity of demand, it is suggested that consumption would have been 8.2 million bales instead of 7.5 million bales a year.

Of course the war baled out the Government and it was no problem to get ride of most of the surplus supplies. The Government nevertheless continued cotton control for a surprisingly long time. In 1944 the CCC also accumulated substantial stocks, but these were largely reduced in 1945.

It can probably be said that from 1941 to 1951 the price-control program on behalf of farmers did very little harm to the textile industry. This is because of the fact that demand was unusually high. But in the postwar period the situation varied to some extent. The Government at times had to absorb large supplies of cotton to keep its price from falling substantially. In fact, by the end of the 1949 season the total carryover, CCC plus private, was about two-thirds of the annual domestic mill consumption. The carryover was so large that growers had to accept marketing quotas for the 1950 crop to receive 90 percent of parity price supports. Despite reductions in the amount to be planted, the increased efficiency more than made it possible to increase supplies. In 1950 the yields were poor and only 10 million bales were produced. In 1950 and 1951 the results of the Korean war were to take large supplies off the hands of the CCC, and the Government made large profits.

By 1953 the Government was again confronted with large surpluses of cotton. The loan rate was 30.8 cents; the crop was very good, and the CCC invested $860 million in cotton by the end of the fiscal year. Though acreage controls were imposed, production because of increased efficiency rose to 13.7 million bales, and Government carryover again increased. In 1955, despite restrictions on acreage, 14.7 billion bales were produced; the yield of 416 pounds per acre was a record. CCC holdings continued to increase. Only the poorest land was retired from cultivation and the remainder was farmed more intensively. With the 14.7 billion bale crop and 11 million bale carryover, the total supply for 1955 harvest year was over 25 million bales. With unsatisfactory export markets this raised serious problems for the American Government, hence the pressure to dump cotton abroad. By 1956 the yield was again at a very high level. Only the beginnings of a substantial export program prevented a large increase in the holdings of the CCC.

In part as a result of the high price policy of the American Government, exports of raw cotton have tended to decline. Whereas in the years 1925–32 (i. e., the harvest years), United States exports were 150 percent of the exports of other countries, in the years 1932–40 and 1945–54, all crop years, the average amount exported from this country was only 52 percent as great as the exports of other countries. In other words, we have suffered a relative loss of two-thirds.

Beginning in 1939 we provided subsidies for the exportation of cotton. Of course these subsidies were not of great importance during the war period because in this period the price was generally above the support level, and the exportation of cotton was largely tied to the problem of financing the war and making materials available to our allies under lend lease and also under UNRRA. But from 1944 to 1947 there were substantial subsidies paid by the Government for the exportation of cotton. Finally, under the Marshall plan large supplies of cotton were moved out of the country. In 1 year 3.4 million bales out of total cotton exports of 5.7 million bales were moved as a result of the aid program; and most of the exports in the years 1950–53 were thus exported. In 1939, 91 percent of total exports were subsidized by the Government, in 1946, 94 percent, and in the fiscal years 1949, 1952, 1953, 1954 about 45 percent.

In 1953 exports declined seriously; they had averaged 5 million bales in the 2 preceding years and fell to less than 3 million. In 1954–55, 1.7 million bales were exported, and in 1955–56 despite the effects of Public Law 480, the Agricultural Trade Development Assistance Act, the International Cooperation Administration, and the efforts of the Export-Import Bank, exports were at the very low level of 2.2 million bales.

Of course, the explanation of the low exports was the high price of American cotton. In August 1955, Broach, Vijay, fine cotton in the Bombay market, was worth 24.2 cents per pound, export tax included, while a roughly equivalent quality of American cotton Middling $1\frac{5}{16}$ inch was worth 34.9 cents at New Orleans, a difference of 10.7 cents. At Alexandria in December, good Ashmouni was worth 34 cents per pound, with tax, while comparable American cotton SM $1\frac{1}{3}$ sold for 40.76 cents per pound.

With this large accumulation of cotton and lost export markets, the Department of Agriculture announced on February 28, 1956, that it was initiating a new export-sales program for Commodity Credit Corporation's stock of upland cotton. All cotton was resold on a competitively bid basis for shipment after July 31, 1956.

On May 28, 1956, the President signed the Agricultural Act of 1956, section 203 which states that CCC should encourage the export of cotton by offering surplus cotton for sale, but at prices not in excess of the level of prices at which cottons of comparable quality are being offered in substantial quantity by other exporting countries.

By November 1956, the CCC had sold about 7.1 million bales of cotton for export. Most of it had been sold at a little more than 25 cents per pound for Middling $1\frac{5}{16}$ inch at average location. This was about 6.6 cents less than the prevailing domestic or support price, and even less than the price of cotton of comparable qualities abroad.

In the 1956–57 marketing year, about 7 million bales would be exported from this country, contrasted with 2.2 million in the previous 12 months. It was announced in February 1957 that the program for the next harvest year would be substantially the same. In addition, various governmental loans were being made to finance the exportation of cotton. Grants and loans to foreign countries for purchases of American cotton amounted to the equivalent of about 1.6 million bales of exports in 1955–56.

Under pressure from the American textile industry, the Department of Agriculture announced on May 21, 1956, that it would pro-

22806—58——59

vide benefits to the exporters of cotton, so that the American industry would be able to purchase cotton for export at the same price as foreigners do from the American market. The Department of Agriculture suggested a payment to exporters of cotton products which would reimburse them for the extra cost in using cotton bought in the supported home market. The State Department suggested that the CCC stocks of cotton be made available to the domestic textile industry for use in products for the export market at the lower price at which raw cotton was dumped abroad. Apparently for administrative reasons, the suggestions of the Department of Agriculture were accepted. The State Department seemed to think that this was too blatant a form of export dumping. From August 1, 1956, through February 1957, exporters of American textiles received up to $7.5 million for exports of about 107 million pounds of cotton products.

Of course, where the American producer feels the burden of the program of the Agriculture Department is in the higher price of cotton as compared to what the farmer pays ·for cotton. These differentials are reflected in a rise of imports of cotton cloth from 2.3 million square yards per month average from 1946 to 1949 to 11.1 million square yards in 1955 and 15.7 million square yards in 1956. Exports, however, had fallen from 84.8 million square yards per month in the 4 years from 1946 through 1949 to 45.2 million square yards in 1955, and remained at a low level in 1956.

The dumping of American cotton abroad, of course, has annoyed countries that produce raw cotton. In September 1955, the International Federation of Cotton & Allied Industries requested that the United States not sell cotton abroad at less than domestic price. The two price system, of course, puts the American producer at a disadvantage in competition with foreign producers. The harm done, however, is probably not nearly so great as the damage that is done as a result of the increase in prices associated with American agricultural policy, for this reduces consumption of cotton and stimulates the production of competing fibers.

A rough estimate suggests that, if American mills were able to buy American cotton at the price it was offered to foreigners, consumption in this country would be about 5 percent or almost half a million bales greater. This loss of 5 percent in business may be a serious factor for textile firms in a precarious position. In fact, in more recent estimates made by the Department of Agriculture, the change in consumption might well be over 700,000 bales, or more than 8 percent. In more recent estimates, the Department of Agriculture puts a higher level of reduction of demand for a given rise of prices than had been assumed earlier.

That the reduction of domestic consumption due to support prices is much more important than the question of imports is suggested by the fact that in 1955 the amount of imports of cotton products was only one-seventieth as much as the amount of cotton used by domestic mills. The raw-cotton equivalent of cotton imports in 1955 amounted to 130,000 bales, while domestic mills consumed 9.1 million bales. In the same year, exports of cotton products included the equivalent of 523,000 bales, a little over 5 percent of domestic mill consumption. Of special importance is the increased consumption of synthetics. From 1925 through 1929, total consumption of synthetics by domestic mills was only 5.46 percent of the total amount of fabrics, while cotton accounted for 86 percent of the total. By 1946, the respective figures were 14 and 74 percent; in 1955, 28 and 66 percent. Of course, the increased use of synthetics should not be related exclusively to the rise in the price of cotton, though it has been a factor of some importance.

Common practice of export subsidies amounts to subsidies for foreign producers (the reverse of a tariff), and thus encourages the penetration of our markets. The price of cotton amounts to about one-half of the finished price of textiles in the United States. But, with foreign low-wage producers, cotton amounts to an even larger percentage of price and consequently gives them a greater advantage. The concession in cotton price to foreign purchasers is of the order of 25–30 percent, or at least 15 percent of the price of the finished textiles. In countries of very low wages, the differential might well be 25 percent of total cost.

An obvious solution would be to sell cotton to American producers at the same price as it is sold to foreigners; namely, the world cotton price. This would at least have the advantage of giving the consumer the benefit of the great rise of productivity in cotton growing. New legislation would be required for the Government at present is not allowed to sell cotton on domestic markets at prices below support levels.

Another suggested method is to impose an additional tariff on cotton goods and apparel imported into the United States to compensate for the difference in price which American mills must pay for cotton and that which foreign mills pay. Exported American cotton is sold at the world price and, consequently, it can be assumed that all cotton textiles and apparel coming into the United States will be made from cotton bought at cheaper prices.

The sale of 9 million bales in export markets in 15 months at world competitive prices and the low level of sales in preceding years, despite sales for domestic currency and grant-financed exports, reflects the disadvantage suffered by American producers in recent years. The large sales under a two-price system have merely clarified a price disadvantage suffered by American producers of textiles and the purchasers of cotton which has prevailed for a long time.

The cotton-textile mills have been forced, as a result of the cotton-farm program, to include in the price of cloth much of the cost of this program. This has seriously hurt their competitive position in the total market for their fabrics. It is generally believed that much of the growth of the synthetic-textile industry, as well as the popularity of many paper substitutes, is due to the relatively high price of cotton caused by farm programs.

It is, therefore, in the interest of the cotton-textile mills, as well as the farmers, to lower the price of cotton or to increase consumption of cotton and cotton textiles and to improve their relative competitive position. It has already been found necessary to lower the price of cotton used in exports in order to restore the export market, and to discourage cotton plantings in foreign countries, stimulated by the high-price umbrella the United States has held over cotton.

From a textile-mill point of view, the price of cotton should be attended by free-market forces so that American mills can buy at world prices and so that the farmer can profit from greater consumption and increased exports.

We are not taking a position against the price-support policy of the Government. We realize that a serious problem of adjustment exists, particularly for the small cotton farmer, and that a completely free market for cotton would bring hardships which should be avoided by a more temperate, long-range program.

Various suggestions have been made for handling this matter, which include either adjustment payments or combination of these, direct subsidy, or an increased acreage allotment. From the textile point of view, there may not be too much difference between these alternatives, although, generally speaking, textile mills would prefer increased acreage.

It is essential, however, to remember that adjustment payments or subsidies must not be loaded onto the price of cotton or onto the textile manufacturers by way of a processing tax or some other device. This would be self-defeating, and would cause great damage to our textile mills. The farm program should not be a tax or a cost added onto textiles.

For this reason we would not be enthusiastic over a certificate plan. Under this plan each grower is given a total crop acreage allotment, and if the farmer does not exceed his allotment he receives a marketing quota in terms of pounds of bales representing his share of the domestic market. For each unit of his quota of that market the cottongrower would receive a certificate which would have a value equal to the difference between the price the farmer received from the sale of the cotton and the domestic price objective. This arrangement would probably protect the United States from the charge of blatant dumping. But an important question is, who pays the bill. The answer is, the cotton-textile industry, and for this reason we are opposed to this particular program.

The difference between a program which would put the burden largely on the textile industry and the consumer and one that would put the burden to a greater extent on the taxpayer can be suggested by the following statistical presentation. Let us assume that Congress legislates that farmers should receive 90 percent of parity, or about $160 per bale (32 cents a pound for 500-pound bales) for middling ⅞-inch cotton. Under the direct income payment type of price support the price in the market is allowed to fall to the free-market level. The difference between the price which prevails in the market, say 65 percent of parity or $115 a bale, i. e., 23 cents a pound, and support price of 90 percent of parity paid direct to the farmer, means the cottongrower receives a payment of $45 for each bale sold. This is to be contrasted with the price support system where the Government buys cotton from the farmer and holds it off the market to raise the price.

If a 10-percent reduction in price means that the quantity consumed is greater by 4 percent, then it can be said if the price fell to $115 a bale with an income-payment scheme rather than being maintained at 32 cents a pound by CCC purchases, the consumption of domestic mills would rise by 1960 from 9.4 million bales a year to about 10.7 million bales. In other words, if farmers were guaranteed 90 percent of parity, and the difference between the free-market price and 90 percent of parity were paid directly to the farmer, consumption would be 1.3 million bales larger than if a market price of 90 percent of parity were maintained by the CCC holding cotton off the market.

The contrast in financial cost is given by the following. Under an income program the Government would have to pay $45 a bale for each bale of cotton consumed. Consumption at the free-market price would be 10.7 million bales. Hence the amount involved would be $480 million, i. e., 10.7 times 45. The cost of the CCC-type program would obviously be the cost of buying the amount of cotton that must be taken off the market to raise the price to 90 percent of parity, or $160 a bale. This would be 10.7 minus 9.41 million bales times 160 or $208 million. Hence the cost to the Government would be 43 percent as great if the Government were to raise the price by destroying 1.3 million bales than if it were to let the price fall and make up the difference through a special payment to farmers. When by taking 4 percent of the cotton supply off the market the price rises 10 percent, it is obvious that a relatively inexpensive way for the Government to support the price is by holding some of the crop off the market.

But what are the costs to the consumer is also a matter of some importance. Under the income-payment program consumers would pay $115 a bale for 10.7 million bales, or a total of $1.2 billion. Under the CCC restriction of supply program, consumers would pay $160 a bale for 9.4 million bales, or $1.5 billion. That is to say, the consumers pay $300 million less for 1.3 million bales more of cotton under the income plan.

Relative burdens are suggested by the following. Under the income-payment plan the Government spends $480 million and consumers spend $1.22 billion, or $1.7 billion in all. With the price-support program the Government spends $208 million and consumers $1.5 billion, the total again $1.7 billion.

It is obvious that under the price-support program a much larger burden is put on the consumer and a smaller burden on the taxpayer. The question may be raised whether the problem of maintaining income of farmers should not be put on the whole economy rather than on one special group, especially one that is having serious problems.

Of course we should consider also the export problem. Under the price-support program the CCC dumps the cotton on foreign markets, but dumping raises the old question which is certainly a serious problem in international relations. Under the income-payment type of price support, with one price there would be no problem of dumping.

## SECTION IX. WOOLENS

Since I was asked to discuss primarily the cotton textiles, I shall be very brief on woolens.

There can be little doubt but that the tariff on raw wool has been a handicap to the woolen industry. It has been particularly unfortunate in view of the large losses of this segment of the textile industry in the last 10 years.

For over 100 years now certain segments of the industry have been against a tariff on raw wool. But in general the textile industry together with the producers of raw materials have cooperated in providing tariff protection for the producer of the raw wool. Indeed there are some arguments to be used in defense of this policy. One reason for the cooperation has been the feeling on the part of the wool manufacturers that they could get a more than compensated rise in their tariff for any increase in the tariff on raw wool.

But in recent years and particularly in the last year or two there has been a changed view on this issue. At last the woolen manufacturers have begun to realize that tariff on raw wool does them more harm than good. Perhaps one reason for this is that they have come to believe they absorb in part the increased cost of raw wool, whether associated with tariffs or any other factor. When the policies were worked out originally there was no question of competition with the manmade fibers. This is no longer true, and therefore the wool manufacturer has to consider the effect of higher prices, associated with the tariff on raw wool, on the greater use of synthetics.

Another factor that has become increasingly important in the discussion of these problems has been the 1954 Wool Tariff Act. This legislation makes it possible to give the domestic producer protection without putting the cost on the textile industry. In other words, the woolgrowers receive the difference between the support level and the market price. In this instance the taxpayer does pay the bill as we have suggested ought to be done in the case of cotton. Indeed the support program through an income deficiency payment has not been very successful in getting the production of domestic wool up to the goals anticipated. Nevertheless it has become clear that it is possible to protect the woolgrowers in the United States without putting the burden on the American producer.

## SECTION X. TRENDS IN WORLD TEXTILE PRODUCTION

(The statistical material used in this section is based on the following: United Nations, Statistical Yearbook, 1956, and earlier editions; United Nations, Statistics of National Income and Expenditures, No. 10, 1957; U. S. Department of Commerce, Business Statistics, 1955 edition; also, National Income Supplement, Survey of Current Business, 1954 edition; Central Statistical Office, Annual Abstract of Statistics, 1956 edition.)

The main purpose of writing this section is to show that in general textiles have had difficulties all over the world, and to attempt to make some comparisons. Table I, for example, shows that in 1950 clothing seemed to take a larger part of the consumer expenditures than in 1938. The United States is, however, an exception. This may be explained partly by the backlog resulting from unavailability during the war. But by 1955 there are reductions in almost every country.

TABLE I.—*Private consumption expenditure, clothing as a percent of total consumer spending*

| | 1938 | 1950 | 1954 | 1955 | | 1938 | 1950 | 1954 | 1955 |
|---|---|---|---|---|---|---|---|---|---|
| Australia | ------ | 16 | 14 | 13 | Ireland | 11 | 15 | 13 | 12 |
| Austria | ------ | 19 | ------ | 13 | Italy | 12 | 13 | 12 | 11 |
| Belgium | ------ | 13 | ------ | 10 | Norway | 13 | 18 | 18 | 17 |
| Canada | 11 | 12 | 11 | 10 | Sweden | 14 | 17 | 14 | 14 |
| Ecuador | ------ | 15 | 16 | ------ | United Kingdom | ------ | 13 | 11 | 12 |
| Germany (West) | 14 | 17 | 14 | 14 | United States | 11 | 10 | 9 | 9 |
| Honduras | 11 | 10 | ------ | ------ | | | | | |

As was true in the United States there was a general tendency for textile prices to rise in the early postwar period. Textile prices, for example, were higher relative to all prices in 1947 in 14 countries and lower in only 6. But by 1955 there was a general decline in textile prices relative to all prices. This was true in virtually every country. The rate of decline was especially large relatively speaking for West Germany, Italy, and the United States. In Spain, France, Egypt and Turkey there were relatively large rises during this post-war period.

This decline in relative textile prices in the postwar period is related to the increased competition particularly from countries which had previously been large importing countries of textiles.

In general, the underdeveloped countries have gained especially in spinning and much more so than in weaving. As a matter of fact, in weaving most of the advanced countries have improved their position relative to 1938, though not nearly so much as such countries as Australia, Egypt, Portugal, Belgium, India, and Pakistan. Of the developed countries Sweden in particular has made a large gain since the early postwar as has West Germany. But in general in comparing prewar and the present situation, that is, the 1955 situation, I find that the largest gains are for Australia, Egypt, Portugal, Yugoslavia, and Belgium and at least satisfactory situation for the United Kingdom, Mexico, and Japan, with France roughly at the prewar level and Italy somewhat above. The United States output also in the weaving area is above prewar.

In wool the general trend was upward during the war, but the rise has clearly been slow in almost all countries. Yarn production has declined in almost every country since 1947. Exceptions are Turkey, Norway, Italy, and West Germany. The United Kingdom has also improved its position since 1947. The United States, of course, experienced a big rise during the war and early postwar and a substantial decline since.

In wool-fabric production the general tendency has been downward. Belgium has improved its position since 1938 and the United States and Canada seem to have suffered the most, with American production much below the 1938 level, as is also true of Australia, Austria, France, and Japan.

In the synthetic-fabric field there have been widespread gains; only the United States has lagged behind in recent years. But this is partly a matter of classification, that is, the exclusion of noncellulosic fibers, nylon, orlon, etc. The largest gains since 1947 and also in relation to 1938 have been made by Norway, Australia, Portugal, Austria, Mexico, the United Kingdom, Colombia, in that order. Japan has made a large recovery since early postwar, but still was below prewar in 1955, as was France.

An interesting approach to this problem is to compare the rise in the real gross national product for numerous countries with the rise in consumption of various textile products. The general picture is that production in general rises much more than textiles.

For example, from prewar to 1955 the real product per capita is up by 55 percent in Austria. The industrial consumption of cotton in 1955 was but 57 percent of prewar, yarn production 74 percent, woven fabric production 122 percent. Industrial consumption of wool was 88 percent, but of rayon and acetate woven fabric production was 418 percent. The last, however, is on the basis of early postwar equals 100, rather than 100 equals prewar as in the other items.

In Belgium, however, the tendency has been in most textile items for output to exceed the rise of real product which was 26 percent in a recent year compared to prewar. The only exception to this is industrial consumption of wool which was 102 and industrial consumption of cotton which was 123, both in relation to 100 for prewar. But it should be noted that compared to an early postwar, generally 1947, the textile items are much below the 1947 level by 1955, that is, relative to the real product. For example, real product rose from 109 to 126, while industrial consumption of cotton fell from 150 to 123, and of wool from 168 to 102.

The same general picture prevails in France. The real product is up to 135 by 1955, but industrial consumption of cotton down to 93, and of wool 101. All other items are at the same level or lower.

The same general pattern prevails for Italy, although industrial consumption of wool was 175 as compared to 125 for the real product in a recent year.

Japan also showed a relative decline of textiles with the exception of yarn production which was at 122 in a recent year as compared to 106 for per capita real product. Industrial consumption of cotton was 62, of woven fabric production of cotton 72, industrial consumption of wool at 88, and rayon and acetate woven fabric production 76.

In the Netherlands the consumption of cotton and yarn production was substantially below the real per capita product. But in wool the rise of industrial consumption was much greater, a rise of 67 percent against 33 percent in the real product.

For Sweden the same general pattern prevails as for most of these countries. Industrial consumption of cotton 86, compared to a real product of 115, and 97 for industrial consumption of wool. Yarn production of wool, however, was 116, and woven fabric production of rayon and acetate is at 218 in a recent year.

Particularly for the United Kingdom have textiles suffered serious declines. Moreover, there has been no significant improvement since the early postwar period except in the industrial consumption of wool and the yarn production of wool, and also in rayon and acetate.

The situation in the United Kingdom is especially a difficult one and unsatisfactory. The per capita real income in relation to prewar is 122. And this suggests a substantial rise since early postwar when the figure was 98. In comparison, industrial consumption of cotton was 68 in an early postwar period and 61 in a recent year; yarn production, 68 and 66; woven-fabric production, 42 and 45.

The record for wool, however, was substantially better. Industrial consumption, 89 in an early postwar period and 101 in a recent year; yarn production 90 and 107; woven-fabric production 196.

It is quite clear from these statistics and from those for the United States that though the United States record is unsatisfactory, it is not so unsatisfactory as the British record. For example, the per capita real income was 142 in the early postwar and 173 in a recent year, with 100 being prewar. Industrial consumption of cotton, however, was 121 and 98—in other words a relative decline by 1955 of more than 70 percent. In yarn production the figures were 107 and 93, in woven-fabric production 105 and 95. In industrial consumption of wool the figures were 184 and 96, reflecting a very marked decline since early postwar for wool, and similarly for yarn production of wool though the decline was not quite so great, the figures being 116 and 92. For woven-fabric production the figures were 121 and 65. Even for rayon and acetate woven-fabric production the totals were only 132 and 109. Hence, though the record is not so dismal as in the United Kingdom, there clearly has been a marked decline in the relative contribution of textiles to the American economy.

In Western Germany the same general situation prevails. Textiles have not kept up with the general economy, though there have been sensational gains since early postwar. Real product in a recent year was 136, industrial consumption of cotton 89, and industrial consumption of wool 72. The rise of industrial consumption of cotton was from 34 in the early postwar to 89 in a recent year, and from 14 to 72 for industrial consumption of wool.

Now let us consider more fully a number of the underdeveloped countries. In general, the picture is different. One will find that textile production has become a larger part of the national product rather than a smaller part as in most of the developed countries. This, of course, explains to a considerable extent the difficulties of the textile industries in the developed countries.

For example, the Argentine, with a per capita real national income of 126 in the early postwar and 120 in a recent year with 100 as prewar, had industrial consumption of cotton of 181 and 230 respectively, and yarn production 230 and 275.

In Australia, the pattern is somewhat similar, with industrial consumption up to 220 and real product for the economy up to 155. Clearly, cotton consumption and yarn production also are gaining. The situation is somewhat different, however, in wool. It might be expected that Australia would gain relative to the economy in consumption of industrial wool and yarn production of wool. Actually the situation was fairly satisfactory until early in the postwar period, but by a recent year industrial consumption of wool was 118 and the real product 155.

Brazil is an exception to the general rule. Its consumption of cotton is relatively small compared to its gain of real income per capita.

Canada, which is in some respects an underdeveloped and in some respects a developed country, follows the pattern more nearly that of the United States.

In Chile, by 1953 real product was 116 and industrial consumption of cotton had risen to 337, a rather spectacular relative rise for cotton textiles.

In Colombia, the picture is mixed. Industrial consumption is up almost three times as much as real product per capita, but yarn production and woven fabric production, both cotton, are down substantially.

For Egypt the rise in consumption of cotton and woven fabric production has been very large, but we have no figures for per capita income.

In Greece, there have been startling rises in textile production, except in the industrial consumption of cotton which has been somewhat less than the rise of per capita real income.

For India and Pakistan no income figures are available, but the consumption of cotton as well as yarn production and woven fabric production of cotton are somewhat higher than prewar level.

The Mexican pattern is a good deal like the United States—a substantial rise of real income though not as much as the United States and a much smaller rise of industrial consumption of cotton, in fact, one of only one-tenth as large as that of the real product. And a very marked decline in the per capita consumption of cotton for yarn production and woven fabric production, only about one-half of the prewar level.

New Zealand, unlike Australia, experienced a much larger rise of yarn production than of real income per capita, in fact, a rise of about 20 times as much relatively speaking, though industrial consumption of wool was roughly at the same relative level as the rise of per capita income.

In Portugal, cotton consumption is up much more than per capita income, and this is also true of wool though not nearly so large a relative rise.

In Spain, the picture is mixed with industrial consumption up more than the rise of real product, but yarn production of cotton below prewar, and the same is true of consumption of wool.

Turkey seems to be expanding its textile industry much more both in cotton and wool than the national product.

Yugoslavia has also experienced a large rise in its textile industry, but national income figures are not available.

Now a few words about textile equipment. As compared to 1939 there have been generally rises in the total amount of spinning spindles. There have been substantial declines, however, for West Germany, the United Kingdom, Japan, France, and the United States in that order, with the United States and Canada having the smallest of these declines. The largest increases relatively in this order have been for Chile, Turkey, Colombia, South Korea, Egypt, Argentina, Portugal, Australia, Peru, Yugoslavia, Mexico, Brazil, India and Pakistan, Greece, Spain, and Italy. The degree of mechanization, and one might say the advance of technology in the industry, is suggested by the following table:

TABLE I.—*Cotton-producing countries ranked by mechanization*

| Spinning (ring spindles as a percent of total, 1955): | Weaving (automatic looms as a percent of total power looms, 1956): |
|---|---|
| Turkey (100) | United States (100) |
| Argentina (100) | Canada (99) |
| West Germany (100) | Turkey (96) |
| Greece (100) | Australia (96) |
| Yugoslavia (100) | Sweden (91) |
| United States (100) | Argentina (84) |
| Brazil (100) | Chile (73) |
| Chile (100) | Italy (67) |
| South Korea (100) | Switzerland (62) |
| Mexico (100) | France (53) |
| Colombia (100) | Greece (47) |
| Austria (100) | Yugoslavia (44) |
| Japan (100) | Egypt (40) |
| Egypt (100) | West Germany (39) |
| Peru (100) | Belgium (36) |
| Italy (99) | Brazil (36) |
| Belgium (99) | Austria (35) |
| Canada (99) | Mexico (32) |
| Netherlands (99) | Colombia (31) |
| India and Pakistan (98) | Netherlands (29) |
| Australia (98) | Peru (28) |
| Portugal (98) | South Korea (19) |
| Sweden (98) | Japan (18) |
| Switzerland (98) | China (15) |
| Spain (93) | United Kingdom (14) |
| France (90) | India and Pakistan (13) |
| United Kingdom (42) | Portugal (12) |

This shows that the United States still rates very high in the degree of mechanization of the industry. It also shows that among the important countries the United Kingdom is very low on the use of ring spindles. And the same holds for a number of the western European countries. On the whole, many of the underdeveloped countries, for example, Yugoslavia, Chile, Brazil, Colombia, have a better record than some of the older textile countries. Again in the use of automatic looms, many of the older textile countries have not an enviable record. This is, for example, true of the United Kingdom, the Netherlands, and is also true of some of the underdeveloped countries, India and Pakistan, for example. Some of the underdeveloped countries have a relatively high degree of mechanization.

Now about cotton looms: The largest decline relative to prewar by 1955–56 was Belgium; next Sweden and Canada, United Kingdom and the United States, the Netherlands and Germany, France, Switzerland, and Italy with the smallest decline. The largest rises occurred in this order: Turkey, Argentina, Egypt, Chile, Colombia, Greece, Australia, Peru, Spain, and Brazil. India and Pakistan and Japan experienced a small rise.

The statistics for machinery also suggest that the largest gains in underdeveloped countries have been in the spinning rather than in the weaving part of the textile industry. The underdeveloped countries have not experienced any large rise of wool spinning capacity.

The United States has experienced the largest decline of wool spinning spindles; France next and Belgium and the United Kingdom and Sweden follow. The largest rises were for Turkey, Austria, Norway, Switzerland, Italy, Spain, the Netherlands, New Zealand, Australia, Canada, and Japan, in that order. Table II suggests the statistics for the degree of mechanization in the woolen industry. Again the United States leads all others. And the United Kingdom now is midway on spinning and also weaving.

TABLE II.—*Wool-producing countries ranked by mechanization*

| Spinning (continuous spindles as a percent of total, 1955): | Weaving (automatic looms as a percent of total power looms, 1955): |
|---|---|
| United States (75) | United States (89) |
| Australia (63) | Canada (72) |
| Japan (63) | Australia (31) |
| Canada (62) | New Zealand (28) |
| United Kingdom (53) | Sweden (26) |
| Sweden (38) | Switzerland (24) |
| Netherlands (37) | United Kingdom (22) |
| France (34) | Norway (20) |
| Italy (32) | France (17) |
| Spain (30) | Netherlands (12) |
| Austria (28) | Austria (6) |
| Switzerland (27) | Spain (4) |
| Portugal (25) | Italy (4) |
| | Portugal (1) |

In woolen looms the largest declines by far since 1938 are for the United States with France, United Kingdom, Spain, Belgium, Netherlands, Japan, Switzerland, Austria, and Canada following. The largest rises are in New Zealand, Norway, Australia, Turkey, Italy, and Sweden, in that order.

In conclusion, I would say that in general the developed countries have suffered severe losses in textiles in relation to 1947. From 1939 to 1947, however, many of them have made substantial gains. In cotton, the United Kingdom's losses were much greater than those of the United States. But in woolens the United States has taken about as great a decline as any country. These trends are evident both in the statistics for output and in the use of machinery. Despite the large losses of the United States in textiles and especially relative to the growth of the economy, the United States still is in the lead in the mechanization of its industry. The United Kingdom was surprisingly low in the degree of mechanization and this is no doubt explained in part by her relatively low wages. Many of the underdeveloped countries starting fresh have been able to obtain much more advanced machinery than many of the developed countries. The gains of the underdeveloped countries have been much larger in the spinning area than in the weaving area, and much more in cotton than in wool. The developed countries have suffered in part because of the changes in the pattern of consumption and in part because of the competition of the underdeveloped countries. Employment has suffered in part also because of the great mechanization.

## SECTION XI. PROBLEM OF SUBSTITUTING FOR BUSINESS LOST [1]

The majority of cotton, woolen, or worsted mills, in fact all mills, in the industry were originally developed to produce yarns and fabrics inside certain specific limitations in respect to counts of yarn, weights of fabric, and different raw materials. In some instances, the permissible range is quite broad, and others equally limited.

In many instances mills initially planned to produce print cloths, balancing spinning equipment to looms, have found it very difficult to compete when circumstances have warranted their trying to manufacture either heavier or lighter fabrics than print cloths. Machinery gets widely out of balance with the changes such as I have mentioned.

Mills which have been initially established to produce combed fabrics at times find it necessary to operate on carded yarns and fabric and as a result their combing equipment is idle and overhead for this equipment goes on and more often than not costs get out of line and the activities are not profitable.

Mills set up to produce coarse carded yarns more often than in fine mills, find it possible to produce a wide variety of fabrics and as a result can successfully compete throughout each full year of perhaps changing styles. (This gives the South an advantage.)

If a mill can operate on a limited number of styles 12 months in the year, their overall machinery production efficiencies will have a minimum of interference and the resulting cost held at a better level than when styles change rapidly and efficiencies become much lower. This is an important consideration when profits are low as they tend to be in textiles.

In the cotton-textile industry as a whole, I believe somewhat in excess of 50 percent of the spindles and looms are geared to operations which do not permit very extensive changing of fabrics without materially increasing production costs and increasing waste.

[1] In writing this section, I had the advice of Mr. Nathaniel Mitchell, of Barnes Textile Associates, Inc. (110 State Street, Boston, Mass.), probably the outstanding textile engineer in the country.

In the woolen industry geared to produce apparel fabrics, I believe in excess of 70 percent of the spindles and looms are set up to produce a rather wide range of yarn counts and fabric weights. In this field the excessive changeovers and resulting losses are more or less a matter of continuous experience.

In the worsted field I would estimate that about 60 percent of the spindles and looms are geared to a rather narrow range of fabrics and as a result they would suffer machine efficiency losses if forced to change to either heavier or lighter fabrics in the respective mills.

There are also mills set up for certain types of decorative fabrics in both the cotton, woolen, and worsted fields where definite hardships would be experienced if they were forced to produce other types of fabric.

Examples of these are the bedspread and blanket industry in cotton, the upholstery and other types of decorative fabrics in woolens and worsted. Woolen blanket mills could not be expected to produce woolen apparel fabrics in competition with mills designed for that purpose.

Mr. Mitchell recollects four woolen blanket mills which were ultimately liquidated after having tried desperately to get into the field of producing apparel fabrics with the same equipment. Sometimes whole organizations have to be changed with the machinery if the basic styles of fabrics are changed.

Mr. Mitchell also recalls his War Production Board experience during World War II. The Armed Forces needed a certain very definite and large yardage of cotton goods during the war period. The analysis which was made indicated it would not be possible to get this production. Members of the industry asked him to serve with others to check the figures and if possible find a way to get production. As a result they bent every effort to allocate the production in such a manner that each mill was assigned fabrics which best fitted its equipment and overall experience. As a result it was found possible to get the production needed and it naturally was at a lower cost than was originally anticipated when fine-goods mills were asked to make coarse goods, and vice versa.

Briefly stated, a plant set up to manufacture velveteens on a competitive basis would find it extremely difficult to compete in almost any other field of production unless the mechanical equipment was changed wherever the change in styles would warrant. Equally, it would be ridiculous for a woolen wearing apparel producing mill to attempt to make velveteens.

A comparison of pictures of spinning and weaving machinery in a carpet mill with those of a worsted mill reflects extreme difference in equipment but indicates that the majority of fabric changes to be considered would be suggested by differences in the machinery of these two plants.

In short, though some substitution is possible and takes place, often it is not practical and, when practical, means increased capital costs and reduced profits or higher prices in an industry where profits are low and price resistance great.

# THE IMPORTATION OF COTTON TEXTILES FROM JAPAN

The American Importers of Japanese Textiles, Inc.

Sam Ishikawa, secretary, and Mike Masaoka, Washington representative

INTRODUCTORY STATEMENT

The American Importers of Japanese Textiles, Inc. (AIJT), is a New York corporation whose members are domestic corporations and companies, partnerships, the majority of whose partners are citizens of the United States, and individual Americans concerned with the national interest involved in textile imports from Japan. Members of this association import approximately 70 percent of all Japanese textiles imported into this country.

AIJT appreciates this opportunity to submit this paper for the compendium of papers on foreign trade policy, which is being prepared by the Subcommittee on Foreign Trade Policy of the Committee on Ways and Means of the House of Representatives, to provide a comprehensive analysis of the many considerations bearing on United States trade and tariff policies and practices.

In the light of the congressional situation on tariff-trade legislation and the alarming growth of so-called protectionist sentiment that may well develop into economic and political isolationism—which we believe to be a threat to our peace and prosperity as a nation—AIJT welcomes this study in the hope that the information and implications developed by this subcommittee will demonstrate anew that our country's self-interests in this troubled world require expanding trade and commerce among the free peoples of the earth.

As importers who daily participate in the handling of Japanese textile products, we believe that much of what appears to be general acceptance of most of the criticisms and protests directed against Japanese imports are based upon the lack of information as to the real impact and contributions of these Japanese commodities to the national economy and welfare. As a matter of fact, as importers, we are convinced that most of the charges and allegations, as well as the emotional and passionate appeals, of that portion of the domestic industry that indulges in these operations are either exaggerated or unfounded.

Moreover, we know from our own painful experience that many relevant and persuasive facts that would cause many Americans to better understand the national advantages in these cotton-textile imports fail to receive the publicity and the acclaim that is commanded by those who often use Japanese textiles as a whipping boy for the ills and the troubles of the domestic textile industry. We refer to such acknowledged facts as that Japan purchases almost twice as much from us as she sells back to us, that Japan is our best customer by far for all our agricultural products and our first or second best customer for all our exportable items, and that Japan buys from 7 to

9 times as much raw cotton in bales as she returns to us in textile manufactures.

Rather than a general discourse on the proven economic, national, and international benefits of a freer trade policy—which, no doubt, experts in the field will expound—our submission will be devoted to the detailing of certain facts and information regarding Japanese textiles which we feel may be useful in more properly evaluating our national trade policy in specific reference to Japanese textile imports.

Understandably, since we represent the American importers and not the Japanese exporters or industry, some information was not available to us and, therefore, was not included in this paper, although it should be pointed out that every effort, within the limits of our facilities and resources, was made in both this country and Japan to secure the latest and pertinent facts on all aspects of this problem.

At the same time, however, it must be made clear that the nature of this submission is such that our primary objective will not be to refute the arguments or challenge the information and the conclusions of both the advocates of more restrictive trade practices and the domestic textile industry. Neither will we concentrate on illustrating the many advantages, such as those to the millions of American consumers, in Japanese textiles. Our purpose will be, instead, to try to supply basic facts and information on Japanese textiles which may enable this subcommittee to understand and appreciate the national interests in these imports.

TRADE PRACTICES IN THE IMPORTATION OF JAPANESE COTTON TEXTILES

Because Japan is a small nation with very limited natural and capital resources, the forces of circumstances have compelled her to develop and adapt trade practices which are uniquely her own throughout her relatively recent history as an industrial and commercial power.

Postwar Japan—following almost complete destruction of her industrial potential, loss of favored foreign markets and sources of supply, and a new awareness of her responsibility and obligations in the partnership of free nations—faces many serious and special problems which, unless properly resolved, may well adversely affect the security of the entire Pacific area and the destiny of that vast mainland of Asia.

Much misunderstanding of Japanese cotton-textile imports, we feel, comes from a lack of basic knowledge of Japanese export operations and United States import practices as they relate to these key goods in the international commerce of these two nations. To make for a better understanding of the normal trade practices that are involved, we shall briefly describe some of these operations.

*Japanese exporters of cotton textiles*

In 1956, Japan exported some 1,262 million square yards of cotton fabrics and 27 million pounds of cotton yarn. These exports were channeled through some 988 business companies. Generally speaking, these exporting firms may be classified into three groups—small, medium, and large-scale exporters.

The small-scale exporters usually are firms which deal with sundry items in addition to their textile business.

The medium-scale exporters usually are companies whose majority business is in cotton yarns and fabrics, but which also handle the importation of raw cotton, raw wool, and other raw materials needed by the manufacturing industry. These medium-scale exporters, for the most part, also serve as merchandisers of made-up textile goods for the home or Japanese market.

The large-scale exporters are better described as "general traders" who engage in both foreign and domestic (Japan) trade. Some of them handle thousands of different items for both export and home consumption—textile products, canned goods, scrap iron, grains, etc.

Another feature of Japanese exporting practices is the clear distinction made between the manufacturing and exporting companies. There are few, if any, manufacturers who operate an export business, and the direct exportation of cotton goods by the manufacturers is very rare indeed.

The standard practice is for the large- or medium-scale exporters to purchase cotton goods from the manufacturers and to export them, or to purchase the yarns or cloths from the spinners and weavers or from the local market and then to assign the materials to be processed by weavers or dyers on a commission basis.

In explanation, it should be noted that the spinners in Japan manufacture items which are suited for mass-production methods in their own mills. For more intricate or complicated products, the spinners usually consign the finishing to independent weavers and dyers on a commission basis. The medium- and large-scale exporters tend to purchase yarns and gray goods from small- and medium-sized spinners and then to have them converted into the more intricate and complicated products by weavers and dyers.

The small-scale exporters, usually lacking capital resources to buy directly from the spinners or weavers, make their purchases for export from the medium- and large-scale exporters.

Of the 988 exporters handling cotton yarn and cloth last year, 22 companies handled only yarn, while 108 firms handled cotton yarn and cloth exclusively. Regular exporters who conducted business throughout the entire year in cotton fabrics numbered 144, with the remaining 844 companies entering the cotton-fabric exporting field only occasionally.

The top-ranking 20 exporters accounted for nearly 65 percent of the total volume of exported cotton cloth last year.

Exporters engaged in secondary products are even more numerous than are those dealing in cotton yarns and cloths. It is estimated that there are perhaps 1,500 such exporters. Their numbers can be explained in the great diversification of textiles exported, as well as in the countless small-lot shipments. These exporters of secondary items, as might be expected, range in size from very small to substantial operations, with some dealing exclusively in only one commodity, such as gloves, and others handling the full range of secondary products.

*Postwar group development*

Following the end of hostilities and the establishment of the allied occupation, dominated by the United States, all control organizations, monopolies, and unwarranted restrictions on business enterprises were dissolved or abolished. The major drive was against the big financial combines, called the Zaibatsu, but it was also carried out against the various trade associations, including those in the cotton-textile exporting trade.

With the destruction of traditional trade patterns and policies, numerous export firms mushroomed to take advantage of what was expected to be occupation benevolence in the rehabilitation and reconstruction of the ravaged nation. Many of these companies were without experienced management and sufficient capital resources to carry out routine export practices. This excessive competition brought complete disorder in the cotton-textile exporting trade.

In signing the San Francisco Treaty of Peace in 1951, Japan pledged herself "to observe internationally recognized fair practices in public and private trade and commerce." To implement this declaration, the National Diet (Parliament) in July 1952 enacted the export transaction law to prevent cutthroat export pricing and unfair trade practices. Subsequently, in 1953, this statute was amended to insure orderly import-trade practices and was redesignated as the "Export-Import Transaction Law."

The export-import transaction law authorized Japanese exporters to organize associations as administrative instrumentalities to supervise the implementation of voluntary regulations as formulated by members of the association.

Taking advantage of this authority, cotton-textile exporters of yarn and cloth reorganized the Japan Cotton Textile Exporters Association in 1952. It was originally organized in 1921. By the end of 1956, it had 147 members, who exported 93 percent of all Japan cloth exported to the United States that year. Also, in 1952, exporters of secondary items reorganized the Japan Textile Products Exporters Association. First established in 1934, at the end of 1956 it had 453 members, who exported more than 95 percent of all cotton made-up goods to the United States.

The sole purpose of these associations was, and is, to assure the orderly export of Japanese cotton textiles. (Elsewhere in this paper, we shall describe their functions in relation to exports to the United States market.)

*Import transaction pattern*

While methods of importing cotton textiles differ among the various importers, the usual transaction follows a pattern something like this: An American buyer interested in purchasing Japanese cotton textiles will, in most instances, contact an importer who specializes in Japanese textiles. Many of these importers serve as agents or affiliates of trading companies in Japan. Most of them are located in New York City.

After the prospective purchaser makes known his specifications, the importer requests quotations on specific items from the exporter in Japan. Following what amounts to bargaining by cables between the importer and the exporter, if agreement is reached between the exporter and the importer representing the purchaser on price, quantity, construction, delivery date, and other terms, contracts are concluded between the importer and the exporter, and the importer and the buyer.

When the letter of credit is received by the exporter, the goods are shipped according to the delivery terms of the contract. In cases where printed or dyed goods are ordered, the Japanese exporters, after receiving the agreed upon specifications as to color, design, and other information, call on spinners and dyers to fabricate the specified articles.

Cost-insurance-freight and cost-and-freight prices are considered the conventional method of quoting prices for exports to the United States. As a general practice, no money is advanced from the importer or buyer. In cases of cost-insurance-freight and cost-and-freight contracts, the importers bear the account and risk of tariffs, while the exporters pay for and bear the risk of ocean freight.

If the merchandise to be imported is printed or yarn-dyed cloth, or cloths with designs, the exporter is obliged to make certain that the importer or the buyer will complete and accept the order; otherwise, he may find himself with what may be unsalable goods manufactured to specifications that cannot be marketed elsewhere. On exports of this type, the Japanese exporter understandably wants to receive the letter of credit as early as possible. On the other hand, the importer or buyer is not anxious to open an early letter of credit, because it may well be months before he receives his shipment. In such cases as these, it is the usual practice for the exporter to receive his letter of credit about 3 weeks before shipment. But in many instances the letter of credit arrives just in time for shipment. The primary reason for this procedure is that the importer does not wish to tie up his capital until the last possible moment. Of course, in certain cases shipments are made that are based on faith and confidence in the importers ordering the merchandise.

Nearly all of the goods are shipped via the Panama Canal and are landed in New York City. In rare instances, cotton goods are shipped via Europe or landed on the west coast. The New York port is the most popular, because it is the center of the American market.

Deliveries of Japanese imports require so much time that it is almost impossible to conduct any spot transactions. The estimated lead time which is required for gray and bleached cloths is from 4 to 6 months, and 6 to 12 months for printed and yarn dyed cloths. This time factor forces the Japanese exporter to solicit future business, rather than relying on spot transactions.

Furthermore, practically no export is done on a consignment basis, although it is not illegal if the Japanese Government approves. As a matter of experience, Japanese exporters discourage consignment transactions because of the numerous difficulties and problems involved, such as selecting buyers, changing fashions, and poor planning.

Although it may be ideal for an importer to be able to stock large inventories, because of the distances separating the manufacturer and the buyer and the risks involved particularly in reference to the time element, most importers are unwilling to make arrangements for goods on consignment. If consignment agreements are reached, it is usually for standard merchandise which is not subject to changes in seasonal or fashion demands. Items subject to fluctuations in demand such as printed cloth, dyed yarn, and other fancy goods are usually exported only on a strict contractual sales basis.

With the imposition of the so-called voluntary quotas for the past 2 years, consignment sales have been even more severely curtailed because the exporter does not care to risk his share of the quota in articles that may not sell.

In spite of the twin facts that there is little activity in spot transactions and that there are few consignment sales, the New York importers have plenty of samples from which buyers may select their goods for import. On the whole, however, the quality of Japanese textiles is so well known among those who are regulars that most buyers do not order on the basis of samples. And, where the buyer desires his own special designs or colors, he is expected to supply the necessary designs or cotton samples.

Generally speaking, cloths for apparels are subject to seasonal fluctuations of demand. Velveteens, for example, are purchased for spring, autumn, and winter sale, while ginghams are for spring, summer, and autumn. An increasing demand for Japanese imports which are not seasonal in character, mostly nonapparel items, has been noticed of late.

*Marketing*

Perhaps the most glaring weakness of Japanese textiles in the United States is the lack of marketing on the part of both the manufacturers and the exporters. What little promotional advertising that is carried on by the manufacturers and exporters is institutional in character, rather than on specific items or on brands. The exporters do almost no packaging or gimmick sales type of merchandising.

The importers too are reluctant to engage in advertising and promotional activities, for the importers are working on the smallest possible margin to sell their goods in the United States market. In most instances, even if only a small allowance were given over to promotion and advertising, items would be priced right out of the American market. Necessarily then, matters of this type are left to the retailer or the wholesaler, which means that, with few exceptions, there is no national advertising or promotional campaign on behalf of Japanese textiles.

On the other hand, the Japanese textile industry for home consumption carries on promotional and advertising campaigns similar to those featured by American industry, where design and fashion trends are promoted.

The easiest explanation for the lack of initiative on the part of the Japanese manufacturer and exporter in the American market is historic. The pre-World War II market for Japanese textiles was primarily in China, India, Indonesia, and the African countries.

In these markets, traditional designs and construction were paramount factors in the sale of textiles. Accordingly, there was no need to seek constantly new designs, colors, fashion, and so forth; only the necessity to fabricate according to the instructions from the importers who themselves were thoroughly conservative and traditional.

Historically too, up until recently, Japanese exports to more economically advanced countries were mainly in gray or bleached goods or shirtings and mulls. Exports to European countries, for example, were primary goods to be finished for reexport to third countries.

Japanese exports of fashionable, stylish printed or dyed yarn articles are a comparatively new factor. It must be conceded, however, that the Japanese seem to be becoming more aware of the need for intensive market research in the United States. No major attempts thus far to lead in fashion trends or to veer demands toward their specific products have been attempted as yet. The principal reason now is their lack of capital for such promotional ventures, although there may also be a lack of confidence in their ability to compete on these grounds.

Summed up, then, it can be said that Japanese exports to the United States are based largely on the specifications listed by the buyer or importer.

*Pricing practices*

Prices of Japanese cotton textile exports to the United States are determined by the negotiations and bargaining that goes on between the exporter and the importer. In many cases, the importers "shop around" for comparative bids to use as bargaining weapons to lower the price. In many cases, admittedly, these tactics are quite successful.

Aside from the bargaining process, the Japanese Government has a procedure for checking on prices.

On most cotton goods, there is no floor price as there are for some other export products to this country. Under the export-import transaction law—which was primarily intended to prevent the escape of precious capital from Japan—the Ministry of International Trade and Industry (MITI), however, has specified that no cotton yarn or fabric may be exported without their approval of the terms of the sales contract. The agreed-upon price is checked in this review by the Japanese Government. If the price of the goods to be exported is considered to be lower than is considered fair, the license necessary for exporting is denied. These MITI determinations of fair price are not made on the basis of a fixed amount, but rather on consideration of the market situation and other germane factors. They serve to prevent unfair prices which might harm Japanese export trade.

*Transactions in secondary products*

The most notable difference between transactions relating to primary and secondary cotton textiles for export is that the American buyer or importer visits Japan for the purpose of placing an order. Scarce though spot transactions are in cotton fabrics, they are even rarer in made-up goods. Transactions, of necessity, are almost always on the basis of future delivery.

The American importer or buyer makes the trip to Japan in order to provide detailed instructions as to materials, sizes, style, design, color, buttons, sewing methods, folding, labeling, etc. In some cases, the basic cutout paper pattern is also provided. Such an importer gives personal supervision and attention to the manufacture of made-up goods from the beginning to the end. Protection is assured for original design and styling.

From the viewpoint of the Japanese manufacturer, however, having the buyer visit Japan is not always beneficial, for at times it has been known that buyers locate stock goods on which they make special deals at unusually low prices. They then terminate their contracts with the original sellers with whom they started business.

In other cases, the American importer may supply the Japanese exporter with raw materials secured in England, Germany, or the United States, etc., to be processed into an article—say, like gloves or brassieres—on a consignment basis.

In still other cases, the American importer is also a manufacturer in the United States. With such apparel wear as blouses and shirts, for instances, the Japanese manufacturer serves as a kind of subcontractor. This, incidentally, appears to be a growing trend.

In the field of made-up goods, the exporters have very few branches or affiliates in the United States, and none are engaged exclusively in the exportation of cotton made-up items. They are usually exporters with a wide variety of export textiles or general merchandise.

As with cotton yarn and cloth, even the large exporting companies with branches in the United States cannot afford to carry extensive overseas inventories to make for more profitable sales by being close to the market with readily available stock. Moreover, made-up articles are highly sensitive to consumer demand and style changes, so stocking of items is a particularly hazardous business at best.

Usually, letters of credit are opened 30 to 60 days before shipment. Since many of the manufacturers need the money for purchases of cloth material and processing charges, the letters of credit are put to use almost immediately after the contracts are signed in such cases.

In pricing of made-up cotton commodities, the manufacturers and exporters are often at the mercy of the buyers. If the buyer discovers that changes in fashion and style have made his order less salable, he often attempts to cancel his contract, leaving the manufacturer or exporter in a very bad bargaining position. Some buyers allege fashion changes as a bargaining device, but most American importers are fair in this regard.

Cancellation of contracts also take place for noncompliance or nonperformance. In nearly all of these events, it is virtually impossible to switch the sale of these products to the Japanese market because the styles may not be suited for Japanese consumption, or the sizes may be too large for the Japanese consumer, etc.

When situations like these arise, the buyer can just about set his own terms, especially with the smaller plants and mills.

As with other cotton goods, MITI has imposed a check on all made-up goods exported to the United States. The same check is made on made-up goods as with other cotton textiles, and for the same reason.

Made-up cotton articles subject to this MITI check include sweaters, cardigans, jackets, finished yarns, braids, tapes and cards, hose, cloth, knit cloth, lace cloth, underwear, nightclothes, shirts, sportswear, polo shirts, blouses, aprons, cooking aprons, business clothes, work clothes, coats, trousers, shirts, dresses and other outerwear, kimono, socks and stockings, tabi, hats, gloves, handkerchiefs, mufflers, scarfs, shawls, neckties, corsets, brassieres, diaper covers, pinafores, cuffs, furoshiki and other personal effects, floor coverings, curtains, blankets, bedsheets, pillowcases and other bedding materials, tablecloths, napkins, towels, Japanese-style towels, dishcloths, cushions, mosquito nets, and other household textiles.

### WORLD MARKET FOR JAPANESE TEXTILES

In any study of the problem of Japanese textiles in the American market, it is important that Japan's position in the total world market for textiles be considered, for one relates to the other in many ways.

*Japan's textiles markets*

As in prewar years—and understandably—the nearby Asian countries remain as Japan's best export market for cotton textiles. In 1956, Asian imports of cotton yarns totaled 92 percent of Japan's exports in the field, or 25 million pounds. Also 60 percent, or 765 million square yards, of Japan's exported cotton fabrics found themselves in the Asian market place.

Japan's export figures to other than Asian markets are as follows: 217 million square yards (17.2 percent) to North and South America, including the United States; 133 million square yards (10.5 percent) to Europe; 90 million square yards to Africa; and 57 million square yards to Oceania.

A comparison with prewar figures reveals a sharp decline in postwar cotton-cloth exports, due to a substantial decrease in shipments to Asian and African countries that has not been offset by increases to European markets.

Japan's prewar average (1934–36) exports were as follows: 1,717 million square yards (64.3 percent) to Asia; 485 million square yards (18.2 percent) to Africa; 306 million square yards (11.4 percent) to North and South America, including the United States; 88 million square yards to Oceania; and 75 million square yards to Europe.

Japanese cotton textiles are exported to nearly all of the countries in the free world, with a small amount of cloth exported to Red China, and some finer count cotton yarn to East Germany on a barter basis. Statistically, Japan's cotton yarn was exported to 59 different markets, while cotton cloth was shipped to 132 markets. For purposes of this breakdown, there are 35 markets in Asia, 18 in Europe, 30 in North and and South America, including the United States, 32 in Africa, and 17 in Oceania.

As for cotton-yarn exports in 1956, the major importers were Hong Kong (7,950,000 pounds), Burma (5,286,000 pounds), and Indochina (4,945,000 pounds), as well as Pakistan, East Germany, etc., in smaller quantities.

Last year, cotton cloth was exported to Indonesia (139 million square yards), Hong Kong (138 million square yards), United States (123 million square yards), Thailand (79 million square yards), and to Ceylon, Australia, Burma, British West Africa, Holland, and the United Kingdom in lesser amounts.

Before the war, China, British India (including Burma), Holland, and the East Indies were Japan's principal markets for cotton yarn, as well as Singapore, Indochina, and the Philippines.

British India (482 million square yards), Dutch East Indies (388 million square yards), China (329 million square yards), Egypt (168 million square yards), British East Asia (98 million square yards), and Australia (77 million square yards), followed by the Philippines, Singapore, Siam, French Morocco, Hong Kong, Iraq, Sudan, Aden, and the United States served as Japan's principal export market for cotton cloth in prewar days.

The most striking aspect of these figures is the great change that has taken place in the textile-trade patterns for Japan from its prewar period. An example which illustrates this startling shift is the prewar total of Japanese exports to British India (including Burma), China, Egypt, and Argentina, as compared with the postwar totals to these same countries. Taken as a group, prewar exports of Japanese cotton totaled 969 million square yards, while in 1956 it had dropped to 68 million square yards. The 1956 breakdown to these countries shows 3,100,000 square yards to India, 12 million square yards to Pakistan, 47,300,000 square yards to Burma, 5 million square yards to China, 200,000 square yards to Egypt, and 5,000 square yards to Argentina.

This decline in Japanese cotton textile exports in the postwar era is attributed to two principal developments: (1) a number of cotton-growing countries, such as India, have now become textile-manufacturing countries, and (2) the countries of the Communist world restrict cotton textile imports in favor of heavy machinery and capital goods.

*Changes in export textile construction*

In the prewar trade, gray goods constituted as much as 30 percent of Japan's total exports of cotton fabrics. By 1956, however, this had dropped to 18.9 percent. As gray goods declined in importance, bleached or dyed-cotton fabric, particularly printed or colored-yarn fabric, has grown in favor in recent years.

*Japanese cotton fabric export by description of process*

[In million square yards]

| | Average 1934–36 | | 1956 | |
|---|---|---|---|---|
| | Amount | Percent | Amount | Percent |
| Total | 2,670.8 | 100.0 | 1,262.0 | 100.0 |
| Gray | 893.7 | 33.5 | 235.3 | 18.7 |
| Bleached | 517.0 | 19.3 | 352.7 | 27.9 |
| Others | 1,260.1 | 47.2 | 674.0 | 53.4 |

Source: Customs Division of the Japanese Ministry of Finance.

The decline in Japan's exports of gray goods and low-quality bleached fabrics can be attributed directly to the emergence in Asia of two countries which have become her greatest competitors—newly independent India and Communist China. These two countries have nearly driven Japan out of the world market for low-grade goods, especially in reference to southeast Asia markets.

The rapid development of the cotton textile industries in India and Red China has forced Japan to emphasize bleached and finished cotton fabrics for the so-called medium or middle class and better trade.

Such bread and butter items as shirtings, sheetings, and drills made up more than 65 percent of Japan's total cotton textile exports in the prewar era. But, by 1956, the percentage of these key items had dropped to 51.2 percent. To partially offset this loss, in recent years such cotton goods as poplin, gingham, velveteen, and corduroy—which require considerable skill and technology—have become increasingly popular.

In cotton yarns, yarns of finer counts are increasing in the export trade, while those with lower counts are decreasing. Cotton fabrics with combed and dyed yarn are finding increasing favor, as are cotton fabrics with fast colors or special resin finishes.

The general trend in Japan indicates that the industry is shifting from cotton goods of low quality to those of higher quality.

Our understanding is that the farsighted textile leaders in Japan believe that only by switching to better quality goods can they compete with the low-price competition of India and Red China. To our way of thinking, this thesis holds true not only for Asia but also for America.

*GATT reservations on Japan*

In the postwar period, especially after she regained her sovereignty in 1952, Japan—stripped of her prewar possessions and prestige—realized that her only hope for economic survival was through international commerce and trade. With a newborn faith in democratic institutions, she embarked on a program to rehabilitate her cotton textile industry from the devastation and destruction of war as the foundation on which an export trade sufficient to enable her to exist could be built.

In this respect, it should be kept in mind that, contrary to popular belief in this country, the Japanese cotton-textile industry was not rebuilt with funds provided by the occupation authorities or by the United States Government. The industry was reconstructed by Japanese funds secured from Japanese sources.

During this difficult period, the United States—from the early days of the occupation to the present—has been an ally and champion of new Japan. It was through American sponsorship that, in September 1955, Japan became a member of the General Agreement on Tariffs and Trade (GATT). Through this membership, Japan expected to receive most-favored-nation treatment from other members of GATT. Fourteen nations, however, invoked article 35, reserving the right not to extend preferential treatment, against Japan. These nations are the United Kingdom, Holland, Belgium, Luxembourg, France, Austria, India, Federation of Rhodesia and Nyasaland, Union of South Africa, Brazil, Cuba, Haiti, Australia, and New Zealand.

The official reason given by these countries at the time article 35 was invoked against Japan was the expressed fear that a most-favored nation treatment would result in excessive imports from Japan, especially in cotton textiles, which would injure their respective domestic industries. The inconsistency of their declarations is exposed, however, when it is observed that many of these nations—United Kingdom, Holland, Belgium, Austria, and Australia, among others—have concluded special treaties with Japan granting near most-favored-nation consideration.

France, Union of South Africa, Federation of Rhodesia and Nyasaland, Cuba, and Haiti are among those which impose higher tariff schedules on Japanese textiles than that which is imposed on certain other countries.

*Japan and the British Commonwealth of nations*

The British Commonwealth of nations grants to each other a special imperial preference in the scheduling of tariff rates.

In some key markets of Africa and Asia, Japan attempts to compete against Indian and British imports at a great disadvantage.

The imperial preference is carried out by two types of schedules: (1) The 2-column, and (2) the 3-column schedules. The first column of tariffs is the imperial preference applied to Commonwealth nations, and the second column in the two-column system applies the maximum duty to non-Commonwealth members. The three-column system divides its tariffs into those for (1) imperial preference, (2) most-favored nation, and (3) general or maximum rates.

Two-column countries include British West Africa and British East Africa, while three-column countries include New Zealand, Union of South Africa, and, until recently, Australia.

Under both of these systems, Japanese textiles are subject to the general or maximum tariffs.

*Quantitative restrictions*

In addition to tariff barriers, many countries impose quantitative restrictions on imports through exchange controls and/or allocation of foreign exchange.

Japanese textile exports face these problems in many sections of the world, but Japan is particularly hard hit by those imposed by the Southeast Asian countries which have developed into important markets in these postwar years.

Southeast Asia nations suffer with their low standard of living, and in many cases their prosperity is dependent almost completely on the price of such primary products as tin, rice, jute, iron ore, rubber, and petroleum. If there is any wide fluctuation on the world market for these items, the economy of these nations is affected. Any decline in their exports forces an immediate decline in their foreign-exchange holdings. Japanese cotton textiles are needed in these areas, but Japan cannot depend on the availability of these markets over the years.

Ceylon, Indonesia, Burma, and Thailand are among the Southeast Asia countries which exercise export-import controls through licensing systems or by allocating foreign-exchange funds. All have been, and are, principal export markets for Japanese textiles.

Another restrictive system that the Japanese must contend with is the open account or bilateral trade arrangement. Under this system, the quantity of cotton textiles, for illustration, is limited by an agreement. If the volume of trade between the two signatories fails to reach expectations, imports are limited to less than the maximum authorized under the arrangement. Japan has such agreements now with Indonesia, Burma, and Thailand.

In other market areas, there may be demand for Japanese textiles but the country involved may not be in a position to purchase the textiles. They have no money with which to pay for the textiles; neither do they have the raw materials that Japan needs to buy in exchange for her textiles. Such situations obviously restrict possible trade. The Belgian Congo is an example. Though there is a recognized demand for Japanese textiles, it has little to sell that Japan needs.

Still other nations limit textile imports in order to protect infant industry. Many of these countries—such as Brazil, Chile, Peru,

India, China, Pakistan, Egypt, and Argentina—were among Japan's best customers in prewar days.

Moreover, such nations as India and Red China have become formidable competitors for the world market in textiles, with a promise that they will become even more successful as their infant industries grow.

*United Kingdom Trade Agreement*

Exports, in the main, to British Commonwealth nations are governed by a payments agreement between Japan and the United Kingdom. The volume of trade between the sterling area, dominated by Britain, and Japan is determined by a separate trade-agreement estimate made on an annual basis. During the past few years, Japanese cotton exports to this sterling bloc amounted to about 500 million square yards.

Under the new agreement promulgated February 1957, the formula for payment has been amended to regulate trade between only Japan and the United Kingdom. In other words, the agreement no longer covers the entire sterling area.

Japan is now free to try to negotiate separately with each of the British dominions and territories to remove trade barriers and to increase trade. This new freedom to try to negotiate directly for market areas, bypassing London, is not expected to cause immediate changes in the traditional trade patterns in this formerly imperial framework.

*Japan and the European common market*

A new factor in the overseas market for Japanese textiles is the recently established European common market.

It is, of course, difficult to estimate its impact on the total world-trade picture as yet. Japanese exporters, as well as those from the United States and other countries, are carefully watching and studying developments in order to ascertain the implications of the European common market for all exporting powers.

Japanese cotton-textile exports to the 6 countries involved in the European common market in 1956 amounted to about 60 million square yards. Most of the fabrics shipped to this market were gray cloth for reprocessing for use in the area and for reexport.

Even greater consequences are expected if the so-called European free-trade area is realized. Last year, Japan's exports of cotton textiles to this area totaled more than 128 million square yards of fabrics, or about 10 percent of all Japanese cotton-fabric exports.

The success and the trade practices developed by both the European common market and the European free-trade area, especially their attitude toward nonmembers in the matter of import duties, import restrictions, and so forth, will have far-reaching consequences throughout the free world, especially with reference to such nations as Japan that must trade to live.

The problem becomes even more complex when considered in the context of textile shipments from India and Hong Kong to the United Kingdom, where the British home industry—even now—is constantly complaining and demanding curbs. If the United Kingdom, for instance, becomes a part of the free-trade area and thereby is compelled to restrict imports from India and Hong Kong, these two rapidly developing textile-exporting areas will be forced to seek other outlets. Their entry into the world market under these circumstances would make for even more intensified competition. Textile exports from Japan would not be alone in its difficulties; the United States and every other country that engages in the export trade will be affected materially.

*Cotton cloth exports from Japan, India, and Hong Kong to Europe in 1956*

| | Japan (1,000 square yards) | | India (1,000 yards) | Hong Kong (million square yards) |
|---|---|---|---|---|
| Belgium and Luxembourg | 2,679 | (2,279) | | |
| France | ------ | ------ | | |
| West Germany | 18,339 | (18,001) | | |
| Holland | 38,232 | (37,393) | | |
| Italy | 1,052 | (977) | | |
| Total (common market) | 60,302 | (58,650) | | |
| United Kingdom | 35,994 | (35,739) | 91,025 | 140.25 |
| Austria | 6,971 | (6,633) | | |
| Denmark | 3,874 | (1,011) | | |
| Norway | 41 | (41) | | |
| Sweden | 15,672 | (13,206) | | |
| Switzerland | 5,706 | (5,403) | | |
| Total (free trade area) | 128,560 | (120,683) | 91,025 | 140.25 |

NOTE.—Figures in parentheses represent gray cotton cloth.
Source: Japan, Ministry of Finance; India, Accounts Relating to the Trade and Navigation of India; Hong Kong, The Cotton Board; England, Quarterly Statistical Review.

Any restrictive action taken by any market area, especially such a large and impressive area as that contemplated in the European free-trade area, will seriously influence the world textile market as such.

What the Japanese cotton-textile exporters fear most, we are informed, is that a liberalization of trade within the European area will bring about severe restrictions against imports from other areas. At this point, we understand, the Japanese industry is not so worried about stronger competition developing from a revitalized European cotton industry as it is that markets will be closed or barred to them by one device or another.

Since it is axiomatic that what happens to the Japanese cotton textile industry, or the industry of any other country, also happens to the United States industry, it seems evident to us that it is in the interests of our country, as a leading exporting power, to use American influence to prevent any restrictive policy against imports by the European trade area from nonarea countries.

After all, the more the United States trades with other countries, the more these other countries may buy from and sell to us. This is as true for Japan as it is for any other free nation, and the end results in this situation are that Japan is by far a better customer for our goods than we are for what she sells to us. This adds up to good business for the United States.

*Prospects of the Red China market*

AIJT is aware of the considerable talk among domestic industry leaders and in the Congress during the past year regarding the possibilities for Japan to open up larger markets in Red China as an alternate solution to her exportation of cotton commodities to the United States. As a matter of fact, a Senator from a textile-producing Southern State suggested during a hearing on American trade policy that the United States should sell raw cotton to Japan to be processed and sold to Communist China. Such possibilities have not only been discussed in this country but also in Japan.

In Japan, particularly since the imposition of the severe quota limitations on velveteens earlier this year, there has been increasing discussion among the velveteen and corduroy manufacturers, as well as among gingham makers, to increase sales to Red China.

In terms of actual shipments of Japanese cotton yarn to Communist China, the volume has increased but still remains small.

What the prospects for the future are remains in the realm of pure guesswork, though certain Japanese exporters envision a rapidly expanding export trade. Our own estimates are that the bright promise for increased trade is illusory.

*Cotton yarn export to Red China*

[In thousand pounds]

| | 1954 | 1955 | 1956 | 1957 January-April |
|---|---|---|---|---|
| Gray, 20s-40s | 34 | 40 | 390 | |
| Bleached, dyed, or mercerized cotton yarn | | | 20 | |
| Total | 34 | 40 | 410 | |

Source: Japanese Ministry of Finance.

If the figures for the first 4 months are projected until the end of the year (1957), there will be a sharp decline in shipments of cotton fabrics to Red China as compared to 1956.

The volume of trade in the past 3 years has been comparatively small, and the prospects for the future seem definitely limited even though Japan has announced increased general trade with the Communist mainland.

The table below reveals comparative figures for cotton fabrics for 1954, 1955, 1956, and the first quarter of 1957.

*Japanese cotton cloth export to Red China*

[In thousand square yards]

| | 1954 | 1955 | 1956 | 1957, January to April |
|---|---|---|---|---|
| Gray: | | | | |
| Shirtings | 5,203 | 1,613 | 3 | |
| Sheetings | 736 | 160 | 600 | |
| Ducks | | | 20 | |
| Others | | | 10 | |
| Total | 5,939 | 1,773 | 633 | |
| Bleached: | | | | |
| Sheetings | | | 8 | 103 |
| Poplins | 508 | 98 | 547 | 147 |
| Jeans | | | 31 | |
| Shirtings | 168 | | | 176 |
| Others | | | | |
| Total | 676 | 98 | 586 | 426 |
| Dyed: | | | | |
| Shirtings | | | 38 | |
| Poplins | 99 | | 97 | |
| Drills | | 172 | 292 | 11 |
| Velveteen and corduroy | | | 638 | |
| Sheetings | | | | 64 |
| Others | | 29 | 330 | 79 |
| Total | 99 | 201 | 1,394 | 154 |
| Printed: | | | | |
| Shirtings | | | 496 | |
| Poplins | | | 1,050 | |
| Velveteen and corduroy | | | 535 | |
| Drills | 43 | | | |
| Others | | | 344 | |
| Total | 43 | | 2,425 | |
| Others: | | | | |
| Others | | | 62 | |
| Velveteen and corduroy | 270 | 674 | | |
| Total | 270 | 674 | 62 | |
| Grand total | 7,027 | 2,746 | 5,100 | 580 |

Source: Japanese Ministry of Finance.

As for "made up" goods, realistically, there seems to be very little prospect for an expanding market, partly due to the embargo imposed by the Chincom (China Committee) list . Even if this embargo were lifted completely, Japanese exporters are under no illusion as to the amount of business that may be developed.

Because there exists in Red China some demand for velveteen, corduroy, waterproof poplin, high-grade satin, and a few other fabrics, it is possible to say that there is a theoretical potential for exporting cotton apparel made from such fabrics, but the greatly improved status of the apparel industry in Communist China makes such a possibility very remote. This is especially so in a controlled economy such as Red China's.

Practically no shipments were made to Red China of "made up" goods as the chart below shows.

*Japanese cotton made-up goods export to Red China*

| | |
|---|---|
| 1954 | Nil. |
| 1955 | Nil. |
| 1956 | Underwears (not knitted), 160 dozens valued at 408,000 yen |
| 1957, January to April | Nil. |

Source: Japanese Ministry of Finance.

Rather than attempting to increase the Red Chinese market for Japanese textiles, leaders of the Japanese industry, we understand, are fearful of the recent and increasingly aggressive efforts of the Communist Chinese to compete in those traditional markets of Southeast Asia, such as Indonesia and Hong Kong. These increases in textile exports have come despite shortages of cotton textiles in the home (Red Chinese) market.

According to a survey of the All Japan Cotton Spinners Association, cotton fabric exports from Communist China is estimated to have increased from 28 million square yards in 1951 to about 260 million square yards in 1956, only 5 years later. Out of this 1956 Red Chinese export total, about 134 million square yards were shipped to Indonesia and 100 million square yards to Hong Kong, both being historic Japanese outlets.

In spite of Red China's rapid growth as a cotton-textile exporter, there are some who hold out hope that Communist China is a potential market for certain fabrics which she may not be able to produce in her present stage of development. Nevertheless, this prospective market of more than 600 million customers means very little to realistic Japanese who are aware that Communist China adheres closely to a barter system of exchange which favors capital over consumer goods. Moreover, Red China may well use her trade as a means to foment political dissension and subversion, rather than as a means of commerce. Some propaganda of this kind is already discerned among Japanese velveteen manufacturers.

The consensus, we have been informed, is that Japanese cotton textile leaders do not anticipate any large-scale trade with Red China; indeed, they fear instead the encroachment of Red China into the traditional Southeast Asia markets of the Japanese.

At best, any textile trade with Red China will be limited to certain constructions.

But most apprehensive are those Japanese textile leaders who see the growing competitive power of Red China as a challenge; they fear that what Japan may lose to Communist Chinese inroads into third markets may be considerably greater than any exports to the China mainland.

Finally, the Japanese have long experience in dealing with the Russians and the Chinese. And, they are cognizant that Communist tactics often utilize trade as a weapon in economic welfare. They do not relish the thought that Japan may be reduced to economic servitude under communism, whether it be under the control of Soviet Russia or Red China, or both.

These are some of the factors which lead us to believe as American importers of Japanese textiles that prospective Japanese trade with Red China has been greatly overrated for one reason or another.

*Future Japanese markets*

Because the Japanese must export to live, Japanese cotton-textile exporters are constantly searching for new outlets and ways in which to expand existing markets. This is especially true at this time when exports have not reached the state of development that marks home consumption.

Frankly put, future prospects for the Japanese cotton textile export industry cannot be described as optimistic and encouraging. If anything, the reverse is true. The development of cotton-textile industries in many nations which heretofore had been profitable markets for Japanese cotton-textile exports and the phenomenal advances in synthetics and other manmade fibers may well foredoom the Japanese industry unless there are new and as yet unforeseen evolutions in the industry.

What the future holds in Europe with the beginnings of a common market and a free-trade area cannot be forecast, but already other areas such as Latin America are thinking in terms of a common market of their own.

All of these developments make it increasingly important that the United States not only provide Japan with a fair share of our own market but also that we exert our leadership for a more liberal trade policy throughout the free world, lest the various geographical and political communities establish tight, self-sufficient economic entities in which there will be no intercourse, commercial or otherwise, between peoples, nations, and trade units. Such economic isolationism presently threatens, and Japan will not be the sole victim if such thinking reaches its ultimate conclusion.

## VOLUNTARY QUOTAS AND THEIR IMPACT

Much has been written and said about the so-called voluntary quotas accepted by the Japanese textile industry.

This section attempts to explain the why and the how of these unprecedented illustrations of international self-restraint.

*Background*

Starting January 1, 1956, the Japanese cotton textile industry imposed what has been described as "voluntary self-restraint quotas" on cotton textile exports to the United States.

There has been much speculation as to the basic motivation for these voluntary controls, but as importers of Japanese textiles we are convinced that the explanation offered by Kojiro Abe, chairman of the All Japan Cotton Spinners Association, speaking not only for his own association but also the Japan Cotton Weavers Association, the Japan

Cotton Textile Exporters Association, and the Japan Textile Products Exporters Association, to the so-called Boggs Subcommittee on Customs, Tariffs, and Reciprocal Trade Agreements last December (1956) in Tokyo, expresses the general sentiments of the Japanese industry.

In his statement Chairman Abe declared:

While much has been said and inferred about the so-called voluntary quotas imposed by the Japanese textile industry early this year, may I state unequivocally on behalf of the four associations (All Japan Cotton Spinners Association, Japan Cotton Weavers Association, Japan Cotton Textile Exporters Association, and the Japan Textile Products Exporters Association) that the underlying inspiration as far as many of us were concerned was our regard for the maintenance of cordial Japanese-American relations. It is conceded, of course, that the clamor and demands for legislative and administrative restrictions on the part of the American industry disturbed many of our members who, quite honestly, could not understand the urgency or necessity for such outcries. We could not comprehend the apprehension of the United States cotton manufacturers because, overall, Japan purchases 4 to 5 times as much raw cotton as we export to the United States in finished or processed goods and because our cotton cloth exports to the United States, for instance, amount to less than 1½ percent of the American production.

On the other hand, it should be known that the Japanese Government, fearful that the mounting vociferousness of the American textile industry would seriously endanger international goodwill between our two nations, urged our industry to take voluntary measures of self-restraint, even at great sacrifice to ourselves, in order to maintain our good relations.

Because our industry has consistently been pro-United States in our attitude, probably more so than any other Japanese industry, we agreed to our Government's suggestion and adopted what have come to be known as voluntary quotas.

We did this, not as an admission of the validity of the charges made against us, but in the spirit that, even though our own industry might suffer materially, the international friendship and comity involved between our two nations transcended the problems of any single industry, no matter how vital to Japan.

Though there may be a tendency in the United States to accept these adjustment measures with cynicism, may I assure you again that these so-called voluntary quotas were adopted in good faith, at great sacrifice and hardship to both management and industry. Proof of our good faith is indicated in our specific procedures and program to implement the provisions of these self-restraint measures.

The voluntary quotas imposed in 1956 limited the overall shipments of cotton fabrics to 150 million square yards, with specific quotas for such individual items as print cloth (20 million square yards), velveteen (5 million square yards), gingham (70 million square yards), blouses (1,500,000 dozen), and other articles like sports shirts, damask tablecloths, and shorts.

Even though these voluntary restrictions were imposed with considerable sacrifice to bring about better Japanese-American understanding and cooperation, the American cotton manufacturers continued their unrelenting attack against Japanese cotton-textile imports. Some cynics might have interpreted these Japanese controls as a sign of weakness or an admission of guilt; at any rate, it seemed to many of us importers that the announcement of these voluntary quotas seemed to be the signal for our domestic industry to accelerate their demands for protection, rather than acceptance of a good-will gesture in the spirit in which it was made.

Representatives of domestic industry bombarded the Congress with demands for mandatory import quotas against Japanese textiles in violation of our expressed foreign-trade policy. They also filed numerous petitions with the United States Tariff Commission under section 7 of the Trade Agreements Extension Act of 1955, requesting escape-clause relief for domestic gingham, blouse, pillowcase, and velveteen industries; demanded recommendations by the Secretary of Agriculture, under section 22 of the Agricultural Adjustment Act of 1935, to the President for the imposition of quotas on cotton-textile imports; organized boycott movements against the purchase of Japanese textiles in a number of communities; and attempted to extend discriminatory Japanese textile sign laws from South Carolina and Alabama to other States, including Georgia, Louisiana, Connecticut, and Rhode Island.

Because of these inspired pressures and a seemingly deteriorating situation in trade relations between Japan and the United States, discussions were held between the United States and Japanese Governments. Through the negotiations carried on by these intergovernmental conversations, a decision was reached that these voluntary quotas should be extended. The announcement of the decision was made by the Japanese Government-sponsored Japan Textile Export Council, in the following public statement:

On September 27, 1956, the export council decided on its basic policy in regard to the voluntary adjustment measures for cotton-textile exports to the United States to be made effective from January 1, 1957.

In accordance with this policy, the council thereafter continued its study of the substance of the measures to be adopted, while at the same time the Japanese Government conducted frank exchanges of views with the United States Government with a view to reflecting American desires in the substances of these measures and thereby securing their effectiveness. Accordingly, in formulating the draft of the present measures, the views and desires of the United States side were fully taken into consideration.

The export council today deliberated upon and adopted the conclusions reached as a result of the above study. The voluntary adjustment measures to be put into effect at the risk of great hardships and sacrifices on the part of the Japanese industry are aimed at eliminating apprehensions held by the American industry toward the importation of Japanese cotton textiles and thereby preventing movements against the import of such goods, especially the materialization of these movements in the form of increased tariffs, discriminatory State legislation and restrictive import legislation, and at maintaining and developing amicable trade relations between Japan and the United States.

For the foregoing reason, the present voluntary control measures are based on the condition that the United States Government would take all feasible steps to solve the problem of discriminatory State textile legislation and to prevent further restrictive action with regard to the importation of Japanese textiles into the United States.

The gist of the measures decided upon with respect to exports to the United States is as follows:

(1) The overall limit for Japanese exports of cotton textiles to the United States shall be 235 million square yards annually, of which the limits for cotton cloth and cotton made-up goods shall be 113 and 122 million square yards, respectively.

(2) As to cotton cloth, with a view to avoiding excessive concentration on any particular item, specific limits shall be established for velveteens, ginghams, combed yarn fabrics, etc. For velveteens and ginghams the limits shall be 2.5 and 35 million square yards, respectively, both for 1957 and 1958, and the limit for combed yarn fabrics shall be 26 million square yards.

(3) With regard to the made-up goods, specific limits for pillowcases, handkerchiefs, brassieres, T-shirts, etc., shall be established in addition to those limits already in effect for blouses, sport shirts, shorts, and damask tablecloths.

(4) Exports from Japan to the United States of particular items shall be distributed equally by quarter as far as practicable and as necessary to meet seasonal demands.

(5) The program shall be of 5 years' duration, beginning 1957, subject, however, to an annual review.

*Quota breakdown*

The overall quota for all Japanese cotton-textile exports to the United States was limited to 235 million square yards, or less than 2½ percent of the total American production of like textiles.

The overall quantitative quota is subdivided into five major groups or categories, as follows:

| | | Square yards |
|---|---|---|
| Group | I. Cotton cloth | 113,000,000 |
| | II. Made-up goods, usually included in United States cotton broad-woven goods production | 30,000,000 |
| | III. Woven apparel | 71,000,000 |
| | IV. Knit goods | 12,000,000 |
| | V. Miscellaneous cotton textiles | 9,000,000 |
| | Total | 235,000,000 |

Within the group I, cotton cloth, category specific quotas were set for ginghams (35 million square yards), velveteens (2,500,000 square yards), and other fabrics (75,500,000 square yards). The gingham and velveteen quotas are effective for 2 years—1957 to 1958.

Within the "other fabrics" limitation, specific quotas were set for sheeting (50 million square yards), shirtings (80-by-80 type) (20 million square yards), other shirtings (43 million square yards), twill and sateen (39 million square yards), poplin (25 million square yards), yarn dyed fabrics (24 million square yards), and other fabrics (44 million square yards). In this category, the total exports of fabrics made from comb warp and filling are not to exceed 26 million yards.

Within the Group II, made-up goods usually included in the United States cotton, broad woven, category, specific quotas were established for pillowcases (plain) (400,000 dozen), dish towels (800,000 dozen), handkerchiefs (1,200,000 dozen), table damask (value of $3,720,000, or an estimated 468,000 dozen sets), and other items (1,875,000 pounds, based on a conversion basis of 4.6 yards to 1 pound of cotton).

Within the group III, woven-apparel, category specific quotas are designated for blouses (1,500,000 dozen), sport shirts (750,000 dozen), dress and work shirts (300,000 dozen), brassieres and other body-supporting garments (600,000 dozen), shorts and trousers (600,000 dozen), and other woven apparel (2,321,000 pounds).

Within the group IV, knit goods, category specific quotas are listed for men's and boys' T-shirts (short sleeve, white, no button, no collar, usually round neck, sometimes V-neck, commonly called marukubi shirt in Japan) (500,000 dozen), gloves and mittens (450,000 dozen), and other knit goods (1,477,000 pounds).

Within the group V, miscellaneous cotton textiles, category no specific quotas are established, but the principle of diversification and avoidance of excessive concentration on any particular item was recognized. Cotton floor coverings, fish nets and netting, cotton thread, etc., are included in this classification.

The Japanese, furthermore, agreed that, with respect to made-up goods, no specific quota would be established, but that the Japanese Government will consult with the United States Government to determine appropriate courses of action whenever it appears that there is—

developing an excessive concentration of exports in a particular item, or if there are other problems (e. g., possible problems resulting from excessive concentration of exports of end items made from a particular type of fabric, such as the

**use of gingham in the manufacture of an excessively large portion of exported blouses, sport shirts, etc.).**

*Operation of voluntary quotas*

The administration of the voluntary quota system is supervised by the Japan Cotton Textile Exporters Association, whose membership exports over 90 percent of all cotton fabrics sent to this country, as far as cotton-fabric exports are concerned, and by the Japan Textile Products Exporters Association, whose membership exports nearly all of the cotton made-up goods, as far as these made-up items are concerned.

These associations are responsible for determining the quota allocations for each exporter. They are, accordingly, in a strategic position to enforce the intent of the voluntary textile agreement. The relatively few exporters who do not belong to these organizations are controlled by MITI, which enforces the voluntary quotas by authority of the export-import transaction law.

The regulations drawn up by the Japan Cotton Textile Exporters Association may be summarized as follows:

1. Coverage: All cotton fabrics exported to the United States.

2. Determination of quotas:

(*a*) An overall annual quota is established for all cotton fabrics exported to the United States. This annual quota is then divided into quarterly quotas.

(*b*) Within the annual and quarterly quotas, separate quotas are established for print cloth, gingham, velveteen, poplin, twill, sateen, sheetings, and others.

(*c*) Individual quotas are determined by the following formula: The percentage of export performance of each individual exporter is measured against the total performance of all members during the base 2½-year period from January 1, 1953, to June 30, 1955. This percentage figure for the individual exporter is multiplied by 70 percent of the overall quota on an annual or quarterly basis. The computed figure is the quota limit that is assigned the individual exporter.

(*d*) The balance of 30 percent (100 percent minus 70 percent of the quota assigned to the individual exporters) of the overall quota is set aside as a reserve for potential exports of new or unspecified items for which demand may develop.

(*e*) Transshipments through third countries are prohibited, and violators are subject to expulsion from the association and the loss of any quota allocation made to them as individual exporters.

2. Administration of quotas:

(*a*) Any member who completes an export contract for sale of cotton fabrics to the United States must report the contents of his contract to the association.

(*b*) The member exporter is also required to submit his application for export approval to MITI, under the provisions of the export trade control ordinance. The application to MITI is also submitted to the association for checks against any discrepancy between the application and the report made to the association.

(*c*) The member exporter is required to submit copies of all shipping documents to the association within 7 days after the actual shipment is made.

In a general way, the export quota administration of the Japan Textile Products Exporters Association is comparable to that of the Japan Cotton Textile Exporters Association, described above. This association not only cooperates in limiting exports under the voluntary quotas but its members voluntarily impose a number of special regulations pertaining to quality, price, terms and conditions of sale, prevention of design copying, and other export matters.

*Attitude on transshipments*

Both the Japan Cotton Textile Exporters Association and the Japan Textile Products Exporters Association are aware that transshipments may well result in such circumvention of the voluntary quota restrictions that United States industry leaders may charge them with bad faith in establishing these controls. They are informed of the comments of domestic textile leaders and of the trade press relating to this subject.

Both associations have strong provisions against transshipments through third countries in their regulations. The violators are subject to expulsion from the association, which is tantamount to the loss of quota allocations.

The enforcement of the prohibition against transshipment is extremely difficult, especially since the importer is under no obligation to observe the quotas imposed by the exporters. Nevertheless, the Japanese control associations are doing everything possible to prevent transshipments. They have stopped shipments of certain goods to such well-known transshipment points as Hong Kong. They have investigated every case of alleged transshipment carefully and honestly. They have even requested the cooperation of our Treasury and Commerce Departments to prevent this practice. They have established special quotas for areas other than the United States for the express purpose of preventing transshipments into this country.

*Transshipments through Central and South America*

Illustrative of the sincerity of the Japanese in trying to discourage and prevent transshipments may be seen in the procedures set up to stop transshipments to this country through such third countries as those in Central and South America.

The Japan Cotton Textile Exporters Association describes their procedure thusly, after stating that its purpose is to prevent cotton textiles exported to Central and South America from being transshipped to the United States in violation of the spirit of the voluntary quotas:

*Before shipment.*—(*a*) When cotton textiles are to be exported to Central and South America, members are required to present their export contract report to the association, prior to submission to MITI. This report is to be checked by the merchandise surveying committee for Central and South America.

(*b*) The exporter must furnish proof that the items in question will not be transshipped to the United States when his shipments include—

(1) All cotton cloth exports to Central and South America shipped via the United States.

(2) All cotton cloth exported directly to these countries which are in great demand in the United States and cloth which is sus-

pected of possible transshipment to the United States by the merchandise surveying committee for Central and South America.

(c) The committee shall investigate and study all reports. It is empowered to determine (1) whether the fabrics in question may enter the United States through transshipment, or (2) whether additional documentary evidence and other information are needed to assure that no transshipment will take place.

(d) If it is decided that additional documents and information are required, the exporter must present such documents as requested by the association before his application for export license is presented to MITI.

(e) Certificates of customs clearance issued by the importing country, including the certificate of reexport when involved, must be submitted to the association within a prescribed period. To signify his good faith, the exporter of suspected shipments must deposit a guaranty bond with the association prior to his application for an export license, as security for his promise to furnish the requested documents.

*After shipment.*—The association checks all invoices and makes certain that shipments have been made in conformity with the issued export license.

*Penalty.*—Violators are subject to a fine equivalent to 5 percent of the export value f. o. b., as described in the application for export license. They may also be expelled from the association.

Experience thus far indicates that importers as a rule have cooperated with the Japanese exporters to prevent transshipments of nonquota textiles to the United States. But, it is evident that the Japanese Government and industry are fully aware of the necessity to stop improper transshipments and are meeting the challenge in an unprecedented manner which denotes their good faith in the matter.

*Impact of quotas on Japanese textile industry*

Although in some of our textile circles the voluntary quotas imposed by the Japanese are ridiculed as meaningless gestures, to our mind they have had real impact on the Japanese textile industry and have caused serious hardships that are little known or appreciated in this country.

As might be expected, the hardest hit are those segments of the Japanese industry whose exports have been most drastically curtailed, notably the manufacturers of velveteens, ginghams, and certain made-up goods.

*Impact on velveteen industry*

The information submitted is taken from a report prepared by the Tenryusha Textile Industry Cooperative Association of Fude-machi in Shizuoka Prefecture, the center of the Japanese velveteen industry.

As of September 1956, the Japanese velveteen and corduroy industry consisted of 1,303 mills equipped with 20,930 looms. Of these mills, 93.9 percent or 1,223 mills with 18,413 looms are concentrated in a small section of Shizuoka Prefecture in central Japan. These small mills average about 18 looms each.

Because of the heavy geographical concentration of small mills whose production is limited to specialty items such as velveteens, any significant fluctuation in demand has a severe effect not only on the mills themselves but also on the surrounding communities. The consequences of the demands of its United States counterpart, consisting of only 3 mills at the most, which resulted in the imposition of a voluntary quota by the Japanese Government of 2,500,000 square yards, was dramatically illustrated when more than 100 representatives of the velveteen industry petitioned the American Embassy last winter for fair consideration and understanding.

Although the closing of velveteen mills may not be attributed to the imposition of the quotas alone, it is, nevertheless, persuasive to note that 4 mills employing some 50 workers closed in a single month, June 1957—the last month reported. In this connection, it should be mentioned in passing that these mills are operated on a paternalistic basis and are not closed down unless there are absolutely no alternatives. It is known, for instance, that a number of mills are kept in operation simply to provide employment, even at a loss to management.

Aside from the weaving mills, several dozen cutting mills were also shut down, presumably because of the voluntary quotas. In Japan, cutting is done by hand by specialists trained for this type of work.

Fortunately, some of the mills were able to shift production to other textiles than velveteens, although, in most cases, some employees had to be dismissed in spite of all efforts made to provide them some employment.

The impact of the quota—which was arbitrarily set at less than half of the exports to the United States in the previous year—on the Japanese velveteen industry is shown in the following table:

*Operation of Japanese velveteen industry (cutting) in 1956*

| | Number of installed machines | Number of workers required | Operating | | Idle | |
|---|---|---|---|---|---|---|
| | | | Machine | Workers | Machine | Workers |
| 1956—January | 5,996 | 6,895 | 3,117 | 3,854 | 2,819 | 3,241 |
| February | 6,016 | 6,918 | 3,068 | 3,618 | 2,948 | 3,300 |
| March | 6,016 | 6,918 | 3,008 | 3,459 | 3,008 | 3,459 |
| April | 6,096 | 7,010 | 3,048 | 3,505 | 3,048 | 3,505 |
| May | 6,096 | 6,975 | 3,048 | 3,505 | 3,048 | 3,505 |
| June | 6,066 | 6,975 | 3,214 | 3,696 | 2,552 | 3,279 |
| July | 6,066 | 6,975 | 4,792 | 5,502 | 1,274 | 1,473 |
| August | 6,066 | 6,975 | 3,942 | 4,533 | 2,124 | 2,442 |
| September | 6,166 | 7,090 | 4,007 | 4,608 | 2,159 | 2,482 |
| October | 5,966 | 6,860 | 3,161 | 3,635 | 2,805 | 3,225 |
| November | 5,946 | 6,839 | 2,616 | 3,008 | 3,330 | 3,829 |
| December | 5,906 | 6,791 | 2,303 | 2,648 | 2,103 | 3,143 |
| January-December average | 6,023 | 6,826 | 3,252 | 3,686 | 2,771 | 3,140 |
| 1957—January | 5,969 | 6,846 | 1,787 | 2,053 | 4,172 | 4,893 |

NOTE 1.—Figures for February, March, April, and May are approximately the same with January 1957.
NOTE 2.—Number of workers required are computed at 1.15 persons per machine.

**According to this report, the figures for February, March, April, and May are approximately the same as those for January. They show that the Japanese velveteen industry is operating at about 35 percent capacity, and that the operating machinery decreased some 50 percent in the year 1957 from 1956. Mill employment in this same period dropped 61 percent. The report concludes the reduction imposed by the quota—from 5 million square yards in 1956 to 2.5 million square yards in 1957 is responsible for these losses.**

*Japanese production in twill-back velveteen*

[In square yards]

| | 1955 | 1956 | 1957 |
|---|---|---|---|
| January | 40,350 | 508,756 | 46,496 |
| February | 84,152 | 355,260 | 40,946 |
| March | 204,516 | 682,641 | 38,571 |
| April | 310,941 | 674,824 | 67,083 |
| May | 369,439 | 300,093 | 53,053 |
| June | 293,298 | 140,856 | 64,505 |
| July | 276,152 | 344,084 | |
| August | 286,836 | 108,075 | |
| September | 208,836 | 79,702 | |
| October | 157,210 | 103,562 | |
| November | 189,078 | 132,694 | |
| December | 198,124 | 112,944 | |
| Total | 2,618,856 | 3,543,491 | 310,654 |

NOTES.—(1) Including other twill velveteens than S/No. 3020. (2) Including both export and domestic. (3) Based on the second inspection volume.

The production figures on twill-back velveteens are particularly meaningful, since this specialized production is geared almost entirely for export to the United States market. The statistics show a 90-percent drop in production in January 1957, compared to January 1956; 88 percent for February; 94 percent for March; 90 percent for April; 82 percent for May; and 47 percent for June.

*Impacts of United States restriction on Japanese velveteen imports*

| Year | Quantitative restriction (million square yards) | Weaving section | | Cutting section | |
|---|---|---|---|---|---|
| | | Idle machines | Jobless workers | Idle machines | Jobless workers |
| 1955 | 7.0 | | | | |
| 1956 | 5.0 | 555 | 185 | 444 | 510 |
| 1957 | 2.5 | 1,333 | 444 | 1,000 | 1,150 |

NOTES.—(1) Calculated in terms of velveteen S/No. 3020. (2) Weaving machine, on the basis of 16-hour working day. (3) Cutting machine, on the basis of 10-hour working day.

These figures are calculated in terms of velveteen S/No. 3020, the operation of weaving machines on a 16-hour day basis, and for cutting on a 10-hour day basis. These figures demonstrate the tremendous impact that the quota restrictions have had on the Japanese industry from the standpoint of production alone. These figures also show that the cutting segment of the industry suffered more than the weaving, in which idle machinery more than doubled in 1957 from 1956, as did the number of unemployed workers.

Last year, two special representations were made to the American consular officials who visited the area. On both occasions, the Japanese industry spokesmen expressed the hope that the United States would recognize the need to import such articles as velveteens which are best suited to small and medium enterprises which can man the mills with adequate labor at minimum cost. They explained that only in these fields of labor intense manufacturing can the Japanese compete with American mass production techniques.

There are reports from the velveteen industry that there is an increasing demand for expanded trade with Red China. Although it should be emphasized that the leaders of the industry have little hope for any large-scale trade with the Chinese mainland, especially since it would have to be on a barter basis, it is, nevertheless, disturbing to us in this country that some of those in the historically most pro-American segment of the Japanese cotton textile industry are beginning to look toward Red China from necessity.

*Impact on gingham industry*

The information on the impact of quotas on the gingham industry is taken from a report by the Banshu Textile Industry Cooperative Association in Hyogo Prefecture, the center of the Japanese industry, where 85 percent of the manufacturing is concentrated. The average size of these mills near Kobe, in Hyogo Prefecture, is small, numbering some 18 looms each.

The Banshu association reports that 70 mills with more than a thousand employees were closed down in 1956, while in 1957 (January to June), 23 mills with 390 employees were shut down. As in the case of velveteens, all of the shutdowns cannot be attributed solely to the imposition of the quota, but the evidence is clear that it was the principal factor. As far as small mill operations are concerned, it should be kept in mind that the cancellation of a single substantial order can force bankruptcy.

***Estimated production of export fabrics in Banshu and percentage of gingham to United States***

[In thousands of square yards]

| | 1955 | | | 1956 | | | 1957 | | |
|---|---|---|---|---|---|---|---|---|---|
| | Total production (A) | Gingham to United States (B) | Percent (B/A) | Total production (A) | Gingham to United States (B) | Percent (B/A) | Total production (A) | Gingham to United States (B) | Percent (B/A) |
| January | 9, 320 | 1, 633 | 17. 5 | 17, 849 | 8, 214 | 46. 0 | 13, 868 | 3, 751 | 27. 0 |
| February | 12, 096 | 2, 354 | 19. 5 | 20, 823 | 9, 316 | 44. 7 | 19, 872 | 4, 630 | 23. 4 |
| March | 14, 384 | 2, 783 | 19. 2 | 23, 893 | 10, 844 | 45. 4 | 16, 342 | 4, 148 | 25. 4 |
| April | 15, 730 | 3, 589 | 22. 8 | 20, 652 | 8, 370 | 40. 5 | 20, 483 | 6, 143 | 30. 0 |
| May | 16, 427 | 5, 584 | 34. 0 | 20, 599 | 8, 907 | 43. 2 | 20, 550 | 5, 107 | 24. 8 |
| June | 18, 077 | 4, 319 | 24. 0 | 20, 107 | 7, 124 | 35. 4 | | | |
| July | 20, 347 | 5, 352 | 26. 3 | 18, 279 | 4, 195 | 22. 9 | | | |
| August | 19, 484 | 5, 344 | 27. 4 | 15, 736 | 2, 818 | 17. 9 | | | |
| September | 20, 380 | 7, 185 | 35. 3 | 11, 679 | 2, 742 | 23. 5 | | | |
| October | 21, 404 | 8, 484 | 39. 6 | 18, 320 | 3, 596 | 19. 6 | | | |
| November | 21, 379 | 9, 747 | 45. 6 | 18, 594 | 3, 949 | 21. 2 | | | |
| December | 23, 398 | 11, 716 | 50. 1 | 19, 889 | 5, 144 | 25. 9 | | | |
| Total | 212, 426 | 68, 092 | 32. 0 | 226, 422 | 75, 219 | 33. 2 | | | |

NOTE.—Data taken from the statistic of Japan Cotton and Staple Fiber Inspecting Foundation on the assumption that among various ginghams those washable and uppers represent export to the United States. This assumption generally holds true before October 1956, but since then includes considerable shipment to Venezuela, etc.

Except for a slight recovery in August to September last year, which is attributed to increased shipments to Venezuela and other markets outside the United States, a steady decline in the production of ginghams for export—almost exclusively for the United States at one time—can be seen.

*Trend of weaving commission*

[Per yard]

| Item and construction | 1955 | 1956 | | | | 1957 | |
|---|---|---|---|---|---|---|---|
| | | January-March | April-June | July-September | October-December | January-March | June |
| Gingham: | | | | | | | |
| 47 inches by 120 yards, 40/s by 40/s, 90 by 60 | ¥22.00-¥22.50 | ¥22.00 | ¥20.00 | ¥18.00 | ¥14.00-¥14.50 | ¥16.00 | ¥16.50 |
| 36 inches by 120 yards, 40/s by 40/s, 70 by 60 | 13.50 | 12.00 | 10.00 | 8.00 | 8.00 | 9.50 | 10.00 |
| Sarong: 48 inches by 2 yards, 40/s by 40/s, 80 by 70 | 22.00 | 21.00-22.00 | 20.00 | 16.00 | 15.00 | 16.50 | 17.50 |
| Handkerchief: 34 inches by 120 yards, 40/s by 40/s, 70 by 60 | 13.00 | 12.00-12.50 | 11.00 | 9.00 | 8.00 | 10.00 | 10.50 |

NOTES.—(1) Survey at a firm in Nishiwaki City (Banshu). (2) Not including commission for yarn dyeing, finishing, preparation, freight, etc.

Nearly all of the gingham exported to this country from the Banshu area are manufactured on a commission basis by local companies which are affiliated with spinners and/or exporters. These affiliates are responsible for ordering and taking delivery and payment of commissions on behalf of the spinners or exporters they represent.

As a direct consequence of the quota restrictions imposed at the end of 1955, the mills in the Banshu district are operating in a most precarious manner. The decline in orders since April and May 1956, brought about cutthroat competition between the traders forcing down the commission rates to a record low for all types of products, irrespective of costs and destination.

The following table reveals the decrease in commissions and the relation of various factors on selected gingham exports to the United States. Commission rates have recovered slightly since the first of the year (1957), but this is due primarily to shipments to markets outside the United States, as well as to the curtailment of production ordered by the association last September to check excessive and unreasonable competition.

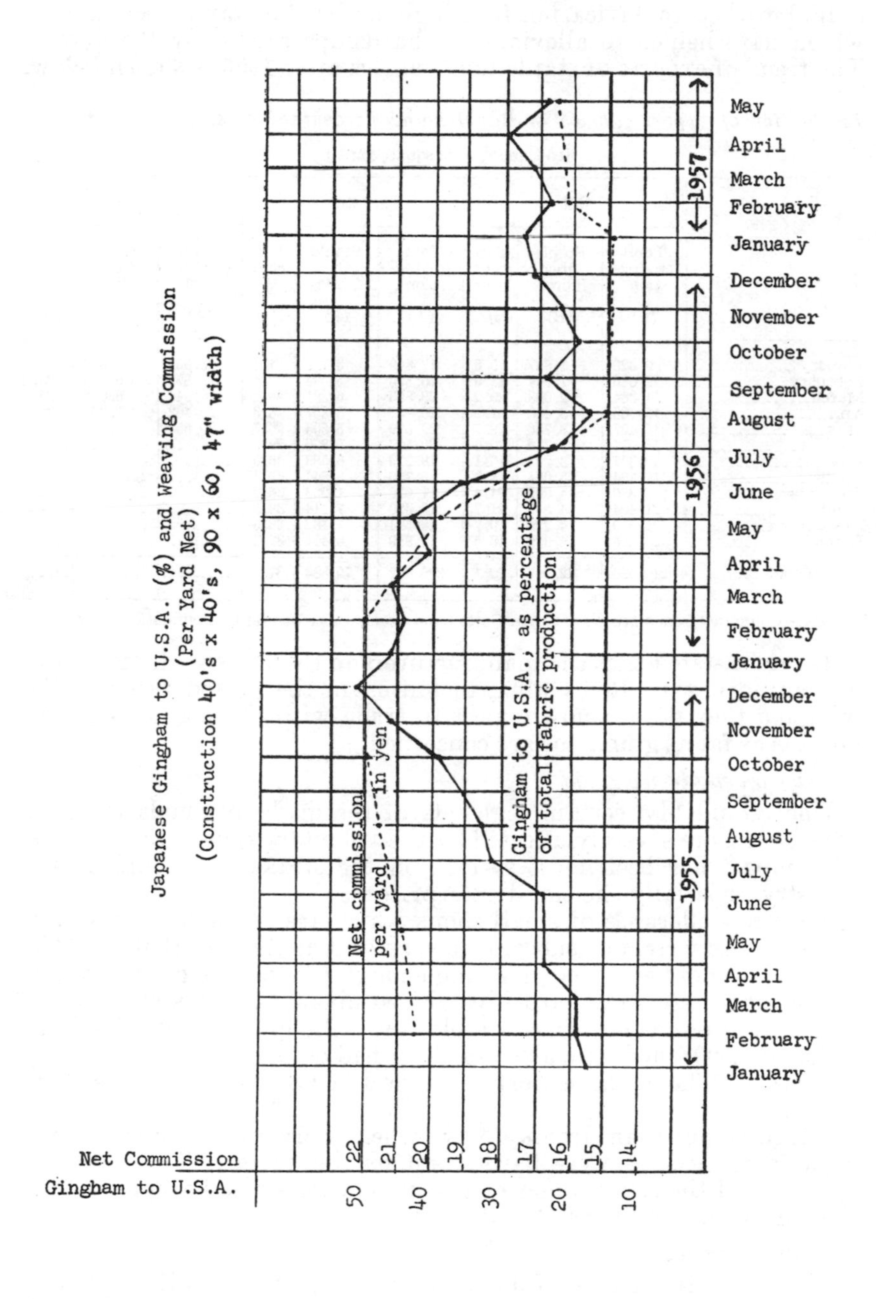
Japanese Gingham to U.S.A. (%) and Weaving Commission
(Per Yard Net)
(Construction 40's x 40's, 90 x 60, 47" width)
Net commission per yard in yen
Gingham to U.S.A., as percentage of total fabric production
Net Commission
Gingham to U.S.A.
22
21
20
19
18
17
16
15
14
50
40
30
20
10
1955
1956
1957
January
February
March
April
May
June
July
August
September
October
November
December
January
February
March
April
May
June
July
August
September
October
November
December
January
February
March
April
May

Prior to the imposition of quotas, these Banshu manufacturers produced largely for the American market. Since the quotas, they have been forced to seek other markets. Fortunately, they have been able to find markets in Africa, not for ginghams but for staple fiber fabrics, which have helped to alleviate the hardships caused by the quotas. The trend of exports of staple fiber fabrics after 1955 is shown below.

*Production of export fabrics in Banshu and percentage of staple fiber fabrics*

[In thousands of square yards]

| | 1955 | | | 1956 | | | 1957 | | |
|---|---|---|---|---|---|---|---|---|---|
| | Total production (A) | Staple fiber fabrics (B) | Percent (B/A) | Total production (A) | Staple fiber fabrics (B) | Percent (B/A) | Total production (A) | Staple fiber fabrics (B) | Percent (B/A) |
| January | 9,320 | 1,827 | 19.6 | 17,849 | 3,778 | 21.1 | 13,868 | 4,559 | 32.8 |
| February | 12,096 | 1,924 | 15.9 | 20,823 | 5,094 | 24.4 | 19,872 | 6,889 | 34.6 |
| March | 14,384 | 2,908 | 20.2 | 23,893 | 6,381 | 26.7 | 16,342 | 6,064 | 37.1 |
| April | 15,730 | 3,460 | 21.9 | 20,652 | 5,857 | 28.3 | 20,482 | 7,093 | 34.6 |
| May | 16,427 | 3,736 | 22.7 | 20,599 | 5,503 | 26.7 | 20,550 | 7,160 | 44.5 |
| June | 18,077 | 3,736 | 20.6 | 20,107 | 5,899 | 29.3 | | | |
| July | 20,347 | 3,293 | 16.1 | 18,279 | 6,583 | 36.0 | | | |
| August | 19,484 | 3,664 | 18.8 | 15,736 | 6,844 | 43.4 | | | |
| September | 20,380 | 4,992 | 24.4 | 11,679 | 4,233 | 36.2 | | | |
| October | 21,404 | 4,662 | 21.7 | 18,320 | 7,114 | 38.8 | | | |
| November | 21,379 | 4,224 | 19.7 | 18,594 | 7,182 | 38.6 | | | |
| December | 23,398 | 4,339 | 18.5 | 19,889 | 6,411 | 32.2 | | | |
| Total | 212,426 | 42,769 | 20.1 | 226,442 | 70,885 | 31.3 | | | |

NOTE.—Computed from statistics of Japan Cotton and Staple Fiber Inspecting Foundation.

It can be stated that the manufacturers in the Banshu district have never traded with Red China, including in the period prior to the war, and they do not now expect to trade with the mainland Communists as far as ginghams are concerned.

*Impact on made-up goods*

Understandably, certain segments of the made-up goods industry have been more severely affected by the voluntary quotas than others. The impact has been most serious on the weaker segments of the industry, especially the small enterprises.

The preponderance of small shops which are affiliated with others in a complex system of subcontracts, as well as the fact that the 1957 quotas have not been operative long enough for reliable guides, makes it difficult to assess the hardships visited upon this industry.

A case in point, however, are blouses. The quota imposed a limitation of 1,500,000 dozen, a year after it had enjoyed exports of 3,500,000 dozen. The actual exports have declined an estimated one-third since 1955.

Rural, rather than urban, areas—where work was done to supplement farm income—were hardest hit by the quotas. The marginal operators of the early stages of production were also harder hit than those in the latter stages of manufacture.

*Personal impact*

Because of the nature of Japan's economy, when a mill or plant is closed down, it is more difficult for the discharged worker to seek employment elsewhere than in the United States. Moreover, the benefits extended to the unemployed in this country by municipal, State and National governments are generally lacking in Japan. Thus, the personal hardships that are visited upon the individual workers by the voluntary-quota system are considerable.

Moreover, especially in reference to the small operations, it is more difficult by far to secure loans to reopen plants or to convert them to manufacturing other products or to establish an entirely new business than it is in the United States. Accordingly, the small operators forced into bankruptcy by these quotas have little opportunity to come back or to enter new fields.

Aside from the individual suffering that must be endured because of these quotas, there is the personal attitude of the displaced Japanese to consider. Unable to comprehend the necessity for the imposition of quotas, and recognizing only that he is unemployed because of the actions of the United States Government, he is more likely to be victimized by those who would foment anti-American sentiment among the Japanese.

*Quota impact on American importers*

Although we believe that the Japanese cotton-textile industry and the Japanese Government should be commended for the spirit in which they have approached the problems raised by American cotton manufacturers, we—as importers—respectfully submit that, in our opinion, quotas, whether mandatory or voluntary, are not the appropriate method to resolve the many problems of the domestic industry, most—if not all—of which are caused by other considerations than imports.

In many ways, the voluntary quotas imposed by Japan are injurious to our own economy. American manufacturers, without the competition of imports, may well raise their prices, and thereby destroy parts of the textile markets which are now available to them by encouraging the development of substitute textiles and synthetics. Marginal manufacturers unwilling to improve management, production, and sales methods are encouraged to remain in the field. But the biggest loser is the American consumer, who no longer will be able to purchase the merchandise of her own selection and who will be forced to either pay higher prices or go without.

It is our contention that American industry should not be allowed to use these voluntary quotas as an excuse to continue inefficient, uneconomic, and unnecessary operations. The domestic industry should be required to improve their techniques and methods or to convert to the manufacturing of other products which are more competitive. American labor and management should not forever be saddled with the manufacturing of certain textile goods which can best be produced in a less-developed economy which has a plentiful supply of labor. Our Government policy should be one to encourage higher wages for the worker and higher profits for management, while, at the same time, providing better quality merchandise at lower prices to the consumer. Artificial and arbitrary barriers to such a policy, based upon local or selfish and temporary considerations, should not be tolerated to impair progress. Such a policy, too, will give inspiration to the less-developed countries of the world to build up their own economies in the hope of trading with us, buying those goods which we can manufacture or grow most efficiently and selling those products which they can manufacture more economically and efficiently than we. Such international commerce would benefit our economy and destiny more than any shortsighted policy of momentary expediency.

We, as importers, found the quotas objectionable enough when the Japanese imposed these quotas voluntarily and, presumably, unilaterally. Now, we have given official sanction to the practice of quotas in violation of American trade and foreign policy for the past quarter century by exchanging official letters and holding discussions on the subject.

Our feeling is that, if the Japanese believe that the imposition of voluntary quotas are required as a matter of their governmental policy, they should be entitled to determine the quantitative limitations themselves, in the light of their own considerations, rather than with official sanction and interference from the United States. As the free world's great leader—in exports and in overseas investments, among other fields—the United States should not be party to any movement or act which may someday be used as a precedent against our own interests.

When the Japanese unilaterally imposed voluntary quotas, it was, of course, a matter of grave concern to us who are engaged in the business of importing textiles from Japan. When our Government acknowledged the quotas and gave it official sanction, however, it became evident that our own Government was interfering with the right of American importers to conduct our own businesses without undue restraint and restrictions. Its action in this matter directly violates the basic American tenet of freedom of enterprise and carries the threat of future Government controls over business and the economy, which we abhor.

A number of importers who have specialized in Japanese textiles have been forced to cancel their orders or to reduce their requirements because of the limited quotas available to the individual exporters. This situation is especially acute in ginghams and velveteens among fabrics and blouses and shirts among made-up goods.

On fabrics such as denims, jeans, corduroys, sateen, twills, and so forth, even if the quotas were lifted entirely, it is doubtful whether American importers of these items could do any substantial volume of business. As will be shown in another section, most fabric imports from Japan do not have any price advantage when the costs of freight and customs duty are added.

For items for which strong demand exists, there are no quota allocations available; they are all used up. On the other hand, for articles for which there is little or no demand, quota allocations remain unused or no quotas are specified against them.

An importer faced with the dilemma created by quotas cannot long continue in business. He is prevented from placing orders for the goods he wants because of the quota. On the other hand, items which he does not want are available because they are not subject to the quota.

During the past 6 months, the general textile market has been in a slump. The demand for imports has, accordingly, been down. But, when business picks up again, because of the restrictions of the quota, textiles to take advantage of the rising market cannot be imported.

As importers, we are faced with this problem: We cannot sell during a slump because no one wants to buy. We cannot import as much as we would like in more prosperous times because of quota limitations. Just when, we ask, are importers of Japanese textiles supposed to do business?

Knowing, however, the intent and the spirit of friendship that motivated the Japanese cotton-textile industry's imposition of voluntary quotas, importers as a class have tried to reciprocate by refraining from protesting too vigorously this infringement on free trade.

But what value is our cooperation if our domestic industry does not join in reciprocating this gesture of international good will by cleaning their own house? Unless our cotton manufacturers, especially the marginal producers, take drastic action to improve their status, the importers will continue to be taxed to support segments of a domestic industry that cannot justify its existence on purely economic grounds.

May we repeat our conviction that, as importers, we are unequivocally opposed to all artificial restraints on trade, including voluntary quotas, mandatory quotas, import quotas, export quotas, and other restrictions on international commerce.

## COMPETITIVENESS OF JAPANESE COTTON TEXTILES

If the anguished cries of some American cotton manufacturers are taken seriously, the Japanese cotton-textile industry is in a position to capture the market now dominated by the domestic industry or a segment thereof whenever it chooses to make the effort. There are also charges that the Japanese industry concentrates their exports in a deliberate attempt to pick off and destroy segments of the local industry one by one as part of a coordinated campaign to seize the entire American market.

Importers, on the other hand, claim that they are hard put to compete in the United States market, that they are slowly being squeezed out of the textile market. They contend that the diversification of products so constantly urged upon Japan is an impossibility under present tariff schedules. They argue that the voluntary quotas have virtually closed the market to them.

This contradiction of analyses raises a number of pertinent questions. Just how competitive are Japanese cotton textiles? What causes them to be competitive? Can American textiles compete with Japanese imports? What about competition in third markets?

### *Cotton-textile purchases from Japan*

Japanese cotton imports into the United States are not a recent phenomenon. As far back as 1887, we have imported cotton textiles from Japan. From the first imports of some 35,000 square yards, we continued to import cotton textiles from Japan at a slowly increasing rate. In certain years of the 1920's, these imports totaled more than 10 million square yards. Most of these imports were made up of piece goods which, in the main, were narrow width cotton crepe. There were also some token shipments of cotton handkerchiefs and floor coverings.

After 1933, substantial increases in imports are recorded, with the prewar peak being reached in 1937, when imports were 124 million square yards, including 109 million square yards of bleached cloth. The following year (1938) because of a depressed United States market, Japanese cotton textile imports dropped to 16 million square yards. In 1939, imports recovered to the extent of 72 million square yards, only to decline in 1940 to 50 million square yards.

With the resumption of trade after the war, imports of cotton textiles from Japan were on a gradual increase until 1954, when some 50 million square yards were imported. In 1955, there was a sharp increase to an alltime high of 140 million square yards. The principal cause for this jump in imports was a strong United States market and a depressed Japan market. In 1956, the imports decreased to 123 million square yards, and this year imports are expected to fall below the 113 million-square-yard limitation of the voluntary quota.

The significance of these figures may be better understood when compared to American production.

At no time in the history of Japanese cotton-textile imports have imports of cotton fabrics exceeded 1.31 percent of our domestic production. The prewar high in 1937 of 124 million square yards represented the highest proportion of imports to domestic production which totaled 9,446 million square yards, or 1.31 percent. The postwar high in 1955 of imports—140 million square yards—represents only 1.24 percent of the domestic output of 11,318 million square yards.

*Handicaps of importers of Japanese textiles*

Importers of Japanese textiles work under many difficult handicaps in competing with domestic products.

First, the importer must hurdle the tariff wall which has been erected to protect the domestic manufacturers. To the importer, these duties represent not protection but discriminatory subsidies which he must overcome.

Although American tariff rates, generally, are not high in relation to other countries, in the case of certain textiles items, especially mass-production goods, they are considered prohibitive. An example in point is corduroy.

Second, ocean freight and insurance are added costs which the domestic manufacturer does not have to assume. Often a single cent can make a difference in the competitive position of a textile item, especially in piece goods.

Third, the importer must take into consideration the lead time required for the delivery of imported textiles. Estimates of some importers are that it takes twice as long for delivery from Japan as it does from domestic mills. This time element often makes the difference between a sale, or none being made. This delivery factor accounts for the inability of Japanese textiles to compete in the field of fashion and style goods which depend upon design and color.

Delivery of imports involves more than just lead time, however. If the delivered item does not meet specifications, sales for an entire season may be lost because of the time factor in bringing in another shipment. The domestic seller has this same problem, it is true, but the great differences in the distances involved make it easier for him to make an adjustment.

Fourth, there are almost no spot transactions which can be made by the importers, again because of the distance factor. This places him under a serious handicap in his ability to take advantage of changing market conditions.

Fifth, the securing of a letter of credit at least 30 days before the shipment is made ties up the money of an importer to his disadvantage. The 30 days before shipment means that money is invested in the imports for a minimum of 70 to 90 days on which he must pay interest.

Sixth, the importer must work on small margins or markups because of the difficulty in meeting the prices on the domestic market. This profit margin limits his ability to merchandise or promote the sale of his commodities. The added expense of advertising, for instance, could price him out of competition with the domestic product.

Seventh, the importer faces difficulties in communications which his domestic competitor does not have to overcome. Inasmuch as the manufacturer in Japan is some 8,000 to 10,000 miles away, communications are not only more difficult but also more expensive and time consuming. To explain the requirements of the market, for example, takes from 10 to 14 days by airmail. A telephone call costs five times more than it does from New York City to any point in the United States. A cablegram costs 30 cents a word. Then, there is the language barrier that also has to be overcome in many instances. All this adds up the cost to the importers.

Eighth, Japanese cotton textiles face market prejudice that infers lower quality and cheaper price. Accordingly, the price differential on certain goods must be considerable, at least 7 to 10 percent, if the imports are to be sold competitively with its domestic counterpart.

Ninth, cultural differences, existing between the importers in many cases and the Japanese manufacturers, make it more difficult to conduct satisfactory business relationships as contrasted with domestic operators or European exporters and manufacturers.

Tenth, the usual business risks that challenge all business enterprise are added to the sometimes extraordinary handicaps that the importer must overcome.

*Importable textile items*

Most importers interviewed for this paper stated that there are only a few Japanese cotton-textile items that can be said to be truly competitive with American products.

Surprisingly, they were able to name only about 3 or 4 types of cotton fabrics that can be imported on a steady basis, and about 6 other types only on a once-in-a-while basis.

For the bulk of the cotton broadwoven cloth, the Japanese products are outpriced by domestic items because of lower American prices, high tariffs, or the inability to compete with domestic fashions, designs, and color.

It is only in a few fabrics such as velveteens, ginghams, and 1 or 2 other fabrics that the Japanese are able to compete with the American commodity. Those once-in-a-while imports are fabrics whose prices become competitive only when the Japanese market is depressed at the same time that the United States market is high. World conditions are such that these twin circumstances seldom occur simultaneously.

Hereafter, we shall present some examples of the breakdown of costs to importers of Japanese cotton textiles that cannot be imported into the United States under ordinary circumstances.

*Example 1*

| Dyed cotton corduroy, No. 3026 (36 inches in width): | Cents |
|---|---|
| F. o. b. (Japan) | 46.0 |
| Ocean freight | 5.0 |
| Insurance | .3 |
| Duty | 23.0 |
| Entry charges (freight-forwarder fees, cartage, etc) | 1.0 |
| Total | 75.3 |
| Brokerage commission | 1.5 |
| Importer's margin | 5.0 |
| Total | 81.8 |
| United States manufacturer's price | 59.0 |
| United States price advantage | 22.8 |

The cost factors cited for Japanese corduroy and the United States manufacturer's price may come as a surprise to many, but it is clear that products like corduroy have very little possibility of entering the American market on a competitive basis. While it is true that there have been some imports of made-up goods, especially baby clothes made of corduroy cloth, for the most part, the price differential of more than 25 percent makes imports of this fabric impossible.

*Example 2*

| 4-Leaf Army uniform twill, dyed, United States type No. 1 (42 inches in width): | Cents |
|---|---|
| F. o. b. (Japan) | 76.5 |
| Insurance and freight | 1.5 |
| Duty | 15.7 |
| Entry charges | .5 |
| Total | 94.2 |
| Broker's commission | 1.8 |
| Total | 96.0 |
| Importer's margin | 4.0 |
| Total | 100.0 |
| United States manufacturer's price | 86.0 |
| United States price advantage | 14.0 |

*Example 3*

| 4-leaf Army uniform twill, gray, United States type No. 1 (42 inches in width): | Cents |
|---|---|
| F. o. b. (Japan) | 60.5 |
| Insurance and freight | 1.5 |
| Duty | 12.0 |
| Entry | .5 |
| Total | 74.5 |
| Broker's commission | 1.5 |
| Total | 76.0 |
| Importer's margin | 3.0 |
| Total | 79.0 |
| United States manufacturer's price | 70.0 |
| United States price advantage | 9.0 |

It is evident that the tariff in the case of twills is too much for Japanese products to overcome.

*Example 4*

| Gray cotton sateen (filling), 46½ inches in width (64 by 104—3.5 yards per pound): | *Cents* |
|---|---|
| F. o. b. (Japan) | 22.5 |
| Insurance and freight | 1.0 |
| Duty | 3.6 |
| Entry charges | .5 |
| Total | 27.6 |
| Broker's commission | .5 |
| Total | 28.1 |
| Importer's margin | .9 |
| Total | 29.0 |
| United States manufacturer's price | 26.0 |
| United States price advantage | 3.0 |

To show how some of the pricing factors operate, we have calculated costs from Japanese import cost-insurance-freight prices landed in New York. We believe this may give some insight as to costs, as calculated by a prospective converter or cutter in New York.

*Example 5*

| Broadcloth, 40 inches (40s by 40s—136t by 60t), combed American cotton: | *Cents* |
|---|---|
| New York price | 26.5 |
| Less: | |
| Duty | —3.6 |
| Entry and other charges | —1.5 |
| Cost-insurance-freight net | 21.4 |
| Less cost-insurance-freight charges | —1.5 |
| Required f. o. b. price | 19.9 |

The actual current Japanese f. o. b. price is 22 cents, which is about 2 cents higher than the required Japanese price to compete on the American market.

*Example 6*

| Print cloth, 37 inches (30s by 40s—100t by 60t): | *Cents* |
|---|---|
| New York price | 17.5 |
| Less: | |
| Duty | —2.4 |
| Entry and other charges | —1.0 |
| Cost-insurance-freight net New York | 14.1 |
| Less cost-insurance-freight charges | 1.1 |
| Required f. o. b. price | 13.0 |

The current Japanese price is approximately 15 cents, or about 2 cents higher than the price which would make this cloth competitive in the United States market.

From the examples used as illustrations, it is clear that on many textile products, even if the duty were reduced considerably, it is doubtful that they could be imported in quantity lots. In other instances, ocean freight and other added costs of imports are more than enough to bar them from the United States.

*Importable garment items*

An erroneous impression exists among many domestic garment manufacturers and others that Japanese-made garments can enter the United States market without any difficulty, and that imports, except for certain highly fashionable goods, can be brought into this country at such low prices as to threaten all American industry.

As with fabrics, the facts are that only a few items which are competitive with domestic products enjoy the opportunity to share the American market.

In the field of made-up goods, not only must the articles compete on a price basis, but also on other aspects such as styles, color, design, and so forth.

For reasons mentioned elsewhere, importers of Japanese cotton made-up goods have many factors to overcome. This has led to the situation in which, essentially, Japanese imports must compete in the secondary, rather than the primary markets. They can only follow, not lead, fashion trends. Because of this, Japanese imports are almost always in competition with American garmentmakers who are also followers, not creators, of trends. In many cases, these companies are either marginal or inefficient, for they do not have the handicaps to overcome that the Japanese imports have, in order to become competitive. The competition is thus confined to the popular price lines of blouses, children's wears, boys' sport shirts, and so forth.

The following are some examples showing the pricing costs of garments, if they were to be imported into the United States:

*Example 1*

| Underwear—(cotton T-shirt, combed yarns—No. 40s): | Per dozen |
|---|---|
| F. o. b. (Japan) | $3.50 |
| Insurance and freight | .50 |
| Duty | .88 |
| Entry charges | .05 |
| C. i. f. (New York) | 4.93 |
| Broker's commission | .15 |
| Importer's margin | .25 |
| Wholesaler's price | 5.33 |
| Wholesaler's markup | .80 |
| Importer's price to retailers | 6.13 |
| United States manufacturer's price to retailers | 5.50 |
| United States price advantage | .63 |

*Example 2*

| Dress shirt (cotton, 40s, 210): | Per dozen |
|---|---|
| F. o. b. (Japan) | $16.00 |
| Insurance and freight | 1.00 |
| Duty | 4.00 |
| Entry charges | .40 |
| C. i. f. New York | 21.40 |
| Broker's commission and importer's margin | 4.28 |
| Retailer's buying price | 25.68 |
| Retailer's markup | 17.12 |
| Consumer's buying price | 42.80 |
| Consumer's buying price per shirt | 3.56 |
| United States price to consumers | 2.98 |
| United States manufacturer's price advantage | .58 |

*Example 3*

| Terry towels (20s): | Per dozen |
|---|---|
| F. o. b. (Japan) | $2.50 |
| Insurance and freight | .20 |
| Duty | .875 |
| Entry charges | .20 |
| C. i. f. New York | 3.775 |
| Broker's commission and importer's margin | .755 |
| Importer's price to retailers | 4.53 |
| Retailer's markup | 2.92 |
| Retailer's selling price, per dozen | 7.45 |
| Per single unit | .62 |
| United States manufactured price | .50 |
| United States price advantage | .12 |

*Example 4*

| Knitted pajamas (30s): | Per dozen |
|---|---|
| F. o. b. (Japan) | $5.00 |
| Insurance and freight | .40 |
| Duty | 1.50 |
| Entry charges | .30 |
| C. i. f. New York | 7.20 |
| Broker's commission and importer's margin | 1.44 |
| Importer's price | 8.64 |
| Retailer's markup | 5.76 |
| Retailer's selling price: | |
| Per dozen | 14.40 |
| Per unit | 1.20 |
| United States manufacturer's product | .99 |
| United States price advantage | .21 |

*Example 5*

| Men's undershorts (20s—30s): | Per dozen |
|---|---|
| F. o. b. (Japan) | $3.10 |
| Insurance and freight | .35 |
| Duty | .62 |
| Entry charges | .50 |
| C. i. f. New York | 4.57 |
| Broker's commission | .07 |
| Importer's margin | .30 |
| Importer's price to retailers or wholesaler | 4.94 |
| United States manufacturer's price | 4.25 |
| United States goods' price advantage | .69 |

*Example 6*

| Ladies' broadcloth pajamas: | Per dozen |
|---|---|
| F. o. b. (Japan) | $11.50 |
| Insurance and freight | 2.10 |
| Duty | 2.30 |
| Entry charges | .20 |
| C. i. f. New York | 16.10 |
| Broker's commission | .58 |
| Importer's margin | 1.15 |
| Importer's price to retailers or wholesaler | 17.83 |
| United States manufactured goods' price | 16.50 |
| United States price advantage | 1.33 |

It should be noted in passing that these examples were collected from a number of importers of Japanese made-up goods with offices in New York City. Naturally, each of the companies interviewed had different methods for computing costs and conducting sales. These examples show, however, that Japanese textiles, whether fabrics or garments, do not enjoy competitive advantages except for a relatively few items in the United States market.

*American textiles in third markets*

Another way in which to determine the competitivity of Japanese textiles with American textiles is to compare their participation in the markets of third countries.

We find that the United States is better able to dominate foreign markets in such items as print cloth and mass-production goods. United States exports of cotton cloths in 1956, for example, far outstrips that of Japan to Canada, Costa Rica, Cuba, Dominican Republic, Guatemala, Haiti, Honduras, Korea, Nicaragua, Panama, the Philippines, Union of South Africa, and Venezuela. The Japanese, on the other hand, export more cotton cloth than this country to Australia, British West Africa, Ceylon, Hong Kong, Indonesia, Thailand, and the United Kingdom.

In certain areas of Latin America and the Philippines, the United States enjoys preferential treatment. In most markets, however, the United States does not receive preferential consideration. Japan is not accorded preferential treatment anywhere over the United States.

To illustrate some of the advantages which preferential treatment gives to the United States in the Philippines, for instance, we are informed that American imports will be assessed for customs duties at the following rates, while Japan is required to pay the full (100 percent) amount:

| | |
|---|---|
| 25 percent of the general rate | Jan. 1, 1956, to Dec. 31, 1958 |
| 50 percent of the general rate | Jan. 1, 1959, to Dec. 31, 1961 |
| 75 percent of the general rate | Jan. 1, 1962, to Dec. 31, 1964 |
| 90 percent of the general rate | Jan. 1, 1965, to Dec. 31, 1973 |
| 100 percent of the general rate | Jan. 1, 1974, to July 3, 1974 |

Summed up, the United States will receive preferential treatment over Japan in the Philippines for another 18 years, unless Japan is granted similar privileges, which is doubtful.

In the matter of export-import control regulations, five commodities in the cotton goods classification have been shifted to unclassified items. This means that the actual import of these items from such general exporting countries as Japan is suspended, while American cotton goods in these categories are extended preferential treatment under the provisions of the preferential trade agreement.

Comparison of American and Japanese exports to foreign markets in which neither is given preferential treatment over the other shows that, other factors being equal—transportation, etc.—the United States can compete favorably with Japan in third countries. In 1956, for example, this country exported 192,060,000 square yards of cotton cloth to Canada, while Japan exported only 16,130,000 square yards. In the same year, the United States shipped 25,150,000 square yards to the Union of South Africa, while Japan shipped only 19,830,000 square yards. In this period the United States sent 32,880,000 square yards to Venezuela and Japan 28,440,000 square yards.

There are two basic reasons that underscore America's ability to outsell Japanese textiles in most third countries. One is that in the field of mass production, the United States is supreme. This means that this country can compete in any foreign market favorably on mass-produced items, especially when transportation costs are not prohibitive. The second is that the United States is superior to Japan in those articles which require design, colors, and fashion.

The United States Tariff Commission summarized the situation in its report to the 84th Congress (1956), in reply to Senate Resolution 236 which directed the Commission to make "an immediate investigation pursuant to section 7 of the Trade Agreements Extension Act of 1951, as amended (escape-clause procedures), to determine whether any textile or textile products are being imported into the United States in such increased quantities, either actual or relative, as to cause or threaten to cause serious injury to the domestic industry producing like or directly competitive products."

The Commission concluded:

> Despite the widespread concern that has developed about imports of textiles from Japan, it appears that such imports are not offering serious competition to most segments of the domestic textile industry. The fact that some such segments are in a relatively strong position vis-a-vis import competition is indicated by the substantial export trade of the United States in textile products. The United States exports go principally to countries such as Canada, Venezuela, the Union of South Africa, Indonesia, and Dominican Republic—in which articles from the United States enjoy no preferential tariff treatment over those imported from other countries, including Japan. The United States exports some cotton manufactures even to Japan.

*American made-up goods in third countries*

As with cotton fabrics, many Americans, including those in the industry, have the notion that Japanese garments can drive American items out of the market of third countries. As with cotton fabrics, this is far from true. Even in Hong Kong, which is Japan's nearby neighbor, relatively speaking, United States exports are giving Japanese products severe competition.

American knit cloth for the manufacture of gloves sells for about 10 cents less per square yard than Japan's competitive product. These cloth imports of knit cotton gloves made from American knit cloth threaten to take away a large portion of the Australian market from Japan, too. This knit-glove example illustrates the handicaps under which the Japanese manufacturer of certain made-up goods must operate. He must first purchase high-priced cloth and then convert the cloth into gloves, while his American competitor both manufactures and converts the cloth.

In Latin America particularly the Japanese are losing their markets to American imports of dressy children's apparel. A big factor in the present trend is the higher freight and insurance costs that the Japanese product must assume. Other factors are the availability of capital to the manufacturers and the efficiency of American mass-production methods. Because of available capital, the American manufacturer can make up goods on a speculative basis and keep them in stock for immediate demands. The Japanese manufacturer, with limited capital, cannot afford to speculate and must operate on the basis of placed orders.

Some United States garments with which the Japanese cannot compete include denim work shirts, khaki shorts, better quality sateen coats, towels, blankets, and T-shirts made of combed yarn.

*Competitive factors relating to Japanese textiles*

Thus far we have developed that American cotton textiles, by and large, can more than hold their own against Japanese imports in both the United States and third-country markets.

At the same time, though, it cannot be denied that certain Japanese cotton textiles do enter the United States market, even though they represent a very small percentage of domestic production. This suggests questions as to what makes certain Japanese products competitive and just why they seem to be concentrated in a relatively few lines.

To present a clearer picture as to the nature of the competition which comes from Japanese textiles, these imported commodities will be segregated into four categories.

In the first category are items which are best suited to mass-production methods, such as twills, denims, sheetings, shirting, sateens, print cloths, ducks, drills, and so forth.

Past records reveal that Japanese imports in this category have been relatively insignificant. The main reasons for this record include (1) high efficiency of the American industry, (2) ocean freight, and (3) insurmountable tariffs.

Business in fabrics in this category is only possible when the Japanese market is depressed and the United States market is booming. An example of what is meant is seen in the 1954 experience with print cloth: The Japanese market was extremely depressed, while the American market was strong. Substantial imports resulted. In the following year, however, when the Japanese market recovered, imports were practically suspended in spite of a tariff concession granted in September 1955.

In the second category are fashion goods.

The Japanese are completely outclassed by the Americans in this field.

The Japanese as yet cannot be expected to compete with American and European designs and fashions. Distance from the United States market is a real cost factor, as is the limited capital available to the Japanese manufacturer which discourages any large-scale experimentation with fashion items. Japanese manufacturers operating some 8,000 miles away from New York City are hardly in a position to know the intimate details and last-minute changes in the market, especially in reference to fashions, colors, designs, and so forth. Basic, too, are the cultural differences, as reflected in tastes and reactions, from the European-American pattern. While the latter is presently a liability for the Japanese manufacturers, it is hoped in time that this can be turned into an asset for turning out unique and unusual fashion ideas acceptable to the western taste.

In the third category are commodities which are imported to take advantage of sudden market changes.

The United States industry is highly specialized, with mill production concentrated on certain items. This makes for more efficient production as well as sales promotion.

Counterbalancing these advantages, their specialized equipment and personnel adds to the difficulty of making sudden shifts to other fabrics to meet unexpected changes in consumer demand. Consequently, a gap in the market is created while the necessary change-over is made. This short supply created by a change in consumer demand is often filled by Japanese imports, and thereby consumer preferences are partially satisfied until the domestic industry can supply the needs.

In the fourth category are the so-called labor intense items, those which require a great deal of labor and for which adequate labor-saving machinery has not been designed.

Velveteen is an example of this type of item.

Although domestic manufacturers have devised machinery to cut labor costs, they have not been developed to the point where they can overcome competition from Italy and Japan, in particular. The same applies generally to ginghams, which also require considerable hand labor.

In this type of competition, Japan can fully challenge the American market, because they enjoy a price advantage in spite of ocean freight and customs duty.

It is a well-accepted thesis that fabrics requiring a considerable amount of hand labor are not appropriate for a highly developed machine economy, such as ours. Only by raising prices can operations be profitable. But, if prices are raised too high, demand drops, or foreign imports are welcomed into the domestic market.

The American velveteen industry today consists of only 1 major manufacturer and 2 others who enter into production only when there is a strong demand.

As importers, we contend that such industry segments as velveteen, which cannot be justified on economic grounds, should be encouraged to shift production to other and more economic products. Such shifts would not only help the textile industry itself rid itself of uneconomic appendages but also benefit the consumer by making available imported fabrics at more reasonable prices.

There is no gainsaying that Japanese cotton textiles are competitive because of low labor costs. But there is also no contradicting that unless Japan can sell cotton textiles—which require considerable hand labor—there is little else they can export to this country. And, without textile exports, Japan would not be able to continue as our best customer for agricultural products and as our first or second best customer for all our exports.

At this point, it should be emphasized that while Japanese labor may be low, in contrast to wages paid in the United States, they are not cheap. Neither is Japanese labor exploited by being worked for coolie wages, as high high-tariff spokesmen have alleged so often and so loudly.

Japanese cotton spinners pay the highest wages in the Japanese economy, while our domestic manufacturers pay among the lowest in our economy. The fringe benefits which the Japanese cotton spinners provide for their workers are much more liberal than those given to American workers in our cotton mills. Moreover, a higher percentage of textile workers in Japan are organized into labor unions than they are in this country, and this includes both New England and the South. These unions, by the way, are affiliated with the International Confederation of Free Trade Unions, with which our own AFL–CIO is also affiliated.

The labor issue, because of its significance and publicity, will be considered in another section.

Another aspect which adds to the competitive ability of the Japanese spinners results from the lower prices they pay for raw cotton.

These lower prices stem not only from the unique situation in which the American manufacturer must purchase United States grown cotton for higher prices than that established as the world market price but also from the years of experience of the Japanese raw-cotton importers, which enables them to take advantage of raw-cotton prices and fluctuations throughout the world. It also stems from the ability of the Japanese manufacturer to mix many types of raw cotton in spinning yarns which are high in quality and yet low in cost.

Although it will be amplified in another section, perhaps it should be stated here that as importers we do not object to a system which will allow American manufacturers to purchase raw cotton at the same prices as others are permitted to purchase the same cotton. Otherwise, we fear that our cotton manufacturers will be priced out of the market by new chemical and synthetic fibers.

To summarize this section, we quote from the concluding paragraphs of the United States Tariff Commission report to the Senate on its Resolution 236, previously referred to, which sustains our general observations and suggests that segments of the domestic industry alleging import injury have available to them "escape clause" procedures to determine the validity of their appeal:

* * * it is clear that textile manufacturers in Japan do not have an across-the-board competitive advantage over the textile manufacturer in the United

States. Such injury as may be caused or threatened by increased imports of textiles or textile manufactures from Japan—or any other country—is bound to be confined to a limited number of categories, most of which, experience has shown, will be narrow. Investigations of such instances of injury are, in the Commission's opinion, best conducted on a selective basis as circumstances warrant. * * *

POTENTIALITIES OF JAPANESE TEXTILE INDUSTRY

Speculation regarding the maximum potentialities of the Japanese textile industry to compete in the United States market has intensified since the increase in textile imports from 1953 to 1955.

Some fears have been expressed by certain industry leaders that the Japanese have the capabilities and the capacity to capture the American market at any time by flooding the country with their textile exports.

Some research into the underlying facts of the Japanese textile industry should serve to allay such alarms and to provide some estimate of the actual maximum prospects for the industry.

*Present productive capacity*

The total number of spindles in place of the Japanese cotton-textile industry was 9,022,000, operated by 149 companies, at the end of 1956. Since 2 of the 149 companies were textile machinery producers, 147 represented the actual number of manufacturing companies.

These spinning mills consumed 1,177,000,000 pounds of raw cotton, or an equivalent of 3,480,000,000 square yards.

Of the 147 cotton-spinning companies, 14 possessed more than 200,000 spindles each, for 65.5 percent of the total. By contrast, spinners with less than 10,000 spindles each represent only 2.4 percent of the total spindleage.

Compared to the prewar situation, the ownership of the cotton-spinning equipment has been diversified considerably. In 1937, 80 companies owned 12,358,000 spindles. Among this 80, 8 companies owned more than 500,000 spindles each, or 54 percent of the total. Only 10 companies owned less than 10,000 spindles. The largest company owned 1,623,000 spindles, while 2 others each owned more than a million spindles each.

The size of these Japanese spinners is important in this context, for the larger spinners are the ones who manufacture for export purposes, while the smaller companies produce for the home (Japan) market.

The trend toward diversification may indicate that manufacturing for the Japanese market is growing in importance.

Many of the cotton manufacturers process other fibers than cotton. Many spin rayon, silk, and wool and even synthetics.

Under the Japanese law, spindles used for rayon must be registered as such and cannot be used for any other purpose.

Of the 2,950,000 spindles registered under the textile equipment law for the spinning of rayon, 1,627,000 spindles are owned by 47 cotton spinners.

Of the 14 major companies with more than 200,000 spindles which engage in the manufacture of manmade fibers, 8 also spin rayon staple, 1 rayon filament, 1 rock wool and glass fiber, and 3 varying types of the latest synthetics.

*Stockholdings*

Instead of a few controlling the major companies, thousands of individual stockholders are listed for the various concerns. In 1956, for instance, 354,000 stockholders held 465 million shares outstanding in 9 of the leading cotton spinning companies.

Small shareholders predominate, with 347,000 owning less than 5,000 shares each. These 347,000 in aggregate own about 51 percent of all the shares.

Japanese holding in terms of numbers may seem large, but in money value they are exceedingly small. For even the largest and more prosperous companies, shares average only about 14 cents each.

*Japanese industry ranking in world*

A study of the International Federation of Cotton and Allied Textile Industries showed the following number of cotton spindles in place for the principal textile countries of the world, as of July 1956: (1) United Kingdom, 28,152,000 spindles; (2) United States, 23,183,000 spindles; (3) Soviet Russia, 12,250,000 spindles; (4) India, 12,068,000 spindles; (5) Japan, 8,501,000 spindles; (6) Red China, 6,290,000 spindles; (7) West Germany, 5,954,000 spindles; (8) Italy, 5,726,000 spindles; and (9) France, 5,547,000 spindles.

Even if the 9,022,000 spindles registered in the latest Japanese report is considered, Japan ranks fifth in the number of cotton spindles in place, behind the United Kingdom, United States, Soviet Russia, and India.

The productive capacity of a nation cannot be measured by a mere recital of the number of spindles in place. A more accurate picture is reflected in the number of hours in which the equipment is operated. In the United States and India, among others, a great number of mills operate on a 3-shift day. Japan, on the other hand, operates her mills on a 2-shift day, while the United Kingdom operates on a 1-shift day.

In addition to shifts per day, the working hours in a week should be considered.

According to the study cited above, the "working hours" (total "working hours" divided by the actual spindles in place) for the year ending July 1956 were (1) United States, 5,792 hours; (2) India, 5,602 hours; (3) Japan, 4,025 hours; (4) West Germany, 3,792 hours; (5) France, 3,325 hours; (6) Italy, 2,499 hours; and (7) United Kingdom, 1,526 hours.

According to this standard, Japan is third in the world, following the United States and India.

Another method of comparison between Japan's productive capacities and those of other countries is in raw cotton consumption.

According to a survey of the International Cotton Advisory Committee (Cotton, January 1957) for the cotton year 1955 to 1956, (1) the United States consumed 9,202,000 bales; (2) India, 4,280,000 bales; (3) Japan, 2,322,000 bales; (4) United Kingdom, 1,545,000 bales; (5) West Germany, 1,318,000 bales; (6) France, 1,215,000 bales; (7) Brazil, 1,050,000 bales; and (8) Italy, 765,000 bales.

Using this criterion, Japan is third in the consumption of raw cotton, again following the United States and India.

From the material cited above, it can be concluded that the Japanese cotton industry has only one-third of America's productive capacity. This proportion holds for both equipment and the operating hours for the machinery.

On this statistical basis, even assuming that Japan completely ignored her home and all foreign markets except the United States, she could export less than a third of our domestic production.

*Japanese dependence on foreign markets*

According to a survey made by the All Japan Cotton Spinners Association, the Japanese cotton textile industry is now less dependent on foreign exports than in prewar years.

Prewar exports of cotton cloth reached an all-time high in 1935, when 2,725 million square yards were exported. Taking an average based on the years 1934 to 1936, exports averaged 2,671 million square yards annually.

In contrast, in the postwar period, the volume of cotton cloth exports reached 1,103 million square yards in 1950, during the Korean conflict. After 1950, exports declined to 762 million square yards in 1952, went up to 914 million square yards in 1953, and reached its postwar peak of 1,278 million square yards in 1954, declining slightly in 1955.

Worldwide exports in the postwar period have tended to average about 1,200 million square yards annually, or less than half of the prewar average of 2,671 million square yards annually.

*Increase in home consumption*

The Japanese textile industry's growth in the postwar era has been remarkable; and yet, exports average less than half of prewar averages. The answer, then, is in the development of the home (Japan) market.

Part of the explanation is in the growth of the population, from some 85 million to 90 million people in the 4 years since 1952. This averages better than a million a year. This increases in population assures an increase in Japanese home consumption of textiles.

Another is the steady rise in the standard of living and in the national income. During this period, too, the average per capita increase in the consumption of all goods was 23 percent, while that for textiles increased 28 percent in the urban areas and 13 percent in the rural districts.

Just as in the United States, the portion of the consumer dollar that goes for clothing has become smaller almost year by year. But, the percentage of decline in Japan is not as large as in this country. And, in 1956, the share of the household budget spent on clothing increased somewhat.

Still another factor is the intensive promotional campaign to encourage greater use of cottons. This program is administered by the Japan Cotton Promotion Institute, which is an outgrowth of an agreement concluded between the National Cotton Council of America and the All Japan Cotton Spinners Association. This institute, composed of the All Japan Cotton Spinners Association, Japan Cotton Traders Association, Japan Cotton Weavers Association, Japan Textile Dyers Association, and Federation of Japan Cotton Yarn Merchants Association, has carried out programs of market research, public relations, and sales promotion of cotton textiles.

Also, the change in clothing habits, especially among the women, from the traditional kimono to western dress, has resulted in greater consumer demand for cotton clothes.

And another part of the explanation is in the reduction of the retail prices of cotton textiles, which encouraged consumption considerably. The lower prices, it might be mentioned, were brought about by the lower raw cotton prices.

A final factor in explaining the increase in the consumption of cotton textiles by the Japanese themselves is, perhaps, found in the general improvement in the quality of cotton textiles. The development of new chemical finishing techniques, for instance, has increased the demand for cottons.

With Japan's economic position improving yearly, and with the increase in population and living standard, the Japanese industry looks rather confidently to their future in their own market. Moreover, if present trends continue, Japan will become less and less dependent upon foreign markets as outlets for her cotton textile production. As a matter of fact, the prewar ratio of exports to sales in the home market of 5 to 3 had been almost completely reversed by 1956.

*Government restrictions on machinery*

To limit production, the Japanese Government has enacted legislation restricting the quantity of equipment and machinery for the textile industry.

The first statute, passed in August 1952, was to stop excessive competition "when it threatens serious damage in the smooth working" of trade, domestic or foreign, in specific industries in which small and medium enterprises were concentrated. Termed the "Small and Medium Business Stabilization Law," by 1956 its jurisdiction extended over 48 industries, including the cotton-weaving industry.

These small and medium businesses employing less than 300 in which a "serious threat" to the stability of the trade exists, are authorized to organize "adjustment associations" empowered to restrict production, equipment, prices, and whatever else is required to stabilize the industry. These associations are under the supervision of MITI which has the authority to order companies outside the associations to comply with the same regulations as those governing members.

Under the provisions of this law, the Federation of Japan Cotton and Staple Fiber Weaving Industry Association was organized, and, in the fall of 1954, its members agreed to the following measures to assure stability in their industry:

(1) Weaving looms for cotton or spun rayon cloth in the hands of the association members were to be registered with the local "adjustment association." The machinery for weaving cotton is interchangeable with those for weaving spun rayon.

(2) No cloth made of cotton or spun rayon was to be woven on unregistered looms.

In November 1954, MITI applied these regulations to nonmember weavers.

Subsequently, the association decided to dismantle 35,000 looms which were considered to be more than was needed. Furthermore, it is expected that this year (1957) 9,000 more looms will be declared to be in surplus and not required. Although not written, there is an understanding that no new equipment will be allowed to be registered, which amounts to a prohibition of new facilities.

Japanese Government statistics at the end of 1956 showed 13,420 cotton and spun rayon weaving mills operating 390,036 looms, not counting those in the very small mills. Of these, 112 mills with 78,210 looms were operated by cotton spinners. Independent weavers numbered 13,308 and operated 311,826 looms.

In 1956, the Japaneses cotton-weaving industry produced 3,462 million square yards of cloth, 1,003,000 square yards of spun rayon, and 194 million square yards of other types of fabrics.

The restriction of cotton-spinning equipment was deferred until 1956, when the National Diet passed the "Textile Industry Equipment Temporary Adjustment Law" to—

rationalize the textile industry by effecting regulation of the equipment of the textile industry in order to contribute to the development of normal export trade of textile products.

The background for this unique statute is an indication of the desire on the part of the Japanese textile industry to avoid situations in which it may be forced to "dump" its production on either or both the domestic and foreign markets.

In a country like Japan, where skilled labor is plentiful and where the prospects for the textile industry look promising, capital investments for expansion of productive facilities attract investors. This type of investment is favored over those for heavy or chemical industries because the amount of capital required for textiles is much less. As investments for capital outlay increase, the productive capacities are increased, creating a situation in which production may exceed demand. Any excessive surplus may cause disorder in the home or foreign markets, or both, with the possibilities for exports greater than those for home sale. This was the situation that was threatened when the law was enacted to cope with the problem.

The rapid expansion of the Japanese textile industry in the postwar period, especially 1950, demanded some checks on unreasonable increases in productive capacities. The textile industry equipment temporary adjustment law covers the growth of spinning equipment, spinning frame, and dying and finishing equipment (cloth tenter) for all fiber types including cotton yarn.

The law provided for (1) the registration of all cotton-spinning machinery with the Government, with the proviso that unregistered machinery was prohibited from spinning cotton; (2) the annual determination by MITI, based upon available equipment and estimates of supply and demand, of the need for additional machinery; and (3) the authority of MITI to order the dismantling or storing of equipment which it considers in excess of overall needs. The law expires in 1960.

The total registry of cotton-spinning machinery now stands at 9,022,000 spindles. No increases in equipment are anticipated in the near future.

*1960 export goal*

MITI's 1960 export goal for cotton cloth is 1,300 million square yards. That objective was almost approximated in 1954, when Japanese exports totaled 1,278 million square yards. In the next 2 years, however, they dropped to 1,138,800,000 square yards in 1955 and then increased slightly to 1,262 million square yards in 1956.

According to our information, there is very little expectation that the goal will be expanded in the near future.

Indeed, with the voluntary quota on exports to the United States and the limited expansion of other markets, there is some doubt that Japan will be able to attain the 1,300 million square yards for export by 1960.

*Competition from synthetics*

The growth of the Japanese cotton textile industry in the future is severely circumscribed by their own Government's so-called 8-year plan. In seeking a solution to the balancing of revenues and needs, the Japanese Government has decided to restrict the expansion of the cotton textile industry in favor of developing synthetics or man-made fibers. This policy decision is in keeping with their determination to develop the Japanese economy with the maximum use of their own natural resources.

The Economic Planning Board issued in January 1956 a publication entitled the "Five Year Plan for Economic Independence," which blueprints the future program for Japanese industries.

As for textiles—

the prospectus stated—

natural fiber goods are to be emphasized as exports whilst chemical and synthetic fibers will be increased in production to meet domestic demands. * * * As a result the ratio of consumption of natural fibers will be 6 to 4 in 1960 as compared with the ratio of 7 to 3 in 1954, so contributing to the self-sufficiency of the fiber industry. * * * In line with long-range trends in the world textile market and demands for a higher level of self-sufficiency in our country in the future, the production of artificial rayon and mixed yarn and fabrics, instead of natural fibers, such as acetate and other synthetic fibers, is to be expanded. The use of artificial rayon and mixed yarn fabrics, instead of natural fibers, is to be encouraged, thereby increasing the domestic consumption and export of artificial textile goods. Domestic consumption of natural fibers is to be gradually reduced and their exports are to be maintained through improvements of quality and reductions in cost. In the branch of spinning and weaving of natural fibers it is necessary to curtail equipment or convert it to other fields, and in this case purchase of surplus facilities by the Government will have to be considered.

Industries such as cotton textiles, which must import their raw materials in its entirety from sources outside the Japanese mainland, will be hard hit by the Government's latest economic decree. This is especially true in view of Japan's decline in exports of cotton textiles from its prewar years.

The inability of the Japanese cotton industry to earn enough foreign exchange to pay for its raw materials seriously threatens the future of Japan's cotton-textile industry. Unless her cotton industry is able to export more items to earn more foreign exchange, especially dollars, chemical and synthetic textile industries will be encouraged at the expense of the cotton industry because the raw materials for manmade fibers are available in Japan except for woodpulp.

The consequences of such an eventuality to the United States grower of cotton should not be overlooked.

MITI revised in July 1956 its goals for 1963, but the fundamental policy of favoring chemical and synthetic textiles over cotton remained. The 1963 production goal for cotton textiles is set at 102 percent of the 1954 level, while that of chemical fiber and yarn are set at 218 percent. The significance of this policy is illustrated in the following table from the United States Department of Agriculture publication, Cotton and Chemical Fibers Competition in Japan, by Bernice M. Hornbeck (Foreign Agricultural Rept. No. 97):

*Rayon and noncellulosic fiber and cotton yarn: Production in Japan for 1954 and 1955 compared with the Japanese Government's goals for 1963*

[In thousand pounds]

| Commodity | Production | | Goal for 1963 | |
|---|---|---|---|---|
| | 1954 | 1955 | Amount | Percent of 1954 |
| Rayon staple fiber, total | 467, 112 | 564, 928 | 949, 999 | 203 |
| Viscose | 461, 579 | 558, 252 | 909, 000 | 197 |
| Acetate | 5, 533 | 6, 676 | 40, 000 | 723 |
| Rayon filament yarn, total | 188, 145 | 200, 348 | 336, 000 | 179 |
| Viscose | 187, 597 | 198, 368 | 296, 000 | 158 |
| Acetate | 548 | 1, 980 | 40, 000 | 7, 299 |
| Noncellulosics, total | 19, 885 | 37, 599 | 184, 000 | 925 |
| Vinylon | 8, 135 | 16, 340 | 120, 000 | 1, 475 |
| Nylon | 11, 750 | 21, 259 | 64, 000 | 545 |
| Rayon and noncellulosica, fiber and yarn, total | 675, 142 | 802, 875 | 1, 469, 000 | 218 |
| Cotton yarn, total | 972, 000 | 905, 000 | 989, 000 | 102 |

Source: Production figures from official records of the Foreign Agricultural Service. Goal figures from the 8-year plan of the Ministry of International Trade and Industry, Japan.

*Japanese foreign investments*

Although a relatively small amount of Japanese capital has been invested in foreign countries, the recent trend shows a gradual increase.

By the end of 1956, according to a study made by the United States Department of Agriculture, it was estimated that there were 5 independently owned Japanese enterprises abroad (outside Japan), 41 jointly owned enterprises, and 39 technical-assistance agreement enterprises.

In the field of textiles, this same trend obtains. Compared to prewar investments overseas, present textile holdings are insignificant.

So far, generally these investments have been made in southeast Asia and Latin America—Ceylon, Thailand, Burma, Brazil, Mexico, and El Salvador. All are small investments, including those in the planning stage, with the largest cotton mill planned for Brazil involving about 24,000 spindles.

Four reasons are given for these investments. They are (1) to encourage investments in raw-cotton growing areas such as Brazil and Mexico, (2) to overcome restrictions in Japan on new spinning and weaving equipment, (3) to help pay for reparations, as with Burma, and (4) to minimize restrictions against Japanese imports, as with Brazil.

In the case of Burma, the Japanese Government is obligated by treaty to implement the reparations agreement by aiding in the economic development of that land. Negotiations are now going on between the Burmese Government and Japanese industry, but many problems remain to be resolved before investments on a business basis will be possible.

Latin American investments can be explained in terms of the experience in Brazil and Mexico. Raw cotton is grown locally. There are few restrictions on remittances of capital and profits. Tax rates are relatively low and equitable for investments. Infant industries are protected by high tariffs and other restrictions. The outlook for markets in the areas are good. And there is little or no race prejudice against either the Japanese as people or Japanese manufactured merchandise.

In summary, there does not seem to be any special significance in these investments by the Japanese cotton-textile industry abroad as far as the international trade in textiles is concerned. For the most part, it is anticipated that the textiles produced in these countries will be for the local markets only. Furthermore, since Japanese exports to these countries are relatively small, Japan-made textiles will not be freed to be shipped to other countries.

The table below shows Japanese exports to Brazil and Mexico:

*Japanese cotton cloth exports to Brazil*

| From— | 1953 | 1954 | 1955 |
|---|---|---|---|
| Japan (1,000 square yards) | | 795 | 1 |
| United States (1,000 square yards) | 12 | 324 | 5 |

*Cotton cloth exports to Mexico*

| From— | 1953 | 1954 | 1955 |
|---|---|---|---|
| Japan (1,000 square yards) | 3,690 | 21,876 | 510 |
| United States (1,000 square yards) | 4,459 | 2,971 | 3,709 |

*Future outlook*

The fears of many of our leading textile spokesmen about Japan's future threat to our American cotton-textile market appear rather unfounded in the light of Japanese restrictions on textile machinery and equipment, of her decreasing dependence on foreign markets, and of her governmental policy of favoring chemical and manmade fibers over cotton.

Added assurance against future competition, at least until 1962, is seen in the voluntary quotas on cotton-textile exports to the United States.

LABOR IN THE JAPANESE TEXTILE INDUSTRY

Probably no other aspect of the Japanese cotton-textile industry has been the subject of more misinformation, misunderstanding, and misapprehension than that relating to Japanese labor—and wages.

Whether maliciously intended or not, emotional invectives, such as "slave labor," "coolie standards," and "sweatshops," coupled with inevitable charges of "cheap wages," have been the principal explanations offered by those who ought to know better in accounting for the popularity of Japanese textile imports in this country.

Much of this distortion arises from the simple, yet unfair, direct comparison of "dollar" or monetary wages paid to the Japanese worker, as contrasted to that of the American worker, without taking into consideration such other factors as fringe benefits, productivity, labor resources, and the textile workers' earnings in comparison with other elements in their economy.

Too often, those who discuss the labor situation in the cotton-textile industry rely on facts which fit prewar conditions, and not the new Japan, whose labor standards and objectives were patterned after those in the United States. Indeed, most of the labor statutes were adopted by the National Diet on the basis of recommendations made by the American occupation authorities.

An effort will be made in this section to present some of the facts which may be helpful in better evaluating the position of labor and its relation to the Japanese cotton-textile industry.

*Source for workers*

Over 80 percent of the Japanese cotton-textile workers are from the farms and rural areas. And 70 percent of all women employed by these mills are from farm families.

More than 40 percent—or some 6,105,000 families—of Japan's population is engaged in agricultural pursuits, a 1954 Government survey shows. And of these rural families, more than 60 percent need to supplement their farm income by working at other occupations. On the average 1 to 2 members of these farm families are employed away from home in other than agricultural industries.

The surplus farm-labor pool provides the principal source of workers for the Japanese cotton-textile industry. Most children of farmers have some knowledge of some skill in textile manufacturing, since most families augment their off-season income with side work, which usually consists of spinning and reeling for the city companies.

Most of these women textile millhands are either or both trying to supplement their family income or earning money for marriage expenses, while learning such marriage arts as cooking, sewing, child care, and so forth. Only 204 of 4,958 women who answered a recent Ministry of Labor questionnaire claimed that they, and not their fathers, were the principal breadwinners in their respective families. Some 41 percent gave as their chief reason for working the need to supplement family income, while 29.5 percent stated that they were working to earn marriage expenses.

That the cotton-textile industry generally enjoys a reputation for excellent working conditions among the entire population is witnessed by the 15 to 20 times as many who apply as there are jobs available. Moreover, those with relatively high scholastic ratings are hired, since employment is usually based on recommendations made by the various high schools.

*Evolution of the dormitory system*

One of the distinguishing characteristics of the cotton-textile industry in Japan is its so-called dormitory system. It is this feature of the industry that makes it difficult to compare wages and labor conditions with those in other countries.

The dormitory system is an outgrowth of the industry's reliance on women workers from agricultural communities far from the mills.

It was to provide living quarters and to give proper protection and guidance to girls where parental supervision was impossible.

According to a survey by the All Japan Cotton Spinners Association, at the beginning of 1957, over 85 percent of the women workers lived in the company compounds, while 49 percent of the men were commuters and 51 percent lived in company houses which were furnished at below-market rentals.

In the prewar period, these dormitories gave rise to much criticism from both domestic and foreign sources. They gave currency to such expressions as "caged labor" and "slave workers." Admittedly, in the early part of the development of the industry, even as in the United States, there were many abuses, but, certainly today, the living and employment conditions are outstanding. Today, conditions are such as to invite competition from applicants for the available job opportunities.

Even the highly critical study, the Japanese Cotton Industry, by Dr. W. T. Korese, a Dutch mill manager, reports the situation thusly:

Without again summing up all the points here, we would mention as improvements, among other things: the prohibition of recruiting girls from remote districts; the abolition of the system of advancing sums to parents, which sums had to be earned by the children; and the fact that they are at liberty now to give notice, their transport to and from home being regulated at the same time. The brand of slave labor, which at one time the Japanese recruiting system so unmistakably bore, has, at any rate, formally disappeared. * * * It is evident that there is a wish to eradicate the legends of millhands living in a state of slavery * * * it must be admitted that the accumulation of laborers in the most important establishments leaves little room for criticism, provided we recall the simple ways of living of the Japanese and the inbred group solidarity of the people.

This study for the Association of the Netherlands Cotton, Rayon, and Linen Industry was published in 1949, almost 10 years ago. Since then, rapid improvements have been noted by visiting officials.

A study released by the Primary Textiles Institute of Canada, in 1956, in commenting on the dormitory system, states:

By Japanese standards, this accommodation is equal to, or better than, that known by employees before they went to the mills, or to that they will have when they leave.

It is this dormitory system which allows the Japanese cotton industry to employ women off the farms. It is this system which helps give the Japanese cotton textile industry a comparative advantage in labor costs over other countries.

*Labor force*

At the beginning of 1955, the textile industry, including all fibers, employed more people than any other industry in Japan. Out of the 5,285,000 workers employed in all manufacturing enterprises, 1,048,000 were employed by the textile industry.

If the 140,000 workers employed by the apparel manufacturers and other finished fiber products and the 65,000 employed by the synthetics manufacturers were added, 23.7 percent, or nearly one-fourth, of the total industrial labor force in Japan would be employed in textiles.

*Number in cotton spinning and weaving*

An All Japan Cotton Spinners Association survey for early 1957 reveals that 120,363 workers were employed in spinning and weaving cotton. This number did not include clerical and supervisory workers.

About 83 percent, or 100,639 workers, were women, as against 17 percent, or 19,727 men. This ratio of men to women of 17 to 83 percent, is high when compared to the 35 percent in all manufacturing and 66 percent for all textile manufacturing. And it is this feature, emphasizing the use of women workers, which partly accounts for lower labor costs in Japan.

It should be noted, however, that men and women are not usually engaged in the same type of employment in the cotton mills. By law, where men and women are engaged in the same operation, they are entitled to the same wage.

*Labor turnover*

Most of the women employees—as previously noted—are selected from middle schools immediately after they have completed 9 years of compulsory education. They are chosen carefully after physical examinations, investigations of references, and family background, and educational and social aptitude tests. By careful screening, only the most suitable employees are hired, thereby reducing training time and the number that has to be dismissed for disciplinary and other reasons. Such selection is possible only because there are many more applicants than there are jobs. Working in the cotton mills is considered to be among the better types of employment available to the women of Japan.

These women remain with the mills until they leave to marry. After marriage, they retire, following the usual Japanese custom. Accordingly, the length of employment among women is much shorter than it is for men.

A 1957 survey covering 61,000 workers by the All Japan Cotton Spinners Association shows the average years of employment for men is 9 years and 6 months, while it is 5 years and 3 months for women. The average for both men and women is 6 years and 1 month.

The average age for men is 33 years and 3 months, and for women 22 years and 2 months. The average for all workers is 24 years and 4 months.

*Comparative wages in terms of economies*

Monetary wage payments in the Japanese cotton-spinning industry have increased substantially in the postwar years, and after 1955 have remained higher than the average of all manufacturing industries in Japan for either men or women workers.

The 1956 monetary wage-payment average per hour for men was ¥166.6, for women ¥61.7, and for both men and women ¥90.8 These wage payments were above the average for all Japanese industries by 56.6 percent for men, 37.4 per cent for women, and 3.9 percent for both. Thus, even with the preponderance of women employees, all textile workers averaged a higher per hour wage than did the average of workers in all manufacturing industries considered together.

On the other hand, monetary wage payments in the United States broad-woven-fabric mill industry were about 25 percent lower than the average of all manufacturing industries in this country. This condition existed before Japanese textile imports entered this country in any substantial amount; that is, prior to the treaty of peace with Japan in 1952.

In the broad-woven-fabric mill industry (including cotton, wool, and synthetic branches), the hourly wage payments in 1950 were $1.23; and in 1955, $1.34. In 1950 the industry's hourly wage payments were 16 percent under the average of all manufacturing industries and 10 percent under the average for non-durable-goods industries. By 1955 the difference increased to 28 percent under the average for all manufacturing and 26 percent below the average for all non-durable-goods industries.

The American cotton textile industry wage average for production workers was $1.19 an hour in 1954, the same as it was in March 1952, when no significent amount of Japanese textiles was exported to the United States during this period.

While the data between the United States and Japanese cotton textile industries is not directly comparative, it is significant that the wage payments as compared with all manufacturing in their respective countries indicate that the Japanese cotton textile mill workers are paid relatively better in their economy than are the broad woven fabric mill industry employees in our American economy.

More significant are figures from the Statistical Abstract of the United States for 1956, which show that the average hourly earnings of all American textile workers are lower than those of the average hourly earnings for all manufacturing workers in this country. As a matter of fact, not 1 of the 17 segments of the domestic textile industry listed have workers whose average hourly wages even equal those for all manufacturing industry in the United States.

Even though in dollar terms Japanese cotton-textile wages may be below those in the United States, they fare much better than do their American counterparts in our economy. This certainly makes the charges of worker exploitation seem farfetched.

Moreover, these statistics should be viewed in the context that Japan's gross national income is about one-tenth that of the United States. In terms of relative standing in their respective economies, as stated previously, the Japanese textile worker is considerably higher than is his United States counterpart.

*Textile labor conditions*

Fringe benefits are especially important nonwage payments made in Japan. When those of the cotton-textile industry are taken into consideration, these particular Japanese workers are even higher paid in terms of their economy. These fringe benefits are of real economic significance because of their magnitude and because, together with the highest wage payments, they exert a leadership role on the entire Japanese economy for better wages and free enterprise.

The standard working day in the Japanese cotton-spinning industry is 8 hours and the workweek is usually 6 days, as is the custom in most countries outside the United States. The mills, by law, may not operate for more than 2 shifts a day.

After a year of employment, the worker must receive at least 6 paid days of vacation and an additional paid day for each subsequent year of employment up to 20 working days for an annual paid vacation. This is provided by statute.

All workers are also granted special leaves for marriage, maternity, and funerals of relatives. These special leaves are usually with full pay and sometimes take a full week when traveling is required. Maternity leaves are much longer.

In addition, all workers receive at least 10 paid holidays a year.

Another benefit to be considered is that the Japanese textile worker is given two bonuses a year, each bonus usually being equal to at least 1 month's wages.

Forced retirement except to those in the very top echelons is dictated at 55 years of age. This is to provide employment for as many as possible in overpopulated Japan.

In the cotton-spinning industry, retirement allowances are equal to 3½ times the monthly wage, not including supplementary allowances such as family and regional dispensations, for 5 years of employment; 8 times for 10 years; 16 times for 15 years; 25 times for 20 years; and 55 times for 30 years. These allowances are not limited to management personnel; they apply equally to those working in the mills.

In cases of retirement for personal reasons, the allowance is 1.8 times the employee's monthly wage after 5 years of employment; about 6 times for 10 years; and 13 times for 15 years. These allowances are relatively low when compared to those who retire because of age. When 20 or more years of service are involved, however, the two rates are almost the same.

When women employees retire to marry, many companies provide them with an extra bonus as a wedding gift.

Workers who are forced to retire at the request of the company receive a considerably higher allowance than that paid to those who retire on account of age or personal reasons. Those who have received special recognition for their services are given special bonuses beyond their regular retirement allowances.

Some retirement allowances are between ¥3,500,000 and ¥3,700,000, a considerable amount in any currency.

Retirement because of accident is adjusted according to the length of service and other factors which have become standardized through usage and custom.

Especially worthwhile are the added and unique fringe benefits based on the Japanese system that can be described as a form of benevolent paternalism. There are virtually no layoffs when new labor-saving machines are installed, or when work is scarce. Many companies have been known to keep workers on their payrolls when their mills have closed down and they are faced with bankruptcy. Because of Japan's chronic unemployment, these paternalistic customs developed over the years provide far greater job security and unemployment benefits than exist elsewhere.

Other unique benefits include free housing in dormitories for unmarried workers, recreational and educational activities, sports and social centers, dining rooms, matrimonial counseling and aid, and medical-hospital-surgical facilities and staff. For some of these benefits, the workers pay only a nominal sum, with the company paying the balance; others are free to the worker, with the compliments of the company.

In 1955, the cotton-spinning industry of Japan estimated that the amount paid by the companies for these special fringe benefits approximated 18 percent of the average worker's annual salary.

Other benefits and rights of workers in the cotton-textile industry of Japan are protected by legislation. Among the protective and beneficent laws are the Labor Standard Law, the Employment Security Law, the Health Insurance Law, the Welfare Pension Insurance Act, the Labor-Relations Adjustment Law, and the Trade-Union Law.

*Labor unions*

Less than a year after the surrender (1945) the Big Ten cotton spinners which were organized during the war, was completely unionized. Since then, the independent spinners have, for the most part, been unionized by the aggressive Japan Federation of Textile Workers Union (JFTWU).

By the end of 1956, JFTWU had organized 99 percent of the cotton-spinning industry. In the cotton division of the union, it had 182,000 members, representing 125,000 employees of the Big Ten and 57,000 of the 59,000 workers of the remaining 119 spinners which were established after the war.

There are 58 unions or locals in the cotton-spinning industry, including the 10 unions of the Big Ten, all of which are affiliated with the JFTWU. This federation covers all of the textile industry, including wool, linen, manmade fibers, cotton, weaving, dyeing, and apparels. The estimated total JFTWU membership is roughly 300,000.

The JFTWU has been affiliated with the non-Communist International Confederation of Free Trade Unions (ICFTU) since July 1950, and with the International Federation of Textile Workers Association (IFTWA) since July 1951. The American Federation of Labor-Congress of Industrial Organizations (AFL-CIO) of the United States is also affiliated with the former, and the Textile Workers Union, AFL-CIO, with the latter.

The union shop principle is recognized in all prevailing labor agreements in the Japanese cotton industry. Other rights of free trade unionism, such as wage and working conditions, union organizing, collective bargaining, grievance-settlement procedures, and other labor-management relations, are recognized in these contracts.

There have been relatively few strikes in the cotton-textile industry because, generally speaking, labor-management relations are among the best in Japan. The only strikes called since August 1945 were two 4-day strikes in December 1951 and a 20-day strike in October 1955.

*Labor conditions in United States textile industry*

A comparison with labor conditions in the United States textile industry is most revealing.

The latest available official statistics are those of the United States Department of Labor, for operations in November 1954. Aside from an increase in wages due to the increase in minimum-wage requirements under the law, this study, though 3 years old, is still considered authoritative.

One of the special cotton-textile industry characteristics noted by the Department of Labor was that in November 1954 employment in the industry was 10 percent lower than it had been in March 1952 and 15 percent below the immediate postwar level early in 1946. The employment loss was proportionately higher in New England than it was in the Southeastern States. Between March 1952 and November 1954, industry employment in the Southeast decreased about 7 percent while the decline in New England was 20 percent.

These employment facts are impressive and pertinent, because they took place before Japanese imports were of any significance, for it was not until 1954 that Japan was able to enter the United States market to any degree worthy of note. And, it was not until 1956 that the first postwar petition to the United States Tariff Commission against any Japanese textile was filed.

The average workweek for the American textile worker in November 1954 was 40 hours.

About one-half of the workers were employed on the second and third (graveyard) shifts. Premium payments for work on the second shift were not common, although third-shift workers were paid about 5 cents an hour in the South and 7 cents in New England extra compensation.

Company-paid vacations were almost universal after a year's service in both New England and the Middle Atlantic States. Only 91 percent of the companies in the Southeast and 82 percent in the Southwest, however, provided paid vacations automatically. Generally, New England mills based vacation benefits on the individuals' annual earnings—about 2 percent (approximately 1 week's pay) after 1 year of service, 3 percent after 3 years, and 4 percent after 5 years or more of service. Southeast cotton-textile workers were usually given a week's paid vacation after the first year of employment and 2 weeks after 5 or more years of service.

In the way of fringe benefits, life insurance and sickness, accident, surgical, and hospitalization insurance, usually financed in part by the company, were available to most workers in all regions. In the South incidentally, insurance benefits had become more widespread by November 1954 than it had been 2 years previously.

Retirement pensions (not including Government social-security benefits) providing regular payments for the remainder of the workers' life after retirement, usually at age 65, were not uniform throughout the textile-manufacturing areas. These pensions applied to 19 percent of the production workers in the Southeast, 6 percent in New England, and 4 percent in the mid-Atlantic region. Lump-sum payment plans were provided to 84 percent of the production workers in New England and to 22 percent in the mid-Atlantic region, but were virtually nonexistent in the South in November 1954.

Unionization of workers in November 1954 covered nearly 30,000 production workers, or nearly 95 percent, in New England. In the Southeast, 50,000 production workers, or nearly 16 percent, were employed by mills with union contracts. About half of the workers in North Carolina, South Carolina, and Virginia who were under union contracts were in the larger mills employing more than a thousand workers, and 50 percent of these were employed by the 10 largest mills.

On an industrywide basis in November 1954, about two-fifths of the cotton-textile-mill workers were paid on an incentive basis, usually piecework. Spinners, weavers, and winders were among the largest groups of piecework workers.

The American industry, unlike its Japanese counterpart, has and is continuing to experience difficulty in securing new workers, especially from the colleges and universities. Harry Reimer, editor of the trade journal Daily News Record, in a lead editorial on March 21, 1957, wrote as follows:

> Are mills satisfied with the supply of trained textile college graduates that is available to them? * * * We are a great industry; we will need trained young men more and more. What does the textile industry plan to do; what does it have in mind about inducing young men to look to it for careers?
>
> How long will it take to overcome the bad publicity of the past 2 years, which has not helped the industry with the public—publicity about poor earnings—publicity about the dire threats of heavy imports of Japanese textiles? What is the industry doing to offset this bad publicity? * * *
>
> The textile industry has been through this type of cycle before—in fact, many times. As a basic industry, it must offer opportunities. Leaders are needed as never before.

The original editorial carried each sentence as a separate paragraph, but we have grouped them together for clarity.

While the Japanese cotton textile industry rates highest in Japan's economy, the American cotton textile industry does not fare too well in our economy. The primary reason is that other industries are outstripping cotton textiles as our total economy expands. Our dynamic economy has moved forward tremendously in the past decade, while our cotton textile industry, although perhaps efficient when compared to foreign countries, has become an inefficient and depressed industry in comparison to such other industries as automobiles, steel, electronics, aviation, etc.

Overall, if the working conditions in Japan are to be compared with those in our domestic cotton textile industry, except for monetary wages, the Japanese cotton textile worker fares relatively well indeed. Certainly, in such items as recreational, medical care, and educational facilities the Japanese have outstripped our textile industry.

*Labor productivity*

Perhaps the most accurate factor in comparing wages or labor between two countries—such as the United States and Japan in this instance—is labor productivity. Unfortunately, any comparison of this nature is a difficult task as best, if not completely impossible. For an accurate comparison, all the many factors which affect productivity must be equal or constant, an impossibility because the size and efficiency of mills, processing of cotton, machinery and other equipment, manufactured product, and so forth—all must be constant and equal in every respect.

The only information we were able to find on the subject is that presented to the Subcommittee on Customs, Tariffs, and Reciprocal Trade Agreements of the Committee on Ways and Means by the Japanese cotton industry last December (see pp. 2103–2104, pt. 4, Overseas Conferences, printed hearings):

> Recognizing the great limitation of any comparison, especially since we have no up-to-date information on United States cotton industry's labor productivity, we make the following comparison in order that we may have some indications as to the relative labor productivity in the two countries.

*Operative hours per 100 pounds production (up to ring spinning)*

| Yarn counts | United Nations standard mills (50,000 spindles) | United States cotton mill | Japanese cotton mill |
|---|---|---|---|
| 20s (carded) | 6.07 | | 7.58 |
| 21s (carded) | | 6.59 | 7.78 |
| 30s (carded) | 8.34 | | 9.40 |
| 31s (combed) | | 10.45 | 14.88 |
| 35s (combed) | 10.83 | | 16.42 |
| 38s (combed) | | 10.05 | 17.30 |
| 40s (combed) | 12.71 | | 17.88 |
| 42s (combed) | | 16.20 | 18.84 |
| 45s (combed) | 14.97 | 12.02 | 20.24 |
| 60s (combed) | 21.40 | 22.99 | 26.90 |
| 65s (combed) | 23.14 | | 28.92 |
| 78s (combed) | | 27.50 | 35.80 |

The United Nations standard mill mentioned above is taken from United Nations Labour Productivity of the Cotton Textile Industry in Five Latin-American Countries, 1951, covering 12 standard mills (modern spinning mills). The United States cotton mill in this table is based on Anglo-American Council on Productivity, Productivity Team Report on Cotton Spinning, March 1950.

The data used for the Japanese cotton mill are taken from actual production figures of the Big Ten spinners for September 1956. Productivity for this group is considered to be the highest among all Japanese cotton mills.

If we compare these figures, we find conclusively that the operative hours per production up to ring spinning in Japanese cotton mills is higher than that of the American mills and the United Nations standard cotton mill.

Furthermore, this is a comparison up to ring spinning, but it is generally believed that if other aspects of the cotton textile industry, such as winding, weaving preparation, weaving, finishing, etc., are taken into consideration, the gap would be even greater. This is because the Japanese cotton industry through modernization of its productive processes has improved its facilities up to ring spinning, but in the later processes it is still far behind the United States.

It is noteworthy, however, that the Report of the Joint (House and Senate) Committee on the Economic Report on Foreign Economic Policy, dated January 5, 1956, does not consider the accurate assessment of real costs and labor productivity to be very important. Except for one Congressman (Henry O. Talle), who did not participate, the report was unanimous. On the subject of real cost comparisons, the joint report declared:

Tariff policy cannot be based on international real cost comparisons and should not even if they could be obtained. There is no meaningful way to compare real costs (inputs of labor and materials) from one country to another, for it is prices, not real costs, that influence trade. Nor is the concept of average cost levels for a whole country either measurable or useful. Although trade actually depends upon price comparisons, these are relatively easy to alter through variation in exchange rates, subsidies, and the normal disparity which may exist at one time between prices and long-run money costs. Although the price of a commodity entering international trade can be and is translated through an exchange rate, it is fallacious to compare internal money costs in different countries through the use of exchange rates. For example, the components of living costs in different countries vary not only in relative prices but in proportional importance to local living standards.

The test of acceptability of foreign imports cannot be in terms of the absolute technical efficiency of their production, even if it could be measured. The market mechanism for allocating resources, which is the basis of a free economy, is a more logical guide. It operates by a principle that we can concentrate on producing those items in which we have the greatest relative advantage and leaves to trade the acquisition of those items in which we have a comparative disadvantage. Departures from the automatic operation of this principle of economic efficiency cost us some of our economic well-being, and have been acceptable to people who understand these principles only because we do not live in a world truly at peace. Surrendering some trade freedom and hence maximum economic advantage has been necessary in a divided world.

Low-wage countries and high-wage countries are not barred from carrying on mutually beneficial trade. This is because wages are only one element in total money costs, and money costs or prices must be compared through an exchange rate which is subject to adjustment. Further, low wages do not necessarily mean cheap labor cost per unit of output, for low wages are generally a sign of low productivity. Relatively plentiful labor is paid low wages, but usually produces so little per capita output that the price of a final product is just as likely to be higher as it is lower than the product price in a high-wage country. But low-wage countries do tend to have a comparative advantage in the production of goods which require much labor, while high-wage countries have a comparative advantage in the production of goods which require a higher proportion of capital or material resources in their manufacture. Absolute advantage in all lines of production is not found in practice and is meaningless as a concept. Low wages abroad tend to limit trade, however, because they usually imply little purchasing power for imports.

The validity of the analysis of the joint committee is witnessed in United States-Japan trade relations, with particular reference to cotton textile imports from Japan. The Japanese cotton textile imports have shown little ability to successfully cope with the American market and are necessarily limited because of cost factors. Elsewhere in this submission, the competitive ability of Japanese imports is clearly demonstrated to be limited at best, even with their lower dollar wages.

*Wages not sole factor*

Wages alone are not the sole or even paramount factor.

It might be noted that if "cheap wages" were the only criterion for trade with the United States, India, Hong Kong, and many other countries and areas would be able to export to our country considerably greater quantities than Japan, for of all the Asian nations Japan has the highest standard of living by far and her workmen are paid the highest wages of all.

Moreover, if wages alone were crucial, how does one account for the fact that in 1955 Japan's postwar high total cotton-fabrics exports to this country equaled less than 1.24 percent of our total domestic production of cotton textiles, while at the same time we were shipping to neighboring Canada that same year an amount equal to approximately 60 percent of her total cotton-textile production?

While it is true that Japanese workers have less purchasing power than do American workers, the fact that our imports of Japanese textiles constitutes one of Japan's most important sources for dollar earnings cannot be ignored. Low as Japanese wages may be, it is still sufficient to generate strong enough demands to constitute Japan as America's usual best customer for all our agricultural products and our first, second, or third overall best customer for all our exports. In this context, we must remember that the poorly paid Japanese cotton-textile worker must pay for his imported-from-the-United States wheat, rice, barley, tobacco, corn, soybeans, and so forth, by selling to us the products of his mills and looms.

IMPORT IMPACT AND AMERICAN INDUSTRY

While the facts are clear that relatively few Japanese imports may compete successfully in the United States market, there are those who argue that the very impact of these few items are such as to threaten the entire domestic industry.

We believe that the threatening nature of this impact has been, and is, grossly exaggerated, for the facts belie the extent to which these relatively few Japanese imports may influence the United States market and industry.

*Statistical impact*

Overall exports of all cotton textiles to the United States by Japan are now limited to a maximum of 235 million square yards annually, including made-up goods. And, as previously pointed out, this maximum amount includes items that Japan cannot export in sufficient quantities to fulfill her subquotas.

This export limitation is equivalent to about 106,000 bales of raw cotton, or about a ninth of the raw cotton that the United States exported to Japan last year (1956).

The impact of these Japanese imports, then, was about 1.2 percent, when compared to the 9,147,000 bales of raw cotton consumed by the domestic mills in 1955.

These 106,000 bales imported into the United States in manufactured cotton textiles are relatively insignificant when contrasted to the 1,725,000 bales of cotton which were lost to other fibers and nonfibers the same year, according to an estimate of M. K. Horne, chief economist for the National Cotton Council of America (NCC).

Greater detail of this alleged impact can be observed by comparing Japanese cotton-fabric exports to the United States with American production, exports, and imports.

*Comparison of American production, export, import, and Japanese export of cotton fabrics, 1936–55*

[Million square yards]

| Year | American cotton fabrics | | | Japan's cotton fabric export to United States (B) | Percent, B/A |
|---|---|---|---|---|---|
| | Production (A) | Export | Import | | |
| 1936 | 8, 614 | 201 | 114 | 73 | 0. 85 |
| 1937 | 9, 446 | 236 | 147 | 124 | 1. 31 |
| 1938 | 7, 549 | 320 | 58 | 16 | . 21 |
| 1939 | 9, 045 | 367 | 112 | 72 | . 80 |
| 1940 | 9, 602 | 358 | 84 | 50 | . 52 |
| 1941 | 11, 328 | 593 | 61 | 48 | . 42 |
| 1942 | 12, 205 | 453 | 18 | | |
| 1943 | 11, 569 | 547 | 20 | | |
| 1944 | 10, 572 | 646 | 11 | | |
| 1945 | 9, 779 | 673 | 80 | | |
| 1946 | 10, 171 | 775 | 45 | | |
| 1947 | 11, 083 | 1, 479 | 16 | 6 | . 05 |
| 1948 | 10, 863 | 940 | 32 | 12 | . 11 |
| 1949 | 9, 392 | 880 | 20 | 5 | . 05 |
| 1950 | 11, 207 | 558 | 48 | 23 | . 21 |
| 1951 | 11, 415 | 802 | 46 | 2 | . 02 |
| 1952 | 10, 593 | 761 | 35 | 7 | . 07 |
| 1953 | 11, 333 | 621 | 64 | 33 | . 29 |
| 1954 | 10, 892 | 605 | 73 | 50 | . 46 |
| 1955 | 11, 319 | 542 | 133 | 140 | 1. 24 |
| 1956 | | | | 123 | |

Sources: Production of cotton fabrics, up to 1954—ACMI, Cotton Textiles Hi-lights, Mid-Century Number, 1900–50; after 1946, the Association of Cotton Textile Merchants of New York, Ten Years of Cotton Textiles.

Export and import of cotton fabrics—ACMI, Cotton Textile Hi-lights, January 1957.

One of the more interesting aspects of this table is that the total American exports in the lowest postwar year (1955) are more than four times that of Japan's highest postwar exports (1955) to the United States.

Thus, as far as general fabrics are concerned, Japanese imports into this country are more than offset by United States exports through the years. Also, it should be noted that Japanese imports fluctuate far less than do United States exports.

The period of high United States exports started during World War II and continued in the postwar era when we were attempting to supply civilian demands built up during hostilities and markets supplied by other countries before the war.

American exports, the table shows, are still substantially greater than they were in 1940, just before the great dislocations caused by World War II.

In the light of this illustration, it is difficult to visualize the impact of Japanese imports on the United States industry; indeed, it would appear that Japanese imports had little, or no, influence on American exports and on the domestic market.

*Selected imports*

While conceding that Japan's total cotton imports into the United States are not large in terms of domestic consumption, it is often alleged that Japanese imports are concentrated on a few selected items and injury is thereby sustained by certain segments of the American industry.

It is only natural, of course, that American buyers of Japanese textiles purchase those particular commodities which are more efficiently produced by Japan in order that the ultimate consumer may receive the best possible bargain—that is quality at a reasonable price.

Since Japan is better able, economically, to manufacture and export certain articles than others, let us examine their individual impact on the American market to determine the validity of allegations made by certain domestic manufacturers.

*Ginghams*

Earlier this year (1957), the United States Tariff Commission terminated its escape-clause investigation (No. 54) on gingham-cloth imports because Japan initiated its 5-year control program on cotton-textile exports to this country. The maximum annual export of gingham cloth to the United States was limited to 35 million square yards.

From submissions to the Tariff Commission in the above-mentioned investigation, it was learned that gingham producers comprise only 3 percent of the domestic cotton mills and account for only 2 percent of the total cotton production.

Other submissions included a table which shows the total of imports as compared to domestic production.

*Domestic production and imports of ginghams*

[In million square yards]

| Year | Production (United States) | Imports | Imports as percent of production |
|---|---|---|---|
| 1951 | 157.7 | | |
| 1952 | 169.7 | | |
| 1953 | 157.4 | 2.8 | 1.2 |
| 1954 | 193.4 | 4.3 | 2.2 |
| 1955 | 260.1 | 32.7 | 13.9 |
| 1956 | [1] 250.0 | [1] 49.0 | 18.4 |

[1] Estimated.

Domestic production of gingham cloth has increased substantially since 1951.

During the Tariff Commission hearings, it was pointed out that the imports increased to meet increasing demands on the part of the consumers, demands which were not filled by domestic production alone.

Under the voluntary export quota, Japanese gingham imports into this country are restricted to 35 million square yards annually, or just about half the increase in domestic production from 1954 to 1955.

*Velveteens*

The entire United States velveteen industry is composed of three companies. One is the major producer, another produces velveteens periodically, and the third limits its activities to processing and finishing. All three companies have other operations and the degree of their dependence on velveteen production is not known.

Overall velveteen production in the United States is relatively low. The average yearly domestic production in the 1930's was 2,479,169 square yards. Production just prior to and during the war, except for 1945, was high, with the yearly average for the 1940's being 4,567,686 square yards. The first 4 years of the 1950's were record-breaking ones, too, since civilian demand following hostilities had to be satisfied.

| | *Square yards* |
|---|---|
| 1930–39 yearly average | 2,479,169 |
| 1940–49 yearly average | 4,567,686 |
| 1949 | 4,502,435 |
| 1950 | 6,883,030 |
| 1951 | 8,094,559 |
| 1952 | 8,246,496 |
| 1953 | 7,683,317 |
| 1954 | 4,322,013 |

Though 1955 and 1956 production figures are not available, it is known that sales of domestic velveteens decreased from 5,458,900 square yards in 1954 to 4,184,000 square yards in 1955. Figures for 1956 are not available.

It is difficult to assess the impact of Japanese velveteen imports on the American industry because of the vagaries of demand on the part of the consumers, the difference in the imported and domestic products, and the influence of various fashion trends.

Imports of Japanese velveteens found eager buyers in the United States and imports increased substantially in 1953, 1954, and 1955—to an all-time high of 6,795,700 square yards. The apparent domestic consumption of all types and constructions of velveteens by the Tariff Commission was estimated to be 12,784,300 square yards in 1955.

The ability and capability of the American velveteen producers to maintain high levels of production are not challenged by import competition. And, the cutback in imports imposed by the Japanese Government now provides American manufacturers an even larger market—partly developed by imports—than they ever enjoyed before.

Japan's annual imports are limited to 2,500,000 square yards, while Italy's are restricted to 1,375,000 square yards (1 year quota for 1957).

United States consumption in 1955 totaled 12,800,000 square yards. Since demand may remain at this level, or increase, American producers are assured the major share of the market because of governmental restrictions on imports imposed by Japan and Italy on their exports to the United States. In a sense, the American producer now enjoys a virtual monopoly.

The high peak of domestic production was reached in 1929, when 8,300,000 square yards were produced. The 8 million square yard mark was reached on only 2 occasions (1951 and 1952), and 7 million square yards only once (1953).

Since the American market consumed 12,800,000 square yards in 1955, after deducting the total that will be imported under current limitations from Japan and Italy, domestic producers need to expand their facilities to produce more than 1,300,000 square yards than their previous high to supply the current market.

*Other fabrics*

Under the Japanese export quotas, "all other fabrics" are limited to 75,500,000 square yards. This category includes sheeting, shirting (80 by 80 type), other shirting, twill and sateen, poplin, yarn dyed fabrics, and other fabrics. In addition, a quota limitation of 30 million square yards is imposed on "made-up goods usually included in United States cotton broad woven production." Items such as pillowcases, dish towels, handkerchiefs, table damask, and others are included.

Added up, Japan's export quota maximum for these 2 categories combined is 105,500,000 square yards annually.

If Japan's quota of 2,500,000 square yards for velveteens and 35 million square yards for ginghams are included, a total of 143 million square yards are arrived at.

This contrasts with United States production in these same categories of 11,298,000,000 square yards, which means that Japan's maximum imports in these classifications cannot exceed 1.26 percent of America's total production in these same items, based on 1956 figures.

*Cotton pillowcases*

Included within the "made-up goods usually in United States cotton broadwoven production" limitation of 30 million square yards annually is plain cotton pillowcases. The quota on this item is 400,000 dozen yearly.

These pillowcase imports from Japan were subject to a Tariff Commission investigation last year (1956). The finding was that "* * * in the judgment of the Commission, no sufficient reason exists for a recommendation to the President" that these specific imports have caused or "threaten" to cause serious injury to the domestic producers.

Part of the summary of the Commission conclusion follows:

The Commission estimates * * * that total domestic production amounted to 9.8 million dozen in 1953, 9.8 million dozen in 1954, and 9.1 million dozen in 1955. The decline in production was accompanied by a rise in imports during that period, but imports were lower in the first 8 months of 1956 than in the corresponding period of 1955.

The decline in production was also accompanied by changes in the volume of exports and in apparent consumption. Exports were higher in 1954 than in 1953, lower in 1955 than in either 1954 or 1953, and at a higher average monthly rate in the first 6 months of 1956 than in any of the 3 preceding years. Apparent consumption rose from 8.5 million dozen in 1953 to 9.4 million in 1954 and to 9.9 million in 1955; and it was at a higher average monthly rate in the first 6 months of 1956 than in the corresponding period of 1955.

From the foregoing, it is apparent that the volume of domestic production does not vary inversely with the volume of imports but rather is a function of an aggregate of variables among which the volume of imports is not even the most important. Moreover, far greater variations in annual production occurred in the years before 1953, when imports were negligible, than have occurred since. The Commission must therefore conclude that there is no significant correlation between the level of production and the level of imports. The Commission also observes that between 1954 and 1955 (the year of highest imports) domestic production of pillowcases made of muslin or percale sheeting declined much more than did the domestic manufacture of printcloth pillowcases. Notwithstanding, no domestic manufacturer of muslin or percale pillowcases claimed serious injury from import competition.

The alleged "concentration" of Japanese pillowcases occurred in 1955, when 977,171 dozen were imported into the United States.

Even though the Tariff Commission officially found that these imports were not injurying or threatening injury to the American industry, the Japanese voluntarily imposed a quota limitation which is less than half the 1955 level of their imports, or 400,000 dozen annually.

*Cotton blouses*

Cotton blouse imports from Japan are now limited to 1,500,000 dozen annually.

The domestic industry, which applied last spring for "escape clause" action with the Tariff Commission, withdrew their petition when the present Japanese quota arrangement was announced later last year.

The unfavorable and unprecedented publicity last summer concerning Japanese "dollar" blouses resulted from an unfortunate circumstance which probably will never be repeated. Too many American buyers ordered far more blouses from Japan than they could reasonably sell on the United States market. This resulted in heavy losses for all concerned—the manufacturers and exporters in Japan and the importers, jobbers, wholesalers, and retailers in this country—with "distress" sales as the ultimate consequence.

About the only beneficial result of last year's experience is that American importers are now on notice that they cannot place orders in Japan indiscriminately and without regard to market trends and conditions. Promiscuous placing of orders in Japan, without adequate study of the factors involved, is not good business practice under any circumstance.

During this period of "distress" selling of Japanese blouses in February 1956, the Tariff Commission was petitioned to investigate. Shortly thereafter, the Japanese Government announced that it would limit blouse exports to this country to about 2,500,000 dozen annually. In the 1957 quota program, this total was reduced to 1,500,000 dozen yearly

In spite of the acrimonious charges of the domestic industry, however, even during this period of "sensational dollar blouses," the American cotton-blouse industry continued to increase its production substantially every year.

Production figures released by the Tariff Commission for women's cotton blouses, waists, and shirt production in this country since 1947 reveal a consistent upward trend in the manufacture of these specialized items:

| | *Dozen* | | *Dozen* |
|---|---|---|---|
| 1947 | 995,000 | 1952 | 5,697,000 |
| 1948 | 1,664,000 | 1953 | 6,653,000 |
| 1949 | 2,690,000 | 1954 | 8,858,000 |
| 1950 | 3,065,000 | 1955 | 9,715,000 |
| 1951 | 3,985,000 | 1956 | [1] |

[1] Not available.

It would appear from these figures of constantly increasing production that Japanese imports of cotton blouses may have helped to develop new markets and new demands for all cotton blouses, domestic as well as imported.

This is often the "true impact" of imports on domestic production that is not mentionel by those involved in American industry.

*Decline in spindles*

The "alarming" decline in the number of spindles is cited by those who allege that Japanese textile imports have injured the domestic industry.

Actually, since the spindle is the most common denominator in the basic manufacture of cotton yarn, the productive capacity of a company or a nation is often expressed in this framework of reference. This measurement, however, may be misleading because the productive capacity of the spindle itself is dependent on both the efficiency of the spindle itself and the intensity of its operation.

The following chart may be revealing in this respect:

| | Date (end of year) | Spindles (thousand units) | Production (metric tons) | Production per spindle (metric tons) |
|---|---|---|---|---|
| United States | 1938 | 29,911 | 1,108.6 | 37.1 |
| Do | 1955 | 22,247 | 1,710.1 | 76.5 |
| Japan | 1938 | 11,502 | 463.0 | 40.0 |
| Do | 1955 | 7,961 | 375.1 | 47.2 |

To repeat, this chart is not intended to show relative efficiency of spindles, or the intensity of their use, but merely to illustrate that production cannot be measured in terms of numbers of spindles alone. There are many other factors to be considered. Nevertheless, it seems clear that an assumption may be made that per spindle productivity has increased over the years, an assumption that is consistent with the improved technology of our times. The dates and the data were selected, incidentally, from the earliest and the latest compilations cited in the World Cotton Statistics, by the International Cotton Advisory Committee in 1956.

The intensity of operation is not reflected in the above figures. Most American mills, it is known, operate on a three-shift day, while Japanese spindles by law may not be operated more than two shifts a day. Also efficiency of operation and the "modernness" of spindles is not mentioned.

The vital fact, however, is that there is no validity to the assumption made by so many domestic producers that simply because there are fewer spindles now in operation as compared to prewar dates there is less production—caused, presumably, by increasing imports.

*"Plight" of domestic industry*

Since it has now been demonstrated that, by and large, the impact of Japanese cotton-textile imports on the United States industry is negligible, perhaps it may be illuminating to examine some of the reasons for the alleged "plight" of the American industry.

In this connection, it should be kept in mind that the economic well-being of the American cotton-textile industry is of serious concern to importers of Japanese cotton textiles, for a strong and prosperous domestic industry reflects an active and profitable market for both imported and homemade products.

As indicated earlier, very few Japanese cotton-textile items by their nature are always competitive with our comparative merchandise; most Japanese articles can be imported and sold competitively only when the American market is "high" and the Japanese market is "low."

It is important, therefore, from the viewpoint of the importers that the domestic industry be healthy and progressive.

*Cyclical fluctuations*

The current alleged straitened condition of the American industry may be explained in part by the so-called cyclical fluctuations which are considered a periodic and rather clearly defined pattern for the industry.

Experience over the years has shown that these major fluctuations have continued within the industry even through such abnormal periods of great demand as those following World War II and the Korean conflict, and imports have little, if any, influence on these cycles.

An outline which suggests the workings of this 2-year cycle, based upon percentages of raw-cotton consumption changes at the mills, is as follows:

CHART I.—Raw-cotton consumption cycle in the United States

[Percent increase or decrease of monthly consumption per day as compared with the corresponding month a year ago]

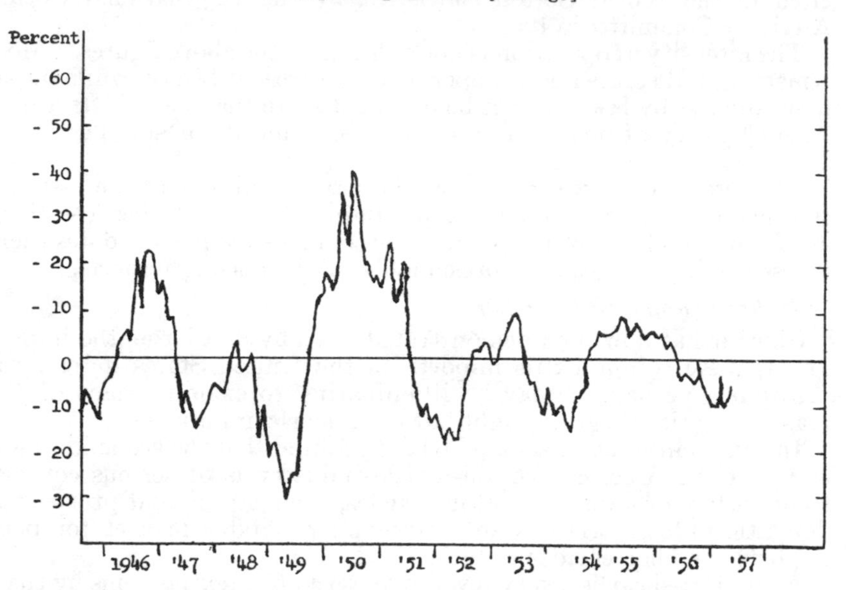


The chart reveals that the cycle of raw-cotton consumption in domestic mills operates, roughly, on a cycle of about 2 years' duration, with a maximum recurrent period of about 3 years. Abnormal postwar conditions during the 1946–48 period and the 1951–52 period illustrates the regularity of the cycle and its existence prior to any significant imports of Japanese cotton textiles.

Chart II reveals the same cyclical pattern in terms of cotton-mill stocks and unfilled orders of cotton broad woven goods and index of cotton consumption. The business activity of the cotton mills can be charted to show repeated "ups and downs" at about 1-year intervals, or at the longest 2 years. Needless to say, when there are many unfilled orders, the industry is relatively prosperous; and, conversely, when there are no unfilled orders, the industry is relatively "depressed."

The ACMI reports that the ratio of unfilled orders of cotton broad woven goods to the current week's production has been smaller successively since June 1956 than the corresponding month a year earlier, while the ratio of stock to average weekly production has been larger during the same period.

CHART II.—Stocks and unfilled orders of cotton broad woven goods and index of cotton consumption

[Stocks and unfilled orders stated in number of current week's production and index of cotton consumption based on 1935–39 as 100]

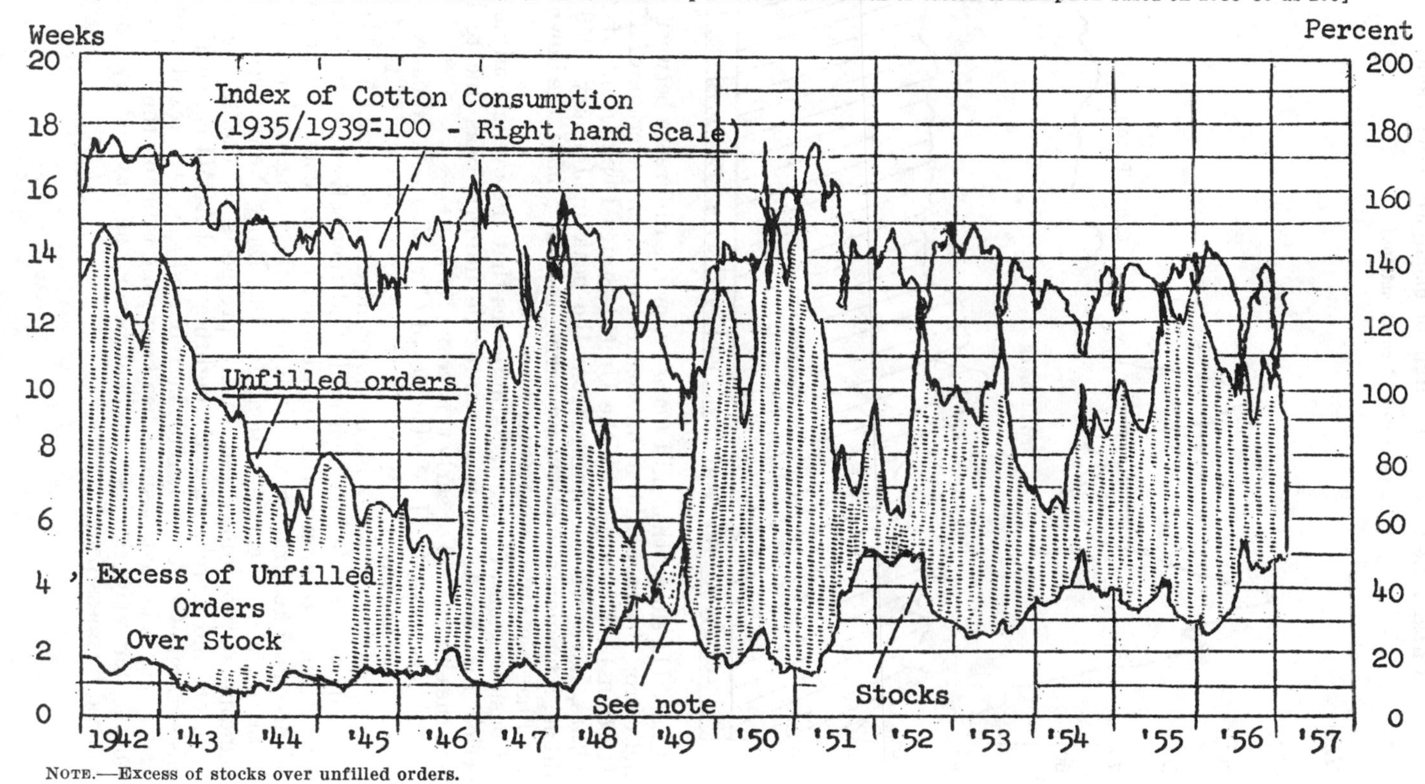


NOTE.—Excess of stocks over unfilled orders.

CHART III.—Gross mill margin of unfinished cotton cloth

[Average of 17 constructions]

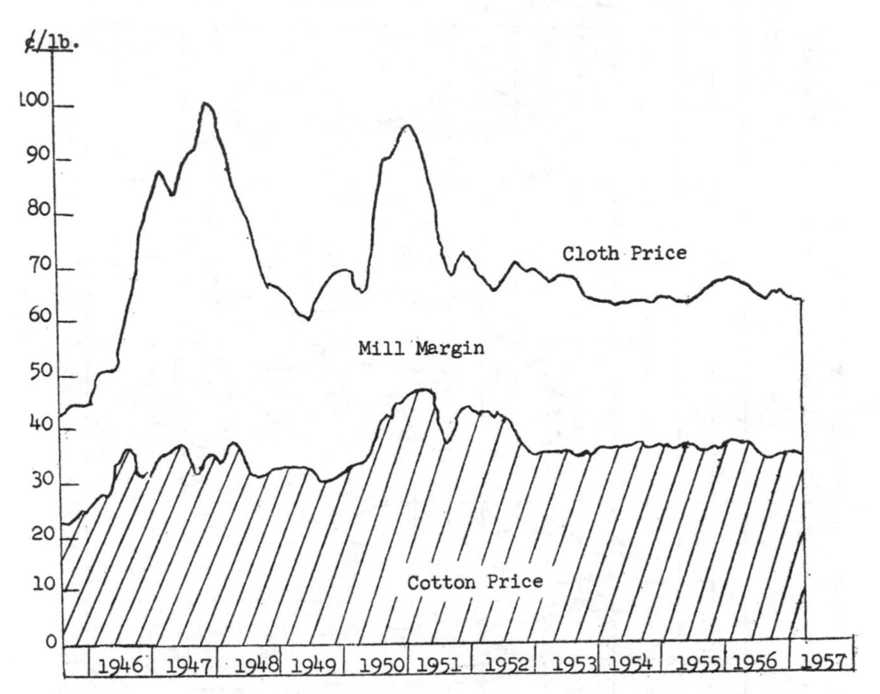


Chart III shows that mill margins, or the difference between cloth and cotton prices, of the unfinished cotton cloth (average of 17 constructions), as reported by the United States Department of Agriculture, have been declining from the peak in January 1956, and although temporarily recovered during the fall (1956), the downward trend has continued apparently into 1957.

Consideration of these facts indicates that the cyclical adjustment period for the American cotton-textile industry was due to begin near the end of 1956 or early this year (1957).

In this context, E. H. Mackenzie, of Carl M. Loeb, Rhoades & Co., who is in charge of the Worth Street Market Review of the Cotton Trade Journal of Memphis, Tenn., pointed out on April 5, 1957, that "the current trouble in which mills find themselves can be traced to their failure to observe the well-defined cotton consumption cycle."

This same realization was independently recognized by Herman S. Shaps, a staff correspondent for the Daily News Record, after sounding out opinions and future prospects of the textile manufacturers and merchants at the eighth annual ACMI convention held this spring. On April 4, 1957, he reported that "the textile-industry leaders concede that business has been rough during the past several months, but view this as a cyclical period, aggravated by generally reduced business pace."

Several important indexes, however, suggest that the current "slump" in the domestic textile industry is not as severe as other post-Korea downswings. In the third quarter of 1956, for example, the latest quarter for which figures are available, the profit on sales still remained higher than any quarter of 1952 or 1954, although it was somewhat less from the peak registered in the first quarter (1956).

The long-run profit on sales is indicated in chart IV.

CHART IV.—Profit rates and current ratios—textile-mill products industry

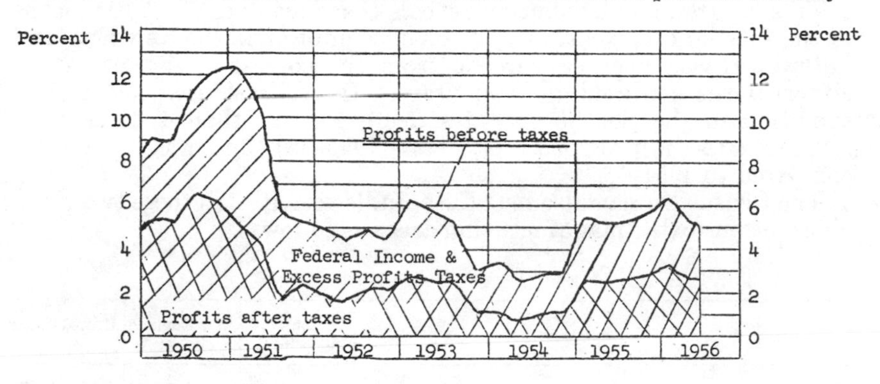


Chart III on mill margins of unfinished cotton cloth shows that the margins are now lower than in the peak of early 1956, but that the margins are higher than the low points in 1952 and 1954. Even recognizing that several cost factors other than raw cotton—such as wages—have risen since then, it can be seen that the current domestic textile situation is in considerably "better shape" than it was in 1952 and 1954.

Another factor is that the average hours per loom per week, as reported by the ACMI, were higher in the early months of 1957 than those for corresponding periods in 1952, 1953, and 1954. The percentage of first-shift loom operations extending into the third shift has also been increasing since the second half of 1956.

All this attests to the prospective and imminent "comeback" of the domestic cotton-textile industry in keeping with its cyclical trends. The alleged "depression" in the industry is almost over, and the period of prosperity seems to be ahead.

*Geographical differences*

While the general situation in the whole industry has been charted, it is also significant that conditions within the industry vary substantially from one area to another in this country. There is not enough information to consider the variations within segments of the industry, but geographical variations as to mill activity can be demonstrated.

The Census Bureau shows the difference in the raw-cotton consumption of the New England and the cotton-growing Southern States during the first 10 months of the 1956–57 crop year as compared to the corresponding periods in preceding years, as follows:

[In thousand bales]

| August-May | Cotton-growing States | New England | United States total |
|---|---|---|---|
| 1956–57 | 7,095 | 309 | 7,449 |
| 1955–56 | 7,347 | 387 | 7,783 |
| 1954–55 | 7,006 | 371 | 7,426 |

This geographic distribution reveals that during the first 10 months of the 1956–57 crop year, raw-cotton consumption in the New England mills decreased over 20 percent from the corresponding period in either of the 2 preceding crop years. In contrast, raw-cotton consumption in the Southern States decreased less than 4 percent, as compared to the previous crop year (1955–56), and was up a little compared to 1954–55.

The Census Bureau also lists the spindle activities in these two principal cotton-textile manufacturing areas as follows:

[In 1,000 spindle units]

| | Cotton-growing States | New England | United States total |
|---|---|---|---|
| May 1957 | 18,103 | 1,552 | 19,781 |
| May 1956 | 18,346 | 2,218 | 20,796 |

This current data indicates that while the decline in active spindles in the cotton-growing South was only 1 percent, it was some 30 percent in the New England States in this same year period.

These breakdowns show that the larger decrease in the activity of the New England mills lowers the operational figures for the entire United States, thereby giving an erroneous impression of the general activity of the southern mills, which now comprise the bulk of the American operation.

Despite the increased raw-cotton consumption of mills in both the North and the South in 1956 over 1955, the historic trend and shift of the cotton-textile industry from New England to the Deep South continues unabated because of the economic forces involved.

*Size of companies*

The cotton-textile industry is universally recognized as one of intense competition. In this day of mass production, however, a certain degree of economic integration is normally necessary to maintain efficient operations.

The question here is not whether the domestic industry is an efficient one. Nevertheless, it cannot be overlooked that the prime reason for many of the consolidations and mergers that have taken place in the industry lately have been for the purpose of integrating smaller units into a more efficient larger operation.

Thus, the often-cited contention that the American industry is suffering because of the ever-decreasing number of companies in operation is misleading in the extreme.

On the other hand, in spite of recent mergers and consolidations, the domestic industry still remains comparatively decentralized and scattered.

As recently as 1949, the Secretary of Commerce testified, before a House Subcommittee on a Study of Monopoly Power that the cotton-textile woven-goods segment of the domestic industry—the basic segment at that—was among the least concentrated of all industries in the Nation. He reported that the 4 largest companies represented only 13.1 percent of the total value of all shipments of the industry. Even with the addition of the next 16 largest companies, the 20 largest companies together controlled only 40.4 percent of the industry's shipment. In contrast, in other industries the 20 major companies controlled such percentages as the following—tires and tubes, 99.3 percent; blast furnaces, 95.5 percent; soap and glycerin, 92.7 percent; copper rolling and drawing, 92.2 percent; and organic chemicals, 86.4 percent.

Davison's Textile Blue Book, July 1952, discloses that the domestic cotton-textile industry was composed of some 607 spinning companies, with a total of 21,160,974 spindles. Of these, 167 companies had 10,000 or less spindles each; 172 had 10,001 to 20,000 spindles each; and 70 had 20,001 to 30,000 spindles each.

This means that, as of July 1952, two-thirds of the American industry operated 30,000 or less spindles per company. By Japanese standards, 30,000 spindle companies are considered small operations.

Recent newspaper and other accounts report that mergers and consolidations are taking place at an accelerated pace. Accordingly, the information provided by both the Secretary of Commerce in 1949 and the Blue Book in 1952 are not up to date.

The fact remains, however, that, generally speaking, the American cotton-textile industry company units are relatively small compared to other major United States industries, which accounts in part for the relative inefficiency of the industry as a whole.

*Consumer preferences*

The Daily News Record on April 4, 1957, reported that J. Craig Smith, president of Avondale Mills, Alabama, declared to a meeting of his fellow executives:

> One of the reasons why our industry hasn't shared in the prosperity of the country is that when most people get through making their monthly payments on automobiles, television sets, refrigerators, and all the other things which are sold on the installment plan, there isn't much money left to buy textiles. Transportation companies and hotels are even selling vacations on the installment plan.

There is little disagreement that textiles have not shared the Nation's general prosperity as much as some other industries in the economy. This does not mean, however, that textiles cannot win a larger part of the consumer dollar.

Avondale's Mr. Smith is reported as admitting, in the same Daily News Record mentioned above, that—

> I don't know what the answer to this problem is. Apparently installment buying is increasing, instead of decreasing—and, if this is so, the textile industry is going to have to find some way to participate more fully in it if we expect to get our share of the consumer dollar.

While the scope of this paper covers only cotton textiles, it goes without saying that the sharing of the consumer dollar more equitably is not the problem of the textile industry alone, but also includes the farmers and other producers of "soft goods" generally.

Consumer preferences between the increasing number of fibers plays an important role in the relative position of cotton textiles to its own prosperity as an industry, as well as to the national economic picture of an expanding economy.

The latest available Department of Agriculture statistics reveal that cotton's share of the textile dollar, which was nearly 90 percent in the 1920's, had declined to about 80 percent in the 1930's and to less than 70 percent in the 1950's, with the single exception of the year 1951. Against this decline, the share of the textile dollar of manmade fibers, which was negligible in the 1920's, has increased from 10 percent in the 1930's to approximately 25 percent in recent years.

Harry C. Mills, vice president, J. C. Penney Co., pointed this out in his statement delivered before the Textile Market-Research Conference of May 29, 1957, in New York City.

In the last 5-year period, with a population increase of 9 percent and an increase of over 28 percent in disposable income, cotton consumption decreased 11 percent. I'm sure everyone here will agree there has been too much ground lost. Let's look at some of the factors that have brought about these losses. One of the threats to the cotton-textile industry is synthetic yarns and fibers. Each day seems to bring along something new in synthetics, with characteristics that appeal to customers. These goods, meeting newly created demands, make sharp inroads into your sales. In addition, great strides have been made in nonwoven fabrics—resin or heat-bonded textile fibers, resin-bonded pulp and paper fibers, plastics. To some extent, glass and aluminum are attempting to make inroads and some day there may be "sprayed-on fabrics" that the American Viscose Corp. is working on at present. Has industry accepted these new fibers and textiles? They certainly have as you know only too well. Take as an example the tremendous falling off in poundage of cotton yarns formerly used as tire cords, the use of cotton in bagging and packaging of food products. In tires, the drop is expressed in a reduction of bales of cotton from 663,000 to 162,000 since 1939. In packing bags from 458,000 bales to 221,000, and I am sure you can think of many more such samples.

M. K. Horne, Jr., chief economist of the National Cotton Council of America, indicated at the same conference that—

If consumer spending was 100 in 1948, it was 132 in 1956. * * * How about the trend in cotton consumption by our domestic mills between 1948 and 1956? If cotton consumption was 100 in 1948, it was down to just a little below 100 in 1956. It declined from 9.1 million bales to a bare 9 million. While the total American market rose—i. e., by 32 percent—the mills last year consumed, not 9 million but 12 million bales. The difference is 3 million bales of domestic mill consumption that cotton did not get.

Questioning himself, "Where did that 3 million go?" he answered in effect that 775,000 bales were lost to other fibers, and 950,000 bales to nontextile materials, among others.

The very substantial and continuing market losses of cotton textiles to other fiber and nonfiber products is based upon both price and nonprice factors. The National Cotton Council of America in 1956 published a report on the Price and the Future of U. S. Cotton, in which these losses are explained.

All prices in the following two charts, reproduced from the same publication, under "Fiber" are for staple fiber (not yarn).

The publication states:

Cotton, you see, is in the same general price range with rayon and also with acetate (which we cotton people usually look upon as another form of rayon, though there's a chemical difference).

*Price of cotton and competing materials*

| | Per pound |
|---|---|
| Fiber: | |
| Cotton (M 15/16 inch) delivered group B mills | $0.3560 |
| Rayon staple (standard) | .34 |
| Rayon staple (carpet quality) | .37 |
| Acetate staple | .37 |
| Nylon | 1.55 |
| Dacron | 1.60 |
| Orlon | 1.50 |
| Acrilan | 1.40 |
| Dynel | 1.28 |
| Vicara | 1.00 |
| | Per unit |
| Feed bags: | |
| Cotton | $0.27 |
| Paper | .12 |
| Burlap | .15 |

When we come to the new fibers (nylon, dacron, and the rest), we have an entirely different situation. Cotton has a great deal of competition with the fibers in this group. It is serious competition but obviously it's not price competition in the usual sense. These new fibers are coming into our markets because of the specialized qualities which they possess, and because of heavy promotion, and in spite of a handicap in price per pound. They are from three to five times as expensive as cotton, pound for pound, and generally from two to three times as expensive after allowance for the extra strength that some of them have.

As for paper and burlap, the only satisfactory way to compare them with cotton is in a product, such as feedbags. We see that cotton is more than twice as expensive as paper, and nearly twice as expensive as burlap. Obviously price is the great weapon that paper and burlap are using against us. As paper improves its quality through research and becomes intrenched in more and more factories by getting the machinery installed for the use of paper bags, cotton's fight for the bag market becomes a harder and harder one. A drastic price cut in cotton would overcome only a fraction of our price disadvantage. This would reduce the odds against us, but would still leave us in a weak position unless combined with a tremendous effort in the fields of promotion and of quality improvement.

You can see why the discussion of price tends to center upon rayon. Not only is this our biggest competitor by far. Not only does it resemble cotton more closely than any other important competitor, and threaten us over a much wider range of markets. In addition it is in our same general price range. Moderate price shifts have a far greater chance of becoming important to us because of any other competing material.

*"One-price cotton"*

Although Japanese cotton textiles are a negligible factor in the overall consumption of cotton textiles in the United States, these imports cannot be ignored as substantial contributors to the holding of domestic consumer preferences for cotton commodities, for they service often marginal and new markets which the domestic industry cannot or will not supply. Many of these new markets especially are built up to the point where the more expensive American cottons may subsequently be sold as the consumers gain a greater appreciation for higher-priced cotton textiles.

The American Importers of Japanese Textiles recognize that the lower the price of raw cotton for the domestic mills the better able will the American industry be to contribute to the holding of the present market in cotton textiles.

Even though AIJT is aware that lower raw-cotton prices for "home" mills mean increased price competition for certain Japanese textile imports, we have not, and do not object to a "one-price cotton" policy on the twofold grounds (1) that the selling price of raw cotton to

American mills should not be artificially controlled, and (2) that there should be no discrimination in the price of raw cotton in favor of foreign purchasers as against our own buyers.

At the present time, raw cotton is at a disadvantage because its price to domestic purchasers is artificially pegged at high levels. Such obvious discrimination favors and encourages the use and development of competing fibers.

We do not believe that a "single price" for raw cotton at world market prices for all would-be purchasers is a panacea for the difficulties of the domestic industry. But, our belief is that such a policy on the part of our Government in reference to surplus and other raw cotton will be of material benefit to the American consumer by making more competitive cotton textiles; would help cotton hold, retain, and regain a portion of the market which has been lost to competing fibers; and would aid in the reestablishment of confidence within the industry itself.

The National Cotton Council of America in 1956 reported that it was difficult to speculate on the results of a price reduction on raw cotton, but, based on a number of assumptions, the council estimated that the short-run effects would be beneficial.

> A price reduction of 5 cents a pound would prevent cotton from losing about 445,000 bales and enable us to gain approximately 315,000 bales for a net improvement in cotton's competitive position of 760,000 bales annually—

the council speculated—

> A price reduction of 7½ cents a pound would prevent cotton from losing 649,000 bales and enable us to gain approximately 460,000 bales for a net improvement in cotton's competitive position of 1,135,000 bales annually.

Since the current United States export subsidy on cotton textiles is about 6 cents per pound, we would not object to a single or "one-price" standard for the sale of American cotton to our own mill operators. This, we feel, is more in keeping with our traditional concepts of free enterprise than the present "two-price" system under which American manufacturers are penalized in favor of foreign purchasers.

## CONCLUSIONS

Too long and too frequently Japanese textile imports into this country have been maligned as scapegoats for the many ills of the domestic industry. Conversely, too seldom are the national interests involved and the economic and other advantages of these same Japanese textile imports espoused.

This submission is an attempt to provide what we believe to be much needed information, which we trust will serve to promote better understanding of the many problems relating to Japanese cotton-textile imports into the United States.

Whenever possible, we have tried to relate our study to the effect or impact these imports have on our American industry and market. Moreover, without unduly burdening our paper with historical facts, we have tried to place the whole question in its proper perspective, in the belief that some insight of the past and present helps to forecast the future.

We have tried to refrain from becoming argumentative, for our primary purpose is to supply such information on Japanese cotton-textile imports as will enable the Subcommittee on Foreign Economic Policy of the Ways and Means Committee of the House of Representatives to formulate American policy for international trade and commerce that is in the best interests and general welfare of our country.

We have neglected, in the main, to emphasize the positive, constructive advantages which derive from the importation of these Japanese cotton textiles, in the hope and expectation that the subcommittee and the committee and the Congress are so well aware of the fundamental benefits that accrue to the United States in such mutually helpful trade as that which exists between this Nation and Japan that they need not be recapitulated here.

*Summary*

This submission may be summarized in the following concepts:

1. Because of the special situations which exist in the Japanese economy, they have developed certain trade practices and organizations in order to more effectively cope with these conditions. Consideration must be given to these practices and organizations in evaluating the problems incidental to the importation of Japanese cotton textiles into the United States. American, European, and other standards cannot be used in assessing the Japanese situation and its resulting practices.

2. Although Japanese exports have aggressively searched for new markets, they are still in great need of additional outlets for their manufactured products. The very nature of Japan's economy makes it necessary that they trade to survive. Trade with Red China is believed to be illusory and the proposed European common market and other "free trade" areas pose threats to some of Japan's present markets. Japan needs, therefore, not only her fair share of the United States market, but also the prestige and influence of this Nation in developing new outlets for her merchandise.

3. In an unprecedented gesture of good will and self-restraint, the Japanese cotton-textile industry voluntarily accepted self-imposed quotas on her exports to the United States at considerable hardship and cost to themselves. The impact of these quota limitations on the Japanese industry has been substantial, especially to her velveteen and gingham producers.

4. Popular thinking to the contrary, Japanese cotton textiles, by and large, do not enjoy competitive advantages over American products. In third countries, American cotton textiles compete most favorably with Japanese textiles. Only those items that require labor intense operations may compete consistently on the domestic market.

5. Dire predictions notwithstanding, the United States cotton-textile industry has little to fear from the Japanese industry in the future. The Japanese industry for the next 5 years at least will remain more or less stable—at present capacity—because of governmental control policies. Other economic factors serve to provide practical limitations on any widespread future expansion.

6. In spite of the common practice, it is not fair or meaningful to directly compare the monetary wages paid to the Japanese workers as contrasted to those paid to American operatives. And what competitive advantages that the Japanese employees enjoy stem, for the most part, from the unique features that are part and parcel of the

historic system that marks Japanese industry. The Japanese textile worker, it must be remembered, is relatively well paid in his economy.

7. Despite publicized and dramatized charges, the impact of Japanese cotton textiles on the United States industry is negligible. The troubles of the domestic industry are not found in imports, but rather in many internal difficulties within the industry which must be overcome if the American cotton-textile industry as such is to become more efficient and more effective in winning a greater share of the consumer dollar.

Briefly, it is our conviction that the American cotton-textile industry as a whole has little to fear from the competition of Japanese cotton-textile imports today, and that the future outlook is not forbidding or ominous. Until 1962 Japanese cotton-textile imports are limited to a fixed total that certainly cannot be claimed to be harmful to our United States industry.

The fundamental problem remains for the American industry itself to recognize the insignificance of imports and to reorganize their industry with vision and courage to cope with the competitive realities of the world and the Nation as they exist today and may exist tomorrow.

It should be emphasized throughout that American importers too have a real stake in keeping the domestic textile market prosperous and expanding, for the importation of Japanese cotton textiles is particularly difficult and uprofitable when the United States market is "depressed" and "sluggish."

*Consumer rights*

It seems to us that in the past Congress has given too much consideration to the welfare of the manufacturer, while neglecting the consumer. "Protection" for industry may be well enough, but it serves to impose a special tax on the consumer to subsidize the manufacturer. Moreover, it violates the fundamental right of the American consumer to buy whatever he wants at the price he is willing to pay.

The report of the Joint Committee on the Economic Report, submitted to Congress on January 5, 1956, which summarizes its recommendations and findings on foreign economic policy, has the following on this subject:

> It is hard to see why consumers should not have the right to choose such goods as are desired, without regard to their origin or their foreign cost. Until we presume to replace freedom with a controlled system where people are no longer their own masters, this must be so. No group of producers should be allowed to have a vested interest in the right to dictate what our people shall consume. The excuse that such a vested interest is essential to maintaining employment is fallacious, and was not allowed to block the introduction in the past of the automobile to the detriment of coachmakers, the electric streetcar to the detriment of horse breeders, or mechanical refrigeration to the detriment of ice deliverers. Some industries can adapt to the will of the consumer, who in a democracy is king. Others have not adapted, and have become extinct.
>
> In a country as rich as ours, with shortened working hours and a complex technology at our command, including modern transport to deliver the luxuries of the world to us, there is no reason why we should not spend our money if we choose for foreign sports cars, lightweight bicycles, handmade laces, particular wines and cheeses, jeweled movement watches, or hand-cut glassware.
>
> Our ability to command exotic products is one measure of our progress and freedom from previous limitations in the pursuit of happiness. Let our home producers use their admitted skills in advertising to compete freely with their foreign rivals. For a Government official to make a moral judgment on how we

ought to spend our money is an invasion of liberty and privacy which is acceptable only where obvious public harm follows, as in the uncontrolled use of narcotics. Interference with free consumer choice must rest upon very compelling grounds, and if these relate to the short-run problems of displacement in certain industries or localities, a solution other than restriction of consumer freedom should be chosen.

If the greatest good for the greatest number is to be our yardstick, then the rights of the consumer should be paramount and all textiles—American made and Japanese imports—should vie on the open market for his trade.

*International considerations*

In this troubled age, we cannot overlook the international implications of trade with Japan.

Japan today is our ally in the Pacific, the key to our defense in Asia, an integral partner in our system of mutual and collective security in the free world. The far-reaching consequences of any defection on the part of Japan to the national security of the United States and to the peace of earth are too well known to need recounting here.

But Japan is a victim of circumstances. Her vast population and her lack of natural resources have combined to force her into a national destiny based upon trade. With an energetic and ambitious people to man her mills and factories, Japan does not covet "aid," but she truly needs trade. Since the end of World War II, she has become one of our best customers for all our exportable items, and especially for agricultural products, most of which are in surplus. In turn, we have become Japan's best customer.

The balances of trade, however, have been consistently in our favor—and for huge amounts.

Japan is already hard put to maintain her high level of commerce with us. Any further restriction or limitation on her ability to export to our markets would impose a severe, perhaps impossible, burden on her people and Government.

Aside from the mutually advantageous two-way trade between Japan and the United States, there are the grim realities of the present-day world to consider. These suggest that the common cause of mankind and freedom dictate expanding trade relations between the two Pacific powers.

*United States Government policy*

In spring of 1956, in response to an inquiry, the United States Ambassador in Tokyo informed the All Japanese Cotton Spinners Association—

(1) That the policy of the United States Government is to effect orderly elimination of unnecessary and artificial restraints on international trade; (2) that the United States Government has made continued efforts to bring about full acceptance of Japan as a member of the world trading community; and (3) that the United States has contributed to higher levels of trade between the two countries through negotiation of mutually advantageous tariff reductions, through the absence of quantitative restrictions on imports, and by the conclusion of a treaty of friendship, commerce, and navigation.

Since this represents our foreign economic policy as it relates to our ally, Japan, it occurs to us as importers that all Americans—including those in the domestic cotton textile industry—should cooperate in the successful implementation of this official pronouncement.

*Cordell Hull's philosophy*

Inasmuch as the Congress will consider next session extension of the reciprocal trade agreements program, and this subcommittee is studying this same program in relation to the continuing foreign economic policy of our Nation, may we recall the basic philosophy of the late Cordell Hull, author of the reciprocal trade agreements program, for its validity today is even more apparent that it was 25 years ago.

In commenting on Tearing Down Tariff Walls, the documentary, The Memoirs of Cordell Hull, published in 1948, sums up his reasoning for the reciprocal trade agreements program in these words:

I did claim, and continue to claim, that:

Economic warfare results in a lowering of living standards throughout the world. It foments internal strife. It offers constant temptation to use force, or threat of force, to obtain what could have been got through normal processes of trade.

A people driven to desperation by unemployment, want, and misery is a constant threat of disorder and chaos, both internal and external. It falls an easy prey to dictators and desperadoes.

Insofar as we make it easier for ourselves and everyone else to live, we diminish the pressure on any country to seek economic betterment through war.

The basic approach to the problem of peace is the ordering of the world's economic life so that the masses of the people can work and live in reasonable comfort.

Nations cannot produce on a level to sustain their people in well-being unless they have reasonable opportunities to trade with one another.

And this cannot happen in a world of extreme economic barriers, political hostility, and recurring wars.

The principles underlying the trade-agreements program are therefore an indispensable cornerstone for the edifice of peace.

When I was a boy on the farm in Tennessee, we had two neighbors—I'll call them Jenkins and Jones—who were enemies of each other. For many years there had been bad feeling between them—I don't know why—and when they met on the road or in town or at church, they stared at each other coldly and didn't speak.

Then one of Jenkins' mules went lame in the spring just when Jenkins needed him most for plowing. At the same time Jones ran short of corn for his hogs. Now it so happened that Jones was through with his own plowing and had a mule to spare, and Jenkins had a bin filled with corn. A friendly third party brought the two men together, and Jones let Jenkins use his mule in exchange for corn for the hogs.

As a result, it wasn't long before the two old enemies were the best of friends. A common-sense trade and ordinary neighborliness had made them aware of their economic need of each other and brought them peace.

Yes, war did come, despite the trade agreements. But it is a fact that war did not break out between the United States and any country with which we had been able to negotiate a trade agreement. It is also a fact that, with very few exceptions, the countries with which we signed trade agreements joined together in resisting the Axis. The political line-up followed the economic line-up.

May we conclude our submission on this note.

# THE AMERICAN TEXTILE INDUSTRY AND COMPETITION FROM JAPAN[1]

Council for Improved United States-Japanese Trade Relations, Nelson A. Stitt, executive director

## INTRODUCTION

*America's stake in a healthy Japan*

The foreign economic policy of the United States is, of course, intended to help build and maintain the kind of world in which America wants to live. These considerations bear most especially upon Japan which, as the most highly industrialized nation of Asia, would be the greatest prize for communism if it could be won by aggression or subversion. Japan is an essential link in the defense of the free world in the Pacific. Notwithstanding plans to remove most of the American ground forces in Japan, there are no present plans to remove the formidable United States Air Force which is based upon Japan or to discontinue its use as an American naval base. The United States can feel confident of Japan's role only so long as the people of Japan are convinced that their interest lies in such cooperation. The people of Japan are now so convinced and their own commitment to the free world and the principles of the United Nations is so great, that they will not easily alter their view. The first consideration, however, in the mind of a Japanese, as in the minds of people the world over, is that he and his family have a decent living. Competing perhaps with this consideration for the first place is self-respect. It is true, therefore, in a very real sense, that the United States can count upon Japan as a friend so long as Japanese are satisfied that on the whole policies of the United States are compatible with Japanese livelihood and Japanese self-respect.

*America's stake in Japan as a market*

For the last 10 years Japan has ranked second or third among all nations of the world as purchasers of exports from the United States. Japan was the leading customer for agricultural exports from the United States during the years 1952 through 1955, and in 1956 (because of Japan's excellent rice crop in 1955) was second only to the United Kingdom. The table on the following page, published by the Department of Agriculture, shows the situation most clearly and shows also the upward incline which imports of United States agricultural commodities have taken in recent years as Japan's economy has grown.

In addition, Japan purchases a wide variety of industrial products (heavy machinery, in particular). The table on page 1000 shows total United States exports to Japan over the period from 1946 to date, as compared with Japan's exports to the United States. The 1957 figure

[1] This study proper (pts. I through V) was prepared at the request of the council by International Economic Consultants of Washington, an independent firm of economists.

of $757 million for the first 5 months will not be sustained for the whole year, because Japan has been experiencing a drain of foreign exchange in 1957 and has had to take measures to halt it. Nevertheless, it is clear that United States exports to Japan in 1957 will far exceed exports in any previous year and that the balance in favor of the United States will be very great.

*Japanese imports: Agricultural commodities, from the United States, averages 1925–29 and 1934–38, annual 1949–56*

[Value at 1952-54 average prices in millions of dollars]

| Commodity | Average | | 1949 | 1950 | 1951 | 1952 | 1953 | 1954 | 1955 | 1956[1] |
|---|---|---|---|---|---|---|---|---|---|---|
| | 1925–29 | 1934–38 | | | | | | | | |
| Cotton | 232.0 | 258.1 | 181.4 | 246.9 | 187.5 | 181.9 | 131.4 | 179.7 | 129.4 | 178.8 |
| Rice | ([2]) | ([2]) | 1.1 | 9.4 | 7.5 | 51.1 | 33.1 | 64.5 | 45.3 | 3.8 |
| Wheat | 13.6 | 2.2 | 159.7 | 72.5 | 100.8 | 99.7 | 77.5 | 91.7 | 96.7 | 90.3 |
| Sugar | ([2]) | ([2]) | .6 | ([2]) | .6 | 2.2 | .1 | .3 | .2 | ([2]) |
| Soybeans | ([2]) | ([2]) | 20.6 | 12.2 | 37.8 | 20.8 | 52.5 | 56.9 | 73.6 | 69.0 |
| Vegetable oils and oilseeds (excluding soybeans) | ([2]) | ([2]) | 3.1 | 3.6 | 1.4 | 1.4 | .6 | 3.3 | 4.2 | 5.8 |
| Barley | ([2]) | ([2]) | 21.9 | 8.1 | 50.3 | 25.6 | 17.2 | 16.7 | 26.4 | 32. |
| Corn | ([2]) | ([2]) | 16.7 | 1.4 | 3.9 | 3.6 | 12.8 | 5.8 | 15.6 | 10.5 |
| Hides and skins | 1.9 | .3 | ([2]) | ([2]) | 5.8 | 8.1 | 17.5 | 16.1 | 23.1 | 22.0 |
| Tallow and lard | ([2]) | ([2]) | 5.0 | 3.3 | 6.7 | 11.7 | 17.5 | 16.7 | 18.1 | 17.3 |
| Tobacco | 4.4 | 3.3 | ([2]) | ([2]) | 2.5 | 4.4 | 3.1 | 4.4 | 6.9 | ([2]) |
| Dried milk | ([2]) | ([2]) | 6.9 | 5.6 | 2.2 | 1.1 | .3 | 6.0 | 6.1 | ([2]) |
| Other commodities | 10.9 | 5.5 | 33.6 | 13.1 | 39.9 | 11.7 | 13.1 | 7.3 | 16.4 | 30.6 |
| Total | 262.8 | 269.4 | 450.6 | 376.1 | 446.9 | 423.3 | 376.7 | 469.4 | 459.2 | 460.5 |

[1] Preliminary.
[2] If any, included in other commodities.

Source: Japan's Agricultural Imports, from the United States—from other countries, U. S. Department of Agriculture, Foreign Agricultural Service, July 1957.

[In millions of dollars]

| | United States exports to Japan | Japanese exports to the United States | United States favorable balance | | United States exports to Japan | Japanese exports to the United States | United States favorable balance |
|---|---|---|---|---|---|---|---|
| 1946 | 102 | 81 | 21 | 1955 | 643 | 432 | 211 |
| 1949 | 468 | 82 | 386 | 1956 | 898 | 558 | 340 |
| 1952 | 622 | 229 | 393 | 1957 (1st 5 months) | 757 | 211 | 546 |
| 1954 | 680 | 279 | 401 | | | | |

Source: U. S. Census Bureau.

*Trade—the lifeblood of Japan*

It is difficult for an inhabitant of a continental country like the United States to grasp the importance of foreign trade to an insular country like Japan which, poor in natural resources, is supporting a growing population of 90 million in a territory no larger than the State of Montana. The Japanese for generations have perfected techniques of intensive agriculture which put every foot of land to use. Measures are being taken at great expense to expand arable land, but Japan must now import at least 20 percent of its food requirements and this percentage is bound to grow as population increases and per capita consumption rises with greater prosperity. What Japan has to export, in the last analysis, is the skills of its people and it must export enough to pay not only for imports needed for consumption but for most of the raw materials to be processed for export. Only a few years ago, it was far from clear how Japan would be able to accomplish this feat but, with the help of a high level of world prosperity, Japan's exports did grow until in 1955 the imbalance in Japan's trade was considerably less than Japan's invisible earnings. The delicate balance of the Japan economy was demonstrated, however, when late in 1956 and early in 1957, the excess of imports over exports began to grow at an alarming rate. In the first 6 months of 1957, Japan lost over $300 million in foreign currencies—a figure representing roughly 30 percent of its available foreign exchange reserves. A series of measures were instituted, designed to slow the rate of import and in August of 1957, for the first time this year, foreign-exchange receipts and expenditures came into balance.

*Japan must trade with the United States*

It has sometimes been suggested that Japan's natural trading area is with the underdeveloped countries of Asia and not with the highly developed economy of the United States. There is a modest amount of truth in this in the sense that Japan—which has risen in less than a century from a feudal agricultural country to the most highly developed industrial nation in the Far East—is best able to furnish materials and equipment which are suited to the needs and pocketbooks of many of its neighbors in Asia. There is an important and a slowly growing trade between Japan and these countries. It is entirely wrong, however, to suppose that this trade can expand at a rate sufficient to meet Japan's needs without economic development in the rest of Asia of explosive proportions. The fact is, as has been often demonstrated, that the greatest rate of economic growth exists in the most highly developed countries and that among such countries are the greatest possibilities for mutual trade. For Japan to sell its manufactures in the United States is thus not an aberration but a normal and healthy development. What has just been said of the underdeveloped countries of Asia is peculiarly true of Communist China, because there, in addition to the other circumstances limiting Japan's markets, the autarchic policies of the Communist China regime inhibit the growth of normal trade. China accounted for a large percentage of Japan's trade when Japan enjoyed special influence in that country. The lowering recently of strategic trade controls upon exports to China will lead to a modest, but only a modest, increase, so that Communist China might account for perhaps at most 4 percent of Japan's exports. In the first 5 months of 1957, the United States bought 19 percent of Japan's exports, and 21 percent in the same period of 1956.

*Some misconceptions*

Japan's wages are, of course, considerably below those of the United States. This is inevitably so, simply because Japan is a poorer country. An arbitrary increase in Japanese wages to the United States level would quickly generate ruinous inflation and economic collapse. If the United States and other strong, wealthy economies were to refuse to receive imports from other countries because they are poorer, world trade—except in a few basic commodities—would dry up and the United States, along with the rest of the world, would be the poorer for it. It is a misconception, in any event, to think of Japanese labor as exploited labor. Conditions of work in Japanese industry, fringe benefits, unionism—all of these things can be compared quite favorably with most nations of the world.

It is also a misconception to think, because Japan's population is growing that the rate of national increase alone is at a level which dooms Japan to poverty. Japan's current rate of population increase is considerably below that of the United States.

Another misconception is the bugaboo often raised that some unprincipled economic geniuses in Japan are singling out areas of the American economy as targets to flood with goods to gain a market. Japan is a free, competitive economy, as is the United States. The reason goods flow from Japan to the United States is almost always that some buyer in the United States, operating under the rules of free enterprise to serve his own interests, conceives of a product which can sell here if made in Japan. He goes to a Japanese seller and explains what he wants and if the latter can supply it, of course, he does. To the extent that the Japanese have organized either in large industry, in trade associations, or in the Government itself, to exercise a directive voice with respect to exports to the United States, it is uniformly on the side of restraint. Measures taken to restrict the exports of cotton textiles are well known. Not so well known are measures taken with respect to plywood, sewing machines, frozen and canned tunafish, chinaware, cigarette lighters, wood screws, and a myriad of other products which are important components of Japan's export trade to the United States.

Indeed, when measures designed to protect against dumping or sales at unduly low prices are taken into account, unofficial controls are applied which affect almost the whole area of Japan's exports. Virtually all of them have as their object avoidance of conflict rather than the exploitation of a foreign market.

A further misconception relates to the quality of Japanese goods. Many Japanese products are made and sold for the American variety stores which cater to the demand for low-price items. The continuing demand for products of this character indicates that wants and needs of American consumers are being met. It is difficult to conceive on what ground objection can be taken to the availability of inexpensive products, especially since a great many of them do not directly compete at all with the comparable American items. Nevertheless, there are many products of Japan which are coming to be better known in the United States which can compete in quality with American products or the products of any other country in the world. Within Japan, in industry after industry, efforts are being made to upgrade exports to the United States so that dollar earnings can be maintained or increased without increasing the competitive impact upon American manufacturers. The reputation of Japanese optical goods is now firmly established. It is well-known in the trade and is becoming well-known to consumers that many of Japan's woolen and worsted textiles are of top quality. Department stores are beginning to realize that "Made in Japan" is a good advertisement for china. And in the fields of the decorative arts, it is difficult to open a magazine or enter a showroom without encountering signs of Japanese influence.

*America's leadership is at stake*

For reasons which have already been indicated, trade relations between the United States and Japan cannot be regarded as exceptional but rather go to the very heart of the foreign economic policy of the United States. The most fundamental of the reasons for the liberal trade policy of the United States apply to Japan with particular force: United States security interests, the interests of the efficient American manufacturer with export potential, the interests of the United States consumer, the interests of the United States farmer, the necessity for markets in the United States if Japan itself is to survive. For the strongest and richest country of the free world to compromise its principles becomes an invitation for all others to do the same.

*The textile industry*

Just as it is wrong to regard any single country as an exception to the principles of the United States in the trade field, so it is a mistake to regard any one industry as exceptional. It is easy to follow one's principles when no one complains. The real test occurs when an industry having many plants, many employees, and many votes is affected. During recent years, official Washington, the press, and the general public have been subjected to a powerful campaign by spokesmen of various sectors of the textile industry for protection against imports. To listen to them, one would have thought that the future of the entire United States textile industry was in mortal danger and that drastic corrective action was imperative to insure its survival. True, there was little agreement on the exact nature of the industry's ills or what constituted adequate corrective action. Labor blamed the industry's difficulties on rapacious promotors juggling with corporate reorganizations for the sake of a quick profit and the failure of management to assert leadership and to display foresight in coping with the industry's problems. Most were ready to agree, however, on one scapegoat: imports were the real threat to the industry and action was needed to stem them.

A veritable campaign was launched against the allegedly dangerous encroachment of imports on the United States textile market—particularly against Japanese textile imports. Four applications for relief under escape-clause provisions were made in the case of special items, for example, blouses, pillowcases, velveteens, ginghams; quotas were sought under section 22 of the Agricultural Adjustment Act; an application under the escape clause for restrictions on all cotton textiles was demanded; discriminatory State legislation, violative of the United States Constitution and treaties was encouraged; "voluntary" export quotas to the United States were urged on foreign countries; a unilaterial import quota was proposed as a rider to the farm bill and to the mutual-security bill; restrictions were sought against woolen and worsted imports under the Geneva reservation, and under section 7 of the trade-agreements legislation on grounds of defense essentiality.

Two of these measures were, in fact, adopted. Elaborate voluntary controls over cotton textile exports to the United States were adopted by Japan after prolonged consultations with the United States Government. This negotiation has been very well described in the statement made by the chairman of this subcommittee to the House of Representatives on March 13, 1957 (Congressional Record, p. 3185). Late in 1956 the President announced the invocation of the Geneva Reservation, raising the duty on woolen fabrics from 25 to 45 percent when imports reach more than 5 percent of United States production for the previous 3 years.

The health of the United States textile industry—one of the Nation's most important—is necessarily a matter of concern to those directly dependent on it for their wages, salaries, and dividends and to those responsible for formulating United States national economic policies. It is also a matter of vital interest to the general public as consumers or as suppliers of goods and services to the hundreds of thousands whose livelihood is, directly or indirectly, dependent on the textile industry. The study which follows is an attempt to assess the extent to which the health of that industry has been affected, if it has been, by imports and to determine the real nature of the difficulties which the industry faces.

Initially, the study treats of the American textile industry as one industry, although differentiations are made in the later sections of the paper. It is not only permissible but essential to do so because a revolution has been underway in the textile industry which is yet ill reflected in its formal organization and in statistical reporting. It is by now a commonplace that the newer synthetics have displaced cotton, wool, and the older man-made fibers to an extraordinary degree since the war. It is not always fully appreciated, first, that the newer fibers are produced by chemical companies and not by traditional spinners, and, second, that weavers are today using a wide variety of combinations of fibers. This is true in particular, of course, of the newer plants which are designed for the new technology. No longer is there a cotton-textile industry, a woolen, a silk, a man-made, etc. There is today *one* American textile industry. The very nature of the fabrics of today and tomorrow rejects the arbitrary segmentation of production into the traditional productive divisions obtaining heretofore. The current problems of United States textile manufacturers, which are conceded to be many, stem from this modern upheaval in the long-set patterns of manufacture and marketing. The more farsighted and statesmanlike leaders of the industry will admit, in moments of frankness, first, that the foregoing is true and, second, that imports play an insignificant role in the present and future of American textile consumption.

## PART I. TRENDS IN THE UNITED STATES TEXTILE INDUSTRY

The United States textile industry is not stagnating as has frequently been alleged. Table I (overleaf) shows the trend in mill consumption of raw fibers from 1900 to 1956. From 3.2 million pounds in 1920 consumption of raw fibers rose to 6.5 million pounds in 1956.

Mill consumption of raw fibers provides an excellent index of the activity of the mills, and while not necessarily indicative of the profitability of their operations, the definite uptrend in fiber consumption over a long period is evidence that the industry has experienced a steady expansion. This is further borne out by movements of the index of United States textile production, as shown in table II.

Consideration of the uses to which textiles are put leaves little doubt that the past uptrend in textile consumption was inevitable and must continue for as long as the United States is experiencing population growth.

TABLE I.—*Total and per capita textile mill consumption of fibers, 1920–56*

| Year beginning Jan. 1 | Population, July 1 [1] | All fibers | | Year beginning Jan. 1 | Population, July 1 [1] | All fibers | |
|---|---|---|---|---|---|---|---|
| | | Total | Per capita [2] | | | Total | Per capita [2] |
| | *Millions* | *Million pounds* | *Pounds* | | *Millions* | *Million pounds* | *Pounds* |
| 1920 | 106.5 | 3,197.8 | 30.0 | 1939 | 130.9 | 4,553.7 | 34.8 |
| 1921 | 108.5 | 3,024.4 | 27.9 | 1940 | 132.1 | 4,913.2 | 37.2 |
| 1922 | 110.1 | 3,412.8 | 31.0 | 1941 | 133.4 | 6,478.7 | 48.6 |
| 1923 | 112.0 | 3,654.7 | 32.6 | 1942 | 134.9 | 6,903.8 | 51.2 |
| 1924 | 114.1 | 3,089.2 | 27.1 | 1943 | 136.7 | 6,611.8 | 48.4 |
| 1925 | 115.8 | 3,572.2 | 30.8 | 1944 | 138.4 | 6,173.3 | 44.6 |
| 1926 | 117.4 | 3,710.2 | 31.6 | 1945 | 139.9 | 5,989.0 | 42.8 |
| 1927 | 119.0 | 4,140.7 | 34.8 | 1946 | 141.4 | 6,501.6 | 46.0 |
| 1928 | 120.5 | 3,721.5 | 30.9 | 1947 | 144.1 | 6,415.1 | 44.5 |
| 1929 | 121.8 | 4,037.6 | 33.1 | 1948 | 146.6 | 6,390.7 | 43.6 |
| 1930 | 123.1 | 3,095.3 | 25.1 | 1949 | 149.2 | 5,435.9 | 36.4 |
| 1931 | 124.0 | 3,222.0 | 26.0 | 1950 | 151.7 | 6,831.0 | 45.0 |
| 1932 | 124.8 | 2,931.8 | 23.5 | 1951 | 154.4 | 6,843.1 | 44.3 |
| 1933 | 125.6 | 3,665.7 | 29.2 | 1952 | 157.0 | 6,421.2 | 40.9 |
| 1934 | 126.4 | 3,157.4 | 25.0 | 1953 | 159.6 | 6,468.0 | 40.5 |
| 1935 | 127.2 | 3,157.1 | 27.6 | 1954 | 162.4 | 6,006.9 | 37.0 |
| 1936 | 128.1 | 4,280.5 | 33.4 | 1955 [3] | 165.3 | 6,666.5 | 40.3 |
| 1937 | 128.8 | 4,410.6 | 34.2 | 1956 [3] | 168.1 | 6,512.1 | 38.7 |
| 1938 | 129.8 | 3,593.2 | 27.7 | | | | |

[1] Bureau of the Census. Population of continental United States July 1, including Armed Forces over seas.
[2] Total consumption divided by population and not a summation of per capita consumption for each fiber.
[3] Preliminary.

Source: The Cotton Situation, CS–169, 1957, U. S. Department of Agriculture (AMS).

TABLE II.—*Index of textile production*

[1935–39=100]

| Year | Index |
|---|---|
| 1919 | 73 |
| 1929 | 94 |
| 1939 | 112 |
| 1947 | 163 |
| 1950 | 182 |
| 1956 | 173 |

Source: Bureau of Census, Historical Series, 1789–1945, p. 180. Figures for 1950–56 are from Survey of Current Business and have been related to the same base as the earlier series.

About two-fifths of the output of the United States textile industry goes to clothing and apparel with another two-fifths for agricultural and industrial purposes and about one-fifth for furnishings. Since the demand for many of the so-called industrial uses—cordage for automobile tires, for instance—is necessarily derivative from and dependent on consumer demand, it must by and large also reflect population growth. Indeed, total annual consumption of textiles by weight has grown in the United States since the 1920's at a more rapid pace than has population. Per capita consumption of all fibers has risen from approximately 30 pounds in the twenties to about 39 pounds in the fifties.

In 1956 the volume of gross sales of the United States textile industry was about $23 billion. Compare these figures with imports of semi- and finished textile products in 1956 which were just under $650 million, or less than 3 percent of domestic sales.[2]

At the risk of getting somewhat ahead of our story, we might remark that it is difficult to see how this small import percentage could constitute a serious threat to the United States industry. As one observer remarked, "The United States textile industry is certainly going to survive." [3]

During the years 1945–56, inclusive, expenditures on new plants and equipment by textile mills amounted to $5.1 billion.[4] This is hardly an indication that a downtrend was anticipated by those who determined the textile companies' investment policies. The annual average rate of investment works out at just under $500 million during this 11-year period. Equally noteworthy is the fact that during the 3 years, 1954, 1955, and 1956, when cries of alarm were repeatedly heard at the dangerous flood of imports, expenditures by the United States textile industry on new plants and equipment were actually on the rise after having declined from their peak in 1948. From $331 million in 1954, they rose to $366 million in 1955, and to $465 million in 1956.[5]

It should be noted, too, that the trend of corporate profits in the industry during the last few years also belies the cries of doom. Net profits after taxes, were as follows:

TABLE III.—*Corporate profits before and after Federal and State taxes: Textile mill products*

[In millions of dollars]

| | Before taxes | After taxes |
|---|---|---|
| 1952 | $526 | $182 |
| 1953 | 533 | 208 |
| 1954 | 326 | 93 |
| 1955 | 709 | 348 |
| 1956 | 694 | 359 |

Source: Survey of Current Business, vol. 37, No. 7, p. 17, and Quarterly Financial Reports for Manufacturing Corporations, FTC/SEC.

With the exception of 1954, there was a generally steady rise in profits earned, the last 2 years showing profits about 40 percent above those in the first 2. While rates of profit for the textile industry as a whole are notoriously low in relation to sales, the point we wish to stress here is the upward direction of net earnings at a time when the industry was allegedly suffering from an inflow of imports.

Why, then, with production trending upward, with new investments taking place, with profits steadily rising does the $20 billion United States textile industry create such a fuss over some 500 to 600 million dollars in imports? Some sectors of the textile industry have, no doubt, been more affected by imports than has the industry as a whole. But the hue and cry against imports of textile products "manufactured by cheap foreign labor" has been out of all proportion to

[2] See table VII, pt. III, below.
[3] The Textile Industry's Troubles, The American Investor, July-August 1957, published by the American Stock Exchange.
[4] Survey of Current Business, vol. 36, No. 6, p. 6, and vol. 37, No. 6, p. 3.
[5] Ibid.

the impact which such imports could possibly have even on those particular sectors. And for the industry as a whole to join in the clamor against textile imports—from Japan in particular—is nothing short of absurd. The attempt to make of imports a scapegoat is no solution to the substantial problems facing the industry. These are discussed in the following sections.

### PART II. CHARACTERISTICS AND PROBLEMS OF THE TEXTILE INDUSTRY

#### *1. The competitive nature of the textile industry*

The industry is essentially competitive in organization. While merger movements in the last two postwar periods—in the early twenties and the late forties and fifties—have increased the proportion of output turned out by the larger, integrated mills, the industry is still characterized by a large number of relatively small units.

"Among our larger industries, the cotton textile industry stands out as the closest approach to the classic conception of competition." [6] This statement is generally true of the textile industry as a whole. While much concern has been expressed at the recent uptrend of mergers in the industry, available information indicates that the ratio of concentration of production in the larger textile plants is not high. The following table illustrates the point:

TABLE IV.—*Textile mill products, by establishments, 1952*

| | Number of establishments | All employees in thousands | Value added in millions |
|---|---|---|---|
| 1 to 99 employees | 4,982 | 136 | $620 |
| 100–249 employees | 1,395 | 196 | 953 |
| 250–499 employees | 637 | 222 | 1,031 |
| 500–999 employees | 387 | 266 | 1,217 |
| 1,000–2,499 employees | 162 | 233 | 1,079 |
| 2,500 or more | 21 | 82 | 356 |
| Total | 7,584 | 1,135 | 5,256 |

Source: The Merger Movement in the Textile Industry, staff report to Subcommittee No. 5 of the Committee on the Judiciary, House of Representatives, 84th Cong., table 11, p. 13.

While the above figures are based on "establishments" which are not necessarily the equivalent of business units, nevertheless, the table is generally indicative of the relative importance of small units in the industry. Just under one-half of the industry's employees were employed, and one-half of the value added by manufacture was performed, by establishments with employees under 500 in number—i. e., by 7,014 establishments out of a total of 7,584. Since about half the industry's output is spread among small establishments, which account for 89 percent of the total number of establishments, competitive conditions almost inevitably prevail. An examination of the degree of concentration of employment in various branches of the textile industry generally confirms the picture of a nonconcentrated industrial structure.

[6] Alderfeder, E. B., Economics of American Industry, 2d edition, McGraw Hill, 1950, p. 372.

TABLE V.—*Concentration of employment in textile mills, 1950*

[100=maximum score for concentration]

| | Employment | Concentration ratio | |
|---|---|---|---|
| | | 1st 4 companies | 1st 8 companies |
| Yarn mills except carpet | 30,000 | 15 | 27 |
| Woolen and worsted fabrics | 113,000 | 29 | 41 |
| Thread mills | 16,000 | 69 | 81 |
| Yarn mills, cotton system | 84,000 | 12 | 20 |
| Cotton broad-woven fabrics | 344,000 | 14 | 22 |
| Rayon and related broad-woven fabrics | 96,000 | 26 | 34 |
| Narrow-fabric mills | 25,000 | 16 | 26 |
| Full-fashioned hosiery mills | 77,000 | 16 | 25 |
| Seamless hosiery mills | 61,000 | 11 | 18 |
| Knit underwear mills | 38,000 | 21 | 37 |
| Wool carpets, rugs, and carpet yarn | 42,000 | 57 | 74 |
| Hard-surface floor coverings | 12,000 | 77 | (1) |
| Fur felt hats and hat bodies | 13,000 | 46 | (1) |

[1] Not available.

Source: Report of the Federal Trade Commission on Changes in Concentration in Manufacturing, 1935 to 1947 and 1950, 1954, p. 132.

From table V above, it can be seen that, in the instances where there appears to be some degree of concentration in a particular branch (i. e., where more than 50 percent of employment is with 4 firms), the amount of employment is low, with the possible exception of wool carpets, rugs, and carpet yarns. In the 2 important branches—woolens and worsteds, and cotton broad-woven fabrics—the top 4 companies account for 29 and 12 percent, respectively, of total employment, and the top 8 companies account for 41 and 20 percent, respectively.

Thus, the available information indicates that there is no heavy concentration in textiles. The staff report of the subcommittee of the House Judiciary Committee recognizes "the highly competitive nature of the industry, at least traditionally." [7] It is significant that it does not draw the conclusion that the recent series of mergers has altered the traditionally competitive nature of the industry, although the study was presumably undertaken with a view to determining whether this, in fact, had been the result. In his research report on New England textiles and the new economy,[8] Dr. Seymour Harris concludes that available material "suggests that the textile industry is not a heavily concentrated one," although, he adds, "It is difficult to draw conclusions concerning textiles in relation to all other manufacturing industries." Unfortunately, a systematic analysis of the concentration ratios in all manufacturing industries has not been undertaken which would permit their weighted classification by degrees of concentration.

*2. Profits in the industry*

The above observations regarding the competitive nature of the textile industry are important. Much has been written about the low profit ratios in textiles, and many have leaped to the easy conclusion that imports have been a major factor. That profit ratios of textile

[7] Ibid., p. 3.
[8] Report by the New England Governors' Textile Committee to the Conference of New England Governors, March 1957, pt. II, p. 82.

firms have, on the average, been low is undeniable. That imports have been, in major part, responsible therefor is a gross distortion of the facts. The competitive nature of the industry almost insures a low rate of profit. In the case of cotton textiles, the staff report of the subcommittee of the House Judiciary Committee,[9] as have most observers, related the industry's low profits and instability to the widely known technology involved, the relatively low capital resources required for entry into the industry, and the consequent tendency for a chronic overcapacity to prevail. Under the circumstances, high profit rates can be expected only in periods of shortages or of unusual demand—in wartime and during early postwar periods (1945–47, for instance), when exports were exceptionally high, since foreign suppliers, many of whose facilities had not yet been restored from wartime destruction, could not meet their normal share of the international market.

As shown in table III, textile-mill profits have been on the rise during the very period in which imports have been increasing; imports can hardly be held, therefore, responsible for the low average profit in the industry. Let it be noted, further, that the average of profits for the industry as a whole disguises a wide range in the profit rates of various firms. Thus, in 1954, which was a poor year for manufacturing earnings generally and for the textile industry in particular, the Bell Co. reported profits equal to 16.19 percent and Wauregan Mills a loss of 19.2 percent of sales.[10]

The fact that some firms could register respectable profits and other sizable losses indicates that, with proper management, capital, and marketing policies, members of the textile industry can make a good showing. In any industry, profits flow more abundantly to firms with the know-how, the resources, and the imagination to keep abreast of and to adapt themselves to technological developments and advances. In extremely competitive industries, the ability to do so spells out the difference, not between low profits and lush profits but between respectable profits and losses.

*3. Competition among fibers and technological advances*

In addition to the normal competitive forces at work in any industry characterized by a low ratio of concentration, the textile industry, or important segments thereof, have had to cope with a high degree of competition among fibers. This has undoubtedly been a factor accounting for a large proportion of the mortality of textile mills. Competition among fibers for the ultimate market does not mean only the displacement of cotton by wool or wool by cotton, or both in various degrees by manmade fibers. Such interfiber displacement is not felt only by the cotton and wool growers or, in the case of synthetics, by the chemical industry. A fact often overlooked is the effect of fiber displacement on various sections and firms of the textile industry. The technology in the use of synthetic fibers, despite the fact that many can be used in combination with cotton or wool is such that many phases—especially the early processing phases of

[9] The Merger Movement in the Textile Industry, staff report to Subcommittee No. 5 of the Committee on the Judiciary, House of Representatives, 84th Cong., p. 3.
[10] Harris, op. cit., pt. II, p. 88. From a sample of 56 textile firms.

cotton or wool—are bypassed in processing the synthetic fibers. Much of the unemployment in the woolen and worsted industries can be traced to the enormous growth in the use of synthetic fibers, either blended or unblended, during the last 20 years. Seymour Harris observed that "the production of these (manmade) fibers mean a diversion of part of the textile industry to the chemical industry."[11]

The older cotton mills have also suffered from the encroachments of manmade fibers. The smaller mills, with inadequate financing, could not easily keep up with the technological pace. These shifts in fiber use were superimposed on the regional migration of the industry from New England to the South. Investments in new plants and equipment tended, by and large, to be the first to introduce the new processes; hence, the southern areas which provided more attractive conditions for new investments were favored.

While no quantitative estimates have been made concerning the impact of the development of new fibers on plant mortality and on unemployment in the older branches of the industry, there can be little doubt that it was substantial. In quantity, the production of manmade fibers in the United States rose from about 20 million pounds in the early twenties to over 1.6 billion pounds in 1956. As a percentage of mill consumption, manmade fibers rose from less than 1 percent in the early twenties to more than 25 percent in 1956, with over half of this increase occurring since the end of World War II.[12]

*4. Increases in productivity*

The textile industry appears to have experienced remarkable technological gains in the postwar period. Harris gives the following data on percentage increases in man-hour output for selected branches of the industry (March 1957 report, pt. II, p. 41):

TABLE VI.—*Changes in man-hour output*

[1954 as a percent of 1947]

| | *Percent* |
|---|---|
| 1. Broad-woven synthetic fabrics | 136.8 |
| 2. Broad-woven cotton fabrics | 130.8 |
| 3. Thrown filament yarn | 146.6 |
| 4. Woolen and worsted fabrics | 118.5 |

Source: TWUA, Textiles, Crisis for America, 1956, p. 6.

Compare the above gains with an estimated increase of 24 percent in per-man output for the United States economy as a whole in the same period (increase in gross national product over increase in civilian population). Or again with an increase of 21 percent in output per worker in all manufacturing industry for the same period (increase in output divided by increase in factory workers). The showing of the textile industry is impressive.

The rise in textile productivity is further supported by estimates of the Textile Workers' Union of America for the period 1950–56. They estimate that output per man-hour during this period rose from 8 to 11½ yards for a 44 percent increase in 6 years.

[11] S. Harris, op. cit., pt. II, p. 104.
[12] The Cotton Situation—CS—169; U. S. Department of Agriculture, 1957.

In view of the inherent limitations on the applicability of automation to the textile industry, the increase it achieved in productivity is surprising.

It is in this development that we must seek a partial explanation for the increase of unemployment in textiles. Growth in textile sales have generally not kept pace with the rise in productivity, although the increase in United States consumption of the newer synthetic fibers has outpaced that of the rest of the industry. Ironically, unemployment is highest in the woolen and worsted industries in the Northeast, where the increase in productivity seems to have been the lowest. (See line 4 of table 5 above.) Competitively, the laggard areas or firms—laggard in keeping up with technological advances—are bound to lose their share of the market, hence the net effect is that technological unemployment (and plant mortality) is heaviest not where the new procedures have been introduced but where they have failed to be introduced.

The above is, like any generalization, to be accepted only with qualifications. While it appears to be generally true as concerns the relative incidence of technological unemployment as between the older and newer regions, unemployment is inevitable wherever a plant introduces radically new labor-saving devices, barring a major increase in its outlets. In his testimony before the House Ways and Means Committee on H. R. 9430, Mr. Edelman of the Textile Workers' Union of America cites the dramatic—and for the workers involved the tragic—example of the effects of technological progress on the labor requirements of a rayon plant in Cumberland, Md. Opened 5 years before and employing a work force of 8,000, the plant by virtue of new processing equipment was able to turn out as much or more with only 4,000 employees.

The point we wish to stress is that all of the technological factors discussed above have had a major impact on the volume of employment provided by the textile industry. Given the fact that outlets for the industry's production have grown less rapidly than its per-man ability to produce—a reduction in employment was unavoidable.

But again, the unions, while recognizing the importance of changes in technology as a factor in the lower level of employment by the textile industry, have laid major stress on the impact of imports without, however, adducing reasonable evidence in support of such contentions. We shall see below that the preponderant evidence is all to the contrary.

## PART III. UNITED STATES TEXTILE PRODUCTION AND FOREIGN TRADE

An examination of the relative insignificance of the volume of United States textile imports in relation to domestic production is the most effective way of disabusing those who may have been impressed by the continuing claims put out by the domestic industry that imports are a serious menace.

Tables VII through XI bring these relative magnitudes into sharp relief. They further reveal that the value of United States exports of textile manufacturers is now of the same general order of magnitude as imports. This point should not be overlooked. Foreign trade is a two-way street. If the United States textile industry is set on inducing the United States Government to restrict the flow of imports, it must be prepared to see similar action taken by other countries against imports from the United States.

A comparison of figures given in table VIII (textile imports) and table IX (textile exports) shows that whereas in the 1936–40 prewar period United States exports of textile products were approximately one-half the volume of imports, they have in the postwar period been consistently higher than imports, until 1956 when they were approximately equal. These facts would appear to indicate that it is in the interests of the United States textile industry to promote the elimination of restrictions on international trade in textiles rather than to encourage protectionist policies.

*1. Textile imports*

During the period 1950–56 the ratio of United States imports to net domestic output of textiles remained the same as in the prewar period. (See table VII and footnote 3 of table VII for an explanation of net domestic output.) In fact, the unweighted average percentage of imports (3.1 percent) to domestic output during 1950–56 was exactly the same as the average for the 1936–40 period.

Table VIII shows the pattern of imports of textile manufacturers during the same period. A comparison of the percentage distribution of the major components of textile imports in the prewar period and in 1956 shows that only one major shift occurred. The value of imports of wool manufactures and semimanufactures rose from 13 percent prewar to 29 percent of the total value of imports in 1956. In fact, the dollar value of semifinished and finished wool products rose from an average of $36 million for 1936–40 to $114 million in 1950 and to $191 million in 1956—for almost a sixfold increase. The BLS index of wool product prices about doubled during this period indicating something like a threefold increase in physical imports of wool manufactures. However, with the exception of wool products, the pattern of imports by 1956 was just about the same as prewar.

The comparison of dollar figures between the prewar periods and the fifties is, of course, not too useful. Prices rose substantially so that physical increases, where they occurred, were far less than indicated by the changes in dollar values. In the case of cotton manufactures, for instance, the BLS wholesale price for cotton products rose 2½ times between 1936–40 and 1950, whereas the value of imports of cotton manufactures rose less than 2 times (see line 1 of table VIII). This would suggest that the quantity of imports of cotton manufactures in 1950 was only about 75 percent of prewar. The same is no doubt true in varying degrees of other textile imports.

**TABLE VII.**—*Comparison of imports and domestic output of textiles and textile products*

[In millions of dollars]

| Average | Col. I [1] United States imports for consumption | Col. II [2] gross domestic sales | Col. III [3] net domestic output | Col. I as percent of col. III |
|---|---|---|---|---|
| 1936-40 | 199.4 | 6,333 | 4,800 | 3.1 |
| 1950 | 451.4 | 21,326 | 16,400 | 2.8 |
| 1951 | 539.0 | 23,138 | 17,800 | 3.0 |
| 1952 | 512.8 | 22,113 | 17,000 | 3.0 |
| 1953 | 464.2 | 21,434 | 16,400 | 2.8 |
| 1954 | 440.0 | 20,586 | 15,800 | 2.8 |
| 1955 | 585.4 | 21,213 | 16,300 | 3.6 |
| 1956 | 648.2 | 23,618 | 18,400 | 3.5 |
| 1950-56 average | | | | 3.1 |

[1] Datum on imports is from line 9, table VIII, United States imports of semi and finished textile manufactures.

[2] Data on domestic sales are:

(*a*) For prewar average and 1950-54 from National Income, 1954 edition, Department of Commerce and Survey of Current Business, July 1957, table 29, corporate sales, by industry: Textile mill products and apparel and other finished fabrics:

(*b*) For 1955 and 1956 figures are from FTC/SEC quarterly financial reports for manufacturing corporations: Textile Mill Products and Apparel and Related Products. Reported sales for the latter groups have been increased by 16 percent to make them comparable with national income data for apparel and other finished fabrics used for previous years.

[3] Net output was calculated as follows: Based on 1947 census data and BLS Interindustry Relationship Study for 1947, inter- and intra-industry shipments were netted out from gross output figures for the following textile industry groups: Spinning, weaving, and dyeing: special textile products: home furnishings: apparel. The net output figure so derived was expressed as a percentage of the gross 1947 corporate sales for the 2 textile categories given in the national income data (see footnote 2 above). This percentage, 77 percent, was then applied to the figures given in col. II and rounded to the nearest 100 million to provide an estimate of the annual net output of the domestic textile industry.

While the procedure does not permit the resulting figures to reflect such major shifts as may have occurred between the various industry groups from year to year, it provides at least a more reasonable basis than would gross sales for comparing the volume of imports to the output of the domestic industry.

**TABLE VIII.**—*United States imports of semifinished and finished textile manufactures* [1]

[In millions of dollars]

| | 1936-40 (average) | Percent | 1950 | 1951 | 1952 | 1953 | 1954 | 1955 | 1956 | Percent |
|---|---|---|---|---|---|---|---|---|---|---|
| 1. Cotton manufactures | 38.7 | 20 | 63.8 | 68.1 | 58.9 | 72.6 | 80.3 | 124.2 | 154.2 | 23 |
| (*a*) Of which cloth | (2) | | (15.1) | (17.5) | (12.3) | (20.8) | (22.4) | (36.1) | (51.5) | |
| 2. Jute burlaps | [3] 47.1 | [3] 23 | 90.6 | 112.1 | 113.7 | 75.5 | 70.9 | 78.7 | 81.4 | [3] 13 |
| 3. Flax, hemp, ramie, and manufactures | 27.4 | 14 | 40.7 | 39.6 | 28.7 | 33.7 | 32.7 | 33.1 | 34.0 | 5 |
| 4. Wool semimanufactures | 6.4 | 3 | 38.3 | 58.9 | 74.9 | 42.2 | 38.1 | 49.3 | 50.3 | 7 |
| 5. Wool manufactures | 19.6 | 10 | 75.5 | 92.7 | 89.7 | 98.1 | 90.3 | 118.7 | 145.5 | 22 |
| (*a*) Of which wool cloth | (2) | | (33.0) | (43.3) | (42.9) | (45.6) | (37.3) | (53.6) | (62.3) | |
| 6. Silk manufactures | 8.2 | 4 | 33.9 | 37.5 | 34.8 | 34.9 | 30.8 | 41.3 | 51.3 | 7 |
| 7. Synthetic fibers and manufactures | 7.8 | 4 | 25.5 | 38.5 | 27.6 | 23.0 | 16.5 | 46.2 | 24.5 | 4 |
| 8. Other semi- and finished manufactures (not elsewhere shown) | 44.3 | 21 | 83.1 | 91.6 | 84.5 | 84.2 | 80.4 | 93.9 | 107.0 | 17 |
| 9. Total, semi-finished and finished textile manufactures | 199.4 | [4] 100 | 451.4 | 539.0 | 512.8 | 464.2 | 440.0 | 585.4 | 648.2 | [4] 100 |

[1] Imports for consumption.

[2] Not available.

[3] For 1936-40 average the category jute burlaps includes also imports of raw fibers and is, therefore, not strictly comparable with the postwar figures.

[4] Percentages are rounded and do not add up to 100.

Source: WTIS, Statistical Reports, pt 3, No. 57-8, U. S. Department of Commerce (1936-40 averages from Statistical Abstract of the United States).

TABLE IX.—*United States domestic exports of textile manufactures*

[In millions of dollars]

| | 1936–40 (Average) | 1950 | 1951 | 1952 | 1953 | 1954 | 1955 | 1956 |
|---|---|---|---|---|---|---|---|---|
| Cotton semimanufactures | 13.9 | 36.6 | 87.9 | 57.7 | 57.4 | 52.4 | 50.7 | 53.8 |
| Cotton manufactures | 47.7 | 226.9 | 390.4 | 312.2 | 271.8 | 264.9 | 242.2 | 239.2 |
| Of which cloth | (1) | (148.9) | (265.2) | (212.6) | (172.5) | (165.2) | (146.6) | (141.9) |
| Synthetic fibers and manufactures | 12.9 | 176.7 | 226.4 | 205.8 | 220.3 | 217.5 | 231.2 | 239.2 |
| Others (not elsewhere shown) | 28.7 | 76.6 | 114.1 | 84.1 | 90.5 | 86.7 | 91.4 | 97.5 |
| Total textile, semifinished and finished manufactures | 103.2 | 516.8 | 818.8 | 659.8 | 640.0 | 621.5 | 615.5 | 629.7 |

[1] Not available.

Source: WTIS, Statistical Reports, pt. 3, No. 57-8, U. S. Department of Commerce (1936–40 averages from Statistical Abstract of the United States).

On the other hand, changes in dollar values registered during the 1950–56 period can be taken as fairly representative of changes in physical imports. Textile prices remained generally steady throughout the period with the exception of a bulge in 1951, which then disappeared.[13] If, therefore, we accept changes in dollar figures as generally equivalent to changes in the volume of imports during the fifties, it is evident that the bulk of the increase during this 7-year period can be accounted for almost entirely by increases in imports of cotton manufactures (about $100 million) and in wool manufactures and semimanufactures (about $80 million).

Each of these major groups is examined below to determine whether such increases as have occurred justify alarm on the part of the domestic industry and whether they can reasonably be interpreted as evidence of a sudden upsurge in the competitive abilities of foreign suppliers which in itself might be cause for concern.

*2. Imported cotton manufactures*

Imports of cotton manufactures, which during the war fell drastically, did not return to 1936–40 levels until about 1954–55.[14] But by 1956 they had risen approximately 50 percent above the 1936–40 average. Most of the increase occurred in the latter half of 1955 and 1956. Of what significance is this increase? How does it compare with changes in domestic production?

An examination of the relative movements in the volume of imports and of domestic output of cotton cloth provides a partial answer, since cotton-cloth imports have been equivalent to approximately one-third of the value of imports of all cotton manufactures.

The figures on cloth imports given in table X confirm generally the picture given by table VIII with respect to cotton manufactures as a whole. Not until 1955 did the quantity of cloth imports regain the 1936–40 levels. Not until 1955 did the ratio of cloth imports to domestic output of cloth return to the 1936–40 average. And, finally. not until 1956 did the ratio of imports to exports of cotton cloth reach the prewar level. Until 1956, imports remained consistently lower relative to exports than in the prewar period. If we exclude the

[13] Silk prices were an exception. They rose well above 1950 levels and remained up through 1956.

[14] If postwar values, as given in table VIII, are deflated by the BLS index of wholesale prices of cotton products.

immediate postwar years when the facilities of foreign suppliers had not been rehabilitated, aggregate United States cloth exports from 1950 to 1956 (amounting to 4.4 billion square yards) were still nearly 7 times the volume of aggregate imports (770 million square yards) during the same 7 years. Note that during the period 1936–40 cotton-cloth exports averaged just under 5 times the volume of cloth imports.

Do these facts indicate that cotton imports present a serious problem for the domestic industry? Hardly. In no postwar year have cotton-cloth imports risen to a figure as high as 2 percent of domestic production. For the period 1945–56 as a whole, imports have averaged just over one-half of 1 percent of domestic output; i. e., about one-half the prewar ratio.

Comment is required on the rise in cotton cloth imports during 1955 and 1956. While cloth imports still totaled only some 1.8 percent of domestic production in the latter year, the percentage increase compared with 1954 imports was nevertheless large. The bulk of the increase was attributable to the one item—ginghams. Imports of this item rose by about 30 million square yards in 1955 and by another 45 million square yards in 1956 over the 1954 level. Had the increase in gingham imports not occurred, total imports of cloth would have remained at about 1 percent of domestic output. This increase in gingham imports did not, however, indicate a sudden collapse in the competitive capabilities of a segment of the domestic industry. It was, rather, a reflection of the inability of the domestic industry to meet a sudden upsurge in demand for a style item.[15]

Gingham is essentially an apparel fabric and therefore subject to alternate swells and declines in demand typical of fashion cycles. Ginghams are not inventory fabrics; they are produced to the specifications of buyers.

TABLE X.—*Domestic production exports and imports of cotton cloth (millons of square yards)*

| Year | Domestic production | United States exports | United States imports [1] | Imports | |
|---|---|---|---|---|---|
| | | | | As percent of production | As percent of exports |
| 1936–40 (annual averages) | [2] 8,651.7 | 286.9 | 98.3 | 0.1 | 34 |
| 1945 | 9,779.2 | 561.3 | 80.0 | .9 | 14 |
| 1946 | 10,171.2 | 774.2 | 43.9 | .4 | 6 |
| 1947 | 11,083.4 | 1,480.7 | 15.9 | .1 | 1 |
| 1948 | 10,863.1 | 940.4 | 31.8 | .3 | 3 |
| 1949 | 9,391.6 | 880.3 | 19.7 | .2 | 2 |
| 1950 | 11,206.7 | 558.7 | 47.8 | .5 | 9 |
| 1951 | 11,415.2 | 802.4 | 35.8 | .3 | 4 |
| 1952 | 10,593.0 | 761.6 | 36.3 | .4 | 5 |
| 1953 | 11,332.6 | 621.0 | 64.3 | .6 | 10 |
| 1954 | 10,892.5 | 605.1 | 73.5 | [illegible] | 12 |
| 1955 | 11,319.3 | 542.4 | 133.1 | 1[illegible] | 24 |
| 1956 | 10,758.0 | 511.6 | 188.2 | 1[illegible] | 37 |
| 1957 | [3] 10,524.0 | [4] 583.2 | [4] 141.4 | 1.4 | 24 |

[1] Countable cloth only.
[2] 1936–39 average; 1940 not available.
[3] Annual rate based on 1st quarter of 1957.
[4] Annual rate based on first 4 months of 1957.

Source: Export and import data compiled from monthly and quarterly data in 1955 Statistical Supplement to Survey of Current Business for 1929–54, and from current issues of the Survey for 1955, 1956, and 1957. Data for domestic production are from data assembled by the Association of Cotton Textile Merchants of New York and published in a table entitled "10 years of cotton textiles."

[15] Cf., Brief of the Japanese Chamber of Commerce of New York, Inc., on Certain Cotton Cloth (Gingham), before the U. S. Tariff Commission, pp. 11 ff.

The increase in imports from Japan occurred because domestic mills could not meet the full demand for gingham. American mills, converters, wholesalers, and apparel manufacturers, therefore, placed orders for gingham with overseas mills, chiefly Japanese. It was not a case of Japanese products flooding the United States market and displacing United States production. While imports from Japan in 1956 were some 70 million square yards higher than in 1954, domestic production was also higher.[16] Imports rose with domestic output and not in its stead. As a matter of fact, the ability of American mills and converters to obtain a large portion of their gingham cloth imports from Japan in loomstate condition for eventual finishing in the United States, actually supported a higher volume of United States employment in finishing operations and a higher level of profits for owners of finishing plants. Both would have been at lower levels had Japanese productive facilities not been available to supplement United States production of gingham cloth.

*3. Other cotton textile imports*

Imports of other cotton fabrics and cotton apparel rose during the 1950–56 period, but on the average did not constitute more than a small percentage of domestic output. Certain exceptions are to be noted. For instance, imports of velveteens, which were the object of an escape-clause action, increased apparently at the expense of domestic production. But the total value of imports of this item in 1955 was less than $6 million—less than 4 percent of all imports of cotton manufactures. The issues raised by imports of velveteens are worth a brief examination. They illustrate the erroneous conclusions that can be drawn from concentrating exclusively on a single, narrowly defined article of import or of production. Velveteens are filling-pile fabrics made wholly of cotton. But as the United States Tariff Commission has stated, "corduroys and certain minor articles are produced in the same plants in which velveteens are made, and to some extent on the same equipment * * *."[17] While domestic production of velveteens fell some 4 million square yards between 1952 and 1955, domestic production of all cotton velvets rose by some 7 million yards, and corduroys by some 38 million yards. The sector of the domestic industry manufacturing these types of fabrics was, therefore, not seriously affected by the decline in the output of one of their items of production which was more than offset by increases in others.

The issues raised by velveteen imports are illuminating on another score. As the Tariff Commission said, "Probably no other cotton fabric requires greater skill and care in the finishing process."[18] The relatively higher labor requirements involved indicates that the economies of mass production and machine operations are not easily adaptable to the finishing operations of velveteens. This suggests, in turn, that velveteens are an item which it would be in the United States interest to import. The United States textile industry can more advantageously concentrate its productive resources on items for the production of which a high ratio of capital to labor yields better returns.

[16] Ibid., p. 41.
[17] Cotton Velveteen Fabrics, Report to the President, escape-clause investigation No. 49, pp. 9 and 10.
[18] Ibid., p. 10.

*4. Imports of woolen textiles*

Imports of woolen textiles present a somewhat different picture from that presented by cotton textile imports. The increase in woolen imports after 1950 was not accompanied by a comparable percentage increase in domestic production. Table XI compares domestic output of wool cloth and wool cloth imports which represent almost one-half of all imports of wool manufactures. However, while the percentage rise in cloth imports was large, their rise had little relationship with the fall in domestic output. Between 1947 and 1956 cloth imports rose by about 15 million pounds but domestic-cloth production fell by 152 million pounds. There can hardly be a cause and effect reltationship here. Further evidence to this effect is seen in the subsequent parallel movement of domestic output and imports of wool cloth between 1954 and 1956 when the first rose by 40 million pounds and the second by 8 million pounds.

TABLE XI.—*Domestic production, exports and imports, of wool fabrics (annual data 1947–56)*[1]

| Year | United States production | | Exports | | | Imports | | | |
|---|---|---|---|---|---|---|---|---|---|
| | 1,000 square yards | 1,000 pounds | Square yards | 1,000 pounds | Percent of United States production | 1,000 square yards | 1,000 pounds | Percent of United States production in square yards | Percent of United States production in pounds |
| 1947 | 755, 286 | 422, 801 | (2) | 17, 165 | 4. 2 | 4, 639 | 2, 515 | 0. 6 | 0. 6 |
| 1948 | 738, 015 | 413, 670 | (2) | 5, 391 | 1. 3 | 9, 243 | 4, 710 | 1. 2 | 1. 1 |
| 1949 | 607, 470 | 340, 497 | (2) | 3, 077 | . 9 | 8, 927 | 4, 289 | 1. 5 | 1. 3 |
| 1950 | 634, 626 | 355, 718 | (2) | 2, 410 | . 7 | 18, 544 | 9, 178 | 2. 9 | 2. 6 |
| 1951 | 533, 188 | 298, 860 | (2) | 2, 565 | . 9 | 18, 726 | 9, 014 | 3. 5 | 3. 0 |
| 1952 | 506, 889 | 284, 119 | (2) | 1, 032 | . 4 | 24, 062 | 12, 516 | 4. 7 | 4. 4 |
| 1953 | 478, 687 | 268, 312 | (2) | 680 | . 3 | 24, 297 | 12, 083 | 5. 1 | 4. 5 |
| 1954 | 421, 053 | 230, 794 | (2) | 609 | . 3 | 19, 550 | 9, 309 | 4. 6 | 4. 0 |
| 1955 | 473, 944 | 259, 782 | (2) | 475 | . 2 | 29, 247 | 14, 345 | 6. 2 | 5. 5 |
| 1956 | 493, 394 | 270, 444 | (2) | 605 | . 2 | 34, 914 | 17, 342 | 7. 1 | 6. 3 |

[1] Data include woven fabrics except felt and blanketing.
[2] Not available.

Source: Unpublished data prepared by the International Economic Analysis Division, Bureau of Foreign Commerce, from basic data of the Bureau of the Census (1957).

Nevertheless, it is evident that imports as a percentage of domestic wool cloth production rose from about 3 percent in 1950 to about 7 percent in 1956, and that United States exports of wool cloth during the same period fell to the vanishing point. The United States woolen exports were, of course, never significant. The postwar recovery of wool imports may have somewhat complicated the adjustment of the domestic industry to postwar conditions but hardly brought these about. Viewed over the longer period, the postwar level of imports did no more than return to earlier levels. Average annual imports in 1951–55 were 23 million square yards. In 1925–29 the average was 20 million square yards.[19] Practically all the foreign manufacturers

[19] Computed from tables appearing on pp. 2–138 and 2–163 in the Bulletin of the Wool Manufacturers, 1954. These figures are not identical with those appearing in table XI since they cover a wider range of cloth.

had succeeded in achieving, was to regain the position in the American market which they had held some 25 years earlier.

The difficulties that the woolen and worsted industries have faced in the postwar period must be appreciated to see the import problem in its proper perspective.

To begin with, the woolen industry faced the problem of contraction from the peak of wartime expansion which had been generated by our huge military requirements. Production of woolen and worsted fabrics rose from 440 million square yards in 1940 to 685 million square yards in 1942, of which 316 million square yards (about one-half) were for the Government's account. By 1946 Government orders had almost disappeared but pent-up civilian demand, which had remained unsatisfied while wartime restrictions were in effect, pushed production to 786 million square yards in 1947 and kept it high for another 2 years.

The Korean war once more brought Government orders into the picture in 1951 and 1952. Thereafter this temporary support disappeared and with a fall in civilian consumption, the industry faced a sharp contraction in the following 2 years.

The woolen and worsted industry was thus exposed to the full force of competition with other fibers from which it had been sheltered during almost 10 years. In this struggle, it has so far waged a losing battle. The woolen and worsted industry was caught between declining demand and stubbornly higher raw material prices than those for other competing products. While the prices of manmade fibers have been steadily falling, and to a lesser extent so have those of cotton, wool prices have remained relatively higher. This has been reflected in the prices of textile products.

The BLS price indexes of wool, synthetic, and cotton textile products show the following situations in 1955 (1947–49 = 100) compared with the index for all commodities.

TABLE XI–A.—*Prices of textile products*

| Year | All commodities | Wool products | Synthetic products | Cotton products |
|---|---|---|---|---|
| 1939 | 50.1 | 56.6 | | 36.6 |
| 1947 | 96.4 | 90.6 | 96.6 | 103.1 |
| 1951 | 114.8 | 144.6 | 97.0 | 111.5 |
| 1955 | 110.7 | 104.7 | 86.5 | 91.5 |

The American woolen and worsted industry was, therefore stuck on a high-price plateau compared with the industry in other countries and compared with American manufacurers of other textile fabrics. In part, this was due to the wool price support policies of the Government which were not abandoned until 1955.

The results are evident in the relative loss which wool has suffered. In 1935–39 the average per capita consumption of wool was 3 pounds and the consumption of manmade fibers was 2.6 pounds out of a total per capita fiber consumption of 28.1 pounds.[20] Thus wool and manmade fibers had about 10 percent each of the total. By 1955 out of a larger total per capita consumption of 36.5 pounds—wool had fallen

[20] Wool, snythetics, and cotton fibers only.

to 2.9 pounds (8 percent of the total) and manmade fibers had risen to 10.3 pounds or to 28 percent of the total.

Imports have clearly had little to do with these developments. Moreover, the industry has been steadily adjusting to the technological changes, and use of blends and of machinery capable of handling varied fibers has reached a point where it is misleading to speak of the woolen and worsted industry as a thing apart. Mill closings in New England are one phase of a process which involves also the construction of new capacity in the South. There has been a steady increase in production since the 1954 low.

It is, of course, always easier to blame some third party for one's difficulties and thereby avoid facing as long as possible the need to put one's own house in order. The temptation to have one's chestnuts pulled out of the fire through legislative action is as old as man and so is the effort to seek protection against the vicissitudes of economic life through tariffs or similar restrictions.

In the 17th century, the howls of the English wool men against the inroads of Indian cottons were louder than the cries of the American textile industry today against foreign competitors. They succeeded in pressuring the Parliament in 1666 to pass a decree that the dead should be buried only in woolen shrouds. To no avail—cotton marched on. The desperate thunderings of the wool men grew even louder and in 1720 Parliament outlawed calico, forbade its use, and decreed a bounty of £5 sterling for all those who informed against their calico-using neighbors. Again to no avail. Economic forces which made of cotton one of the leading British textiles prevailed. It was only when the British wool industry buckled down to the job of improving its own manufactures and faced up to the requirements of the situation that it was able to hold its own and to become one of the mainstays of the British textile industry during the next two centuries. The lesson is worth noting.

## PART IV. THE COMPETITIVE POSITION OF JAPAN

In its campaign to restrict imports, the domestic textile industry has directed its fire chiefly against Japan. Imports made with cheap Japanese labor have been particularly singled out as a threat to the American industry and to American labor. The rise in Japanese textile imports during the past few years has been misrepresented as only the beginning of a dangerous flood. Not only has there been silence regarding the fact that the Japanese Government and Japanese textile industry have adopted measures to curtail exports to the United States of those textile items which appear to be especially competitive with domestic output in the American market, but absurd charges have been made that the Japanese textile industry is deliberately concentrating on certain textile exports with a view to taking over the United States market.

Let us examine the facts. How dangerous, actually or potentially, is the Japanese textile industry to its American counterpart?

### 1. *Prewar versus postwar*

The Japanese textile industry has not recovered its prewar position either in volume of production or in its relative share of world trade in textiles. Compared with the United States, whose output of cloths and fabrics (other than wool) has been running well ahead of prewar, Japanese textile-cloth output is today well below the prewar average, except only in the production of rayon fabrics.

Table XII shows the relative prewar and postwar position of the world's principal textile countries. Compared with prewar, Japan's production of cotton and wool fabrics is running at about 75 percent. Its exports of cotton fabrics are about one-half and its exports of wool about two-thirds of prewar levels. India and the United States, on the other hand, have shown increases in both the production and export of cotton. Compared with prewar, there has been, of course, a general shrinkage in the international volume of trade in textiles, but Japan's share of this reduced total is still smaller than before the war.

Table XIII shows the changing export position in cotton cloth of the major producing countries. Japan dropped from a prewar position of just under 40 percent of total trade in 1937 to about 24 percent in 1955; the United Kingdom from 28 to 11 percent. On the other hand, the United States and India rose from 3.5 and 3.3 percent, respectively, to 11.3 and 15.6 percent, respectively. These facts hardly suggest that the United States cotton industry is at a serious competitive disadvantage relative to the Japanese industry.

TABLE XII.—*Fabric production and exports of principal textile countries*

[Million yards]

| PRODUCTION | 1937 | 1954 | 1955 |
|---|---|---|---|
| United States: | | | |
| Cotton | 8,785 | 9,816 | [1] 11,319 |
| Synthetic | 1,002 | 2,351 | -------- |
| Wool | 471 | 445 | [2] 473 |
| United Kingdom: | | | |
| Cotton | 3,640 | 1,994 | -------- |
| Synthetic | 482 | 780 | -------- |
| Wool | 477 | 441 | -------- |
| India: Cotton | 3,952 | 4,996 | [3] 5,089 |
| Japan: | | | |
| Cotton | 4,794 | 3,193 | 3,000 |
| Synthetic | 1,297 | 1,340 | 1,670 |
| Wool | 279 | 154 | 183 |

| EXPORTS | 1937 | 1954 | 1955 |
|---|---|---|---|
| United States: | | | |
| Cotton | 227 | 613 | 547 |
| Synthetic | 19 | 225 | -------- |
| United Kingdom: | | | |
| Cotton | 1,921 | 637 | [3] 555 |
| Synthetic | 80 | 175 | [3] 134 |
| Wool | 130 | 92 | [3] 71 |
| India: Cotton | 221 | 861 | [3] 875 |
| Japan: | | | |
| Cotton | 2,643 | 1,278 | 1,121 |
| Synthetic | 502 | 636 | 907 |
| Wool | 35 | 12 | 11 |

[1] From table X. Figures given for 1954 are not similar to those given in table X for United States production and exports.
[2] From table XI. Figures given for 1954 are not strictly comparable with those in table XI.
[3] Estimated.

Source: The Textile Industry in Japan, Primary Textiles Institute, Toronto, 1956, p. 91.

TABLE XIII.—*Exports of cotton cloth in free world*

[1,000 yards/1,000 square yards/or quintals]

| | Percent of total in 1937 | 1937 | 1955 | Percent of total in 1955 |
|---|---|---|---|---|
| 1. Japan | 39.2 | 2,643,429 | 1,138,829 | 23.7 |
| 2. United Kingdom | 28.5 | 1,921,320 | 554,537 | 11.6 |
| 3. United States | 3.5 | 236,151 | 542,400 | 11.3 |
| 4. India | 3.3 | 221,360 | 747,148 | 15.6 |
| 5. All others | 25.5 | 1,721,800 | 1,809,530 | 37.8 |
| Total | 100.0 | 6,744,060 | 4,792,444 | 100.0 |

Source: Trend of the World Cotton Industry, prepared by All Japan Cotton Spinners Association, Osaka, September 1956, table VI.

If the United States industry has succeeded in increasing its share of the market in third countries at the expense of both Japan and the United Kingdom, it can hardly be vulnerable in the protected United States market. This is even more evident in the case of man-made fibers and manufactures. Japanese and United States exports of these items were about $240 million each in 1956.[21] But in the case of Japan, this represents only a doubling of prewar performance, whereas in the case of the United States it represents a nearly ten-fold increase. The only textile sector in which the United States is practically read out of world markets is in the production of woolens and worsteds. This, however, is virtually inevitable, as we have seen earlier. Given the artificial maintenance of high raw-wool prices in the United States, American producers of wool manufactures are automatically priced out of world markets, except in periods of world shortages.

*2. Hard currency markets*

The competitive resilience of the United States textile industry in the face of Japanese competition is best tested in third countries which are also hard-currency markets. In soft-currency areas, quotas and restrictions against dollar imports constitute a discrimination against United States products, which makes it difficult to measure the relative competitive abilities of soft-yen products and hard-dollar goods.

The following table showing the dollar value of Japanese and American textile exports to major dollar markets in 1955 is strong evidence of the ability of the United States industry to hold its own.

TABLE XIV.—*Value of United States and Japanese textile imports in 1955 to certain dollar markets*

[In thousands of dollars]

| Exported to— | Exports by United States | Exports by Japan |
|---|---|---|
| Canada | $127,745 | $13,733 |
| Philippines | 69,540 | 13,297 |
| Cuba | 36,293 | 146 |
| Venezuela | 28,793 | 8,375 |
| Union of South Africa | 38,868 | 20,736 |

Source: Harris, op. cit., pt. II, pp. 122, 128.

*3. Japanese costs*

Japan is frequently alleged to derive unfair competitive advantages from cheap labor. It is true that Japanese wage rates are low. They are not as low as frequently cited. Cash wages are supplemented by noncash earnings. In the cotton spinning industry, these were equivalent to about 18 percent of monetary wages in 1955. Additional fringe benefits and facilities provided to Japanese workers would raise the total even higher. But the major factor which a simple wage comparison obscures is the much greater productivity of the United States industry. Across-the-board figures for purposes of comparison are not easily come by. However, the following table on man-hour output

[21] See table IX for United States data. Japanese data are from Annual Japanese Textiles Export Statistics—Institute of Textile Trade Research and Statistics, Osaka.

for cotton spinning operations suggests the much greater productivity of American mills.

TABLE XV.—*Comparative efficiency ring spinning operative hours per 100 pounds production*

| Yarn counts | United Nations standard mill [1] 50,000 spindles | United States cotton mill [2] | Japanese cotton mill [3] |
|---|---|---|---|
| 20s (carded) | 6.07 | - | 7.58 |
| 21s (carded) | - | 6.59 | 7.78 |
| 30s (carded) | 8.34 | - | 9.40 |
| 31s (combed) | - | 10.45 | 14.88 |
| 35s (combed) | 10.83 | - | 16.42 |
| 38s (combed) | - | 10.05 | 17.30 |
| 40s (combed) | 12.71 | - | 17.88 |
| 42s (combed) | - | 16.20 | 18.84 |
| 45s (combed) | 14.97 | 12.02 | 20.24 |

[1] United Nations: Labor productivity of the cotton textile industry in five Latin-American countries, 1951.
[2] Anglo-American Council on Productivity: Productivity team report on cotton spinning, March 1950.
[3] Actual production figures of the Japanese Big 10 spinners for September 1956.

The figure probably understate the United States margin of superiority since United States figures relate to 1950 data while Japanese data are for 1956. More up-to-date figures on the United States would almost certainly show an increase in the margin. Moreover, these data refer only to spinning operations. The Japanese industry lags considerably more behind the advanced industrial countries in the later stages of production, especially in dying and finishing. Japanese productivity in finished textile products is, therefore, much lower than indicated by comparisons of performance in the spinning sections alone.[22]

An interesting statistical study which appeared in the United Nations World Economic Survey, 1956, suggests that the rise in Japanese exports between 1950 and 1956—which one should recall are still well below prewar levels—did not rest on extensive price cutting. It is reproduced in table XVI.

The table shows an average rise of 1 percent in the unit values of the textile exports of 7 countries during the 1950–55 period. The rise in the unit value of United States exports was only 91 percent of the average increase for the group, whereas the rise in the unit value of Japanese exports lagged the average by only 1 percent. At the same time, however, the rise in the volume of Japanese exports was 60 percent more than the average volume rise for the group as a whole compared with an increase in the United States export volume of only 12 percent more than the average.

The performance of the United Kingdom was considerably different. Unit values rose 10 percent more than the average rise of the group while the increase in the volume of her exports was only 71 percent as great as for the group.

[22] Cf., Seki, Keizo. The Cotton Industry of Japan, Japan Society for the Promotion of Science, Tokyo, 1956.

The changes in unit values could mean either price changes or a shift in exports into a higher or lower price class. The relative increase in the unit values of the United Kingdom's exports most probably reflects a shift into higher priced goods since United Kingdom textile prices remained generally depressed throughout the period. As suggested in the Economic Survey,[23] it is probable that as Japanese goods began moving into commonwealth markets when restrictions were reduced, British exports tended to become more concentrated in the quality (and therefore higher priced classes). In any case, such inroads as the Japanese exports may have made in third markets appear to have occurred primarily at the expense of the United Kingdom and not of the United States. Secondly, they seem to have been accomplished without severe price reductions.

*4. Japanese textile policies*

Japan has been accused of overconcentration on the export of textiles in its attempt to balance its trade. This concentration, it has been alleged, has resulted in heavy pressures on the textile industries of other countries. The contention is not borne out by the facts.

TABLE XVI.—*Textile manufactures:*[1] *Relative changes in export unit value, quantum and value for 7 countries, 1950–55*

| Country | Change in export unit value relative to average change for group | Country | Change in quantum relative to average change for group | Country | Change in value relative to average change for group |
|---|---|---|---|---|---|
| United Kingdom | 110 | Germany | 258 | Germany | 280 |
| Germany | 108 | Japan | 160 | Japan | 159 |
| France | 103 | Netherlands | 151 | Netherlands | 136 |
| Japan | 99 | United States | 112 | United States | 102 |
| United States | 91 | Italy | 82 | France | 83 |
| Netherlands | 90 | France | 80 | United Kingdom | 76 |
| Italy | 87 | United Kingdom | 71 | Italy | 72 |
| Average for group | 101 | Average for group | 112 | Average for group | 113 |

[1] Covers standard international trade classification division 65.

Source: World Economic Survey, 1956—U. N.

In 1956 the value of Japanese textile exports was only 34 percent of the value of all Japanese exports in that year as compared with an average of 52 percent for the period 1934–36. Not only are the Japanese aware of the desirability of not putting all their export eggs in the textile basket, but these changing ratios indicate that such awareness is being translated into action. Further evidence is seen in the lower postwar ratio of Japanese textile exports to domestic Japanese production of textiles compared with prewar years.

[23] U. N. World Economic Survey, 1956, p. 78.

TABLE XVII.—*Export ratio of major textiles to total Japanese output (based on quantities)*

| | Average, 1934–36 | 1954 |
|---|---|---|
| | *Percent* | *Percent* |
| Cotton: | | |
| Yarn | 3.7 | 2.9 |
| Fabrics | 75.7 | 40.1 |
| Rayon: | | |
| Yarn | 16.7 | 9.4 |
| Fabrics | 70.3 | 41.0 |
| Wool: | | |
| Yarn | 5.2 | 7.0 |
| Fabrics | [1] 12.6 | 7.9 |
| Raw silk | 12.4 | 29.4 |
| Silk, fabrics | 29.1 | 14.2 |

[1] 1937 only.

Source: The Textile Industry in Japan. Primary Textile Institute, p. 107. Montreal, 1956.

With the exception of wool yarn, which showed a slight rise, and with the notable exception of raw silk, which more than doubled, Japanese exports of all other textile items in 1956 showed a lower ratio to domestic output than prewar. Raw silk, of course, is not competitive with United States industry—it is one of its essential raw materials.

In any case, it is difficult to see why the United States textile industry has been so alarmed by Japanese exports to the United States. In 1956 United States imports of Japanese semifinished and finished textile manufactures amounted to $152 million out of total imports of $648 million from all sources. (Voluntary restrictions imposed in late 1956 should bring the proportion of Japanese goods even lower in 1957.) As one of the major textile exporting nations this performance should not be cause for alarm. We have seen that imports of textiles in 1956 amounted to about 3.5 percent of total net domestic production (see table VII). This is small enough cause for concern. Imports from Japan (less than 25 percent of total imports) were, therefore, less than 1 percent of net domestic output in the United States. To sound the alarm on this account borders on the ridiculous.

*5. Balanced capacity and balanced exports*

In a statement prepared for a congressional hearing, the chairman of the All Japan Cotton Textile Spinners Association said—

> * * * if we, Japanese, are the hard and realistic businessmen we are often accused of being, most certainly we would not jeopardize our market in the United States by measures calculated to kill the goose that lays the golden egg, so to speak. As we have repeated over and over again, the Japanese textile industry is so important to the Japanese economy that we cannot afford to take the short-range view but must always emphasize the long-range program.[24]

The statement aptly summarizes the Japanese approach to international economic trade policy. The Japanese undoubtedly find it hard to understand the clamor against Japanese exports that has been raised in the United States. Nevertheless, they realize that, however ill-founded, the American reaction risks souring the political and economic relations between the two countries and have had sufficient industrial statesmanship to take the steps to remove the al-

[24] Hearings before the Subcommittee on Customs, Tariffs, and Reciprocal Trade Agreements of the House Ways and Means Committee, 84th Cong., pt. 4.

leged grievances. The Japanese textile industry accordingly took measures last year to restrict voluntarily their exports to the United States, which are fully described elsewhere. Beyond this, the Japanese Government has obtained legislative authority to control the volume of textile production. Two basic acts are controlling. The first is the Small and Medium Enterprise Stabilization Act of 1953, and the second is the Textile Industry Temporary Adjustment Act of 1956. The first act provides for an industry board made up of representatives of industry, labor, and government to establish production goals and where necessary to curtail production. Whenever it appears probable that production will exceed demand and lead to uneconomic price-cutting or other means of disposing of output, the board is authorized to limit output. This has in fact occurred. In 1955, for example, cuts in spinning ranging from 12 to 18 percent were ordered. When compliance was less than fully effective, seals were actually placed on machines to assure their inactivity.

The second act is even more drastic. It authorizes the industry board to establish equipment goals for the longer term and to take related steps to assure that production goals are adhered to. Overall production goals and export goals have been set for the next few years. Export goals for 1956, for instance, are generally at the same level as actual exports for 1954. These goals will require a shrinkage of the textile industry's capacity. This will entail the sealing of a substantial number of looms and the actual scrapping of many more. It is estimated that the following number of machines will have to be scrapped by 1960:

| | |
|---|---|
| Spindles | 1,200,000 |
| Cotton looms | 110,000 |
| Silk-rayon looms | 33,000 |

In 1957, 9,000 looms are scheduled to be scrapped and the pace will pick up in following years. With this shrinkage in sight, additions of modern, new machinery will be less frequent. An industry already less efficient than that in the United States will continue to lag.

These far-reaching steps are hardly indicative of indifference to foreign reaction or of a desire to flood the world market with Japanese goods at whatever cost. It is doubtful that the United States industry would in peacetime accept such controls as an accommodation to foreign outcries. The steps taken by the Japanese industry and Government were not, of course, taken solely out of consideration for United States interests. They have as an objective the creation of a balanced Japanese textile industry. At the same time, this constitutes even greater assurance for the United States industry that the measures taken by Japan will not be lightly abandoned.

## PART V. POLICY ISSUES FOR THE UNITED STATES

What can we conclude from the foregoing? First, that there is no basis in fact for believing that domestic textile industry is threatened by imports generally or by imports from Japan in particular. Low profits in the industry are not related to imports but to its essentially competitive organization. In this respect the textile industry is more to be compared with retail business than with other major manufacturing industries. Certain segments are faced with problems that are serious but which are also unrelated to imports. As a matter of fact, the industry as a whole shows no sign of stagnation. It makes no more sense to look at certain problem sectors of the industry and proclaim it a sick one than it would to call the automobile industry sick because Studebaker-Packard has gone through the wringer.

There is one problem faced by the cotton-textile manufacturers which does deserve the careful scrutiny which it is bound to receive in the next session of Congress—the price of raw cotton. It is hard to defend a differential between the price paid by the domestic manufacturers and the price paid by foreign competitors. Elements of the problem which must be considered, however, are the extent to which the differential is presently equalized in the United States market by import duties on cotton textiles and with respect to United States textile exports by the existing subsidies.

For the rest, the problems of the domestic industry are largely problems of adjustment to technological change and geographic relocation within the United States. This is not to minimize these problems, which are very real to the localities and firms concerned. But imports should not be made the scapegoat for unprogressive management and competition from lower wage areas of the United States. There are much more suitable means than trade limitations open to the Government to lend assistance in making necessary adjustments.

The United States is committed to a liberal international economic policy, having the expansion of world trade through the lowering of restrictions as an objective. The United States textile industry, more than most, should appreciate the importance of discouraging protectionist tactics by foreign importers of American textile products. The issue is whether the United States will continue to encourage international trade in textiles or whether it will reverse its course. The world textile trade has shrunk compared with the prewar period. The less developed countries aspire to greater self-sufficiency in the production of textile products and apparel. The United States, in the face of this trend, can accelerate the rate of decline or attempt to moderate it. If the United States restricts imports, so will others in retaliation. The result will not, on balance, benefit the United States textile industry. Furthermore, United States interests as a major exporter of raw cotton transcend those of the textile industry proper. Policies designed to pressure the Japanese and others to curb the volume of their textile exports will, to the extent they are effective, lead to an abnormal reduction in their production of cotton textiles and to a diversion of their resources into other industries. This can only lead to lower United States exports of raw cotton.

In the final analysis, the question is whether the textile industry has some particular claim to special treatment. Should the broad policies and objectives of the United States Government in the international field and the interests of the general public as consumers bow to some special consideration in the case of textile imports? The facts we have reviewed in earlier sections suggest that this is not the case.

There is no point in denying that, except in periods of a general increase in business activity, imports will tread on someone's toes.

But so will the sales of American competitors. There is no basic difference. The displacement of a domestic sale by an item produced overseas by one of the more efficient foreign manufacturers is in no real sense different from the displacement of a sale by an item produced by one of the more efficient American firms. The tag "foreign" becomes a handy veil to disguise the fact that the plea for protection is, in fact, a plea for reduced competition. The American economic system and its tremendous technological and industrial progress has been based largely on the preservation of competitive conditions. A certain degree of insecurity is the price it has paid and must continue to pay for free enterprise. This applies to world trade as well. The United States aspires to the removal of shackles on international commerce. The ingenuity, technical competence, and the productive efficiency of American industry are counted on to enable it to hold its own in this broader arena. But it must also expect to allow others to sell in the American market those items for which they show particular skills, efficiencies, or lower costs. This is a corollary that is easy to forget but which is fundamental.

The United States has expended millions in aiding foreign countries to rebuild their war-damaged industries. It has expended millions to help close the dollar gap, and millions more in providing technical know-how and competence to foreign countries in order to increase their productivity. All this has been done with the objective of seeing them ultimately become independent of extraordinary United States assistance, an objective which, in the final analysis, can only be achieved by larger United States imports. Obviously, foreign products which succeed in coming into the United States market will tend to be those items produced by foreign firms who, in conformity with United States precepts, have performed most efficiently. To restrict their importation is to stultify America's entire postwar economic policy.

# XI

# THE CHEMICAL INDUSTRY AND FOREIGN TRADE POLICY

## THE UNITED STATES CHEMICAL INDUSTRY AND IMPORT COMPETITION[1]

The Manufacturing Chemists' Association, Inc., J. E. Hull, president

### INTRODUCTION

The Manufacturing Chemists' Association, Inc., is a national trade organization of 160 member companies which manufacture and sell chemicals. These companies account for more than 90 percent of the chemical productive capacity of the United States. The characteristics of the chemical industry and the nature of the foreign competition to which it has been and continues to be subjected have led this association to its consistently expressed belief that the United States should maintain selective tariff protection for those products, chemical and other, which are essential to the economy and defense of our Nation.

The chemical industry is a creative industry and one which is proud of its accomplishments. The production of fertilizers and explosives from the air, of synthetic rubber from petroleum, and of delicate fabrics, dainty perfumes, and lifegiving medicinals from crude coal tar are real achievements. But the ability to fashion scientific miracles does not, necessarily, include the ability to circumvent economic obstacles. And a chemical company must do both in order to be successful.

The United States is fortunate in having an abundant supply of a wide variety of raw materials, fertile agricultural lands, a large supply of electric energy, a moderate climate, free public education, an intelligent work force, a high standard of living, and a large market. In varying degree these characteristics tend to distinguish the United States from other industrial countries. So also do our antitrust laws, our minimum-wage laws, our high wage rates, our agricultural price supports, and dozens of other regulations. While these regulations have created floors under domestic costs, and imposed conditions of equality under which all domestic industry must compete, they have also made it more difficult for American producers to compete abroad, and have made the American market—the largest single market in the world—more attractive to foreign producers who are beyond the reach of United States laws. As a result, the United States discriminates against domestic manufacturers in favor of foreign manufacturers by permitting access to the American market of foreign-made goods which are produced under conditions we would not tolerate. Basically, it is the purpose of our customs tariff laws to offset this discrimination.

---

[1] In transmitting this paper to the subcommittee, the association reported that it hopes to be able to present to the subcommittee at a later date a more comprehensive study comparing wage rates and other elements of manufacturing costs in the United States with such rates and costs in a number of foreign countries.

Schedule 1 of the Tariff Act of 1930, covering substantially all dutiable chemicals, and portions of schedule 16 (the free list) embrace over 11,000 articles of commerce now produced in commercial quantities by the domestic chemical industry, and a multitude of others which might become important in years to come.[2] Obviously this broad spectrum of related products of mines, wells, fields, forests, streams, sea water and the atmosphere, permits of few hard and fast generalizations as to the need for tariff protection. Production ranges from millions of tons to a few milligrams. Processes vary from the simplest chemical reaction vessels to the most intricate complexes of multiple-stage equipment. Some lend themselves to a high degree of automation; others require vast amounts of skilled labor per unit of output. Some are continuous; many involve batch operations. Some products are inevitably produced in relatively fixed proportions as byproducts of other operations, yet must be used or marketed.

For these reasons, this association has consistently advocated appropriate measures to offset differences in the cost of producing chemicals at home and abroad. It believes that customs duties assessed on imports constitute the most efficacious means of providing such protection, and that rates of duty should be established selectively in accordance with need. Hence, it has opposed, and will continue to oppose, across-the-board changes—increases or reductions—in tariff rates.

This memorandum outlines principal features of the chemical industry and presents examples of import competition which illustrate the continuing need for selective tariff protection (appendixes A, B, C, and D).

## CHEMICAL MANUFACTURE IS IMPORTANT TO THE ECONOMY

The domestic chemical industry embraces both big and small businesses. It represents an investment of billions of dollars of private capital at some 12,000 plant locations. It gives direct employment to over 830,000 people. Its sales exceed $24 billion per year. Its products have created employment for additional millions, e. g., the plastics and aerosol industries. The industry invests about $450 million per year in research and development and has added new plant construction at an average annual rate of $1 billion per year for the last 12 years. In all, chemical production accounts for 6 percent of total manufacturing in the United States.

## A STRONG AND COMPREHENSIVE CHEMICAL INDUSTRY IS ESSENTIAL IN PEACE AND WAR

The dependence of every major industry of the country upon products of the chemical industry is shown in exhibit A, and by the following examples of the use of various chemicals by several of the principal industries:

Steel: 1.5 million tons of sulfuric acid per year.

Petroleum: More than 100 different chemicals, including more than 1 million pounds of cracking catalysts (chemicals) per day; 49,000 tons hydrochloric acid per year.

---

[2] Man in a Chemical World, Morrison, A. Cressy, pp. 274–275, Scribner, New York, 1937.

Electrical equipment: Synthetic rubbers, such as silicone butyl, and nitrile; numerous other chemicals for insulating materials, surface coatings, etc.

Pulp and paper: Over 400,000 short tons of chlorine per year; over 300,000 short tons of soda ash per year; over 170,000 tons of caustic soda per year; sulfur dioxide, sodium sulfate, and other chemicals.

The rapid pace of research in chemicals is developing new products every day. Rubber products, for instance, are, to an ever-increasing extent, products of chemistry. In 1956 the rubber industry, employing chemical techniques and products of the chemical industry, produced the first 100-percent "synthetic natural" rubber. This step was hailed by the President of the United States as a development which would "vastly simplify the maintenance of security."

Chemical companies have played a leading role in the development of nonferrous metals which have recently come into prominence and have promise of increasingly important uses, such as columbium, titanium, lithium, boron, zirconium, and beryllium. Some are important in the construction of atomic reactors. Others are said to be key materials in still secret fuels for propelling jet aircraft and guided missiles. The recovery of these metals has been made practical through the employment of chemical procedures and techniques developed within the chemical industry.

In the field of public health, the chemical industry has developed numerous drugs and medicinals for the protection and preservation of the health of the Nation, such as vaccines, hormones, antibiotics, and vitamins. Of recent national interest are Salk vaccine and Asiatic-flu vaccine.

Perhaps the most dramatic contribution of the chemical industry to national defense and to the whole economy has been the development of fissionable material. The nuclear installations at Hanford, Wash., and Oak Ridge, Tenn., have been operated from the beginning by chemical producers at the request of the United States Government. Only the chemical industry possessed the operating techniques and technical personnel essential to produce nuclear materials.

These are but a token few of the thousands of important uses which make chemicals vital in our highly industrialized economy. They point up how a strong and well-rounded chemical industry is indispensable to a sound, flourishing industrial economy.

The difficulties which the United States faced at the beginning of World War I, when the blockade cut off foreign supplies of vital chemicals from Germany, are well known. Under the protection of the Tariff Acts of 1922 and 1930, a healthy domestic chemical industry developed in the United States. When World War II broke out, America had an integrated chemical industry ready to switch from peace to war. Every essential branch of the chemical industry was ready and well equipped to sustain the war effort.

In evaluating the defense potential, of this industry, it must be viewed as far more than a collection of physical plants. Fully as important as the plants, if not more so, are the chemists and other scientists who are actively employed in production and research. This industry and its scientific and engineering personnel provided the necessary chemical know-how which solved many of the technical defense problems during and since World War II. Without a dynamic chemical industry in being, with its reservoir of trained scientific and technical manpower, it would have been impossible to build and successfully operate the plants which produced synthetic rubber, aviation gasoline, explosives, drugs, pharmaceuticals, and, perhaps most important of all, atomic energy. Today the work of these scientists and this industry is making a major contribution to the development of guided missiles and other ultramodern weapons.

### THE CHEMICAL INDUSTRY IS CHARACTERIZED BY A MULTIPLICITY OF PRODUCTS, PROCESSES, AND RAW MATERIALS

Some industries start with many raw and semifinished materials and make them into a single product, such as an automobile or a refrigerator. Other industries take a single raw material, such as petroleum, and make from it a number of end products.

The chemical industry is far more complex. It uses virtually every substance which occurs in nature. It produces over 11,000 commercial products. It markets about 400 new chemicals each year. During early stages of commercial manufacture many of the new products are subjected to the same economic pressures which affect infant industries. Lack of adequate tariff protection, in our opinion, will tend to stifle research efforts and discourage further growth of the industry.

The field of chemicals is too comprehensive and too complex to be characterized by unqualified generalizations. With this reservation, however, the Tariff Act impliedly recognizes three overlapping general classes by the degree of the protection it accords:

1. Basic chemicals, such as acids, alkalies, salts, and some organic chemicals. The following characteristics apply to their production and distribution: Large quantities of materials are handled; mass-production techniques are employed; a high degree of automation exists; there is relative uniformity of products; the labor-cost factor is not relatively high; long-distance transportation is generally uneconomic. Basic chemicals have accordingly received little or no tariff protection.

2. Chemical products for use in further chemical manufacturing. Included in this classification are thousands of chemicals known as intermediates. As basic chemicals are upgraded they are subjected to more and more processing steps such as oxidation, reduction, halogenation, fusion, alkylation, carboxylation, nitration, sulfonation, etc. These successive steps result in a greater and greater number of products produced in smaller and smaller quantities for the respective individual products. With this reduction in the quantity of production there also occurs greater variation in quality, strength, etc., since production of the more highly upgraded products requires closer conformity to purchaser specifications. As the process of upgrading becomes further removed from the basic chemicals, mass-production techniques become less feasible. Generally, all of these factors combine to make labor costs a much larger component of product costs for this class of chemicals than for basic chemicals. Moreover, as unit-product values become higher, transportation over longer distances becomes economically more feasible. In consequence, this broad class of products has been recognized as meriting a higher degree of tariff protection than basic chemicals.

3. Finished chemical products, such as pharmaceuticals, dyes, man-made fibers, cosmetics, detergents, plastics, and perfumes. Products in this category, although finished products of the chemical industry, are commonly the raw materials for other industries. In the manufacture of this class of products, the process of chemical upgrading reaches its culmination. With notable exceptions, some of the principal economic consequences are: Automation is relatively less frequent and even where technically possible often becomes impractical because of the need to vary production schedules to accommodate differing specifications as to strength, quality, etc.; batch processes, often employing what are pot and kettle techniques, are common; because of product variations and limited quantities, packaging and special handling become important operations; both production and distribution involve a substantially higher degree of human effort resulting in greatly increased labor costs. For this class of products, unit values are high, and transportation over long distances (e. g., from one country to another) becomes a relatively insignificant economic factor. These chemicals, accordingly, have been recognized as requiring a somewhat higher degree of tariff protection, which takes the form not only of higher rates but, in the case of the coal-tar and related chemicals, a special valuation basis known as the American selling price. (This basis will be specially discussed, infra.)

As the process of chemical upgrading proceeds from step to step, wage rates, fringe benefits, and governmental controls over hours of work, safety standards, sanitation, etc., have an increasingly greater impact upon product costs. These costs, in consequence, tend more and more to reflect the standards of living and of social control in the respective countries of manufacture.

Each of the three categories contain both organic and inorganic chemicals. Organic chemicals are defined generally as compounds which, like plant and animal matter, contain the carbon atom. Compounds other than organic, and largely obtained from minerals and atmospheric gases, are termed "inorganic chemicals."

THE INTERDEPENDENCE OF CHEMICAL COMPOUNDS COMPLICATES THE ECONOMICS OF CHEMICAL PRODUCTION

Characteristically, chemical processes result in two or more different compounds. Consequently, the marketability of one of the resulting products is affected by the economic factors which affect the other product resulting from the operation.

A typical example in the inorganic field is the production of chlorine and caustic soda, two of the most widely used basic chemicals. When an electric current is passed through salt brine under controlled conditions, both chlorine and caustic soda are produced. Except for a few specialized byproduct processes, chlorine cannot be commercially produced without the accompanying manufacture of caustic soda. Any economic disturbance of the market for either of these products will directly affect the profitability of the overall process and, therefore, of the other product. Thus, if there were excessive imports of low-cost caustic soda into the United States, the economy of chlorine production and sales would necessarily be affected.

The production of coproducts in the organic field is far more complicated than the simple illustration of inorganic production already recited. The interrelationships of intermediates themselves and the economics of their production and use have a direct bearing on the overall equilibrium of organic chemical production.

For example, chlorobenzene is an organic intermediate used in manufacture of DDT and other insecticides, dyestuffs, explosives, and other organic chemicals. In manufacture of a dye intermediate, chlorobenzene is nitrated with mixed acid and not 1 but 2 principal products, ortho-nitrochlorobenzene (ONCB) and para-nitrochlorobenzene (PNCB) are produced, as well as small amounts of still other products. The difference between ONCB and PNCB is only a matter of the relative positions of the nitro group and the chlorine atom in the molecule as shown in the following structural formulas:

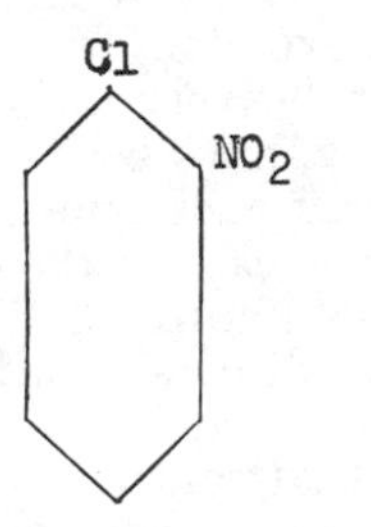


Ortho-Nitrochlorobenzene

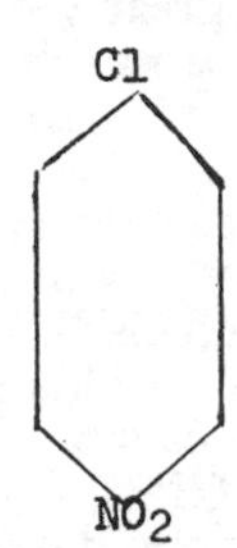


Para-Nitrochlorobenzene

This difference of position produces different chemical properties and, therefore, controls the uses to which these two materials may be put. The ratio of ONCB to PNCB is approximately 1:2 and very little can be done to alter this ratio. Economic production of one of these materials, therefore, depends upon the development of profitable uses for the other, and the use ratio must necessarily be about the same as the production ratio. Otherwise, production of one in excess of demand will result in a surplus having a lower unit value, and more of the total cost of manufacture would have to be applied against the other.

Likewise, imports of ONCB, for example, will tend to depress the domestic price of that product and necessitate assigning all or a greater proportion of the nitration and separation costs to PNCB. And, as the cost of manufacturing PNCB rises, it too will become vulnerable to foreign imports.

The only way to maintain American production in this situation is adequate tariff rates on both of these products, on other coproducts, on the intermediate chlorobenzene from which this process started, and possibly on the end products. This illustration can be multiplied many times in the organic chemical industry.

### THERE IS A CLEAR NEED FOR AMERICAN SELLING-PRICE PROVISIONS

The branch of the industry based on products derived from coal tar is highly complex and interdependent (see exhibit B). For 35 years it has been recognized by Congress as needing special treatment. The only tariff protection found practical to foster the growth and protect this industry has been the American selling-price basis for valuing imports of these chemicals.

There is no dependable foreign price data covering any of the 1,200 commercially important dyes and the thousands of intermediates now dutiable under the American selling-price provision Experience has shown that if the products were dutiable on foreign values, foreign producers would be in a position to manipulate the values for duty purposes. In this connection, a Tariff Commission investigation disclosed that determination of reasonably equivalent rates of duty applicable to other bases of evaluation would consume 2 years or more and require the exercise of broad discretion.[3] Also, experience has shown that the American selling price provision is particularly important in its application to new products. Their initial domestic costs are high yet continued development is of paramount importance to the economy.

Other countries which have a coal-tar chemical industry recognize the importance of these chemicals by imposing drastic import restrictions. For instance, the United Kingdom, France, Germany, Italy, India, and Japan control imports of coal-tar products by requiring import permits and by issuing them almost exclusively for noncompetitive items or for needs in excess of their domestic production.

Customs administration in the United States has been well handled and reasonably effective under the American selling price provisions.

THE CHEMICAL INDUSTRY IS CHARACTERIZED BY VIGOROUS COMPETITION

An outstanding feature of the chemical industry is robust competition. The high degree of competition among companies is reflected in the fact that in 1956 total sales of the 3 largest chemical producers amounted to only 17 percent of total chemical industry sales.

The chemical industry is replete with examples of the classic competition which occurs when several sellers of the same product seek to sell to the same buyer. This is greatly intensified by competition between different chemical products, between manufacturing processes, and between raw materials. Here are a few of the many examples which could be cited:

1. Competition between products for similar markets: Man-made fiber competes with natural fiber; high tenacity rayon competes with nylon; cellophane competes with polyethylene film, and wax paper competes with both of the latter as well as with aluminum foil.

2. Competition between processes: Acetic acid is made from 3 different raw materials by 5 different processes; ethylene glycol, widely used as an antifreeze, is made by 3 different processes.

3. Competition between raw materials: Petroleum is competitive with natural fats in making detergents; coal is competitive with petroleum as a source of phthalic anhydride; petroleum is competitive with molasses for production of ethyl alcohol.

The number of chemical companies competing in certain fields are: Plastic materials, 166; sulfuric acid, 77; photo chemicals, 17; explo-

---

[3] Memorandum of Tariff Commission on H. R. 8304, 81st Cong., printed in hearings on H. R. 1535, Committee on Ways and Means, 82d Cong., pp. 222, 236; testimony of W. R. Johnson, Assistant to the Commissioner of Customs, p. 90.

sives, 19; dyes, 53; organic intermediates, 138; paints, 850; synthetic ammonia, 35; oxygen, 90.

Many benefits have accrued to the American public from the highly competitive conditions which exist in the chemical industry. These benefits include the availability of ample supplies of an ever-widening range of new materials and products at favorable prices—prices which in many cases either have declined actually or relatively below the level of earlier years. For example, during the past 30 years prices of most necessities have more than doubled. In this same period of time the price of ammonia—nitrogen plant food for farm use—has gone down from $108 per ton to its present price of about $80 per ton. Penicillin dropped from $86 per million units to 5 cents per million units in 12 years' time (1944–56).

In the last 30 years the Wholesale Price Index (of the Bureau of Labor Statistics, United States Department of Labor) for industrial chemicals has increased 47.6 percent while the index for all commodities other than farm products and food increased nearly twice as much—86 percent. During 1956 the BLS Wholesale Price Index for chemicals rose only 0.5 percent while all commodities rose 3.2 percent during the same period. (See exhibit C for comparison of chemical prices with other commodities for the period 1940–56.)

The low level of chemical prices compared to other prices and the current decline in the earnings of chemical manufacturers result from the fact that the American chemical industry is vigorously competitive and demonstrate that the tariff rates applicable to imports of chemical products have not fostered monopoly in this country.

The competitive race for putting new chemical-industry products on the market accounts for the high level of research and development expenditures. As a corollary, peacetime employment of scientists in industrial research activities is a vital factor in maintaining a scientific manpower reserve which is available in national emergencies.

THE FOREIGN CHEMICAL INDUSTRY IS GROWING RAPIDLY

The interruption of chemical production which World War II caused in Europe and Japan has ended. Not only has European domestic chemical production been fully restored but by 1951 Western Europe's chemical exports had increased half again in volume over prewar. Great Britain's chemical exports were running 165 percent over prewar. Italy, France, and the Benelux nations shows a similar pattern of chemical exports.

The increase of exports from these nations has been attributed to the disappearance of Germany from the world chemical market in the years which followed World War II, but this statement does not hold true today.

German chemical production has grown rapidly in the last decade, achieving twice its pre-World War II volume by 1954. In 1956, 21 percent of West German sales of chemicals were foreign sales.[4]

---

[4] Die Industrie der Bundesrepublik Deutschland, 1956, pt. III, No. 4, p. 17.

The establishment of the European common market undoubtedly will alter materially the productive pattern of the chemical industry in the member nations. In general, European manufacturers construct producing facilities with built-in export capacity. There is no reason to believe that the industrial concentration and rearrangement to be developed within the common market countries will alter this habit. Although it is not known precisely how the economic union will affect the union's chemical industry, it is expected that considerably increased export competition will develop. The announced purposes of the common market are to increase trade among member nations and decrease imports from outside the area. The European Economic Union (common market) member nations are Belgium, France, West Germany, Italy, Luxembourg, and the Netherlands.

The traditional chemical importing nations—such as Poland, Spain, Yugoslavia, India—have also been expanding their chemical production. Portugal, for example, began its first production of ammonia in 1952. Sweden has more than doubled its chemical production since 1947.

Switzerland and Japan have become major exporters of chemicals.

No review of foreign chemical production, however brief, would be complete without reference to the U. S. S. R. and satellite nations.

Fifteen percent of the U. S. S. R. budget for 1956 was allotted to its chemical industry. A recent report[5] announced that under Russia's coordinated chemical production plan finished industrial chemicals will be turned out in Eastern Germany and Poland, and Southeastern countries will concentrate on raw and semifinished products. Rumania now has under construction a $12 million plant for making caprolactam for nylon fiber which is due on stream in 1958. Capacity will be 15,000 pounds per day.

## LOW WAGES LOWER FOREIGN MANUFACTURING COSTS

Wages and living standards of industrial workers in foreign countries are substantially lower than the wage and living standards prevalent in the United States. Since wage rates for chemical workers in many foreign countries are not available, direct comparisons of foreign and American chemical wages cannot be listed for all countries. The following tables show the low average rates paid to industrial workers in certain countries which are producers of chemicals exported to the United States, a comparison of wages paid chemical workers in the United States and three foreign countries, and the ratio of these wage rates and costs per man-hour.

---

[5] Chemical Week, August 10, 1957, p. 3.

TABLE I.—*Wage rates for industrial labor, 1956* [1]

| Country | Average hourly earnings (United States dollars) | Percentage of United States rate |
|---|---|---|
| United States | $1.98 | 100 |
| United Kingdom | .59 | 30 |
| West Germany | .47 | 24 |
| France | .43 | 22 |
| Italy | .31 | 16 |
| Sweden | .82 | 41 |
| Denmark | .68 | 34 |
| Netherlands | .39 | 20 |
| Switzerland [2] | .76 | 38 |
| Belgium [3] | .50 | 25 |
| Japan [4] | .22 | 11 |

[1] Wage rates and exchange rates from the Monthly Bulletin of Statistics, United Nations, April 1957, pp. 123, 124 and 164–166.
[2] From Swiss consulate general: 3.28 Swiss francs per hour average for 1955.
[3] From Belgian consulate general: First quarter 1957 semiskilled industrial labor.
[4] Hourly rate for all manufacturing based on $46.40 for average month of 207 hours. Average chemical wage earner receives equivalent of $52.54 per month for average of 189 hours' work or $0.26 per hour. Japanese Government publication, Population, Labor Food Supply, and Prices, November 1956.

TABLE II.—*1957 wages and fringe benefits for chemical production workers, United States versus other countries* [1]

| | Estimated hourly wage | Fringe benefits | Total estimated cost per man-hour |
|---|---|---|---|
| | | *Percent* | |
| Japan, April 1957 | 24⅗ cents | 35–50 | 33⅕ to 36⁹⁄₁₀ cents. |
| Great Britain, April 1957 | 63 cents | 10–12 | 69³⁄₁₀ to 75⅗ cents. |
| West Germany, February 1957 | 50 cents | 35–40 | 52½ to 70 cents. |
| United States, April 1957 | $2.17 | [2] 21.8 | $2.64. |

[1] Information furnished by Bureau of Labor Statistics, U. S. Department of Labor.
[2] Source: Fringe Benefits, 1955, a survey by Economic Research Department, United States Chamber of Commerce, table 5: Distribution of fringe benefits as percentage of payroll; chemical and allied products.

NOTE.—Average supplementary benefits paid by chemical companies have increased since 1955 as indicated in Bureau of Labor Statistics, Review of Major 1956 Wage Developments.

TABLE III

Estimated hourly wage:
- United States equals 8.8 times Japan
- United States equals 3.4 times Great Britain
- United States equals 4.3 times West Germany

Estimated cost per man-hour:
- United States equals 7.1 to 7.9 times Japan
- United States equals 3.4 to 3.8 times Great Britain
- United States equals 3.7 to 5 times West Germany

While direct labor costs are only one element of the total cost of manufacture, wage levels have a definite bearing on the level of product unit cost, even in modern, highly automated plants. Chemical production processes, techniques, and plant systems are much the same in foreign countries as in the United States. The same level of technical proficiency prevails. Many processes used in the United States, such as the mercury cell for producing chlorine, a nylon process, a polyethylene process, and numerous others were developed in Europe and are operated in the United States under license or other arrangement. Wage differentials between countries are reflected not only in direct labor costs but also in cumulative labor costs—the wages paid for developing, designing, and constructing manufacturing plants as well as research and distribution costs.

As chemical products are upgraded from basic materials to finished products the value added by manufacture reflects an increasing differential when low-wage countries are compared with high-wage countries.

Imports from countries having lower wage levels and lower standards of living reflect those factors in their production costs.

A national policy of selective tariff protection is essential in order to insure that appropriate evaluation of such differentials will be made whenever American tariff rates are being considered.

EXCESSIVE IMPORTATION OF COMPETING CHEMICALS FROM LOW-WAGE COUNTRIES IS ADVERSE TO THE BEST INTERESTS OF THE UNITED STATES

A healthy, profitable domestic chemical industry is vital to the welfare of the United States. As has been pointed out, chemicals are needed by every other domestic industry, and the scientific and technical personnel of the industry are essential to a sound national defense.

While the desirability of competition is recognized, there is no reason why a foreign producer should receive an unfair advantage because he has lower costs.

Our system of laws protects consumers and producers alike from unfair domestic competition in the United States. We do not permit a domestic producer to take unfair advantage of his domestic competitor. In agriculture, the farmer is protected by price supports. The industrial worker is protected by minimum-wage laws. It is only reasonable, therefore, that we protect domestic producers and consumers from unfair foreign competition. If we permit foreign imports from low-wage countries to drive domestic prices below a point where reasonably efficient American producers can compete, the effect would be to deprive American consumers of the competitive protection resulting from the availability of domestically made products, and to subject our consumers to price manipulations over which we could exercise no control. This would also have the dangerous result of depriving our economy (as well as our national defense potential) of reliable and competitive domestic sources for essential chemical products.

CONCLUSION

1. The chemical industry is a dynamic industry. It is in a constant state of flux and subject to an extremely high rate of obsolescence, as new products and processes replace the old.

2. A comprehensive domestic chemical industry, embracing all branches of chemistry and vigorous in all its parts, is of prime importance to the defense and general welfare of the United States. Failure of any segment of the industry to survive would weaken the whole in geometric proportions.

3. Cost of production of many chemical products in the United States substantially exceeds the cost of production in other countries, not by reason of any inadequacy on the part of domestic industry but

because of the cost of the higher social standards to which the domestic economy is committed. Unless means are provided to offset differences in domestic and foreign costs, domestic production of many chemicals may cease and the United States would then become dependent upon foreign sources for them.

4. To the extent that American producers withdraw from certain product fields our peacetime economy and our national defense potential will suffer.

5. The American chemical industry spends about $450 million each year on research and development. This results in about 400 new products coming on the market each year. Unless these products are protected in their "infant" stage, we must expect that new product research will be reduced accordingly.

6. Any consideration of tariff increases or reductions should be considered on a product-by-product rather than on an across-the-board basis. National policies in this area can be worked out consistent with the international interests and responsibilities of the United States.

EXHIBIT A

# BROAD SCOPE OF THE CHEMICAL INDUSTRY TODAY

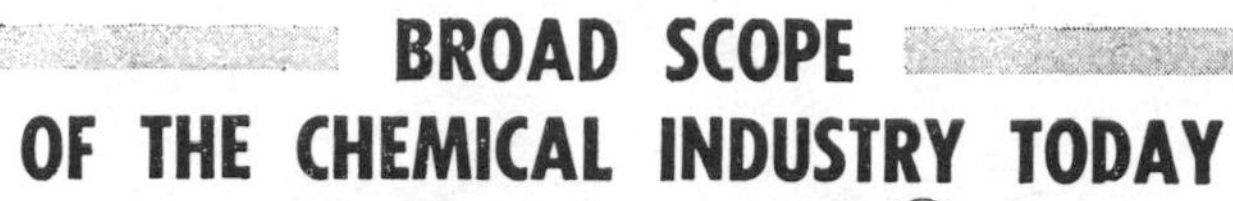

ABUNDANT RAW MATERIALS
from Mine, Forest, Sea, Air, Farm, Oil, Brine and Gas Wells

THE CHEMICAL INDUSTRY
converts them into more than 8,850 compounds in more than 12,000 plants operated by hundreds of chemical manufacturers.

CHEMICALS
Chemicals such as acids and alkalies, salts, organic compounds, solvents, compressed gases, pigments and dyes are used

BY THE CHEMICAL INDUSTRY ITSELF
To Produce

Explosives
Fertilizers
Paints
Pesticides
Plastic Materials
Sanitizing Chemicals
Synthetic Fibers
Synthetic Rubber
And many others
Cosmetics
Detergents & Soap
Drugs & Medicines
Dyes & Inks

BY OTHER INDUSTRIES
In the Production of

| Durable Goods | Non-durable Goods |
|---|---|
| Building Materials | Beverages |
| Electrical Equipment | Food Products |
| Furniture & Fixtures | Leather & Leather Products |
| Hardware | Packaging |
| Lumber Products | Paper & Paper Products |
| Machinery | Petroleum & Coal Products |
| Metal Products | Rubber Products |
| Motor Vehicles & Equipment | Textiles |
| Transportation Equipment | |

And other products of metal, glass, paper and wood

THE ULTIMATE MARKET
(Fundamental human needs)

Health, Food, Clothing, Shelter, Transportation, Communication, Defense and Other Needs

Reproduced from "The Chemical Industry Facts Book", Manufacturing Chemists' Association, Inc.

EXHIBIT B

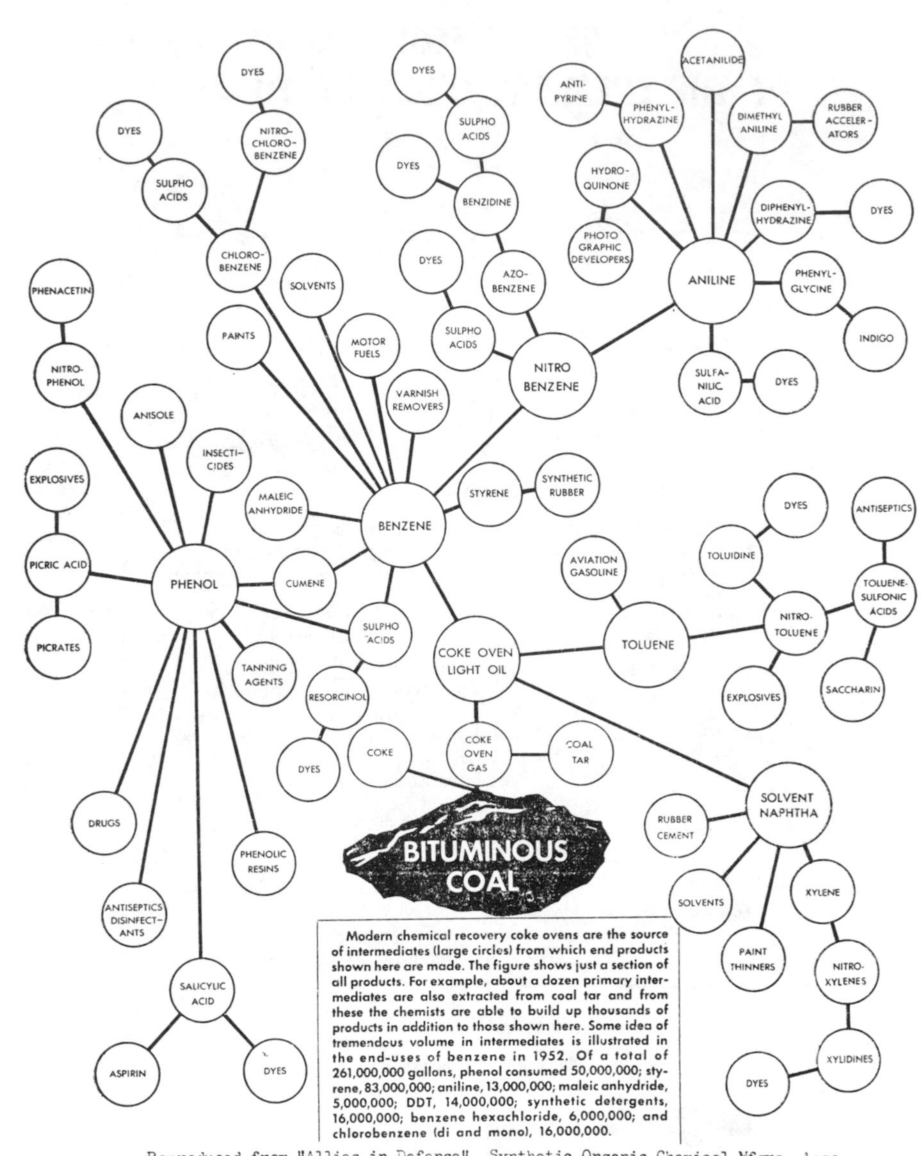


Reproduced from "Allies in Defense", Synthetic Organic Chemical Mfgrs. Asso.

EXHIBIT C-1

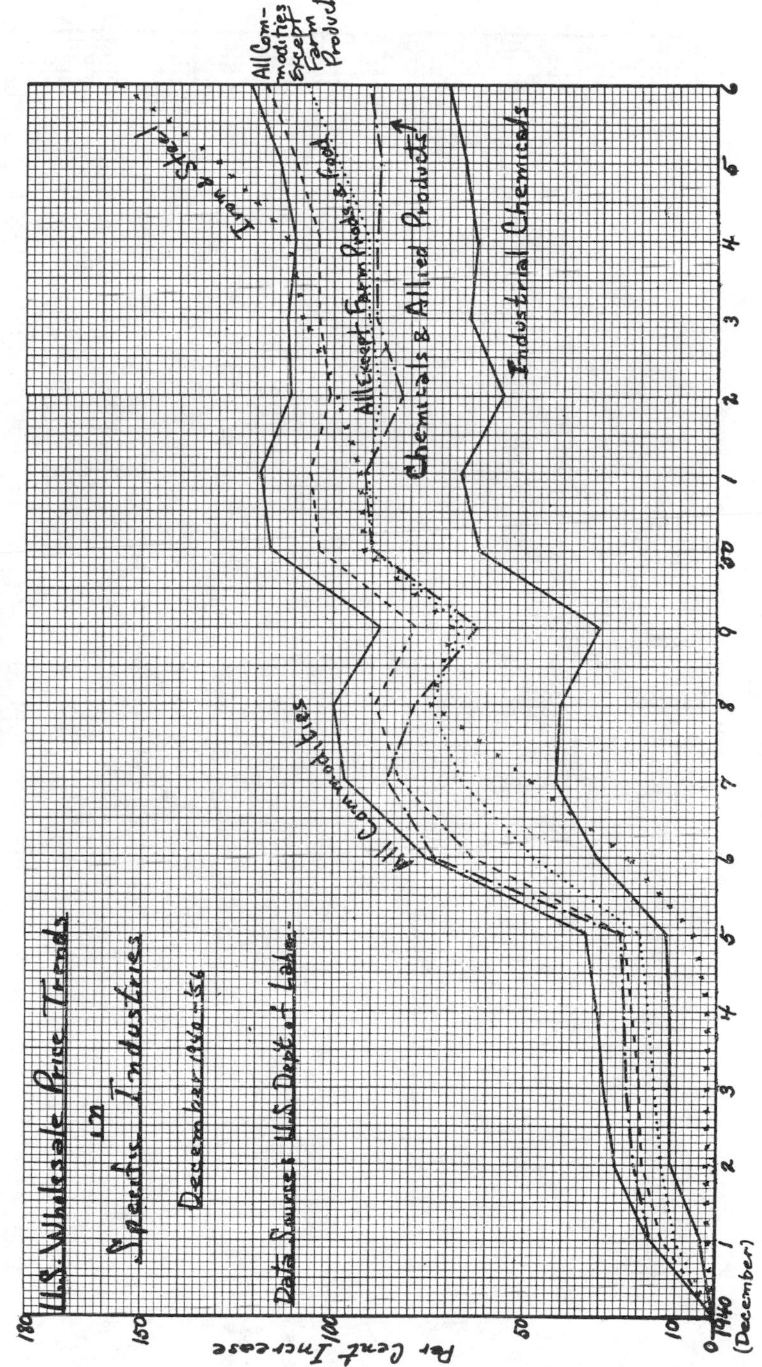
U.S. Wholesale Price Trends
in
Specific Industries
December 1940–56
Data Source: U.S. Dept. of Labor
All Commodities Except Farm Products
Iron & Steel
All Commodities
All Except Farm Products & food
Chemicals & Allied Products
Industrial Chemicals
Per Cent Increase
180
150
100
50
10
0
1940
(December)
1
2
3
4
5
6
7
8
9
'50
1
2
3
4
5
6

EXHIBIT C-2

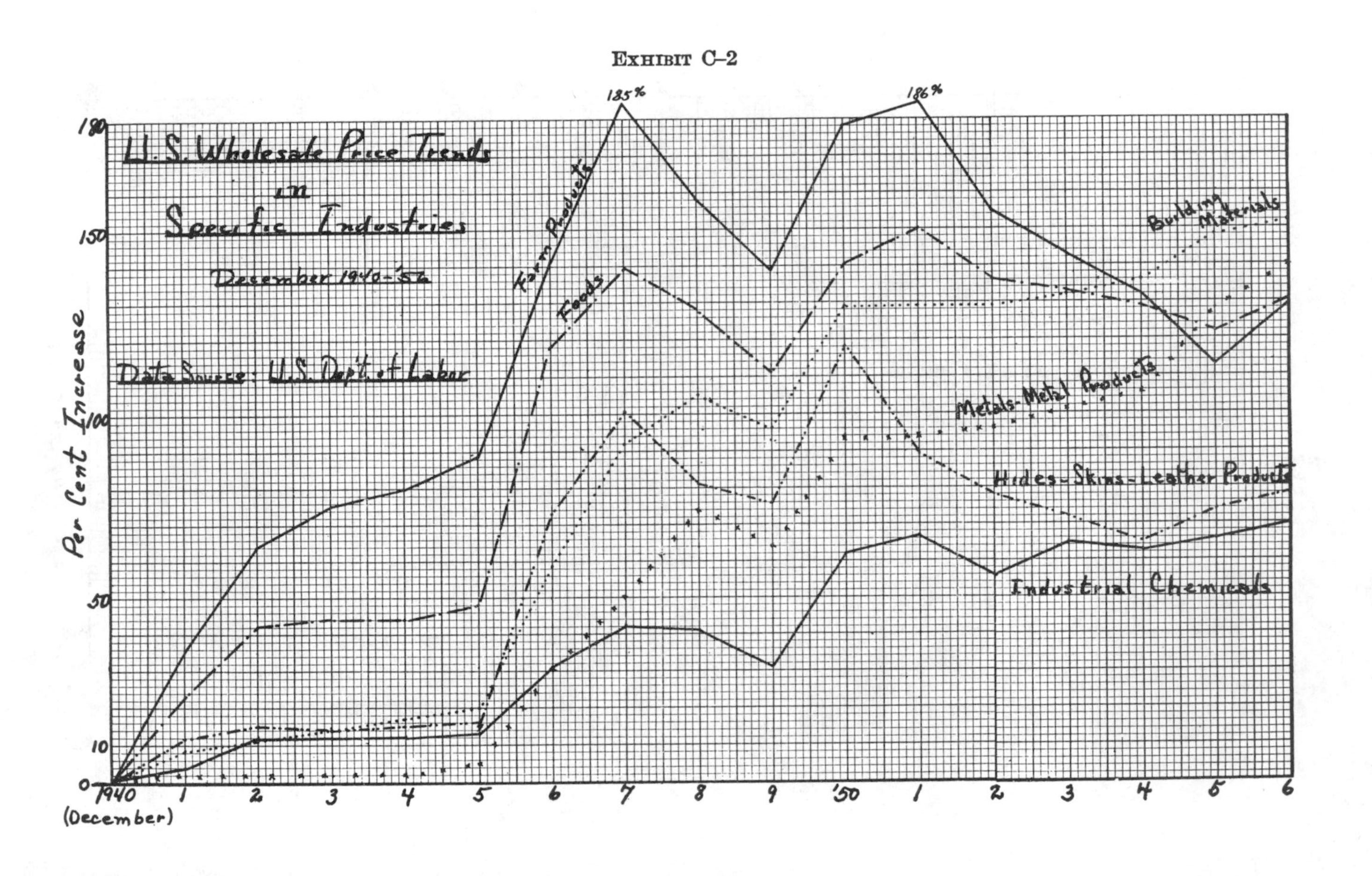
U.S. Wholesale Price Trends
in
Specific Industries
December 1940-'56
Data Source: U.S. Dep't of Labor
Per Cent Increase
Farm Products
Foods
Building Materials
Metals-Metal Products
Hides-Skins-Leather Products
Industrial Chemicals
185%
186%
(December)

The following appendixes contain examples which illustrate the continuing need for selective tariff protection.

## APPENDIX A

## DYES

Coal-tar dyes provide an illuminating example of the effect of foreign competition.

### DECLINING PRODUCTION AND SALES

During the period 1948 through 1956, United States production of dyes declined from 201,376,000 to 151,575,000 pounds, or nearly 25 percent, and sales of domestic dyes dropped from 186,782,000 to 154,547,000 pounds, or nearly 17 percent. Moreover, this drop in production and sales was accompanied by an increase in capacity, which the Government found to be necessary for national defense reasons. Under Government auspices, anthraquinone vat dye capacity in the United States was increased from 37 million to 47 million pounds. Sales of these dyes in 1956 amounted to only 28,576,000 pounds, leaving idle capacity of 18,600,000 pounds, 40 percent of capacity projected for defense requirements.

### INCREASING IMPORTS

While production and sale of American-made dyes were declining approximately 20 percent between 1948 and 1956, imports of foreign-made dyes increased 190 percent by weight and 124 percent by value, *at a time when the United States had substantial idle capacity and 1 domestic producer alone had ample capacity to make and ship every pound of dye that was imported.*

The explanation for this situation is brief and clear. Foreign costs were (and are) so much lower than domestic costs that foreign producers paying standard wage rates in their own countries could (and still can) make the products, ship them here, pay all costs of transportation, insurance, brokerage, and duties, and still undersell the domestic producer and make a profit.

### FOREIGN VERSUS DOMESTIC PRODUCTION COSTS

Exact figures on foreign versus American costs of production are difficult to obtain, but there are excellent grounds for believing that in Germany and Switzerland, the principal exporters of dyes to the United States, total costs of production probably amount to approximately 50 percent of United States costs, on the average.

1. It is known—from visits of American employees to German plants and from German consultants—that the facilities, techniques, and labor requirements for most dyes are substantially identical in both countries, and that the most important item of cost, there as here, is labor, both in technical operations and in research.

2. It is known that the average hourly earnings of chemical-plant workers in Western Germany are less than one-fourth as much as in the United States, and that research chemists with doctor of philosophy degrees receive less than one-third as much as in this country.

3. It is known that a single dye frequently requires as many as 20 prior and successive processing steps in which the physical influences of heat, pressure, and mixing are combined with the chemical reactions of oxidation, reduction, chlorination, hydrolysis, halogenation, caustic fusion, alkylation, carboxylation, nitration, sulfonation, condensation, liming, diazotizing, and coupling. Painstaking research, close attention, and expert manipulation by highly trained chemists, engineers, and skilled workmen are standard requirements. A single dye may be in process for weeks, and may weigh as little as one-eightieth as much as the materials used in making it.

4. It is known that several American companies have been sending research work to Germany to take advantage of the lower rates paid there to highly qualified research chemists.

5. It is known that a German corporation which specializes in plant design and engineering and is affiliated with one of the largest dye producers in Germany has offered to perform such work in Germany for American companies because, as it stated, "reductions in the final cost of a plant can be effected by taking advantage of the considerably lower cost of engineering when accomplished, in part, in Germany."

22806—58——68

LOSS OF RESEARCH AND PRODUCTION TO FOREIGN COUNTRIES

American dye producers may be compelled, as some have, to export research work, and even dye-production facilities, to foreign lands. The consequence of such a move would be (1) to deprive this country of a resource far exceeding the value of all the dyes and dye plants in this country; (2) to force this country to rely, increasingly, on foreign sources for a highly essential segment of technological manpower; and (3) to finance discoveries and developments abroad, at our expense, of which we would be fair-weather beneficiaries.

As the Tariff Commission has reminded us, "the development of synthetic dyes has been the keystone of the modern organic-chemical industry, not only in the United States but throughout the world" (Dyes, War Changes in Industry Series, Report No. 19, United States Tariff Commission, 1946, p. 1).

This is the industry that supplied the chemists and performed the research and operated plants that made possible the atomic bomb; that produced the napalm bomb, dye markers, and high explosives; that synthesized cortisone; and that purified and made possible the mass production of streptomycin and penicillin. It is inconceivable that this Nation would be willing to give up so much. Its own best interests would dictate the contrary.

---

## Appendix B

### Formic Acid

Although not a large-volume chemical, this acid is important for a variety of uses including dyeing and finishing textiles, laundry sour, insecticide manufacture, tanning, medicines, food preservative, and rubber coagulant.

There are three manufacturers in the United States. At the beginning of World War II, the only production in the world was in the United States and Germany. When the Dutch East Indies, where it was used for rubber coagulant, were cut off from normal sources from Germany, the United States Government encouraged the two producers in this country to expand facilities and rush supplies to the Far East.

In tariff negotiations in 1950, the duty on formic acid was reduced from 3 cents to 2.4 cents per pound. Representations were made at that time that manufacture of this acid was not profitable and tariff reductions were not warranted. Imports have increased steadily and domestic production has decreased materially since then.

One producer reports that he has had to reduce prices in order to compete with imports in spite of the fact that actual costs have increased 30 percent in the past 4 years; he no longer offers his product on the west coast. Sales are now the lowest since 1949; a deflated price structure, due to import competition helped at least in part by tariff reductions, and low production further increase his loss on this operation.

All available information indicates that formic acid is produced in Europe by essentially the same processes used in the United States. European costs are believed to be lower through lower wages, both direct and indirect.

## Appendix C

### Calcium Hypochlorite

This chemical, containing a minimum of 70 percent available chlorine, is essential for use as a germicide, disinfectant, deodorant, and for bleaching applications such as in the laundry and textile industries. During war emergencies, calcium hypochlorite was under 100 percent allocation for the military and essential civilian uses. There are three producers in the United States; in recent years there have been substantial imports from Japan.

As a result of GATT negotiations in 1951, the 25 percent ad valorem duty was reduced to 12½ percent which now applies to this chemical. Since this reduction, the imports of calcium hypochlorite have been substantial and are reported as follows:

| | Pounds |
|---|---|
| 1954 | 275,000 |
| 1955 | 550 to 850,000 |
| 1956 | 1,000,000 |
| 1957 | [1] 1,200,000 |

[1] Based on first 5 months.

All domestic producers report substantial import competition from Japan offered in the domestic market at 11 to 20 percent below their prices and wholly without regard to geographical locations in the United States. This imported material is going to domestic users and the Army Chemical Corps; the latter formerly purchased all its requirements from domestic sources but in 5 months of 1957 has already made 41 percent of its purchases from foreign sources.

The lower prices offered by foreign producers have materially reduced export sales by United States manufacturers. Producers report loss of markets in Puerto Rico, Cuba, Canada, and South Africa due to Japanese production.

This loss of sales in the export market and to the Government, together with lower domestic sales has injured the total sales efforts of domestic companies resulting in higher costs, lower profits, and lower plant employment.

---

## Appendix D

### Caffeine

Caffeine, first produced in the United States in 1895, is one of our oldest pharmaceuticals. Today it is still an important pharmaceutical but its major outlet is now in cola-type soft drinks.

Except for the period of World War II domestic producers have been able to supply this country's needs, but in the period of 1943–46 and even until 1951 Brazil furnished a large supply as imports, then dropped out of the picture. Beginning with 1952 West Germany, having reestablished its chemical industry to a large degree, started exporting to the United States in a serious way, increasing its shipments from 131,939 pounds in 1952 to 611,086 pounds in 1956, practically 100 percent of total imports of this product in 1956 or one-third of the estimated domestic consumption.

The increased entries of caffeine into the United States have been aided, if not made possible, by reductions in the import duty under the Trade Agreements Act. The duty of $1.25 a pound in the Tariff Act of 1930 has been reduced to 90 cents, then to 60 cents, and today it is 54 cents a pound, a total reduction of 56.8 percent. Beginning with July 1, 1958, the duty will be 51 cents, equal to a reduction 59.2 percent from the original duty of $1.25 a pound in the Tariff Act of 1930.

Not only has the import duty been reduced and imports increased but the prices for the imported material have been below prevailing domestic prices. The result is that domestic producers' profit margin has been cut to almost zero. The competition from imported caffeine is not limited to the eastern seaboard. It is experienced also in Indiana, Michigan, Missouri, and other States.

# THE SYNTHETIC ORGANIC CHEMICAL INDUSTRY AND UNITED STATES FOREIGN TRADE POLICY

**P. K. Lawrence, chairman, International Commercial Relations Committee, Synthetic Organic Chemical Manufacturers Association of the United States**

In response to the invitation of the Subcommittee on Foreign Trade Policy to submit a paper for inclusion in the subcommittee's planned compendium, the Synthetic Organic Chemical Manufacturers Association, on June 13, 1957, transmitted considerable material which it had prepared and filed with executive department agencies, as well as with the appropriate committees of Congress. This material set forth the position of the synthetic organic chemical industry concerning the appropriateness of existing tariff and trade legislation. The staff of the subcommittee indicated that the material submitted would be very useful to it in connection with the work which the subcommittee had undertaken, but was too voluminous for inclusion in the proposed compendium, and a suggestion was made that a paper be prepared adapting the material for this purpose. The association feels sure that the subcommittee is cognizant of the inherent inadequacies of a digest or adaptation of this kind. These comments therefore should be considered only as a succinct outline of the pertinent views which the association has previously advanced and supported in discussion of tariff and trade legislation and policies.

## THE SYNTHETIC ORGANIC CHEMICAL INDUSTRY

The association consists of 95 manufacturers of synthetic organic chemicals whose products, it is estimated, amount to more than 90 percent of the total production of such chemicals in the United States. The industry developed through the manufacture of chemical products from coal-tar crudes. These crudes were a byproduct of coke manufactured for the steel industry. Synthetic organic compounds in intermediate form were later derived from petrochemicals and from acetylene. Other sources also have been opened up to the organic chemist, and the industry is constantly engaged in research programs in an attempt to utilize other materials and processes.

The industry's operations are conducted essentially on a "batch" process basis. The chemicals which begin the processing stage may remain in process for months before emerging in finished form. They are carried through various steps in appropriate containers or apparatus. Complete processing may require many separate steps. Relatively high labor costs per unit of production are incurred in this type of manufacture. Few organic chemicals lend themselves to the continuous process of manufacture where materials are added and finished products are constantly removed in a manufacturing vehicle.

The products of this industry are either directly utilized, or are combined and converted into explosives, medicinals, dyes, plastics, synthetic rubber, insecticides, detergents, photographic chemicals, soil conditioners, flavor and perfume materials, synthetic fibers, fuel additives and a host of other useful products.

The organic chemical industry of the United States sustained its first real development after the conclusion of World War I. Military necessity dictated that the interests of the United States required the establishment and continued expansion of an organic chemical industry if this Nation were to provide for its defense and maintain its security, or resist foreign attack or invasion.

The industry has made phenomenal progress in the last 40 years by reason of tremendous expenditures for research and development programs. Today practicaly every industry, as well as agriculture, is dependent upon organic chemicals for use in the some stage of manufacturing operations or in the growing, handling, or preserving of agriculture commodities. The needs of the industry for raw materials is of extreme importance to the economic stability of the coal, petroleum, and natural gas industries; byproducts of agriculture also find increasing use in the processing and combination of organic chemicals. Finished products manufactured or produced from organic chemicals enter into the lives of every person in the United States. They are indispensable to the production of the amazing stream of new products, processes, and uses which have spurred the expansion rate of growth of the entire United States economy.

Literally thousands of chemicals are annually produced by the industry, and this production is so interrelated that a decline in output of a particular chemical adversely affects the production of many other chemicals.

THE ROLE OF THE INDUSTRY IN WORLD WAR II

As a result of World War I experience the United States was painfully aware of the necessity of establishing and fostering the growth of an organic chemical industry as an instrument of military importance. The Nation suffered when German chemicals necessary to produce explosives, medicines, dyes, and similar products were cut off. At the end of the war the Congress, in the formation of a national defense policy enacted legislation designed to establish and safeguard a synthetic organic chemical industry in the United States. As an interim measure an embargo was placed upon the importation of organic chemicals until Congress could devise an adequate tariff policy for this purpose. The chemical schedule of the Tariff Act of 1922, repeated and expanded in the Tariff Act of 1930, was adopted as the means for safeguarding national security by providing adequate tariff protection to this industry. Under this policy the industry developed rapidly. In 1921 it consisted of 201 companies and approximately 13,000 employees producing 144 million pounds of organic chemicals; by 1939, 236 companies comprised the industry and approximately 52,000 employees produced over 4 billion pounds of organic chemicals. By 1941 the industry had grown to 335 companies producing almost 7 billion pounds of organic chemicals.

Military and essential production needs of World War II absorbed the entire productive capacity of the industry and required a further expansion of nearly 300 percent over 1939. In 1944 the industry produced 15 billion pounds of chemicals all of which were regarded as required for military or essential civilian production. Included among these chemicals were synthetic drugs and medicinals, chemical warfare products, synthetic rubber, fibers, plastics and resins, high-powered aviation fuels, and more powerful explosives.

The Korean emergency, although calling only for limited mobilization, found the industry equipped to handle demands. It then consisted of 564 companies and approximately 153,000 employees, which produced over 27 billion pounds of organic chemicals in 1951. Almost half of such production consisted of chemicals for which the mobilization agencies of Government programed plant expansions. New military uses for organic chemicals included bulletproof vests, rockets, napalm bombs, jet fuels, and the antibiotic drugs.

The Nation's dependence on the industry for future military and essential civilian needs is apparent. The ability of the industry to serve such needs is, of course, dependent upon the maintenance of its productive capacity and retention of its technically trained manpower through production and sale of its products for home consumption in the United States and for export to other countries.

THE SYNTHETIC ORGANIC INDUSTRY AND THE DOMESTIC ECONOMY

We have adverted to the interrelationship among the coal, steel, and petroleum industries and the organic chemical industry. We have also pointed out that the products in this industry enter into practically every civilian manufacturing operation, as well as being of importance to the agricultural segment of our economy.

From another standpoint, the importance of the industry to the domestic economy may be measured by the effect of expansion and growth of the industry upon the strength of the general domestic economy. The industry is expanding at a rate of 4 times that of all United States industry; while the gross national product during the period 1939 to 1952 merely doubled, the value of the industry's sales increased 10 times. Total production of the industry increased 6 times during that period, while total industrial production for the Nation merely doubled. Total employment in the industry tripled and payrolls increased from $100 million to $717 million—an increase of more than 7 times.

Average hourly earnings increased from 77½ cents in 1939 to $2.08 in 1952, an average in excess of all manufacturing industries.

Despite inflationary trends, the industry's average unit sales prices held remarkably well during this period, increasing only 44 percent, while the wholesale price index of all commodities increased 120 percent. Insofar as the rate of expansion and growth is concerned, the status of the organic chemical industry is believed to be without equal. Growth and expansion have been fostered through industry practices of devoting exceptionally large portions of sales dollars to research and development; a large portion of annual profits is expected to increase capacity. The progress and sustained growth of the industry have attracted large amounts of equity capital which have been expended each year for new plant and equipment.

During the 1939–52 period, however, the congressional tariff policy of safeguarding and encouraging the growth of this most essential industry has been weakened by the administration of the trade-agreements program. More than 90 of the 116 tariff rates applying to organic chemicals have been reduced in bilateral trade agreements or in the multilateral agreement known as GATT. The effect upon the industry generally of these reductions in tariff is, with the resurgence of the European chemical industry, becoming a matter of grave concern to the association and its members.

Such concern is predicated upon several cost-of-production factors. Since the products of the industry are essentially those of batch processes rather than so-called continuous processes, domestic producers are at a distinct disadvantage when compared to foreign organic chemical industries. It is the view of the association that insofar as raw materials and technology are concerned foreign organic chemical industries and that of the United States are on substantially equivalent terms. In many instances, however, where there is comparable productivity, foreign labor costs are from one-fourth to one-tenth those of the United States industry.

Increased imports manufactured under the competitive advantage which comparable productivity but lower wage levels provide directly affect many products of this industry. Indirectly, their effect is to encroach upon the portion of sale dollars devoted to research or plowed back by the industry for expansion of capacity found necessary to meet mobilization bases.

The overall objectives of trade expansion are ill-served by policies or actions which directly affect or indirectly retard the growth of any segment of this complex and interrelated industry whose continued healthy condition is essential not only to the economic well-being of the United States in time of peace but imperative in time of war or national emergency.

## THE GENERAL AGREEMENT ON TARIFFS AND TRADE SHOULD BE DISAPPROVED BY THE CONGRESS

In 1947 the United States embarked upon a policy of entering into multilateral contractual obligations pertaining to tariffs and trade which was formalized in the agreement commonly known as GATT. Beginning in 1951 and continuing to date, the Congress, in extending the provisions and effectiveness of the Trade Agreements Act has included a provision to the effect that such extensions of the law shall not be construed as approval or disapproval of GATT.

The association has consistently supported the view that even provisional membership of the United States in GATT is not sanctioned by the provisions of the act and is contrary to the intent of Congress.

Many substantive provisions of GATT paralleled provisions of the defunct ITO charter and concern policies unrelated to the specified and limited powers delegated by the Congress to the President in the Trade Agreements Act: modifying, by raising or lowering existing tariff rates and altering forms of duties, and imposing, modifying, or removing other import restrictions. There is nothing in the act which permits the President, or an unnamed subordinate in the Department of State, to bind the United States contractually to engage in a permanent program of tariff reductions, or to conform existing statutes of the United States in the field of tariffs, internal taxation, wages, aid to underdeveloped countries, use of our natural resources, or other laws or policies of this country to those of an international organization—GATT.

We believe the act should explicitly declare that the purpose sought to be attained is the making of mutually advantageous and beneficial trade agreements which are concerned solely with tariff rates and other import restrictions as now defined in the law and such agreements should be negotiated and concluded on a bilateral basis directly with the countries with whom the United States seeks to increase trade.

The practice of granting compensatory concessions whenever the United States withdraws or modifies a concession previously granted pursuant to the escape-clause remedy, or national-security needs, finds no support in the existing language of the act. It is a GATT concept which the Congress should explicitly condemn as outside the scope of the law. The effect often is to injure or threaten injury to segments of American industry other or different from those segments which have been afforded escape clause or other relief and to upset orderly and stable marketing and sale of other products.

### LEGISLATION PERTAINING TO TARIFFS AS WELL AS OTHER ASPECTS OF OUR FOREIGN TRADE POLICY SHOULD CLEARLY INDICATE THAT AUTHORITY DELEGATED TO THE EXECUTIVE DEPARTMENT IS MINISTERIAL IN NATURE

The administration of the trade-agreements program has been dominated by the Department of State which has treated tariff and trade issues as belonging to the field of foreign relations. Proposals that the United States become party to an international organization such as GATT, or the defunct International Trade Organization, or its successor, the Organization for Trade Cooperation, have been aggressively sponsored by the State Department.

These efforts are contrary to the authority vested in the President by that act. Congress and Congress alone, has been vested with constitutional authority to levy and collect taxes and import duties and regulate commerce with foreign nations (U. S. Constitution, art. 1, sec. 6, clauses 1 and 3). This authority cannot be divested by the Congress and be reposed in the Executive. Congress may delegate to the Executive, or to a specially created legislative agency, authority to administer tariff policies which have been enacted into legislation. Such delegated authority, however, is ministerial in nature and should be clearly restricted to actions designed to implement and put into effect specific purposes which the Congress has spelled out in appropriate legislation.

In the administration of the trade-agreements program the several committees established by Executive orders, under the leadership of the Department of State, have misconceived their functions as administrators of delegated congressional authority. It is the view of this association that the trade-agreements program as it has been administered, particularly during the period 1947 to date, has been treated as a device for putting into effect broad foreign relations policies which are not directly related to tariff problems as they concern foreign trade or the economic needs of the United States.

Accordingly, trade-agreement legislation which may be enacted by the Congress should clearly and distinctly restrict the actions of the Executive to specific subject matter as to which Congress has delegated ministerial functions of administration.

The provisions of GATT itself furnish cogent evidence of departure from the delegated and limited authority given the President in the Trade Agreements Act. It is submitted that existing administrative practices and procedures have been the vehicle for embarking upon extralegal contractual arrangements with an international organization. The Congress should prevent future expeditions of this character by carefully and completely setting forth in the law, practices and procedures which should be followed in the negotiation, the making and administration of trade agreements.

DEFENSE AND SECURITY NEEDS OF THE UNITED STATES MUST NOT BE SACRIFICED OR JEOPARDIZED BY THE ADMINISTRATION OF THE TRADE-AGREEMENTS PROGRAM

Although the Congress in the Trade Agreement Extension Acts of 1954 and 1955 included national-defense amendments in the law, vesting in ODM the responsibility of safeguarding our national defense and security needs, the soundly conceived legislative provisions cannot be effectively enforced unless ODM itself be given authority to determine whether proposed reductions in duty threaten essential defense industries. As administered, the first national-defense amendment requires the Trade Agreements Committee, rather than ODM, initially to determine whether proposed reductions in duty may create serious problems warranting attention of ODM. The Congress has determined ODM is best equipped to handle such matters, and it is submitted that ODM should be authorized to establish lists of products essential to our defense or security needs which the Trade Agreement Committee or other agencies of the Government may not thereafter include in any list of tariff items which would be made the subject of trade-agreement negotiations or concessions. The agency charged with this responsibility should be equipped with background information which would enable it to recognize the dangers of domestic productive capacity and skilled manpower which increased imports could pose as a threat to national defense. The Trade Agreements Committee is not so equipped.

The other so-called national-defense amendment relates to the limited authority of ODM to inquire whether national security has been threatened by reason of imports of a particular commodity on which a trade-agreement concession has been made. A determination that injury or threatened injury exists can only be reported to the President, who then may order a full investigation of the facts pertaining to a threat to national security. Upon the completion of such investigation, a report is made to the President who, if he finds that imports are threatening to impair national security, is directed to take appropriate action to remedy the situation.

Existing legislation should be amended so as to require that both ODM and the President act promptly in disposing of any "national security" case. To that end, the statute should provide that once ODM has advised the President of the possibility that imports threaten to impair national security, an investigation ordered by the President shall be concluded within 90 days, and the President shall, within 30 days thereafter, act upon the findings and recommendations made as a result of the investigation.

The subcommittee, from the material previously filed, is well aware of the fact that the synthetic organic chemical industry of the United States is in the forefront of industries which are most essential to our national security. The administration of the trade agreements program, insofar as this industry is concerned, reflects an inability to comprehend this essential fact. The industry cannot continue to efficiently serve defense needs if the "permanent" program of tariff reductions permits foreign makers to export low-cost organic chemicals to the United States and displace domestic, peacetime production of "bread and butter" items. The capacity to produce, the availability of skills, and the sale of peacetime products create the capital funds, know-how, and facilities essential to the production of wartime needs. The interrelationship among organic chemicals is so intimate that competitive impact is not single in nature; secondary effects are as drastic, if not more devastating, than those produced directly as a result of a specific tariff concession.

### THE INTERESTS OF THIS CRITICAL DEFENSE INDUSTRY SHOULD BE SAFEGUARDED BY MORE EFFECTIVE ANTIDUMPING ACT PROVISIONS, ESCAPE-CLAUSE PROVISIONS AND BY REALISTIC PERIL-POINT DETERMINATIONS

The association in July 1957 appeared before the Ways and Means Committee in support of the then pending bills, H. R. 6006 and H. R. 6007, to amend the Antidumping Act of 1921. It suggested certain changes so as to promote greater certainty, speed, and efficiency in the enforcement of the Antidumping Act. We refer to the statement filed with the Ways and Means Committee for details of the association views. It suffices here to state that the association disagreed with the views of the Treasury Department that the terms "injury" and "industry" should not be defined in the antidumping statute for the reason that injury to domestic industry under that law cannot be decided "without reference to the economics of the situation." The Treasury Department suggests that these terms be left to "interpretation" by the Tariff Commission in administering the provisions of the antidumping law. The association cannot understand how the congressional directive of providing "greater certainty" in the administration of the Antidumping Act could be attained without spelling out in the statute some definitions of these most essential terms.

It is submitted that the criteria for measuring "injury" for Trade Agreement Act purposes might well form a basis for the guidance of the Tariff Commission in ascertaining whether injury exists under the antidumping statute. For the particular purposes of the dumping statute, we also suggest, in accordance with the comment of the Senate Finance Committee that injury "in a particular geographical area may be sufficient for a finding of injury under the Antidumping Act" (S. Rept. No. 2326, August 6, 1954, to accompany H. R. 10009).

So, too, the term "industry" as defined in the trade agreements law might well serve as a model for defining that term in the antidumping statute, The clarifying language used by the Congress in the 1955

Trade Agreement Extension Act to define "industry" so as to mean any "portion or subdivision" of an organization producing a particular product should be made applicable to dumping cases and should be incorporated into the antidumping statute.

The administration of the escape-clause provisions of the Trade Agreements Act has resulted in a series of differences of opinion between the Tariff Commission and the President which should be resolved by the Congress. These differences apparently arise from the fact that the Congress has expressly directed the Commission to recommend withdrawal or modification of a trade agreement concession when imports cause or threaten serious injury to a domestic industry. However, another statement of congressional purpose permits the President, in his discretion, to follow or refuse to follow the Commission's recommendations. The only direction furnished the President is to act in a manner consistent with "the national interest." In practice, it is the State Department which dominates the administration of the escape-clause provisions and that Department ignores the specific statement of congressional purpose that a concession should be withdrawn when a determination of injury has been made. In practice the President has construed the term "national interest" in a broad and sweeping manner so as to deny relief to an affected industry which has suffered injury, for the reason that continuance of the concession supports the expansion of our export markets, protects American consumers against price rises, and withdrawal of the concession might affect our national security and also that adequate compensation for such concessions could not be made to nations affected by the withdrawal or modification of a concession.

It is submitted that none of these factors, whether they be logically comprehended by the term "national interest," should outweigh the clear statement of congressional policy that escape-clause relief should be allowed an industry injured by a trade agreement concession. Limitations upon the actions of the President under the national-interest concept which permit him to ignore escape-clause determinations of the Tariff Commission should be spelled out clearly in the statute, otherwise the explicit purpose of the Congress is to be thwarted by a variety of reasons, most of which are wholly irrelevant in the administration of a statute concerned with foreign trade.

It is particularly important that provisions be made in the statute for the prompt withdrawal of concessions in situations where defense productive capacity is or likely will be impaired by increased imports. Where such productive capacity may affect the defense mobilization base ODM should advise the Tariff Commission as to the essentiality of the industry or segment of the industry complaining of injury. Following this determination if the Tariff Commission therefore finds that defense productive capacity was being or likely would be impaired, a prompt report should be made to the President recommending that the national interest requires the withdrawal of the concession and requires an increase in duty or other modification of customs treatment necessary to prevent such impairment.

The administration of the peril-point provisions of the statute, as the association has on many occasions previously commented, leaves much to be desired. It is submitted that insofar as the chemical industry is concerned, it is almost impossible, under existing tariff classifications of chemicals, adequately to prepare material for presentation to the Tariff Commission in peril-point hearings. It is also submitted that the Commission's obligations in the peril-point proceedings are incapable of performance under the conditions laid down in the act. Sufficient time should be accorded all interested persons to make representations concerning peril points and the Commission should be furnished with the investigative means and the afforded adequate time within which to complete studies of peril-point questions.

The subcommittee is aware of the many products of the organic chemical industry which are essential to the establishment and maintenance of an adequate defense mobilization productive capacity. In the administration of the peril-point provisions of the statute, the association suggests that any producer of synthetic organic chemicals who believes that an item has been included in a public list which is intended to be the subject of negotiation for trade agreement concessions, shall notify ODM that such item is or is likely to be one which is essential to the establishment or maintenance of the defense mobilization base. Within 60 days after the receipt of such notice ODM shall notify the agency responsible for trade agreement negotiations whether any or all of the productive capacity of the chemical industry of the United States manufacturing or producing such item is regarded by ODM as an essential part of the mobilization base. An affirmative finding by ODM will require that the affected item be deleted from the public list of commodities eligible for negotiation. In the event that only a portion of such productive capacity is considered as an essential part of the mobilization base, ODM should advise the Tariff Commission of such fact and the Commission should then be required to determine the minimum level to which customs duty or other treatment of imports could be modified without endangering the productive capacity essential to the mobilization base.

## CONCLUSION

Space limitations placed upon the association by the subcommittee permit making only general observations. The material submitted with our letter of June 13, 1957, fully discusses the matters which have been referred to herein. It is believed essential that the detailed material previously submitted be carefully examined if the position of the association is to be fully considered in the development of a report concerning problems of tariffs and foreign trade which the subcommittee is preparing for the use of the Congress.

We appreciate the opportunity of participating in this most important work of the subcommittee. Immediate as well as long-term needs of the synthetic organic chemical industry call for a most searching examination by the Congress of the administration of the trade agreements program; the Congress must reassume the duties and responsibilities vested in it by the Constitution in all matters pertaining to tariffs and foreign trade, leaving to the Executive, or to a specially created legislative agency, the ministerial task of putting a soundly conceived congressional program into operation.

It is submitted that national-defense needs are inextricably linked with the status of tariffs and the products of this industry must be safeguarded from threats of injury arising out of ill-considered and hasty duty concessions. The industry possesses ample capacity to serve peacetime requirements of the domestic economy; its ability to meet wartime emergencies depends upon the maintenance and continued growth of such capacity. It is also submitted that the vital interests of the United States require that establishment of a tariff policy, negotiation, and making, as well as the administration of trade agreements not be under the control of, or be subject to the mandates of an international organization like GATT.

# XII

# THE PETROLEUM INDUSTRY AND FOREIGN TRADE POLICY

# UNITED STATES IMPORTS OF PETROLEUM AND THE DOMESTIC INDUSTRY

Russell B. Brown, general counsel, Independent Petroleum Association of America

## INTRODUCTION

The Independent Petroleum Association of America, hereinafter referred to as IPAA, is a national organization representing independent producers of crude petroleum and natural gas, including land and royalty owners, with membership located in every oil-producing area of the Nation.

Domestic oil producers learned very early that one of the greatest deterrents to the creation and growth of a strong domestic oil industry lies in the flood of foreign oil which, as history has proven, is with us when not needed and noticeably absent when most needed—in times of emergency.

IPAA was thus organized in 1929 principally to foster and preserve a strong domestic petroleum industry within the borders of the United States. It has sought to promulgate a healthy and expanding industry which could be, and which has been, called upon to produce the petroleum needed to successfully prosecute wars, stave off and deter war threats, help other friendly nations in times of crisis, and supply the petroleum products for an ever-expanding national economy.

From its inception the IPAA has dedicated its efforts to establishing a proper relation between domestically produced oil and imported oil. When imported oil is in proper balance with domestic production, this Nation is oilwise safe. When not, it is in grave peril.

IPAA, over the past quarter of a century, has used every opportunity to bring to the attention of the legislative and executive branches of Government, and the public as well, the wisdom in having a healthy domestic oil industry for reasons of national security. In addition to fostering a strong domestic oil industry for our Nation's defense, IPAA has also worked diligently to show the economic dangers to the American economy and consumer in peacetime, if this Nation should become dependent on foreign oil largely under the control of a few companies.

As will be seen later, this has been an uphill battle. It has been necessary to combat a philosophy espoused by some that this Nation could afford to become dependent on foreign oil sources. Also during this period, the domestic oil industry has been faced with a policy, advocated by many at the administrative level of Government, which has had the effect of encouraging the development of overseas oil to the detriment of the domestic producer and this Nation's security.

Fortunately, the Congress has repeatedly reviewed the oil import problem and similar problems of other industries, with resulting enactments designed to encourage domestic industries. In spite of these pronouncements of congressional policy, through administrative practices the laws in many instances have been ignored or ineffectively implemented. As a result, through the years, the problem has needlessly continued and worsened.

There are evident now, however, with respect to the oil-import problem, definite indications that many of the proponents of the unsound policy leading to dependency on uncertain foreign sources are beginning to recognize that "there is no security in foreign oil for the defense of our own borders."

Recent dramatic confirmation of the dangers of a policy that would make this Nation dependent on foreign oil was provided by the Suez crisis. This made helpless our allies in Western Europe, which avoided suffering and serious economic disruption by being able to turn to a strong domestic industry in the United States.

The following is a review of the background developments and of the experiences of the domestic oil industry which have brought about a new administrative policy with respect to imported oil.

## RECOGNITION OF IMPORT THREAT

Congress in 1955 gave careful consideration to the very serious problem caused by excessive oil imports. At that time, Congress wisely adopted the so-called national security provision of the Trade Agreements Extension Act of 1955, which authorized the President, whenever he deemed it necessary, to reduce the level of imports of a commodity whenever that level threatens national security. The congressional policy (see appendix A) inherent in this provision was finally recognized on July 29, 1957, in a unanimous report by the President's Special (Cabinet) Committee To Investigate Crude Oil Imports (see appendix B). In its report, the Committee stated:

> * * * if we are to have enough oil to meet our national security needs, there must be a limitation on imports that will insure a proper balance between imports and domestic production.

This constructive action, which is an administrative recognition of the principle of the longstanding position of the IPAA, has been long in reaching the stature of the official policy of the United States. It is to be hoped that this policy, which has been developed under the national security provision, will be properly implemented to achieve its announced goal.

## UNITED STATES TRADE POLICY—HOW IT HAS AFFECTED THE PETROLEUM INDUSTRY

In 1934 the President was authorized to enter into foreign trade agreements. Just prior to enactment of the original Trade Agreements Act, Congress in 1932 placed an excise tax on petroleum imports at one-half cent per gallon on crude oil, kerosene, and fuel oil; 2½ cents per gallon on gasoline; and 4 cents per gallon on lubricating oil.

The legislative history of the 1934 trade act in clear and unambiguous language stated that excise taxes imposed by Congress on imports were not to be reduced through trade agreement concessions. In its report accompanying this act, House Report No. 1000, 73d Congress, 2d session, the House Ways and Means Committee stated:

> In order that the necessary reciprocity may be accorded, the President is empowered to promise that existing excise duties which affect imported goods will

**not be increased during the term of any particular agreement. It should be carefully noted, however, that the President is given no right to reduce or incerase any excise duty. His power of reduction of duties is limited to those which are in fact customs duties.**

Yet, in spite of this direct and unequivocal statement of congressional intent, the United States entered into the Venezuelan and Mexican trade agreements and GATT which, as will be seen, have made largely meaningless the excise tax on petroleum imports. This has been done through unauthorized administrative actions.

*Venezuelan trade agreement*

In 1939 the United States Government entered into a trade agreement with Venezuela, a great oil-producing nation. This agreement reduced the excise taxes as established by Congress in 1932 on crude, topped crude, and fuel oil from one-half cent per gallon to one-fourth cent per gallon on imports equal to 5 percent of the refinery runs in the United States during the preceding calendar year. This agreement brought about significant increases in petroleum imports from Venezuela.

*Mexican trade agreement*

In an agreement entered into with Mexico in 1943, the 5 percent of refinery runs quota restriction contained in the Venezuelan agreement was superseded and, in addition to the reductions made by the Venezuelan agreement, the excise tax on kerosene and liquid asphalt was reduced from one-half cent to one-fourth cent per gallon.

*GATT*

Further pursuing a policy of encouraging greater and greater oil imports, the United States in 1947 entered into a multilateral agreement with some 20 nations covering all oil products not included in the Mexican or Venezuelan agreements which, among other things, reduced the import tax on gasoline from 2½ to 1¼ cents per gallon.

Thus, as a result of these three agreements, the excise duties on crude and all petroleum products established by Congress in 1932 were reduced by 50 percent, and as a result of the most-favored-nation clause became applicable to all oil imports.

*Renegotiation of Venezuelan agreement*

Following the abrogation of the Mexican agreement in 1951, which restored the terms of the 1939 Venezuelan agreement, the United States Government renegotiated the Venezuelan agreement and further reduced the excise tax on crude oil and residual fuel oil. It is now generally recognized that the small portion remaining of the original excise tax on oil imports has little or no effect on curbing imports. The trade-agreements program thus whittled away any effective brakes on foreign oil imports with the net effect encouraging greater dependency on undependable foreign sources for this vital product, oil.

Thus, partly as a result of these agreements and partly due to other governmental encouragement, oil imports have risen steadily over the past 20 years except for the submarine-tanker debacle during World War II. As a result today oil imports amount to more than 20 percent of domestic production as contrasted to 5 percent during the period from 1935 to 1939 just prior to the Venezuelan trade agreement. This long experience (see chart, appendix C) shows that stern measures must now be taken lest our national security be placed in further jeopardy.

*Escape-clause treatment*

The experience of IPAA in seeking escape-clause relief from excessive oil imports further shows that the spirit and congressional intent laid down in the basic trade law and subsequent "relief" measures have been repeatedly circumvented or ignored by the executive branch of our Government.

The general purpose and subsequent experience under the escape-clause procedures by industry in general is all too well known to recite here.

It is important to note, however, that IPAA very early sought relief under the escape clauses that were contained in the Venezuelan and Mexican trade agreements. During negotiations of the Mexican agreement, the domestic oil producers had expressed great concern over proposed further reductions in the excise tax on oil. Assurances were then made that the escape clause (which later became the standard escape clause) in the Mexican agreement and also a comparable clause in the Venezuelan agreement were placed there to "safeguard the interests of our domestic producers."

Accordingly, IPAA in February 1949 filed a petition with the United States Tariff Commission for relief under these clauses from a damaging and rising tide of oil imports.

Its application and petition for such relief was turned down in May 1949 on the grounds "* * * that because of some scaling down of both production and imports." As a matter of fact, there was no "scaling down" of imports. The records show clearly that imports before and since that time increased rapidly. For example, in 1948 average daily imports were 514,000 barrels. For 1949 the daily average had risen to 645,000 barrels and they have risen steadily each year to an alltime high of 1,426,000 for 1956.

Thus it can be easily seen that, as applied to oil, this "relief" measure has been made completely ineffective through administrative practices.

*Peril-point provisions*

In the Trade Agreements Act of 1948, Congress wrote into the law a peril-point procedure which provided that trade commitments should not be made that may be seriously injurious to domestic producers. This provision was repealed in 1949, but later reenacted in 1951.

In 1951 the United States set about to renegotiate the 1939 Venezuelan trade agreement. Under the peril-point provision, the Tariff Commission held hearings to determine the peril point for oil import duties, below which serious injury may result to the domestic oil industry. At this hearing, IPAA urged that no further reductions be made in the excise tax on petroleum imports, and that the excise-tax levels established by Congress in 1932 be restored in order to avoid further serious injury to domestic oil producers.

As a result of the hearing, the Tariff Commission divided equally on the proper peril point for oil imports.

The executive department, however, ignored the peril-point findings of both groups of Commissioners and in fact established its own peril point which was lower than the peril points set by either group of the Commissioners.

Here again a congressional mandate for the protection of domestic producers was ignored.

*Buy American Act*

Another prime example of how the executive branch overlooks statutory pronouncement when so minded, lies in the treatment of the oil industry under the Buy American Act. This law required the Federal Government when making purchases for public use to give preference if the product (crude oil in this instance) is produced "in the United States in sufficient and reasonably available commercial quantities and of a satisfactory quality."

If enforced, this law would aid materially in meeting the damage being done to domestic industry from excessive oil imports. Unfortunately, experience has shown that by administrative action the heart has been removed from this act. As an example, on April 5, 1954, the General Services Administration issued a directive which, among other things, stated:

15. Buy American exemption: The regional director, region 7, General Services Administration, having been duly authorized thereunto, has determined that crude petroleum is not produced in the United States in sufficient and reasonably available commercial quantities and, therefore, has exempted from the Buy American Act petroleum fuels and petroleum lubricants.

This finding was clearly without foundation and in the fall of 1954 GSA rescinded the directive in part, modifying the exemption so as to apply only to the east coast. Nowhere in the act does Congress authorize the Buy American Act to be ignored on a regional basis.

The law declares simply that petroleum products purchased by the Government anywhere in the United States be made "substantially" from crude oil produced in the United States unless crude oil is not produced "in the United States in sufficient and reasonably available commercial quantities and of a satisfactory quality."

In its directive, the General Services Administration also stated:

In addition, imports serve to maintain a flow of foreign crude into this country. If this flow ceases, a marketing pattern for foreign crude would develop which would make it difficult or unduly expensive for this country to acquire supplemental crude when and as needed.

Thus the purpose of the Buy American Act is reversed. Although Congress passed the act so as to encourage American industry the GSA is now administering that law so as to encourage oil imports.

As recently as March 11, 1957, GSA reiterated its policy as set forth above.

It is now fairly clear from the report of the President's Special Committee to Investigate Crude Oil Imports (cited earlier) that this line of thought by GSA is without foundation and is in conflict with higher policy.

It is hoped that GSA in light of the report of the President's Special Committee will review its policies under the Buy American Act. It is further hoped that GSA will then more strictly follow the intent and purpose behind Congress in adopting this act—namely, encourage American industry.

*Anti-Dumping Act—Domestic oil industry experience*

The Anti-Dumping Act was enacted to prohibit imports of foreign commodities into the United States at prices less than the foreign exporter sells his commodity at home or other world markets.

Experience demonstrates that there are basic weaknesses in the act which need strengthening if it is to be effective in carrying out its intended purposes.

The broad discretionary authority permitted the Treasury Department in determining whether to investigate alleged breaches of this law has resulted in ineffective administration. The agencies concerned are not required to make public their findings of fact or conclusions of law and are not required to publicly account for their decisions. IPAA has recently urged in a hearing before the House Ways and Means Committee that the antidumping law be amended to require the agencies concerned to make a public record in each case and to publicize a report setting forth their findings and reasons for any action taken.

One experience of the domestic oil industry which points up the inadequacy of the present law occurred in 1952. At that time in a press release dated August 22, 1952, a Senate Small Business Subcommittee on Monopoly, issued a press release announcing a report from the MSA on ECA and MSA relations with international oil companies concerning petroleum prices. This release stated that according to the report "quantities of Middle East oil were dumped in the United States at net prices far below those realized on shipments to Europe." In spite of this and other responsible indications of "dumping" of oil, no action under the law was required by the Treasury Department nor any action taken by it to determine if there was in fact any dumping of oil into the United States.

It is also submitted that proof of injury as a result of dumping under the present law standards is unnecessary and imposes an undue burden upon domestic industries. Dumping is an unfair and undesirable trade practice. An aggrieved industry should not be required to prove that it has been injured before governmental action is taken to stop such practices.

## HISTORY OF OIL TRADE

Each time petroleum was made the subject of a trade agreement or other protective laws were circumvented, oil imports increased.

During 1935–39 oil imports averaged 153,000 barrels daily or 4.8 percent of domestic production. Following World War II (imports for 1942 were lowest since 1928), imports grew progressively until last year they amounted to 19.9 percent of domestic production. In contrast, many consuming nations of United States petroleum products have turned to other sources of supply to such an extent that domestic oil supplying this market has decreased from 13.9 percent of domestic crude oil production for the years 1935–39 to 6 percent for 1956.

It is thus apparent that due to governmental policies which have encouraged exploitation of overseas sources together with the elimination, for all practical purposes, of all trade barriers on oil imports, this Nation has reached the point where both "oil security" and adequate consumer supplies for a dynamic national economy could become dependent on oil from sources that might dry up overnight as a result of a "Suez" or submarine warfare. If this Nation should become dependent on unstable foreign sources for its oil needs, a would-be aggressor or power-hungry despot could force the United States to its knees without firing a shot merely by cutting off our oil supplies.

It is encouraging that under the sound congressional policy laid down in the national-security amendment the United States Governmet is now taking steps to correct this dangerous trend.

OIL'S CONTRIBUTION TO FOREIGN TRADE

The petroleum industry recognizes the important role of international trade. The industry as a whole agrees that there is a proper place for imports which will supplement but not supplant domestic production. However, let's take a look at the relative position of oil in total trade say for 1956 and compare this with 1934, the year the foreign trade agreement program was authorized. In 1956 oil provided $1,269 million or 10.2 percent of total imports. In 1934 these figures were $36 million or 2.2 percent of this Nation's import trade.

Looking at the matter strictly on the basis of encouraging international trade, it is submitted that it is unfair to ask one industry, particularly one vital to national security, to contribute more than its fair share in trade dollars.

Since World War II more than three-fourths of all oil imported into the United States came from four countries—Venezuela, Netherlands Antilles, Kuwait and Saudi Arabia. The value of oil imports from these four countries in 1956 was almost five times the total value in 1947. In contrast, total exports of United States merchandise to these same countries in 1956 was less than 50 percent higher than in 1947. This clearly shows that the amount of goods these countries buy from us is not directly related to or dependent on the amount of oil we import from them.

NATIONAL SECURITY PROVISION REESTABLISHES CONGRESSIONAL INTENT

As can be seen from the foregoing experiences of the petroleum industry, it became necessary in 1955 for Congress to take affirmative action above and beyond the then existing law to curb excessive imports of a commodity which were causing serious injury to an industry so vital to our Nation's security. Accordingly, Congress wrote into law the so-called national security amendment. In so doing Congress once again reiterated that our liberalized trade laws must not be used to cripple domestic industry—particularly an industry vital to the security of the United States. This affirmative congressional action was necessary as a result of a longstanding administrative policy of encouraging imports at any price.

In adopting the national security amendment, the Senate Finance Committee stated in its report (Rept. 232, 84th Cong., 1st sess.):

The committee had before it several proposals dealing with specific commodities; namely, petroleum, fluorspar, lead, and zinc. In lieu of specific action on each of these the committee adopted an amendment which specifies that the Director of the Office of Defense Mobilization shall report to the President when he has reason to believe that imports of a commodity are entering the United States in such quantities as to threaten to impair the national security; that the President shall cause an immediate investigation to be made if he feels there is reason for such belief; and that the President, if he finds a threat to the national security exists, shall take whatever action is necessary to adjust imports to a level that will not threaten to impair the national security.

The committee believes that this amendment will provide a means for assistance to the various national defense industries which would have been affected by the individual amendments presented.

The White House issued on February 26, 1955, a report based on a study by the President's Advisory Committee on Energy Supplies and Resources Policy which indicates the importance of a strong domestic petroleum industry.

In taking this action, Congress had before it a report based on a study by the President's Advisory Committee on Energy Supplies and Resources Policy. This report pointed out the importance of a strong domestic petroleum industry and the committee declared that exceptions from the trade program should be taken to protect the industry essential to the national security. That Congress fully intended that the Cabinet Fuels Committee report serve as a basis for implementing the national security amendment can be seen by statements made by congressional leaders at the time of its adoption (see appendix A). With respect to oil imports, the report states:

An expanding domestic oil industry, plus a healthy oil industry in friendly countries which help to supply the United States market, constitute basically important elements in the kind of industrial strength which contributes most to a strong national defense. Other energy industries, especially coal, must also maintain a level of operation which will make possible rapid expansion in output should that become necessary. In this complex picture both domestic production and imports have important parts to play; neither should be sacrificed to the other.

Since World War II importation of crude oil and residual fuel oil into the United States has increased substantially, with the result that today these oils supply a significant part of the United States market for fuels.

The committee believes that if the imports of crude and residual oils should exceed significantly the respective proportions that these imports of oils bore to the production of domestic crude oil in 1954, the domestic fuels situation could be so impaired as to endanger the orderly industrial growth which assures the military and civilian supplies and reserves that are necessary to the national defense. There would be an inadequate incentive for exploration and the discovery of new sources of supply.

In view of the foregoing, the committee concludes that in the interest of national defense imports should be kept in the balance recommended above. It is highly desirable that this be done by voluntary, individual action of those who are importing or those who become importers of crude or residual oil. The committee believes that every effort should be made and will be made to avoid the necessity of governmental intervention.

The committee recommends, however, that if in the future the imports of crude oil and residual fuel oils exceed significantly the respective proportions that such imported oils bore to domestic production of crude oil in 1954, appropriate action should be taken.

The committee recommends further that the desirable proportionate relationships between imports and domestic production be reviewed from time to time in the light of industrial expansion and changing economic and national-defense requirements.

In arriving at these conclusions and recommendations, the committee has taken into consideration the importance to the economies of friendly countries of their oil exports to the United States as well as the importance to the United States of the accessibility of foreign oil supplies both in peace and war.

Adoption of the national security amendment was a milestone in the struggle for adequate and proper protection of the domestic petroleum industry from excessive oil imports. The recent report by the President's Special Committee To Investigate Crude Oil Imports (see Appendix B) graphically points up the wisdom of the action taken by Congress in 1955. This report which came about as a result of the machinery set in motion under the national security provision determined the following:

In summary, unless a reasonable limitation of petroleum imports is brought about, your committee believes that:

(*a*) Oil imports will flow into this country in ever-mounting quantities, entirely disproportionate to the quantities needed to supplement domestic supply.

(*b*) There will be a resultant discouragement of, and decrease in, domestic production.

(*c*) There will be a marked decline in domestic exploration and development.

(*d*) In the event of a serious emergency, this Nation will find itself years away from attaining the level of petroleum production necessary to meet our national security needs.

In its report, the committee also stated:

Domestic consumers are utilizing an increasing amount of petroleum products for transportation, fuel, heating, and many other aspects of consumer life. In the event of a national emergency, it is essential to these consumers that there be adequate supplies at reasonable cost, both now and in the future. The low cost of imported oil is attractive, but excessive reliance upon it in the short run may put the Nation in a long-term vulnerable position. Imported supplies could be cut off in an emergency and might well be diminished by events beyond our control. This vulnerability could easily result in a much higher cost, or even in the unavailability, of oil to consumers. It is therefore believed that the best security will be served if a reasonable balance is maintained between domestic and foreign supplies.

* * * * * * *

Your committee recognizes that there are important foreign policy aspects to the problem of limiting petroleum imports. The oil reserves and production capacities of other free nations, as well as our own, are important to our national security. A number of countries inevitably depend in varying degree upon access to our domestic market for their petroleum exports and it must be recognized that it is also in the interest of our national security that our allies and friends have healthy and expanding economies. It is believed, however, that taking all factors into consideration, our national security requires the maintenance of some reasonable balance between imports and domestic production at this time. In light of the foregoing considerations, our recommendations are framed with the objective of limiting imports in order to maintain such a balance and yet to allow other nations to participate in the growth of our domestic demand to a degree consistent with our national security.

As a result of its findings, the Cabinet Committee recommended to the President that he establish quotas on oil imports for each importing company to be complied with on a voluntary basis (see Appendix B). The President approved this recommendation and directed that machinery be set in motion to carry out the oil import quota program.

In its concluding recommendation to the President, the Cabinet Committee warned:

Increased volume of crude oil imports and the proposed imports for the latter half of 1957 threaten to impair the national security. This threat, under existing conditions, requires a limitation on imports. The committee recommends, therefore, that unless the importing companies comply voluntarily with the import limitation plan hereinafter set forth, you find that there is a threat to the national security within the meaning of section 7 of the Trade Agreements Extension Act of 1955. Pending the outcome of this voluntary program, this committee should continue as now constituted.

It is obvious that the domestic petroleum industry desires to have this action taken by the President prove successful. We have every reason to believe that it will work, however, we agree with the words of the Cabinet committee when it stated—

Unless the importing companies comply voluntarily with the import limitation plan, * * * the President should find that * * * there is a threat to the national security within the meaning of section 7 of the Trade Agreements Extension Act of 1955.

The special Cabinet committee report also states—

It is clear that there is a direct relationship between the Nation's security and adequate and available sources of energy. Oil and gas account for two-thirds of all the energy that is consumed in this country. Furthermore, there is no adequate substitute in sight for the foreseeable future. Therefore, we must have available adequate supply of oil.

The Cabinet committee reports in 1955 and 1957 remove all doubt as to the importance of oil's place in national defense.

In addition to these findings of the Cabinet committees, noted military authorities have reiterated the importance of oil in the successful prosecution of any military action. Not long ago the famous World War II military expert, Gen. Carl Spaatz, declared—

Oil is the essential ingredient of modern warfare. Even supermodern atomic weapons amount to nothing unless the means of their delivery are fueled with oil.

Further evidence as to the need for action to preserve a healthy and going domestic petroleum industry is contained in a statement by Prof. Edward S. Mason, Harvard University, presented before this subcommittee of the Committee on Ways and Means in September 1956. At that time Professor Mason stated—

The only points I want to emphasize here are that oil may well represent a special case justifying import limitation for defense purposes. * * *

It is thus recognized by leading authorities both in and out of Government that this Nation can ill afford to become dependent on oil from overseas sources.

A more recent example of the vital importance of a strong domestic oil industry is that of the success of the "oil lift" brought about by the Suez situation. Who can say when there may be another Suez or a similar crisis which will again prove the importance of a strong and healthy petroleum industry within the borders of the United States.

### IMPORT COMPETITION, COST AND PRICES

This review has dealt primarily with United States foreign-trade policies as they have been applied to oil imports. In considering these trade policies, it is important to keep in mind certain unique characteristics of United States foreign trade in petroleum.

In many, if not most, cases, commodities imported into this country are produced by nationals of foreign countries, with relatively low labor costs a primary factor in competing at lower prices in the United States markets. The dollars received from such imports go directly into normal foreign exchange, where they are available for the purchase of exported goods produced in the United States.

The situation as to oil is quite different in a number of important respects. Most of the oil imported into this country is produced by a few large American oil companies in a few foreign areas—principally

Venezuela and the Middle East. The cost of finding, developing, and producing foreign oil is only a fraction of the cost in this country. This is particularly true in the Middle East, where only a part of the import dollar goes into foreign exchange or benefits the nationals of these countries. A large part of the advantage gained by lower costs of foreign oil are reflected in increased profits for these American companies, rather than benefits to the general economy of Middle East countries or in lower prices to the American consumer.

In general, lower costs to the oil companies operating in foreign areas are due to the huge deposits of oil that have been found in relation to the funds invested and the prolific productivity as compared with average operations in the United States. Lower labor rates are a relatively minor factor.

The cost advantage for companies with foreign oil production is illustrated by the following summary tabulation:

*Producing wells, reserves, and production per well in principal producing countries, 1956*

| | Number of producing wells | Proved reserves per well | Production per well |
|---|---|---|---|
| | | *Barrels* | *Barrels* |
| United States | 537,682 | 56,600 | 13 |
| Venezuela | 12,815 | 1,092,500 | 176 |
| Saudi Arabia | 154 | 272,727,000 | 8,650 |
| Kuwait | 185 | 270,270,000 | 5,179 |

Source: World Oil.

The average proved reserves underlying each well in Venezuela are more than 20 times as large as in the United States, while the average well in Saudi Arabia and Kuwait has 3,000 to 4,000 times the volume of reserves of the average United States producing well. The daily production in the United States, averaging 13 barrels per well, compares with almost 200 barrels daily per well in Venezuela and more than 5,000 barrels daily in the Middle East. These tremendous differences in productivity are attributable to the physical characteristics of oil deposits, and result in cost advantages to the oil companies distinct from and overriding normal business costs such as labor rates, depreciation, supplies, equipment, etc.

Further evidence of the basic cost factors in foreign oil operations was provided in a 1956 report by the Arabian-American Oil Co. entitled "Middle East Oil Development" which contained the following significant information:

| | |
|---|---|
| Total investment to develop Middle East oil reserves, 10 years, 1946–55 | Approximately $2,000,000,000. |
| Estimated increase in Middle East oil reserves, 10 years, 1946–55 | 107,000,000,000 barrels. |
| Total 1955 oil production in Middle East | 1,168,000,000 barrels. |
| Middle East governments' income from oil operations in 1955 | About $900,000,000. |

The investment of $2 billion to develop 107 billion barrels of reserves indicates a cost of finding and development averaging approximately $0.02 per barrel. Other authoritative estimates show a much larger volume of reserves found and developed, indicating a cost of

$0.01 per barrel or less. As further evidence of the extremely low costs, the governments' yearly income of about $900 million indicates total profits of approximately $1,800 million based on the general policy of paying 50 percent of the profits to the governments. Total profits of $1,800 million on 1,168 million barrels produced in 1955 would be equivalent to an average profit of about $1.50 per barrel as compared with an average crude-oil price of approximately $1.80 per barrel, indicating that the total cost of finding, developing, and producing Middle East oil does not exceed 30 cents per barrel. These cost figures are necessarily rough approximations, but it is likely that actual costs are even lower than indicated by the above figures. In any event, there is no doubt that the cost of Middle East oil is a very small fraction of the cost of domestic oil.

If the relatively low costs of imported oil to the few large companies that dominate foreign oil operations were the only factor involved, it could appear in the best interest of the American consumer to use this oil to the maximum extent without regard to the effect on domestic oil supplies. As pointed out previously in this statement, however, the vulnerability of imported oil was recognized in the July 29 report and recommendations of President Eisenhower and his Cabinet Committee. The long history of incidents, such as expropriation of American oil interests in Mexico, tanker sinkings during World War II, the shutdown of Iranian production, and the Suez crisis provide ample and conclusive evidence that reliance on uncertain foreign sources can easily result in much higher costs or the disastrous unavailability of essential oil supplies.

Experience over a long period of years shows that a dependable and abundant supply of domestic oil has been, and should continue to be, the best guaranty of low prices to the consumer.

For example, during the period from 1948 to 1957, the domestic oil-producing industry found and developed more than 35 billion barrels of oil in the United States, or 50 percent more than the amount produced during that period. The capacity to produce oil in the United States was expanded from less than 6 million barrels daily in 1948 to an estimated 10,150,000 barrels daily in 1957, an increase of about 70 percent. This expansion of capacity exceeded the increase of 60 percent in consumption of oil in the United States.

Thus, the consumer has had the assurance of ample supplies from domestic sources during the past decade. He has enjoyed low prices for oil, as shown by the fact that, despite inflation and higher costs since 1948, the retail price of gasoline (excluding taxes) has increased less than the Government's index of all retail prices. Crude-oil prices have lagged behind prices for other basic materials, being only 22.4 percent above the 1948 level, while steel prices, for example, have risen by more than 70 percent. The average consumer's hourly wage will now buy one-fourth more gasoline than 10 years ago, including the increased taxes on gasoline. These facts demonstrate the benefits of ample supplies produced by thousands of competing companies and individuals in the domestic oil industry.

Both past experiences and the future outlook provide a firm basis for confidence that domestic oil producers can continue to supply plenty of oil at reasonable prices. Authoritative estimates of the undiscovered oil in United States areas yet to be explored run into the hundreds of billions of barrels, and there is every reason to believe that these estimates will prove to be too low as scientific techniques are developed. Advances in technology are making possible a greater and greater recovery from underground reserves, which could increase domestic supplies by additional hundreds of billions of barrels.

The welfare of the consumer requires an assured supply of oil at reasonable price. It is a fact—and not theory—that an abundance of domestic oil, produced by an expanding, competitive oil industry in the United States, is the best safeguard for the consumer in peace or in time of emergency.

## Appendix A

### Legislative History and Subsequent Expressions of Congressional Intent of the National Security Amendment, Section 7 of the Trade Agreements Extension Act of 1955

#### SENATOR BYRD

Senator Harry F. Byrd, Virginia, commented as follows (pp. 4494 and 4495 of the Congressional Record, May 2, 1955):

"Mr. Byrd. * * * The committee believes that this amendment will provide a means for assistance to the various national-defense industries which would have been affected by the individual amendments presented.

* * * * * *

"Congress can initiate and adopt such legislation as it might deem advisable should the action needed to protect these essential industries not be taken."

#### SENATORS DANIEL AND MILLIKIN

On May 2 and 4, 1955, Senator Price Daniel, Texas, and Senator Eugene Millikin, Colorado, discussed the defense amendment. This discussion, from pages 4500, 4501, and 4760 of the Congressional Record, is in part, as follows:

*May 2*

"Mr. Daniel. Does the Senator feel that there was sufficient evidence before the committee to indicate that an increase of imports over the 1954 ratio might endanger the national security?

"Mr. Millikin. That is my personal opinion. The judgment of the committee never focused on that question, but that is my personal judgment.

"Mr. Daniel. Does the Senator feel that action would be taken if over an extended period imports should be in excess of the ratio which existed in 1954?

"Mr. Millikin. I do; and while I do not propose to put a jinx on the processes we have recommended, if those processes do not work, I shall be among the first actively to support special measures.

"Mr. Daniel. I thank the Senator. I am glad to have his statement. I know of the Senator's interest in this subject. I take it he believes that the national security should be protected, insofar as it would be adversely affected by imports of oil and other products mentioned in the committee report.

"Mr. Millikin. That is my feeling. My own State of Colorado is an oil producer. It produces fluorspar; it produces coal; it produces many items which are essential to our national defense. If I did not think this amendment would protect us, I would be urging something else.

"Mr. Daniel. At least it is the intention of the Committee on Finance that this amendment shall be used to protect us in the matter of oil imports and the importation of other commodities which are necessary to our national defense.

"Mr. Millikin. The Committee on Finance did not make a direct decision to that effect. I can say, however, that the Senator from Colorado believes it should be used for that purpose.

* * * * * * *

"I am convinced that the proposal can and will work. It grants to the President authority to take whatever action he deems necessary to adjust imports if they should threaten to impair the national security. He may use tariffs, quotas, import taxes, or other methods of import restriction. He is not limited as far as commodities are concerned except that they must be involved in our national security.

*May 4*

"Mr. DANIEL. Mr. President, on Monday of this week, the distinguished senior Senator from Colorado [Mr. Millikin] was kind enough to answer several questions put to him by me. I appreciate his courtesy. However, I noticed that the Record, as printed, shows an answer to my last question which I did not understand to have been given, and which I do not believe the senior Senator from Colorado intended.

"I should like to repeat the question, noting that the Senator from Colorado is on the floor.

"The question is set forth on page 4501 of the Congressional Record of May 2, 1955; and I ask the Senator from Colorado to comment on it, after I repeat it. The question is this—and I now address it again to the senior Senator from Colorado:

" 'At least it is the intention of the Committee on Finance that this amendment'—we were talking about section 7 (b)—'shall be used to protect us in the matter of oil imports and the importation of other commodities which are necessary to our national defense.'

"Mr. MILLIKIN. Mr. President, I am very sorry if my answer was not as clear and specific as it should have been, when we had our exchange the other day.

"I wish to say that was the intention of the Senate Finance Committee. That was the purpose of writing the amendment and of adopting it in the committee.

"Mr. DANIEL. I thank the Senator from Colorado.

"Did the committee hear evidence to the effect that an increase of oil imports above the 1954 ratio between imports and domestic production would endanger the national security?

"Mr. MILLIKIN. The committee heard such evidence.

"Mr. DANIEL. Does the Senator from Colorado remember any evidence to the contrary?

"Mr. MILLIKIN. I do not.

"Mr. DANIEL. I thank the Senator from Colorado."

### SENATOR CARLSON

On May 3, 1955, Senator Frank Carlson, Kansas, commented on the defense amendment. His remarks, from page 4641 of the Congressional Record of that date, are as follows:

"* * * The Senate Finance Committee, in approving H. R. 1, specifically recognized the problem and inserted in its report a portion of the report of the President's Advisory Committee on Energy Supplies and Resources which had been submitted by the White House. In addition, the committee added section 7 delegating to the President specific authority to act with relation to the restriction of imports of certain commodities, which I understand to include petroleum. Under this provision the Director of Defense Mobilization, when he has reason to believe that any article is being imported in such quantities as to threaten or impair the national security, may so advise the President. Then, if the President agrees, he may cause an investigation to be made and, if the investigation supports the findings of the Director, the President is required to take such action as he deems necessary to adjust the imports of such article to a level which will not threaten to impair the national security.

"As a member of the Finance Committee, I supported this proposal as a substitute for various amendments providing limitations upon the importation of specific commodities, one of which amendments was the one which I had supported in regard to petroleum. I supported the proposal adopted by the committee because I was assured by those in the administration responsible for the administration of the trade-agreements program that if such amendment were adopted by the committee and by Congress action would immediately follow, and that imports of petroleum and its products would be definitely restricted.

"I was further assured that such restriction would be based upon the study previously made, to which reference was made by the committee; that the basis of the limitation would be in accordance with the recommendation of that study. This study indicated the necessity of limiting imports of petroleum and its products to an amount and in the relative position of the imports of petroleum in 1954 as related to domestic production of crude oil in 1954.

"I was further assured that the Director of Defense Mobilization would take the action indicated as necessary to adjust imports of petroleum and its products to the level and relationship of 1954.

* * * * * * *

"It is my judgment that, if these assurances can be supported by such further evidence as this body may think proper, we can all rely upon these assurances and that the importation of petroleum and its products will forthwith be limited to a relationship to our domestic production and in an amount equal to the 1954 position.

"Since the report of the Finance Committee, I have further explored this situation with administrative agencies charged with the responsibility for the application of this program, and I can say to the Senate that again I have complete assurance of compliance of these agencies with the direction set forth in that amendment.

"Based on these assurances, I heartily support the report of the Finance Committee.

"* * * There can be no doubt in my mind as to the intent of the committee, nor, do I believe, as to the intent of the Senate in regard to limiting the oil imports to the average daily imports of the year 1954, based on the report of the President's Commission on Energy Supplies and Resources Policy.

"I can assure the Senate that I would not have agreed to the amendment in H. R. 1, dealing with imports of commodities which are of national defense interest, had I not been assured that it would be the policy of those who administer the act to follow the intent of those who participated in preparing the report of the Advisory Committee.

* * * * * * *

"I think, as the senior Senator from Colorado [Mr. Millikin], the ranking minority member of the Senate Finance Committee, stated yesterday, that we expect those in authority to administer this program on the basis of a limitation of imports; and if it develops, and we find that the program is not being so administered, then it will become the duty of the Senate Finance Committee, the House Ways and Means Committee, or individual Senators or Members of Congress to demand full compliance with this intent."

#### SENATORS ANDERSON AND CARLSON

On May 3, 1955, Senator Clinton Anderson, New Mexico, inquired of Senator Carlson as to the purposes of the defense amendment. This discussion, from page 4641 of the Congressional Record, is as follows:

"Mr. ANDERSON. As the Senator from Kansas knows, some oil is produced in my State, and the oil producers there are very anxious about this question of oil imports. At the same time I value the stand and the opinion of the Senator from Kansas very highly. Does he feel that the oil producers of my State would be justified in taking the assurances given as guaranties that the oil industry is not going to be disrupted by unusual and devastating amounts of oil imports?

"Mr. CARLSON. I am pleased to state to the distinguished Senator from New Mexico, who always follows closely the interests of not only the people of his own State, but of the people of the Nation, that had I not believed that the amendment we approved in committee, which was recommended by a very substantial vote, would protect the oil industry from ever-increasing imports, I certainly would not have voted to report the bill to the Senate, and I certainly would not be on the floor today stating I favored it and would vote for it.

"Mr. ANDERSON. I appreciate the statement of the Senator from Kansas, in whose State there have been oil operations of long standing. Some of us were somewhat worried by the situation, so far as reducing importations of fuel oil was concerned, because we felt it was crude oil which was causing a great deal of the trouble. At the same time, if there is only one amendment before the Senate, the easy and natural thing is to vote for the amendment, if it is in the interest and welfare of one's own State. With the proposal in the present language, I should like to ask the Senator from Kansas, for whom I have great respect, if he feels that, along with other Senators who come from oil-producing States, we are doing all we can be expected to do if we vote for this type of amendment.

"Mr. CARLSON. I will say to the Senator from New Mexico that I believe that this amendment will establish a standard on which we can rely; that it will limit oil imports, as recommended by the Advisory Committee on Energies Supplies and Resources Policy, to 13.6, and we expect that recommendation to be carried out.

"Mr. ANDERSON. I thank the Senator from Kansas for that information. It is reassuring to me.

SENATORS DANIEL AND CARLSON

On May 3, 1955, Senator Price Daniel, Texas and Senator Frank Carlson, Kansas, discussed the Defense Amendment. Their discussion appeared on Pages 4642 and 4643 of the Congressional Record as follows:

"Mr. DANIEL. * * * If imports are allowed to exceed the ratio they bore to market demand or production in 1954, the national security would be endangered. Is that not correct?

"Mr. CARLSON. I thoroughly agree with the distinguished Senator from Texas. It was for that reason that the junior Senator from Kansas and the junior Senator from Texas and many other Senators cosponsored an amendment making the limit 10 percent. I say very honestly and sincerely, had it not been that I was satisfied with the amendment adopted by the committee, after days and days of hard work and conferences, I would still have supported a limitation on oil imports of 10 percent.

"* * * There is no question that excess importation will affect not only our national defense, but our economy, and it is important that we have an economy that is thriving and growing.

"Mr. DANIEL. Based on that evidence, is it the Senator's understanding that if oil imports should exceed the 1954 ratio, there would be injury to our national security?

"Mr. CARLSON. There can be no question about that.

"Mr. DANIEL. Was there any reason why the committee included the amendment at all, if the committee did not feel that the national security would suffer if oil imports were in excess of the 1954 ratio?

"Mr. CARLSON. As I said earlier in my remarks, the Finance Committee spent much time on this amendment and on other amendments dealing with quota imports and their effect on the national defense. We were seriously concerned about the matter. For that reason, we have assurances that those administering the act will act in accordance with the proposals submitted by the President's Advisory Committee on Energy Supplies and Resources Policy and the evidence submitted to our committee. I have no doubt of it.

"Mr. DANIEL. As a member of the committee, is it the opinion of the Senator from Kansas that a majority of the committee, which supported the amendment, intended that the necessary action be taken to keep imports from exceeding the 1954 ratio, which has been interpreted by the President's advisory committee as the ratio beyond which injury would be done to the national security?

"Mr. CARLSON. One reason why I say that is very definitely the opinion of the committee, or at least the intent of the committee, is the fact that the chairman of the Finance Committee included in the report of the committee a part of the Advisory Committee's report, which, after all, in my opinion, gives the intent of the Finance Committee.

" * * * we expect the administrative agencies to carry out the intent of the Senate and of the Finance Committee; and I feel confident they will do so. In fact, I think I can say we had definite assurances that they intend to do so.

"Mr. DANIEL. A moment ago I understood the Senator from Kansas to say that, as a member of the committee he has received such assurances.

"Mr. CARLSON. I have.

"Mr. DANIEL. I wish to say that I, also, have today received such assurances. However, I think it is more important for us to consider the assurances made to the Senator from Kansas, who is a member of the Finance Committee. Further, he is a coauthor of the Neely amendment. Is that correct?

"Mr. CARLSON. That is correct.

"Mr. DANIEL. Since the Senator from Kansas was an original coauthor of the Neely amendment, I think his statement as to what the administrative official will do with the committee substitute for the Neely amendment is very important.

* * * * * * *

"Mr. DANIEL. I hope that action will be taken, and I am sure the Senator from Kansas will be one of the first to support enactment of a stronger provision requiring the reduction of excessive oil imports, if the administrative officials fail to carry out the intent of the amendment.

"Mr. CARLSON. There is no question about that.

"Mr. DANIEL. Does the Senator from Kansas understand that after the Cabinet report was issued, administrative officials expressed themselves to importing companies as feeling that the recommendations of the Cabinet committee should be followed, and that the importing companies should voluntarily cut their imports to the 1954 ratio?

"Mr. CARLSON. I think that is a very fair statement. As a matter of fact, during the hearings, when we had before us some of the presidents of and other witnesses representing the larger importing companies, I brought out the fact that I did not like to have imports limited by means of a rigid percentage basis, and that I hoped they would voluntarily make an effort to hold the imports within the limits set forth in the advisory committee's report. They assured us they would. So we are taking them on faith. If they do not do so, I assure the Senator from Texas that, insofar as I am concerned, I shall propose that action be taken to have them comply.

"Mr. DANIEL. I should like to ask one more question, which may appear to be somewhat technical: As I understand, under the amendment the Director of the Office of Defense Mobilization would be the Government official who would report to the President that imports might be at such a ratio that they would endanger the national security.

"Mr. CARLSON. That is correct.

"Mr. DANIEL. Since the same official was on the Cabinet committee—as a matter of fact, he was chairman of the committee, was he not?

"Mr. CARLSON. He was.

"Mr. DANIEL. Since he was on that committee, and since his committee has already made one investigation and report as to a ratio of oil imports which would endanger the national security, is it the understanding of the Senator from Kansas that that official already has sufficient information to report to the President, and to justify action by the President under this amendment?

"Mr. CARLSON. Not only is it my understanding but it is most reasonable that he should do so, and I so stated earlier in my remarks.

"Mr. DANIEL. In other words, there would be necessity now to make a further examination of the evidence, insofar as oil is concerned. If it continues to exceed the danger point there is no need for a new investigation.

"Mr. CARLSON. That is correct.

"Mr. DANIEL. I thank the Senator from Kansas.

Subsequent to the enactment of the Trade Agreements Extension Act of 1955 numerous Members of Congress have made statements which clearly show that the intent of the defense amendment, as applied to oil, was to provide statutory authority in the President to keep petroleum imports within the 1954 relationship.

On July 30, 1955, 27 members of the Senate[1] addressed a letter to the Director of the Office of Defense Mobilization which unmistakably reflects the intent of Congress with respect to the defense amendment. This letter read in part as follows:

"As you know, the 1955 extension of the Trade Agreements Act contains a new provision commonly referred to as the national defense amendment, authorizing the President to take such action as he deems necessary to adjust imports of any commodity when such imports threaten to impair the national security. Responsibility for initiating such action under that provision of the law rests with your Office.

"In adopting the national defense amendment one of the principal factors considered by the Congress was the problem created by the large and increasing importation of foreign oil into the United States. In this connection the Congress gave particular attention to the findings of the Cabinet Committee, that in the interest of national defense oil imports should not exceed significantly the ratio that these imports bore to the production of domestic crude oil in 1954,

[1] Allott (Colorado); Anderson (New Mexico); Barrett (Wyoming); Bender (Ohio); Bible (Nevada); Capehart (Indiana); Case (South Dakota); Chavez (New Mexico); Curtis (Nebraska); Daniel (Texas); Dirksen (Illinois); Goldwater (Arizona); Jenner (Indiana); Kerr (Oklahoma); Kilgore (West Virginia); Langer (North Dakota); Long (Louisiana); Mansfield (Montana); Martin (Pennsylvania); Monroney (Oklahoma); Neely (West Virginia); O'Mahoney (Wyoming); Schoeppel (Kansas); Scott (North Carolina); Welker (Idaho); and Young (North Dakota).

"The legislative record of the Trade Agreements Extension Act in the Senate Finance Commmittee and in the Senate itself shows that the new provision of the act was adopted in the light of assurances that the executive branch of the Government would take action under this new authority to assure that oil imports would not exceed the levels recommended by the special Cabinet Committee. In the case of oil imports, therefore, the executive and legislative branches of the Government are in agreement, without the need for further study, as to specific standards to be applied in implementing the policy contained in the national defense amendment."

More recently on July 27, 1956, 31 members of the Senate[2] addressed a letter to the Director of the Office of Defense Mobilization further making unmistakably clear that the intent of Congress in adopting the defense amendment was that petroleum imports should not be permitted to exceed the 1954 relationship in order to protect the national security. In this letter it was stated as follows:

"In a letter to you on July 30, 1955, signed by several Members of the Senate, it was pointed out that section 7 of the Trade Agreements Extension Act of 1955 was adopted in the light of assurances that the executive branch of the Government would take action under this authority to assure that oil imports would not exceed the 1954 relationship to domestic production. Responsibility for initiating such action has rested with your office.

"It is our understanding that oil imports have continuously exceeded the 1954 ratio to domestic production, and that these excesses have been increasing despite the efforts by your office during the past year to obtain a voluntary restraint on these imports through a number of appeals to the importing companies. It is our further understanding that the future programs of these companies, as submitted to the Texas Railroad Commission, show greater excesses in scheduled imports at a time when domestic production is being curtailed. In short, no evidence is available to us that oil imports have been, or are being, restricted within the limits determined to be necessary in the interest of national defense.

"In view of this situation, we are concerned with regard to your letters of May 11 and June 26, 1956, to the importing companies. Analysis of these letters indicates that you are now excluding from any restriction, or approving at increased levels, about three-fourths of the total volume of crude oil and refined products imports as currently scheduled. The voluntary restraints requested in your letters apply to a relatively small portion of the increasing imports and would seem to delay a restriction of imports within the standard recognized by the Senate in amending the trade agreements law. Your plans to reexamine this basic standard indicate a further delay in accomplishing such restriction.

"As Senators interested in assuring that oil imports do not impair the necessary developments of domestic fuel resources, we would appreciate any further advice or information you can furnish us as to this matter, including whatever assurances you can give us that action will be taken to carry out the intent of the defense amendment to hold oil imports to the 1954 relationship."

The intent of the United States House of Representatives is equally clear. The defense amendment was adopted in the Senate in lieu of several proposals to limit petroleum imports to 10 percent of domestic consumption. Similar proposals were at that time pending also in the House. Since the defense amendment was incorporated by the Senate, it was necessary that this bill, in its amended form, be approved by the House before it became law. In so doing the House of Representatives accepted the purposes and objectives of the defense amendment as intended by the Senate.

The following subsequent statements by Members of the House of Representatives further makes it unmistakably clear that it was the intent of the House in adopting the defense amendment that petroleum imports should be limited to the 1954 relationship:

---

[2] Allott (Colorado), Anderson (New Mexico), Barrett (Wyoming), Beall (Maryland), Bible (Nevada), Capehart (Indiana), Carlson (Kansas), Case (South Dakota), Chavez (New Mexico), Clements (Kentucky), Curtis (Nebraska), Daniel (Texas), Dirksen (Illinois), Ellender (Louisiana), Goldwater (Arizona), Humphreys (Kentucky), Jenner (Indiana), Kerr (Oklahoma), Laird (West Virginia), Langer (North Dakota), Long (Louisiana), Martin (Pennsylvania), Mansfield (Montana), Monroney (Oklahoma), Murray (Montana), McClellan (Arkansas), Neely (West Virginia), Schoeppel (Kansas), Scott (North Carolina), Welker (Idaho), and Young (North Dakota).

CONGRESSMAN JOHN JARMAN (OKLAHOMA), CONGRESSIONAL RECORD, JUNE 12, 1956

"Mr. JARMAN. * * * In adopting this amendment what yardstick did the Congress expect would be employed in dealing with the oil import problem? It was made imminently clear, Mr. Speaker, that the Congress expected—and in fact had assurances—that the Cabinet Committee formula, holding imports to their 1954 relationship to domestic production, would be the criterion for effectuating this amendment."

Following the speech by Congressman Jarman, which included the above statement, several Members of the House made comments which clearly show that they agree with Congressman Jarman concerning the intent of Congress in adopting the defense amendment.

Excerpts from these comments, Congressional Record, June 12, 1956, are as follows:

CONGRESSMAN PAGE BELCHER (OKLAHOMA)

"Mr. BELCHER. * * * I want to commend the gentleman on his statement and join with him in his remarks."

CONGRESSMAN GEORGE H. MAHON (TEXAS)

"Mr. MAHON. * * * I have gone along with the theory it would be best to avoid further legislation if adequate results can be achieved otherwise. I think the administration has all the power it needs to cope with the situation and I am sure the gentleman agrees. The percentage of oil of foreign origin which we are using has sharply increased. It has reached the danger point for the United States."

CONGRESSMAN EDGAR W. HIESTAND (CALIFORNIA)

"Mr. HIESTAND. I would like to state that I have carefully studied the gentleman's statement. It should be called a study because it it very effective. It is commended to all of those interested in the oil industry it is commended especially to the members of the Department and the Office of Defense Mobilization for careful study. It depicts a serious situation."

CONGRESSMAN CARL ALBERT (OKLAHOMA)

"Mr. ALBERT. Mr. Speaker, I desire to avail myself of this opportunity to compliment my colleague on his fine statement. * * * Increasing imports are hurting the oil industry in this country, and the time has come when specific legislative restrictions on imports or quotas should be imposed by law. Again I want to commend my friend for his statement."

CONGRESSMAN OMAR BURLESON (TEXAS)

"Mr. BURLESON. * * * I am sure the gentleman agrees that in the Trade Agreements Act passed in 1955, it was the clear intent of the Congress that all imports should be held to the 1954 level."

CONGRESSMAN FRANK IKARD (TEXAS)

"Mr. IKARD. * * * I was very happy to see the gentleman so clearly point out in his remarks what was, without question, the intent of this Congress last year when we passed H. R. 1, the Reciprocal Trade Act, the so-called national defense amendments, which were designed to take care of this situation and without any shadow of doubt, according to the record before the committees and on the floor of the Congress, the intention of Congress was clearly expressed."

More recently in a statement in the Congressional Record, July 5, 1956, page A5584, Congressman Charles W. Vursell (Illinois) said:

"Mr. VURSELL. * * * We continued our fight against excessive imports in the Congress until in 1955 the President appointed a Cabinet-level committee, headed by Dr. Flemming, Director of the Office of Defense Mobilization, to study energy supplies and resources including oil. That committee, after making a thorough study, rendered a decision that in the future the proportion of oil imports to domestic production be held at the 1954 level. Since that time, Dr. Flemming, acting for the executive department, and the Congress have been making every effort to get the seven major oil importing oil companies to voluntarily reduce their imports and comply with the expressed will of the Congress and the executive department.

* * * * * * *

"Unless voluntary compliance is met which will result in the proportion of oil imports to domestic production being held at the 1954 level, as recommended by the President's Cabinet Committee at the close of their study, I shall join with other Members of the Congress in introducing and supporting legislation which I predict will be passed by the Congress in the next session to accomplish this."

On July 27, 1956, Congressman Frank Ikard (Texas), Congressional Record, July 27, 1956, page 13860, made the following statement:

"Mr. IKARD. * * * The defense amendment, as applied to oil, was made clear during the congressional debate. The legislative history clearly shows that it was the intent of Congress that oil imports should be limited to the 1954 relationship. The legislative history is clear that with respect to oil imports, the Congress determine that imports in excess of the 1954 relationship would threaten to impair the national security."

### SENATORS NEELY AND CARLSON

On July 27, 1956, Senator Matthew M. Neely, West Virginia, and Senator Frank Carlson, Kansas, discussed the intent of Congress in adopting the defense amendment. The following excerpts are from the Congressional Record, July 27, 1956, pages 13705, 13706, and 13707:

"Mr. NEELY. * * * White House bill No. 1, to extend the authority of the President to enter into reciprocal trade agreements, was before the Senate or its Committee on Finance in the spring of 1955, I offered an amendment to the bill to restrict petroleum imports into the United States to 10 percent of the domestic petroleum demand for the corresponding quarter of the previous year.

"When the bill and the proposed amendments reached the floor of the Senate in May 1955, the bill was passed but my amendment, which was supported by 38 Members of this body on a rising vote, was defeated, upon assurances from spokesmen or friends of the administration that if voluntary action by the petroleum industry should prove ineffectual the President would take immediate action to restrict imports to the 1954 level.

* * * * * * *

"The solemn pledges of immediate and decisive action by the President were given in support of a substitute amendment to the bill mentioned which gave the President specific authority to impost and enforce limitations upon oil imports. That substitute amendment was accepted by the Senate and became a part of the House bill No. 1.

"No one can read the debate on that substitute amendment particularly the statements of friends and spokesmen of the administration without reaching the conclusion that it was not merely permissive but directive. Certainly not even the most vigorous advocate of unlimited oil imports can or will deny that it was the purpose of the Congress to place drastic restraints upon this flood of foreign oil.

"The positive assurances that the President would act immediately to keep oil imports at their 1954 levels were given to the Senate by two of the most illustrious Republicant Members of this body, the Senator from Kansas [Mr. Carlson] and the Senator from Colorado [Mr. Millikin].

* * * * * * *

"Mr. CARLSON. I do not want to break into the excellent statement the Senator is making. It is a statement which should be made. I was one of the cosponsors of Resolution No. 1, which would have limited the importations of oil to 10 percent. I think it can be very definitely stated that the Senate Finance Committee, which considered that proposal, decided that if we could work out a program of voluntary reduction of imports, to keep it within the 16.6 percent of the 1954 domestic production, it would be much better than to tie the hands of the administration by enacting restrictive legislation.

"I share the views of the Senator from West Virginia. I want to commend him for calling this matter to the attention of the Senate. We are now importing oil to the extent of approximately 20 percent of domestic production. I can assure the Senator that when I made the statement that he was quoted, I had assurance then and still contend they will be carried out. There is no doubt in my mind as to the intent of the Senate Finance Committee, and the United States Senate felt that oil imports would be held to the 16.6 percent level as recommended by the Presidential Commission on Energy Supplies and Resources Policy. I say to the Senator I still stand on that statement.

* * * * * * *

"I call that to the attention of the Senator from West Virginia and to the Senate for the reason that I am in full accord that if this does not result in limiting imports to 16.6 percent of domestic production, on which we had an agreement, I shall in the next session be urging legislation that will restrict imports by legislative or congressional enactment. Again, in view of my commitment to the Senate, that if oil imports are not voluntarily limited, I will press for enactment of legislation that will limit these imports."

---

## APPENDIX B

### RECOMMENDATIONS OF THE SPECIAL COMMITTEE TO INVESTIGATE CRUDE OIL IMPORTS—JULY 29, 1957

THE WHITE HOUSE,
*Washington, July 29, 1957.*

Memorandum for the Secretary of the Interior and the Director of the Office of Defense Mobilization:

I have approved the recomendations of the Special Committee To Investigate Crude Oil Imports as set forth in the attached report. I direct you to put these recommendations into effect as rapidly as possible.

DWIGHT D. EISENHOWER.

---

WASHINGTON, D. C., *July 29, 1957.*

The PRESIDENT,
*The White House.*

DEAR MR. PRESIDENT: On June 26, 1957, you established the Special Committee To Investigate Crude Oil Imports. You directed the Committee to report its findings and recommendations at the earliest practicable date.

The Committee's report is attached herewith.

Respectfully yours,

SINCLAIR WEEKS,
*The Secretary of Commerce.*

---

### PETROLEUM IMPORTS

#### *I. Background*

The problem of oil imports, and their effect upon the domestic petroleum industry, was one of the primary reasons that caused President Eisenhower to establish the Cabinet Committee on Energy Supplies and Resources Policy in July 1954. The President directed the Committee to study and evaluate all factors pertaining to the continued development of energy supplies and resources in the United States, "with the aim of strengthening the national defense, providing orderly industrial growth, and assuring supplies for our expanding national economy and for any future emergency."

On February 26, 1955, the White House released a report on energy supplies and resources policy in which the Cabinet Committee concluded that in the interest of national security imports of crude and residual oils should be kept in balance with the domestic production of crude oil at the proportionate relationships that existed in 1954. The Committee also recommended that these ratios should be reevaluated from time to time in the light of changing circumstances.

As a result of this study the importing companies were requested to restrict imports of petroleum to the United States on a voluntary, individual basis in conformity with the policies enunciated by the Committee. The voluntary method was chosen as a matter of basic policy in preference to tariffs, quotas, or other methods of mandatory limitation in order to avoid regulatory controls wherever possible.

As a result of considerable debate in Congress upon the subject of petroleum imports, the Trade Agreements Extension Act of 1955 included the following section (7):

"(b) In order to further the policy and purpose of this section, whenever the Director of the Office of Defense Mobilization has reason to believe that any article is being imported into the United States in such quantities as to threaten to impair the national security, he shall so advise the President, and if the President agrees that there is reason for such belief, the President shall cause an immediate investigation to be made to determine the facts. If, on the basis of such investigation, and the report to him of the findings and recommendations made in connection therewith, the President finds that the article is being imported into the United States in such quantities as to threaten to impair the national security, he shall take such action as he deems necessary to adjust the imports of such article to a level that will not threaten to impair the national security."

The policy of voluntary restriction worked with reasonable success until the middle of 1956. At that time the schedules submitted to ODM by the importing companies for the last half of 1956 and the first half of 1957 indicated that there would be a sharp rise in imports, and that the volume would be substantially in excess of the proportional relationship that had been recommended by the Committee.

As a consequence of the increased level of imports scheduled for the last half of 1956, the Independent Petroleum Association of America (IPAA) filed a petition on August 7, requesting action under section 7 of the Trade Agreements Extension Act of 1955.

After the petition had been filed, the Director of Defense Mobilization announced that a public hearing would be held at which all interested parties would be provided with the opportunity of presenting their points of view. This hearing began on October 22, 1956, and was conducted by the General Counsel of ODM. Representatives of persons and groups favoring and opposing action under section 7 were heard. In addition, at the request of ODM, representatives of oil importing companies made statements relative to their plans for the future. The hearing was concluded on October 24, 1956. Information developed in the hearing has been considered by this Committee.

Early in December 1956, the Director of Defense Mobilization announced that he was suspending action on the case because of the changed conditions growing out of the Suez crisis. At the same time he made this statement:

"Import programs of the importing companies recently filed with the ODM show that the plans they had formulated for 1957, if carried out, would be contrary to the Committee's recommendations and would constitute a threat to our national security. This situation, without other intervening circumstances (the Suez crisis), would have left no course for me but to make a certification to the President under section 7 of the Trade Agreements Extension Act of 1955."

In a letter dated March 6, 1957, the Director requested the importing companies to furnish ODM with more recent estimates of their import plans for the balance of 1957, assuming that normal oil movements could be resumed in the near future.

The estimates for imports during the last half of 1957 were compiled and presented a situation of even greater seriousness than that which prevailed prior to the Suez crisis, for the new schedules were considerably higher than those that were submitted for the fall of 1956.

On April 23, 1957, the new Director, Mr. Gordon Gray, advised the President pursuant to section 7 of the Trade Agreements Extension Act of 1955 that he had reason to believe that crude oil is being imported into the United States in such quantities as to threaten to impair the national security.

The analysis of the petroleum import situation that follows is made, therefore, in the light of the foregoing events.

*II. Recent events*

Review of the oil import levels year by year does not indicate that through the first half of 1956 crude oil imports had reached such a high level as to constitute a threat to the national security. Imports scheduled for the last half of 1956 and for the first half of 1957 were of such a magnitude that in the judgment of the then Director of the Office of Defense Mobilization they would have constituted a threat to national security. However, the interruption of petroleum transportation from the Middle East to the area west of Suez which occurred in November 1956 disrupted the normal pattern of petroleum movements over a period of several months, and, as a result, the schedule of imports for the last half of 1956, as well as the one for the first half of 1957, was never put into effect.

The program of imports for the last half of 1957, as presented to the Director of the Office of Defense Mobilization during March and April, indicated that the importers planned to increase materially the import levels over those of 1956 (see table I).

*III. Effect on national security*

Your committee's investigation of the oil import problem has been confined to the effect of the present trend of imports on national security.

It is clear that there is a direct relationship between the Nation's security and adequate and available sources of energy. Oil and gas account for two-thirds of all the energy that is consumed in this country. Furthermore, there is no adequate substitute in sight for the foreseeable future. Therefore, we must have available adequate supplies of oil.

We have concluded, for reasons that are set forth later in this section of the report, that if we are to have enough oil to meet our national security needs, there must be a limitation on imports that will insure a proper balance between imports and domestic production.

Before arriving at this conclusion, we considered and rejected, for the reasons noted below, the following three proposals that are based on a policy of permitting imports to follow whatever course they may take:

1. *Import foreign crude oil and store it in this country within depleted fields or elsewhere.*—The practical problems of cost and the physical problems connected with the storage of crude oil would make this solution impracticable from the standpoint of industry and Government alike.

2. *Enlarge Government participation in exploring for oil reserves which, when discovered, would not be put into production.*—Such a course would be costly to an already overburdened government and would be contrary to the principles of free enterprise which characterize American industry.

3. *Encourage increased importations in order that our own natural resources might be conserved.*—Your committee has concluded that for the following reasons such a policy would be unsound:

(*a*) It would result in a sharp decline in domestic exploration by private enterprise because the industry would have no assurance of an adequate market for domestic oil after discoveries had been made and, as a result, would reduce its exploratory operations. Barring Government operations which would be undesirable, adequate exploration and the development of additional reserves can only be generated by a healthy domestic production industry.

(*b*) Consequently, as the extent of the Nation's useful reserves are not known until they are discovered and developed, the United States would be unable to make a sound appraisal of its petroleum resources because it would not know the extent to which our reserve capacity could be developed.

(*c*) Furthermore, in the event of an emergency which denied the United States access to oil in other countries and which called for additional availability of domestic oil, the Nation would be faced with the long delays that characterize exploratory activity, as well as with the possible necessity of making large expenditures of public funds for exploration, production, and transportation. In this connection, it should be borne in mind that no matter how large the expenditures might be, it would be impossible to recover the momentum of a vigorous domestic industry.

(*d*) In brief, such a policy of encouraging importation as a means of conserving our petroleum resources would mean that in an emergency the Nation would be confronted with all of the liabilities inherent in a static, as contrasted with a dynamic, mobilization base, including the delays, waste, and inefficiency that accompany efforts to strengthen any part of the mobilization base on a crash basis.

In the light of the above examination of suggestions looking toward a policy of unrestricted imports, your committee has concluded that if we are to have a vigorous program of exploration in this country by private enterprise in order to care for increasing domestic consumption and to meet emergency needs, and if we are to know what our reserve potential is in this country, it is essential that we follow a policy which will encourage continuation of free enterprise exploration at a rate consistent with the demands of a growing economy.

The latest available figures demonstrate that the amount of oil we are adding to our reserves is not keeping pace with the increase in domestic consumption, in spite of the fact that our services are at an alltime high. Indeed, there has been some recent indication of a decrease in exploratory drilling, notwithstanding an increase in domestic demand for petroleum. There has also been a decrease in the number of exploratory crews in operation. It is not possible to attribute this decline to any single cause. The sharp increase in imports programed by the importers in their report to ODM indicates such a trend of increase in relation to domestic production as will bring about a further decline in domestic exploratory and development activities. This should not be permitted. This timelag between exploration and production requires that we explore today for tomorrow's usable reserves. Any other course will impair industrial expansion, availability of supplies for consumer use, and preparedness for an emergency.

In summary, unless a reasonable limitation of petroleum imports is brought about, your committee believes that—

(*a*) Oil imports will flow into this country in ever-mounting quantities, entirely disproportionate to the quantities needed to supplement domestic supply.

(*b*) There will be a resultant discouragement of, and decrease in, domestic production.

(*c*) There will be a marked decline in domestic exploration and development.

(*d*) In the event of a serious emergency, this Nation will find itself years away from attaining the level of petroleum production necessary to meet our national security needs.

Your committee recognizes that there are important foreign policy aspects to the problem of limitating petroleum imports. The oil reserves and production capacities of other free nations, as well as our own, are important to our national security. A number of countries inevitably depend in varying degree upon access to our domestic market for their petroleum exports and it must be recognized that it is also in the interest of our national security that our allies and friends have healthy and expanding economies. It is believed, however, that, taking all factors into consideration, our national security requires the maintenance of some reasonable balance between imports and domestic production at this time. In light of the foregoing considerations, our recommendations are framed with the objective of limiting imports in order to maintain such a balance and yet to allow other nations to participate in the growth of our domestic demand to a degree consistent with our national security.

It is our conviction that as a nation we must pursue a careful, considered course that will permit reasonable imports into our country and still stimulate a dynamic and vigorous exploratory and development effort in this country.

*IV. Effect on consumers*

Domestic consumers are utilizing an increasing amount of petroleum products for transportation, fuel, heating, and many other aspects of consumer life. In the event of a national emergency, it is essential to these consumers that there be adequate supplies at reasonable cost, both now and in the future. The low cost of imported oil is attractive, but excessive reliance upon it in the short run may put the Nation in a long-term vulnerable position. Imported supplies could be cut off in an emergency and might well be diminished by events beyond our control. This vulnerability could easily result in a much higher cost, or even in the unavailability, of oil to consumers. It is, therefore, believed that the best interests of domestic consumers, as well as of national security, will be served if a reasonable balance is maintained between domestic and foreign supplies.

*V. Conclusions and recommendations*

1. Increased volume of crude-oil imports and the proposed imports for the latter half of 1957 threaten to impair the national security. This threat, under existing conditions, requires a limitation on imports. The Committee recommends, therefore, that unless the importing companies comply voluntarily with the import limitation plan hereinafter set forth, you find that there is a threat to the national security within the meaning of section 7 of the Trade Agreements Extension Act of 1955. Pending the outcome of this voluntary program, this Committee should continue as now constituted.

2. For the initial phase of such a program of limitation, in the interest of national security, the following plan is recommended to cover the period of the last half of 1957 and the first half of 1958:[8]

[8] The term "crude oil" as used throughout this plan is oil at the wellhead.

(*a*) *Districts I–IV:*

i. All importing companies, except those referred to in (ii) below, should be requested to cut back 10 percent below their average crude-oil imports for the years 1954, 1955, and 1956.

ii. In order that small 1954 importers and companies that have started to import since 1954 should have the opportunity to participate in the United States market on a basis more equitable than if the above cutback were applied to them, it is recommended that companies having crude-oil imports of less than 20,000 barrels per day in 1954 should be allowed to import the amounts set forth in the schedules submitted by them to ODM in July 1957, but in no instance to exceed an increase of over 12,000 barrels per day over their actual 1956 imports. (See table II for analysis of effect of this formula on importing companies.)

(*b*) District V:[4]

Imports should be determined on a semiannual basis. Pending a change in the deficit condition now pending in the area by, for example, the development of an economical means of interregional transportation, the level of imports must be such as to make up the difference between the demand and the quantity of domestic crude oil available to the area, as established by the Department of the Interior. The schedule of imports for the last half of 1957, as submitted by the companies to the Director of Defense Mobilization, appears to be slightly higher than would be called for by the foregoing formula. However, there is reason to believe that the imports for this period will not exceed 275,000 barrels per day and, consequently, no voluntary import limitations are proposed for this district at the present time. This situation should be reviewed, however, during the latter part of 1957 from the point of view of the plans of importers for the first half of 1958, in view of the fact that additional pipeline capacity to the west coast is scheduled to become available during the first half of 1958. (See table III.)

(*c*) Imports under proposed plan:

| | | |
|---|---|---|
| Districts I–IV, barrels per day | | 756,000 |
| Percentage ratio, imports to production | 12.0 | |
| Percentage ratio, imports to demand | 9.6 | |
| District V, barrels per day | | 275,000 |
| Percentage ratio, imports to production | 29.8 | |
| Percentage ratio, imports to demand | 23.3 | |
| Total, barrels per day | | 1,031,000 |

(*d*) New importers should have the opportunity to enter and share in a reasonable manner in the United States market. Companies planning to become importers should present their plans to the Department of the Interior at least 6 months before their plans are to become operative. A determination should then be made as to the extent these importers should share in the market initially, and as to whether room can be made for them as a result of the increase in permissible imports arising out of the increase in domestic demand or whether it will be necessary for older importers to decrease their imports in order to make room for the new companies.

(*e*) All imports into the United States should be for the direct account of the importers, and no importer should be allowed to increase its imports through oil sale and product purchase agreements, by transfer of allotments, or by other indirect means.

(*f*) The Committee recognizes that it would be possible to circumvent this plan by companies entering into certain types of arrangements for the importation of distilled products. We recommend that the Office of Defense Mobilization and the Department of the Interior follow this situation very closely.

3. The plan above outlined should be reviewed by this or some comparable committee at least once a year. Under normal peacetime conditions we believe that such a review should proceed on the assumption that in districts I–IV an effort will be made to maintain a ratio between imports and domestic production of approximately 12 percent[5] and that in district V imports will be restricted

[4] See appendix A–1 for reasons for separating districts I–IV and district V.

[5] The relationship between imports and domestic demand would be approximately 9.6 percent. In this report we have referred to the ratio between imports and production in order to be consistent with the report made by the Presidential Advisory Committee on Energy Supplies and Resources Policy in February 1955. In the future it is recommended that the statistics dealing with this problem be compiled on the basis of the relationship between imports and demand, instead of between imports and production.

to the difference between demand and the domestic crude oil that can be made available to the area on a reasonably competitive basis.

4. The plan above outlined should be administered by the Department of the Interior under policy guidance from the Office of Defense Mobilization. In the administration of the plan, provision should be made for the hearing and consideration of cases where it is alleged that inequities would result from the application of the plan, with the understanding that the Administrator will have authority to establish the necessary administrative procedures and act in such a manner as to alleviate inequities when they are found to exist, including any showing that the plan does not provide competitive opportunities for newer importers.

Respectfully submitted.

JOHN FOSTER DULLES,
*Secretary of State.*
DONALD A. QUARLES,
(For the Secretary of Defense).
GEORGE M. HUMPHREY,
*Secretary of the Treasury.*
FRED A. SEATON,
*Secretary of the Interior.*
JAMES T. O'CONNELL,
(For the Secretary of Labor).
SINCLAIR WEEKS,
*Secretary of Commerce, Chairman.*

---

## APPENDIX A-1

### SEPARATION OF DISTRICTS I-IV FROM DISTRICT V

The effect of imports into the United States on national security is entirely different in the eastern area of the country (districts I-IV) than it is in the Pacific region (district V). The facts may be set forth briefly as follows:

1. Districts I-IV have a substantial production capacity which is in excess of actual production because the volume of production is controlled by certain of the State regulatory commissions in the interest of conserving the volatile components which would be lost in storage. Texas, for example, produces approximately one-half of the crude oil in this area, and the State commission has recently limited production to 13 days per month to prevent waste. Stocks are in excess of the seasonal normal.

2. Commercial production in district V, which is represented almost entirely by California oilfields, is not controlled by regulatory bodies and is at as high a level as is consistent with sound engineering practices. Nevertheless, production is declining steadily and imports are necessary to meet the demand.

3. The geographic separation of districts I-IV and district V is such that transportation of crude oil or refined products from one region to the other is not being provided in such quantities as to meet the total demands of district V. Crude oil produced in the intermountain territory tends to flow westward to the Pacific slope, and is an increasingly important source of domestic supply for the area.

The problems of the two regions are at the present time sufficiently different, so that the Committee's plan, as outlined hereafter, takes into account the separate and distinct features of each.

### DISTRICTS I-IV (AREA EAST OF THE ROCKY MOUNTAINS)

An analysis of table I shows that in 1954 crude oil imported into districts I-IV represented 11.3 percent of the domestic production in the same area.[6] Imports increased slightly in 1955 and the first half of 1956 to bring the ratio up to 11.9 percent in the latter period. In the third quarter of 1956 imports increased sharply and the ratio increased to 13.5 percent. It would have been even higher in the fourth quarter if the Suez situation had not intervened in the last 2 months of the year. Following the reopening of the Suez Canal, the importing companies filed scheduled estimates aggregating 970,700 barrels per day for the last half of 1957 for an import ratio of 16 percent.[6]

---

[6] In 1954, imports of residual fuel oil into districts I-IV represented additional imports equal to 6.6 percent of the domestic production. Residual imports have remained relatively steady from 1954 to date.

DISTRICT V (AREA WEST OF THE ROCKY MOUNTAINS)

As indicated in table I, the 1954 crude-oil imports to district V amounted to only 51,000 barrels per day, or 5.2 percent of the amount which was produced in that area. Imports increased steadily, as domestic production declined, until they are scheduled to average 296,000 barrels per day in the last half of 1957. This would result in an import ratio of 32.1 percent for the area. The industry has followed the practice of using all of the domestic crude that has been available on a competitive basis. The scheduled imports are slightly higher than the estimated requirement. However, there is reason to believe that the imports for this period actually will not exceed 275,000 barrels per day. This would result in an import ratio of 29.8 percent for the area.

TABLE I.—*Percentage ratio of crude-oil imports to United States crude-oil production*

[In thousands of barrels daily]

| | 1954 | 1955 | 1st half, 1956 | 3d quarter, 1956 | 4th quarter, 1956 | 2d half, 1957 |
|---|---|---|---|---|---|---|
| Districts I-IV: | | | | | | |
| Imports | 605 | 689 | 735 | 830 | 718 | [1] 971 |
| Production | 5,367 | 5,835 | 6,199 | 6,155 | 6,212 | [2] 6,079 |
| Percentage ratio | 11.3 | 11.8 | 11.9 | 13.5 | 11.6 | 16.0 |
| District V: | | | | | | |
| Imports | 51 | 93 | 153 | 212 | 198 | [1] 275 |
| Production | 975 | 972 | 967 | 959 | 949 | [2] 923 |
| Percentage ratio | 5.2 | 9.6 | 15.8 | 22.1 | 20.9 | 29.8 |
| Total United States: | | | | | | |
| Imports | 656 | 782 | 888 | 1,042 | 916 | [1] 1,246 |
| United States production | 6,342 | 6,807 | 7,166 | 7,114 | 7,161 | [2] 7,002 |
| Percentage ratio | 10.34 | 11.5 | 12.4 | 14.7 | 12.8 | 17.8 |

[1] The importing companies, in filing reports with the Office of Defense Mobilization, estimated that their imports into district V for this period would be 296,000 barrels per day. There is reason to believe, however, that these imports will not exceed 275,000 barrels per day and, as a result, this figure is being used throughout the report.

[2] Estimated, Office of Oil and Gas, Department of the Interior.

TABLE II.—*District I-IV crude-oil imports*

[In thousands of barrels daily]

| | 1954 | 1955 | 1956 | 3-year average | Programed, last half, 1957 | Imports per formula |
|---|---|---|---|---|---|---|
| Established importers: | | | | | | |
| Atlantic | 62.7 | 64.1 | 69.4 | 65.4 | 75.7 | 58.9 |
| Gulf | 117.9 | 125.2 | 129.0 | 124.0 | 153.0 | 111.6 |
| Sinclair | 65.1 | 68.8 | 73.5 | 69.1 | 74.6 | 62.2 |
| Socony | 87.2 | 71.5 | 65.0 | 74.6 | 78.9 | 67.1 |
| Standard (California) | 70.6 | 76.7 | 75.3 | 74.2 | 86.0 | 66.8 |
| Standard (New Jersey) | 80.7 | 79.4 | 79.9 | 80.0 | 87.0 | 72.0 |
| Texas | 52.2 | 65.1 | 64.2 | 60.5 | 74.9 | 54.5 |
| Subtotal | 536.4 | 550.8 | 556.3 | 547.8 | 630.1 | 493.1 |
| New mporters: | | | | | | |
| Cities Service | 11.3 | 29.2 | 25.8 | --------- | 32.6 | 32.6 |
| Eastern States | 4.3 | 17.2 | 18.6 | --------- | 18.3 | 18.3 |
| Gabriel | -------- | -------- | 5.7 | --------- | 7.5 | 7.5 |
| Great Northern [1] | -------- | 6.0 | 21.1 | --------- | 33.0 | 33.0 |
| International Refineries [1] | 2.0 | 2.0 | 9.2 | --------- | 10.9 | 10.9 |
| Lakehead [1] | -------- | -------- | .3 | --------- | .3 | .3 |
| Lake Superior [1] | 2.0 | 2.0 | 5.0 | --------- | 5.0 | 5.0 |
| Northwestern | -------- | 2.0 | 6.0 | --------- | 10.0 | 10.0 |
| Phillips | 7.0 | 10.6 | 11.1 | --------- | 12.0 | 12.0 |
| Shell [1] | -------- | .5 | .8 | --------- | 7.5 | 7.5 |
| Standard of Indiana | 15.5 | 15.0 | 17.8 | --------- | 49.4 | 29.8 |
| Standard of Ohio | -------- | .7 | 1.9 | --------- | 8.2 | 8.2 |
| Sun | 15.1 | 24.4 | 38.4 | --------- | 58.4 | 50.4 |
| Tidewater | 5.1 | 12.9 | 22.2 | --------- | 84.6 | 34.2 |
| Southwestern | 1.5 | 5.6 | 2.1 | --------- | 2.9 | 2.9 |
| Subtotal | 63.8 | 128.1 | 186.0 | --------- | 340.6 | 262.6 |
| Miscellaneous | 4.8 | 10.1 | 12.7 | --------- | --------- | --------- |
| Total, districts I-IV | 605.0 | 689.0 | 755.0 | --------- | [2] 970.7 | [3] 755.7 |

[1] Importer of Canadian crude.
[2] District I-IV production required, 6,079.
[3] District I-IV production required, 6,294.

TABLE III.—*District V crude-oil imports*

[In thousands of barrels daily]

| | 1954 | 1955 | 1956 | 3-year average | Programed last half, 1957 | Imports per formula |
|---|---|---|---|---|---|---|
| District V: | | | | | | |
| Douglas | -------- | 1.6 | 1.0 | 0.9 | (1) | (1) |
| Socony (General Petroleum) | 3.5 | 26.4 | 32.5 | 20.8 | 26.5 | 26.5 |
| Standard (California) | 21.0 | 17.7 | 22.1 | 20.3 | 68.0 | 68.0 |
| Shell | -------- | 6.6 | 28.1 | 11.6 | 56.9 | 56.9 |
| Texas | 10.6 | 9.4 | 21.9 | 14.0 | 19.0 | 19.0 |
| Tidewater | 13.7 | 25.0 | 43.1 | 27.3 | 53.0 | 53.0 |
| Union | -------- | -------- | 11.7 | 3.9 | 24.5 | 24.5 |
| United States Oil Refining Co | -------- | -------- | -------- | --------- | 7.5 | 7.5 |
| Richfield | -------- | -------- | 1.5 | .5 | 16.6 | 16.6 |
| Wilshire | -------- | -------- | 12.2 | 4.0 | 24.0 | 24.0 |
| Others (to balance) | 2.2 | 6.3 | 4.9 | 4.4 | --------- | --------- |
| Total | 51.0 | 93.0 | 179.0 | 107.7 | [2] 296.0 | [2] 296.0 |

[1] Not reported.
[2] There is reason to believe that the total imports for this period will not exceed 275,000 barrels per day.

## Appendix O

### United States Petroleum Imports, 1928–56

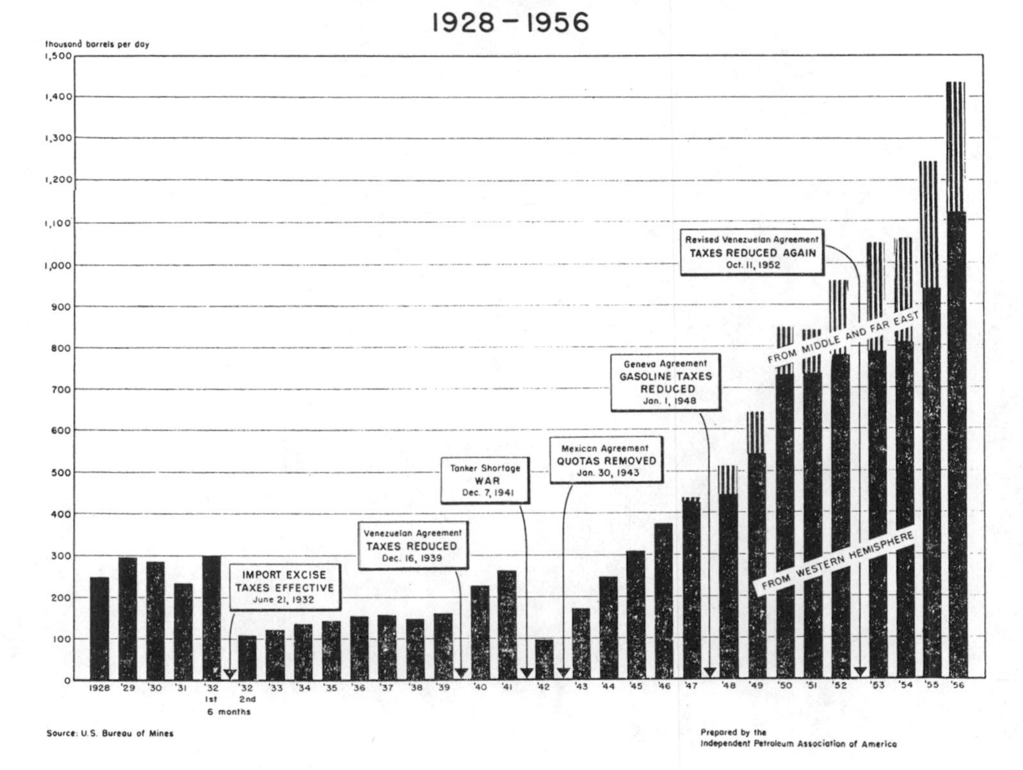
U.S. PETROLEUM IMPORTS
1928 – 1956
thousand barrels per day
1,500
1,400
1,300
1,200
1,100
1,000
900
800
700
600
500
400
300
200
100
0
1928
'29
'30
'31
'32 1st
'32 2nd
6 months
'33
'34
'35
'36
'37
'38
'39
'40
'41
'42
'43
'44
'45
'46
'47
'48
'49
'50
'51
'52
'53
'54
'55
'56
IMPORT EXCISE TAXES EFFECTIVE June 21, 1932
Venezuelan Agreement TAXES REDUCED Dec. 16, 1939
Tanker Shortage WAR Dec. 7, 1941
Mexican Agreement QUOTAS REMOVED Jan. 30, 1943
Geneva Agreement GASOLINE TAXES REDUCED Jan. 1, 1948
Revised Venezuelan Agreement TAXES REDUCED AGAIN Oct. 11, 1952
FROM MIDDLE AND FAR EAST
FROM WESTERN HEMISPHERE
Source: U.S. Bureau of Mines
Prepared by the Independent Petroleum Association of America

# XIII

# THE PLYWOOD INDUSTRY AND FOREIGN TRADE POLICY

# HARDWOOD PLYWOOD IMPORTS UNFAIR COMPETITION FOR AMERICAN INDUSTRY

Hardwood Plywood Institute, Robert N. Hawes, general counsel

SECTION I. HARDWOOD PLYWOOD

Plywood consists of panels or assemblies that are made up of wood veneers on the face and back usually with a center or core of wood veneer; lumber or other material, all bonded together with an adhesive. The plies are laid up with the grain of the wood running at right angles to the adjoining ply. Plywood panels are manufactured in various types and grades, depending primarily on the use for which required; they may be constructed for either utility or decorative purposes.

Depending on the species of wood used in the face ply, plywood may be either softwood or hardwood. The terms "softwood" and "hardwood" relate to the botanical classification of the species of tree from which the wood veneer is derived. Hardwood is used to designate wood from a deciduous tree and softwood is applied to wood from a coniferous tree.

This statement is concerned only with hardwood plywood. Hardwood plywood is designated in the trade according to the species of wood used in the face ply. The principal hardwood used to make hardwood plywood by the domestic industry are: Gum, birch, oak, walnut, maple, ash, beech, cherry, elm, magnolia, cottonwood, sycamore, African and Honduras mahogany and lauan (Philippine mahogany) are also used.

Hardwood plywood production in the United States may be classified into two distinct categories: (1) Container and packaging plywood; and (2) other than container and packaging. The second category is broken down into a further division of (1) market hardwood plywood, and (2) plywood produced in a plant as a material for a product which is the plant's specialty of manufacture, called captive hardwood plywood.

In regard to container plywood, the Tariff Commission in its report of June 1955, said:

> Container plywood is produced for a particular use, i. e., for the production of a wide variety of containers and boxes for shipping, storage, and dispensing. In the manufacture of container plywood it is not necessary to meet the quality standards required of noncontainer types, e. g., qualities of appearance and smoothness and the absence of defects. There is little or no competition between container plywood and other hardwood plywood.
>
> Container type hardwood plywood produced predominantly in plants which produce container plywood exclusively. Because of this fact, together with the fact that it is essentially a different product from noncontainer plywood, for all practical purposes, the domestic producers constitute a separate industry from that engaged in the production of noncontainer type.

The noncontainer type hardwood plywood production is divided into two separate and distinct industries. Plants producing hardwood plywood to be sold in commercial channels, hereafter referred to as market hardwood plywood. The second, plants that are engaged primarily and specially in the production of a product in which plywood is a material, which produces hardwood plywood to be used as a component but not for sale in commercial channels, called captive plywood.

Plants making captive plywood are not in the plywood business but are engaged primarily in production of some other product. The captive plywood is made as a component for the fabrication of the plants principal product. The producers of capitive plywood are no more in the plywood business than in the sawmill business, as they make dimension lumber in amounts equal to or greater than the amount of plywood produced.

Another factor that is of the utmost importance is that captive plywood is produced for a particular use; in many, if not most instances, it would not be suitable for other uses without alteration. Captive plywood is usually of an odd size, special construction, flat or curved to serve a special purpose. The last and most important factor is that it is not made for sale in commercial channels, therefore does not compete with market hardwood plywood or imports.

The criteria set up by the Tariff Commission for the finding that the container plywood producers were a separate and distinct industry is equally applicable to captive plywood. Captive plywood is produced for a particular use, as a component of the primary specialty of the producer. It is not made for sale in commercial channels. The producing plants are engaged in production of products other than hardwood plywood. Captive plywood is essentially a different product, being produced as a component for another product. It is not manufactured in the standard sizes nor the thicknesses of market hardwood plywood. The producers of captive hardwood plywood and producers of market hardwood plywood are not in competition.

In spite of the fact that the criteria for exclusion of container plywood was also applicable to captive plywood, the Tariff Commission included captive plywood in calculation of domestic shipments and consumption. The only places in the Tariff Commission report where captive plywood statistics are used are in shipments and consumption, all other statistical data on the domestic industry relates only to market hardwood plywood.

The Tariff Commission accepted the fallacious argument of the representatives of the importers and foreign producers. Their obvious purpose was to show that the imports of hardwood plywood have taken a smaller proportion of the domestic market. To accept the argument that all production of a product (not shipments) must be included in determining the ratio of imports to domestic shipments would result in producers for sale in the market being destroyed where there was both market and captive production in an industry. It is quite clear that the importers and foreign producers are not concerned with the producers of captive hardwood plywood; those companies produce their own plywood and are not buyers. The competition for the importers and foreign producers comes from the domestic plants which make hardwood plywood to sell, the market hardwood plywood producers.

The importers and foreign producers are desirous of confusing the real issues and the advocating of the inclusion of captive plywood into consumption figures is a part of that purpose. The importers and foreign producers know that the captive production reduces the domestic market, as neither they or the domestic producers can sell to a company which produces its own plywood. If all captive producers discontinued production of hardwood plywood but continued to manufacture their primary specialty, then a new market would open for hardwood plywood which would constitute a part of the domestic consumption. The inclusion of captive hardwood plywood production in determining consumption would create a false picture of the domestic market and would constitute the acceptance of an intentionally misleading premise put forth to further the purpose of destroying the market hardwood plywood producers.

SECTION II. DOMESTIC HARDWOOD PLYWOOD INDUSTRY

Accurate statistics on the domestic hardwood plywood industry setting out the number of plants, production, and financial data are not available. The Census of Manufactures, 1954, Hardwood Millwork, Plywood, and Prefabricated Structural Wood Products does not contain pure figures on the market hardwood plywood industry, because container plywood and captive plywood are included.

The shipment figures in the Department of Commerce Facts for Industry, Hardwood Plywood—Market Shipments and Inventories, published quarterly, have been revised in subsequent quarters and in subsequent years. The revisions have been questioned, as well as the comparability of coverage from quarter to quarter. At the suggestion of the domestic producers, the Census Bureau is undertaking a survey of the years 1951 through 1956 for the purpose of securing complete accurate statistics. It is believed that the survey will be complete early in the fall of 1957.

The Bureau of Census in its second quarter, 1957, issue of Hardwood Market Shipments and Inventories makes this statement:

> Preliminary coverage checks being made against the 1954 census of manufacturers and other sources, indicate that further checks should be made to assure comparability of this quarterly statistical series. It is anticipated that the coverage checks will be completed before release of the data for the third quarter and until this analysis is completed the data presented in this series must necessarily be considered preliminary.

For the purpose of this presentation, the Bureau of Census latest published figures are used for market hardwood plywood. The revised figures have been issued since the publication of the domestic industry's statements on domestic shipments. The revision issued by the Bureau of Census has caused concern and embarrassment to the domestic industry, which relied on the published figures.

The static condition of the market hardwood plywood industry is illustrated by the shipment figures contained in table 1 following:

TABLE 1.—*Domestic shipments market hardwood plywood, 1951–56; and 1st 2 quarters 1957* [1]

[Thousand square feet]

| | 1st quarter | 2d quarter | 3d quarter | 4th quarter | Annual |
|---|---|---|---|---|---|
| 1951 | 234,733 | 215,038 | 176,518 | 178,960 | 805,249 |
| 1952 | 188,004 | 185,205 | 197,070 | 224,578 | 794,857 |
| 1953 | 236,368 | 220,357 | 176,637 | 172,270 | 805,632 |
| 1954 | 167,888 | 169,857 | 178,411 | 201,989 | { 713,145<br>[2] 799,124 |
| 1955 | 209,912 | 220,908 | 225,867 | 244,220 | { 900,407<br>[3] 917,784 |
| 1956 | 257,473 | 225,764 | 188,529 | 212,701 | 884,567 |
| 1957 | 196,022 | 186,936 | | | |

[1] In view of revisions and variance of figures with other census tabulations, a survey is now being made for the years 1951 through 1957 to determine a correct series of figures for these years.
[2] Census of manufacturers, 1954.
[3] Annual figures shown are 900,407 equal unadjusted sum of quarterly figures and 917,784 equal annual adjusted figures.

Source: U. S. Bureau Census Facts for Industry—Hardwood Plywood: Market Shipments and Inventories.

The only financial statistics available for the domestic hardwood plywood industry are those collected by Seidman & Seidman, certified public accountants. The companies covered by the survey of Seidman & Seidman represent the most efficient companies in the industry and from 40 to 50 percent of the total shipments of the market hardwood plywood industry.

Table 2, following, is a consolidated operating statement prepared by Seidman & Seidman for the years and number of companies indicated.

TABLE 2.—*Consolidated operating statement for United States concerns producing market hardwood plywood, 1939, 1948, and 1951–56*

| Item | 1939 (9 companies) | 1948 (33 companies) | 1951 (46 companies) | 1952 (46 companies) | 1953 (46 companies) | 1954 (46 companies) | 1955 (30 companies) | 1956 (35 companies) |
|---|---|---|---|---|---|---|---|---|
| | Amount (in thousands of dollars) | | | | | | | |
| Net sales | 4,081 | 50,972 | 78,191 | 67,219 | 77,342 | 63,933 | 106,804 | 108,641 |
| Manufacturing cost of goods sold | 3,371 | 41,456 | 64,642 | 59,279 | 67,971 | 57,332 | 92,930 | 96,088 |
| General administrative and selling expense | 457 | 3,242 | 5,020 | 4,659 | 5,170 | 4,877 | 7,734 | 8,095 |
| Net operating profit | 253 | 6,274 | 8,529 | 3,281 | 4,201 | 1,724 | 6,140 | 4,458 |
| Net income before Federal income taxes [1] | 264 | 6,491 | 8,770 | 3,291 | 4,414 | 2,006 | 5,800 | 4,314 |
| | Ratio to net sales (percent) | | | | | | | |
| Net sales | 100.0 | 100.0 | 100.0 | 100.0 | 100.0 | 100.0 | 100.0 | 100.0 |
| Manufacturing cost of goods sold | 82.6 | 81.3 | 82.7 | 88.2 | 87.9 | 89.7 | 87.01 | 88.45 |
| General administrative and selling expense | 11.2 | 6.4 | 6.4 | 6.9 | 6.7 | 7.6 | 7.24 | 7.45 |
| Net operating profit | 6.2 | 12.3 | 10.9 | 4.9 | 5.4 | 2.7 | 5.75 | 4.10 |
| Net income before Federal income taxes [1] | 6.5 | 12.7 | 11.2 | 4.9 | 5.7 | 3.1 | 5.75 | 3.97 |

[1] Net income, before Federal income taxes, includes, in addition to net operating profit, net income not associated with manufacturing operations. It will be seen that the ratio of net operating profit to net sales is not significantly different from the ratio of net income to net sales.

Source: Compiled from financial data supplied to the Tariff Commission by concerns for which market hardwood plywood represents the predominant or exclusive product. Data covering 30 companies in 1955 and 35 companies in 1956 from reports by Seidman & Seidman, certified public accountants.

Table 3, following, is based on the Seidman & Seidman report in table 1, and is a percentage breakdown of the costs and profit on sales. This table shows the increases in the various cost factors on a percentage basis. It should be noted that the increase in costs is fairly evenly distributed between all cost items.

TABLE 3.—*Domestic market hardwood plywood industry, ratio of costs and profits to sales* [1]

[Expressed in percentages of sales]

| | 1950 (49 companies) | 1951 (51 companies) | 1952 (51 companies) | 1953 (52 companies) | 1955 (30 companies) | 1956 (35 companies) | Change, 1956 from 1950 |
|---|---|---|---|---|---|---|---|
| Net sales | 100.00 | 100.00 | 100.00 | 100.00 | 100.00 | 100.00 | |
| Cost of goods sold | 81.24 | 82.37 | 87.64 | 87.70 | 87.01 | 88.45 | +7.21 |
| Composition: | | | | | | | |
| Material consumed | 51.87 | 59.21 | 53.58 | 53.98 | 55.35 | 54.50 | +2.63 |
| Direct labor | 19.14 | 19.12 | 21.29 | 21.42 | 20.00 | 21.76 | +2.62 |
| Manufacturing overhead | 10.23 | 11.04 | 12.77 | 12.30 | 11.66 | 12.19 | +1.96 |
| Gross profit on sales | 18.76 | 17.63 | 12.36 | 12.30 | 12.99 | 11.55 | −7.21 |
| Administrative and selling expense | 6.50 | 6.41 | 7.06 | 7.10 | 7.24 | 7.45 | +.95 |
| Operating profit before taxes | 12.26 | 11.22 | 5.30 | 5.20 | 5.75 | 3.97 | −8.29 |

[1] Figures available for only 1st half of 1954 do not permit extension to annual basis.

Source: Seidman & Seidman, certified public accountants.

The figures for 1954 were available only for the first half, which did not reflect the entire year and, therefore, have been omitted.

Tables 2 and 3 illustrate the condition of the domestic market hardwood-plywood industry on an annual basis. A comparison of the quarterly domestic shipment figures of all market hardwood plywood with the quarterly dollar-sales and profits-before-taxes figures for the 35 companies covered by the Seidman & Seidman report for the year 1956 shows the direct effect of the reduction in shipments in dollar sales and profits.

| | Shipments market hardwood plywood [1] 1,000 sq. ft. | Dollar sales market hardwood plywood [2] | Profit before taxes [2] (percent) |
|---|---|---|---|
| 1st quarter 1956 | 257,573 | $32,884,756 | 5.60 |
| 2d quarter 1956 | 225,764 | 33,653,064 | 4.89 |
| 3d quarter 1956 | 188,529 | 19,959,425 | 2.89 |
| 4th quarter 1956 | 212,701 | 22,144,011 | 1.15 |

[1] See table 1.
[2] Seidman & Seidman report for 1956.

The above figures show that the industry requires shipments of approximately 1 billion square feet annually to earn a return of 5.6 percent before taxes. Shipments in the area of 850 million square feet on an annual basis will put the industry as a whole at a break-even point.

Profits before taxes for the market hardwood plywood industry for 1956 of 3.9 percent compares unfavorably with the average profit before taxes for all manufacturing companies for 1956 which is 9.4 percent. Table 4, which follows, shows the decline in profits before taxes for the market hardwood plywood industry from 12.3 percent in 1951 to 3.9 percent in 1956. This table also shows the comparable profit before taxes for all manufacturing and the lumber and wood products industry. The profit before taxes of all manufacturing companies reflects the expansion that has occurred in American industry which has not been permitted to the market hardwood plywood industry.

TABLE 4.—*Ratios of net operating profit*[1] *to net sales for companies producing market hardwood plywood, all manufacturing corporations, and producers of lumber and wood prdoucts, 1948 and 1951–56*

[In percentages]

| Year | Producers of market hardwood plywood [2] | All manufacturing corporations [3] | Producers of lumber and wood products [3] |
|---|---|---|---|
| 1948 | 12.3 | 11.0 | 14.7 |
| 1951 | 10.9 | 11.0 | 10.4 |
| 1952 | 4.9 | 9.0 | 7.0 |
| 1953 | 5.4 | 9.0 | 5.9 |
| 1954 | 2.7 | 8.2 | 5.8 |
| 1955 | 5.7 | 9.9 | 9.0 |
| 1956 | 3.9 | 9.4 | 6.3 |

[1] Before Federal income taxes.
[2] Based on financial data supplied to the U. S. Tariff Commission by 33 companies for 1948; 46 companies for the years 1951–54. Data covering 30 companies for 1955, and 35 companies for 1956 from reports by Seidman & Seidman, certified public accountants.
[3] Compiled from the official statistics of the Federal Trade Commission and the U. S. Securities and Exchange Commission.

*Labor costs in the domestic industry*

As shown by table 2 above, direct labor costs in 1956 represent 21.76 percent of the dollar sales return. Direct labor in relation to the cost of goods sold represented 24.60 percent of the cost in 1956.

A survey of 55 companies producing market hardwood plywood in plants located east of the Rockies shows that the average hourly base rate for plant workers in 1956 is ts follows:

| | |
|---|---|
| Northeastern area | $1.46 |
| Southeastern area | 1.18 |
| South-central area | 1.22 |
| Southern area | 1.26 |
| Lake States area | 1.45 |
| Pacific Northwest area | 1.86 |

A survey of 32 plants in the areas set out above shows an average cost per 1,000 square feet, one-fourth-inch hardwood plywood of $38.50 per 1,000 square feet. The average fringe benefits now an integral part of the wage structure are, on the average, $3.62 per 1,000 square feet. The $3.62 fringe benefit compares with a Japanese total labor cost of $4.17 per 1,000 square feet in 1953 and $5.50 per 1,000 square feet in 1955.[1]

The domestic market hardwood plywood industry sells its products in commercial channels for many uses. Tables 5 and 6 show the percentages developed in an end-use survey conducted by the Hardwood Plywood Institute at both the producer and distributor level. Retail

[1] Importers exhibit 19, Tariff Commission hearing—hardwood plywood.

dealers buy a substantial portion of all shipments which are in turn resold by them for home construction, paneling, do-it-yourself, and to small fabricators.

TABLE 5.—*Hardwood Plywood Institute, market hardwood plywood end use—Production report, 30 identical trade-promotion mills, Feb. 11, 1957*

[Percent of volume]

| | 1954 | 1955 | 1956 |
|---|---|---|---|
| Furniture: | | | |
| Case goods, suites, etc | 21.5 | 21.5 | 17.7 |
| TV, radio, hi-fi | 3.5 | 3.1 | 1.8 |
| Tables and desks | 8.5 | 7.8 | 7.0 |
| Total | 33.5 | 32.4 | 26.5 |
| Millwork—commercial and home: | | | |
| Fixtures and millwork | 16.4 | 17.8 | 13.9 |
| Kitchen cabinets | 9.5 | 11.3 | 13.0 |
| Flush doors | 12.0 | 9.5 | 6.1 |
| Total | 37.9 | 38.6 | 33.0 |
| Other home construction: | | | |
| Retail lumber dealers | 10.2 | 14.6 | 17.0 |
| Project housing | 1.6 | 1.1 | 1.3 |
| Total | 11.8 | 15.7 | 18.3 |
| Industrial uses: | | | |
| Mobile homes and transportation | 3.4 | 3.9 | 8.3 |
| Boats and marine | 1.0 | 1.4 | 3.9 |
| Industrial | 10.3 | 5.6 | 8.4 |
| Toys and luggage | 2.1 | 2.4 | 1.6 |
| Total | 16.8 | 13.3 | 22.2 |

TABLE 6.—*Hardwood Plywood Institute, distributor survey (based on mill and distributor sales analysis), January 1957*

Market hardwood plywood-use study

[Percent]

| End-use classification | January 1955 | January 1956 | January 1957 |
|---|---|---|---|
| Furniture, including radio, hi-fi and TV | 6.8 | 8.4 | 3.6 |
| Tabletops | 3.1 | 2.4 | .8 |
| Fixtures and millwork | 30.4 | 35.5 | 22.6 |
| Kitchen cabinets | 16.4 | 17.7 | 21.1 |
| Industrial | 7.7 | 4.3 | 3.0 |
| Dealers | 23.3 | 24.5 | 34.1 |
| Project housing | 2.8 | .8 | 1.8 |
| Department stores | 3.4 | .3 | 1.8 |
| Trailers and transportation | 4.5 | 3.5 | 4.3 |
| Boats | 1.6 | 2.6 | 6.9 |
| Total | 100.0 | 100.0 | 100.0 |

THICKNESS STUDY

[Percent]

| Year | 3 and 5 ply | 7 ply and thicker | Lumber core |
|---|---|---|---|
| 1956 | 60 | 25 | 15 |
| 1957 | 68 | 27 | 5 |

*Price trend of domestic market hardwood plywood*

Market hardwood plywood has sold at depressed prices since 1951, the year beginning the influx of imports of plywood. The trend of prices of market hardwood plywood has been the reverse of that of all commodities which has risen almost 10 index points since 1951. With demand high, as evidenced by the consumption figures hereafter set out in table 17, the depressed prices in the industry are the direct result of the low-priced imports.

Table 7 following, gives the Bureau of Labor Wholesale Price Index for hardwood plywood, lumber and wood products, and all commodities other than farm products and food.

TABLE 7.—*Hardwood plywood wholesale price index, 1951–57, comparison with categories lumber and wood products and all commodities other than farm products and food*

[1947–49—100]

| Year | All hardwood plywood | Birch | Gum | Lumber and wood products | All commodities other than farm products and food |
|---|---|---|---|---|---|
| 1951 | 110.8 | 117.3 | 107.1 | 123.9 | 115.9 |
| 1952 | 101.3 | 115.1 | 93.3 | 120.3 | 113.2 |
| 1953 | 108.4 | 121.5 | 100.9 | 120.2 | 114.0 |
| 1954 | 100.3 | 115.0 | 91.9 | 118.0 | 114.5 |
| 1955 | 102.6 | 116.8 | 94.5 | 123.5 | 117.0 |
| 1956 | 104.7 | 117.0 | 97.8 | 125.4 | 122.2 |
| 1957, monthly breakdown: | | | | | |
| January | 104.2 | 114.5 | 98.4 | 121.3 | 125.2 |
| February | 103.4 | 112.4 | 98.4 | 120.7 | 125.5 |
| March | 103.4 | 112.4 | 98.4 | 120.0 | 125.4 |
| April | 103.4 | 112.4 | 98.4 | 120.2 | 125.4 |
| May | 103.4 | 112.4 | 98.4 | 119.7 | 125.2 |
| June | 103.4 | 112.4 | 98.4 | 119.7 | 125.2 |
| July | 103.4 | 112.4 | 98.4 | 119.3 | 125.6 |

Source: U. S. Department of Labor, Bureau of Labor Statistics.

SECTION III. HARDWOOD PLYWOOD IMPORTS

Plywood imports (98 percent or more hardwood, 2 percent or less, softwood) have increased since 1951 from 74 million square feet to 706 million square feet in 1956, or 854 percent. In the first half of 1957, imports amounted to 423 million square feet, an annual rate of 846 million square feet, or an increase of 1,043 percent over 1951.

Hardwood plywood imports from Japan have increased from 13 million square feet in 1951 to 527 million square feet in 1956 or 3,954 percent. The first half 1957, imports from Japan amounted to 339 million square feet, or an estimated total of 675 million square feet for 1957, an increase over 1951 of 5,092 percent.

Table 8 is a Business Service Bulletin prepared by the Business and Defense Services Administration, Department of Commerce, which gives the complete overall statistics on plywood imports, including within it in table 6 Changes in United States Rates of Duty on Plywood, 1922–58.

**TABLE 8.—*Foreign trade information on plywood, United States imports, 1934–56***

TABLE 1.—*United States imports of plywood, by country of origin, 1954–56*

[Quantity in square feet, surface measure; value in dollars]

| Country | 1956 [1] | | 1955 | | 1954 | |
|---|---|---|---|---|---|---|
| | Quantity | Value | Quantity | Value | Quantity | Value |
| Japan | 527, 020, 882 | 33, 916, 570 | 428, 625, 825 | 27, 562, 501 | 289, 012, 910 | 16, 666, 239 |
| Canada | 81, 244, 276 | 10, 466, 661 | 99, 338, 280 | 12, 702, 938 | 71, 074, 806 | 9, 577, 789 |
| Finland | 33, 876, 284 | 4, 033, 762 | 40, 560, 133 | 4, 407, 503 | 32, 188, 564 | 3, 273, 247 |
| Philippine Republic | 14, 904, 978 | 1, 221, 994 | 9, 785, 038 | 1, 025, 061 | 1, 503, 447 | 118, 908 |
| French Equatorial Africa | 13, 086, 754 | 1, 218, 433 | 9, 239, 340 | 729, 346 | 4, 575, 973 | 358, 505 |
| New Guinea | 9, 306, 229 | 619, 392 | 6, 829, 213 | 442, 249 | 6, 065, 718 | 357, 542 |
| West Germany | 4, 734, 006 | 588, 558 | 3, 673, 440 | 486, 929 | 4, 885, 700 | 530, 905 |
| Surinam | 3, 894, 244 | 404, 504 | 3, 919, 137 | 423, 236 | 4, 276, 192 | 401, 540 |
| Italy | 3, 068, 217 | 165, 953 | 4, 847, 478 | 255, 188 | 6, 042, 273 | 325, 931 |
| Netherlands | 2, 710, 662 | 393, 967 | 2, 309, 431 | 391, 696 | 772, 177 | 138, 305 |
| Belgium and Luxembourg | 2, 520, 923 | 851, 784 | 1, 129, 575 | 174, 074 | 664, 660 | 97, 342 |
| United Kingdom | 1, 675, 161 | 343, 089 | 1, 844, 760 | 347, 103 | 287, 336 | 62, 860 |
| France | 1, 573, 700 | 205, 471 | 4, 462, 242 | 334, 493 | 4, 903, 678 | 390, 741 |
| Denmark | 1, 249, 099 | 100, 780 | 1, 170, 412 | 97, 500 | 276, 528 | 21, 481 |
| Spain | 1, 048, 867 | 124, 458 | 1, 375, 423 | 129, 533 | 649, 291 | 67, 213 |
| Israel | 826, 689 | 52, 621 | 707, 273 | 51, 424 | 1, 124, 899 | 66, 028 |
| Mexico | 436, 443 | 58, 279 | 3, 618, 275 | 359, 241 | 3, 389, 217 | 286, 780 |
| Taiwan | 416, 157 | 27, 969 | 81, 359 | 7, 800 | 103, 870 | 4, 201 |
| Panama | 394, 381 | 58, 234 | 929, 661 | 140, 537 | 105, 822 | 14, 172 |
| Switzerland | 304, 239 | 37, 486 | | | | |
| Guatemala | 301, 430 | 28, 004 | 341, 590 | 28, 492 | 36, 420 | 2, 356 |
| Sweden | 282, 232 | 21, 660 | 389, 911 | 28, 568 | 782, 026 | 75, 094 |
| Austria | 236, 856 | 67, 751 | 431, 700 | 102, 054 | 678, 181 | 86, 476 |
| Honduras | 185, 794 | 23, 301 | | | 4, 800 | 375 |
| Belgian Congo | 133, 536 | 16, 164 | 1, 145, 270 | 93, 970 | 479, 572 | 46, 829 |
| Portugal | 67, 812 | 4, 320 | | | | |
| Nansei and Nanpo Islands, not elsewhere classified | 64, 000 | 4, 429 | | | | |
| Canal Zone | 42, 741 | 4, 519 | 80, 637 | 14, 881 | 78, 273 | 12, 419 |
| Brazil | 31, 172 | 996 | 10, 609 | 411 | 113, 146 | 4, 410 |
| Cuba | 25, 000 | 2, 077 | | | | |
| Hong Kong | 15, 000 | 1, 650 | | | | |
| British Guiana | 12, 800 | 1, 090 | | | | |
| Union of South Africa | 9, 600 | 773 | | | | |
| Ecuador | 8, 100 | 1, 582 | | | | |
| Poland and Danzig | 6, 737 | 334 | 140, 165 | 15, 041 | 26, 575 | 3, 708 |
| Australia | 3, 675 | 1, 159 | 58, 880 | 5, 196 | 136, 000 | 7, 041 |
| Gold Coast | 3, 328 | 295 | | | | |
| French West Africa | | | 544, 304 | 48, 097 | 7, 850 | 943 |
| Norway | | | 144, 726 | 6, 175 | | |
| Yugoslavia | | | 34, 344 | 2, 208 | 99, 952 | 7, 440 |
| India | | | | | 19, 803 | 2, 353 |
| French Morocco | | | | | 272, 160 | 20, 176 |
| Total | 705, 722, 004 | 54, 570, 069 | 627, 767, 431 | 50, 413, 445 | 434, 637, 819 | 33, 029, 349 |

[1] Preliminary.

Source: Bureau of the Census.

TABLE 2.—*United States imports of plywood, by country of origin, 1934–53*

[Quantity in square feet, surface measure; value in dollars]

| Country | Quantity | Value | Quantity | Value | Quantity | Value | Quantity | Value |
|---|---|---|---|---|---|---|---|---|
| | 1953 | | 1952 | | 1951 | | 1950 | |
| Japan | 104, 978, 697 | 6, 870, 873 | 17, 342, 330 | 1, 099, 778 | 12, 924, 820 | 1, 026, 997 | 5, 127, 411 | 305, 008 |
| Canada | 50, 847, 400 | 7, 618, 155 | 57, 094, 327 | 8, 714, 459 | 47, 242, 126 | 6, 944, 007 | 50, 048, 990 | 5, 977, 780 |
| Finland | 31, 893, 812 | 2, 690, 004 | 4, 665, 133 | 351, 186 | 3, 440, 292 | 269, 525 | 1, 308, 322 | 64, 206 |
| Philippine Republic | 521, 767 | 16, 650 | 117, 122 | 14, 231 | 71, 312 | 8, 586 | 304, 214 | 37, 711 |
| French Equatorial Africa | 3, 384, 873 | 293, 351 | 591, 136 | 46, 404 | | | | |
| Germany [1] | 2, 200, 709 | 277, 853 | 877, 324 | 121, 458 | 405, 452 | 42, 784 | | |
| Surinam | 4, 393, 856 | 378, 800 | 2, 528, 912 | 240, 844 | 1, 908, 491 | 169, 008 | 627, 510 | 59, 748 |
| Italy | 6, 716, 858 | 367, 458 | 34, 169 | 3, 114 | 418, 430 | 79, 691 | 109, 824 | 31, 131 |
| Netherlands | 977, 120 | 147, 977 | 110, 645 | 19, 260 | 151, 074 | 15, 430 | 961 | 78 |
| Belgium | 178, 876 | 22, 262 | 10, 368 | 1, 343 | 165, 697 | 14, 231 | | |
| United Kingdom | 119, 208 | 23, 343 | | | 31, 938 | 813 | | |
| France | 7, 594, 365 | 620, 316 | 377, 929 | 23, 152 | 19, 507 | 2, 521 | 33, 307 | 3, 450 |
| Denmark | 8, 730 | 1, 876 | | | 9, 998 | 850 | | |
| Spain | 400, 419 | 48, 313 | 128, 537 | 16, 001 | 5, 716 | 790 | | |
| Israel and Palestine | 377, 181 | 26, 426 | | | 128, 632 | 18, 510 | | |
| Mexico | 2, 130, 220 | 187, 531 | 928, 380 | 109, 803 | 732, 442 | 81, 035 | 824, 987 | 93, 736 |
| Taiwan | 440, 885 | 26, 805 | 95, 363 | 4, 905 | | | | |
| Panama | 1, 512, 003 | 241, 648 | 56, 096 | 10, 442 | 60, 000 | 11, 998 | | |
| Switzerland | 134, 736 | 6, 868 | 35, 295 | 1, 496 | | | 513 | 95 |
| Guatemala | 319, 272 | 26, 974 | 12, 236 | 1, 212 | | | | |
| Sweden | 615, 868 | 40, 698 | 57, 485 | 4, 718 | 307, 056 | 36, 421 | 136, 721 | 10, 345 |
| Austria | 149, 755 | 29, 232 | 111, 680 | 9, 511 | | | | |
| Belgian Congo | 118, 072 | 11, 106 | | | 354, 525 | 38, 409 | | |
| Canal Zone | 102, 311 | 17, 897 | 75, 612 | 1, 890 | | | | |
| Brazil | 521, 075 | 33, 506 | 414, 434 | 22, 652 | 5, 444, 245 | 161, 811 | 4, 822, 934 | 86, 704 |
| Cuba | 2, 042 | 1, 009 | | | | | | |
| Union of South Africa | | | | | | | 20 | 18 |
| Australia | | | | | 24, 934 | 1, 397 | | |
| Norway | | | 150 | 38 | 1, 298 | 469 | | |
| Yugoslavia | 89, 998 | 12, 216 | | | 17, 843 | 2, 066 | | |
| Nigeria | 99, 050 | 11, 057 | | | | | | |
| Chile | 17, 469 | 1, 398 | 76, 101 | 3, 146 | 4, 641 | 853 | | |
| Netherland Antilles | | | | | | | 16, 320 | 1, 482 |
| British Malaya | | | 41, 160 | 2, 891 | | | | |
| Total | 220, 846, 627 | 20, 051, 602 | 85, 781, 924 | 10, 823, 934 | 73, 870, 469 | 8, 928, 202 | 63, 362, 034 | 6, 671, 492 |
| | 1949 | | 1948 | | 1947 | | 1946 | |
| Japan | 858, 761 | 69, 760 | 21, 952 | 1, 716 | | | | |
| Canada | 16, 849, 468 | 2, 043, 108 | 39, 535, 461 | 5, 091, 582 | 22, 894, 649 | 3, 615, 937 | 8, 202, 785 | 1, 152, 638 |
| Finland | 674, 601 | 47, 618 | 306, 901 | 28, 534 | 10, 911, 910 | 392, 440 | 13, 569, 381 | 837, 699 |

| | | | | | | | | |
|---|---|---|---|---|---|---|---|---|
| Philippine Republic | 50, 400 | 8, 253 | 23, 170 | 2, 021 | | | | |
| Germany | 200 | 40 | | | | | | |
| Surinam | 9, 984 | 1, 148 | | | | | | |
| Belgium | 13, 857 | 3, 203 | | | | | | |
| France | 95 | 110 | | | | | | |
| Denmark | | | 7, 632 | 1, 080 | | | | |
| Mexico | 417, 876 | 42, 231 | 795, 679 | 108, 626 | 2, 714, 901 | 333, 745 | 1, 863, 144 | 222, 063 |
| Sweden | | | 771, 723 | 54, 803 | 570, 638 | 157, 903 | 5, 900 | 483 |
| Brazil | 732, 582 | 25, 270 | 882, 479 | 20, 977 | 57, 000 | 5, 142 | 592, 866 | 73, 685 |
| Cuba | | | | | 1, 530 | 252 | | |
| Yugoslavia | | | 16 | 5 | | | | |
| Chile | | | | | | | 115, 951 | 12, 423 |
| China | 136, 800 | 6, 559 | 46, 820 | 4, 026 | | | | |
| Venezuela | 6, 024 | 524 | | | | | | |
| New Zealand | 1, 368 | 194 | | | | | | |
| Total | 19, 752, 016 | 2, 248, 018 | 42, 391, 833 | 5, 313, 370 | 37, 150, 628 | 4, 505, 419 | 24, 350, 027 | 2, 298, 991 |
| | 1945 | | 1944 | | 1943 | | 1942 | |
| Canada | 732, 799 | 73, 562 | 1, 156 | 278 | 3, 897 | 4, 414 | 222, 285 | 7, 366 |
| United Kingdom | | | | | 83 | 24 | | |
| Mexico | 55, 630 | 15, 816 | | | | | | |
| Brazil | | | | | 1, 282 | 122 | | |
| China | | | | | 4, 050 | 115 | | |
| Total | 788, 429 | 89, 378 | 1, 156 | 278 | 9, 312 | 4, 675 | 222, 285 | 7. 366 |
| | 1941 | | 1940 | | 1939 | | 1938 | |
| Japan | 1, 641, 935 | 25, 531 | 1, 889, 504 | 27, 097 | 1, 406, 801 | 19, 620 | 1. 207, 589 | 26, 087 |
| Canada | 1, 564, 989 | 39, 204 | 66, 548 | 1, 884 | 3, 931 | 105 | | |
| Finland | | | 592, 808 | 12, 260 | 1, 069, 930 | 20, 074 | 1, 152, 506 | 20, 846 |
| Philippine Republic | | | | | | | 2, 700 | 173 |
| Germany | | | | | | | 8, 400 | 840 |
| United Kingdom | | | | | | | 3, 487 | 839 |
| France | | | | | 22, 989 | 991 | 10, 685 | 941 |
| Sweden | | | | | 1, 600 | 40 | | |
| Belgian Congo | 58, 352 | 1, 300 | | | | | | |
| China | 204, 394 | 2, 944 | 74, 321 | 1, 241 | 9, 149 | 260 | 16, 270 | 478 |
| Latvia | | | | | 260, 684 | 6, 881 | 173, 582 | 3, 662 |
| Poland and Danzig | | | | | 84, 192 | 1, 683 | 64, 874 | 2, 227 |
| U. S. S. R. | | | | | | | 238, 179 | 5, 558 |
| Total | 3, 469, 670 | 68, 979 | 2. 623, 181 | 42, 482 | 2, 859, 276 | 49, 654 | 2, 878, 272 | 61, 651 |

See footnote at end of table, p. 1100,

TABLE 2.—*United States imports of plywood, by country of origin, 1934–53*—Continued

[Quantity in square feet, surface measure; value in dollars]

| Country | Quantity | Value | Quantity | Value | Quantity | Value | Quantity | Value |
|---|---|---|---|---|---|---|---|---|
| | 1937 | | 1936 | | 1935 | | 1934 | |
| Japan | 3,293,974 | 55,768 | 519,126 | 9,829 | 8,853 | 314 | | |
| Canada | 17,515 | 246 | 4,366 | 71 | | | 3,703 | 120 |
| Finland | 569,954 | 17,364 | 12,983 | 278 | | | | |
| Germany | 31,500 | 1,306 | | | | | 1,266 | 140 |
| United Kingdom | | | | | | | 5,400 | 149 |
| France | 4,363 | 246 | | | | | | |
| Denmark | 1,200 | 49 | | | 2,292 | 27 | 6,112 | 76 |
| Australia | 11,709 | 530 | 3,276 | 336 | | | | |
| China | 422,006 | 10,770 | 84,543 | 1,822 | | | | |
| Latvia | 8,725 | 361 | | | | | 25,950 | 519 |
| Poland and Danzig | 171,191 | 2,227 | 19,680 | 267 | 19,184 | 236 | 53,594 | 715 |
| U. S. S. R. | | | 34,336 | 3,850 | | | 18,104 | 251 |
| Total | 4,532,137 | 88,867 | 678,310 | 16,453 | 30,329 | 577 | 114,129 | 1,970 |

[1] Beginning in 1952, separate classifications were established for West Germany and East Germany. The plywood imports in 1952–53 were all from West Germany.

Source: Bureau of the Census.

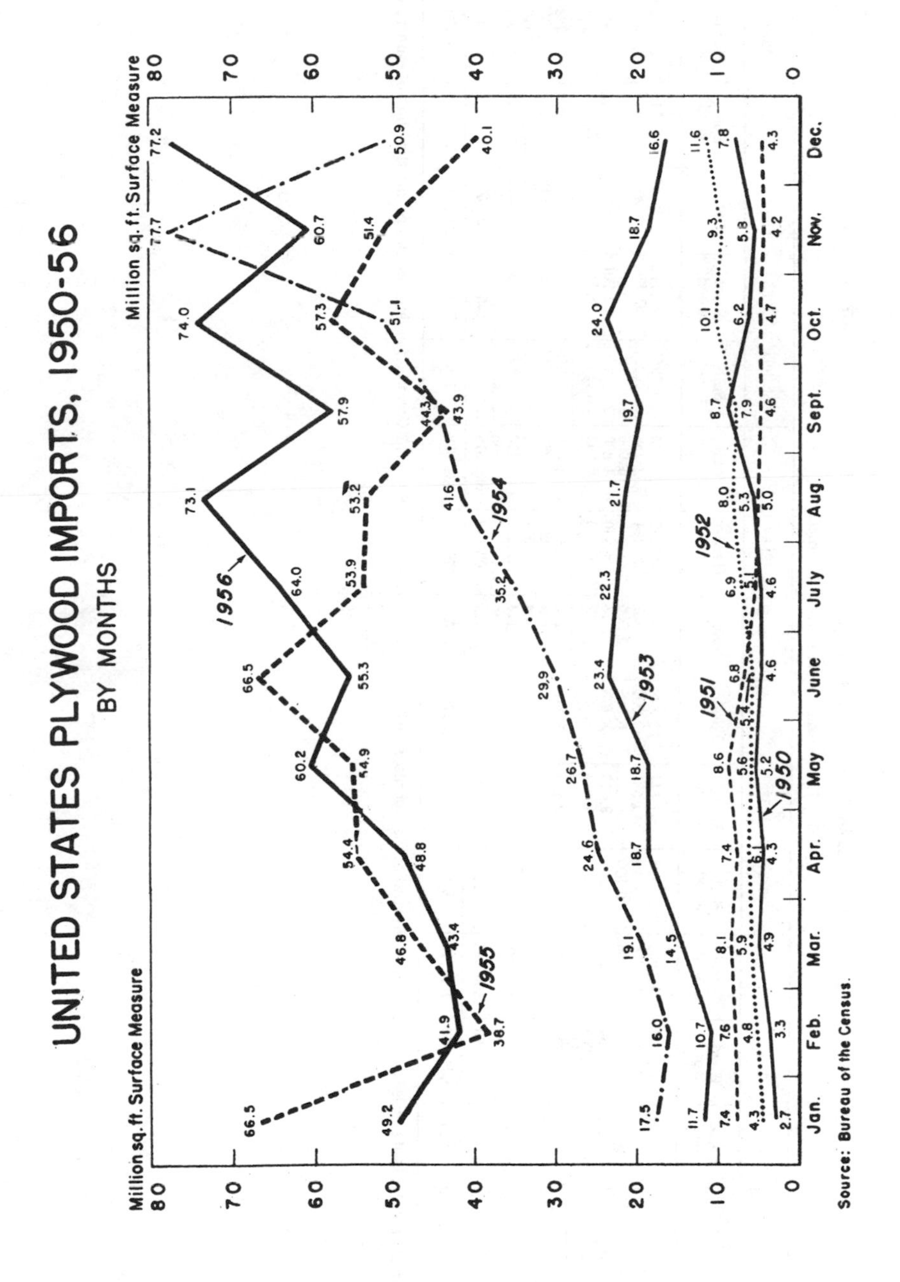
UNITED STATES PLYWOOD IMPORTS, 1950-56
BY MONTHS
Million sq. ft. Surface Measure
Million sq. ft. Surface Measure
80
70
60
50
40
30
20
10
0
Jan.
Feb.
Mar.
Apr.
May
June
July
Aug.
Sept.
Oct.
Nov.
Dec.
1956
1955
1954
1953
1952
1951
1950
49.2 41.9 43.4 48.8 60.2 55.3 64.0 73.1 57.9 74.0 60.7 77.2
66.5 38.7 46.8 54.4 44.9 66.5 53.9 53.2 44.3 57.3 51.4 40.1
17.5 16.0 19.1 24.6 26.7 29.9 35.2 41.6 43.9 51.1 77.7 50.9
11.7 10.7 14.5 18.7 18.7 23.4 22.3 21.7 19.7 24.0 18.7 16.6
Source: Bureau of the Census.

TABLE 3.—*Estimated breakdown of plywood imports between softwoods and hardwoods, 1952–56* [1]

[Thousand square feet, surface measure]

| Country | 1956 | | | 1955 | | | 1954 | | | 1953 | | | 1952 | | |
|---|---|---|---|---|---|---|---|---|---|---|---|---|---|---|---|
| | Softwood | Hardwood | Total | Softwood | Hardwood | Total | Softwood | Hardwood | Total | Softwood | Hardwood | Total | Softwood | Hardwood | Total |
| Canada | 502 | 80,742 | 81,244 | 794 | 98,544 | 99,338 | 833 | 70,242 | 71,075 | 251 | 50,596 | 50,847 | 119 | 56,975 | 57,094 |
| Finland | -------- | 33,876 | 33,876 | 29 | 40,531 | 40,560 | 7 | 32,181 | 32,188 | -------- | 31,894 | 31,894 | 115 | 4,550 | 4,665 |
| New Guinea | 9,306 | -------- | 9,306 | 6,829 | -------- | 6,829 | 6,066 | -------- | 6,066 | -------- | -------- | -------- | -------- | -------- | -------- |
| West Germany | -------- | 4,734 | 4,734 | -------- | 3,673 | 3,673 | 76 | 4,810 | 4,886 | -------- | 2,201 | 2,201 | -------- | 877 | 877 |
| Italy | -------- | 3,068 | 3,068 | -------- | 4,847 | 4,847 | 7 | 6,035 | 6,042 | -------- | 6,717 | 6,717 | -------- | 34 | 34 |
| Belgium | -------- | 2,521 | 2,521 | 8 | 1,122 | 1,130 | -------- | 665 | 665 | -------- | 179 | 179 | -------- | 10 | 10 |
| Mexico | 87 | 349 | 436 | 724 | 2,894 | 3,618 | 749 | 2,640 | 3,389 | 253 | 1,877 | 2,130 | 200 | 728 | 928 |
| Sweden | 243 | 39 | 282 | 357 | 33 | 390 | 529 | 253 | 782 | 517 | 99 | 616 | -------- | 57 | 57 |
| Austria | -------- | 237 | 237 | -------- | 432 | 432 | 64 | 614 | 678 | -------- | 150 | 150 | -------- | 112 | 112 |
| Brazil | 31 | -------- | 31 | 11 | -------- | 11 | 113 | -------- | 113 | 491 | 30 | 521 | 414 | -------- | 414 |
| Australia | 4 | -------- | 4 | 59 | -------- | 59 | 136 | -------- | 136 | -------- | -------- | -------- | -------- | -------- | -------- |
| All others | -------- | 569,983 | 569,983 | -------- | 466,880 | 466,880 | -------- | 308,618 | 308,618 | -------- | 125,592 | 125,592 | -------- | 21,591 | 21,591 |
| Total | 10,173 | 695,549 | 705,722 | 8,811 | 618,956 | 627,767 | 8,580 | 426,058 | 434,638 | 1,512 | 219,335 | 220,847 | 848 | 84,934 | 85,782 |

[1] Estimated on basis of species data reported by Bureau of the Census, supplemental data from the U. S. Tariff Commission, and species production data of country of origin.

TABLE 4.—*United States imports of plywood by species, 1952–56*

[Quantity in square feet, surface measure; value in dollars]

| Country | 1956 | | 1955 | | 1954 | | 1953 | | 1952 | |
|---|---|---|---|---|---|---|---|---|---|---|
| | Quantity | Value | Quantity | Value | Quantity | Value | Quantity | Value | Quantity | Value |
| Red pine plywood: | | | | | | | | | | |
| Finland | | | | | | | | | 114, 912 | 11, 703 |
| Italy | | | | | 6, 400 | 339 | | | | |
| Belgium | | | 7, 868 | 450 | | | | | | |
| Mexico | | | | | 25, 000 | 2, 722 | | | | |
| Sweden | | | 45, 000 | 2, 659 | 400, 824 | 32, 178 | 68, 862 | 3, 805 | | |
| Total | | | 52, 868 | 3, 109 | 432, 224 | 35, 239 | 68, 862 | 3, 805 | 114, 912 | 11, 703 |
| Birch plywood: | | | | | | | | | | |
| Japan | 31, 007, 193 | 3, 855, 559 | 17, 082, 802 | 1, 894, 336 | 7, 509, 725 | 836, 402 | 7, 358, 485 | 768, 835 | 802, 846 | 88, 838 |
| Canada | 80, 742, 355 | 10, 360, 629 | 98, 544, 347 | 12, 630, 948 | 69, 929, 972 | 9, 444, 251 | 50, 595, 783 | 7, 561, 136 | 56, 904, 634 | 8, 681, 313 |
| Finland | 33, 672, 220 | 4, 015, 138 | 40, 530, 666 | 4, 405, 489 | 32, 180, 584 | 3, 270, 559 | 31, 893, 812 | 2, 690, 004 | 4, 372, 165 | 326, 474 |
| West Germany | 11, 553 | 1, 583 | 7, 721 | 733 | | | 1, 040 | 230 | | |
| Italy | | | 40, 008 | 3, 532 | 125, 476 | 11, 460 | 6, 800 | 1, 475 | | |
| Belgium | 42, 249 | 3, 611 | | | | | | | | |
| France | | | | | | | 9, 612 | 1, 027 | | |
| Denmark | | | 55, 778 | 4, 120 | | | | | | |
| Israel and Palestine | | | | | | | 24, 967 | 1, 718 | | |
| Mexico | | | | | 289, 506 | 20, 779 | | | | |
| Switzerland | 209, 781 | 26, 419 | | | | | 134, 736 | 6, 868 | 35, 295 | 1, 496 |
| Sweden | 39, 185 | 6, 542 | 32, 670 | 7, 257 | 253, 083 | 31, 993 | 98, 512 | 8, 473 | 55, 881 | 4, 557 |
| Cuba | 25, 000 | 2, 077 | | | | | | | | |
| Poland | | | 140, 165 | 15, 041 | 26, 575 | 3, 708 | | | | |
| Norway | | | 144, 726 | 6, 175 | | | | | | |
| Total | 145, 749, 536 | 18, 271, 558 | 156, 578, 883 | 18, 967, 631 | 110, 314, 921 | 13, 619, 152 | 90, 123, 747 | 11, 039, 766 | 62, 170, 821 | 9, 102, 678 |
| Alder and Parana pine plywood: | | | | | | | | | | |
| Brazil | 2, 650 | 498 | 10, 609 | 411 | 61, 677 | 2, 803 | 429, 524 | 27, 704 | 414, 434 | 22, 652 |
| Total | 2, 650 | 498 | 10, 609 | 411 | 61, 677 | 2, 803 | 429, 524 | 27, 704 | 414, 434 | 22, 652 |
| Spanish cedar plywood: | | | | | | | | | | |
| Mexico | | | 40, 980 | 4, 423 | 155, 700 | 14, 564 | 867, 539 | 65, 170 | 236, 692 | 19, 842 |
| Brazil | | | | | | | 709 | 168 | | |
| Total | | | 40, 980 | 4, 423 | 155, 700 | 14, 564 | 868, 248 | 65, 338 | 236, 692 | 19, 842 |

NOTES.—Imports of plywood are classified by the Bureau of the Census in the following schedule A classifications: 4209100, red pine; 4209300, birch; 4209450, Alder and Parama pine; 4209550, Spanish cedar; 4209590, other. Imports of the species shown separately, 1952–56, are given in table 4. The balance of the plywood imported in those years was included in the classification 4209590, other. In previous years, plywood imports have been classified under the following separate classifications: 1934–47: Birch, alder, other. 1948–March 1950: Birch, alder, western redcedar, other. April 1950–May 1951: Birch, alder, western redcedar, red pine, other. June 1951–53: Birch, alder, western redcedar, red pine, Spanish cedar, Parama pine, other. (Imports of western redcedar, not shown in table 4, were recorded as 8 square feet ($1) in 1952, none in 1953.) 1954: Birch, alder and Parama pine, red pine, Spanish cedar, other.

Source: Bureau of the Census.

TABLE 5.—*United States imports of plywood by customs districts, 1956*

| Customs district | Square feet | Customs district | Square feet | Customs district | Square feet |
|---|---|---|---|---|---|
| Maine-New Hampshire | 6,100 | Georgia | 508,554 | Washington | 52,167,014 |
| Vermont | 1,098,098 | Florida | 13,456,575 | Hawaii | 1,089,849 |
| Massachusetts | 9,487,948 | Mobile | 2,047,174 | Montana and Idaho | 3,460 |
| St. Lawrence | 5,720,274 | New Orleans | 9,632,447 | Wisconsin | 17,593 |
| Rochester | 62,928 | Sabine | 46,200 | Michigan | 73,715,151 |
| Buffalo | 386,114 | Galveston | 12,690,200 | Chicago | 4,916,510 |
| New York | 85,506,313 | Laredo | 21,619 | Ohio | 166,834 |
| Philadelphia | 7,569,310 | El Paso | 52,256 | Tennessee | 2,969,972 |
| Maryland | 21,485,133 | San Diego | 586,822 | St. Louis | 191,472 |
| Virginia | 29,567,075 | Los Angeles | 205,766,279 | Puerto Rico | 5,249,381 |
| South Carolina | 2,511,425 | San Francisco | 80,677,877 | | |
| | | Oregon | 76,348,047 | Total | 705,722,004 |

Source: Bureau of the Census.

TABLE 6.—*Changes in United States rates of duty on plywood, 1922–58*

[Percent ad valorem]

| Species | Tariff rate in— | | | | | | | | | |
|---|---|---|---|---|---|---|---|---|---|---|
| | Act of 1922 | Act of 1930 | 1936 [1] | GATT, Geneva, 1948 | GATT, Annecy, 1949 | GATT, Torquay, 1950 | 1954 | 1956 [2] | 1957 [2] | 1958 [2] |
| Western redcedar | 33⅓ | 40 | ------ | [3] 20 | ------ | ------ | 20 | ------ | ------ | ------ |
| Birch | 33⅓ | 50 | [1] 25 | ------ | [4] 20 | [3] 15 | 15 | ------ | ------ | ------ |
| Alder | 33⅓ | 50 | ------ | ------ | [5] 25 | ------ | 25 | ------ | ------ | ------ |
| Parana pine | (6) | (6) | ------ | ------ | ------ | [7] 25 | 25 | ------ | ------ | ------ |
| Red pine | (6) | (6) | ------ | ------ | [5] 20 | ------ | 20 | [5] 19 | [5] 18 | [5] 17 |
| Spanish cedar | (6) | (6) | ------ | ------ | ------ | 40 | 40 | ------ | ------ | ------ |
| Other | 33⅓ | 40 | ------ | ------ | ------ | [8] 20 | 20 | ------ | ------ | ------ |

1 Trade agreement with Finland, effective November 1936.
2 Effective July 1. Negotiated at Geneva, Switzerland, January–May 1956.
3 Concession granted to Canada.
4 Concession granted to Finland.
5 Concession granted to Sweden.
6 Included in "Other."
7 Concession granted to Brazil.
8 Concession granted to Canada, Benelux (Belgium, Netherlands, Luxembourg), and France.

NOTES.—From Oct. 26, 1946, to Aug. 15, 1947, imports of plywood, because of the housing emergency, were exempt from duties in accordance with Presidential Proclamation No. 2708. Trade Agreements Act of June 12, 1934, as amended, and Trade Agreements Extension Act of 1951, as amended, provide for generalization of trade-agreement concessions to all countries except Soviet-bloc countries. Article II of the General Agreement on Tariffs and Trade (GATT) provides for generalization of GATT concessions to GATT members.

Source: Summaries of Tariff Information, vol. 4, Wood and Manufactures; General Agreement on Tariffs and Trade Schedule XX; Annecy protocol; Torquay protocol; 6th protocol. Geneva.

TABLE 7.—*World production of plywood, 1946–55* [1]

[Thousand cubic meters; 1,000 cubic meters equal 1,131 square feet, ⅜-inch basis, or 1,696 square feet, ¼-inch basis]

| Region | 1946 | 1951 | 1952 | 1953 | 1954 | 1955 |
|---|---|---|---|---|---|---|
| Europe | 480 | 1,470 | 1,360 | 1,505 | 1,885 | 2,040 |
| Finland | 150 | 314 | 233 | 270 | 346 | 363 |
| France | 44 | 144 | 144 | 147 | 191 | 226 |
| Germany, West | 60 | 480 | 419 | 484 | 630 | 649 |
| Italy | 25 | 140 | 140 | 140 | 150 | 150 |
| Portugal | [2] 5 | 25 | 30 | 32 | 31 | [2] 40 |
| Spain | [2] 10 | 30 | 30 | 35 | 40 | [2] 40 |
| Sweden | 42 | 57 | 50 | 45 | 56 | [2] 60 |
| United Kingdom | 38 | 39 | 29 | 34 | 51 | 54 |
| Yugoslavia | 10 | 22 | 22 | 24 | 36 | 41 |
| U. S. S. R. | [2] 400 | [2] 850 | 883 | 946 | 1,024 | [2] 1,070 |
| North America | 1,990 | 4,090 | 4,240 | 4,930 | 5,020 | 6,110 |
| Canada | 192 | 344 | 351 | 460 | 524 | 611 |
| United States | 1,800 | 3,750 | 3,890 | 4,470 | [2] 4,500 | [2] 5,500 |
| Latin America | 145 | 150 | 140 | 160 | 180 | 185 |
| Argentina | [2] 20 | 48 | 33 | 29 | 31 | [2] 35 |
| Brazil | 110 | 67 | 63 | 79 | 93 | [2] 100 |
| Africa | 15 | 80 | 50 | 80 | 80 | 80 |
| Asia | 90 | 310 | 415 | 515 | 655 | 830 |
| India | 13 | 26 | 34 | 23 | 29 | 35 |
| Israel | | | 8 | 11 | 16 | 20 |
| Japan | 67 | 228 | 298 | 409 | 535 | 700 |
| Philippines | | 23 | 34 | 30 | 40 | 45 |
| Pacific area | 58 | 83 | 64 | 81 | 95 | 105 |
| Australia | 48 | 68 | 50 | 67 | 81 | 90 |
| New Zealand | 10 | 15 | 14 | 14 | 14 | 15 |
| World total | 3,180 | 7,030 | 7,150 | 8,220 | 8,940 | 10,420 |

[1] Regional and world totals include some country estimates. No estimate is available for China.
[2] Estimated figures.

Source. Unasylva, vol. 10, No. 3, September 1956 (publication of the Food and Agricultural Organization of the United Nations).

Tables 9 and 10 are a continuation of tables 1 and 4, respectively, and of table 8 through the first half of 1957.

TABLE 9.—*United States imports of plywood by country of origin, January–June 1957*

[Quantity, thousand square feet, surface measure]

| Country | Quantity | Value |
|---|---|---|
| Japan | 338, 538 | $21, 808, 195 |
| Canada | 31, 895 | 3, 894, 225 |
| Finland | 12, 528 | 1, 398, 777 |
| Philippine Republic | 13, 906 | 1, 038, 109 |
| French Equatorial Africa | 5, 339 | 484, 392 |
| New Guinea | 2, 510 | 179, 511 |
| West Germany | 2, 358 | 274, 155 |
| Surinam | 3, 159 | 318, 331 |
| Italy | 812 | 40, 656 |
| Netherlands | 1, 670 | 283, 059 |
| Belgium and Luxembourg | 2, 922 | 275, 189 |
| United Kingdom | 1, 086 | 260, 276 |
| France | 740 | 98, 268 |
| Denmark | 690 | 48, 643 |
| Spain | 705 | 74, 438 |
| Israel | 276 | 19, 622 |
| Mexico | 1, 002 | 127, 998 |
| Taiwan | 1, 221 | 47, 624 |
| Panama | 106 | 22, 208 |
| Switzerland | 41 | 4, 804 |
| Guatemala | 269 | 10, 315 |
| Sweden | 96 | 6, 164 |
| Austria | 40 | 13, 727 |
| Honduras | 201 | 25, 052 |
| Belgian Congo | | |
| Portugal | 14 | $1, 800 |
| Nansei and Nanpo Islands | 490 | 15, 240 |
| Canal Zone | | |
| Brazil | 13 | 749 |
| Cuba | | |
| Hong Kong | | |
| British Guiana | | |
| Union of South Africa | | |
| Ecuador | | |
| Poland and Danzig | | |
| Australia | | |
| Gold Coast | 55 | 5, 471 |
| French West Africa | | |
| Norway | | |
| Yugoslavia | | |
| India | | |
| French Morocco | | |
| Netherland Antilles | 14 | 1, 127 |
| Anglo-Egypt Sudan | 181 | 15, 792 |
| Thailand | 27 | 1, 370 |
| Costa Rica | 176 | 2, 653 |
| El Salvador | 149 | 20, 350 |
| Total | 423, 229 | 30, 818, 290 |

Source: Bureau of Census.

TABLE 10.—*United States imports, birch plywood, January–June 1957*

[Quantity, 1,000 square feet surface measure]

| Country | Quantity | Value |
|---|---|---|
| Japan | 12, 239 | $1, 597, 973 |
| Canada | 31, 767 | 3, 873, 641 |
| Finland | 12, 482 | 1, 395, 219 |
| Switzerland | 41 | 4, 804 |
| Thailand | 23 | 959 |
| Sweden | 2 | 606 |
| Total | 56, 554 | 6, 873, 202 |

Source: Bureau of Census.

Table 11 is a table contained in the report of the Tariff Commission on hardwood plywood, June 1955, which has been continued through the first half of 1957. This table gives the hardwood plywood United States imports for consumption by country of origin and quantity.

TABLE 11.—*Hardwood plywood: United States imports for consumption, by kinds and by specified sources, specified years 1937–56; and 1st 6 months 1957*

[Quantity, thousand square feet, surface measure]

| Type of plywood, and country | 1937 [1] | 1939 [1] | 1946 [1] | 1947 [1] | 1948 [1] | 1949 [1] | 1950 [1] | 1951 [1] | 1952 [1] | 1953 [1] | 1954 [2] | 1955 [2] | 1956 [2] | 1957 [2] (1st 6 months) |
|---|---|---|---|---|---|---|---|---|---|---|---|---|---|---|
| Birch plywood: | | | | | | | | | | | | | | |
| Japan | 21 | 24 | | | | | 230 | 803 | 803 | 7,358 | 7,510 | 17,083 | 31,007 | 12,239 |
| Canada | 16 | 1 | 4,587 | 12,115 | 17,811 | 15,529 | 49,683 | 46,907 | 56,905 | 50,596 | 69,930 | 98,544 | 80,742 | 31,767 |
| Finland | 561 | 1,070 | 13,569 | 10,912 | 307 | 675 | 1,308 | 2,566 | 4,372 | 31,890 | 32,181 | 40,531 | 33,672 | 12,482 |
| Surinam | | | | | | | | | | | | | | |
| France | | | | | | | | | | 10 | | | | |
| Italy | | | | | | | | 20 | | 7 | 125 | 40 | | |
| Mexico | | | | | | | | | | | 290 | | | |
| All other | 10 | 346 | 6 | 291 | 772 | | | 132 | 91 | 259 | 280 | 382 | 328 | 41 |
| Total | 608 | 1,441 | 18,162 | 23,318 | 18,890 | 16,204 | 51,221 | 50,428 | 62,171 | 90,120 | 110,316 | 156,580 | 145,749 | 56,529 |
| All other hardwood plywood: | | | | | | | | | | | | | | |
| Japan | 3,273 | 1,383 | | | 22 | 859 | 4,898 | 12,091 | 16,539 | 97,620 | 281,503 | 411,543 | 496,014 | 326,299 |
| Canada | 2 | 3 | 164 | 447 | 195 | 168 | 39 | 99 | 70 | 31 | 312 | | 502 | (3) |
| Finland | 9 | | | | | | | 8 | 178 | | | | 204 | (3) |
| Surinam | | | | | | 10 | 644 | 1,908 | 2,529 | 4,394 | 4,276 | 3,919 | 3,894 | 3,159 |
| France | 4 | 23 | | | | | 33 | 20 | 378 | 7,585 | 4,904 | 4,462 | 1,574 | 740 |
| Italy | | | | | | | 110 | 398 | 34 | 6,710 | 6,042 | 4,807 | 3,068 | 812 |
| Mexico | | | 1,863 | 2,715 | 794 | 418 | 825 | 532 | 728 | 1,830 | 2,640 | 2,894 | 349 | (3) |
| All other | 625 | 9 | 116 | 2 | 78 | 208 | 306 | 1,277 | 2,304 | 10,572 | 16,165 | 34,751 | 44,195 | 31,872 |
| Total | 3,913 | 1,418 | 2,143 | 3,164 | 1,089 | 1,663 | 6,855 | 16,333 | 22,760 | 128,742 | 315,742 | 462,376 | 695,549 | [4] 362,892 |
| All hardwood plywood: | | | | | | | | | | | | | | |
| Japan | 3,294 | 1,407 | | | 22 | 859 | 5,128 | 12,894 | 17,342 | 104,978 | 289,013 | 428,626 | 527,021 | 338,538 |
| Canada | 18 | 4 | 4,751 | 12,562 | 18,006 | 15,697 | 49,722 | 47,006 | 56,975 | 50,627 | 70,242 | 98,544 | 81,244 | 31,767 |
| Finland | 570 | 1,070 | 13,569 | 10,912 | 307 | 675 | 1,308 | 2,574 | 4,550 | 31,890 | 32,181 | 40,531 | 33,876 | 12,482 |
| Surinam | | | | | | 10 | 644 | 1,908 | 2,529 | 4,394 | 4,276 | 3,919 | 3,894 | 3,159 |
| France | 4 | 23 | | | | | 33 | 20 | 378 | 7,595 | 4,904 | 4,462 | 1,574 | 740 |
| Italy | | | | | | | 110 | 418 | 34 | 6,717 | 6,167 | 4,847 | 3,068 | 812 |
| Mexico | | | 1,863 | 2,715 | 794 | 418 | 825 | 532 | 728 | 1,830 | 2,640 | 2,894 | 349 | |
| All other | 635 | 355 | 122 | 293 | 850 | 208 | 306 | 1,409 | 2,395 | 10,831 | 16,445 | 35,133 | 44,523 | 31,913 |
| Total | 4,521 | 2,859 | 20,305 | 26,482 | 19,979 | 17,867 | 58,076 | 66,761 | 84,931 | 218,862 | 426,058 | 618,956 | 695,549 | 419,421 |

[1] U. S. Tariff Commission Hardwood Plywood Report, 1955.
[2] U. S. Bureau of Census.
[3] This figure not available.
[4] Figure reflects all hardwood plywood except unavilable figures for Canada, Mexico, Brazil, Sweden, Finland, and New Guinea.

Table 12 is a table contained in the report of the Tariff Commission on hardwood plywood, June 1955, which has been continued through the first half of 1957. The table gives the hardwood plywood United States imports for consumption by value per 1,000 square feet of birch and other species.

From the statistics set out in tables 11 and 12, the Department of Commerce, Forest Products Division, Business and Defense Service Administration, has compiled the following tables which show the average dutiable value or sales price, f. o. b. exporting country:

Table 13, which follows, covers the period 1951–56 and shows two facts of extreme importance; (1) the average price of all the Japanese plywood, door panels, all sizes and thicknesses, fancy face, grooved, special construction, etc., was $63.20 whereas the average price for plywood imported from other countries was $117.85; and (2) the average price of imports from other countries has gone down steadily from an average in 1951 of $129.51 to $115.84 in 1956.

Table 14 is a continuation of table 13 for the first half of 1957. This table also shows two significant facts: (1) The prices of Japanese plywood have increased somewhat since 1956, which fact is not to be attributed to an increase in unit price but rather to an increase in the percentage of thicker panels imported from Japan; (2) the average prices from countries other than Japan have fallen from $115.84 in 1956 to $106.26 for the first half of 1957. With Japan steadily increasing its shipments to the United States at prices approximately one-half the average for other exporting countries, the countries other than Japan have been forced to make steadily increasing reductions in price. This has been extremely detrimental to the domestic industry, as the forcing down of the prices of imports from countries other than Japan have increased the differential between the domestic prices and the prices of imports from countries other than Japan.

Table 15, set out below, was compiled by the Forest Products Division, BDSA, Department of Commerce, from reports of foreign trade of Japan and Foreign Service dispatches. It should be noted that in 1956 Japan changed its method of reporting so that the thickness groupings for quantity and price do not correspond with prior years. In addition, all thickness reporting for plywood other than lauan was discontinued. The change in reporting came after the domestic industry had questioned the Japanese quota. The present method of reporting precludes checking of exports against published quota figures.

Table 15 is significant in that it shows the extremely low prices of the Japanese plywood.

Table 16 also was compiled by the Forest Products Division, BDSA, from the same sources used in compilation of table 14. Table 16 gives the percentages by species and thickness. Again we are confronted with the change in method of reporting in 1956, which prevents a comparative analysis of 1956 with prior years.

TABLE 12.—*Hardwood plywood: United States imports for consumption, by kinds and by specified sources, specified years 1937 to 1956; and 1st 6 months of 1957*

[Unit value, per 1,000 square feet]

| Type of plywood, and country | 1937 [1] | 1939 [1] | 1946 [1] | 1947 [1] | 1948 [1] | 1949 [1] | 1950 [1] | 1951 [1] | 1952 [1] | 1953 [1] | 1954 [2] | 1955 [2] | 1956 [2] | 1957 [2] (1st 6 months) |
|---|---|---|---|---|---|---|---|---|---|---|---|---|---|---|
| Birch plywood: | | | | | | | | | | | | | | |
| Japan | $34 | $26 | | | | | $97 | $124 | $111 | $104 | $111 | $110 | $121 | $130 |
| Canada | 11 | 49 | $149 | $164 | $144 | $124 | 120 | 147 | 153 | 149 | 135 | 128 | 128 | 122 |
| Finland | 30 | 19 | 62 | 36 | 93 | 71 | 49 | 72 | 75 | 84 | 102 | 108 | 119 | 112 |
| Surinam | | | | | | | | | | | | | | |
| France | | | | | | | | | | 107 | | | | |
| Italy | | | | | | | | 72 | | 217 | 91 | | | |
| Mexico | | | | | | | | | | | 71 | | | |
| All other | 41 | 25 | 82 | 112 | 71 | | | 142 | 66 | 67 | 127 | 87 | 122 | 117 |
| Average | 30 | 20 | 84 | 103 | 140 | 122 | 118 | 142 | 146 | 122 | 124 | 108 | 123 | 120 |
| All other hardwood plywood: | | | | | | | | | | | | | | |
| Japan | 17 | 14 | | | 78 | 81 | 58 | 77 | 61 | 62 | 56 | 62 | 60 | 62 |
| Canada [3] | 38 | 20 | 142 | 173 | 132 | 97 | 130 | 173 | 117 | 169 | | | | |
| Finland | 45 | | | | | | | 218 | 73 | | | | | |
| Surinam | | | | | | 115 | 95 | 89 | 95 | 86 | 94 | 108 | 54 | 100 |
| France | 56 | 43 | | | | | 104 | 129 | 61 | 82 | 79 | 75 | 130 | 134 |
| Italy | | | | | | | 283 | 196 | 91 | 55 | 53 | 52 | 126 | 169 |
| Mexico [3] | | | 119 | 123 | 136 | 101 | 114 | 127 | 133 | 92 | | | | |
| All other | 23 | 29 | 107 | 126 | 91 | 90 | 124 | 107 | 110 | 116 | 153 | 108 | 100 | 91 |
| Average | 18 | 14 | 120 | 130 | 131 | 89 | 75 | 86 | 72 | 69 | | | | |
| All hardwood plywood: | | | | | | | | | | | | | | |
| Japan | 17 | 14 | | | 78 | 81 | 59 | 80 | 63 | 65 | 66 | 64 | 64 | 64 |
| Canada [3] | 14 | 26 | 149 | 164 | 144 | 123 | 120 | 147 | 152 | 149 | | | | |
| Finland | 30 | 19 | 62 | 36 | 93 | 71 | 49 | 72 | 75 | 84 | | | | |
| Surinam | | | | | | 115 | 95 | 89 | 95 | 86 | 94 | 108 | 54 | 100 |
| France | 61 | 43 | | | | | 105 | 126 | 61 | 82 | 79 | 75 | 130 | 134 |
| Italy | | | | | | | 283 | 191 | 92 | 55 | 53 | 52 | 126 | 169 |
| Mexico [3] | | | 119 | 123 | 136 | 101 | 114 | 128 | 133 | 92 | | | | |
| All other | 23 | 25 | 106 | 112 | 73 | 90 | 124 | 111 | 108 | 115 | 153 | 108 | 100 | 110 |
| Average | 20 | 17 | 88 | 107 | 140 | 119 | 113 | 129 | 127 | 91 | | | | |

[1] U. S. Tariff Commission hardwood plywood report, 1955.
[2] U. S. Bureau of Census.
[3] In the "All other" category "Other" hardwoods not separated from softwoods, so average value is not set out for Canada or Mexico.

TABLE 13.—*United States imports of plywood, 1951–56, dutiable value or sales price f. o. b. exporting country*

[Quantity, millions of square feet, surface measure; value, millions of dollars]

| Year | Imports from Japan | | | | Imports from countries other than Japan | | | | Total imports | | | |
|---|---|---|---|---|---|---|---|---|---|---|---|---|
| | Quantity | Value | Percent of total quantity | Price per thousand square feet surface measure [1] | Quantity | Value | Percent of total quantity | Price per thousand square feet surface measure [1] | Quantity | Value | Percent of total quantity | Price per thousand square feet surface measure [1] |
| 1951 | 12.9 | 1.0 | 17.5 | $77.52 | 61.0 | 7.9 | 82.5 | $129.51 | 73.9 | 8.9 | 100.0 | $120.43 |
| 1952 | 17.3 | 1.1 | 20.2 | 63.58 | 68.5 | 9.7 | 79.8 | 141.61 | 85.8 | 10.8 | 100.0 | 125.87 |
| 1953 | 105.0 | 6.9 | 47.6 | 65.71 | 115.8 | 13.2 | 52.4 | 113.99 | 220.8 | 20.1 | 100.0 | 100.10 |
| 1954 | 289.0 | 16.7 | 66.5 | 57.79 | 145.6 | 16.3 | 33.5 | 111.95 | 434.6 | 33.0 | 100.0 | 75.93 |
| 1955 | 428.6 | 27.6 | 68.3 | 64.40 | 199.2 | 22.8 | 31.7 | 114.46 | 627.8 | 50.4 | 100.0 | 80.28 |
| 1956 | 527.0 | 33.9 | 74.7 | 64.33 | 178.7 | 20.7 | 25.3 | 115.84 | 705.7 | 54.6 | 100.0 | 77.37 |
| Weighted average | | | | 63.20 | | | | 117.85 | | | | 82.75 |

[1] In general, prices are based on market or selling price and are f. o. b. the exporting country. United States import duties are excluded.

Source: Bureau of the Census.

Prepared in: Forest Products Division, Business and Defense Services Administration, Department of Commerce, Feb. 14, 1957.

TABLE 14.—*United States plywood imports, 1957 (1st 6 months), dutiable value or sales price f. o. b. exporting country*

[Quantity in million square feet, surface measure; value in million dollars]

| Month | Japan | | | | Other than Japan | | | | All countries | | | |
|---|---|---|---|---|---|---|---|---|---|---|---|---|
| | Quantity | Value | Percent of total quantity | Price per thousand square feet [1] | Quantity | Value | Percent of total quantity | Price per thousand square feet [1] | Quantity | Value | Percent of total quantity | Price per thousand square feet [1] |
| January | 53.2 | $3.2 | 81.0 | $60.66 | 12.5 | $1.3 | 19.0 | $102.13 | 65.7 | $4.5 | 100.0 | $68.55 |
| February | 45.8 | 2.9 | 80.2 | 63.51 | 11.3 | 1.2 | 19.8 | 107.41 | 57.1 | 4.1 | 100.0 | 72.20 |
| March | 62.1 | 4.0 | 80.7 | 64.34 | 14.8 | 1.6 | 19.3 | 109.46 | 76.9 | 5.6 | 100.0 | 73.04 |
| April | 60.8 | 4.0 | 80.4 | 65.58 | 14.9 | 1.7 | 19.6 | 114.24 | 75.7 | 5.7 | 100.0 | 75.13 |
| May | 63.2 | 4.1 | 81.7 | 64.87 | 14.2 | 1.6 | 18.3 | 112.68 | 77.4 | 5.7 | 100.0 | 73.64 |
| June | 53.4 | 3.6 | 75.9 | 67.42 | 17.0 | 1.6 | 24.1 | 94.12 | 70.4 | 5.2 | 100.0 | 73.86 |
| Weighted average | 338.5 | 21.8 | 80.0 | 64.40 | 84.7 | 9.0 | 20.0 | 106.26 | 423.2 | 30.8 | 100.0 | 72.78 |
| Annual rate, 1957 | 677.0 | | | | 169.4 | | | | 846.4 | | | |
| Actual, 1956 | 527.0 | | | | 178.7 | | | | 705.7 | | | |
| Increase (percent) | | | +28.5 | | | | | | | | +19.9 | |
| Decrease (percent) | | | | | | | −5.2 | | | | | |

[1] In general, prices are based on market or selling price and are f. o. b. the exporting country. United States import duties are excluded.

Source: Bureau of the Census.

Prepared in: Forest Products Division, Business and Defense Services Administration Department of Commerce, Aug. 21, 1957.

TABLE 15.—*Plywood exports from Japan, 1951–56, by species and thickness*

[Quantity in thousand square feet; value in thousand dollars]

| Species and thickness | 1951 | | | | | | 1952 | | | | | |
|---|---|---|---|---|---|---|---|---|---|---|---|---|
| | World | | | United States [1] | | | World | | | United States [1] | | |
| | Quantity | Value | Price per thousand square feet | Quantity | Value | Price per thousand square feet | Quantity | Value | Price per thousand square feet | Quantity | Value | Price per thousand square feet |
| Lauan | 102, 328 | 6, 273 | $61. 30 | 7, 374 | 561 | $76. 08 | 47, 257 | 2, 182 | $46. 17 | 18, 508 | 928 | $50. 14 |
| Other | 37, 064 | 2, 211 | 59. 65 | 4, 556 | 373 | 81. 87 | 10, 669 | 823 | 77. 14 | 5, 259 | 436 | 82. 90 |
| Total, plywood | 139, 392 | 8, 484 | 60. 86 | 11, 930 | 934 | 78. 29 | 57, 926 | 3, 005 | 51. 88 | 23, 767 | 1, 364 | 57. 39 |
| | 1953 [2] | | | | | | 1954 | | | | | |
| Lauan, total | 128, 571 | 7, 068 | $54. 97 | 85, 185 | 4, 994 | $58. 63 | 391, 635 | 20, 760 | $53. 01 | 228, 634 | 12, 951 | $56. 65 |
| Not over 3/16 inch | 100, 460 | 4, 687 | 46. 66 | 67, 859 | 3, 477 | 51. 24 | 336, 978 | 15, 930 | 47. 27 | 198, 060 | 10, 073 | 50. 86 |
| Over 3/16 inch but not 7/8 inch | 27, 807 | 2, 342 | 84. 22 | 17, 224 | 1, 504 | 87. 32 | 54, 448 | 4, 802 | 88. 19 | 30, 431 | 2, 863 | 94. 08 |
| Over 7/8 inch | 304 | 39 | 128. 29 | 102 | 13 | 127. 45 | 209 | 28 | 133. 97 | 143 | 15 | 104. 90 |
| Other, total | 28, 263 | 2, 443 | 86. 44 | 23, 396 | 2, 093 | 89. 46 | 51, 774 | 4, 756 | 91. 86 | 35, 181 | 3, 430 | 97. 50 |
| Not over 3/16 inch | 22, 093 | 1, 621 | 73. 37 | 18, 214 | 1, 371 | 75. 27 | 40, 935 | 3, 035 | 74. 14 | 27, 869 | 2, 154 | 77. 29 |
| Over 3/16 inch but not 7/8 inch | 6, 126 | 817 | 133. 37 | 5, 182 | 722 | 139. 33 | 10, 839 | 1, 721 | 158. 78 | 7, 312 | 1, 276 | 174. 51 |
| Over 7/8 inch | 44 | 5 | 113. 64 | | | | 0. 5 | 0. 4 | 800. 00 | | | |
| Total, plywood | 156, 834 | 9, 511 | 60. 64 | 108, 581 | 7, 087 | 65. 27 | 443, 409 | 25, 516 | 57. 55 | 263, 815 | 16, 381 | 62. 09 |

| | 1955 | | | | | | 1956 [2] | | | | | |
|---|---|---|---|---|---|---|---|---|---|---|---|---|
| Lauan, total | 542,508 | 27,755 | $51.16 | 367,293 | 19,692 | $53.61 | 559,405 | 28,653 | $51.22 | 429,003 | 22,542 | $52.55 |
| Not over 3/16 inch | 455,251 | 20,454 | 44.93 | 307,242 | 14,451 | 47.03 | | | | | | |
| Over 3/16 inch but not 7/8 inch | 86,534 | 7,197 | 83.17 | 59,889 | 5,202 | 86.86 | | | | | | |
| Over 7/8 inch | 723 | 104 | 143.85 | 162 | 39 | 240.74 | | | | | | |
| Not over 1/8 inch | | | | | | | 360,274 | 14,967 | 41.54 | 308.819 | 13,102 | 42.43 |
| 1/8 to 5/32 inch | | | | | | | 15,073 | 642 | 42.59 | 4,816 | 232 | 48.17 |
| 5/32 to 1/4 inch | | | | | | | 161,775 | 9,708 | 60.00 | 99,111 | 6,673 | 67.33 |
| 1/4 to 3/4 inch | | | | | | | 21,758 | 3,244 | 149.09 | 15,833 | 2,465 | 155.69 |
| Over 3/4 inch | | | | | | | 524 | 93 | 177.48 | 425 | 69 | 162.35 |
| Other, total | 87,002 | 8,782 | 100.94 | 71,674 | 7,640 | 106.59 | 141,504 | 14,097 | 99.62 | 127,291 | 13,119 | 103.06 |
| Not over 3/16 inch | 64,380 | 4,887 | 75.91 | 51,567 | 4,051 | 78.56 | | | | | | |
| Over 3/16 inch but not 7/8 inch | 22,378 | 3,868 | 172.85 | 19,865 | 3,562 | 179.31 | | | | | | |
| Over 7/8 inch | 244 | 27 | 110.66 | 242 | 27 | 111.57 | | | | | | |
| Total, plywood | 629,510 | 36,537 | 58.04 | 438,967 | 27,332 | 62.26 | 700,909 | 42,750 | 60.99 | 556,294 | 35,661 | 64.10 |

[1] Includes Puerto Rico, Virgin Islands, Hawaii.
[2] Thickness classifications were revised in 1953 and 1956.

Prepared by Forest Products Division, BDSA, Department of Commerce, based on annual returns of the foreign trade of Japan, 1951–55; 1956 data from Foreign Service Dispatch 1051, Tokyo, Apr. 4, 1957.

TABLE 16.—*Plywood exports from Japan to United States, 1953–56, ratio by species and thickness*

[Quantity, thousand square feet; value in thousand dollars]

| | 1953 | | | | 1954 | | | |
|---|---|---|---|---|---|---|---|---|
| | Quantity | Percent by thickness [1] | Value | Price per thousand square feet | Quantity | Percent by thickness [1] | Value | Price per thousand square feet |
| Lauan, total | 85,185 | 78.5 (100.0) | 4,994 | $58.63 | 228,634 | 86.7 (100.0) | 12,951 | $56.65 |
| Not over 3/16 inch | 67,859 | 62.5 (79.7) | 3,477 | 51.24 | 198,060 | 75.1 (86.6) | 10,073 | 50.86 |
| Over 3/16 inch but not 7/8 inch | 17,224 | 15.9 (20.2) | 1,504 | 87.32 | 30,431 | 11.5 (13.3) | 2,863 | 94.08 |
| Over 7/8 inch | 102 | .1 (.1) | 13 | 127.45 | 143 | .1 (.1) | 15 | 104.90 |
| Other, total | 23,396 | 21.5 (100.0) | 2,093 | 89.46 | 35,181 | 13.3 (100.0) | 3,430 | 97.50 |
| Not over 3/16 inch | 18,214 | 16.7 (77.9) | 1,371 | 75.27 | 27,869 | 10.5 (79.2) | 2,154 | 77.29 |
| Over 3/16 inch but not 7/8 inch | 5,182 | 4.8 (22.1) | 722 | 139.33 | 7,312 | 2.8 (20.8) | 1,276 | 174.51 |
| Over 7/8 inch | | | | | | | | |
| Total plywood | 108,581 | 100.0 | 7,087 | 65.27 | 263,815 | 100.0 | 16,381 | 62.09 |
| | 1955 | | | | 1956 [2] | | | |
| Lauan, total | 367,293 | 83.7 (100.0) | 19,692 | $53.61 | 429,003 | 77.1 (100.0) | 22,542 | $52.55 |
| Not over 3/16 inch | 307,242 | 70.0 (83.6) | 14,451 | 47.03 | | | | |
| Over 3/16 inch but not 7/8 inch | 59,889 | 13.6 (16.3) | 5,202 | 86.86 | | | | |
| Over 7/8 inch | 162 | .1 (.1) | 39 | 240.74 | | | | |
| Not over 1/8 inch | | | | | 308,819 | 55.5 (72.0) | 13,102 | 42.43 |
| 1/8 inch to 5/32 inch | | | | | 4,816 | .9 (1.1) | 232 | 48.17 |
| 5/32 inch to 1/4 inch | | | | | 99,111 | 17.8 (23.1) | 6,673 | 67.33 |
| 1/4 inch to 3/4 inch | | | | | 15,833 | 2.8 (3.7) | 2,465 | 155.69 |
| Over 3/4 inch | | | | | 425 | .1 (.1) | 69 | 162.35 |
| Other, total | 71,674 | 16.3 (100.0) | 7,640 | 106.59 | 127,291 | 22.9 (100.0) | 13,119 | 103.06 |
| Not over 3/16 inch | 51,567 | 11.7 (71.9) | 4,051 | 78.56 | | | | |
| Over 3/16 inch but not 7/8 inch | 19,865 | 4.5 (27.7) | 3,562 | 179.31 | | | | |
| Over 7/8 inch | 242 | .1 (.4) | 27 | 11.57 | | | | |
| Total plywood | 438,967 | 100.0 | 27,332 | 62.26 | 556,294 | 100.0 | 35,661 | 64.10 |

[1] Percent of species by thickness shown in parentheses.
[2] Thickness classifications revised, 1956.

Prepared by Forest Products Division, BDSA, Department of Commerce, based on Annual Returns of the Foreign Trade of Japan 1951–55; 1956 Data From Foreign Service Dispatch 1051, Tokyo, Apr. 4, 1957.

## SECTION IV. RATIO OF PLYWOOD IMPORTS TO DOMESTIC SHIPMENTS AND CONSUMPTION

Plywood imports have steadily taken an increasing portion of the domestic market. In 1951 imports represented only 8 percent of the total hardwood plywood sold in the domestic market. In the first half of 1957, imports represented 53 percent of all the hardwood plywood sold in the United States.

The following table 17 gives the quantitative figures on domestic shipments, imports, consumption, and the ratio of imports to domestic shipments and consumption.

TABLE 17.—*Ratio of plywood imports to domestic shipments and consumption, 1951–56 and 1st 6 months 1957* [1]

[Quantities in thousand square feet surface measure; ratios in percentage]

| Year | Imports | Domestic shipments | Consumption | Ratio of imports to domestic shipments | Ratio of imports to consumption | Percent increase in ratio of imports to domestic shipments over 1951 | Percent increase in ratio of imports to consumption over 1951 |
|---|---|---|---|---|---|---|---|
| 1951 | 73, 870 | 805, 249 | 879, 119 | 9. 2 | 8. 4 | | |
| 1952 | 85, 782 | 794, 857 | 880, 639 | 10. 8 | 9. 7 | 17. 4 | 15. 5 |
| 1953 | 220, 847 | 805, 632 | 1, 026, 479 | 27. 4 | 21. 5 | 197. 8 | 156. 0 |
| 1954 | 434, 638 | [2] 799, 124 | 1, 233, 762 | 54. 4 | 35. 2 | 491. 3 | 319. 0 |
| 1955 | 627, 767 | [3] 917, 784 | 1, 545, 551 | 68. 4 | 40. 6 | 643. 5 | 383. 0 |
| 1956 | 705, 722 | 884, 567 | 1, 590, 507 | 79. 8 | 44. 4 | 767. 4 | 428. 6 |
| 1st 6 months 1957 | 423, 229 | 382, 958 | 806, 187 | 110. 5 | 52. 5 | 1, 101. 1 | 525. 0 |

[1] All figures used in this table represent revisions made by Bureau of Census as recently as Sept. 11, 1957.
[2] Census of manufacturers, 1954.
[3] Sum of quarterly figures adjusted on an annual basis.

Source: U. S. Bureau of Census.

Table 18, which follows, is a graph illustrating the static condition of domestic market hardwood plywood shipments while imports soar from the bottom of the graph to exceed the domestic shipments in the first half of 1957.

TABLE 18

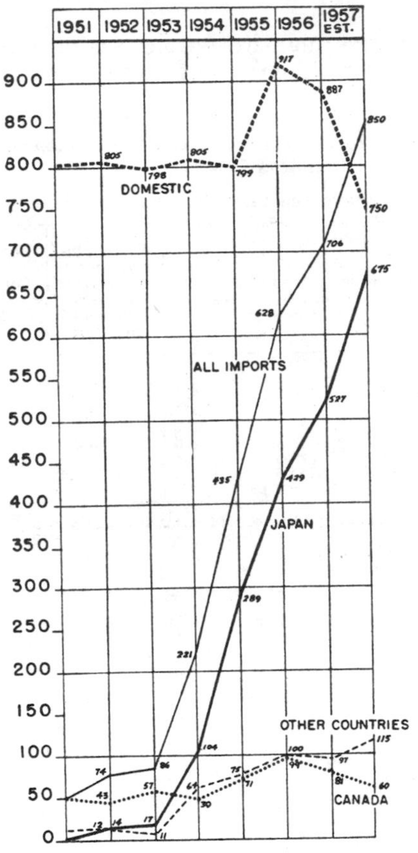


**DOMESTIC MARKET HARDWOOD PLYWOOD SHIPMENTS**

**PLYWOOD IMPORTS ***

**1951 - 1956**

* SOFTWOOD PLYWOOD IMPORTS REPRESENT LESS than 2 % OF TOTAL

SOURCE: U.S. BUREAU OF CENSUS

Tables 19 and 20 graphically illustrate the proportion of the domestic market which has been absorbed by imports. The eroding effect of the imports from Japan is disclosed by these charts, as we can see how the Japanese have constantly increased their proportion of the domestic market. A study of these circles in relation to the total quantity representing consumption, conclusively demonstrates that the American market hardwood plywood industry has not been permitted to share in the growth curve of consumption.

TABLE 19

# U.S. MARKET HARDWOOD PLYWOOD CONSUMPTION*
# 1951-1956

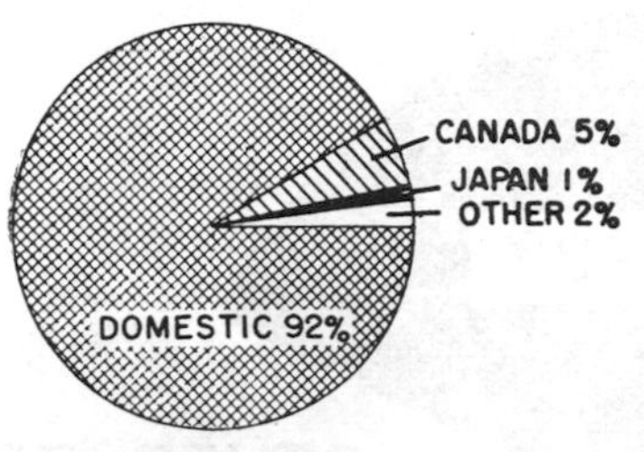


*1951 = 879 MILLION SQ. FT.*

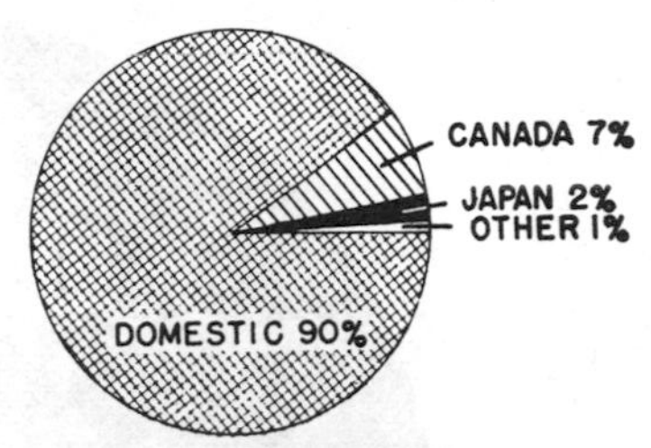


*1952 = 884 MILLION SQ. FT.*

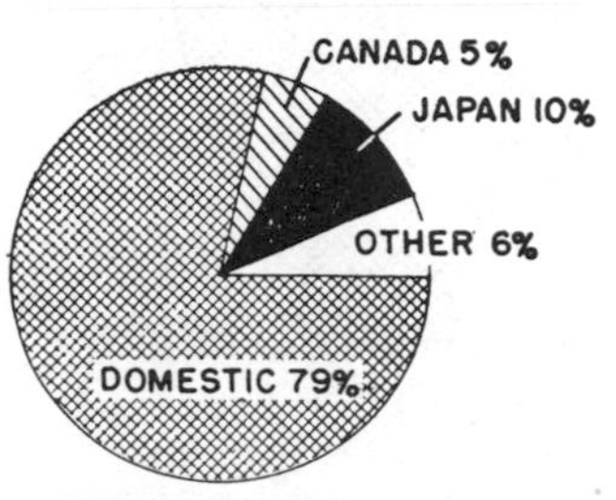


*1953 = 1026 MILLION SQ. FT.*

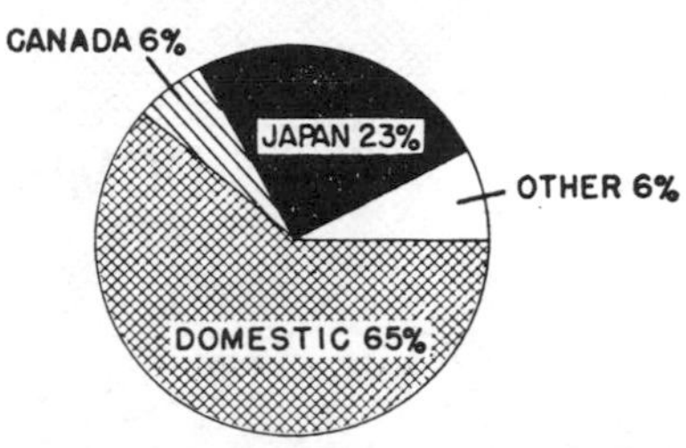


*1954 = 1234 MILLION SQ. FT.*

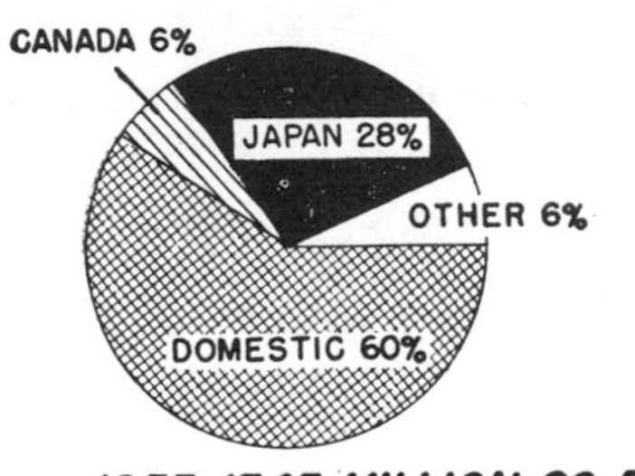

*1955 = 1545 MILLION SQ. FT.*

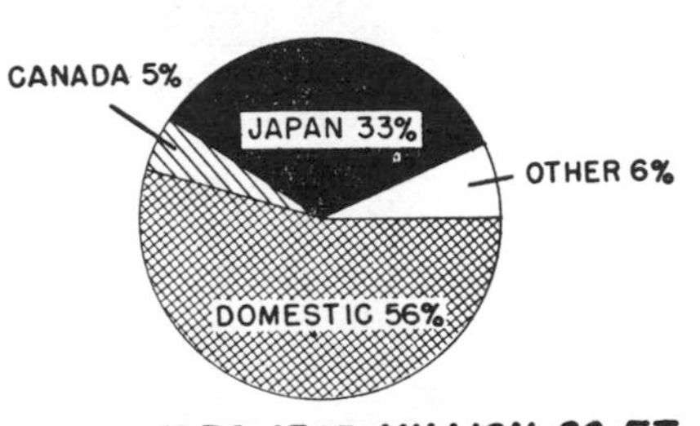


*1956 = 1593 MILLION SQ. FT.*

**Each circle equals 100% domestic hardwood plywood consumption in the United States in the year indicated.*

SOURCE: U.S. BUREAU OF CENSUS

TABLE 20

## U.S. MARKET HARDWOOD PLYWOOD CONSUMPTION FIRST HALF 1957

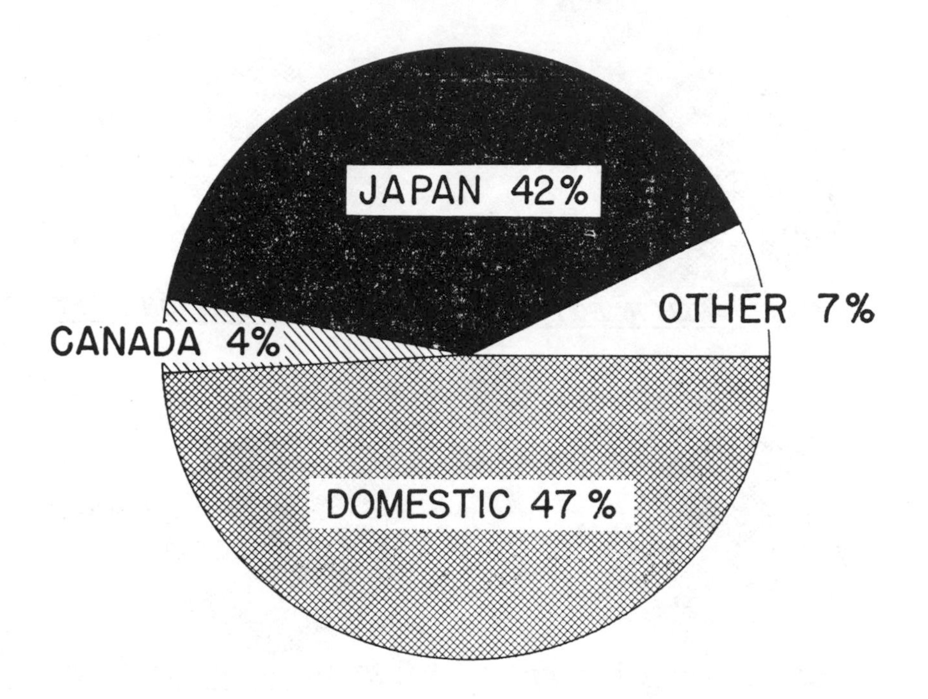


*FIRST HALF 1957 = 806 MILLION SQ.FT.*

SOURCE: U. S. BUREAU OF CENSUS

### SECTION V. IMPORTED PLYWOOD IS LOW PRICED

There is no dispute that imported plywoods are priced substantially below comparable plywood produced in the United States. The price differential between imported plywood and domestic market hardwood plywood establishes the unfair competition of the imported plywoods. This differential is attributable to the low wages in the foreign countries.

The Bureau of the Census in tabulating imports statistics on hardwood plywood reports the quantity in square feet surface measure and the price or value in dollars. Japan, however, reports exports of plywood on a thickness basis with values for each of the thickness groups. These figures establish a base which shows the very low price of the Japanese plywood exported to the United States.

The following table on comparative price figures on hardwood plywood imported from Japan and domestic market hardwood plywood, pinpoints this substantial price differential. Because Japan in 1956 changed its method of reporting, the figures for 1955 must be used. The prices quoted for domestic panels are based on an average for early 1957, a period following a reduction, consequently, the prices quoted are less than the prices in 1955. (Confirmed by BLS Wholesale Price Index, Hardwood Plywood.)

[Prices per thousand square feet, veneer core]

(Species listed on comparable grades and types and compete for same end-use application)

| *Average United States prices (f. o. b. mill)* | | *Average Japan prices (f. o. b. Japan)* [1] | |
|---|---|---|---|
| Gum: | | Lauan: | |
| ⅛ inch | $127.50 | ⅛ inch to 3/16 inch | [2] $47.03 |
| ¼ inch | 137.50 | ¼ inch to ⅞ inch | [2] 86.86 |
| ¾ inch | 312.50 | | |
| Lauan: | | Average all thicknesses | 53.61 |
| ⅛ inch | 135.00 | See above. | |
| ¼ inch | 150.00 | | |
| ¾ inch | 314.00 | | |
| Birch: | | | |
| ⅛ inch | 145.00 | See above. | |
| ¼ inch | 240.00 | | |
| ¾ inch | 467.00 | | |

[1] Plywood exports from Japan, Department of Commerce.
[2] Average.

Cost of production of the American producer exceeds the sales price of most imported plywoods. Tables 8, 9, and 10 show the country of origin, the quantity, and price or value of hardwood-plywood imports for the years 1939 through the first half of 1957.

Tables 13 and 14 show the average sales price or f. o. b. price of Japanese hardwood-plywood and plywood from other countries for the period 1951 through the first half of 1957.

The average production costs of the domestic producers can be obtained by breaking down the sales price into its cost factors. Table 3, prepared from reports received by Seidman & Seidman, certified public accountants, from 34 companies in the first half of 1956 and 36 companies in the second half of 1956 (averaged at 35) shows the ratio of costs to net dollar sales (100) as follows:

Using the ratios shown by the Seidman & Seidman report, the following table breaks down the average f. o. b. domestic mill price to its cost factors.

| | Thickness | | |
|---|---|---|---|
| | ⅛ inch | ¼ inch | ¾ inch |
| Gum plywood veneer core: | | | |
| F. o. b. mill price, thousand square feet | $127.50 | $137.50 | $312.50 |
| Materials consumed | 69.48 | 74.93 | 170.31 |
| Direct labor | 27.73 | 29.90 | 67.84 |
| Manufacturing overhead | 15.54 | 16.76 | 38.09 |
| General administrative and selling costs | 9.70 | 10.25 | 23.27 |
| Total costs | 122.25 | 131.84 | 299.51 |
| Profit before taxes | 5.25 | 5.66 | 12.99 |
| Birch veneer core: | | | |
| F. o. b. mill price, thousand square feet | 145.00 | 240.00 | 467.00 |
| Materials consumed | 79.02 | 130.80 | 264.52 |
| Direct labor | 31.55 | 52.22 | 101.62 |
| Manufacturing overhead | 17.68 | 29.26 | 56.92 |
| General administrative and selling costs | 10.80 | 17.88 | 34.79 |
| Total costs | 139.05 | 230.16 | 447.85 |
| Profit before taxes | 5.95 | 9.84 | 19.15 |
| Lauan veneer core: | | | |
| F. o. b. mill price, thousand square feet | 135.00 | 150.00 | 314.00 |
| Materials consumed | 73.57 | 81.75 | 170.82 |
| Direct labor | 29.38 | 32.64 | 68.32 |
| Manufacturing overhead | 16.46 | 17.29 | 38.07 |
| General administrative and selling costs | 10.05 | 10.17 | 23.39 |
| Total costs | 129.46 | 141.85 | 300.60 |
| Profit before taxes | 5.54 | 8.15 | 13.40 |

In the final analysis, the differential between the sales price of imported plywood and the production costs of domestic plywood must be considered in light of the present f. o. b. dock, duty-paid prices for imported hardwood plywood. The following table emphasizes this differential between the sales price of hardwood plywood imported from Japan and the domestic manufacturing production costs for a similar panel.

*Prices from L. V. Pease, Ltd., San Francisco, Calif., Aug. 15, 1957*

| | F. o. b. dock, duty-paid price of plywood from Japan | United States manufacturers' production cost |
|---|---|---|
| Lauan (rotary cut): | | |
| ⅛ inch by 4 feet by 8 feet | $76 | $129.46 |
| ¼ inch by 4 feet by 8 feet | 100 | 141.85 |
| ¾ inch by 4 feet by 8 feet | 280 | 300.60 |
| Sen (ash) ¼ inch by 4 feet by 8 inches | 125 | 230.10 |

SECTION VI. JAPANESE PLYWOOD INDUSTRY

Plants March 1957, 224; annual production capacity 3 billion square feet.[2] It is reported from Japan that new equipment installed or

[2] Foreign Service Dispatch 865.

being installed will increase capacity by at least 20 percent by the end of 1957 (3.6 billion square feet).

Japanese plywood production has increased from 619 million square feet in 1951 to 2.2 billion square feet in 1956 (360 percent greater). The Japanese domestic demand has increased from 382 million square feet in 1951 to 1.4 billion square feet in 1956. In 1951 there was 237 million square feet available for export, whereas in 1956 there was an exportable surplus of 784 million square feet (330 percent greater than 1951).[3]

The principal wood used for manufacturing export plywood is lauan, 77 percent, a wood not grown in Japan but imported from the Philippines and southeast Asia.

The domestic woods used for manufacturing export plywood are: Oak, birch, elm, basswood, ash and beech.

Sizes and thicknesses of Japanese plywood available for export conform to the hardwood plywood commercial standard CS35–56.[4]

Owing to modernized equipment, streamlined enterprise, and the improvement of manufacturing technique to the international level, the standard size has been enlarged from usual 3 by 6 feet to 4 by 8 feet (panel) (p. 38).[5]

*Japanese plywood exports to the world* [1]

| | Thousand square feet | Percent of production |
|---|---|---|
| 1951 | 153,422 | 19.1 |
| 1952 | 57,893 | 7.3 |
| 1953 | 154,251 | 14.8 |
| 1954 | 443,405 | 30.7 |
| 1955 | 629,510 | 33.5 |
| 1956 (estimate) | 784,444 | 35.4 |

[1] The Japan Lumber Industries, March 1957.

*Foreign markets for Japanese plywood exports* [1]

| | 1951 | 1952 | 1953 | 1954 | 1955 | 1956 |
|---|---|---|---|---|---|---|
| Asia | 4.9 | 21.1 | 6.1 | 2.7 | 2.5 | 3.4 |
| Europe | 30.4 | 18.9 | 10.7 | 17.4 | 15.3 | 7.6 |
| North America | 13.1 | 49.3 | 79.2 | 76.9 | 80.2 | 88.5 |
| South America | | .5 | .9 | 1.2 | .3 | .1 |
| Africa | 2.0 | 4.5 | .9 | .4 | .5 | .1 |
| Oceanic | 48.2 | 5.7 | 1.2 | 1.4 | 1.2 | .3 |
| Unknown | 1.4 | | .3 | | | |

[1] The Japan Lumber Industries, March 1957.

*Organizations and structure of plywood industry* [6]

There are five national organizations in the plywood industry in Japan. They are:

Japan Plywood Industry Association
Japan Plywood Adjustment Association
Japan Plywood Export Association
Japan Plywood Inspection Corp.
Japan Veneer Commercial Foundation

[3] The Japan Lumber Industries, March 1957.
[4] Id.
[5] Id.
[6] The Japan Lumber Industries, March 1957.

22806—58——73

*Japan Plywood Industry Association.*—Its activities include the study how to improve manufacturing technique, modernization of equipment, naturalization of management, better standardization, securing raw materials, preparation of statistical data, mapping out of general plan and policy in production and research work.

*Japan Plywood Adjustment Association.*—This was organized in April 1956 by plywood manufacturers throughout the country, and *its purpose is to adjust demand and supply.* Its membership comprises more than 90 percent of plywood manufacturers in Japan. Since May 1956, *it has successfully stabilized the market by regulating the entire* production *of plywood. In the coming 1957 fiscal year starting April the association plans to stabilize demand and supply of both foreign and domestic markets by restricting the production amounts for export and home consumption respectively.* (Emphasis supplied.)

*Japan Plywood Export Association.*—This is organized by plywood exporters with a membership of 88. *With a view of stabilizing oversea markets* * * *. (Emphasis supplied.)

*Japan Plywood Inspection Corp.*—This is an organ to grade and inspect plywood.

*Japan Veneer Commercial Foundation.*—Its main function is publicity work.

### SECTION VII. FAILURE OF THE JAPANESE EXPORT QUOTA ON PLYWOOD

The Japanese Plywood Exporters Association, in the latter part of 1955, formulated a regulation establishing a quota on the export of plywood to the continents of North and South America and to England.[7] The association's regulation affected exports during the last half of the Japanese fiscal year 1955 (October 1, 1955–March 31, 1956). On October 28, 1955, the Ministry of International Trade and Industry (MITI) issued order 54 which complemented the association's regulation.[8]

MITI Order 54 announced a quota on plywood made of lauan, sen, and birch except prefabricated case board. Prefabricated case board referred to plywood and veneer boards which were precut and formed in Japan to be assembled by the foreign importer or buyer into finished products, such as various types of furniture and boxes. The quantitative limitations of the quota were established on a 4-millimeter thickness basis. On March 3, 1956, a new plywood quota covering the fiscal year 1956 (April 1, 1956–March 31, 1957) was announced. MITI Order 54 applied to this quota and it included the plywood mentioned above on a 4-millimeter basis. This 4-millimeter basis is important, because all plywood thicker than 4 millimeters has to be converted under the quota, to 4-millimeter basis. This conversion affects the square footage allowable under the quota; i. e., 1 square foot, 8 millimeters (approximately one-third inch thickness) equals 2 square feet 4 millimeters (approximately one-eighth inch thickness).

Subsequently important changes were made in the quota, many of which were not reported until several months after the changes had been put into effect. In March 1956 [9] United Kingdom and Ireland

---

[7] Dispatch No. 360, October 19, 1955.
[8] Dispatch No. 414, November 9, 1955.
[9] Dispatch No. 864, March 27, 1956.

were excluded from the controls. In December 1956,[10] 15 months after the quota had been in effect, the following important changes were announced:

(*a*) Effective April 1, 1956, a change was made in the method of calculating the quantity of plywood to be exported under the quota allocation system. Square-footage measurement of plywood was no longer calculated on a thickness basis of 4 millimeters. The thickness basis was eliminated entirely and surface-measure basis employed, which permitted the Japanese to increase their plywood exports.

(*b*) Beginning July 1956, sen and birch plywood were removed from the quota. United States import statistics showed a fantastic increase in the imports of birch plywood from Japan for the last 6 months of 1956 compared with any previous 6-month period. Because sen plywood is not separately listed in United States import statistics, no statement can be made as to the effect of the removal of sen plywood from the quota.

(*c*) The Japanese announced that special types of plywood, such as fancy face, curved, strengthened, scarf-joint, 2-ply, 3-ply lumber core, ribbon grain, etc., had never been under quota control. If such were true, then any hardwood plywood could be classified in one of the above categories and could be exported outside the quota. For instance, fancy face could include all plywood with a grain figure, such as rotary-cut lauan, the principal item of Japanese plywood for export. MITI Order 54 did not provide for the exception of the above types of plywood.

These amendments had the effect of limiting the applicability of, if not abolishing, the quota. Obviously, at best only a portion of the plywood was covered by the quota, which was so flexible as to permit rapid adjustments to change the portion covered. In actual operation, the quota has been meaningless. The purpose of bringing these facts before the committee is to meet the repeated assertions that Japanese plywood exports are under strict export quota control.

The following tabulation illustrates the operation of the Japanese plywood export quota.

[Quantity, thousand square feet]

| Period | MITI [1] | Dispatch 626 [2] | United States imports [3] of plywood from Japan | Japan's [4] exports to United States, Canada, and South America |
|---|---|---|---|---|
| October-December 1955 | 98,400 | 124,137 | 104,198 | 124,856 |
| January-March 1956 | 108,000 | 131,947 | 91,130 | 111,415 |
| April-June 1956 | 100,000 | 104,896 | 115,785 | 144,042 |
| July-September 1956 | 100,000 | 89,359 | 152,329 | 159,717 |
| October-December 1956 | 100,000 | 89,200 | 167,777 | 199,138 |
| Total, 1956 | 408,000 | 415,402 | 527,021 | 614,312 |

[1] Dispatch No. 360, Oct. 19, 1955.
[2] Dispatch No. 626, Dec. 21, 1956.
[3] Bureau of Census.
[4] Japan's export statistics.

[10] Dispatch No. 626, December 21, 1956.

An analysis of the following tabulation will emphasize that the export quota was without meaning. United States import statistics show that the United States imports of plywood from Japan exceeded the quota; and Japan's export statistics show that plywood exports to the quota countries exceeded the quota. Although the quota was established to limit exports of plywood, exports climbed rapidly.

Amendments, revisions, deletions, and free interpretation were employed at will by Japan to liberalize the export of plywood, but at the same time to insist to the United States industry and others that Japan was adhering to the quota.

The most recent revision of the quota covering the period of January–June 1957 is most illustrative of how Japan controls the export of plywood under its quota system.

[Quantity in thousands of square feet]

| Period | Quota | United States imports of plywood from Japan |
|---|---|---|
| January–March 1957 | 89,993 | 161,097 |
| April–June 1957 | 91.800 | 177,441 |

Under the quota, Japan has increased plywood exports to the United States (on basis of United States import data) from 91 million square feet in the first quarter 1956 to 177 million square feet during the second quarter 1957, an increase of 95 percent. Obviously, the echoed and reechoed intent of the quota is without foundation.

In addition to the export quota, which is promulgated by the Japanese Plywood Exporters Association with the blessing of Ministry of International Trade and Industry, the Japanese plywood production is controlled by the Japaneses Adjustment Association, the membership of which number 178 producers out of the total of 226.[11] The most recent production quota specifically earmarked for export to the United States and other countries of the Western Hemisphere covers the period [12] April–September 1957 and is as follows:

[Thousand square feet]

| | |
|---|---|
| Class A: Door sizes, lauan | 100,108 |
| Class B: 4 feet by 8 feet, 1/4 inch and up, lauan | 80,622 |
| Class C: Lauan other than A and B | 73,102 |
| Class D: Domestic woods | 112,606 |
| Total | 366,438 |

On an annual basis this production quota of 178 companies destined for export to the United States and other countries of the Western Hemisphere would total 733 million square feet. Fantastic, yes, but this is not all—arrangements will be made to provide an additional amount for the 48 producers, who are not members of the association.

On the basis of United States imports of plywood from Japan during the period April–June 1957 and the historical record of Japan's plywood exports to Western Hemisphere countries other than

[11] Dispatch No. 1334, June 7, 1957.
[12] Ibid.

the United States, the new quota provides for increased exports to the United States.

The announced quota for July–September 1957[13] for the United States, Hawaii, and other countries of North and South America is as follows:

[Quantity, thousand square feet]

| | |
|---|---|
| Class A: Lauan less than 4.5 millimeter | 59,000 |
| Class B: Lauan 4.5 millimeter and more | 32,800 |
| Class C: Lauan less than 4.5 millimeter, 16 inches and over wide, 78 inches and over long | 7,170 |
| Total | 98,970 |

A new quota has been announced for both the October–December 1957 period and the January–March 1958 period. It is as follows:[14]

*Quarterly quota*

[In thousand square feet]

| Description | October to December 1957 | January to March 1958 |
|---|---|---|
| Class A: Lauan door panels | 50,000 | 50,000 |
| Class B: Lauan 4 feet by 8 feet, ¼ inch and up | 30,000 | 30,000 |
| Class C: Lauan other than A and B | 39,000 | 39,000 |
| Class D: Domestic woods | 36,000 | 36,000 |
| Total | 155,000 | 155,000 |

The above quota would restore the domestic woods and excluded lauan panels to the quota, however, it has not yet been ascertained what exclusions there are, such as prefinished, grooved and other specialties. In any event, this quota if all inclusive, would exceed the 1956 shipments into the United States by 93 million square feet.

## SECTION VIII. TARIFF COMMISSION DECISION ON THE HARDWOOD PLYWOOD ESCAPE-CLAUSE CASE

The hardwood-plywood manufacturers applied for escape-clause relief in September 1954. The hearings were held by the Tariff Commission in March 1955. At this time the State Department was negotiating a new trade agreement with Japan. The decision of the Tariff Commission denying relief to the domestic industry was handed down on June 2, 1955. In June, the new trade agreement with Japan was announced by the State Department. In that the hardwood-plywood industry's case was directed primarily at Japan because of the tremendous increase in shipments from Japan and the low prices based on the low-wage scale in Japan, the escape-clause hearings could not have come at a more unfavorable time for the American industry.

The decision of the Tariff Commission is inexplicable to the domestic industry and others.

The conclusions of the Tariff Commission were contrary to the record and findings of serious injury in conformity with the criteria established by Congress in section 7 (b) of the Trade Agreements Act of 1951, as amended.

[13] Dispatch No. 161, August 13, 1957.
[14] Bulletin, August 15, 1957, Pease, Ltd., San Francisco, Calif.

The factors set up by Congress and the Commission's findings are as follows:

| Trade Agreements Act, sec. 7 (b): | Findings of commission[1] | | |
|---|---|---|---|
| | Domestic production (thousand square feet) | | |
| | 1953 | 1954 | Decrease |
| (a) Downward trend of production (table 5) | 1,242,171 | 1,093,481 | 148,691 |
| | BLS price index | | |
| | 1953 | 1954 | Decrease |
| (b) Downward trend of prices (table 13) | 97 | 90 | 7 |
| | Operating profit (percent of sales) | | |
| | 1953 | 1954 | Decrease |
| (c) Downward trend of profits (table 14) | 5.4 | 2.7 | [2] 2.7 |
| | Producers of hardwood plywood | All manufacturing corporations | Lumber and wood products |
| (d) Decline in ratio of profits to net sales (report, p. 21): | | | |
| 1953 | 5.4 | 9.0 | 5.9 |
| 1954 | 2.7 | 8.3 | 5.8 |
| | Aggregate earnings (1951 base year=100), percent | | |
| | 1953 | 1954 | Decrease |
| (e) Downward trend wages (table 14) | 106 | 93 | 13 |
| | Sales 46 companies | | |
| | 1953 | 1954 | Decrease |
| (f) Downward trend sales (table 14) | $77,342,000 | $63,933,000 | [3] $13,409,000 |
| | Imports (thousand square feet) | | |
| | 1953 | 1954 | Increase |
| (g) Increase in imports (table 7) | 218,862 | 425,898 | [4] 207,036 |
| | Ratio of inventory to production, percent | | |
| | 1953 | 1954 | Increase |
| (h) Higher or growing inventory (table 10) | 4.4 | 5.1 | 0.7 |
| | Ratio of imports to consumption, percent | | |
| | 1953 | 1954 | Decline |
| (i) Decline in proportion of domestic market supplied by domestic producers (table 3) | 14.9 | 28.0 | 13.1 |

[1] Reference tables are contained in U. S. Tariff Commission report, Hardwood Plywood, June 1955.
[2] A decrease of 50 percent. [3] A decrease of 17.5 percent. [4] An increase of 95 percent.

The statement of the Tariff Commission that the hardwood-plywood industry had experienced a rapid and continuous expansion was not supported by the record. The report of the Tariff Commission, tables 3 and 5,[15] show what purports to be production for the hardwood-plywood industry, both market and captive. The figures are a composite of market hardwood-plywood shipments and producers of other products which produced plywood as a component for their specialty product. These figures disclose the following:

[Thousand square feet]

| | Market hardwood plywood | Captive hardwood plywood |
|---|---|---|
| 1951 | 805, 249 | 367, 760 |
| 1952 | 794, 857 | 381, 490 |
| 1953 | 805, 632 | 436, 539 |
| 1954 | 716, 481 | [1] 377, 000 |

[1] Estimated.

The above figures demonstrate that for the 1951–54 period the market hardwood plywood industry not only did not show an increase of any kind or an expansion; the average was down almost to the 1947 level. Captive hardwood plywood showed a slight increase over 1951, the maximum being 14 percent in 1953. As the above are the only facts in the record on which the statement of the Commission could be based, the statement is in error.

The statement of the Tariff Commission (p. 11)[16] that the expansion of consumption in flush doors would not have been possible if the producers had been entirely dependent on domestic plywood was unsupported by the facts adduced at the hearings and was mere conjecture, based on opinions rather than evidence.

The following facts establish the erroneousness of this statement:

(*a*) The capacity of the domestic producer has never been reached, due to cheap imports. This capacity far exceeds the demands of domestic users of hardwood plywood, including producers of flush doors.

(*b*) The domestic producers manufactured door skins until forced out of the market by low-priced, imported plywood. The Bureau of Census industry figures show that, in 1951, 62 percent of the production of market hardwood plywood was in thicknesses of three-sixteenths inch or less; this amounted to 500 million square feet, a quantity more than sufficient to meet twice the demand of the door industry.

(*c*) The flush-door manufacturers switched from domestic plywood because of the lower prices of the imported plywood produced in low-wage-scale countries.

The Tariff Commission's statement that the injury to the domestic industry was attributable to "a marked decline in production in those industries which constitute the principal markets for ordinary plywood" is in error, in that the finding and conclusion is not supported by the record, or the Commission staff findings; was contradictory of

[15] U. S. Tariff Commission Report, Hardwood Plywood, June 1955.
[16] Id.

and in direct conflict with other findings of the Commission, for the following reasons, to wit:

The Commission found (p. 10) [17] "a marked and continuous expansion of consumption of ordinary hardwood plywood." Table 3 [18] shows 1954 to be the peak year, with consumption 58,378,000 square feet over 1953, and 1953, 221,253,000 square feet over 1951.

A marked and continuous expansion of consumption is the direct result of increased production by the industries which constitute the principal markets for ordinary hardwood plywood. Increased consumption indicates a marked increase in production and use rather than a decline in demand. The Commission finding that imports were double the amount in 1953 establishes a high demand by the principal users of ordinary plywood.

The statement that there was a decline in the market demand for hardwood plywood is contradictory of the Commission finding that plywood imports increased due to "high-level domestic construction, a high level of national income, the increased popularity of flush doors" (report, p. 12).[19]

The conclusion of the Tariff Commission that the deterioration in the domestic hardwood plywood industry was due to the general recession in industry in 1953–54 was not supported by the record, and contrary to findings of the Commission, for the following reasons, to wit:

The production-index figures cited by the Commission for furniture and radio-TV industries refer to the high and low months of 1953 and 1954, respectively, and do not reflect the averages for the years 1953 and 1954. (See above.) The selection of a high month against a low month is not representative.

The general-production index may not be used to attribute a recession to a particular industry (hardwood plywood) where the facts establish a peak consumption and demand for the product of the industry.

A decline in a general-production index cannot be fairly used to explain injury to the hardwood plywood industry in light of record consumption, high production by principal users, and tremendous increases in imports at unfairly low prices.

The conclusion of the Tariff Commission in the hardwood plywood case that a general industry recession in the United States negates injury from imports to a particular industry and must be considered determinative on the question of injury, without regard to the criteria established by section 7 of the Trade Agreements Act, nullifies the intent of Congress to protect American industry from increased imports causing or threatening serious injury to a domestic industry.

### SECTION IX. FUTURE OF THE AMERICAN MARKET HARDWOOD PLYWOOD INDUSTRY

The American market hardwood plywood industry has been teetering on the brink of disaster for the past 4 years. Plywood imports have taken over an increasing percent of the domestic market each year, while domestic producers' shipments have remained static;

---

[17] Id.
[18] Id.
[19] Id.

prices have been depressed, and production costs have increased. The domestic industry has exhausted its ingenuity to find new outlets for its product. With earnings too low to attract new capital or credit, or to support research and development, or to finance recently developed mechanical improvements as they come on the market, the industry will be destroyed unless a fair and reasonable measure of relief is provided by Congress.

The American market hardwood plywood producers have established themselves as competent, aggressive, and ingenious American businessmen. They have long withstood the assault by low-priced, imported plywood from countries with a wage scale only a fraction of the minimum wage required by law in the United States. Only with great reluctance, and at a sacrifice of the inherent pride that all American businessmen have in their ability to take care of themselves, do the hardwood plywood manufacturers come to Congress for assistance on their problem.

In order to gain a proper perspective for measuring the adverse effect of plywood imports on the domestic industry, we must consider the imports from Japan, the Japanese plywood industry, and the trading methods of the Japanese. It should not be concluded that imports of plywood from countries other than Japan do not add to the damage created by the imports from Japan. The Japanese producers now have taken over 82 percent of all United States plywood imports, which represents 42 percent of domestic consumption. This domination of the United States imports gives control to Japan of the domestic hardwood plywood market. In fact, 42 percent of all domestic-market sales assures to Japan an effective control over the prices and shipments in the American market. The eroding effects of the plywood imports from Japan have brought the domestic industry to its present depressed condition.

Japan's dominant position in the United States market has been achieved in the last 6 years. Plywood imports from Japan have increased from 13 million square feet in 1951 to 527 million square feet in 1956, and to an estimated 675 million square feet in 1957, an increase of 5,100 percent in 1957 over 1951. The average price or value of United States plywood imports from Japan per 1,000 square feet was $77.52 in 1951 and $64.33 in 1956 (table 13). The low price for the 6-year period was $57.39 in 1954, the year when the American industry was in such dire straits.[20] In 1956, the average Japanese export price for lauan (Philippine mahogany) was $51.22, and for other species (birch, sen (ash), and oak), $99.62 (table 15). In considering these prices, it must be remembered that the average includes plywood of all thicknesses, from one-eighth inch to over seven-eighths inch and from the lowest to the highest priced.

In 1955, at the time of the American industry's escape-clause hearing, the Japanese announced a voluntary quota on exports of plywood. Section VII herein explains the failure of this quota in detail. It is quite obvious that announcements on the promulgation of the quota were made to mislead the American industry into a false sense of security and to furnish the State Department with an answer to the criticism from persons concerned with the effect of the plywood

[20] Id.

imports on the American industry. A published quota did not disclose all the exceptions, and therefore, was misleading. The Japanese had what they termed "escape clauses" in their quota regulations, which were not disclosed. The point considered is that the noncompliance with the terms of the published quota indicates the plan of the Japanese to monopolize the market hardwood plywood sales in the United States.

It has been, and will be again, contended by the Japanese producers and the importers of Japanese plywood that (1) Japanese plywood has merely supplemented the domestic supply and (2) the American consumer has benefited. These contentions have not been supported by evidence and both contentions are misleading. The basis of the first contention is that the imports supplied a demand for door panels (door skins) to the flush-door industry when such panels were not procurable from American producers. Door panels are thin plywood, three-sixteenths inch and less in thickness. Flush doors made from plywood door panels were becoming important in the United States market in 1951. Until that time, panel doors were the principal type used. In 1951 the domestic hardwood plywood industry produced 510 million square feet of hardwood plywood in panels three-sixteenths inch or less in thickness, which represented 62 percent of its total production. With 62 percent of its production in panels of a thickness suitable for door panels, the American industry not only could have, but would have, supplied the demand of the flush-door industry. Domestic producers were prevented from taking full advantage of this market by the influx of low-priced, door-panel plywood from Japan. After 1951 offers of door-panel business were conditioned on domestic producers supplying the panels at less than the price of the Japanese panels. Such a low price could not be met, and domestic producers lost the business. The domestic producer did not participate in the growth created by the flush-door business except, to a limited extent, where species was a requisite.

The American consumer of hardwood plywood has reaped little benefit from the low price of imported plywood. The profits have accrued to the importers and others selling the imported plywood. With the wide differential between the Japanese price and the domestic producers' prices, the sellers of Japanese plywood set a price only sufficiently lower than that of the American producers which would assure the obtaining of the business. Any contention that the importers would waive an opportunity for a larger profit so that the American consumer can benefit is without factual substance.

In reviewing the past 6 years of the ascendance of Japan to a dominating position in the United States hardwood plywood market, a very definite pattern of operation is evident which conclusively shows that the Japanese do not desire merely to have a fair and equitable portion of the market, but wish to have control of the market.

It has been contended by the Japanese producers and importers that they were interested only in the door-panel market. There is no question that the thin-panel market was the first objective of the Japanese plan. During the years 1951 through 1954, tables 15 and 16 show that a major portion of Japan's exports were in thin panels destined for the United States flush-door industry. The first objective of the Japanese plan was achieved when many domestic producers of door panels were forced to withdraw from the door-panel market. During Japan's concentration on the door-panel industry, domestic producers of thin panels turned their sales efforts to the furniture and trailer industries. Thus, the second objective of the Japanese became the furniture and trailer industries. In 1954, the door-panel market was nearing saturation. Japanese exports of plywood to the United States had reached 263.8 million square feet (table 15), more than the door industry could absorb.

Since 1955, a large portion of the thin panels imported from Japan have continued to enter the domestic furniture and trailer industries. In 1956, the Japanese also increased its shipments of one-fourth inch and thicker panels and entered a new plywood end-use market in the United States. At the same time, Japan broadened its pattern of plywood exports to include increased quantities of species other than lauan (Philippine mahogany), such as birch, sen (ash), oak, cherry, and so forth. Table 15 shows this changing pattern in Japan's plywood exports.

The Japanese export quota reported by L. Pease, Ltd., for October–December 1957 and January–March 1958 (see footnote 9, sec. VII), provides only 32 percent of the quota for lauan door panels; 19 percent for one-fourth inch lauan, 22 percent for other sizes of lauan, and 31 percent for domestic woods (not lauan). This is conclusive proof of invasion of other markets by the Japanese. This is confirmed by the production quota of the Japanese Adjustment Association (sec. VII).

If the Japanese do not plan to take over our markets, these questions must be answered: Why did they disregard the quota? Why is the sales price of the Japanese plywood approximately one-half the price from other countries? Why are the quantities exported to the United States constantly increased when the injury to the domestic industry is well known? Why are the Japanese increasing their shipments of thicker panels and specialties, such as grooved and prefinished panels, which were first developed and first promoted by the domestic producers?

The Japanese could, by increasing their prices, remain competitive, reduce the quantities shipped, and still earn the same amount of dollars, with higher profits to themselves. It is not erroneous to assume that the Japanese are willing to wait for the higher profit until such time as there is no longer any domestic industry. Foreign countries exporting to the United States do not concern the Japanese. The Japanese have established that they can drive down the plywood export prices of other foreign countries (tables 13 and 14), so that soon there will be no profit for those countries.

The invasion by the imports into the customary markets of domestic producers resulted in companies affected by the unfair price competition moving into new market areas. This movement brought about a scrambling for business. Domestic producers have been forced to accept the unattractive, profitless orders, such as less-than-carload lots and difficult-size specification. Such orders were and are continually accepted in order to maintain the plants in operation. Unless such orders are mixed with the more profitable orders, this business is a slow death.

This scrambling, plus the development of some new uses, has permitted the domestic producer to maintain shipments at or slightly higher than the 1951 level. In his effort to keep operating, and thus maintain the quantity of shipments, the domestic producer has been forced to sacrifice profits. The domestic-industry profits before taxes have dropped from 12.3 percent in 1947 to 3.9 percent in 1956. Profit on sales in the first half of 1956 were only 5.24 percent, before taxes. In the second half of 1956, the industry's profits on sales, before taxes, were only 1.8 percent. It is evident that, if the domestic industry is to survive, it must be permitted to have a larger portion of the increased consumption of the domestic markets or much higher prices.

Neither of these objectives can be obtained so long as plywood imports, particularly from Japan, remain uncontrolled. The proportion of the domestic market absorbed by plywood imports has steadily increased from 8 percent in 1951 to 53 percent in the first half of 1957 (tables 9 and 20). Efforts of the domestic producers to regain a portion of the market growth have been frustrated by the steadily increasing plywood imports from Japan at low prices.

The profit factor referred to above is substantiated by the Bureau of Labor Statistics Wholesale Price Index (table 7), which shows that the 1957 hardwood plywood prices are 7.4 index points lower than 1951.

The domestic hardwood plywood producers have been denied the right to participate in the growth of the hardwood plywood market, which has increased from 879 million square feet in 1951 to 1,600 million square feet in 1956, approximately 100 percent increase. The increase in the market has been the result of the sales promotional efforts of the domestic industry. New uses have been found, markets broadened, new panels developed such as grooved and prefinished panels, and the buying public have been sold on the use of wood paneling and cabinets for the homes. Large sums of money have been spent by individual companies in developing markets. In addition, the trade promotion members of the Hardwood Plywood Institute have spent nearly $1 million since 1953 in a quality control and sales promotion program. The foreign producers and importers have not contributed to these promotional efforts. The development of the large market has been an achievement solely of the domestic industry. The domestic industry has not been permitted to profit from its efforts and expenditures, but the foreign producers and importers have had a free ride and creamed off the profits. To illustrate, grooved and prefinished plywood panels were developed by domestic producers at great expense. Sales campaigns were launched and the markets developed. Following the typical pattern of Japanese trade of letting the domestic industry develop a market. the Japanese have waited until within the last year to start shipping grooved and prefinished panels with price tags so low in comparison with the domestic costs that the domestic sales are being seriously affected. A new market was developed only to be invaded by low-priced imports from Japan.

An American industry should be entitled to grow with its markets. To say that American industry has no complaint against imports so long as it has not suffered a loss in shipments although the market has grown, is to discriminate against American industry in favor of foreign countries. The denial of the right to grow and to profit from the markets developed, is unjust and contrary to American principles. Why should foreign countries have a disproportionate share of the domestic market when that market was made by American industry? The hardwood plywood industry has not been allowed to grow with its own market nor has it been permitted to operate profitably with no increase in sales. If it is to be the foreign-trade policy of the United States that growth in consumption shall belong to foreign producers, then our economic and national welfare is in serious danger.

What is the future for the American hardwood plywood industry? It is at the crossroads today, not through any fault of its own, but due solely to a foreign-trade policy which has disregarded the interests and rights of the domestic industries in the home market. Our industry can maintain itself as a modern economic production unit only if permitted sufficient earnings to meet increasing costs for material and payrolls, cost of research and development, the continued purchase of newly developed equipment and a reasonable profit. The market hardwood plywood industry has the unused capacity to produce at least twice as much plywood as produced in 1956. The labor force many of which have grown up in the business, is well trained and efficient. The plants are modern, well equipped, but some may not be as well equipped as the Japanese plants. The domestic plants have been kept modern by the producer's dollar, not by use of the American taxpayer's dollar. There are only four publicly owned companies in the industry and for these hardwood plywood represents only a small part of their total sales. All other plans are privately owned, many having been in the same family and community for all the years of their existence. They are small business.

The market for the domestic producers is the United States. Exports of hardwood plywood have been, for all practical purposes, nonexistent for several years. The domestic producer is unable to compete abroad. The industry problems will be solved, if it is permitted a fair share in the market growth. So long as imports are permitted to enter the United States unrestricted in quantity, the domestic producer will not be able to secure a sufficient portion of the market to maintain the industry as a sound economic segment of our national economy.

An increase in tariff will not accomplish the required relief. The differential between the price of Japanese plywood and the costs of production of domestic hardwood plywood is so great that an increase in the duty to the 1930 rate of 40 percent would not dent this differential. Any increase in duty would increase the differential between the price of Japanese plywood and the prices of plywood from other countries. For example, in 1956, the average price value per 1,000 square feet of Canadian plywood was $128, the Japanese $63, a 20-percent increase in duty would add $25.60 to the Canadian price and $12.60 to the Japanese price and the differential would go up from $65 to $78. The Canadians have lost a substantial part of their plywood market in the United States due to Japanese prices. A further differential would only improve the Japanese position at the expense of the Canadians and other countries. The domestic industry is not advocating the cause of any foreign plywood producer, but the fact that the Japanese plywood is unfairly priced compared to world prices should not be ignored. The domestic industry also feels that it would be unjust to advocate a course which would discriminate against one or more countries and at the same time create an advantage for one other country.

The quota on imports is the only fair and equitable means of providing relief for the domestic industry. A quota would permit the domestic industry to share in the growth of the domestic market thereby securing sufficient sales to maintain the industry in a sound financial condition. A quota based on the foreign country's historical shipments to the domestic market with a set-aside for newcomers would assure fair treatment for all foreign countries. It is true that Japan would protest such a quota on the ground that it would be unfair to roll back the quantities imported from Japan. Such a protest from Japan is without a semblance of merit. Japan has created the problem by its plan to take over the domestic market.

The State Department has taken the position that quotas on products, except agricultural products under support programs, are contrary to the commitments of the United States to the General Agreement on Tariffs and Trade (GATT). The President has accepted the State Department views and announced that he will not approve quotas on industrial products. The State Department is of the view that Congress has transferred its power to control foreign trade and tariffs to GATT. This contention we deem completely without merit and sincerely hope Congress will reaffirm its authority under the Constitution.

The administration's position on quotas has nullified the provisions of the escape-clause section of the Trade Agreements Act which authorizes the Tariff Commission to recommend quotas. So long as this administration maintains its objection to quotas, application for relief through the Tariff Commission is useless, when quotas are required.

On behalf of the domestic manufacturers of market hardwood plywood, we respectfully request that a recommendation be made by your committee for the enactment of a law providing a quota on hardwood plywood imports.

# HARDWOOD PLYWOOD IMPORTS AND UNITED STATES FOREIGN TRADE POLICY

William J. Barnhard, Sharp and Bogan, Washington, D. C.[1]

## I. Introduction

The problem of hardwood plywood imports sheds light on many of the most significant aspects of United States foreign trade policy. Examination of the problems involved in the case of this specific commodity is therefore uniquely appropriate in any general consideration of the objectives, policies, and procedures of a trade program.

For one thing, the activities of the domestic hardwood plywood industry typify the many United States industries which have engaged in an incessant search for protection against competition. The trade association purporting to speak for the industry has, during a period of only the past 3 years, attacked these imports by way of the escape clause, the Antidumping Act, the Buy American Act, quota legislation, and even local fire laws and building ordinances.

The hardwood plywood situation also reflects the rapid emergence of the United States as a have-not nation, dependent in sharply increasing degree on the availability of foreign raw materials and industrial supplies.

Hardwood plywood imports demonstrate vividly the not uncommon situation where entire United States manufacturing industries and thousands of American jobs are largely or completely dependent upon imports of a particular commodity.

Hardwood plywood imports are typical of the many imports which satisfy consumer needs that cannot be met by domestic production, and thus supplement rather than supplant domestic production.

Hardwood plywood imports typify the foreign-made goods that create new markets in the United States, thus opening new areas for expansion of domestic sales as well as imports.

The hardwood plywood industry follows a standard pattern by ignoring the competitive impact of plastics, hardboard, chipboard, and other domestically produced competitive products, and attempting to make imports the scapegoat for any adjustments necessitated by normal economic growth.

The spokesmen for the domestic plywood industry are typical also in their callous disregard of the interests of the American consumer, both industrial and ultimate, and in their subordination of the national interest to the selfish interests of their own industry.

---

[1] Counsel for Imported Hardwood Plywood Association, San Francisco; Plywood Group, National Council of American Importers, New York; and American Association of Hardwood Plywood Users, Washington, D. C.

Finally, the problems which have arisen over imports of hardwood plywood follow a pattern that has reached such proportions as to demand a new emphasis and a new direction in the formulation of a proper and an effective foreign trade policy.

## II. Hardwood Plywood: A Case Study in Protection

### A. THE COMMODITY

Hardwood plywood consists of plywood of various sizes and thicknesses faced with a veneer of hardwood—i. e., generally, the wood from a broadleaved or deciduous tree. Most domestic hardwood veneers are made of oak, walnut, gum, birch, mahogany, and similar woods. Most imported hardwood plywood is faced with a veneer of lauan (Philippine mahogany), birch, poplar, oak, beech, and mahogany.

The bulk of domestic hardwood plywood is made in thicknesses of one-fourth inch or greater. The bulk of imported plywood is in one-eighth inch thickness, generally made and cut for use in the making of flush doors and known in the trade as "doorskins."

The major American plywood is not hardwood plywood, but softwood—principally Douglas-fir and pine. Softwood plywood differs substantially from hardwood plywood in texture, composition, price, and use. There is virtually no softwood plywood imported. In this report, therefore, as in the recent Tariff Commission report on hardwood plywood imports, there will be no discussion of the impact on the softwood plywood industry, since this is an industry producing a different product not effected by imports.

Similarly, there is excluded from the scope of this report, as from the Tariff Commission report, a particular type of hardwood plywood known as container or packaging plywood. This is a specific type of plywood, produced for a limited purpose, greatly inferior in quality and cheaper in price than ordinary hardwood plywood. The United States container plywood is substantially less expensive than the cheapest of the hardwood plywood imports. Moreover, there are no imports of container plywood.

The report therefore deals with all of the hardwood plywood imports and with domestic hardwood plywood other than container plywood, thus limiting the study to those commodities which are like or directly competitive with the imports.

### B. THE DOMESTIC INDUSTRY

The domestic hardwood plywood industry is made up of two major elements—about two-thirds of the hardwood plywood producers who sell their production to distributors or industrial consumers (market plywood), and about one-third of the industry that produces hardwood plywood consumed in its own finishing or processing plants (captive plywood). The producers of captive plywood include door manufacturers, cabinetmakers, furniture manufacturers, and others who produce finished articles incorporating the hardwood plywood they produce. There are about 20 hardwood plywood manufacturers who are producers of both market and captive plywood, selling some of their output to distributors or other industrial consumers, and consuming a part of their output in their own processing plants. The market plywood and the captive plywood are identical in every respect, being used for the same purposes and produced in the identical manner.

There are also several manufacturers of hardwood plywood who, either in separate plants or as part of their ordinary hardwood plywood production, produce container plywood. The Atlas Plywood Corp., for example, while one of the major producers and distributors of ordinary hardwood plywood, is also the country's leading producer of container plywood. Sales of container plywood have been reduced almost 50 percent in the last 5 years, because of the competition of corrugated paper and other substitute packaging materials. This segment of the plywood industry, therefore, is in an increasingly difficult position. However, as explained above, since there are no imports of container plywood or of any other plywood which is competitive with container plywood, these difficulties are admittedly attributable to causes other than import competition.

Table No. 1, attached hereto, shows the levels of production of domestic hardwood plywood. Note that during the past 2 years, that is, since the Tariff Commission unanimously found that the increased imports of hardwood plywood were not causing or threatening any injury to the domestic industry, domestic production has increased by about 30 percent. This very substantial increase in domestic production was achieved in the face of sharp competition from domestic hardboard and chipboard, and in the face of a substantial decline in residential construction, which forms one of the major markets for sales of ordinary hardwood plywood.

Many of the larger producers of ordinary hardwood plywood are also manufacturers or distributors of softwood plywood. The softwood plywood industry, which is not affected by plywood imports, has suffered a substantial price relapse during the past 18 months, principally because of the vast overexpansion of the softwood plywood industry. All of the major producers have shown a substantial decline in earnings or in net operating profits in their softwood plywood sales, because of the price drop, and many of them report a substantial increase in the returns from sales of hardwood plywood, often completely offsetting the softwood plywood losses. (See table No. 2.) For example, the financial statement of the Roddis Plywood Corp., which breaks down its sales into the various categories handled by the company, reflects a substantial increase in hardwood plywood sales and profits, more than offsetting a decrease in sales and profits of softwood plywood. (See table 3.)

The domestic hardwood plywood industry is dominated by a handful of major companies which are usually both manufacturers and distributors of plywood products, including both hardwood and softwood plywood. The financial position of the four leading companies in the industry is indicated in table No. 2. While the growth evidenced by these giants of the domestic hardwood plywood industry is generally applicable to the industry as a whole, it must also be noted that the rate of growth among the giants is substantially greater than the growth among the smaller independent nonintegrated producers in the industry. This pattern of greater concentration in the hardwood plywood industry follows the pattern of American industry generally, as detailed in the report of the Small Business Committee of the United States Senate (Rept. No. 129, 84th Cong., 1st sess.), which notes this most disturbing trend among manufacturing corporations.

C. HARDWOOD PLYWOOD IMPORTS

*1. Tariff treatment*

The Tariff Act of 1930 provided for a duty of 50 percent ad valorem on birch and alder plywood, and a 40 percent duty on all other types of plywood. As a result of tariff concessions, the existing duty on birch plywood is 15 percent, on alder plywood 25 percent, and on all other imported plywood (except Spanish cedar) 20 percent.

Since Japan accounts for about three-fourths of all hardwood plywood imports, and the great bulk of Japanese plywood is of lauan (Philippine mahogany), the effective rate of duty on most hardwood plywood imports is 20 percent.

*2. History*

The sharp increase in hardwood plywood imports over the past 5 years finds its origin in the architectural and structural changes that came about in American residential and commercial construction soon after World War II. The developing style and trend toward flat surfaces in furniture and interior finishing opened up a tremendous market for decorative hardwood plywood. Builders and furniture makers had little difficulty obtaining from the domestic hardwood plywood industry the ¼-inch and thicker panels necessary for wall paneling, desk tops, and other types of furniture. However, with the style trend dictating a change from the traditional panel door to the modern flush door, domestic door manufacturers found it impossible to obtain from United States plywood mills the doorskins they needed for the natural wood veneer of their flush doors.

Domestic plywood manufacturers in 1950 and 1951 indicated that they either could not or would not provide the independent door manufacturers with the ⅛-inch doorskins necessary for the production of flush doors. There are on file with the Tariff Commission numerous letters from plywood mills to door manufacturers, indicating that the door manufacturers must look elsewhere for the doorskins they need.

It was at this time that the west coast regional manager of the United States Plywood Corp., the Nation's leading plywood distributor, turned to the already well-established Japanese plywood industry to find a source of doorskins for the rapidly growing flush-door market. Over a period of at least 18 months, this representative of our Nation's leading plywood company pleaded with the Japanese plywood mills to produce the type of plywood needed in the United States market and not available domestically. He worked with the production experts, explained the needs of the United States consumers, helped in the analysis of the United States market, coached them in meeting United States specifications, and provided the impetus to the Japanese industry to fill the tremendous need arising in the United States, a need which had not been and could not be filled by the domestic producers of hardwood plywood.

At the time of the Tariff Commisson hearing, it was pointed out that 81 percent of the hardwood plywood imported from Japan was in the form of doorskins, and that a smaller but still significant proportion of the imported hardwood plywood from other countries was also in the form of doorskins, including birch skins from Canada and Finland. At that time, also, the National Woodwork Manufacturers Association, of Chicago, Ill., published a list of 127 hardwood-flush-door manufacturers operating in the United States. The production figures available from the leaders of this industry indicate that the total United States production of hardwood-plywood doorskins would have been almost sufficient to supply the needs of 3 out of the 127 flush-door manufacturers. It was to meet the needs of this industry, which had increased its production of flush doors from a few hundred thousand in 1947 to an estimated 13 to 15 million currently, that hardwood-plywood imports have sustained their great growth.

As the Tariff Commission points out in its 1955 reports—

imports have been supplemental to the domestic supply of hardwood plywood. Indeed, the availability of imports has helped to develop new markets for the product. The great expansion in consumption of hardwood plywood in the production of flush doors would not have been possible if producers had been dependent entirely on domestic plywood. Domestic supplies either would not have been adequate or would have been available only at prices that would have retarded their use.

*3. Types and volume*

As indicated above, the great bulk of hardwood-plywood imports have consisted of ⅛-inch doorskins, specifically cut and produced for sale to flush-door manufacturers. Most of the remaining volume of hardwood-plywood imports consists of one-quarter-inch standard panels, usually in the standard 4 by 8 size. There is also some importation of ⅛-inch plywood used for backing or drawer bottoms in furniture manufacture.

However, the imports have never been able to develop any significant volume of hardwood plywood suitable for furniture making, construction, or the other major outlets for hardwood plywood. In furniture making, which is perhaps the greatest outlet for hardwood plywood in the South and Southeastern States, the inevitable requirements for special cut-to-size plywood to fit particular needs of the moment make the use of imported hardwood plywood virtually impossible. Plywood for such purposes must be produced locally and in accordance with specifications subject to constant change. In such circumstances, there is little opportunity for imports to develop any significant market.

The volume of imports of hardwood plywood and the major countries providing such imports are listed in table No. 4. A comparison of this volume of imports with the volume of domestic production, however, requires some adjustment in order to obtain a true picture of the relationship. As indicated above, the great bulk of hardwood plywood imports is ⅛-inch plywood, while the great bulk of domestic hardwood plywood is in thicknesses of ¼ up to 1½ inches. In order to obtain a true picture of the relationship of imports to the total United States market, it is necessary to convert these widely varying commodities to a common denominator. This is what the domestic industry itself does in its annual figures when it states the capacity of individual plants on a 1/4-inch basis. Thus, a plant which produces 1 million square feet of 1/8-inch plywood would have a rated capacity of 500,000 square feet, while a plant which produced 1 million square feet of 1/2-inch plywood would have a rated capacity of 2 million feet on a 1/4-inch basis.

Table No. 5 is an attempt to compare domestic hardwood plywood production with hardwood plywood imports on a similar basis of a common denominator. The figures admittedly are based on general estimates, since there are no figures available which detail the thicknesses of domestic production and no recent figures on the details of imports. In terms of volume and value, however, the table presents a much more accurate picture of the relationship between imports and domestic production than a mere comparison of the surface measure of imports as against the surface measure of hardwood plywood made and sold in the United States. The latter ratio, which has been used by the domestic hardwood plywood industry in its propaganda, not only ignores the necessary adjustment because of differing thicknesses and values, but also ignores at least one-third of the domestic hardwood plywood industry which is the segment producing captive plywood.

*4. Comparative wages*

There is no doubt that wages in Japan are substantially lower than they are in the United States. However, there is also no doubt that the difference in wage costs is not reflected in the alleged Japanese wage rate of 11 1/2 cents per hour which has been the basis of the recent Hardwood Plywood Institute propaganda. This comparison is improper and unfair for several reasons. For one thing, the labor cost to a Japanese employer is considerably more than the hourly wage rate indicates, for it includes social benefits, unemployment benefits, full-employment requirements, and other normal labor costs which raise the actual labor expense substantially. Furthermore, the only true basis of labor cost comparison is in the labor content of the completed product, rather than in a paper comparison of wage rates.

The Hardwood Plywood Institute has provided information to the Tariff Comission showing that the labor content of domestically produced hardwood plywood is about 20 percent of the value of the products. Detailed data compiled by the investigators of the Treasury Department during an antidumping investigation of the Japanese plywood industry contain verified figures showing that the labor content of Japanese hardwood plywood is approximately 13 percent of the total cost of production. The relationship between this 13 percent figure and the 20 percent labor content of United States plywood is a much more realistic basis for comparison of relative labor costs than a comparison of basic wage rates.

It is interesting to note that the effective rate of duty on imported hardwood plywood has also been fixed at 20 percent, a figure which corresponds exactly to the labor content of domestically produced plywood.

It is interesting to note also that, as in the case of most protectionist claims, the complaint against cheap foreign labor is here made by one of the low-wage industries of the United States. As recently as 1955, the Hardwood Plywood Institute pointed out that two-thirds of the companies in the domestic hardwood plywood industry were paying wages below 90 cents an hour. The extremely low wage rates paid in the domestic hardwood plywood industry were even significantly lower prior to the time that imported plywood became a recognizable factor in the United States market .

D. THE UNCEASING SEARCH FOR PROTECTION

The domestic hardwood plywood industry has become a prime example of the United States industries who feel that in order to gain protection from import competition they need not be right, only persistent. The number and variety of attacks made by this industry against imports attests to the vigor and ingenuity of the industry leaders, or at least of the trade association executives they maintain in Washington.

For several years now the United States importers of hardwood plywood, their American customers who rely on these imports, and their foreign suppliers have been operating under a persistent cloud. The constant harassment by the domestic industry through various Government channels has created almost as much disturbance and uncertainty to the import trade as an unfavorable governmental decision might have done.

*2. The escape clause*

The first discernible action by the domestic industry looking to protection of their market was the filing of an escape-clause complaint by the Hardwood Plywood Institute with the Tariff Commission in 1954. Its purpose was to have the Tariff Commission recommend and the President impose a quota on future hardwood plywood imports. In June 1955 the Tariff Commission unanimously found that, although imports of hardwood plywood had increased at a great rate, these imports were neither causing nor threatening any injury to the domestic industry.

The Tariff Commission pointed out in detail the facts which have already been outlined, demonstrating that imports were supplemental to domestic production, that they opened up new markets for hardwood plywood, that they were essential to the continued existence of the flush-door manufacturing industry and other American prcessing industries, and that the domestic industry had been able to maintain a high rate of hardwood plywood production.

*2. The Antidumping Act*

During this same period, the Hardwood Plywood Institute also filed a complaint with the Treasury Department under the Antidumping Act, charging that Japanese plywood was being sold in the United States at a dumping price and was thereby injuring the domestic industry. The Treasury Department conducted an exhaustive investigation in Japan as well as at Washington and various ports of entry, and early in 1956 concluded that Japanese hardwood plywood was not being sold in the United States at a dumping price. During the extensive period of the investigation, of course, none of the entries of Japanese hardwood plywood could obtain customs clearance, since the Secretary had taken the usual step at the beginning of the investigation by ordering a withholding of appraisements on all imports subject to the investigation.

*3. The Buy American Act*

Soon thereafter, additional activity by the Hardwood Plywood Institute under the terms of the Buy American Act resulted in an order by the Corps of Engineers barring the use of imported hardwood plywood in the construction of residences on several Army posts. In at least one case, where the Army specifications called for Philippine mahogany plywood, the restrictions of the Buy American Act were applied even though domestically produced plywood meeting the specifications was not readily available and, when it became available, it was only at a cost at least 30 to 40 percent higher than the imported panels originally contracted for.

*4. Local action*

Additional activity by the domestic industry includes a wide variety of local and State pressure and propaganda, designed to impose additional and artificial restrictions on the use of imported hardwood plywood. In one case, local fire laws were rewritten in such a way as to place imported plywoods in a separate category, and building ordinances were then interpreted as prohibiting the use of imported panels in local construction.

*5. Legislative quota*

The most recent activity of the Hardwood Plywood Institute, and the most intensive, has been its attempt to persuade Congress to impose by legislation the import quota which the Tariff Commission ruled was not necessary or proper. By an intensive program of lobbying, including many misrepresentations and evidencing a viciousness rarely seen even in the heat of tariff controversies (see exhibits A and B), the lobbying group for the domestic industry induced many Senators and Representatives to introduce quota legislation.

The drastic effect of the proposed legislative quota is detailed in table No. 8, which shows that if the quota had been in effect for 1957, all hardwood plywood imports would have been cut by 67 percent, Japan would have been cut by 77 percent and the Philippines by 95 percent. In addition, aside from the havoc this would wreak on the American processing industries requiring such imports, the quota legislation would mean a loss in steamship revenues of between $4 million and $5 million a year, and a loss to American agriculture and other major American exporters of at least $36 million in annual sales abroad.

The heart of the propaganda campaign supporting the legislative quota was the claim by the domestic industry that 28 hardwood plywood mills have been shut down by import competition since the June 1955 decision of the Tariff Commission. An on-the-spot survey of the 28 mills alleged to have been shut down because of import competition revealed that 9 of them are still in operation, 5 of them never existed, 3 of them burned to the ground, 1 was closed before imports became significant, 4 were merged with other operations of the parent company as part of a program of consolidation, and the 6 remaining were closed for a variety of reasons including a shortage of timber resources, undercapitalization, labor difficulties and other factors having no relation to import competition. Several of the plants on the list of 28 produced only container plywood which, as has been pointed out, is not imported at all and is not competitive at all with any imported plywood. (See tables 6 and 7.)

### E. ARE IMPORTS INJURIOUS TO THE DOMESTIC INDUSTRY?

Only 2 years ago, after a complete investigation of the industry, the Tariff Commission unanimously determined that imports were not causing, or even threatening, any injury to the domestic hardwood plywood industry. This finding was made in the face of an increase in Japanese imports of more than 2,000 percent over a 4-year period.

Since 1955 there has been no significant change in the circumstances found by the Commission. Imports have continued to increase, although at a much slower pace than in 1951–54. Doorskins still constitute the bulk of the plywood imports, particularly those from Japan. The domestic industry continues to expand, although at a much faster rate than in 1951–54.

The United States flush-door manufacturing industry continues to depend for its very existence on the maintenance of imports. To a lesser degree, this is also true of the cabinetmakers, boatbuilders and others whose market depends in significant part on the availability of exotic plywoods at a realistic price.

Some domestic plywood has always been available to fill the particular needs of those industries, but only at a price that precluded their entrance into the low-cost and medium-cost home, boat, or cabinet. In the construction industry, the great expansion in recent years has been in just those price fields. In that price range, domestic hardwood plywood doors were not economically feasible, or even possible. If imported doorskins had not become available, the builders could not have turned to domestic hardwood plywood doorskins, but would have had to find a less expensive substitute. It was for this reason that the Tariff Commission found that imports had created a new market, supplementing domestic production, and actually opening up new areas of sales for domestic wall paneling and other plywood products made possible only because imports permitted the construction of this type of home.

The only domestic hardwood plywood available at anything close to the price of imported doorskins was gum, which is the principal plywood of the South. But gum, in the ordinary course of production, is not an exotic wood suitable for a clear finish, which is what the present style trend demands. It can be suitably stained or carefully selected to present an attractive finish, but this adds substantially to the cost. It is for this reason that gum is classed in the trade as a paint-grade doorskin. These paint-grade doorskins of gum are experiencing severe competition, but not from imports. Hardboard (masonite) takes paint as well as gum does and is 40 or 50 percent less expensive. A builder who is planning to paint his flush door, therefore, will often prefer a hardboard door to a plywood door. This competition from domestic products, rather than from imports, is the chief cause of local difficulties that exist among some of the smaller hardwood plywood manufacturers.

A similar development is found in the rapid growth of the chipboard and particle board industry, which uses hitherto waste material as the core of a board faced with attractive exotic hardwood panels. In the thicker grades of plywood, chiefly one-half inch and up, these low-cost boards are providing stiff competition.

The greatest problem facing the domestic hardwood plywood industry, as in all timber industries, is the inability of the small producer to obtain maximum utilization of the log. The large manufacturers are using the waste chips for particle board, the sawdust for paper or hardboard, the fine grades for face veneers, the cheaper lumber for other wood products. The small producer cannot expect to compete successfully with this type of integrated efficient operation.

The result has been, in this industry as in others, a greater concentration of production and profits in the hands of the few giants with the financial ability to integrate their operations. Only a solution to this problem can help the small hardwood plywood producer. A cessation of imports would not help him, and might even hurt him.

F. ARE IMPORTS INJURIOUS TO THE NATIONAL INTEREST?

In general, all commercial imports benefit the national economy. If they did not meet a commercial need, they would not be imported. In the case of hardwood plywood, as in so many other products, the imports fill a gap that cannot be met from domestic production. The choice is not between imports and domestic products, it is between imports and nothing.

This gap in United States production may be caused by several factors, although the principal element is undoubtedly the labor cost. Our wage scales are fixed by the assembly-line industries, the major industries, rather than the high-labor-content handicraft industries. If the glove, lens, and felt-hat industries, for example, are to retain any labor at all they must match the pay scales of the automobile and electric appliance industries. But this inevitably prices the handicraft products out of the market, at least out of a substantial part of the market. That gap in the low and medium-income market just cannot be met from United States production. Some people just cannot or will not pay $8 for a pair of gloves, or $12 for a hat, or $20 for a flush door. They either do without or they find a cheaper substitute, unless their market needs can be met by imports having a lower cost of production. Filling this need is one of the major commercial purposes of the import trade and one of its major contributions to the national economy.

In the case of hardwood plywood, this gap is most apparent in the flush-door industry. The entire United States door manufacturing industry, including hundreds of companies, many of them small concerns in one-company towns, is completely dependent on imports to fill the gap left by domestic production. The continued existence and prosperity of this door industry, and the many others dependent in some degree on imports, is certainly in the national interest.

There is no need in this paper to belabor the benefits of competition, the need for a two-way flow of trade, our national interest in maintaining strong allies and secure alliances, the rights of the American consumer, the interest of the American taxpayer in fostering mutually beneficial trade instead of giveaway aid programs, and the other general but still vital aspects of our foreign trade policy. It is necessary only to point out that imports of hardwood plywood have not injured the domestic industry, have in certain respects aided that industry in expanding to record levels of production, have filled a vital need of the American economy, and have provided essential materials for several American industries and thousands of jobs within those industries. Continued expansion in this trade, it seems clear, is eminently in the national interest.

## III. Stability: A Foreign Trade Program of Moderation

### A. YESTERDAY'S TRADE POLICY—TARIFF REDUCTION

The heart of the reciprocal trade agreements program, which has been our Nation's consistent trade policy for the past 23 years, has been the mutual reduction of tariff levels.

The customs duties on many of our imports have been cut by 75 percent or more from the levels fixed by the Smoot-Hawley Tariff Act of 1930. Some have been cut by half, as hardwood plywood was reduced from 40 to 20 percent. Except for the imports from Soviet bloc countries, which are a negligible factor in our world trade, there are few dutiable imports that have not been the object of substantial tariff reduction.

It is not always remembered that these tariff concessions by the United States have not been sacrifices, grudgingly accepted by us in order to wring concessions from other nations. On the contrary, the tariff concessions we have granted have usually been of even greater benefit to our Nation and its economy than the reciprocal concessions we have received. By encouraging more imports into our markets, these tariff reductions have reduced prices or kept them stable, reduced taxes (for the tariff is, after all, nothing but an excise tax), stimulated competition, opened new markets, fostered new processing and finishing industries, created new industrial and commercial jobs, and provided the American consumer with a wider variety of attractively priced products. These have been the chief direct benefits to us from our own concessions.

Several indirect benefits have also accrued to us by reason of our tariff concessions. They have reduced foreign aid expenditures by limiting the need for economic assistance abroad; they have strengthened the bonds of the free world through a program of economic interdependence; they have contributed to the strength and security of our free world allies; and they have stimulated our own export sales by removing part of the greatest limiting factor on United States sales abroad—the short supply of dollars.

In addition to these direct and indirect benefits resulting from the tariff concessions that we ourselves have granted, our economy has benefited substantially from the tariff concessions that other nations have granted reciprocally on the products we sell abroad. However, these benefits have been less extensive and less direct for the simple reason that foreign tariff levels have not been the major stumbling block to American exports. The greatest limiting factor on those exports has been the supply of dollars available to purchase United States goods. Occasionally, therefore, trading nations of the free world have lowered their tariff on American-made goods only to find that there were not enough dollars in their country to pay for the increased United States exports that should have resulted from the tariff concession. As a result, the tariff concessions abroad frequently cause no actual increase in the volume of American exports to a particular market.

One of the principal activities of the General Agreement on Tariffs and Trade (GATT) has been to secure for the United States and other trading nations the practical benefits that the tariff concessions were intended to achieve. Despite the lack of any formalized personnel or machinery, the GATT Secretariat has been able to accomplish this objective to some extent and has thus aided substantially in the exports of American coal, apples, textiles, leather products, motorcycles, tobacco, and many other United States export commodities.

These limitations, which usually take the form of exchange quotas, are gradually being dissipated. They can be completely removed, with resulting benefits to American export sales, only by increasing the supply of dollars abroad (that is, letting our friends and allies abroad earn more dollars by sales to the United States market) and by the Organization for Trade Cooperation (OTC) which would operate as a watchdog to see that the GATT terms are lived up to by all signatory parties. To the extent, however, that such limitations still exist, American exporters have not reaped the full harvest intended for them by the reciprocal trade concessions.

It is for this reason that the tariff concessions granted by other nations, while beneficial to our economy, have been of less direct benefit to our country and somewhat less stimulating to our economy than the concessions we ourselves have granted.

### B. TODAY'S TRADE POLICY—FRINGE PROTECTION

Concurrently with the last few years of the period of tariff reduction, the United States has entered upon an era of fringe protection. During these past few years, the basic objective of the reciprocal trade program has remained unchanged and has been accepted by both the executive and the legislative branches of our Government. The vitality of that program, however, has been dissipated by a variety of attitudes and decisions that threaten the entire trade policy.

The escape clause (sec. 7 of the Trade Agreements Extension Act of 1951) has become a sword of Damocles hanging over the heads of manufacturers and exporters desiring to enter the American market and to take advantage of the concessions we have granted. As the escape clause has been administered in recent years, it says to the foreign manufacturers and exporters: "You may enter the American market and pay only the low tariff that we have negotiated, but if you are successful in selling here, your imports will be stopped." Under these circumstances, a foreign exporter is extremenly reluctant to invest substantial sums in promotion, advertising, establishment of sales outlets, or other necessary and expensive steps needed to develop a market. The constant harassment under the "escape clause" of imports of bicycles, watches, spring clothespins, wood screws and other commodities has been sufficient to discourage both American and foreign businessmen from taking advantage of the trade concessions we have negotiated.

The Antidumping Act of 1921 has threatened to become an even greater stumbling block to imports, because of the unfair and uncertain way in which it has been administered. Because of the retroactive penalties permitted under the Antidumping Act and the withholding of customs appraisements ordered at the start of an antidumping investigation, the continuation of imports is greatly discouraged even before it is known whether dumping actually exists. This circumstance, plus the recent decisions of the Treasury Department and the Tariff Commission, have encouraged more protectionist industries in the United Sates to file dumping complaints. There are now more dumping investigations underway (and therefore more imports which are automatically denied customs clearance) than at any time in recent commercial history, and more than twice as many as there were before the Tariff Commission's decision in the cast-iron soil-pipe case. This decision, which found that an expanding and prosperous industry was being injured by imports that amounted to less than four-tenths of 1 percent of domestic production, has encouraged a plethora of domestic industries to seek protection against import competition, however small it may be.

The Buy American Act, a relic of the depression of the 1930's, has been applied with some elements of realism and equity to direct Government purchases, but is still a complete and unncessary bar to the use of imported materials in the performance of Government contracts. Recent decisions have threatened prime contractors with blacklisting because a minute portion of the contract involved the purchase and use of imported materials by one of the sub-sub-contractors. The rule of reason proclaimed by the President in the case of Government purchases, allowing the Government and the taxpayers to benefit from substantially lower prices, now has no applicability to expenditures under Government contracts.

Section 22 of the Agricultural Adjustment Act, in which Congress authorized the President to reduce certain agricultural imports by 50 percent, has recently been used by the President to impose a complete embargo on certain dairy products. Section 22 is obviously necessary so long as United States farm prices are maintained at artificial levels far above world prices. But recent decisions appear to have gone beyond its language and its purpose, and provided a new area for protection on the fringes of the trade program.

The national security amendment (sec. 7 of the Reciprocal Trade Agreements Extension Act of 1955) offers an additional opportunity to domestic industries to harass imports. Aside from such harassment, this amendment appears to offer no additional protection to domestic industries beyond that already available under the escape clause. Despite this, more than 15 complaints have already been filed with the Office of Defense Mobilization, many of them by industries which have already been found to require no relief from import competition. So far, there has been only one formal decision under this national security amendment, and the official actions following this decision indicate that the persisent harassment of imports will be as common to ODM proceedings as they are to other Government procedures. The specific action referred to is the ODM decision to reopen the investigation of cordage and twine imports less than 6 months after its decision of March 7, 1957, that such imports were not threatening the national security under the terms of section 7.

The administration's action in the lead and zinc case, where it sponsored restrictive legislation only a few years after it had refused to adopt the Tariff Commission's recommendation for a similar restriction, seems to be part of the overall pattern.

The inevitable result of such activity has been to create uncertainty and reluctance on the part of foreign exporters, United States importers, and the American manufacturers consuming imported materials, to develop a significant trade in any but the most essential commodities. Many have believed that the repeated avowals of a liberal trade policy have done little more than pay lipservice to our reciprocal trade program. Whether or not this is so, it seems certain that the trade objectives which have been adopted by both political parties and by all executive and legislative leaders in recent years cannot be revitalized as a major instrument of national policy unless these fringe areas are administered in accordance with the objectives of that policy.

With recognition of the fact that excesses must be avoided and that certain precautionary measures are necessary, even in the most beneficial legislation, the foreign economic policy has properly been "we are in favor of liberal trade, but * * *." In recent years, however, through the various administrative actions described above, the "buts" seem to have dominated the program.

### C. TOMORROW'S TRADE POLICY—STABILITY

*1. Objectives*

The tariff-cutting authority which has been the heart of the reciprocal-trade program has just about accomplished its purpose. With very few individual exceptions, tariffs in the United States are generally admitted to be at a reasonable level. The scope of further tariff-cutting authority is so limited that it offers few prospects for either successful negotiation or further stimulation of trade. A reduction of the existing tariff on hardwood plywood, for example, from the present 20 percent to 19½ percent next year and then to 19 percent the following year, would have no significant effect on the import and export program.

What is needed instead is a program of stability, which would provide greater certainty and greater prosperity both to the world traders and the domestic producers.

To the United States importers, their suppliers and customers, a program of stability would provide a guaranty against constant harassment through myriad Government procedures. These traders would know that, so long as they engaged in fair competition and avoided flooding the domestic market, their chief concern need only be with the competitive circumstances of the market place rather than the artificial impediments that prevent normal operation of the market place.

To the domestic producer facing import competition, a program of stability would provide a guaranty of gradualism and fair competition. By preventing excessive increases in imports, the program of stability would guarantee to the domestic producer an opportunity to adjust his production and sales operations to the developing circumstances of the market. By effectively preventing predatory dumping and other unfair methods of competition, the program would guarantee that the circumstances of the market would involve fair competition.

Although it is normal and natural for a domestic producer to desire freedom from competition, he has no right to such freedom and the nation has no interest in granting it to him. Competition, whether originating with a more efficient domestic producer, imports, or newly developed products, will inevitably force the producer into either more economical operations or into production of a new more profitable commodity. So long as he has the opportunity to make such adjustments, without being forced into bankruptcy by a sudden and unexpected competitive onslaught, he has a right to ask no more.

There is no national purpose served in subsidizing uneconomic operations, marginal production, or low-grade mining. By the same token, there is no national purpose served in forcing many American businesses into sudden bankruptcy. A constantly expanding level of world trade, with gradualism prescribed where it is necessary, can be a vital spur to national prosperity and international security.

*2. Essential elements*

(*a*) *Escape clause.*—The proper purpose of an escape clause is not to prevent an increase in imports, but to prevent an excessive increase that does not offer the domestic industry an opportunity to adjust to the new circumstances of the market. There is no justification or need for a "share of the market" doctrine, for where a domestic industry has actually increased its sales it does not require relief from import competition, even though the imports have increased at a somewhat faster rate.

Retention of the segmentation clause appears to be proper, but within reasonable limitations. For example, if the wood-screw industry included one plant owned by Generals Motors, it would be improper to deny needed relief to the wood-screw industry because of the profitability of the automobile industry. However, where an industry produces several related products, such as wood screws, steel screws, lag bolts, etc., the decision of the industry managers to shift their productive facilities away from a less profitable item into a more profitable item should not warrant any import restrictions. This is the type of adjustment which is the proper purpose of a program of stability, and results in greater prosperity both to the domestic industry and the import trade, as well as the consuming public.

Since the escape clause is only a retraction of a tariff reduction, the relief to be granted should be limited to a tariff increase. There is no need or justification for the imposition of quotas, the most unfair and the most difficult administratively of all import restrictions. Further, since the uneconomic operations of a domestic industry should not be permanently subsidized, any relief granted under the escape clause should be on a sliding-scale basis, over a sufficient period of time to allow the domestic industry to adjust to the new economic conditions. Discretion should be given to the Tariff Commission as to the need for instituting a full-scale investigation, in order to discourage frivolous complaints and persistent harassment.

(*b*) *Dumping.*—The Antidumping Act is essential to prevent unfair and injurious price discrimination in world trade, and its administration should be limited to that purpose, It should not be used to penalize American businessmen who are in a position to drive a harder bargain than businessmen in other countries. It should not be used to penalize low prices, since low prices are an advantage, not a disadvantage, to the buying country. It should be administered in such a way that penalties will be imposed only on those imports which are actually being dumped, instead of the present system which unjustly penalizes all imports subject to investigation, even though 96 percent of those investigations have determined that there was no dumping present.

(*c*) *Buy American.*—The Buy American Act, which adds substantially to the cost of government and imposes unnecessary restrictions on our free-world trading partners, should probably be repealed. However, if this is not deemed advisable, the present policy which sets reasonable limitations on the Buy American principle as applied to direct Government purchases, should at least be extended to Government contracts as well.

(*d*) *Section 22.*—Some import restriction similar to that now contained in section 22 of the Agricultural Adjustment Act is essential, so long as the United States farm prices are maintained at levels above the world prices. If there were no barrier to the importation of these agricultural commodities, it is obvious that the great bulk of the world products would flood the American market in order to obtain the artificially high price. The result would be disaster to the farm price-support program. However, section 22 is intended to be a compromise between the Government program to support farm prices and the equally vital Government program to encourage our world trade. Administration of the program in such a spirit of compromise would not only foster these twin objectives, but would be of tremendous benefit to the American farm community, which finds major outlets in export markets. The establishment of complete embargoes under the provisions of section 22 does not accord with these objectives.

(*e*) *Peril point.*—With the tariff-cutting authority no longer a significant factor in the reciprocal trade program, the provision for peril points loses most of its early significance. To the extent that future rate cutting is necessary, the peril-point procedure should be retained. It seems reasonable also to broaden this proceeding to include consideration not only of tariff rates but also of trade rules which will be the subject of negotiation. Moreover, consideration should be given to applications by importers or domestic consumers of imported material who believe that the existing rate on a particular commodity is too high, and who might seek a determination from the Tariff Commission that the peril point for such commodity is substantially below the existing tariff level.

(*f*) *Miscellaneous.*—A variety of other pertinent statutory provisions require similar treatment. The program of customs simplification should be continued, to eliminate all unnecessary redtape and delays in the handling of world trade commodities. Countervailing duties should be imposed only where they cause injury to a domestic industry, since there is no purpose in raising import prices unless they cause injury. The national security amendment, if it is necessary at all as a supplement to the escape clause, should be strictly limited to its proper purpose instead of being used as an additional means of creating uncertainty in the import trade.

(*g*) *OTC.*—Creation of the Organization for Trade Cooperation is a significant factor in a program of trade stability, offering tremendous benefits to American businessmen, whether importers, exporters, or domestic producers facing import competition. The very purpose of OTC is in full accord with a program of stability, rather than tariff cutting, since OTC would have no power to change any tariff levels but would merely inspect the operation of the trade agreements that had been signed to see whether their terms are being observed. OTC would help protect the domestic producer against unfair import competition, by helping to guarantee that the fair-trade rules incorporated into the international trade agreements are not violated by foreign suppliers. To the American manufacturers and exporters, particularly those like textiles, coal, chemicals, electrical goods, and others who face intensive international competition, OTC would help to remove the exchange quotas and other restrictions placed on our exports in foreign countries. In short, the stability which a proper trade act can achieve in the United States, can be achieved on an international level primarily through an organization like OTC operating within the framework and the limitations of the contracts into which we have entered.

(*h*) *Limited rate authority.*—Although this program of stability envisages no general rate-cutting authority, it may be necessary and advantageous to recognize that some specific tariff cutting authority might be of tremendous benefit to the national interest. Certainly, there should be some authority to take action in specific cases where existing tariff levels are out of line with the general program. More important, however, is the developing problem involving the European common market and similar customs union developments throughout the world. In order to protect the position of the United States in world trade, it may be necessary for our negotiators to work out a modus operandi with the common market authorities. In such negotiations, it might be necessary for our negotiators to have some rate-cutting authority in order to strengthen their position vis-a-vis the common market. To enter into such negotiations from a position of weakness might seriously jeopardize a substantial portion of our export market.

## IV. Conclusion

The United States importer, together with his American customer and foreign supplier, has no right to demand an uncontrolled flow of imports into the United States market. He is entitled, however, to the certainty and stability of a foreign trade program that will make his business depend on the fair competition of the market place rather than the vacillations of Government policy or administration.

The United States producer facing import competition has no right to demand freedom from such competition. He is entitled, however, to the assurance that any significant change in competitive circumstances resulting from a change in Government policy will produce the gradualism necessary to permit adjustment to the new situation.

The United States as a whole has a vital national interest in maintaining the highest possible level of free world trade as an essential element of our national prosperity and our international security.

These objectives can be achieved only by a program of stability in America's world trade—stability that will reconcile the conflicting demands of the commercial interests in a program that provides the optimum benefits to the United States and all its citizens, whether as businessmen, workers, farmers, consumers, or taxpayers.

EXHIBIT A

JAPANESE PLYWOOD
IMPORT OF FOREIGN PLYWOOD
● WHAT IT MEANS TO YOU AND YOUR FAMILY
Hardwood Plywood Manufacturers Committee
Suite 601, 1145 19th Street, N. W.
Washington 6, D. C.
National 8-4905

EXHIBIT B

[The Saturday Evening Post, August 10, 1957]

ARE WE DRIVING JAPAN INTO RED CHINA'S ARMS?—A FAMOUS AUTHOR REPORTS FROM TOKYO ON THE AMERICAN POLICY WHICH MAY COST US OUR BULWARK IN THE PACIFIC

(By Cameron Hawley)

* * * * * *

**Yesterday, in one of my last interviews, I talked to a venerable captain of industry who has come through purging, bankruptcy, and depurging to emerge as a chairman of the board of one of the big trading companies. Huddled in one of the white slipcovered chairs that furnish every Japanese conference room, he sipped his pale tea and said, "Japan's best future is with the United States, there's no doubt about that, but whether you will allow us to realize upon that future—well, that's something else again. Have you seen this?"**

**He put down his teacup and, with a tremor that I suspect may not have been caused by palsy, handed me a small booklet. "This was put out by some association in your country that is trying to cut our exports of hardwood plywood."**

**The cover of the booklet was illustrated with a bucktoothed, slant-eyed monster, carbon copied from the hate-inspiring cartoons of World War II, towering over three cringing little American workers about to be smashed down by a sheet of plywood in the hands of the ogre.**

**"Your manufacturers may have a just cause for tariff protection," he went on. "I won't comment on that—my views are prejudiced—but it does seem that this is the sort of thing that will, in the end, force us to believe that if anyone is driving a wedge between the United States and Japan, it is some of your own people."**

**He may be right.**

TABLE No. 1.—*United States production of hardwood plywood (other than container plywood)*

[In million square feet, surface measure]

| Year | Market | Captive | Total |
|---|---|---|---|
| 1947 | 727 | [1] 320 | [1] 1,047 |
| 1951 | [1] 805 | [1] 368 | 1,173 |
| 1952 | 795 | 381 | 1,176 |
| 1953 | 806 | 436 | 1,242 |
| 1954 | 716 | [1] 377 | [1] 1,093 |
| 1955 | 918 | 445 | [1] 1,363 |
| 1956 | 884 | [1] 442 | [1] 1,326 |

[1] Estimates based on Census Bureau figures on relation of market to captive, 1953–55.

Source: U. S. Census Bureau, except as indicated.

TABLE No. 2.—*Sales and earnings of leading plywood companies*

[In thousands]

| Year | United States Plywood | | Georgia-Pacific | | Atlas Plywood | | Roddis Plywood | |
|---|---|---|---|---|---|---|---|---|
| | Sales | Income | Sales | Income | Sales | Income | Sales | Income |
| 1956 | $202,832 | $25,984 | $121,305 | $7,429 | $58,433 | $2,273 | $55,199 | $1,403 |
| 1955 | 150,565 | 17,432 | 91,966 | 6,203 | 55,342 | (1) | 50,456 | 1,420 |
| 1954 | 124,067 | 11,373 | 68,874 | 1,795 | 36,314 | 2,050 | 40,236 | 957 |
| 1953 | 116,200 | 13,279 | 66,368 | 1,205 | 42,497 | 3,872 | 34,026 | 735 |
| 1952 | 107,642 | 13,723 | 63,056 | 1,916 | 32,579 | 1,771 | 31,778 | 608 |
| 1051 | 108,450 | 22,409 | 62,739 | 3,177 | 32,300 | 6,114 | 33,429 | 2,046 |
| 1950 | 69,235 | 8,757 | 58,193 | 3,874 | 19,065 | 1,868 | 27,887 | 1,893 |

[1] Not available.

## NOTES

From Roddis 1956 report: "Gains were made in sales of hardwood plywood, solid core doors, lumber and hardwood veneer. Fir plywood, which accounted for 43 percent of your company's total sales in 1955, declined to 35 percent in 1956."

From Atlas 1956 report: "Products which previously had provided the backbone of our profitable sales were being displaced by other products such as paper and corrugated containers. * * * The consolidated net earnings * * * reflect the drop in current market prices of fir plywood to the lowest level in years."

From Georgia-Pacific 1956 report: "We have under construction an addition to our Savannah, Ga., hardwood plywood and specialty plant, which will about double our productive capacity at that location. * * * The current economic picture is fairly bright, but one disturbing factor is the decline in housing starts."

From United States Plywood 1956 report: "A decline in softwood plywood prices * * * was reflected in year-end inventory values. As a result, the earnings were adversely affected to the extent of 18 cents per common share."

TABLE 3.—*Breakdown of plywood sales of leading producer, Roddis Plywood Corp.*[1] *sales for years ending Oct. 31*

[All figures and announcements from official periodic reports]

| | Hardwood plywood | Percent of sales | Hardwood doors | Percent of sales | Fir plywood | Percent of sales | Total sales |
|---|---|---|---|---|---|---|---|
| 1956 | $11,790 | 21 | $6,969 | 13 | $19,370 | 35 | $55,199 |
| 1955 | 8,357 | 17 | 6,938 | 14 | 21,897 | 43 | 50,456 |
| 1954 | 6,720 | 17 | 7,586 | 19 | 16,955 | 41 | 40,753 |
| 1953 | 5,856 | 17 | 3,876 | 11 | 11,415 | 33 | 34,590 |
| 1952 | 4,864 | 15 | 6,241 | 19 | 10,136 | 31 | 32,262 |
| 1951 | 5,540 | 18 | 6,825 | 21 | 10,029 | 31 | 32,403 |
| 1950 | 5,293 | 19 | 6,526 | 23 | 8,715 | 31 | 27,887 |

[1] Similar figures are not generally available from other producers, although the annual reports to stockholders (see table No. 2) indicate an identical trend.

TABLE No. 4.—*Imports of hardwood plywood*

[In million square feet, surface measure]

| Country | 1956 | 1955 | 1954 | 1953 | 1952 | 1951 |
|---|---|---|---|---|---|---|
| Japan | 527.0 | 429.0 | 289.0 | 105.0 | 17.0 | 13.0 |
| Canada | 81.0 | 99.0 | 70.0 | 51.0 | 57.0 | 47.0 |
| Finland | 34.0 | 41.0 | 32.0 | 32.0 | 5.0 | 3.0 |
| Philippines | 15.0 | 10.0 | 2.0 | .5 | .1 | .1 |
| French Africa | 13.0 | 9.0 | 5.0 | 3.0 | .6 | |
| West Germany | 5.0 | 4.0 | 5.0 | 2.0 | .9 | |
| Surinam | 4.0 | 4.0 | 4.0 | 4.0 | 3.0 | .2 |
| Italy | 3.0 | 5.0 | 6.0 | 7.0 | | .4 |
| Netherlands | 3.0 | 2.0 | .8 | 1.0 | .1 | .2 |
| Belgium and Luxembourg | 3.0 | 1.0 | .7 | .2 | | .2 |
| United Kingdom | 2.0 | 2.0 | .3 | .1 | | |
| France | 2.0 | 5.0 | 5.0 | 8.0 | .4 | |
| Denmark | 1.0 | 1.0 | .3 | | | |
| Spain | 1.0 | 1.0 | .6 | .4 | .1 | |
| Israel | .8 | .7 | 1.0 | .4 | | .1 |
| Mexico | .3 | 3.0 | 3.0 | 2.0 | .7 | .7 |
| All others | 1.0 | 2.0 | 1.0 | 2.0 | | 2.0 |
| Total | 696.0 | 619.0 | 426.0 | 219.0 | 85.0 | 67.0 |

Source: U. S. Department of Commerce.

TABLE No. 5. *Comparison of imports and United States production of hardwood plywood (other than container plywood)*

[In million square feet, converted to estimated ¼-inch basis]

| Year | United States | Imports | Total market | Percent of United States | Percent of imports |
|---|---|---|---|---|---|
| 1956 | 3, 315 | 522 | 3, 837 | 86 | 14 |
| 1955 | 3, 408 | 464 | 3, 872 | 88 | 12 |
| 1954 | 2, 733 | 320 | 3, 053 | 89 | 11 |

TABLE No. 6.—*Summary of 28 plywood plants claimed to have shut down because of imports*

1. Meyercord Compound Lumber Co., Mobile, Ala.; closed, replaced by Meyercord Door Manufacturing Co.
2. Jefferson Lumber Co., Monticello, Fla.; operating under different name.
3. Monticello Manufacturing Co., Boyd, Fla.; closed, lack of capital, lack of timber.
4. Atlas Plywood Corp., Brunswick, Ga.; closed before imports were significant.
5. Toccoa Manufacturing Co., Toccoa, Ga.; operating as subsidiary.
6. Georgia Veneer & Lumber Co., Toomsboro, Ga.; operating as subsidiary.
7. Plywood Products, Inc., Toccoa, Ga.; closed, consolidation with parent.
8. Waynesboro Veneer & Plywood Co., Waynesboro, Ga.; demolished by fire in 1952.
9. Southern Plywood Co., Thomasville, N. C.; no such plant.
10. Standard Plywood Co., Fairmont, N. C.; demolished by fire in 1954.
11. Atlantic Plywood Co., Florence, S. C.; closed, labor difficulties.
12. Atlas Plywood Corp., Goldsboro, N. C.; closed, consolidated with parent.
13. Peerless Plywood Co., High Point, N. C.; closed for personal reasons.
14. Fairmont Plywood Co., Fairmont, N. C.; not separate plant (same as No. 10 above).
15. Syncor, Inc., Alma, N. C.; not separate plant (same as No. 17 below).
16. Southern Plywood Co., High Point, N. C.; demolished by fire in 1954.
17. Daystrom Corp., Alma, N. C.; operating as subsidiary.
18. Atlantic Plywood Co., Atlantic, N. C.; no such plant.
19. Waccamaw Co., Whiteville, N. C.; operating.
20. Plywood Plastics, Hampton, S. C.; operating as subsidiary.
21. Varnville Door Co., Varnville, S. C.; closed, lack of capital.
22. Standard Plywood Co., Hampton, S. C.; no such plant.
23. Atlas Plywood Corp., Newport, Vt.; closed, consolidation.
24. Atlas Plywood Corp., Richford, Vt.; closed, consolidation, Container Plywood.
25. Moorefield Plywood Co., Moorefield, W. Va.; closed, financial operations.
26. Shawano Laminating Co., Shawano, Wis.; closed, inefficient management (softwood).
27. Jolin Corp., Shawano, Wis.; operating in receivership, overexpansion.
28. Baldwin Plywood Co., Gillett, Wis.; operating on lease.

TABLE No. 7.—*Breakdown of 28 plywood plants claimed to have shut down because of imports (28 plants identified by number)*

| Still operating | No plant | Burned down | Closed | | | |
|---|---|---|---|---|---|---|
| | | | Before imports | Consolidated | Undercapitalized | Other |
| 1 | 9 | 8 | ------ | ------ | ------ | ------ |
| 2 | 14 | 10 | 4 | 7 | 3 | [1] 11 |
| 5 | 15 | 16 | ------ | 12 | 21 | [2] 13 |
| 6 | 18 | ------ | ------ | 23 | ------ | [3] 25 |
| 17 | 22 | ------ | ------ | 24 | ------ | [4] 26 |
| 19 | ------ | ------ | ------ | ------ | ------ | ------ |
| 20 | ------ | ------ | ------ | ------ | ------ | ------ |
| 27 | ------ | ------ | ------ | ------ | ------ | ------ |
| 28 | ------ | ------ | ------ | ------ | ------ | ------ |
| 9 | 5 | 3 | 1 | 4 | 2 | 4 |

[1] Labor.
[2] Personal.
[3] Financial.
[4] Management.

TABLE No. 8.—*Hardwood plywood imports under the proposed legislative quota, if it were in effect for 1957*

[In million square feet]

| Country | Actual imports 1956 | Quota for 1957 | Percent change |
|---|---|---|---|
| Japan | 527.0 | 123.0 | −77 |
| Canada | 81.0 | 54.0 | −33 |
| Finland | 34.0 | 21.0 | −38 |
| Philippines | 15.0 | .7 | −95 |
| Surinam | 3.8 | 3.0 | −21 |
| France | 1.6 | 4.0 | +250 |
| Italy | 3.1 | 4.0 | +130 |
| Mexico | .4 | 1.5 | +375 |
| All others who have shipped plywood in the past | 40.0 | 8.0 | −80 |
| Reserve for all new exporters, including Formosa, etc. | | 12.0 | |
| Total | 706.0 | 232.0 | −67 |

TABLE No. 9.—*Growth in United States hardwood plywood plants producing for sale (noncaptive)*

| Year | All plywood plants [1] | Western softwood plants [2] | Estimated number of hardwood plants [3] |
|---|---|---|---|
| 1939 | 98 | 26 | 72 |
| 1947 | 163 | 39 | 124 |
| 1954 | 255 | 100 | 155 |

[1] From the U. S. Bureau of Census.
[2] From Douglas-Fir Plywood Association.
[3] Estimated from other figures.

TABLE No. 10

*Uses of United States market hardwood plywood, 1953 (other than container plywood)*

| | |
|---|---|
| Market hardwood plywood: 1953 production, million square feet (surface measure) | 806 |
| Distribution: | *Percent* |
| To distributors and dealers | 17 |
| To industrial consumers and fabricators | 83 |
| Furniture manufacturers | 49 |
| Cabinetmakers, TV, kitchen, etc | 14 |
| Door manufacturers | 8 |
| Others (trailers, toys, luggage, etc.) | 12 |
| | 83 |

Source: U. S. Tariff Commission.

*Uses of United States hardwood plywood, 1953*

| | *Percent* |
|---|---|
| All hardwood plywood, market and captive (other than container plywood): | |
| Construction purposes | 43 |
| Furniture and cabinets | 37 |
| Other industrial uses | 18 |
| Miscellaneous | 2 |

Source: Forestry Products Research Society, veneer and plywood committee.

O